# Contents

II European driving: cut through the confusion
IV Driving regulations
VIII Ski resorts
X Sights of Europe
XXIV European politics and economics

**1 Route planning maps**

1 Key to route planning map pages

**24 Road maps**

24 Key to road map pages · Distance table

**201 City plans and approach maps**

| | | | | |
|---|---|---|---|---|
| Alicante C | 201 | Luxembourg C | 215 |
| Amsterdam CU | 202 | Lyon CU | 215 |
| Antwerpen C | 201 | Madrid UC | 215 |
| Athina UC | 202 | Málaga C | 216 |
| Barcelona CU | 203 | Marseille C | 216 |
| Basel C | 203 | Milano CU | 217 |
| Beograd C | 205 | Moskva CU | 218 |
| Berlin CU | 204 | München CU | 218 |
| Bordeaux CU | 205 | Nápoli CU | 219 |
| Bruxelles UC | 205 | Oslo UC | 219 |
| Budapest CU | 206 | Paris CU | 220 |
| Dublin CU | 207 | Praha CU | 222 |
| Düsseldorf CU | 207 | Roma CU | 223 |
| Edinburgh C | 207 | Rotterdam C | 222 |
| Firenze Florence C | 209 | Sankt Peterburg U | 222 |
| Frankfurt C | 209 | Sevilla C | 224 |
| Genève Geneva C | 209 | Stockholm CU | 225 |
| Génova Genoa C | 209 | Strasbourg CU | 224 |
| Göteborg C | 210 | Stuttgart C | 224 |
| Granada C | 210 | Torino UC | 226 |
| Hamburg CU | 210 | Venézia C | 226 |
| Helsinki CU | 211 | Warszawa CU | 227 |
| İstanbul U | 211 | Wien UC | 227 |
| København CU | 212 | Zagreb C | 228 |
| Köln Cologne C | 212 | Zürich C | 228 |
| Lisboa CU | 213 | C City street plan | |
| London CU | 213 | U Urban area map | |

**229 Index to road maps**

www.philips-maps.co.uk

First published in 2007 as Philip's EasyRead Europe by
Philip's, a division of Octopus Publishing Group Ltd
www.octopusbooks.co.uk
Carmelite House, 50 Victoria Embankment
London EC4Y 0DZ
An Hachette UK Company · www.hachette.co.uk

Sixth edition 2015, first impression 2015

 **Ordnance Survey®** This product includes mapping
data licensed from Ordnance
Survey®, with the permission
of the Controller of Her Majesty's Stationery Office
© Crown copyright 2015. All rights reserved.
Licence number 100011710.

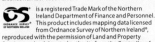 is a registered Trade Mark of the Northern
Ireland Department of Finance and Personnel.
This product includes mapping data licensed
from Ordnance Survey of Northern Ireland®,
reproduced with the permission of Land and Property
Services under delegated authority from the Controller of
Her Majesty's Stationery Office, © Crown Copyright 2015.

The maps of Ireland on pages 26 to 30 and the urban
area map and town plan of Dublin are based upon the
Crown Copyright and are reproduced with the permission
of Land & Property Services under delegated authority from
the Controller of Her Majesty's Stationery Office, © Crown
Copyright and database right 2015, PMLPA No 100503,
and on Ordnance Survey Ireland by permission of the
Government © Ordnance Survey Ireland / Government of
Ireland Permit number 8982.

Cartography by Philip's, Copyright © Philip's 2015

*Nielsen BookScan Travel Publishing Year Book 2014 data
**Independent research survey, from research carried out
by Outlook Research Limited, 2005/06

**Photographic acknowledgements:**
Page II, top imageBROKER / Alamy ·
right mladen61 / iStockphoto · bottom Mode Images / Alamy
Page III centre zstock / Shutterstock ·
right Nathan Wright / Shutterstock

## Legend to route planning maps pages 2–23

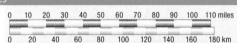

| | |
|---|---|
| | Motorway with selected junctions |
| | tunnel, under construction |
| | Toll motorway, pre-pay motorway |
| | Main through route, other major road, other road |
| 25  56 | European road number, motorway number |
| 55 | National road number |
| 56 | Distances – in kilometres |
| | International boundary, national boundary |
| LE HAVRE | Car ferry and destination |
| ✈ 1089 ▲ | Mountain pass, international airport, height (metres) |

**Town – population**

| | | | | |
|---|---|---|---|---|
| MOSKVA ■ ■ | 5 million + | | Gävle ⊙ ⊚ | 50000–100000 |
| BERLIN ▣ ▣ | 2–5 million | | Nybro ○ ○ | 20000–50000 |
| MINSK ▣ ▣ | 1–2 million | | Ikast ○ ○ | 10000–20000 |
| Oslo ◉ ⊚ | 500000–1 million | | Skjern ○ ⊚ | 5000–10000 |
| Århus ⊙ ⊚ | 200000–500000 | | Lillesand ○ ○ | 0–5000 |
| Turku ⊚ ⊚ | 100000–200000 | | | |

The green version of the symbol indicates towns with
Low Emission Zones

### Scale · pages 2–23

1:3 200 000
1 in = 50.51 miles
1 cm = 32km

0 10 20 30 40 50 60 70 80 90 100 110 miles
0 20 40 60 80 100 120 140 160 180 km

## Legend to road maps pages 26–200

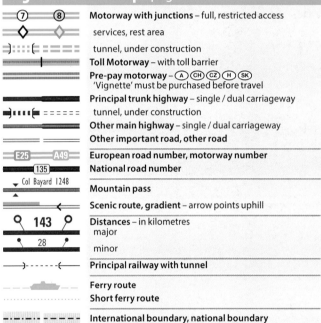

| | |
|---|---|
| ⑦  ⑧ | Motorway with junctions – full, restricted access |
| ◇ | services, rest area |
| | tunnel, under construction |
| | Toll Motorway – with toll barrier |
| | Pre-pay motorway – A CH CZ H SK 'Vignette' must be purchased before travel |
| | Principal trunk highway – single / dual carriageway |
| | tunnel, under construction |
| | Other main highway – single / dual carriageway |
| | Other important road, other road |
| E25  A49 | European road number, motorway number |
| 135 | National road number |
| Col Bayard 1248 | Mountain pass |
| | Scenic route, gradient – arrow points uphill |
| 143 | Distances – in kilometres major |
| 28 | minor |
| | Principal railway with tunnel |
| | Ferry route |
| | Short ferry route |
| | International boundary, national boundary |
| | National park, natural park |

| | | | |
|---|---|---|---|
| ✈ Airport | | ⛷ Ski resort | |
| �🏛 Ancient monument | | 🎡 Theme park | |
| ⚲ Beach | | ◉ World Heritage site | |
| H Castle or house | | 1754▲ Spot height | |
| ∩ Cave | | **Sevilla** World Heritage town | |
| ✦ Other place of interest | | **Verona** Town of tourist interest | |
| ⁂ Park or garden | | ■ ● City or town with Low Emission Zone | |
| ✢ Religious building | | | |

### Scale · pages 26–181

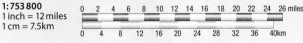

1:753 800
1 inch = 12 miles
1 cm = 7.5km

0 2 4 6 8 10 12 14 16 18 20 22 24 26 miles
0 4 8 12 16 20 24 28 32 36 40km

### Scale · pages 182–200

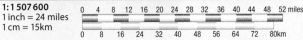

1:1 507 600
1 inch = 24 miles
1 cm = 15km

0 4 8 12 16 20 24 28 32 36 40 44 48 52 miles
0 8 16 24 32 40 48 56 64 72 80km

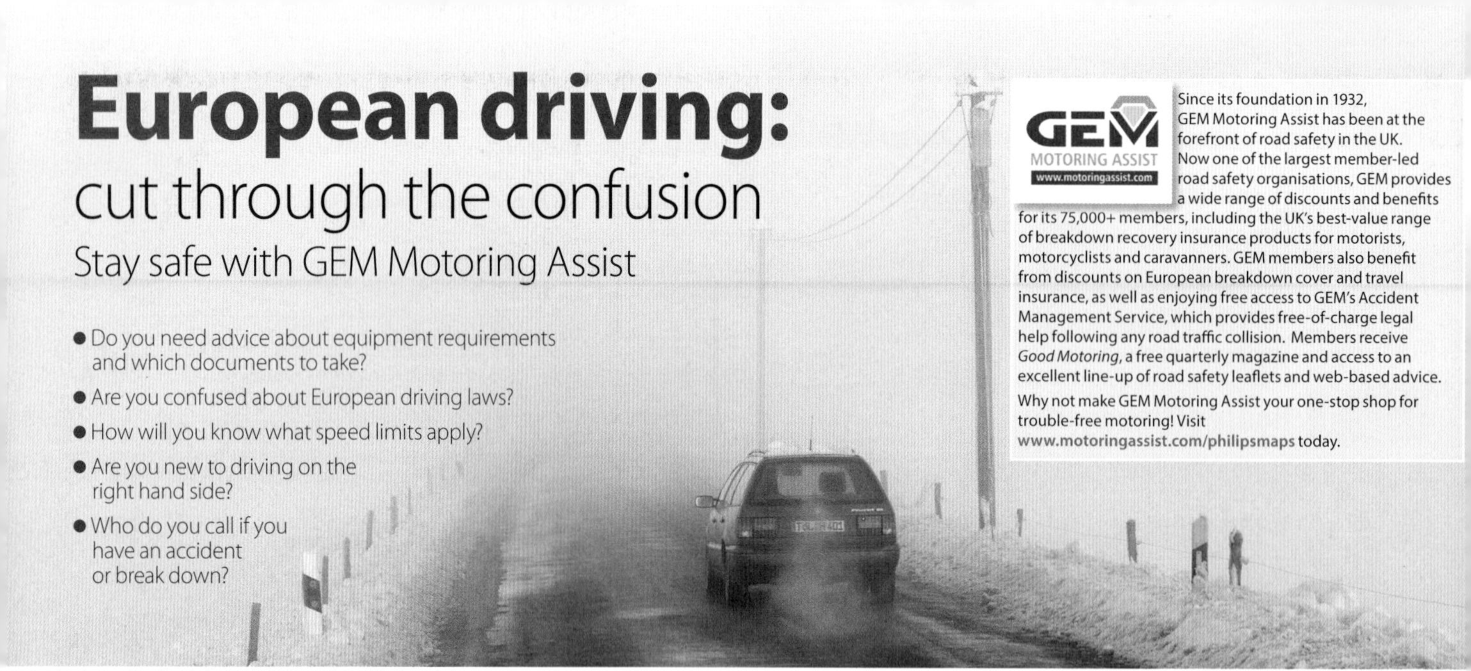

# European driving:
## cut through the confusion
### Stay safe with GEM Motoring Assist

- Do you need advice about equipment requirements and which documents to take?
- Are you confused about European driving laws?
- How will you know what speed limits apply?
- Are you new to driving on the right hand side?
- Who do you call if you have an accident or break down?

**M**illions of us drive abroad on holiday each year. Perhaps it's a long motorway trip to the Mediterranean, a selection of historic cities and sites or a gentle tour along quiet country lanes. Whatever the purpose, it makes sense to ensure that both we and our vehicles are properly prepared for the journey.

It's not easy getting to grips with the finer points of driving in other countries, however experienced you may be as a motorist. Whether you have notched up thousands of miles of European driving or are preparing to make your first journey, the chances are you will always manage to find some road sign or legal requirement that will cause confusion.

What's more, 'driving in Europe' covers such a huge area. There are 28 countries in the European Union alone, each with its own set of road traffic laws and motoring customs. Driving in Europe can mean a spectacular and sunny coastal road that's within sight of Africa, or a snowy track amid the biting cold of the Arctic Circle, where the only others on the road are reindeer. Add to this some of the world's most congested cities, dense clusters of motorways (many with confusing numbers) and a big variation in safety standards and attitudes to risk. No wonder we often risk getting lost, taking wrong turnings or perhaps stopping where we shouldn't.

Depending on the country we're in, our errors at the wheel or our lack of familiarity with the rules of the road can sometimes bring unwelcome consequences. In any country, foreign drivers are subject to the same traffic rules as residents, enforceable in many situations by hefty on-the-spot fines and other sanctions. The situation across Europe is complex, simply because of the number of different sets of rules. For example, failure to carry a specific piece of breakdown equipment may be an offence in one country, but not in another. It's easy to see why the fun and excitement of a road trip in Europe could be spoilt by a minefield of regulations.

But we want to ensure that doesn't happen. Preparation and planning are key to a great holiday. It certainly pays to do a bit of research before you go, just to ensure you and your vehicle are up to the journey, your documents are in order and you're carrying the correct levels of equipment to keep the law enforcers happy.

## Before you go
Some sensible planning will help make sure your European journey is enjoyable and – we hope – stress-free. So take some time before departure to ensure everything is in good shape: and that includes you, your travelling companions and your vehicle.

## For you:
Try to become familiar with the driving laws of your holiday destination, including the local speed limits and which side of the road to drive on. You will be subject to these laws when driving abroad and if you are stopped by the police, it is not an excuse to say that you were unaware of them. Police officers in many countries have the power to impose (and collect) substantial on-the-spot fines for motoring offences, whether you are a resident or a visitor.

The European Commission's 'Driving Abroad' website http://ec.europa.eu/transport/road_safety/going_abroad gives detailed information on different road traffic rules in different European countries.

The Foreign and Commonwealth Office also gives country-specific travel advice www.gov.uk/driving-abroad with information on driving.

### Passports
Check everyone's passport to make sure they are all valid.

Don't wait for your passport to expire. Unused time, rounded up to whole months (minimum one month, maximum nine months), will usually be added to your new passport.

New passports usually take two weeks to arrive. The Passport Office (0300 222 0000, www.gov.uk/renew-adult-passport) offers a faster service if you need a replacement passport urgently, but you'll have to pay a lot more.

### Driving Licence
The new style photocard driving licence is valid in all European Union countries. However, you must ensure you carry both parts: the credit card-size photocard and the paper licence. The previously used pink EU format UK licence is also valid, though it may not be recognized in some areas. So if you haven't already done so, now is the time to update your old licence. For more information, contact the DVLA (0300 790 6802, www.dft.gov.uk/dvla)

### Travel Insurance
Travel insurance is vital as it covers you against medical emergencies, accidents, thefts and cancellations, and repatriation. Ask for details before buying any travel insurance policy. Find out what it covers you for, and to what value. More important, check what's not covered. One of the key benefits of GEM membership is the excellent discount you can get on travel insurance. For more details, please visit: www.motoringassist.com/philipsmaps

### European Breakdown Cover
Don't risk letting a breakdown ruin your European trip. Ensure you purchase a policy that will cover you for roadside assistance, emergency repair and recovery of your vehicle to the UK, wherever in Europe you may be heading. Once again, GEM members enjoy a specially discounted rate. You'll find the details at www.motoringassist.com/philipsmaps

### EHIC
The E111 medical treatment form is no longer valid. Instead, you need an EHIC card for everyone travelling. These are free and cover you for any medical treatment you may need during a trip to another EU country or Switzerland. However, do check at the time of requiring assistance that your EHIC will be accepted. Apply online (www.ehic.org.uk), by telephone (0300 3301350) or complete an application form, available from a Post office. Allow up to 14 days for the cards to arrive.

## For your vehicle:

### Service
It makes sense to get your car serviced before you travel. As a minimum, ensure the tyres have plenty of tread left and that water and oil levels are checked and topped up if required. Check them regularly during your time away.

### Vehicle Registration Document
Police in many countries can demand that you prove you have the right to be driving your car. That means you need to show the registration document, or a suitable letter of authorization if the registration document is not in your name. Remember you should never leave the registration document in the car.

### Nationality plate
Your vehicle must display a nationality plate of an approved pattern, design and size.

### MOT
If your car is more than three years old, make sure you take its current MOT test certificate with you.

### Insurance
If you are planning a trip to Europe, you should find that your car insurance policy provides you with the minimum amount of cover you need. But it's important to contact your insurer before you go, to confirm exactly what level of cover you have and for how many days it will be valid.

### Mechanical adjustments
Check the adjustments required for your headlights before you go. Beam deflectors are a legal requirement if you drive in Europe. They are generally sold at the ports, on ferries and in the Folkestone Eurotunnel terminal, but be warned – the instructions can be a little confusing! The alternative is to ask a local garage to do the job for you before you go. If you choose this, then make sure you shop around as prices for undertaking this very simple task vary enormously.

### Equipment check-list
This checklist represents GEM's suggestions for what you should take with you in the car. Different countries have different rules about what's compulsory and these rules change from time to time. So it's important to check carefully before you set out. For country-by-country guidance, visit www.motoringassist.com/europe or see page IV of this atlas.

- Fire extinguisher
- First aid kit
- High-visibility jacket – one for each occupant
- Two warning triangles
- Replacement bulbs and fuses
- Spare spectacles (if worn) for each driver
- Snow chains for winter journeys into the mountains
- Camera and notebook. Keep in your glove compartment and record any collisions or damage for insurance purposes (if it is safe).

### Contact details
Make sure you have all relevant emergency helpline numbers with you, including emergency services, breakdown assistance, the local British consulate and your insurance company. There are links to embassies and consulates around the world from the Foreign Office website. (www.fco.gov.uk) For information, the European emergency telephone number (our equivalent of 999) is 112.

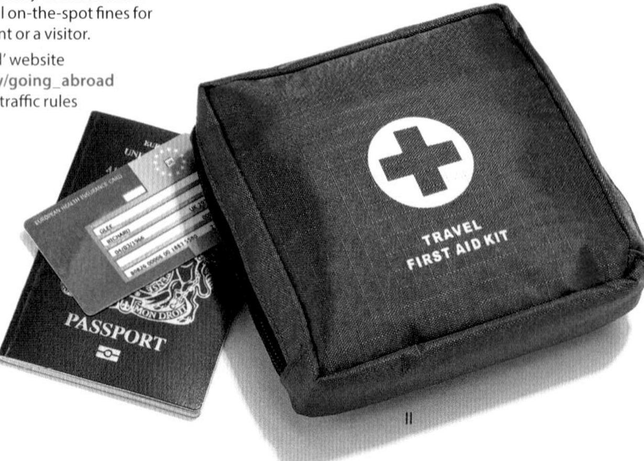

## STOP AND GIVE WAY

**Who has priority?**
Make sure you keep a watchful eye on signs telling you who has priority on the road. Look for a yellow diamond sign, which tells you that traffic already on the road has priority. If you see the yellow diamond sign crossed out, then you must give way to traffic joining the road.

**Priorité a droite**
Despite the use of the yellow diamond signs, be aware that on some French roads (especially roundabouts in Paris), the traditional 'priorité a droite' practice is followed, even though it may no longer be legal. In theory these days, the rule no longer applies unless it is clearly signed. In practice, though, it makes sense to anticipate a driver pulling out in front of you, even though the priority may be yours.

**Headlight flash**
Bear in mind that the practice of flashing headlights at a junction in France does not mean the same thing as it might in the UK. If another motorists flashes his headlights at you, he's telling you that he has priority and will be coming through in front of you.

**Stop means stop!**
If you come to a solid white line with an octagonal 'STOP' sign, then you must come to a complete stop. In other words your wheels must stop turning. Adherence to the 'STOP' sign is generally much more rigorously enforced in European countries than you may be used to here.

## HELP ME, PLEASE!

**If you're in a difficult situation and need local help, then the following words and phrases might prove useful if language is a problem:**

| English | French | Spanish | Italian | German |
|---|---|---|---|---|
| **Do you speak English?** | Parlez-vous anglais? | ¿Habla usted inglés? | Parla inglese? | Sprechen Sie Englisch? |
| **Thank you (very much)** | Merci (beaucoup) | (Muchas) Gracias | Grazie (mille) | Danke (sehr) |
| **Is there a police station near here?** | Est-ce qu'il y a un commissariat de police près d'ici? | ¿Hay una comisaría cerca? | C'e' un commissariato qui vicino? | Gibt es ein Polizeirevier hier in der Nähe? |
| **I have lost my passport.** | J'ai perdu mon passeport. | He perdido mi pasaporte | Ho perso il mio passaporto. | Ich have meinen Reisepass verloren. |
| **I have broken down.** | Je suis tombé en panne | Mi coche se ha averiado. | Ho un guasto. | Ich habe eine Panne. |
| **I have run out of fuel.** | Je suis tombé en panne d'essence. | Me he quedado sin gasolina. | Ho terminato la benzina. | Ich habe kein Benzin mehr. |
| **I feel ill.** | Je me sens malade. | Me siento mal. | Mi sento male. | Mir ist schlecht. |

## WORTH KNOWING

**You will need a separate GB sticker in EU countries** if your car doesn't have a registration plate containing the GB euro-symbol.

**Fuel** is generally most expensive at motorway service areas and cheapest at supermarkets. However, these are usually shut on Sundays and Bank Holidays. So-called '24 hour' regional fuel stations in France seldom accept payment by UK credit card, so don't rely on them if your tank is running low during a night-time journey.

**If you see several fuel stations** in short succession before a national border, it's likely that fuel on the other side will be more expensive, so take the opportunity to fill up.

**Radar speed camera detectors** are illegal in most European countries.

**The insurance 'green card'** is no longer required for journeys in Europe, but it is important to make sure you have contact details for your insurer in case of an accident or claim.

**Speed limits in France are enforced rigorously.** Radar controls are frequent, and any driver (including non-residents) detected at more than 25km/h above the speed limit can have their licence confiscated on the spot. Furthermore, if you are caught exceeding the speed limit by 50km/h, even on a first offence, you will face a term of imprisonment. • New legislation introduced in France in 2012 required every driver to carry a self-breathalyser test kit. However, the imposition of a €11 fine for failing to produce a breathalyser when required has been postponed indefinitely. So, in theory, you are required to carry a breathalyser kit, but no fine can be imposed if you don't.

**In Spain you must carry two warning triangles,** plus a spare pair of glasses for every driver who needs to use them.

**In Luxembourg,** there are specific rules relating to how you fix a satnav device to your windscreen. Get it wrong and you could be fined on the spot.

**In Germany** it is against the law to run out of fuel on the motorway. If you do run out, then you face an on-the-spot fine.

**Norway and Sweden have particularly low limits for drink-driving:** just 20mg per 100ml of blood (compared to 80 in the UK). In Slovakia, the limit is zero.

**In Hungary, the limit is also zero.** If you are found to be drink-driving, your driving licence will be withdrawn by police officers on the spot.

**In most countries**, maps and signs will have the European road number (shown in white on a green background) alongside the appropriate national road number. However, in Sweden and Belgium only the E-road number will be shown.

## Other laws and motoring advice to be aware of across Europe:

**Austria** Recent rules require the mandatory use of winter tyres between 1 November and 15 April.

**Belgium** You will have to pay to use most public toilets – including those at motorway service stations • You are not permitted to use cruise control on motorways when traffic is heavy • There are also specific penalties for close-following on motorways • Roadside drug-testing of drivers (using oral fluid testing devices) forms a regular part of any police controls.

**Cyprus** There have been important changes in how speeding and drink-driving are sanctioned. Cyprus now has a graduated system of speeding fines, ranging from one euro per km/h over the limit in marginal cases through to fines of up to €5,000 and a term of imprisonment for the most severe infringements. There are also graduated fines for drink-driving, ranging from fixed penalties for being slightly over the limit to terms of imprisonment and fines of up to €5,000 for the most severe.

**Denmark** Cars towing caravans and trailers are prohibited from overtaking on motorways at certain times of day.

**Finland** Speeding fines are worked out according to your income. Access to a national database allows police at the roadside to establish a Finnish resident's income and number of dependants. Officers then impose a fine based on a specific number of days' income. The minimum speeding fine is 115 euros • If you hit an elk or deer, you must report the collision to the police.

**France** Any driver must be in possession of a valid breathalyser (displaying an 'BF' number), either electronic or chemical, to be shown to a police officer in case of control • Motorcyclist's helmets must have four reflective stickers fitted, and there is an on-the-spot fine of €135 for non-compliance (by foreign riders as well as French) • Jail terms for drivers caught at more than 50km/h above the speed limit – even first time offenders • Radar detectors, are banned with fines of €1500 for anyone using them • There are stiff penalties for driving while using a mobile phone.

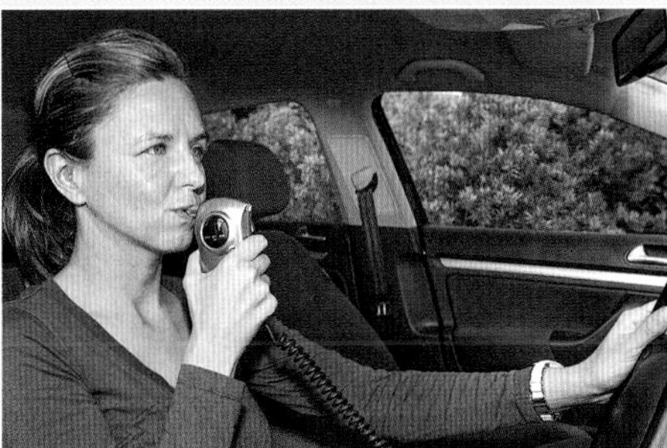

**Germany** Check your fuel contents regularly as it's an offence to run out of fuel on a German motorway • It's also an offence to make rude signs to other road users.

**Greece** has Europe's highest accident rate in terms of the number of crashes per vehicle. Pay particular attention at traffic light junctions, as red lights are frequently ignored • All drivers detected with more than 1.10 g/l of alcohol in blood, or more than 0.60mg/l in breath will be prosecuted for the offence • Carrying a petrol can in a vehicle is forbidden.

**Ireland** The drink-drive limit was reduced in 2011 from 0.8 mg per ml to 0.5. • Beware of rural three-lane roads, where the middle overtaking lane is used by traffic travelling in both directions. On wider rural roads it's the accepted practice for slower vehicles to pull over to let faster traffic through.

**Italy** Police can impound your vehicle if you cannot present the relevant ownership documents when requested • You will need a red and white warning sign if you plan to use any rear-mounted luggage rack such as a bike rack • Zero alcohol tolerance is now applied for drivers who have held a driving licence for less than three years, as well as to drivers aged 18 to 21, professional drivers, taxi drivers and truckers.

**Norway** Under new legislation, police officers can perform roadside drug impairment saliva tests. There are specific limits set for the presence of 20 common non-alcohol drugs. • You'll find what amounts to a zero tolerance where drinking and driving is concerned. Only 0.1mg of alcohol per millilitre of blood is permitted (compared to 0.8 in the UK) • Speeding fines are high. For example, a driver caught at 25 km/h over the 80 km/h speed limit on a national road could expect a fine of around £600.

**Portugal** If you are towing a caravan, you must have a current inventory of the caravan's contents to show a police officer if requested.

**Slovakia** It is mandatory to use dipped headlights on every road journey, regardless of the time of day, season or weather conditions.

**Spain** Motorway speed limits in Spain are 120km/h • If you need glasses for driving, then the law requires you to carry a spare pair with you in the car • It's compulsory to carry two spare warning triangles, spare bulbs for your car and reflective jackets.

**Turkey** Take great caution if you're driving at dusk. Many local drivers put off using their lights until it's properly dark, so you may find oncoming traffic very hard to spot • During the time of Ramadan, many people will not eat or drink between the hours of sunrise and sunset. This can seriously reduce levels of alertness, especially among people driving buses, trucks and taxis.

## TOP TIPS FOR STAYING SAFE

**Collisions abroad occur not just because of poor driving conditions locally, but also because we do not always take the same safety precautions as we might expect to take at home, for example by not wearing a seatbelt or by drinking and driving.**

**1. Plan your route before you go.** That includes the journey you make to reach your destination (with sufficient breaks built in) and any excursions or local journeys you make while you're there.

**2. Remember that, wherever you drive, you will be subject to the same laws as local drivers.** Claiming ignorance of these laws will not be accepted as an excuse.

**3. Take extra care at junctions** when you re driving on the 'right side' of the road. If driving in a family group, involve every member in a quick 'junction safety check' to help reduce the risk of a collision. Having everybody in the car call out a catchphrase such as "DriLL DriLL DriLL" (Driver Look Left) on the approach to junctions and roundabouts is a small but potentially life-saving habit.

**4. Take fatigue seriously.** The excellent European motorway network means you can cover big distances with ease. But you must also make time for proper breaks (experts recommend a break of at least 15 minutes after every two hours of driving). If possible, share the driving and set strict daily limits to the number of driving hours. Watch a short video that explains the risks of driver fatigue: www.motoringassist.com/fatigue

**5. Drink-driving limits across Europe are lower than those in the UK.** The only exception is Malta, where the limit is the same (0.8mg per ml). Bear this in mind if you're flying to a holiday or business destination and plan to have a drink on the plane, as the combination of unfamiliar roads and alcohol in your bloodstream is not a safe one. It's also worth remembering that drivers who cause collisions because they were drinking are likely to find their insurance policy will not cover them.

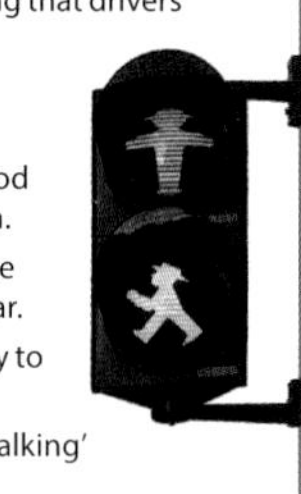

**6. Expect the unexpected.** Styles of driving in your destination country are likely to be very different from those you know in the UK. Drive defensively and certainly don't get involved in any altercations on the road.

**7. Don't overload your car** while away, however tempting the local bargains may appear. Make sure you have good all-round visibility by ensuring you don't pile up items on the parcel shelf or boot, and keep your windscreen clean.

**8. Always wear a seatbelt** and ensure everyone else on board wears one. Check specific regulations regarding the carriage of children: in some countries children under the age of 12 are not permitted to travel in the front of the car.

**9. Don't use your mobile phone while driving**. Even though laws on phone use while driving differ from country to country, the practice is just as dangerous wherever you are.

**10. When you're exploring on foot, be wise to road safety as a pedestrian**. You may get into trouble for 'jay-walking' so don't just wander across a road. Use a proper crossing, but remember that drivers may not stop for you! Don't forget that traffic closest to you approaches from the LEFT.

# Driving regulations

**Vehicle** A national vehicle identification plate is always required when taking a vehicle abroad. Fitting headlamp converters or beam deflectors when taking a right-hand drive car to a country where driving is on the right (every country in Europe except the UK and Ireland) is compulsory. Within the EU, if not driving a locally hired car, it is compulsory to have either Europlates or a country of origin (e.g. GB) sticker. Outside the EU (and in Andorra) a sticker is compulsory, even with Europlates.

**Documentation** All countries require that you carry a valid passport, vehicle registration document, hire certificate or letter of authority for the use of someone else's vehicle, full driving licence/International Driving Permit and insurance documentation/green card. Some non-EU countries also require a visa. Minimum driving ages are often higher for people holding foreign licences. New exit checks at the Eurotunnel and ferry terminals mean that drivers taking vehicles from the UK should allow extra time.

**Licence** A photo licence is preferred; with an old-style paper licence, an International Driving Permit (IDP) should also be carried. In some countries, an IDP is compulsory, whatever form of licence is held. Non-EU drivers should always have both a licence and and IDP. UK (except NI) drivers with photo licences should check in advance whether a hire company will wish to check for endorsements and vehicle categories. If so, visit *www.gov.uk/view-driving-licence* to create a digital code (valid for 72 hours) that allows licence details to be shared.

**Insurance** Third-party cover is compulsory across Europe. Most insurance policies give only basic cover when driving abroad, so you should check that your policy provides at least third-party cover for the countries in which you will be driving and upgrade it to the level that you require. You may have to take out extra cover at the frontier if you cannot produce acceptable proof of adequate insurance. Even in countries in which a green card is not required, carrying one is recommended for extra proof of insurance.

**Motorcycles** It is compulsory for all motorcyclists and passengers to wear crash helmets.

**Other** In countries in which visibility vests are compulsory, one for each person should be carried in the passenger compartment, or panniers on a motorbike, where they can be reached easily. Warning triangles should also be carried in the passenger compartment • The penalties for infringements of regulations vary considerably from one country to another. In many countries the police may impose on-the-spot fines (ask for a receipt). Penalties can be severe for serious infringements, particularly for exceeding the blood-alcohol limit; in some countries this can result in immediate imprisonment • In some countries, vignettes for toll roads are being replaced by electronic tags.

The publishers have made every effort to ensure that the information given here was correct at the time of going to press. No responsibility can be accepted for any errors or their consequences. Please note that driving regulations may change, and that it has not been possible to cover all the information for every type of vehicle.

## Symbols

- Motorway
- Dual carriageway
- Single carriageway
- Surfaced road
- Unsurfaced / gravel road
- Urban area
- Speed limit in kilometres per hour (kph)
- Seat belts
- Children
- Blood alcohol level
- Warning triangle
- First aid kit
- Spare bulb kit
- Fire extinguisher
- Minimum driving age
- Additional documents required
- Mobile phones
- **LEZ** Low Emission Zone
- Dipped headlights
- Winter driving
- ★ Other information

## Andorra (AND)

| | 🚗 | 🚙 | 🚛 | 🏙 |
|---|---|---|---|---|
| | n/a | 90 | 60/90 | 50 |

- Compulsory
- Under 10 and below 150 cm must travel in an EU-approved restraint system adapted to their size in the rear. Airbag must be deactivated if a child is in the front passenger seat.
- 0.05%
- △ Compulsory / Recommended
- Compulsory / Recommended
- 18
- Not permitted whilst driving
- Compulsory for motorcycles during day and for other vehicles during poor daytime visibility.
- Winter tyres or snow chains compulsory in poor conditions or when indicated by signs
- ★ On-the-spot fines imposed
- ★ Visibility vests compulsory

## Austria (A)

| | 🚗 | 🚙 | 🚛 | 🏙 |
|---|---|---|---|---|
| | 130 | 100 | 100 | 50 |
| **If towing trailer under 750kg / over 750 kg** | | | | |
| | 100 | 100 | 100/80 | 50 |

- Compulsory
- Under 14 and under 150cm cannot travel as a front or rear passenger unless they use a suitable child restraint; under 14 over 150cm must wear adult seat belt
- 0.049% • 0.01% if licence held less than 2 years
- △ Compulsory / Compulsory
- Recommended / Recommended
- 18 (16 for motorbikes under 50 cc, 20 for over 50 cc)
- Only allowed with hands-free kit
- **LEZ** LEZ On A12 motorway non-compliant vehicles banned and certain substances banned, night-time speed restrictions; Steermark province has LEZs affecting lorries
- Must be used during the day by all road users. Headlamp converters compulsory
- Winter tyres compulsory 1 Nov–15 Apr
- ★ On-the-spot fines imposed

- ★ Radar detectors and dashboard cameras prohibited
- ★ To drive on motorways or expressways, a motorway sticker must be purchased at the border or main petrol station. These are available for 10 days, 2 months or 1 year. Vehicles 3.5 tonnes or over must display an electronic tag.
- ★ Visibility vests compulsory

## Belarus (BY)

| | 🚗 | 🚙 | 🚛 | 🏙 |
|---|---|---|---|---|
| | 110 | 90 | 90 | 60* |
| **If towing trailer under 750kg** | | | | |
| | 90 | 70 | 70 | |

*In residential areas limit is 20 km/h • Vehicle towing another vehicle 50 kph limit • If full driving licence held for less than two years, must not exceed 70 kph

- Compulsory in front seats, and rear seats if fitted
- Under 12 not allowed in front seat and must use appropriate child restraint
- 0.00%
- △ Compulsory
- Compulsory
- Recommended
- Compulsory
- 18
- Visa, vehicle technical check stamp, international driving permit, green card, health insurance. Even with a green card, local third-party insurance may be imposed at the border
- Use prohibited
- Compulsory during the day Nov–Mar and at all other times in conditions of poor visibility or when towing or being towed.
- Winter tyres compulsory; snow chains recommended
- ★ A temporary vehicle import certificate must be purchased on entry and driver must be registered
- ★ Fees payable for driving on highways
- ★ It is illegal for vehicles to be dirty
- ★ On-the-spot fines imposed
- ★ Radar-detectors prohibited

- Vehicles registered outside Eurasion Economic Union or over 3.5 tons are required to use BelToll device for automatic payment of motorway tolls. See www.beltoll.by/index.php/en/faq/

## Belgium (B)

| | 🚗 | 🚙 | 🚛 | 🏙 |
|---|---|---|---|---|
| | 120* | 120* | 90 | 50** |
| **If towing trailer** | | | | |
| | 90 | 90 | 60 | 50 |
| **Over 3.5 tonnes** | | | | |
| | 90 | 90 | 60 | 50 |

*Minimum speed of 70kph may be applied in certain conditions on motorways and some dual carriageways **Near schools, hospitals and churches the limit may be 30kph

- Compulsory
- All under 19s under 135 cm must wear an appropriate child restraint. Airbags must be deactivated if a rear-facing child seat is used in the front
- 0.049% △ Compulsory
- Recommended / Recommended
- Compulsory / 18
- Only allowed with a hands-free kit
- Mandatory at all times for motorcycles and advised during the day in poor conditions for other vehicles
- ★ Cruise control must be deactivated on motorways where indicated
- ★ On-the-spot fines imposed
- ★ Radar detectors prohibited
- ★ Sticker indicating maximum recommended speed for winter tyres must be displayed on dashboard if using them
- ★ Visibility vest compulsory

## Bosnia and Herzegovina (BIH)

| | 🚗 | 🚙 | 🚛 | 🏙 |
|---|---|---|---|---|
| | 130 | 100 | 80 | 50 |

- Compulsory if fitted
- Under 12s must sit in rear using an appropriate child restraint. Under-2s may travel in a rear-facing child seat in the front only if the airbags have been deactivated.
- 0.03% △ Compulsory
- Compulsory

- Compulsory
- Compulsory for LPG vehicles
- 18
- Visa, International Driving Permit, green card
- Prohibited
- Compulsory for all vehicles at all times
- Winter tyres compulsory 15 Nov–15 Apr; snow chains recommended
- ★ GPS must have fixed speed camera function deactivated; radar detectors prohibited.
- ★ On-the-spot fines imposed
- ★ Visibility vest, tow rope or tow bar compulsory
- ★ Spare wheel compulsory, except for two-wheeled vehicles

## Bulgaria (BG)

| | 🚗 | 🚙 | 🚛 | 🏙 |
|---|---|---|---|---|
| | 130 | 90 | 90 | 50 |
| **If towing trailer** | | | | |
| | 100 | 70 | 70 | 50 |

- Compulsory in front and rear seats
- Under 3s not permitted in vehicles with no child restraints; 3–10 year olds must sit in rear
- 0.05% △ Compulsory
- Compulsory
- Recommended
- Compulsory / 18
- Photo driving licence preferred; a paper licence must be accompanied by an International Driving Permit. Green card or insurance specific to Bulgaria.
- Only allowed with a hands-free kit
- Compulsory
- Snow chains should be carried from 1 Nov–1 Mar.
- ★ Fee at border
- ★ GPS must have fixed speed camera function deactivated; radar detectors prohibited
- ★ On-the-spot fines imposed
- ★ Road tax stickers (annual, monthly or weekly) must be purchased at the border and displayed prominently with the vehicle registration number written on them.
- ★ Visibility vest compulsory

# Croatia (HR)

| ⏱ | 130 | 110 | 90 | 50 |
|---|---|---|---|---|
| **Under 24** | | | | |
| ⏱ | 120 | 100 | 80 | 50 |
| **If towing** | | | | |
| ⏱ | 110 | 80 | 80 | 50 |

- 🚗 Compulsory if fitted
- 👶 Children under 12 not permitted in front seat and must use appropriate child seat or restraint in rear.
- 🍷 0.00% △ Compulsory
- 🔺 Compulsory
- 💡 Compulsory
- 🦺 Recommended
- 🔞 18
- 📇 Green card recommended
- 📞 Only allowed with a hands-free kit
- 💡 Compulsory
- ❄ Snow chains and shovel compulsory in winter
- ★ On-the-spot fines imposed
- ★ Radar detectors prohibited
- ★ Tow bar and rope compulsory
- ★ Visibility vest compulsory

# Czech Republic (CZ)

| ⏱ | 130 | 90 | 90 | 50 |
|---|---|---|---|---|
| **If towing** | | | | |
| ⏱ | 80 | 80 | 80 | 50 |

- 🚗 Compulsory in front seats and, if fitted, in rear
- 👶 Children under 36 kg and 150 cm must use appropriate child restraint. Only front-facing child retraints are permitted in the front in vehicles with airbags fitted. Airbags must be deactivated if a rear-facing child seat is used in the front.
- 🍷 0.00% △ Compulsory
- 💡 Compulsory 🔦 Compulsory
- 🔦 Compulsory
- 🔞 18 (17 for motorcycles under 125 cc)
- 📞 Only allowed with a hands-free kit
- **LEZ** Two-stage LEZ in Prague for vehicles over 3.5 and 6 tonnes. Permit system.
- 💡 Compulsory at all times
- ❄ Winter tyres or snow chains compulsory between Nov and Apr
- ★ GPS must have fixed speed camera function deactivated; radar detectors prohibited
- ★ On-the-spot fines imposed
- ★ Replacement fuses must be carried
- ★ Spectacles or contact lens wearers must carry a spare pair in their vehicle at all times
- ★ Vignette needed for motorway driving, available for 1 year, 60 days, 15 days. Toll specific to lorries introduced 2006, those over 12 tonnes must buy an electronic tag
- ★ Visibility vest compulsory

# Denmark (DK)

| ⏱ | 110-130 | 80-90 | 80 | 50 |
|---|---|---|---|---|
| **If towing** | | | | |
| ⏱ | 80 | 70 | 70 | 50 |

- 🚗 Compulsory front and rear
- 👶 Under 135cm must use appropriate child restraint; in front permitted only in an appropriate rear-facing seat with any airbags disabled.
- 🍷 0.05% △ Compulsory
- 🔺 Recommended 🔦 Recommended
- 🔦 Recommended 🔞 18
- 📞 Only allowed with a hands-free kit
- **LEZ** Aalborg, Arhus, Copenhagen, Frederiksberg and Odense. Proofs of emissions compliance / compliant filter needed to obtain sticker. Non-compliant vehicles banned.
- 💡 Must be used at all times
- ★ On-the-spot fines imposed
- ★ Radar detectors prohibited
- ★ Tolls apply on the Storebaeltsbroen and Oresundsbron bridges.
- ★ Visibility vest recommended

# Estonia (EST)

| ⏱ | n/a | 90* | 90 | 50 |
|---|---|---|---|---|

**If full driving licence held for less than two years**

| ⏱ | 90 | 90 | 90 | 50 |
|---|---|---|---|---|

*In summer, the speed limit on some dual carriageways may be raised to 100/110 kph

- 🚗 Compulsory if fitted
- 👶 Children too small for adult seatbelts must wear a seat restraint appropriate to their size. Rear-facing safety seats must not be used in the front if an air bag is fitted, unless this has been deactivated.
- 🍷 0.00%
- △ 2 compulsory
- 💡 Compulsory
- 🔦 Recommended
- 🔦 Compulsory 🔞 18
- 📞 Only allowed with a hands-free kit
- 💡 Compulsory at all times
- ❄ Winter tyres are compulsory from Dec–Mar. Studded winter tyres are allowed from 15 Oct–31 Mar, but this can be extended to start 1 October and/or end 30 April
- ★ A toll system is in operation in Tallinn
- ★ On-the-spot fines imposed

# Finland (FIN)

| ⏱ | 120 | 100 | 80-100 | 20/50 |
|---|---|---|---|---|
| **Vans, lorries and if towing** | | | | |
| ⏱ | 80 | 80 | 60 | 20/50 |

*100 in summer • If towing a vehicle by rope, cable or rod, max speed limit 60 kph.
- Maximum of 80 kph for vans and lorries
- Speed limits are often lowered in winter

- 🚗 Compulsory in front and rear
- 👶 Below 135 cm must use a child restraint or seat
- 🍷 0.05%
- △ Compulsory
- 🔺 Recommended
- 🔦 Recommended
- 🔦 Recommended
- 🔞 18 (motorbikes below 125cc 16)
- 📞 Only allowed with a hands-free kit
- 💡 Must be used at all times
- ❄ Winter tyres compulsory Dec–Feb
- ★ On-the-spot fines imposed
- ★ Radar-detectors are prohibited
- ★ Visibility vest compulsory

# France (F)

| ⏱ | 130 | 110 | 90 | 50 |
|---|---|---|---|---|

**On wet roads or if full driving licence held for less than 2 years**

| ⏱ | 110 | 100 | 80 | 50 |
|---|---|---|---|---|

**If towing below / above 3.5 tonnes gross**

| ⏱ | 110/90 | 100/90 | 90/80 | 50 |
|---|---|---|---|---|

50kph on all roads if fog reduces visibility to less than 50m • Licence will be lost and driver fined for exceeding speed limit by over 40kph

- 🚗 Compulsory in front seats and, if fitted, in rear
- 👶 In rear, 4 or under must have a child safety seat (rear facing if up to 9 months); if 5–10 must use an appropriate restraint system. Under 10 permitted in the front only if rear seats are fully occupied by other under 10s or there are no rear safety belts. In front, if child is in rear-facing child seat, any airbag must be deactivated.
- 🍷 0.05%. If towing or with less than 2 years with full driving licence, 0.00% • All drivers/motorcyclists must carry 2 unused breathalysers to French certification standards, showing an NF number.
- △ Compulsory
- 💡 Recommended
- 🔦 Recommended
- 🔞 18

- 📱 Use not permitted whilst driving
- **LEZ** An LEZ operates in the Mont Blanc tunnel
- 💡 Compulsory in poor daytime visibility and at all times for motorcycles
- ❄ Winter tyres recommended. Carrying snow chains recommended in winter as these may have to be fitted if driving on snow-covered roads, in accordance with signage.
- ★ GPS must have fixed speed camera function deactivated; radar-detection equipment is prohibited
- ★ It is compulsory to carry a French-authority-recognised (NF) breathalyser.
- ★ On-the-spot fines imposed
- ★ Tolls on motorways. Electronic tag needed if using automatic tolls.
- ★ Visibility vests compulsory except for motorcyclists and passengers, who must have reflective stickers on their helmets (front, back and both sides).

# Germany (D)

| ⏱ | * | * | 100 | 50 |
|---|---|---|---|---|
| **If towing** | | | | |
| ⏱ | 80 | 80 | 80 | 50 |

*no limit, 130 kph recommended

- 🚗 Compulsory
- 👶 Under 150 cm and 12 or under must use an appropriate child seat or restraint. In front if child is in rear-facing child seat, airbags must be deactivated.
- 🍷 0.05% • 0.0% for drivers 21 or under or with less than two years full licence
- △ Compulsory
- 💡 Compulsory
- 🔦 Recommended
- 🔦 Recommended
- 🔞 18 (motorbikes: 16 if under 50cc)
- 📞 Use permitted only with hands-free kit – also applies to drivers of motorbikes and bicycles
- **LEZ** More than 60 cities have or are planning LEZs. Proof of compliance needed to acquire sticker. Non-compliant vehicles banned.
- 💡 Compulsory during poor daytime visibility and tunnels; recommended at other times. Compulsory at all times for motorcyclists.
- ❄ Winter tyres compulsory in all winter weather conditions; snow chains recommended
- ★ GPS must have fixed speed camera function deactivated; radar detectors prohibited
- ★ On-the-spot fines imposed
- ★ Tolls on autobahns for lorries
- ★ Visibility vest compulsory

# Greece (GR)

| ⏱ | 130 | 110 | 90 | 50 |
|---|---|---|---|---|
| **Motorbikes, and if towing** | | | | |
| ⏱ | 90 | 70 | 70 | 40 |

- 🚗 Compulsory in front seats and, if fitted, in rear
- 👶 Under 12 or below 135cm must use appropriate child restraint. In front if child is in rear-facing child seat, any airbags must be deactivated.
- 🍷 0.05% • 0.00% for drivers with less than 2 years' full licence and motorcyclists
- △ Compulsory
- 💡 Compulsory
- 🔦 Recommended
- 🔦 Compulsory
- 🔞 18
- 📱 Not permitted.
- 💡 Compulsory during poor daytime visibility and at all times for motorcycles
- ❄ Snow chains permitted on ice- or snow-covered roads
- ★ On-the-spot fines imposed
- ★ Radar-detection equipment is prohibited
- ★ Tolls on several newer motorways.

# Hungary (H)

| ⏱ | 130 | 110 | 90 | 50 |
|---|---|---|---|---|
| **If towing** | | | | |
| ⏱ | 80 | 70 | 70 | 50 |

- 🚗 Compulsory in front seats and if fitted in rear seats
- 👶 Under 135cm and over 3 must be seated in rear and use appropriate child restraint. Under 3 allowed in front only in rear-facing child seat with any airbags deactivated.
- 🍷 0.00% △ Compulsory
- 💡 Compulsory 🔦 Compulsory
- 🔦 Recommended
- 🔞 17
- 📞 Only allowed with a hands-free kit
- **LEZ** Budapest has vehicle restrictions on days with heavy dust and is planning an LEZ.
- 💡 Compulsory during the day outside built-up areas; compulsory at all times for motorcycles
- ❄ Snow chains compulsory where conditions dictate
- ★ Electronic vignette system in use for tolls on several motorways
- ★ Many motorways are toll and operate electronic vignette system with automatic number plate recognition, tickets are available for 4 days, 7 days, 1 month, 1 year
- ★ On-the-spot fines issued
- ★ Radar detectors prohibited
- ★ Tow rope recommended
- ★ Visibility vest compulsory

# Iceland (IS)

| ⏱ | n/a | 90 | 80 | 50 |
|---|---|---|---|---|

- 🚗 Compulsory in front and rear seats
- 👶 Under 12 or below 150cm not allowed in front seat and must use appropriate child restraint.
- 🍷 0.05%
- △ Compulsory 💡 Compulsory
- 🔦 Compulsory 🔦 Compulsory
- 🔞 18; 21 to drive a hire car; 25 to hire a jeep
- 📞 Only allowed with a hands-free kit
- 💡 Compulsory at all times
- ❄ Winter tyres compulsory c.1 Nov–14 Apr (variable)
- ★ Driving off marked roads is forbidden
- ★ Highland roads are not suitable for ordinary cars
- ★ On-the-spot fines imposed

# Ireland (IRL)

| ⏱ | 120 | 100 | 80 | 50 |
|---|---|---|---|---|
| **If towing** | | | | |
| ⏱ | 80 | 80 | 80 | 50 |

- 🚗 Compulsory where fitted. Driver responsible for ensuring passengers under 17 comply
- 👶 Children 3 and under must be in a suitable child restraint system. Airbags must be deactivated if a rear-facing child seat is used in the front. Those under 150 cm and 36 kg must use appropriate child restraint in cars with seatbelts.
- 🍷 0.05% • 0.02% for novice and professional drivers
- △ Compulsory
- 💡 Recommended
- 🔦 Recommended
- 🔦 Recommended
- 🔞 17 (16 for motorbikes up to 125cc; 18 for over 125cc; 18 for lorries; 21 bus/minibus)
- 📞 Only allowed with a hands-free kit
- 💡 Compulsory for motorbikes at all times and in poor visibility for other vehicles
- ★ Driving is on the left
- ★ GPS must have fixed speed camera function deactivated; radar detectors prohibited
- ★ On-the-spot fines imposed
- ★ Tolls are being introduced on some motorways; the M50 Dublin has barrier-free tolling with number-plate recognition.

## Italy (I)

| ⏱ | 🏛 130 | 🛣 110 | ⚠ 90 | 🏭 50 |
|---|---|---|---|---|
| **If towing** | | | | |
| ⏱ | 80 | 70 | 70 | 50 |
| **Less than three years with full licence** | | | | |
| ⏱ | 100 | 90 | 90 | 50 |
| **When wet** | | | | |
| ⏱ | 100 | 90 | 80 | 50 |

Some motorways with emergency lanes have speed limit of 150 kph

- Compulsory in front seats and, if fitted, in rear
- Under 12 not allowed in front seats except in child safety seat; children under 3 must have special seat in the back. For foreign-registered cars, the country of origin's legislation applies.
- 0.05%, but 0.00% for professional drivers or with less than 3 years full licence
- △ Compulsory
- Recommended
- Compulsory
- Recommended
- 18 (14 for mopeds, 16 up to 125cc, 20 up to 350cc)
- Only allowed with hands-free kit
- **LEZ** Most northern and several southern regions operate seasonal LEZs and many towns and cities have various schemes that restrict access. There is an LEZ in the Mont Blanc tunnel
- Compulsory outside built-up areas, in tunnels, on motorways and dual carriageways and in poor visibility; compulsory at all times for motorcycles
- Snow chains compulsory where signs indicate 15 Oct–15 Apr
- ★ On-the-spot fines imposed
- ★ Radar-detection equipment is prohibited
- ★ Tolls on motorways. Blue lanes accept credit cards; yellow lanes restricted to holders of Telepass pay-toll device.
- ★ Visibility vest compulsory

## Kosovo (RKS)

| ⏱ | 🏛 130 | 🛣 80 | ⚠ 80 | 🏭 50 |
|---|---|---|---|---|

- Compulsory
- Under 12 must sit in rear seats
- 0.03% • 0.00% for professional, business and commercial drivers
- △ Compulsory
- Compulsory
- Compulsory
- Compulsory
- 18 (16 for motorbikes less than 125 cc, 14 for mopeds)
- International driving permit, locally purchased third-party insurance (green card is not recognised), documents with proof of ability to cover costs and valid reason for visiting. Visitors from many non-EU countries require a visa.
- Only allowed with a hands-free kit
- Compulsory at all times
- Winter tyres or snow chains compulsory in poor winter weather conditions

## Latvia (LV)

| ⏱ | 🏛 n/a | 🛣 100 | ⚠ 90 | 🏭 50 |
|---|---|---|---|---|
| **If towing** | | | | |
| ⏱ | n/a | 80 | 80 | 50 |

In residential areas limit is 20kph • If full driving licence held for less than two years, must not exceed 80 kph

- Compulsory in front seats and if fitted in rear
- If under 12 years and 150cm must use child restraint in front and rear seats
- 0.05% • 0.02% with less than 2 years experience
- △ Compulsory
- Compulsory
- Recommended
- Compulsory

## Lithuania (LT)

| ⏱ | 🏛 130 | 🛣 110 | ⚠ 90 | 🏭 50 |
|---|---|---|---|---|
| **If towing** | | | | |
| ⏱ | n/a | 70 | 70 | 50 |

In winter speed limits are reduced by 10–20 km/h

- Compulsory in front seats and if fitted in rear seats
- Under 12 or below 135 cm not allowed in front seats unless in a child safety seat, under 3 must use appropriate child seat and sit in rear
- 0.04% • 0.02% if full licence held less than 2 years
- △ Compulsory Compulsory
- Recommended Compulsory
- 18
- Licences without a photograph must be accompanied by photographic proof of identity, e.g. a passport
- Only allowed with a hands-free kit
- Must be used at all times
- Winter tyres compulsory 10 Nov–1 Apr
- ★ On-the-spot fines imposed
- ★ Visibility vest compulsory

## Luxembourg (L)

| ⏱ | 🏛 130/110 | 🛣 90 | ⚠ 90 | 🏭 50 |
|---|---|---|---|---|
| **If towing** | | | | |
| ⏱ | 90 | 75 | 75 | 50 |

If full driving licence held for less than two years, must not exceed 75 kph • In 20 km/h zones, pedestrians have right of way.

- Compulsory
- Children under 3 must use an appropriate restraint system. Airbags must be disabled if a rear-facing child seat is used in the front. Children 3–18 and/or under 150 cm must use a restraint system appropriate to their size. If over 36kg a seatbelt may be used in the back only
- 0.05% • 0.02% for young drivers, drivers with less than 2 years experience and drivers of taxis and commercial vehicles
- △ Compulsory Compulsory (buses)
- Compulsory 18
- Compulsory (buses, transport of dangerous goods)
- Use permitted only with hands-free kit
- Compulsory for motorcyclists and in poor visibility for other vehicles
- Winter tyres compulsory in winter weather
- ★ On-the-spot fines imposed
- ★ Visibility vest compulsory

## Macedonia (MK)

| ⏱ | 🏛 120 | 🛣 100 | ⚠ 80 | 🏭 50 |
|---|---|---|---|---|
| **Newly qualified drivers or if towing** | | | | |
| ⏱ | 100 | 80 | 80 | 50 |

- Compulsory in front seats and, if fitted, in rear
- Under 12 not allowed in front seats
- 0.05% • 0.00% for business, commercial and professional drivers and with less than 2 years experience
- △ Compulsory Compulsory
- Compulsory 18 (mopeds 16)
- Recommended; compulsory for LPG vehicles
- International driving permit; visa
- Use not permitted whilst driving
- Compulsory at all times
- Winter tyres or snow chains compulsory 15 Nov–15 Mar

## (unlabelled column — continuation)

- 18
- Only allowed with hands-free kit
- Must be used at all times all year round
- Winter tyres compulsory for vehicles up to 3.5 tonnes Dec–Feb, but illegal May–Sept
- ★ On-the-spot fines imposed
- ★ Pedestrians have priority
- ★ Radar-detection equipment prohibited
- ★ Visibility vests compulsory

## (top of column 3)

- ★ GPS must have fixed speed camera function deactivated; radar detectors prohibited
- ★ Novice drivers may only drive between 11pm and 5am if there is someone over 25 with a valid licence in the vehicle.
- ★ On-the-spot fines imposed
- ★ Tolls apply on many roads
- ★ Tow rope compulsory
- ★ Visibility vest must be kept in the passenger compartment and worn to leave the vehicle in the dark outside built-up areas

## Moldova (MD)

| ⏱ | 🏛 90 | 🛣 90 | ⚠ 90 | 🏭 60 |
|---|---|---|---|---|
| **If towing or if licence held under 1 year** | | | | |
| ⏱ | 70 | 70 | 70 | 60 |

- Compulsory in front seats and, if fitted, in rear seats
- Under 12 not allowed in front seats
- 0.00% △ Compulsory
- Compulsory Recommended
- Compulsory
- 18 (mopeds and motorbikes, 16; vehicles with more than eight passenger places, taxis or towing heavy vehicles, 21)
- International Driving Permit (preferred), visa
- Only allowed with hands-free kit
- Must use dipped headlights at all times
- Winter tyres recommended Nov–Feb

## Montenegro (MNE)

| ⏱ | 🏛 n/a | 🛣 100 | ⚠ 80 | 🏭 50 |
|---|---|---|---|---|

80kph speed limit if towing a caravan

- Compulsory in front and rear seats
- Under 12 not allowed in front seats. Under-5s must use an appropriate child seat.
- 0.03 % △ Compulsory
- Compulsory Compulsory
- Compulsory Prohibited
- 18 (16 for motorbikes less than 125cc; 14 for mopeds)
- Must be used at all times
- From mid-Nov to March, driving wheels must be fitted with winter tyres
- ★ An 'eco' tax vignette must be obtained when crossing the border and displayed in the upper right-hand corner of the windscreen
- ★ On-the-spot fines imposed
- ★ Tolls on some primary roads and in the Sozina tunnel between Lake Skadar and the sea
- ★ Visibility vest compulsory

## Netherlands (NL)

| ⏱ | 🏛 130 | 🛣 80/100 | ⚠ 80/100 | 🏭 50 |
|---|---|---|---|---|

- Compulsory
- Under 3 must travel in the back, using an appropriate child restraint; 3–18 and under 135cm must use an appropriate child restraint
- 0.05% • 0.02% with less than 5 years experience or moped riders under 24
- △ Compulsory
- Recommended Recommended
- Recommended 18
- Only allowed with a hands-free kit
- **LEZ** About 20 cities operate or are planning LEZs. A national scheme is planned.
- Recommended in poor visibility and on open roads. Compulsory for motorcycles.
- ★ On-the-spot fines imposed
- ★ Radar-detection equipment is prohibited

## Norway (N)

| ⏱ | 🏛 90/100 | 🛣 80 | ⚠ 80 | 🏭 30/50 |
|---|---|---|---|---|
| **If towing trailer with brakes** | | | | |
| ⏱ | 80 | 80 | 80 | 50 |
| **If towing trailer without brakes** | | | | |
| ⏱ | 60 | 60 | 60 | 50 |

## (column 4 continuation)

- Compulsory in front seats and, if fitted, in rear
- Children less than 150cm tall must use appropriate child restraint. Under 4 must use child safety seat or safety restraint (cot)
- 0.01% △ Compulsory Recommended
- Recommended Recommended
- 18 (heavy vehicles 18/21)
- Only allowed with a hands-free kit
- **LEZ** Planned for Bergen, Oslo and Trondheim
- Must be used at all times
- Winter tyres or summer tyres with snow chains compulsory for snow- or ice-covered roads
- ★ On-the-spot fines imposed
- ★ Radar-detectors are prohibited
- ★ Tolls apply on some bridges, tunnels and access roads into Bergen, Oslo, Trondheim and Stavangar. Several use electronic fee collection only.
- ★ Visibility vest compulsory

## Poland (PL)

| | 🏛 | 🛣 | ⚠ | 🏭 |
|---|---|---|---|---|
| **Motor-vehicle only roads[1], under/over 3.5 tonnes** | | | | |
| ⏱ | 130[2]/80[2] | 110/80 | 100/80 | n/a |
| **Motor-vehicle only roads[1] if towing** | | | | |
| ⏱ | n/a | 80 | 80 | n/a |
| **Other roads, under 3.5 tonnes** | | | | |
| ⏱ | n/a | 100 | 90 | 50/60[3] |
| **Other roads, 3.5 tonnes or over** | | | | |
| ⏱ | n/a | 80 | 70 | 50/60[3] |
| **Other roads, if towing** | | | | |
| ⏱ | n/a | 60 | 60 | 30 |

[1]Indicated by signs with white car on blue background. [2]Minimum speed 40 kph. [3]50 kph 05.00–23.00; 60 kph 23.00–05.00; 20 kph in marked residential areas

- Compulsory in front seats and, if fitted, in rear
- Under 12 and below 150 cm must use an appropriate child restraint. Rear-facing child seats not permitted in vehicles with airbags.
- 0.02% △ Compulsory
- Recommended Recommended
- Compulsory
- 18 (mopeds and motorbikes under 125cc – 16)
- Only allowed with a hands-free kit
- Compulsory for all vehicles
- Snow chains permitted only on roads completely covered in snow
- ★ On-the-spot fines imposed
- ★ Radar-detection equipment is prohibited
- ★ Vehicles over 3.5 tonnes (including cars towing caravans) must have a VIAbox for the electronic toll system
- ★ Visibility vests compulsory for drivers of Polish-registered vehicles

## Portugal (P)

| ⏱ | 🏛 120* | 🛣 90/100 | ⚠ 90 | 🏭 50/20 |
|---|---|---|---|---|
| **If towing** | | | | |
| ⏱ | 100* | 90 | 80 | 50 |

*40kph minimum; 90kph maximum if licence held under 1 year

- Compulsory in front seats and, if fitted, in rear
- Under 12 and below 135cm must travel in the rear in an appropriate child restraint; rear-facing child seats permitted in front only if airbags deactivated
- 0.05% • 0.02% for drivers with less than 3 years with a full licence
- △ Compulsory Recommended
- Recommended Recommended
- 18 (motorcycles under 50cc 17)
- MOT certificate for vehicles over 3 years old, photographic proof of identity (e.g. driving licence or passport) must be carried at all times.
- Only allowed with a hands-free kit
- **LEZ** An LEZ prohibits vehicles without catalytic converters from certain parts of Lisbon. There are plans to extend the scheme city-wide

## Column 1

- Compulsory for motorcycles, compulsory for other vehicles in poor visibility and tunnels
- Visibility vest compulsory
- On-the-spot fines imposed
- Radar-detectors prohibited
- Tolls on motorways; do not use green lanes, these are reserved for auto-payment users. Some motorways require an automatic toll device.
- Wearers of spectacles or contact lenses should carry a spare pair

### Romania (RO)

| | 🏛 | ⛟ | ⚠ | 🏭 |
|---|---|---|---|---|
| **Cars and motorcycles** | | | | |
| ⊙ | 120/130 | 100 | 90 | 50 |
| **Vans** | | | | |
| ⊙ | 110 | 90 | 80 | 40 |
| **Motorcycles** | | | | |
| ⊙ | 100 | 80 | 80 | 50 |

For motor vehicles with trailers or if full driving licence has been held for less than one year, limits are 20kph lower than listed above • Jeep-like vehicles: 70kph outside built-up areas but 50kph in all areas if diesel • Mopeds 45 kph.

- Compulsory
- Under 12s not allowed in front and must use an appropriate restraint in the rear
- 0.00%
- △ Compulsory
- Compulsory ⚷ Compulsory
- Compulsory ⊖ 18
- Only allowed with hands-free kit
- Compulsory outside built-up areas, compulsory everywhere for motorcycles
- Winter tyres compulsory Nov–Mar if roads are snow- or ice-covered, especially in mountainous areas
- Electronic road tax system; price depends on emissions category and length of stay
- Compulsory road tax can be paid at the border, post offices and some petrol stations
- It is illegal for vehicles to be dirty
- On-the-spot fines imposed
- Tolls on motorways
- Visibility vest compulsory

### Russia (RUS)

| | 🏛 | ⛟ | ⚠ | 🏭 |
|---|---|---|---|---|
| ⊙ | 110 | 90 | 90 | 60 |
| **If licence held for under 2 years** | | | | |
| ⊙ | 70 | 70 | 70 | 60 |

- Compulsory if fitted
- Under 12 permitted in front seat only in an appropriate child restraint
- 0.03% △ Compulsory
- Compulsory
- Compulsory
- Compulsory
- ⊖ 18
- International Driving Permit with Russian translation, visa, green card endorsed for Russia, International Certificate for Motor Vehicles
- Only allowed with a hands-free kit
- Compulsory during the day
- On-the-spot fines imposed
- Picking up hitchhikers is prohibited
- Radar detectors/blockers prohibited
- Road tax payable at the border

### Serbia (SRB)

| | 🏛 | ⛟ | ⚠ | 🏭 |
|---|---|---|---|---|
| ⊙ | 120 | 100 | 80 | 60 |

- Compulsory in front and rear seats
- Age 3–12 must be in rear seats and wear seat belt or appropriate child restraint; under 3 in rear-facing child seat permitted in front only if airbag deactivated
- 0.03%, but 0.0% for commercial drivers, motorcyclists, or if full licence held less than 1 year
- △ Compulsory
- Compulsory ⚷ Compulsory
- Compulsory

## Column 2

- 18 (16 for motorbikes less than 125cc; 14 for mopeds)
- International Driving Permit, green card or locally bought third-party insurance
- Compulsory
- Winter tyres compulsory Nov–Apr for vehicles up to 3.5 tonnes. Carrying snow chains recommended in winter as these may have to be fitted if driving on snow-covered roads, in accordance with signage.
- 3-metre tow bar or rope
- 80km/h speed limit if towing a caravan
- Spare tyre compulsory
- On-the-spot fines imposed
- Radar detectors prohibited
- Tolls on motorways and some primary roads
- Visibility vest compulsory

### Slovak Republic (SK)

| | 🏛 | ⛟ | ⚠ | 🏭 |
|---|---|---|---|---|
| ⊙ | 130/90 | 90 | 90 | 50 |

- Compulsory
- Under 12 or below 150cm must be in rear in appropriate child restraint
- 0.0% △ Compulsory
- Compulsory ⚷ Compulsory
- Recommended
- ⊖ 18 (15 for mopeds)
- International driving permit, proof of health insurance
- Only allowed with a hands-free kit
- Compulsory at all times
- Winter tyres compulsory
- On-the-spot fines imposed
- Radar-detection equipment is prohibited
- Tow rope compulsory
- Vignette required for motorways, car valid for 1 year, 30 days, 7 days; lorry vignettes carry a higher charge.
- Visibility vests compulsory

### Slovenia (SLO)

| | 🏛 | ⛟ | ⚠ | 🏭 |
|---|---|---|---|---|
| ⊙ | 130 | 90* | 90* | 50 |
| **If towing** | | | | |
| ⊙ | 80 | 80* | 80* | 50 |

*70kph in urban areas

- Compulsory in front seats and, if fitted, in rear
- Under 12 and below 150cm must use appropriate child restraint; babies must use child safety seat
- 0.05%, but 0.0% for commercial drivers, under 21s or with less than one year with a full licence
- △ Compulsory
- Compulsory ⚷ Compulsory
- Recommended
- ⊖ 18 (motorbikes up to 125cc – 16, up to 350cc – 18)
- Licences without photographs must be accompanied by an International Driving Permit
- Only allowed with hands-free kit
- Must be used at all times
- Visibility vest compulsory
- On-the-spot fines imposed
- Snow chains or winter tyres compulsory mid-Nov to mid-March, and in wintery conditions at other times
- Vignettes valid for variety of periods compulsory for vehicles below 3.5 tonnes for toll roads. Write your vehicle registration number on the vignette before displaying it. For heavier vehicles electronic tolling system applies; several routes are cargo-traffic free during high tourist season.

### Spain (E)

| | 🏛 | ⛟ | ⚠ | 🏭 |
|---|---|---|---|---|
| ⊙ | 120* | 100* | 90 | 50 |
| **If towing** | | | | |
| ⊙ | 80 | 80 | 70 | 50 |

*Urban motorways and dual carriageways 80 kph

## Column 3

- Compulsory in front seats and if fitted in rear seats
- Under 135cm and below 12 must use appropriate child restraint
- 0.05% • 0.03% if less than 2 years full licence or if vehicle is over 3.5 tonnes or carries more than 9 passengers
- △ Two compulsory (one for in front, one for behind)
- Recommended ⚷ Compulsory
- Recommended
- ⊖ 18 (21 for heavy vehicles; 16 for motorbikes up to 125cc)
- Only allowed with hands-free kit
- Compulsory for motorcycles and in poor daytime visibility for other vehicles.
- Snow chains recommended for mountainous areas in winter
- It is recommended that spectacles or contact lens wearers carry a spare pair.
- Radar-detection equipment is prohibited
- Spare tyre compulsory
- Tolls on motorways
- Visibility vest compulsory

### Sweden (S)

| | 🏛 | ⛟ | ⚠ | 🏭 |
|---|---|---|---|---|
| ⊙ | 90–120 | 80 | 70–100 | 30–60 |
| **If towing trailer with brakes** | | | | |
| ⊙ | 80 | 80 | 70 | 50 |

- Compulsory in front and rear seats
- Under 15 or below 135cm must use an appropriate child restraint and may sit in the front only if airbag is deactivated; rear-facing baby seat permitted in front only if airbag deactivated.
- 0.02% △ Compulsory
- Recommended ⚷ Recommended
- Recommended ⊖ 18
- Licences without a photograph must be accompanied by photographic proof of identity, e.g. a passport
- **LEZ** Gothenberg, Helsingborg, Lund, Malmo, Mölndal and Stockholm have LEZs, progressively prohibiting vehicles 6 or more years old.
- Must be used at all times
- 1 Dec–31 Mar winter tyres, anti-freeze and shovel compulsory
- On-the-spot fines imposed
- Radar-detection equipment is prohibited

### Switzerland (CH)

| | 🏛 | ⛟ | ⚠ | 🏭 |
|---|---|---|---|---|
| ⊙ | 120 | 80 | 80 | 50/30 |
| **If towing up to 1 tonne / over 1 tonne** | | | | |
| ⊙ | 80 | 80 | 60/80 | 30/50 |

- Compulsory in front and, if fitted, in rear
- Up to 12 years or below 150 cm must use an appropriate child restraint. Children 6 and under must sit in the rear.
- 0.05%, but 0.0% for commercial drivers or with less than three years with a full licence
- △ Compulsory
- Recommended ⚷ Recommended
- Recommended
- ⊖ 18 (mopeds up to 50cc – 16)
- Only allowed with a hands-free kit
- Compulsory
- Winter tyres recommended Nov–Mar; snow chains compulsory in designated areas in poor winter weather
- GPS must have fixed speed camera function deactivated; radar detectors prohibited
- Motorways are all toll and for vehicles below 3.5 tonnes a vignette must be purchased at the border. The vignette is valid for one calendar year. Vehicles over 3.5 tonnes must have an electronic tag for travel on any road.
- On-the-spot fines imposed
- Pedestrians have right of way
- Picking up hitchhikers is prohibited on motorways and main roads
- Spectacles or contact lens wearers must carry a spare pair in their vehicle at all times

## Column 4

### Turkey (TR)

| | 🏛 | ⛟ | ⚠ | 🏭 |
|---|---|---|---|---|
| ⊙ | 120 | 90 | 90 | 50 |
| **If towing** | | | | |
| ⊙ | 80 | 80 | 80 | 40 |

- Compulsory if fitted
- Under 150 cm and below 36kg must use suitable child restraint. If above 136 cm may sit in the back without child restraint. Under 3s can only travel in the front in a rear facing seat if the airbag is deactivated. Children 3–12 may not travel in the front seat.
- 0.00%
- △ Two compulsory (one in front, one behind)
- Compulsory ⚷ Compulsory
- Compulsory ⊖ 18
- International driving permit advised, and required for use with licences without photographs; note that Turkey is in both Europe and Asia, green card/UK insurance that covers whole of Turkey or locally bought insurance, e-visa obtained in advance.
- Prohibited
- Compulsory in daylight hours
- Spare tyre compulsory
- On-the-spot fines imposed
- Several motorways, and the Bosphorus bridges are toll roads
- Tow rope and tool kit must be carried

### Ukraine (UA)

| | 🏛 | ⛟ | ⚠ | 🏭 |
|---|---|---|---|---|
| ⊙ | 130 | 110 | 90 | 60 |
| **If towing** | | | | |
| ⊙ | 80 | 80 | 80 | 60 |

Speed limit in pedestrian zone 20 kph

- Compulsory in front and rear seats
- Under 12 and below 145cm must use an appropriate child restraint and sit in rear
- 0.02% – if use of medication can be proved. Otherwise 0.00%
- △ Compulsory
- Compulsory ⚷ Optional
- Compulsory ⊖ 18
- International Driving Permit, visa, International Certificate for Motor Vehicles, green card
- No legislation
- Compulsory in poor daytime and from Oct–Apr
- Winter tyres compulsory Nov–Apr in snowy conditions
- Road tax is payable on entry to the country.
- On-the-spot fines imposed
- Tow rope and tool kit recommended

### United Kingdom (GB)

| | 🏛 | ⛟ | ⚠ | 🏭 |
|---|---|---|---|---|
| ⊙ | 112 | 112 | 96 | 48 |
| **If towing** | | | | |
| ⊙ | 96 | 96 | 80 | 48 |

- Compulsory in front seats and if fitted in rear seats
- Under 3 not allowed in front seats except with appropriate restraint, and in rear must use child restraint if available; in front 3–12 or under 135cm must use appropriate child restraint, in rear must use appropriate child restraint (or seat belt if no child restraint is available, e.g. because two occupied restraints prevent fitting of a third).
- 0.08% (England, Northern Ireland, Wales), 0.05% (Scotland)
- △ Recommended
- Recommended ⚷ Recommended
- Recommended ⊖ 17 (16 for mopeds)
- Only allowed with hands-free kit
- **LEZ** London's LEZ operates by number-plate recognition; non-compliant vehicles face hefty daily charges. Foreign-registered vehicles must register.
- Driving is on the left
- On-the-spot fines imposed
- Smoking is banned in all commercial vehicles
- Some toll motorways and bridges

# Ski resorts

The resorts listed are popular ski centres, therefore road access to most is normally good and supported by road clearing during snow falls. However, mountain driving is never predictable and drivers should make sure they take suitable snow chains as well as emergency provisions and clothing. Listed for each resort are: the atlas page and grid square; the resort/minimum piste altitude (where only one figure is shown, they are at the same height) and maximum altitude of its own lifts; the number of lifts and gondolas (the total for lift-linked resorts); the season start and end dates (snow cover allowing); whether snow is augmented by cannon; the nearest town (with its distance in km) and, where available, the website and/or telephone number of the local tourist information centre or ski centre ('00' prefix required for calls from the UK).

The ❄ symbol indicates resorts with snow cannon

## Andorra
### Pyrenees
**Pas de la Casa / Grau Roig 146 B2** ❄
2050–2640m • 77 lifts • Dec–Apr • Andorra La Vella (30km) 🖳 www.pasdelacasa-andorra.com • *Access via Envalira Pass (2407m), highest in Pyrenees, snow chains essential.*

## Austria
### Alps
**Bad Gastein 109 B4** ❄ 1050/1100–2700m • 50 lifts • Dec–Mar • St Johann im Pongau (45km) 🛈 +43 6432 3393 0 🖳 www.gastein.com

**Bad Hofgastein 109 B4** ❄ 860–2295m • 50 lifts • Dec–Mar • St Johann im Pongau (40km) 🛈 +43 6432 3393 0 🖳 www.gastein.com/en/region-orte/bad-hofgastein

**Bad Kleinkirchheim 109 C4** ❄ 1070–2310m • 27 lifts • Dec–Mar • Villach (35km) 🛈 +43 4240 8212 🖳 www.badkleinkirchheim.at

**Ehrwald 108 B1** ❄ 1000–2965m • 24 lifts • Dec–Apr • Imst (30km) 🛈 +43 5673 2395 🖳 www.wetterstein-bahnen.at/en

**Innsbruck 108 B2** ❄ 574/850–3200m • 59 lifts • Dec–Apr • Innsbruck 🛈 +43 512 56 2000 🖳 www.innsbruck-pauschalen.com • *Motorway normally clear. The motorway through to Italy and through the Arlberg Tunnel are both toll roads.*

**Ischgl 107 B5** ❄ 1340/1380–2900m • 101 lifts • Dec–May • Landeck (25km) 🛈 +43 50990 100 🖳 www.ischgl.com • *Car entry to resort prohibited between 2200hrs and 0600hrs.*

**Kaprun 109 B3** ❄ 885/770–3030m • 53 lifts • Nov–Apr • Zell am See (10km) 🛈 +43 6542 770 🖳 www.zellsee-kaprun.com

**Kirchberg in Tirol 109 B3** 860–2000m • 60 lifts • Nov–Apr • Kitzbühel (6km) 🖳 www.kitzbueheler-alpen.com/en 🛈 +43 57507 2000 • *Easily reached from Munich International Airport (120 km)*

**Kitzbühel (Brixen im Thale) 109 B3** ❄ 800/1210–2000m • 12 lifts • Dec–Apr • Wörgl (40km) 🛈 +43 57057 2200 🖳 www.kitzbueheler-alpen.com/en

**Lech/Oberlech 107 B5** ❄ 1450–2810m • 97 lifts • Dec–Apr • Bludenz (50km) 🛈 +43 5583 2161 0 🖳 www.lechzuers.com • *Roads normally cleared but keep chains accessible because of altitude.*

**Mayrhofen 108 B2** ❄ 630–2500m • 30 lifts • Dec–Apr • Jenbach (35km) 🛈 +43 5285 6760 🖳 www.mayrhofen.at • *Chains rarely required.*

**Obertauern 109 B4** ❄ 1740/1640–2350m • 26 lifts • Dec–Apr • Radstadt (20km) 🛈 +43 6456 7252 🖳 www.obertauern.com • *Roads normally cleared but chain accessibility recommended. Camper vans and caravans not allowed; park these in Radstadt*

**Saalbach Hinterglemm 109 B3** ❄ 1030/1100–2100m • 70 lifts • Nov–Apr • Zell am See (19km) 🛈 +43 6541 6800-68 🖳 www.saalbach.com • *Both village centres are pedestrianised and there is a good ski bus service during the daytime*

**St Anton am Arlberg 107 B5** ❄ 1300–2810m • 94 lifts • Dec–Apr • Innsbruck (104km) 🖳 www.stantonamarlberg.com 🛈 +43 5446 22690

**Schladming 109 B4** ❄ 745–1900m • 65 lifts • Dec–Mar • Schladming 🛈 +43 36 87 233 10 🖳 www.schladming-dachstein.at

**Serfaus 108 B1** ❄ 1427/1200–2820m • 67 lifts • Dec–Apr • Landeck (30km) 🛈 +43 5476 6239 🖳 www.serfaus-fiss-ladis.at • *Private vehicles banned from village. Use Dorfbahn Serfaus, an underground funicular which runs on an air cushion.*

**Sölden 108 C2** ❄ 1380–3250m, • 33 lifts • Sep–Apr (glacier); Nov–Apr (main area) • Imst (50km) 🛈 +43 57200 200 🖳 www.soelden.com • *Roads normally cleared but snow chains recommended because of altitude. The route from Italy and the south over the Timmelsjoch via Obergurgl is closed Oct–May and anyone arriving from the south should use the Brenner Pass motorway.*

**Zell am See 109 B3** ❄ 750–1950m • 53 lifts • Dec–Mar • Zell am See 🛈 +43 6542 770 🖳 www.zellamsee-kaprun.com • *Low altitude, so good access and no mountain passes to cross.*

**Zell im Zillertal (Zell am Ziller) 109 B3** ❄ 580/930–2410m • 22 lifts • Dec–Apr • Jenbach (25km) 🛈 +43 5282 7165–226 🖳 www.zillertalarena.com

**Zürs 107 B5** ❄ 1720/1700–2450m • 97 lifts • Dec–Apr • Bludenz (30km) 🛈 +43 5583 2245 🖳 www.lech-zuers.at • *Roads normally cleared but keep chains accessible because of altitude. Village has garage with 24-hour self-service gas/petrol, breakdown service and wheel chains supply.*

## France
### Alps
**Alpe d'Huez 118 B3** ❄ 1860–3330m • 85 lifts • Dec–Apr • Grenoble (63km) 🖳 www.alpedhuez.com • *Snow chains may be required on access road to resort.*

**Avoriaz 118 A3** ❄ 1800/1100–2280m • 35 lifts • Dec–May • Morzine (14km) 🛈 +33 4 50 74 72 72 🖳 www.morzine-avoriaz.com • *Chains may be required for access road from Morzine. Car-free resort, park on edge of village. Horse-drawn sleigh service available.*

**Chamonix-Mont-Blanc 119 B3** ❄ 49 lifts • 1035–3840m • Dec–Apr • Martigny (38km) 🛈 +33 4 50 53 75 50 🖳 www.chamonix.com

**Chamrousse 118 B2** ❄ 1700–2250m • 26 lifts • Dec–Apr • Grenoble (30km) 🖳 www.chamrousse.com • *Roads normally cleared, keep chains accessible because of altitude.*

**Châtel 119 A3** ❄ 1200/1110–2200m • 41 lifts • Dec–Apr • Thonon-Les-Bains (35km) 🛈 +33 4 50 73 22 44 🖳 http://info.chatel.com/english-version.html

**Courchevel 118 B3** ❄ 1750/1300–2470m • 67 lifts • Dec–Apr • Moûtiers (23km) 🖳 www.courchevel.com • *Roads normally cleared but keep chains accessible. Traffic 'discouraged' within the four resort bases.*

**Flaine 118 A3** ❄ 1600–2500m • 26 lifts • Dec–Apr • Cluses (25km) 🛈 +33 4 50 90 80 01 🖳 www.flaine.com • *Keep chains accessible for D6 from Cluses to Flaine. Car access for depositing luggage and passengers only. 1500-space car park outside resort. Near Sixt-Fer-á-Cheval.*

**La Clusaz 118 B3** ❄ 1100–2600m • 55 lifts • Dec–Apr • Annecy (32km) 🛈 +33 4 50 32 65 00 🖳 www.laclusaz.com • *Roads normally clear but keep chains accessible for final road from Annecy.*

**La Plagne 118 B3** ❄ 2500/1250–3250m • 109 lifts • Dec–Apr Moûtiers (32km) 🛈 +33 4 79 09 79 79 🖳 www.la-plagne.com • *Ten different centres up to 2100m altitude. Road access via Bozel, Landry or Aime normally cleared. Linked to Les Arcs by cablecar.*

**Les Arcs 119 B3** ❄ 1600/1200–3230m • 77 lifts • Dec–May • Bourg-St-Maurice (15km) 🛈 +33 4 79 07 12 57 🖳 www.lesarcs.com • *Four base areas up to 2000 metres; keep chains accessible. Pay parking at edge of each base resort. Linked to La Plagne by cablecar*

**Les Carroz d'Araches 118 A3** ❄ 1140–2500m • 80 lifts • Dec–Apr • Cluses (13km) 🛈 +33 4 50 90 00 04 🖳 www.lescarroz.com

**Les Deux-Alpes 118 C3** ❄ 1650/1300–3600m • 55 lifts • Dec–Apr • Grenoble (75km) 🛈 +33 4 76 79 22 00 🖳 www.les2alpes.com • *Roads normally cleared, however snow chains recommended for D213 up from valley road (D1091).*

**Les Gets 118 A3** ❄ 1170/1000–2000m • 52 lifts • Dec–Apr • Cluses (18km) 🖳 www.lesgets.com

**Les Ménuires 118 B3** ❄ 1815/1850–3200m • 40 lifts • Dec–Apr • Moûtiers (27km) 🖳 www.lesmenuires.com • *Keep chains accessible for D117 from Moûtiers.*

**Les Sept Laux Prapoutel 118 B3** ❄ 24 lifts • 1350–2400m, • Dec–Apr • Grenoble (38km) 🖳 www.les7laux.com • *Roads normally cleared, however keep chains accessible for mountain road up from the A41 motorway. Near St Sorlin d'Arves.*

**Megève 118 B3** ❄ 1100/1050–2350m • 79 lifts • Dec–Apr • Sallanches (12km) 🛈 +33 4 50 21 27 28 🖳 www.megeve.com • *Horse-drawn sleigh rides available.*

**Méribel 118 B3** ❄ 1400/1100–2950m • 61 lifts • Dec–May • Moûtiers (18km) 🛈 +33 4 79 08 60 01 🖳 www.meribel.net • *Keep chains accessible for 18km to resort on D90 from Moûtiers.*

**Morzine 118 A3** ❄ 1000–2460m • 67 lifts, • Dec–Apr • Thonon-Les-Bains (30km) 🛈 +33 4 50 74 72 72 🖳 www.morzine-avoriaz.com

**Pra Loup 132 A2** ❄ 1600/1500–2500m • 53 lifts • Dec–Apr • Barcelonnette (10km) 🛈 +33 4 92 84 10 04 🖳 www.praloup.com • *Roads normally cleared but chains accessibility recommended.*

**Risoul 118 C3** ❄ 1850/1650–2750m • 59 lifts • Dec–Apr • Briançon (40km) 🛈 +33 4 92 46 02 60 🖳 www.risoul.com • *Keep chains accessible. Near Guillestre. Linked with Vars Les Claux.*

**St-Gervais Mont-Blanc 118 B3** ❄ 850/1150–2350m • 27 lifts • Dec–Apr • Sallanches (10km) 🛈 +33 4 50 47 76 08 🖳 www.st-gervais.com

**Serre Chevalier 118 C3** ❄ 1350/1200–2800m • 77 lifts • Dec–Apr • Briançon (10km) 🛈 +33 4 92 24 98 98 🖳 www.serre-chevalier.com • *Made up of 13 small villages along the valley road, which is normally cleared.*

**Tignes 119 B3** ❄ 2100/1550–3450m • 87 lifts • Jan–Dec • Bourg St Maurice (26km) 🛈 +33 4 79 40 04 40 🖳 www.tignes.net • *Keep chains accessible because of altitude.*

**Val d'Isère 119 B3** ❄ 1850/1550–3450m • 87 lifts • Dec–Apr • Bourg-St-Maurice (30km) 🛈 +33 4 79 06 06 60 🖳 www.valdisere.com • *Roads normally cleared but keep chains accessible.*

Background photo: Schladming ski resort, Austria
nikolpetr / Shutterstock

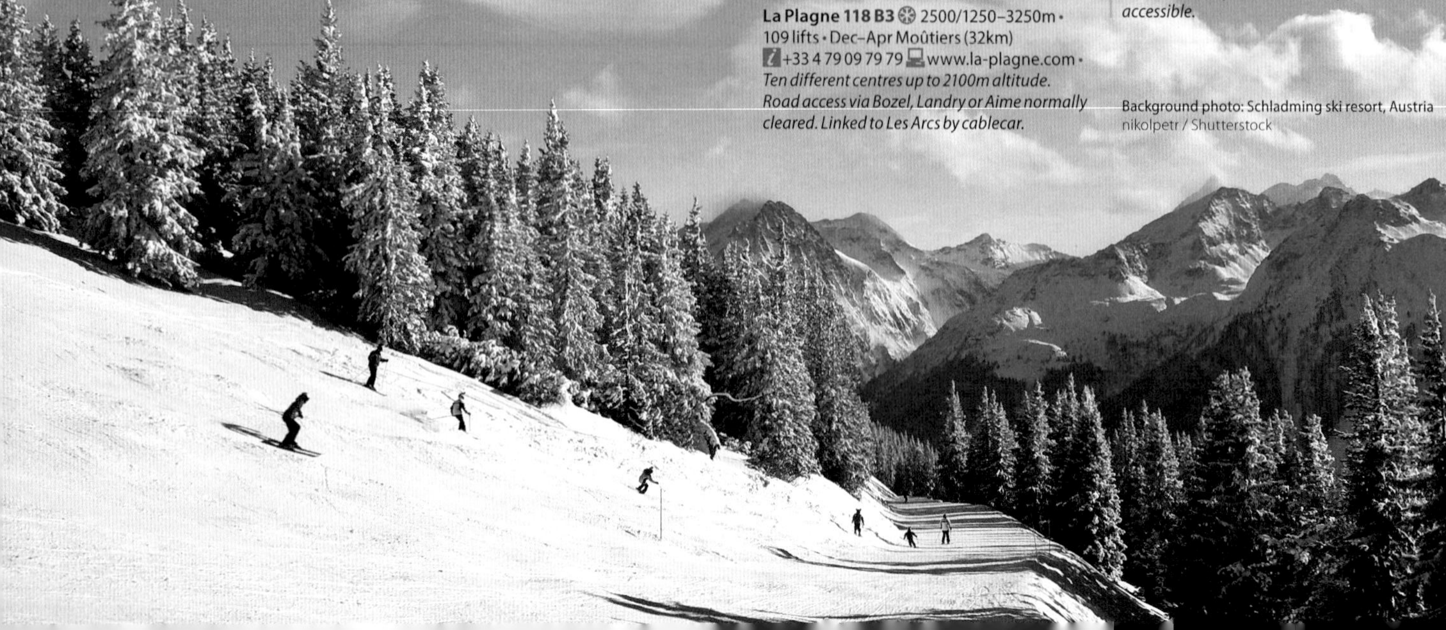

**Val Thorens 118 B3** 2300/1850–3200m • 29 lifts • Dec–Apr • Moûtiers (37km) www.valthorens.com • *Chains essential – highest ski resort in Europe. Obligatory paid parking on edge of resort.*

**Valloire 118 B3** 1430–2600m • 34 lifts • Dec–Apr • Modane (20km) +33 4 79 59 03 96 www.valloire.net • *Road normally clear up to the Col du Galbier, to the south of the resort, which is closed from 1st November to 1st June. Linked to Valmeinier.*

**Valmeinier 118 B3** 1500–2600m • 34 lifts • Dec–Apr • St Michel de Maurienne (47km) +33 4 79 59 53 69 www.valmeinier.com • *Access from north on D1006 / D902. Col du Galbier, to the south of the resort closed from 1st November to 1st June. Linked to Valloire.*

**Valmorel 118 B3** 1400–2550m • 90 lifts • Dec–Apr • Moûtiers (15km) +33 4 79 09 85 55 www.valmorel.com • *Near St Jean-de-Belleville. Linked with ski areas of Doucy-Combelouvière and St François-Longchamp.*

**Vars Les Claux 118 C3** 1850/1650–2750m • 59 lifts • Dec–Apr • Briançon (40km) +33 4 92 46 51 31 www.vars-ski.com • *Four base resorts up to 1850 metres. Keep chains accessible. Linked with Risoul.*

**Villard de Lans 118 B2** 1050/1160–2170m • 28 lifts • Dec–Apr • Grenoble (32km) +33 4 76 95 10 38 www.villarddelans.com

### Pyrenees

**Font-Romeu 146 B3** 1800/1600–2200m • 25 lifts • Nov–Apr • Perpignan (87km) +33 4 68 30 68 30 www.font-romeu.fr • *Roads normally cleared but keep chains accessible.*

**Saint-Lary Soulan 145 B4** Dec–Mar • 830/1650/1700–2515m • 31 lifts • Tarbes (75km) +33 5 62 39 50 81 www.saintlary.com • *Access roads constantly cleared of snow.*

### Vosges

**La Bresse-Hohneck 106 A1** 500/900–1350m • 33 lifts • Dec–Mar • Cornimont (6km) +33 3 29 25 41 29 www.labresse.net

## Germany

### Alps

**Garmisch-Partenkirchen 108 B2** 700–2830m • 38 lifts • Dec–Apr • Munich (95km) +49 8821 180 700 www.gapa.de • *Roads usually clear, chains rarely needed.*

**Oberaudorf 108 B3** 480–1850m • 30 lifts • Dec–Apr • Kufstein (15km) www.oberaudorf.de • *Motorway normally kept clear. Near Bayrischzell.*

**Oberstdorf 107 B5** 815m • 26 lifts • Dec–Apr • Sonthofen (15km) +49 8322 7000 http://oberstdorf.de

### Rothaargebirge

**Winterberg 81 A4** 700/620–830m • 19 lifts • Dec–Mar • Brilon (30km) +49 2981 925 00 www.winterberg.de • *Roads usually cleared, chains rarely required.*

## Greece

### Central Greece

**Mount Parnassos: Kelaria-Fterolakka 182 E4** 1640–2260m • 17 lifts • Dec–Apr • Amfiklia +30 22340 22694-5 www.parnassos-ski.gr

**Mount Parnassos: Gerondovrahos 182 E4** 1800–1900m • 3 lifts • Dec–Apr • Amfiklia +30 29444 70371

### Peloponnisos

**Mount Helmos: Kalavrita Ski Centre 184 A3** 1650–2100m • 5 lifts • Dec–Mar • Kalavrita +30 26920 2261 www.kalavrita-ski.gr

**Mount Menalo: Ostrakina 184 B3** 1500–1600m • 4 lifts • Dec–Mar • Tripoli +30 27960 22227

### Macedonia

**Mount Falakro: Agio Pneuma 183 B6** 1720/1620–2230m • 9 lifts • Dec–Apr • Drama + 30 25210 23691 www.falakro.gr (Greek only)

**Mount Vasilitsa: Vasilitsa 182 C3** 1750/1800–2113m • 8 lifts • Dec–Mar • Konitsa + 30 24620 26100 www.vasilitsa.com (Greek only)

**Mount Vermio: Seli 182 C4** 1500–1900m • 11 lifts • Dec–Mar • Kozani + 30 23320 71234 www.seli-ski.gr (in Greek)

**Mount Vermio: Tria-Pente Pigadia 182 C3** 1420–2005m • 7 lifts • Dec–Mar • Ptolemaida +30 23320 44464

**Mount Verno: Vigla 182 C3** 1650–1900m • 5 lifts • Dec–Mar • Florina +30 23850 22354 www.vigla-ski.gr (in Greek)

**Mount Vrondous: Lailias 183 B5** 1600–1850m • 3 lifts • Dec–Mar • Serres +30 23210 53790

### Thessalia

**Mount Pilio: Agriolefkes 183 D5** 1300–1500m • 4 lifts • Dec–Mar • Volos +30 24280 73719

## Italy

### Alps

**Bardonecchia 118 B3** 1312–2750m • 21 lifts • Dec–Apr • Bardonecchia + 39 122 99032 www.bardonecchiaski.com • *Resort reached through the 11km Frejus tunnel from France, roads normally cleared.*

**Bórmio 107 C5** 1200/1230–3020m • 24 lifts • Dec–Apr • Tirano (40km) www.bormio.com • *Tolls payable in Ponte del Gallo Tunnel, open 0800hrs–2000hrs.*

**Breuil-Cervinia 119 B4** 2050–3500m • 21 lifts • Jan–Dec • Aosta (54km) +39 166 944311 www.cervinia.it • *Snow chains strongly recommended. Bus from Milan airport.*

**Courmayeur 119 B3** 1200–2760m • 21 lifts • Dec–Apr • Aosta (40km) +39 165 841612 www.courmayeurmontblanc.it • *Access through the Mont Blanc tunnel from France. Roads constantly cleared.*

**Limone Piemonte 133 A3** 1000/1050–2050m • 29 lifts • Dec–Apr • Cuneo (27km) + 39 171 925281 www.limonepiemonte.it • *Roads normally cleared, chains rarely required.*

**Livigno 107 C5** 1800–3000m • 31 lifts • Nov–May • Zernez (CH) (27km) +39 342 052200 www.livigno.com • *Keep chains accessible. The direction of traffic through Munt la Schera Tunnel to/from Zernez is regulated on Saturdays. Check in advance.*

**Sestrière 119 C3** 2035/1840–2840m • 92 lifts • Dec–Apr • Oulx (22km) +39 122 755444 www.visitsestriere.com • *One of Europe's highest resorts; although roads are normally cleared keep chains accessible.*

### Appennines

**Roccaraso – Aremogna 169 B4** 1285/1240–2140m • 24 lifts • Dec–Apr • Castel di Sangro (7km) +39 864 62210 www.roccaraso.net (in Italian)

### Dolomites

**Andalo – Fai della Paganella 121 A3** 1042/1050/2125m • 19 lifts • Dec–Apr • Trento (40km) www.visitdolomitipaganella.it +39 461 585836

**Arabba 108 C2** 1600/1450–2950m • 29 lifts • Dec–Mar • Brunico (45km) +39 436 780019 www.arabba.it • *Roads normally cleared but keep chains accessible.*

**Cortina d'Ampezzo 108 C3** 1224/1050–2930m • 37 lifts • Dec–Apr • Belluno (72km) www.cortina.dolomiti.org • +39 436 869086 • *Access from north on route 51 over the Cimabanche Pass may require chains.*

**Corvara (Alta Badia) 108 C2** 1568–2500m • 56 lifts • Dec–Apr • Brunico (38km) +39 471 836176 www.altabadia.it • *Roads normally clear but keep chains accessible.*

**Madonna di Campiglio 121 A3** 1550/1500–2600m • 72 lifts • Dec–Apr • Trento (60km) +39 465 447501 www.campigliodolomiti.it/homepage • *Roads normally cleared but keep chains accessible. Linked to Folgarida and Marilleva.*

**Moena di Fassa (Sorte/Ronchi) 108 C2** 1184/1450–2520m • 8 lifts • Dec–Apr • Bolzano (40km) +39 462 609770 www.fassa.com

**Selva di Val Gardena/Wolkenstein Groden 108 C2** 1563/1570–2450m • 81 lifts • Dec–Apr • Bolzano (40km) +39 471 777777 www.valgardena.it • *Roads normally cleared but keep chains accessible.*

## Norway

**Hemsedal 47 B5** 700/640–1450m • 24 lifts • Nov–May • Honefoss (150km) +47 32 055030 www.hemsedal.com • *Be prepared for extreme weather conditions.*

## Slovak Republic

**Chopok (Jasna-Chopok) 99 C3** 900/950–1840m • 17 lifts • Dec–Apr • Jasna +421 907 886644 www.jasna.sk (in Slovak only)

**Donovaly 99 C3** 913–1360m • 17 lifts • Nov–Apr • Ruzomberok +421 48 4199900 www.parksnow.sk/zima

**Martinské Hole 98 B2** 1250/1150–1456m • 8 lifts • Nov–May • Zilina +421 43 430 6000 www.martinky.com

**Plejsy 99 C4** 470–912m • 9 lifts • Dec–Mar • Krompachy +421 53 429 8015 www.plejsy.sk

**Strbske Pleso 99 B4** 1380–1825m • 7 lifts • Dec–Mar • Poprad +421 917 682 260 www.vt.sk (in Slovak only)

## Slovenia

### Julijske Alpe

**Kanin (Bovec) 122 A2** 460/1600–2389m • 12 lifts • Dec–Apr • Bovec +386 5 384 1919 www.boveckanin.si

**Kobla (Bohinj) 122 A2** 512/530–1495m • 6 lifts • Dec–Mar • Bohinjska Bistrica +386 4 5747 100 www.bohinj.si/kobla/en/naprave.html

**Kranjska Gora 122 A2** 800–1210m • 19 lifts • Dec–Mar • Kranjska Gora +386 4 5809 440 www.kranjska-gora.si

**Vogel 122 A2** 570–1800m • 8 lifts • Dec–Apr • Bohinjska Bistrica +386 4 5729 712 www.vogel.si

### Kawiniške Savinjske Alpe

**Krvavec 122 A3** 1450–1970m • 10 lifts • Dec–Apr • Kranj 386 4 25 25 911 www.rtc-krvavec.si

### Pohorje

**Rogla 123 A4** 1517/1050–1500m • 13 lifts • Dec–Apr • Slovenska Bistrica +386 3 75 77 100 www.rogla.eu

## Spain

### Pyrenees

**Baqueira-Beret/Bonaigua 145 B4** 1500–2500m • 33 lifts • Dec–Apr • Vielha (15km) +34 902 415 415 www.baqueira.es • *Roads normally clear but keep chains accessible. Near Salardú.*

### Sistema Penibetico

**Sierra Nevada 163 A4** 2100–3300m • 24 lifts • Dec–May • Granada (32km) +34 902 70 80 90 http://sierranevada.es • *Access road designed to be avalanche safe and is snow cleared.*

## Sweden

**Idre Fjäll 199 D9** 590–890m • 33 lifts • Nov–Apr • Mora (140km) +46 253 41000 www.idrefjall.se • *Be prepared for extreme weather conditions.*

**Sälen 49 A5** 360m • 15 lifts • Nov–Apr • Malung (70km) +46 771 84 00 00 www.skistar.com/salen • *Be prepared for extreme weather conditions.*

## Switzerland

### Alps

**Adelboden 106 C2** 1353m • 55 lifts • Dec–Apr • Frutigen (15km) +41 33 673 80 80 www.adelboden.ch • *Linked with Lenk.*

**Arosa 107 C4** 1800m • 16 lifts • Dec–Apr • Chur (30km) +41 81 378 70 20 www.arosa.ch (German only) • *Roads cleared but keep chains accessible due to high altitude.*

**Crans Montana 119 A4** 1500–3000m • 34 lifts • Dec–Apr, Jul–Oct • Sierre (15km) www.crans-montana.ch • *Roads normally cleared but keep chains accessible for ascent from Sierre.*

**Davos 107 C4** 1560/1100–2840m • 55 lifts • Nov–Apr • Davos. Linked with Klosters +41 81 415 21 21 www.davos.ch

**Engelberg 106 C3** 1000/1050–3020m • 26 lifts • Nov–May • Luzern (39km) +41 41 639 77 77 www.engelberg.ch • *Straight access road normally cleared.*

**Flums (Flumserberg) 107 B4** 1400/1000–2220m • 17 lifts • Dec–Apr • Buchs (25km) +41 81 720 18 18 www.flumserberg.ch • *Roads normally cleared, but 1000-metre vertical ascent; keep chains accessible.*

**Grindelwald 106 C3** 1050–2950m • 20 lifts • Dec–Apr • Interlaken (20km) +41 33 854 12 50 www.jungfrauregion.ch

**Gstaad – Saanenland 106 C2** 1050/950–3000m • 74 lifts • Dec–Apr • Gstaad +41 33 748 81 81 www.gstaad.ch • *Linked to Anzère.*

**Klosters 107 C4** 1191/1110–2840m • 55 lifts • Dec–Apr • Davos (10km). Linked with Davos +41 81 410 20 20 www.davos.ch/klosters • *Roads normally clear but keep chains accessible.*

**Leysin 119 A4** 2263/1260–2330m • 16 lifts • Dec–Apr • Aigle (6km) +41 24 493 33 00 www.leysin.ch

**Mürren 106 C2** 1650–2970m • 12 lifts • Dec–Apr • Interlaken (18km) +41 33 856 86 86 www.mymuerren.ch • *No road access. Park in Strechelberg (1500 free places) and take the two-stage cable car.*

**Nendaz 119 A4** 1365/1400–3300m • 20 lifts • Nov–Apr • Sion (16km) +41 27 289 55 89 www.nendaz.ch • *Roads normally cleared, however keep chains accessible for ascent from Sion. Near Vex.*

**Saas-Fee 119 A4** 1800–3500m • 23 lifts • Jan–Dec • Brig (35km) +41 27 958 18 58 http://old.saas-fee.ch/en/ • *Roads normally cleared but keep chains accessible because of altitude.*

**St Moritz 107 C4** 1856/1730–3300m • 24 lifts • Nov–May • Chur (89km) +41 81 837 33 33 www.stmoritz.ch • *Roads normally clear but keep chains accessible.*

**Samnaun 107 C5** 1846/1400–2900m • 40 lifts • Dec–May • Scuol (30km) +41 81 861 88 30 www.engadin.com • *Roads normally clear but keep chains accessible.*

**Verbier 119 A4** 1500–3330m • 17 lifts • Nov–Apr • Martigny (27km) +41 27 775 38 70 www.verbier.ch • *Roads normally cleared.*

**Villars-Gryon 119 A4** 1253/1200–2100m • 16 lifts • Dec–Apr, Jun–Jul • Montreux (35km) +41 24 495 32 32 www.villars.ch • *Roads normally cleared but keep chains accessible for ascent from N9. Near Bex.*

**Wengen 106 C2** 1270–2320m • Dec–Apr • 19 lifts • Interlaken (12km) +41 33 856 85 85 http://wengen.ch • *No road access. Park at Lauterbrunnen and take mountain railway.*

**Zermatt 119 A4** 1620–3900m • 40 lifts, • all year • Brig (42km) +41 27 966 81 00 www.zermatt.ch • *Cars not permitted in resort, park in Täsch (3km) and take shuttle train.*

## Turkey

### North Anatolian Mountains

**Uludag 186 B4** 1770–2320m • 15 lifts • Dec–Mar • Bursa (36km) +90 224 285 21 11 http://skiingturkey.com/resorts/uludag.html

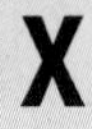

# 300 greatest sights of Europe

For entries with no website listed, use that given for the national tourist board.

## Albania Shqipëria
www.albania.al

### Berat
Fascinating old town with picturesque Ottoman Empire buildings and traditional Balkan domestic architecture.
www.albania.al/region/berat 182 C1

### Tirana Tiranë
Capital of Albania. Skanderbeg Square has main historic buildings. Also: 18c Haxhi Ethem Bey Mosque; Art Gallery (Albanian); National Museum of History. Nearby: medieval Krujë; Roman monuments.
www.albania.al/region/tirane 182 B1

## Austria Österreich
www.austria.info

### Bregenz
Lakeside town bordering Germany, Liechtenstein, Switzerland. Locals, known as Vorarlbergers, have their own dialect. The Martinsturm Roman to 17c tower, 17c town hall and Seekapelle, Kunsthaus modern art museum, Vorarlberger Landesmuseum, Festspielhaus.
www.bregenz.travel 107 B4

### Graz
University town, seat of imperial court to 1619. Historic centre around Hauptplatz. Imperial monuments: Burg; mausoleum of Ferdinand II; towers of 16c schloss; 17c Schloss Eggenberg (with Old Gallery). Also: 16c Town Hall; Zeughaus; 15c cathedral; New Gallery (good 19–20c); Kunsthaus (modern art).
www.graztourismus.at 110 B2

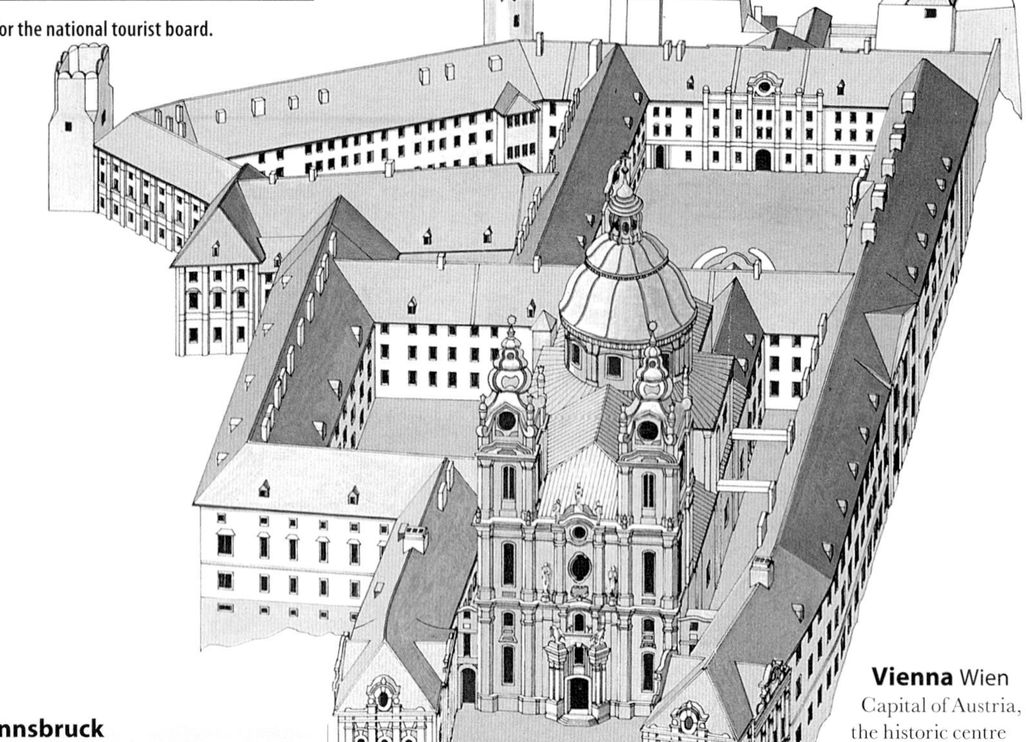

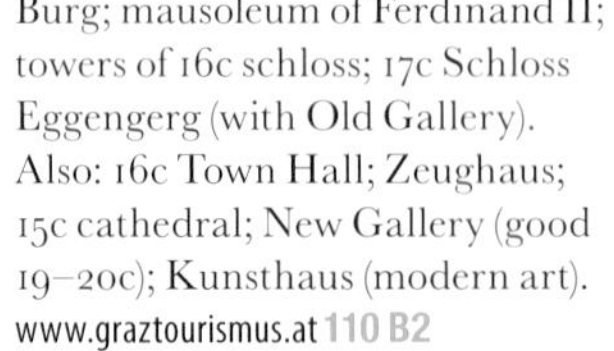

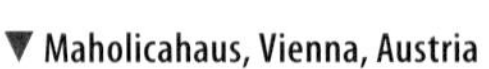

▼ Maholicahaus, Vienna, Austria

### Innsbruck
Old town is reached by Maria-Theresien-Strasse with famous views. Buildings: Goldenes Dachl (1490s); 18c cathedral; remains of Hofburg imperial residence; 16c Hofkirche (tomb of Maximilian I).
www.innsbruckaustria.co.uk 108 B2

### Krems
On a hill above the Danube, medieval quarter has Renaissance mansions. Also: Gothic Piaristenkirche; Museumkrems; Kunsthalle (modern art). www.krems.gv.at 97 C3

### Linz
Port on the Danube. Historic buildings are concentrated on Hauptplatz below the imperial 15c schloss.

▲ Melk Abbey, Austria

Notable: Baroque Old Cathedral; 16c Town Hall; Old Castle Museum; Lentos Art Museum. www.linz.at 96 C2

### Melk
Set on a rocky hill above the Danube, the fortified abbey is the greatest Baroque achievement in Austria – particularly the Grand Library and abbey church. www.stiftmelk.at 110 A2

### Salzburg
Set in subalpine scenery, the town was associated with powerful 16–17c prince-archbishops. The 17c cathedral has a complex of archiepiscopal buildings: the Residence and its gallery (19c); the 13c Franciscan Church (notable altar). Also: Mozart's birth-place; Schloss Mirabell; Salzburg Museum; the Hohensalzburg fortress; the Collegiate Church of St Peter (cemetery, catacombs); Museum of Modern Art at the Mönschberg and Rupertinum.
www.salzburg.info/en 109 B4

### Salzkammergut
Natural beauty with 76 lakes (Wolfgangersee, Altersee, Traunsee, Grundlsee) in mountain scenery. Attractive villages (St Wolfgang) and towns (Bad Ischl, Gmunden) include Hallstatt, famous for Celtic remains.
www.salzkammergut.at 109 B4

### Vienna Wien
Capital of Austria, the historic centre lies within the Ring. Churches: Gothic St Stephen's Cathedral; 17c Imperial Vault; 14c Augustine Church; 14c Church of the Teutonic Order (treasure); 18c Baroque churches (Jesuit Church, Franciscan Church, St Peter, St Charles). Imperial residences: Hofburg; Schönbrunn. Architecture of Historicism on Ringstrasse (from 1857). Art Nouveau: station pavilions, Secession Building, Postsparkasse, Looshaus, Majolicahaus. Museums: Art History Museum (antiquities, old masters), Cathedral and Diocesan Museum (15c), Albertina (graphic arts), Liechtenstein Museum (old masters), Museum of Applied Arts, Museum of Modern Art (MUMOK), Leopold Museum, Belvedere (Gothic, Baroque, 19–20c); AzW (architecture); Vienna Museum.
www.wien.info 111 A3

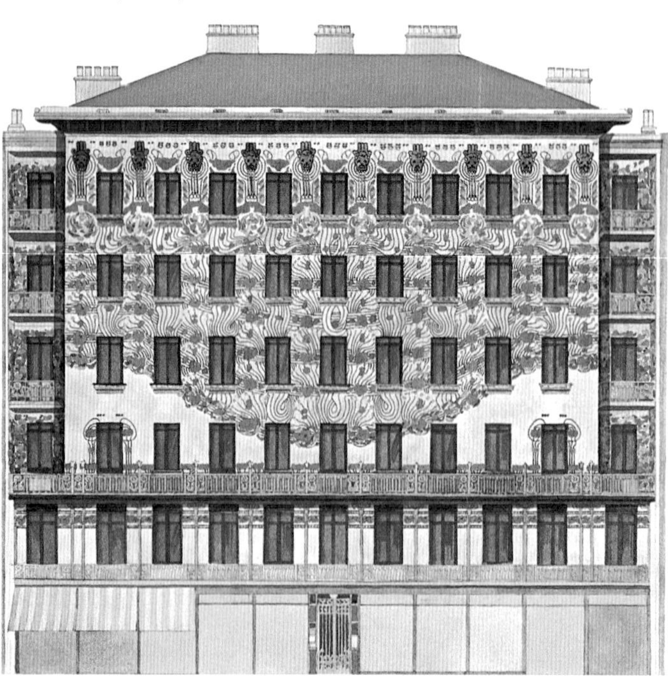

## Belgium Belgique
www.visitbelgium.com

### Antwerp Antwerpen
City with many tall gabled Flemish houses on the river. Heart of the city is Great Market with 16–17c guildhouses and Town Hall. Charles Borromeus Church (Baroque). 14–16c Gothic cathedral has Rubens paintings. Rubens also at the Rubens House and his burial place in St Jacob's Church. Excellent museums: Mayer van den Bergh Museum (applied arts); Koninklijk Museum of Fine Arts (Flemish, Belgian); MAS (ethnography, folklore, shipping); Muhka (modern art).
www.visitantwerpen.be 79 A4

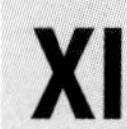

## Bruges Brugge

Well-preserved medieval town with narrow streets and canals. Main squares: the Market with 13c Belfort and covered market; the Burg with Basilica of the Holy Blood and Town Hall. The collections of Groeninge Museum and Memling museum in St Jans Hospital include 15c Flemish masters. The Onze Lieve Vrouwekerk has a famous *Madonna and Child* by Michelangelo
https://bezoekers.brugge.be/en 78 A3

## Brussels Bruxelles

Capital of Belgium. The Lower Town is centred on the enormous Grand Place with Hôtel de Ville and rebuilt guildhouses. Symbols of the city include the 'Manneken Pis' and Atomium (giant model of a molecule). The 13c Notre Dame de la Chapelle is the oldest church. The Upper Town contains: Gothic cathedral; Neo-classical Place Royale; 18c King's Palace; Royal Museums of Fine Arts (old and modern masters) Magritte Museum; MRAH (art and historical artefacts); BELvue museum (in the Bellevue Residence). Also: much Art Nouveau (Horta Museum, Hôtel Tassel, Hôtel Solvay); Place du Petit Sablon and Place du Grand Sablon; 19c Palais de Justice.
http://visitbrussels.be 79 B4

## Ghent Gent

Medieval town built on islands surrounded by canals and rivers. Views from Pont St-Michel. The Graslei and Koornlei quays have Flemish guild houses. The Gothic cathedral has famous Van Eyck altarpiece. Also: Belfort; Cloth Market; Gothic Town Hall; Gravensteen. Museums: STAM Museum in Bijloke Abbey (provincial and applied art); Museum of Fine Arts (old masters). www.visitgent.be 79 A3

## Namur

Reconstructed medieval citadel is the major sight of Namur, which also has a cathedral and provincial museums.
www.namurtourisme.be/index.php 79 B4

## Tournai

The Romanesque-Gothic cathedral is Belgium's finest (much excellent art). Fine Arts Museum has a good collection (15–20c). www.tournai.be 78 B3

▼ Town Hall, Antwerp, Belgium

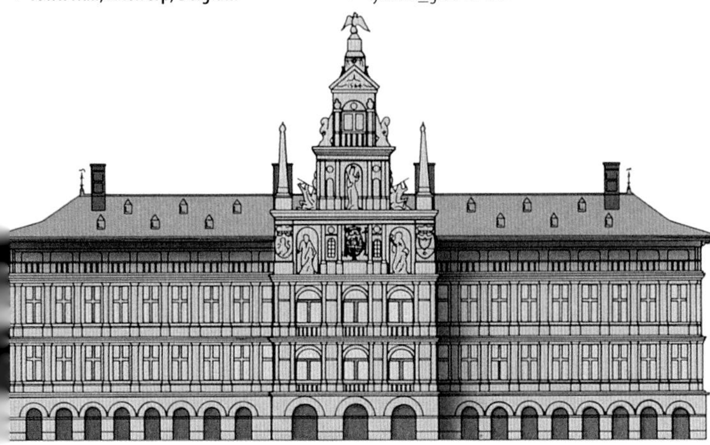

**Bulgaria** Bulgariya
http://bulgariatravel.org

### Black Sea Coast

Beautiful unspoiled beaches (Zlatni Pyasŭtsi). The delightful resort Varna is popular. Nesebŭr is famous for Byzantine churches. Also: Danube Delta in Hungary. 17 D7

### Koprivshtitsa

Beautiful village known both for its half-timbered houses and links with the April Rising of 1876. Six house museums amongst which the Lyutov House and the Oslekov House, plus the birthplaces of Georgi Benkovski, Dimcho Debelyanov, Todor Kableshkov, and Lyuben Karavelov.
www.eng.koprivshtitza.com

### Plovdiv

City set spectacularly on three hills. The old town has buildings from many periods: 2c Roman stadium and amphitheatre; 14c Dzumaiya Mosque; Archaeological Museum; 19c Ethnographic Museum. Nearby: Bačkovo Monastery (frescoes). 183 A6 http://bulgariatravel.org/en/object/306/plovdiv_grad

### Rila

Bulgaria's finest monastery, set in the most beautiful scenery of the Rila mountains. The church is richly decorated with frescoes.
www.rilamonastery.pmg-blg.com 183 A5

### Sofia Sofiya

Capital of Bulgaria. Sights: exceptional neo-Byzantine cathedral; Church of St Sofia; St Alexander Nevsky Cathedral; Boyana church; 4c rotunda of St George (frescoes); Byzantine Boyana Church (frescoes) on panoramic Mount Vitoša. Museums: National Historical Museum (particularly for Thracian artefacts); National Art Gallery (icons, Bulgarian art). http://bulgariatravel.org/en/object/234/sofia 17 D5

### Veliko Tŭrnovo

Medieval capital with narrow streets. Notable buildings: House of the Little Monkey; Hadji Nicoli Inn; ruins of medieval citadel; Baudouin Tower; churches of the Forty Martyrs and of SS Peter and Paul (frescoes); 14c Monastery of the Transfiguration.
http://bulgariatravel.org/en/object/15/veliko_tyrnovo_grad 17 D6

**Croatia** Hrvatska
http://croatia.hr/en-GB/Homepage

### Dalmatia Dalmacija

Exceptionally beautiful coast along the Adriatic. Among its 1185 islands, those of the Kornati Archipelago and Brijuni Islands are perhaps the most spectacular. Along the coast are several attractive medieval and Renaissance towns, most notably Dubrovnik, Split, Šibenik, Trogir, Zadar. 138 B2

### Dubrovnik

Surrounded by medieval and Renaissance walls, the city's architecture dates principally from 15–16c. Sights: many churches and monasteries including Church of St Blaise and Dominican monastery (art collection); promenade street of Stradun, Dubrovnik Museums; Renaissance Rector's Palace; Onofrio's fountain; Sponza Palace. The surrounding area has some 80 16c noblemen's summer villas.
http://experience.dubrovnik.hr/eng 139 C4

### Islands of Croatia

There are over 1,000 islands off the coast of Croatia among which there is Brač, known for its white marble and the beautiful beaches of Bol (www.bol.hr); Hvar (www.tzhvar.hr/en/) is beautifully green with fields of lavender, marjoram, rosemary, sage and thyme; Vis (www.tz-vis.hr) has the beautiful towns of Komiža and Vis Town, with the Blue Cave on nearby Biševo. 123 & 137–138

### Istria Istra

Peninsula with a number of ancient coastal towns (Rovinj, Poreč, Pula, Piran in Slovene Istria) and medieval hill-top towns (Motovun). Pula has Roman monuments (exceptional 1c amphitheatre). Poreč has narrow old streets; the mosaics in 6c Byzantine basilica of St Euphrasius are exceptional. See also Slovenia.
www.istra.hr 122 B2

### Plitvička Jezera

Outstandingly beautiful world of water and woodlands with 16 lakes and 92 waterfalls interwoven by canyons. Archaeological museums; art gallery; Gallery of Ivan Meštrović.
www.tzplitvice.hr 123 C4

### Split

Most notable for the exceptional 4c palace of Roman Emperor Diocletian, elements of which are incorporated into the streets and buildings of the town itself. The town also has a cathedral (11c baptistry) and a Franciscan monastery.
www.split.info 138 B2

## Trogir

The 13–15c town centre is surrounded by medieval city walls. Romanesque-Gothic cathedral includes the chapel of Ivan the Blessed. Dominican and Benedictine monasteries house art collections; Ćipiko palace; Lučić palace. http://tztrogir.hr 138 B2

## Zagreb

Capital city of Croatia with cathedral and Archbishop's Palace in Kaptol and to the west Gradec with Baroque palaces. Donji Grad – The Lower Town - is home to the Archaological Museum, Art Pavilion, Museum of Arts and Crafts, Ethnographic Museum, Mimara Museum and National Theatre; Modern Gallery; Museum of Contemporary Art.
www.zagreb-touristinfo.hr 124 B1

**Czech Republic** Česka Republica
www.czechtourism.com

### Brno

Capital of Moravia. Sights: Vegetable Market and Old Town Hall; Capuchin crypt decorated with bones of dead monks; hill of St Peter with Gothic cathedral; Church of St James; Mies van der Rohe's buildings (Bata, Avion Hotel, Togendhat House). Museums: Moravian Museum; Moravian Gallery; City Art Gallery; Brno City Museum in Spilberk Castle. www.brno.cz 97 B4

### České Budějovice

Famous for Budvar beer, the medieval town is centred on náměsti Přemysla Otokara II. The Black Tower gives fine views. Nearby: medieval Český Krumlov. www.c-budejovice.cz/en 96 C2

### Kutná Hora

A town with strong silver mining heritage shown in the magnificent Cathedral of sv Barbara which was built by the miners. See also the ossuary with 40,000 complete sets of bones moulded into sculptures and decorations.
www.czechtourism.com/t/kutna-hora 97 B3

### Olomouc

Well-preserved medieval university town of squares and fountains. The Upper Square has the Town Hall. Also: 18c Holy Trinity; Baroque Church of St Michael. http://tourism.olomouc.eu 98 B1

### Pilsen Plzeň

Best known for Plzeňský Prazdroj (Pilsener Urquell), beer has been brewed here since 1295. An industrial town with eclectic architecture shown in the railway stations and the namesti Republiky (main square).
www.czechtourism.com/a/pilsen-area 96 B1

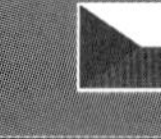

## Prague Praha

Capital of Czech Republic and Bohemia. The Castle Quarter has a complex of buildings behind the walls (Royal Castle; Royal Palace; cathedral). The Basilica of St George has a fine Romanesque interior. The Belvedere is the best example of Renaissance architecture. Hradčani Square has aristocratic palaces and the National Gallery. The Little Quarter has many Renaissance (Wallenstein Palace) and Baroque mansions and the Baroque Church of St Nicholas. The Old Town has its centre at the Old Town Square with the Old Town Hall (astronomical clock), Art Nouveau Jan Hus monument and Gothic Týn church. The Jewish quarter has 14c Staranova Synagogue and Old Jewish Cemetery. The Charles Bridge is famous. The medieval New Town has many Art Nouveau buildings and is centred on Wenceslas Square. www.prague.cz 84 B2

## Spas of Bohemia

Spa towns of Karlovy Vary (Carlsbad: www.karlovyvary.cz/en), Márianske Lázně (Marienbad: www.marianskelazne.cz) and Frantiskovy Lázně 83 B4

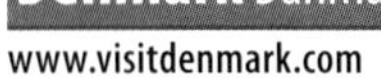

## Denmark Danmark

www.visitdenmark.com

## Århus

Second largest city in Denmark with a mixture of old and new architecture that blends well, Århus has been dubbed the culture capital of Denmark with the Gothic Domkirke; Latin Quarter; 13th Century Vor Frue Kirke; Den Gamle By, open air museum of traditional Danish life; ARoS (art museum).
www.visitaarhus.com 59 B3

## Copenhagen København

Capital of Denmark. Old centre has fine early 20c Town Hall. Latin Quarter has 19c cathedral. 18c Kastellet has statue of the Little Mermaid nearby. The 17c Rosenborg Castle was a royal residence, as was the Christianborg (now government offices). Other popular sights: Nyhavn canal; Tivoli Gardens. Excellent art collections: Ny Carlsberg Glypotek; National Gallery; National Museum.
www.visitcopenhagen.dk 61 D2

## Hillerød

Frederiskborg (home of the national history museum) is a fine red-brick Renaissance castle set among three lakes. www.visitnorthsealand.com/ln-int/north-sealand/hilleroed 61 D2

## Roskilde

Ancient capital of Denmark. The marvellous cathedral is a burial place of the Danish monarchy. The Viking Ship Museum houses the remains of five 11c Viking ships excavated in the 1960s. www.visitroskilde.com 61 D2

## Estonia Eesti

www.visitestonia.com

## Kuressaare

Main town on the island of Saaremaa with the 14c Kuressaare Kindlus. 8 C3

## Pärnu

Sea resort with an old town centre. Sights: 15c Red Tower; neoclassical Town Hall; St Catherine's Church. www.visitparnu.com 8 C4

## Tallinn

Capital of Estonia. The old town is centred on Town Hall Square. Sights: 15c Town Hall; Toompea Castle; Three Sisters houses. Churches: Gothic St Nicholas; 14c Church of the Holy Spirit; St Olaf's Church; Kumu Art Museum; Maritime Museum. www.tourism.tallinn.ee/eng 8 C4

## Tartu

Historic town with 19c university. The Town Hall Square is surrounded by neoclassical buildings. Also: remains of 13c cathedral; Estonian National Museum. www.visittartu.com 8 C5

## Finland Suomi

www.visitfinland.com

## Finnish Lakes

Area of outstanding natural beauty covering about one third of the country with thousands of lakes, of which Päijänne and Saimaa are the most important. Tampere, industrial centre of the region, has numerous museums, including the Tampere Art Museum (modern). Savonlinna has the medieval Olavinlinna Castle. Kuopio has the Orthodox and Regional Museums. 8 A5

## Helsinki

Capital of Finland. The 19c neo-classical town planning between the Esplanade and Senate Square includes the Lutheran cathedral. There is also a Russian Orthodox cathedral. The Constructivist Stockmann Department Store is the largest in Europe. The main railway station is Art Nouveau. Gracious 20c buildings in Mannerheimintie avenue include Finlandiatalo by Alvar Aalto. Many good museums: Art Museum of the Ateneum (19–20c); National Museum; Design Museum; Helsinki City Art Museum (modern Finnish); Open Air Museum (vernacular architecture); 18c fortress of Suomenlinna has several museums. www.visithelsinki.fi/en 8 B4

## Lappland (Finnish)

Vast unspoiled rural area. Lappland is home to thousands of nomadic Sámi living in a traditional way. The capital, Rovaniemi, was rebuilt after WWII; museums show Sámi history and culture. Nearby is the Arctic Circle with the famous Santa Claus Village. Inari is a centre of Sámi culture. See also Norway and Sweden. www.lapland.fi/en/travel 192–193

## France

http://us.rendezvousenfrance.com/

## Albi

Old town with rosy brick architecture. The vast Cathédrale Ste-Cécile (begun 13c) holds some good art. The Berbie Palace houses the Toulouse-Lautrec museum. www.albi-tourisme.fr 130 B1

## Alps

Grenoble (www.grenoble-tourisme.com/en/), capital of the French Alps, has a good 20c collection in the Museum of Grenoble. The Vanoise Massif has the greatest number of resorts (Val d'Isère, Courchevel). Chamonix has spectacular views on Mont Blanc, France's and Europe's highest peak. 118 B2

## Amiens

France's largest Gothic cathedral has beautiful decoration. The Museum of Picardy has unique 16c panel paintings. www.visit-amiens.com 90 B2

## Arles

Ancient, picturesque town with Roman relics (1c amphitheatre), 11c cathedral, Archaeological Museum (Roman art); Van Gogh centre. www.arlestourisme.com 131 B3

## Avignon

Medieval papal capital (1309–77) with 14c walls and many ecclesiastical buildings. Vast Palace of the Popes has stunning frescoes. The Little Palace has fine Italian Renaissance painting. The 12–13c Bridge of St Bénézet is famous. www.ot-avignon.fr 131 B3

## Bourges

The Gothic Cathedral of St Etienne, one of the finest in France, has a superb sculptured choir. Also notable is the House of Jacques Coeur. www.bourgestourisme.com 103 B4

## Brittany Bretagne

Brittany is famous for cliffs, sandy beaches and wild landscape. It is also renowned for megalithic monuments (Carnac) and Celtic culture. Its capital, Rennes, has the Palais de Justice and good collections in the Museum of Brittany (history) and Museum of Fine Arts. Also: Nantes; St-Malo. www.bretagne.com 100–101

## Burgundy Bourgogne

Rural wine region with a rich Romanesque, Gothic and Renaissance heritage. The 12c cathedral in Autun and 12c basilica in Vézelay have fine Romanesque sculpture. Monasteries include 11c L'Abbaye de Cluny (ruins) and L'Abbaye de Fontenay. Beaune has beautiful Gothic Hôtel-Dieu and 15c Nicolas Rolin hospices. www.burgundy-tourism.com 104 B3

## Caen

City with two beautiful Romanesque buildings: Abbaye aux Hommes; Abbaye aux Dames. The château has

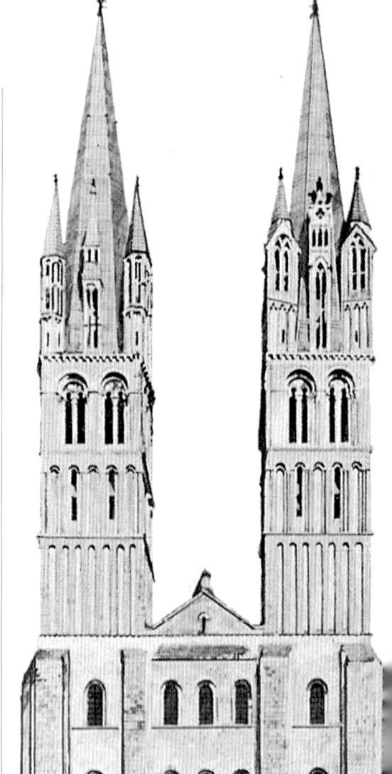

▲ Abbaye aux Hommes, Caen, France

two museums (15–20c painting; history). The *Bayeux Tapestry* is displayed in nearby Bayeux. www.tourisme.caen.fr 89 A3

## Carcassonne

Unusual double-walled fortified town of narrow streets with an inner fortress. The fine Romanesque Church of St Nazaire has superb stained glass. www.tourism-carcassonne.co.uk 130 B1

## Chartres

The cathedral is an exceptional example of Gothic architecture (Royal Doorway, stained glass, choir screen). The Fine Arts Museum has a good collection. www.chartres.com 90 C1

## Clermont-Ferrand

The old centre contains the cathedral built out of lava and Romanesque basilica. The Puy de Dôme and Puy de Sancy give spectacular views over some 60 extinct volcanic peaks (*puys*). www.clermontferrandtourism.com 116 B3

## Colmar

Town characterised by Alsatian half-timbered houses. The Unterlinden Museum has excellent German religious art including the famous Isenheim altarpiece. The Dominican church also has a fine altarpiece. Espace André Malraux (contemporary arts). www.ot-colmar.fr 106 A2

## Corsica Corse

Corsica has a beautiful rocky coast and mountainous interior. Napoleon's birthplace of Ajaccio has: Fesch Museum with Imperial Chapel and a large collection of Italian art; Maison Bonaparte; cathedral. Bonifacio, a medieval town, is spectacularly set on a rock over the sea. www.visit-corsica.com 180

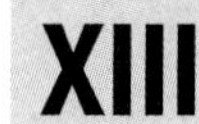

## Côte d'Azur

The French Riviera is best known for its coastline and glamorous resorts. There are many relics of artists who worked here: St-Tropez has Musée de l'Annonciade; Antibes has 12c Château Grimaldi with the Picasso Museum; Cagnes has the Renoir House and Mediterranean Museum of Modern Art; St-Paul-de-Vence has the excellent Maeght Foundation and Matisse's Chapelle du Rosaire. Cannes is famous for its film festival. Also: Marseille, Monaco, Nice.
www.frenchriviera-tourism.com 133 B3

## Dijon

Great 15c cultural centre. The Palais des Ducs et des Etats is the most notable monument and contains the Museum of Fine Arts. Also: the Charterhouse of Champmol.
www.visitdijon.com 105 B4

## Disneyland Paris

Europe's largest theme park follows in the footsteps of its famous predecessors in the United States.
www.disneylandparis.com 90 C2

## Le Puy-en-Velay

Medieval town bizarrely set on the peaks of dead volcanoes. It is dominated by the Romanesque cathedral cloisters). The Romanesque chapel of St-Michel is dramatically situated on the highest rock.
www.ot-lepuyenvelay.fr 117 B3

## Loire Valley

The Loire Valley has many 15–16c châteaux built amid beautiful scenery by French monarchs and members of their courts. Among the most splendid are Azay-le-Rideau, Chenonceaux and Loches. Also: Abbaye de Fontévraud. www.loirevalleytourism.com 102 B2

## Lyon

France's third largest city has an old centre and many museums including the Museum of the History of Textiles and the Museum of Fine Arts (old masters). www.lyon-france.com 117 B4

## Marseilles Marseille

Second lagest city in France. Spectacular views from the 19c Notre-Dame-de-la-Garde. The Old Port has 11-12c Basilique St Victor crypt, catacombs). Cantini Museum has major collection of 20c French art. Château d'If was the setting of Dumas' *The Count of Monte Cristo*.
www.marseille-tourisme.com 131 B4

## Mont-St-Michel

Gothic pilgrim abbey (11–12c) set dramatically on a steep rock island rising from mud flats and connected to the land by a road covered by the tide. The abbey is made up of a complex of buildings.
www.ot-montsaintmichel.com 101 A4

## Nancy

A centre of Art Nouveau. The 18c Place Stanislas was constructed by dethroned Polish king Stanislas.

Museums: School of Nancy Museum (Art Nouveau furniture); Fine Arts Mus. http://en.nancy-tourisme.fr/home/ 92 C2

## Nantes

Former capital of Brittany, with the 15c Château des ducs de Bretagne. The cathedral has a striking interior.
www.nantes-tourisme.com
101 B4

## Nice

Capital of the Côte d'Azur, the old town is centred on the old castle on the hill. The seafront includes the famous 19c Promenade des Anglais. The aristocratic quarter of the Cimiez Hill has the Marc Chagall Museum and the Matisse Museum. Also: Museum of Modern and Contemporary Art (especially neo-Realism and Pop Art).
www.nicetourism.com 133 B3

## Paris

Capital of France, one of Europe's most interesting cities. The Île de la Cité area, an island in the River Seine has the 12–13c Gothic Notre Dame (wonderful stained glass) and La Sainte-Chapelle (1240–48), one of the jewels of Gothic art. The Left Bank area: Latin Quarter with the famous Sorbonne university; Museum of Cluny housing medieval art; the Panthéon; Luxembourg Palace and Gardens; Montparnasse, interwar artistic and literary centre; Eiffel Tower; Hôtel des Invalides with Napoleon's tomb. Right Bank: the great boulevards (Avenue des Champs-Élysées joining the Arc de Triomphe and Place de la Concorde); 19c Opéra Quarter; Marais, former aristocratic quarter of elegant mansions (Place des Vosges); Bois de Boulogne, the largest park in Paris; Montmartre, centre of 19c bohemianism, with the Basilique Sacré-Coeur. The Church of St Denis is the first gothic church and the mausoleum of the French monarchy. Paris has three of the world's greatest art collections: The Louvre (to 19c, *Mona Lisa*), Musée d'Orsay (19–20c) and National Modern Art Museum in the Pompidou Centre. Other major museums include: Orangery Museum; Paris Museum of Modern Art; Rodin Museum; Picasso Museum. Notable cemeteries with graves of the famous: Père-Lachaise, Montmartre, Montparnasse. Near Paris are the royal residences of Fontainebleau and Versailles.
www.parisinfo.com 90 C2

▲ Château de Chenonceaux,
Châteaux of the Loire, France

## Pyrenees

Beautiful unspoiled mountain range. Towns include: delightful sea resorts of St-Jean-de-Luz and Biarritz; Pau, with access to the Pyrenees National Park; pilgrimage centre Lourdes.
144–145

## Reims

Together with nearby Epernay, the centre of champagne production. The 13c Gothic cathedral is one of the greatest architectural achievements in France (stained glass by Chagall). Other sights: Palais du Tau with cathedral sculpture, 11c Basilica of St Rémi; cellars on Place St-Niçaise and Place des Droits-des-Hommes.
www.reims-tourisme.com 91 B4

## Rouen

Old centre with many half-timbered houses and 12–13c Gothic cathedral and the Gothic Church of St Maclou with its fascinating remains of a dance macabre on the former cemetery of Aître St-Maclou. The Fine Arts Museum has a good collection.
www.rouentourisme.com 89 A5

## St-Malo

Fortified town (much rebuilt) in a fine coastal setting. There is a magnificent boat trip along the river Rance to Dinan, a splendid well-preserved medieval town.
www.saint-malo-tourisme.com 101 A3

## Strasbourg

Town whose historic centre includes a well-preserved quarter of medieval half-timbered Alsatian houses, many of them set on the canal. The cathedral is one of the best in France. The Palais Rohan contains several museums. www.otstrasbourg.fr 93 C3

## Toulouse

Medieval university town characterised by flat pink brick (Hôtel Assézat). The Basilique St Sernin, the largest Romanesque church in France, has many art treasures. Marvellous Church of the Jacobins holds the body of St Thomas Aquinas.
www.toulouse-tourisme.com 129 C4

## Tours

Historic town centred on Place Plumereau. Good collections in the Guilds Museum and Fine Arts Museum. www.tours-tourisme.fr 102 B2

## Versailles

Vast royal palace built for Louis XIV, primarily by Mansart, set in large formal gardens with magnificent fountains. The extensive and much-imitated state apartments include the famous Hall of Mirrors and the exceptional Baroque chapel.
www.chateauversailles.fr 90 C2

## Vézère Valley Caves

A number of prehistoric sites, most notably the cave paintings of Lascaux (some 17,000 years old), now only seen in a duplicate cave, and the cave of Font de Gaume. The National Museum of Prehistory is in Les Eyzies.
www.lascaux-dordogne.com/en 129 B4

## Germany Deutschland

www.germany.travel

### Northern Germany

## Aachen

Once capital of the Holy Roman Empire. Old town around the Münsterplatz with magnificent cathedral. An exceptionally rich treasure is in the Schatzkammer. The Town Hall is on the medieval Market. www.aachen.de 80 B2

## Berlin

Capital of Germany. Sights include: the Kurfürstendamm avenue; Brandenburg Gate, former symbol of the division between East and West Germany; Tiergarten; Unter den

Linden; 19c Reichstag. Berlin has many excellent art and history collections. Museum Island: Pergamon Musem (classical antiquity, Near and Far East, Islam; Bode Museum (sculpture, Byzantine art); Altes Museum (Greek and Roman); New National Gallery (20th-c European); Old National Gallery (19th-c German); New Museum (Egyptian, prehistoric). Dahlem: Museum of Asian Art; Museum of European Cultures; Muesum of Ethnology; Die Brücke Museum (German Expressionism). Tiergarten: Picture Gallery (old masters); Decorative Arts Museum (13–19c); New National Gallery (19–20c);

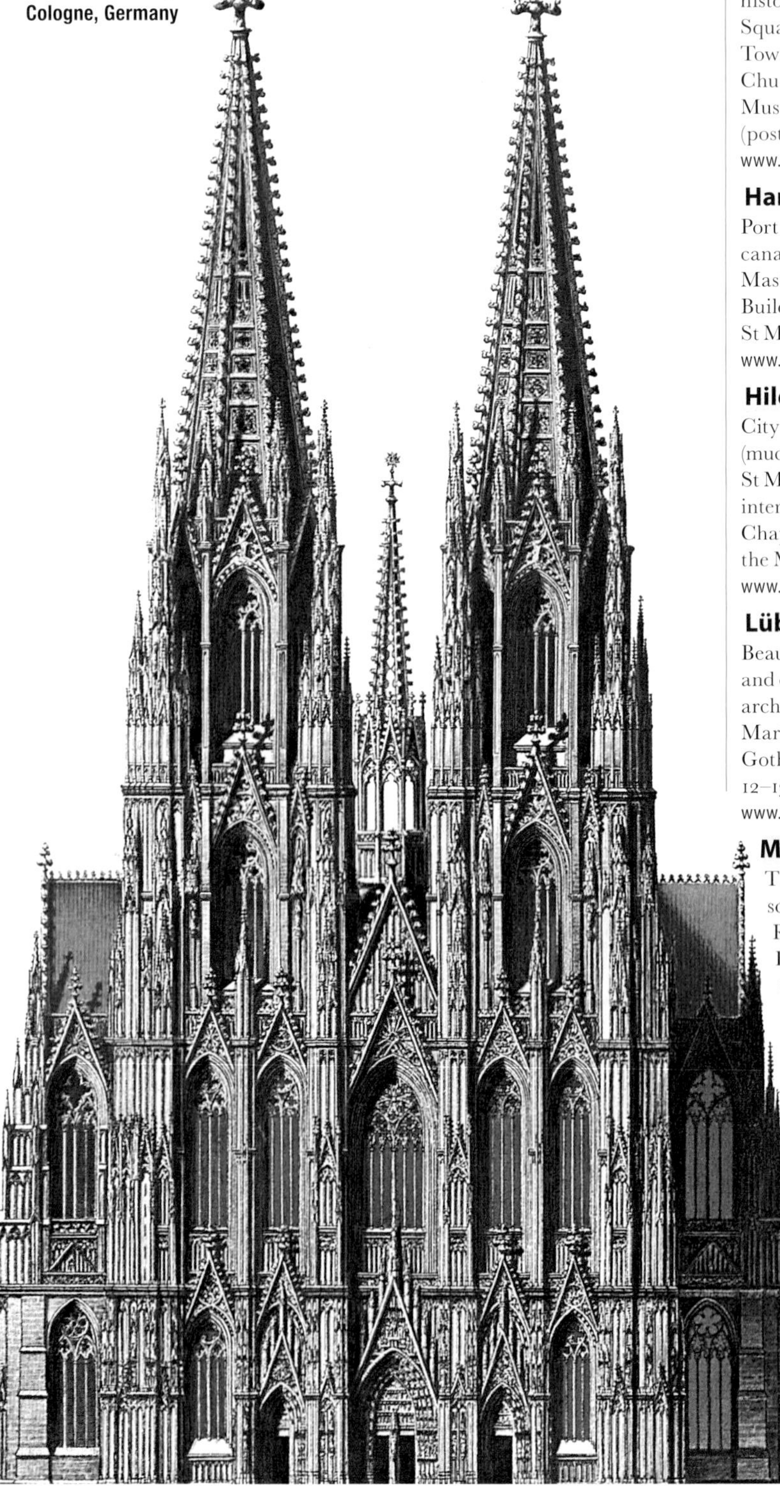

Gothic cathedral, Cologne, Germany

Bauhaus Archive. Kreuzberg: Gropius Building with Jewish Museum and Berlin Gallery; remains of Berlin Wall and Checkpoint Charlie House. Unter den Linden: German Guggenheim (commissioned contemporary works). http://visitberlin.de **74 B2**

### Cologne Köln

Ancient city with 13–19c cathedral (rich display of art). In the old town are the Town Hall and many Romanesque churches (Gross St Martin, St Maria im Kapitol, St Maria im Lyskirchen, St Ursula, St Georg, St Severin, St Pantaleon, St Apostolen). Museums: Diocesan

Museum (religious art); Roman-German Museum (ancient history); Wallraf-Richartz and Ludwig Museum (14–20c art). www.cologne-tourism.com **80 B2**

### Dresden

Historic centre with a rich display of Baroque architecture. Major buildings: Castle of the Electors of Saxony; 18c Hofkirche; Zwinger Palace with fountains and pavilions (excellent old masters); Albertinum with excellent Gallery of New Masters; treasury of Grünes Gewölbe. The Baroque-planned New Town contains the Japanese Palace and Schloss Pillnitz. www.dresden.de **84 A1**

### Frankfurt

Financial capital of Germany. The historic centre around the Römerberg Square has 13–15c cathedral, 15c Town Hall, Gothic St Nicholas Church, Saalhof (12c chapel). Museums: Museum of Modern Art (post-war); State Art Institute. www.frankfurt-tourismus.de **81 B4**

### Hamburg

Port city with many parks, lakes and canals. The Kunsthalle has Old Masters and 19-20c German art. Buildings: 19c Town Hall; Baroque St Michael's Church. www.hamburg-tourism.de **72 A3**

### Hildesheim

City of Romanesque architecture (much destroyed). Principal sights: St Michael's Church; cathedral (11c interior, sculptured doors, St Anne's Chapel); superb 15c Tempelhaus on the Market Place. www.hildesheim.de **72 B2**

### Lübeck

Beautiful old town built on an island and characterised by Gothic brick architecture. Sights: 15c Holsten Gate; Market with the Town Hall and Gothic brick St Mary's Church; 12–13c cathedral; St Ann Museum. www.luebeck-tourism.de **65 C3**

### Mainz

The Electoral Palatinate schloss and Market fountain are Renaissance. Churches: 12c Romanesque cathedral; Gothic St Steven's (with stained glass by Marc Chagall). www.mainz.de **93 A4**

### Marburg

Medieval university town with the Market Place and Town Hall, St Elizabeth's Church (frescoes, statues, 13c shrine), 15–16c schloss. www.marburg.de **81 B4**

### Münster

Historic city with well-preserved Gothic and Renaissance buildings: 14c Town Hall; Romanesque-Gothic cathedral. The Westphalian Museum holds regional art. www.muenster.de/stadt/tourismus/en **71 C4**

### Potsdam

Beautiful Sanssouci Park contains several 18–19c buildings including: Schloss Sanssouci; Gallery (European masters); Orangery; New Palace; Chinese Teahouse. www.potsdam-tourism.com **74 B2**

### Rhein Valley Rheintal

Beautiful 80km gorge of the Rhein Valley between Mainz and Koblenz with rocks (Loreley), vineyards (Bacharach, Rüdesheim), white medieval towns (Rhens, Oberwesel) and castles. Some castles are medieval (Marksburg, Rheinfles, island fortress Pfalzgrafenstein) others were built or rebuilt in the 19c (Stolzenfles, Rheinstein). **80 B3**

### Weimar

The Neoclassical schloss, once an important seat of government, now houses a good art collection. Church of SS Peter and Paul has a Cranach masterpiece. Houses of famous people: Goethe, Schiller, Liszt. The famous Bauhaus was founded at the School of Architecture and Engineering. www.weimar.de **82 B3**

## Southern Germany

### Alpine Road
Deutsche Alpenstrasse

German Alpine Road in the Bavarian Alps, from Lindau on Bodensee to Berchtesgaden. The setting for 19c fairy-tale follies of Ludwig II of Bavaria (Linderhof, Hohenschwangau, Neuschwanstein), charming old villages (Oberammergau) and Baroque churches (Weiss, Ottobeuren). Garmisch-Partenkirchen has views on Germany's highest peak, the Zugspitze. **108 B2**

### Augsburg

Attractive old city. The Town Hall is one of Germany's finest Renaissance buildings. Maximilianstrasse has several Renaissance houses and Rococo Schaezler Palace (good art collection). Churches: Romanesque-Gothic cathedral; Renaissance St Anne's Church. The Fuggerei, founded 1519 as an estate for the poor, is still in use. www.augsburg-tourismus.de **94 C2**

### Bamberg

Well-preserved medieval town. The island, connected by two bridges, has the Town Hall and views of Klein Venedig. Romanesque-Gothic cathedral (good art) is on an exceptional square of Gothic, Renaissance and Baroque buildings – Alte Hofhalttung; Neue Residenz with State Gallery (German masters); Ratstube. http://en.bamberg.info **94 B2**

### Black Forest Schwarzwald

Hilly region between Basel and Karlsruhe, the largest and most picturesque woodland in Germany, with the highest summit, Feldberg, lake resorts (Titisee), health resorts (Baden-Baden) and clock craft (Triberg). Freiburg is the regional capital. www.schwarzwald.de **93 C4**

## Freiburg

Old university town with system of streams running through the streets. The Gothic Minster is surrounded by the town's finest buildings. Two towers remain of the medieval walls. The Augustine Museum has a good collection.
www.freiburg.de/pb/,Len/225797.html 106 B2

## Heidelberg

Germany's oldest university town, majestically set on the banks of the river and romantically dominated by the ruined schloss. The Gothic Church of the Holy Spirit is on the Market Place with the Baroque Town Hall. Other sights include the 16c Knight's House and the Baroque Morass Palace with the Museum of the Palatinate.
www.tourism-heidelberg.com 93 B4

## Lake Constance Bodensee

Lake Constance, with many pleasant lake resorts. Lindau, on an island, has numerous gabled houses. Birnau has an 18c Rococo church. Konstanz (Swiss side) has the Minster set above the Old Town. www.bodensee.eu 107 B4

## Munich München

Old town centred on the Marienplatz with 15c Old Town Hall and 19c New Town Hall. Many richly decorated churches: St Peter's (14c tower); Gothic red-brick cathedral; Renaissance St Michael's (royal portraits on the façade); Rococo St Asam's. The Residenz palace consists of seven splendid buildings holding many art objects. Schloss Nymphenburg has a palace, park, botanical gardens and four beautiful pavilions. Superb museums: Old Gallery (old masters), New Gallery (18–19c), Lenbachhaus (modern German). Many famous beer gardens.
www.munich-touristinfo.de 108 A2

## Nuremberg Nürnberg

Beautiful medieval walled city dominated by the 12c Kaiserburg. Romanesque-Gothic St Sebaldus Church and Gothic St Laurence Church are rich in art. On Hauptmarkt is the famous 14c Schöner Brunnen. Also notable is 15c Dürer House. The German National Museum has excellent German medieval and Renaissance art.
http://tourismus.nuernberg.de/no_cache/en/home.html 94 B3

## Regensburg

Medieval city set majestically on the Danube. Views from 12c Steinerne Brücke. Churches: Gothic cathedral; Romanesque St Jacob's; Gothic St Blaisius; Baroque St Emmeram. Other sights: Old Town Hall (museum); Haidplatz; Schloss Thurn und Taxis; State Museum.
www.regensburg.de 95 B4

## Romantic Road Romantische Strasse

Romantic route between Aschaffenburg and Füssen, leading through picturesque towns and villages of medieval Germany. The most popular section is the section between Würzburg and Augsburg, centred on Rothenburg ob der Tauber. Also notable are Nördlingen, Harburg Castle, Dinkelsbühl, Creglingen.
www.romantischestrasse.de 94 B2

## Rothenburg ob der Tauber

Attractive medieval walled town with tall gabled and half-timbered houses on narrow cobbled streets. The Market Place has Gothic-Renaissance Town Hall, Rattrinke-stubbe and Gothic St Jacob's Church (altarpiece).
www.tourismus.rothenburg.de 94 B2

## Speyer

The 11c cathedral is one of the largest and best Romanesque buildings in Germany. 12c Jewish Baths are well-preserved.
www.speyer.de/sv_speyer/en/Tourism 93 B4

## Stuttgart

Largely modern city with old centre around the Old Schloss, Renaissance Alte Kanzlei, 15c Collegiate Church and Baroque New Schloss. Museums: Regional Museum; Old and New State Galleries. The 1930s Weissenhofsiedlung is by several famous architects.
www.stuttgart-tourist.de/en 94 C1

## Trier

Superb Roman monuments: Porta Nigra; Aula Palatina (now a church); Imperial Baths; amphitheatre. The Regional Museum has Roman artefacts. Also, Gothic Church of Our Lady; Romanesque cathedral.
www.trier-info.de 92 B2

## Ulm

Old town with half-timbered gabled houses set on a canal. Gothic 14–19c minster has tallest spire in the world (161m). www.tourismus.ulm.de 94 C1

## Würzburg

Set among vineyard hills, the medieval town is centred on the Market Place with the Rococo House of the Falcon. The 18c episcopal princes' residence (frescoes) is magnificent. The cathedral is rich in art. Work of the great local Gothic sculptor, Riemenschneider, is in Gothic St Mary's Chapel, Baroque New Minster, and the Mainfränkisches Museum. www.wuerzburg.de 94 B1

## Greece Ellas

www.visitgreece.gr

## Athens Athina

Capital of Greece. The Acropolis, with 5c BC sanctuary complex (Parthenon, Propylaia, Erechtheion, Temple of Athena Nike), is the greatest architectural achievement of antiquity in Europe. The Agora was a public meeting place in ancient Athens. Plaka has narrow streets and small Byzantine churches (Kapnikarea). The Olympeum was the largest temple in Greece. Also: Olympic Stadium; excellent collections of ancient artefacts (Museum of Cycladic and Ancient Greek Art; New Acropolis Museum; National Archeological Museum; Benaki Museum).
www.visitgreece.gr 185 B4

## Corinth Korinthos

Ancient Corinth (ruins), with 5c BC Temple of Apollo, was in 44 BC made capital of Roman Greece by Julius Caesar. Set above the city, the Greek-built acropolis hill of Acrocorinth became the Roman and Byzantine citadel (ruins). 184 B3

## Crete Kriti

Largest Greek island, Crete was home to the great Minoan civilization (2800–1100 BC). The main relics are the ruined Palace of Knossos and Malia. Gortys was capital of the Roman province. Picturesque Rethimno has narrow medieval streets, a Venetian fortress and a former Turkish mosque. Matala has beautiful beaches and famous caves cut into cliffs. Iraklio (Heraklion), the capital, has a good Archeological Museum. 185 D6

## Delphi

At the foot of the Mount Parnassos, Delphi was the seat of the Delphic Oracle of Apollo, the most important oracle in Ancient Greece. Delphi was also a political meeting place and the site of the Pythian Games. The Sanctuary of Apollo consists of: Temple of Apollo, led to by the Sacred Way; Theatre; Stadium. The museum has a display of objects from the site (5c BC Charioteer). 182 E4

## Epidavros

Formerly a spa and religious centre focused on the Sanctuary of Asclepius (ruins). The enormous 4c BC theatre is probably the finest of all ancient theatres. 184 B4

## Greek Islands

Popular islands with some of the most beautiful and spectacular beaches in Europe. The many islands are divided into various groups and individual islands: The major groups are the Kiklades and Dodekanisa in the Aegean Sea, the largest islands are Kerkyra (Corfu) in the Ionian Sea and Kriti. 182–185 & 188

## Meteora

The tops of bizarre vertical cylinders of rock and towering cliffs are the setting for 14c Cenobitic monasteries, until recently only accessible by baskets or removable ladders. Mega Meteoro is the grandest and set on the highest point. Roussánou has the most extraordinary site. Varlaám is one of the oldest and most beautiful, with the Ascent Tower and 16c church with frescoes. Aghiou Nikolaou also has good frescoes.
www.meteora-greece.com 182 D3

## Mistras

Set in a beautiful landscape, Mistras is the site of a Byzantine city, now in ruins, with palaces, frescoed churches, monasteries and houses. 184 B3

## Mount Olympus Oros Olymbos

Mount Olympus, mythical seat of the Greek gods, is the highest, most dramatic peak in Greece. 182 C4

## Mycenae Mikines

The citadel of Mycenae prospered between 1950 BC and 1100 BC and consists of the royal complex of Agamemnon: Lion Gate, royal burial site, Royal Palace, South House, Great Court. 184 B3

## Olympia

In a stunning setting, the Panhellenic Games were held here for a millennium. Ruins of the sanctuary of Olympia consist of the Doric temples of Zeus and Hera and the vast Stadium. There is also a museum (4c BC figure of Hermes). 184 B2

## Rhodes

One of the most attractive islands with wonderful sandy beaches. The city of Rhodes has a well-preserved medieval centre with the Palace of the Grand Masters and the Turkish Süleymaniye Mosque
www.rhodestravels.com 188 C2

## Salonica Thessaloniki

Largely modern city with Byzantine walls and many fine churches: 8c Aghia Sofia; 11c Panaghia Halkeo; 14c Dodeka Apostoli; 14c Aghios Nikolaos Orfanos; 5c Aghios Dimitrios (largest in Greece, 7c Mosaics). 183 C5

## Hungary Magyarorszàg

http://gotohungary.com

## Balaton

The 'Hungarian sea', famous for its holiday resorts: Balatonfüred, Tihany, Badasconytomaj, Keszthely.
http://gotohungary.com 111 C4

## Budapest

Capital of Hungary on River Danube, with historic area centring on the Castle Hill of Buda district. Sights include: Matthias church; Pest district with late 19c architecture, centred on Ferenciek tere; neo-Gothic Parliament Building on river; Millennium Monument. The Royal Castle houses a number of museums: Hungarian National Gallery, Budapest History Museum; Ludwig Collection. Other museums: National Museum of Fine Arts (excellent Old and Modern masters); Hungarian National Museum (Hungarian history). Famous for public thermal baths: Király and Rudas baths, both made under Turkish rule; Gellért baths, the most visited.
http://budapest.gotohungary.com/budapest-and-surroundings 112 B3

## Esztergom

Medieval capital of Hungary set in scenic landscape. Sights: Hungary's largest basilica (completed 1856); royal palace ruins. 112 B2

## Pécs

Attractive old town with Europe's fifth oldest university (founded 1367). Famous for Turkish architecture (Mosque of Gazi Kasim Pasha, Jakovali Hassan Mosque). www.iranypecs.hu/en/index.html 125 A4

## Sopron

Beautiful walled town with many Gothic and Renaissance houses. Nearby: Fertöd with the marvellous Eszergázy Palace. http://portal.sopron.hu 111 B3

## Ireland

www.discoverireland.com

## Aran Islands

Islands with spectacular cliffs and notable pre-Christian and Christian sights, especially on Inishmore. www.aranislands.ie 26 B2

## Cashel

Town dominated by the Rock of Cashel (61m) topped by ecclesiastical ruins including 13c cathedral; 15c Halls of the Vicars; beautiful Romanesque 12c Cormac's Chapel (fine carvings). www.cashel.ie 29 B4

## Connemara

Beautiful wild landscape of mountains, lakes, peninsulas and beaches. Clifden is the capital. www.connemara.ie/en 28 A1

## Cork

Pleasant city with its centre along St Patrick's Street and Grand Parade lined with fine 18c buildings. Churches: Georgian St Anne's Shandon (bell tower); 19c cathedral. www.corkcity.ie/traveltourism 29 C3

## County Donegal

Rich scenic landscape of mystical lakes and glens and seascape of cliffs (Slieve League cliffs are the highest in Europe). The town of Donegal has a finely preserved Jacobean castle. www.govisitdonegal.com 26 B2

## Dublin

Capital of Ireland. City of elegant 18c neoclassical and Georgian architecture with gardens and parks (St Stephen's Green, Merrion Square with Leinster House – now seat of Irish parliament). City's main landmark, Trinity College (founded 1591), houses in its Old Library fine Irish manuscripts (7c Book of Durrow, 8c Book of Kells). Two Norman cathedrals: Christ Church; St Patrick's. Other buildings: originally medieval Dublin Castle with State Apartments; James Gandon's master-pieces: Custom House; Four Courts. Museums: National Museum (archaeology, decorative arts, natural history); National Gallery (old masters, Impressionists); Museum of Modern Art; Dublin Writers' Museum. www.visitdublin.com 30 A2

## Glendalough

Impressive ruins of an important early Celtic (6c) monastery with 9c cathedral, 12c St Kevin's Cross, oratory of St Kevin's Church. www.glendalough.ie 30 A2

## Kilkenny

Charming medieval town, with narrow streets dominated by 12c castle (restored 19c). The 13c Gothic cathedral has notable tomb monuments. www.kilkennytourism.ie 30 B1

## Newgrange

Part of a complex that also includes the sites of Knowth, Dowth, Fourknocks, Loughcrew and Tara, Newgrange is one of the best passage graves in Europe, the massive 4500-year-old tomb has stones richly decorated with patterns. www.knowth.com/newgrange.htm 30 A2

## Ring of Kerry

Route around the Iveragh peninsula with beautiful lakes (Lough Leane), peaks overlooking the coastline and islands (Valencia Island, Skelling). Also: Killarney; ruins of 15c Muckross Abbey. www.ringofkerrytourism.com 29 B2

## Italy Italia

www.italia.it

### Northern Italy

## Alps

Wonderful stretch of the Alps running from the Swiss and French borders to Austria. The region of Valle d'Aosta is one of the most popular ski regions, bordered by the highest peaks of the Alps. 108–109 & 119–120

## Arezzo

Beautiful old town set on a hill dominated by 13c cathedral. Piazza Grande is surrounded by medieval and Renaissance palaces. Main sight: Piero della Francesca's frescoes in the choir of San Francesco. 135 B4

## Assisi

Hill-top town that attracts crowds of pilgrims to the shrine of St Francis of Assisi at the Basilica di San Francesco, consisting of two churches, Lower and Upper, with superb frescoes. www.assisi-info.com 136 B1

## Bologna

Elegant city with oldest university in Italy. Historical centre around Piazza Maggiore and Piazza del Nettuno with the Town Hall, Palazzo del Podestà, Basilica di San Petronio. Other churches: San Domenico; San Giacomo Maggiore. The two towers (one incomplete) are symbols of the city. Good collection in the National Gallery (Bolognese). www.bolognawelcome.com 135 A4

## Dolomites Dolomiti

Part of the Alps, this mountain range spreads over the region of Trentino-Alto Adige, with the most picturesque scenery between Bolzano and Cortina d'Ampezzo. www.dolomiti.it 121 A4

## Ferrara

Old town centre around Romanesque-Gothic cathedral and Palazzo Communale. Also: Castello Estense; Palazzo Schifanoia (frescoes); Palazzo dei Diamanti housing Pinacoteca Nazionale. www.ferraraterraeacqua.it 121 C4

## Florence Firenze

City with exceptionally rich medieval and Renaissance heritage. Piazza del Duomo has:13–15c cathedral (first dome since antiquity); 14c campanile; 11c baptistry (bronze doors). Piazza della Signoria has: 14c Palazzo Vecchio (frescoes); Loggia della Signoria (sculpture); 16c Uffizi Gallery with one of the world's greatest collections (13–18c). Other great paintings: Museo di San Marco; Palatine Gallery in 15–16c Pitti Palace surrounded by Boboli Gardens. Sculpture: Cathedral Works Museum; Bargello Museum; Academy Gallery (Michelangelo's *David*). Among many other Renaissance palaces: Medici-Riccardi; Rucellai; Strozzi. The 15c church of San Lorenzo has Michelangelo's tombs of the Medici. Many churches have richly frescoed chapels: Santa Maria Novella, Santa Croce, Santa Maria del Carmine. The 13c Ponte Vecchio is one of the most famous sights. www.firenzeturismo.it 135 B4

## Italian Lakes

Beautiful district at the foot of the Alps, most of the lakes with holiday resorts. Many lakes are surrounded by aristocratic villas (Maggiore, Como, Garda). 120–121

## Mantua Mántova

Attractive city surrounded by three lakes. Two exceptional palaces: Palazzo Ducale (Sala del Pisanello; Camera degli Sposi; Castello San Giorgio); luxurious Palazzo Tè (brilliant frescoes). Also: 15c Church of Sant'Andrea; 13c law courts. www.turismo.mantova.it 121 B3

## Milan Milano

Modern city, Italy's fashion and design capital (Corso and Galleria Vittoro Emmanuelle II). Churches include: Gothic cathedral (1386–1813), the world's largest (4c baptistry); Romanesque St Ambrose; 15c San Satiro; Santa Maria delle Grazie with Leonardo da Vinci's *Last Supper* in the convent refectory. Great art collections, Brera Gallery, Ambrosian Library, Museum of Modern Art. Castello Sforzesco (15c, 19c) also has a gallery. The famous La Scala opera house opened in 1778. Nearby: monastery at Pavia. www.visitamilano.it/turismo 120 B2

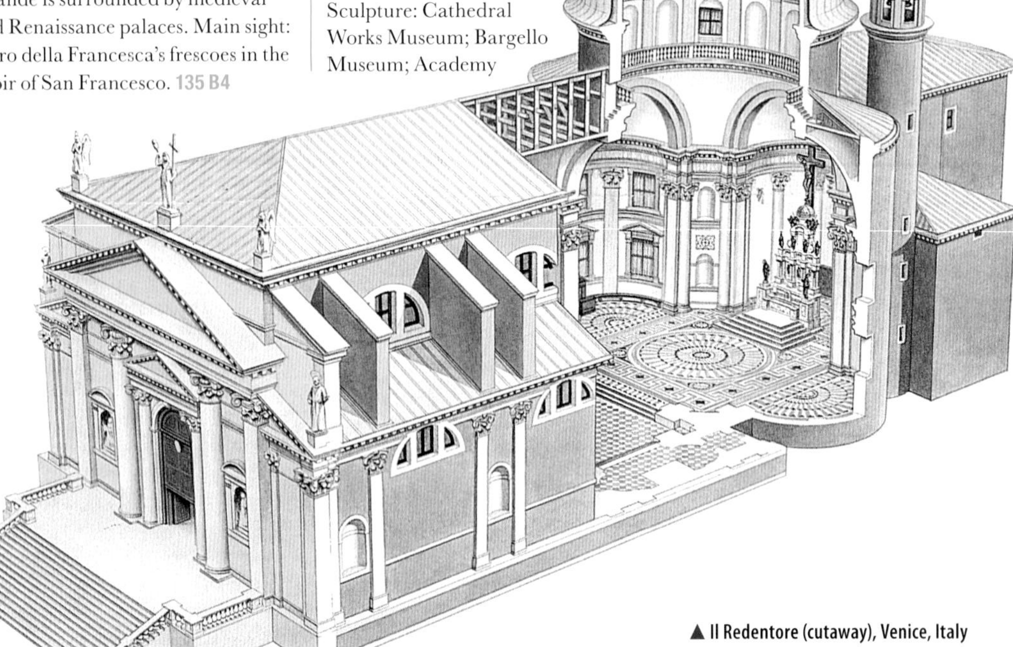

▲ Il Redentore (cutaway), Venice, Italy

## Padua Pádova

Pleasant old town with arcaded streets. Basilica del Santo is a place of pilgrimage to the tomb of St Anthony. Giotto's frescoes in the Scrovegni Chapel are exceptional. Also: Piazza dei Signori with Palazzo del Capitano; vast Palazzo della Ragione; church of the Eremitani (frescoes).
www.turismopadova.it **121 B4**

## Parma

Attractive city centre, famous for Corregio's frescoes in the Romanesque cathedral and church of St John the Evangelist, and Parmigianino's frescoes in the church of Madonna della Steccata. Their works are also in the National Gallery.
www.turismo.comune.parma.it **120 C3**

## Perúgia

Hill-top town centred around Piazza Quattro Novembre with the cathedral, Fontana Maggiore and Palazzo dei Priori. Also: Collegio di Cambio (frescoes); National Gallery of Umbria; many churches.
www.perugiaonline.com **136 B1**

## Pisa

Medieval town centred on the Piazza dei Miracoli. Sights: famous Romanesque Leaning Tower, Romanesque cathedral (excellent façade, Gothic pulpit); 12–13c baptistry; 13c Camposanto cloistered cemetery (fascinating 14c frescoes).
www.turismo.pisa.it **134 B3**

## Ravenna

Ancient town with exceptionally well-preserved Byzantine mosaics. The finest are in 5c Mausoleo di Galla Placidia and 6c Basilica di San Vitale. Good mosaics also in the basilicas of Sant'Apollinare in Classe and Sant'Apollinare Nuovo.
www.turismo.ra.it/eng **135 A5**

▼ Romanesque cathedral, Pisa, Italy

## Siena

Outstanding 13–14c medieval town centred on beautiful Piazza del Campo with Gothic Palazzo Publico (frescoes of secular life). Delightful Romanesque-Gothic Duomo (Libreria Piccolomini, baptistry, art works). Many other richly decorated churches. Fine Sienese painting in Pinacoteca Nazionale and Museo dell'Opera del Duomo.
www.sienaonline.com **135 B4**

## Turin Torino

City centre has 17-18c Baroque layout dominated by twin Baroque churches. Also: 15c cathedral (holds Turin Shroud); Palazzo Reale; 18c Superga Basilica; Academy of Science with rich Egyptian Museum.
www.turismotorino.org **119 B4**

## Urbino

Set in beautiful hilly landscape, Urbino's heritage is mainly due to the 15c court of Federico da Montefeltro at the magnificent Ducal Palace (notable Studiolo), now also a gallery.
www.turismo.pesarourbino.it **136 B1**

## Venice Venezia

Stunning old city built on islands in a lagoon, with some 150 canals. The Grand Canal is crossed by the famous 16c Rialto Bridge and is lined with elegant palaces (Gothic Ca'd'Oro and Ca'Foscari, Renaissance Palazzo Grimani, Baroque Rezzonico). The district of San Marco has the core of the best known sights and is centred on Piazza San Marco with 11c Basilica di San Marco (bronze horses, 13c mosaics); Campanile (exceptional views) and Ducal Palace (connected with the prison by the famous Bridge of Sighs). Many churches (Santa Maria Gloriosa dei Frari, Santa Maria della Salute, Redentore, San Giorgio Maggiore, San Giovanni e

Paolo) and scuole (Scuola di San Rocco, Scuola di San Giorgio degli Schiavoni) have excellent works of art. The Gallery of the Academy houses superb 14–18c Venetian art. The Guggenheim Museum holds 20c art.
http://en.turismovenezia.it **122 B1**

## Verona

Old town with remains of 1c Roman Arena and medieval sights including the Palazzo degli Scaligeri; Arche Scaligere; Romanesque Santa Maria Antica; Castelvecchio; Ponte Scaliger. The famous 14c House of Juliet has associations with *Romeo and Juliet*. Many churches with fine art works (cathedral; Sant'Anastasia; basilica di San Zeno Maggiore).
www.tourism.verona.it **121 B4**

## Vicenza

Beautiful town, famous for the architecture of Palladio, including the Olympic Theatre (extraordinary stage), Corso Palladio with many of his palaces, and Palazzo Chiericati. Nearby: Villa Rotonda, the most influential of all Palladian buildings. www.vicenzae.org **121 B4**

## Southern Italy

## Naples Napoli

Historical centre around Gothic cathedral (crypt). Spaccanapoli area has numerous churches (bizarre Cappella Sansevero, Gesù Nuovo, Gothic Santa Chiara with fabulous tombs). Buildings: 13c Castello Nuovo; 13c Castel dell'Ovo; 15c Palazzo Cuomo.

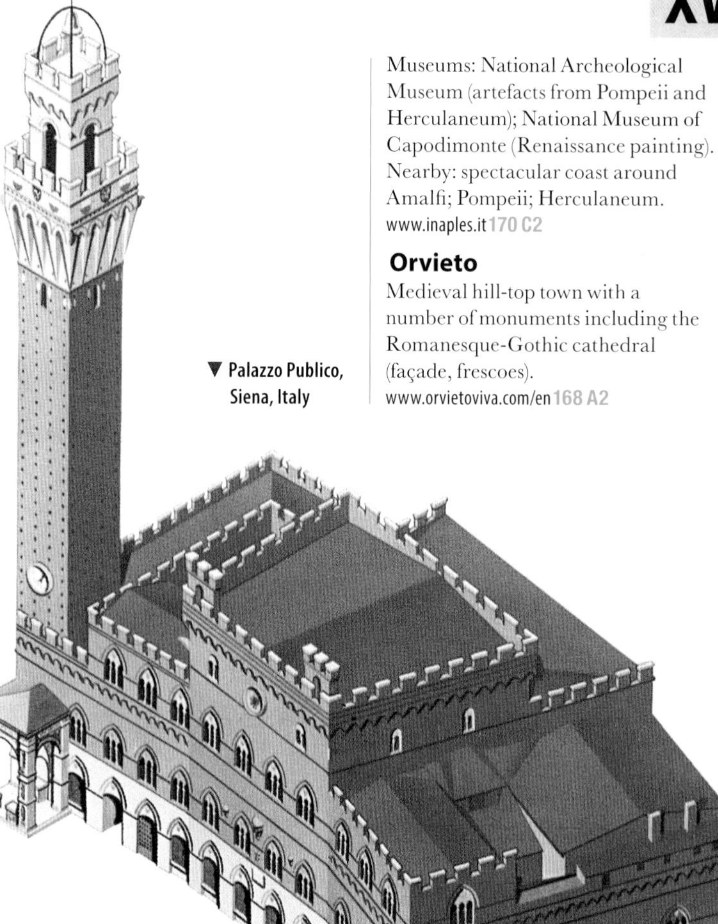

▼ Palazzo Publico, Siena, Italy

Museums: National Archeological Museum (artefacts from Pompeii and Herculaneum); National Museum of Capodimonte (Renaissance painting). Nearby: spectacular coast around Amalfi; Pompeii; Herculaneum.
www.inaples.it **170 C2**

## Orvieto

Medieval hill-top town with a number of monuments including the Romanesque-Gothic cathedral (façade, frescoes).
www.orvietoviva.com/en **168 A2**

## Rome Roma

Capital of Italy, exceptionally rich in sights from many eras. Ancient sights: Colosseum; Arch of Constantine; Trajan's Column; Roman and Imperial fora; hills of Palatino and Campidoglio (Capitoline Museum shows antiquities); Pantheon; Castel Sant' Angelo; Baths of Caracalla). Early Christian sights: catacombs (San Calisto, San Sebastiano, Domitilla); basilicas (San Giovanni in Laterano, Santa Maria Maggiore, San Paolo Fuori le Mura). Rome is known for richly decorated Baroque churches: il Gesù, Sant'Ignazio, Santa Maria della Vittoria, Chiesa Nuova. Other churches, often with art treasures: Romanesque Santa Maria in Cosmedin, Gothic Santa Maria Sopra Minerva, Renaissance Santa Maria del Popolo, San Pietro in Vincoli. Several Renaissance and Baroque palaces and villas house superb art collections (Palazzo Barberini, Palazzo Doria Pamphilj, Palazzo Spada, Palazzo Corsini, Villa Giulia, Galleria Borghese) and are beautifully frescoed (Villa Farnesina). Fine Baroque public spaces with fountains: Piazza Navona; Piazza di Spagna with the Spanish Steps; also Trevi Fountain. Nearby: Tivoli; Villa Adriana. Rome also contains the Vatican City (Città del Vaticano).
www.turismoroma.it **168 B2**

## Volcanic Region

Region from Naples to Sicily. Mount Etna is one of the most famous European volcanoes. Vesuvius dominates the Bay of Naples and has at its foot two of Italy's finest Roman sites, Pompeii and Herculaneum, both destroyed by its eruption in 79AD. Stromboli is one of the beautiful Aeolian Islands.

## Sardinia Sardegna

Sardinia has some of the most beautiful beaches in Italy (Alghero). Unique are the nuraghi, some 7000 stone constructions (Su Nuraxi, Serra Orios), the remains of an old civilization (1500–400 BC). Old towns include Cagliari and Sássari.
www.sardi.it 178–179

## Sicily Sicilia

Surrounded by beautiful beaches and full of monuments of many periods, Sicily is the largest island in the Mediterranean. Taormina with its Greek theatre has one of the most spectacular beaches, lying under the mildly active volcano Mount Etna. Also: Agrigento; Palermo, Siracusa.
www.sicilytourism.com 176–177

### Agrigento

Set on a hill above the sea and famed for the Valley of the Temples. The nine originally 5c BC Doric temples are Sicily's best-preserved Greek remains. www.agrigento-sicilia.it 176 B2

### Palermo

City with Moorish, Norman and Baroque architecture, especially around the main squares (Quattro Canti, Piazza Pretoria, Piazza Bellini). Sights: remains of Norman palace (12c Palatine Chapel); Norman cathedral; Regional Gallery (medieval); some 8000 preserved bodies in the catacombs of the Cappuchin Convent. Nearby: 12c Norman Duomo di Monreale.
www.palermotourism.com 176 A2

### Syracuse Siracusa

Built on an island connected to the mainland by a bridge, the old town has a 7c cathedral, ruins of the Temple of Apollo; Fountain of Arethusa; archaeological museum. On the mainland: 5c BC Greek theatre with seats cut out of rock; Greek fortress of Euralus; 2c Roman amphitheatre; 5–6c Catacombs of St John. 177 B4

## Latvia Latvija

www.latvia.travel/en

### Riga

Well-preserved medieval town centre around the cathedral. Sights: Riga Castle; medieval Hanseatic houses; Great Guild Hall; Gothic Church of St Peter; Art Nouveau buildings in the New Town. Nearby: Baroque Rundale Castle.
www.latvia.travel/en/riga 8 D4

## Lithuania Lietuva

http://lietuva.lt/en/tourism

### Vilnius

Baroque old town with fine architecture including: cathedral; Gediminas Tower; university complex; Archbishop's Palace; Church of St Anne. Also: remains of Jewish life; Vilnius Picture Gallery (16–19c regional); Lithuanian National Museum. www.vilnius.com 13 A6

## Luxembourg

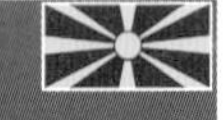

www.visitluxembourg.com

### Luxembourg

Capital of Luxembourg, built on a rock with fine views. Old town is around the Place d'Armes. Buildings: Grand Ducal Palace; fortifications of Rocher du Bock; cathedral. Museum of History and Art holds an excellent regional collection. 92 B2

## Macedonia Makedonija

www.exploringmacedonia.com

### Ohrid

Old town, beautifully set by a lake, with houses of wood and brick, remains of a Turkish citadel, many churches (two cathedrals; St Naum south of the lake).
www.ohrid.com.mk 182 B2

### Skopje

Historic town with Turkish citadel, fine 15c mosques, oriental bazaar, ancient bridge. Superb Byzantine churches nearby. 182 A3

## Malta

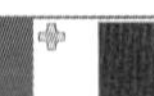

www.visitmalta.com

### Valletta

Capital of Malta. Historic walled city, founded in 16c by the Maltese Knights, with 16c Grand Master's Palace and a richly decorated cathedral. 175 C3

## Monaco

www.visitmonaco.com

### Monaco

Major resort area in a beautiful location. Sights include: Monte Carlo casino, Prince's Palace at Monaco-Ville; 19c cathedral; oceanographic museum. 133 B3

## Netherlands Nederland

http://holland.com

### Amsterdam

Capital of the Netherlands. Old centre has picturesque canals lined with distinctive elegant 17–18c merchants' houses. Dam Square has 15c New Church and Royal Palace. Other churches include Westerkerk. The Museumplein has three world-famous museums: the newly restored Rijksmuseum (several art collections including 15–17c painting); Van Gogh Museum; Municipal Museum (art from 1850 on). Other museums: Anne Frank House; Jewish Historical Museum; Rembrandt House; Hermitage Museum (exhibitions). http://holland.com 70 B1

### Delft

Well-preserved old Dutch town with gabled red-roofed houses along canals. Gothic churches: New Church; Old Church. Famous for Delftware (two museums).
www.delft.nl 70 B1

### Haarlem

Many medieval gabled houses centred on the Great Market with 14c Town Hall and 15c Church of St Bavon. Museums: Frans Hals Museum; Teylers Museum.
www.haarlemmarketing.co.uk 70 B1

### The Hague Den Haag

Seat of Government and of the royal house of the Netherlands. The 17c Mauritshuis houses the Royal Picture Gallery (excellent 15–18c Flemish and Dutch). Other museums: Escher Museum; Meermanno Museum (books); Municipal Museum. 70 B1

### Het Loo

Former royal palace and gardens set in a vast landscape (commissioned by future the future King and Queen of England, William and Mary).
www.paleishetloo.nl 70 B2

### Keukenhof

In spring, landscaped gardens, planted with bulbs of many varieties, are the largest flower gardens in the world. www.keukenhof.nl 70 B1

### Leiden

University town of beautiful gabled houses set along canals. The

▼ Westerkerk, Amsterdam, Netherlands

Rijksmuseum Van Oudheden is Holland's most important home to archaeological artefacts from the Antiquity. The 16c Hortus Botanicus is one of the oldest botanical gardens in Europe. The Cloth Hall with van Leyden's *Last Judgement*.
http://leidenholland.com 70 B1

### Rotterdam

The largest port in the world. The Boymans-van Beuningen Museum has a huge and excellent decorative and fine art collection (old and modern). Nearby: 18c Kinderdijk with 19 windmills.
https://en.rotterdam.info/visitors 79 A4

### Utrecht

Delightful old town centre along canals with the Netherlands' oldest university and Gothic cathedral. Good art collections: Central Museum; National Museum.
www.utrecht.nl 70 B2

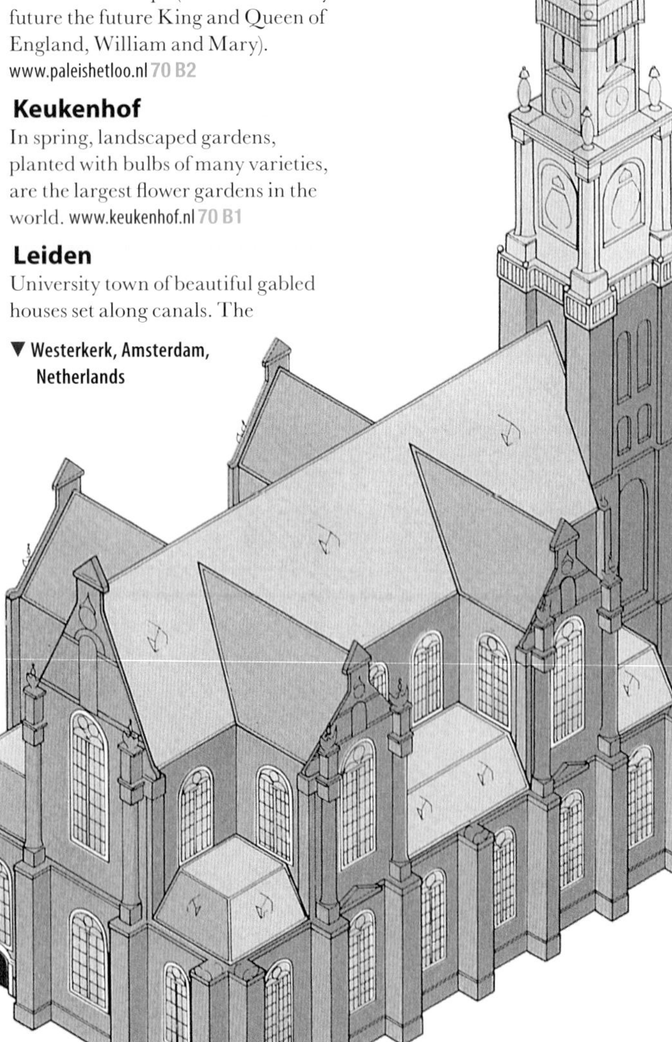

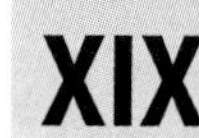

## Norway Norge

www.visitnorway.com

### Bergen
Norway's second city in a scenic setting. The Quay has many painted wooden medieval buildings. Sights: 12c Romanesque St Mary's Church; Bergenhus fortress with 13c Haakon's Hall; Rosenkrantz Tower; Grieghallen; Bergen Art Museum (Norwegian art); Bryggens Museum. www.visitbergen.com 46 B2

### Lappland (Norwegian)
Vast land of Finnmark is home to the Sámi. Nordkapp is the northern point of Europe. Also Finland, Sweden. 192–193

### Norwegian Fjords
Beautiful and majestic landscape of deep glacial valleys filled by the sea. The most thrilling fjords are between Bergen and Ålesund. www.fjords.com 46 & 198

### Oslo
Capital of Norway with a modern centre. Buildings: 17c cathedral; 19c city hall, 19c royal palace; 19c Stortinget (housing parliament); 19c University; 13c Akershus (castle); 12c Akerskirke (church). Museums: National Gallery; Munch Museum; Viking Ship Museum; Folk Museum (reconstructed buildings). www.visitoslo.com 48 C2

### Stavkirker
Wooden medieval stave churches of bizarre pyramidal structure, carved with images from Nordic mythology. Best preserved in southern Norway.

### Tromsø
Main arctic city of Norway with a university and two cathedrals. www.visittromso.no 192 C3

### Trondheim
Set on the edge of a fjord, a modern city with the superb Nidaros cathedral (rebuilt 19c). Also: Stiftsgaard (royal residence); Applied Arts Museum. www.trondheim.com 199 B7

## Poland Polska
www.poland.travel/en-gb

### Częstochowa
Centre of Polish Catholicism, with the 14c monastery of Jasna Góra a pilgrimage site to the icon of the Black Madonna for six centuries. www.jasnagora.pl 86 B3

### Gdańsk
Medieval centre with: 14c Town Hall (state rooms); Gothic brick St Mary's Church, Poland's largest; Long Market has fine buildings (Artus Court); National Museum. www.gdansk.pl/en 69 A3

### Kraków
Old university city, rich in architecture, centred on superb 16c Marketplace with Gothic-Renaissance Cloth Hall containing the Art Gallery (19c Polish), Clock Tower, Gothic redbrick St Mary's Church (altarpiece). Czartoryski Palace has city's finest art collection. Wawel Hill has the Gothic cathedral and splendid Renaissance Royal Palace. The former Jewish ghetto in Kazimierz district has 16c Old Synagogue, now a museum. www.krakow.pl/english 99 A3

### Poznań
Town centred on the Old Square with Renaissance Town Hall and Baroque mansions. Also: medieval castle; Gothic cathedral; National Museum (European masters). www.poznan.pl 76 B1

### Tatry
One of Europe's most delightful mountain ranges with many beautiful ski resorts (Zakopane). Also in Slovakia. 99 B3

### Warsaw Warszawa
Capital of Poland, with many historic monuments in the Old Town with the Royal Castle (museum) and Old Town Square surrounded by reconstructed 17–18c merchants' houses. Several churches including: Gothic cathedral; Baroque Church of the Nuns of Visitation. Richly decorated royal palaces and gardens: Neoclassical Łazienki Palace; Baroque palace in Wilanów. The National Museum has Polish and European art. www.warsawtour.pl/en 77 C6

### Wrocław
Historic town centred on the Market Square with 15c Town Hall and mansions. Churches: Baroque cathedral; St Elizabeth; St Adalbert. National Museum displays fine art. Vast painting of Battle of Racławice is specially housed. www.wroclaw.pl 85 A5

## Portugal

www.visitportugal.com

### Alcobaça
Monastery of Santa Maria, one of the best examples of a Cistercian abbey, founded in 1147 (exterior 17–18c). The church is Portugal's largest (14c tombs). www.mosteiroalcobaca.pt/en 154 A1

### Algarve
Modern seaside resorts among picturesque sandy beaches and rocky coves (Praia da Rocha). Old towns: Lagos; Faro. www.visitalgarve.pt/visitalgarve/vEN 160 B1

### Batalha
Abbey is one of the masterpieces of French Gothic and Manueline architecture (tombs, English Perpendicular chapel, unfinished pantheon). www.mosteirobatalha.pt/en 154 A2

### Braga
Historic town with cathedral and large Archbishop's Palace. 148 A1

### Coimbra
Old town with narrow streets set on a hill. The Romanesque cathedral is particularly fine (portal). The university (founded 1290) has a fascinating Baroque library. Also: Museum of Machado de Castro; many monasteries and convents. http://turismodecoimbra.pt/en 148 B1

### Évora
Centre of the town, surrounded by walls, has narrow streets of Moorish character and medieval and Renaissance architecture. Churches: 12–13c Gothic cathedral; São Francisco with a chapel decorated with bones of some 5000 monks; 15c Convent of Dos Lóis. The Jesuit university was founded in 1559. Museum of Évora holds fine art (particularly Flemish and Portugese). http://www.evora-portugal.com 154 C3

### Guimarães
Old town with a castle with seven towers on a vast keep. Churches: Romanesque chapel of São Miguel; São Francisco. Alberto Sampaio Museum and Martins Sarmento Museum are excellent. http://whc.unesco.org/en/list/1031 148 A1

### Lisbon Lisboa
Capital of Portugal. Baixa is the Neoclassical heart of Lisbon with the Praça do Comércio and Rossio squares. São Jorge castle (Visigothic, Moorish, Romanesque) is surrounded by the medieval quarters. Bairro Alto is famous for *fado* (songs). Monastery of Jerónimos is exceptional. hurches: 12c cathedral; São Vicente de Fora; São Roque (tiled chapels); Torre de Belém; Convento da Madre de Deus. Museums: Gulbenkian Museum (ancient, oriental, European), National Museum of Ancient Art; Design Museum; Modern Art Centre; Azulego Museum (decorative tiles). Nearby: palatial monastic complex Mafra; royal resort Sintra. www.visitlisboa.com 154 B1

### Porto
Historic centre with narrow streets. Views from Clérigos Tower. Churches: São Francisco; cathedral. Soares dos Reis Museum holds fine and decorative arts (18–19c). The suburb of Vila Nova de Gaia is the centre for port wine. www.visitporto.travel 148 A1

### Tomar
Attractive town with the Convento de Cristo, founded in 1162 as the headquarters of the Knights Templar (Charola temple, chapter house, Renaissance cloisters). 154 A2

## Romania

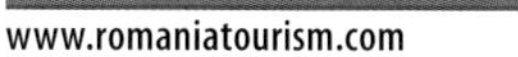

www.romaniatourism.com

### Bucovina
Beautiful region in northern Romanian Moldova renowned for a number of 15–16c monasteries and their fresco cycles. Of particular note are Moldovita, Voroneţ and Suceviţa. 17 B6

### Bucharest Bucureşti
Capital of Romania with the majority of sites along the Calea Victoriei and centring on Piaţa Revoluţei with 19c Romanian Athenaeum and 1930s Royal Palace housing the National Art Gallery. The infamous 1980s Civic Centre with People's Palace is a symbol of dictatorial aggrandisement. www.romaniatourism.com/bucharest.html 17 C7

### Carpathian Mountains Carpaţii
The beautiful Carpathian Mountains have several ski resorts (Sinaia) and peaks noted for first-rate mountaineering (Făgă raşuiui, Rodnei). Danube Delta Europe's largest marshland, a spectacular nature reserve. Travel in the area is by boat, with Tulcea the starting point for visitors. The Romanian Black Sea Coast has a stretch of resorts (Mamaia, Eforie) between Constantaţ and the border, and well-preserved Roman remains in Histria. 17 B6

### Transylvania Transilvania
Beautiful and fascinating scenic region of medieval citadels (Timişoara, Sibiu) provides a setting for the haunting image of the legendary Dracula (Sighişoara, Braşov, Bran Castle). Cluj-Napoca is the main town. 17 B5

## Russia Rossiya
www.russia-travel.com

### Moscow Moskva
Capital of Russia, with many monuments. Within the Kremlin's red walls are: 15c Cathedral of the Dormition; 16c Cathedral of the Archangel; Cathedral of the Annunciation (icons), Armour Palace. Outside the walls, Red Square has the Lenin Mausoleum and 16c St Basil's Cathedral. There are a number of monasteries (16c Novodevichi). Two superb museums: Tretiakov Art Gallery (Russian); Pushkin Museum of Fine Art (European); also State Historical Museum. Kolomenskoe, once a royal summer retreat, has the Church of the Ascension. www.visitrussia.org.uk/travel-to-Russia/moscow 9 E10

### Novgorod
One of Russia's oldest towns, centred on 15c Kremlin with St Sophia Cathedral (iconostasis, west door). Two other cathedrals: St Nicholas; St George. Museum of History, Architecture and Art has notable icons and other artefacts. http://visitnovgorod.com 9 C7

### Peterhof (Petrovdorets)
Also known as Petrovdorets, Peterhof is a grand palace with numerous pavilions (Monplaisir) set in beautiful parkland interwoven by a system of fountains, cascades and waterways connected to the sea. www.peterhofmuseum.ru 9 C6

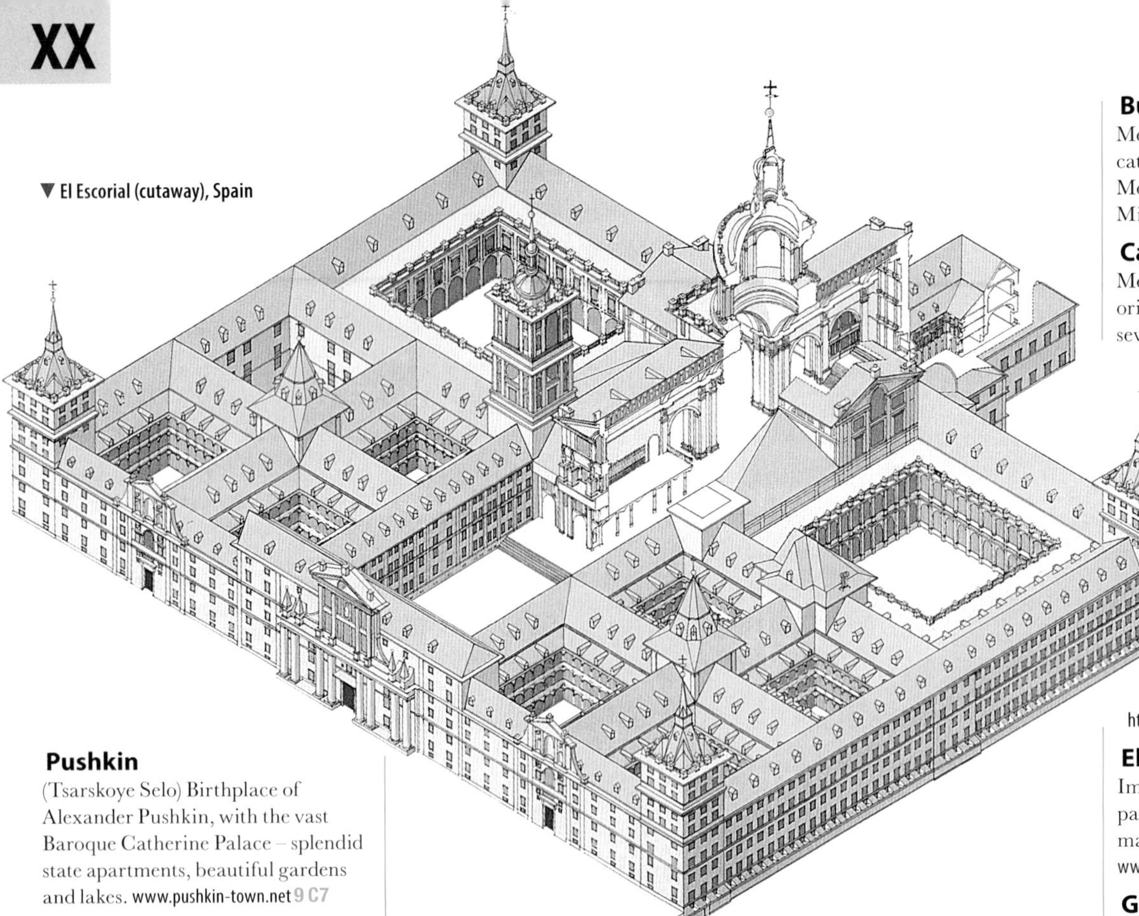

▼ El Escorial (cutaway), Spain

## Pushkin

(Tsarskoye Selo) Birthplace of Alexander Pushkin, with the vast Baroque Catherine Palace – splendid state apartments, beautiful gardens and lakes. www.pushkin-town.net 9 C7

## Saint Petersburg
Sankt Peterburg

Founded in 1703 with the SS Peter and Paul Fortress and its cathedral by Peter the Great, and functioning as seat of court and government until 1918. Many of the most famous sights are around elegant Nevski Prospekt. The Hermitage, one of the world's largest and finest art collections is housed in several buildings including the Baroque Winter and Summer palaces. The Mikhailovsky Palace houses the Russian Museum (Russian art). Other sights: neoclassical Admiralty; 19c St Isaac's Cathedral and St Kazan Cathedral; Vasilievsky Island with 18c Menshikov Palace; Alexander Nevsky Monastery; 18c Smolny Convent. www.saint-petersburg.com 9 C7

## Sergiev Posad

(Zagorsk) Trinity St Sergius monastery with 15c cathedral. 9 D11

## Serbia Srbija

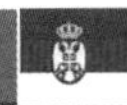

www.serbia.travel

## Belgrade Beograd

Capital of Serbia. The largely modern city is set between the Danube and Sava rivers. The National Museum holds European art. To the south there are numerous fascinating medieval monasteries, richly embellished with frescoes. www.tob.co.rs/en/index.php 127 C2

## Slovak Republic
Slovenska Republika

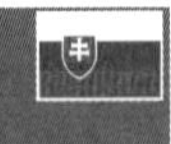

www.slovakia.travel

## Bratislava

Capital of Slovakia, dominated by the castle (Slovak National Museum, good views). Old Town centred on the Main Square with Old Town Hall and Jesuit Church. Many 18–19c palaces (Mirbach Palace, Pálffy Palace, Primate's Palace), churches (Gothic cathedral, Corpus Christi Chapel) and museums (Slovak National Gallery). http://visit.bratislava.sk/en 111 A4

## Košice

Charming old town with many Baroque and neoclassical buildings and Gothic cathedral. http://visitkosice.eu 12 D4

## Spišské Podhradie

Region, east of the Tatry, full of picturesque medieval towns (Levoča, Kežmarok, Prešov) and architectural monuments (Spišský Castle). 99 B4

## Tatry

Beautiful mountain region. Poprad is an old town with 19c villas. Starý Smokovec is a popular ski resort. See also Poland. 99 B3

## Slovenia Slovenija

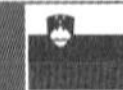

www.slovenia.info

## Istria Istra

Two town centres, Koper and Piran, with medieval and Renaissance squares and Baroque palaces. See also Croatia. 122 B2

## Julian Alps Julijske Alpe

Wonderfully scenic section of the Alps with lakes (Bled, Bohinj), deep valleys (Planica, Vrata) and ski resorts (Kranjska Gora, Bohinjska Bistrica). 122 A2

## Karst Caves

Numerous caves with huge galleries, extraordinary stalactites and stalagmites, and underground rivers. The most spectacular are Postojna (the most famous, with Predjamski Castle nearby) and Škocjan. http://www.postojnska-jama.eu/en 123 B3

## Ljubljana

Capital of Slovenia. The old town, dominated by the castle (good views), is principally between Prešeren Square and Town Hall (15c, 18c), with the Three Bridges and colonnaded market. Many Baroque churches (cathedral, St Jacob, St Francis, Ursuline) and palaces (Bishop's Palace, Seminary, Gruber Palace). Also: 17c Križanke church and monastery complex; National Gallery and Modern Gallery show Slovene art. www.visitljubljana.si 123 A3

## Spain España

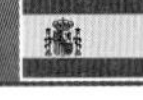

www.spain.info

## Ávila

Medieval town with 2km-long 11c walls. Pilgrimage site to shrines to St Teresa of Ávila (Convent of Santa Teresa, Convent of the Incarnation). www.avila.com/avila_tourism 150 B3

## Barcelona

Showcase of Gothic ('Barri Gòtic': cathedral; Santa María del Mar; mansions on Carrer de Montcada) and *modernista* architecture ('Eixample' area with Manzana de la Discòrdia; Sagrada Familia, Güell Park, La Pedrera). Many elegant boulevards (La Rambla, Passeig de Gràcia). Museums: Modern Catalan Art, Catalan Archaeology, Picasso Museum, Miró Museum, Tàpies Museum. Nearby: monastery of Montserrat (Madonna); Figueres (Dali Museum). www.barcelonaturisme.com 147 C3

## Burgos

Medieval town with Gothic cathedral, Moorish-Gothic Royal Monastery and Charterhouse of Miraflores. 143 B3

## Cáceres

Medieval town surrounded by originally Moorish walls and with several aristocratic palaces with solars. 155 A4

## Córdoba

Capital of Moorish Spain with a labyrinth of streets and houses with tile-decorated patios. The 8–10c Mezquita is the finest mosque in Spain. A 16c cathedral was added at the centre of the building and a 17c tower replaced the minaret. The old Jewish quarter has 14c synagogue http://english.turismodecordoba.org 156 C3

## El Escorial

Immense Renaissance complex of palatial and monastic buildings and mausoleum of the Spanish monarchs. www.patrimonionacional.es 151 B3

## Granada

The Alhambra was hill-top palace-fortress of the rulers of the last Moorish kingdom and is the most splendid example of Moorish art and architecture in Spain. The complex has three principal parts: Alcazaba fortress (11c); Casa Real palace (14c, with later Palace of Carlos V); Generalife gardens. Also: Moorish quarter; gypsy quarter; Royal Chapel with good art in the sacristy. www.turgranada.es 163 A4

## León

Gothic cathedral has notable stained glass. Royal Pantheon commemorates early kings of Castile and León. 142 B1

## Madrid

Capital of Spain, a mainly modern city with 17–19c architecture at its centre around Plaza Mayor. Sights: Royal Palace with lavish apartments; Descalzas Reales Convent (tapestrics and other works); Royal Armoury museum. Spain's three leading galleries: Prado (15–18c); Queen Sofia Centre (20c Spanish, Picasso's *Guernica*); Thyssen-Bornemisza Museum (medieval to modern). www.turismomadrid.es/en 151 B4

## Oviedo

Gothic cathedral with 12c sanctuary. Three Visigoth (9c) churches: Santullano, Santa María del Naranco, San Miguel de Lillo. 141 A5

## Palma

Situated on Mallorca, the largest and most beautiful of the Balearic islands, with an impressive Gothic cathedral. www.palmademallorca.es 166 B2

## Picos de Europa
Mountain range with river gorges and peaks topped by Visigothic and Romanesque churches. 142 A2

## Pyrenees
Unspoiled mountain range with beautiful landscape and villages full of Romanesque architecture (cathedral of Jaca). The Ordesa National Park has many waterfalls and canyons. 144–145

## Salamanca
Delightful old city with some uniquely Spanish architecture: Renaissance Plateresque is famously seen on 16c portal of the university (founded 1215); Baroque Churrigueresque on 18c Plaza Mayor; both styles at the Convent of San Esteban. Also: Romanesque Old Cathedral; Gothic-Plateresque New Cathedral; House of Shells. www.salamanca.es 150 B2

## Santiago di Compostela
Medieval city with many churches and religious institutions. The famous pilgrimage to the shrine of St James the Apostle ends here in the magnificent cathedral, originally Romanesque with many later elements (18c Baroque façade). www.santiagodecompostela.org 140 B2

## Segovia
Old town set on a rock with a 1c Roman aqueduct. Also: 16c Gothic cathedral; Alcázar (14–15c, rebuilt 19c); 12-sided 13c Templar church of Vera Cruz. 151 B3

## Seville Sevilla
City noted for festivals and flamenco. The world's largest Gothic cathedral (15c) retains the Orange Court and minaret of a mosque. The Alcazar is a fine example of Moorish architecture. The massive 18c tobacco factory, now part of the university, was the setting for Bizet's *Carmen*. Barrio de Santa Cruz is the old Jewish quarter with narrow streets and white houses. Casa de Pilatos (15–16c) has a fine domestic patio. The Museum of Fine Arts is in a former convent. Nearby: Roman Italica with amphitheatre. 162 A2

## Tarragona
The city and its surroundings have some of the best-preserved Roman heritage in Spain. Also: Gothic cathedral (cloister); Archaeological Museum. www.tarragonaturisme.cat 147 C2

## Toledo
Historic city with Moorish, Jewish and Christian sights. The small 11c mosque of El Cristo de la Luz is one of the earliest in Spain. Two synagogues have been preserved: Santa María la Blanca; El Tránsito. Churches: San Juan de los Reyes; Gothic cathedral (good artworks). El Greco's *Burial of the Count of Orgaz* is in the Church of Santo Tomé. More of his works are in the El Greco house and, with other art, in Hospital de Santa Cruz. 151 C3

## Valencia
The old town has houses and palaces with elaborate façades. Also: Gothic cathedral and Lonja de la Seda church. www.turisvalencia.es 159 B3

## Zaragoza
Town notable for Moorish architecture (11c Aljafería Palace). The Basilica de Nuestra Señora del Pilar, one of two cathedrals, is highly venerated. www.zaragoza.es/turismo 153 A3

## Sweden Sverige
www.visitsweden.com/sweden

## Abisko
Popular resort in the Swedish part of Lapland set in an inspiring landscape of lakes and mountains. www.visitabisko.com 194 B9

## Gothenburg Göteborg
Largest port in Sweden, the historic centre has 17–18c Dutch architectural character (Kronhuset). The Art Museum has interesting Swedish works. www.goteborg.com 60 B1

## Gotland
Island with Sweden's most popular beach resorts (Ljugarn) and unspoiled countryside with churches in Baltic Gothic style (Dahlem, Bunge). Visby is a pleasant walled medieval town. http://gotland.com/en 57 C4

## Lappland (Swedish)
Swedish part of Lappland with 18c Arvidsjaur the oldest preserved Sámi village. Jokkmokk is a Sámi cultural centre, Abisko a popular resort in fine scenery. Also Finland, Norway. www.kirunalapland.se 192–193

## Lund
Charming university city with medieval centre and a fine 12c Romanesque cathedral (14c astronomical clock, carved tombs). www.visitlund.se/en 61 D3

## Malmö
Old town centre set among canals and parks dominated by a red-brick castle (museums) and a vast market square with Town Hall and Gothic Church of St Peter. www.malmotown.com/en 61 D3

## Mora
Delightful village on the shores of Siljan Lake in the heart of the Dalarna region, home to folklore and traditional crafts. 50 A1

## Stockholm
Capital of Sweden built on a number of islands. The Old Town is largely on three islands with 17–18c houses, Baroque Royal Castle (apartments and museums), Gothic cathedral, parliament. Riddarholms church has tombs of the monarchy. Museums include: National Museum; Modern Museum (one of world's best modern collections); Nordiska Museet (cultural history); open-air Skansen (Swedish houses). Baroque Drottningholm Castle is the residence of the monarchy. www.visitstockholm.com 57 A4

▼ Château de Chillon, Switzerland

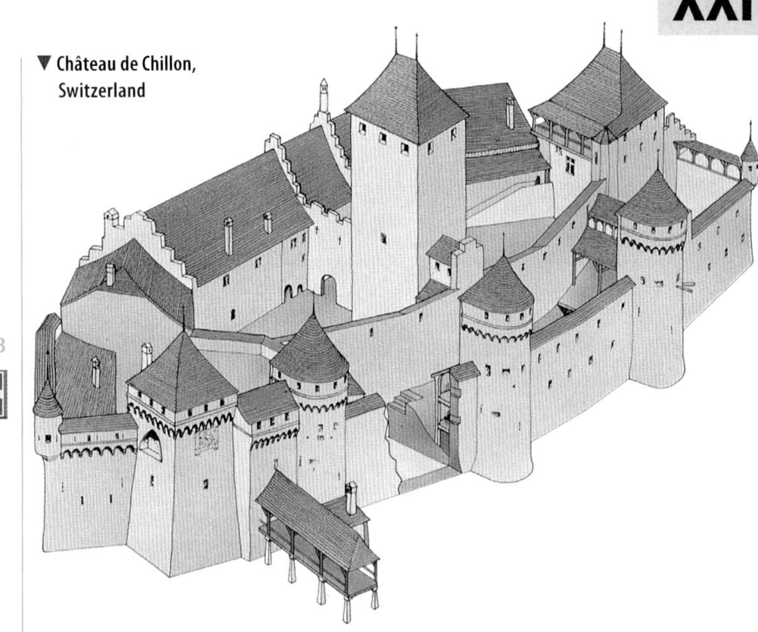

## Swedish Lakes
Beautiful region around the Vättern and Vänern Lakes. Siljan Lake is in the Dalarna region where folklore and crafts are preserved (Leksand, Mora, Rättvik). 55 B4

## Uppsala
Appealing university town with a medieval centre around the massive Gothic cathedral. www.destinationuppsala.se/en 51 C4

## Switzerland Schweiz
www.myswitzerland.com

## Alps
The most popular Alpine region is the Berner Oberland with the town of Interlaken a starting point for exploring the large number of picturesque peaks (Jungfrau). The valleys of the Graubünden have famous ski resorts (Davos, St Moritz). Zermatt lies below the most recognizable Swiss peak, the Matterhorn. 119 A4

## Basle Basel
Medieval university town with Romanesque-Gothic cathedral (tomb of Erasmus). Superb collections: Art Museum; Museum of Contemporary Art. www.basel.com/en 106 B2

## Bern
Capital of Switzerland. Medieval centre has fountains, characteristic streets (Spitalgasse) and tower-gates. The Bärengraben is famed for its bears. Also: Gothic cathedral; good Fine Arts Museum. www.bern.com/en 106 C2

## Geneva Genève
The historic area is centred on the Romanesque cathedral and Place du Bourg du Four. Excellent collections: Art and History Museum; new Museum of Modern and Contemporary Art. On the lake shore: splendid medieval Château de Chillon. www.geneve-tourisme.ch 118 A3

## Interlaken
Starting point for excursions to the most delightful part of the Swiss Alps, the Bernese Oberland, with Grindelwald and Lauterbrunnen – one of the most thrilling valleys leading up to the ski resort of Wengen with views on the Jungfrau. www.interlaken.ch 106 C2

## Lucerne Luzern
On the beautiful shores of Vierwaldstättersee, a charming medieval town of white houses on narrow streets and of wooden bridges (Kapellbrücke, Spreuerbrücke). It is centred on the Kornmarkt with the Renaissance Old Town Hall and Am Rhyn-Haus (Picasso collection). www.luzern.com 106 C1

## Zürich
Set on Zürichsee, the old quarter is around Niederdorf with 15c cathedral. Gothic Fraumünster has stained glass by Chagall. Museums: Swiss National Museum (history); Art Museum (old and modern masters); Rietberg Museum (non-European cultures). www.zuerich.com 107 B3

## Turkey Türkiye
www.gototurkey.co.uk

## Istanbul
Divided by the spectcular Bosphorus, the stretch of water that separates Europe from Asia, the historic district is surrounded by the Golden Horn, Sea of Marmara and the 5c wall of Theodosius. Major sights: 6c Byzantine church of St Sophia (converted first to a mosque in 1453 and then a museum in 1934); 15c Topkapi Palace; treasury and Archaeological Museum; 17c Blue Mosque; 19c Bazaar; 16c Süleymaniye Mosque; 12c Kariye Camii; European district with Galata Tower and 19c Dolmabahçe Palace. http://english.istanbul.com 186 A3

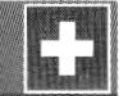

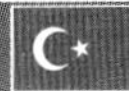

## Ukraine Ukraina
www.ukraine.com

### Kiev Kyïv
Capital of Ukraine, known for its cathedral (11c, 17c) with Byzantine frescoes and mosaics. The Monastery of the Caves has churches, monastic buildings and catacombs.
www.kiev.info **13 C9**

## United Kingdom
www.visitbritain.com

### England
www.visitengland.com

### Bath
Elegant spa town with notable 18c architecture: Circus, Royal Crescent, Pulteney Bridge, Assembly Rooms; Pump Room. Also: well-preserved Roman baths; superb Perpendicular Gothic Bath Abbey. Nearby: Elizabethan Longleat House; exceptional 18c landscaped gardens at Stourhead. http://visitbath.co.uk **43 A4**

### Brighton
Resort with a sea-front of Georgian, Regency and Victorian buildings, Palace Pier and old town of narrow lanes. The main sight is the Oriental-style Royal Pavilion. Nearby: South Downs National Park.
www.visitbrighton.com **44 C3**

### Bristol
Old port city with the fascinating Floating Harbour. Major sights include Gothic 13–14c Church of St Mary Redcliffe and 19c Clifton Suspension Bridge.
http://visitbristol.co.uk **43 A4**

### Cambridge
City with university founded in the early 13c. Peterhouse (1284) is the oldest college. Most famous colleges were founded in 14–16c: Queen's, King's (with the superb Perpendicular Gothic 15–16c King's College Chapel), St John's (with famous 19c Bridge of Sighs), Trinity, Clare, Gonville and Caius, Magdalene. Museums: excellent Fitzwilliam Museum (classical, medieval, old masters). Kettle's Yard (20c British).
www.visitcambridge.org **45 A4**

### Canterbury
Medieval city and old centre of Christianity. The Norman-Gothic cathedral has many sights and was a major medieval pilgrimage site (as related in Chaucer's *Canterbury Tales*). St Augustine, sent to convert the English in 597, founded St Augustine's Abbey, now in ruins.
www.canterbury.co.uk **45 B5**

### Chatsworth
One of the richest aristocratic country houses in England (largely 17c) set in a large landscaped park. The palatial interior has some 175 richly furnished rooms and a major art collection. www.chatsworth.org **40 B2**

### Chester
Charming medieval city with complete walls. The Norman-Gothic cathedral has several abbey buildings. www.visitchester.com **38 A4**

### Cornish Coast
Scenic landscape of cliffs and sandy beaches with picturesque villages (Fowey, Mevagissey). St Ives has the Tate Gallery with work of the St Ives Group. St Michael's Mount is reached by causeway at low tide.
www.visitcornwall.com **42 B1**

### Dartmoor
Beautiful wilderness area in Devon with tors and its own breed of wild pony as well as free-ranging cattle and sheep.
www.dartmoor.gov.uk **42 B3**

### Durham
Historic city with England's finest Norman cathedral and a castle, both placed majestically on a rock above the river. www.thisisdurham.com **37 B5**

### Eden Project
Centre showing the diversity of plant life on the planet, built in a disused clay pit. Two biomes, one with Mediterranean and Southern African focus and the larger featuring a waterfall, river and tropical trees plants and flowers. Outdoors also features plantations including bamboo and tea. www.edenproject.com **42 B2**

### Hadrian's Wall
Built to protect the northernmost border of the Roman Empire in the 2c AD, the walls originally extended some 120km with castles every mile and 16 forts. Best-preserved walls around Hexam; forts at Housesteads and Chesters. www.visithadrianswall.co.uk **37 A4**

### Lake District
Beautiful landscape of lakes (Windermere, Coniston) and England's high peaks (Scafell Pike, Skiddaw, Old Man), famous for its poets, particularly Wordsworth.
www.lakedistrict.gov.uk **36 B3**

### Leeds Castle
One of the oldest and most romantic English castles, standing in the middle of a lake. Most of the present appearance dates from 19c.
www.leeds-castle.com **45 B4**

### Lincoln
Old city perched on a hill with narrow streets, majestically dominated by the Norman-Gothic cathedral and castle.
www.visitlincolnshire.com **40 B3**

### Liverpool
City on site of port founded in 1207 and focused around 1846 Albert Dock, now a heritage attraction. Croxteth Hall and Country Park; Speke Hall; Sudley House; Royal Liver Building; Liverpool Cathedral; Walker Art Gallery; Tate Liverpool; University of Liverpool Art Gallery.
www.visitliverpool.com **38 A4**

### London
Capital of UK and Europe's largest city. To the east of the medieval heart of the city – now the largely modern financial district and known as the City of London – is the Tower of London (11c White Tower, Crown Jewels) and 1880s Tower Bridge. The popular heart of the city and its entertainment is the West End, around Piccadilly Circus, Leicester Square and Trafalgar Square (Nelson's Column). Many sights of political and royal power: Whitehall (Banqueting House, 10 Downing Street, Horse Guards); Neo-Gothic Palace of Westminster (Houses of Parliament) with Big Ben; The Mall leading to Buckingham Palace (royal residence, famous ceremony of the Changing of the Guard). Numerous churches include: 13–16c Gothic Westminster Abbey (many tombs, Henry VII's Chapel); Wren's Baroque St Paul's Cathedral, St Mary-le-Bow, spire of St Bride's, St Stephen Walbrook. Museums of world fame: British Museum (prehistory, oriental and classical antiquity, medieval); Victoria and Albert Museum (decorative arts); National Gallery (old masters to 19c); National Portrait Gallery (historic and current British portraiture); Tate – Britain and Modern; Science Museum; Natural History Museum. Madame Tussaud's waxworks museum is hugely popular. Other sights include: London Eye, Kensington Palace; Greenwich with Old Royal Observatory (Greenwich meridian), Baroque Royal Naval College, Palladian Queen's House; Tudor Hampton Court Palace; Syon House. Nearby: Windsor Castle (art collection, St George's Chapel).
www.visitlondon.com **44 B3**

◀ Salisbury Cathedral, England

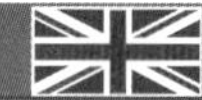

## Longleat

One of the earliest and finest Elizabethan palaces in England. The palace is richly decorated. Some of the grounds have been turned into a pleasure park, with the Safari Park, the first of its kind outside Africa. www.longleat.co.uk **43 A4**

## Manchester

Founded on a Roman settlement of 79AD and a main player in the Industrial Revolution. Victorian Gothic Town Hall; Royal Exchange; Cathedral. Many museums including Imperial War Museum North, Lowry Centre and Manchester Art Gallery. www.visitmanchester.com **40 B1**

## Newcastle upon Tyne

A key player in the Industrial Revolution with 12th century cathedral and many museums as well as strong railway heritage. www.newcastlegateshead.com **37 B5**

## Norwich

Medieval quarter has half-timbered houses. 15c castle keep houses a museum and gallery. Many medieval churches include the Norman-Gothic cathedral. www.visitnorwich.co.uk **41 C5**

## Oxford

Old university city. Earliest colleges date from 13c: University College; Balliol; Merton. 14–16c colleges include: New College; Magdalen; Christ Church (perhaps the finest). Other buildings: Bodleian Library; Radcliffe Camera; Sheldonian Theatre; cathedral. Good museums: Ashmolean Museum (antiquity to 20c); Museum of the History of Science; Museum of Modern Art; Christ Church Picture Gallery

(14–17c). Nearby: outstanding 18c Blenheim Palace. www.visitoxfordandoxfordshire.com **44 B2**

## Petworth

House (17c) with one of the finest country-house art collections (old masters), set in a huge landscaped park. www.nationaltrust.org.uk **44 C3**

## Salisbury

Pleasant old city with a magnificent 13c cathedral built in an unusually unified Gothic style. Nearby: Wilton House. www.visitwiltshire.co.uk **44 B2**

## Stonehenge

Some 4000 years old, one of the most famous and haunting Neolithic monuments in Europe. Many other Neolithic sites are nearby. www.english-heritage.org.uk **44 B2**

## Stourhead

Early 18c palace famous for its grounds, one of the finest examples of neoclassical landscaped gardening, consisting of a lake surrounded by numerous temples. www.nationaltrust.org.uk **43 A4**

## Stratford-upon-Avon

Old town of Tudor and Jacobean half-timbered houses, famed as the birth and burial place of William Shakespeare and home of the Royal Shakespeare Company. www.shakespeare-country.co.uk **44 A2**

## Wells

Charming city with beautiful 12–16c cathedral (west facade, scissor arches, chapter house, medieval clock). Also Bishop's Palace; Vicar's Close. www.wellssomerset.com **43 A4**

## Winchester

Historic city with 11–16c cathedral. Also: 13c Great Hall, Winchester College, St Cross almshouses. Western gateway to the South Downs National Park. www.visitwinchester.co.uk **44 B2**

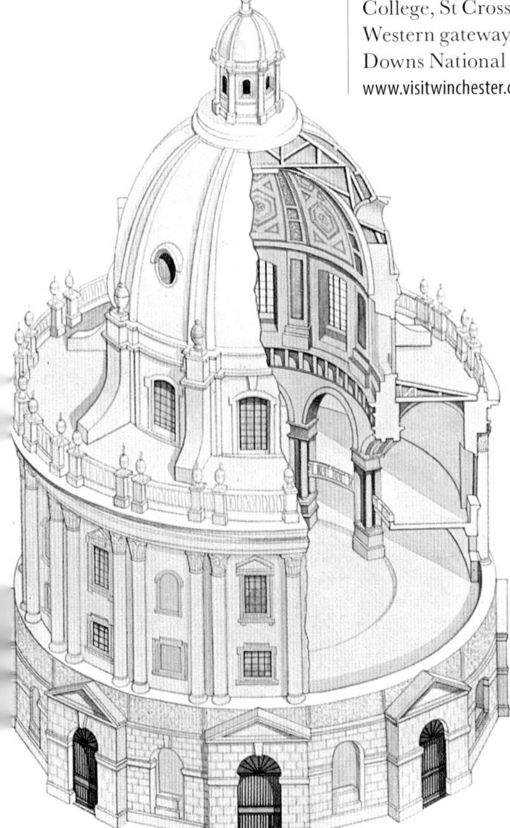

◀ Radcliffe Camera), Oxford, England

## York

Attractive medieval city surrounded by well-preserved walls with magnificent Gothic 13–15c Minster. Museums: York City Art Gallery (14–19c); Jorvik Viking Centre. Nearby: Castle Howard. www.visityork.org **40 B2**

### Northern Ireland
www.discovernorthernireland.com

## Antrim Coast

Spectacular coast with diverse scenery of glens (Glenarm, Glenariff), cliffs (Murlough Bay) and the famous Giant's Causeway, consisting of some 40,000 basalt columns. Carrickefergus Castle is the largest and best-preserved Norman castle in Ireland. http://antrimcoastandglensaonb.ccght.org http://causewaycoastaonb.ccght.org **27 A4**

## Belfast

Capital of Northern Ireland. Sights: Donegall Square with 18c Town Hall; neo-Romanesque Protestant cathedral; University Square; Ulster Museum (European painting). http://visit-belfast.com **27 B5**

## Giant's Causeway

Spectacular and unique rock formations in the North Antrim coast, formed by volcanic activity 50–60 million years ago. World Heritage Site. www.nationaltrust.org.uk **27 A4**

### Scotland
www.visitscotland.com

## Edinburgh

Capital of Scotland, built on volcanic hills. The medieval Old Town is dominated by the castle set high on a volcanic rock (Norman St Margaret's Chapel, state apartments, Crown Room). Holyrood House (15c and 17c) has lavishly decorated state apartments and the ruins of Holyrood Abbey (remains of Scottish monarchs). The 15c cathedral has the Crown Spire and Thistle Chapel. The New Town has good Georgian architecture (Charlotte Square, Georgian House). Excellent museums: Scottish National Portrait Gallery, National Gallery of Scotland; Scottish National Gallery of Modern Art. **35 C4**

## Glamis Castle

In beautiful, almost flat landscaped grounds, 14c fortress, rebuilt 17c, gives a fairy-tale impression. www.strathmore-estates.co.uk **35 B5**

## Glasgow

Scotland's largest city, with centre around George Square and 13–15c Gothic cathedral. The Glasgow School of Art (currently closed for repair after a fire) is the masterpiece of Charles Rennie Mackintosh. Fine art collections: Glasgow Museum and Art Gallery; Hunterian Gallery; Burrell Collection; Kelvingrove Art Gallery and Museum. **35 C3**

## Loch Ness

In the heart of the Highlands, the lake forms part of the scenic Great Glen running from Inverness to Fort William. Famous as home of the fabled Loch Ness Monster (exhibition at Drumnadrochit). Nearby: ruins of 14–16c Urquhart Castle. www.lochness.com **32 D2**

### Wales
www.visitwales.com

## Caernarfon

Town dominated by a magnificent 13c castle, one of a series built by Edward I in Wales (others include Harlech, Conwy, Beaumaris, Caerphilly). www.visitcaernarfon.com **38 A2**

## Cardiff

Capital of Wales, most famous for its medieval castle, restored 19c in Greek, Gothic and Oriental styles. Also: National Museum and Gallery. www.visitcardiff.com **39 C3**

### Vatican City
### Città del Vaicano
www.vatican.va

## Vatican City Città del Vaticano

Independent state within Rome. On Piazza San Pietro is the 15–16c Renaissance-Baroque Basilica San Pietro (Michelangelo's dome and *Pietà*), the world's most important Roman Catholic church. The Vatican Palace contains the Vatican Museums with many fine art treasures including Michelangelo's frescoes in the Sistine Chapel. **168 B2**

▼ The facade of Basilica San Pietro, Vatican City

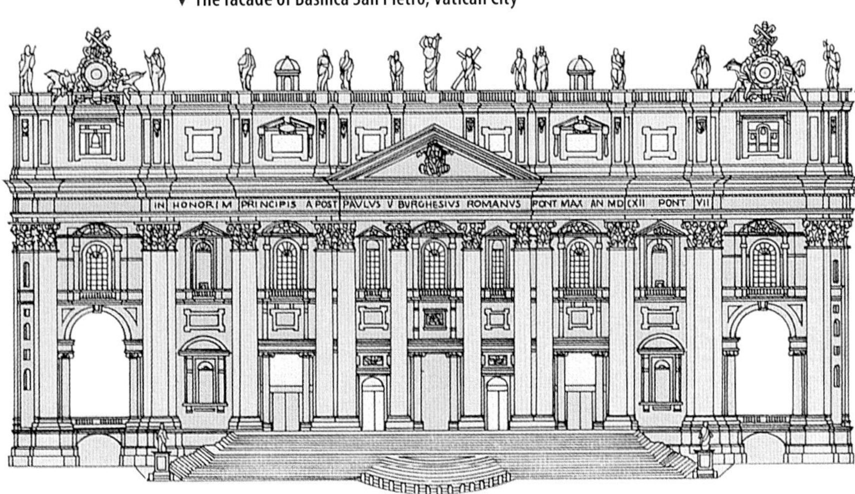

# European politics and economics

**The figures given for capitals' populations are for the whole metropolitan area.**

## Albania Shqipëria

**Area** 28,748 km² (11,100 mi²)
**Population** 3,011,000
**Capital** Tirana / Tiranë (764,000)
**Languages** Albanian (official), Greek, Vlach, Romani and Slavic
**GDP** $4,781 (2014)
**Currency** Lek = 100 Quindars
**Government** multiparty republic
**Head of state** Bujar Nishani, 2012
**Head of government** Prime Minister Edi Rama, Socialist Party, 2013
**Website** www.km.gov.al/?gj=gj2
**Events** In the 2005 general elections, the Democratic Party and its allies won a decisive victory on pledges of reducing crime and corruption, promoting economic growth and decreasing the size of government. The party retained power by a narrow margin in 2009, amid disputes over electoral procedure. After three years of talks, a Stabilisation and Association Agreement was signed with the EU in June 2006, and the country formally applied for membership in April 2009, the same month as it became a member of NATO. Protests at alleged official corruption and vote-rigging led to violent clashes in 2011. The Socialist Party won 53% of the vote in 2013 elections. Albania became an EU candidate member in June 2014.
**Economy** Although economic growth has begun, Albania is still one of the poorest countries in Europe. 56% of the workforce are engaged in agriculture. Private ownership of land has been encouraged since 1991 and foreign investment is encouraged. Public debt stands at over 70%.

## Andorra Principat d'Andorra

**Area** 468 km² (181 mi²)
**Population** 85,000
**Capital** Andorra la Vella (44,000)
**Languages** Catalan (official), French, Castilian and Portuguese **GDP** $46,418 (2012)
**Currency** Euro = 100 cents
**Government** independent state and co-principality
**Head of state** co-princes: Joan Enric Vives i Sicilia, Bishop of Urgell, 2003 and François Hollande (see France), 2012
**Head of government** Chief Executive Antoni Martí Petit, Democrats for Andorra, 2011
**Website** http://visitandorra.com
**Events** In 1993 a new democratic constitution was adopted that reduced the roles of the President of France and the Bishop of Urgell to constitutional figureheads. In 2010, the OECD removed Andorra from its list of uncooperative tax havens. The introduction of personal income tax was approved in 2013, and came into force in 2015.
**Economy** About 80% of the work force are employed in the services sector, but tourism accounts for about 80% of GDP with an estimated 9 million visiting annually, attracted by its duty-free status and its summer and winter resorts. Agricultural production is limited (2% of the land is arable) and most food has to be imported. The principal livestock activity is sheep rearing. Manufacturing output consists mainly of cigarettes, cigars and furniture.

## Austria Österreich

**Area** 83,859 km² (32,377 mi²)
**Population** 8,505,000
**Capital** Vienna / Wien (2,419,000)
**Languages** German (official)
**GDP** $46,420 (2014)
**Currency** Euro = 100 cents
**Government** federal republic
**Head of state** President Heinz Fischer, 2004
**Head of government** Federal Chancellor Werner Faymann, Social Democratic Party, 2008
**Website** www.austria.gv.at
**Events** Since general elections in 1999, the extreme right Freedom Party has made gains at the expense of the Social Democrats and their successive coalition partners. In 2013 parliamentary elections, the coalition received just over 50% of the vote and the Freedom Party 21%.
**Economy** Has a well-developed market economy and high standard of living. The economy continued to grow in 2014. The leading economic activities are the manufacture of metals and tourism. Dairy and livestock farming are the principal agricultural activities.

## Belarus

**Area** 207,600 km² (80,154 mi²)
**Population** 9,609,000
**Capital** Minsk (2,002,000)
**Languages** Belarusian, Russian (both official)
**GDP** $8,042 (2014)
**Currency** Belarussian ruble = 100 kopek
**Government** Republic
**Head of state** President Alexander Lukashenko, 1994
**Head of government** Andrei Kobyakov, independent, 2014
**Website** www.belarus.by/en/government
**Events** Belarus attained its independence in 1991. As a result of a referendum in 1996 the president increased his power at the expense of parliament. In 1997, Belarus signed a Union Treaty committing it to political and economic integration with Russia. Since his election in July 1994 as the country's first president, Alexander Lukashenko, has steadily consolidated his power through authoritarian means. Government restrictions on freedom of speech, the press and religion continue and in early 2005, the US listed Belarus as an outpost of tyranny. Belarus joined the EU's Eastern Partnership in 2009. In 2010, it signed a customs union with Russia and Kazakhstan. Alexander Lukashenko was declared to have won a fourth term as president in December 2010 in elections, described internationally as flawed, which provoked protests. The arrests and beatings of opposition candidates and protesters led to EU sanctions, but clamp-downs on personal and political freedoms have continued.
**Economy** Belarus has faced problems in the transition to a free-market economy. After relaxation of currency rules in early 2011, the value of the ruble dropped sharply and the country's large foreign debts and lack of hard currency led to negotiations with Russia over substantial loans. Agriculture, especially meat and dairy farming, is important. In 2011, the country was forced to apply to the IMF for funds and for a Russian-led bailout.

## Belgium Belgique

**Area** 30,528 km² (11,786 mi²)
**Population** 12,000,000
**Capital** Brussels/Bruxelles (1,830,000)
**Languages** Dutch, French, German (all official)
**GDP** $47,722 (2014)
**Currency** Euro = 100 cents
**Government** federal constitutional monarchy
**Head of state** King Philippe I, 2013
**Head of government** Prime Minister Charles Michel, Reformist Movement, 2014
**Website** www.belgium.be/en
**Events** In 1993 Belgium adopted a federal system of government. Elections in June 2007 led to the Christian Democrats gaining almost 30% of the vote in Flanders. An uneasy coalition was eventually formed in March 2008, but negotiations for constitutional reform stalled. Former PM Leterme replaced Herman van Rompuy when the latter became President of the European Council. The coalition collapsed in April 2010. Elections in June resulted in gains for the pro-separatist New Flemish Alliance and the Socialist Party in Wallonia. Negotiations to form a coalition lasted until December 2011. After parliamentary elections in May 2014, a coalition was formed in October, led by Charles Michel, leader of the Francophone Reformist Movement.
**Economy** Belgium is a major trading nation with a modern, private-enterprise economy, which grew slightly in 2014. The leading activity is manufacturing i.e. steel and chemicals. With few natural resources, it imports substantial quantities of raw materials and export a large volume of manufactures.

## Bosnia-Herzegovina Bosna i Hercegovina

**Area** 51,197 km² (19,767 mi²)
**Population** 3,872,000
**Capital** Sarajevo (608,000)
**Languages** Bosnian/Croatian/Serbian
**GDP** $4,644 (2014)
**Currency** Convertible Marka = 100 convertible pfenniga
**Government** federal republic
**Head of state** Chairman of the Presidency – rotates between Presidency members Bakir Izetbegović (Party of Democratic Action), Mladen Ivanić (Party of Democratic Progress) and Dragan Čović (Croatian Democratic Union of Bosnia and Herzegovina)
**Head of government** Prime Minister Denis Zvizdić, Party of Democratic Action, 2015
**Website** www.fbihvlada.gov.ba/english/index.php
**Events** In 1992 a referendum approved independence from the Yugoslav federation. The Bosnian Serb population was against independence and in the resulting war occupied over two-thirds of the land. Croat forces seized other parts of the area. The 1995 Dayton Peace Accord ended the war and set up the Bosnian Muslim/Croat Federation and the Bosnian Serb Republic, each with their own president, government, parliament, military and police. There is also a central Bosnian government and rotating presidency. The office of High Representative has the power to impose decisions where the authorities are unable to agree or where political or economic interests are affected; the current incumbent, Valentin Inzko took charge in 2009. EUFOR troops took over from the NATO-led force in 2004. In late 2005, agreement was reached to set up state-wide police defence and security forces, a state court and state taxation system, and the EU initiated its Stabilisation and Association Agreement with Bosnia in 2007. In 2005, agreement was reached to set up state-wide police, defence and security forces, a state court and state taxation system. In 2006, Bosnia joined NATO's Partnership for Peace programme and received its membership action plan in 2010. In 2007, the EU initiated its Stabilisation and Association Agreement with Bosnia, which was eventually signed in March 2015.
**Economy** Excluding Macedonia, Bosnia was the least developed of the former republics of Yugoslavia. Currently receiving substantial aid, though this will be reduced. The country attracts considerable foreign direct investment and the Convertible Marka is Euro-pegged. The economy grew slightly in 2014.

## Bulgaria Bulgariya

**Area** 110,912 km² (42,822 mi²)
**Population** 6,925,000 **Capital** Sofia (1,454,000)
**Languages** Bulgarian (official), Turkish
**GDP** $7,753 (2014) **Currency** Lev = 100 stotinki
**Government** multiparty republic
**Head of state** President Rosen Asenov Plevneliev, Citizens for European Development of Bulgaria GERB, 2012
**Head of government** Prime Minister Boiko Borisov, Citizens for European Development of Bulgaria (GERB), 2014.
**Website** www.government.bg
**Events** In 1990 the first non-communist president for 40 years, Zhelyu Zhelev, was elected. A new constitution in 1991 saw the adoption of free-market reforms. Bulgaria joined NATO in 2004. The president was re-elected in 2006. Bulgaria joined the EU in January 2007, but lack of progress in tackling corruption has led to the delay, then scrapping of a large proportion of EU funding. The GERB-led coalition fell in early 2012 after street protests and was replaced in May 2013 by a technocratic government. Parliamentary elections of 2014 saw GERB win over 32% of the vote, returning former PM Boiko Borisov to power, despite allegations of systemic corruption.
**Economy** The Lev has been pegged to the Euro since 2002. The economy has begun to attract significant amounts of foreign direct investment. Bulgaria experienced macroeconomic stability and strong growth from 1996 to early 2008, and after a sharp decline in GDP in 2009, the economy returned to slight growth from 2010. Manufacturing is the leading economic activity but has outdated technology. The main products are chemicals, metals, machinery and textiles. The valleys of the Maritsa are ideal for winemaking, plums and tobacco. Tourism is increasing rapidly.

## Croatia Hrvatska

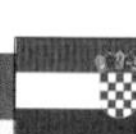

**Area** 56,538 km² (21,829 mi²)
**Population** 4,471,000
**Capital** Zagreb (1,111,000)
**Languages** Croatian **GDP** $13,494 (2014)
**Currency** Kuna = 100 lipa
**Government** multiparty republic
**Head of state** President Kolinda Grabar-Kitarović, Croatian Democratic Union, 2015
**Head of government** Prime Minister Zoran Milanović, Social Democratic Party of Croatia (SDP), 2011.
**Website** http://croatia.hr
**Events** A 1991 referendum voted overwhelmingly in favour of independence from Yugoslavia. Serb-dominated areas took up arms to remain in the federation. Serbia armed Croatian Serbs, war broke out between Serbia and Croatia, and Croatia lost much territory. In 1992 United Nations peacekeeping troops were deployed. Following the Dayton Peace Accord of 1995, Croatia and Yugoslavia established diplomatic relations. An agreement between the Croatian government and Croatian Serbs provided for the eventual reintegration of Krajina into Croatia in 1998. PM Kosor leads a minority government. Presidential elections of 2014/15 saw former Assistant Secretary General of NATO for Public Diplomacy, Kolinda Grabar-Kitarović, win after a run-off against incumbent Ivo Josipović. Croatia joined NATO in 2009 and, after a referendum in 2012, joined the EU in 2013.
**Economy** The wars badly disrupted Croatia's economy but it emerged from a mild recession in 2000, with tourism, banking and public investment leading the way. The economy continues to struggle and unemployment is high.

## Czech Republic Česka Republica

**Area** 78,864 km² (30,449 mi²)
**Population** 10,627,000
**Capital** Prague/Praha (2,300,000)
**Languages** Czech (official), Moravian
**GDP** $19,563 (2014)
**Currency** Czech Koruna = 100 haler
**Government** multiparty republic
**Head of state** President Milos Zeman, 2013
**Head of government** Prime Minister Bohuslav Sobotka, SDP, 2014
**Website** www.vlada.cz/en/
**Events** In 1992 the government agreed to the secession of the Slovak Republic, and on 1 January 1993 the Czech Republic was created. The Czech Republic was granted full membership of NATO in 1999 and joined the EU in May 2004. Governments have been characterized by short-lived coalitions. PM Petr Nečas was forced to resign in June 2013 over allegations of corruption. After early parliamentary elections in October, Bohuslav Sobotka of the Social Democrats was appointed head of a coalition government in January 2014.
**Economy** The country has deposits of coal, uranium, iron ore, tin and zinc. Industries include chemicals, beer, iron and steel. Private ownership of land is gradually being restored. Agriculture employs 12% of the workforce. Inflation is under control. Intensified restructuring among large enterprises, improvements in the financial sector and effective use of available EU funds served to strengthen output growth until the onset of the worldwide economic downturn, because of reduced exports. Prague is now a major tourist destination.

## Denmark Danmark

**Area** 43,094 km² (16,638 mi²)
**Population** 5,627,000
**Capital** Copenhagen / København (1,997,000)
**Languages** Danish (official)
**GDP** $60,564 (2014)
**Currency** Krone = 100 øre
**Government** parliamentary monarchy
**Head of state** Queen Margrethe II, 1972
**Head of government** Prime Minister Lars Lokke Rasmussen, Venstre, 2015
**Website** www.denmark.dk/en
**Events** In 1992 Denmark rejected the Maastricht Treaty, but reversed the decision in a 1993 referendum. In 1998 the Amsterdam Treaty was ratified by a further referendum. In 2009 Greenland assumed responsibility for many domestic competencies. Former PM Lars Lokke Rasmussen was returned to power in parliamentary elections in 2015.
**Economy** Danes enjoy a high standard of living with a thoroughly modern market economy

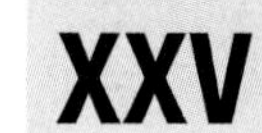

featuring high-tech agriculture, up-to-date small-scale and corporate industry, comfortable living standards and a stable currency, which is pegged to the Euro, but still independent. Economic growth gained momentum in 2004, but slowed in 2007. GDP has continued to grow slightly since 2012. Denmark is self-sufficient in oil and natural gas. Services, including tourism, form the largest sector (63% of GDP). Farming employs only 4% of the workforce but is highly productive. Fishing is also important.

## Estonia Eesti

**Area** 45,100 km² (17,413 mi²)
**Population** 1,314,000
**Capital** Tallinn (543,000)
**Languages** Estonian (official), Russian
**GDP** $19,671 (2014)
**Currency** Euro = 100 cents
**Government** multiparty republic
**Head of state**
President Toomas Hendrik Ilves, 2006
**Head of government** Prime Minister Taavi Roivas, Reform Party, 2014
**Website** http://valitsus.ee/en
**Events** In 1992 Estonia adopted a new constitution and multiparty elections were held. Estonia joined NATO in March 2004 and the EU in May 2004. In 2005 a treaty defining the border with Russia was signed, but Russia refused to ratify it after Estonia introduced a reference to the Russian occupation of Estonia. Long-standing coalition PM Andrus Ansip resigned as leader in early 2014 and was replaced by 34-year-old Taavi Roivas, who went on to win elections in 2015. Estonia joined the OECD in 2010 and adopted the Euro in January 2011. Strict language laws are regarded by Russian-speakers as discriminatory.
**Economy** Privatisation and free-trade reforms after independence increased foreign investment and trade. Chief natural resources are oil shale and forests. Manufactures include petrochemicals, fertilisers and textiles. Estonia has led the way among new EU states with a strong electronics and communications sector. Since the country emerged from the global financial crisis in 2010, the economy has grown erratically.

## Finland Suomi

**Area** 338,145 km² (130,557 mi²)
**Population** 5,457,000
**Capital** Helsinki (1,403,000)
**Languages** Finnish, Swedish (both official)
**GDP** $49,497 (2014)
**Currency** Euro = 100 cents
**Government** multiparty republic
**Head of state** President Sauli Niinistö, National Coalition Party, 2012
**Head of government** Prime Minister Juha Sipilä, Centre Party, 2015
**Events** In 1986 Finland became a member of EFTA and in 1995 joined the EU. A new constitution was established in March 2000. The Finnish Parliament voted for the EU constitution in 2006. Successive governments have been in the form of multi-party coalitions. In the presidential election of 2012, Sauli Niinistö defeated Pekka-Haavisto of the Green Party.
**Economy** Forests are Finland's most valuable resource, with wood and paper products accounting for 35% of exports. Engineering, shipbuilding and textile industries have grown. Finland excels in high-tech exports and is a leading light in the telecoms industry. Farming employs 9% of the workforce. Unemployment remains high, although the economy returned to growth in 2011.

## France

**Area** 551,500 km² (212,934 mi²)
**Population** 66,616,000
**Capital** Paris (12,162,000)
**Languages** French (official), Breton, Occitan
**GDP** $44,538 (2014)
**Currency** Euro = 100 cents
**Government** multiparty republic
**Head of state** President François Hollande, Socialist Party, 2012
**Head of government** Prime Minister Manuel Valls, Socialist Party, 2014
**Website** www.diplomatie.gouv.fr/en/
**Events** Early 2015 saw multiple attacks by Islamist terrorists, most notably on the offices of the satirical magazine Charlie Hebdo.
**Economy** France is a leading industrial nation. Industries include chemicals and steel. It is the leading producer of farm products in western

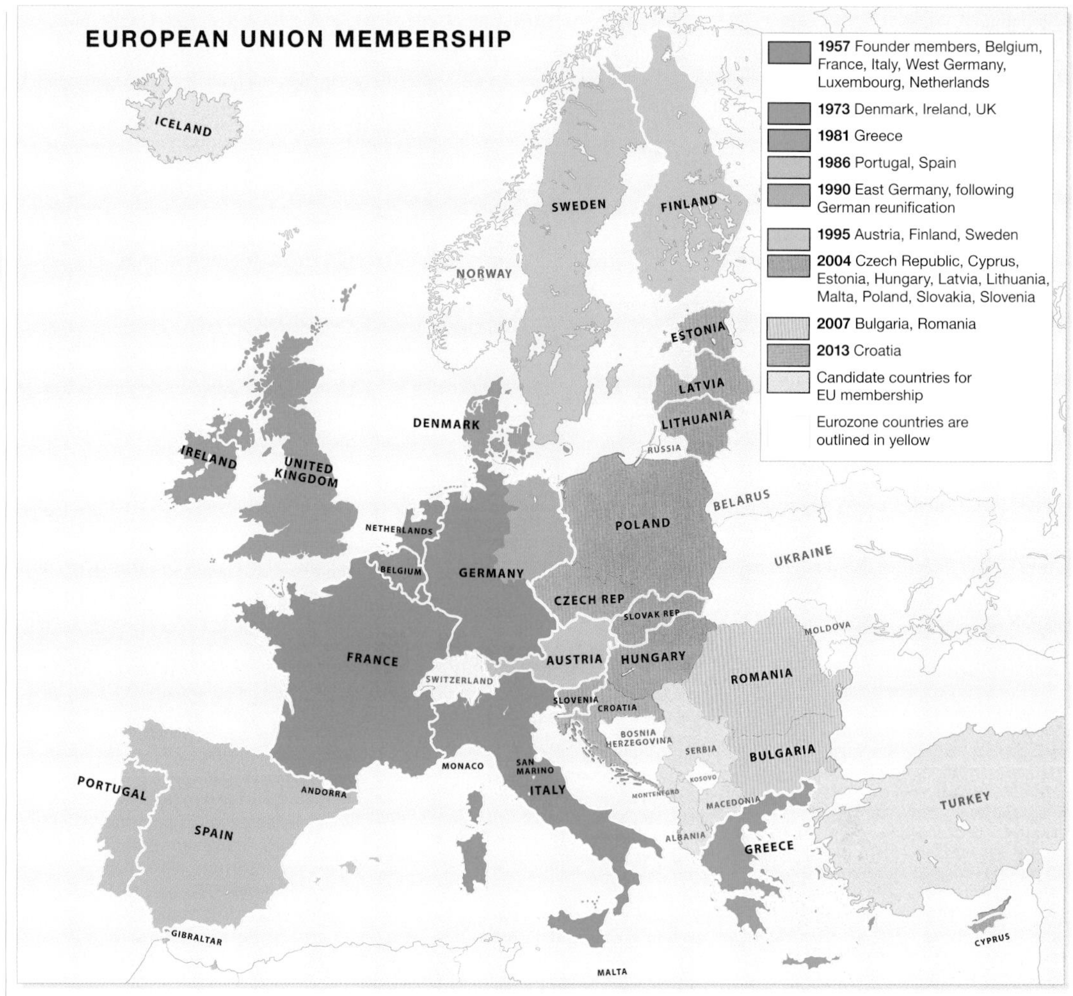

**EUROPEAN UNION MEMBERSHIP**

- **1957** Founder members, Belgium, France, Italy, West Germany, Luxembourg, Netherlands
- **1973** Denmark, Ireland, UK
- **1981** Greece
- **1986** Portugal, Spain
- **1990** East Germany, following German reunification
- **1995** Austria, Finland, Sweden
- **2004** Czech Republic, Cyprus, Estonia, Hungary, Latvia, Lithuania, Malta, Poland, Slovakia, Slovenia
- **2007** Bulgaria, Romania
- **2013** Croatia
- Candidate countries for EU membership
- Eurozone countries are outlined in yellow

Europe. Livestock and dairy farming are vital sectors. Despite a degree of recovery, unemployment remains high. It is the world's second largest producer of cheese and wine. Tourism is a major industry.

## Germany Deutschland

**Area** 357,022 km² (137,846 mi²)
**Population** 80,716,000
**Capital** Berlin (6,000,000)
**Languages** German (official)
**GDP** $47,590 (2014)
**Currency** Euro = 100 cents
**Government** federal multiparty republic
**Head of state** President Joachim Gauck, independent, 2012
**Head of government** Chancellor Angela Merkel, Christian Democratic Union, 2005
**Website** www.bundesregierung.de
**Events** Germany is a major supporter of the European Union, and former chancellor Helmut Köhl was the driving force behind the creation of the Euro. The grand coalition government formed in 2005 between the CDU, CSU and Social Democrats was replaced by one of the CDU, CSU and FDP after elections in 2009. Repeated calls upon German funds in support of weaker Eurozone economies have caused widespread anger. In 2012, after Christian Wulff was forced to resign because of corruption charges the consensus candidate former Lutheran pastor and civil rights activist Joacham Glauk was elected president. Angela Merkel's CDU only narrowly missed winning an outright majority in 2013 elections.
**Economy** Germany has long been one of the world's greatest economic powers. The economy returned to growth in 2014. Services form the largest economic sector. Machinery and transport equipment account for 50% of exports. It is the world's third-largest car producer. Other major products include ships, iron, steel, petroleum and tyres. It has the world's second-largest lignite mining industry. Other minerals are copper, potash, lead, salt, zinc and aluminium. Germany is the world's second-largest producer of hops and beer, and fifth-largest of wine. Other products are cheese and milk, barley, rye and pork.

## Greece Ellas

**Area** 131,957 km² (50,948 mi²)
**Population** 10,816,000
**Capital** Athens / Athina (3,758,000)
**Languages** Greek (official)
**GDP** $21,653 (2014)
**Currency** Euro = 100 cents
**Government** multiparty republic
**Head of state** President Prokopis Pavlopoulos, New Democracy, 2015
**Head of government** Prime Minister Alexis Tsipras, Syriza, 2015
**Website** www.primeminister.gr/english
**Events** In 1981 Greece joined the EU, and Andreas Papandreous became Greece's first Socialist prime minister. The coalition led by Antonis Samaras fell in early 2015 because of continued discontent over the economy. The left-wing Syriza, under Alexis Tsipras, came to power on a ticket of rejecting the international donors' austerity measures. Months of negotiations over extra loans or deferment of repayments failed to reach a compromise, culminating in the Greek PM opting for a referendum on the donor's proposals, making a Greek exit from the Eurozone more probable.
**Economy** Greece is one of the poorest members of the European Union. Manufacturing is important. Products: textiles, cement, chemicals, metallurgy. Minerals: lignite, bauxite, chromite. Farmland covers 33% of Greece, grazing land 40%. Major crops: tobacco, olives, grapes, cotton, wheat. Livestock are raised. Tourism provides 15% of GDP. In receipt of multiple loans from Eurozone funds and the IMF, Greece has repeatedly been in danger of defaulting on debt repayments, with the possible result that it would be forced to give up the currency. Austerity measures imposed by the international community have depressed economic activity. Unemployment remains at over 25% and over one-third of the population is below the poverty line.

## Hungary Magyarorszàg

**Area** 93,032 km² (35,919 mi²)
**Population** 9,879,000
**Capital** Budapest (3,284,000)
**Languages** Hungarian (official)
**GDP** $13,881 (2014)
**Currency** Forint = 100 filler
**Government** multiparty republic
**Head of state** President János Áder, Fidesz, 2012.
**Head of government** Prime Minister Viktor Orban, Fidesz, 2010
**Website** www.kormany.hu/en
**Events** In 1990 multiparty elections were held for the first time. In 1999 Hungary joined NATO and in 2004 it acceded to the EU. In 2012 attempts to change the electoral system led to widespread protests, as have austerity measures imposed by successive governments. Relations with the EU bodies and IMF remain fractious because of the effect of terms imposed for Euro accession and financial bailouts.
**Economy** Since the early 1990s, Hungary has adopted market reforms and partial privatisation programmes. High levels of public debt meant that Hungary had to appeal for repeated loans from the IMF and EU to prevent economic collapse when the world economic crisis struck. The manufacture of machinery and transport is the most valuable sector. Hungary's resources include bauxite, coal and natural gas. Major crops include grapes for wine-making, maize, potatoes, sugar beet and wheat. Tourism is a growing sector.

## Iceland Ísland

**Area** 103,000 km² (39,768 mi²)
**Population** 326,000
**Capital** Reykjavik (209,000)
**Languages** Icelandic **GDP** $51,262 (2014)
**Currency** Krona = 100 aurar
**Government** multiparty republic
**Head of state** President Olafur Ragnar Grimmson, 1996
**Head of government** Prime Minister Sigmundur Gunnlaugsson, Progresssive Party, 2013
**Website** www.government.is/
**Events** In 1944, a referendum decisively voted to sever links with Denmark, and Iceland became a fully independent republic. In 1946 it joined NATO. In 1970 Iceland joined the European Free Trade Association. The last postwar US military personnel left in September 2006, the same year that the government voted to resume commercial whaling. There are concerns among environmentalists about

## LANGUAGES

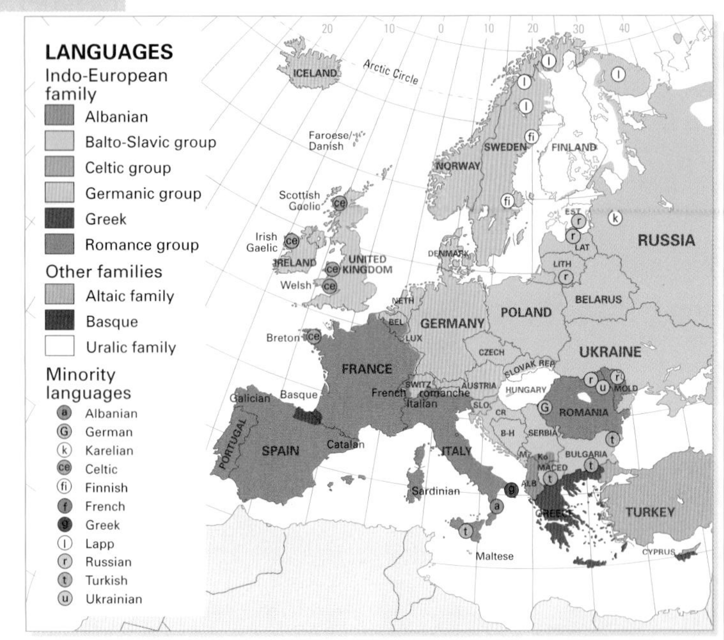

**Indo-European family**
- Albanian
- Balto-Slavic group
- Celtic group
- Germanic group
- Greek
- Romance group

**Other families**
- Altaic family
- Basque
- Uralic family

**Minority languages**
- (a) Albanian
- (G) German
- (k) Karelian
- (ce) Celtic
- (fi) Finnish
- (f) French
- (g) Greek
- (l) Lapp
- (r) Russian
- (t) Turkish
- (u) Ukrainian

the impact of major new industrial complexes powered by Iceland's abundant thermal energy. Even though Sigurdardottir's Social Democratic Alliance had returned some stability to the economy, the Social Democrats were defeated in 2013 parliamentary elections. In March 2015, the government withdrew the country's application to join the EU.

**Economy** The economy has long been sensitive to declining fish stocks as well as to fluctuations in world prices for its main exports: fish and fish products, aluminum and ferrosilicon. There has traditionally been low unemployment, and remarkably even distribution of income. Risky levels of investment in overseas companies left Iceland's banks with high debts when the global credit crunch hit, and the government had to apply for IMF funding. The economy returned to its pre-crash size in early 2015.

## Ireland Eire

**Area** 70,273 km² (27,132 mi²)
**Population** 4,5893,000
**Capital** Dublin (1,804,000)
**Languages** Irish, English (both official)
**GDP** $53,462 (2014) **Currency** Euro = 100 cents
**Government** multiparty republic
**Head of state** President Michael Higgins, Independent (formerly Labour Party), 2011
**Head of government** Taoiseach Enda Kenny, Fine Gael, 2011
**Website** www.gov.ie/en/
**Events** In 1948 Ireland withdrew from the British Commonwealth and joined the European Community in 1973. The Anglo-Irish Agreement (1985) gave Ireland a consultative role in the affairs of Northern Ireland. Following a 1995 referendum, divorce was legalised. Abortion remains a contentious political issue. In the Good Friday Agreement of 1998 the Irish Republic gave up its constitutional claim to Northern Ireland and a North-South Ministerial Council was established. Sinn Fein got its first seats in the European elections of June 2004. In 2008, long-standing PM Bertie Ahern stood down and Brian Cowen of Fianna Fáil formed a coalition. This fell in early 2011 because of public anger at the bailout from the EU and IMF.
**Economy** Ireland benefited greatly from its membership of the European Union. It joined in circulating the Euro in 2002. Grants have enabled the modernisation of farming, which employs 14% of the workforce. Major products include cereals, cattle and dairy products, sheep, sugar beet and potatoes. Fishing is important. Traditional sectors, such as brewing, distilling and textiles, have been supplemented by high-tech industries, such as electronics. Tourism is the most important component of the service industry. The economy also benefited from a rise in consumer spending, construction and business investment, but growth slowed in 2007 and the country went into recession in 2008, and the joint banking and debt crisis eventually led to the government of Brian Cowen requesting a bailout from the EU and IMF. In 2013, Ireland was the first country to exit from its EU bailout programme and the economy grew strongly in 2014.

## Italy Italia

**Area** 301,318 km² (116,338 mi²)
**Population** 60,783,000
**Capital** Rome / Roma (4,194,000)
**Languages** Italian (official)
**GDP** $35,823 (2014)
**Currency** Euro = 100 cents
**Government** social democracy
**Head of state** President Sergio Mattarella, 2015
**Head of government** Prime Minister Matteo Renzi, Democratic Party, 2014
**Website** www.italia.it
**Events** Since World War II Italy has had a succession of unstable, short-lived governements. In February 2014, Matteo Renzi, former mayor of Florence was appointed PM at the head of a coalition. In 2014, more than 190,000 refugees from north Africa and beyond arrived in Italy.
**Economy** Italy's main industrial region is the north-western triangle of Milan, Turin and Genoa. It is the world's eighth-largest car and steel producer. Machinery and transport equipment account for 37% of exports. Agricultural production is important. Italy is the world's largest producer of wine. Tourism is a vital economic sector. Italy emerged from a two-year recession at the end of 2013, but unemployment remains high.

## Kosovo (Republika e Kosoves/Republika Kosovo)

**Area** 10,887 km² (4203 mi²)
**Population** 1,859,000
**Capital** Pristina (465,000)
**Languages** Albanian, Serbian (both official), Bosnian, Turkish, Roma
**GDP** $3,898 (2014)
**Currency** Euro (Serbian dinar in Serb enclaves)
**Government** Multipalty republic
**Head of state** President Atifete Jahjaga (2011)
**Head of government** Prime Minister Isa Mustafa, Democratic League of Kosovo, 2014
**Website** www.kryeministri-ks.net/?page=2,1
**Events** An autonomous province with a mainly ethnic Albanian Muslim popluation, Kosovo first declared independence from Serbia in 1990, leading to years of increased ethnic tension and violence. In 1998 conflict between Serb police and the Kosovo Liberation Army led to a violent crackdown by Serbia, which ceased only after more than two months' aerial bombardment by Nato in 1999, during which hundreds of thousands of Kosovo Albanians were massacred or expelled before Serbia agreed to withdraw and a UN peacekeeping force and administration were sent in, which remained in place until 2008. Talks on the status of the province took place in 2003 and 2006. In 2008, independence was declared again and a new constitution was adopted that transferred power from the UN to the ethnic Albanian government, a move that was rejected by Serbia and Russia but recognised by the US and major European countries. The UN referred Kosovo's declaration of independence to the International Court of Justice, which declared in 2010 that it was not illegal. In March 2011, direct talks between Serbia and Kosovo began. In 2013, the EU brokered

an agreement on policing for the Serb minority. PM Thaci claimed victory after early results of parliamentary elections in June 2014, but after months of wrangling Isa Mustafa formed a coalition government.
**Economy** Kosovo is one of the poorest areas of Europe, with a high proportion of the population classed as living in poverty. It possesses some mineral resources but the chief economic activity is agriculture.

## Latvia Latvija

**Area** 64,589 km² (24,942 mi²)
**Population** 1,998,000
**Capital** Riga (1,018,000)
**Languages** Latvian (official), Russian
**GDP** $15,783 (2014)
**Currency** Euro = 100 cents
**Government** multiparty republic
**Head of state** President Andris Bērziņš, Independent, 2011
**Head of government** Prime Minister Laimdota Straujuma, People's Party 2014
**Website** www.mk.gov.lv/en
**Events** Latvia became a member of NATO and the EU in spring 2004. People applying for citizenship are now required to pass a Latvian language test, which has caused much upset amongst the one third of the population who are Russian speakers. After Ivars Godmanis resigned in February 2009 over his handling of the economic crisis, including having to apply for aid from the IMF, a 6-party coalition was approved by parliament. After the resignation of Valdis Dombrovskis in early 2014, Laimdota Straujuma was appointed PM, and the governing coalition increased its majority in elections in October. Latvia adopted the Euro on 1 January 2014.
**Economy** Latvia has to import many of the materials needed for manufacturing. It produces only 10% of the electricity it needs, and the rest has to be imported from Belarus, Russia and Ukraine. Manufactures include electronic goods, farm machinery and fertiliser. Farm exports include beef, dairy products and pork. The majority of companies, banks, and real estate have been privatised. Unemployment remains very high.

## Liechtenstein

**Area** 157 km² (61 mi²)
**Population** 36,000
**Capital** Vaduz (5,300)
**Languages** German (official)
**GDP** $134,617 (2012)
**Currency** Swiss franc = 100 centimes
**Government** independent principality
**Head of state** Prince Hans Adam II (1989)
**Head of government** Prime Minister Adrian Hasler, Progressive Citizens Party, 2013
**Website** www.liechtenstein.li
**Events** Women finally got the vote in 1984. The principality joined the UN in 1990. In 2003 the people voted in a referendum to give Prince Hans Adam II new political powers, rendering the country Europe's only absolute monarchy with the prince having power of veto over the government. Its status as a tax haven has been criticised as it has been alleged that many billions are laundered there each year. The law has been reformed to ensure that anonymity is no longer permitted when opening a bank account. In August 2004 Prince Hans Adam II transferred the day-to-day running of the country to his son Prince Alois, though he did not abdicate and remains titular head of state. The OECD removed Liechtenstein from its list of uncooperative tax havens in 2010. In 2013, the Progressive Citizens Party came first in parliamentary elections.
**Economy** Liechtenstein is the fourth-smallest country in the world and one of the richest per capita. Since 1945 it has rapidly developed a specialised manufacturing base. It imports more than 90% of its energy requirements. The economy is widely diversified with a large number of small businesses. Tourism is increasingly important.

## Lithuania Lietuva

**Area** 65,200 km² (25,173 mi²)
**Population** 2,944,000
**Capital** Vilnius (806,000)
**Languages** Lithuanian (official), Russian, Polish
**GDP** $16,386 **Currency** Euro = 100 cents
**Government** multiparty republic
**Head of state** President Dalla Grybauskaite, 2009
**Head of government** Prime Minister Algirdas Butkevicius, Social Democratic Party, 2012
**Website** www.lrvk.lt/en
**Events** The Soviet Union recognised Lithuania's independence in September 1991. Lithuania joined NATO in March 2004 and the EU that May. Elections in autumn 2012 led to a change in the make-up of the ruling coalition. Lithuania adopted the Euro on 1 January 2015.
**Economy** Lithuania is dependent on Russian raw materials. Manufacturing is the most valuable export sector and major products include chemicals, electronic goods and machine tools. Dairy and meat farming and fishing are also important activities. More than 80% of enterprises have been privatised. The economy was badly hit by the 2008 global economic crisis.

## Luxembourg

**Area** 2,586 km² (998 mi²)
**Population** 550,000
**Capital** Luxembourg (165,000)
**Languages** Luxembourgian / Letzeburgish (official), French, German
**GDP** $111,716 (2014) **Currency** Euro = 100 cents
**Government** constitutional monarchy (or grand duchy)
**Head of state** Grand Duke Henri, 2000
**Head of government** Prime Minister Xavier Bettel, Democratic Party, 2013
**Website** www.visitluxembourg.com
**Events** Governments have mostly been coalitions led by the Christian Social People's Party under Jean-Claude Juncker. In July 2013, the Social Workers Party withdrew from the latest coalition, provoking early elections. These resulted in a coalition between the Social Democrats, Socialists and Greens.
**Economy** It has a stable, high-income economy, benefiting from its proximity to France, Germany and Belgium. The city of Luxembourg is a major centre of European administration and finance. In 2009, it implemented stricter laws on transparency in the banking sector. There are rich deposits of iron ore, and is a major producer of iron and steel. Other industries include chemicals, textiles, tourism, banking and electronics.

## Macedonia Makedonija

**Area** 25,713 km² (9,927 mi²)
**Population** 2,100,000
**Capital** Skopje (669,000)
**Languages** Macedonian (official), Albanian
**GDP** $5,481 (2014)
**Currency** Denar = 100 deni
**Government** multiparty republic
**Head of state** President Gjorge Ivanov, VMRO-DPMNE, 2009
**Head of government** Prime Minister Nikola Gruevski, VMRO-DPMNE, 2006
**Website** www.vlada.mk/?language=en-gb
**Events** In 1993 the UN accepted the new republic as a member. It formally retains the FYR prefix because of Greek fears that the name implies territorial ambitions towards the Greek region named Macedonia. In August 2004, proposed expansion of rights and local autonomy for Albanians provoked riots by Macedonian nationalists, but the measures went through. In December 2005, EU leaders agreed that Macedonia should become a candidate for membership, if corruption was stamped out, but in February 2007 expressed alarm at political developments during 2006 and continuing problems about rights for ethnic Albanians. In 2008 Greece vetoed NATO's invitation of membership to Macedonia, in a move ruled illegal by the International Court of Justice in 2011. After snap elections in 2014, Gruevski's VMRO-DPMNE won a fourth successive term in government.
**Economy** Macedonia is a developing country. The poorest of the six former republics of Yugoslavia, its economy was devastated by UN trade sanctions against Yugoslavia and by the Greek embargo. The economy returned to growth in 2013. Manufactures, especially metals, dominate exports. Agriculture employs 17% of the workforce. Major crops include cotton, fruits, maize, tobacco and wheat.

XXVII

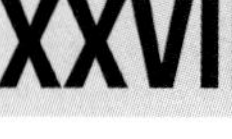
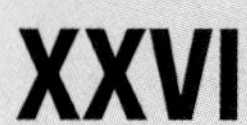

## Malta

**rea** 316 km² (122 mi²)
**opulation** 453,000
**apital** Valetta (6,700)
**anguages** Maltese, English (both official)
**DP** $24,876 (2014) **Currency** Euro = 100 cents
**iovernment** multiparty republic
**lead of state** President Marie Louise Coleiro
reca, Labour Party, 2014
**lead of government** Prime Minister
oseph Muscat, Labour Party, 2013
**Vebsite** www.gov.mt
**vents** In 1990 Malta applied to join the EU.
1997 the newly elected Malta Labour Party
ledged to rescind the application. The
hristian Democratic Nationalist Party, led
y the pro-European Edward Fenech Adami,
egained power in 1998 elections and won
gain by a narrow margin in March 2008. Malta
ined the EU in May 2004 and adopted the
uro on 1 January 2008. In 2013, the Labour
arty defeated Lawrence Gonzi's Nationalists to
turn to power for the first time in 15 years.
**conomy** Malta produces only about 20%
f its food needs, has limited fresh water
upplies and has few domestic energy sources.
lachinery and transport equipment account
or more than 50% of exports. Malta's historic
aval dockyards are now used for commercial
iipbuilding and repair. Manufactures include
nemicals, electronic equipment and textiles.
ne largest sector is services, especially tourism.
ne economy remains at risk from the Eurozone
risis.

## Moldova

**rea** 33,851 km² (13,069 mi²)
**opulation** 3,600,000
**apital** Chisinau (metropolitan 801,000)
**anguages** Moldovan / Romanian (official)
**DP** $2,233 (2014) **Currency** Leu = 100 bani
**overnment** multiparty republic
**ead of state** President Nicolae Timofti,
dependent, 2012.
**ead of government** Prime Minister
atalia Gherman (acting),
beral Democratic Party, 2015
**Vebsite** www.moldova.md
**vents** In 1994 a referendum rejected reunifica-
on with Romania and Parliament voted to
in the CIS. A new constitution established
presidential parliamentary republic. The
ansnistria region mainly inhabited by Russian
nd Ukrainian speakers declared independ-
nce in 1990. This independence has never
een recognised and a regional referendum
Transnistria in 2006 that supported eventual
nion of the region with Russia is similarly
eing ignored. Relations between Chisinau and
oscow remain strained. Moldova joined the
J's Eastern Partnership in 2009 and signed its
ssociation Agreement in June 2014. Elections
November resulted in pro-European parties
maining in power, although the pro-Russian
ocialist Party made major gains. New PM Chiril
aburici resigned after only a few weeks.
**conomy** There is a favourable climate and
ood farmland but no major mineral deposits.
griculture is important and major products
clude fruits and grapes for wine-making.
armers also raise livestock, including dairy
attle and pigs. Moldova has to import
aterials and fuels for its industries. Exports
clude food, wine, tobacco and textiles. The
conomy remains vulnerable to high fuel prices
nd poor agricultural weather. The economy
agnated in 2014.

## Monaco

**rea** 1.5 km² (0.6 mi²)
**opulation** 36,000
**apital** Monaco-Ville (1150)
**anguages** French (official), Italian,
onegasque
**DP** 163,026 (2012) **Currency** Euro = 100 cents
**overnment** principality
**ead of state** Prince Albert II, 2005
**ead of government** Minister of State
ichel Roger, independent, 2010
**'ebsite** www.gouv.mc
**vents** Monaco has been ruled by the Grimaldi
mily since the end of the 13th century and
een under the protection of France since 1860.
**conomy** The chief source of income is tour-
n. The state retains monopolies in tobacco,
e telephone network and the postal service.
here is some light industry, including print-
g, textiles and postage stamps. Also a major
anking centre, residents live tax free. Prince
bert wishes to attract high-tech industries
and to prove that Monaco is not a haven for money-launderers, and in 2010 the OECD removed Monaco from its list of uncooperative tax havens.

## Montenegro Crna Gora

**Area** 13,812 km² (5,333 mi²)
**Population** 625,000
**Capital** Podgorica (186,000)
**Languages** Serbian (of the Ijekavian dialect)
**GDP** $7,419 (2014) **Currency** Euro = 100 cents
**Government** federal republic
**Head of state** President Filip Vujanovic, 2003
**Head of government** Prime Minister
Milo Djukanovich, Democratic Party of Socialists, 2012
**Website** www.gov.me/en/homepage
**Events** In 1992 Montenegro went into federation with Serbia, first as Federal Republic of Yugoslavia, then as a looser State Union of Serbia and Montenegro. Montenegro formed its own economic policy and adopted the Deutschmark as its currency in 1999. It currently uses the Euro, though it is not formally part of the Eurozone. In 2002, Serbia and Montenegro came to a new agreement regarding continued cooperation. On 21 May 2006, the status of the union was decided as 55.54% of voters voted for independence of Montenegro, narrowly passing the 55% threshold needed to validate the referendum under rules set by the EU. On 3 June 2006 the Parliament of Montenegro declared independence. Montenegro was rapidly admitted to the UN, the World Bank and the IMF, joined NATO's Partnership for Peace and applied for EU membership. It was formally named as an EU candidate country in 2010 and accession negotiations started in 2012, just after it joined the WTO.
**Economy** A rapid period of urbanisation and industrialisation was created within the communism era of Montenegro. During 1993, two thirds of the Montenegrin population lived below the poverty line. Financial losses under the effects of the UN sanctions on the economy of Montenegro are estimated to be $6.39 billion. Today there is faster and more efficient privatisation, introduction of VAT and usage of the Euro.

## The Netherlands Nederland

**Area** 41,526 km² (16,033 mi²)
**Population** 16,820,000
**Capital** Amsterdam (2,400,000); administrative capital 's-Gravenhage (The Hague) (1,051,000)
**Languages** Dutch (official), Frisian
**GDP** $51,373 **Currency** Euro = 100 cents
**Government** constitutional monarchy
**Head of state** King Willem-Alexander, 2013
**Head of government** Prime Minister
Mark Rutte, People's Party for Freedom and Democracy, 2010
**Website** www.government.nl
**Events** A founding member of NATO and the EU. Jan Peter Balkenende's coalition cabinet with the Labour Party and the Christian Union collapsed in early 2010 after Labour refused to sanction continued military deployment in Afghanistan. In 2010 the former junior coalition partner, the Party for Freedom and Democracy, took power, winning again in 2012. In 2013, Queen Beatrix abdicated.
**Economy** The Netherlands has prospered through its close European ties. Private enterprise has successfully combined with progressive social policies. It is highly industrialised. Products include aircraft, chemicals, electronics and machinery. Agriculture is intensive and mechanised, employing only 5% of the workforce. Dairy farming is the leading agricultural activity. It continues to be one of the leading European nations for attracting foreign direct investment.

## Norway Norge

**Area** 323,877 km² (125,049 mi²)
**Population** 5,138,000
**Capital** Oslo (1,503,000)
**Languages** Norwegian (official), Lappish, Finnish
**GDP** $97,013 (2014) **Currency** Krone = 100 øre
**Government** constitutional monarchy
**Head of state** King Harald V, 1991
**Head of government** Prime Minister
Erna Solberg, Conservative Party, 2013
**Website** www.norway.org.uk
**Events** In referenda in 1972 and 1994 Norway rejected joining the EU. A centre-left coalition, the Labour-led 'Red-Green Alliance' won closely contested elections in September 2005, and retained power in 2009. It was ousted by a Conservative-led minority government in 2013.
**Economy** Norway has one of the world's highest standards of living. Discovery of oil and gas in adjacent waters in the late 1960s boosted its economic fortunes, with its chief exports now oil and natural gas. Per capita, it is the world's largest producer of hydroelectricity. It is possible oil and gas will begin to run out in Norway in the next two decades but it has been saving its oil budget surpluses and is invested abroad in a fund, valued at more than $250 billion at its height, although this fell rapidly as a result of the global financial crisis. Major manufactures include petroleum products, chemicals, aluminium, wood pulp and paper.

## Poland Polska

**Area** 323,250 km² (124,807 mi²)
**Population** 38,545,000
**Capital** Warsaw / Warszawa (metropolitan 2,666,000)
**Languages** Polish (official) **GDP** $14,379 (2014)
Currency Zloty = 100 groszy
**Government** multiparty republic
**Head of state** President Andrzej Duda, Law and Justice, 2015
**Head of government** Prime Minister
Ewa Kopacz, Civic Platform, 2014
**Website** http://en.polska.pl
**Events** Poland joined the OECD in 1996, NATO in 1999 and the EU in 2004. Ewa Kopacz became PM when her predecessor, Donald Tusk, was appointed President of the European Council. Andrzej Duda narrowly beat Bronislaw Komorowski in presidential elections in May 2015.
**Economy** Of the workforce, 27% is employed in agriculture and 37% in industry. Poland is the world's fifth-largest producer of lignite and ships. Copper ore is also a vital resource. Manufacturing accounts for 24% of exports. Agriculture remains important. Economic growth began to speed up in 2013 in response to record low interest rates.

## Portugal

**Area** 88,797 km² (34,284 mi²)
**Population** 10,427,000
**Capital** Lisbon / Lisboa (3,035,000)
**Languages** Portuguese (official)
**GDP** $22,130 (2014) **Currency** Euro = 100 cents
**Government** multiparty republic
**Head of state** President Anibal Cavaco Silva, Social Democratic Party, 2006
**Head of government** Pedro Passos Coelho, social Democratic Party, 2011
**Website** www.portugal.gov.pt/en.aspx
**Events** In 1986 Portugal joined the EU. In 2002 the Social Democrat Party won the election and formed a coalition government with the Popular Party. The opposition Socialist Party were clear victors in European elections of June 2004, a result attributed in part to the ruling party's support for the war in Iraq. The Socialist Party's minority government collapsed in 2011 when Parliament rejected further austerity measures. Since their return to power they have instigated several further tranches of cuts, leading to instability in both the coalition and the country.
**Economy** Portugal was badly hit by the economic downturn and in April 2011 requested a financial bailout from the IMF and Eurozone funds. Despite budget cuts, public debt remained high, but Portugal exited its bailout in May 2014. Manufacturing accounts for 33% of exports. Textiles, footwear and clothing are major exports. Portugal is the world's fifth-largest producer of tungsten and eighth-largest producer of wine. Olives, potatoes and wheat are also grown. Tourism is very important.

## Romania

**Area** 238,391 km² (92,042 mi²)
**Population** 20,122,000
**Capital** Bucharest / Bucuresti (2,272,000)
**Languages** Romanian (official), Hungarian
**GDP** $10,035 (2014)
**Currency** Romanian leu = 100 bani
**Government** multiparty republic
**Head of state** President Klaus Iohannis, National Liberal Party, 2014
**Head of government** Prime Minister
Gabriel Oprea (acting), National Union for the Progress of Romania, 2015
**Website** www.gov.ro
**Events** A new constitution was introduced in 1991. Ion Iliescu, a former communist official, was re-elected in 2000, but barred from standing again in 2004, when he was replaced by Traian Basescu. After losing a vote of no confidence after just 10 months as PM, Boc was reappointed in December 2009. Romania joined NATO in 2004 and joined the EU in January 2007 after making progress towards tackling corruption, although because of this issue France and Germany blocked its Schengen area accession in December 2010. Protests in 2012 led to PM Emil Boc's resignation. Klaus Iohannis beat PM Victor Ponta in presidential elections in late 2014. The latter was forced to resign in June 2015 after investigators questioned him about tax evasion, money laundering and fraud. Adoption of the Euro has been postponed until at least 2019.
**Economy** The currency was re-valued in 2005. Despite a period of strong economic growth, Romania's large public debt led to the need for substantial IMF loans in 2009, necessitating severe cuts in public services.

## Russia Rossiya

**Area** 17,075,000 km² (6,592,800 mi²)
**Population** 143,700,000
**Capital** Moscow / Moskva (metropolitan 11,511,000)
**Languages** Russian (official), and many others
**GDP** $12,926 (2014)
**Currency** Russian ruble = 100 kopeks
**Government** federal multiparty republic
**Head of state** President Vladimir Putin 2012
**Head of government** Prime Minister
Dimitry Medvedev, 2012
**Website** http://government.ru/en/
**Events** In 1992 the Russian Federation became a co-founder of the CIS (Commonwealth of Independent States). A new Federal Treaty was signed between the central government and the autonomous republics within the Russian Federation, Chechnya refused to sign and declared independence. In December 1993 a new democratic constitution was adopted. From 1994 to 1996, Russia fought a civil war in Chechnya which flared up again in 1999. Putin's chosen successor, Medvedev, was elected by a landslide in elections that were criticised by outside observers for biased media coverage. In 2011 Putin was re-elected as President, after the law that prevented serving a third term was revoked. He appointed former president Medvedev as PM. Critics allege that freedom of speech and dissent are being repressed amid crackdowns on NGOs and opponents of the ruling party. Russia joined the WTO in 2012. In February 2014, in response to events in Ukraine, Russian forces took over the Crimean Peninsula and Sevastopol, leading to accusations of illegal annexation from the West (see Ukraine) and international sanctions.
**Economy** In 1993 mass privatisation began. By 1996, 80% of the Russian economy was in private hands. A major problem remains the size of Russia's foreign debt. It is reliant on world oil prices to keep its economy from crashing and the sudden fall in oil prices in the second half of 2008 forced it to devalue the ruble several times. The drop in oil prices in 2014 and international sanctions caused the ruble to halve in value against the US dollar. Industry employs 46% of the workforce and contributes 48% of GDP. Mining is the most valuable activity. Russia is the world's leading producer of natural gas and nickel, the second largest producer of aluminium and phosphates, and the third-largest of crude oil, lignite and brown coal. Most farmland is still government-owned or run as collectives, with important products barley, oats, rye, potatoes, beef and veal. In 2006, the ruble became a convertible currency.

## San Marino

**Area** 61 km² (24 mi²)
**Population** 33,000
**Capital** San Marino (4,100)
**Languages** Italian (official)
**GDP** $56,820 (2014) **Currency** Euro = 100 cents
**Government** multiparty republic
**Head of state** co-Chiefs of State:
Andrea Belluzzi and Roberto Venturini
**Head of government** Secretary of State for Foreign and Political Affairs and Economic Planning Pasquale Valentini, 2012
**Website** www.visitsanmarino.com
**Events** World's smallest republic and perhaps Europe's oldest state, San Marino's links with Italy led to the adoption of the Euro. Its 60-member Great and General Council is elected every five years and headed by two captains regent, who are elected by the council every six months. In 2013 a narrow majority of

recorded votes were in favour of joining the EU, but the low turnout invalidated the result.
**Economy** The economy is largely agricultural. Tourism is vital to the state's income, contributing over 50% of GDP. The economy is generally stable.

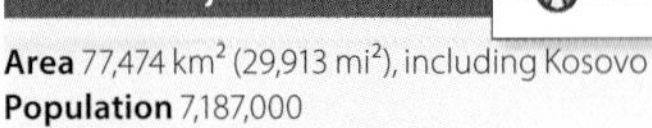

## Serbia Srbija

**Area** 77,474 km² (29,913 mi²), including Kosovo
**Population** 7,187,000
**Capital** Belgrade / Beograd (metropolitan 1,659,000)
**Languages** Serbian
**GDP** $6,123 (2014)
**Currency** Dinar = 100 paras
**Government** federal republic
**Head of state** President Tomislav Nikolić, Serbian Progresssive Party,
**Head of government** Prime Minister Aleksandar Vucic, Progressive Party, 2014
**Website** www.srbija.gov.rs
**Events** Serbian attempts to control the Yugoslav federation led to the secession of Slovenia and Croatia in 1991 and to Bosnia-Herzegovina's declaration of independence in 1992 and the three-year war that ended only with the signing of the Dayton Peace Accord. Slobodan Milosovic became president of Yugoslavia in 1997. Kostunica won the elections of September 2000: Milosevic refused to hand over power, but was ousted after a week. From 2003 to 2006, Serbia was part of the State Union of Serbia and Montenegro, After a referendum in May 2006, the Parliament of Montenegro declared Montenegro independent. Serbia assumed the State Union's UN membership. In 2006 Serbia joined the NATO Partnership for Peace programme and in 2008 signed a Stability and Association Agreement with the EU, to which it applied formally for membership in December 2009. Serbia became a candidate member of the EU in 2012 and accession talks began in early 2014. In May of the latter year, the pro-EU Progressive Party scored a landslide victory in parliamentary elections.
**Economy** The lower-middle income economy was devastated by war and economic sanctions. Industrial production collapsed. Natural resources include bauxite, coal and copper. There is some oil and natural gas. Manufacturing includes aluminium, cars, machinery, plastics, steel and textiles. Agriculture is important. In 2008 Serbia and Russia signed an energy deal, and in October 2009 the latter granted the former a 1 billion Euro loan to ease its budgetary problems.

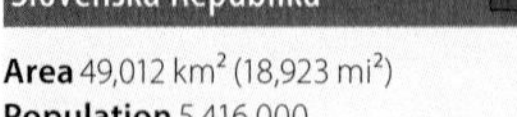

## Slovak Republic Slovenska Republika

**Area** 49,012 km² (18,923 mi²)
**Population** 5,416,000
**Capital** Bratislava (metropolitan 660,000)
**Languages** Slovak (official), Hungarian
**GDP** $18,454 (2014)
**Currency** Euro = 100 cents
**Government** multiparty republic
**Head of state** President Andrej Kiska, independent, 2014
**Head of government** Prime Minister Robert Fico, Direction - Social Democracy (Smer), 2012.
**Website** www.government.gov.sk
**Events** In 1993 the Slovak Republic became a sovereign state, breaking peaceably from the Czech Republic, with whom it maintains close relations. In 1996 the Slovak Republic and Hungary ratified a treaty confirming their borders and stipulating basic rights for the 560,000 Hungarians in the country. The Slovak Republic joined NATO in March 2004 and the EU two months later. There is still a problem with the Romany population. The country adopted the Euro in January 2009. In elections in April 2012 Smer returned to power with a parliamentary majority. Former businessman and philanthropist Andrej Kiska won the presidential election against PM Fico in 2014.
**Economy** The transition from communism to private ownership was initially painful with industrial output falling, unemployment and inflation rising, but the economy has become more stable. Manufacturing employs 33% of the workforce. Bratislava and Košice are the chief industrial cities. Major products include ceramics, machinery and steel. Farming employs 12% of the workforce. Crops include barley and grapes. Tourism is growing.

## Slovenia Slovenija

**Area** 20,256 km² (7,820 mi²)
**Population** 2,062,000
**Capital** Ljubljana (275,000)
**Languages** Slovene
**GDP** $24,019 (2014)
**Currency** Euro = 100 cents
**Government** multiparty republic
**Head of state** President Borut Pahor, Social Democratic Party, 2012
**Head of government** Prime Minister Miro Cerar, Modern Centre Party, 2014
**Website** www.gov.si
**Events** In 1990 Slovenia declared itself independent, which led to brief fighting between Slovenes and the federal army. In 1992 the EU recognised Slovenia's independence. Janez Drnovsek was elected president in December 2002. Slovenia joined NATO in March 2004 and the EU two months later. In June 2004 the value of the Tolar was fixed against the Euro, which it joined in 2007. The 2008 general election resulted in a coalition government led by the Social Democratic Party. A referendum in June 2010 narrowly approved the settlement of the border dispute with Croatia. After two years of political instability, Ivan Janša was appointed PM in February 2012, leading a centre-right coalition, but his government fell the following year. The succeeding administration fell in May 2014 leading to early elections, which led to a coalition government headed by the newly founded Modern Centre Party led by lawyer Miro Cerar.
**Economy** The transformation of a centrally planned economy and the fighting in other parts of former Yugoslavia caused problems for Slovenia but the economy eventually experienced strong growth in per capita GDP until this was badly hit by the gobal financial crisis. Manufacturing is the leading activity. Major manufactures include chemicals, machinery, transport equipment, metal goods and textiles. Major crops include maize, fruit, potatoes and wheat.

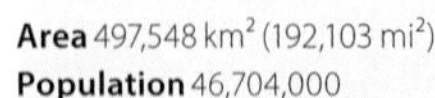

## Spain España

**Area** 497,548 km² (192,103 mi²)
**Population** 46,704,000
**Capital** Madrid (metropolitan 6,369,000)
**Languages** Castilian Spanish (official), Catalan, Galician, Basque
**GDP** $30,278 (2014)
**Currency** Euro = 100 cents
**Government** constitutional monarchy
**Head of state** King Felipe VI, 2014
**Head of government** Prime Minister Mariano Rajoy, Spanish People's Party, 2011
**Website** www.lamoncloa.gob.es/home.htm
**Events** From 1959-98 the militant Basque organisation ETA waged a campaign of terror. Its first ceasefire was broken in 2000 and a second - declared in 2006 - with a bomb attack on Madrid airport at the end of the year. A third ceasefire was declared in September 2010. In March 2004 Al qaeda-related bombers killed 191 people in Madrid, resulting in an election win for the opposition Socialist Party. In the 2008 elections, the socialists increased their numbers in Parliament, but did not gain a majority. Austerity measures brought in to tackle public debt, and as condition of the country's financial bailout, changes to pensions and benefits and rising unemployment led to widespread protests in 2010 and 2011. Local and regional elections in May 2011 resulted in heavy losses for the socialists and the Popular Party won a sweeping majority in general elections in November. King Juan Carlos abdicated in favour of Prince Felipe in 2014.
**Economy** Spain's transformation from a largely poor, agrarian society to a prosperous nation came to an end with the economic downturn of 2008. The country's debt burden became untenable and financial bailouts from the international community in 2010 and the Eurozone in 2012 were necessary. Unemployment is more than double the European average. Agriculture now employs only 10% of the workforce and the sector is shrinking further because of recurrent droughts. Spain is the world's third-largest wine producer. Other crops include citrus fruits, tomatoes and olives. Industries: cars, ships, chemicals, electronics, metal goods, steel and textiles.

## Sweden Sverige

**Area** 449,964 km² (173,731 mi²)
**Population** 9,658,000
**Capital** Stockholm (2,127,000)
**Languages** Swedish (official), Finnish
**GDP** $58,491 (2014)
**Currency** Swedish krona = 100 ore
**Government** constitutional monarchy
**Head of state** King Carl Gustaf XVI, 1973
**Head of government** Prime Minister Stefan Löfvén, Social Democrats, 2014
**Website** www.sweden.gov.se
**Events** In 1995 Sweden joined the European Union. The cost of maintaining Sweden's extensive welfare services has become a major political issue. In 2003 Sweden rejected adoption of the Euro. Parliamentary elections in October 2014 led to a fragile minority government being formed by the Social Democrats.
**Economy** Sweden is a highly developed industrial country. It has rich iron ore deposits. Privately owned firms account for about 90% of industrial output. Steel is a major product, used to manufacture aircraft, cars, machinery and ships. Forestry and fishing are important. Agriculture accounts for 2% of GDP and jobs. The Swedish central bank focuses on price stability with its inflation target of 2%.

## Switzerland Schweiz

**Area** 41,284 km² (15,939 mi²)
**Population** 8,014,000 **Capital** Bern (356,000)
**Languages** French, German, Italian, Romansch (all official) **GDP** $87,475 (2014)
**Currency** Swiss Franc = 100 centimes / rappen
**Government** federal republic
**Head of state** President of the Swiss Confederation Simonetta Sommaruga, Social Democratic Party, 2015
**Website** www.admin.ch
**Events** Priding themselves on their neutrality, Swiss voters rejected membership of the UN in 1986 and the EU in 1992 and 2001. However, Switzerland finally became a partner country of NATO in 1997 and joined the organisation in 2002, when it also joined the UN. The federal council is made up of seven federal ministers from whom the president is chosen on an annual basis. A 2005 referendum backed membership of EU Schengen and Dublin agreements, bringing Switzerland into the European passport-free zone and increasing co-operation on crime and asylum seekers. Immigration is becoming an increasingly divisive issue.
**Economy** Switzerland is a wealthy and stable modern market economy with low unemployment, and per capita GDP grew strongly in 2014. Manufactures include chemicals, electrical equipment, machinery, precision instruments, watches and textiles. Livestock, notably dairy farming, is the chief agricultural activity. Tourism is important, and Swiss banks remain a safe haven for investors. In early 2015, the rapid fall of the value of the Euro on international markets led the Swiss National Bank to reverse the decision of 2011 to peg the Franc to the Euro.

## Turkey Türkiye

**Area** 774,815 km² (299,156 mi²)
**Population** 76,668,000
**Capital** Ankara (metropolitan 5,045,000)
**Languages** Turkish (official), Kurdish
**GDP** $10,482 (2014)
**Currency** New Turkish lira = 100 kurus
**Government** multiparty republic
**Head of state** Recep Tayyip Erdogan, Justice and Development Party (AK), 2014
**Head of government** Ahmet Davutoğlu, Justice and Development Party (AK), 2014
**Website** www.mfa.gov.tr/default.en.mfa
**Events** The Kurdistan Workers Party (PKK) carried out terrorist activities throughout the 1980s and 1990s, but declared a ceasefire in 1999, changed their name to Congress for Freedom and Democracy in Kurdistan (KADEK) and said they wanted to campaign peacefully for Kurdish rights. In September 2003 they ended a 4-year ceasefire, but declared another in 2006, although this did not hold. In October 2005, the EU opened accession negotiations with Ankara. Membership of the EU is an aim but human rights, the Cyprus issue and the hostility of successive French and Austrian governments are barriers, but it was announced in October that talks would recommence the following month. The PM and President are both former Islamists, although they say they are committed to secularism. The escalating civil war in Syria has caused a refugee crisis on the border. In 2014 elections, PM Erdogan won the first direct presidential election. However, in 2015's parliamentary elections, the AK lost its majority, thus preventing the controversial proposed referendum that would have given him executive powers.
**Economy** Turkey is an upper-middle-income country, as classified by the World Bank. Agriculture employs 47% of the workforce, but is becoming less important to the economy. Turkey is a leading producer of citrus fruits, barley, cotton, wheat, tobacco and tea. It is a major producer of chromium and phosphate fertilisers. Tourism is a vital source of foreign exchange. In January 2005, the New Turkish lira was introduced at a rate of 1 to 1,000,000 old Turkish lira. The economy shrank slightly in 2014

## Ukraine Ukraina

**Area** 603,700 km² (233,088 mi²)
**Population** 44,573,000
**Capital** Kiev / Kyviv (3,275,000)
**Languages** Ukrainian (official), Russian
**GDP** $3,055 (2014)
**Currency** Hryvnia = 100 kopiykas
**Government** multiparty republic
**Head of state** Petro Poroshenko, independent 2014 **Head of government** Arseniy Yatsenyuk, People's Front, 2014
**Website** www.kmu.gov.ua/control/en
**Events** The Chernobyl disaster of 1986 contaminated large areas of Ukraine. Independence was achieved in 1991 with the dissolution of the USSR. Leonid Kuchma was elected president in 1994. He continued the policy of establishing closer ties with the West and sped up the pace of privatisation. In 2010, the coalition government of Yulia Tymoshenko fell, and the Party of the Regions formed a coalition with the Communists and the centrist Lytvyn Bloc. Former PM Victor Yanukovic beat Tymoshenko in the presidential elections. Ukraine joined the EU's Eastern Partnership in 2009, but has abandoned plans to join NATO. President Yanukovich's decision to abandon plans for closer ties with the EU led to riots from late 2013, followed by his escape to Russia in February 2014. The following month, Russia sent forces into the Crimean Peninsula to assist separatists. A few days later, after a partially boycotted referendum, the administrations of Crimea and Sevastopol asked Russia for the right to accede, which Russia granted and annexed the region and cit[y]. Parliamentary elections in late 2014 resulted in a resounding win for pro-Western parties. Fighting continues in the east despite a fragile ceasefire brokered by France and Germany in February 2015.
**Economy** Ukraine is a lower-middle-income economy. Agriculture is important. It is the world's leading producer of sugar beet, the second-largest producer of barley, and a major producer of wheat. Ukraine has extensive raw materials, including coal (though many mines are exhausted), iron ore and manganese ore. Ukraine is reliant on oil and natural gas imports. The economy's dependence on steel exports made it vulnerable to the 2008 global economic downturn and it was offered a massive loan by the IMF.

## United Kingdom

**Area** 241,857 km² (93,381 mi²)
**Population** 63,705,000
**Capital** London (metropolitan 15,011,000)
**Languages** English (official), Welsh (also official in Wales), Gaelic **GDP** $45,653 (2014)
**Currency** Sterling (pound) = 100 pence
**Government** constitutional monarchy
**Head of state** Queen Elizabeth II, 1952
**Head of government** Prime Minister David Cameron, Conservative Party, 2010
**Website** www.gov.uk
**Events** The United Kingdom of Great Britain and Northern Ireland is a union of four countries – England, Northern Ireland, Scotland and Wales. Since 1997, Scotland and Wales have had their own legislative assemblies. In 2005 the IRA anounced a permanent cessation of hostilities and the Northern Ireland Assembly was finally reinstated in early 2007. Scotland voted against independence from the UK in September 2014. The Conservative Party won a majority in the parliamentary elections of 2015.
**Economy** The UK is a major industrial and trading nation. A producer of oil, petroleum products, natural gas, potash, salt and lead. Financial services and tourism are leading service industries. The economic downturn of 2008 led to the government effectively nationalising several banks and bailing out others with huge loans. Economic growth continues to improve

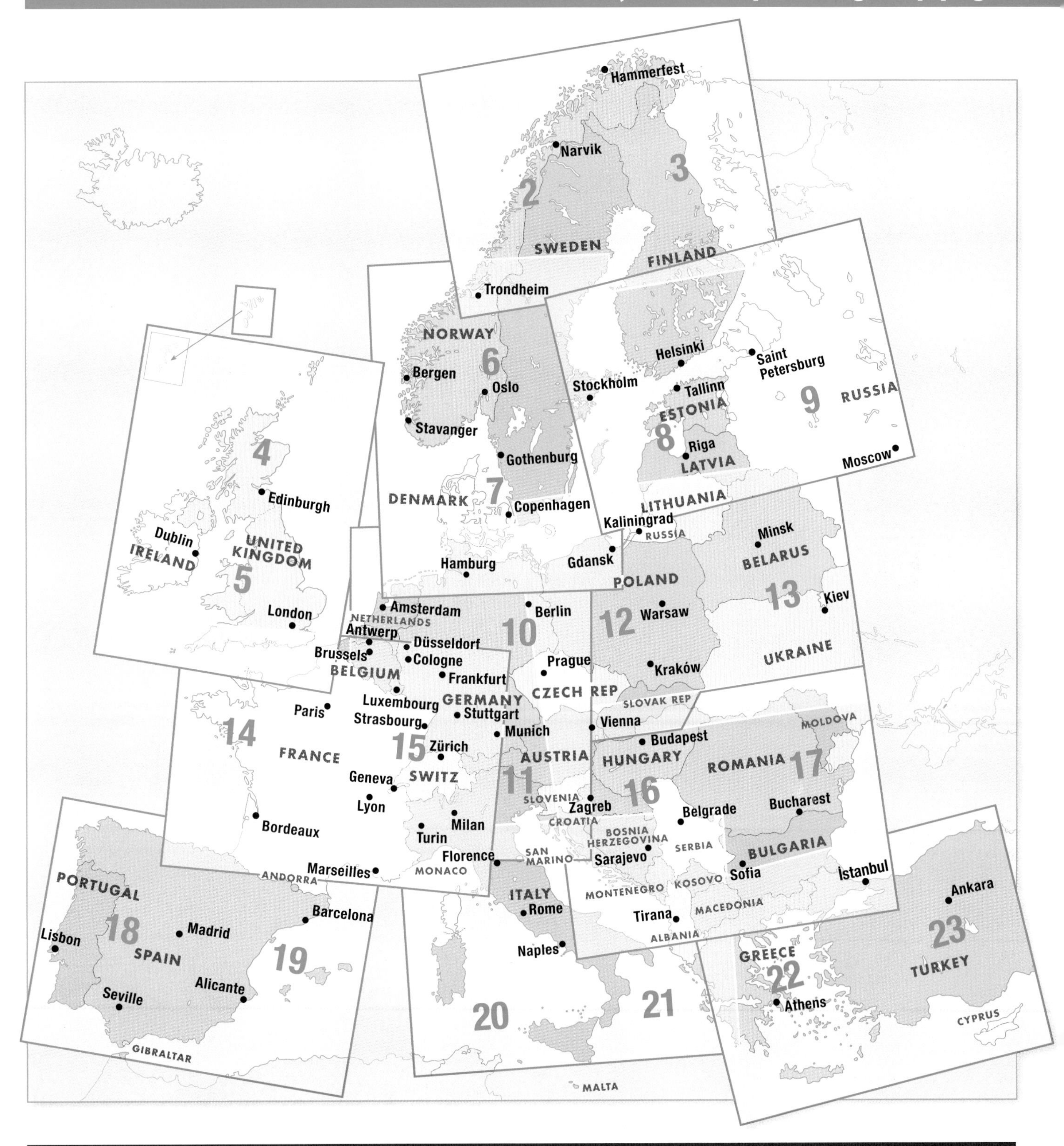

## Motorway vignettes

**Some countries require you to purchase (and in some cases display) a vignette before using motorways.**

**In Austria** you will need to purchase and display a vignette on the inside of your windscreen. Vignettes are available for purchase at border crossings and petrol stations. More details from www.asfinag.at/toll/toll-sticker

**In Belarus** all vehicles over 3.5 tonnes and cars and vans under 3.5 tonnes registered outside the Eurasion Economic Union are required to have a *BelToll* unit installed. This device exchanges data with roadside gantries, enabling motorway tolls to be automatically deducted from the driver's account. www.beltoll.by/index.php/en/faq

**In the Czech Republic**, you can buy a vignette at the border and also at petrol stations. Make sure you write your vehicle registration number on the vignette before displaying it. The roads without toll are indicated by a traffic sign saying 'Bez poplatku'. More details from www.motorway.cz

**In Hungary** a new e-vignette system was introduced in 2008. It is therefore no longer necessary to display the vignette, though you should make doubly sure the information you give on your vehicle is accurate. Vignettes are sold at petrol stations throughout the country. Buy online at www.toll-charge.hu

**In Slovakia**, a vignette is also required to be purchased before using the motorways. This is sold in two kinds at the Slovak border and petrol stations. You will need to write your vehicle registration plate on the vignette before displaying it. More details from www.slovakia.com/travel/car

**In Switzerland**, you will need to purchase and display a 'vignette' before you drive on the motorway. Bear in mind you will need a separate vignette if you are towing a caravan. www.ezv.admin.ch/zollinfo_privat/04338/index.html?lang=en

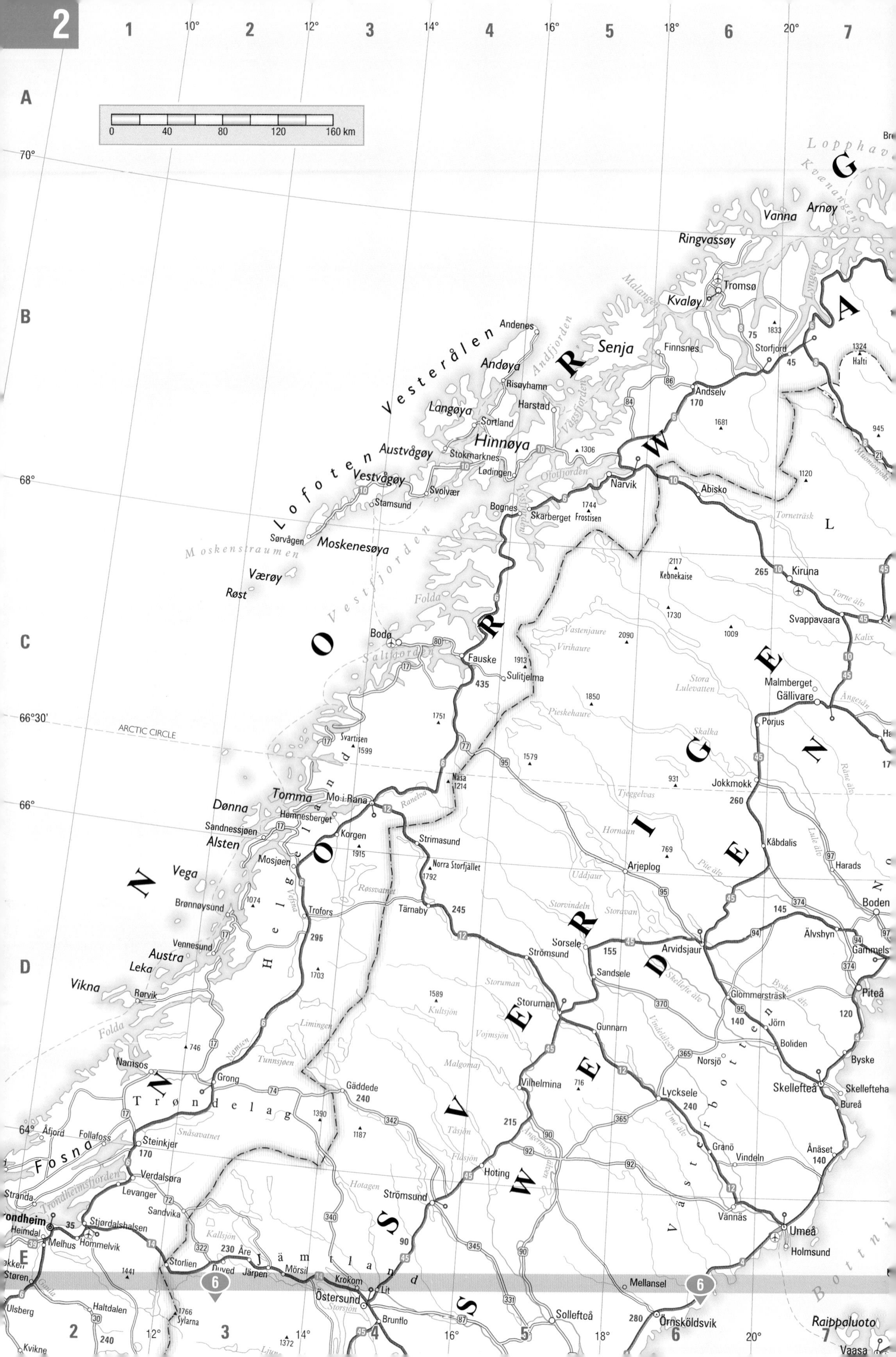
2
0 40 80 120 160 km
ARCTIC CIRCLE
NORWAY
SWEDEN
NOREG
SVERIGE
Lofoten
Vesterålen
Senja
Hinnøya
Andøya
Langøya
Austvågøy
Vestvågøy
Moskenesøya
Værøy
Røst
Ringvassøy
Kvaløy
Vanna
Arnøy
Tromsø
Narvik
Bodø
Fauske
Mo-i-Rana
Mosjøen
Namsos
Steinkjer
Trondheim
Kiruna
Gällivare
Jokkmokk
Arjeplog
Arvidsjaur
Storuman
Vilhelmina
Lycksele
Skellefteå
Umeå
Östersund
Örnsköldsvik
Luleå
Piteå
Helgeland
Trøndelag
Jämtland
Västerbotten
Norrbotten
Fosna
Vestfjorden
Moskenstraumen
Saltfjorden
Trondheimsfjorden
Kebnekaise
Svartisen
Sulitjelma
Andenes
Harstad
Sortland
Stokmarknes
Svolvær
Lødingen
Bognes
Finnsnes
Andselv
Storfjord
Abisko
Svappavaara
Malmberget
Porjus
Kåbdalis
Harads
Boden
Älvshyn
Sorsele
Strömsund
Gäddede
Hoting
Vännäs
Holmsund
Sollefteå
Åre
Storlien
Levanger
Verdalsøra
Brønnøysund
Sandnessjøen
Trofors
Tärnaby
Vaasa
Raippaluoto

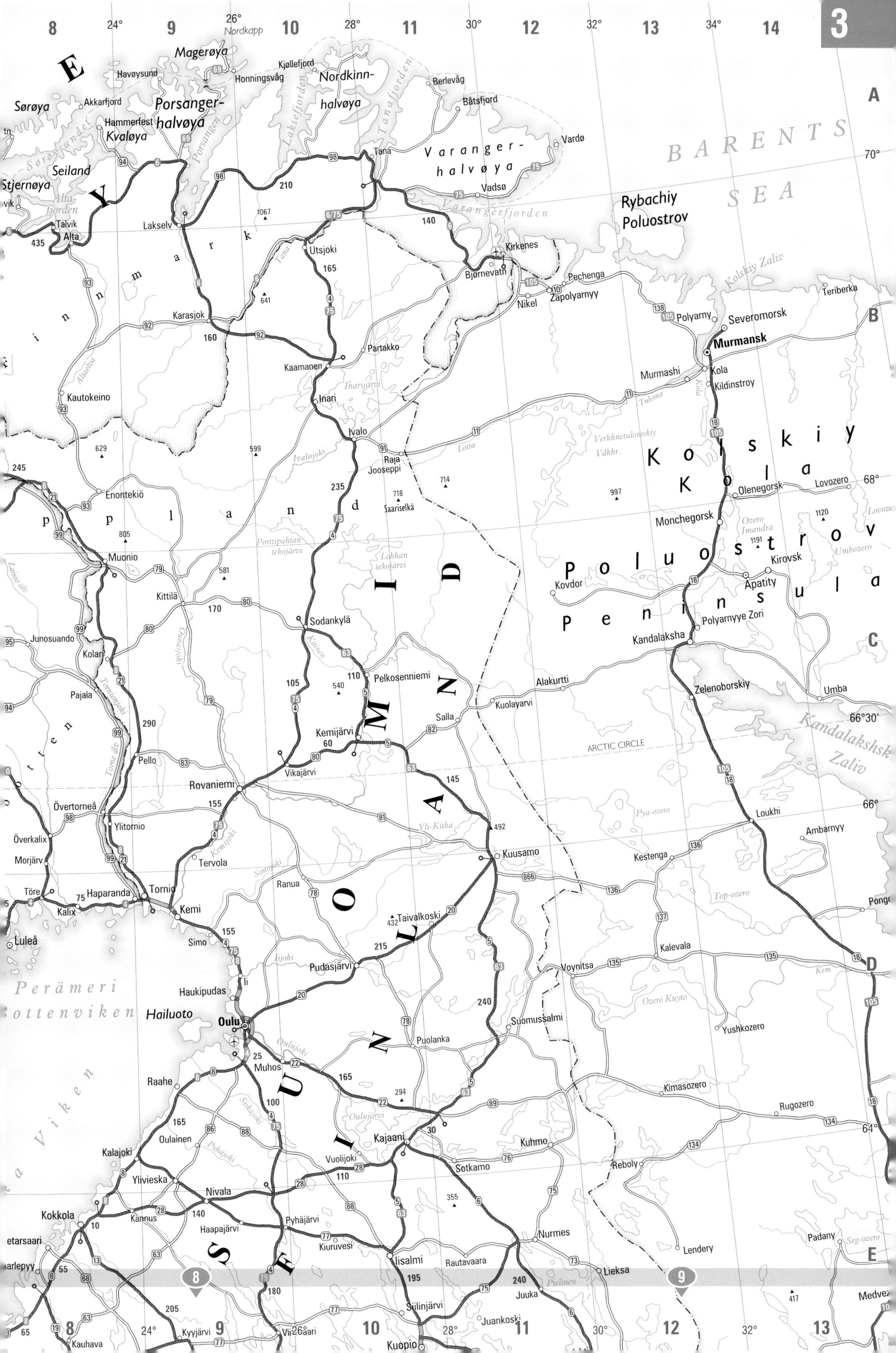
Nordkapp
Magerøya
Havøysund
Honningsvåg
Kjøllefjord
Nordkinn-halvøya
Berlevåg
Båtsfjord
Sørøya
Akkarfjord
Porsanger-halvøya
Hammerfest
Kvaløya
Varanger-halvøya
Vardø
Tana
Seiland
Stjernøya
Vadsø
Varangerfjorden
BARENTS SEA
Rybachiy Poluostrov
Talvik
Alta
Lakselv
Utsjoki
Kirkenes
Bjørnevatn
Pechenga
Nikel
Zapolyarnyy
Teriberka
Polyarny
Severomorsk
Murmansk
Karasjok
Partakko
Kaamanen
Inari
Murmashi
Kola
Kildinstroy
Kautokeino
Ivalo
Raja Jooseppi
Kolskiy Poluostrov
Kola Peninsula
Enontekiö
Saariselkä
Olenegorsk
Lovozero
Monchegorsk
Muonio
Kittilä
Apatity
Kirovsk
Kovdor
Sodankylä
Polyarnyye Zori
Kandalaksha
Junosuando
Kolari
Pelkosenniemi
Alakurtti
Pajala
Zelenoborskiy
Umba
Kuolayarvi
Salla
Kemijärvi
Pello
Vikajärvi
ARCTIC CIRCLE
Kandalakshskiy Zaliv
Rovaniemi
Övertorneå
Ylitornio
Loukhi
Ambarnyy
Överkalix
Kuusamo
Morjärv
Tervola
Kestenga
Ranua
Töre
Haparanda
Tornio
Kalix
Kemi
Taivalkoski
Luleå
Simo
Kalevala
Pudasjärvi
Voynitsa
Perämeri
Bottenviken
Haukipudas
Hailuoto
Oulu
Suomussalmi
Yushkozero
Muhos
Puolanka
Raahe
Kimasozero
Rugozero
Oulainen
Kajaani
Kalajoki
Kuhmo
Vuolijoki
Sotkamo
Ylivieska
Reboly
Nivala
Kokkola
Kannus
Haapajärvi
Pyhäjärvi
Nurmes
Kiuruvesi
Lendery
Padany
Iisalmi
Rautavaara
Lieksa
Juuka
Siilinjärvi
Juankoski
Kyyjärvi
Kauhava
Kuopio
Medvez
FINNMARK
LAPPLAND
SUOMI FINLAND
Pietarsaari
Jakobstad

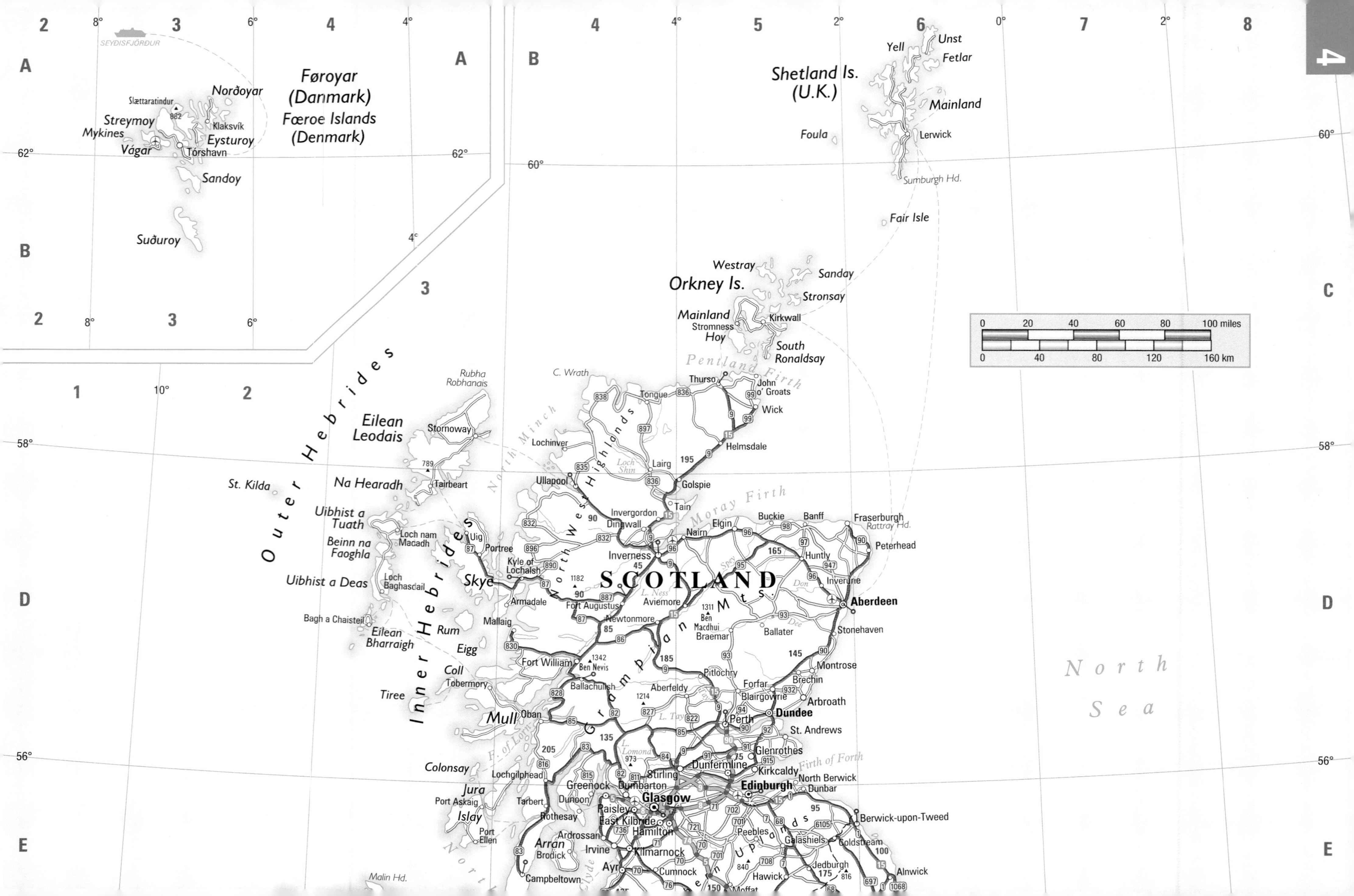
Føroyar
(Danmark)
Færoe Islands
(Denmark)
Norðoyar
Slættaratindur
882
Streymoy
Mykines
Klaksvík
Eysturoy
Vágar
Tórshavn
Sandoy
Suðuroy
SEYÐISFJÖRÐUR
Shetland Is.
(U.K.)
Yell
Unst
Fetlar
Mainland
Foula
Lerwick
Sumburgh Hd.
Fair Isle
Orkney Is.
Westray
Sanday
Stronsay
Mainland
Kirkwall
Stromness
Hoy
South
Ronaldsay
Pentland Firth
0 20 40 60 80 100 miles
0 40 80 120 160 km
Outer Hebrides
Eilean
Leodais
Rubha
Robhanais
Stornoway
Na Hearadh
Tairbeart
St. Kilda
Uibhist a
Tuath
Loch nam
Madadh
Beinn na
Faoghla
Uibhist a Deas
Loch
Baghasdail
Bagh a Chaisteil
Eilean
Bharraigh
Inner Hebrides
Skye
Uig
Portree
Rum
Eigg
Coll
Tobermory
Tiree
Mull
Oban
Colonsay
Jura
Port Askaig
Islay
Port
Ellen
Malin Hd.
C. Wrath
Thurso
John
o' Groats
Wick
Tongue
Helmsdale
Lairg
Golspie
Tain
Lochinver
Ullapool
North Minch
North West Highlands
Invergordon
Dingwall
Inverness
Kyle of
Lochalsh
Armadale
Mallaig
Fort Augustus
Fort William
Ben Nevis
SCOTLAND
Grampian Mts.
Moray Firth
Elgin
Nairn
Buckie
Banff
Fraserburgh
Rattray Hd.
Peterhead
Huntly
Inverurie
Aberdeen
Stonehaven
Ballater
Braemar
Ben
Macdhui
Aviemore
Newtonmore
Pitlochry
Aberfeldy
Ballachulish
Montrose
Brechin
Forfar
Blairgowrie
Arbroath
Dundee
Perth
St. Andrews
Glenrothes
Dunfermline
Kirkcaldy
Firth of Forth
North Berwick
Dunbar
Edinburgh
Stirling
Dumbarton
Greenock
Dunoon
Glasgow
Paisley
East Kilbride
Hamilton
Lochgilphead
Tarbert
Rothesay
Ardrossan
Irvine
Kilmarnock
Arran
Brodick
Ayr
Cumnock
Campbeltown
Peebles
Galashiels
Coldstream
Berwick-upon-Tweed
Jedburgh
Hawick
Moffat
Alnwick
Southern Uplands
North Sea

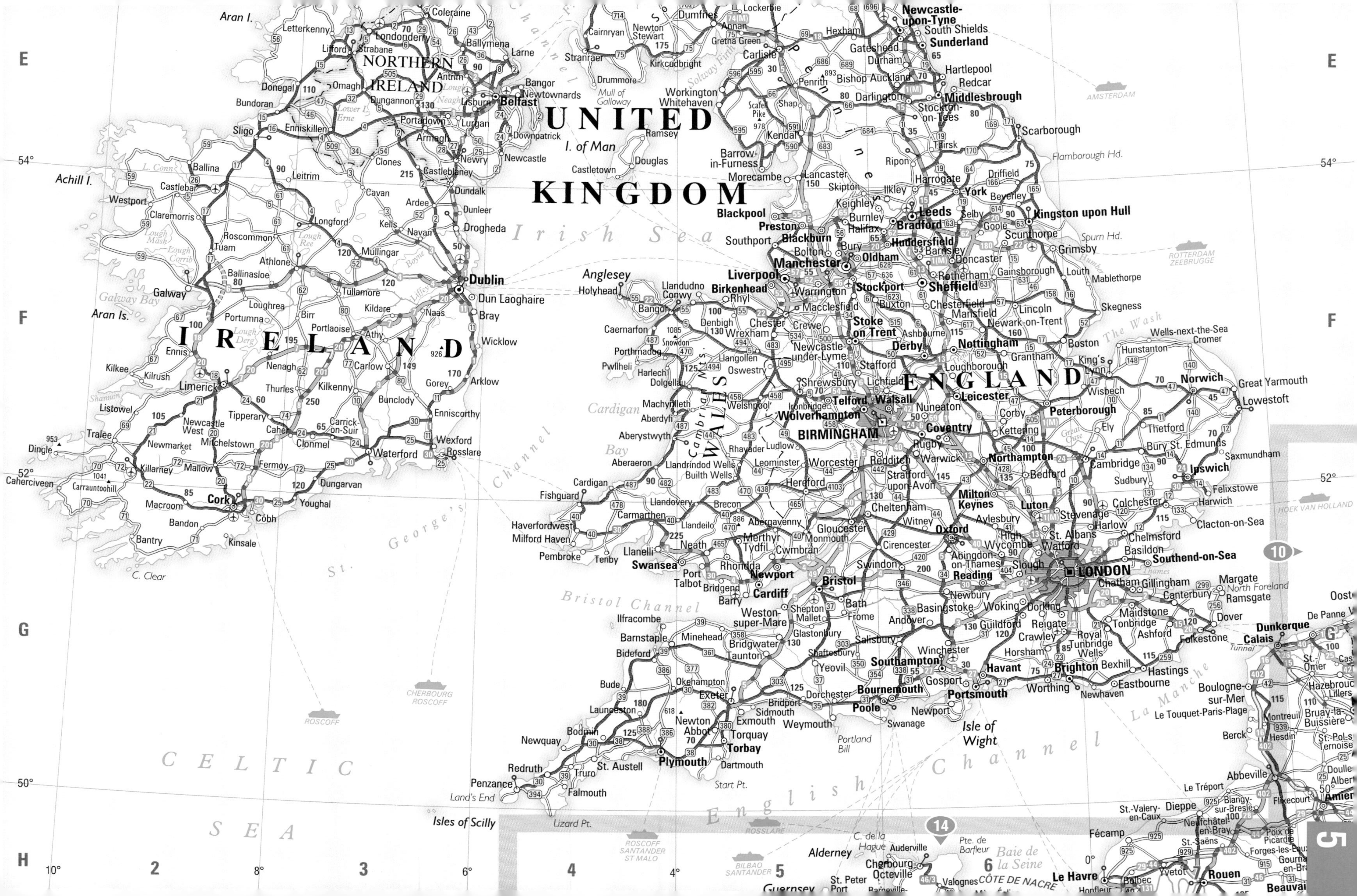

UNITED KINGDOM
IRELAND
NORTHERN IRELAND
ENGLAND
WALES
Irish Sea
St. George's Channel
Bristol Channel
English Channel
La Manche
CELTIC SEA
Cardigan Bay
Galway Bay
The Wash
I. of Man
Isle of Wight
Anglesey
Isles of Scilly
Aran I.
Achill I.
Aran Is.
Alderney
Guernsey
Flamborough Hd.
Spurn Hd.
Land's End
Lizard Pt.
Start Pt.
Portland Bill
C. Clear
North Foreland
Cambrian Mts.
Pennines
Dublin
Belfast
Cork
Limerick
Galway
Waterford
Wexford
Rosslare
Londonderry
Coleraine
Ballymena
Larne
Bangor
Newtownards
Lisburn
Armagh
Newry
Dundalk
Drogheda
Dun Laoghaire
Bray
Wicklow
Arklow
Sligo
Donegal
Letterkenny
Enniskillen
Omagh
Athlone
Mullingar
Tralee
Killarney
Dingle
Kinsale
Cobh
Youghal
LONDON
BIRMINGHAM
Manchester
Liverpool
Leeds
Sheffield
Bradford
Newcastle-upon-Tyne
Sunderland
Middlesbrough
York
Kingston upon Hull
Nottingham
Leicester
Derby
Coventry
Wolverhampton
Stoke on Trent
Cardiff
Swansea
Newport
Bristol
Plymouth
Southampton
Portsmouth
Bournemouth
Brighton
Oxford
Reading
Cambridge
Norwich
Ipswich
Peterborough
Northampton
Luton
Milton Keynes
Southend-on-Sea
Dover
Folkestone
Canterbury
Great Yarmouth
Lowestoft
Carlisle
Blackpool
Preston
Scarborough
Dunkerque
Calais
Boulogne-sur-Mer
Le Havre
Rouen
Dieppe
Cherbourg-Octeville
Abbeville
Baie de la Seine
CÔTE DE NACRE
AMSTERDAM
ROTTERDAM ZEEBRUGGE
HOEK VAN HOLLAND
CHERBOURG ROSCOFF
ROSCOFF
ROSCOFF SANTANDER ST MALO
BILBAO SANTANDER
ROSSLARE
54°
52°
50°
10°
8°
6°
4°
0°
E
F
G
H
2
3
4
5
6
7
10
14

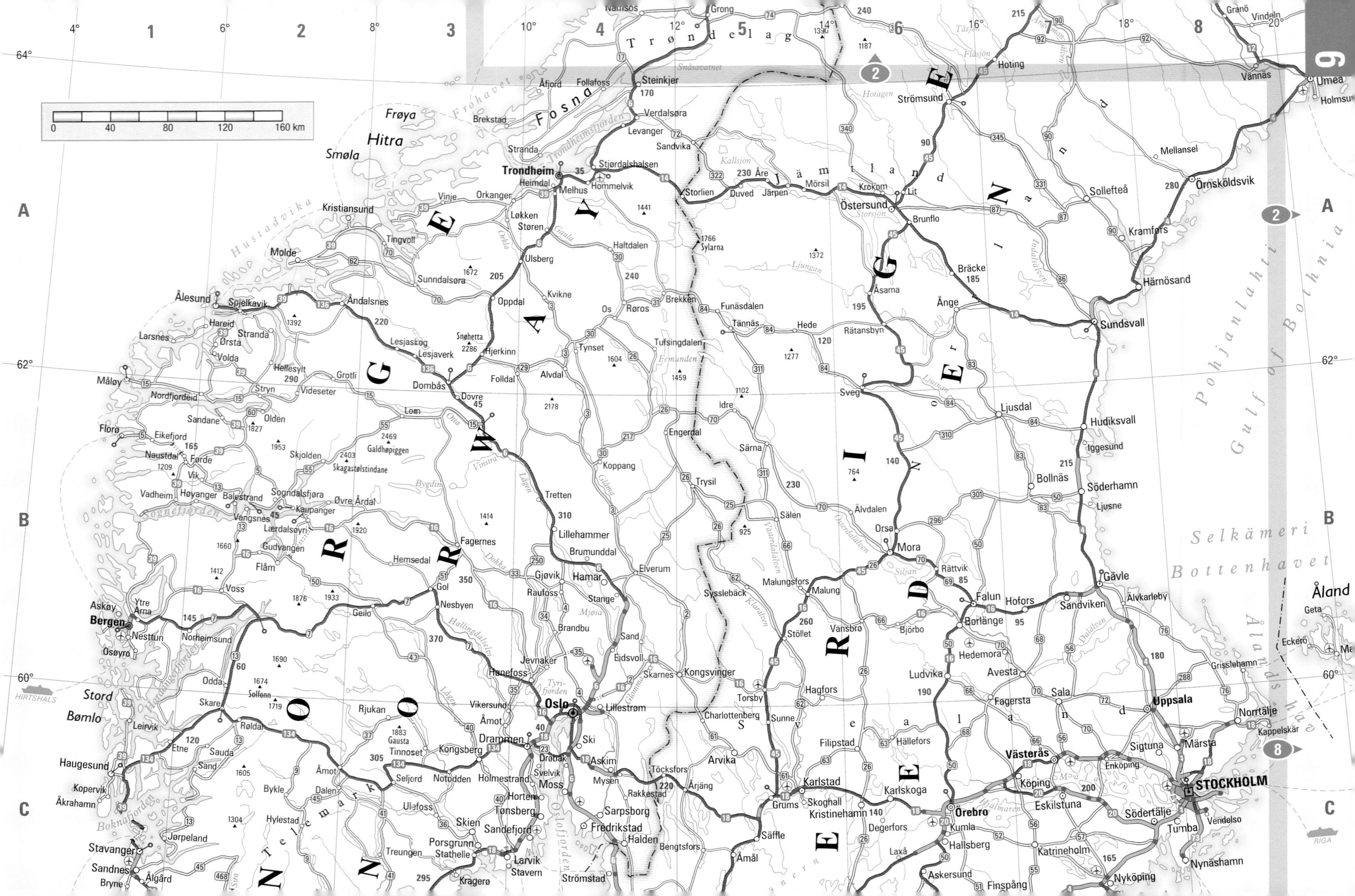
NORGE
SVERIGE
Trøndelag
Jämtland
Ångermanland
Hälsingland
Dalarna
Värmland
Västmanland
Uppland
Telemark
Fosna
Gulf of Bothnia
Pohjanlahti
Selkämeri
Bottenhavet
Ålands hav
Åland
Hustadvika
Frohavet
Oslofjorden
Sognefjorden
Hardangerfjorden
Boknafjorden
Trondheimsfjorden
Frøya
Hitra
Smøla
Stord
Bømlo
Trondheim
Steinkjer
Namsos
Grong
Verdalsøra
Levanger
Stjørdalshalsen
Hommelvik
Melhus
Heimdal
Orkanger
Løkken
Støren
Ulsberg
Oppdal
Kristiansund
Molde
Ålesund
Spjelkavik
Åndalsnes
Lesjaskog
Lesjaverk
Dombås
Dovre
Hjerkinn
Folldal
Alvdal
Tynset
Røros
Os
Brekken
Haltdalen
Kvikne
Sunndalsøra
Tingvoll
Måløy
Florø
Førde
Stryn
Olden
Lom
Sandane
Volda
Ørsta
Stranda
Hellesylt
Geiranger
Grotli
Videseter
Sogndalsfjøra
Kaupanger
Lærdalsøyri
Gudvangen
Flåm
Voss
Bergen
Ytre Arna
Askøy
Nesttun
Osøyro
Norheimsund
Odda
Skare
Røldal
Haugesund
Kopervik
Åkrahamn
Stavanger
Sandnes
Bryne
Ålgård
Jørpeland
Sauda
Etne
Leirvik
Geilo
Gol
Nesbyen
Hemsedal
Fagernes
Lillehammer
Tretten
Gjøvik
Hamar
Elverum
Brumunddal
Stange
Raufoss
Brandbu
Jevnaker
Hønefoss
Eidsvoll
Sand
Kongsvinger
Skarnes
Lillestrøm
Oslo
Ski
Askim
Mysen
Drøbak
Moss
Sarpsborg
Fredrikstad
Halden
Drammen
Kongsberg
Notodden
Rjukan
Gausta
Tinnoset
Seljord
Åmot
Dalen
Bykle
Hylestad
Skien
Porsgrunn
Larvik
Sandefjord
Tønsberg
Horten
Kragerø
Stavern
Trysil
Engerdal
Koppang
Idre
Särna
Sälen
Malung
Malungsfors
Mora
Orsa
Älvdalen
Rättvik
Falun
Borlänge
Hofors
Sandviken
Gävle
Söderhamn
Hudiksvall
Iggesund
Ljusne
Bollnäs
Ljusdal
Sveg
Funäsdalen
Tännäs
Hede
Rätansbyn
Åsarna
Östersund
Krokom
Storlien
Duved
Åre
Järpen
Mörsil
Brunflo
Bräcke
Ånge
Sundsvall
Härnösand
Kramfors
Sollefteå
Örnsköldsvik
Strömsund
Hoting
Vännäs
Umeå
Holmsund
Vindeln
Granö
Mellansel
Sysslebäck
Torsby
Hagfors
Stöllet
Vansbro
Sunne
Charlottenberg
Arvika
Årjäng
Töcksfors
Karlstad
Skoghall
Kristinehamn
Karlskoga
Filipstad
Degerfors
Grums
Säffle
Åmål
Bengtsfors
Strömstad
Ludvika
Hällefors
Avesta
Hedemora
Fagersta
Sala
Västerås
Köping
Örebro
Kumla
Hallsberg
Eskilstuna
Katrineholm
Nyköping
Laxå
Askersund
Finspång
Uppsala
Enköping
Sigtuna
Märsta
Norrtälje
Kappelskär
Grisslehamn
Älvkarleby
Stockholm
Södertälje
Tumba
Nynäshamn
Vendelso
Geta
Eckerö
Hirtshals
Riga
Galdhøpiggen
Skagastølstindane
Snøhetta
Sylarna
Solfonn
0 40 80 120 160 km

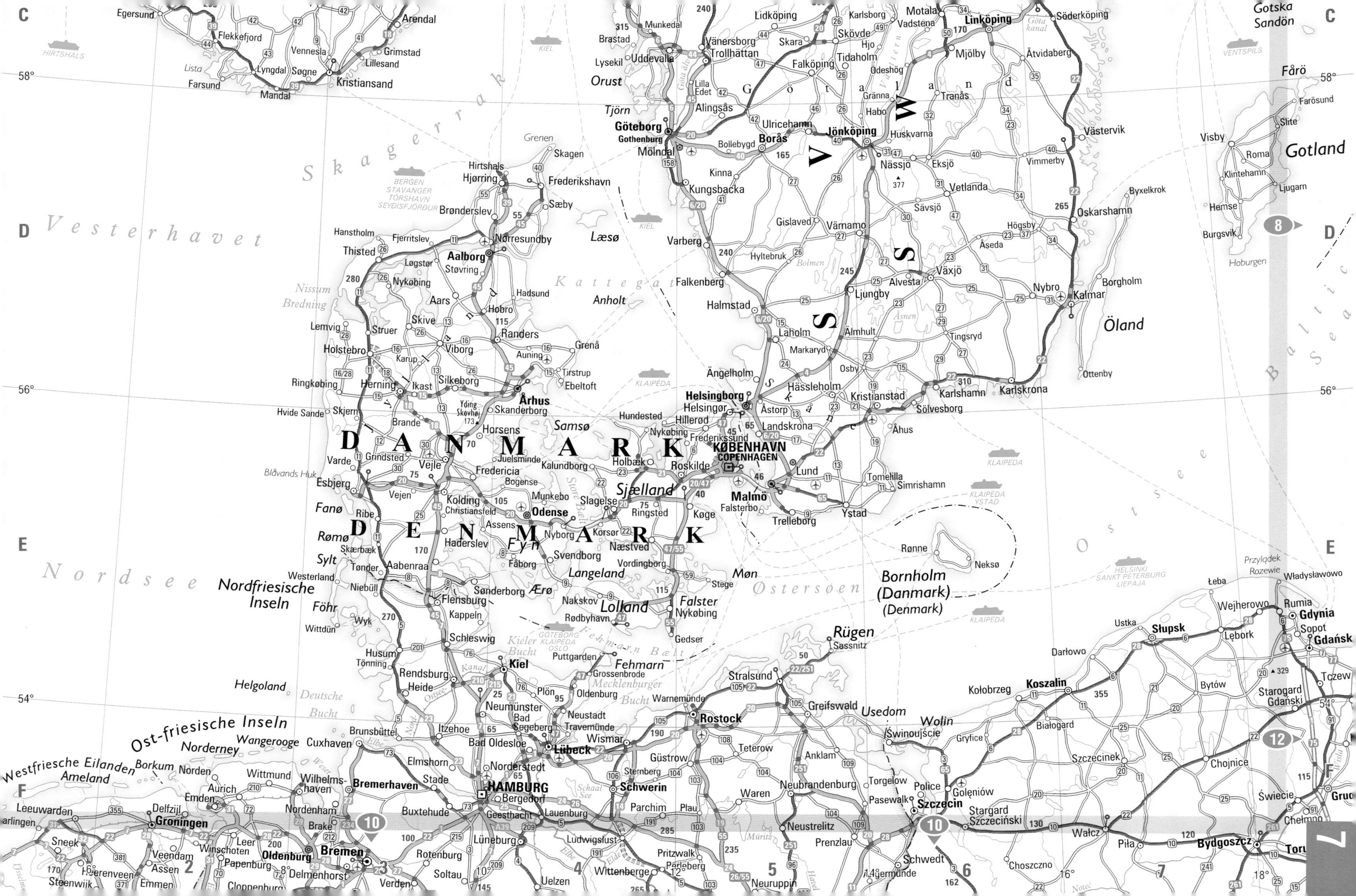

Vesterhavet
Skagerrak
Kattegat
Nordsee
Østersøen
Ostsee
Baltic Sea
DANMARK
DENMARK
Göteborg
Gothenburg
København
Copenhagen
Malmö
Helsingborg
Aalborg
Århus
Odense
Sjælland
Fyn
Lolland
Falster
Møn
Langeland
Ærø
Samsø
Anholt
Læsø
Bornholm (Danmark) (Denmark)
Rønne
Nexø
Öland
Gotland
Fårö
Gotska Sandön
Visby
Kalmar
Karlskrona
Växjö
Jönköping
Linköping
Borås
Halmstad
Varberg
Kristiansand
Arendal
Mandal
Egersund
Hirtshals
Skagen
Frederikshavn
Hjørring
Esbjerg
Vejle
Kolding
Randers
Viborg
Herning
Holstebro
Silkeborg
Horsens
Fredericia
Roskilde
Køge
Næstved
Slagelse
Trelleborg
Ystad
Lund
Kristianstad
Nordfriesische Inseln
Ost-friesische Inseln
Westfriesche Eilanden
Helgoland
Sylt
Föhr
Rømø
Fanø
Flensburg
Kiel
Lübeck
Hamburg
Bremen
Bremerhaven
Cuxhaven
Oldenburg
Groningen
Rostock
Stralsund
Rügen
Usedom
Wolin
Schwerin
Wismar
Szczecin
Koszalin
Słupsk
Gdynia
Gdańsk
Bydgoszcz
Fehmarn
Mecklenburger Bucht
Deutsche Bucht
Kieler Bucht
Fehmarn Bælt
58°
56°
54°
C
D
E
F

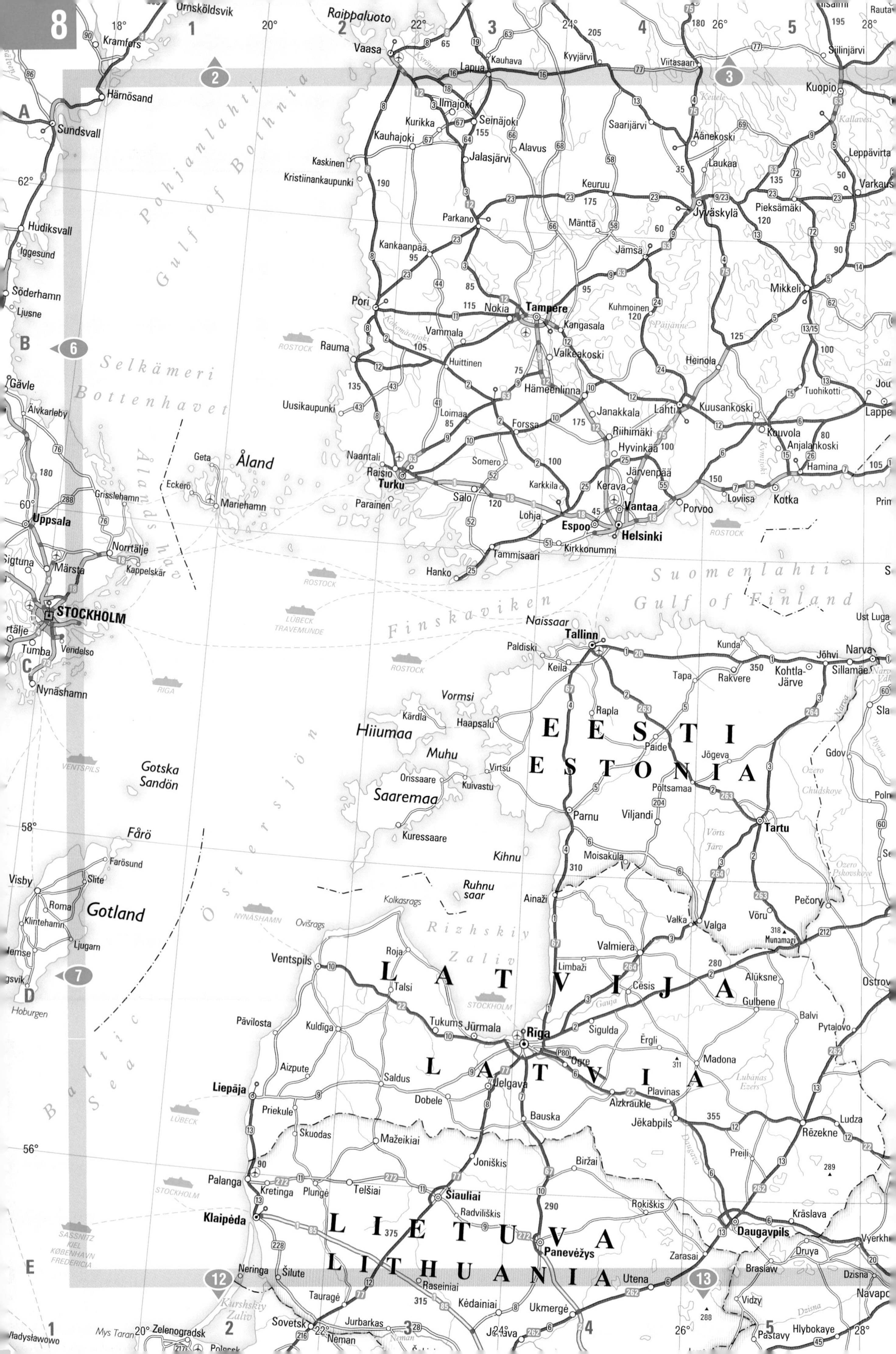

8
Örnsköldsvik
Raippaluoto
Kramfors
Vaasa
Lapua
Kauhava
Kyyjärvi
Viitasaari
Siilinjärvi
Härnösand
Ilmajoki
Seinäjoki
Kurikka
Kauhajoki
Alavus
Jalasjärvi
Saarijärvi
Äänekoski
Kuopio
Kallavesi
Sundsvall
Kaskinen
Kristiinankaupunki
Laukaa
Leppävirta
Varkaus
Pohjanlahti
Gulf of Bothnia
Keuruu
Jyväskylä
Pieksämäki
Parkano
Mänttä
Hudiksvall
Iggesund
Kankaanpää
Jämsä
Mikkeli
Söderhamn
Ljusne
Pori
Nokia
Tampere
Kuhmoinen
Kangasala
Päijänne
Vammala
Rauma
ROSTOCK
Valkeakoski
Heinola
Selkämeri
Bottenhavet
Huittinen
Hämeenlinna
Tuohikotti
Gävle
Älvkarleby
Uusikaupunki
Loimaa
Forssa
Janakkala
Lahti
Kuusankoski
Kouvola
Anjalankoski
Riihimäki
Hyvinkää
Åland
Geta
Ålands hav
Naantali
Raisio
Turku
Somero
Järvenpää
Hamina
Eckerö
Mariehamn
Grisslehamn
Karkkila
Kerava
Salo
Parainen
Loviisa
Kotka
Vantaa
Porvoo
Uppsala
Lohja
Espoo
Helsinki
Norrtälje
Kappelskär
Tammisaari
Kirkkonummi
Sigtuna
Märsta
Hanko
Suomenlahti
Gulf of Finland
STOCKHOLM
Finskaviken
LÜBECK TRAVEMÜNDE
Naissaar
Tallinn
Ust Luga
Södertälje
Tumba
Vendelso
Paldiski
Keila
Kunda
Narva
Jõhvi
Sillamäe
Kohtla-Järve
Tapa
Rakvere
Nynäshamn
RIGA
Vormsi
Rapla
Kärdla
Haapsalu
Hiiumaa
EESTI
ESTONIA
Paide
Jõgeva
Gdov
Muhu
Virtsu
VENTSPILS
Gotska Sandön
Orissaare
Kuivastu
Põltsamaa
Saaremaa
Pärnu
Viljandi
Tartu
Vörts Järv
Ozero Chudskoye
Fårö
Kuressaare
Kihnu
Moisaküla
Fårösund
Slite
Visby
Ruhnu saar
Ainaži
Ozero Pskovskoye
Kolkasrags
Roma
Gotland
Pečory
Klintehamn
NYNÄSHAMN
Ovišrags
Östersjön
Võru
Valka
Valga
Munamagi
Rizhskiy Zaliv
Ljugarn
Valmiera
Ventspils
Roja
Limbaži
Alūksne
LATVIJA
Talsi
Cēsis
Gauja
Gulbene
Ostrov
Hoburgen
Pāvilosta
Kuldīga
Tukums
Jūrmala
STOCKHOLM
Sigulda
Balvi
Pytalovo
Rīga
Ērgli
Aizpute
LATVIA
Ogre
Madona
Saldus
Jelgava
Lubānas Ezers
Liepāja
Dobele
Pļaviņas
Aizkraukle
Baltic Sea
Bauska
Jēkabpils
Ludza
Priekule
Rēzekne
LÜBECK
Skuodas
Mažeikiai
Preiļi
Daugava
Joniškis
Biržai
Palanga
Kretinga
Plungė
Telšiai
Šiauliai
Radviliškis
Rokiškis
Krāslava
Klaipėda
LIETUVA
Daugavpils
SASSNITZ KIEL KØBENHAVN FREDERICIA
Panevėžys
Zarasai
Vyerkhnyadzvinsk
Druya
Neringa
Šilutė
LITHUANIA
Utena
Braslaw
Dzisna
Raseiniai
Navapolatsk
Kurshskiy Zaliv
Tauragė
Kėdainiai
Ukmergė
Vidzy
Dzisna
Sovetsk
Jurbarkas
Jonava
Pastavy
Hlybokaye
Władysławowo
Mys Taran
Zelenogradsk
Neman
Polessk

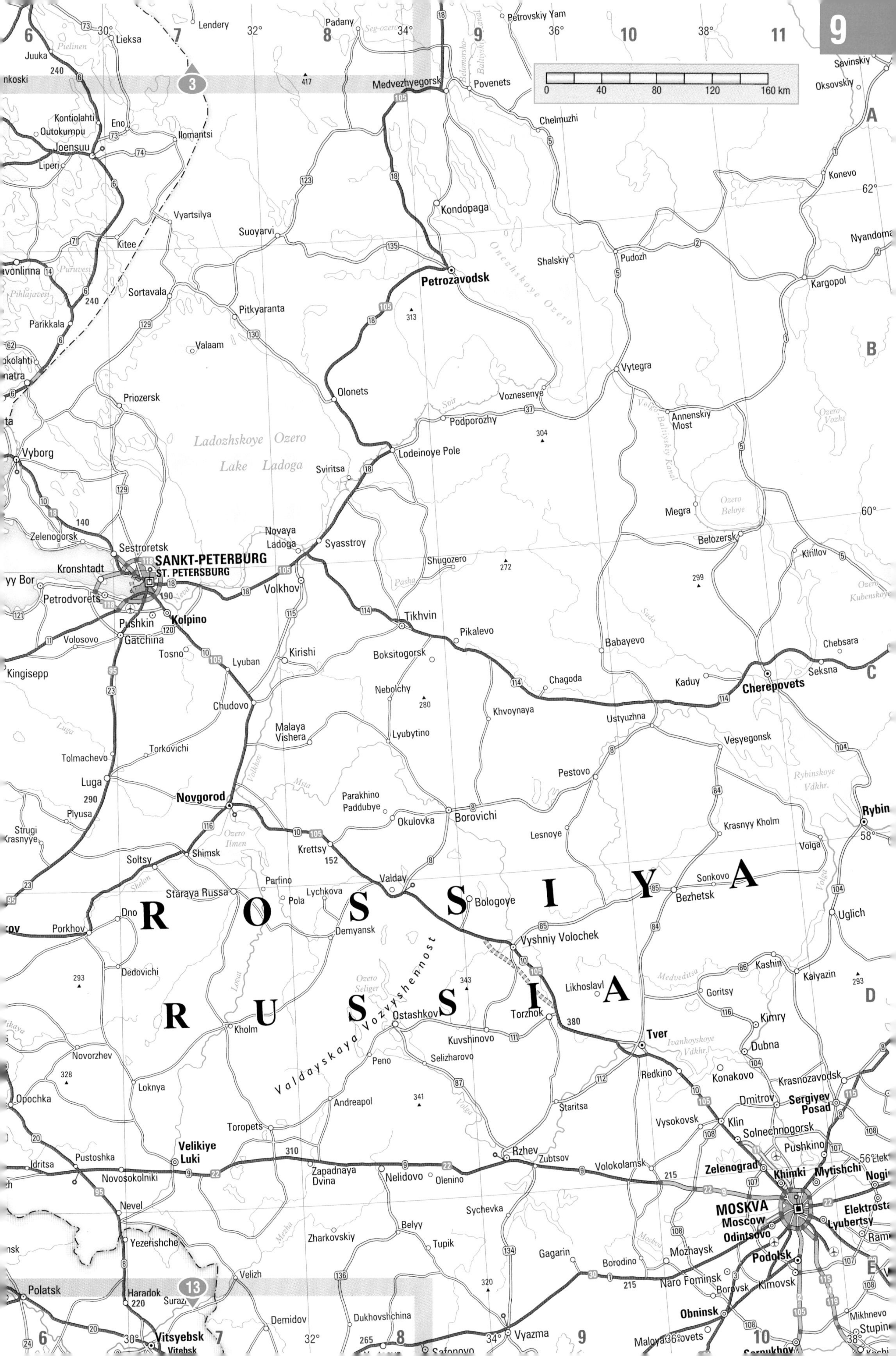

ROSSIYA
RUSSIA
SANKT-PETERBURG
ST. PETERSBURG
MOSKVA
Moscow
Ladozhskoye Ozero
Lake Ladoga
Onezhskoye Ozero
Valdayskaya Vozvyshennost
Petrozavodsk
Medvezhyegorsk
Povenets
Kondopaga
Suoyarvi
Pitkyaranta
Sortavala
Valaam
Priozersk
Vyborg
Zelenogorsk
Sestroretsk
Kronshtadt
Petrodvorets
Pushkin
Gatchina
Kolpino
Tosno
Lyuban
Kirishi
Volkhov
Novaya Ladoga
Syasstroy
Sviritsa
Lodeinoye Pole
Podporozhy
Voznesenye
Olonets
Vytegra
Pudozh
Shalskiy
Chelmuzhi
Kargopol
Konevo
Nyandoma
Savinskiy
Oksovskiy
Annenskiy Most
Megra
Belozersk
Kirillov
Babayevo
Chebsara
Seksna
Cherepovets
Kaduy
Chagoda
Pikalevo
Tikhvin
Boksitogorsk
Shugozero
Nebolchy
Lyubytino
Khvoynaya
Ustyuzhna
Vesyegonsk
Pestovo
Borovichi
Okulovka
Parakhino Paddubye
Malaya Vishera
Chudovo
Novgorod
Luga
Torkovichi
Tolmachevo
Plyusa
Strugi Krasnyye
Kingisepp
Volosovo
Shimsk
Soltsy
Staraya Russa
Parfino
Pola
Lychkova
Krettsy
Valday
Bologoye
Demyansk
Dno
Porkhov
Dedovichi
Kholm
Ostashkov
Peno
Selizharovo
Kuvshinovo
Torzhok
Vyshniy Volochek
Likhoslavl
Lesnoye
Sonkovo
Bezhetsk
Krasnyy Kholm
Rybin
Volga
Uglich
Kalyazin
Kashin
Goritsy
Kimry
Dubna
Tver
Redkino
Konakovo
Krasnozavodsk
Sergiyev Posad
Dmitrov
Klin
Solnechnogorsk
Vysokovsk
Staritsa
Rzhev
Zubtsov
Volokolamsk
Zelenograd
Khimki
Mytishchi
Pushkino
Elektrostal
Lyubertsy
Odintsovo
Podolsk
Mozhaysk
Borodino
Naro Fominsk
Borovsk
Kimovsk
Obninsk
Maloyaroslavets
Serpukhov
Stupino
Mikhnevo
Gagarin
Vyazma
Sychevka
Belyy
Tupik
Nelidovo
Olenino
Zapadnaya Dvina
Andreapol
Toropets
Velikiye Luki
Novosokolniki
Pustoshka
Idritsa
Nevel
Yezerishche
Loknya
Novorzhev
Opochka
Velizh
Demidov
Dukhovshchina
Safonovo
Polatsk
Haradok
Surazh
Vitsyebsk
Vitebsk
Joensuu
Outokumpu
Kontiolahti
Eno
Ilomantsi
Liperi
Lieksa
Juuka
Pielinen
Lendery
Padany
Seg-ozero
Petrovskiy Yam
Vyartsilya
Kitee
Puruvesi
Parikkala
Pihlajavesi
Imatra
Rybinskoye Vdkhr.
Ozero Beloye
Ozero Kubenskoye
Ozero Ilmen
Ozero Seliger
Ivankovskoye Vdkhr.
Medveditsa
Volkhov
Msta
Sheksna
Suda
Pasha
Svir
Volgo-Baltiyskiy Kanal
Belomorsko-Baltiyskiy Kanal
Lovat
Shelon
Mezha
Moskva
0 40 80 120 160 km
A B C D E
6 7 8 9 10 11
30° 32° 34° 36° 38°
56° 58° 60° 62°

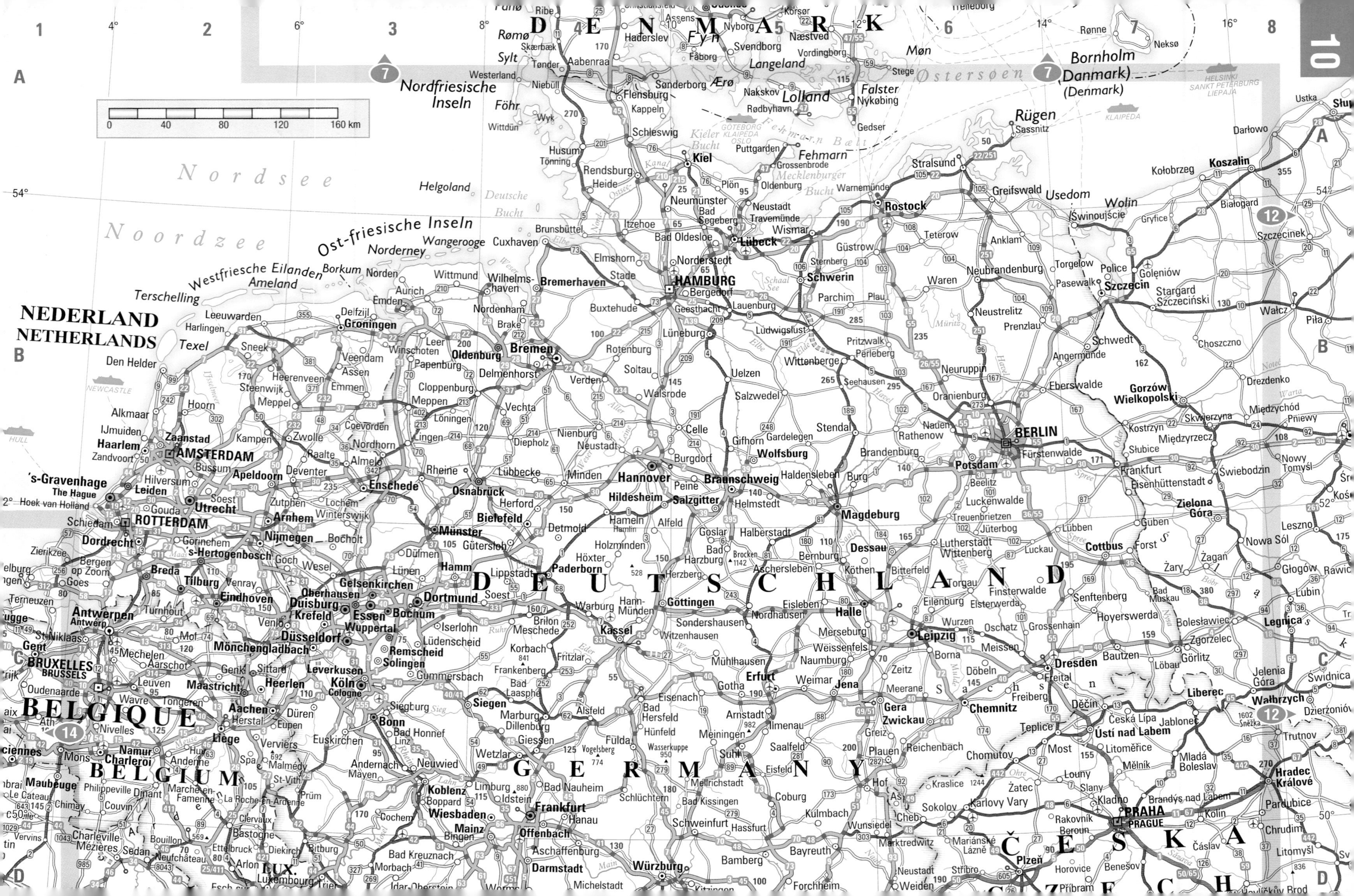
DANMARK
NEDERLAND
NETHERLANDS
DEUTSCHLAND
GERMANY
BELGIQUE
BELGIUM
ČESKÁ
LUX.
Nordsee
Noordzee
Østersøen
Nordfriesische Inseln
Ost-friesische Inseln
Westfriesche Eilanden
Bornholm
(Danmark)
(Denmark)
Rügen
Usedom
Wolin
Fehmarn
Lolland
Falster
Langeland
Fyn
Ærø
Møn
Helgoland
Texel
Terschelling
Ameland
Borkum
Norderney
Wangerooge
Föhr
Sylt
Rømø
0
40
80
120
160 km
BERLIN
HAMBURG
Bremen
Hannover
Hamburg
Magdeburg
Leipzig
Dresden
Kiel
Lübeck
Rostock
Schwerin
Szczecin
Köln
Cologne
Düsseldorf
Dortmund
Essen
Frankfurt
AMSTERDAM
ROTTERDAM
's-Gravenhage
The Hague
BRUXELLES
BRUSSELS
PRAHA
PRAGUE

11
SWITZERLAND
SCHWEIZ
ÖSTERREICH
AUSTRIA
SLOVENIJA
SLOVENIA
LIECHTENSTEIN
SAN MARINO
MONACO
MÜNCHEN
MUNICH
Stuttgart
Nürnberg
Zürich
Bern
Basel
Genève
Lausanne
Innsbruck
Salzburg
Linz
Graz
Ljubljana
Trieste
Venézia
Verona
MILANO
TORINO
Génova
Bologna
LYON
Grenoble
Dijon
Strasbourg
Karlsruhe
Heidelberg
Augsburg
Regensburg
Ingolstadt
Bolzano
Trento
Pádova
Golfo di Venézia

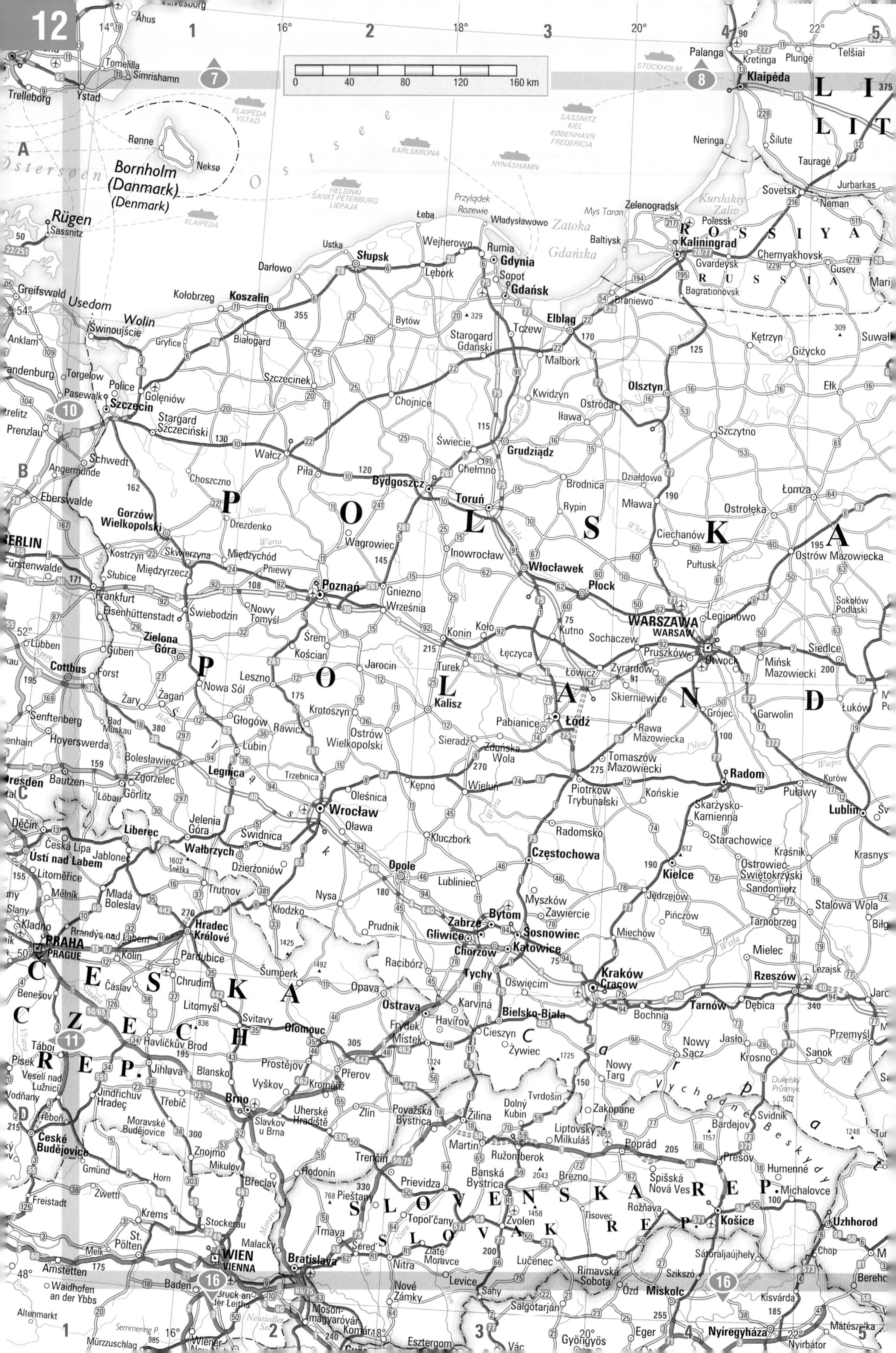
Åhus
Tomelilla
Simrishamn
Trelleborg
Ystad
Rønne
Bornholm
(Danmark)
(Denmark)
Neksø
Østersøen
Ostsee
KLAIPĖDA
YSTAD
KARLSKRONA
NYNÄSHAMN
SASSNITZ
KIEL
KØBENHAVN
FREDERICIA
HELSINKI
SANKT PETERBURG
LIEPAJA
KLAIPEDA
STOCKHOLM
0
40
80
120
160 km
Palanga
Kretinga
Plungė
Telšiai
Klaipėda
Neringa
Šilute
Tauragė
Jurbarkas
Sovetsk
Neman
Kurshskiy Zaliv
Zelenogradsk
Polessk
Mys Taran
Baltiysk
Kaliningrad
Chernyakhovsk
Gvardeysk
Gusev
Bagrationovsk
ROSSIYA
RUSSIA
LIETUVA
Rügen
Sassnitz
Greifswald
Usedom
Wolin
Świnoujście
Anklam
Torgelow
Pasewalk
Police
Goleniów
Szczecin
Prenzlau
Schwedt
Angermünde
Eberswalde
Stargard Szczeciński
Kołobrzeg
Koszalin
Białogard
Gryfice
Darłowo
Ustka
Słupsk
Łeba
Lębork
Wejherowo
Rumia
Gdynia
Sopot
Gdańsk
Przylądek Rozewie
Władysławowo
Zatoka Gdańska
Bytów
Starogard Gdański
Tczew
Elbląg
Malbork
Braniewo
Szczecinek
Chojnice
Kwidzyn
Iława
Ostróda
Olsztyn
Kętrzyn
Giżycko
Ełk
Szczytno
Wałcz
Piła
Bydgoszcz
Świecie
Grudziądz
Chełmno
Toruń
Brodnica
Działdowo
Rypin
Mława
Łomża
Ostrołęka
Ciechanów
Pułtusk
Ostrów Mazowiecka
Choszczno
Gorzów Wielkopolski
Drezdenko
Wągrowiec
Inowrocław
Włocławek
Płock
Kostrzyn
Skwierzyna
Międzychód
Pniewy
Słubice
Międzyrzecz
Frankfurt
Eisenhüttenstadt
Świebodzin
Nowy Tomyśl
Poznań
Gniezno
Września
Konin
Koło
Kutno
Sochaczew
WARSZAWA
WARSAW
Legionowo
Pruszków
Otwock
Mińsk Mazowiecki
Siedlce
Sokołów Podlaski
Zielona Góra
Guben
Cottbus
Forst
Lübben
Śrem
Kościan
Leszno
Jarocin
Turek
Łęczyca
Łowicz
Żyrardów
Skierniewice
Nowa Sól
Żary
Żagań
Senftenberg
Bad Muskau
Hoyerswerda
Głogów
Rawicz
Krotoszyn
Kalisz
Pabianice
Łódź
Rawa Mazowiecka
Grójec
Garwolin
Łuków
Ostrów Wielkopolski
Sieradz
Zduńska Wola
Tomaszów Mazowiecki
Radom
Kurów
Puławy
Lublin
Lubin
Bolesławiec
Legnica
Trzebnica
Kępno
Wieluń
Piotrków Trybunalski
Końskie
Skarżysko-Kamienna
Dresden
Bautzen
Zgorzelec
Görlitz
Löbau
Oleśnica
Wrocław
Oława
Jelenia Góra
Świdnica
Wałbrzych
Dzierżoniów
Kluczbork
Radomsko
Starachowice
Kraśnik
Krasnystaw
Děčín
Liberec
Česká Lípa
Jablonec
Ústí nad Labem
Litoměřice
Mělník
Mladá Boleslav
Trutnov
Śnieżka
Opole
Lubliniec
Częstochowa
Kielce
Ostrowiec Świętokrzyski
Sandomierz
Stalowa Wola
Nysa
Kłodzko
Prudnik
Zabrze
Bytom
Gliwice
Chorzów
Katowice
Sosnowiec
Myszków
Zawiercie
Jędrzejów
Pińczów
Tarnobrzeg
Miechów
Mielec
Kladno
Slaný
Brandýs nad Labem
PRAHA
PRAGUE
Kolín
Hradec Králové
Pardubice
Šumperk
Racibórz
Tychy
Oświęcim
Kraków
Cracow
Tarnów
Dębica
Rzeszów
Leżajsk
Benešov
Čáslav
Chrudim
Litomyšl
Svitavy
Opava
Ostrava
Karviná
Havířov
Frýdek-Místek
Bielsko-Biała
Cieszyn
Żywiec
Bochnia
Nowy Sącz
Jasło
Krosno
Sanok
Przemyśl
Tábor
Havlíčkův Brod
Olomouc
Nowy Targ
Písek
Jihlava
Blansko
Prostějov
Přerov
Vyškov
Kroměříž
Veselí nad Lužnicí
Jindřichův Hradec
Vodňany
Třebíč
Brno
Slavkov u Brna
Uherské Hradiště
Zlín
Považská Bystrica
Žilina
Dolný Kubín
Tvrdošín
Zakopane
Dukelský Průsmyk
Svidník
Bardejov
Třeboň
Moravské Budějovice
České Budějovice
Znojmo
Mikulov
Břeclav
Hodonín
Trenčín
Martin
Ružomberok
Liptovský Mikuláš
Poprad
Prešov
Humenné
Michalovce
Gmünd
Horn
Prievidza
Banská Bystrica
Brezno
Spišská Nová Ves
Freistadt
Zwettl
Krems
Stockerau
Piešťany
Topoľčany
Zvolen
Tisovec
Rožňava
Košice
Uzhhorod
Chop
St. Pölten
Melk
Amstetten
WIEN
VIENNA
Malacky
Trnava
Sereď
Nitra
Zlaté Moravce
Levice
Lučenec
Rimavská Sobota
Sátoraljaújhely
Bratislava
Szikszó
Miskolc
Ózd
Kisvárda
Berehove
Waidhofen an der Ybbs
Baden
Bruck an der Leitha
Mosonmagyaróvár
Nové Zámky
Šahy
Salgótarján
Eger
Nyíregyháza
Mátészalka
Nyírbátor
Altenmarkt
Mürzzuschlag
Semmering P.
Neusiedler See
Komárom
Esztergom
Vác
Gyöngyös
Wiener
POLSKA
POLAND
ČESKÁ REP.
CZECH REP.
SLOVENSKÁ REP.
SLOVAK REP.
Sudety
Karpaty
Východné Beskydy
Oder
Warta
Noteć
Wisła
Bug
Narew
Wkra
Pilica
Prosna
Wieprz
San
Bóbr
Nysa
Spree
Jihlava
Morava
Váh
Sázava
Vltava
Enns
Lyna
BERLIN
Fürstenwalde
Brandenburg
Tur

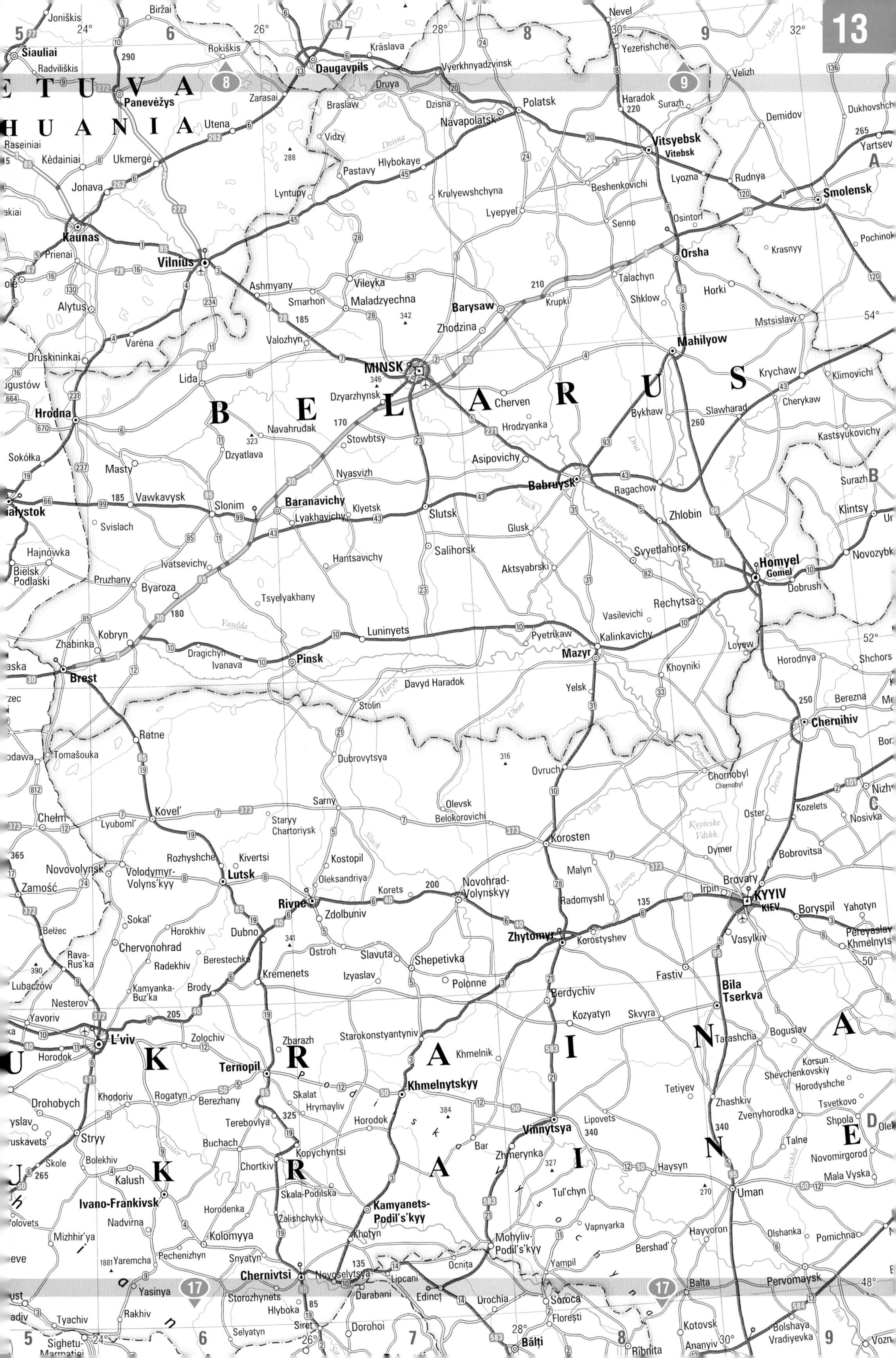
LIETUVA
LITHUANIA
BELARUS
UKRAINA
Podil's'ka Vysochyna
Joniškis
Biržai
Šiauliai
Radviliškis
Rokiškis
Daugavpils
Krāslava
Panevėžys
Zarasai
Utena
Raseiniai
Kėdainiai
Ukmergė
Jonava
Kaunas
Prienai
Vilnius
Alytus
Varėna
Druskininkai
Nevel
Yezerishche
Vyerkhnyadzvinsk
Druya
Braslaw
Dzisna
Polatsk
Navapolatsk
Haradok
Surazh
Velizh
Demidov
Dukhovshchina
Yartsev
Vitsyebsk
Vitebsk
Vidzy
Pastavy
Hlybokaye
Lyntupy
Krulyewshchyna
Beshenkovichi
Lyozna
Rudnya
Smolensk
Lyepyel
Senno
Osintorf
Orsha
Krasnyy
Pochinok
Ashmyany
Vileyka
Smarhon
Maladzyechna
Barysaw
Krupki
Talachyn
Shklow
Horki
Zhodzina
Valozhyn
Mstsislaw
Mahilyow
MINSK
Dzyarzhynsk
Lida
Krychaw
Klimovichi
Cherven
Hrodzyanka
Bykhaw
Slawharad
Cherykaw
Kastsyukovichy
Hrodna
Sokółka
Navahrudak
Stowbtsy
Dzyatlava
Masty
Nyasvizh
Asipovichy
Babruysk
Ragachow
Surazh
Vawkavysk
Slonim
Baranavichy
Klyetsk
Lyakhavichy
Slutsk
Zhlobin
Klintsy
Białystok
Svislach
Glusk
Hajnówka
Bielsk Podlaski
Ivatsevichy
Hantsavichy
Salihorsk
Svyetlahorsk
Homyel
Gomel
Novozybkov
Aktsyabrski
Dobrush
Pruzhany
Byaroza
Tsyelyakhany
Rechytsa
Vasilevichi
Zhabinka
Kobryn
Luninyets
Pyetrikaw
Kalinkavichy
Mazyr
Loyew
Dragichyn
Ivanava
Pinsk
Brest
Horodnya
Shchors
Khoyniki
Davyd Haradok
Yelsk
Stolin
Berezna
Chernihiv
Ratne
Tomašouka
Dubrovytsya
Ovruch
Chornobyl
Chernobyl
Nizhyn
Chełm
Lyuboml'
Kovel'
Sarny
Staryy Chartoriysk
Olevsk
Belokorovichi
Oster
Kozelets
Nosivka
Korosten
Dymer
Bobrovitsa
Novovolynsk
Rozhyshche
Kivertsi
Volodymyr-Volyns'kyy
Kostopil
Zamość
Lutsk
Oleksandriya
Malyn
Brovary
Irpin
KYYIV
KIEV
Rivne
Korets
Novohrad-Volynskyy
Radomyshl
Boryspil
Yahotyn
Zdolbuniv
Pereyaslav-Khmelnytskyy
Sokal'
Horokhiv
Dubno
Zhytomyr
Korostyshev
Vasylkiv
Bełżec
Chervonohrad
Ostroh
Slavuta
Shepetivka
Rava-Rus'ka
Radekhiv
Berestechko
Kremenets
Izyaslav
Polonne
Fastiv
Lubaczów
Kamyanka-Buz'ka
Brody
Berdychiv
Bila Tserkva
Nesterov
Yavoriv
Kozyatyn
Skvyra
L'viv
Zolochiv
Zbarazh
Starokonstyantyniv
Tarashcha
Boguslav
Horodok
Ternopil
Khmelnik
Korsun-Shevchenkovskiy
Horodyshche
Drohobych
Khodoriv
Rogatyn
Berezhany
Skalat
Hrymayliv
Khmelnytskyy
Tetiyev
Zhashkiv
Tsvetkovo
Terebovlya
Horodok
Vinnytsya
Lipovets
Zvenyhorodka
Shpola
Stryy
Buchach
Kopychyntsi
Bar
Talne
Skole
Bolekhiv
Chortkiv
Zhmerynka
Haysyn
Novomirgorod
Kalush
Mala Vyska
Ivano-Frankivsk
Skala-Podilska
Tul'chyn
Uman
Horodenka
Kamyanets-Podil's'kyy
Nadvirna
Zalishchyky
Vapnyarka
Hayvoron
Olshanka
Pomichna
Mizhhir'ya
Kolomyya
Khotyn
Mohyliv-Podil's'kyy
Bershad'
Yaremcha
Pechenizhyn
Snyatyn
Yampil
Chernivtsi
Novoselytsya
Ocnița
Lipcani
Balta
Pervomaysk
Yasinya
Storozhynets
Darabani
Edineț
Drochia
Soroca
Hlyboka
Florești
Kotovsk
Bolshaya Vradiyevka
Rakhiv
Tyachiv
Siret
Dorohoi
Bălți
Rîbnița
Ananyiv
Voznesensk
Selyatyn
Sighetu Marmației
Dzisna
Viliya
Yaselda
Pripyat
Drut
Sozh
Byarezina
Pitsich
Horyn
Ubort
Uzh
Desna
Sluch
Teterev
Kyyivske Vdskh.
Dnister
Southern Buh
Ros
5
6
7
8
9
24°
26°
28°
30°
32°
54°
52°
50°
48°
A
B
C
D
E
17

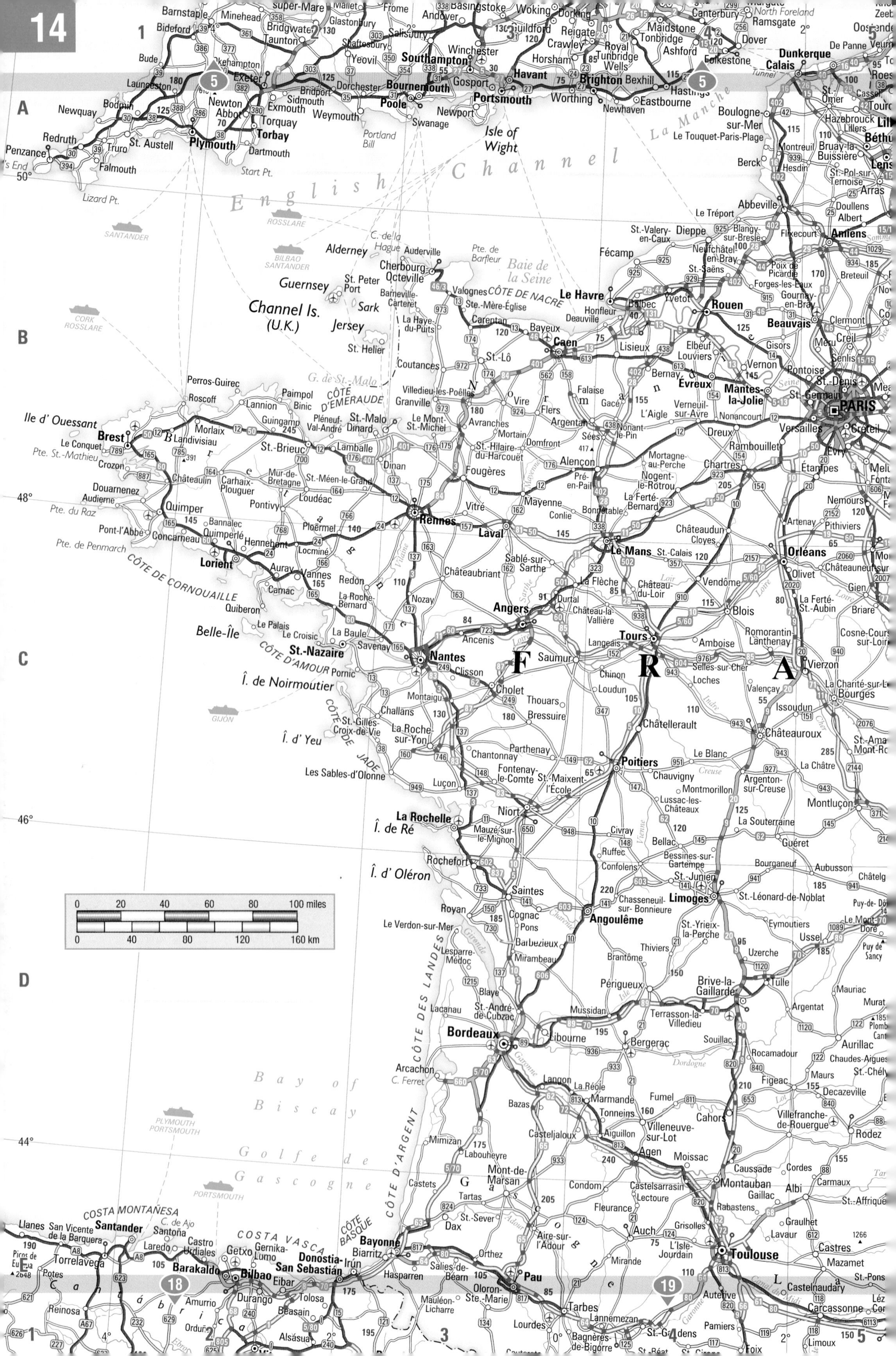

Barnstaple
Minehead
Bideford
Bridgwater
Taunton
Glastonbury
Frome
Andover
Basingstoke
Woking
Dorking
Guildford
Reigate
Crawley
Horsham
Royal Tunbridge Wells
Maidstone
Tonbridge
Ashford
Canterbury
North Foreland
Ramsgate
Dover
Folkestone
Shaftesbury
Salisbury
Yeovil
Southampton
Winchester
Bude
Okehampton
Exeter
Launceston
Newton Abbot
Torquay
Torbay
Dartmouth
Plymouth
Sidmouth
Exmouth
Bridport
Dorchester
Weymouth
Poole
Bournemouth
Swanage
Portland Bill
Newport
Isle of Wight
Gosport
Portsmouth
Havant
Worthing
Brighton
Newhaven
Bexhill
Hastings
Eastbourne
Newquay
Bodmin
Redruth
Truro
St. Austell
Penzance
Falmouth
Start Pt.
Lizard Pt.
50°
English Channel
La Manche
Dunkerque
Calais
Tunnel
Boulogne-sur-Mer
Le Touquet-Paris-Plage
St.-Omer
Hazebrouck
Béthune
Lens
Arras
Bruay-la-Buissière
St.-Pol-sur-Ternoise
Montreuil
Hesdin
Berck
Abbeville
Doullens
Albert
Amiens
Le Tréport
Dieppe
St.-Valery-en-Caux
Fécamp
Neufchâtel-en-Bray
St.-Saëns
Forges-les-Eaux
Poix de Picardie
Breteuil
Gournay-en-Bray
Beauvais
Clermont
Creil
Senlis
Méru
Gisors
Vernon
Pontoise
St.-Denis
St.-Germain
PARIS
Versailles
Créteil
Évry
Étampes
Rouen
Yvetot
Bolbec
Le Havre
Honfleur
Deauville
Lisieux
Elbeuf
Louviers
Évreux
Bernay
Mantes-la-Jolie
Verneuil-sur-Avre
Nonancourt
Dreux
Rambouillet
Chartres
L'Aigle
Gacé
Nonant-le-Pin
Sées
Argentan
Falaise
Flers
Vire
Caen
Bayeux
Carentan
Ste.-Mère-Église
Valognes
CÔTE DE NACRE
Baie de la Seine
Pte. de Barfleur
Cherbourg-Octeville
C. de la Hague
Auderville
Barneville-Carteret
La Haye-du-Puits
St.-Lô
Coutances
Villedieu-les-Poêles
Granville
Avranches
Mortain
Domfront
Le Mont-St.-Michel
St.-Hilaire-du-Harcouët
Fougères
Alençon
Pré-en-Pail
Mortagne-au-Perche
Nogent-le-Rotrou
La Ferté-Bernard
Bonnétable
Mayenne
Conlie
Laval
Vitré
Rennes
Alderney
Guernsey
St. Peter Port
Sark
Channel Is. (U.K.)
Jersey
St. Helier
G. de St.-Malo
CÔTE D'EMERAUDE
St.-Malo
Dinard
Dinan
Lamballe
St.-Brieuc
Paimpol
Binic
Pléneuf-Val-André
Perros-Guirec
Roscoff
Lannion
Guingamp
Morlaix
Landivisiau
Brest
Le Conquet
Pte. St.-Mathieu
Crozon
Ile d' Ouessant
Châteaulin
Carhaix-Plouguer
Mûr-de-Bretagne
St.-Méen-le-Grand
Loudéac
Pontivy
Douarnenez
Audierne
Pte. du Raz
Quimper
Pont-l'Abbé
Concarneau
Bannalec
Quimperlé
Hennebont
Lorient
Pte. de Penmarch
CÔTE DE CORNOUAILLE
Ploërmel
Locminé
Auray
Vannes
Carnac
Quiberon
Belle-Île
Le Palais
Le Croisic
La Baule
St.-Nazaire
Savenay
Redon
La Roche-Bernard
Nozay
Châteaubriant
Sablé-sur-Sarthe
Le Mans
St.-Calais
La Flèche
Château-du-Loir
Angers
Durtal
Château-la-Vallière
Ancenis
Nantes
Clisson
Pornic
CÔTE D'AMOUR
Î. de Noirmoutier
Montaigu
Cholet
Challans
St.-Gilles-Croix-de-Vie
La Roche-sur-Yon
Î. d' Yeu
CÔTE DE JADE
Les Sables-d'Olonne
Luçon
Chantonnay
Fontenay-le-Comte
Bressuire
Thouars
Parthenay
Saumur
Chinon
Loudun
Tours
Langeais
Amboise
Blois
Vendôme
Châteaudun
Cloyes
Orléans
Olivet
Pithiviers
Nemours
Artenay
Châteauneuf-sur
Gien
La Ferté-St.-Aubin
Briare
Cosne-Cours-sur-Loire
Romorantin-Lanthenay
Selles-sur-Cher
Loches
Vierzon
Valençay
La Charité-sur-Loire
Bourges
Issoudun
Châteauroux
Châtellerault
Poitiers
Le Blanc
Chauvigny
Montmorillon
Lussac-les-Châteaux
Argenton-sur-Creuse
La Châtre
Montluçon
La Souterraine
Guéret
Bourganeuf
Aubusson
St.-Maixent-l'École
Niort
Mauzé-sur-le-Mignon
La Rochelle
Î. de Ré
Rochefort
Î. d' Oléron
Civray
Ruffec
Confolens
Bellac
Bessines-sur-Gartempe
St.-Junien
Limoges
St.-Léonard-de-Noblat
Eymoutiers
St.-Yrieix-la-Perche
Ussel
Saintes
Royan
Cognac
Pons
Le Verdon-sur-Mer
Angoulême
Chasseneuil-sur-Bonnieure
Barbezieux
Lesparre-Médoc
Gironde
Mirambeau
Blaye
Brantôme
Thiviers
Uzerche
Tulle
Brive-la-Gaillarde
Périgueux
St.-André-de-Cubzac
Lacanau
Bordeaux
Libourne
Mussidan
Bergerac
Terrasson-la-Villedieu
Souillac
Argentat
Mauriac
Aurillac
Arcachon
C. Ferret
CÔTE DES LANDES
Langon
La Réole
Marmande
Tonneins
Bazas
Fumel
Cahors
Figeac
Rocamadour
Decazeville
Villefranche-de-Rouergue
Rodez
Casteljaloux
Aiguillon
Villeneuve-sur-Lot
Agen
Moissac
Montauban
Caussade
Cordes
Carmaux
Gaillac
Albi
Rabastens
Graulhet
Lavaur
Castres
Mazamet
Toulouse
Mimizan
Labouheyre
Mont-de-Marsan
Castets
Tartas
Dax
St.-Sever
Aire-sur-l'Adour
Condom
Castelsarrasin
Lectoure
Fleurance
Auch
L'Isle-Jourdain
Grisolles
Mirande
Bayonne
Biarritz
Irún
Donostia-San Sebastián
Hasparren
Salies-de-Béarn
Orthez
Pau
Oloron-Ste.-Marie
Mauléon-Licharre
Tarbes
Lourdes
Lannemezan
Bagnères-de-Bigorre
St.-Gaudens
Auterive
Pamiers
Foix
Castelnaudary
Carcassonne
Limoux
Bay of Biscay
Golfe de Gascogne
CÔTE D'ARGENT
CÔTE BASQUE
COSTA VASCA
COSTA MONTAÑESA
Santander
Llanes
San Vicente de la Barquera
Torrelavega
Santoña
C. de Ajo
Laredo
Castro Urdiales
Barakaldo
Getxo
Bilbao
Gernika-Lumo
Durango
Eibar
Amurrio
Tolosa
Beasain
Alsásua
Reinosa
Potes
Picos de Europa
FRANCE
46°
48°
44°
0
20
40
60
80
100 miles
0
40
80
120
160 km

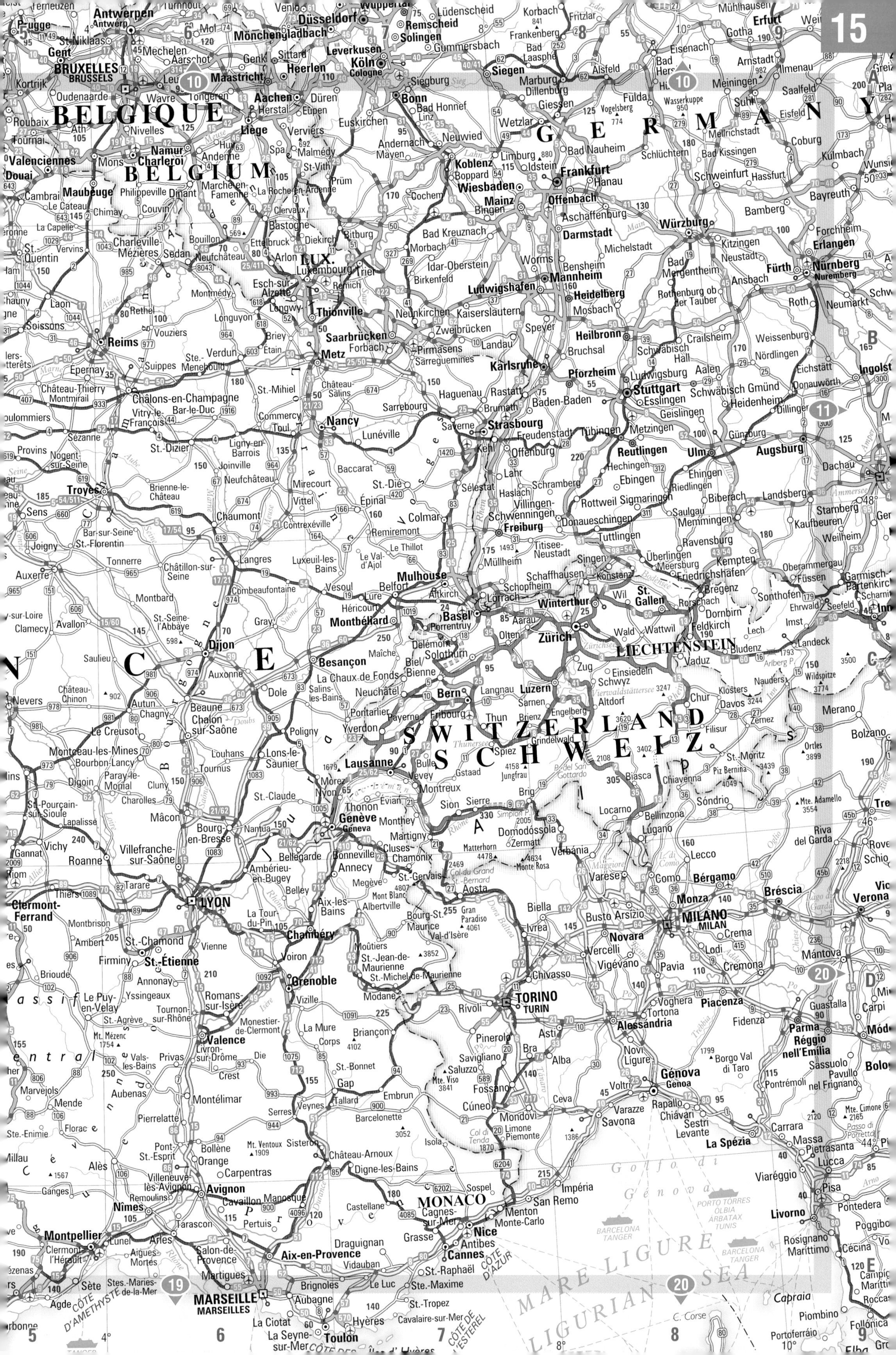
BELGIQUE
BELGIUM
GERMANY
SWITZERLAND
SCHWEIZ
LIECHTENSTEIN
LUX.
MONACO
MARE LIGURE
LIGURIAN SEA
Golfo di Génova
CÔTE D'AZUR
CÔTE DE L'ESTEREL
CÔTE D'AMETHYSTE
Antwerpen
Antwerp
Brugge
Gent
BRUXELLES
BRUSSELS
Mechelen
Aarschot
Genk
Maastricht
Kortrijk
Oudenaarde
Wavre
Tongeren
Leuven
Mönchengladbach
Düsseldorf
Wuppertal
Remscheid
Solingen
Leverkusen
Köln
Cologne
Heerlen
Sittard
Aachen
Herstal
Eupen
Düren
Bonn
Bad Honnef
Siegburg
Siegen
Gummersbach
Lüdenscheid
Korbach
Fritzlar
Frankenberg
Bad Laasphe
Marburg
Dillenburg
Giessen
Alsfeld
Fulda
Vogelsberg
Eisenach
Bad Hersfeld
Gotha
Erfurt
Mühlhausen
Arnstadt
Ilmenau
Meiningen
Suhl
Saalfeld
Eisfeld
Coburg
Kulmbach
Bayreuth
Bamberg
Forchheim
Erlangen
Fürth
Nürnberg
Nuremberg
Ansbach
Roth
Neumarkt
Weissenburg
Eichstätt
Ingolstadt
Donauwörth
Dillingen
Augsburg
Dachau
Landsberg
Starnberg
Kaufbeuren
Weilheim
Kempten
Füssen
Oberammergau
Garmisch-Partenkirchen
Sonthofen
Imst
Landeck
Innsbruck
Ulm
Günzburg
Memmingen
Biberach
Riedlingen
Ehingen
Saulgau
Ravensburg
Friedrichshafen
Überlingen
Meersburg
Konstanz
Bodensee
Singen
Tuttlingen
Donaueschingen
Sigmaringen
Rottweil
Schramberg
Villingen-Schwenningen
Titisee-Neustadt
Freiburg
Müllheim
Lörrach
Schopfheim
Schaffhausen
Winterthur
Zürich
St. Gallen
Wil
Wattwil
Bregenz
Dornbirn
Feldkirch
Bludenz
Vaduz
Rorschach
Lech
Wald
Zürichsee
Einsiedeln
Schwyz
Altdorf
Vierwaldstättersee
Zug
Luzern
Sarnen
Engelberg
Chur
Klosters
Davos
Filisur
Zernez
St.-Moritz
Piz Bernina
Chiavenna
Sóndrio
Merano
Bolzano
Ortles
Mte. Adamello
Riva del Garda
Rovereto
Trento
Verona
Lago di Garda
Bréscia
Bérgamo
Lecco
Como
Lago di Como
Monza
MILANO
MILAN
Varese
Lago Maggiore
Lugano
Bellinzona
Locarno
Biasca
P. del San Gottardo
Verbánia
Domodóssola
Simplon P.
Brig
Sierre
Sion
Matterhorn
Zermatt
Monte Rosa
Jungfrau
Grindelwald
Brienz
Spiez
Thun
Thunersee
Gstaad
Bern
Langnau
Fribourg
Payerne
Neuchâtel
Biel/Bienne
Solothurn
Olten
Aarau
Basel
Delémont
Porrentruy
La Chaux de Fonds
Pontarlier
Yverdon
Lausanne
Vevey
Montreux
Bulle
Morez
Nyon
Genève
Geneva
Lac Léman
Thonon
Evian
Monthey
Martigny
Chamonix
Cluses
Bonneville
Annecy
St.-Gervais
Col du Grand St.-Bernard
Aosta
Mont Blanc
Megève
Albertville
Bourg-St.-Maurice
Gran Paradiso
Val-d'Isère
Moûtiers
St.-Jean-de-Maurienne
St.-Michel-de-Maurienne
Modane
Biella
Ivrea
Vercelli
Novara
Busto Arsizio
Vigévano
Pavia
Lodi
Crema
Cremona
Mantova
Piacenza
Voghera
Tortona
Alessandria
Asti
Chivasso
TORINO
TURIN
Rívoli
Pinerolo
Savigliano
Saluzzo
Mte. Viso
Bra
Alba
Fossano
Cúneo
Mondovì
Ceva
Limone Piemonte
Col di Tenda
Savona
Varazze
Voltri
Génova
Genoa
Novi Ligure
Rapallo
Chiávari
Sestri Levante
La Spézia
Carrara
Massa
Pietrasanta
Viaréggio
Lucca
Pisa
Livorno
Pontedera
Rosignano Marittimo
Cécina
Piombino
Follonica
Portoferráio
Capraia
C. Corse
Parma
Réggio nell'Emília
Módena
Carpi
Guastalla
Fidenza
Borgo Val di Taro
Pontrémoli
Sassuolo
Pavullo nel Frignano
Bologna
Mte. Cimone
Impéria
San Remo
Menton
Monte-Carlo
Nice
Antibes
Cannes
Grasse
Cagnes-sur-Mer
Sospel
Castellane
Draguignan
Vidauban
Le Luc
St.-Raphaël
Ste.-Maxime
St.-Tropez
Cavalaire-sur-Mer
Hyères
Toulon
La Seyne-sur-Mer
La Ciotat
Aubagne
Brignoles
MARSEILLE
MARSEILLES
Martigues
Aix-en-Provence
Salon-de-Provence
Pertuis
Manosque
Cavaillon
Avignon
Carpentras
Orange
Bollène
Pont-St.-Esprit
Villeneuve-lès-Avignon
Remoulins
Nîmes
Tarascon
Arles
Aigues-Mortes
Stes.-Maries-de-la-Mer
Lunel
Montpellier
Clermont-l'Hérault
Sète
Agde
Béziers
Ganges
Millau
Alès
Mende
Florac
Marvejols
Aubenas
Montélimar
Pierrelatte
Crest
Die
Privas
Valence
Livron-sur-Drôme
Romans-sur-Isère
Tournon-sur-Rhône
Annonay
Yssingeaux
Le Puy-en-Velay
Mt. Mézenc
Brioude
St.-Étienne
St.-Chamond
Firminy
Montbrison
Ambert
Thiers
Clermont-Ferrand
Vichy
Gannat
Riom
Roanne
Tarare
LYON
Vienne
Villefranche-sur-Saône
Ambérieu-en-Bugey
Bourg-en-Bresse
Nantua
Bellegarde
Belley
Aix-les-Bains
Chambéry
La Tour-du-Pin
Voiron
Grenoble
Vizille
La Mure
Corps
Briançon
Embrun
Gap
Tallard
Barcelonnette
Veynes
Sisteron
Serres
Digne-les-Bains
Château-Arnoux
Mt. Ventoux
Mâcon
Cluny
Charolles
Paray-le-Monial
Digoin
Bourbon-Lancy
Montceau-les-Mines
Le Creusot
Chalon-sur-Saône
Beaune
Chagny
Autun
Louhans
Tournus
Lons-le-Saunier
Poligny
St.-Claude
Oyonnax
Dole
Auxonne
Dijon
Besançon
Montbéliard
Belfort
Héricourt
Lure
Vesoul
Gray
Langres
Luxeuil-les-Bains
Le Val-d'Ajol
Remiremont
Le Thillot
Mulhouse
Altkirch
Colmar
Sélestat
Épinal
St.-Dié
Baccarat
Lunéville
Nancy
Toul
Commercy
Bar-le-Duc
St.-Dizier
Vitry-le-François
Châlons-en-Champagne
Épernay
Reims
Soissons
Laon
St.-Quentin
Chauny
Verdun
Ste.-Menehould
Suippes
St.-Mihiel
Metz
Briey
Étain
Thionville
Longwy
Esch-sur-Alzette
Luxembourg
Arlon
Neufchâteau
Bastogne
Clervaux
Diekirch
Ettelbruck
Bouillon
Sedan
Charleville-Mézières
Rethel
Vouziers
Montmédy
Longuyon
Saarbrücken
Forbach
Sarreguemines
Pirmasens
Zweibrücken
Kaiserslautern
Neunkirchen
Landau
Speyer
Ludwigshafen
Mannheim
Heidelberg
Worms
Bensheim
Darmstadt
Frankfurt
Offenbach
Hanau
Aschaffenburg
Wiesbaden
Mainz
Bingen
Bad Kreuznach
Idar-Oberstein
Birkenfeld
Morbach
Trier
Bitburg
Prüm
St.-Vith
Malmédy
Spa
Verviers
Liège
Huy
Namur
Charleroi
Mons
Nivelles
Ath
Tournai
Roubaix
Valenciennes
Douai
Maubeuge
Cambrai
Le Cateau
Chimay
Couvin
Philippeville
Dinant
Marche-en-Famenne
La Roche-en-Ardenne
Euskirchen
Andernach
Mayen
Neuwied
Koblenz
Boppard
Limburg
Idstein
Wetzlar
Bad Nauheim
Cochem
Linz
Schlüchtern
Bad Kissingen
Schweinfurt
Hassfurt
Würzburg
Kitzingen
Bad Mergentheim
Neustadt
Rothenburg ob der Tauber
Crailsheim
Nördlingen
Aalen
Schwäbisch Gmünd
Heidenheim
Schwäbisch Hall
Heilbronn
Mosbach
Michelstadt
Bruchsal
Karlsruhe
Pforzheim
Ludwigsburg
Stuttgart
Esslingen
Geislingen
Reutlingen
Metzingen
Tübingen
Hechingen
Ebingen
Freudenstadt
Baden-Baden
Rastatt
Brumath
Haguenau
Strasbourg
Kehl
Offenburg
Lahr
Haslach
Saverne
Sarrebourg
Château-Salins
Mirecourt
Vittel
Contrexéville
Neufchâteau
Chaumont
Joinville
Ligny-en-Barrois
Brienne-le-Château
Troyes
Bar-sur-Seine
Sens
St.-Florentin
Joigny
Tonnerre
Auxerre
Châtillon-sur-Seine
Montbard
Combeaufontaine
St.-Seine-l'Abbaye
Avallon
Clamecy
Saulieu
Château-Chinon
Nevers
Sézanne
Provins
Nogent-sur-Seine
Château-Thierry
Montmirail
Le Val
Massif Central
Cévennes
Jura
Vosges
Lorraine
Bourgogne
Provence
Alpes
Ardennes
Champagne
FRANCE

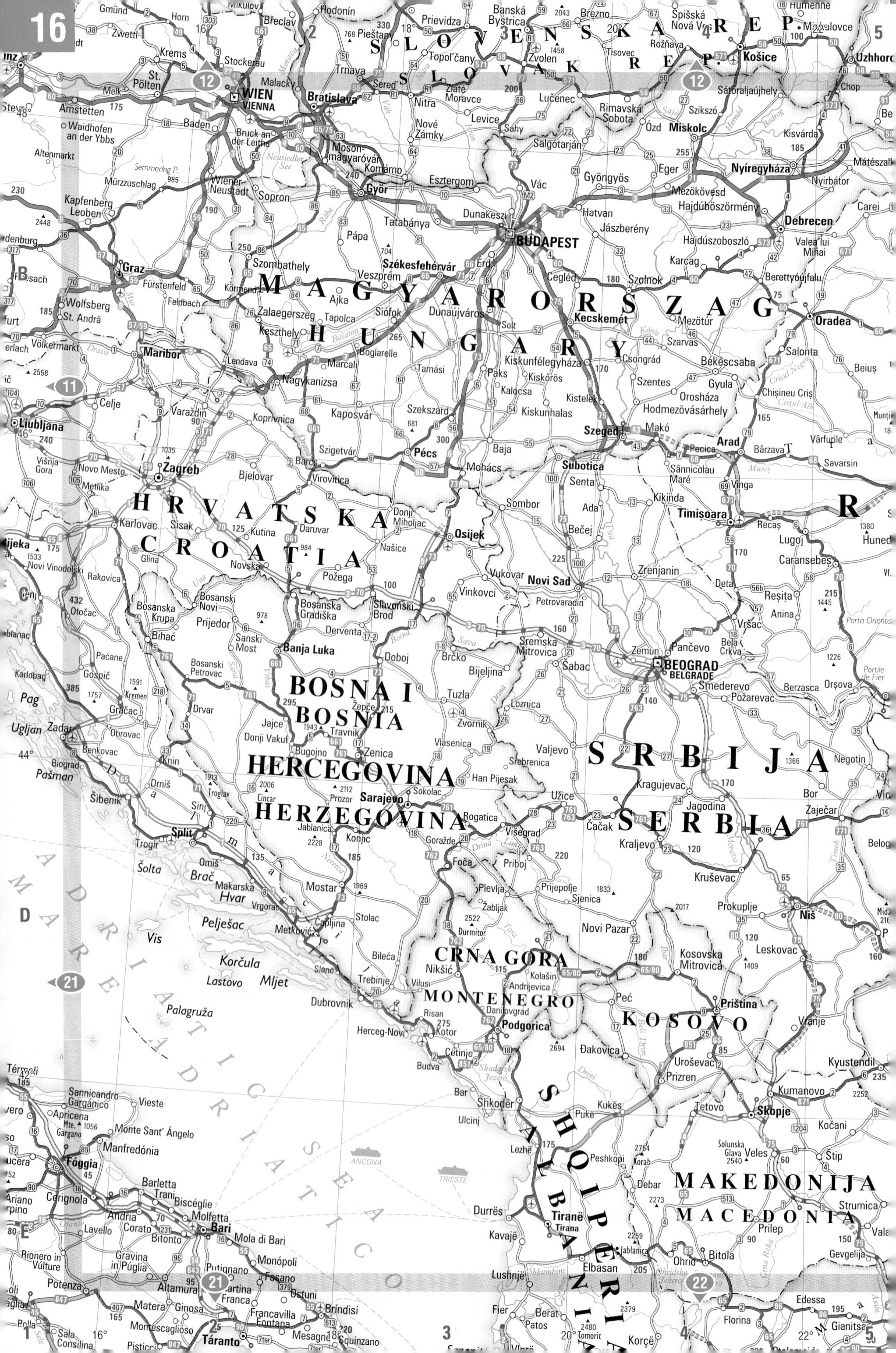

SLOVENSKÁ REP.
SLOVAK REP.
MAGYARORSZÁG
HUNGARY
HRVATSKA
CROATIA
BOSNA I HERCEGOVINA
BOSNIA HERZEGOVINA
SRBIJA
SERBIA
CRNA GORA
MONTENEGRO
KOSOVO
SHQIPËRIA
ALBANIA
MAKEDONIJA
MACEDONIA
MARE ADRIATICO
ADRIATIC SEA
Gmünd
Horn
Zwettl
Krems
Stockerau
St. Pölten
Melk
Amstetten
Steyr
Waidhofen an der Ybbs
Altenmarkt
WIEN
VIENNA
Baden
Bruck an der Leitha
Wiener Neustadt
Mürzzuschlag
Semmering P.
Kapfenberg
Leoben
Graz
Fürstenfeld
Feldbach
Wolfsberg
St. Andrä
Völkermarkt
Hodonín
Breclav
Malacky
Bratislava
Piešťany
Trnava
Sereď
Prievidza
Topoľčany
Nitra
Zlaté Moravce
Nové Zámky
Levice
Šahy
Banská Bystrica
Zvolen
Lučenec
Brezno
Rimavská Sobota
Spišská Nová Ves
Rožňava
Tisovec
Košice
Michalovce
Uzhhorod
Humenne
Moson-magyaróvár
Komárno
Neusiedler See
Győr
Sopron
Szombathely
Körmend
Esztergom
Tatabánya
Pápa
Veszprém
Ajka
Székesfehérvár
Érd
Dunakeszi
BUDAPEST
Vác
Salgótarján
Gyöngyös
Hatvan
Eger
Ózd
Miskolc
Sátoraljaújhely
Szikszó
Kisvárda
Nyíregyháza
Mátészalka
Nyírbátor
Mezőkövesd
Hajdúböszörmény
Debrecen
Hajdúszoboszló
Jászberény
Karcag
Berettyóújfalu
Valea lui Mihai
Carei
Cegléd
Szolnok
Kecskemét
Mezőtúr
Oradea
Szarvas
Békéscsaba
Salonta
Beiuş
Gyula
Orosháza
Chişineu Criş
Szentes
Csongrád
Kiskunfélegyháza
Kiskőrös
Kalocsa
Paks
Dunaújváros
Solt
Siófok
Tapolca
Zalaegerszeg
Keszthely
Balaton
Boglarelle
Marcali
Tamási
Nagykanizsa
Lendava
Kaposvár
Szekszárd
Kiskunhalas
Kistelek
Hódmezővásárhely
Szeged
Makó
Pecica
Arad
Bârzava
Vârfurile
Savarsin
Mureş
Sânnicolau Mare
Vinga
Timişoara
Recaş
Lugoj
Hunedoara
Caransebeş
Reşiţa
Anina
Deta
Vršac
Bela Crkva
Berzasca
Orşova
Portile de Fier
Baja
Mohács
Pécs
Szigetvár
Barcs
Maribor
Ptuj
Celje
Ljubljana
Varaždin
Koprivnica
Zagreb
Novo Mesto
Višnja Gora
Metlika
Karlovac
Sisak
Kutina
Bjelovar
Virovitica
Daruvar
Donji Miholjac
Osijek
Našice
Požega
Novska
Slavonski Brod
Vinkovci
Vukovar
Novi Sad
Petrovaradin
Subotica
Senta
Ada
Sombor
Bečej
Kikinda
Zrenjanin
Sremska Mitrovica
Zemun
Pančevo
BEOGRAD
BELGRADE
Smederevo
Požarevac
Šabac
Loznica
Valjevo
Kragujevac
Jagodina
Bor
Zaječar
Negotin
Čačak
Kraljevo
Kruševac
Užice
Prokuplje
Niš
Leskovac
Pirot
Vranje
Novi Pazar
Sjenica
Prijepolje
Priboj
Višegrad
Rijeka
Novi Vinodolski
Senj
Otočac
Rakovica
Glina
Bosanski Novi
Bosanska Krupa
Prijedor
Bihać
Bosanska Gradiška
Derventa
Sanski Most
Banja Luka
Doboj
Brčko
Bijeljina
Tuzla
Zvornik
Vlasenica
Srebrenica
Han Pijesak
Bosanski Petrovac
Drvar
Jajce
Donji Vakuf
Travnik
Zenica
Žepče
Bugojno
Prozor
Sarajevo
Sokolac
Rogatica
Goražde
Foča
Jablanica
Konjic
Mostar
Stolac
Čapljina
Metković
Bileća
Trebinje
Pag
Ugljan
Zadar
Biograd
Pašman
Benkovac
Obrovac
Gračac
Gospić
Karlobag
Knin
Drniš
Šibenik
Sinj
Trogir
Split
Omiš
Šolta
Brač
Makarska
Hvar
Vrgorac
Pelješac
Vis
Korčula
Lastovo
Mljet
Palagruža
Slano
Dubrovnik
Herceg-Novi
Risan
Kotor
Budva
Cetinje
Podgorica
Danilovgrad
Nikšić
Vilusi
Žabljak
Durmitor
Pljevlja
Kolašin
Andrijevica
Peć
Đakovica
Prizren
Uroševac
Priština
Kosovska Mitrovica
Kumanovo
Kyustendil
Skopje
Tetovo
Kočani
Štip
Veles
Solunska Glava
Prilep
Strumica
Gevgelija
Bitola
Ohrid
Struga
Debar
Peshkopi
Kukës
Pukë
Shkodër
Bar
Ulcinj
Lezhë
Durrës
Tiranë
Tirana
Kavajë
Elbasan
Librazhd
Lushnjë
Fier
Berat
Patos
Korçë
Tomorit
Florina
Edessa
Gianitsa
Axios
Termoli
Sannicandro Garganico
Vieste
Apricena
Mte. Gargano
Monte Sant' Angelo
Manfredónia
Fóggia
Lucera
Ariano Irpino
Cerignola
Barletta
Trani
Bisceglie
Molfetta
Andria
Corato
Bitonto
Bari
Mola di Bari
Monópoli
Lavello
Gravina in Púglia
Altamura
Rionero in Vúlture
Potenza
Matera
Ginosa
Putignano
Fasano
Ostuni
Martina Franca
Brindisi
Francavilla Fontana
Mesagne
Squinzano
Táranto
Montescaglioso
Sala Consilina
Pisticci
Polla
Ofanto
ANCONA
TRIESTE
Sava
Drava
Dunav
Tisa
Drina
Mur
Raba
Neretva
Morava
Bosna
Vrbas
Una
Kupa
Ibar
Timok
Crni Drim
Skadarsko Jezero
Ohridsko Jezero
Prespansko Jezero
Szamos
Körös
Hernád
Sajó
Bodrog
Váh
Nitra
Hron
Enns
Crişul Negru
Crişul Alb

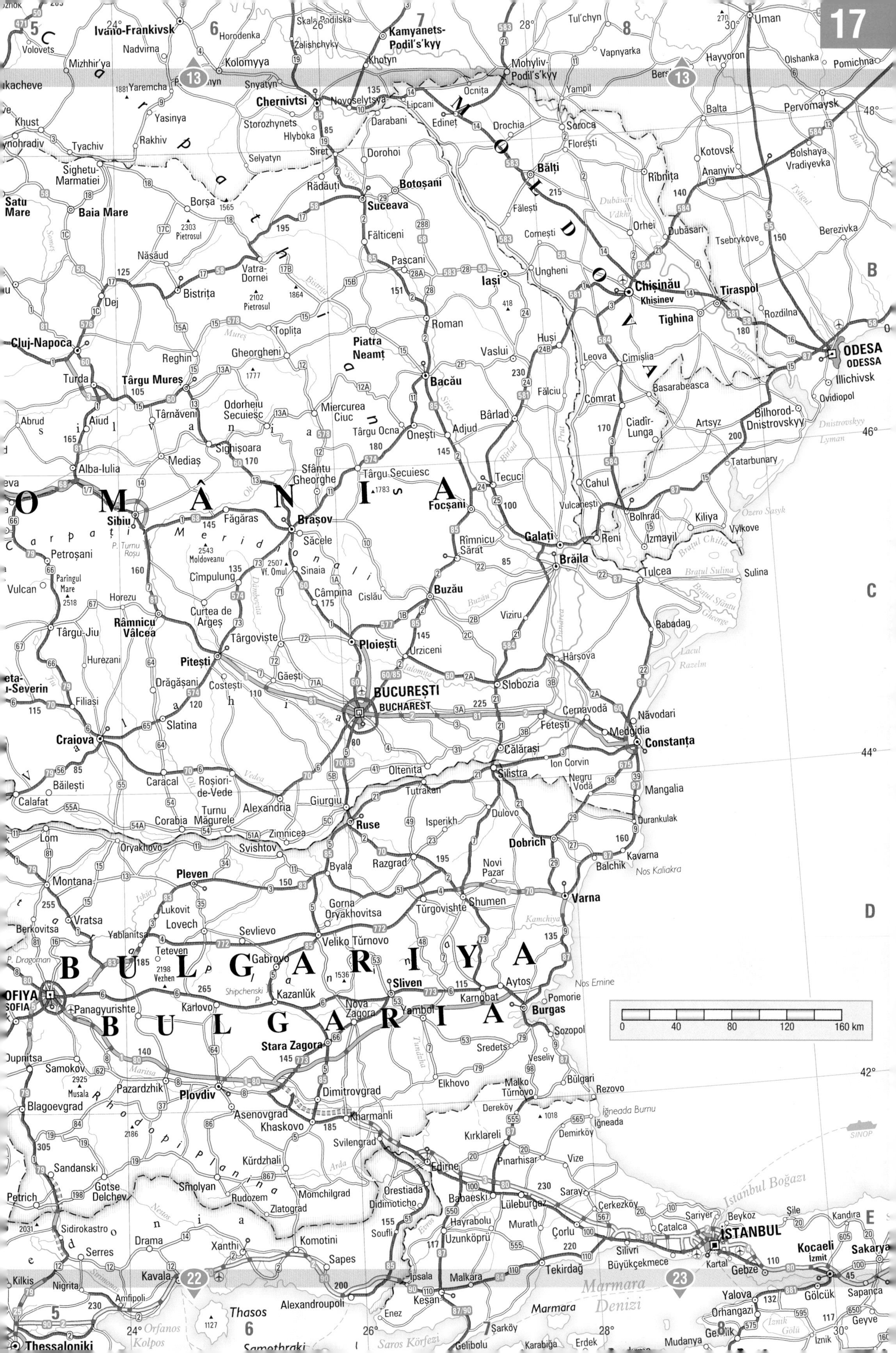
Ivano-Frankivsk
Kamyanets-Podil's'kyy
Uman
Volovets
Nadvirna
Horodenka
Skala-Podilska
Zalishchyky
Tul'chyn
Vapnyarka
Hayvoron
Olshanka
Pomichna
Mizhhir'ya
Kolomyya
Khotyn
Mohyliv-Podil's'kyy
Yaremcha
Snyatyn
Ocnița
Yampil
Balta
Pervomaysk
Chernivtsi
Novoselytsya
Lipcani
Khust
Storozhynets
Darabani
Edineț
Drochia
Soroca
Yasinya
Hlyboka
Florești
Kotovsk
Rakhiv
Tyachiv
Siret
Dorohoi
Selyatyn
Bălți
Ribnița
Ananyiv
Bolshaya Vradiyevka
Sighetu-Marmatiei
Satu Mare
Baia Mare
Borșa
Rădăuți
Botoșani
Suceava
Pietrosul
Fălești
Dubăsari
Orhei
Tsebrykove
Berezivka
Năsăud
Fălticeni
Cornești
Pașcani
Ungheni
Chișinău
Khisinev
Tiraspol
Dej
Bistrița
Vatra-Dornei
Iași
Tighina
Rozdilna
Cluj-Napoca
Toplița
Piatra Neamț
Roman
Hușí
Odesa
ODESSA
Reghin
Gheorgheni
Vaslui
Leova
Cimișlia
Illichivsk
Turda
Târgu Mureș
Bacău
Fălciu
Comrat
Basarabeasca
Ovidiopol
Odorheiu Secuiesc
Miercurea Ciuc
Bârlad
Ciadîr-Lunga
Artsyz
Bilhorod-Dnistrovskyy
Abrud
Aiud
Târnăveni
Târgu Ocna
Onești
Adjud
Sighișoara
Mediaș
Alba-Iulia
Sfântu Gheorghe
Târgu Secuiesc
Tecuci
Tatarbunary
Cahul
R O M Â N I A
Sibiu
Făgăraș
Brașov
Focșani
Vulcănești
Bolhrad
Kiliya
Vylkove
Săcele
Rîmnicu Sărat
Galați
Reni
Izmayil
Petroșani
Moldoveanu
Vf. Omul
Sinaia
Brăila
Tulcea
Sulina
Vulcan
Parângul Mare
Cîmpulung
Câmpina
Cislău
Buzău
Horezu
Curtea de Argeș
Viziru
Babadag
Râmnicu Vâlcea
Târgu-Jiu
Târgoviște
Ploiești
Urziceni
Hurezani
Pitești
Găești
Hârșova
Drăgășani
Costești
Slobozia
Filiași
BUCUREȘTI
BUCHAREST
Năvodari
Cernavodă
Fetești
Medgidia
Constanța
Craiova
Slatina
Călărași
Ion Corvin
Oltenița
Silistra
Negru Vodă
Băilești
Caracal
Roșiori-de-Vede
Mangalia
Calafat
Turnu Măgurele
Alexandria
Giurgiu
Tutrakan
Corabia
Zimnicea
Ruse
Isperikh
Dulovo
Durankulak
Lom
Oryakhovo
Svishtov
Dobrich
Kavarna
Razgrad
Byala
Novi Pazar
Balchik
Nos Kaliakra
Montana
Pleven
Varna
Shumen
Gorna Oryakhovitsa
Tŭrgovishte
Vratsa
Lovech
Lukovit
Berkovitsa
Yablanitsa
Sevlievo
Veliko Tŭrnovo
Teteven
Gabrovo
B U L G A R I Y A
Vezhen
Sliven
Aytos
Nos Emine
Pomorie
Kazanlŭk
Karnobat
Burgas
SOFIYA
SOFIA
Panagyurishte
Karlovo
Nova Zagora
Yambol
B U L G A R I A
Sozopol
Stara Zagora
Sredets
Dupnitsa
Samokov
Veseliy
Musala
Pazardzhik
Plovdiv
Elkhovo
Malko Tŭrnovo
Bŭlgari
Rezovo
Blagoevgrad
Dimitrovgrad
Asenovgrad
Kharmanli
Khaskovo
Dereköy
İğneada Burnu
İğneada
Demirköy
Svilengrad
Kırklareli
Sandanski
Kŭrdzhali
Edirne
Pınarhisar
Vize
Petrich
Gotse Delchev
Smolyan
Rudozem
Momchilgrad
Zlatograd
Orestiada
Didimoticho
Babaeski
Lüleburgaz
Saray
Çerkezköy
İstanbul Boğazı
Sariyer
Beykoz
Şile
Kandıra
Sidirokastro
Hayrabolu
Muratlı
Çatalca
İSTANBUL
Kocaeli
İzmit
Sakarya
Drama
Serres
Xanthi
Komotini
Soufli
Uzunköprü
Çorlu
Silivri
Büyükçekmece
Sapes
Kartal
Gebze
Kilkis
Kavala
Nigrita
Amfipoli
İpsala
Malkara
Tekirdağ
Marmara Denizi
Yalova
Gölcük
Sapanca
Thasos
Alexandroupoli
Keşan
Enez
Marmara
Orhangazi
Geyve
Orfanos Kolpos
Şarköy
Gelibolu
Karabiğa
Erdek
Mudanya
Gemlik
İznik
Saros Körfezi
Thessaloniki
M O L D O V A
0 40 80 120 160 km
44°
42°
46°
48°
30°
28°
26°
24°
A
B
C
D
E
5
6
7
8
13
22
23

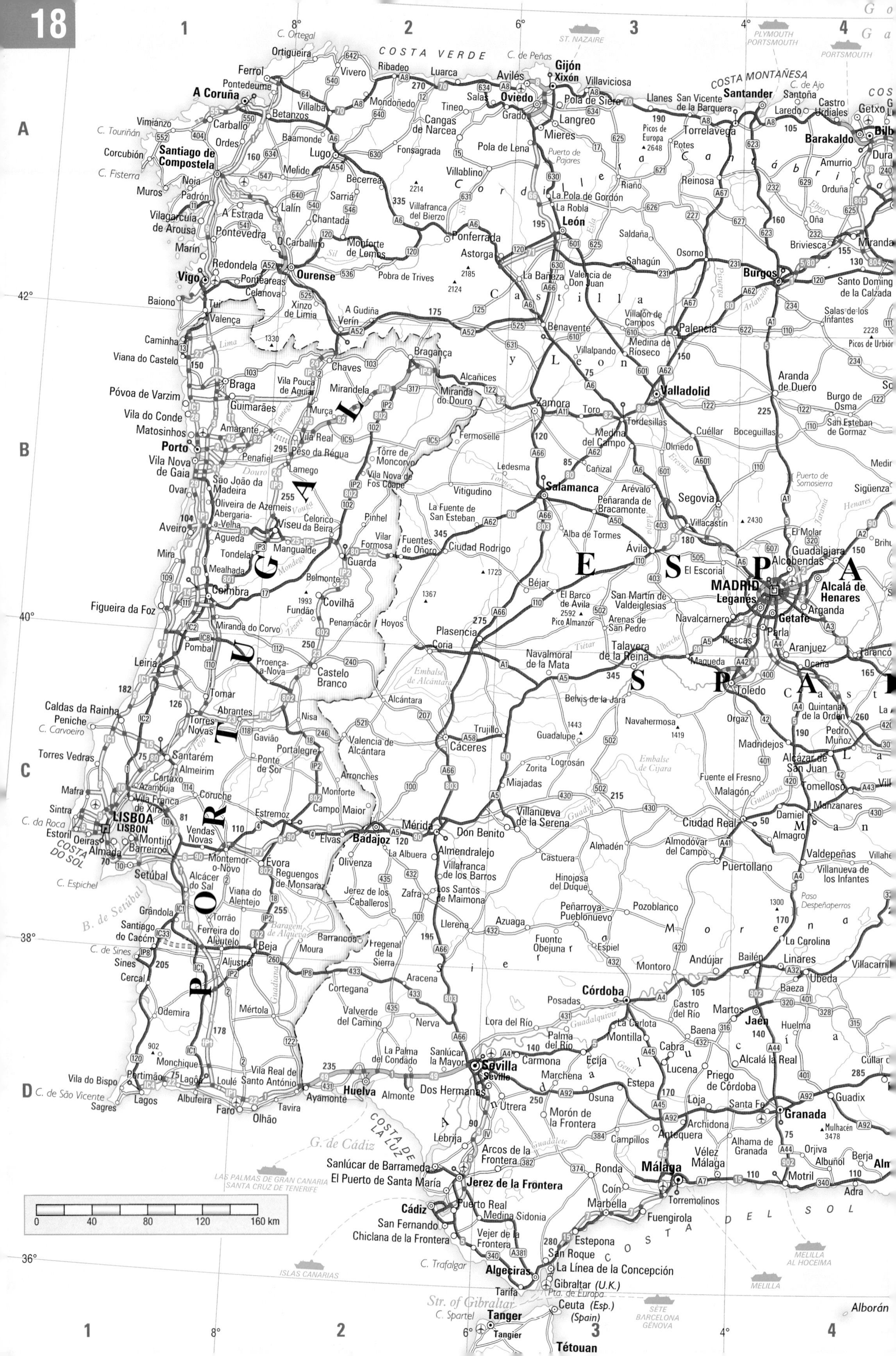
COSTA VERDE
COSTA MONTAÑESA
C. Ortegal
C. de Peñas
C. de Ajo
ST. NAZAIRE
PLYMOUTH
PORTSMOUTH
Ortigueira
Ferrol
Pontedeume
A Coruña
Vivero
Ribadeo
Luarca
Avilés
Gijón
Xixón
Villaviciosa
Oviedo
Pola de Siero
Llanes
San Vicente de la Barquera
Santander
Santoña
Laredo
Castro Urdiales
Getxo
Barakaldo
Carballo
Betanzos
Villalba
Mondoñedo
Tineo
Salas
Grado
Langreo
Mieres
Torrelavega
Reinosa
Vimianzo
C. Touriñán
Corcubión
Santiago de Compostela
C. Fisterra
Muros
Noia
Ordes
Baamonde
Lugo
Fonsagrada
Cangas de Narcea
Pola de Lena
Puerto de Pajares
Picos de Europa
Potes
Amurrio
Orduña
Oña
Padrón
Melide
Becerreá
Villablino
Cordillera Cantábrica
La Pola de Gordón
La Robla
Riaño
Vilagarcía de Arousa
A Estrada
Pontevedra
Lalín
Chantada
Sarria
Villafranca del Bierzo
Ponferrada
León
Saldaña
Osorno
Briviesca
Miranda
Marín
O Carballiño
Monforte de Lemos
Astorga
La Bañeza
Sahagún
Burgos
Santo Domingo de la Calzada
Redondela
Vigo
Ponteareas
Ourense
Pobra de Trives
Valencia de Don Juan
Baiona
Celanova
Xinzo de Limia
A Gudiña
Verín
Benavente
Villalón de Campos
Palencia
Salas de los Infantes
Picos de Urbión
Tui
Valença
Caminha
Viana do Castelo
Chaves
Bragança
Villalpando
Medina de Rioseco
Castilla y León
Póvoa de Varzim
Braga
Vila Pouca de Aguiar
Mirandela
Alcañices
Miranda do Douro
Valladolid
Aranda de Duero
Burgo de Osma
Vila do Conde
Guimarães
Matosinhos
Porto
Amarante
Murça
Vila Real
Peso da Régua
Zamora
Toro
Tordesillas
Medina del Campo
Cuéllar
Boceguillas
San Esteban de Gormaz
Vila Nova de Gaia
Penafiel
Lamego
Torre de Moncorvo
Fermoselle
Olmedo
Ovar
São João da Madeira
Vila Nova de Foz Côa
Ledesma
Cañizal
Puerto de Somosierra
Sigüenza
Oliveira de Azeméis
Vitigudino
Salamanca
Arévalo
Peñaranda de Bracamonte
Segovia
Aveiro
Albergaria-a-Velha
Viseu
Celorico da Beira
Pinhel
La Fuente de San Esteban
Villacastín
Águeda
Mangualde
Vilar Formosa
Fuentes de Oñoro
Ciudad Rodrigo
Alba de Tormes
Ávila
El Molar
Guadalajara
Alcobendas
Mira
Tondela
Guarda
El Escorial
MADRID
Leganés
Alcalá de Henares
Mealhada
Belmonte
Béjar
El Barco de Avila
San Martín de Valdeiglesias
Getafe
Arganda
Coimbra
Covilhã
Fundão
Pico Almanzor
Arenas de San Pedro
Navalcarnero
Figueira da Foz
Penamacôr
Hoyos
Plasencia
Parla
Miranda do Corvo
Pombal
Coria
Navalmoral de la Mata
Talavera de la Reina
Illescas
Aranjuez
Leiria
Proença-a-Nova
Castelo Branco
Embalse de Alcántara
Maqueda
Ocaña
Toledo
Tomar
Alcántara
Belvis de la Jara
Quintanar de la Orden
Caldas da Rainha
Peniche
C. Carvoeiro
Abrantes
Torres Novas
Nisa
Trujillo
Guadalupe
Navahermosa
Orgaz
Pedro Muñoz
Gavião
Valencia de Alcántara
Cáceres
Madridejos
Torres Vedras
Santarém
Portalegre
Ponte de Sor
Zorita
Logrosán
Embalse de Cijara
Alcázar de San Juan
Almeirim
Arronches
Miajadas
Fuente el Fresno
Malagón
Tomelloso
Mafra
Cartaxo
Azambuja
Coruche
Monforte
Villanueva de la Serena
Manzanares
Sintra
Vila Franca de Xira
C. da Roca
LISBOA
LISBON
Estremoz
Campo Maior
Mérida
Don Benito
Ciudad Real
Daimiel
Almagro
Estoril
Oeiras
Almada
Montijo
Barreiro
Vendas Novas
Elvas
Badajoz
Almendralejo
Almadén
Almodóvar del Campo
Valdepeñas
COSTA DO SOL
Montemor-o-Novo
Évora
Olivenza
La Albuera
Villafranca de los Barros
Castuera
Puertollano
Setúbal
Alcácer do Sal
Reguengos de Monsaraz
Jerez de los Caballeros
Zafra
Los Santos de Maimona
Hinojosa del Duque
Villanueva de los Infantes
C. Espichel
Viana do Alentejo
Paso Despeñaperros
Grândola
B. de Setúbal
Torrão
Peñarroya-Pueblonuevo
Pozoblanco
Sierra Morena
Santiago do Cacém
Ferreira do Alentejo
Barragem de Alqueva
Barrancos
Llerena
Azuaga
Fuente Obejuna
La Carolina
C. de Sines
Sines
Beja
Moura
Fregenal de la Sierra
Espiel
Bailén
Linares
Cercal
Aljustrel
Aracena
Montoro
Andújar
Villacarrillo
Úbeda
Cortegana
Córdoba
Baeza
Odemira
Mértola
Valverde del Camino
Nerva
Posadas
Castro del Río
Martos
Lora del Río
La Carlota
Jaén
Huelma
Palma del Río
Montilla
Baena
Monchique
La Palma del Condado
Sanlúcar la Mayor
Sevilla
Carmona
Écija
Cabra
Alcalá la Real
Cúllar
Vila do Bispo
Portimão
Lagoa
Loulé
Vila Real de Santo António
Huelva
Almonte
Dos Hermanas
Marchena
Lucena
Priego de Córdoba
C. de São Vicente
Sagres
Lagos
Albufeira
Faro
Olhão
Tavira
Ayamonte
Utrera
Osuna
Estepa
Loja
Santa Fe
Granada
Guadix
COSTA DE LA LUZ
Morón de la Frontera
Archidona
Antequera
Alhama de Granada
Mulhacén
G. de Cádiz
Lebrija
Arcos de la Frontera
Campillos
Vélez Málaga
Orjiva
Albuñol
Berja
Sanlúcar de Barrameda
El Puerto de Santa María
Jerez de la Frontera
Ronda
Málaga
Motril
Adra
LAS PALMAS DE GRAN CANARIA
SANTA CRUZ DE TENERIFE
Coín
Torremolinos
Cádiz
Puerto Real
Medina Sidonia
Marbella
Fuengirola
San Fernando
Chiclana de la Frontera
Vejer de la Frontera
COSTA DEL SOL
Estepona
San Roque
La Línea de la Concepción
C. Trafalgar
Algeciras
Gibraltar (U.K.)
ISLAS CANARIAS
MELILLA
AL HOCEIMA
Tarifa
Pta. de Europa
Str. of Gibraltar
Ceuta (Esp.)
(Spain)
SÈTE
BARCELONA
GENOVA
Alborán
C. Spartel
Tanger
Tangier
Tétouan
PORTUGAL
ESPAÑA
SPAIN
CASTILLA LA MANCHA
Andalucía
0 40 80 120 160 km

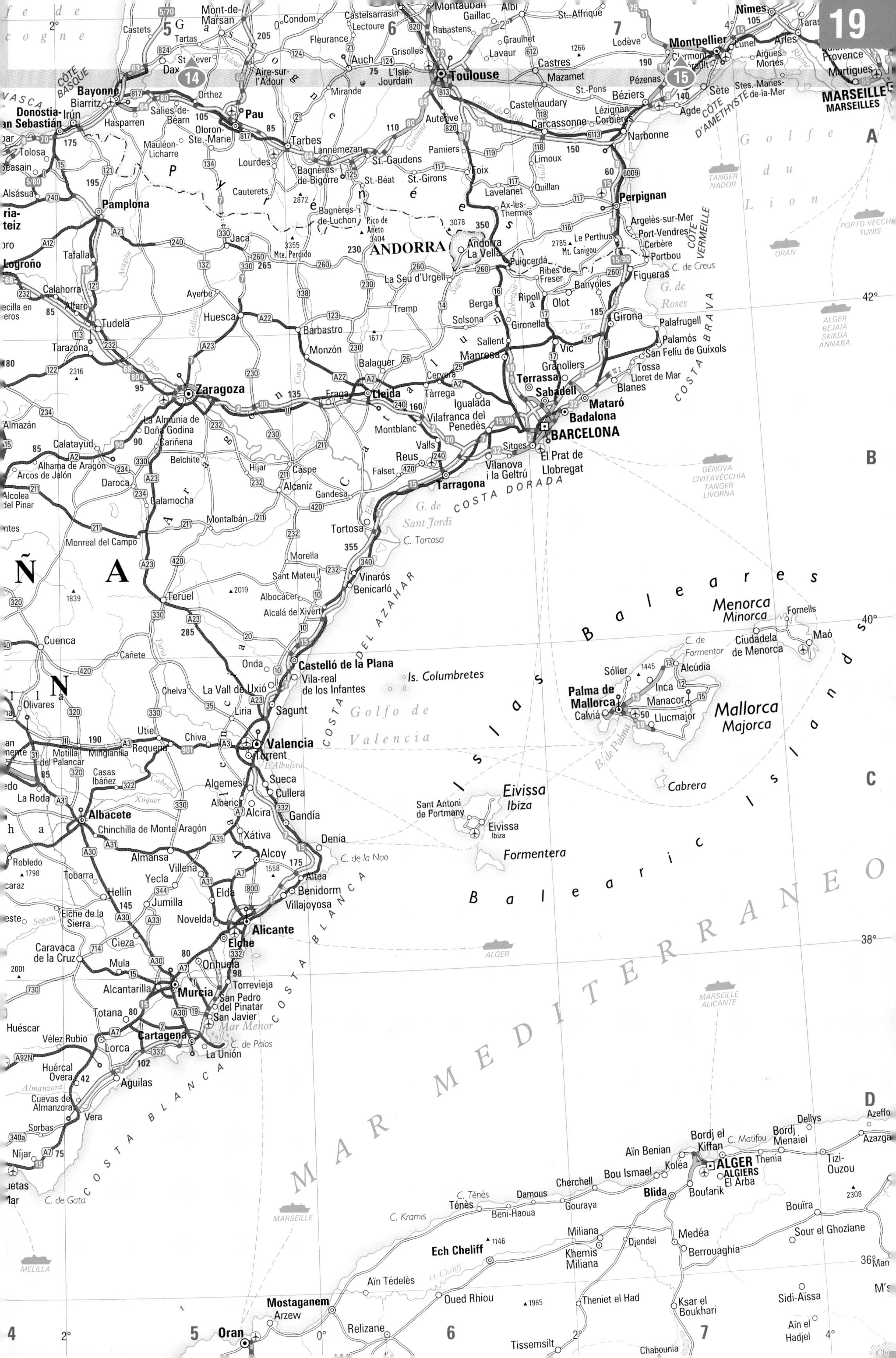

Mont-de-Marsan
Castelsarrasin
Montauban
Albi
St.-Affrique
Nîmes
Arles
Castets
Tartas
Condom
Lectoure
Fleurance
Rabastens
Gaillac
Graulhet
Lavaur
Lodève
Montpellier
Lunel
Aigues-Mortes
Provence
Martigues
Dax
Aire-sur-l'Adour
Auch
Grisolles
L'Isle-Jourdain
Toulouse
Castres
Mazamet
Pézenas
Sète
Stes.-Maries-de-la-Mer
MARSEILLE
MARSEILLES
Bayonne
Biarritz
Orthez
Pau
Mirande
St.-Pons
Béziers
Agde
Donostia-San Sebastián
Irún
Salies-de-Béarn
Hasparren
Oloron-Ste.-Marie
Tarbes
Auterive
Castelnaudary
Lézignan-Corbières
Carcassonne
Narbonne
CÔTE D'AMÉTHYSTE
Golfe du Lion
CÔTE BASQUE
Tolosa
Mauléon-Licharre
Lourdes
Lannemezan
St.-Gaudens
Pamiers
Limoux
Beasain
Bagnères-de-Bigorre
St.-Béat
St.-Girons
Foix
Quillan
Perpignan
Alsásua
Pamplona
Cauterets
Lavelanet
Ax-les-Thermes
Argelès-sur-Mer
Port-Vendres
Cerbère
Portbou
Bagnères-de-Luchon
Pico de Aneto
ANDORRA
Andorra La Vella
Le Perthus
Mt. Canigou
CÔTE VERMEILLE
Tafalla
Jaca
Mte. Perdido
Puigcerdà
Ribes de Freser
C. de Creus
Logroño
La Seu d'Urgell
Banyoles
Figueras
Calahorra
Alfaro
Ayerbe
Tremp
Berga
Ripoll
Olot
G. de Roses
Tudela
Huesca
Barbastro
Solsona
Gironella
Girona
Palafrugell
Palamós
Tarazona
Monzón
Sallent
Vic
San Felíu de Guíxols
COSTA BRAVA
Balaguer
Manresa
Granollers
Tossa
Lloret de Mar
Blanes
Zaragoza
Fraga
Lleida
Cervera
Tàrrega
Terrassa
Sabadell
Igualada
Mataró
Badalona
BARCELONA
La Almunia de Doña Godina
Cariñena
Almazán
Calatayud
Montblanc
Vilafranca del Penedès
Valls
Reus
Sitges
Vilanova i la Geltrú
El Prat de Llobregat
Alhama de Aragón
Arcos de Jalón
Belchite
Híjar
Caspe
Alcañiz
Falset
Tarragona
COSTA DORADA
Daroca
Gandesa
Calamocha
Montalbán
G. de Sant Jordi
Tortosa
C. Tortosa
Monreal del Campo
Morella
Sant Mateu
Vinaròs
Benicarló
COSTA DEL AZAHAR
Teruel
Albocàcer
Alcalá de Xivert
Islas Baleares
Menorca
Minorca
Fornells
Ciudadela de Menorca
Maó
C. de Formentor
Cuenca
Cañete
Onda
Castelló de la Plana
Vila-real de los Infantes
Is. Columbretes
Sóller
Alcúdia
Inca
Palma de Mallorca
Calvià
Manacor
Llucmajor
Mallorca
Majorca
Chelva
La Vall de Uixó
Liria
Sagunt
Golfo de Valencia
Olivares
Utiel
Requena
Chiva
Valencia
Torrent
Motilla del Palancar
Minglanilla
Casas Ibáñez
Algemesí
Sueca
Cullera
B. de Palma
Cabrera
La Roda
Alberic
Alcira
Gandía
Sant Antoni de Portmany
Eivissa
Ibiza
Albacete
Chinchilla de Monte Aragón
Xàtiva
Denia
Formentera
Almansa
Alcoy
C. de la Nao
Robledo
Tobarra
Villena
Yecla
Altea
Benidorm
Villajoyosa
Balearic Islands
Hellín
Jumilla
Elda
Novelda
Elche de la Sierra
Alicante
Elche
COSTA BLANCA
Caravaca de la Cruz
Cieza
Mula
Orihuela
Torrevieja
Alcantarilla
Murcia
San Pedro del Pinatar
San Javier
Mar Menor
Totana
Cartagena
C. de Palos
La Unión
Huéscar
Vélez Rubio
Lorca
Huércal Overa
Aguilas
Cuevas de Almanzora
Vera
Sorbas
Níjar
C. de Gata
MAR MEDITERRANEO
Dellys
Azeffoun
Bordj el Kiffan
C. Matifou
Bordj Menaiel
Azazga
Aïn Benian
Koléa
ALGER
ALGIERS
Thenia
Tizi-Ouzou
Cherchell
Bou Ismaël
El Arba
Blida
Boufarik
C. Ténès
Ténès
Damous
Gouraya
Beni-Haoua
C. Kramis
Bouïra
Miliana
Djendel
Médéa
Sour el Ghozlane
Ech Cheliff
Khemis Miliana
Berrouaghia
Aïn Tédelès
Oued Rhiou
Mostaganem
Arzew
Theniet el Had
Ksar el Boukhari
Sidi-Aïssa
Oran
Relizane
Tissemsilt
Chabounia
Aïn el Hadjel
TANGER NADOR
PORTO-VECCHIO TUNIS
ORAN
ALGER BEJAIA SKIKDA ANNABA
GENOVA CIVITAVECCHIA TANGER LIVORNA
ALGER
MARSEILLE ALICANTE
MARSEILLE
MELILLA

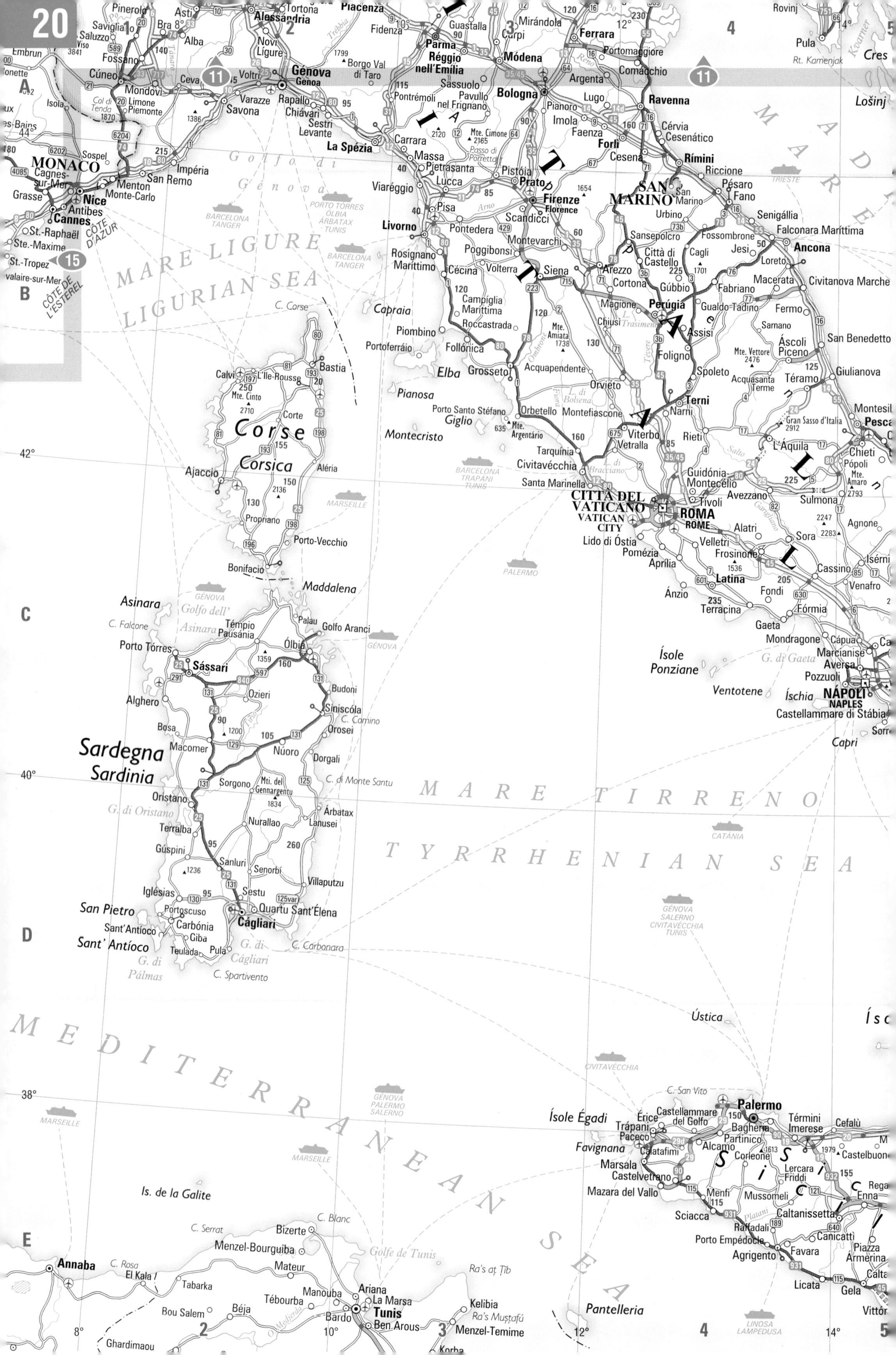
1
2
3
4
5
A
B
C
D
E
Pinerolo
Asti
Alessandria
Tortona
Piacenza
Fidenza
Guastalla
Mirándola
Ferrara
Rovinj
Saluzzo
Savigliano
Bra
Alba
Novi Ligure
Parma
Réggio nell'Emília
Módena
Portomaggiore
Pula
Cres
Fossano
Borgo Val di Taro
Embrun
Cúneo
Ceva
Voltri
Génova
Genoa
Sassuolo
Bologna
Argenta
Comacchio
Rt. Kamenjak
Mondovì
Limone Piemonte
Col di Tenda
Isola
Varazze
Savona
Rapallo
Chiávari
Sestri Levante
Pontrémoli
Pavullo nel Frignano
Lugo
Ravenna
Lošinj
Pianoro
Imola
Faenza
Forlì
Cérvia
Cesenático
Mte. Cimone
Passo di Porretta
La Spézia
Carrara
Massa
Cesena
Rímini
Riccione
Sospel
MONACO
Cagnes-sur-Mer
Impéria
San Remo
Menton
Monte-Carlo
Pietrasanta
Pistóia
Prato
Lucca
Viaréggio
Firenze
Florence
SAN MARINO
San Marino
Pésaro
Fano
Grasse
Nice
Antibes
Cannes
St.-Raphaël
Ste.-Maxime
St.-Tropez
CÔTE D'AZUR
CÔTE DE L'ESTÉREL
Golfo di Génova
Pisa
Livorno
Pontedera
Scandicci
Montevarchi
Urbino
Senigállia
Falconara Maríttima
Ancona
Sansepolcro
Fossombrone
Città di Castello
Cagli
Jesi
Loreto
Rosignano Maríttimo
Poggibonsi
Volterra
Siena
Arezzo
Cortona
Gúbbio
Macerata
Civitanova Marche
Fabriano
Cécina
Campíglia Maríttima
Roccastrada
Magione
Perúgia
Gualdo Tadino
Fermo
Chiusi
L. Trasimeno
Assisi
Sarnano
MARE LIGURE
LIGURIAN SEA
C. Corse
Capraia
Piombino
Portoferráio
Follónica
Elba
Grosseto
Mte. Amiata
Acquapendente
Foligno
Spoleto
Mte. Vettore
Áscoli Piceno
San Benedetto
Bastia
Calvi
L'Île-Rousse
Mte. Cinto
Corte
Corse
Corsica
Aléria
Ajaccio
Propriano
Porto-Vecchio
Bonifacio
Pianosa
Porto Santo Stéfano
Giglio
Montecristo
Orbetello
Mte. Argentário
Orvieto
L. di Bolsena
Montefiascone
Viterbo
Vetralla
Tarquínia
Civitavécchia
L. di Bracciano
Santa Marinella
Terni
Narni
Rieti
Acquasanta Terme
Téramo
Giulianova
Montesil
Pesca
Gran Sasso d'Italia
L'Áquila
Chieti
Pópoli
Mte. Amaro
Sulmona
Guidónia-Montecélio
Tívoli
Avezzano
CITTÀ DEL VATICANO
VATICAN CITY
ROMA
ROME
Lido di Óstia
Pomézia
Aprília
Velletri
Frosinone
Alatri
Sora
Agnone
Isérnia
Cassino
Venafro
Latina
Fondi
Ánzio
Terracina
Gaeta
Fórmia
Maddalena
Asinara
Golfo dell' Asinara
C. Falcone
Tempio Pausánia
Palau
Golfo Aranci
Porto Tórres
Sássari
Ólbia
Alghero
Ozieri
Budoni
Siniscola
C. Comino
Orosei
Bosa
Macomer
Núoro
Dorgali
Sardegna
Sardinia
Sorgono
Mti. del Gennargentu
C. di Monte Santu
Oristano
G. di Oristano
Terralba
Nurallao
Arbatax
Lanusei
Gúspini
Sanluri
Senorbì
Villaputzu
Iglésias
Sestu
Quartu Sant'Élena
Cágliari
San Pietro
Portoscuso
Carbónia
Sant'Antíoco
Giba
Teulada
Pula
G. di Cágliari
C. Carbonara
G. di Pálmas
C. Spartivento
Ísole Ponziane
Ventotene
Mondragone
Cápua
Marcianise
G. di Gaeta
Aversa
Pozzuoli
Íschia
NÁPOLI
NAPLES
Castellammare di Stábia
Capri
MARE TIRRENO
TYRRHENIAN SEA
MEDITERRANEAN SEA
Ústica
C. San Vito
Palermo
Ísole Égadi
Érice
Castellammare del Golfo
Trápani
Paceco
Bagheria
Términi Imerese
Cefalù
Partinico
Alcamo
Favignana
Calatafimi
Corleone
Castelbuono
Marsala
Castelvetrano
Lercara Friddi
Mazara del Vallo
Menfi
Mussomeli
Enna
Sciacca
Caltanissetta
Sicilia
Raffadali
Canicattì
Porto Empédocle
Agrigento
Favara
Piazza Armerina
Licata
Gela
Vittória
Is. de la Galite
C. Blanc
C. Serrat
Bizerte
Menzel-Bourguiba
Golfe de Tunis
Annaba
C. Rosa
El Kala
Mateur
Ra's at Tib
Tabarka
Manouba
Ariana
La Marsa
Kelibia
Tunis
Ben Arous
Ra's Mustafá
Menzel-Temime
Bou Salem
Béja
Bardo
Téboursa
Pantelleria
Ghardimaou
Korba
Medjerda
42°
40°
38°
8°
10°
12°
14°
MARSEILLE
GÉNOVA
PALERMO
TRIESTE
CATÁNIA
CIVITAVÉCCHIA
BARCELONA TANGER
PORTO TÓRRES ÓLBIA ÁRBATAX TUNIS
BARCELONA TRAPANI TUNIS
GÉNOVA SALERNO CIVITAVÉCCHIA TUNIS
GÉNOVA PALERMO SALERNO
LINOSA LAMPEDUSA

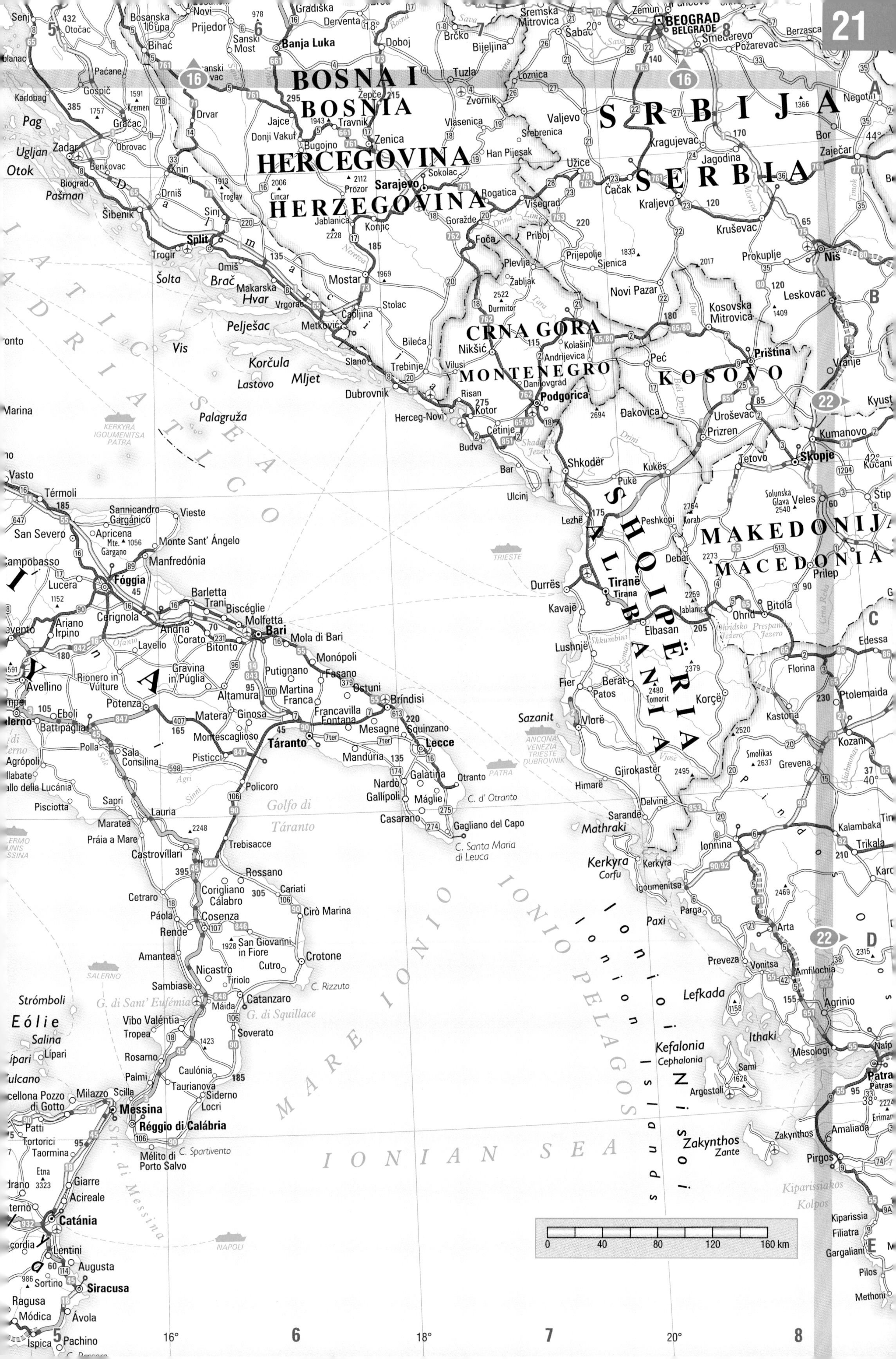

BOSNA I BOSNIA
HERCEGOVINA HERZEGOVINA
SRBIJA SERBIA
CRNA GORA MONTENEGRO
KOSOVO
SHQIPËRIA ALBANIA
MAKEDONIJA MACEDONIA
BEOGRAD BELGRADE
Sarajevo
Podgorica
Priština
Skopje
Tiranë Tirana
Banja Luka
Bari
Táranto
Lecce
Bríndisi
Fóggia
Messina
Réggio di Calábria
Catánia
Siracusa
Split
Zadar
Šibenik
Dubrovnik
Mostar
Zenica
Tuzla
Doboj
Bihać
Prijedor
Knin
Kotor
Budva
Cetinje
Nikšić
Shkodër
Durrës
Elbasan
Vlorë
Korçë
Gjirokastër
Ohrid
Bitola
Prilep
Kumanovo
Tetovo
Niš
Kraljevo
Kragujevac
Čačak
Užice
Valjevo
Novi Pazar
Peć
Prizren
Uroševac
Kosovska Mitrovica
Ioannina
Kerkyra Corfu
Igoumenitsa
Preveza
Arta
Agrinio
Patra
Pirgos
Lefkada
Kefalonia Cephalonia
Zakynthos Zante
Ithaki
Paxi
Brač
Hvar
Vis
Korčula
Lastovo
Mljet
Pelješac
Pag
Ugljan
Pašman
Šolta
Palagruža
Vasto
Térmoli
Vieste
Manfredónia
Barletta
Trani
Molfetta
Monópoli
Potenza
Matera
Cosenza
Catanzaro
Crotone
Rossano
Golfo di Táranto
MARE IONIO
IONIO PELAGOS
IONIAN SEA
Ionioi Nisoi
Ionian Islands
Strómboli
Eólie
Salina
Lípari
Vulcano
Etna 3323
Str. di Messina
C. d' Otranto
C. Santa Maria di Leuca
C. Spartivento
C. Rizzuto
G. di Sant' Eufémia
G. di Squillace
Kiparissiakos Kolpos
0 40 80 120 160 km
16°
18°
20°
6
7
8

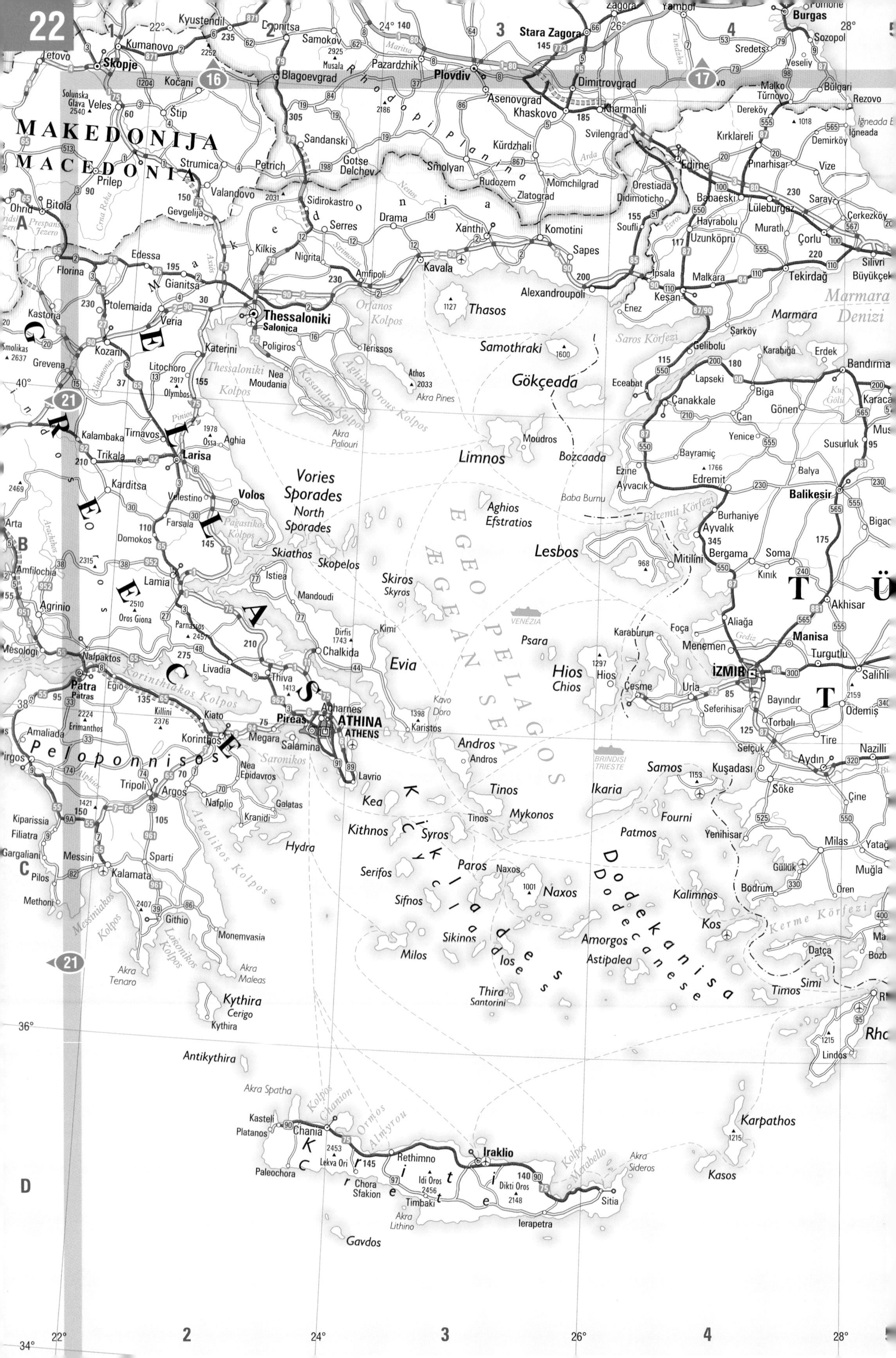
MAKEDONIJA
MACEDONIA
GREECE
ELLAS
Skopje
Kumanovo
Tetovo
Kyustendil
Kočani
Štip
Veles
Strumica
Prilep
Bitola
Ohrid
Gevgelija
Valandovo
Florina
Edessa
Kastoria
Ptolemaida
Veria
Kozani
Grevena
Gianitsa
Kilkis
Thessaloniki
Salonica
Serres
Drama
Kavala
Xanthi
Komotini
Alexandroupoli
Sapes
Nigrita
Amfipoli
Sidirokastro
Blagoevgrad
Sandanski
Petrich
Gotse Delchev
Smolyan
Plovdiv
Pazardzhik
Samokov
Stara Zagora
Asenovgrad
Khaskovo
Kŭrdzhali
Dimitrovgrad
Kharmanli
Svilengrad
Burgas
Sozopol
Sredets
Yambol
Edirne
Orestiada
Didimoticho
Soufli
Kırklareli
Pınarhisar
Babaeski
Lüleburgaz
Uzunköprü
Hayrabolu
Çorlu
Tekirdağ
Silivri
Keşan
Ipsala
Malkara
Marmara Denizi
Thasos
Samothraki
Gökçeada
Limnos
Moudros
Bozcaada
Çanakkale
Gelibolu
Lapseki
Eceabat
Biga
Çan
Bandırma
Balıkesir
Edremit
Ayvalık
Bergama
Lesbos
Mitilini
Aghios Efstratios
Vories Sporades
North Sporades
Skiathos
Skopelos
Skiros
Skyros
Evia
Chalkida
Kimi
Karistos
Katerini
Larisa
Volos
Trikala
Kalambaka
Karditsa
Farsala
Lamia
Agrinio
Mesologi
Nafpaktos
Patra
Patras
Egio
Kiato
Korinthos
Megara
Livadia
Thiva
Pireas
ATHINA
ATHENS
Salamina
Lavrio
Peloponnisos
Tripoli
Argos
Nafplio
Kalamata
Sparti
Pirgos
Kiparissia
Filiatra
Pilos
Methoni
Githio
Monemvasia
Kythira
Antikythira
AIGAIO PELAGOS
AEGEAN SEA
Andros
Tinos
Mykonos
Kea
Kithnos
Syros
Serifos
Sifnos
Paros
Naxos
Milos
Sikinos
Ios
Thira
Santorini
Amorgos
Astipalea
Kiklades
Dodekanisa
Dodecanese
Ikaria
Samos
Fourni
Patmos
Kalimnos
Kos
Simi
Rhodes
Lindos
Karpathos
Kasos
Hios
Chios
Psara
İZMIR
Manisa
Akhisar
Aliağa
Foça
Menemen
Çeşme
Urla
Seferihisar
Torbalı
Selçuk
Kuşadası
Aydın
Söke
Milas
Bodrum
Muğla
Datça
Marmaris
Kriti
Chania
Rethimno
Iraklio
Agios Nikolaos
Sitia
Ierapetra
Paleochora
Chora Sfakion
Timbaki
Gavdos
Kasteli
Platanos
Hydra
Argolikos Kolpos
Saronikos
Korinthiakos Kolpos
Thessaloniki Kolpos
Orfanos Kolpos
Saros Körfezi
Edremit Körfezi
Kerme Körfezi
Athos 2033
Olymbos 2917
Ossa 1978
Parnassos 2457
Idi Oros 2456
Dikti Oros 2148
21
16
17
D
22°
24°
26°
28°
36°
40°
34°
2
3
4

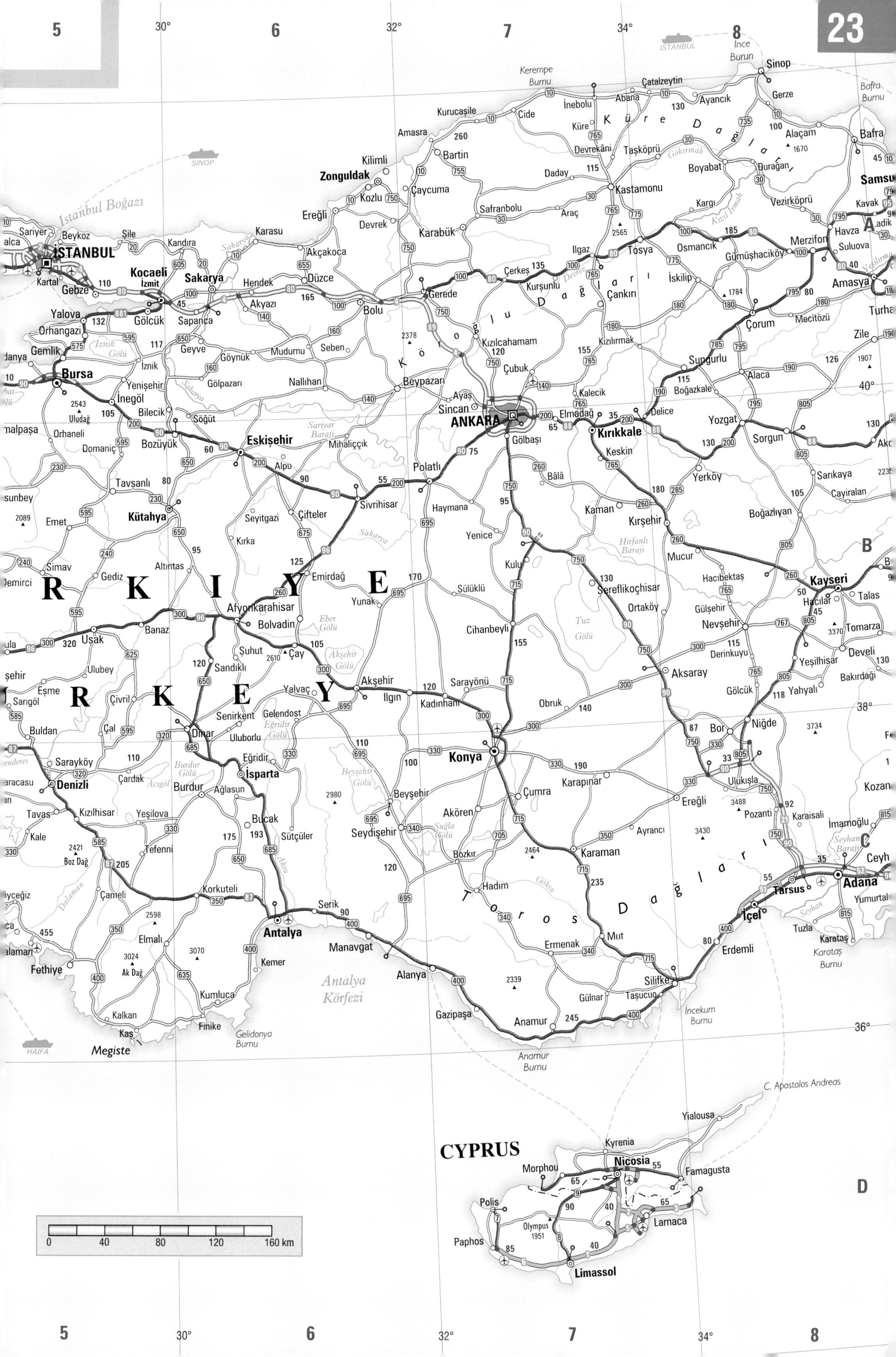

5
6
7
8
30°
32°
34°
36°
38°
40°
A
B
C
D
İSTANBUL
SINOP
HAIFA
İstanbul Boğazı
Kerempe Burnu
İnce Burun
Sinop
Bafra Burnu
Bafra
Samsun
Çatalzeytin
Abana
İnebolu
Ayancık
Gerze
Kurucaşile
Cide
Küre
Küre Dağları
Amasra
Bartın
Devrekâni
Taşköprü
Alaçam
Boyabat
Durağan
Kilimli
Zonguldak
Kozlu
Çaycuma
Daday
Kastamonu
Vezirköprü
Kavak
Ereğli
Devrek
Safranbolu
Araç
Kargı
Kızılırmak
Karabük
Ilgaz
Tosya
Osmancık
Merzifon
Havza
Suluova
Amasya
Sarıyer
Beykoz
Şile
Karasu
Akçakoca
Kandıra
Kartal
Gebze
Kocaeli
İzmit
Sakarya
Hendek
Düzce
Çerkeş
Kurşunlu
Gümüşhacıköy
İskilip
Çankırı
Yalova
Gölcük
Sapanca
Akyazı
Bolu
Gerede
Çorum
Mecitözü
Turhal
Orhangazi
İznik Gölü
Gemlik
Mudanya
Geyve
Göynük
Mudurnu
Seben
Köroğlu Dağları
Kızılcahamam
Kızılırmak
Zile
Bursa
İznik
Yenişehir
Gölpazarı
Nallıhan
Beypazarı
Çubuk
Sungurlu
Alaca
Uludağ
İnegöl
Bilecik
Söğüt
Ayaş
Sincan
ANKARA
Kalecik
Elmadağ
Boğazkale
Delice
Yozgat
Mustafakemalpaşa
Orhaneli
Domaniç
Bozüyük
Eskişehir
Sarıyar Barajı
Mihalıççık
Kırıkkale
Gölbaşı
Keskin
Sorgun
Alpu
Polatlı
Bâlâ
Yerköy
Sarıkaya
Çayıralan
Tavşanlı
Sivrihisar
Haymana
Kaman
Kırşehir
Boğazlıyan
Emet
Kütahya
Seyitgazi
Çifteler
Sakarya
Yenice
Hirfanlı Barajı
Kırka
Kulu
Mucur
Simav
Demirci
Gediz
Altıntaş
Emirdağ
Şereflikoçhisar
Hacıbektaş
Kayseri
Talas
Hacılar
TÜRKIYE
Yunak
Sülüklü
Ortaköy
Gülşehir
Nevşehir
Afyonkarahisar
Bolvadin
Eber Gölü
Tuz Gölü
Tomarza
Uşak
Banaz
Cihanbeyli
Derinkuyu
Develi
Şuhut
Çay
Akşehir Gölü
Yeşilhisar
Ulubey
Sandıklı
Aksaray
Bakırdağı
Eşme
Sarıgöl
Çivril
Yalvaç
Akşehir
Sarayönü
Ilgın
Kadınhanı
Gölcük
Yahyalı
Obruk
Senirkent
Gelendost
Eğirdir Gölü
Buldan
Çal
Dinar
Uluborlu
Bor
Niğde
Sarayköy
Eğirdir
Konya
Burdur Gölü
Isparta
Çardak
Acıgöl
Burdur
Ağlasun
Beyşehir Gölü
Karapınar
Ulukışla
Kozan
Denizli
Beyşehir
Çumra
Ereğli
Tavas
Kızılhisar
Yeşilova
Bucak
Akören
Pozantı
Karaisali
İmamoğlu
Kale
Seydişehir
Suğla Gölü
Sütçüler
Ayrancı
Seyhan Barajı
Boz Dağ
Tefenni
Bozkır
Karaman
Ceyhan
Hadım
Toros Dağları
Tarsus
Adana
Köyceğiz
Çameli
Korkuteli
Göksu
Yumurtalık
Serik
İçel
Dalaman
Elmalı
Antalya
Manavgat
Ermenak
Mut
Tuzla
Karataş
Erdemli
Karataş Burnu
Fethiye
Ak Dağ
Kemer
Alanya
Antalya Körfezi
Silifke
Taşucu
Gülnar
Kumluca
Kalkan
Kaş
Finike
Gazipaşa
Anamur
İncekum Burnu
Megiste
Gelidonya Burnu
Anamur Burnu
C. Apostolos Andreas
Yialousa
CYPRUS
Kyrenia
Morphou
Nicosia
Famagusta
Polis
Olympus
Larnaca
Paphos
Limassol
0
40
80
120
160 km

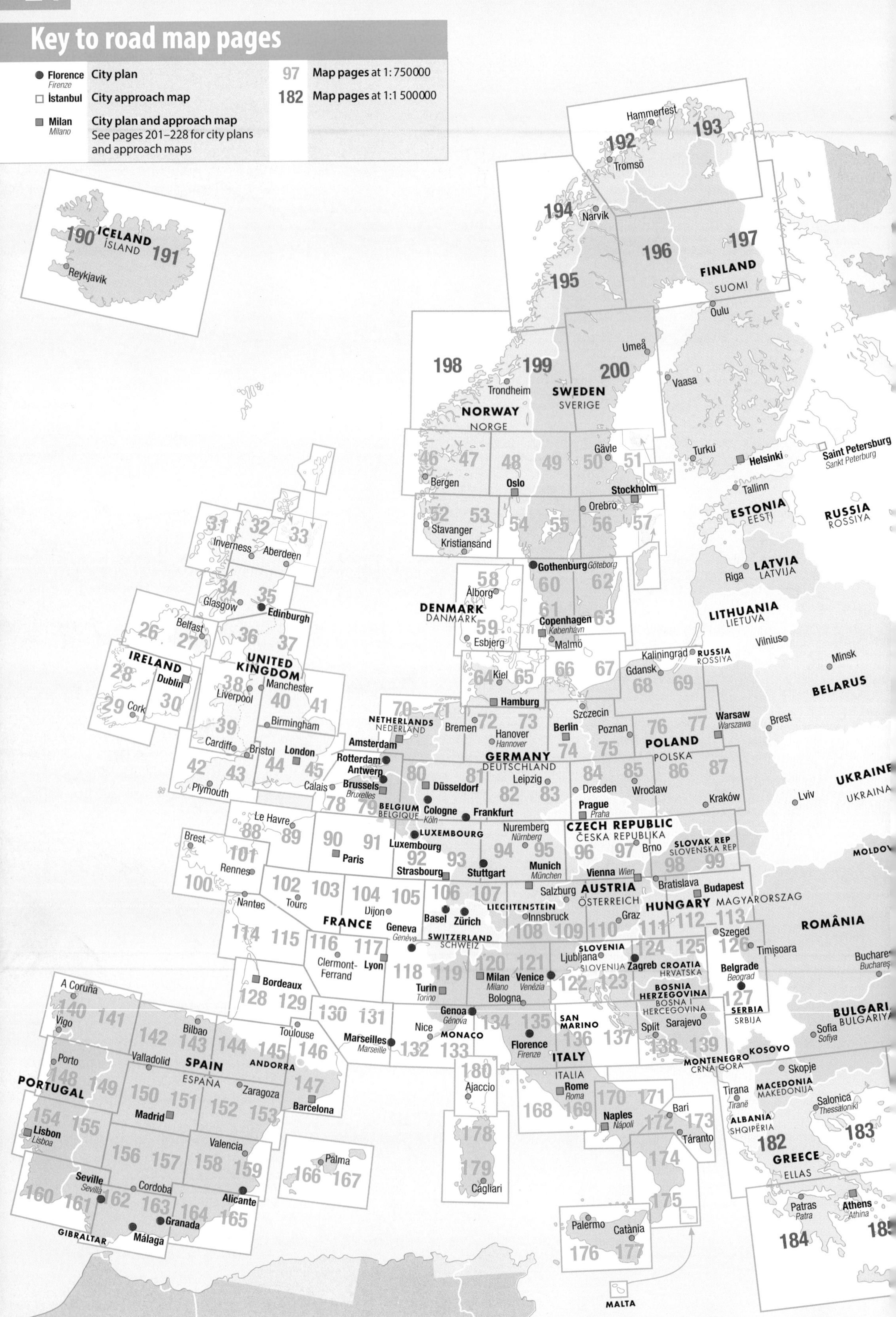

● **Florence** **City plan**
*Firenze*

□ **İstanbul** **City approach map**

▢ **Milan** **City plan and approach map**
*Milano* See pages 201–228 for city plans and approach maps

**97** **Map pages** at 1:750 000

**182** **Map pages** at 1:1 500 000

**190** **ICELAND** **191**
ÍSLAND

Reykjavik

Hammerfest
**192** **193**
Tromsö

**194** Narvik

**196** **197**
**195** **FINLAND**
SUOMI

Oulu

**198** **199** **200**
Umeå
Trondheim **SWEDEN**
SVERIGE
Vaasa
**NORWAY**
NORGE
Gävle
Turku Helsinki Saint Petersburg
Sankt Peterburg
**46** **47** **48** **49** **50** **51**
Bergen Oslo Stockholm
Tallinn
Örebro **ESTONIA** **RUSSIA**
**52** **53** **54** **55** **56** **57** EESTI ROSSIYA
Stavanger
Kristiansand
Gothenburg Göteborg
**31** **32** **33** **58** Riga **LATVIA**
Inverness Aberdeen **60** **62** LATVIJA
Ålborg
**34** **35** **DENMARK** **61** **LITHUANIA**
Glasgow DANMARK Copenhagen **63** LIETUVA
Belfast Edinburgh **59** København Vilnius
**26** **36** **37** Esbjerg Malmö Minsk
**27** Kaliningrad **RUSSIA** **BELARUS**
**IRELAND** **64** **65** **66** **67** Gdansk ROSSIYA
**28** Dublin **UNITED** Kiel **68** **69** Warsaw
**KINGDOM** Hamburg **POLAND** Warszawa Brest
**29** **30** **38** Manchester **70** **71** **72** **73** **POLSKA**
Cork Liverpool Bremen **74** **75** **76** **77** **UKRAINE**
**39** Birmingham **NETHERLANDS** Hanover Berlin Poznan UKRAINA
Cardiff NEDERLAND Hannover Kraków
**42** **43** **44** **45** Amsterdam **80** **GERMANY** **84** **85** **86** **87** Lviv
Bristol London Rotterdam DEUTSCHLAND Leipzig Wroclaw **MOLDOV**
Plymouth Antwerp **81** **82** **83** Dresden
**78** Brussels Düsseldorf **CZECH REPUBLIC**
Calais Bruxelles **79** Cologne Frankfurt **96** **97** Brno
**88** **89** **BELGIUM** Köln Nuremberg ČESKA
Le Havre BELGIQUE **93** Nürnberg **94** **95** REPUBLIKA **98** **99** **SLOVAK REP**
Brest **90** **91** LUXEMBOURG **96** Prague SLOVENSKA REP
**101** Luxembourg Stuttgart Munich **96** **97** Praha
Rennes **92** München Vienna Wien **ROMÂNIA**
**100** **102** **103** **104** **105** Strasbourg **106** **107** Salzburg **AUSTRIA** Bratislava Budapest
Nantes Dijon Basel Zürich ÖSTERREICH **HUNGARY** MAGYARORSZAG
**FRANCE** Geneva LIECHTENSTEIN Innsbruck Graz **111** **112** **113** Szeged
**114** **115** **116** **117** Genève **108** **109** **110** **124** **125** **126**
Clermont- SWITZERLAND **SLOVENIA** **CROATIA** Timişoara
Ferrand Lyon SCHWEIZ Ljubljana **HRVATSKA** Belgrade
**118** **119** **120** **121** SLOVENIJA Zagreb Beograd Buchare
A Coruña Bordeaux Milan Venice **122** **123** **BOSNIA** Bucharş
**140** **128** **129** Turin Milano Venézia **HERZEGOVINA** **SERBIA**
Vigo **141** **130** **131** Torino Bologna BOSNA I SRBIJA **BULGARI**
Porto Bilbao Genoa **134** **135** **SAN** HERCEGOVINA **127** Sofia BULGARIYA
**142** **143** Toulouse Nice Génova **MARINO** Split Sarajevo Sofiya
**148** **144** **145** **146** Marseilles **136** **137** **MONTENEGRO** **KOSOVO**
**PORTUGAL** **149** Valladolid **ANDORRA** Marseille MONACO Florence **138** **139** CRNA GORA Skopje
Lisbon **150** **151** **SPAIN** **147** **132** **133** Firenze **MACEDONIA**
Lisboa **155** Madrid ESPAÑA Zaragoza **ITALY** Tirana MAKEDONIJA
**154** Barcelona **180** ITALIA Tiranë **183**
Valencia Ajaccio **168** **169** **170** **171** **ALBANIA**
**156** **157** **158** **159** Rome Bari SHQIPËRIA
Seville **166** **167** Palma Roma **172** **173**
Sevilla Naples **GREECE** Salonica
**160** **162** Cordoba Alicante **178** Nápoli Táranto **182** ELLAS Thessaloníki
**161** **163** **164** **165** **179** **174** **GREECE**
GIBRALTAR Granada Cágliari ELLAS
Málaga **175** Patras Athens
Palermo **184** Patra Athína **185**
Catánia
**176** **177**

**MALTA**

# Distance table

**Amsterdam**

| City | Distances (km) |
|---|---|
| **Athina** | 2945 |
| **Barcelona** | 1505 3192 |
| **Bergen** | 1484 3742 2803 |
| **Berlin** | 650 2412 1863 1309 |
| **Bruxelles** | 197 2895 1308 1586 764 |
| **Bucuresti** | 2245 1219 2644 3037 1707 2181 |
| **Budapest** | 1420 1530 1999 2212 882 1358 852 |
| **Calais** | 367 3100 1269 1783 956 215 2398 1573 |
| **Dublin** | 533 3630 1817 270 1504 763 3021 2196 548 |
| **Edinburgh** | 1093 3826 1995 176 1696 941 3124 2299 726 346 |
| **Frankfurt** | 441 2499 1313 1508 550 383 1804 979 575 1123 1301 |
| **Göteborg** | 1029 3080 2362 819 668 1145 1734 1550 1342 477 176 1067 |
| **Hamburg** | 447 2719 1780 1023 286 563 2014 1189 760 477 1486 485 582 |
| **Helsinki** | 1560 2539 2338 1063 475 1239 1834 1009 1431 1318 1236 1598 505 1113 |
| **İstanbul** | 2756 1145 2990 3653 2223 2706 690 1341 2911 3537 3657 2314 2891 2530 2350 |
| **København** | 965 2782 2090 1103 370 1081 2077 1252 1278 752 479 795 284 518 803 2593 |
| **Köln** | 256 2684 1376 1427 566 198 1983 1158 390 938 1116 180 986 404 1517 2499 714 |
| **Lisboa** | 2331 4460 1268 3723 2869 3141 3917 3222 2069 2617 2795 2400 3282 2700 3817 4342 3014 2339 |
| **London** | 480 3200 1387 458 1074 333 2591 1766 118 430 608 693 122 878 1991 3107 1188 508 2187 |
| **Luxembourg** | 406 2661 1190 1613 749 209 2052 1227 424 972 1150 240 1172 590 1703 2472 900 186 2160 542 |
| **Madrid** | 1790 3809 617 3183 2364 1600 3262 2622 1528 1634 2254 1930 2742 2160 3276 3589 2473 1798 651 1646 1628 |
| **Marseille** | 1210 2683 509 2435 1541 1030 2154 1505 1063 1588 1789 1023 1994 1412 2525 2479 1722 1006 1777 1182 822 1126 |
| **Milano** | 1085 2182 1038 2141 1060 890 1668 992 1072 1620 1798 683 1700 1118 1535 1993 1428 868 2315 1190 679 1655 538 |
| **Moskva** | 2457 2930 3655 2223 1821 2585 1761 2099 2800 3348 3526 2312 1665 2115 1160 2605 2325 2387 4875 2918 2852 4224 3270 3027 |
| **München** | 839 2106 1340 1788 594 789 1497 672 994 1524 1720 398 1347 765 1069 1907 969 580 2545 1094 555 2010 1011 473 2305 |
| **Oslo** | 1347 3372 2680 503 960 1463 2667 1842 1660 773 729 1385 316 900 697 3089 590 1304 3604 1778 1490 3063 2312 2018 1823 1559 |
| **Paris** | 510 2917 988 1922 1051 320 2307 1482 281 829 1007 591 1481 899 2012 2727 1209 495 1821 399 351 1280 782 857 2903 810 1799 |
| **Praha** | 950 2067 1750 1675 345 888 1362 537 1097 1635 1816 512 1013 652 770 1878 715 690 2870 1205 753 2329 1399 853 1853 388 1305 1061 |
| **Roma** | 1691 1140 1385 2706 1502 1520 1904 1263 1678 2226 2404 1289 2265 1683 1977 2237 1993 1474 2653 1796 1285 2002 876 606 3362 918 2583 1389 1309 |
| **Sevilla** | 2347 4223 1031 3736 2894 2150 3709 3010 2078 2626 2804 2344 3295 2713 3826 4034 3023 2318 401 2196 2178 550 1540 2078 4774 2371 3613 1830 2781 2446 |
| **Sofiya** | 2206 828 2453 3103 1673 2156 391 790 2361 2891 3087 1764 2341 1980 1800 550 2043 1949 3706 2461 1922 3037 1929 1443 2252 1367 2632 2177 1328 1687 3484 |
| **Stockholm** | 1393 3418 2726 1063 1006 1509 2713 1888 1673 2254 1069 1431 505 946 167 3185 590 1350 3650 1824 3109 2358 2064 1228 1600 530 1845 1351 2629 3659 2679 |
| **Warszawa** | 1256 2128 2366 1909 606 1350 1473 648 1542 2110 2268 1136 1274 886 361 1989 956 1152 3480 1680 1345 2960 2015 1469 1245 996 1506 1677 616 1853 3397 1439 1612 |
| **Wien** | 1168 1772 1856 1970 640 1114 1067 242 1308 1954 2034 731 1308 947 1088 1583 1010 916 3100 1524 993 2473 1353 818 2137 430 1600 1240 295 1126 2876 1033 1646 727 |
| **Zürich** | 816 2426 1030 1938 863 619 1810 985 804 1352 1530 464 1497 915 2164 2323 1433 589 2296 922 410 1647 699 292 2552 303 1815 592 691 898 2061 1173 1861 1307 743 |

**Legend example:**

| | Dublin ▶ Göteborg = 477 km |
|---|---|
| 548 **Dublin** | |
| 726 346 **Edinburgh** | |
| 575 1123 1301 **Frankfurt** | |
| 1342 477 176 1067 **Göteborg** | |
| 760 477 1486 485 582 **Hamburg** | |

Distances shown in blue involve at least one ferry journey

**km**

RUSSIA
ROSSIYA

Moscow
Moskva

Kiev
Kyyiv

UKRAINE
UKRAINA

MOLDOVA

İstanbul

Ankara

186  187

TURKEY
TÜRKIYE

İzmir

Antalya

188  189

181

Nicosia CYPRUS
KYPROS

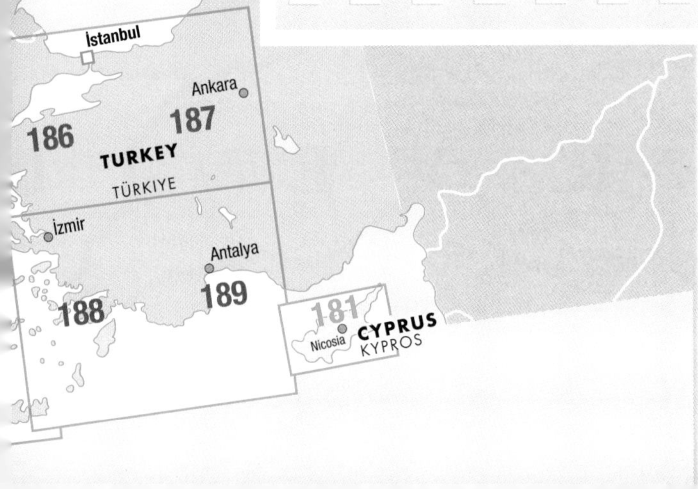

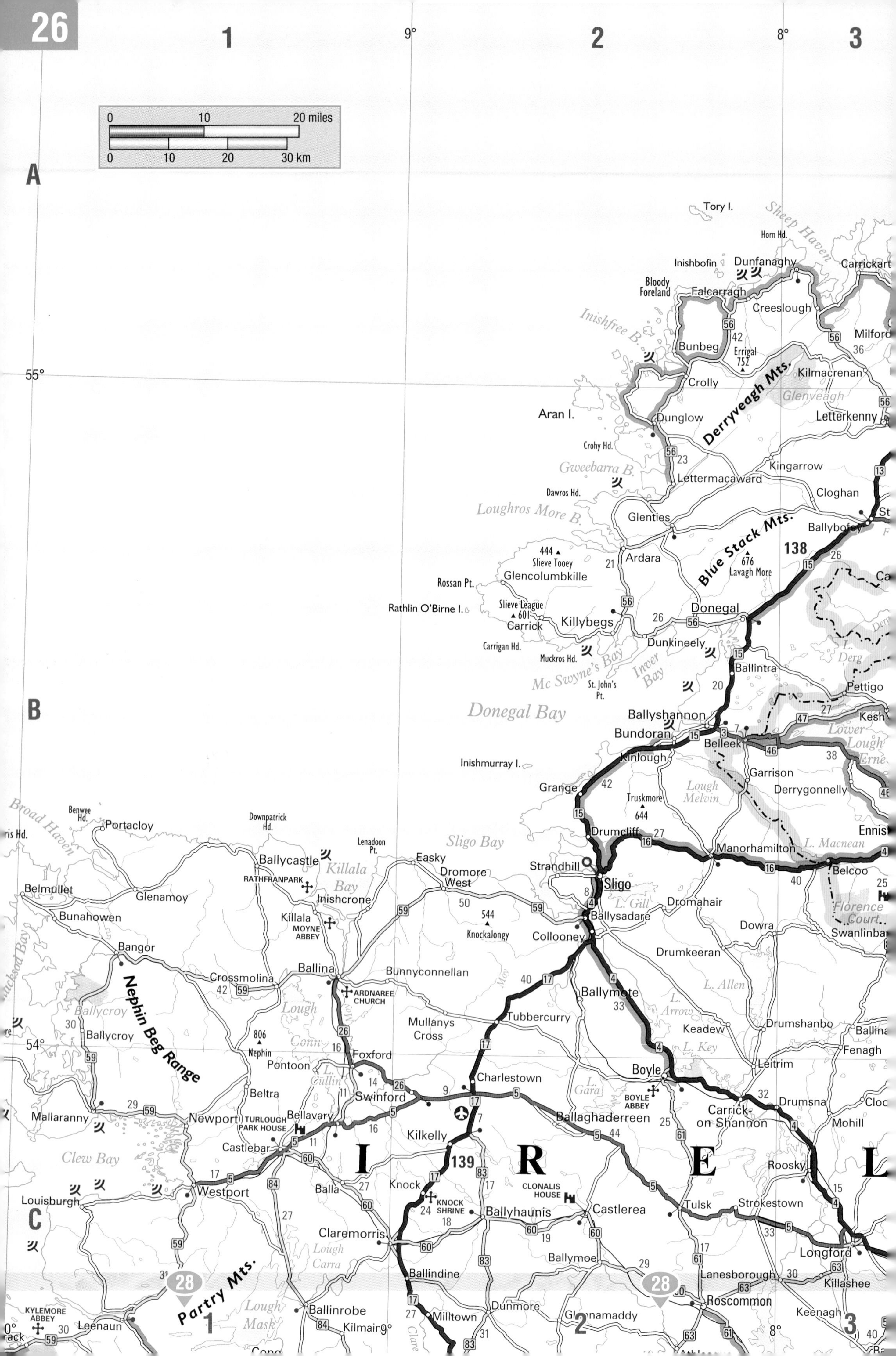

1
2
3
A
B
C
9°
8°
55°
54°
0 10 20 miles
0 10 20 30 km
Tory I.
Sheep Haven
Horn Hd.
Inishbofin
Dunfanaghy
Carrickart
Bloody Foreland
Falcarragh
Creeslough
Inishfree B.
Bunbeg
Errigal 752
Milford
Crolly
Derryveagh Mts.
Kilmacrenan
Glenveagh
Aran I.
Dunglow
Letterkenny
Crohy Hd.
Gweebarra B.
Lettermacaward
Kingarrow
Dawros Hd.
Cloghan
Loughros More B.
Glenties
Blue Stack Mts.
Ballybofey
444 Slieve Tooey
Ardara
676 Lavagh More
138
Rossan Pt.
Glencolumbkille
Rathlin O'Birne I.
Slieve League 601
Carrick
Killybegs
Donegal
Carrigan Hd.
Muckros Hd.
Dunkineely
Mc Swyne's Bay
Inver Bay
St. John's Pt.
L. Derg
Ballintra
Pettigo
Donegal Bay
Ballyshannon
Bundoran
Belleek
Kesh
Lower Lough Erne
Inishmurray I.
Kinlough
Garrison
Derrygonnelly
Grange
Lough Melvin
Truskmore 644
Drumcliff
Ennis
Manorhamilton
L. Macnean
Benwee Hd.
Broad Haven
Portacloy
Downpatrick Hd.
Lenadoon Pt.
Sligo Bay
Ballycastle
Killala Bay
RATHFRANPARK
Easky
Dromore West
Strandhill
Sligo
Belcoo
Belmullet
Glenamoy
Inishcrone
L. Gill
Dromahair
Florence Court
Bunahowen
Killala
MOYNE ABBEY
544 Knockalongy
Ballysadare
Collooney
Dowra
Swanlinbar
Bangor
Drumkeeran
Crossmolina
Ballina
Bunnyconnellan
Nephin Beg Range
ARDNAREE CHURCH
Ballymote
L. Allen
Ballycroy
Lough Conn
806 Nephin
Tubbercurry
L. Arrow
Mullanys Cross
Drumshanbo
Keadew
Ballinamore
Pontoon
Foxford
L. Key
Fenagh
Boyle
Leitrim
L. Cullin
Charlestown
L. Gara
Mallaranny
Beltra
Swinford
BOYLE ABBEY
Carrick-on Shannon
Drumsna
Newport
Bellavary
TURLOUGH PARK HOUSE
Ballaghaderreen
Mohill
Castlebar
Kilkelly
Clew Bay
I
R
E
L
139
Roosky
Louisburgh
Westport
Balla
Knock
CLONALIS HOUSE
KNOCK SHRINE
Ballyhaunis
Castlerea
Tulsk
Strokestown
Claremorris
Lough Carra
Longford
Ballymoe
Ballindine
Lanesborough
Killashee
Partry Mts.
Lough Mask
Ballinrobe
Dunmore
Glennamaddy
Roscommon
Keenagh
KYLEMORE ABBEY
Leenaun
Kilmaine
Milltown

28
28

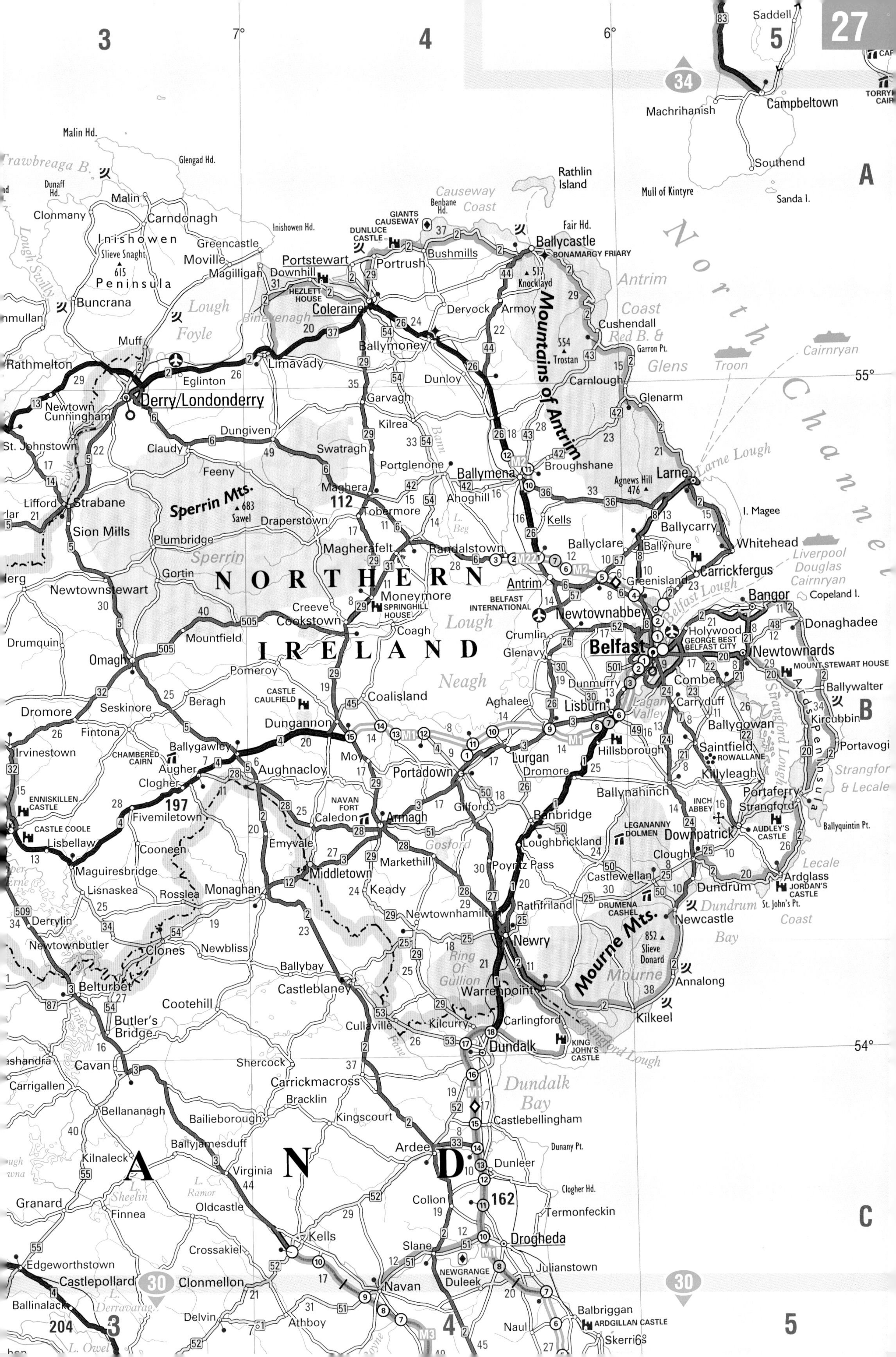

NORTHERN IRELAND
North Channel
Malin Hd.
Glengad Hd.
Trawbreaga B.
Dunaff Hd.
Malin
Clonmany
Carndonagh
Inishowen Peninsula
Slieve Snaght 615
Inishowen Hd.
Greencastle
Moville
Magilligan
Buncrana
Lough Swilly
Lough Foyle
Muff
Rathmelton
Eglinton
Derry/Londonderry
Newtown Cunningham
St. Johnstown
Lifford
Strabane
Sion Mills
Claudy
Dungiven
Feeny
Sperrin Mts.
Sawel 683
Draperstown
Plumbridge
Gortin
Newtownstewart
Omagh
Mountfield
Drumquin
Dromore
Seskinore
Fintona
Irvinestown
Beragh
Pomeroy
Castle Caulfield
Coalisland
Dungannon
Ballygawley
Chambered Cairn
Augher
Clogher
Aughnacloy
Fivemiletown
Enniskillen Castle
Castle Coole
Lisbellaw
Cooneen
Maguiresbridge
Lisnaskea
Rosslea
Monaghan
Derrylin
Newtownbutler
Clones
Newbliss
Belturbet
Cootehill
Butler's Bridge
Cavan
Carrigallen
Bellananagh
Kilnaleck
Granard
Finnea
Edgeworthstown
Castlepollard
Ballinalack
L. Sheelin
L. Ramor
L. Derravarag
L. Owel
Ballyjamesduff
Virginia
Bailieborough
Shercock
Carrickmacross
Bracklin
Kingscourt
Oldcastle
Crossakiel
Kells
Clonmellon
Delvin
Athboy
Navan
Slane
Collon
Ardee
Dunleer
Castlebellingham
Dunany Pt.
Clogher Hd.
Termonfeckin
Drogheda
Julianstown
Newgrange
Duleek
Balbriggan
Ardgillan Castle
Naul
Skerries
Dundalk
Dundalk Bay
King John's Castle
Carlingford
Carlingford Lough
Kilcurry
Cullaville
Castleblaney
Ballybay
Emyvale
Middletown
Keady
Newtownhamilton
Markethill
Armagh
Navan Fort
Caledon
Moy
Portadown
Gilford
Banbridge
Loughbrickland
Poyntz Pass
Newry
Rathfriland
Ring of Gullion
Warrenpoint
Mourne Mts.
Slieve Donard 852
Newcastle
Annalong
Kilkeel
Castlewellan
Drumena Cashel
Dundrum
Dundrum Bay
Clough
Downpatrick
Inch Abbey
Legananny Dolmen
Ballynahinch
Saintfield
Rowallane
Killyleagh
Strangford Lough
Strangford
Portaferry
Audley's Castle
Ardglass
Jordan's Castle
St. John's Pt.
Lecale Coast
Ballyquintin Pt.
Ards Peninsula
Portavogie
Kircubbin
Ballywalter
Mount Stewart House
Newtownards
Donaghadee
Bangor
Copeland I.
Holywood
George Best Belfast City
Belfast
Belfast Lough
Comber
Carryduff
Ballygowan
Lisburn
Lagan Valley
Hillsborough
Dromore
Lurgan
Dunmurry
Aghalee
Glenavy
Crumlin
Lough Neagh
Belfast International
Antrim
Newtownabbey
Greenisland
Carrickfergus
Whitehead
Ballycarry
Ballynure
Ballyclare
Kells
Larne
Larne Lough
I. Magee
Agnews Hill 476
Broughshane
Ballymena
Ahoghill
Randalstown
L. Beg
Portglenone
Magherafelt
Moneymore
Springhill House
Cookstown
Coagh
Creeve
Tobermore
Maghera
Swatragh
Kilrea
Garvagh
Bann
Dunloy
Ballymoney
Limavady
Coleraine
Binevenagh
Hezlett House
Downhill
Portstewart
Portrush
Dunluce Castle
Giants Causeway
Bushmills
Benbane Hd.
Causeway Coast
Dervock
Armoy
Ballycastle
Bonamargy Friary
Fair Hd.
Rathlin Island
Knocklayd 517
Mountains of Antrim
Trostan 554
Antrim Coast
Cushendall
Red B. & Garron Pt.
Glens
Carnlough
Glenarm
Troon
Cairnryan
Liverpool Douglas Cairnryan
Saddell
Machrihanish
Campbeltown
Southend
Mull of Kintyre
Sanda I.
55°
54°
7°
6°

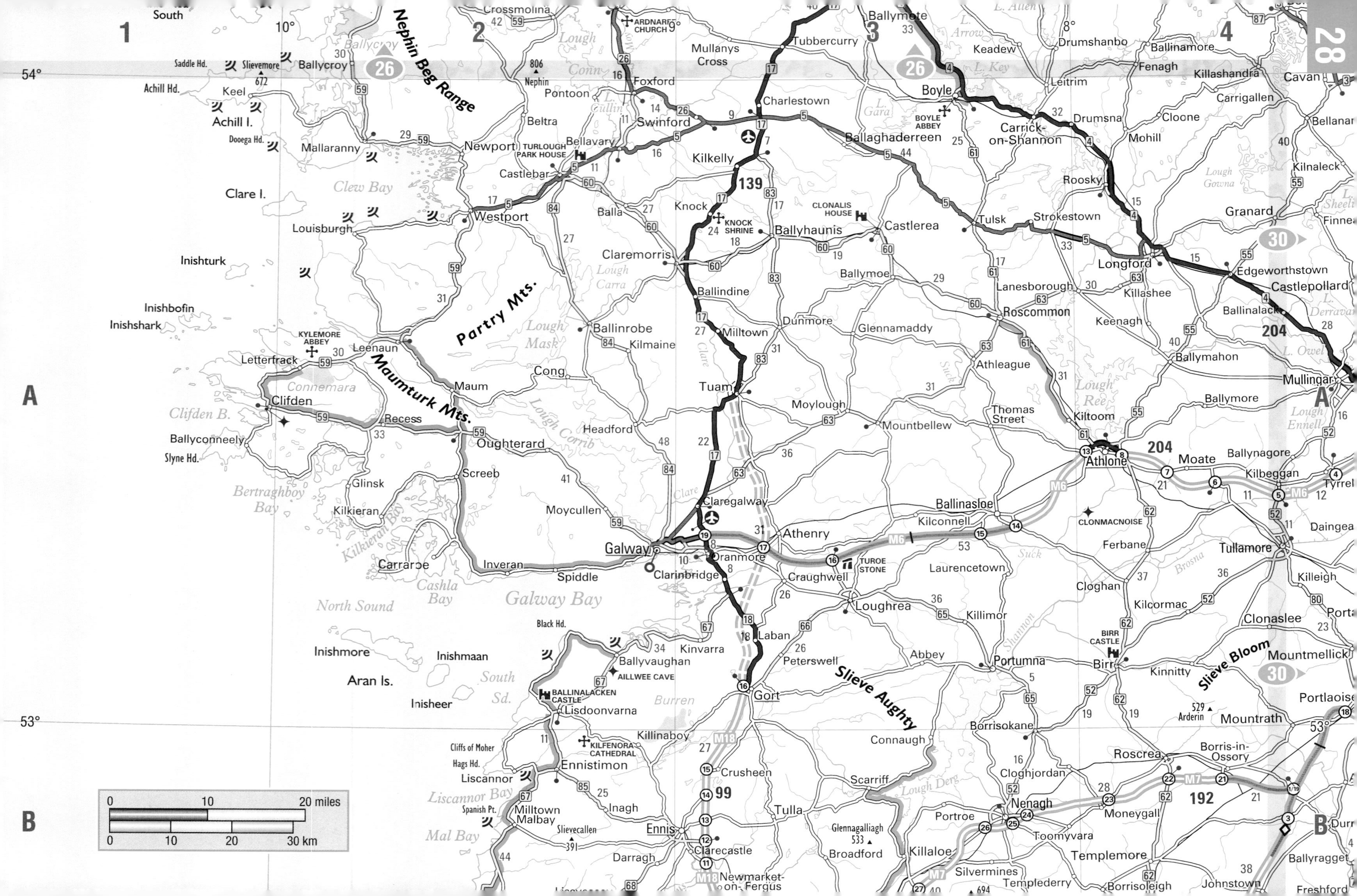
Nephin Beg Range
Partry Mts.
Maumturk Mts.
Slieve Aughty
Slieve Bloom
Saddle Hd.
Slievemore
Ballycroy
Achill Hd.
Keel
Achill I.
Dooega Hd.
Mallaranny
Clare I.
Clew Bay
Inishturk
Inishbofin
Inishshark
Louisburgh
Westport
Newport
Castlebar
Crossmolina
Nephin
Pontoon
Beltra
TURLOUGH PARK HOUSE
Bellavary
Foxford
Swinford
ARDNAREE CHURCH
Mullanys Cross
Tubbercurry
Charlestown
Kilkelly
Knock
KNOCK SHRINE
Balla
Claremorris
Ballyhaunis
CLONALIS HOUSE
Castlerea
Ballaghaderreen
Ballymote
Boyle
BOYLE ABBEY
Keadew
Drumshanbo
Ballinamore
Fenagh
Leitrim
Carrick-on-Shannon
Drumsna
Cloone
Mohill
Carrigallen
Killashandra
Cavan
Bellanar
Kilnaleck
Granard
Finnea
Rooskty
Tulsk
Strokestown
Longford
Edgeworthstown
Castlepollard
Killashee
Lanesborough
Roscommon
Keenagh
Ballinalack
Ballymahon
Mullingar
Ballymore
Ballymoe
Glennamaddy
Dunmore
Ballindine
Milltown
Tuam
Athleague
Moylough
Mountbellew
Thomas Street
Kiltoom
Athlone
Moate
Ballynagore
Kilbeggan
Tyrrel
Daingea
Kylemore Abbey
Letterfrack
Leenaun
Connemara
Clifden
Clifden B.
Ballyconneely
Slyne Hd.
Recess
Maum
Cong
Lough Mask
Lough Carra
Ballinrobe
Kilmaine
Lough Corrib
Headford
Oughterard
Screeb
Glinsk
Kilkieran
Bertraghboy Bay
Kilkieran Bay
Carraroe
Cashla Bay
Inveran
Spiddle
Moycullen
Claregalway
Galway
Clarinbridge
Oranmore
Athenry
Craughwell
TUROE STONE
Loughrea
Ballinasloe
Kilconnell
Laurencetown
Killimor
CLONMACNOISE
Ferbane
Cloghan
Tullamore
Killeigh
Kilcormac
Clonaslee
Mountmellick
Portlaoise
Galway Bay
North Sound
Inishmore
Inishmaan
Aran Is.
Inisheer
South Sd.
Black Hd.
Kinvarra
Ballyvaughan
AILLWEE CAVE
BALLINALACKEN CASTLE
Lisdoonvarna
Burren
Laban
Peterswell
Gort
Abbey
Portumna
BIRR CASTLE
Birr
Kinnitty
Arderin
Mountrath
Borris-in-Ossory
Cliffs of Moher
Hags Hd.
Liscannor
Liscannor Bay
Spanish Pt.
Milltown Malbay
Mal Bay
Ennistimon
KILFENORA CATHEDRAL
Killinaboy
Crusheen
Inagh
Slievecallen
Ennis
Clarecastle
Darragh
Newmarket-on-Fergus
Tulla
Scarriff
Connaugh
Lough Derg
Glennagalliagh
Broadford
Killaloe
Borrisokane
Cloghjordan
Nenagh
Portroe
Toomyvara
Silvermines
Templederry
Roscrea
Moneygall
Templemore
Borrisoleigh
Johnstown
Ballyragget
Freshford
Durr
0 10 20 miles
0 10 20 30 km

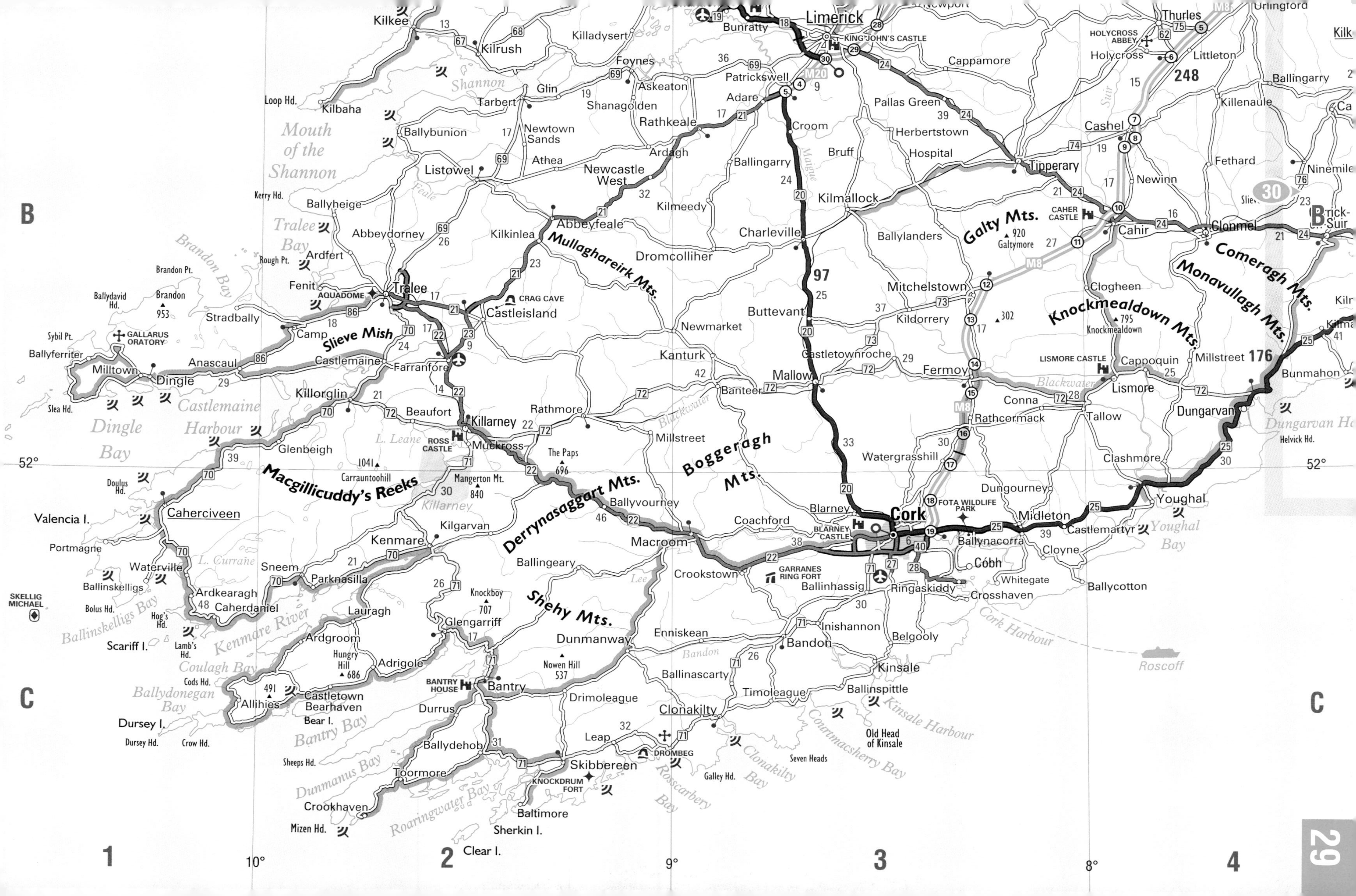

C 4 · 8° · 3 · 9° · 2 · 10° · 1

B · 52° · B · 52° · C · C

Kilkee
Urlingford
Kilkenny
Ballingarry
Ninemilehouse
Brick-
Carrick-
Suir
Ballinaule
Kilmac...
Killenaule
Fethard
Bunmahon
Helvick Hd.
Dungarvan Harbour
Comeragh Mts.
Monavullagh Mts.
Clonmel
Slie...
Littleton
Thurles
Holycross
HOLYCROSS ABBEY
248
Newinn
Cahir
Millstreet 176
Dungarvan
Youghal
Youghal Bay
Roscoff
Cashel
Clogheen
Knockmealdown Mts.
795
Knockmealdown
Cappoquin
Lismore
Clashmore
Castlemartyr
Ballycotton
Tipperary
CAHER CASTLE
Galty Mts.
920 Galtymore
LISMORE CASTLE
Tallow
Midleton
Castlemacorra
Cloyne
Whitegate
Crosshaven
Cork Harbour
Pallas Green
Herbertstown
Hospital
Ballylanders
Mitchelstown
302
Kildorrery
Fermoy
Conna
Rathcormack
Dungourney
Ballynacorra
Cóbh
FOTA WILDLIFE PARK
Limerick
KING JOHN'S CASTLE
Kilmallock
Castletownroche
Watergrasshill
Cork
Ringaskiddy
Belgooly
Kinsale
Old Head of Kinsale
Kinsale Harbour
Courtmacsherry Bay
Croom
Bruff
Charleville
97
Buttevant
Mallow
Banteer
Blarney
BLARNEY CASTLE
Ballinhassig
GARRANES RING FORT
Coachford
Ballincollig
Bandon
Inishannon
Adare
Patrickswell
Ballingarry
Newmarket
Kanturk
Boggeragh Mts.
Millstreet
Crookstown
Macroom
Enniskean
Ballinascarty
Timoleague
Seven Heads
Clonakilty
Clonakilty Bay
Galley Hd.
Rosscarbery Bay
DROMBEG
Foynes
Askeaton
Shanagolden
Rathkeale
Ardagh
Newcastle West
Dromcolliher
Mullaghareirk Mts.
Abbeyfeale
Ballyvourney
Ballingeary
Derrynasaggart Mts.
Shehy Mts.
Dunmanway
Nowen Hill 537
Drimoleague
Leap
Skibbereen
KNOCKDRUM FORT
Baltimore
Sherkin I.
Killadysert
Kilrush
Glin
Newtown Sands
Athea
Shannon
Tarbert
Listowel
CRAG CAVE
Castleisland
Rathmore
The Paps 696
Killarney
MUCKROSS
Kilgarvan
Glengarriff
Knockboy 707
Bantry
BANTRY HOUSE
Durrus
Ballydehob
Toormore
Mizen Hd.
Crookhaven
Kilkee
Ballybunion
Kilbaha
Loop Hd.
Mouth of the Shannon
Ballyheige
Abbeydorney
Fenit
AQUADOME
Tralee
Tralee Bay
Slieve Mish Mts.
Camp
Castlemaine
Farranfore
Beaufort
ROSS CASTLE
L. Leane
Killarney
L. Guitane
Mangerton Mt. 840
Macgillicuddy's Reeks
Carrauntoohil 1041
Kenmare
Kenmare River
Parknasilla
Ardgroom
Hungry Hill 686
Castletown Bearhaven
Bear I.
Sheeps Hd.
Dunmanus Bay
Bantry Bay
Roaringwater Bay
Clear I.
Kerry Hd.
Rough Pt.
Brandon Bay
Brandon 953
Brandon Pt.
GALLARUS ORATORY
Dingle
Milltown
Anascaul
Stradbally
Castlemaine Harbour
Killorglin
Glenbeigh
Dingle Bay
Ballydavid Hd.
Ballyferriter
Sybil Pt.
Sea Hd.
Slea Hd.
Cahersiveen
Valencia I.
Portmagne
Waterville
Ballinskelligs
Bolus Hd.
Hog's Hd.
Ballinskelligs Bay
Scariff I.
Lamb's Hd.
Cods Hd.
Sneem
Caherdaniel
491
Allihies
Dursey I.
Dursey Hd.
Crow Hd.
Coulagh Bay
Ballydonegan Bay
SKELLIG MICHAEL

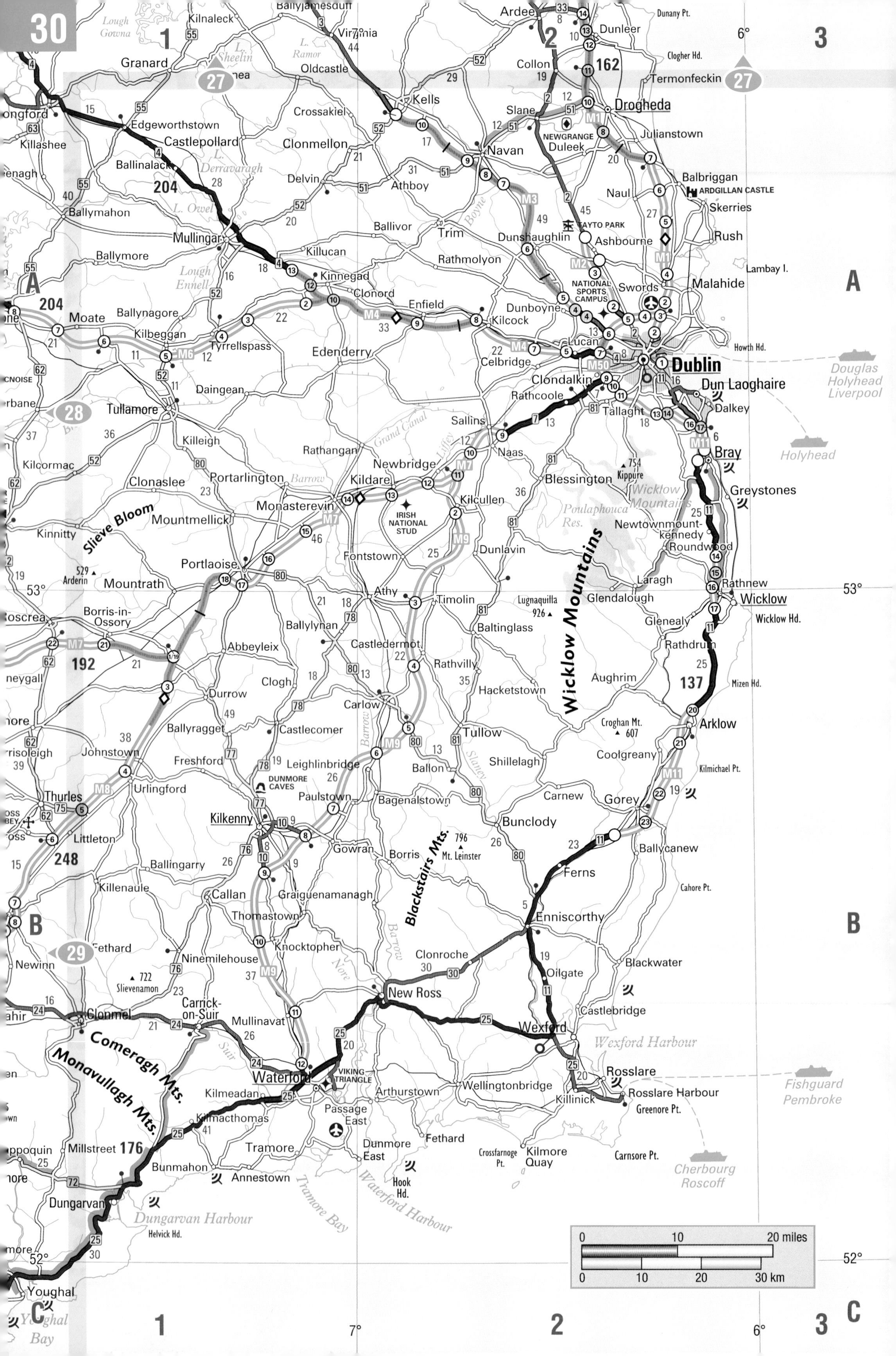
Ballyjamesduff
Ardee
Dunany Pt.
Lough Gowna
Kilnaleck
Virginia
Dunleer
L. Sheelin
L. Ramor
Clogher Hd.
Granard
Oldcastle
Collon
Termonfeckin
Kells
Drogheda
Longford
Edgeworthstown
Crossakiel
Slane
Killashee
Castlepollard
Clonmellon
NEWGRANGE
Julianstown
Duleek
Navan
L. Derravaragh
Ballinalack
Delvin
Athboy
Balbriggan
ARDGILLAN CASTLE
Naul
Skerries
Ballymahon
L. Owel
Boyne
TAYTO PARK
Ballivor
Trim
Dunshaughlin
Ashbourne
Rush
Mullingar
Killucan
Ballymore
Rathmolyon
Lambay I.
Lough Ennell
Kinnegad
NATIONAL SPORTS CAMPUS
Swords
Malahide
Clonord
Enfield
Dunboyne
Moate
Ballynagore
Kilbeggan
Kilcock
Tyrrellspass
Edenderry
Lucan
Howth Hd.
Celbridge
Dublin
Douglas
Holyhead
Liverpool
Clondalkin
Dun Laoghaire
Daingean
Rathcoole
Dalkey
Tullamore
Tallaght
Sallins
Grand Canal
Killeigh
Rathangan
Liffey
Naas
Bray
Holyhead
Newbridge
Kippure
Kilcormac
Portarlington
Barrow
Kildare
Blessington
Clonaslee
Wicklow Mountains
Greystones
Monasterevin
IRISH NATIONAL STUD
Kilcullen
Poulaphouca Res.
Mountmellick
Slieve Bloom
Newtownmount-kennedy
Kinnitty
Roundwood
Fontstown
Dunlavin
Portlaoise
Arderin
Mountrath
Laragh
Rathnew
Athy
Timolin
Lugnaquilla
Glendalough
Wicklow
Borris-in-Ossory
Ballylynan
Baltinglass
Gleneal y
Wicklow Hd.
Abbeyleix
Castledermot
Rathdrum
Rathvilly
Clogh
Aughrim
Mizen Hd.
Durrow
Hacketstown
Carlow
Arklow
Ballyragget
Castlecomer
Croghan Mt.
Johnstown
Tullow
Coolgreany
Freshford
Leighlinbridge
Shillelagh
Kilmichael Pt.
Thurles
DUNMORE CAVES
Ballon
Slaney
Urlingford
Paulstown
Bagenalstown
Carnew
Gorey
Kilkenny
Bunclody
Littleton
Gowran
Borris
Blackstairs Mts.
Mt. Leinster
Ballycanew
Ballingarry
Ferns
Killenaule
Callan
Graiguenamanagh
Cahore Pt.
Thomastown
Enniscorthy
Fethard
Knocktopher
Barrow
Newinn
Ninemilehouse
Clonroche
Blackwater
Oilgate
Slievenamon
Nore
New Ross
Carrick-on-Suir
Mullinavat
Castlebridge
Clonmel
Wexford
Wexford Harbour
Comeragh Mts.
Suir
Monavullagh Mts.
Waterford
VIKING TRIANGLE
Rosslare
Fishguard
Pembroke
Kilmeadan
Arthurstown
Wellingtonbridge
Rosslare Harbour
Kilmacthomas
Passage East
Killinick
Greenore Pt.
Millstreet
Tramore
Dunmore East
Fethard
Crossfarnoge Pt.
Kilmore Quay
Carnsore Pt.
Bunmahon
Annestown
Hook Hd.
Cherbourg
Roscoff
Tramore Bay
Waterford Harbour
Dungarvan
Dungarvan Harbour
Helvick Hd.
Youghal
Youghal Bay
0 10 20 miles
0 10 20 30 km
53°
52°
7°
6°

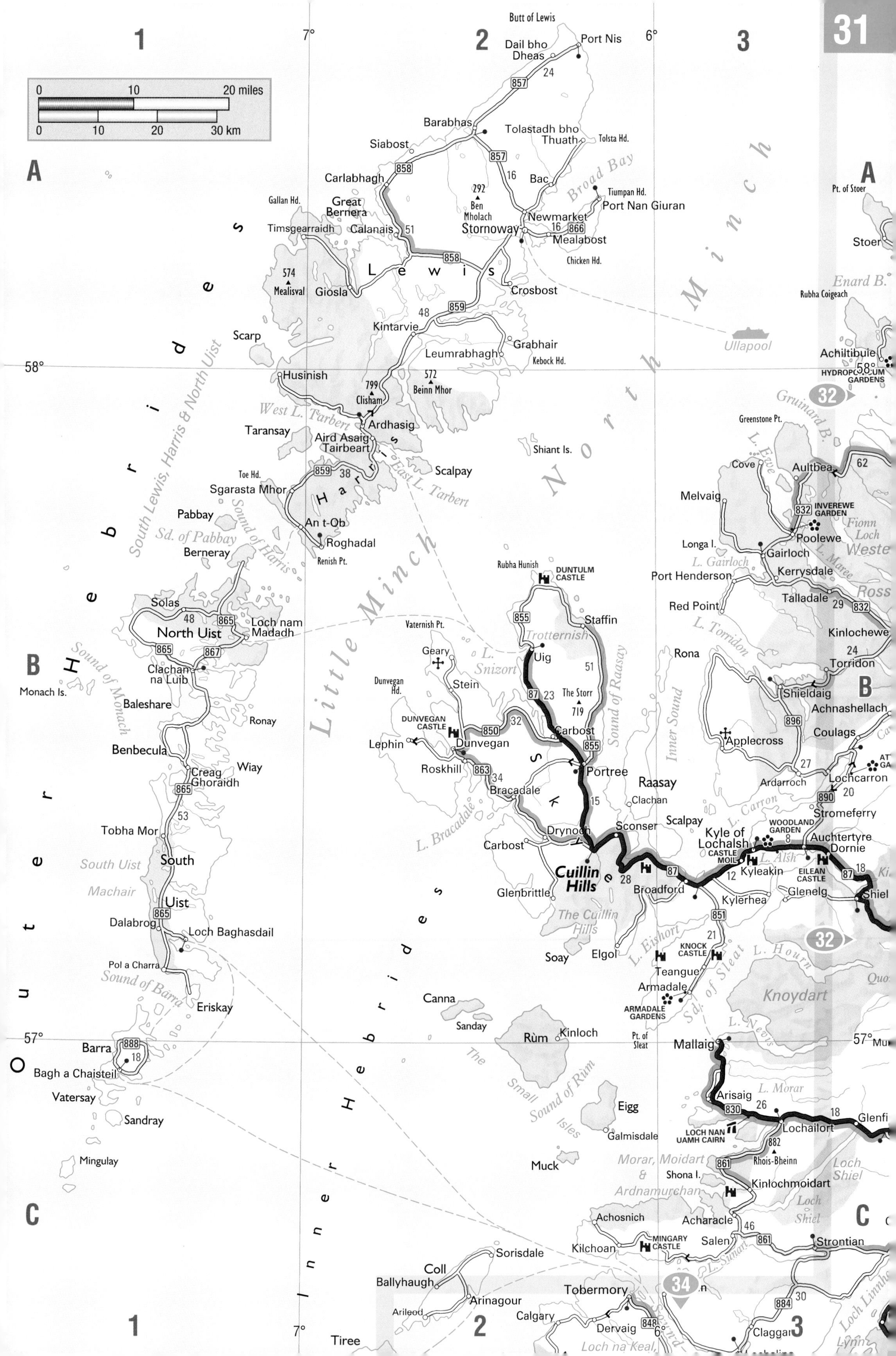

Butt of Lewis
Port Nis
Dail bho Dheas
Barabhas
Siabost
Tolastadh bho Thuath
Tolsta Hd.
Carlabhagh
Great Bernera
Gallan Hd.
Timsgearraidh
Calanais
Ben Mholach
Stornoway
Newmarket
Port Nan Giuran
Tiumpan Hd.
Bac
Broad Bay
Mealabost
Chicken Hd.
Lewis
Mealisval
Giosla
Crosbost
Kintarvie
Grabhair
Leumrabhagh
Kebock Hd.
Scarp
Husinish
Clisham
Beinn Mhor
Ardhasig
West L. Tarbert
Taransay
Aird Asaig
Tairbeart
Scalpay
East L. Tarbert
Shiant Is.
Toe Hd.
Sgarasta Mhor
Harris
Pabbay
Sd. of Pabbay
Sound of Harris
An t-Ob
Roghadal
Renish Pt.
Berneray
Outer Hebrides
South Lewis, Harris & North Uist
Little Minch
North Minch
The Minch
Ullapool
Solas
North Uist
Loch nam Madadh
Clachan na Luib
Monach Is.
Sound of Monach
Baleshare
Ronay
Benbecula
Wiay
Creag Ghoraidh
Tobha Mor
South Uist
South Uist Machair
Dalabrog
Loch Baghasdail
Pol a Charra
Sound of Barra
Eriskay
Barra
Bagh a Chaisteil
Vatersay
Sandray
Mingulay
Rubha Hunish
DUNTULM CASTLE
Staffin
Trotternish
Vaternish Pt.
Geary
L. Snizort
Uig
Stein
Dunvegan Hd.
DUNVEGAN CASTLE
Lephin
Dunvegan
Roskhill
The Storr
Carbost
Portree
Sound of Raasay
Raasay
Bracadale
L. Bracadale
Skye
Clachan
Sconser
Scalpay
Drynoch
Carbost
Cuillin Hills
The Cuillin Hills
Glenbrittle
Broadford
Kyle of Lochalsh
CASTLE MOIL
Kyleakin
Kylerhea
Soay
Elgol
L. Eishort
KNOCK CASTLE
Teangue
Armadale
ARMADALE GARDENS
Sd. of Sleat
Pt. of Sleat
Canna
Sanday
Rùm
Kinloch
Inner Hebrides
The Small Isles
Sound of Rùm
Eigg
Galmisdale
Muck
Mallaig
L. Nevis
L. Hourn
Knoydart
Arisaig
L. Morar
Lochailort
LOCH NAN UAMH CAIRN
Rhois-Bheinn
Morar, Moidart & Ardnamurchan
Shona I.
Kinlochmoidart
Loch Shiel
Achosnich
Acharacle
Kilchoan
MINGARY CASTLE
Salen
L. Sunart
Strontian
Sorisdale
Coll
Ballyhaugh
Arinagour
Arileod
Tobermory
Calgary
Dervaig
Loch na Keal
Claggan
Tiree
Loch Linnhe
Glenfi
Pt. of Stoer
Stoer
Enard B.
Rubha Coigeach
Achiltibuie
HYDROPONICUM GARDENS
Gruinard B.
Greenstone Pt.
L. Ewe
Cove
Aultbea
Melvaig
INVEREWE GARDEN
Fionn Loch
Poolewe
Longa I.
L. Gairloch
Gairloch
L. Maree
Kerrysdale
Port Henderson
Talladale
Wester Ross
Red Point
L. Torridon
Kinlochewe
Rona
Inner Sound
Torridon
Shieldaig
Achnashellach
Applecross
Coulags
Ardarroch
Lochcarron
L. Carron
Stromeferry
WOODLAND GARDEN
Auchtertyre
Dornie
L. Alsh
EILEAN CASTLE
Glenelg
Shiel
Mu
0
10
20 miles
10
20
30 km
1
2
3
A
B
C
7°
6°
58°
57°

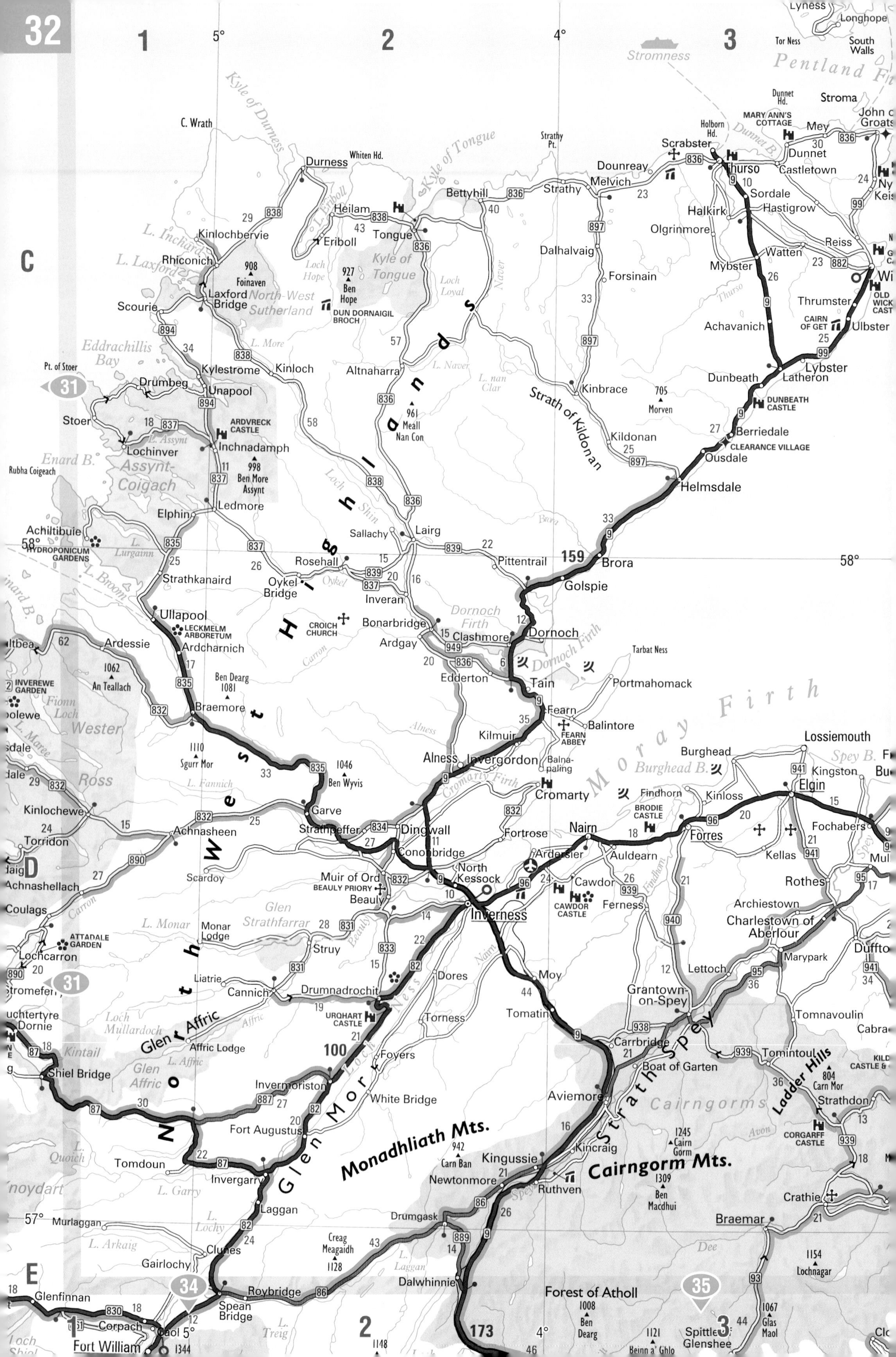

Stromness
Pentland Firth
Lyness
Longhope
Tor Ness
South Walls
Dunnet Hd.
Stroma
John o' Groats
MARY ANN'S COTTAGE
Mey
Holborn Hd.
Dunnet B.
Scrabster
Dunnet
Thurso
Castletown
Dounreay
Melvich
Strathy
Strathy Pt.
C. Wrath
Kyle of Durness
Durness
Whiten Hd.
Kyle of Tongue
Bettyhill
Heilam
L. Eriboll
Eriboll
Tongue
Kinlochbervie
L. Inchard
Rhiconich
L. Laxford
Laxford Bridge
908 Foinaven
927 Ben Hope
DUN DORNAIGIL BROCH
North-West Sutherland
Loch Hope
Loch Loyal
Scourie
Eddrachillis Bay
L. More
Kylestrome
Kinloch
Altnaharra
L. Naver
L. nan Clar
Pt. of Stoer
Drumbeg
Unapool
Stoer
ARDVRECK CASTLE
Inchnadamph
L. Assynt
Lochinver
998 Ben More Assynt
Enard B.
Rubha Coigeach
Assynt-Coigach
961 Meall Nan Con
Elphin
Ledmore
Achiltibuie
HYDROPONICUM GARDENS
L. Lurgainn
L. Broom
Strathkanaird
Oykel Bridge
Rosehall
Sallachy
Lairg
Loch Shin
Pittentrail
Inveran
Ullapool
LECKMELM ARBORETUM
Ardcharnich
Ardessie
CROICH CHURCH
Bonarbridge
Ardgay
Clashmore
Dornoch Firth
Dornoch
Edderton
Tain
Tarbat Ness
Portmahomack
1062 An Teallach
INVEREWE GARDEN
Fionn Loch
Wester Ross
Ben Dearg 1081
Braemore
Fearn
FEARN ABBEY
Balintore
Kilmuir
Alness
Invergordon
Balnapaling
Cromarty Firth
Cromarty
1110 Sgurr Mor
L. Fannich
1046 Ben Wyvis
Garve
Strathpeffer
Dingwall
Kinlochewe
Torridon
Achnasheen
Scardoy
Conon Bridge
North Kessock
Fortrose
Muir of Ord
BEAULY PRIORY
Beauly
Inverness
Ardersier
Nairn
Auldearn
Cawdor
CAWDOR CASTLE
Ferness
Forres
Findhorn
BRODIE CASTLE
Kinloss
Burghead
Burghead B.
Lossiemouth
Kingston
Elgin
Spey B.
Fochabers
Kellas
Rothes
Archiestown
Charlestown of Aberlour
Marypark
Dufftown
Moray Firth
Achnashellach
Coulags
L. Monar
Monar Lodge
Glen Strathfarrar
Struy
ATTADALE GARDEN
Lochcarron
Stromeferry
Liatrie
Cannich
Drumnadrochit
Dores
Moy
Tomatin
Grantown-on-Spey
Lettoch
Tomnavoulin
Dornie
Loch Mullardoch
Glen Affric
Affric Lodge
URQUHART CASTLE
Torness
Foyers
Carrbridge
Boat of Garten
Tomintoul
Ladder Hills
804 Carn Mor
Kintail
Shiel Bridge
Invermoriston
Loch Ness
White Bridge
Aviemore
Strath Spey
Cairngorms
Strathdon
CORGARFF CASTLE
Fort Augustus
Glen Mor
Monadhliath Mts.
942 Carn Ban
1245 Cairn Gorm
Cairngorm Mts.
1309 Ben Macdhui
Kincraig
Kingussie
Newtonmore
Ruthven
L. Quoich
Tomdoun
Invergarry
Knoydart
L. Garry
Laggan
Crathie
Braemar
57°
Murlaggan
L. Lochy
L. Arkaig
Clunes
Gairlochy
Creag Meagaidh 1128
Drumgask
Dalwhinnie
L. Laggan
1154 Lochnagar
Dee
Glenfinnan
Corpach
Fort William
Caol
Spean Bridge
Roybridge
L. Treig
Forest of Atholl
1008 Ben Dearg
1121 Beinn a' Ghlo
Spittle of Glenshee
1067 Glas Maol
Halkirk
Hastigrow
Sordale
Olgrinmore
Reiss
Watten
Mybster
Dalhalvaig
Forsinain
Thrumster
Ulbster
OLD WICK CASTLE
CAIRN OF GET
Achavanich
Lybster
Latheron
Dunbeath
DUNBEATH CASTLE
705 Morven
Kinbrace
Strath of Kildonan
Kildonan
Berriedale
CLEARANCE VILLAGE
Ousdale
Helmsdale
Brora
Golspie
58°
North West Highlands

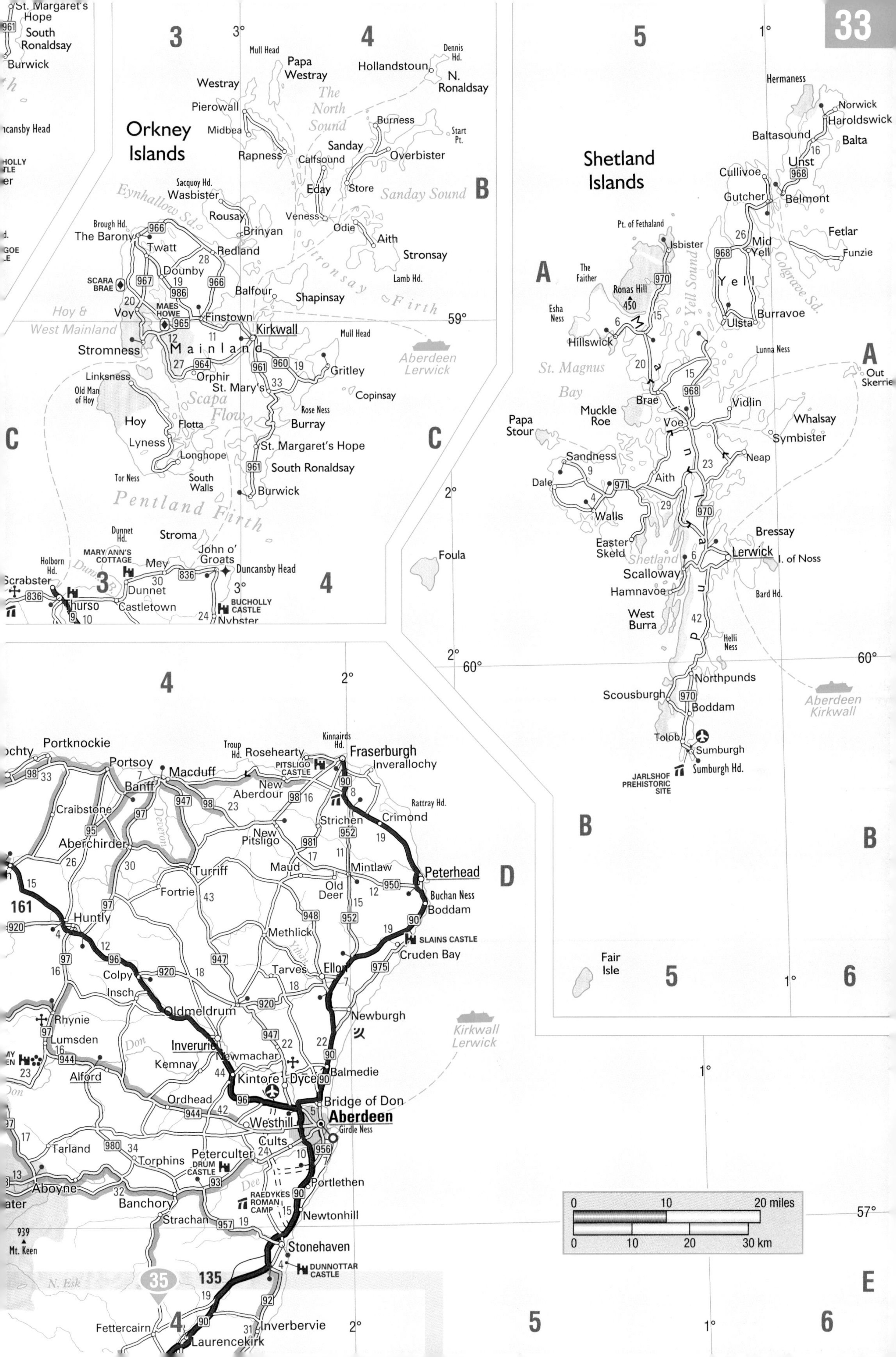
Orkney Islands
Westray
Papa Westray
Hollandstoun
N. Ronaldsay
Pierowall
The North Sound
Sanday
Overbister
Stronsay
Shapinsay
Kirkwall
Mainland
Stromness
Finstown
Orphir
St. Mary's
Hoy
Flotta
Lyness
Longhope
Burray
St. Margaret's Hope
South Ronaldsay
Burwick
Scapa Flow
Pentland Firth
Stroma
John o' Groats
Duncansby Head
Thurso
Castletown
Dunnet
Mey
Shetland Islands
Unst
Baltasound
Haroldswick
Yell
Fetlar
Mainland
Lerwick
Scalloway
Brae
Voe
Whalsay
Foula
Fair Isle
Sumburgh
Aberdeen Lerwick
Aberdeen Kirkwall
Kirkwall Lerwick
Fraserburgh
Peterhead
Banff
Macduff
Portsoy
Turriff
Huntly
Inverurie
Ellon
Aberdeen
Stonehaven
Banchory
Aboyne
Alford
Laurencekirk
Inverbervie
0 10 20 miles
0 10 20 30 km

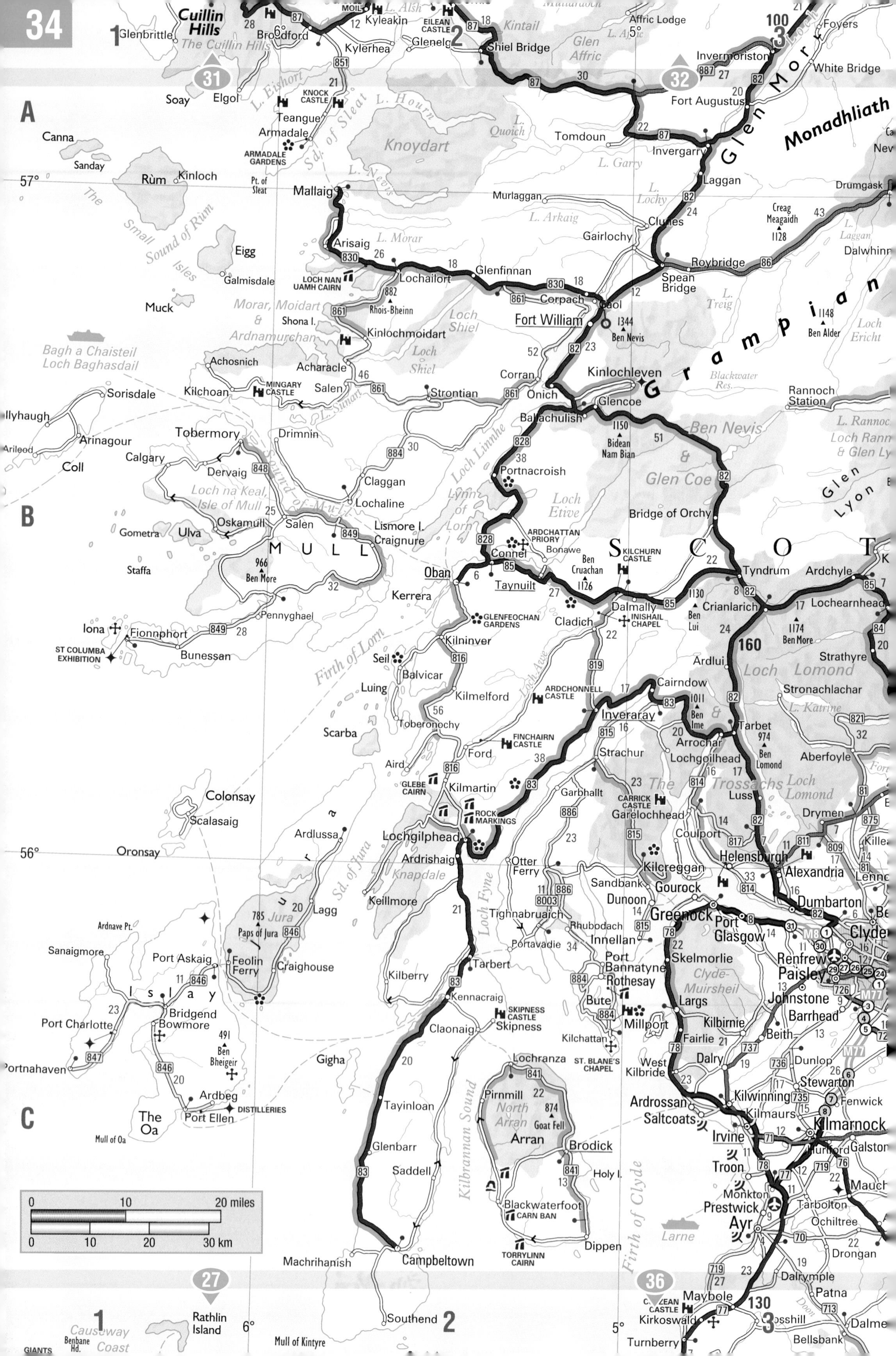

Cuillin Hills
Glenbrittle
The Cuillin Hills
Broadford
Kyleakin
Eilean Castle
Kylerhea
Glenelg
Kintail
Shiel Bridge
Glen Affric
Affric Lodge
Invermoriston
Foyers
White Bridge
Fort Augustus
Glen Mor
Monadhliath
Soay
Elgol
L. Eishort
Knock Castle
L. Hourn
Teangue
Armadale
Armadale Gardens
Sd. of Sleat
Knoydart
L. Quoich
Tomdoun
Invergarry
L. Garry
Canna
Sanday
Rùm
Kinloch
Pt. of Sleat
Mallaig
L. Nevis
57°
Murlaggan
Laggan
L. Lochy
Drumgask
L. Arkaig
Clunes
Creag Meagaidh
1128
The Small Isles
Sound of Rum
Eigg
Arisaig
L. Morar
Gairlochy
Galmisdale
Loch nan Uamh Cairn
Lochailort
Glenfinnan
Corpach
Roybridge
Spean Bridge
Dalwhinnie
Muck
Morar, Moidart & Ardnamurchan
Shona I.
Rhois-Bheinn
Kinlochmoidart
Loch Shiel
Fort William
Caol
Ben Nevis
1344
L. Treig
Ben Alder
1148
Loch Ericht
Grampian
Bagh a Chaisteil
Loch Baghasdail
Achosnich
Acharacle
Corran
Kinlochleven
Blackwater Res.
Rannoch Station
Sorisdale
Kilchoan
Mingary Castle
Salen
Strontian
Onich
Glencoe
L. Sunart
Ballachulish
Bidean Nam Bian
1150
Ben Nevis & Glen Coe
L. Rannoch
Loch Rannoch & Glen Lyon
Arinagour
Coll
Arileod
Tobermory
Drimnin
Calgary
Dervaig
Loch na Keal, Isle of Mull
Sound of Mull
Loch Linnhe
Claggan
Lochaline
Portnacroish
Loch Etive
Glen Lyon
Lynn of Lorn
Bridge of Orchy
Gometra
Ulva
Oskamull
Salen
Lismore I.
Craignure
Ardchattan Priory
Bonawe
Mull
Connel
Ben Cruachan
1126
Kilchurn Castle
Tyndrum
Ardchyle
Staffa
Ben More
966
Oban
Taynuilt
Kerrera
Scotland
Dalmally
Crianlarich
Ben Lui
1130
Lochearnhead
Iona
Fionnphort
Pennyghael
Bunessan
St Columba Exhibition
Glenfeochan Gardens
Cladich
Inishail Chapel
Ben More
1174
Kilninver
Seil
Balvicar
Firth of Lorn
Ardlui
Loch Lomond
Strathyre
Luing
Kilmelford
Loch Awe
Ardchonnell Castle
Cairndow
Inveraray
Ben Ime
1011
Stronachlachar
L. Katrine
Scarba
Toberonochy
Arrochar
Tarbet
Ben Lomond
974
Finchairn Castle
Ford
Strachur
Lochgoilhead
Aberfoyle
Aird
Glebe Cairn
Kilmartin
Rock Markings
The Trossachs
Loch Lomond
Luss
Colonsay
Scalasaig
Garbhallt
Carrick Castle
Garelochhead
Drymen
Oronsay
Ardlussa
Lochgilphead
Ardrishaig
Coulport
Killearn
56°
Jura
Knapdale
Otter Ferry
Helensburgh
Alexandria
Sd. of Jura
Keillmore
Kilcreggan
Sandbank
Dunoon
Gourock
Dumbarton
Lagg
Greenock
Port Glasgow
Clydebank
Ardnave Pt.
Paps of Jura
785
Loch Fyne
Tighnabruaich
Rhubodach
Innellan
Skelmorlie
Renfrew
Glasgow
Sanaigmore
Port Askaig
Feolin Ferry
Craighouse
Portavadie
Port Bannatyne
Rothesay
Clyde-Muirsheil
Paisley
Islay
Kilberry
Tarbert
Bute
Largs
Johnstone
Barrhead
Port Charlotte
Bridgend
Bowmore
Kennacraig
Skipness Castle
Skipness
Millport
Kilbirnie
Beith
Claonaig
Kilchattan
St. Blane's Chapel
Fairlie
Ben Bheigeir
491
Portnahaven
Gigha
Lochranza
West Kilbride
Dalry
Dunlop
Stewarton
Ardbeg
Pirnmill
North Arran
Goat Fell
874
Kilwinning
Fenwick
The Oa
Port Ellen
Distilleries
Tayinloan
Kilbrannan Sound
Ardrossan
Saltcoats
Kilmaurs
Kilmarnock
Mull of Oa
Arran
Brodick
Irvine
Hurlford
Galston
Glenbarr
Troon
Saddell
Holy I.
Mauchline
Firth of Clyde
Monkton
Prestwick
Tarbolton
0
10
20 miles
30 km
Blackwaterfoot
Carn Ban
Larne
Ayr
Ochiltree
Torrylinn Cairn
Dippen
Drongan
Campbeltown
Machrihanish
Dalrymple
Patna
Culzean Castle
Maybole
Kirkoswald
Crosshill
Dalmellington
Rathlin Island
Southend
Turnberry
Bellsbank
Causeway Coast
Giants
Benbane Hd.
Mull of Kintyre
6°
5°
A
B
C
1
2
3
31
32
27
36

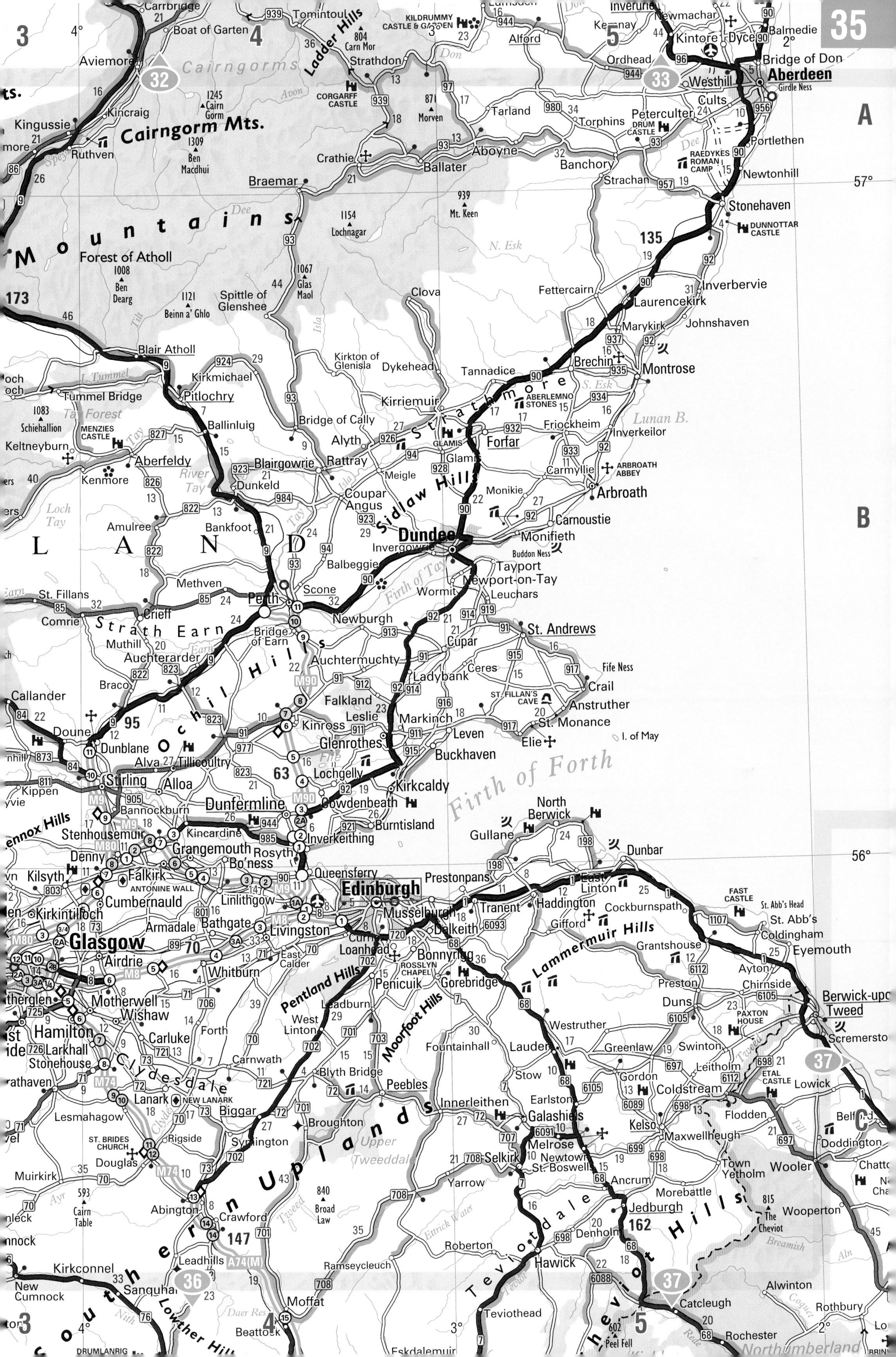
Aberdeen
Dundee
Edinburgh
Glasgow
Perth
Stirling
Cairngorm Mts.
Grampian Mountains
Forest of Atholl
Strathmore
Sidlaw Hills
Ochil Hills
Strath Earn
Firth of Forth
Firth of Tay
Lammermuir Hills
Pentland Hills
Moorfoot Hills
Southern Uplands
Cheviot Hills
Clydesdale
Teviotdale
Montrose
Arbroath
St. Andrews
Kirkcaldy
Dunfermline
Falkirk
Galashiels
Hawick
Jedburgh
Peebles
Stonehaven
Berwick-upon-Tweed
Northumberland

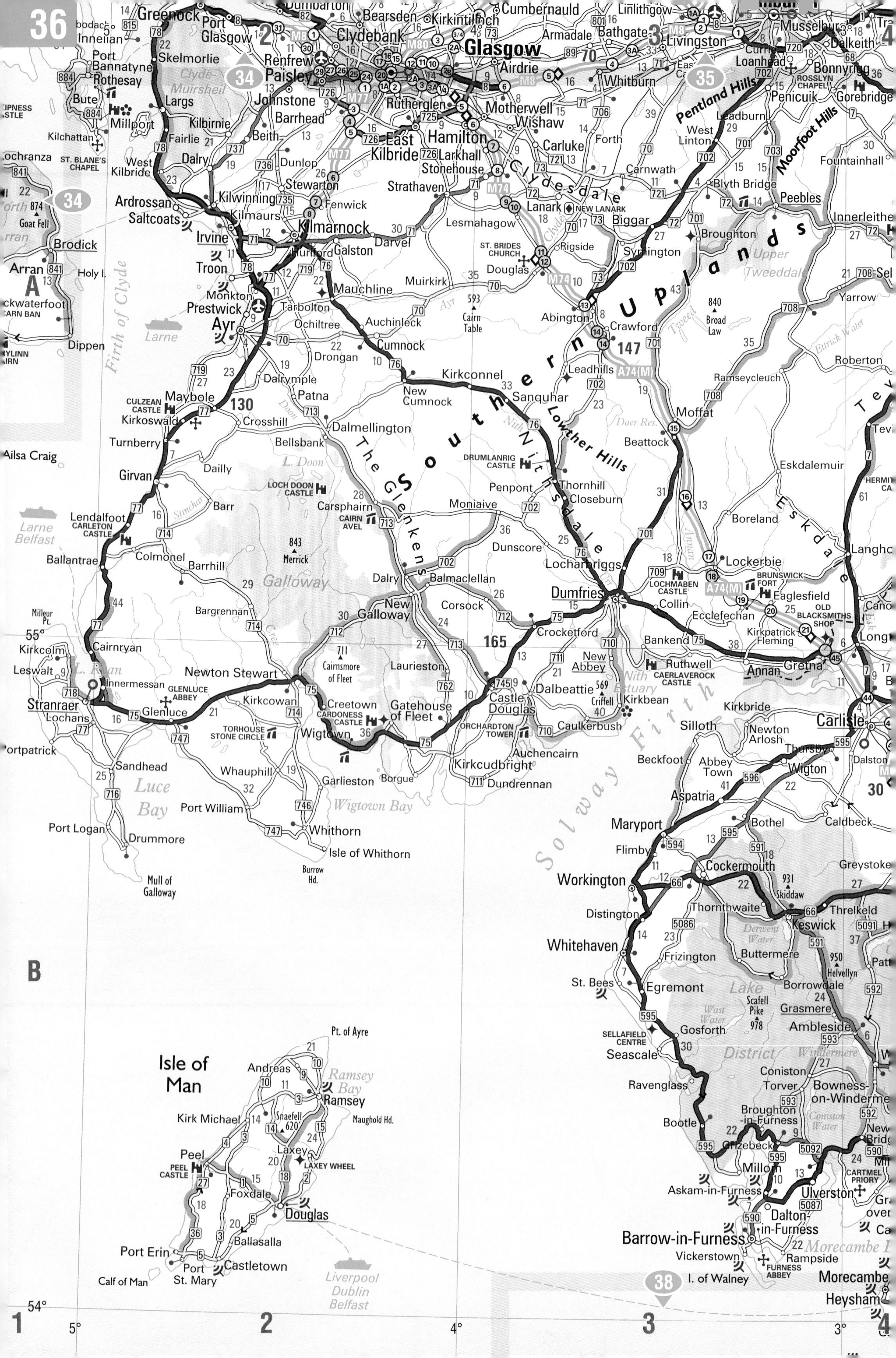

Greenock
Port Glasgow
Dumbarton
Bearsden
Kirkintilloch
Cumbernauld
Linlithgow
Musselburgh
Dalkeith
Clydebank
Glasgow
Armadale
Bathgate
Livingston
Renfrew
Paisley
Airdrie
Whitburn
Loanhead
Bonnyrigg
Rosslyn Chapel
Johnstone
Rutherglen
Motherwell
Penicuik
Gorebridge
Barrhead
Wishaw
Pentland Hills
Moorfoot Hills
East Kilbride
Hamilton
Carluke
Forth
West Linton
Larkhall
Stonehouse
Clydesdale
Carnwath
Fountainhall
Strathaven
Lanark
New Lanark
Blyth Bridge
Peebles
Biggar
Innerleithen
Innellan
Port Bannatyne
Rothesay
Bute
Skelmorlie
Clyde-Muirsheil
Largs
Kilbirnie
Millport
Fairlie
Beith
Kilchattan
St. Blane's Chapel
West Kilbride
Dalry
Dunlop
Stewarton
Lochranza
Goat Fell
Arran
Ardrossan
Saltcoats
Kilwinning
Kilmaurs
Fenwick
Kilmarnock
Irvine
Hurlford
Galston
Darvel
Lesmahagow
St. Brides Church
Rigside
Douglas
Symington
Broughton
Upper Tweeddale
Brodick
Holy I.
Troon
Monkton
Prestwick
Tarbolton
Mauchline
Muirkirk
Cairn Table
Abington
Crawford
Broad Law
Yarrow
Whiting Bay
Ayr
Ochiltree
Auchinleck
Cumnock
Drongan
Dippen
Firth of Clyde
Larne
Southern Uplands
Leadhills
Moffat
Roberton
Ramseycleuch
Dalrymple
Patna
Kirkconnel
New Cumnock
Sanquhar
Lowther Hills
Maybole
Culzean Castle
Kirkoswald
Crosshill
Dalmellington
Bellsbank
Beattock
Turnberry
Ailsa Craig
Girvan
Dailly
L. Doon
Drumlanrig Castle
Loch Doon Castle
Nithsdale
Thornhill
Closeburn
Penpont
Eskdalemuir
Barr
Carsphairn
Cairn Avel
The Glenkens
Moniaive
Eskdale
Boreland
Lendalfoot
Carleton Castle
Larne Belfast
Colmonel
Ballantrae
Barrhill
Merrick
Galloway
Dunscore
Lochmaben Castle
Lockerbie
Brunswick Fort
Eaglesfield
Dalry
Balmaclellan
Lincluden
Dumfries
Collin
Corsock
Old Blacksmiths Shop
Millieur Pt.
Bargrennan
New Galloway
Ecclefechan
Kirkcolm
Cairnryan
Crocketford
Bankend
Kirkpatrick Fleming
Leswalt
L. Ryan
Stranraer
Innermessan
Newton Stewart
Cairnsmore of Fleet
Laurieston
New Abbey
Ruthwell
Caerlaverock Castle
Annan
Gretna
Dalbeattie
Criffell
Nith Estuary
Kirkbean
Glenluce Abbey
Glenluce
Kirkcowan
Creetown
Cardoness Castle
Gatehouse of Fleet
Castle Douglas
Kirkbride
Carlisle
Lochans
Portpatrick
Torhouse Stone Circle
Wigtown
Orchardton Tower
Caulkerbush
Silloth
Newton Arlosh
Thursby
Solway Firth
Sandhead
Whauphill
Auchencairn
Kirkcudbright
Beckfoot
Abbey Town
Wigton
Dalston
Luce Bay
Garlieston
Borgue
Dundrennan
Port William
Aspatria
Wigtown Bay
Port Logan
Drummore
Whithorn
Isle of Whithorn
Maryport
Bothel
Caldbeck
Burrow Hd.
Flimby
Mull of Galloway
Workington
Cockermouth
Skiddaw
Greystoke
Distington
Thornthwaite
Threlkeld
Keswick
Derwent Water
Whitehaven
Frizington
Buttermere
Helvellyn
St. Bees
Egremont
Borrowdale
Lake District
Scafell Pike
Grasmere
Ambleside
Sellafield Centre
Gosforth
Wast Water
Seascale
Windermere
Coniston
Torver
Ravenglass
Bowness-on-Windermere
Broughton-in-Furness
Coniston Water
Bootle
Grizebeck
Millom
Cartmel Priory
Askam-in-Furness
Ulverston
Dalton-in-Furness
Barrow-in-Furness
Morecambe Bay
Vickerstown
Rampside
Furness Abbey
I. of Walney
Morecambe
Heysham
Pt. of Ayre
Isle of Man
Andreas
Ramsey Bay
Ramsey
Maughold Hd.
Kirk Michael
Snaefell
Laxey
Laxey Wheel
Peel
Peel Castle
Foxdale
Douglas
Ballasalla
Port Erin
Port St. Mary
Castletown
Calf of Man
Liverpool Dublin Belfast
54°
55°
5°
4°
3°
1
2
3
4
A
B

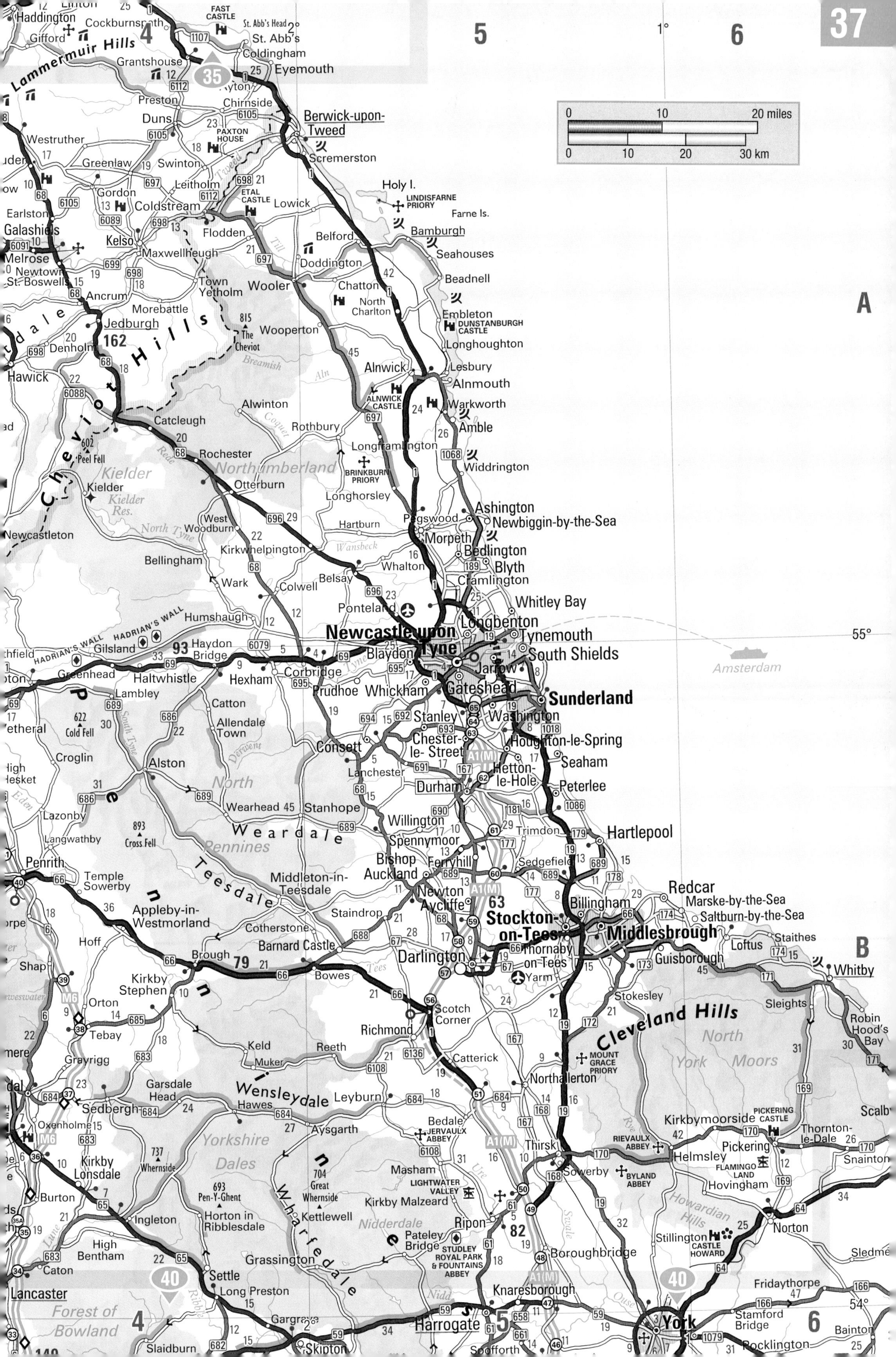
37
4
5
6
1°
0 10 20 miles
0 10 20 30 km
A
B
55°
54°
Haddington
Gifford
Cockburnspath
Lammermuir Hills
FAST CASTLE
St. Abb's Head
St. Abb's
Coldingham
Eyemouth
Grantshouse
Ayton
Preston
Chirnside
Duns
PAXTON HOUSE
Berwick-upon-Tweed
Scremerston
Westruther
Greenlaw
Swinton
Tweed
Gordon
Leitholm
ETAL CASTLE
Lowick
Holy I.
LINDISFARNE PRIORY
Farne Is.
Earlston
Coldstream
Galashiels
Kelso
Flodden
Belford
Bamburgh
Seahouses
Melrose
Newtown St. Boswells
Maxwellheugh
Doddington
Beadnell
Town Yetholm
Wooler
Chatton
North Charlton
Till
Ancrum
Morebattle
Embleton
DUNSTANBURGH CASTLE
Jedburgh
Cheviot Hills
The Cheviot
Wooperton
Longhoughton
Denholm
Breamish
Alnwick
Lesbury
Aln
Alnmouth
Hawick
ALNWICK CASTLE
Warkworth
Alwinton
Amble
Catcleugh
Rothbury
Coquet
Longframlington
Peel Fell
Rochester
Rede
Widdrington
BRINKBURN PRIORY
Kielder
Northumberland
Otterburn
Kielder Res.
Longhorsley
Ashington
Newbiggin-by-the-Sea
West Woodburn
Hartburn
Pegswood
North Tyne
Morpeth
Newcastleton
Kirkwhelpington
Wansbeck
Bedlington
Bellingham
Whalton
Blyth
Belsay
Cramlington
Wark
Colwell
Whitley Bay
Ponteland
Humshaugh
Longbenton
HADRIAN'S WALL
Newcastle upon Tyne
Tynemouth
Gilsland
Haydon Bridge
South Shields
Amsterdam
Blaydon
Jarrow
Greenhead
Haltwhistle
Hexham
Corbridge
Tyne
Gateshead
Sunderland
Lambley
Prudhoe
Whickham
Catton
Washington
Stanley
Cold Fell
Allendale Town
South Tyne
Chester-le-Street
Houghton-le-Spring
Consett
Seaham
Croglin
Alston
Derwent
Lanchester
Hetton-le-Hole
North
Durham
Peterlee
Eden
Lazonby
Wearhead
Stanhope
Willington
Trimdon
Hartlepool
Weardale
Cross Fell
Langwathby
Pennines
Spennymoor
Bishop Auckland
Ferryhill
Sedgefield
Penrith
Temple Sowerby
Middleton-in-Teesdale
Teesdale
Newton Aycliffe
Redcar
Marske-by-the-Sea
Billingham
Saltburn-by-the-Sea
Appleby-in-Westmorland
Staindrop
Stockton-on-Tees
Middlesbrough
Cotherstone
Loftus
Staithes
Hoff
Barnard Castle
Thornaby on-Tees
Darlington
Guisborough
Whitby
Shap
Brough
Tees
Yarm
Kirkby Stephen
Bowes
Orton
Scotch Corner
Stokesley
Sleights
Cleveland Hills
Robin Hood's Bay
Tebay
Richmond
North York Moors
Keld
Muker
Reeth
Catterick
MOUNT GRACE PRIORY
Grayrigg
Garsdale Head
Northallerton
Wensleydale
Leyburn
Sedbergh
Hawes
Bedale
Aysgarth
JERVAULX ABBEY
Kirkbymoorside
PICKERING CASTLE
Scalby
Oxenholme
Yorkshire Dales
Thornton-le-Dale
Thirsk
RIEVAULX ABBEY
Helmsley
Pickering
Snainton
Kirkby Lonsdale
Whernside
Great Whernside
Masham
FLAMINGO LAND
Sowerby
Rye
BYLAND ABBEY
Hovingham
LIGHTWATER VALLEY
Burton
Pen-Y-Ghent
Wharfedale
Kirkby Malzeard
Howardian Hills
Ingleton
Horton in Ribblesdale
Kettlewell
Nidderdale
Ripon
Norton
Pateley Bridge
Stillington
CASTLE HOWARD
High Bentham
STUDLEY ROYAL PARK & FOUNTAINS ABBEY
Boroughbridge
Sledmere
Caton
Grassington
Swale
Ure
Lune
Lancaster
Settle
Knaresborough
Fridaythorpe
Long Preston
Ribble
Nidd
Ouse
Forest of Bowland
Gargrave
Harrogate
York
Stamford Bridge
Slaidburn
Skipton
Spofforth
Pocklington
Bainton

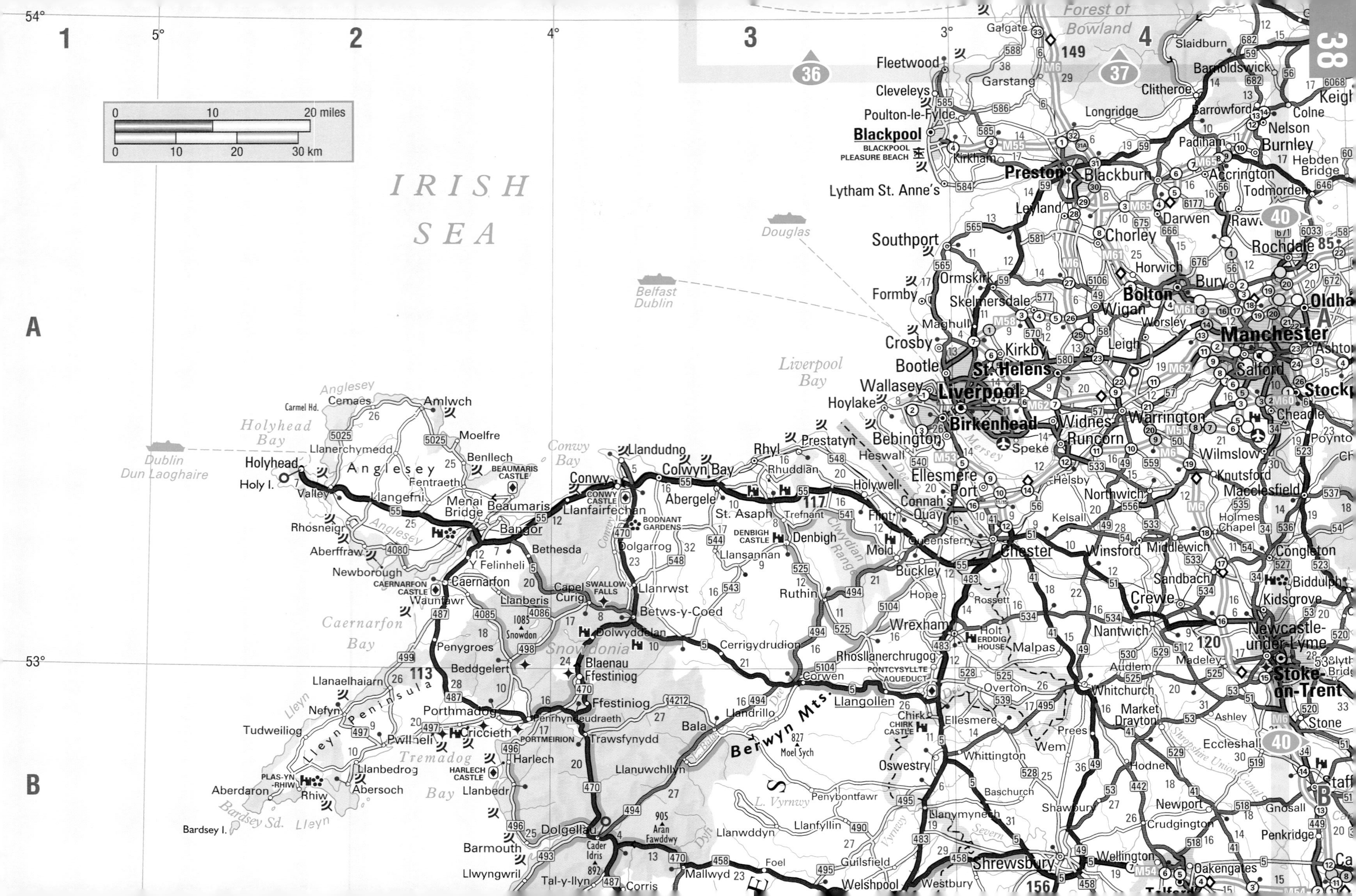
IRISH SEA
Liverpool Bay
Caernarfon Bay
Tremadog Bay
Holyhead Bay
Conwy Bay
Douglas
Belfast Dublin
Dublin Dun Laoghaire
Anglesey
Lleyn Peninsula
Snowdonia
Clwydian Range
Berwyn Mts.
Forest of Bowland
Holyhead
Holy I.
Valley
Llangefni
Menai Bridge
Beaumaris
Bangor
Amlwch
Cemaes
Moelfre
Benllech
Rhosneigr
Aberffraw
Newborough
Caernarfon
Waunfawr
Llanberis
Bethesda
Capel Curig
Betws-y-Coed
Llanrwst
Conwy
Llandudno
Colwyn Bay
Abergele
Rhyl
Prestatyn
St. Asaph
Denbigh
Ruthin
Mold
Flint
Holywell
Wrexham
Llangollen
Corwen
Bala
Blaenau Ffestiniog
Ffestiniog
Porthmadog
Criccieth
Pwllheli
Nefyn
Abersoch
Aberdaron
Harlech
Barmouth
Dolgellau
Tal-y-llyn
Corris
Mallwyd
Welshpool
Oswestry
Shrewsbury
Whitchurch
Market Drayton
Newport
Wellington
Stoke-on-Trent
Newcastle-under-Lyme
Crewe
Nantwich
Chester
Northwich
Runcorn
Widnes
Warrington
Liverpool
Birkenhead
St. Helens
Wigan
Bolton
Manchester
Salford
Stockport
Oldham
Rochdale
Bury
Preston
Blackpool
Blackburn
Burnley
Southport
Fleetwood
Lytham St. Anne's
Macclesfield
Knutsford
Wilmslow
Congleton
Sandbach
Ellesmere Port
Connah's Quay
Queensferry
Bebington
Wallasey
Hoylake
Bootle
Crosby
Formby
Ormskirk
Skelmersdale
Kirkby
Chorley
Leyland
Darwen
Accrington
Clitheroe
Longridge
Garstang
Speke
0 10 20 miles
0 10 20 30 km

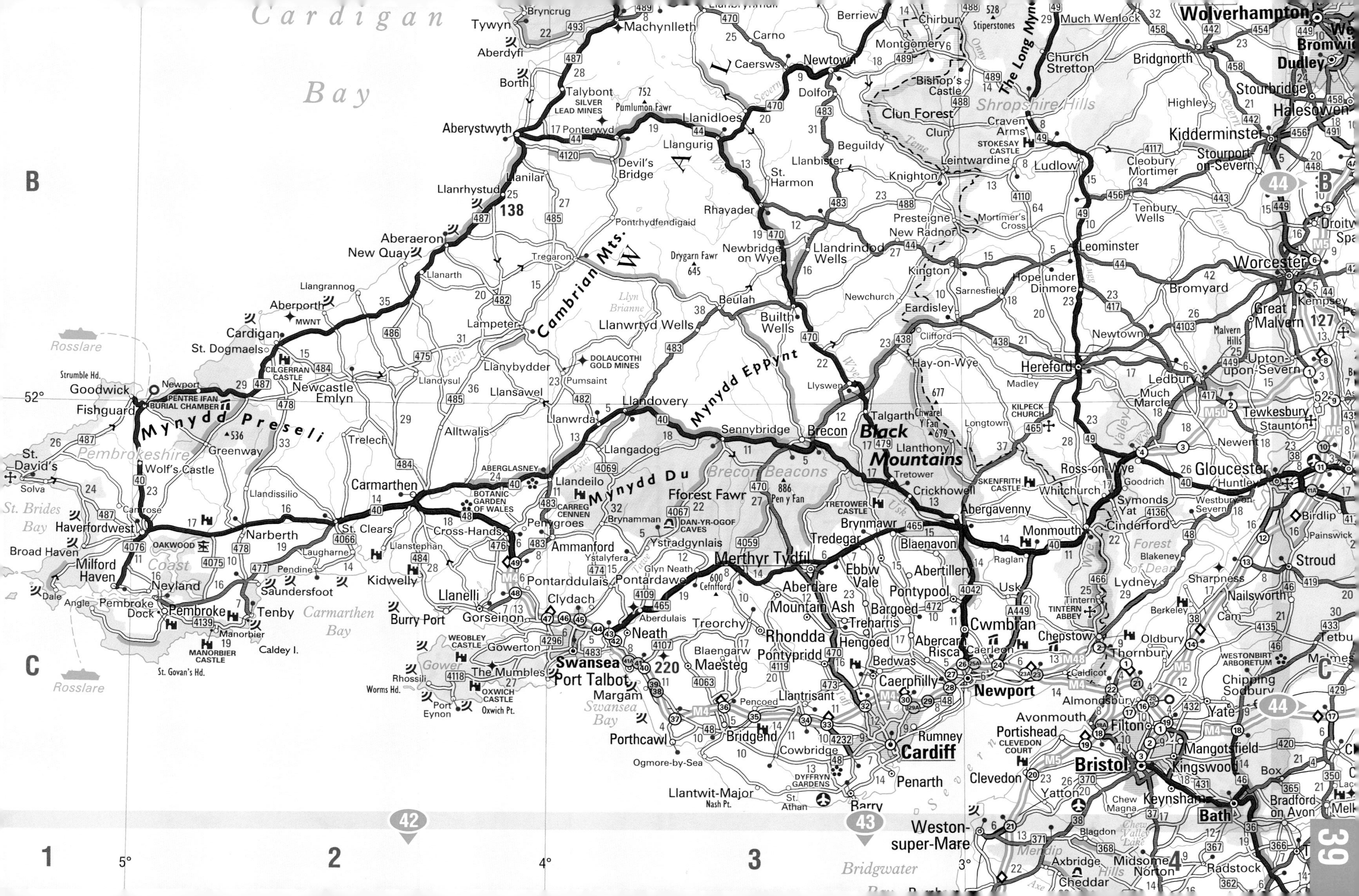

Cardigan Bay
Tywyn
Aberdyfi
Machynlleth
Borth
Talybont
Aberystwyth
Devil's Bridge
Llanidloes
Llangurig
Newtown
Caersws
Carno
Berriew
Montgomery
Bishop's Castle
Clun Forest
Shropshire Hills
The Long Mynd
Church Stretton
Much Wenlock
Bridgnorth
Wolverhampton
Dudley
Stourbridge
Halesowen
Kidderminster
Stourport-on-Severn
Cleobury Mortimer
Ludlow
Craven Arms
Leintwardine
Knighton
Presteigne
New Radnor
Tenbury Wells
Leominster
Worcester
Bromyard
Great Malvern
Llanrhystud
Aberaeron
New Quay
Cambrian Mts.
Rhayader
Llandrindod Wells
Newbridge on Wye
Kington
Hope under Dinmore
Llangrannog
Aberporth
Cardigan
St. Dogmaels
Newcastle Emlyn
Lampeter
Llanwrtyd Wells
Builth Wells
Hay-on-Wye
Hereford
Ledbury
Upton-upon-Severn
Tewkesbury
Goodwick
Fishguard
Newport
Mynydd Preseli
Mynydd Eppynt
Llandovery
Sennybridge
Brecon
Black Mountains
Talgarth
Ross-on-Wye
Gloucester
St. David's
Pembrokeshire
Wolf's Castle
Haverfordwest
Milford Haven
Pembroke Dock
Pembroke
Tenby
Saundersfoot
Narberth
St. Clears
Carmarthen
Llandeilo
Mynydd Du
Brecon Beacons
Fforest Fawr
Crickhowell
Abergavenny
Monmouth
Ammanford
Merthyr Tydfil
Tredegar
Blaenavon
Llanelli
Swansea
Port Talbot
Neath
Rhondda
Pontypridd
Caerphilly
Cwmbran
Newport
Chepstow
Cardiff
Penarth
Barry
Bridgend
Porthcawl
Llantwit-Major
Weston-super-Mare
Clevedon
Portishead
Bristol
Bath
Keynsham
Stroud
Cinderford
Lydney
Carmarthen Bay
Swansea Bay
Bridgwater
Rosslare
52°
5°
4°
3°

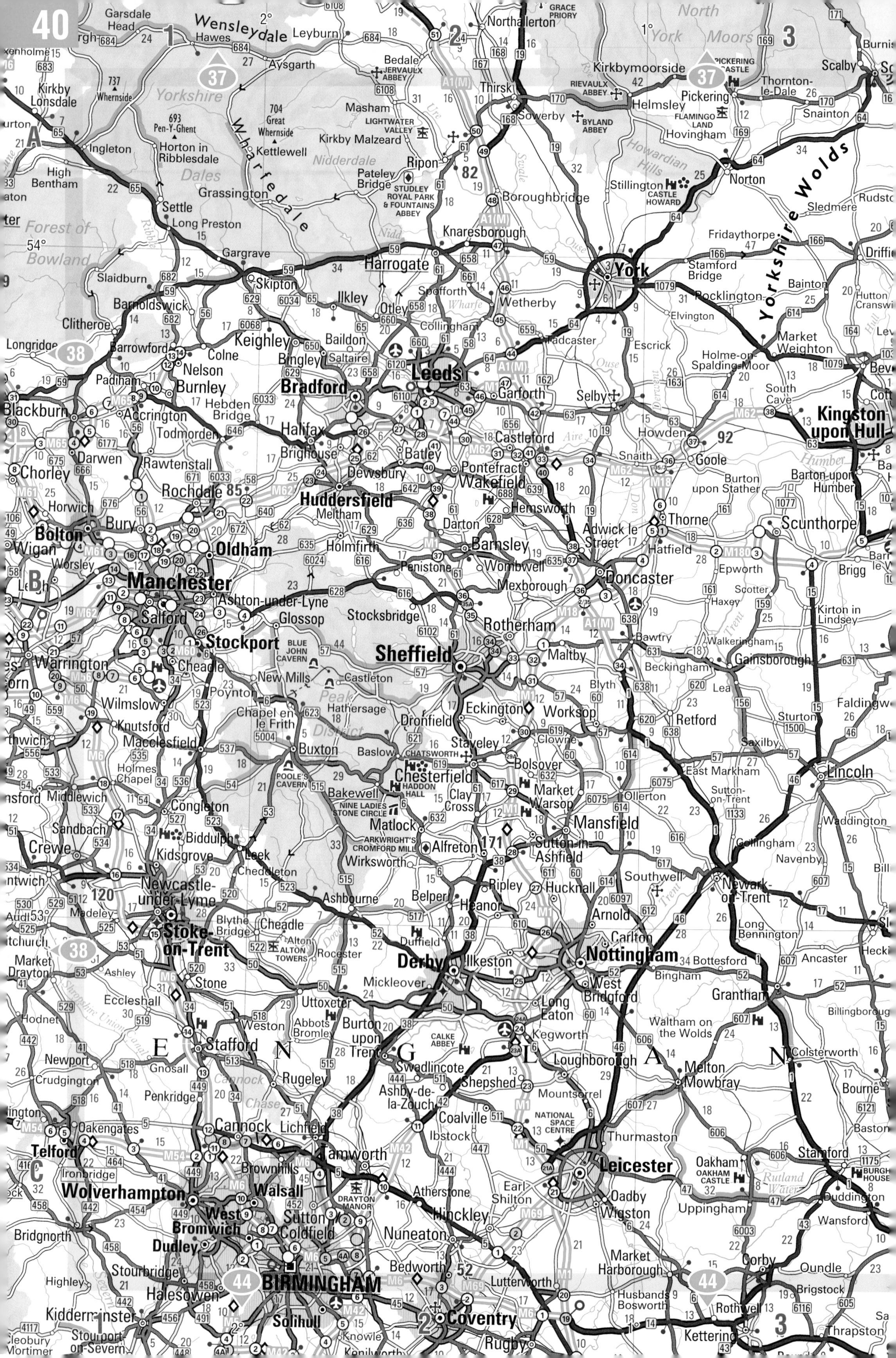
Wensleydale
Hawes
Leyburn
Northallerton
North York Moors
Kirkbymoorside
Pickering
Scalby
Thornton-le-Dale
Snainton
Helmsley
Thirsk
Sowerby
Bedale
Aysgarth
Kirkby Lonsdale
Yorkshire Dales
Whernside
Pen-Y-Ghent
Great Whernside
Horton in Ribblesdale
Kettlewell
Ingleton
High Bentham
Wharfedale
Nidderdale
Masham
Kirkby Malzeard
Ripon
Pateley Bridge
Hovingham
Howardian Hills
Stillington
Castle Howard
Norton
Yorkshire Wolds
Sledmere
Settle
Long Preston
Grassington
Forest of Bowland
Boroughbridge
Knaresborough
Harrogate
Gargrave
Skipton
Slaidburn
Barnoldswick
Ilkley
Otley
Spofforth
Wetherby
York
Stamford Bridge
Pocklington
Fridaythorpe
Bainton
Clitheroe
Keighley
Bingley
Baildon
Collingham
Tadcaster
Escrick
Elvington
Market Weighton
Holme-on-Spalding-Moor
Longridge
Barrowford
Colne
Nelson
Burnley
Padiham
Bradford
Leeds
Garforth
Selby
South Cave
Blackburn
Accrington
Hebden Bridge
Todmorden
Halifax
Castleford
Howden
Kingston upon Hull
Darwen
Rawtenstall
Brighouse
Batley
Pontefract
Snaith
Goole
Chorley
Rochdale
Dewsbury
Wakefield
Huddersfield
Hemsworth
Burton upon Stather
Barton-upon-Humber
Horwich
Bury
Meltham
Darton
Thorne
Scunthorpe
Bolton
Wigan
Oldham
Holmfirth
Barnsley
Adwick le Street
Hatfield
Worsley
Manchester
Penistone
Wombwell
Doncaster
Epworth
Brigg
Ashton-under-Lyne
Mexborough
Salford
Glossop
Stockbridge
Rotherham
Kirton in Lindsey
Stockport
Sheffield
Maltby
Bawtry
Beckingham
Gainsborough
Warrington
Cheadle
New Mills
Castleton
Blyth
Wilmslow
Poynton
Chapel en le Frith
Hathersage
Peak District
Dronfield
Eckington
Worksop
Retford
Knutsford
Buxton
Staveley
Clowne
Saxilby
Macclesfield
Baslow
Chatsworth
Chesterfield
Bolsover
East Markham
Lincoln
Holmes Chapel
Middlewich
Poole's Cavern
Bakewell
Clay Cross
Market Warsop
Ollerton
Sutton-on-Trent
Sandbach
Congleton
Matlock
Mansfield
Waddington
Crewe
Biddulph
Kidsgrove
Leek
Wirksworth
Alfreton
Sutton-in-Ashfield
Navenby
Cheddleton
Ripley
Hucknall
Southwell
Newark-on-Trent
Newcastle-under-Lyme
Ashbourne
Belper
Heanor
Arnold
Madeley
Stoke-on-Trent
Blythe Bridge
Cheadle
Alton Towers
Rocester
Duffield
Carlton
Long Bennington
Market Drayton
Ashley
Derby
Ilkeston
Nottingham
Bottesford
Ancaster
Stone
Mickleover
West Bridgford
Bingham
Grantham
Eccleshall
Uttoxeter
Long Eaton
Hodnet
Weston
Abbots Bromley
Burton upon Trent
Calke Abbey
Kegworth
Waltham on the Wolds
Newport
Stafford
Swadlincote
Loughborough
Melton Mowbray
Colsterworth
Gnosall
Rugeley
Shepshed
Bourne
Crudgington
Penkridge
Cannock Chase
Ashby-de-la-Zouch
Mountsorrel
Coalville
Ibstock
National Space Centre
Thurmaston
Oakengates
Cannock
Lichfield
Telford
Brownhills
Tamworth
Leicester
Oakham
Stamford
Rutland Water
Ironbridge
Wolverhampton
Walsall
Drayton Manor
Atherstone
Earl Shilton
Oadby
Uppingham
West Bromwich
Sutton Coldfield
Hinckley
Wigston
Wansford
Bridgnorth
Dudley
Nuneaton
Market Harborough
Corby
Oundle
Stourbridge
Bedworth
Lutterworth
Halesowen
Birmingham
Husbands Bosworth
Brigstock
Kidderminster
Solihull
Coventry
Rothwell
Stourport-on-Severn
Knowle
Rugby
Kettering
Thrapston
ENGLAND

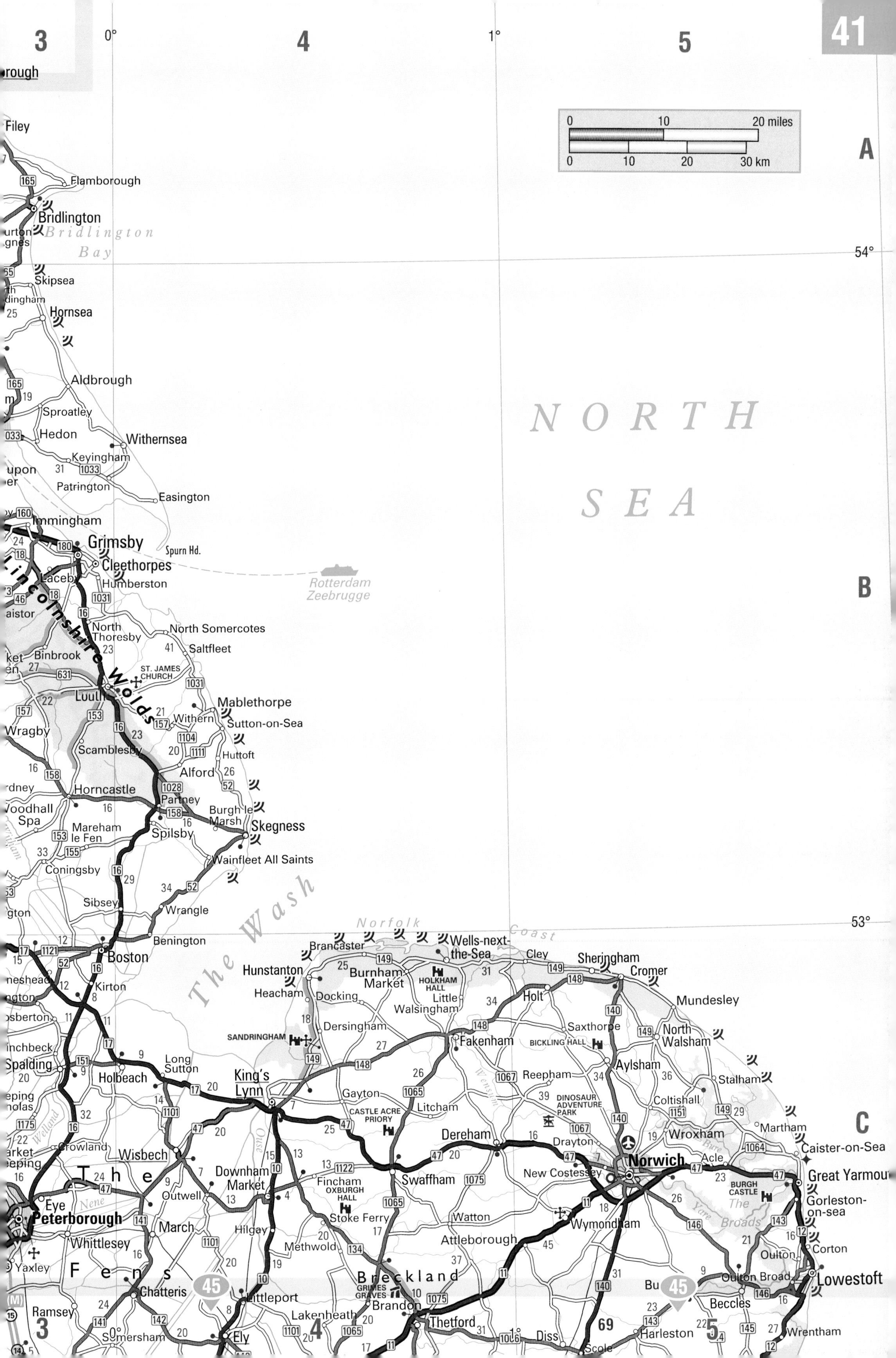

0  10  20 miles

0  10  20  30 km

**A**

Filey

165 Flamborough

Bridlington

urton
gnes

*Bridlington
Bay*

**54°**

55 Skipsea

dingham
25 Hornsea

Aldbrough

165
m  19 Sproatley

*N O R T H*

033 Hedon  Withernsea

upon   Keyingham
er     31 1033  **B**

Patrington  Easington

*S E A*

160
mmingham

24 180 **Grimsby**  Spurn Hd.

18     Laceby **Cleethorpes**

3 46        Humberston  *Rotterdam*
aistor  18                  *Zeebrugge*

16  1031

North  North Somercotes
ket   Thoresby
en  Binbrook  27  Saltfleet
     631        41
157  22  ST. JAMES
              CHURCH  1031

153 **Louth**  Mablethorpe

Wragby  21  Withern  Sutton-on-Sea
     16  157  1104
     23  111
Scamblesby  20  Huttoft
rdney  16  158  Alford  26
                    1028  52
Woodhall  Horncastle  Partney
Spa         158  Burgh le
Mareham  16  Marsh
153 le Fen  Spilsby  **Skegness**
33  155

Coningsby  16  29  Wainfleet All Saints

**53°**
Sibsey  34  52
ton  Wrangle

12  Benington  *Norfolk*  *Coast*
17 1121        *The*  Brancaster
15           **Boston**  Wells-next-  Cley  Sheringham
52  16              the-Sea  149  149  **Cromer**
nesnead  Hunstanton  25  Burnham  31  148
ing  12  Kirton  Market  HOLKHAM  Holt  Mundesley
sberton  11  8  Heacham  Docking  HALL  34  140
inchbeck  11  Little  148  Saxthorpe  North
osberton        Walsingham  148  149  Walsham
                18  Dersingham  BICKLING HALL
**Spalding**  151  9  SANDRINGHAM  27  Fakenham  Aylsham
20  9  Holbeach  Long  149  148  26  1067  Reepham  34  Coltishall
                Sutton  King's  Gayton  1065  39  1151  149  29
eping  16  14  17  20  Lynn  7  Litcham  DINOSAUR  1067  Wroxham  Martham  **C**
nolas  1101  47  20  CASTLE ACRE  ADVENTURE  140  19  Acle  1064  Caister-on-Sea
1175  32  PRIORY  25  47  PARK  47  **Norwich**  23  47  Great Yarmou
22  Crowland  Wisbech  15  13  Dereham  47  20  New Costessey  BURGH  Gorleston-
rket  16  Downham  13  1122  Swaffham  1075  CASTLE  on-sea
eping  47  Market  10  Fincham  1065  Watton  11  18  26  *The*  143
Eye  Nene  141  Outwell  4  OXBURGH  Stoke Ferry  17  Wymondham  146  *Broads*  12
**Peterborough**  March  13  HALL  Attleborough  45  21  Corton
Whittlesey  1101  Hilgay  Methwold  134  37  31  Bu  45  Oulton
Yaxley  *F*  *e*  *n*  *s*  20  19  *B*  *r*  *e*  *c*  *k*  *l*  *a*  *n*  *d*  11  140  Oulton Broad  **Lowestoft**
14  Ramsey  24  Chatteris  10  Littleport  GRIMES  Brandon  1075  **69**  23  143  Beccles  145  16
141  142  Somersham  20  Lakenheath  GRAVES  20  Thetford  31  10  6  Diss  Harleston  22  Wrentham
M  3  50°  Ely  4  1101  2u  1065  1  Scole  5  12

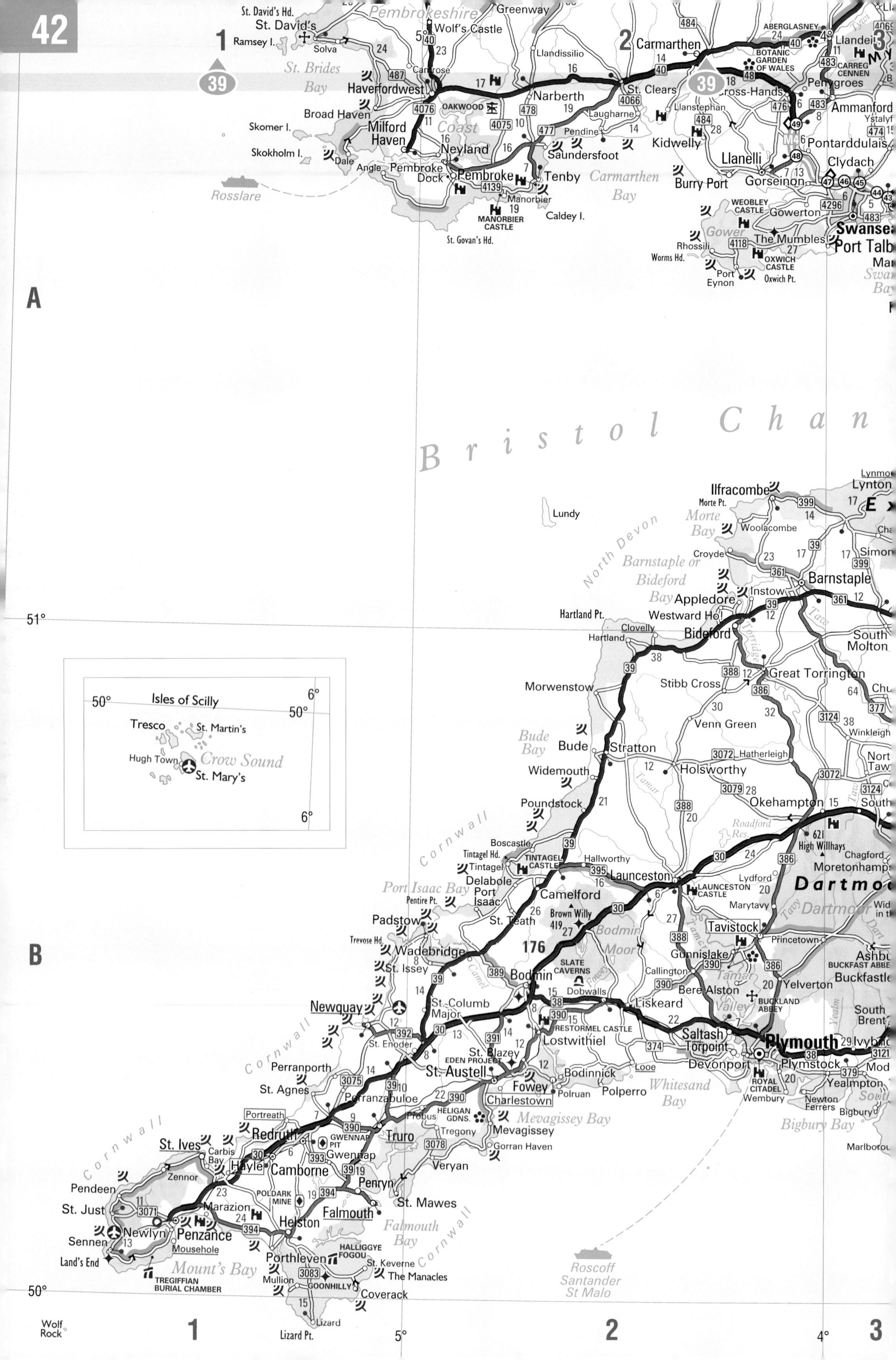
Pembrokeshire
St. David's Hd.
St. David's
Ramsey I.
Solva
Wolf's Castle
Greenway
St. Brides Bay
Haverfordwest
Broad Haven
Skomer I.
Skokholm I.
Dale
Milford Haven
Angle
Pembroke Dock
Neyland
Pembroke
Coast
OAKWOOD
Narberth
Llandissilio
St. Clears
Laugharne
Pendine
Saundersfoot
Tenby
Manorbier
MANORBIER CASTLE
St. Govan's Hd.
Caldey I.
Carmarthen Bay
Rosslare
Carmarthen
Llanstephan
Kidwelly
Burry Port
Llanelli
Gorseinon
Cross-Hands
BOTANIC GARDEN OF WALES
ABERGLASNEY
Llandeilo
CARREG CENNEN
Penygroes
Ammanford
Ystalyfera
Pontarddulais
Clydach
WEOBLEY CASTLE
Gower
Gowerton
The Mumbles
Swansea
Port Talbot
Rhossili
Worms Hd.
Port Eynon
OXWICH CASTLE
Oxwich Pt.
Bristol Channel
Lundy
North Devon
Ilfracombe
Morte Pt.
Morte Bay
Woolacombe
Croyde
Barnstaple or Bideford Bay
Barnstaple
Lynmouth
Lynton
Instow
Appledore
Westward Ho!
Hartland Pt.
Hartland
Clovelly
Bideford
South Molton
Great Torrington
Stibb Cross
Morwenstow
Venn Green
Winkleigh
Bude Bay
Bude
Stratton
Hatherleigh
Widemouth
Holsworthy
Poundstock
Okehampton
Roadford Res.
High Willhays
Chagford
Moretonhampstead
Boscastle
Tintagel Hd.
Tintagel
TINTAGEL CASTLE
Hallworthy
Launceston
LAUNCESTON CASTLE
Lydford
Marytavy
Dartmoor
Delabole
Port Isaac Bay
Port Isaac
Pentire Pt.
Camelford
Brown Willy 419
Bodmin Moor
Padstow
St. Teath
Tavistock
Princetown
Trevose Hd.
Wadebridge
SLATE CAVERNS
Gunnislake
St. Issey
Bodmin
Callington
Tamar Valley
BUCKFAST ABBEY
Buckfastleigh
Yelverton
Bere Alston
Dobwalls
Newquay
St. Columb Major
Liskeard
BUCKLAND ABBEY
South Brent
RESTORMEL CASTLE
Lostwithiel
Saltash
Torpoint
Plymouth
Ivybridge
St. Enoder
St. Blazey
EDEN PROJECT
Perranporth
St. Austell
Bodinnick
Looe
Plymstock
Devonport
Yealmpton
Fowey
Polruan
Polperro
Whitesand Bay
ROYAL CITADEL
Wembury
Newton Ferrers
Bigbury
St. Agnes
Charlestown
Perranzabuloe
Portreath
Probus
HELIGAN GDNS.
Mevagissey Bay
Mevagissey
Bigbury Bay
Redruth
GWENNAP PIT
Truro
Tregony
Gorran Haven
Marlborough
St. Ives
Carbis Bay
Gwennap
Hayle
Camborne
Veryan
Zennor
Penryn
Pendeen
POLDARK MINE
St. Mawes
St. Just
Marazion
Falmouth
Newlyn
Penzance
Helston
Falmouth Bay
Sennen
Mousehole
Porthleven
HALLIGGYE FOGOU
Land's End
Mount's Bay
St. Keverne
The Manacles
TREGIFFIAN BURIAL CHAMBER
Mullion
GOONHILLY
Coverack
Roscoff
Santander
St Malo
Lizard
Lizard Pt.
Wolf Rock
Cornwall
Isles of Scilly
Tresco
St. Martin's
Hugh Town
Crow Sound
St. Mary's
50°
6°
51°
5°
4°
A
B
1
2
3

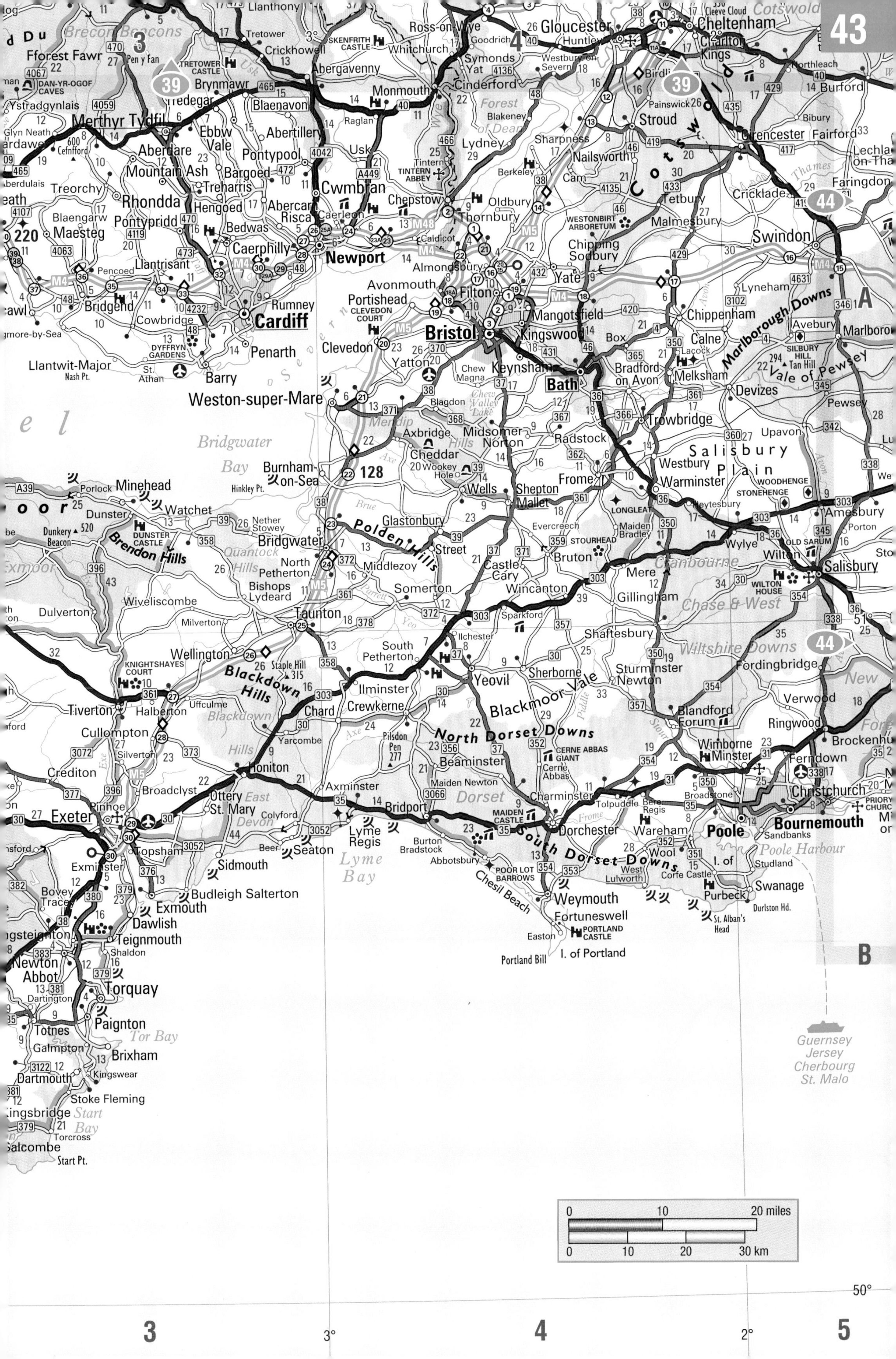
Brecon Beacons
Fforest Fawr
Pen y Fan
Tretower
Crickhowell
TRETOWER CASTLE
Brynmawr
Tredegar
Blaenavon
DAN-YR-OGOF CAVES
Ystradgynlais
Merthyr Tydfil
Glyn Neath
Cefnfford
Aberdare
Mountain Ash
Ebbw Vale
Abertillery
Pontypool
Bargoed
Treharris
Hengoed
Treorchy
Rhondda
Blaengarw
Maesteg
Pontypridd
Abercarn
Risca
Bedwas
Caerphilly
Llantrisant
Pencoed
Bridgend
Cowbridge
Cardiff
Rumney
Penarth
DYFFRYN GARDENS
Llantwit-Major
Nash Pt.
St. Athan
Barry
Llanthony
Abergavenny
SKENFRITH CASTLE
Ross-on-Wye
Whitchurch
Goodrich
Symonds Yat
Monmouth
Raglan
Usk
Cwmbran
Caerleon
Newport
Chepstow
TINTERN ABBEY
Tintern
Forest of Dean
Cinderford
Blakeney
Lydney
Gloucester
Huntley
Westbury-on-Severn
Cheltenham
Cleeve Cloud
Charlton Kings
Northleach
Burford
Painswick
Birdlip
Stroud
Bibury
Cirencester
Fairford
Lechlade-on-Thames
Faringdon
Cotswolds
Sharpness
Berkeley
Nailsworth
Cam
Tetbury
Cricklade
Thames
Oldbury
Thornbury
WESTONBIRT ARBORETUM
Malmesbury
Swindon
Caldicot
Almondsbury
Chipping Sodbury
Yate
Lyneham
Avonmouth
Portishead
CLEVEDON COURT
Filton
Bristol
Mangotsfield
Kingswood
Chippenham
Marlborough Downs
Avebury
Marlborough
SILBURY HILL
Tan Hill
Vale of Pewsey
Clevedon
Yatton
Chew Magna
Keynsham
Bath
Box
Bradford on Avon
Lacock
Calne
Melksham
Devizes
Pewsey
Weston-super-Mare
Blagdon
Chew Valley Lake
Mendip Hills
Axbridge
Cheddar
Midsomer Norton
Radstock
Trowbridge
Upavon
Salisbury Plain
Bridgwater Bay
Burnham-on-Sea
Wookey Hole
Wells
Shepton Mallet
Frome
Westbury
Warminster
WOODHENGE
STONEHENGE
Heytesbury
Amesbury
Porton
Hinkley Pt.
Porlock
Minehead
Dunster
Watchet
Dunkery Beacon
DUNSTER CASTLE
Brendon Hills
Exmoor
Nether Stowey
Quantock Hills
Bridgwater
Glastonbury
Polden Hills
Street
Evercreech
LONGLEAT
Maiden Bradley
STOURHEAD
Bruton
Mere
Wylye
Wilton
OLD SARUM
Salisbury
North Petherton
Middlezoy
Castle Cary
Wincanton
Cranborne Chase & West Wiltshire Downs
Gillingham
WILTON HOUSE
Dulverton
Wiveliscombe
Bishops Lydeard
Somerton
Milverton
Taunton
Sparkford
Ilchester
Shaftesbury
Wellington
Staple Hill
Blackdown Hills
South Petherton
Yeovil
Sherborne
Sturminster Newton
Fordingbridge
KNIGHTSHAYES COURT
Uffculme
Ilminster
Crewkerne
Chard
Blackmoor Vale
Verwood
New Forest
Tiverton
Halberton
Yarcombe
Pilsdon Pen
North Dorset Downs
Blandford Forum
Ringwood
Cullompton
Silverton
Beaminster
CERNE ABBAS GIANT
Cerne Abbas
Wimborne Minster
Ferndown
Brockenhurst
Crediton
Honiton
Axminster
Maiden Newton
Dorset
Christchurch
Broadclyst
Ottery St. Mary
East Devon
Colyford
Bridport
MAIDEN CASTLE
Charminster
Tolpuddle
Bere Regis
Broadstone
PRIORY CHURCH
Exeter
Pinhoe
Topsham
Beer
Seaton
Lyme Regis
Lyme Bay
Burton Bradstock
Abbotsbury
POOR LOT BARROWS
Dorchester
South Dorset Downs
Wareham
Poole
Bournemouth
Sandbanks
Poole Harbour
Exminster
Sidmouth
Chesil Beach
Wool
West Lulworth
I. of Purbeck
Corfe Castle
Studland
Swanage
Bovey Tracey
Budleigh Salterton
Exmouth
Weymouth
Fortuneswell
Durlston Hd.
St. Alban's Head
Dawlish
Teignmouth
Shaldon
Easton
PORTLAND CASTLE
Portland Bill
I. of Portland
Newton Abbot
Torquay
Dartington
Paignton
Tor Bay
Totnes
Galmpton
Brixham
Dartmouth
Kingswear
Stoke Fleming
Kingsbridge
Start Bay
Torcross
Salcombe
Start Pt.
Guernsey
Jersey
Cherbourg
St. Malo
0 10 20 miles
0 10 20 30 km
50°
3°
2°
3
4
5
A
B

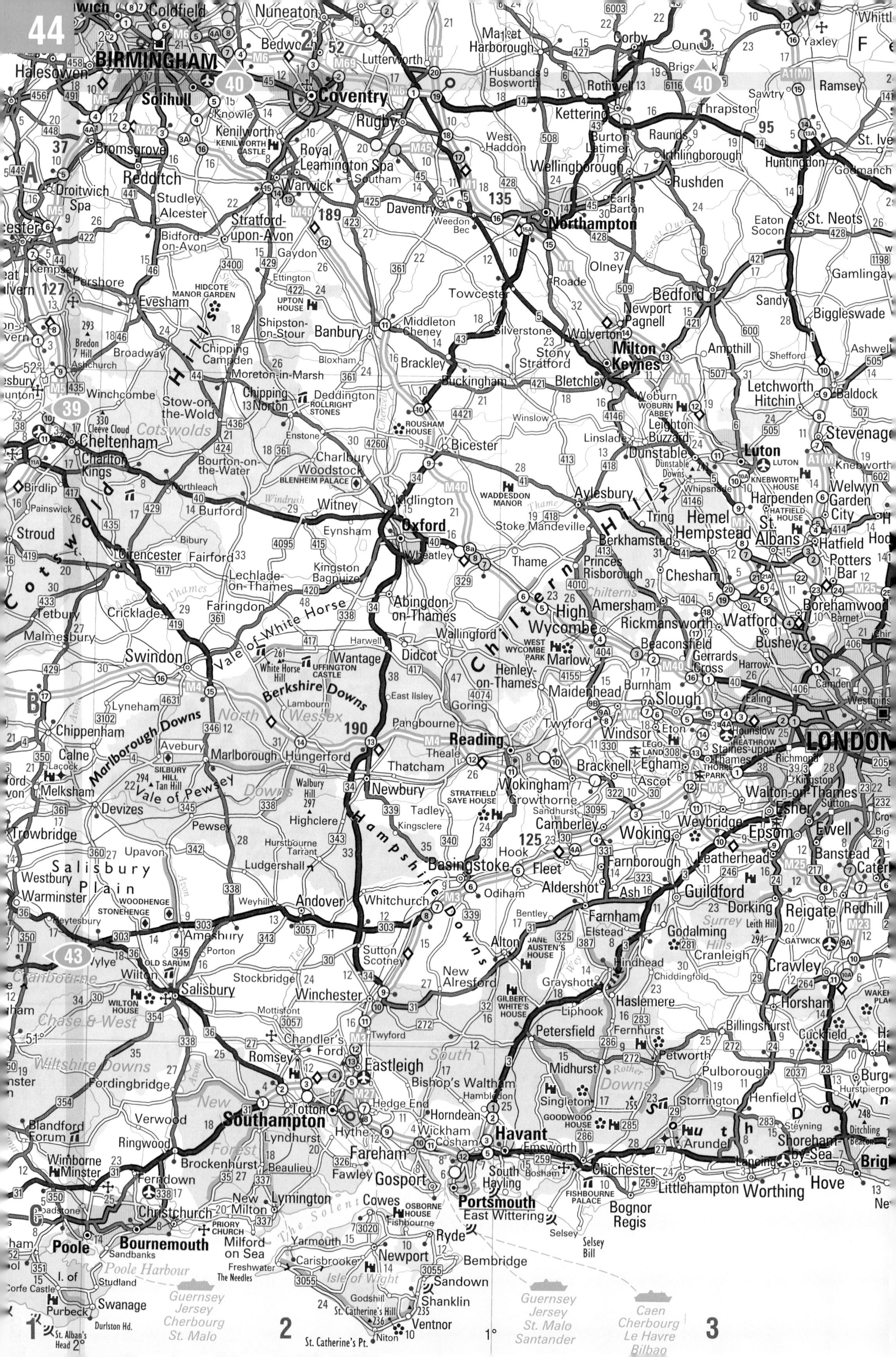

Coldfield
Nuneaton
Market Harborough
Corby
Oundle
Yaxley
BIRMINGHAM
Halesowen
Solihull
Coventry
Lutterworth
Husbands Bosworth
Rothwell
Sawtry
Ramsey
Knowle
Kenilworth
KENILWORTH CASTLE
Rugby
Kettering
Thrapston
Bromsgrove
Royal Leamington Spa
Southam
West Haddon
Burton Latimer
Raunds
Irthlingborough
Huntingdon
Redditch
Warwick
Wellingborough
Rushden
Droitwich Spa
Studley
Alcester
Daventry
Weedon Bec
Northampton
Earls Barton
Eaton Socon
St. Neots
Stratford-upon-Avon
Bidford-on-Avon
Gaydon
Olney
Roade
Kempsey
Pershore
Ettington
HIDCOTE MANOR GARDEN
UPTON HOUSE
Towcester
Bedford
Gamlingay
Evesham
Shipston-on-Stour
Banbury
Middleton Cheney
Newport Pagnell
Sandy
Biggleswade
Bredon Hill
Ashchurch
Broadway
Chipping Campden
Silverstone
Stony Stratford
Wolverton
Milton Keynes
Ampthill
Shefford
Ashwell
Bloxham
Brackley
Buckingham
Bletchley
Moreton-in-Marsh
Winchcombe
Stow-on-the-Wold
Chipping Norton
Deddington
ROLLRIGHT STONES
Woburn
WOBURN ABBEY
Letchworth
Hitchin
Baldock
Cleeve Cloud
Cheltenham
Cotswolds
Enstone
ROUSHAM HOUSE
Bicester
Winslow
Leighton Buzzard
Linslade
Stevenage
Charlton Kings
Bourton-on-the-Water
Charlbury
Woodstock
BLENHEIM PALACE
Dunstable
Dunstable Downs
Luton
KNEBWORTH HOUSE
Knebworth
Birdlip
Northleach
Kidlington
WADDESDON MANOR
Aylesbury
Whipsnade
Harpenden
Welwyn Garden City
Painswick
Burford
Witney
Oxford
Stoke Mandeville
Tring
Hemel Hempstead
St. Albans
HATFIELD HOUSE
Hatfield
Stroud
Bibury
Eynsham
Wheatley
Berkhamsted
Cirencester
Fairford
Lechlade-on-Thames
Kingston Bagpuize
Thame
Princes Risborough
Chesham
Potters Bar
Tetbury
Cricklade
Faringdon
Abingdon-on-Thames
Chilterns
Amersham
Borehamwood
Barnet
Malmesbury
Vale of White Horse
High Wycombe
Rickmansworth
Watford
Harwell
Wallingford
WEST WYCOMBE PARK
Beaconsfield
Bushey
Swindon
Wantage
White Horse Hill
UFFINGTON CASTLE
Didcot
Marlow
Gerrards Cross
Harrow
Camden
Henley-on-Thames
Maidenhead
Burnham
Slough
Ealing
Westminster
Berkshire Downs
Lambourn
East Ilsley
Goring
Lyneham
North Wessex
Pangbourne
Twyford
Windsor
Eton
Hounslow
HEATHROW
Chippenham
Marlborough Downs
Reading
Theale
LEGOLAND
Staines-upon-Thames
LONDON
Calne
Lacock
Avebury
Marlborough
Hungerford
Thatcham
Bracknell
Egham
Richmond
SILBURY HILL
Tan Hill
Vale of Pewsey
Walbury Hill
Newbury
Wokingham
Ascot
THORPE PARK
Kingston
Melksham
Downs
STRATFIELD SAYE HOUSE
Crowthorne
Sandhurst
Walton-on-Thames
Esher
Sutton
Devizes
Pewsey
Highclere
Tadley
Kingsclere
Camberley
Woking
Weybridge
Epsom
Ewell
Trowbridge
Upavon
Hurstbourne Tarrant
Hampshire Downs
Hook
Farnborough
Leatherhead
Banstead
Salisbury Plain
Westbury
Ludgershall
Basingstoke
Fleet
Warminster
WOODHENGE
STONEHENGE
Weyhill
Andover
Whitchurch
Odiham
Aldershot
Ash
Guildford
Dorking
Reigate
Redhill
Heytesbury
Amesbury
Bentley
Farnham
Elstead
Surrey Hills
Leith Hill
Godalming
GATWICK
Porton
Sutton Scotney
Alton
JANE AUSTEN'S HOUSE
Cranleigh
Wylye
Wilton
OLD SARUM
Stockbridge
Hindhead
Chiddingfold
Crawley
Cranborne
New Alresford
Grayshott
Salisbury
WILTON HOUSE
Winchester
GILBERT WHITE'S HOUSE
Haslemere
Horsham
Cranborne Chase & West
Mottisfont
Twyford
Liphook
Billingshurst
Cuckfield
Chandler's Ford
Petersfield
Fernhurst
Petworth
Romsey
Eastleigh
Bishop's Waltham
Midhurst
Pulborough
Burgess Hill
Wiltshire Downs
Fordingbridge
Hambledon
Singleton
Storrington
Henfield
Hurstpierpoint
New Forest
Totton
Hedge End
Horndean
GOODWOOD HOUSE
South Downs
Steyning
Ditchling Beacon
Verwood
Southampton
Hythe
Wickham
Havant
Emsworth
Arundel
Shoreham-by-Sea
Brighton
Blandford Forum
Ringwood
Lyndhurst
Fareham
Cosham
Chichester
Lancing
Wimborne Minster
Brockenhurst
Beaulieu
Fawley
Gosport
South Hayling
Bosham
Littlehampton
Worthing
Hove
Ferndown
Portsmouth
Newhaven
New Milton
Lymington
Cowes
OSBORNE HOUSE
Fishbourne
East Wittering
FISHBOURNE PALACE
Bognor Regis
Christchurch
PRIORY CHURCH
Milford on Sea
Selsey
Poole
Bournemouth
Sandbanks
Yarmouth
Ryde
Selsey Bill
Poole Harbour
Freshwater
The Needles
Carisbrooke
Newport
Bembridge
I. of Purbeck
Studland
Corfe Castle
Isle of Wight
Sandown
Swanage
Godshill
Shanklin
Guernsey Jersey Cherbourg St. Malo
Guernsey Jersey St. Malo Santander
Caen Cherbourg Le Havre Bilbao
St. Catherine's Hill
Durlston Hd.
St. Alban's Head
Ventnor
St. Catherine's Pt.
Niton
The Solent

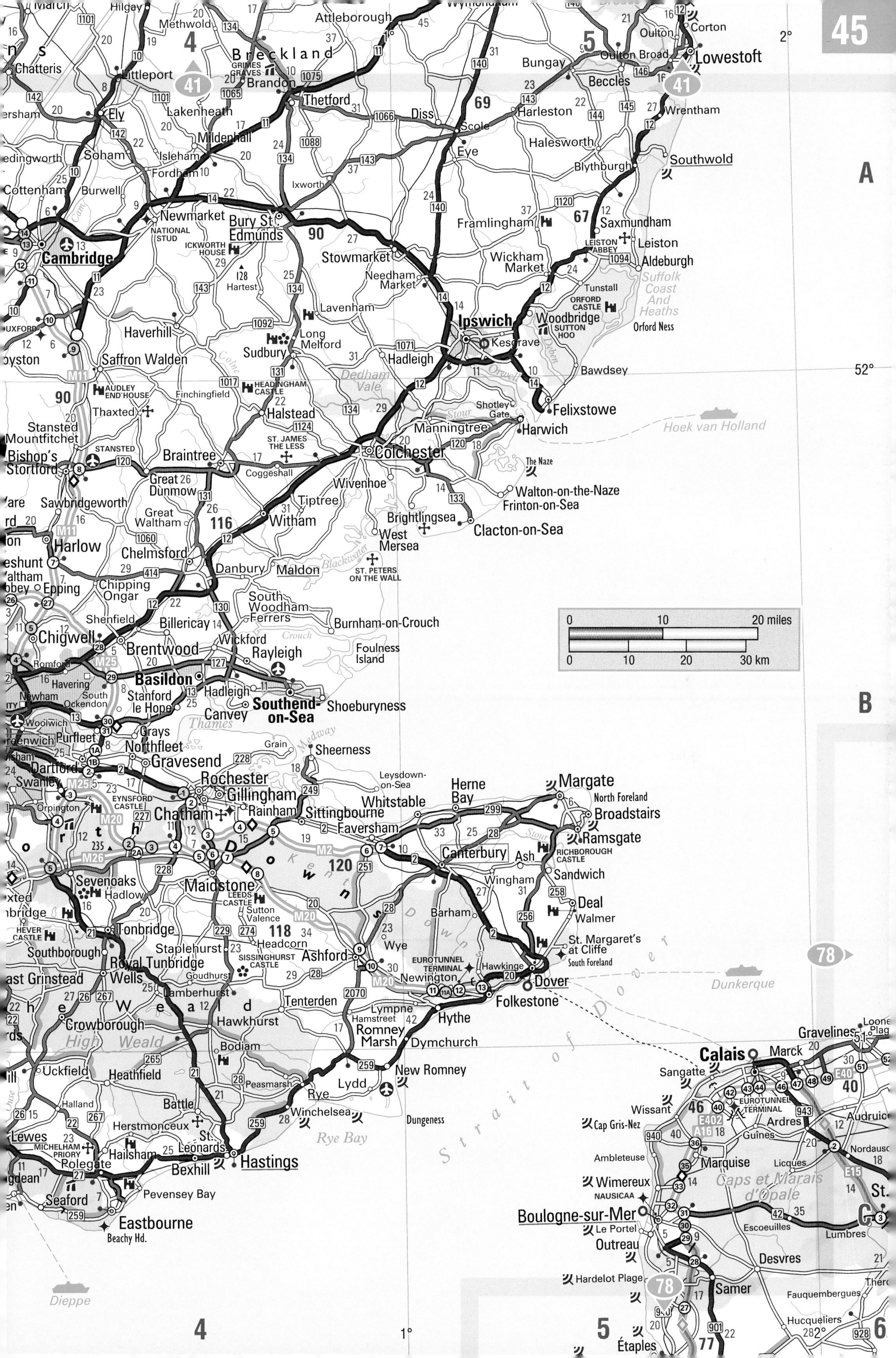
Hilgay
Methwold
Attleborough
Breckland
GRIMES GRAVES
Brandon
Thetford
Littleport
Chatteris
Ely
Lakenheath
Mildenhall
Isleham
Soham
Fordham
Cottenham
Burwell
Newmarket
NATIONAL STUD
Cambridge
Bury St. Edmunds
ICKWORTH HOUSE
Hartest
Ixworth
Diss
Scole
Eye
Bungay
Harleston
Halesworth
Beccles
Oulton
Oulton Broad
Corton
Lowestoft
Wrentham
Southwold
Blythburgh
Saxmundham
LEISTON ABBEY
Leiston
Aldeburgh
Framlingham
Wickham Market
Tunstall
ORFORD CASTLE
Suffolk Coast And Heaths
Orford Ness
Woodbridge
SUTTON HOO
Stowmarket
Needham Market
Lavenham
Long Melford
Sudbury
Hadleigh
Ipswich
Kesgrave
Deben
Orwell
Bawdsey
Felixstowe
Harwich
Hoek van Holland
Shotley Gate
Manningtree
Stour
Dedham Vale
Haverhill
DUXFORD
Royston
Saffron Walden
AUDLEY END HOUSE
Thaxted
Finchingfield
HEADINGHAM CASTLE
Halstead
Colne
Stansted Mountfitchet
STANSTED
Bishop's Stortford
Braintree
ST. JAMES THE LESS
Coggeshall
Colchester
Wivenhoe
The Naze
Walton-on-the-Naze
Frinton-on-Sea
Clacton-on-Sea
Brightlingsea
West Mersea
Tiptree
Great Dunmow
Sawbridgeworth
Great Waltham
Witham
Harlow
Chelmsford
Cheshunt
Epping
Chipping Ongar
Danbury
Maldon
Blackwater
ST. PETERS ON THE WALL
South Woodham Ferrers
Burnham-on-Crouch
Crouch
Shenfield
Billericay
Wickford
Rayleigh
Foulness Island
Chigwell
Brentwood
Romford
Havering
Basildon
Hadleigh
Southend-on-Sea
Shoeburyness
Newham
South Ockendon
Stanford le Hope
Canvey
Thames
Woolwich
Greenwich
Purfleet
Grays
Northfleet
Dartford
Gravesend
Grain
Medway
Sheerness
Swanley
Orpington
EYNSFORD CASTLE
Rochester
Gillingham
Chatham
Rainham
Sittingbourne
Leysdown-on-Sea
Whitstable
Herne Bay
Margate
North Foreland
Broadstairs
Ramsgate
Faversham
Canterbury
RICHBOROUGH CASTLE
Ash
Sandwich
Wingham
North Downs
Kent Downs
Sevenoaks
Hadlow
Maidstone
LEEDS CASTLE
Sutton Valence
Barham
Deal
Walmer
St. Margaret's at Cliffe
South Foreland
Tonbridge
HEVER CASTLE
Southborough
Royal Tunbridge Wells
Staplehurst
Headcorn
SISSINGHURST CASTLE
Ashford
Wye
EUROTUNNEL TERMINAL
Hawkinge
Newington
Dover
Folkestone
Dunkerque
East Grinstead
Goudhurst
Lamberhurst
Weald
Tenterden
Hawkhurst
Crowborough
High Weald
Lympne
Hamstreet
Hythe
Romney Marsh
Dymchurch
Strait of Dover
Bodiam
Uckfield
Heathfield
Peasmarsh
Lydd
New Romney
Rye
Battle
Halland
Winchelsea
Dungeness
Rye Bay
Herstmonceux
St. Leonards
Lewes
MICHELHAM PRIORY
Hailsham
Polegate
Bexhill
Hastings
Newhaven
Seaford
Pevensey Bay
Eastbourne
Beachy Hd.
Dieppe
Calais
Gravelines
Marck
Sangatte
EUROTUNNEL TERMINAL
Wissant
Cap Gris-Nez
Ardres
Audruicq
Guînes
Nordausques
Ambleteuse
Marquise
Licques
Caps et Marais d'Opale
Wimereux
NAUSICAA
Boulogne-sur-Mer
Le Portel
Outreau
Escoeuilles
Lumbres
Desvres
Hardelot Plage
Samer
Fauquembergues
Hucqueliers
Étaples
0 10 20 miles
0 10 20 30 km
52°
2°
1°
A
B
4
5
6
41
78
77

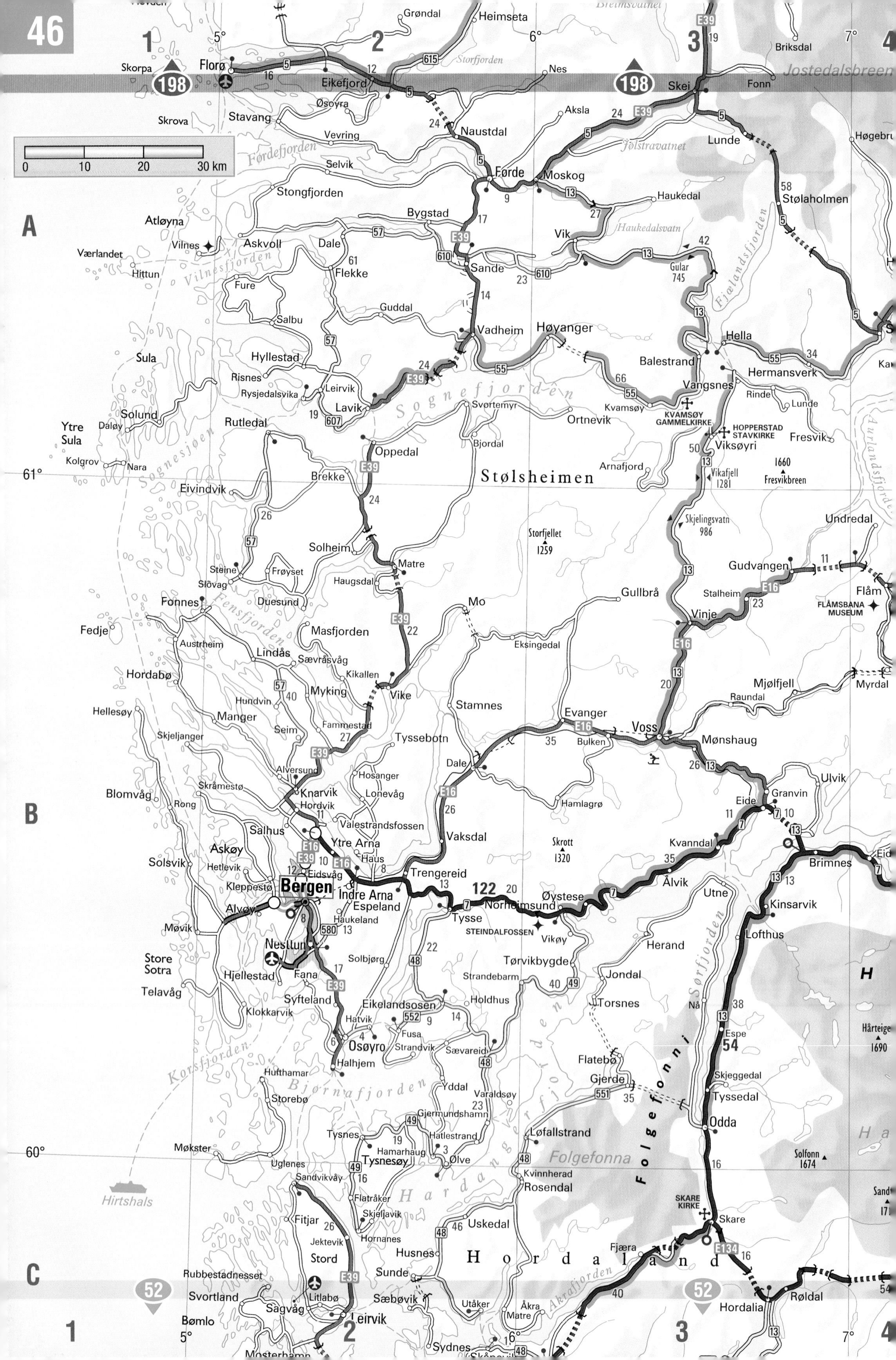
Florø
Skorpa
198
Eikefjord
Grøndal
Heimseta
Storfjorden
Nes
Skei
Fonn
Jostedalsbreen
Briksdal
Øsoyra
Stavang
Skrova
Naustdal
Aksla
Lunde
Høgebru
0
10
20
30 km
Vevring
Førdefjorden
Jølstravatnet
Selvik
Førde
Moskog
Haukedal
Stongfjorden
Stølaholmen
Bygstad
Haukedalsvatn
Atløyna
Askvoll
Dale
Vik
Værlandet
Vilnes
Vilnesfjorden
Hittun
Sande
Gular
745
Flekke
Fjælandsfjorden
Fure
Guddal
Salbu
Vadheim
Høyanger
Hella
Sula
Hyllestad
Balestrand
Hermansverk
Risnes
Rysjedalsvika
Leirvik
Vangsnes
Rinde
Lunde
Lavik
Sognefjorden
Svortemyr
Ortnevik
Kvamsøy
KVAMSØY GAMMELKIRKE
Solund
Ytre Sula
Daløy
Rutledal
HOPPERSTAD STAVKIRKE
Viksøyri
Fresvik
Bjordal
Oppedal
Aurlandsfjorden
Kolgrov
Nara
Sognesjøen
Arnafjord
1660
Fresvikbreen
61°
Brekke
Stølsheimen
Vikafjell
1281
Eivindvik
Skjelingsvatn
986
Undredal
Storfjellet
1259
Solheim
Gudvangen
Steine
Frøyset
Matre
Slövag
Haugsdal
Stalheim
Flåm
FLÅMSBANA MUSEUM
Fonnes
Duesund
Fensfjorden
Mo
Gullbrå
Vinje
Fedje
Austrheim
Masfjorden
Lindås
Eksingedal
Sævråsvåg
Hordabø
Kikallen
Myking
Vike
Mjølfjell
Myrdal
Raundal
Hundvin
Hellesøy
Manger
Seim
Stamnes
Evanger
Fammestad
Skjeljanger
Voss
Bulken
Mønshaug
Tyssebotn
Alversund
Hosanger
Dale
Skråmestø
Lonevåg
Knarvik
Ulvik
Granvin
Blomvåg
Rong
Hordvik
Hamlagrø
Eide
Salhus
Vålestrandsfossen
Vaksdal
Ytre Arna
Askøy
Skrott
1320
Kvanndal
Brimnes
Solsvik
Hetlevik
Haus
Eidsvåg
Trengereid
Ålvik
Kleppestø
Bergen
Indre Arna
Espeland
Øystese
Utne
Alvøy
Norheimsund
Tysse
Kinsarvik
Haukeland
STEINDALFOSSEN
Vikøy
Møvik
Lofthus
Nesttun
Herand
Store Sotra
Solbjørg
Tørvikbygde
Hjellestad
Fana
Strandebarm
Jondal
Telavåg
Syfteland
Holdhus
Torsnes
Klokkarvik
Eikelandsosen
Nå
Hatvik
Fusa
Espe
Hårteigen
1690
Osøyro
Strandvik
Sævareid
Sørfjorden
Korsfjorden
Halhjem
Flatebø
Hufthamar
Bjørnafjorden
Yddal
Gjerde
Skjeggedal
Folgefonni
Storebø
Varaldsøy
Tyssedal
Gjermundshamn
Odda
Tysnes
Hatlestrand
Løfallstrand
60°
Møkster
Hamarhaug
Tysnesøy
Ølve
Folgefonna
Solfonn
1674
Uglenes
Hardangerfjorden
Sandvikvåg
Kvinnherad
Rosendal
Hirtshals
Flatråker
Skjeljavik
SKARE KIRKE
Skare
Fitjar
Uskedal
Jektevik
Hornanes
Stord
Husnes
Hordaland
Fjæra
Rubbestadnesset
Sunde
Akrafjorden
Svortland
Litlabø
Sæbøvik
52
Røldal
Sagvåg
Utåker
Åkra
Matre
Hordalia
Bømlo
Leirvik
Sydnes
Mosterhamn
5°
6°
7°
1
2
3
4
A
B
C

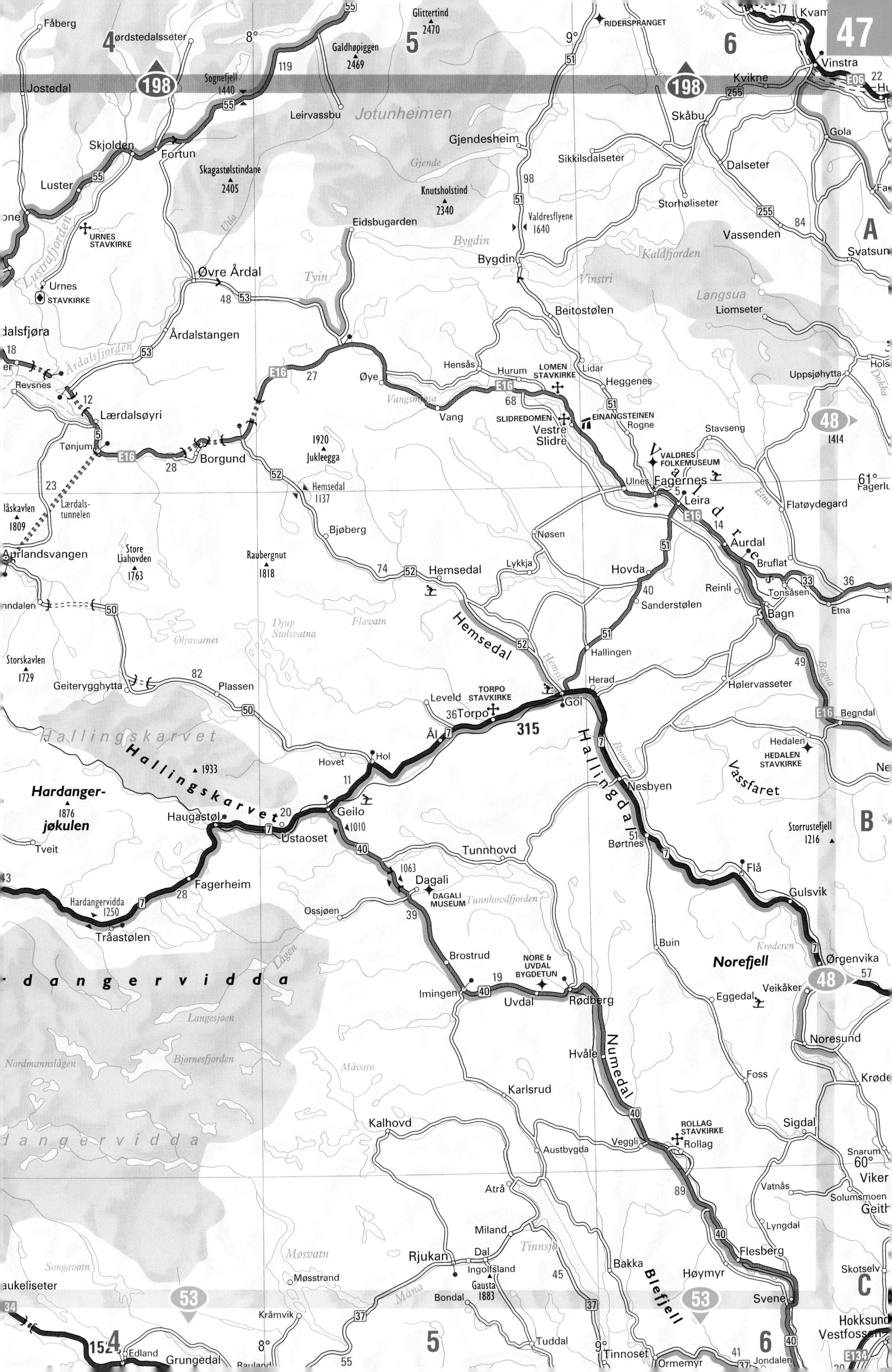
Fåberg
Jostedal
Fortun
Skjolden
Luster
Urnes
Lustrafjorden
Sognefjell
1440
Galdhøpiggen
2469
Glittertind
2470
Leirvassbu
Jotunheimen
Gjendesheim
Gjende
Skagastølstindane
2405
Knutsholstind
2340
Eidsbugarden
Bygdin
Tyin
Øvre Årdal
Årdalstangen
Årdalsfjorden
Revsnes
Lærdalsøyri
Tønjum
Borgund
Lærdalstunnelen
Aurlandsvangen
Store Liahovden
1763
Raubergnut
1818
Jukleegga
1920
Hemsedal
1137
Bjøberg
Øye
Vangsmjøsa
Vang
Hensås
Hurum
LOMEN STAVKIRKE
SLIDREDOMEN
Vestre Slidre
EINANGSTEINEN
Rogne
Heggenes
Lidar
Beitostølen
Vinstri
Kaldfjorden
Langsua
Liomseter
RIDERSPRANGET
Sjoa
Kvam
Vinstra
Kvikne
Skåbu
Gola
Dalseter
Sikkilsdalseter
Storhøliseter
Valdresflyene
1640
Vassenden
Svatsum
Uppsjøhytta
Dokka
Stavseng
VALDRES FOLKEMUSEUM
Valdres
Ulnes
Fagernes
Leira
Etna
Flatøydegard
Aurdal
Bruflat
Tonsåsen
Reinli
Bagn
Begna
Sanderstølen
Hovda
Nøsen
Lykkja
Hemsedal
Hallingen
Herad
Gol
TORPO STAVKIRKE
Torpo
Leveld
Ål
Hol
Hovet
Hallingdal
Hølervasseter
Begndal
Hedalen
HEDALEN STAVKIRKE
Vassfaret
Nesbyen
Børtnes
Storrustefjell
1216
Flå
Gulsvik
Krøderen
Norefjell
Ørgenvika
Veikåker
Eggedal
Noresund
Foss
Sigdal
Snarum
Vatnås
Viker
Solumsmoen
Lyngdal
Flesberg
Skotselv
Svene
Hokksund
Vestfossen
Djup Stolsvatna
Flævatn
Øljuvatnet
Storskavlen
1729
Geiterygghytta
Plassen
Hallingskarvet
1933
Hardangerjøkulen
1876
Haugastøl
Tveit
Ustaoset
Geilo
1010
Tunnhovd
Dagali
DAGALI MUSEUM
Tunnhovdfjorden
Ossjøen
Brostrud
NORE & UVDAL BYGDETUN
Imingen
Uvdal
Rødberg
Numedal
Hvåle
Karlsrud
Kalhovd
Austbygda
Veggli
ROLLAG STAVKIRKE
Rollag
Fagerheim
Hardangervidda
1250
Tråastølen
Hardangervidda
Langesjøen
Nordmannslågen
Bjornesfjorden
Måvatn
Møsvatn
Møsstrand
Songavatn
Haukeliseter
Atrå
Miland
Rjukan
Dal
Ingolfsland
Tinnsjø
Gausta
1883
Bondal
Bakka
Blefjell
Høymyr
Måna
Kråmvik
Edland
Grungedal
Tuddal
Tinnoset
Ormemyr
Jondalen

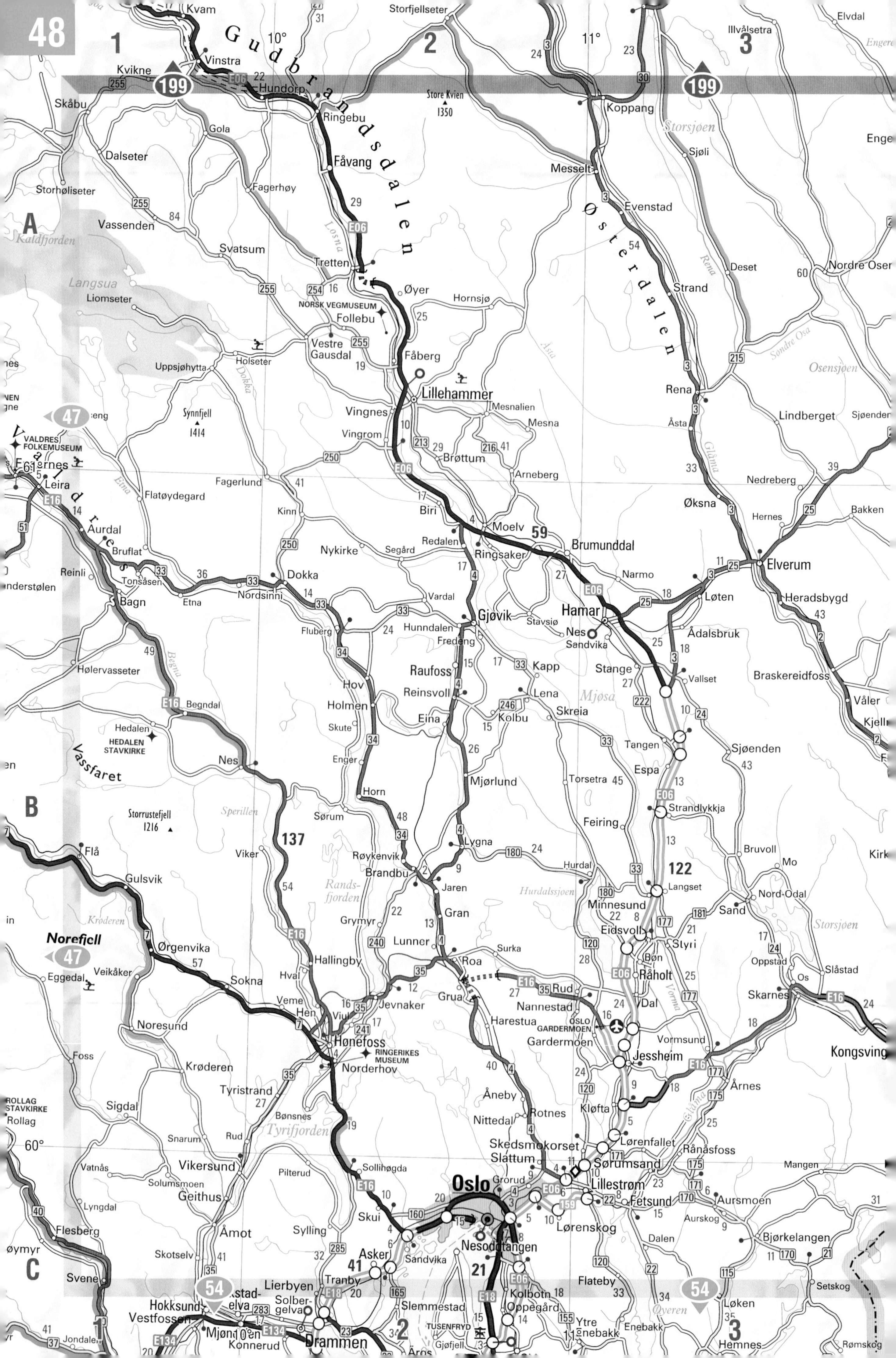
Gudbrandsdalen
Østerdalen
Valdres
Lillehammer
Hamar
Gjøvik
Elverum
Hønefoss
Oslo
Lillestrøm
Drammen
Mjøsa
Tyrifjorden
Randsfjorden
Vassfaret
Kvam
Vinstra
Kvikne
Hundorp
Ringebu
Fåvang
Tretten
Øyer
Fåberg
Follebu
NORSK VEGMUSEUM
Vestre Gausdal
Koppang
Messelt
Evenstad
Strand
Rena
Deset
Skåbu
Dalseter
Gola
Storhøliseter
Fagerhøy
Vassenden
Svatsum
Liomseter
Langsua
Kaldfjorden
Holseter
Uppsjøhytta
Synnfjell 1414
Store Kvien 1350
Storfjellseter
Illvålsetra
Elvdal
Storsjøen
Sjøli
Nordre Osen
Osensjøen
Lindberget
Sjøenden
Mesnalien
Mesna
Vingnes
Vingrom
Brøttum
Arneberg
Biri
Moelv
Brumunddal
Ringsaker
Redalen
Nykirke
Segård
Dokka
Nordsinni
Etna
Bagn
Tonsåsen
Bruflat
Aurdal
Leira
Fagernes
VALDRES FOLKEMUSEUM
Fagerlund
Flatøydegard
Reinli
Hølervasseter
Begndal
Hedalen
HEDALEN STAVKIRKE
Nes
Storrustefjell 1216
Sperillen
Flå
Gulsvik
Krøderen
Norefjell
Ørgenvika
Eggedal
Veikåker
Sokna
Noresund
Foss
Sigdal
Rollag
ROLLAG STAVKIRKE
Snarum
Vikersund
Geithus
Åmot
Lyngdal
Flesberg
Svene
Vestfossen
Hokksund
Mjøndalen
Konnerud
Drammen
Lierbyen
Solbergelva
Tranby
Asker
Sandvika
Slemmestad
Nesoddtangen
Kolbotn
Oppegård
TUSENFRYD
Ytre Enebakk
Flateby
Øyeren
Lørenskog
Fetsund
Aurskog
Aursmoen
Bjørkelangen
Setskog
Løken
Hemnes
Rømskog
Sørumsand
Rånåsfoss
Lørenfallet
Skedsmokorset
Slattum
Grorud
Nittedal
Rotnes
Åneby
Kløfta
Jessheim
Gardermoen
OSLO GARDERMOEN
Nannestad
Harestua
Gran
Jaren
Brandbu
Lunner
Grua
Roa
Jevnaker
Hallingby
Viul
Hen
Norderhov
RINGERIKES MUSEUM
Tyristrand
Sollihøgda
Skui
Sylling
Pilterud
Bønsnes
Krøderen
Raufoss
Reinsvoll
Eina
Kolbu
Lena
Skreia
Kapp
Hunndalen
Fredeng
Vardal
Fluberg
Hov
Holmen
Skute
Enger
Horn
Sørum
Røykenvik
Lygna
Mjørlund
Torsetra
Feiring
Hurdal
Hurdalssjøen
Minnesund
Eidsvoll
Styri
Bøn
Råholt
Dal
Vormsund
Ånes
Kongsvinger
Skarnes
Slåstad
Oppstad
Sand
Nord-Odal
Storsjøen
Bruvoll
Langset
Strandlykkja
Espa
Tangen
Sjøenden
Stange
Vallset
Ådalsbruk
Løten
Heradsbygd
Braskereidfoss
Våler
Nes
Sandvika
Stavsjø
Narmo
Øksna
Nedreberg
Hernes
Bakken
Åsta
Mangen
Kirkenær
Viker
Dalen

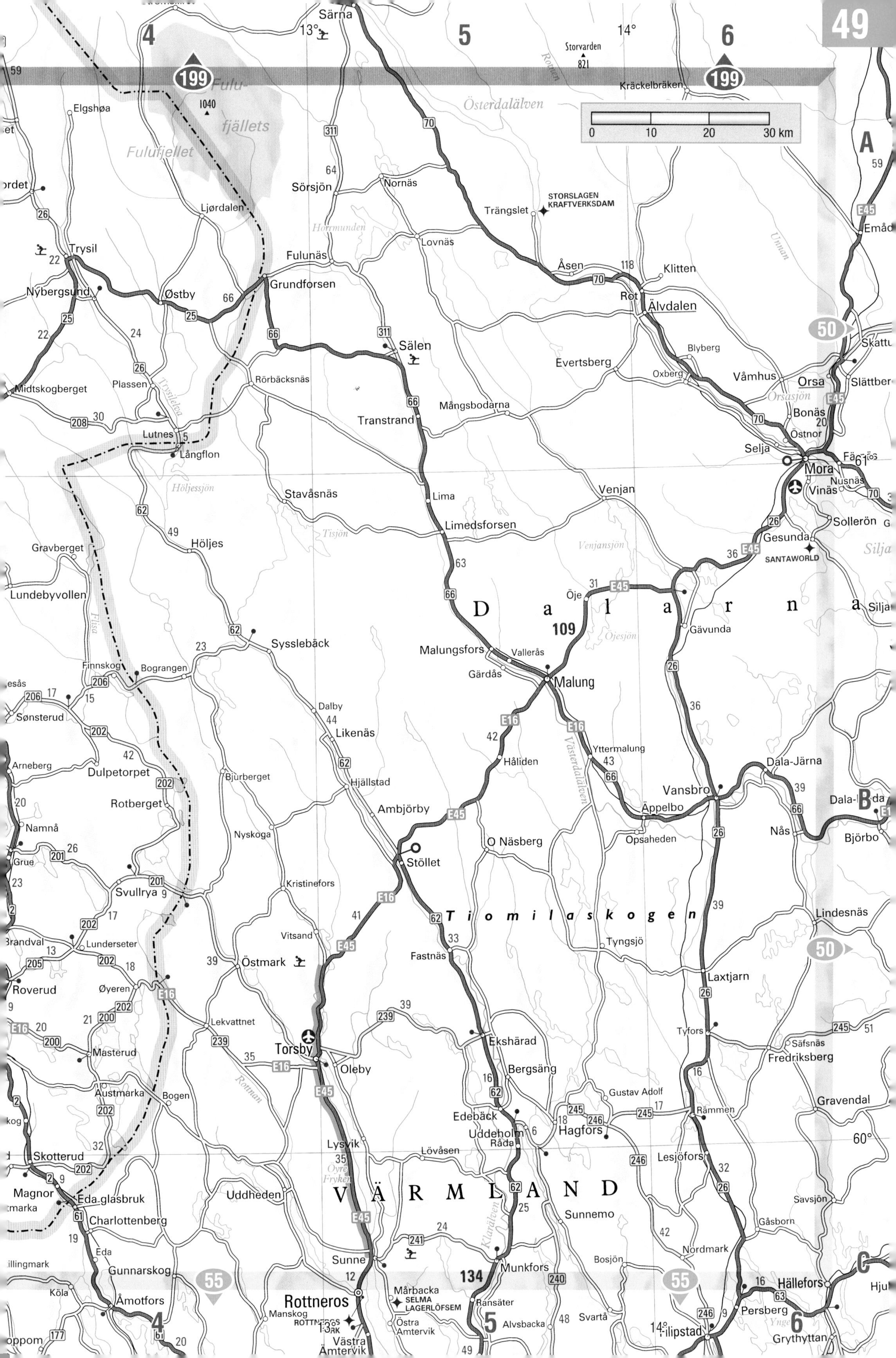
Särna
Fulufjällets
Fulufjellet
Trysil
Sälen
Grundforsen
Transtrand
Älvdalen
Orsa
Mora
Malung
Dalarna
Tiomilaskogen
Vansbro
Torsby
Ekshärad
Hagfors
Uddeholm
Värmland
Sunne
Rottneros
Munkfors
Filipstad
Hällefors
Charlottenberg
Eda glasbruk
Österdalälven
Storvarden 821
Kräckelbräken
Trängslet
STORSLAGEN KRAFTVERKSDAM
SANTAWORLD
SELMA LAGERLÖFSEM
0 10 20 30 km

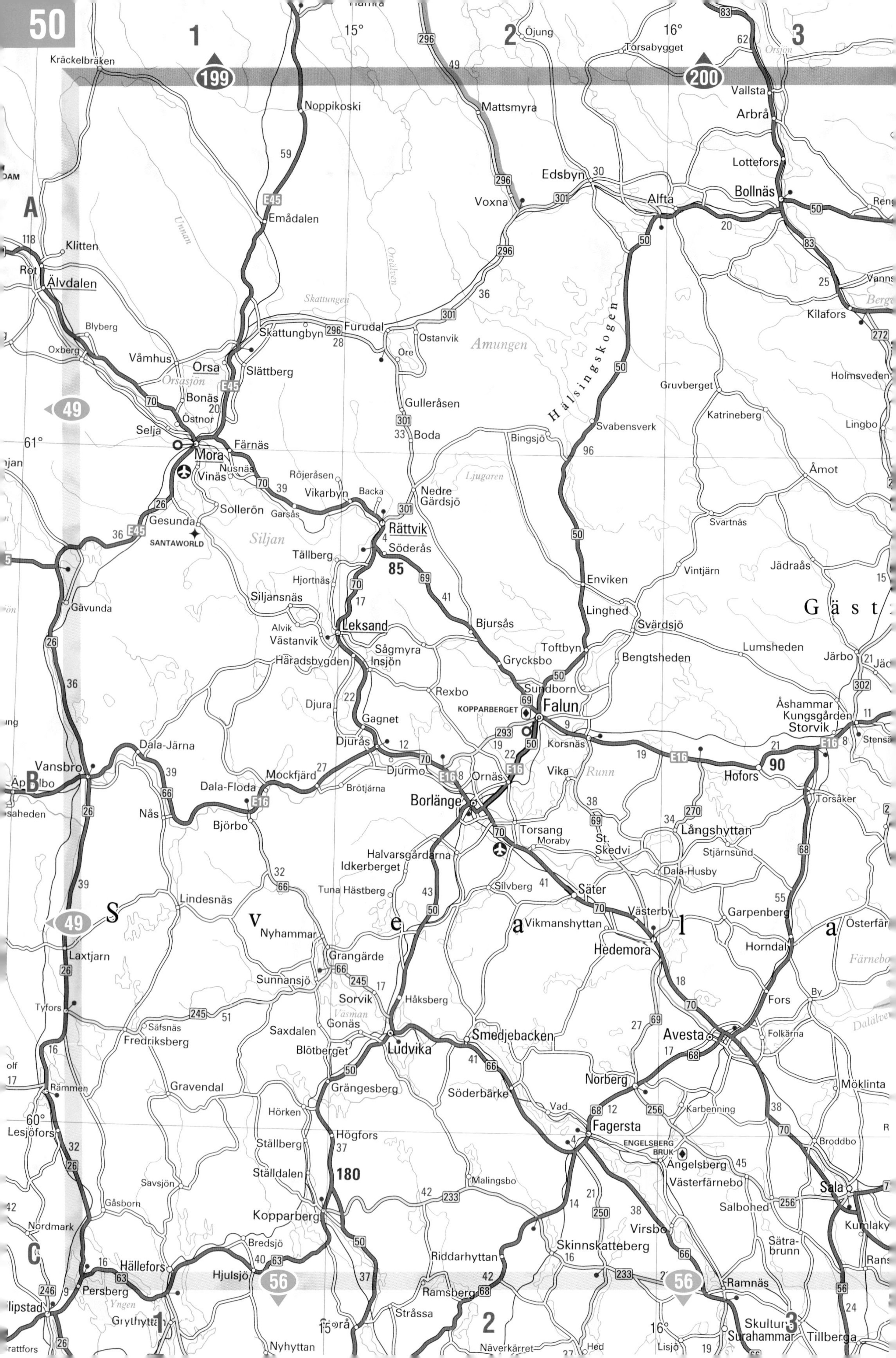

199
200
49
56
Kräckelbräken
Noppikoski
Mattsmyra
Öjung
Torsabygget
Vallsta
Arbrå
Lottefors
Edsbyn
Voxna
Alfta
Bollnäs
Emådalen
Unnan
Oreälven
Klitten
Rot
Älvdalen
Blyberg
Oxberg
Våmhus
Orsa
Orsasjön
Bonäs
Östnor
Selja
Mora
Färnäs
Nusnäs
Vinäs
Sollerön
Garsås
Gesunda
SANTAWORLD
Siljan
Skattungen
Skattungbyn
Slättberg
Furudal
Ostanvik
Ore
Amungen
Gulleråsen
Boda
Röjeråsen
Vikarbyn
Backa
Nedre Gärdsjö
Rättvik
Söderås
Tällberg
Hjortnäs
Siljansnäs
Alvik
Västanvik
Leksand
Sågmyra
Insjön
Häradsbygden
Djura
Gagnet
Djurås
Djurmo
Brötjärna
Mockfjärd
Dala-Floda
Dala-Järna
Vansbro
Äppelbo
Nås
Björbo
Gävunda
Hälsingskogen
Svabensverk
Bingsjö
Ljugaren
Enviken
Linghed
Svärdsjö
Toftbyn
Bengtsheden
Grycksbo
Bjursås
Rexbo
Sundborn
Falun
KOPPARBERGET
Korsnäs
Ornäs
Borlänge
Vika
Runn
Torsang
Moraby
St. Skedvi
Säter
Silvberg
Halvarsgårdarna
Idkerberget
Tuna Hästberg
Gruvberget
Katrineberg
Svartnäs
Vintjärn
Jädraås
Åmot
Lingbo
Holmsveden
Kilafors
Lumsheden
Järbo
Åshammar
Kungsgården
Storvik
Hofors
Torsåker
Långshyttan
Stjärnsund
Dala-Husby
Garpenberg
Västerby
Hedemora
Vikmanshyttan
Horndal
Österfärnebo
Färnebofjärden
Fors
By
Folkärna
Dalälven
Avesta
Möklinta
Norberg
Karbenning
Fagersta
ENGELSBERG BRUK
Ängelsberg
Västerfärnebo
Broddbo
Sala
Salbohed
Kumlaky
Sätra-brunn
Virsbo
Skinnskatteberg
Ramnäs
Skultuna
Surahammar
Tillberga
Lisjö
Hed
Näverkärret
Riddarhyttan
Ramsberg
Stråssa
Malingsbo
Söderbärke
Vad
Smedjebacken
Ludvika
Håksberg
Grängesberg
Högfors
Hörken
Ställberg
Ställdalen
Kopparberg
Bredsjö
Hjulsjö
Hällefors
Persberg
Yngen
Grythyttan
Nyhyttan
Fjällbo
Filipstad
Rattfors
Nordmark
Gåsborn
Savsjön
Lesjöfors
Rämmen
Gravendal
Fredriksberg
Säfsnäs
Tyfors
Laxtjärn
Lindesnäs
Nyhammar
Grangärde
Sunnansjö
Sorvik
Vasman
Gonäs
Saxdalen
Blötberget
Svealand
Gästrikland

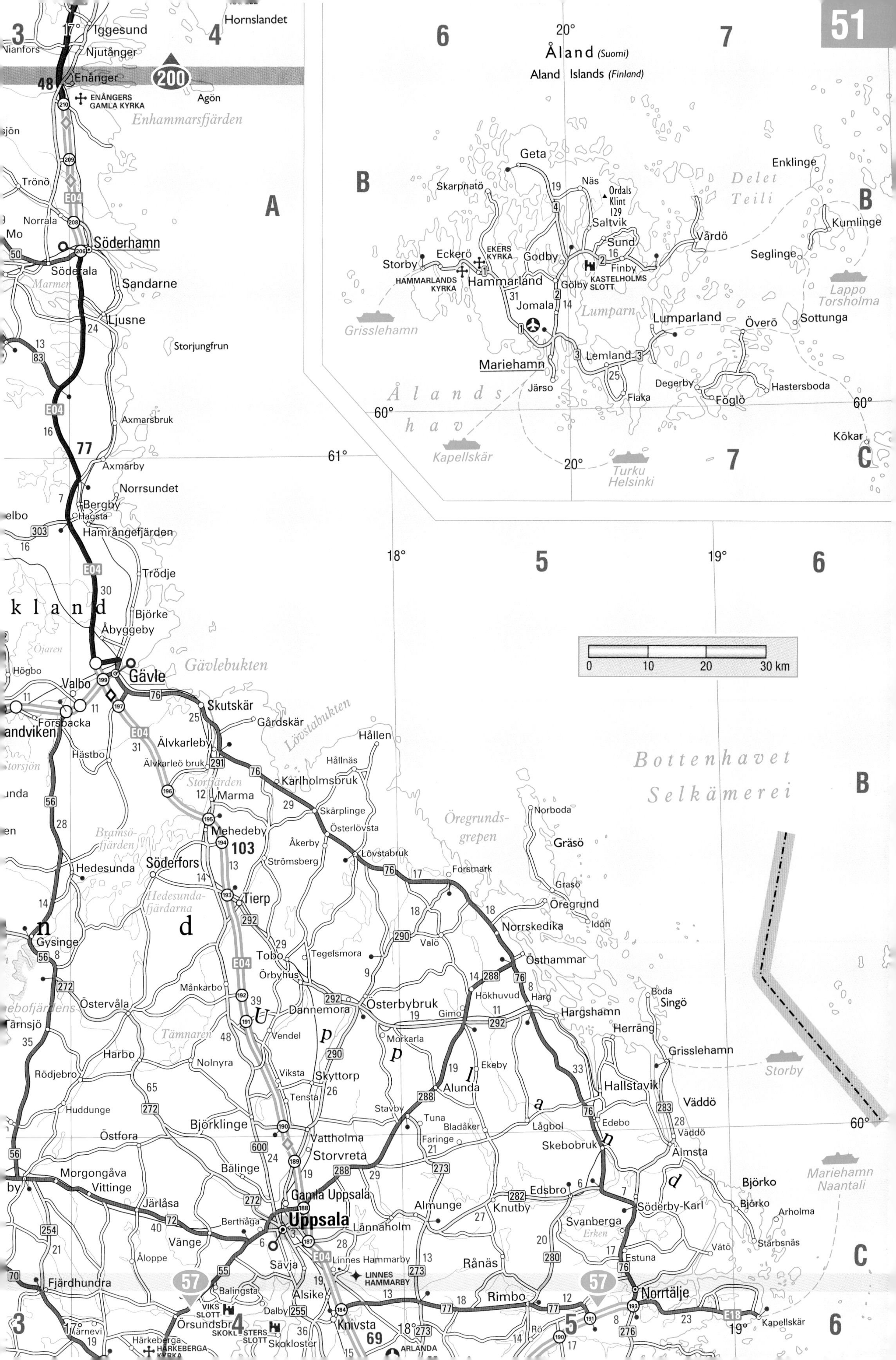

Åland (Suomi)
Aland Islands (Finland)
Geta
Skarpnatö
Näs
Ordals Klint 129
Saltvik
Sund
Vårdö
Enklinge
Delet Teili
Kumlinge
Seglinge
Storby
Eckerö
EKERS KYRKA
Godby
Finby
KASTELHOLMS SLOTT
HAMMARLANDS KYRKA
Hammarland
Gölby
Jomala
Lumparn
Lumparland
Överö
Sottunga
Lappo Torsholma
Grisslehamn
Mariehamn
Lemland
Järso
Flaka
Degerby
Föglö
Hastersboda
Ålands hav
Kapellskär
Turku Helsinki
Kökar
Bottenhavet
Selkämerei
Iggesund
Njutånger
Hornslandet
Enånger
ENÅNGERS GAMLA KYRKA
Agön
Enhammarsfjärden
Trönö
Norrala
Söderhamn
Söderala
Marmen
Sandarne
Ljusne
Storjungfrun
Axmarsbruk
Axmarby
Norrsundet
Bergby
Hagsta
Hamrångefjärden
Trödje
Björke
Åbyggeby
Gävlebukten
Högbo
Valbo
Gävle
Skutskär
Gårdskär
Lövstabukten
Forsbacka
Sandviken
Hästbo
Älvkarleby
Älvkarleö bruk
Storfjärden
Marma
Hållen
Hållnäs
Karlholmsbruk
Skärplinge
Österlövsta
Öregrundsgrepen
Norboda
Gräsö
Åkerby
Lövstabruk
Strömsberg
Forsmark
Mehedeby
Bramsöfjärden
Hedesunda
Söderfors
Tierp
Hedesundafjärdarna
Öregrund
Idön
Norrskedika
Gysinge
Tobo
Tegelsmora
Valö
Östhammar
Örbyhus
Månkarbo
Hökhuvud
Harg
Östervåla
Dannemora
Österbybruk
Gimo
Hargshamn
Boda
Singö
Tämnaren
Vendel
Morkarla
Herräng
Harbo
Nolnyra
Ekeby
Grisslehamn
Storby
Rödjebro
Viksta
Skyttorp
Alunda
Hallstavik
Tensta
Väddö
Huddunge
Stavby
Tuna
Bladåker
Edebo
Björklinge
Vattholma
Faringe
Lågbol
Östfora
Skebobruk
Älmsta
Storvreta
Bälinge
Morgongåva
Vittinge
Gamla Uppsala
Edsbro
Söderby-Karl
Björko
Arholma
Mariehamn Naantali
Järlåsa
Almunge
Knutby
Svanberga
Erken
Berthåga
Uppsala
Lännaholm
Starbsnäs
Vänge
Vätö
Åloppe
Linnes Hammarby
Estuna
Sävja
Rånäs
LINNES HAMMARBY
Fjärdhundra
Balingsta
Alsike
Rimbo
Norrtälje
VIKS SLOTT
Dalby
Örsundsbro
Knivsta
SKOKLOSTERS SLOTT
Skokloster
Härkeberga
HÄRKEBERGA KYRKA
ARLANDA
Kapellskär
Rö
Tärnsjö
Uppland
0 10 20 30 km

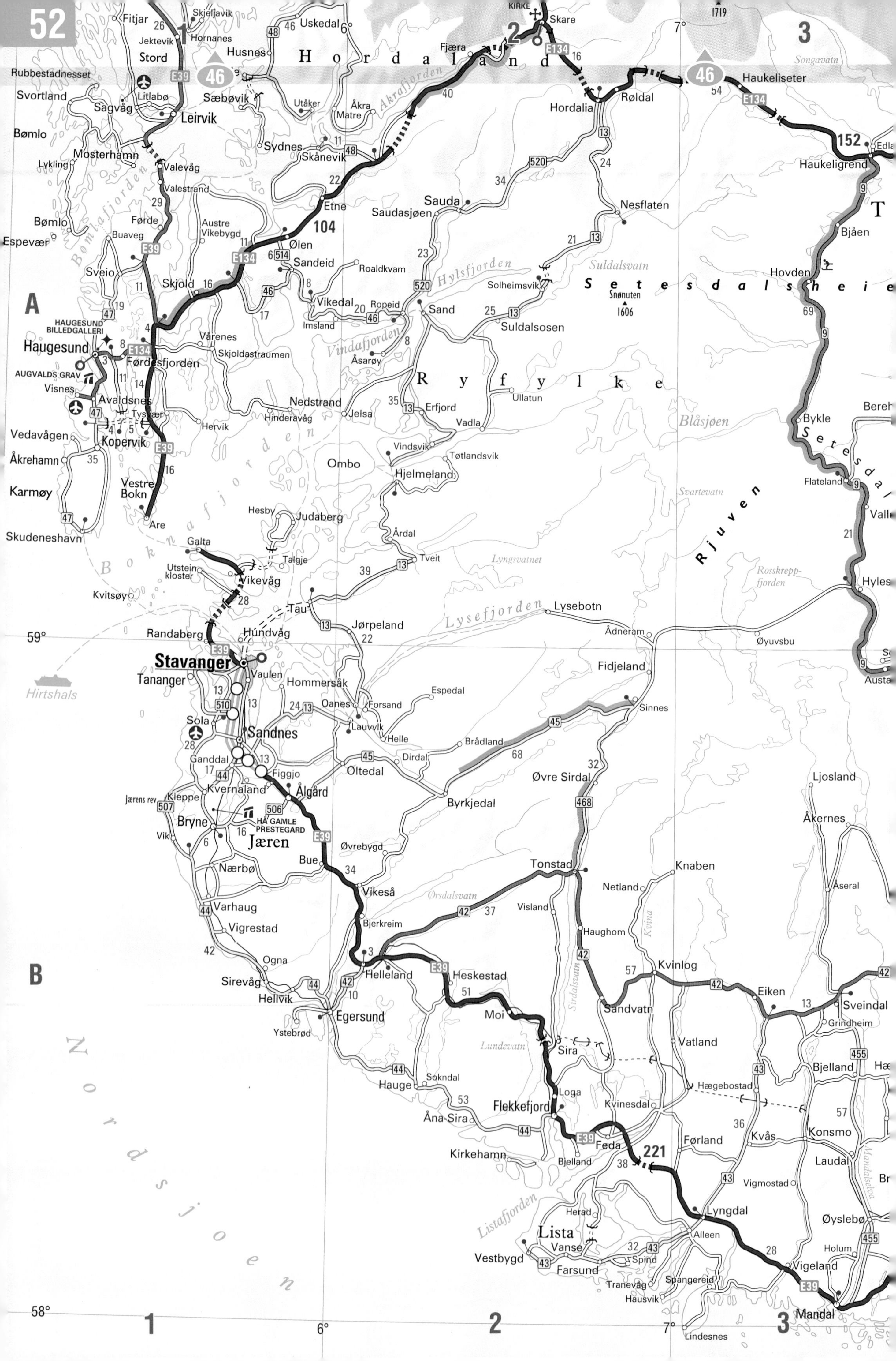
Hordaland
Ryfylke
Setesdalsheie
Setesdal
Rjuven
Jæren
Nordsjøen
Boknafjorden
Stavanger
Haugesund
HAUGESUND BILLEDGALLERI
AUGVALDS GRAV
HÅ GAMLE PRESTEGARD
Sandnes
Egersund
Flekkefjord
Mandal
Lista
Farsund
Lyngdal
Kopervik
Karmøy
Skudeneshavn
Stord
Leirvik
Fitjar
Bømlo
Husnes
Uskedal
Skånevik
Etne
Ølen
Sauda
Røldal
Haukeliseter
Haukeligrend
Hovden
Bykle
Suldalsosen
Sand
Hjelmeland
Jørpeland
Tau
Randaberg
Tananger
Sola
Bryne
Egersund
Hirtshals
Lysefjorden
Lysebotn
Sirdalsvatn
Tonstad
Kvinesdal
Vigeland
Lindesnes
59°
58°
6°
7°
1
2
3
A
B
E39
E134
46
13
42
43
44
45
9
104
152
221

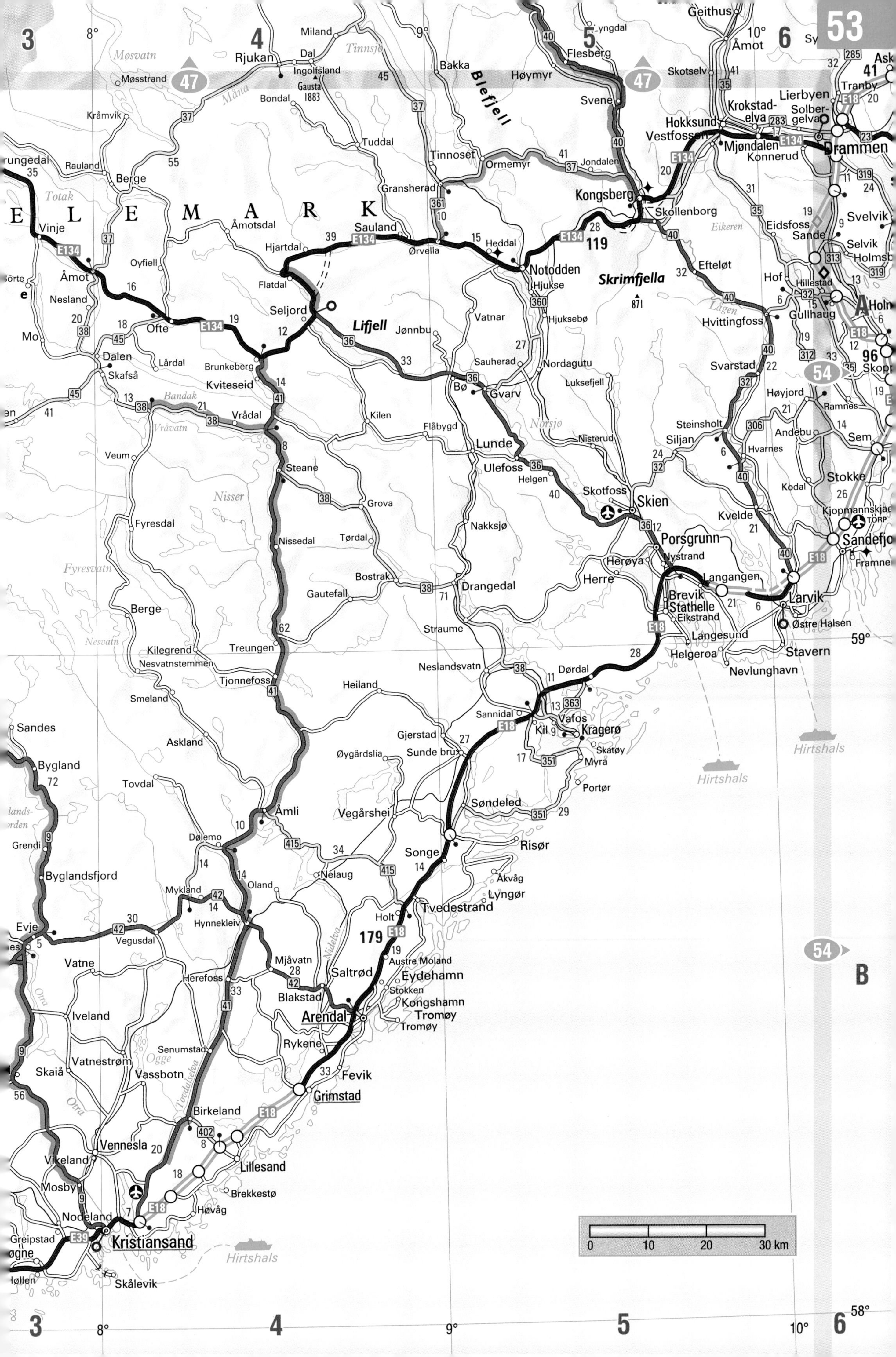
Møsvatn
Møsstrand
Rjukan
Miland
Dal
Ingolfsland
Gausta 1883
Tinnsjø
Bondal
Kråmvik
Rauland
Berge
Totak
TELEMARK
Vinje
Åmot
Oyfiell
Nesland
Ofte
Dalen
Skafså
Lårdal
Brunkeberg
Kviteseid
Bandak
Vråvatn
Vrådal
Hjartdal
Flatdal
Seljord
Lifjell
Sauland
Tuddal
Bakka
Blefjell
Høymyr
Tinnoset
Ormemyr
Gransherad
Heddal
Ørvella
Notodden
Hjukse
Hjuksebø
Vatnar
Jønnbu
Sauherad
Nordagutu
Bø
Gvarv
Lunde
Ulefoss
Helgen
Norsjø
Luksefjell
Nisterud
Skrimfjella 871
Flesberg
Svene
Jondalen
Kongsberg
Skollenborg
Efteløt
Hvittingfoss
Lågen
Eikeren
Geithus
Åmot
Skotselv
Krokstad-elva
Hokksund
Vestfossen
Mjøndalen
Konnerud
Drammen
Lierbyen
Solbergelva
Tranby
Eidsfoss
Sande
Svelvik
Selvik
Holmsb
Hof
Hillestad
Gullhaug
Holm
Svarstad
Skopp
Høyjord
Ramnes
Andebu
Sem
Steinsholt
Siljan
Hvarnes
Kodal
Stokke
Kvelde
Kjopmannskjær
TORP
Sandefjord
Framnes
Skotfoss
Skien
Porsgrunn
Nystrand
Herøya
Herre
Langangen
Brevik
Stathelle
Eikestrand
Larvik
Østre Halsen
Langesund
Helgeroa
Stavern
Nevlunghavn
Kilen
Flåbygd
Steane
Veum
Nisser
Grova
Fyresdal
Nissedal
Tørdal
Nakksjø
Fyresvatn
Bostrak
Gautefall
Drangedal
Berge
Straume
Nesvatn
Kilegrend
Treungen
Nesvatnstemmen
Tjonnefoss
Neslandsvatn
Dørdal
Heiland
Smeland
Sannidal
Vafos
Kil
Kragerø
Skatøy
Myra
Portør
Gjerstad
Sunde bru
Øygardslia
Sandes
Askland
Bygland
Tovdal
Hirtshals
Søndeled
Åmli
Vegårshei
Dølemo
Risør
Songe
Åkvåg
Lyngør
Nelaug
Oland
Mykland
Hynnekleiv
Tvedestrand
Holt
Byglandsfjord
Evje
Vegusdal
Vatne
Herefoss
Mjåvatn
Saltrød
Austre Moland
Eydehamn
Stokken
Kongshamn
Tromøy
Blakstad
Arendal
Iveland
Rykene
Senumstad
Ogge
Vatnestrøm
Skaiå
Vassbotn
Fevik
Grimstad
Birkeland
Vennesla
Vikeland
Lillesand
Mosby
Brekkestø
Høvåg
Nodeland
Greipstad
Kristiansand
Skålevik
Søgne
Høllen
Grendi
Otra
Tovdalselva
Nidelva
0 10 20 30 km
8° 9° 10° 59° 58°
3 4 5 6 A B
47 54

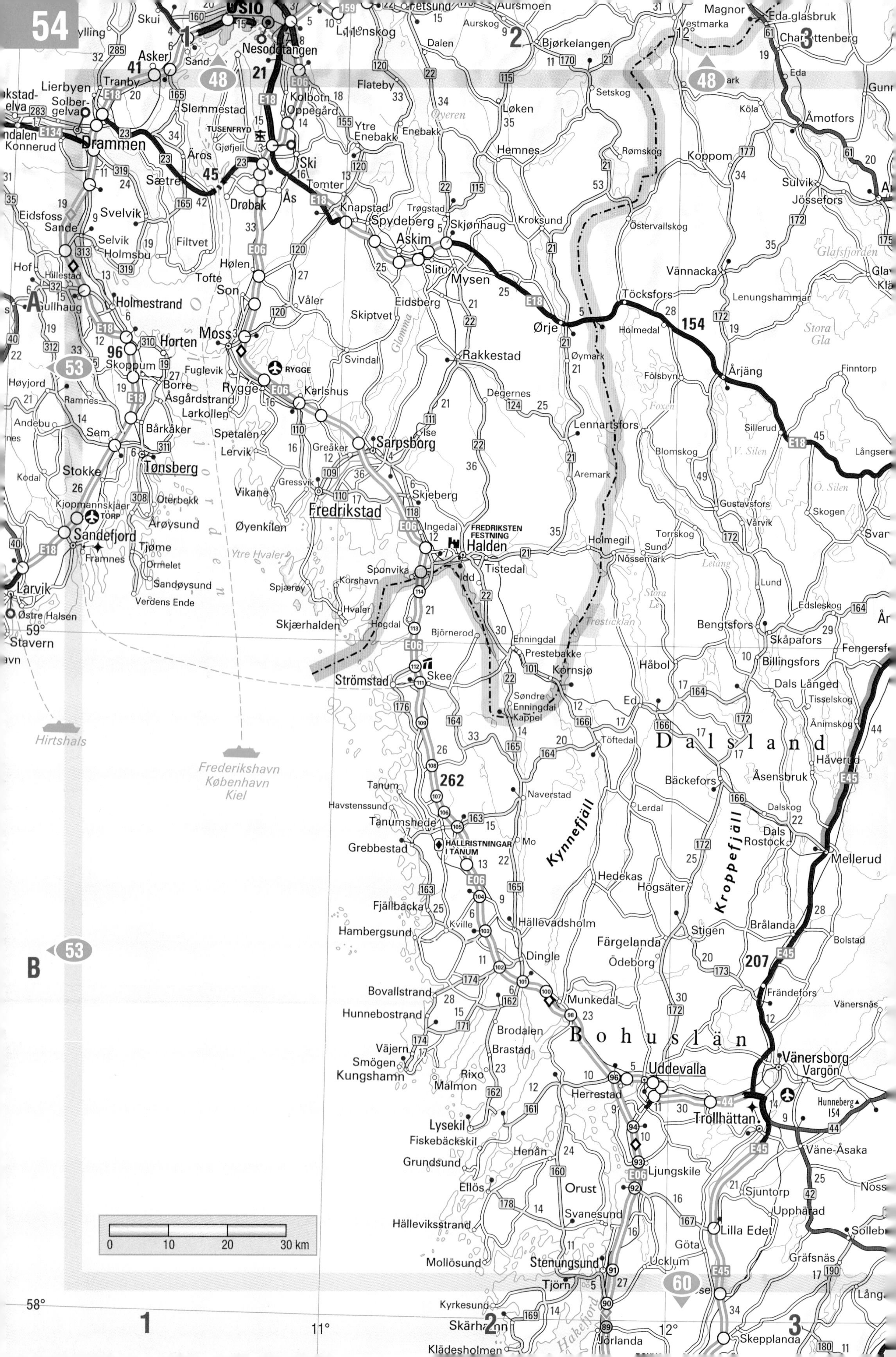

Oslo
Nesoddtangen
Asker
Lierbyen
Tranby
Solbergelva
Drammen
Konnerud
Slemmestad
Tusenfryd
Gjøfjell
Åros
Sætre
Drøbak
Ås
Ski
Kolbotn
Oppegård
Ytre Enebakk
Enebakk
Flateby
Lillestrøm
Fetsund
Aursmoen
Aurskog
Bjørkelangen
Magnor
Eda glasbruk
Vestmarka
Charlottenberg
Eda
Köla
Åmotfors
Koppom
Sulvik
Jössefors
Setskog
Løken
Øyeren
Hemnes
Rømskog
Tomter
Knapstad
Spydeberg
Trøgstad
Skjønhaug
Askim
Slitu
Mysen
Eidsberg
Kroksund
Östervallskog
Vännacka
Glafsfjorden
Töcksfors
Holmedal
Lenungshammar
Ørje
Øymark
Stora Gla
Årjäng
Finntorp
Svelvik
Selvik
Sande
Eidsfoss
Holmsbu
Filtvet
Hølen
Tofte
Son
Våler
Skiptvet
Hof
Hillestad
Gullhaug
Holmestrand
Moss
Horten
Fuglevik
Rygge
Svindal
Glomma
Rakkestad
Degernes
Skoppum
Borre
Åsgårdstrand
Larkollen
Karlshus
Høyjord
Ramnes
Andebu
Sem
Bårkåker
Spetalen
Lervik
Sarpsborg
Greåker
Ise
Lennartsfors
Fölsbyn
Foxen
Blomskog
Sillerud
V. Silen
Långserud
Tønsberg
Stokke
Kodal
Gressvik
Vikane
Fredrikstad
Skjeberg
Aremark
Ö. Silen
Gustavsfors
Vårvik
Skogen
Kjopmannskjaer
Torp
Sandefjord
Framnes
Tjøme
Ormelet
Sandøysund
Verdens Ende
Årøysund
Øyenkilen
Oterbekk
Ytre Hvaler
Ingedal
Fredriksten Festning
Halden
Tistedal
Holmegil
Sund
Nössemark
Torrskog
Letang
Larvik
Østre Halsen
Stavern
Sponvika
Korshavn
Spjærøy
Hvaler
Skjærhalden
Idd
Stora Le
Lund
Edsleskog
Hogdal
Björnerod
Enningdal
Prestebakke
Kornsjø
Tresticklan
Bengtsfors
Skåpafors
Fengersfors
Håbol
Billingsfors
Dals Långed
Tisselskog
Ånimskog
Strömstad
Skee
Søndre Enningdal
Kappel
Ed
Töftedal
Dalsland
Håverud
Åsensbruk
Bäckefors
Hirtshals
Frederikshavn
København
Kiel
Tanum
Havstenssund
Tanumshede
Grebbestad
Hällristningar i Tanum
Naverstad
Lerdal
Kynnefjäll
Kroppefjäll
Mo
Dalskog
Dals Rostock
Mellerud
Hedekas
Högsäter
Fjällbacka
Kville
Hambergsund
Hällevadsholm
Färgelanda
Ödeborg
Stigen
Brålanda
Bolstad
Dingle
Bovallstrand
Munkedal
Frändefors
Vänersnäs
Hunnebostrand
Brodalen
Bohuslän
Väjern
Smögen
Kungshamn
Brastad
Rixo
Malmon
Uddevalla
Vänersborg
Vargön
Herrestad
Trollhättan
Hunneberg
Lysekil
Fiskebäckskil
Grundsund
Henån
Väne-Åsaka
Ljungskile
Ellös
Orust
Sjuntorp
Upphärad
Hälleviksstrand
Svanesund
Lilla Edet
Sollebrunn
Göta
Mollösund
Stenungsund
Ucklum
Gräfsnäs
Tjörn
Kyrkesund
Skärhamn
Klädesholmen
Jörlanda
Hakefjord
Skepplanda
Långed
0
10
20
30 km
59°
58°
11°
12°
1
2
3
A
B
48
53
60

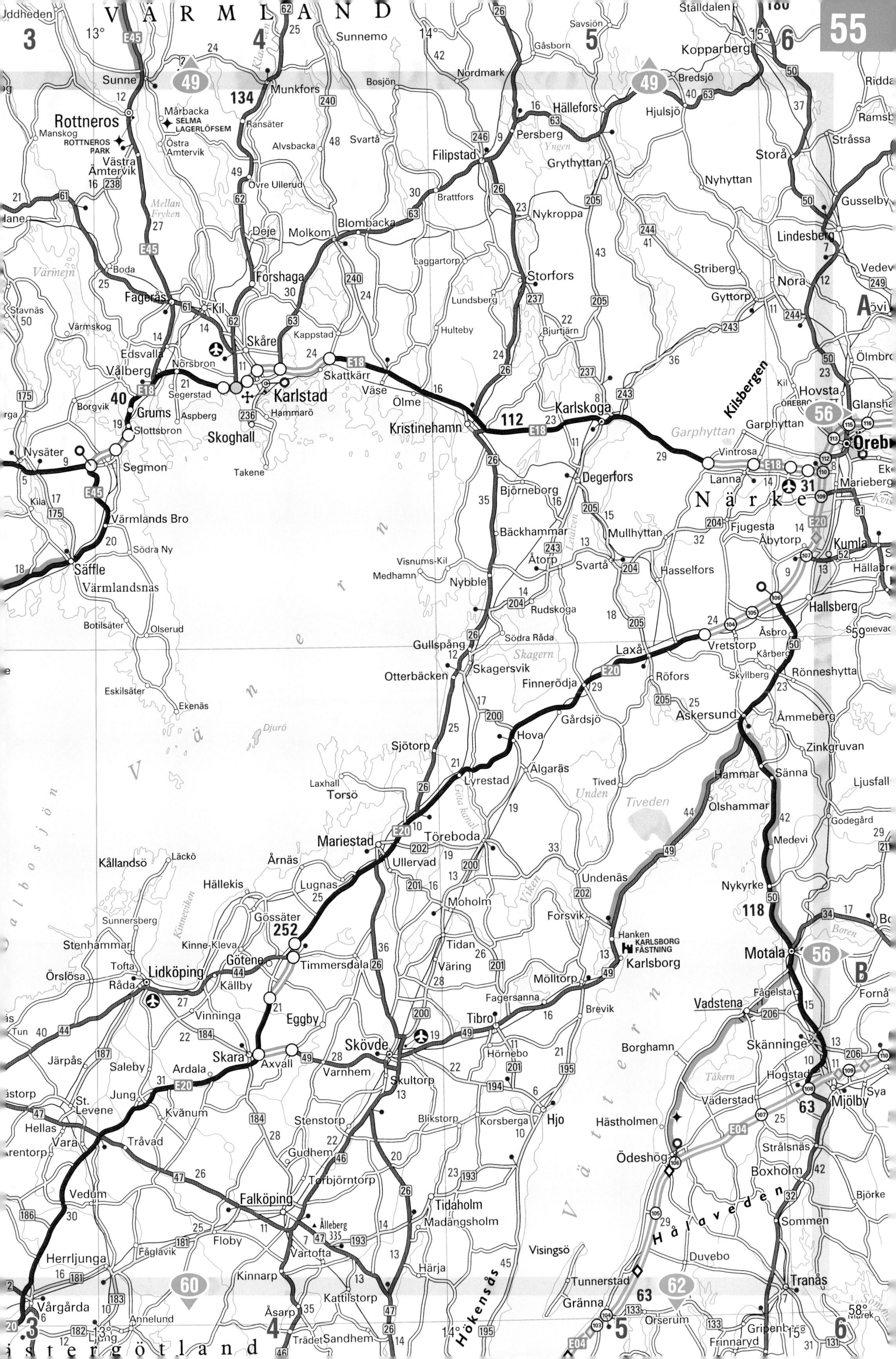
VÄRMLAND
Närke
Västergötland
Vänern
Vättern
Karlstad
Kristinehamn
Karlskoga
Örebro
Filipstad
Mariestad
Lidköping
Skövde
Falköping
Motala
Askersund
Hallsberg
Säffle
Sunne
Rottneros
Munkfors
Hällefors
Lindesberg
Nora
Degerfors
Laxå
Hova
Töreboda
Skara
Götene
Tidaholm
Hjo
Tibro
Karlsborg
Vadstena
Mjölby
Skänninge
Ödeshög
Gränna
Tranås
Vårgårda
Herrljunga
Grums
Kil
Forshaga
Skoghall
Storfors
Gullspång
Kopparberg
Kumla
Kilsbergen
Tiveden
Hålaveden
Hökensås
Kinnekulle

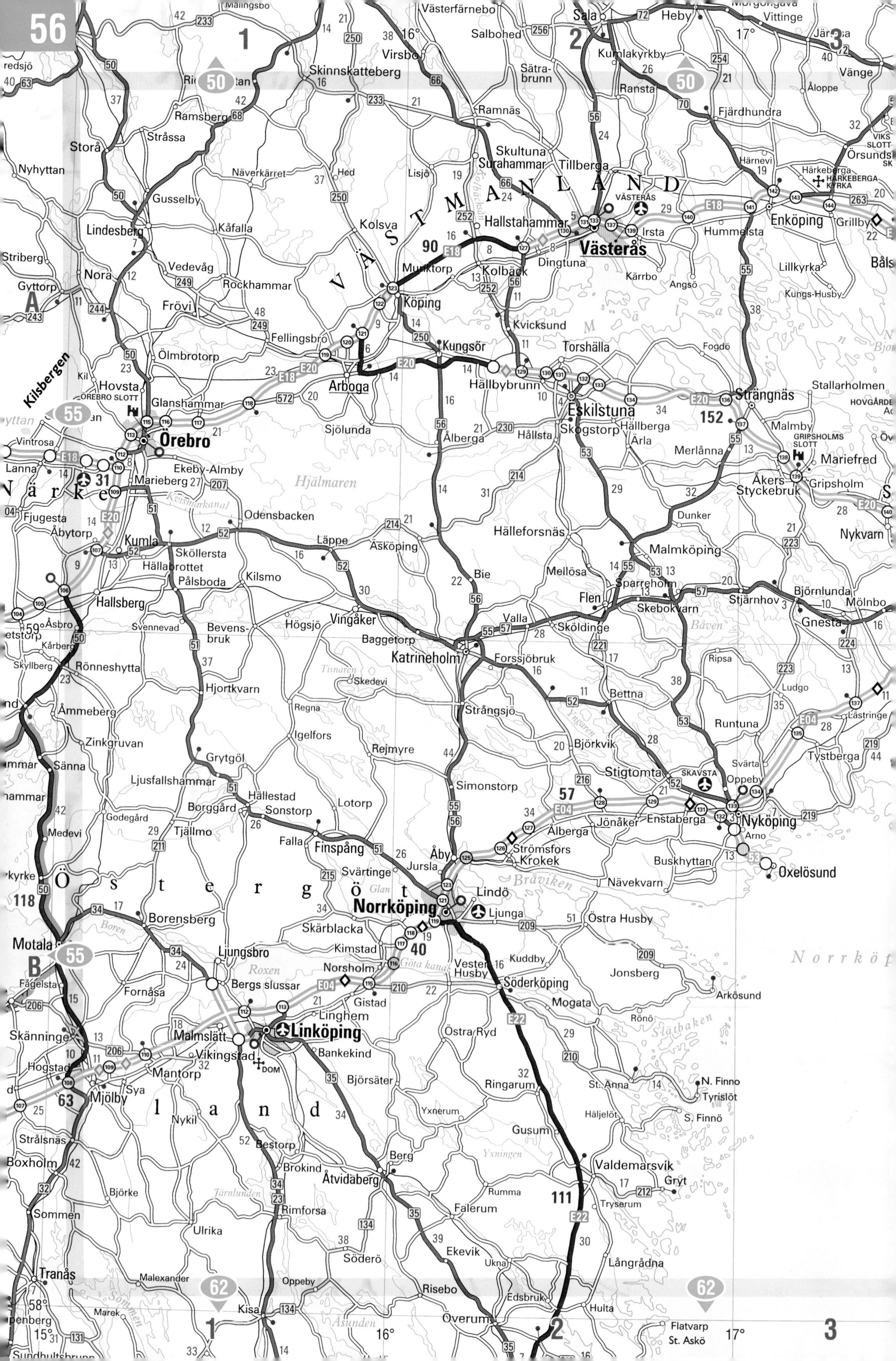
Västerfärnebo
Sala
Heby
Vittinge
Salbohed
Virsbo
Skinnskatteberg
Kumlakyrkby
Vänge
Ramsberg
Sätra-brunn
Ransta
Åloppe
Stråssa
Ramnäs
Fjärdhundra
Storå
Skultuna
Surahammar
Tillberga
Härnevi
Örsundsbro
Nyhyttan
Näverkärret
Hed
Lisjö
Härkeberga
HÄRKEBERGA KYRKA
Gusselby
V Ä S T M A N L A N D
VÄSTERÅS
Lindesberg
Kåfalla
Kolsva
Hallstahammar
Enköping
Grillby
Irsta
Hummelsta
Västerås
Striberg
Nora
Vedevåg
Munktorp
Kolbäck
Dingtuna
Lillkyrka
Bålsta
Gyttorp
Rockhammar
Köping
Kärrbo
Angsö
Kungs-Husby
Frövi
Fellingsbro
Kungsör
Kvicksund
Mälaren
Ölmbrotorp
Torshälla
Fogdö
Kilsbergen
Kil
Hovsta
ÖREBRO SLOTT
Arboga
Hällbybrunn
Strängnäs
Stallarholmen
HOVGÅRDEN
Glanshammar
Sjölunda
Eskilstuna
Hällberga
Malmby
Örebro
Ålberga
Hållsta
Skogstorp
Ärla
GRIPSHOLMS SLOTT
Vintrosa
Lanna
Ekeby-Almby
Merlånna
Mariefred
Marieberg
Hjälmaren
Åkers Styckebruk
Gripsholm
N ä r k e
Kvismarkanal
Fjugesta
Odensbacken
Dunker
Nykvarn
Åbytorp
Kumla
Läppe
Äsköping
Hälleforsnäs
Sköllersta
Malmköping
Hällabrottet
Pålsboda
Kilsmo
Bie
Mellösa
Sparreholm
Hallsberg
Flen
Skebokvarn
Stjärnhov
Björnlunda
Mölnbo
Gnesta
Åsbro
Vingåker
Bevens-bruk
Svennevad
Högsjö
Valla
Sköldinge
Kårberg
Baggetorp
Båven
Skyllberg
Rönneshytta
Katrineholm
Forssjöbruk
Ripsa
Tisnaren
Skedevi
Hjortkvarn
Bettna
Ludgo
Åmmeberg
Regna
Strångsjö
Runtuna
Lästringe
Zinkgruvan
Igelfors
Yngaren
Björkvik
Rejmyre
Tystberga
Grytgöl
Stigtomta
SKAVSTA
Svärta
Sänna
Ljusfallshammar
Simonstorp
Oppeby
Hällestad
Borggård
Sonstorp
Lotorp
Ålberga
Jönåker
Entaberga
Nyköping
Godegård
Arno
Medevi
Tjällmo
Falla
Finspång
Strömsfors
Krokek
Åby
Jursla
Buskhyttan
Oxelösund
Svärtinge
Bråviken
Nävekvarn
Ö s t e r g ö t l a n d
Glan
Lindö
Norrköping
Ljunga
Östra Husby
Borensberg
Boren
Skärblacka
Motala
Kimstad
Ljungsbro
Vester-Husby
Kuddby
Norrköpingsdjupet
Fågelsta
Roxen
Norsholm
Göta kanal
Jonsberg
Bergs slussar
Söderköping
Arkösund
Fornåsa
Gistad
Mogata
Linghem
Rönö
Skänninge
Malmslätt
Linköping
Östra Ryd
Slätbaken
Vikingstad
Bankekind
DOM
Hogstad
Mantorp
Sya
Björsäter
Ringarum
St. Anna
N. Finno
Mjölby
Tyrislöt
Yxnerum
Häljelöt
S. Finnö
Nykil
Gusum
Strålsnäs
Bestorp
Boxholm
Berg
Yxningen
Valdemarsvik
Brokind
Åtvidaberg
Järnlunden
Gryt
Björke
Rumma
Tryserum
Sommen
Rimforsa
Falerum
Ulrika
Ekevik
Söderö
Ukna
Långrådna
Tranås
Malexander
Oppeby
Risebo
Edsbruk
Hulta
Marek
Kisa
Åsunden
Överum
Flatvarp
St. Askö
Sundhultsbrunn
16°
17°
15°
58°
1
2
3
A
B
E18
E20
E04
E22

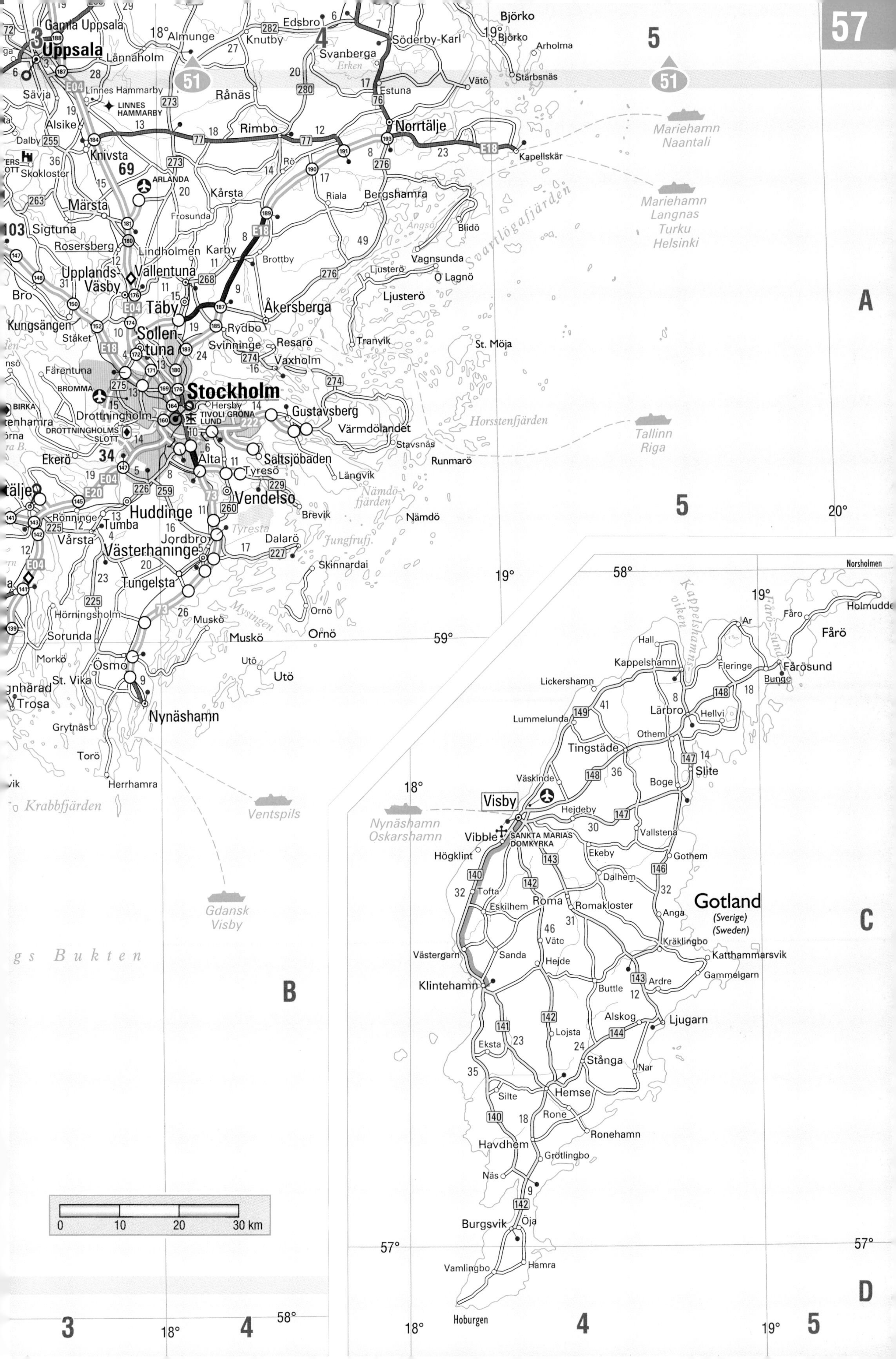
Gamla Uppsala
Uppsala
Lännaholm
Almunge
Knutby
Edsbro
Söderby-Karl
Svanberga
Erken
Björko
Arholma
Stärbsnäs
Vätö
Estuna
Savja
Linnés Hammarby
LINNES HAMMARBY
Rånäs
Alsike
Rimbo
Norrtälje
Mariehamn
Naantali
Dalby
Knivsta
Kapellskär
Skokloster
Rö
ARLANDA
Kårsta
Riala
Bergshamra
Mariehamn
Langnas
Turku
Helsinki
Märsta
Frösunda
Ängsö
Blidö
Sigtuna
Rosersberg
Lindholmen
Karby
Svartlögafjärden
Brottby
Vagnsunda
Ljusterö
Ö Lagnö
Upplands-Väsby
Vallentuna
Bro
Täby
Åkersberga
Kungsängen
Stäket
Sollentuna
Rydbo
Svinninge
Resarö
Tranvik
St. Möja
Vaxholm
Färentuna
BROMMA
Stockholm
BIRKA
Drottningholm
DROTTNINGHOLMS SLOTT
Hersby
TIVOLI GRÖNA LUND
Gustavsberg
Värmdölandet
Horsstenfjärden
Tallinn
Riga
Stavsnäs
Ekerö
Älta
Saltsjöbaden
Runmarö
Tyresö
Längvik
Nämdöfjärden
Huddinge
Vendelso
Brevik
Nämdö
Rönninge
Tumba
Tyresta
Jordbro
Vårsta
Västerhaninge
Dalarö
Jungfrufj.
Skinnardai
Tungelsta
Hörningsholm
Muskö
Mysingen
Ornö
Sorunda
Muskö
Ornö
Morkö
Ösmo
Utö
St. Vika
Trosa
Nynäshamn
Grytnäs
Torö
Herrhamra
Krabbfjärden
Ventspils
Gdansk
Visby
Nynäshamn
Oskarshamn
0
10
20
30 km
Norsholmen
Kappelshamnsviken
Fårösund
Holmudden
Fårö
Hall
Kappelshamn
Fleringe
Fårösund
Bunge
Lickershamn
Lärbro
Hellvi
Lummelunda
Othem
Tingstäde
Slite
Väskinde
Boge
Visby
Hejdeby
Vibble
SANKTA MARIAS DOMKYRKA
Vallstena
Högklint
Ekeby
Gothem
Dalhem
Tofta
Roma
Eskilhem
Romakloster
Anga
Gotland
(Sverige)
(Sweden)
Väte
Kräklingbo
Västergarn
Sanda
Hejde
Katthammarsvik
Gammelgarn
Klintehamn
Ardre
Buttle
Alskog
Ljugarn
Lojsta
Eksta
Stånga
Nar
Hemse
Silte
Rone
Ronehamn
Havdhem
Grötlingbo
Näs
Burgsvik
Öja
Vamlingbo
Hamra
Hoburgen
A
B
C
D
3
4
5

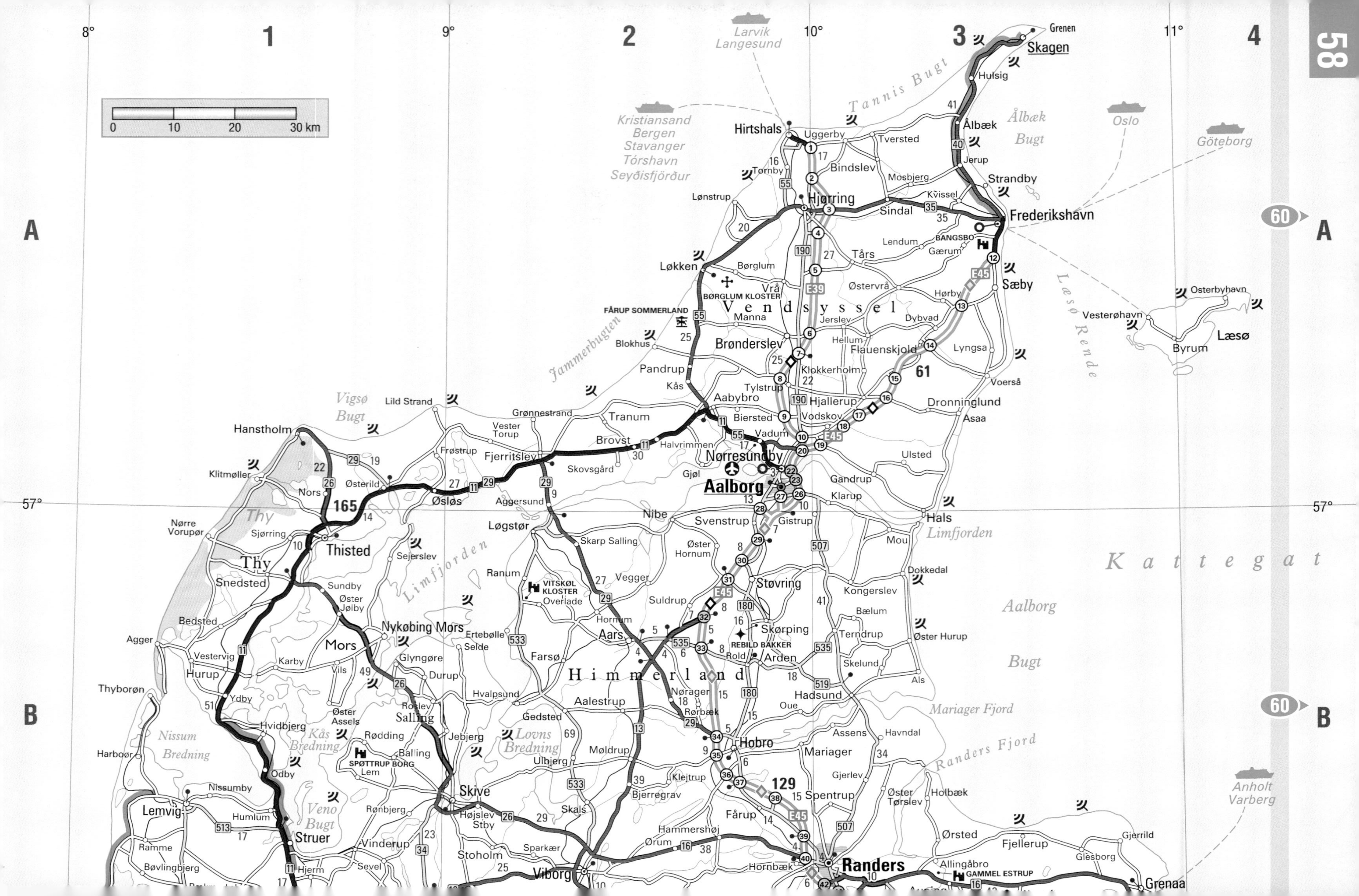

8°
9°
10°
11°
57°
1
2
3
4
A
B
60
0 10 20 30 km
Skagen
Grenen
Hulsig
Tannis Bugt
Ålbæk
Ålbæk Bugt
Jerup
Strandby
Frederikshavn
Kvissel
Bangsbo
Gærum
Sæby
Hirtshals
Uggerby
Tversted
Bindslev
Mosbjerg
Tornby
Hjørring
Sindal
Lønstrup
Lendum
Tårs
Løkken
Børglum
Børglum Kloster
Vrå
Østervrå
Hørby
Vendsyssel
Manna
Jersley
Dybvad
Fårup Sommerland
Blokhus
Brønderslev
Hellum
Flauenskjold
Lyngsa
Jammerbugten
Pandrup
Kås
Klokkerholm
Tylstrup
Voerså
Aabybro
Hjallerup
Dronninglund
Asaa
Biersted
Vodskov
Vadum
Halvrimmen
Nørresundby
Aalborg
Gjøl
Gandrup
Klarup
Ulsted
Hals
Limfjorden
Mou
Gistrup
Svenstrup
Nibe
Øster Hornum
Kattegat
Aalborg Bugt
Dokkedal
Kongerslev
Bælum
Øster Hurup
Terndrup
Skelund
Als
Støvring
Skørping
Rebild Bakker
Rold
Arden
Suldrup
Hadsund
Oue
Mariager Fjord
Havndal
Assens
Mariager
Randers Fjord
Gjerlev
Spentrup
Øster Tørslev
Holbæk
Randers
Ørsted
Fjellerup
Gjerrild
Glesborg
Allingåbro
Gammel Estrup
Grenaa
Anholt
Varberg
Læsø
Læsø Rende
Vesterøhavn
Østerbyhavn
Byrum
Oslo
Göteborg
Larvik
Langesund
Kristiansand
Bergen
Stavanger
Tórshavn
Seyðisfjörður
Hanstholm
Vigsø Bugt
Lild Strand
Klitmøller
Nors
Østerild
Frøstrup
Vester Torup
Grønnestrand
Tranum
Brovst
Fjerritslev
Skovsgård
Øsløs
Aggersund
Løgstør
Thy
Nørre Vorupør
Sjørring
Thisted
Sejerslev
Snedsted
Sundby
Øster Jølby
Bedsted
Agger
Vestervig
Hurup
Karby
Mors
Nykøbing Mors
Vils
Ertebølle
Selde
Glyngøre
Durup
Thyborøn
Ydby
Hvidbjerg
Øster Assels
Kås Bredning
Roslev
Salling
Rødding
Balling
Spøttrup Borg
Lem
Jebjerg
Hvalpsund
Ranum
Vitskøl Kloster
Overlade
Skarp Salling
Vegger
Hornum
Aars
Farsø
Himmerland
Nørager
Rørbæk
Aalestrup
Gedsted
Løvns Bredning
Møldrup
Ulbjerg
Hobro
Kleitrup
Bjerregrav
Fårup
Hammershøj
Ørum
Hornbæk
Harboør
Nissum Bredning
Odby
Nissumby
Lemvig
Humlum
Struer
Veno Bugt
Ramme
Bøvlingbjerg
Hjerm
Rønbjerg
Vinderup
Sevel
Skive
Højslev Stby
Stoholm
Sparkær
Skals
Viborg
E45
E39

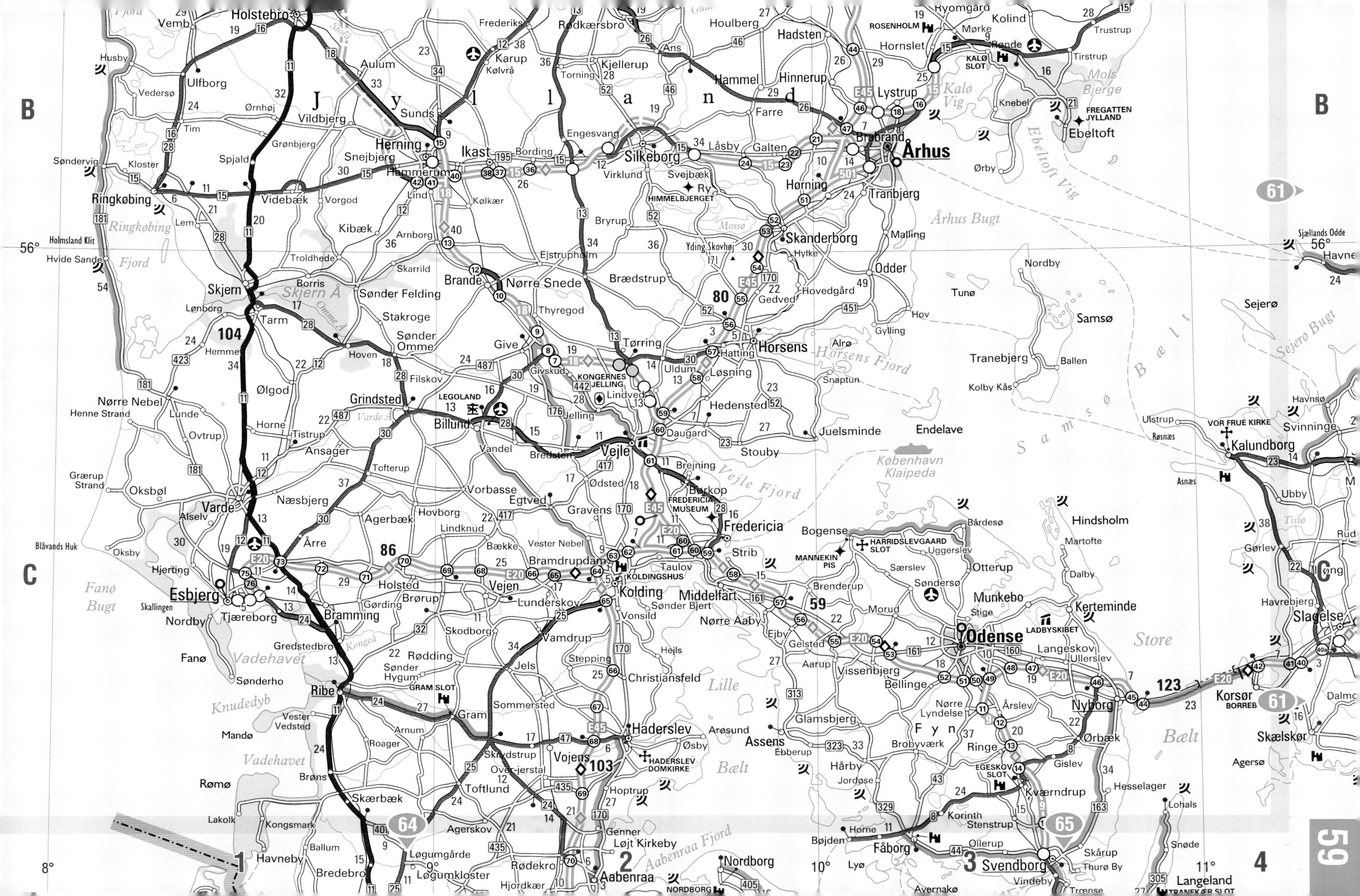

B
C
1
2
3
4
8°
9°
10°
11°
56°
Holstebro
Vemb
Husby
Ulfborg
Vedersø
Søndervig
Kloster
Ringkøbing
Ringkøbing Fjord
Holmsland Klit
Hvide Sande
Tim
Ørnhøj
Spjald
Videbæk
Vorgod
Lem
Skjern
Skjern Å
Borris
Troldhede
Lønborg
Tarm
Hemmet
Ølgod
Nørre Nebel
Henne Strand
Lunde
Ovtrup
Horne
Tistrup
Ansager
Grærup Strand
Oksbøl
Varde
Alslev
Blåvands Huk
Oksby
Hjerting
Esbjerg
Fanø Bugt
Skallingen
Nordby
Tjæreborg
Fanø
Vadehavet
Sønderho
Knudedyb
Mandø
Vester Vedsted
Rømø
Lakolk
Kongsmark
Havneby
Ballum
Bredebro
Brøns
Skærbæk
Ribe
Gredstedbro
Bramming
Gørding
Holsted
Brørup
Vejen
Årre
Næsbjerg
Agerbæk
Hovborg
Lindknud
Vorbasse
Egtved
Gravens
Vester Nebel
Bække
Bramdrupdam
Kolding
KOLDINGSHUS
Lunderskov
Vonsild
Skodborg
Rødding
Sønder Hygum
GRAM SLOT
Gram
Arnum
Roager
Vamdrup
Jels
Sommersted
Skodstrup
Over-Jerstal
Toftlund
Agerskov
Løgumgårde
Løgumkloster
Rødekro
Hjordkær
Aabenraa
Aabenraa Fjord
Løjt Kirkeby
Genner
Hoptrup
Vojens
Haderslev
HADERSLEV DOMKIRKE
Øsby
Stepping
Christiansfeld
Hejls
Sønder Bjert
Taulov
Fredericia
FREDERICIA MUSEUM
Børkop
Brejning
Vejle
Vejle Fjord
Ødsted
Bredsten
Vandel
Billund
LEGOLAND
Grindsted
Varde Å
Filskov
Give
Givskud
KONGERNES JELLING
Jelling
Lindved
Uldum
Tørring
Hatting
Horsens
Horsens Fjord
Løsning
Hedensted
Daugard
Stouby
Juelsminde
Snaptun
Endelave
Gylling
Hov
Alrø
Odder
Hovedgård
Gedved
Nørre Snede
Brande
Thyregod
Sønder Felding
Stakroge
Sønder Omme
Hoven
Skarrild
Arnborg
Kibæk
Ejstrupholm
Brædstrup
Bryrup
Ikast
Bording
Herning
Hammerum
Snejbjerg
Lind
Kølkær
Sunds
Aulum
Vildbjerg
Grønbjerg
Frederiks
Karup
Kølvrå
Rødkærsbro
Kjellerup
Torning
Engesvang
Silkeborg
Virklund
Svejbæk
Ry
HIMMELBJERGET
Mossø
Yding Skovhøj
Skanderborg
Hylke
Hørning
Tranbjerg
Malling
Århus Bugt
Århus
Brabrand
Galten
Låsby
Farre
Hammel
Hinnerup
Hadsten
Houlberg
Ans
Lystrup
Hornslet
ROSENHOLM
Ryomgård
Mørke
Kolind
Rønde
KALØ SLOT
Kalø Vig
Knebel
Mols Bjerge
Tirstrup
Trustrup
FREGATTEN JYLLAND
Ebeltoft
Ebeltoft Vig
Ørby
Tunø
Nordby
Samsø
Tranebjerg
Ballen
Kolby Kås
Samsø Bælt
Sejerø
Sejerø Bugt
Sjællands Odde
Havnsø
Svinninge
Ulstrup
Røsnæs
VOR FRUE KIRKE
Kalundborg
Asnæs
Ubby
Tissø
Gørlev
København Klaipeda
Hindsholm
Martofte
Bårdesø
Dalby
Bogense
HARRIDSLEVGAARD SLOT
MANNEKIN PIS
Uggerslev
Særslev
Otterup
Søndersø
Munkebo
Stige
Kerteminde
LADBYSKIBET
Odense
Langeskov
Ullerslev
Store Bælt
Nyborg
Korsør
BORREB
Slagelse
Havrebjerg
Skælskør
Agersø
Strib
Middelfart
Nørre Aaby
Brenderup
Morud
Ejby
Gelsted
Aarup
Vissenbjerg
Bellinge
Glamsbjerg
Lille Bælt
Assens
Ebberup
Arøsund
Fyn
Nørre Lyndelse
Årslev
Ringe
Brobyværk
Hårby
Jordøse
Ørbæk
Gislev
EGESKOV SLOT
Kværndrup
Hesselager
Lohals
Korinth
Stenstrup
Ollerup
Horne
Bøjden
Fåborg
Lyø
Svendborg
Vindeby
Skårup
Thurø By
Avernakø
Nordborg
Snøde
Langeland
E20
E45
61
64
65

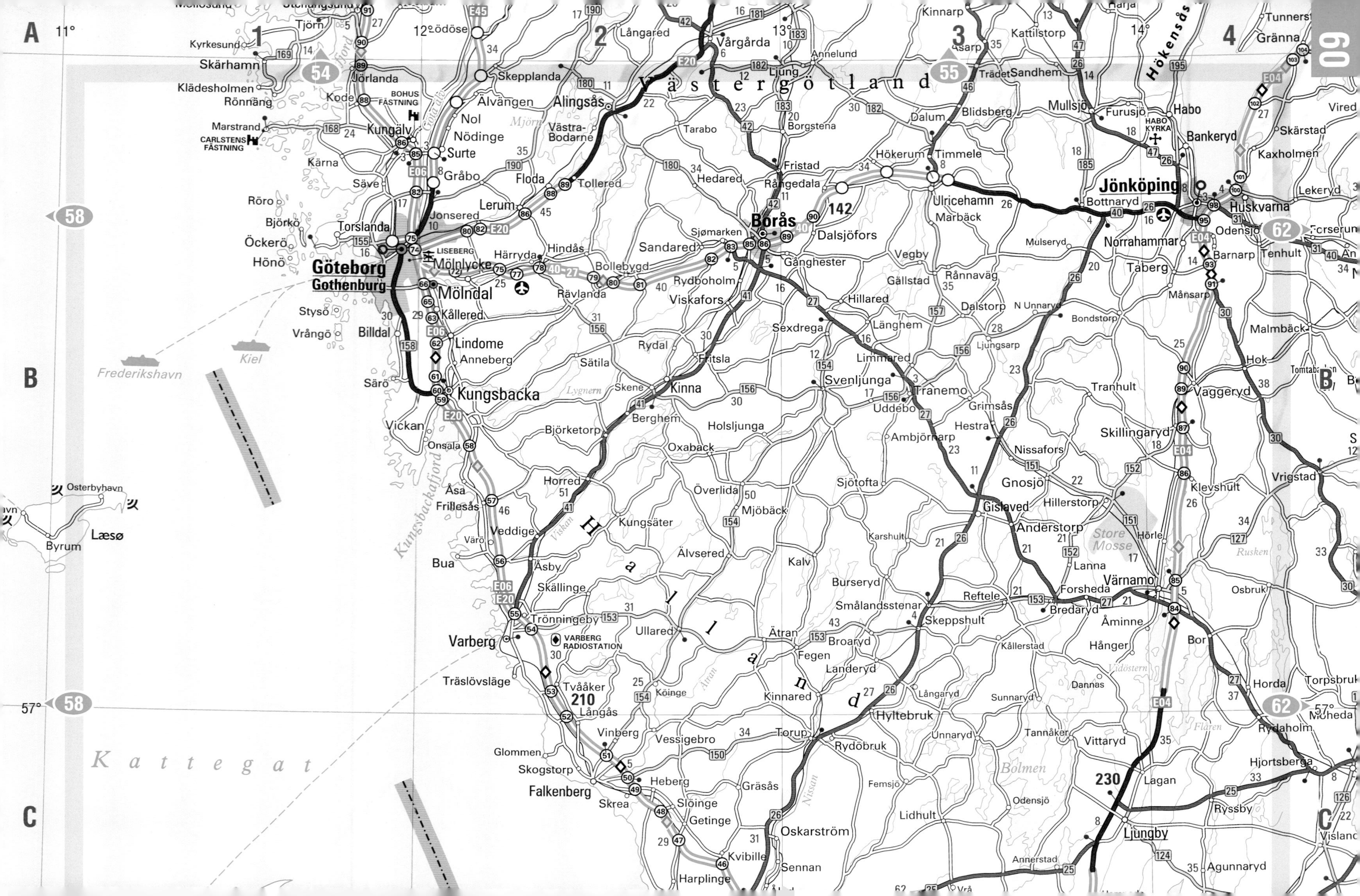

Västergötland
Halland
Kattegat
Göteborg
Gothenburg
Borås
Jönköping
Varberg
Falkenberg
Kungsbacka
Mölndal
Alingsås
Kungälv
Huskvarna
Värnamo
Ljungby
Gislaved
Ulricehamn
Skillingaryd
Vaggeryd
Hyltebruk
Oskarström
Torsland
Lerum
Floda
Kinna
Svenljunga
Tranemo
Anderstorp
Gnosjö
Smålandsstenar
Lindome
Onsala
Vargårda
Tjörn
Skärhamn
Marstrand
Stenungsund
Læsø
Byrum
Osterbyhavn
Frederikshavn
Kiel
Store Mosse
Bolmen
Hökensås
Tvååker
Torup
Kungsäter
Ullared
Fegen
Landeryd
Horred
Rydal
Sätila
Björketorp
Veddige
Frillesås
Åsa
Skrea
Bua
Glommen
Träslövsläge
Dalsjöfors
Sandared
Härryda
Landvetter
Mullsjö
Habo
Bankeryd
Gränna
Taberg
Norrahammar
Bredaryd
Forsheda
Reftele
Skeppshult
Rydöbruk
Lidhult
Lagan
Ryssby
Agunnaryd
VARBERG RADIOSTATION
BOHUS FÄSTNING
CARLSTENS FÄSTNING
HABO KYRKA
LISEBERG

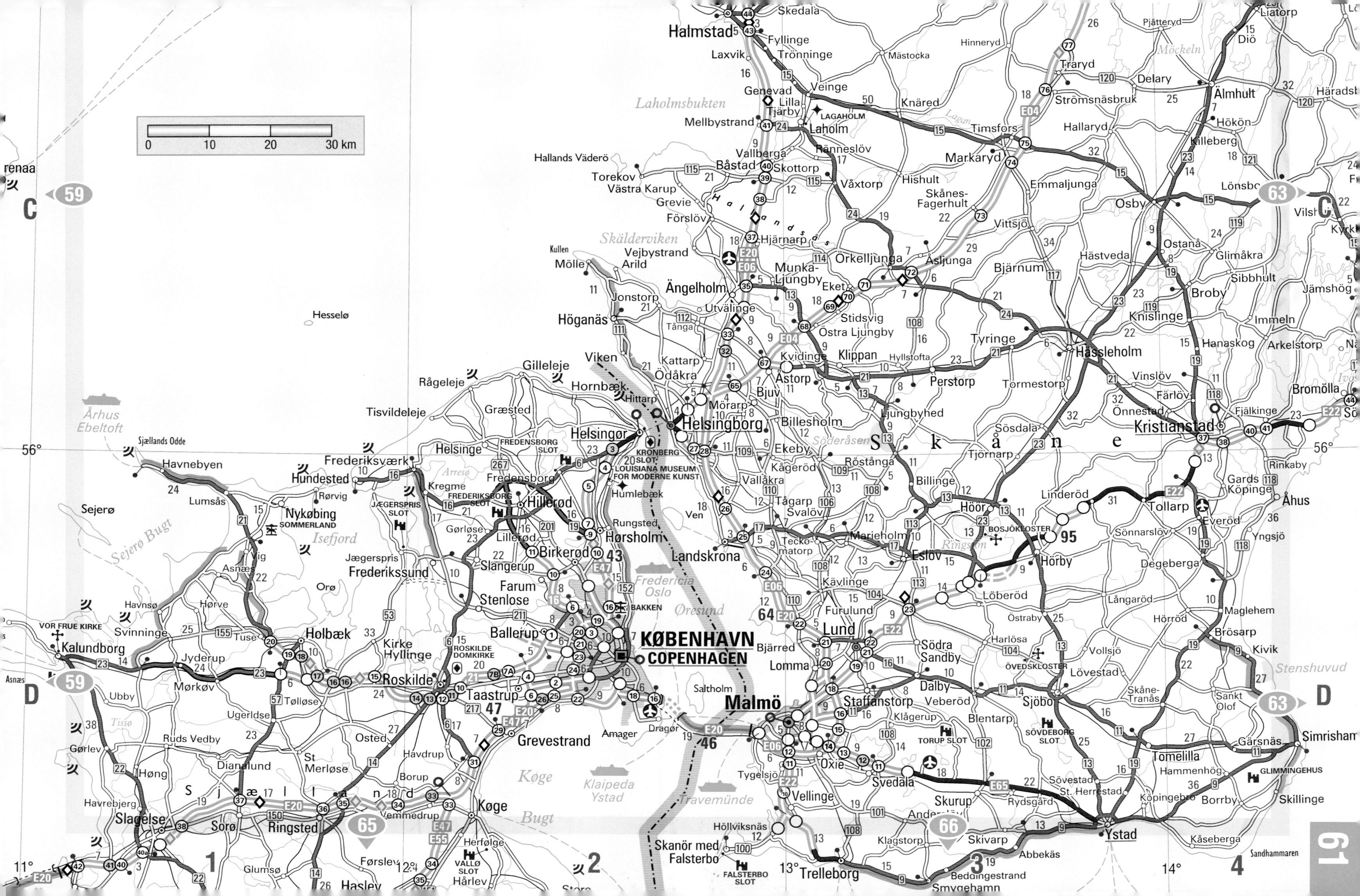
Halmstad
Laholmsbukten
Laholm
Båstad
Ängelholm
Höganäs
Helsingborg
Helsingør
Landskrona
KØBENHAVN
COPENHAGEN
Malmö
Lund
Trelleborg
Ystad
Kristianstad
Hässleholm
Eslöv
Hörby
Sjöbo
Simrishamn
Skåne
Öresund
Køge Bugt
Sejerø Bugt
Isefjord
Skälderviken
Roskilde
Hillerød
Frederikssund
Holbæk
Kalundborg
Slagelse
Sorø
Ringsted
Køge
Taastrup
Ballerup
Frederiksværk
Hundested
Nykøbing
Sjællands Odde
Hesselø
Sejerø
Klippan
Åstorp
Örkelljunga
Markaryd
Älmhult
Osby
Tomelilla
Svedala
Skanör med Falsterbo
Kullen
0 10 20 30 km
56°
11°
12°
13°
14°

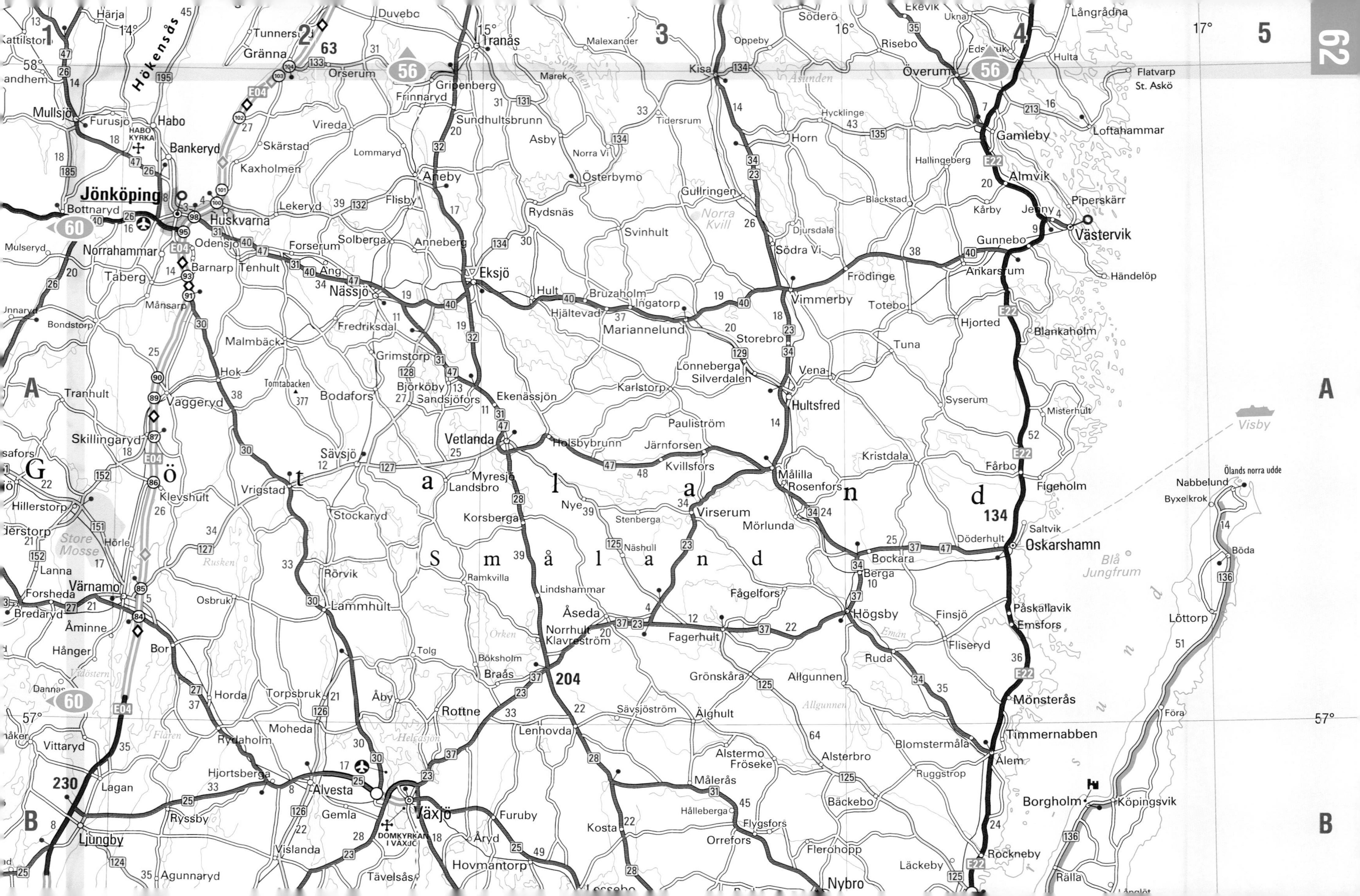
Småland
Götaland
Jönköping
Huskvarna
Bankeryd
Habo
Habo Kyrka
Mullsjö
Furusjö
Bottnaryd
Norrahammar
Taberg
Barnarp
Tenhult
Odensjö
Månsarp
Mulseryd
Bondstorp
Hökensås
Härja
Gränna
Tunnerstad
Orserum
Duvebo
Vireda
Skärstad
Kaxholmen
Lommaryd
Lekeryd
Forserum
Solberga
Flisby
Aneby
Frinnaryd
Gripenberg
Tranås
Sundhultsbrunn
Asby
Marek
Malexander
Sommen
Norra Vi
Österbymo
Rydsnäs
Tidersrum
Kisa
Oppeby
Söderö
Åsunden
Horn
Hycklinge
Risebo
Överum
Ukna
Gamleby
Loftahammar
Hulta
Långrådna
Flatvarp
St. Askö
Hallingeberg
Almvik
Kårby
Jenny
Piperskärr
Västervik
Händelöp
Gunnebo
Ankarsrum
Blackstad
Djursdala
Norra Kvill
Gullringen
Svinhult
Södra Vi
Vimmerby
Frödinge
Totebo
Hjorted
Blankaholm
Tuna
Storebro
Lönneberga
Silverdalen
Vena
Hultsfred
Syserum
Misterhult
Eksjö
Nässjö
Ång
Hult
Bruzaholm
Ingatorp
Hjältevad
Mariannelund
Fredriksdal
Grimstorp
Björköby
Sandsjöfors
Ekenässjön
Karlstorp
Pauliström
Malmbäck
Hok
Tomtabacken
Bodafors
Vaggeryd
Tranhult
Skillingaryd
Klevshult
Hillerstorp
Store Mosse
Hörle
Lanna
Värnamo
Forsheda
Bredaryd
Åminne
Hånger
Bor
Vidöstern
Dannäs
Vittaryd
Flaren
Ljungby
Lagan
Agunnaryd
Ryssby
Hjortsberga
Rydaholm
Horda
Torpsbruk
Moheda
Alvesta
Gemla
Vislanda
Växjö
Domkyrkan i Växjö
Tävelsås
Hovmantorp
Åryd
Furuby
Helgasjön
Åby
Rottne
Tolg
Braås
Böksholm
Orken
Lammhult
Rörvik
Osbruk
Rusken
Vrigstad
Stockaryd
Sävsjö
Vetlanda
Holsbybrunn
Myresjö
Landsbro
Korsberga
Ramkvilla
Nye
Stenberga
Näshult
Kvillsfors
Järnforsen
Målilla
Rosenfors
Virserum
Mörlunda
Lindshammar
Åseda
Norrhult
Klavreström
Fagerhult
Fågelfors
Kristdala
Bockara
Berga
Högsby
Emån
Finsjö
Fliseryd
Ruda
Allgunnen
Grönskåra
Sävsjöström
Älghult
Lenhovda
Alstermo
Fröseke
Alsterbro
Blomstermåla
Måleras
Hälleberga
Flygsfors
Orrefors
Kosta
Bäckebo
Flerohopp
Nybro
Läckeby
Ruggstrop
Döderhult
Saltvik
Oskarshamn
Figeholm
Fårbo
Påskallavik
Emsfors
Mönsterås
Timmernabben
Ålem
Rockneby
Blå Jungfrun
Visby
Ölands norra udde
Nabbelund
Byxelkrok
Böda
Löttorp
Föra
Borgholm
Köpingsvik
Rälla
Kalmarsund
15°
16°
17°
57°
58°
E04
E22
56
60
63
134
204
230

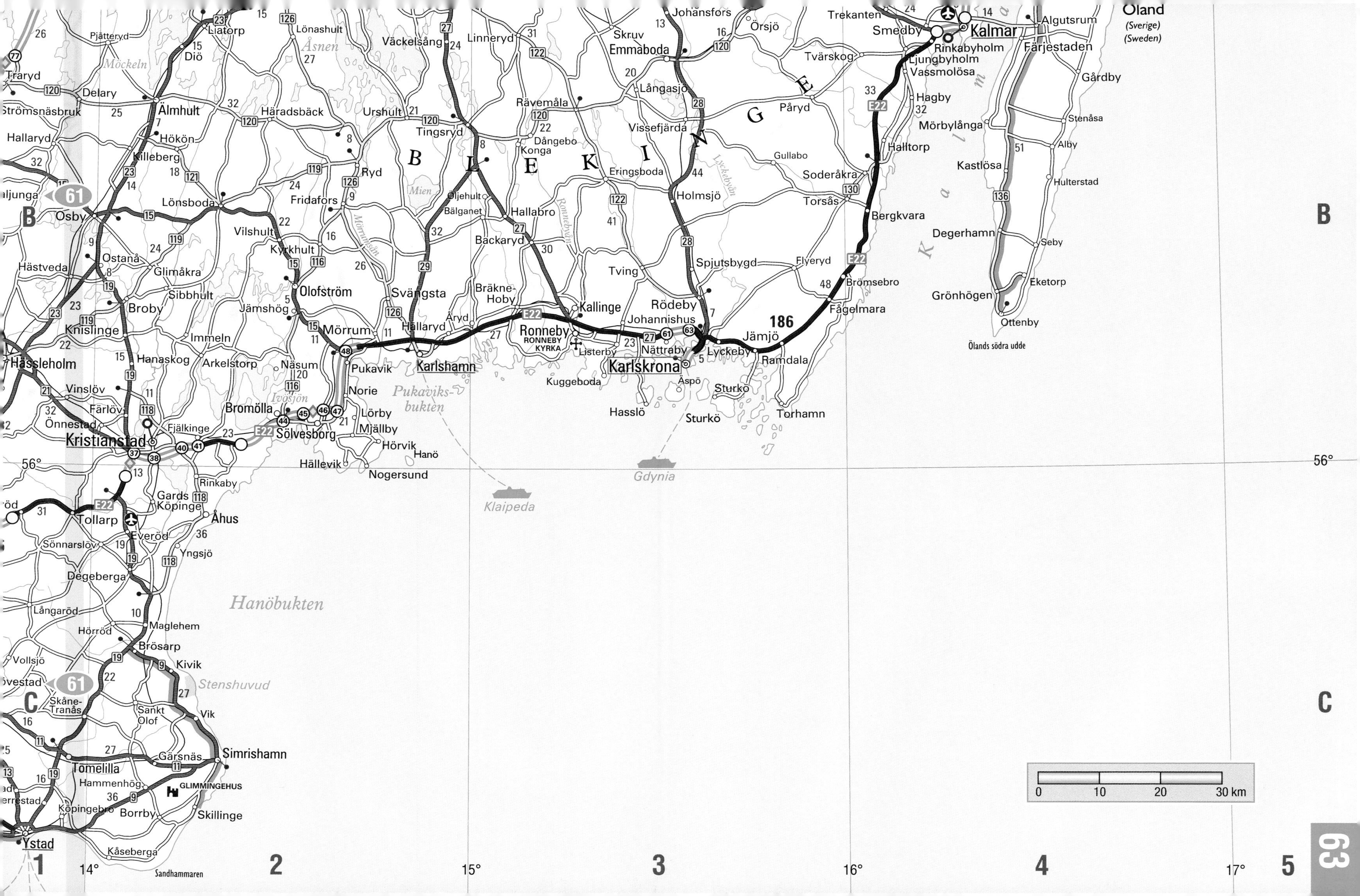

63
Öland
(Sverige)
(Sweden)
Kalmar
Färjestaden
Algutsrum
Gårdby
Stenåsa
Alby
Hulterstad
Seby
Eketorp
Ottenby
Ölands södra udde
Grönhögen
Degerhamn
Kastlösa
Mörbylånga
Smedby
Trekanten
Rinkabyholm
Ljungbyholm
Vassmolösa
Hagby
Halltorp
Bergkvara
Söderåkra
Torsås
Brömsebro
Fågelmara
Jämjö
Ramdala
Torhamn
Sturkö
Aspö
Lyckeby
Karlskrona
Nättraby
Johannishus
Rödeby
Kallinge
Ronneby
RONNEBY KYRKA
Listerby
Kuggeboda
Hasslö
Gdynia
Klaipeda
Karlshamn
Pukaviksbukten
Pukavik
Norie
Lörby
Mjällby
Hörvik
Hanö
Hällevik
Nogersund
Sölvesborg
Bromölla
Ivösjön
Näsum
Mörrum
Olofström
Jämshög
Kyrkhult
Vilshult
Svängsta
Hällaryd
Äryd
Bräkne-Hoby
Backaryd
Hallabro
Öljehult
Bälganet
Mien
Mörrumsån
Ronnebyån
Lyckebyån
Tving
Spjutsbygd
Flyeryd
Holmsjö
Eringsboda
Gullabo
Påryd
Vissefjärda
Långasjö
Emmaboda
Skruv
Johansfors
Örsjö
Tvärskog
Rävemåla
Dångebo
Konga
Tingsryd
Linneryd
Väckelsång
Urshult
Ryd
Fridafors
Häradsbäck
Lönashult
Åsnen
Liatorp
Diö
Älmhult
Hökön
Killeberg
Lönsboda
Osby
Delary
Pjätteryd
Möckeln
Traryd
Strömsnäsbruk
Hallaryd
Hästveda
Ostanå
Glimåkra
Sibbhult
Broby
Knislinge
Immeln
Arkelstorp
Hanaskog
Hässleholm
Vinslöv
Färlöv
Önnestad
Kristianstad
Fjälkinge
Rinkaby
Gards Köpinge
Åhus
Yngsjö
Tollarp
Everöd
Sönnarslöv
Degeberga
Långaröd
Hörröd
Maglehem
Hanöbukten
Brösarp
Kivik
Stenshuvud
Vik
Sankt Olof
Vollsjö
Skåne-Tranås
Simrishamn
Gärsnäs
Tomelilla
Hammenhög
GLIMMINGEHUS
Köpingebro
Borrby
Skillinge
Kåseberga
Ystad
Sandhammaren
B L E K I N G E
K a l m a r
186
E22
56°
14°
15°
16°
17°
1
2
3
4
5
B
C
0
10
20
30 km

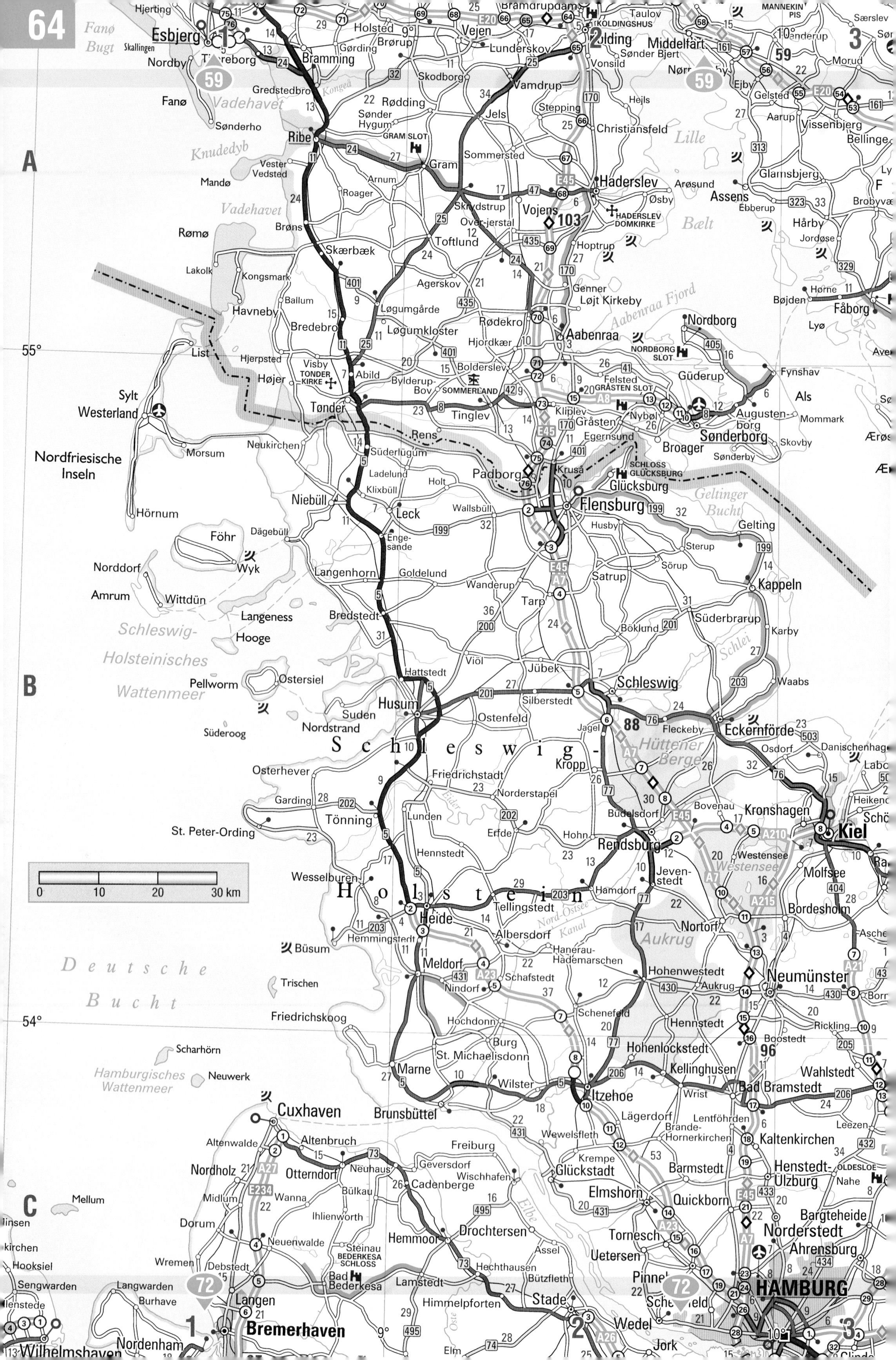

Fanø Bugt
Skallingen
Esbjerg
Hjerting
Nordby
Tjæreborg
Bramming
Gredstedbro
Fanø
Vadehavet
Sønderho
Ribe
Knudedyb
Vester Vedsted
Mandø
Vadehavet
Rømø
Brøns
Skærbæk
Lakolk
Kongsmark
Havneby
Ballum
Bredebro
List
Hjerpsted
Højer
Visby
TØNDER KIRKE
Abild
Tønder
Sylt
Westerland
Nordfriesische Inseln
Morsum
Neukirchen
Hörnum
Föhr
Dägebüll
Wyk
Norddorf
Amrum
Wittdün
Langeness
Hooge
Schleswig-Holsteinisches Wattenmeer
Pellworm
Ostersiel
Süderoog
Nordstrand
Suden
Husum
Holsted
Gørding
Brørup
Vejen
Lunderskov
Kolding
KOLDINGSHUS
Taulov
Bramdrupdam
Middelfart
Sønder Bjert
Vonsild
Skodborg
Rødding
Sønder Hygum
GRAM SLOT
Gram
Vamdrup
Jels
Stepping
Christiansfeld
Sommersted
Haderslev
HADERSLEV DOMKIRKE
Arøsund
Øsby
Vojens
Skrydstrup
Over-jerstal
Toftlund
Roager
Arnum
Hoptrup
Genner
Løjt Kirkeby
Agerskov
Løgumgårde
Løgumkloster
Rødekro
Hjordkær
Aabenraa
Aabenraa Fjord
Bolderslev
Bylderup-Bov
SOMMERLAND
Tinglev
Rens
Kliplev
Gråsten
GRÅSTEN SLOT
Felsted
Egernsund
Padborg
Kruså
Nordborg
NORDBORG SLOT
Güderup
Fynshav
Als
Nybøl
Broager
Augustenborg
Sønderborg
Mommark
Skovby
Sønderby
SCHLOSS GLÜCKSBURG
Glücksburg
Lille Bælt
Assens
Ebberup
Hårby
Jordløse
Glamsbjerg
Vissenbjerg
Aarup
Gelsted
Ejby
Bellinge
Brobyvæ
Bøjden
Hørne
Fåborg
Lyø
Søndersø
Morud
Særslev
MANNEKIN PIS
Süderlügum
Ladelund
Klixbüll
Holt
Niebüll
Leck
Wallsbüll
Flensburg
Husby
Gelting
Geltinger Bucht
Enge-Sande
Sterup
Langenhorn
Goldelund
Wanderup
Satrup
Sörup
Kappeln
Tarp
Bredstedt
Süderbrarup
Böklund
Karby
Schlei
Viöl
Jübek
Hattstedt
Schleswig
Waabs
Silberstedt
Ostenfeld
Jagel
Fleckeby
Eckernförde
Osdorf
Danischenhagen
Hüttener Berge
Kropp
Schleswig-Holstein
Osterhever
Friedrichstadt
Norderstapel
Garding
Tönning
Lunden
St. Peter-Ording
Erfde
Hohn
Büdelsdorf
Bovenau
Kronshagen
Kiel
Rendsburg
Westensee
Molfsee
Hennstedt
Jevenstedt
Hamdorf
Wesselburen
Tellingstedt
Heide
Albersdorf
Nord-Ostsee Kanal
Nortorf
Bordesholm
Hemmingstedt
Büsum
Meldorf
Hanerau-Hademarschen
Aukrug
Neumünster
Hohenwestedt
Schafstedt
Nindorf
Trischen
Deutsche Bucht
Friedrichskoog
Schenefeld
Hennstedt
Boostedt
Rickling
Hochdonn
Burg
St. Michaelisdonn
Hohenlockstedt
Scharhörn
Hamburgisches Wattenmeer
Neuwerk
Marne
Wilster
Kellinghusen
Wahlstedt
Itzehoe
Wrist
Bad Bramstedt
Cuxhaven
Brunsbüttel
Lägerdorf
Lentföhrden
Brande-Hornerkirchen
Kaltenkirchen
Leezen
Altenbruch
Altenwalde
Freiburg
Wewelsfleth
Krempe
Glückstadt
Barmstedt
Henstedt-Ulzburg
OLDESLOE
Nahe
Nordholz
Otterndorf
Neuhaus
Geversdorf
Cadenberge
Wischhafen
Elmshorn
Quickborn
Bargteheide
Norderstedt
Mellum
Midlum
Wanna
Bülkau
Ihlienworth
Drochtersen
Dorum
Neuenwalde
Steinau
BEDERKESA SCHLOSS
Hemmoor
Elbe
Tornesch
Uetersen
Ahrensburg
Hooksiel
Wremen
Debstedt
Bad Bederkesa
Lamstedt
Hechthausen
Assel
Bützfleth
Pinneberg
HAMBURG
Sengwarden
Langwarden
Burhave
Langen
Himmelpforten
Stade
Schenefeld
Wedel
Bremerhaven
Wilhelmshaven
Nordenham
Jork
Elm
Oste

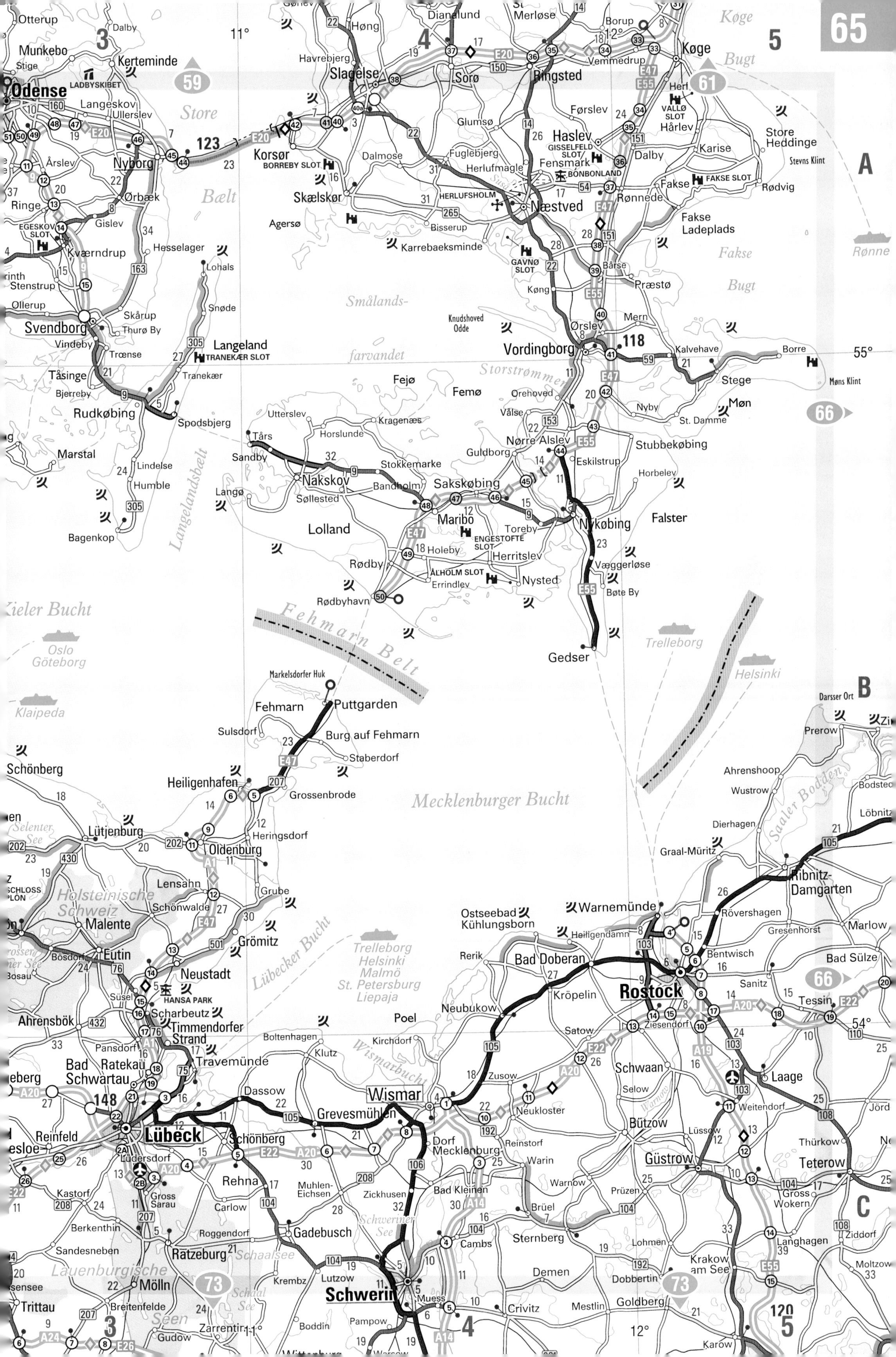
Otterup
Dalby
Munkebo
Kerteminde
Stige
Odense
LADBYSKIBET
Langeskov
Ullerslev
Årslev
Nyborg
Ringe
Ørbæk
Gislev
EGESKOV SLOT
Kværndrup
Hesselager
Lohals
Stenstrup
Ollerup
Svendborg
Skårup
Thurø By
Vindeby
Snøde
Langeland
TRANEKÆR SLOT
Trænse
Tåsinge
Tranekær
Bjerreby
Rudkøbing
Spodsbjerg
Marstal
Lindelse
Humble
Bagenkop
Langelandsbælt
Store
Bælt
Korsør
BORREBY SLOT
Skælskør
Agersø
Slagelse
Havrebjerg
Høng
Dianalund
Sorø
Dalmose
Glumsø
Fuglebjerg
Herlufmagle
HERLUFSHOLM
Bisserup
Karrebaeksminde
Næstved
Fensmark
BONBONLAND
GISSELFELD SLOT
GAVNØ SLOT
Ringsted
Merløse
Borup
Vemmedrup
Køge
Køge Bugt
Herfølge
VALLØ SLOT
Hårlev
Førslev
Haslev
Dalby
Karise
Store Heddinge
Stevns Klint
Fakse
FAKSE SLOT
Rønnede
Rødvig
Fakse Ladeplads
Fakse Bugt
Rønne
Bårse
Præstø
Køng
Smålands-
farvandet
Knudshoved Odde
Mern
Ørslev
Vordingborg
Kalvehave
Borre
Møns Klint
Storstrømmen
Stege
Møn
Nyby
St. Damme
Fejø
Femø
Orehoved
Vålse
Utterslev
Kragenæs
Horslunde
Tårs
Sandby
Nørre Alslev
Guldborg
Eskilstrup
Stubbekøbing
Stokkemarke
Nakskov
Bandholm
Sakskøbing
Horbelev
Søllested
Langø
Maribo
Toreby
Nykøbing
Falster
Lolland
ENGESTOFTE SLOT
Holeby
Herritslev
Rødby
ÅLHOLM SLOT
Errindlev
Nysted
Vægggerløse
Bøte By
Rødbyhavn
Fehmarn Belt
Gedser
Trelleborg
Helsinki
Kieler Bucht
Oslo
Göteborg
Klaipeda
Markelsdorfer Huk
Fehmarn
Puttgarden
Sulsdorf
Burg auf Fehmarn
Staberdorf
Schönberg
Heiligenhafen
Grossenbrode
Mecklenburger Bucht
Darsser Ort
Prerow
Ahrenshoop
Wustrow
Saaler Bodden
Dierhagen
Graal-Müritz
Ribnitz-Damgarten
Lütjenburg
Selenter See
Heringsdorf
Oldenburg
Lensahn
Holsteinische Schweiz
Schönwalde
Grube
Malente
Eutin
Bösdorf
Grömitz
Neustadt
HANSA PARK
Süsel
Scharbeutz
Timmendorfer Strand
Ahrensbök
Pansdorf
Bad Schwartau
Ratekau
Travemünde
Lübecker Bucht
Trelleborg
Helsinki
Malmö
St. Petersburg
Liepaja
Ostseebad Kühlungsborn
Warnemünde
Heiligendamm
Rövershagen
Gresenhorst
Marlow
Rerik
Bad Doberan
Bentwitsch
Bad Sülze
Kröpelin
Rostock
Sanitz
Tessin
Neubukow
Poel
Satow
Ziesendorf
Boltenhagen
Klutz
Kirchdorf
Wismarbucht
Zusow
Schwaan
Selow
Laage
Dassow
Wismar
Neukloster
Weitendorf
Lübeck
Reinfeld
Gadebusch
Grevesmühlen
Schönberg
Dorf Mecklenburg
Bützow
Lüssow
Thürkow
Rehna
Reinstorf
Warin
Güstrow
Teterow
Kastorf
Carlow
Muhlen-Eichsen
Zickhusen
Bad Kleinen
Warnow
Prüzen
Gross Wokern
Berkenthin
Lüdersdorf
Gross Sarau
Brüel
Sandesneben
Roggendorf
Ratzeburg
Schaalsee
Schweriner See
Cambs
Sternberg
Lohmen
Langhagen
Ziddorf
Lauenburgische Seen
Mölln
Krembz
Lutzow
Demen
Dobbertin
Krakow am See
Moltzow
Breitenfelde
Schwerin
Crivitz
Mestlin
Goldberg
Trittau
Zarrentin
Muess
Pampow
Boddin
Gudow
Karow

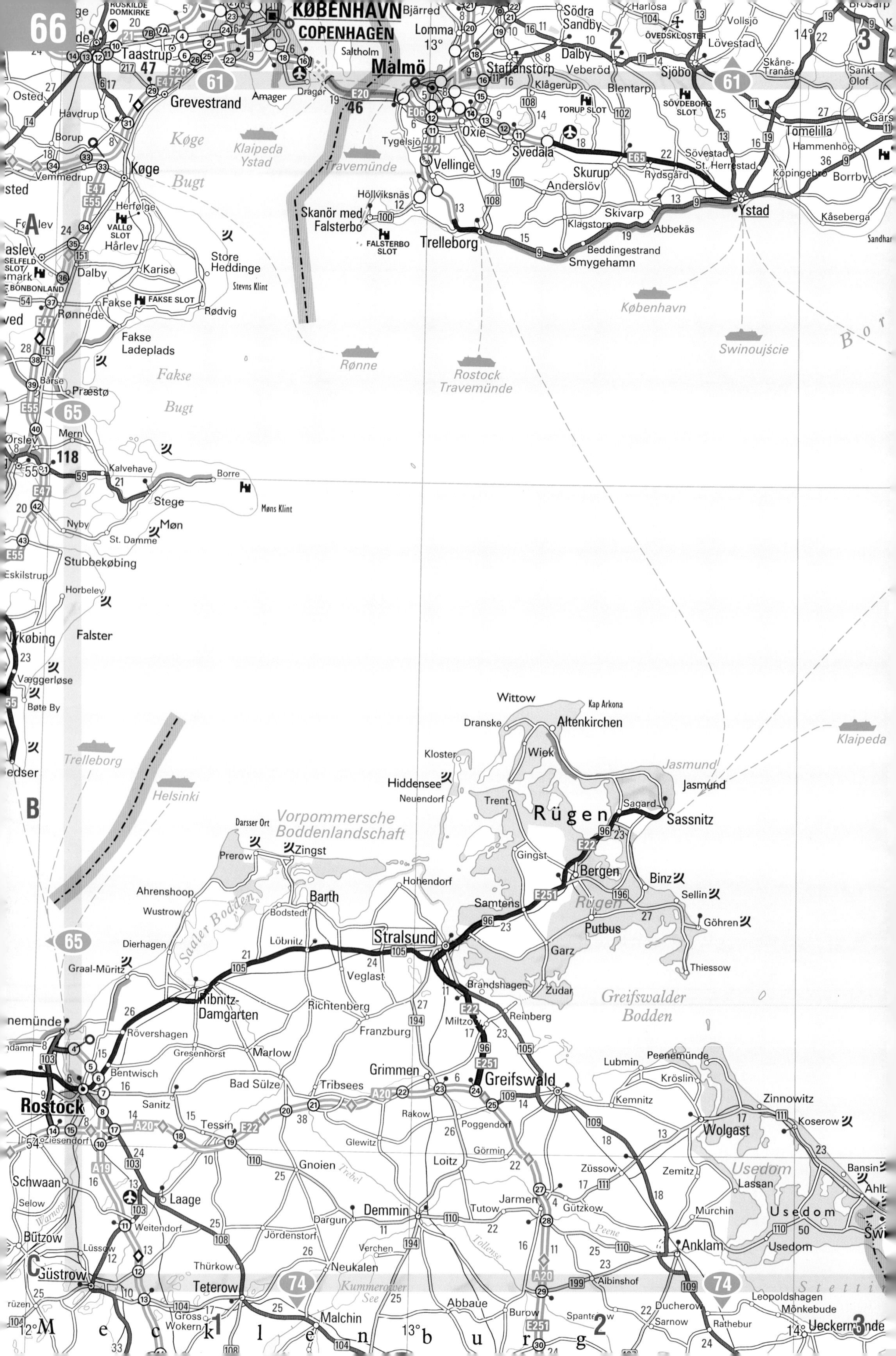
KØBENHAVN
COPENHAGEN
Malmö
Taastrup
Grevestrand
Amager
Dragør
Saltholm
Bjärred
Lomma
Södra Sandby
Dalby
Staffanstorp
Veberöd
Blentarp
Sjöbo
Lövestad
Vollsjö
Harlösa
ÖVEDSKLOSTER
Skåne-Tranås
Sankt Olof
Tomelilla
Hammenhög
Borrby
Kåseberga
Ystad
Sövestad
St. Herrestad
Köpingebro
Rydsgård
Skurup
Svedala
Oxie
Klågerup
TORUP SLOT
SÖVDEBORG SLOT
Tygelsjö
Vellinge
Höllviksnäs
Skanör med Falsterbo
FALSTERBO SLOT
Trelleborg
Anderslöv
Skivarp
Klagstorp
Abbekäs
Beddingestrand
Smygehamn
Køge
Køge Bugt
Havdrup
Borup
Vemmedrup
Herfølge
VALLØ SLOT
Hårlev
Karise
Store Heddinge
Stevns Klint
Dalby
Fakse
FAKSE SLOT
Rødvig
Rønnede
Fakse Ladeplads
Fakse Bugt
Præstø
Mern
Ørslev
Kalvehave
Stege
Borre
Møns Klint
Møn
Nyby
St. Damme
Stubbekøbing
Horbelev
Nykøbing
Falster
Væggerløse
Bøte By
Klaipeda
Ystad
Travemünde
Rønne
Rostock
Travemünde
København
Swinoujście
Trelleborg
Helsinki
Wittow
Kap Arkona
Dranske
Altenkirchen
Wiek
Kloster
Hiddensee
Neuendorf
Jasmund
Sassnitz
Sagard
Trent
Rügen
Gingst
Bergen
Binz
Sellin
Samtens
Putbus
Göhren
Garz
Thiessow
Zudar
Brandshagen
Greifswalder Bodden
Darsser Ort
Vorpommersche Boddenlandschaft
Prerow
Zingst
Ahrenshoop
Wustrow
Saaler Bodden
Barth
Bodstedt
Hohendorf
Stralsund
Löbnitz
Veglast
Dierhagen
Graal-Müritz
Ribnitz-Damgarten
Richtenberg
Franzburg
Miltzow
Reinberg
Röversshagen
Gresenhorst
Marlow
Bentwisch
Bad Sülze
Tribsees
Grimmen
Greifswald
Lubmin
Peenemünde
Kröslin
Kemnitz
Zinnowitz
Koserow
Wolgast
Rostock
Sanitz
Tessin
Rakow
Poggendorf
Glewitz
Görmin
Gnoien
Loitz
Züssow
Zemitz
Usedom
Lassan
Bansin
Ahlbeck
Schwaan
Ziesendorf
Selow
Laage
Bützow
Weitendorf
Demmin
Dargun
Jördenstorf
Verchen
Tutow
Jarmen
Gützkow
Murchin
Anklam
Lüssow
Güstrow
Thürkow
Neukalen
Teterow
Kummerower See
Malchin
Abbaue
Burow
Albinshof
Spantekow
Ducherow
Sarnow
Rathebur
Leopoldshagen
Mönkebude
Ueckermünde
Gross Wokern
Mecklenburg
Stettin

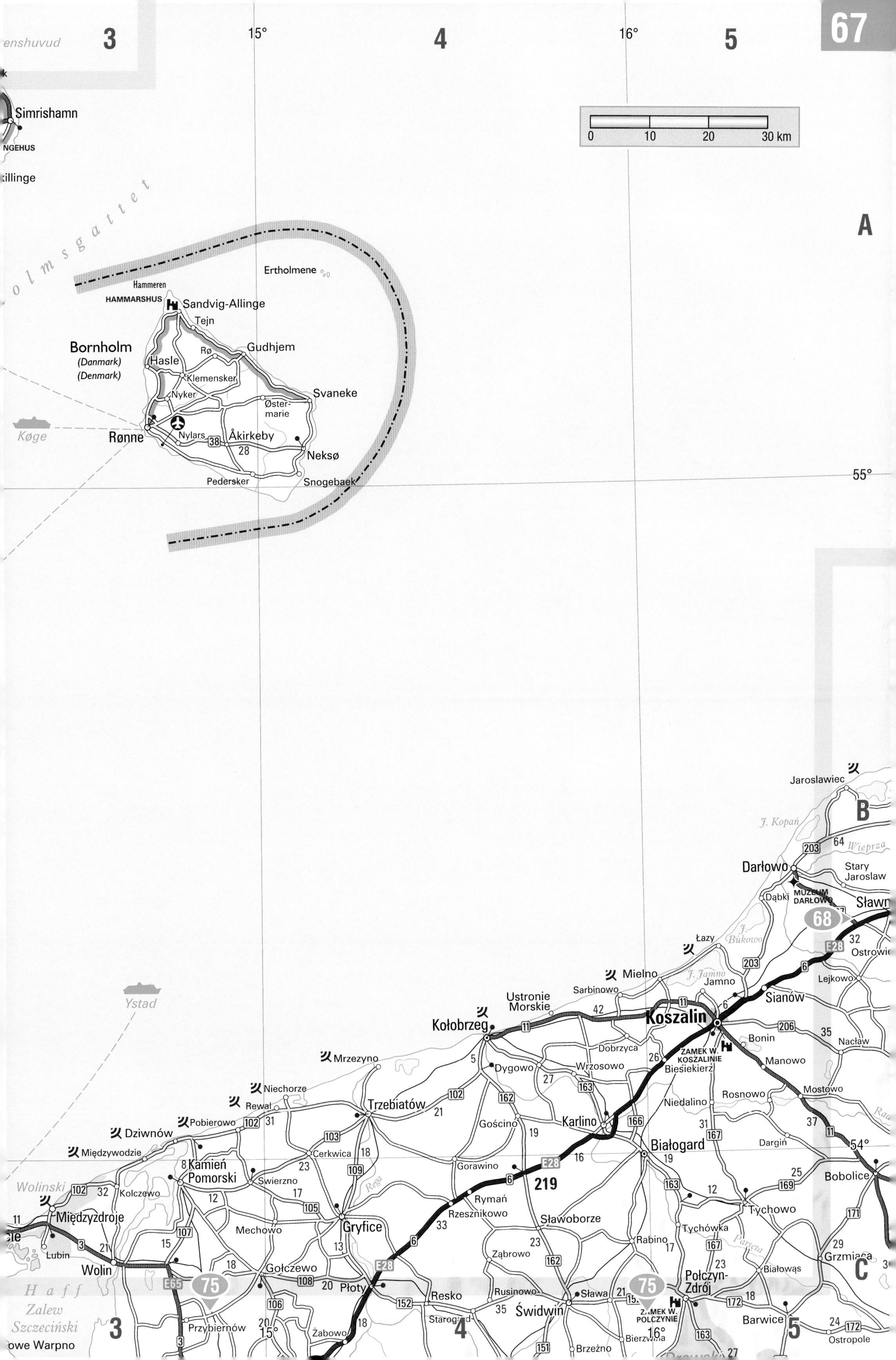

enshuvud

**3**   15°   **4**   16°   **5**

**A**

Simrishamn

NGEHUS

killinge

Køge

*olmsgattet*

Ertholmene °₀

Hammeren
**HAMMARSHUS**   Sandvig-Allinge

Tejn

**Bornholm**   Rø   Gudhjem
*(Danmark)*
*(Denmark)*   Hasle
Klemensker
Nyker   Svaneke
Øster-
marie

Rønne   Nylars   38   Åkirkeby   Neksø
28

Pederster   Snogebaek

55°

Ystad

Jaroslawiec

**B**   *J. Kopań*

203   64   *Wieprza*

Darłowo   Stary
Jaroslaw

**MUZEUM
DARŁOWO**   Sławn

Dąbki   **68**

Łazy   *J.*   E28   32
*Bukowo*   6   Ostrowie
203

Mielno   *J. Jamno*   Lejkowo

Sarbinowo   Jamno
Ustronie   42   **Koszalin**   11   Sianów
Morskie   206   35   Nacław
Kołobrzeg   11   Dobrzyca   **ZAMEK W.**   6
KOSZALINIE   Bonin
Mrzezyno   5   Dygowo   26   Manowo
Wrzosowo   Biesiekierz   Niedalino   Mostowo   37
Niechorze   27   163   Rosnowo
102   162   Karlino   31   167
Rewal   21   Gościno   19   166   Dargiń   *Radew*
Pobierowo   102   31   Trzebiatów   16   Białogard   25
Dziwnów   103   Cerkwica   18   E28   19   163   Bobolice
Międzywodzie   23   6   219   163   12   169
Wolinski   109   Gorawino   Sławoborze   Tychowo   171
102   32   Kolczewo   Swierzno   17   Rymań   Tychówka   167
8 **Kamień**   12   105   Rzeszńikowo   162   Rabino   17   Białowąs   29
Międzyzdroje   **Pomorski**   Mechowo   33   Zabrowo   23   163   Grzmiąca
107   **Gryfice**   6   167
3   21   15   13   162   Sława   21   Połczyn-   18   **C**
Wolin   18   Gołczewo   108   20   Resko   Zdrój   172
*Haff*   106   Płoty   152   Rusinowo   **ZAMEK W.**   Barwice
*Zalew*   E65   **75**   E28   Starogard   **Świdwin**   **POŁCZYNIE**   163   24   172
*Szczeciński*   Przybiernów   20   Żabowo   Bierzwnia   172   Ostropole
owe Warpno   **3**   3   15°   18   **4**   Brzeźno   16°   **5**
151   27

0   10   20   30 km

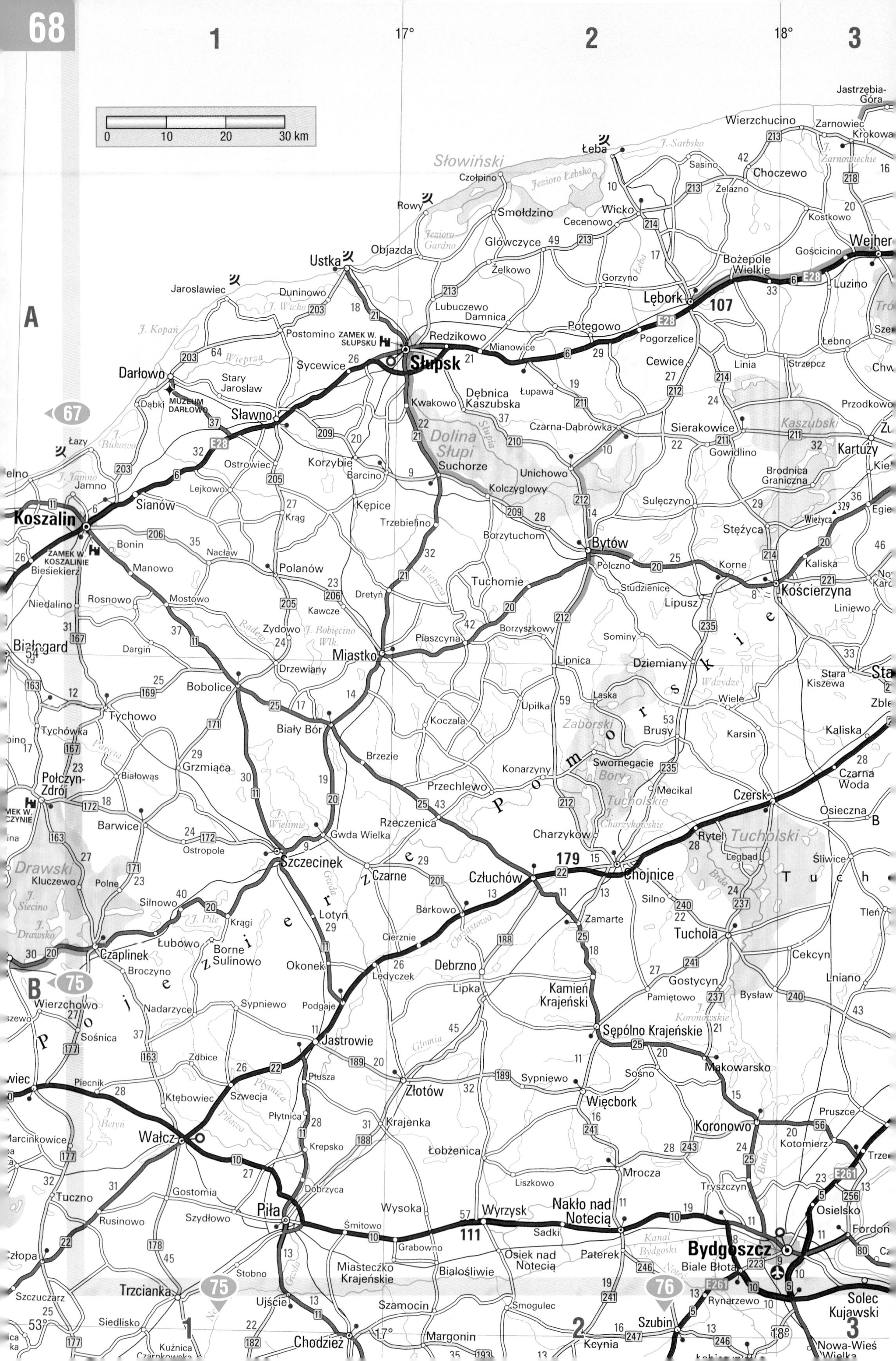
1
17°
2
18°
3
A
B
0 10 20 30 km
Słowiński
Jezioro Łebsko
Jezioro Gardno
Łeba
Wierzchucino
Jastrzębia-Góra
Zarnowiec
Krokowa
Choczewo
Sasino
Żelazno
Czołpino
Rowy
Smołdzino
Wicko
Cecenowo
Główczyce
Kostkowo
Wejherowo
Ustka
Objazda
Żelkowo
Gorzyno
Bożepole Wielkie
Gościcino
Luzino
Jarosławiec
Duninowo
Lubuczewo
Damnica
Lębork
J. Wicko
J. Kopań
Postomino
ZAMEK W. SŁUPSKU
Redzikowo
Potęgowo
Pogorzelice
Łebno
Darłowo
Stary Jarosław
Sycewice
Słupsk
Mianowice
Cewice
Linia
Strzepcz
MUZEUM DARŁOWO
Dąbki
Sławno
Kwakowo
Dębnica Kaszubska
Łupawa
Przodkowo
Łazy
J. Bukowo
Dolina Słupi
Czarna-Dąbrówka
Sierakowice
Kaszubski
Kartuzy
Ostrowiec
Korzybie
Barcino
Suchorze
Gowidlino
Unichowo
Brodnica Graniczna
J. Jamno
Jamno
Lejkowo
Kolczygłowy
Sulęczyno
Koszalin
Sianów
Kępice
Trzebielino
Stężyca
Wieżyca
Krąg
Borzytuchom
Bonin
Nacław
Bytów
Kaliska
ZAMEK W. KOSZALINIE
Manowo
Polanów
Półczno
Korne
Biesiekierz
Tuchomie
Studzienice
Kościerzyna
Niedalino
Rosnowo
Mostowo
Kawcze
Dretyń
Lipusz
Liniewo
Zydowo
J. Bobięcino Wlk.
Borzyszkowy
Białogard
Dargiń
Radew
Piaszczyna
Miastko
Sominy
Lipnica
Dziemiany
Drzewiany
Stara Kiszewa
J. Wdzydze
Bobolice
Wiele
Tychowo
Koczała
Upiłka
Laska
Zaborski
Brusy
Karsin
Kaliska
Tychówka
Biały Bór
Parsęta
Brzezie
Grzmiąca
Swornegacie
Połczyn-Zdrój
Białowąs
Konarzyny
Bory Tucholskie
Mecikal
Przechlewo
Czersk
Czarna Woda
Barwice
Rzeczenica
J. Wielimie
J. Charzykowskie
Charzykowy
Osieczna
Rytel
Tucholski
Ostropole
Gwda Wielka
Szczecinek
Czarne
Człuchów
Chojnice
Legbąd
Śliwice
Drawski
Kluczewo
Polne
J. Siecino
J. Drawsko
Silnowo
Lotyń
Silno
Brda
Zamarte
Tleń
J. Pile
Krągi
Cierznie
Chrząstowa
Tuchola
Czaplinek
Łubowo
Borne Sulinowo
Okonek
Lędyczek
Debrzno
Cekcyn
Broczyno
Lipka
Kamień Krajeński
Gostycyn
Lniano
Wierzchowo
Nadarzyce
Sypniewo
Podgaje
Pamiętowo
J. Koronowskie
Bysław
Sośnica
Jastrowie
Glomia
Sępólno Krajeńskie
Zdbice
Ptusza
Sypniewo
Sośno
Makowarsko
Piecnik
Kłębowiec
Szwecja
Płytnica
Złotów
Więcbork
Pruszce
J. Betyń
Piława
Krajenka
Koronowo
Marcinkowice
Wałcz
Krepsko
Łobżenica
Kotomierz
Mrocza
Tuczno
Gostomia
Dobrzyca
Liszkowo
Tryszczyn
Osielsko
Rusinowo
Szydłowo
Piła
Wysoka
Wyrzysk
Nakło nad Notecią
Fordon
Śmiłowo
Sadki
Kanał Bydgoski
Człopa
Stobno
Grabowno
Osiek nad Notecią
Paterek
Bydgoszcz
Miasteczko Krajeńskie
Białośliwie
Biale Błota
Trzcianka
Solec Kujawski
Szczuczarz
Ujście
Szamocin
Smogulec
Rynarzewo
Siedlisko
Szubin
Chodzież
Margonin
Kcynia
Nowa-Wieś Wielka
Kuźnica Czarnkowska
Noteć
Gwda
Wieprza
Łeba
Słupia
E28
E261
179
107
111
67
75
76
P o j e z i e r z e
P o m o r s k i e
T u c h

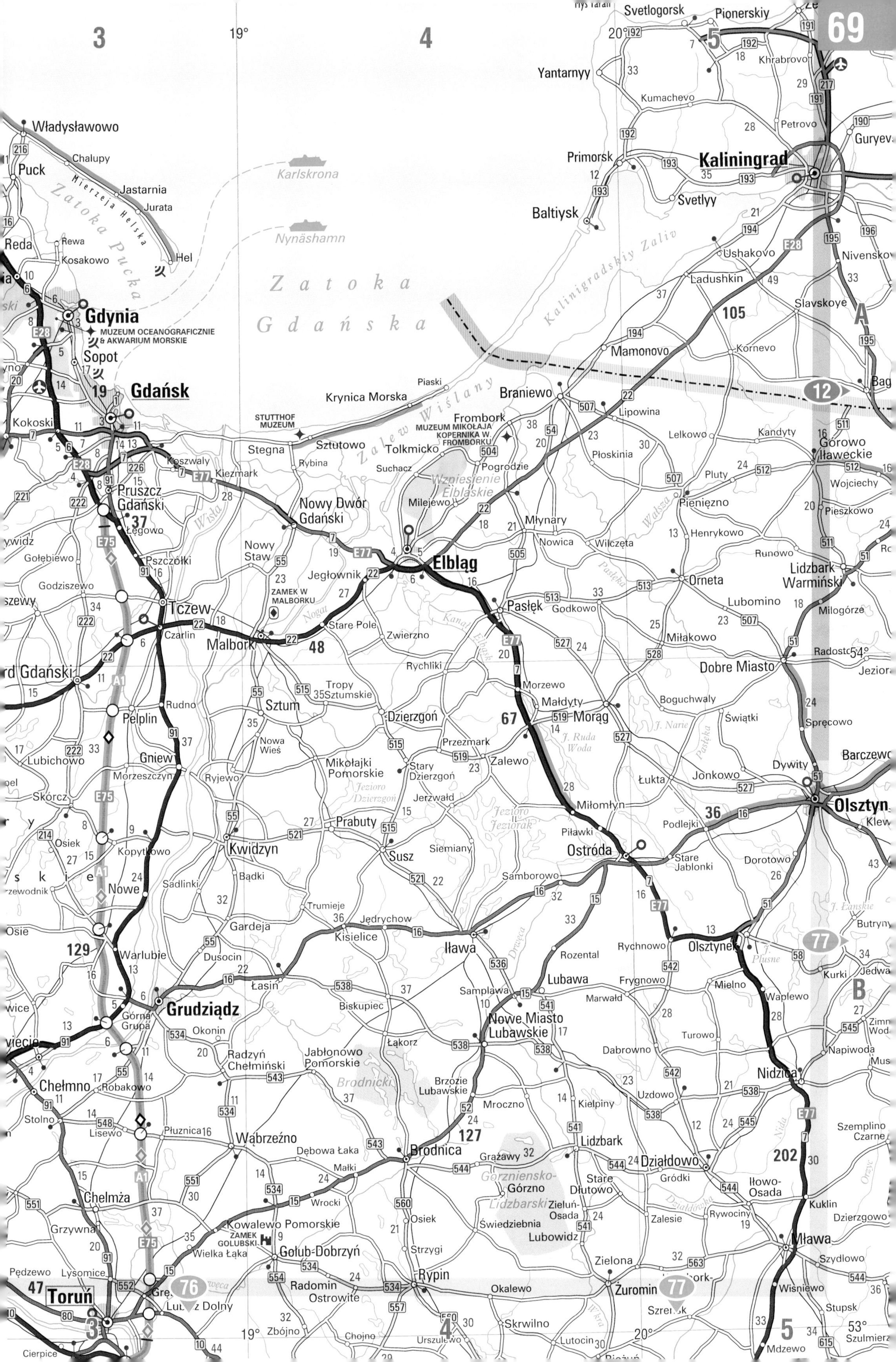
Zatoka Gdańska
Zatoka Pucka
Mierzeja Helska
Zalew Wiślany
Kaliningradskiy Zaliv
Karlskrona
Nynäshamn
Gdynia
Gdańsk
Sopot
MUZEUM OCEANOGRAFICZNIE & AKWARIUM MORSKIE
Władysławowo
Puck
Jastarnia
Jurata
Hel
Chałupy
Reda
Rewa
Kosakowo
Kokoski
Pruszcz Gdański
Pszczółki
Tczew
Czarlin
Pelplin
Gniew
Rudno
Morzeszczyn
Skórcz
Lubichowo
Osiek
Nowe
Kopytkowo
Warlubie
Grudziądz
Górna Grupa
Chełmno
Robakowo
Stolno
Lisewo
Płużnica
Chełmża
Grzywna
Toruń
Lysomice
Pędzewo
Cierpice
Malbork
Sztum
Nowy Staw
Nowy Dwór Gdański
Stegna
Sztutowo
Krynica Morska
Piaski
STUTTHOF MUZEUM
ZAMEK W MALBORKU
Elbląg
Tolkmicko
Frombork
MUZEUM MIKOŁAJA KOPERNIKA W FROMBORKU
Pogrodzie
Wzniesienie Elbląskie
Milejewo
Jegłownik
Stare Pole
Zwierzno
Rychliki
Dzierzgoń
Tropy Sztumskie
Mikołajki Pomorskie
Stary Dzierzgoń
Prabuty
Kwidzyn
Susz
Iława
Kisielice
Gardeja
Łasin
Biskupiec
Radzyń Chełmiński
Jabłonowo Pomorskie
Wąbrzeźno
Brodnica
Kowalewo Pomorskie
ZAMEK GOLUBSKI
Golub-Dobrzyń
Rypin
Radomin
Ostrowite
Pasłęk
Młynary
Morąg
Miłomłyn
Ostróda
Zalewo
Lubawa
Nowe Miasto Lubawskie
Lidzbark
Działdowo
Mława
Nidzica
Olsztynek
Olsztyn
Dobre Miasto
Orneta
Lidzbark Warmiński
Pieniężno
Braniewo
Górowo Iławeckie
Mamonovo
Kaliningrad
Baltiysk
Primorsk
Svetlyy
Yantarnyy
Svetlogorsk
Pionerskiy
Khrabrovo
Guryevsk
Slavskoye
Ushakovo
Ladushkin
Kornevo
Żuromin
Zielona
Lubowidz
Gorznieńsko-Lidzbarski
E28
E75
E77
A1
76
77
12
3
4
5
A
B
19°
20°
54°
53°

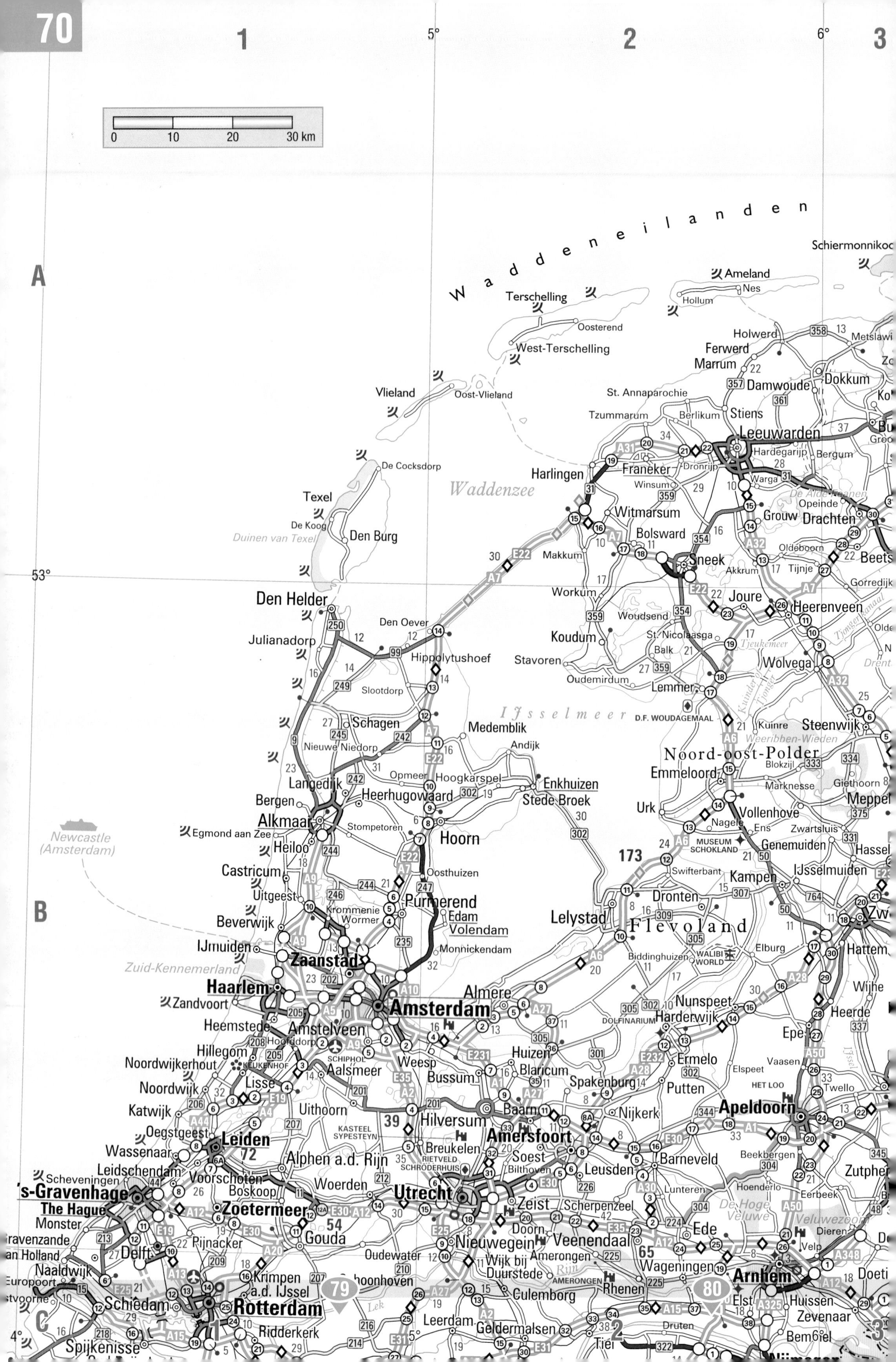
Waddeneilanden
Waddenzee
IJsselmeer
Flevoland
Noord-oost-Polder
Amsterdam
Rotterdam
's-Gravenhage
The Hague
Utrecht
Haarlem
Leiden
Leeuwarden
Apeldoorn
Amersfoort
Arnhem
0 10 20 30 km

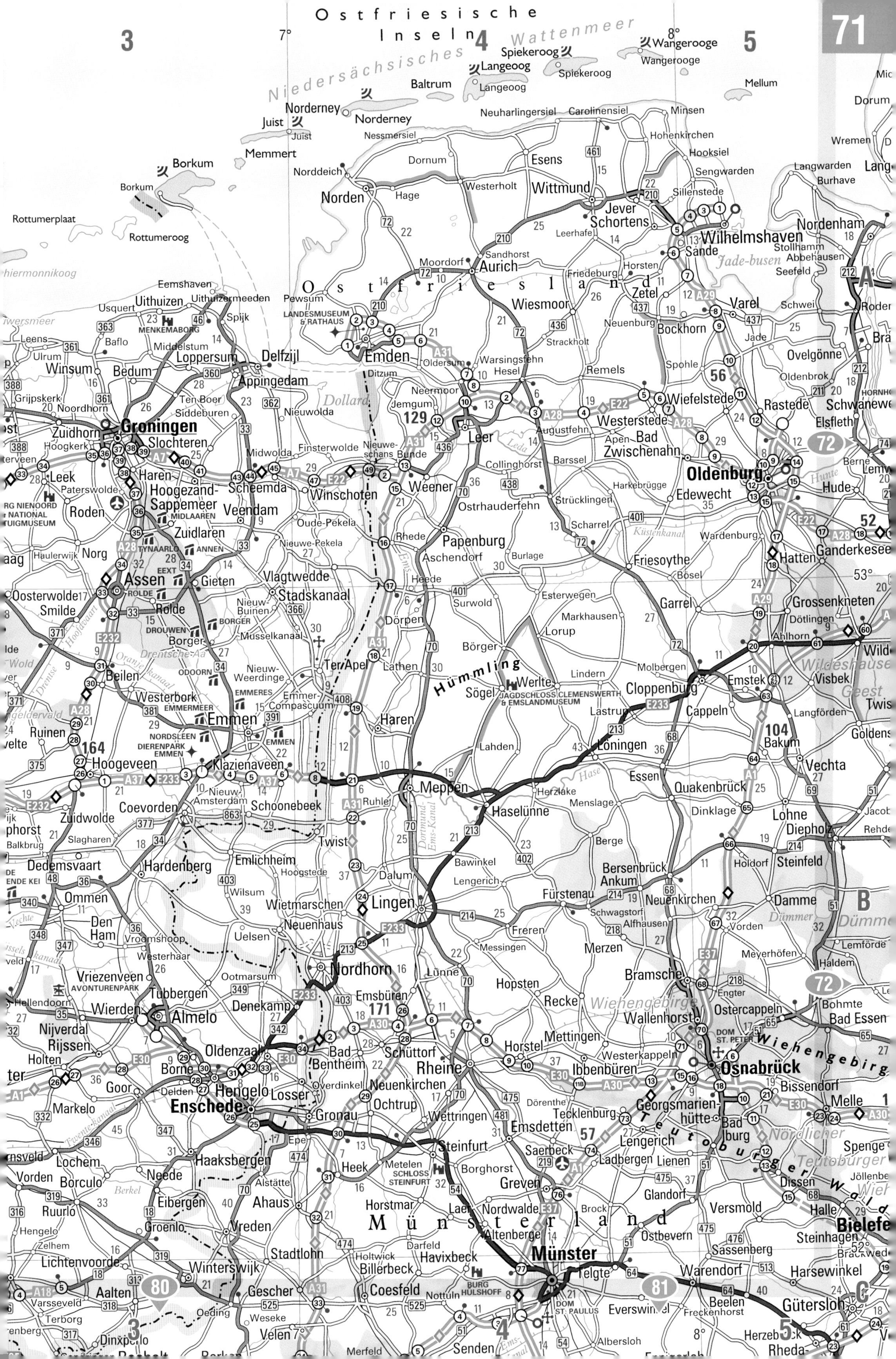
Ostfriesische Inseln
Niedersächsisches Wattenmeer
Wangerooge
Spiekeroog
Langeoog
Baltrum
Norderney
Juist
Memmert
Borkum
Rottumerplaat
Rottumeroog
Mellum
Dorum
Wremen
Minsen
Carolinensiel
Neuharlingersiel
Nessmersiel
Hohenkirchen
Hooksiel
Sengwarden
Langwarden
Burhave
Norddeich
Dornum
Esens
Norden
Hage
Westerholt
Wittmund
Jever
Schortens
Sillenstede
Wilhelmshaven
Nordenham
Stollhamm
Abbehausen
Seefeld
Sande
Jade-busen
Leerhafe
Horsten
Friedeburg
Sandhorst
Moordorf
Aurich
Ostfriesland
Eemshaven
Uithuizen
Uithuizermeeden
Usquert
Pewsum
LANDESMUSEUM & RATHAUS
Zetel
Varel
Schwei
Wiesmoor
Neuenburg
Bockhorn
Jade
MENKEMABORG
Spijk
Leens
Baflo
Middelstum
Ulrum
Winsum
Bedum
Loppersum
Delfzijl
Appingedam
Emden
Oldersum
Warsingsfehn
Hesel
Strackholt
Remels
Spohle
Ovelgönne
Oldenbrok
Rastede
Schwanewede
Elsfleth
Wiefelstede
Westerstede
Apen
Bad Zwischenahn
Oldenburg
Hude
Berne
Edewecht
Harkebrügge
Grijpskerk
Noordhorn
Ten Boer
Siddeburen
Nieuwolda
Dollard
Ditzum
Neermoor
Jemgum
Leer
Leda
Augustfehn
Zuidhorn
Hoogkerk
Groningen
Slochteren
Midwolda
Finsterwolde
Nieuweschans
Bunde
Weener
Collinghorst
Barssel
Leek
Haren
Paterswolde
Hoogezand-Sappemeer
Scheemda
Winschoten
Ostrhauderfehn
Strücklingen
Küstenkanal
Wardenburg
Roden
MIDLAARDEN
Veendam
Oude-Pekela
Rhede
Papenburg
Scharrel
Hatten
Ganderkesee
Zuidlaren
Nieuwe-Pekela
Aschendorf
Burlage
Friesoythe
Bösel
Haulerwijk
Norg
TYNAARLO
ANNEN
Eext
Gieten
Vlagtwedde
Heede
Assen
ROLDE
Rolde
Stadskanaal
Surwold
Esterwegen
Garrel
Grossenkneten
Dötlingen
Ahlhorn
Oosterwolde
Smilde
Nieuw-Buinen
Dörpen
Markhausen
Lorup
BORGER
DROUWEN
Borger
Musselkanaal
Drentsche Aa
Ter Apel
Lathen
Börger
Hümmling
Molbergen
Lindern
Cloppenburg
Emstek
Visbek
Wildeshausen
Beilen
ODOORN
Nieuw-Weerdinge
Werlte
Sögel
JAGDSCHLOSS CLEMENSWERTH & EMSLANDMUSEUM
EMMERES
Westerbork
EMMERMEER
Emmer-Compascuum
Cappeln
Langförden
Emmen
Haren
Lastrup
Ruinen
NORDSLEEN
DIERENPARK EMMEN
Lahden
Löningen
Bakum
Vechta
Hoogeveen
Klazienaveen
Meppen
Essen
Quakenbrück
Zuidwolde
Coevorden
Nieuw-Amsterdam
Schoonebeek
Ruhle
Dortmund-Ems-Kanal
Herzlake
Haselünne
Menslage
Dinklage
Lohne
Diepholz
Slagharen
Balkbrug
Twist
Berge
Holdorf
Steinfeld
Dedemsvaart
Hardenberg
Emlichheim
Hoogstede
Dalum
Bawinkel
Lengerich
Bersenbrück
Ankum
Ommen
Wilsum
Wietmarschen
Lingen
Fürstenau
Schwagstorf
Neuenkirchen
Damme
Dümmer
Den Ham
Vroomshoop
Uelsen
Neuenhaus
Freren
Alfhausen
Vorden
Lemförde
Westerhaar
Messingen
Merzen
Meyerhöfen
Haldem
Vriezenveen
AVONTURENPARK
Ootmarsum
Nordhorn
Lünne
Hopsten
Bramsche
Engter
Hellendoorn
Tubbergen
Denekamp
Emsbüren
Recke
Wiehengebirge
Wallenhorst
Ostercappeln
Bohmte
Bad Essen
Wierden
Almelo
Nijverdal
Rijssen
Oldenzaal
Bad Bentheim
Schüttorf
Rheine
Horstel
Mettingen
Westerkappeln
DOM ST. PETER
Osnabrück
Holten
Borne
Hengelo
Losser
Overdinkel
Neuenkirchen
Ibbenbüren
Bissendorf
Goor
Delden
Enschede
Gronau
Ochtrup
Wettringen
Dörenthe
Tecklenburg
Georgsmarienhütte
Bad Iburg
Melle
Markelo
Emsdetten
Teutoburger Wald
Nördlicher Teutoburger Wald
Spenge
Lochem
Haaksbergen
Epe
Heek
Metelen
SCHLOSS STEINFURT
Steinfurt
Borghorst
Saerbeck
Ladbergen
Lienen
Lengerich
Vorden
Borculo
Neede
Alstätte
Greven
Glandorf
Dissen
Jöllenbeck
Berkel
Eibergen
Ahaus
Horstmar
Laer
Nordwalde
Brock
Versmold
Halle
Bielefeld
Ruurlo
Hengelo
Zelhem
Groenlo
Vreden
Münsterland
Altenberge
Ostbevern
Steinhagen
Lichtenvoorde
Winterswijk
Stadtlohn
Darfeld
Holtwick
Havixbeck
Münster
Sassenberg
Brackwede
Billerbeck
BURG HULSHOFF
Telgte
Warendorf
Harsewinkel
Aalten
Varsseveld
Gescher
Coesfeld
Nottuln
DOM ST. PAULUS
Everswinkel
Freckenhorst
Beelen
Gütersloh
Terborg
Oeding
Weseke
Velen
Senden
Albersloh
Herzebrock
Rheda
Dinxperlo
Merfeld
72
80
81

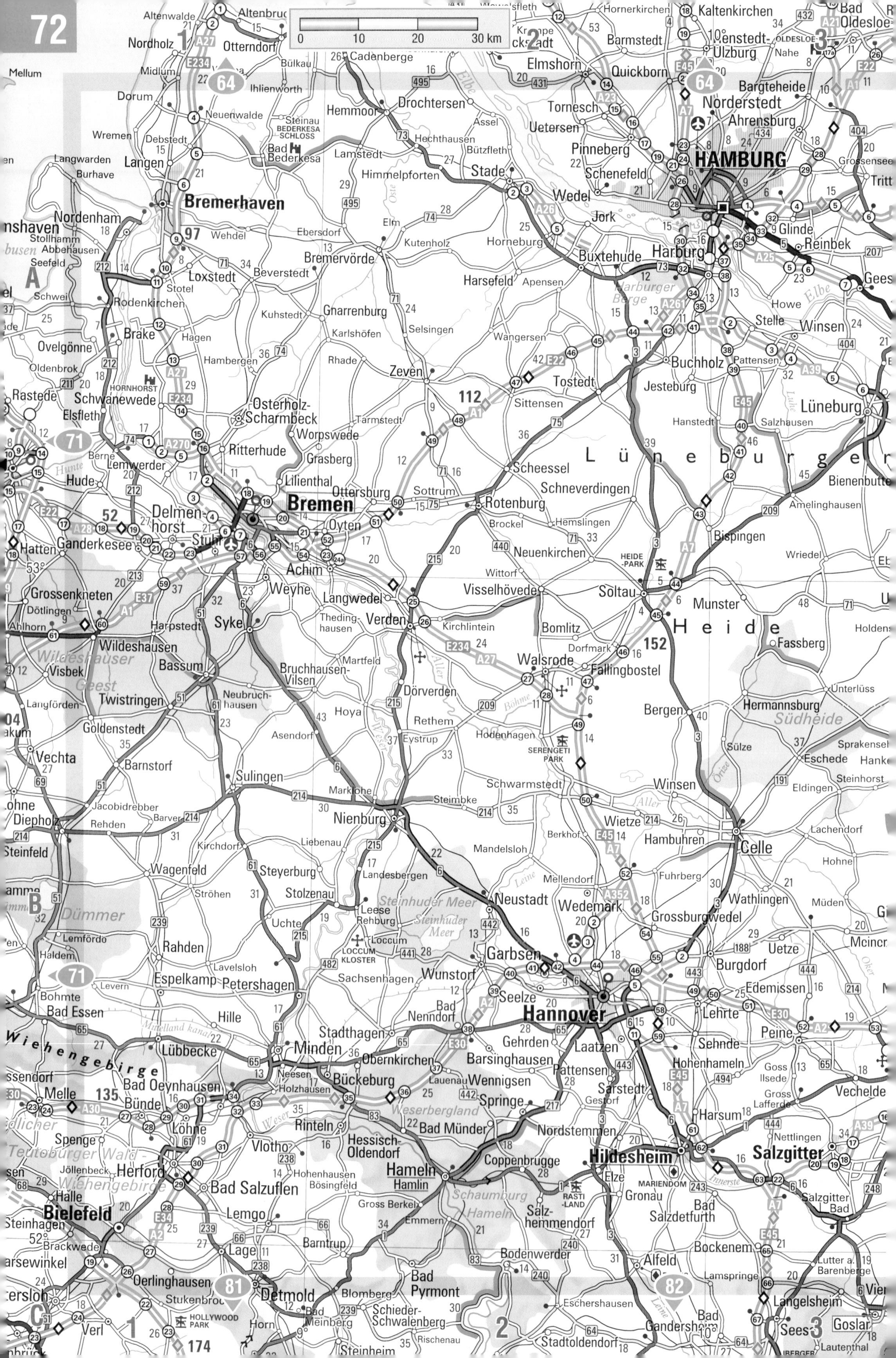

72
0 10 20 30 km
Altenwalde
Altenbruch
Nordholz
Otterndorf
Cadenberge
Mellum
Midlum
Dorum
Ihlienworth
Bülkau
Neuenwalde
Steinau
BEDERKESA SCHLOSS
Bad Bederkesa
Wremen
Debstedt
Langen
Langwarden
Burhave
Bremerhaven
Nordenham
Stollhamm
Abbehausen
Seefeld
Wehdel
Loxstedt
Stotel
Beverstedt
Schwei
Rodenkirchen
Brake
Hagen
Ovelgönne
Oldenbrok
Rastede
Elsfleth
Schwanewede
HORNHORST
Hambergen
Osterholz-Scharmbeck
Ritterhude
Berne
Lemwerder
Hude
Delmenhorst
Stuhr
Ganderkesee
Hatten
Grossenkneten
Dötlingen
Ahlhorn
Wildeshausen
Wildeshauser Geest
Visbek
Langförden
Harpstedt
Bassum
Twistringen
Goldenstedt
Vechta
Barnstorf
Lohne
Diepholz
Steinfeld
Rehden
Jacobidrebber
Barver
Dümmer
Lemförde
Haldem
Bohmte
Bad Essen
Wiehengebirge
Melle
Spenge
Jöllenbeck
Herford
Bünde
Löhne
Halle
Bielefeld
Steinhagen
Brackwede
Harsewinkel
Gütersloh
Verl
Oerlinghausen
Stukenbrock
HOLLYWOOD PARK
Teutoburger Wald
Bremen
Lilienthal
Worpswede
Grasberg
Ottersburg
Oyten
Achim
Weyhe
Syke
Langwedel
Theding-hausen
Verden
Bruchhausen-Vilsen
Martfeld
Neubruchhausen
Hoya
Asendorf
Sulingen
Wagenfeld
Ströhen
Kirchdorf
Steyerburg
Stolzenau
Uchte
Rahden
Espelkamp
Lavelsloh
Petershagen
Levern
Hille
Lübbecke
Minden
Bad Oeynhausen
Vlotho
Bad Salzuflen
Lemgo
Lage
Detmold
Horn
Bad Meinberg
Blomberg
Schieder-Schwalenberg
Bad Pyrmont
Barntrup
Steinheim
Rischenau
Hameln
Hamlin
Emmern
Gross Berkel
Hohenhausen
Bösingfeld
Rinteln
Hessisch-Oldendorf
Bückeburg
Obernkirchen
Stadthagen
Neesen
Holzhausen
Weserbergland
Bad Münder
Coppenbrügge
Lauenau
Wennigsen
Springe
Barsinghausen
Gehrden
Bad Nenndorf
Wunstorf
Sachsenhagen
Loccum
LOCCUM KLOSTER
Leese
Rehburg
Steinhuder Meer
Landesbergen
Liebenau
Nienburg
Marklohe
Eystrup
Rethem
Dörverden
Hodenhagen
Steimbke
Schwarmstedt
Neustadt
Mandelsloh
Garbsen
Seelze
Hannover
Laatzen
Pattensen
Sarstedt
Gestorf
Nordstemmen
Hildesheim
Elze
Gronau
Salzhemmendorf
Schaumburg
RASTI-LAND
Bodenwerder
Eschershausen
Stadtoldendorf
Alfeld
Bad Gandersheim
Lamspringe
Bockenem
Bad Salzdetfurth
MARIENDOM
Harsum
Hohenhameln
Sehnde
Lehrte
Burgdorf
Uetze
Edemissen
Peine
Vechelde
Salzgitter
Salzgitter Bad
Nettlingen
Lutter a. Barenberge
Langelsheim
Goslar
Seesen
Lautenthal
Wedemark
Mellendorf
Berkhof
Wietze
Hambühren
Celle
Fuhrberg
Wathlingen
Grossburgwedel
Winsen
Bergen
Hermannsburg
Südheide
Sülze
Eschede
Unterlüss
Faßberg
Munster
Lüneburger Heide
Soltau
HEIDE-PARK
Bispingen
Wriedel
Amelinghausen
Bienenbüttel
Fallingbostel
Walsrode
Dorfmark
Bomlitz
Visselhövede
Kirchlinteln
Wittorf
Neuenkirchen
Hemslingen
Brockel
Rotenburg
Sottrum
Scheessel
Schneverdingen
Sittensen
Tostedt
Wangersen
Zeven
Tarmstedt
Selsingen
Karlshöfen
Rhade
Gnarrenburg
Kuhstedt
Bremervörde
Ebersdorf
Elm
Kutenholz
Himmelpforten
Lamstedt
Hechthausen
Hemmoor
Drochtersen
Assel
Bützfleth
Stade
Horneburg
Harsefeld
Apensen
Buxtehude
Jork
Wedel
Schenefeld
Pinneberg
Uetersen
Tornesch
Elmshorn
Glückstadt
Barmstedt
Quickborn
Hornerkirchen
Kaltenkirchen
Henstedt-Ulzburg
Nahe
Bad Oldesloe
Bargteheide
Norderstedt
Ahrensburg
HAMBURG
Grossensee
Trittau
Glinde
Reinbek
Harburg
Harburger Berge
Geesthacht
Howe
Stelle
Winsen
Buchholz
Jesteburg
Pattensen
Hanstedt
Salzhausen
Lüneburg
SERENGETI PARK
Mühlen
Elbe
Weser
Aller
Leine
Hunte
Oste
Böhme
Örtze
Innerste
Mittelland kanal

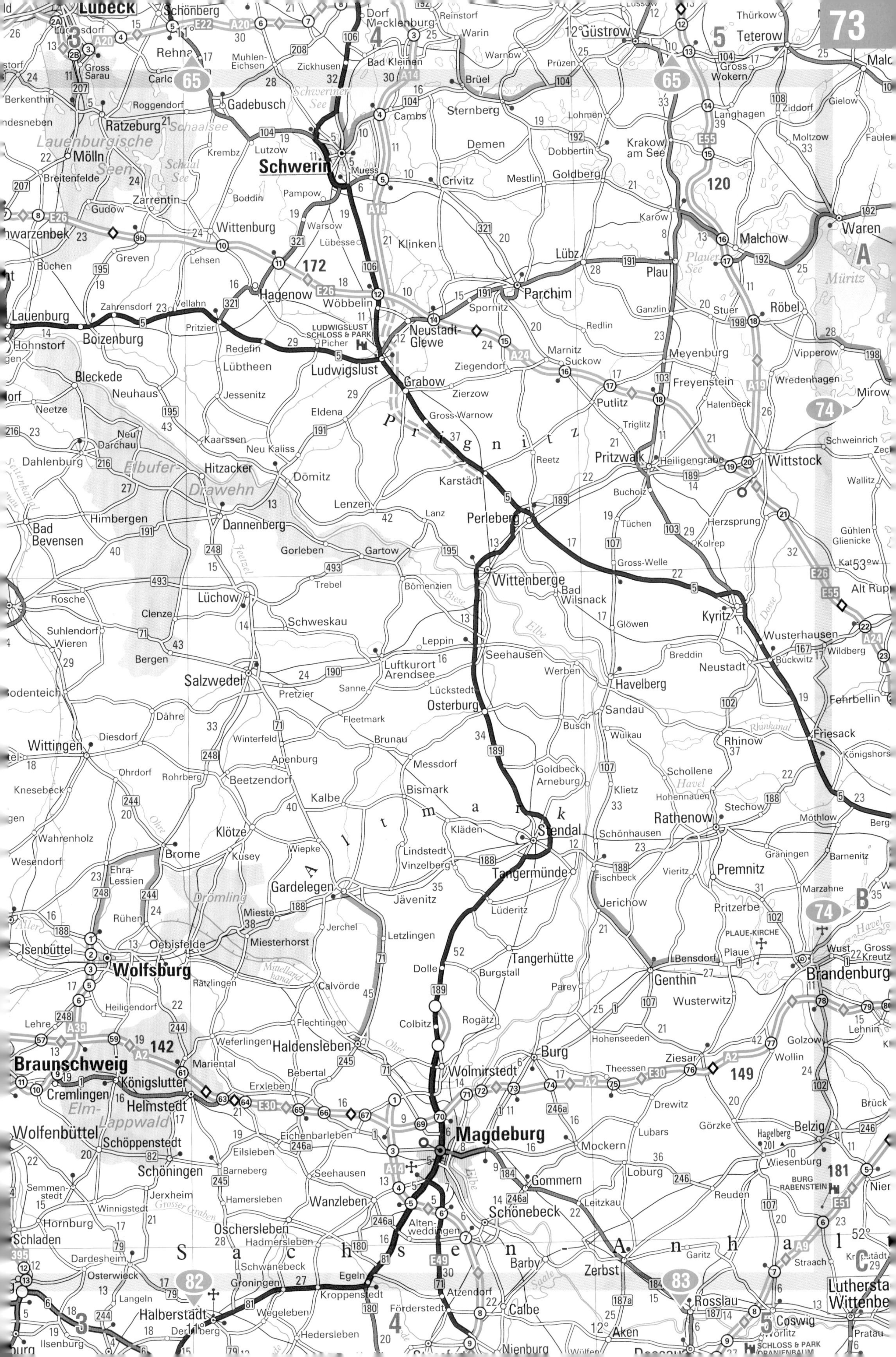
Lübeck
Schönberg
Dorf Mecklenburg
Reinstorf
Warin
Güstrow
Thürkow
Teterow
Malchin
Rehna
Carlow
Gross Sarau
Muhlen-Eichsen
Zickhusen
Bad Kleinen
Warnow
Prüzen
Gross Wokern
Berkenthin
Roggendorf
Gadebusch
Schweriner See
Brüel
Sternberg
Langhagen
Ziddorf
Gielow
Ratzeburg
Schaalsee
Cambs
Lohmen
Lauenburgische Seen
Mölln
Krembz
Lutzow
Demen
Dobbertin
Krakow am See
Moltzow
Faulenrost
Breitenfelde
Schaal See
Schwerin
Muess
Crivitz
Mestlin
Goldberg
Zarrentin
Boddin
Pampow
Gudow
Warsow
Karow
Waren
Schwarzenbek
Wittenburg
Lübesse
Klinken
Malchow
Greven
Lehsen
Lübz
Plau
Plauer See
Büchen
Hagenow
Wöbbelin
Parchim
Müritz
Lauenburg
Zahrensdorf
Vellahn
Spornitz
Ganzlin
Stuer
Röbel
Hohnstorf
Boizenburg
Pritzier
Redefin
Picher
Ludwigslust Schloss & Park
Neustadt-Glewe
Redlin
Marnitz
Suckow
Meyenburg
Vipperow
Bleckede
Lübtheen
Ludwigslust
Ziegendorf
Freyenstein
Wredenhagen
Mirow
Neuhaus
Jessenitz
Grabow
Zierzow
Putlitz
Halenbeck
Neetze
Eldena
Gross Warnow
Prignitz
Triglitz
Neu Darchau
Kaarssen
Neu Kaliss
Reetz
Pritzwalk
Heiligengrabe
Wittstock
Schweinrich
Dahlenburg
Elbufer-Drawehn
Hitzacker
Dömitz
Karstädt
Wallitz
Bucholz
Lenzen
Lanz
Perleberg
Tüchen
Herzsprung
Bad Bevensen
Himbergen
Dannenberg
Jeetzel
Kolrep
Gühlen Glienicke
Gorleben
Gartow
Gross-Welle
Trebel
Bömenzien
Wittenberge
Bad Wilsnack
Kyritz
Alt Ruppin
Rosche
Lüchow
Biese
Elbe
Clenze
Schweskau
Glöwen
Wusterhausen
Suhlendorf
Wieren
Leppin
Seehausen
Breddin
Wildberg
Bergen
Salzwedel
Luftkurort Arendsee
Werben
Havelberg
Neustadt
Bückwitz
Bodenteich
Pretzier
Sanne
Lückstedt
Osterburg
Sandau
Fehrbellin
Dähre
Fleetmark
Busch
Wulkau
Rhinkanal
Wittingen
Diesdorf
Winterfeld
Brunau
Rhinow
Friesack
Apenburg
Messdorf
Goldbeck
Arneburg
Schollene
Havel
Ohrdorf
Rohrberg
Beetzendorf
Klietz
Hohennauen
Königshorst
Knesebeck
Kalbe
Bismark
Altmark
Stechow
Rathenow
Ohre
Klötze
Kläden
Stendal
Schönhausen
Möthlow
Wahrenholz
Wiepke
Lindstedt
Gräningen
Barnewitz
Wesendorf
Brome
Kusey
Vinzelberg
Tangermünde
Fischbeck
Vieritz
Premnitz
Ehra-Lessien
Gardelegen
Jävenitz
Marzahne
Drömling
Mieste
Lüderitz
Jerichow
Pritzerbe
Rühen
Jerchel
Letzlingen
Plaue-Kirche
Havel
Isenbüttel
Oebisfelde
Miesterhorst
Tangerhütte
Bensdorf
Plaue
Wust
Gross Kreutz
Wolfsburg
Rätzlingen
Mittellandkanal
Calvörde
Dolle
Burgstall
Genthin
Brandenburg
Heiligendorf
Parey
Wusterwitz
Lehre
Flechtingen
Colbitz
Rogätz
Lehnin
Braunschweig
Weferlingen
Haldensleben
Hohenseeden
Ziesar
Golzow
Wollin
Mariental
Bebertal
Burg
Theessen
Königslutter
Cremlingen
Erxleben
Wolmirstedt
Elm-Lappwald
Helmstedt
Drewitz
Brück
Wolfenbüttel
Schöppenstedt
Eilsleben
Eichenbarleben
Magdeburg
Lübars
Görzke
Belzig
Hagelberg
Schöningen
Barneberg
Seehausen
Mockern
Wiesenburg
Loburg
Semmenstedt
Jerxheim
Hamersleben
Wanzleben
Gommern
Burg Rabenstein
Niemegk
Winnigstedt
Grosser Graben
Reuden
Hornburg
Oschersleben
Altenweddingen
Schönebeck
Leitzkau
Schladen
Hadmersleben
Sachsen-Anhalt
Dardesheim
Osterwieck
Schwanebeck
Barby
Zerbst
Garitz
Straach
Egeln
Groningen
Kroppenstedt
Atzendorf
Saale
Lutherstadt Wittenberg
Langeln
Halberstadt
Wegeleben
Förderstedt
Calbe
Rosslau
Coswig
Derenburg
Hedersleben
Aken
Wörlitz
Schloss & Park Oranienbaum
Ilsenburg
Nienburg
Pratau
65
74
82
83
172
120
142
149
181
A
B
C

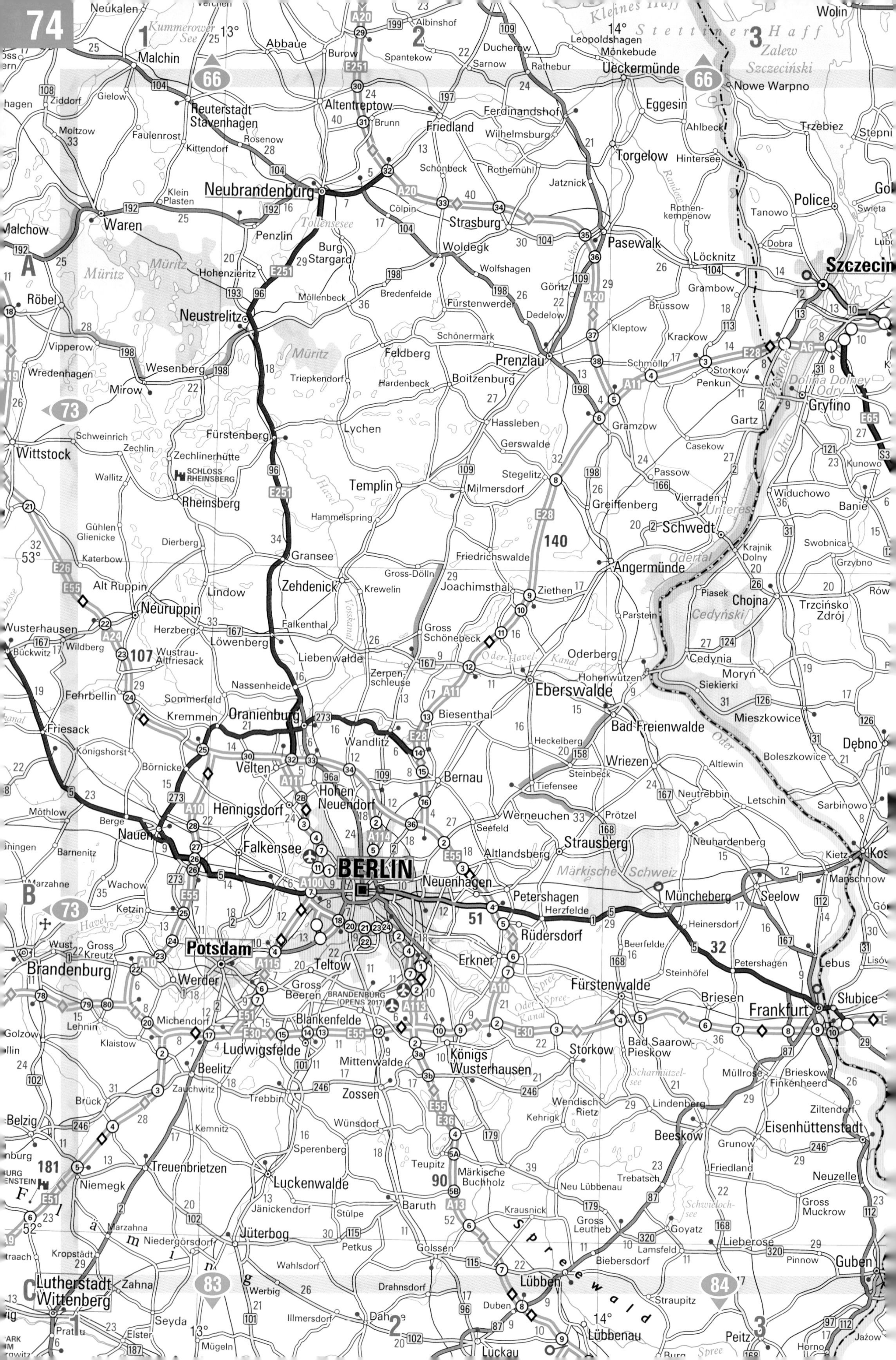
Neukalen
Malchin
Reuterstadt Stavenhagen
Neubrandenburg
Altentreptow
Friedland
Ueckermünde
Eggesin
Torgelow
Stettiner Haff
Zalew Szczeciński
Nowe Warpno
Wolin
Police
Pasewalk
Strasburg
Woldegk
Löcknitz
Szczecin
Waren
Müritz
Penzlin
Burg Stargard
Neustrelitz
Röbel
Vipperow
Mirow
Wesenberg
Feldberg
Prenzlau
Gartz
Gryfino
Wittstock
Fürstenberg
Lychen
Templin
Rheinsberg
Schloss Rheinsberg
Schwedt
Angermünde
Chojna
Gransee
Zehdenick
Joachimsthal
Neuruppin
Lindow
Löwenberg
Liebenwalde
Oderberg
Eberswalde
Cedynia
Moryń
Fehrbellin
Oranienburg
Bad Freienwalde
Mieszkowice
Dębno
Friesack
Velten
Hennigsdorf
Hohen Neuendorf
Bernau
Wriezen
Nauen
Falkensee
BERLIN
Neuenhagen
Strausberg
Märkische Schweiz
Müncheberg
Seelow
Kostrzyn
Petershagen
Rüdersdorf
Erkner
Potsdam
Brandenburg
Werder
Teltow
Fürstenwalde
Frankfurt
Słubice
Michendorf
Ludwigsfelde
Blankenfelde
Königs Wusterhausen
Storkow
Bad Saarow-Pieskow
Beelitz
Mittenwalde
Zossen
Beeskow
Eisenhüttenstadt
Belzig
Treuenbrietzen
Luckenwalde
Teupitz
Märkische Buchholz
Niemegk
Jüterbog
Baruth
Lieberose
Guben
Golssen
Lübben
Spreewald
Lutherstadt Wittenberg
Zahna
Dahme
Lübbenau
Peitz
Luckau
Seyda
Fläming

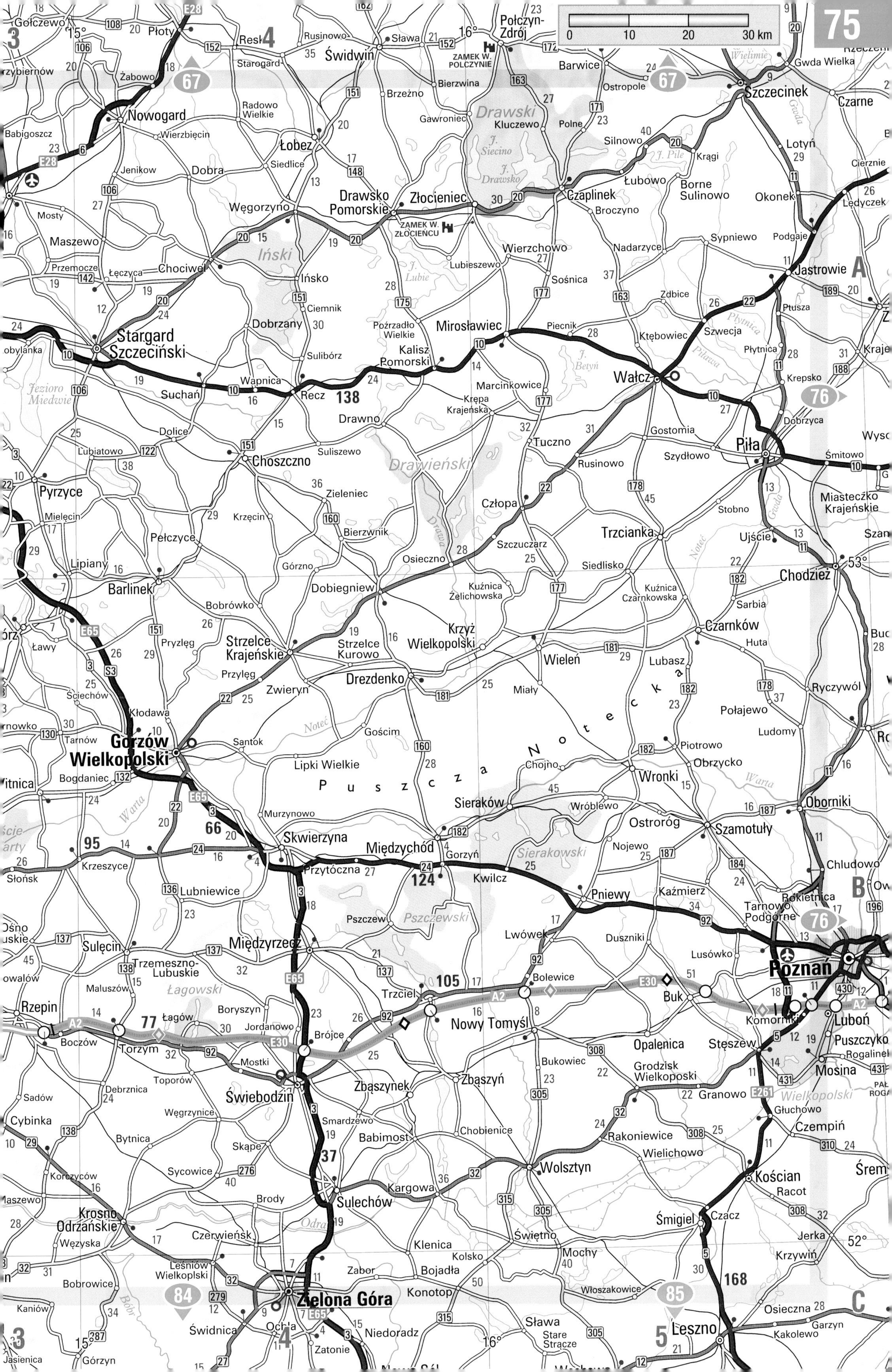
0
10
20
30 km
Gołczewo
Płoty
Resko
Rusinowo
Sława
Świdwin
Połczyn-Zdrój
ZAMEK W. POŁCZYNIE
Barwice
Wielimie
Gwda Wielka
Szczecinek
Czarne
Żabowo
Starogard
Bierzwina
Ostropole
Nowogard
Radowo Wielkie
Brzeżno
Gawroniec
Drawski
Kluczewo
Polne
Babigoszcz
Wierzbięcin
Łobez
J. Siecino
Silnowo
J. Pile
Krągi
Lotyń
Jenikow
Dobra
Siedlice
J. Drawsko
Czaplinek
Lubowo
Borne Sulinowo
Okonek
Cierznie
Lędyczek
Mosty
Węgorzyno
Drawsko Pomorskie
Złocieniec
ZAMEK W. ZŁOCIEŃCU
Broczyno
Maszewo
Iński
Wierzchowo
Nadarzyce
Sypniewo
Podgaje
Przemocze
Łęczyca
Chociwel
Lubieszewo
J. Lubie
Sośnica
Jastrowie
Ińsko
Zdbice
Ciemnik
Stargard Szczeciński
Dobrzany
Poźrzadło Wielkie
Mirosławiec
Piecnik
Kłębowiec
Szwecja
Płytnica
Płusza
Krajenka
Kalisz Pomorski
Sulibórz
J. Betyń
Piława
Jezioro Miedwie
Wapnica
Marcinkowice
Wałcz
Krępsko
Suchań
Recz
Krępa Krajeńska
Dobrzyca
Drawno
Gostomia
Dolice
Tuczno
Piła
Śmitowo
Lubiatowo
Suliszewo
Rusinowo
Szydłowo
Choszczno
Drawieński
Pyrzyce
Zieleniec
Człopa
Miasteczko Krajeńskie
Mielęcin
Krzęcin
Bierzwnik
Drawa
Stobno
Trzcianka
Pełczyce
Szczuczarz
Ujście
Lipiany
Górzno
Osieczno
Siedlisko
Chodzież
Barlinek
Dobiegniew
Kuźnica Żelichowska
Kuźnica Czarnkowska
Bobrówko
Sarbia
Czarnków
Ławy
Pyrzyce
Strzelce Krajeńskie
Strzelce Kurowo
Krzyż Wielkopolski
Wieleń
Huta
Lubasz
Ściechów
Przyłęg
Zwierzyn
Drezdenko
Miały
Ryczywół
Kłodawa
Noteć
Połajewo
Tarnów
Santok
Gościm
Ludomy
Gorzów Wielkopolski
Piotrowo
Bogdaniec
Lipki Wielkie
Chojno
Obrzycko
Puszcza Notecka
Wronki
Warta
Sieraków
Wróblewo
Oborniki
Murzynowo
Ostroróg
Szamotuły
Skwierzyna
Międzychód
Nojewo
Krzeszyce
Gorzyń
Sierakowski
Słońsk
Przytoczna
Kwilcz
Chludowo
Lubniewice
Pniewy
Kaźmierz
Rokietnica
Tarnowo Podgórne
Ośno Lubuskie
Pszczew
Pszczewski
Lwówek
Duszniki
Sulęcin
Międzyrzecz
Lusówko
Poznań
Trzemeszno-Lubuskie
Bolewice
Maluszów
Łagowski
Trzciel
Buk
Rzepin
Boryszyn
Komorniki
Luboń
Łagów
Jordanowo
Nowy Tomyśl
Boczów
Torzym
Brójce
Opalenica
Stęszew
Puszczykowo
Mostki
Rogalinek
Toporów
Bukowiec
Grodzisk Wielkopolski
Mosina
Świebodzin
Zbąszynek
Zbąszyń
Sadów
Debrznica
Granowo
Wielkopolski
Węgrzynice
Głuchowo
Cybinka
Smardzewo
Czempiń
Bytnica
Babimost
Chobienice
Rakoniewice
Skąpe
Wielichowo
Korczyców
Sycowice
Wolsztyn
Kościan
Śrem
Kargowa
Racot
Brody
Sulechów
Krosno Odrzańskie
Odra
Śmigiel
Czacz
Węzyska
Czerwieńsk
Świętno
Jerka
Klenica
Mochy
Krzywiń
Leśniów Wielkopolski
Kolsko
Zabór
Bojadła
Bobrowice
Zielona Góra
Konotop
Włoszakowice
Kaniów
Bóbr
Osieczna
Garzyn
Ochla
Sława
Niedoradz
Stare Strącze
Leszno
Kakolewo
Świdnica
Zatonie
Górzyn
Jasienica
E28
E65
E30
E261
A2
S3
15°
16°
53°
52°

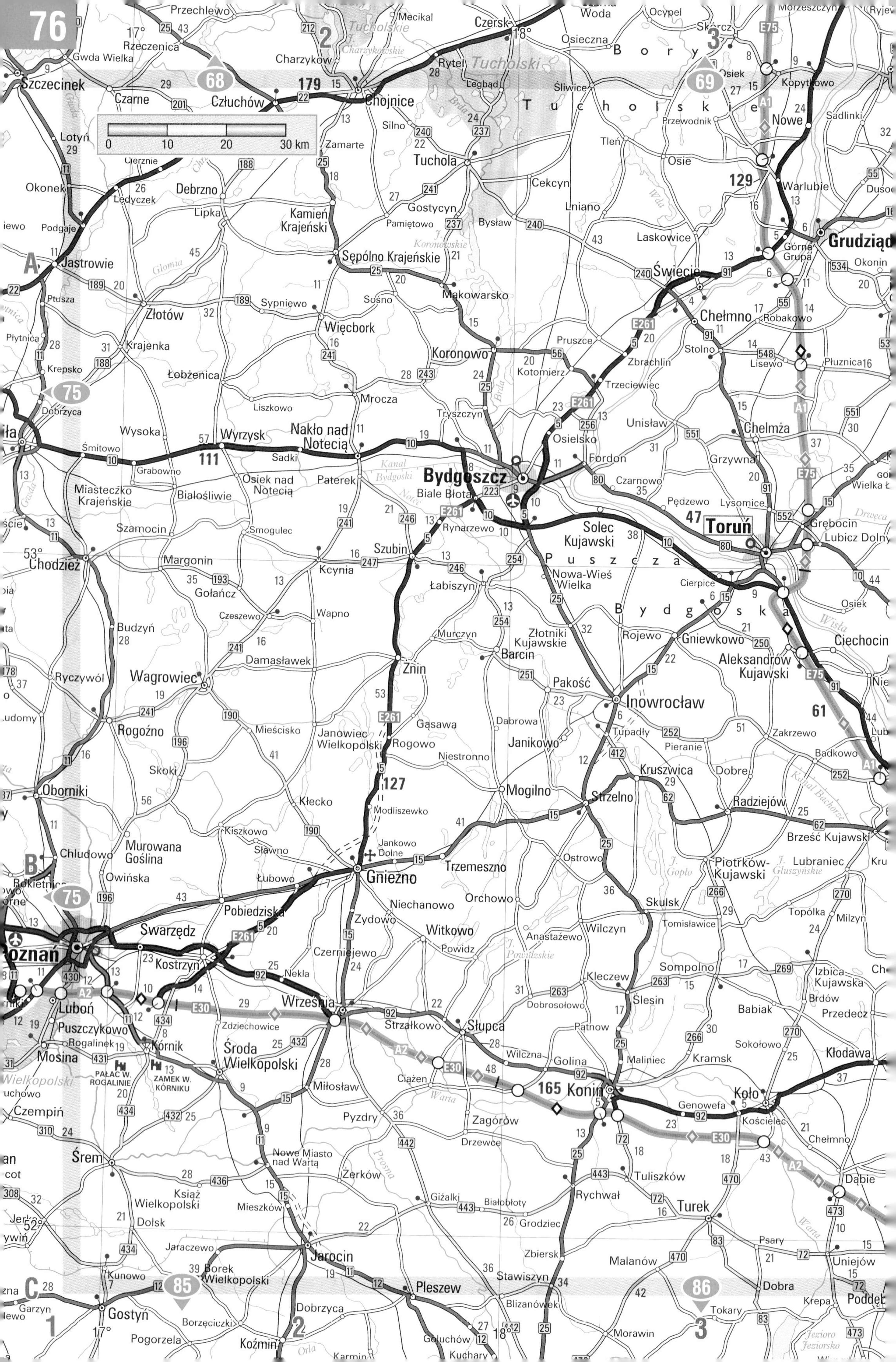

Przechlewo
Mecikal
Tucholskie
Charzykowskie
Czersk
18°
Woda
Ocypel
Skórcz
Morzeszczyn
17°
Rzeczenica
Gwda Wielka
Charzykowy
Rytel
Tucholski
Osieczna
B o r y
68
69
Osiek
Kopytkowo
Szczecinek
Czarne
Człuchów
179
Chojnice
Legbąd
Śliwice
T u c h o l s k i e
Przewodnik
Nowe
Sadlinki
0 10 20 30 km
Lotyń
Zamarte
Silno
Tuchola
Tleń
Osie
Okonek
Lędyczek
Debrzno
Lipka
Kamień Krajeński
Gostycyn
Pamiętowo
Cekcyn
Lniano
Bysław
129
Warlubie
Podgaje
J. Koronowskie
Laskowice
Grudziądz
Górna Grupa
Jastrowie
Sępólno Krajeńskie
Świecie
Okonin
A
Ptusza
Złotów
Sypniewo
Sośno
Makowarsko
Chełmno
Robakowo
Płytnica
Krajenka
Więcbork
Koronowo
Pruszce
Zbrachlin
Stolno
Lisewo
Płużnica
Krepsko
Łobżenica
Kotomierz
Trzeciewiec
75
Dobrzyca
Liszkowo
Mrocza
Tryszczyn
Unisław
Wysoka
Wyrzysk
Nakło nad Notecią
Osielsko
Chełmża
Śmiłowo
111
Sadki
Fordon
Grzywna
Grabowno
Kanał Bydgoski
Bydgoszcz
Czarnowo
Miasteczko Krajeńskie
Białośliwie
Osiek nad Notecią
Paterek
Białe Błota
Lysomice
Pędzewo
Szamocin
Smogulec
Rynarzewo
Solec Kujawski
47
Toruń
Grębocin
Lubicz Dolny
53°
Chodzież
Margonin
Szubin
Kcynia
P u s z c z a
Gołańcz
Łabiszyn
Nowa Wieś Wielka
Cierpice
Czeszewo
Wapno
B y d g o s k a
Osiek
Budzyń
Murczyn
Złotniki Kujawskie
Rojewo
Gniewkowo
Ciechocin
Barcin
Aleksandrów Kujawski
Damasławek
Żnin
Pakość
Ryczywół
Wągrowiec
Inowrocław
61
Rogoźno
Mieścisko
Janowiec Wielkopolski
Gąsawa
Dąbrowa
Janikowo
Tupadły
Pieranie
Zakrzewo
Rogowo
Niestronno
Skoki
127
Kruszwica
Dobre
Badkowo
Oborniki
Kłecko
Mogilno
Strzelno
Radziejów
Modliszewko
Kanał Bachorze
Kiszkowo
Brześć Kujawski
Chludowo
Murowana Goślina
Sławno
Jankowo Dolne
Trzemeszno
Ostrowo
Piotrków-Kujawski
Lubraniec
J. Gopło
J. Gluszyńskie
B
Owińska
Łubowo
Gniezno
Orchowo
Skulsk
Topólka
Milżyn
Pobiedziska
Niechanowo
Tomisławice
Swarzędz
Żydowo
Witkowo
Wilczyn
Anastazewo
Poznań
Kostrzyn
Czerniejewo
Powidz
J. Powidzkie
Sompolno
Izbica Kujawska
Kleczew
Brdów
Luboń
Nekla
Września
Ślesin
Babiak
Przedecz
Puszczykowo
Zdziechowice
Strzałkowo
Słupca
Dobrosołowo
Pątnów
Rogalinek
Kórnik
Środa Wielkopolski
Sokołowo
Mosina
Pałac w Rogalinie
Zamek w Kórniku
Wilczna
Golina
Kramsk
Kłodawa
Ciążeń
Maliniec
Miłosław
165
Konin
Koło
Czempiń
Pyzdry
Warta
Zagórów
Genowefa
Kościelec
Chełmno
Drzewce
Śrem
Nowe Miasto nad Wartą
Żerków
Prosna
Tuliszków
Dąbie
Książ Wielkopolski
Giżałki
Białobłoty
Rychwał
Mieszków
Turek
Dolsk
Grodziec
Jaraczewo
Psary
Jarocin
Zbiersk
Malanów
Uniejów
Borek Wielkopolski
Kunowo
Stawiszyn
85
86
Pleszew
Dobra
C
Gostyń
Garzyn
Dobrzyca
Blizanów
Krępa
Tokary
Poddębice
Borzęciczki
Pogorzela
Koźmin
Gołuchów
Kuchary
Morawin
Jezioro Jeziorsko
Orla
Karmin
1
2
3

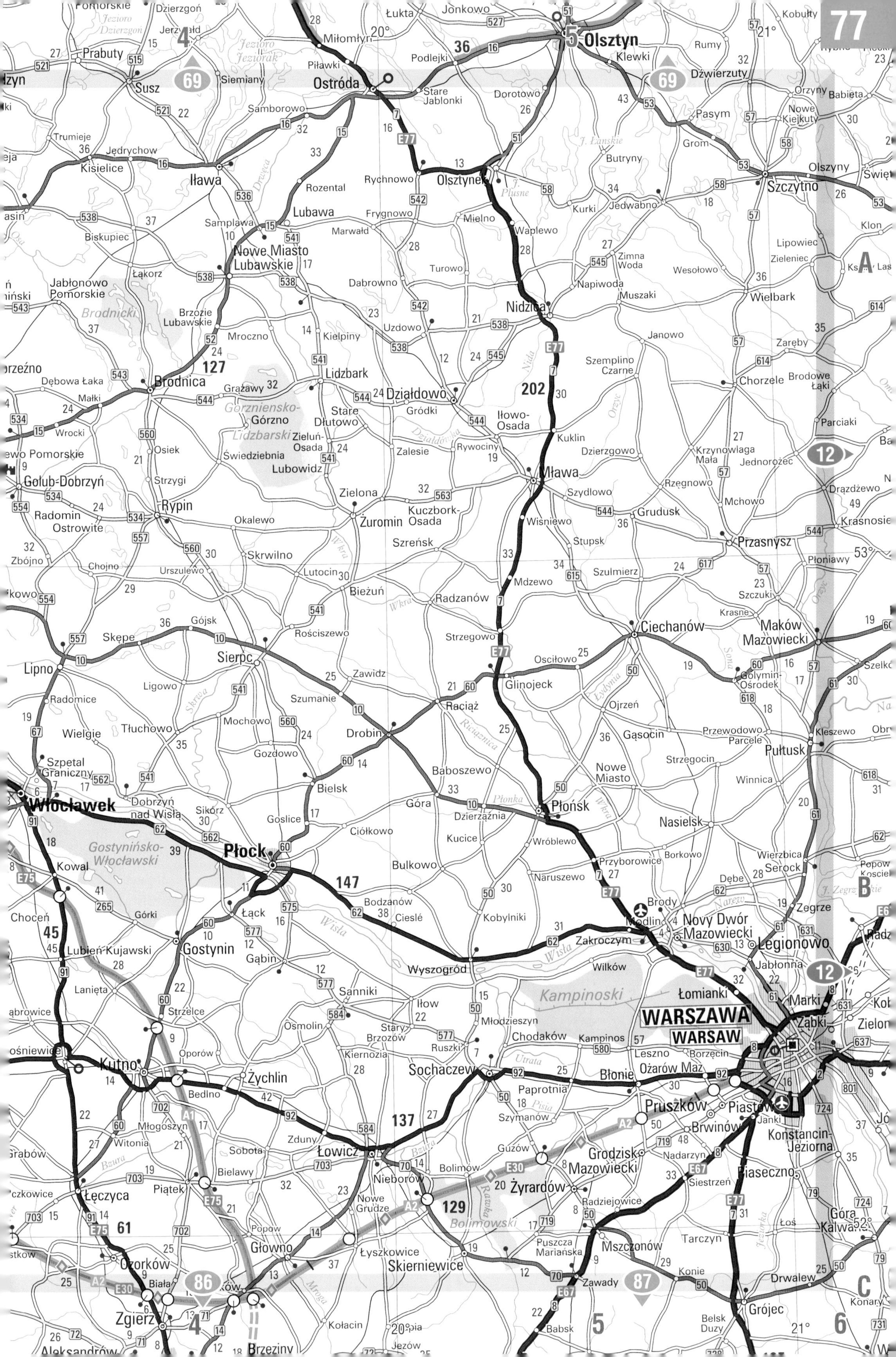
Pomorskie
Dzierzgoń
Jezioro Dzierzgoń
Jerzwałd
Prabuty
Susz
Siemiany
Jezioro Jeziorak
Samborowo
Trumieje
Kisielice
Jędrychowo
Iława
Łukta
Jonkowo
Miłomłyn
Piławki
Ostróda
Podlejki
Stare Jabłonki
Olsztyn
Klewki
Rumy
Dźwierzuty
Kobułty
Dorotowo
Pasym
Orzyny
Babięta
Nowe Kiejkuty
Grom
J. Łańskie
Butryny
Olsztynek
Rychnowo
Rozental
J. Pluszne
Kurki
Jedwabno
Szczytno
Olszyny
Lubawa
Frygnowo
Mielno
Marwałd
Waplewo
Samplawa
Biskupiec
Nowe Miasto Lubawskie
Łąkorz
Turowo
Zimna Woda
Wesołowo
Lipowiec
Zieleniec
Klon
Jabłonowo Pomorskie
Dabrowno
Napiwoda
Muszaki
Wielbark
Brodnicki
Brzozie Lubawskie
Mroczno
Kielpiny
Uzdowo
Nidzica
Janowo
Zaręby
Szemplino Czarne
Brodnica
Dębowa Łąka
Małki
Grążawy
Lidzbark
Działdowo
Chorzele
Brodowe Łąki
Gorznieńsko-Lidzbarski
Górzno
Stare Dłutowo
Gródki
Iłowo-Osada
Parciaki
Wrocki
Zieluń-Osada
Zalesie
Rywociny
Kuklin
Dzierzgowo
Krzynowłoga Mała
Jednorożec
Osiek
Świedziebnia
Lubowidz
Mława
Golub-Dobrzyń
Strzygi
Rzęgnowo
Szydłowo
Radomin
Ostrowite
Rypin
Zielona
Żuromin
Kuczbork-Osada
Grudusk
Mchowo
Drążdżewo
Krasnosielc
Okalewo
Wiśniewo
Stupsk
Przasnysz
Płoniawy
Zbójno
Chojno
Skrwilno
Szreńsk
Urszulewo
Lutocin
Mdzewo
Szulmierz
Szczuki
Bieżuń
Radzanów
Krasne
Maków Mazowiecki
Lipno
Skępe
Gójsk
Rościszewo
Strzegowo
Ciechanów
Sierpc
Zawidz
Osciłowo
Gołymin-Ośrodek
Ligowo
Szumanie
Raciąż
Glinojeck
Radomice
Ojrzeń
Wielgie
Tłuchowo
Mochowo
Drobin
Gąsocin
Przewodowo Parcele
Kleszewo
Szpetal Graniczny
Gozdowo
Pułtusk
Strzegocin
Nowe Miasto
Winnica
Baboszewo
Bielsk
Włocławek
Dobrzyń nad Wisłą
Sikórz
Góra
Dzierzążnia
Płońsk
Nasielsk
Goślice
Ciółkowo
Kucice
Wróblewo
Gostynińsko-Włocławski
Płock
Bulkowo
Przyborowice
Borkowo
Wierzbica
Serock
Kowal
Naruszewo
Dębe
Zegrze
Choceń
Łąck
Bodzanów
Cieślé
Kobylniki
Brody
Modlin
Nowy Dwór Mazowiecki
Legionowo
Górki
Gostynin
Gąbin
Zakroczym
Lubień Kujawski
Wyszogród
Wilków
Jabłonna
Lanięta
Sanniki
Iłów
Kampinoski
Łomianki
Marki
WARSZAWA
WARSAW
Ząbki
Strzelce
Osmolin
Stary Brzozów
Młodzieszyn
Chodaków
Kampinos
Oporów
Kiernozia
Ruszki
Leszno
Borzęcin
Kutno
Żychlin
Sochaczew
Błonie
Ożarów Maz.
Bedlno
Paprotnia
Pruszków
Piastów
Janki
Konstancin-Jeziorna
Młogoszyn
Zduny
Szymanów
Brwinów
Witonia
Sobota
Łowicz
Guzów
Grodzisk Mazowiecki
Nadarzyn
Grabów
Bielawy
Nieborów
Bolimów
Żyrardów
Piaseczno
Piątek
Łęczyca
Nowe Grudze
Radziejowice
Siestrzeń
Bolimowski
Góra Kalwaria
Głowno
Popów
Łyszkowice
Skierniewice
Puszcza Mariańska
Mszczonów
Tarczyn
Ozorków
Biała
Zawady
Konie
Drwalew
Zgierz
Kołacin
Babsk
Grójec
Belsk Duży
Konary
Aleksandrów
Brzeziny
Jeżów
Wisła
Narew
Wkra
Bzura
Rawka
Pilica
Utrata
Mroga
Skrwa
Płonka
Orzyc
Drwęca
Działdówka
Sona
Łydynia
Raciążnica
Nida
Jeziorka
Pisia
E77
E75
E30
E67
A1
A2
20°
21°
53°
52°
A
B
C
4
5
6
69
86
87
12
36
127
202
147
137
129
129
45
61

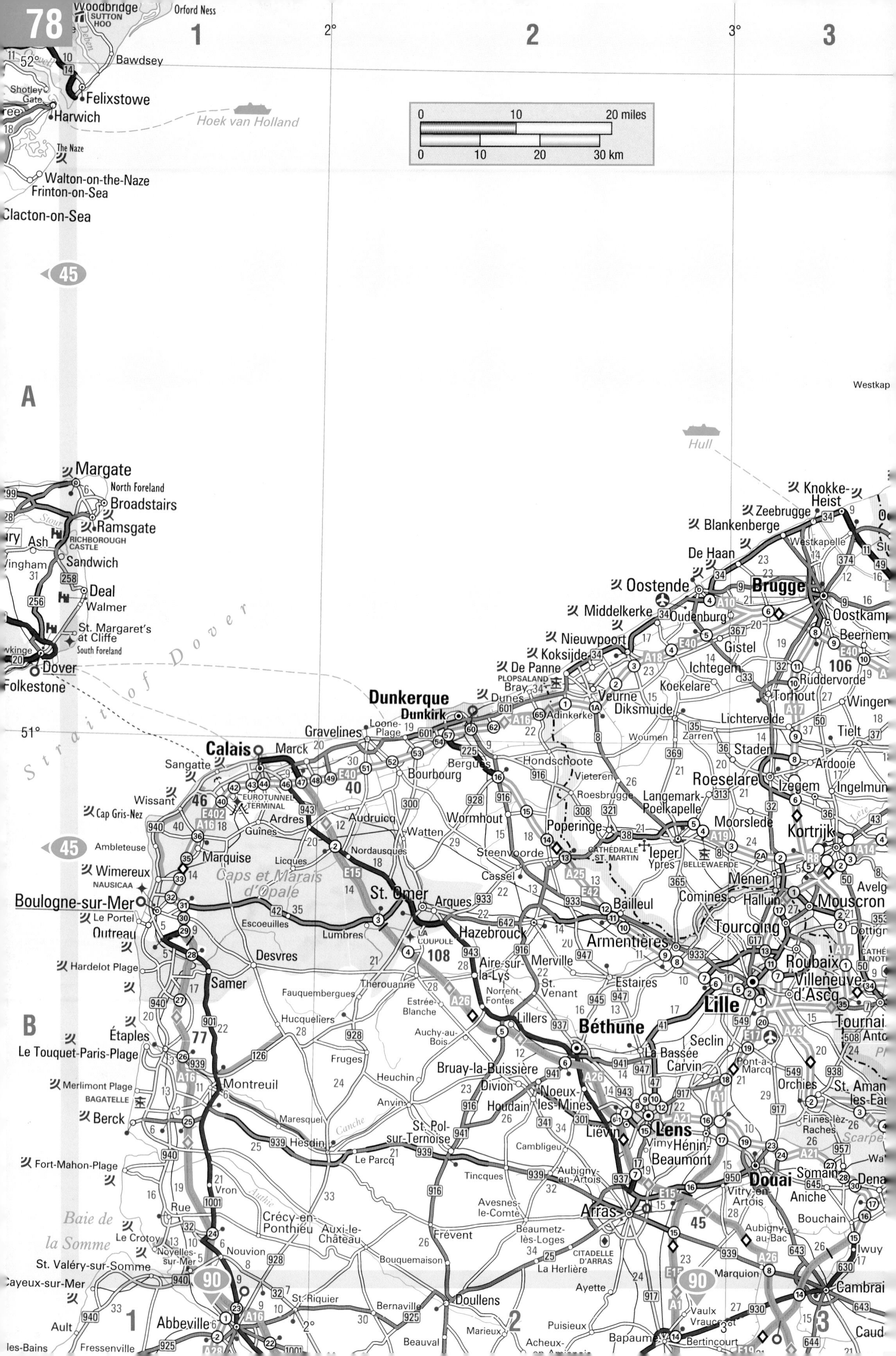

Woodbridge
SUTTON HOO
Orford Ness
Deben
Bawdsey
Felixstowe
Shotley Gate
Harwich
Hoek van Holland
The Naze
Walton-on-the-Naze
Frinton-on-Sea
Clacton-on-Sea
0
10
20 miles
0
10
20
30 km
1
2
3
2°
3°
52°
51°
A
B
45
Westkap
Hull
Margate
North Foreland
Broadstairs
Ramsgate
RICHBOROUGH CASTLE
Ash
Sandwich
Deal
Walmer
St. Margaret's at Cliffe
South Foreland
Dover
Folkestone
Strait of Dover
Knokke-Heist
Zeebrugge
Blankenberge
Westkapelle
De Haan
Oostende
Brugge
Middelkerke
Oudenburg
Oostkamp
Beernem
Nieuwpoort
Gistel
Koksijde
Ichtegem
De Panne
PLOPSALAND
Koekelare
Ruddervoorde
Bray Dunes
Veurne
Diksmuide
Torhout
Wingene
Adinkerke
Lichtervelde
Tielt
Dunkerque
Dunkirk
Woumen
Zarren
Gravelines
Loone-Plage
Staden
Ardooie
Calais
Marck
Bergues
Hondschoote
Vleteren
Roeselare
Izegem
Ingelmunster
Sangatte
Bourbourg
Roesbrugge
Langemark-Poelkapelle
Wissant
EUROTUNNEL TERMINAL
Wormhout
Cap Gris-Nez
Ardres
Audruicq
Poperinge
Moorslede
Kortrijk
Guînes
Watten
CATHÉDRALE ST. MARTIN
Ieper
Ypres
BELLEWAERDE
Ambleteuse
Marquise
Licques
Nordausques
Steenvoorde
Wimereux
Caps et Marais d'Opale
Cassel
Menen
NAUSICAA
St. Omer
Comines
Halluin
Mouscron
Boulogne-sur-Mer
Arques
Bailleul
Le Portel
Escoeuilles
Hazebrouck
Tourcoing
Outreau
Lumbres
LA COUPOLE
Armentières
Dottignies
Desvres
Merville
Roubaix
Hardelot Plage
Aire-sur-la-Lys
Villeneuve-d'Ascq
Samer
Thérouanne
St. Venant
Estaires
Fauquembergues
Norrent-Fontes
Lille
Estrée-Blanche
Étaples
Hucqueliers
Lillers
Béthune
Tournai
Le Touquet-Paris-Plage
Auchy-au-Bois
Seclin
Fruges
La Bassée
Carvin
Pont-a-Marcq
Orchies
St. Amand-les-Eaux
Merlimont Plage
Montreuil
Heuchin
Bruay-la-Buissière
BAGATELLE
Divion
Noeux-les-Mines
Berck
Anvin
Houdain
Maresquel
Liévin
Lens
Flines-lèz-Raches
St. Pol-sur-Ternoise
Vimy
Hénin-Beaumont
Hesdin
Canche
Camblignéul
Fort-Mahon-Plage
Le Parcq
Tincques
Aubigny-en-Artois
Douai
Somain
Vron
Authie
Vitry-en-Artois
Aniche
Rue
Avesnes-le-Comte
Arras
Baie de la Somme
Crécy-en-Ponthieu
Auxi-le-Château
Frévent
Aubigny-au-Bac
Bouchain
Le Crotoy
Beaumetz-lès-Loges
Noyelles-sur-Mer
Nouvion
CITADELLE D'ARRAS
St. Valéry-sur-Somme
Bouquemaison
La Herlière
Marquion
Cayeux-sur-Mer
Ayette
Cambrai
St. Riquier
Bernaville
Doullens
Vaulx Vraucourt
Ault
Abbeville
Marieux
Puisieux
Bapaume
Bertincourt
Caudry
Fressenville
Beauval
Acheux
90
106
108
77

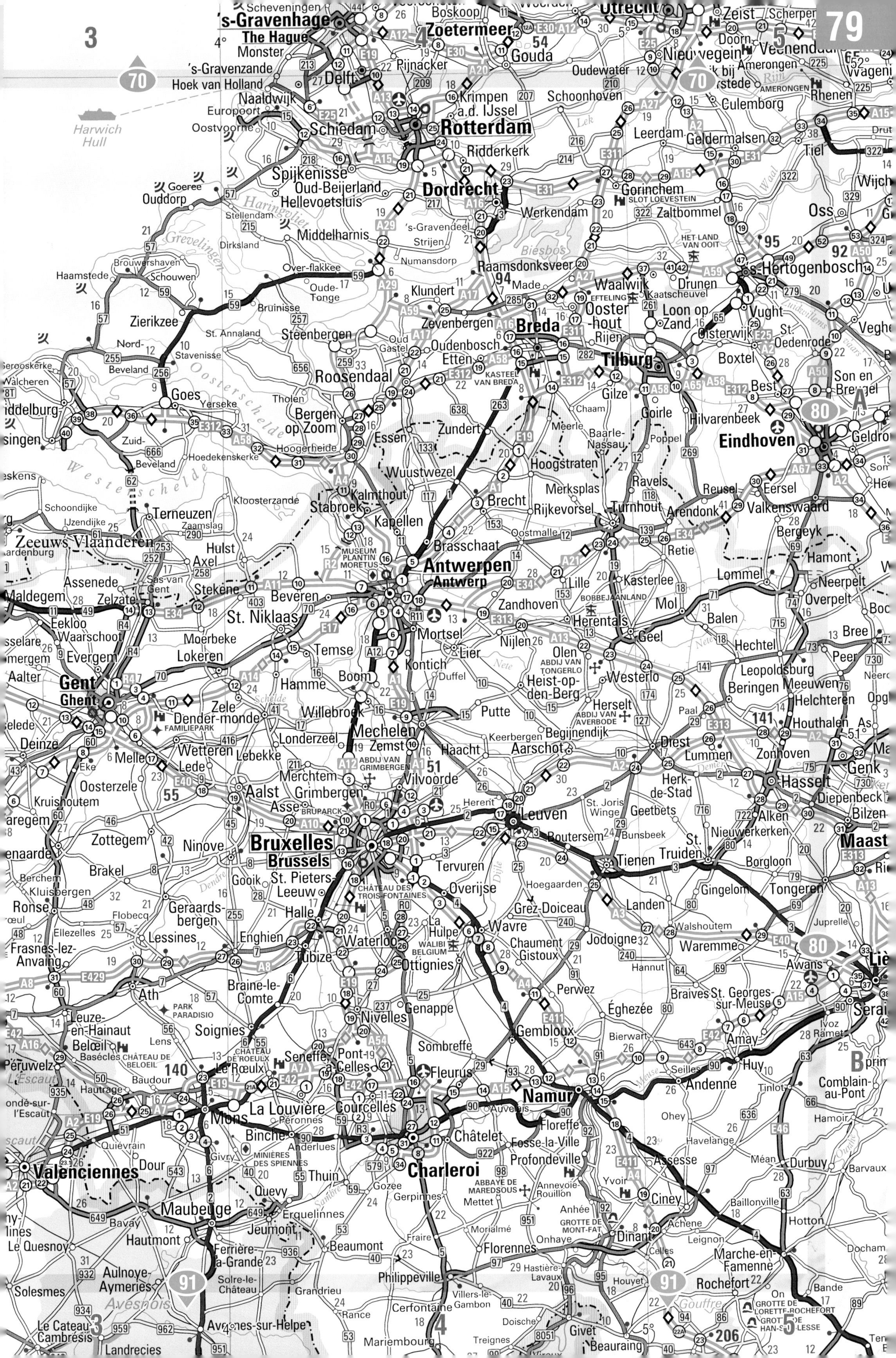

's-Gravenhage
The Hague
Scheveningen
Monster
's-Gravenzande
Hoek van Holland
Naaldwijk
Delft
Europoort
Oostvoorne
Schiedam
Rotterdam
Krimpen a.d. IJssel
Zoetermeer
Boskoop
Gouda
Rijnacker
Utrecht
Zeist
Doorn
Nieuwegein
Veenendaal
Amerongen
Rhenen
Culemborg
Oudewater
Schoonhoven
Leerdam
Geldermalsen
Tiel
Ridderkerk
Dordrecht
Spijkenisse
Oud-Beijerland
Hellevoetsluis
Goeree
Ouddorp
Gorinchem
Slot Loevestein
Zaltbommel
Werkendam
Biesbos
Middelharnis
's-Gravendeel
Strijen
Numansdorp
Over-flakkee
Oude-Tonge
Stellendam
Dirksland
Grevelingen
Haringvliet
Brouwershaven
Haamstede
Schouwen
Zierikzee
Bruinisse
Klundert
Raamsdonksveer
Made
Waalwijk
Efteling
Kaatsheuvel
Drunen
Het Land van Ooit
Oss
's-Hertogenbosch
Vught
Oosterhout
Zevenbergen
Breda
Rijen
Loon op Zand
Tilburg
Oisterwijk
St. Oedenrode
Boxtel
Best
Son en Breugel
Eindhoven
Geldrop
Veghel
Wijchen
Steenbergen
St. Annaland
Oud Gastel
Oudenbosch
Etten
Kasteel van Breda
Gilze
Goirle
Hilvarenbeek
Roosendaal
Tholen
Bergen op Zoom
Hoogerheide
Essen
Zundert
Baarle-Nassau
Poppel
Chaam
Meerle
Hoogstraten
Goes
Yerseke
Nord-Beveland
Zuid-Beveland
Stavenisse
Oosterschelde
Walcheren
Middelburg
Vlissingen
Hoedekenskerke
Westerschelde
Terneuzen
Schoondijke
IJzendijke
Zaamslag
Kloosterzande
Zeeuws Vlaanderen
Hulst
Axel
Sas-van Gent
Assenede
Zelzate
Maldegem
Eekloo
Waarschoot
Evergem
Aalter
Gent
Ghent
Deinze
Stekene
St. Niklaas
Beveren
Moerbeke
Lokeren
Temse
Hamme
Stabroek
Kalmthout
Kapellen
Wuustwezel
Brecht
Merksplas
Rijkevorsel
Turnhout
Ravels
Reusel
Eersel
Arendonk
Valkenswaard
Bergeyk
Retie
Hamont
Lommel
Neerpelt
Overpelt
Brasschaat
Museum Plantin Moretus
Antwerpen
Antwerp
Mortsel
Lier
Kontich
Duffel
Boom
Zandhoven
Lille
Kasterlee
Mol
Herentals
Bobbejaanland
Geel
Balen
Olen
Westerlo
Nijlen
Heist-op-den-Berg
Herselt
Hechtel
Leopoldsburg
Beringen
Bree
Peer
Meeuwen
Helchteren
Houthalen
Zonhoven
Genk
Hasselt
Diepenbeek
Bilzen
Maastricht
Zele
Dender-monde
Familiepark
Wetteren
Lede
Melle
Oosterzele
Willebroek
Mechelen
Zemst
Londerzeel
Lebbeke
Merchtem
Grimbergen
Abdij van Grimbergen
Vilvoorde
Haacht
Keerbergen
Putte
Begijnendijk
Aarschot
Diest
Lummen
Herk-de-Stad
Aalst
Asse
Bruparck
Bruxelles
Brussels
Ninove
Zottegem
Kruishoutem
Brakel
Oudenaarde
Ronse
Kluisbergen
Geraardsbergen
Gooik
St. Pieters-Leeuw
Halle
Herent
Leuven
Tervuren
Overijse
Château des Trois-Fontaines
Boutersem
Tienen
St. Truiden
Bunsbeek
Geetbets
Nieuwerkerken
Alken
Borgloon
Tongeren
Gingelom
Landen
Hoegaarden
Grez-Doiceau
Wavre
La Hulpe
Waterloo
Walibi Belgium
Chaumont Gistoux
Jodoigne
Waremme
Hannut
Walshoutem
Awans
Liège
Seraing
Enghien
Lessines
Flobecq
Ellezelles
Frasnes-lez-Anvaing
Ath
Tubize
Braine-le-Comte
Ottignies
Genappe
Nivelles
Perwez
Éghezée
Braives
St. Georges-sur-Meuse
Amay
Huy
Leuze-en-Hainaut
Belœil
Château de Beloeil
Péruwelz
Basècles
Park Paradisio
Lens
Soignies
Le Rœulx
Château de Rœulx
Seneffe
Pont-à-Celles
Sombreffe
Fleurus
Gembloux
Bierwart
Namur
Andenne
Seilles
Tinlot
Comblain-au-Pont
Baudour
Hautrage
Mons
La Louvière
Courcelles
Auvelais
Floreffe
Ohey
Binche
Péronnes
Anderlues
Châtelet
Fosse-la-Ville
Profondeville
Quiévrain
Dour
Valenciennes
Givry
Minières des Spiennes
Charleroi
Thuin
Gozee
Gerpinnes
Abbaye de Maredsous
Mettet
Annevoie-Rouillon
Anhée
Grotte de Mont-Fat
Yvoir
Assesse
Ciney
Havelange
Méan
Durbuy
Barvaux
Quevy
Maubeuge
Bavay
Erquelinnes
Jeumont
Hautmont
Le Quesnoy
Ferrière-la-Grande
Beaumont
Morialmé
Florennes
Onhaye
Dinant
Achêne
Leignon
Celles
Marche-en-Famenne
Hotton
Baillonville
Aulnoye-Aymeries
Solesmes
Avesnois
Solre-le-Château
Grandrieu
Philippeville
Villers-le-Gambon
Hastière-Lavaux
Houyet
Rochefort
Grotte de Lorette-Rochefort
Grotte de Han-sur-Lesse
Bande
Le Cateau Cambrésis
Landrecies
Avesnes-sur-Helpe
Rance
Cerfontaine
Mariembourg
Doische
Treignes
Givet
Beauraing
Gouffre
Harwich
Hull
Dijle
Demer
Nete
Schelde
Dendre
Sambre
Meuse
L'Escaut
Rijn
Lek
Waal

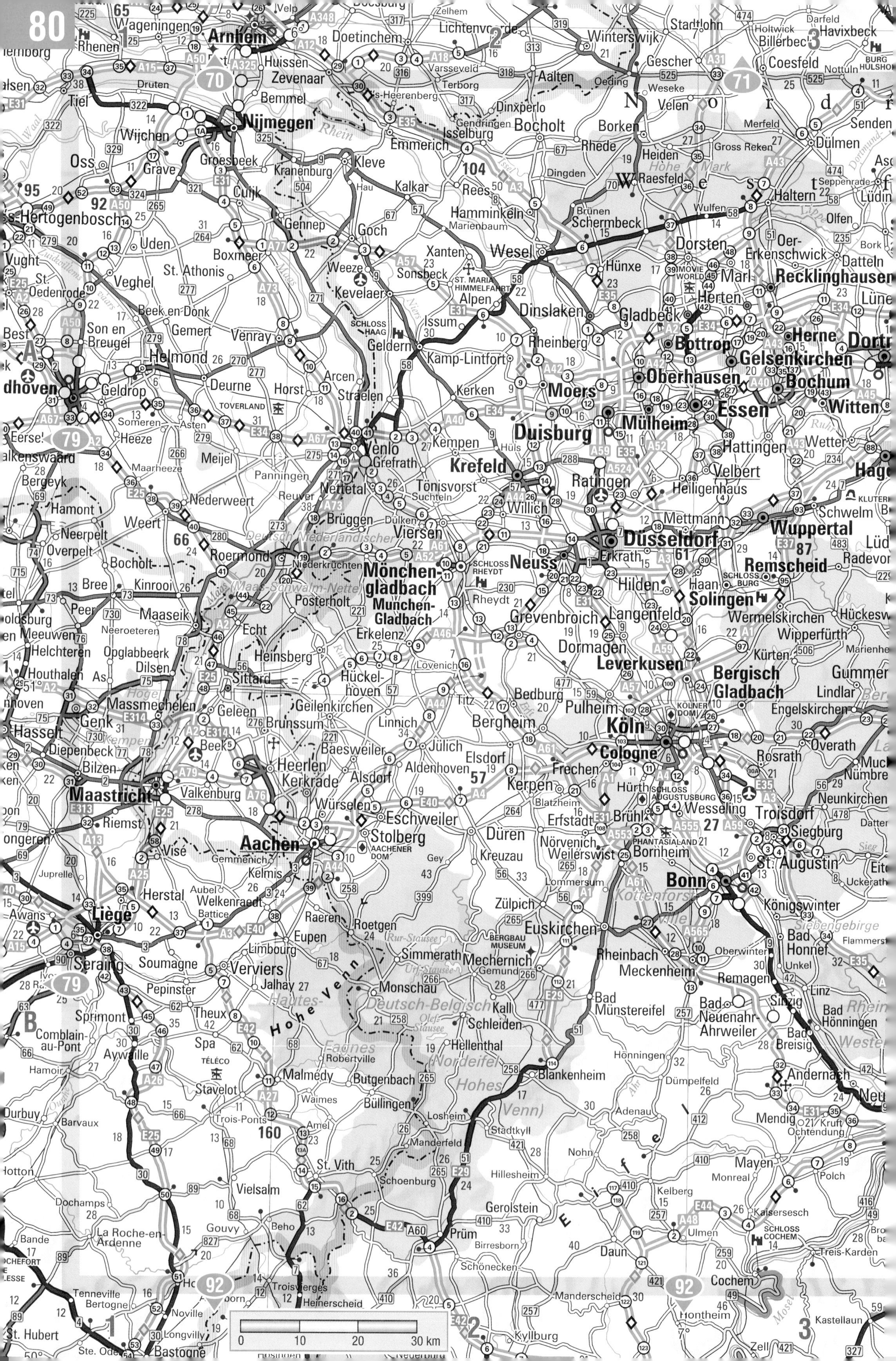

80
Wageningen
Arnhem
Rhenen
Doetinchem
Lichtenvoorde
Winterswijk
Stadtlohn
Billerbeck
Havixbeck
Coesfeld
Huissen
Zevenaar
Varsseveld
Aalten
Gescher
Oeding
Tiel
Druten
Bemmel
Terborg
Dinxperlo
Velen
Nijmegen
Wijchen
Emmerich
Isselburg
Bocholt
Borken
Merfeld
Senden
Dülmen
Oss
Grave
Groesbeek
Kranenburg
Kleve
Rhede
Heiden
Gross Reken
Hohe Mark
Kalkar
Rees
Raesfeld
Haltern
Cuijk
Hamminkeln
Schermbeck
's-Hertogenbosch
Uden
Boxmeer
Gennep
Goch
Dorsten
Marl
Oer-Erkenschwick
Datteln
Vught
St. Athonis
Weeze
Xanten
Wesel
Hünxe
Recklinghausen
St. Oedenrode
Veghel
Kevelaer
Sonsbeck
Alpen
Herten
Beek en Donk
Dinslaken
Gladbeck
Best
Son en Breugel
Gemert
Venray
Geldern
Issum
Rheinberg
Bottrop
Herne
Gelsenkirchen
Helmond
Deurne
Kamp-Lintfort
Oberhausen
Bochum
Eindhoven
Geldrop
Horst
Arcen
Straelen
Kerken
Moers
Essen
Witten
Someren
Asten
Duisburg
Mülheim
Eersel
Heeze
Venlo
Kempen
Hattingen
Wetter
Valkenswaard
Maarheeze
Meijel
Grefrath
Krefeld
Ratingen
Velbert
Bergeyk
Panningen
Reuver
Nettetal
Tönisvorst
Heiligenhaus
Hamont
Nederweert
Brüggen
Willich
Mettmann
Schwelm
Weert
Wuppertal
Neerpelt
Overpelt
Roermond
Viersen
Düsseldorf
Erkrath
Bocholt
Niederkrüchten
Mönchengladbach
Neuss
Remscheid
Bree
Kinrooi
Posterholt
Rheydt
Hilden
Haan
Solingen
Peer
Maaseik
Echt
Wermelskirchen
Hückeswagen
Meeuwen
Heinsberg
Erkelenz
Grevenbroich
Langenfeld
Wipperfürth
Helchteren
Opglabbeek
Dilsen
Dormagen
Kürten
Houthalen
Sittard
Hückelhoven
Lövenich
Leverkusen
Bergisch Gladbach
Gummersbach
Genk
Massmechelen
Geleen
Geilenkirchen
Bedburg
Pulheim
Lindlar
Hasselt
Brunssum
Linnich
Bergheim
Köln
Engelskirchen
Diepenbeek
Beek
Baesweiler
Jülich
Elsdorf
Cologne
Overath
Bilzen
Heerlen
Kerkrade
Alsdorf
Aldenhoven
Kerpen
Frechen
Hürth
Rosrath
Maastricht
Valkenburg
Würselen
Eschweiler
Brühl
Wesseling
Troisdorf
Neunkirchen
Tongeren
Riemst
Aachen
Stolberg
Düren
Erftstadt
Siegburg
Visé
Gemmenich
Kreuzau
Nörvenich
Weilerswist
Bornheim
St. Augustin
Kelmis
Herstal
Welkenraedt
Zülpich
Bonn
Königswinter
Liège
Battice
Raeren
Roetgen
Eupen
Euskirchen
Siebengebirge
Seraing
Soumagne
Limbourg
Simmerath
Mechernich
Rheinbach
Bad Honnef
Verviers
Jalhay
Monschau
Meckenheim
Remagen
Pepinster
Hautes-Fagnes
Hohe Venn
Deutsch-Belgischer
Kall
Bad Münstereifel
Sinzig
Linz
Sprimont
Theux
Schleiden
Bad Neuenahr-Ahrweiler
Bad Hönningen
Comblain-au-Pont
Aywaille
Spa
Hellenthal
Bad Breisig
Robertville
Malmedy
Bütgenbach
Blankenheim
Dümpelfeld
Andernach
Stavelot
Büllingen
Losheim
Adenau
Mendig
Ochtendung
Trois-Ponts
Amel
Stadtkyll
Durbuy
Nohn
Mayen
St. Vith
Manderfeld
Hillesheim
Monreal
Polch
Vielsalm
Schoenburg
Hotton
Dochamps
Gerolstein
Kelberg
Gouvy
Prüm
Daun
Ulmen
Kaisersesch
La Roche-en-Ardenne
Beho
Birresborn
Cochem
Treis-Karden
Schönecken
Troisvierges
Manderscheid
Tenneville
Bertogne
Heinerscheid
Noville
Hontheim
Kastellaun
St. Hubert
Longvilly
Bastogne
Kyllburg
Zell
Eifel
Rhein
Maas
Mosel
0
10
20
30 km

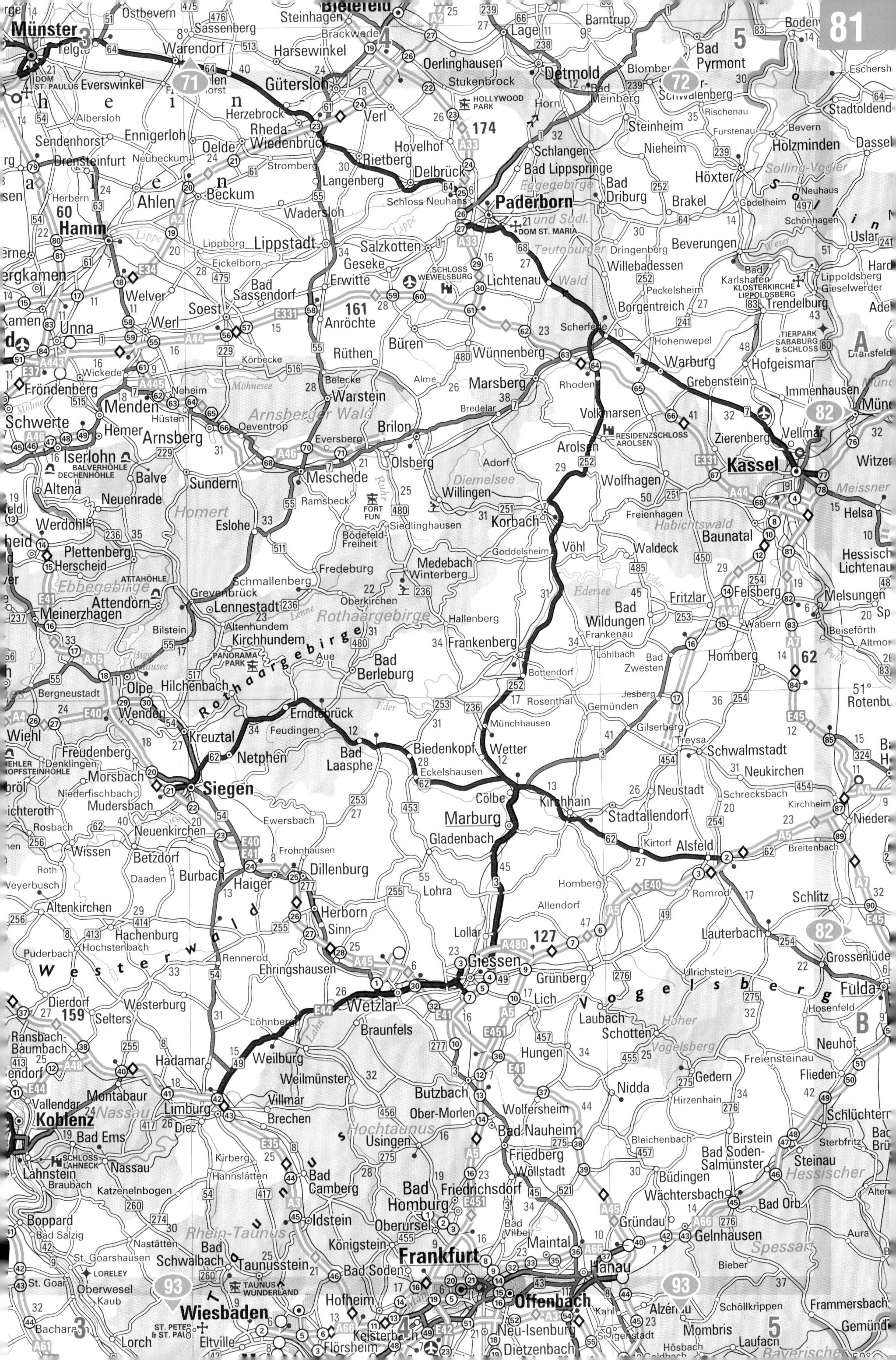
Münster
Telgte
Ostbevern
Sassenberg
Warendorf
Everswinkel
Albersloh
Sendenhorst
Ennigerloh
Drensteinfurt
Neubeckum
Oelde
Ahlen
Beckum
Herbern
Hamm
Bielefeld
Steinhagen
Brackwede
Harsewinkel
Gütersloh
Herzebrock
Rheda-
Wiedenbrück
Verl
Rietberg
Stromberg
Langenberg
Delbrück
Hovelhof
Oerlinghausen
Stukenbrock
HOLLYWOOD
PARK
Lage
Detmold
Bad Meinberg
Horn
Barntrup
Blomberg
Bad
Pyrmont
Schwalenberg
Steinheim
Nieheim
Schlangen
Bad Lippspringe
Eggegebirge
Bad
Driburg
Paderborn
DOM ST. MARIA
Schloss Neuhaus
Wadersloh
Lippstadt
Lippborg
Salzkotten
Geseke
Erwitte
Eickelborn
Bad
Sassendorf
Soest
Werl
Welver
Unna
Kamen
Bergkamen
Wickede
Fröndenberg
Menden
Neheim
Hüsten
Arnsberg
Oeventrop
Möhnesee
Körbecke
Arnsberger Wald
Belecke
Warstein
Rüthen
Anröchte
Büren
SCHLOSS
WEWELSBURG
Lichtenau
Wünnenberg
Alme
Marsberg
Bredelar
Brilon
Eversberg
Olsberg
Meschede
Schwerte
Hemer
Iserlohn
BALVERHÖHLE
DECHENHÖHLE
Balve
Altena
Neuenrade
Sundern
Werdohl
Plettenberg
Herscheid
Ebbegebirge
ATTAHÖHLE
Attendorn
Meinerzhagen
Homert
Eslohe
Ramsbeck
FORT
FUN
Siedlinghausen
Bödefeld-
Freiheit
Fredeburg
Schmallenberg
Grevenbrück
Lennestadt
Altenhundem
Kirchhundem
Bilstein
PANORAMA
PARK
Rothaargebirge
Oberkirchen
Winterberg
Medebach
Hallenberg
Willingen
Diemelsee
Adorf
Korbach
Goddelsheim
Vöhl
Edersee
Höxter
Holzminden
Brakel
Beverungen
Dringenberg
Willebadessen
Peckelsheim
Borgentreich
Bad
Karlshafen
KLOSTERKIRCHE
LIPPOLDSBERG
Lippoldsberg
Trendelburg
TIERPARK
SABABURG
& SCHLOSS
Hofgeismar
Warburg
Hohenwepel
Scherfede
Rhoden
Volkmarsen
Grebenstein
Immenhausen
Vellmar
Zierenberg
Kassel
RESIDENZSCHLOSS
AROLSEN
Arolsen
Wolfhagen
Freienhagen
Habichtswald
Baunatal
Waldeck
Helsa
Hessisch
Lichtenau
Melsungen
Felsberg
Fritzlar
Bad
Wildungen
Frankenau
Wabern
Homberg
Bad
Zwesten
Löhlbach
Rotenburg
Frankenberg
Bottendorf
Rosenthal
Gemünden
Jesberg
Gilserberg
Treysa
Schwalmstadt
Neukirchen
Bad
Berleburg
Aue
Olpe
Hilchenbach
Erndtebrück
Feudingen
Bad
Laasphe
Biedenkopf
Eckelshausen
Wetter
Münchhausen
Cölbe
Marburg
Kirchhain
Neustadt
Stadtallendorf
Schrecksbach
Kirtorf
Alsfeld
Romrod
Bergneustadt
Wenden
Wiehl
Kreuztal
Netphen
Freudenberg
Siegen
Morsbach
Mudersbach
Wissen
Betzdorf
Neuenkirchen
Daaden
Burbach
Haiger
Dillenburg
Frohnhausen
Eversbach
Gladenbach
Lohra
Herborn
Sinn
Altenkirchen
Hachenburg
Westerwald
Rennerod
Ehringshausen
Lollar
Giessen
Grünberg
Lich
Laubach
Schotten
Hungen
Vogelsberg
Lauterbach
Schlitz
Grossenlüder
Fulda
Hosenfeld
Neuhof
Flieden
Schlüchtern
Steinau
Bad Soden-
Salmünster
Birstein
Gedern
Nidda
Büdingen
Wächtersbach
Bad Orb
Gelnhausen
Spessart
Dierdorf
Selters
Westerburg
Hadamar
Weilburg
Wetzlar
Braunfels
Weilmünster
Villmar
Brechen
Butzbach
Ober-Mörlen
Wölfersheim
Bad Nauheim
Friedberg
Wöllstadt
Friedrichsdorf
Bad
Homburg
Oberursel
Usingen
Hochtaunus
Bad
Camberg
Idstein
Königstein
Limburg
Diez
Montabaur
Vallendar
Koblenz
Bad Ems
SCHLOSS
LAHNECK
Nassau
Lahnstein
Braubach
Katzenelnbogen
Kirberg
Hahnstätten
Boppard
Bad Salzig
Nastätten
Rhein-Taunus
Bad
Schwalbach
Taunusstein
St. Goarshausen
LORELEY
St. Goar
Oberwesel
Kaub
Bacharach
Lorch
Eltville
Wiesbaden
TAUNUS
WUNDERLAND
Hofheim
Bad Soden
Frankfurt
Offenbach
Neu-Isenburg
Dietzenbach
Kelsterbach
Flörsheim
Bad
Vilbel
Maintal
Hanau
Gründau
Alzenau
Mombris
Schöllkrippen
Laufach
Frammersbach

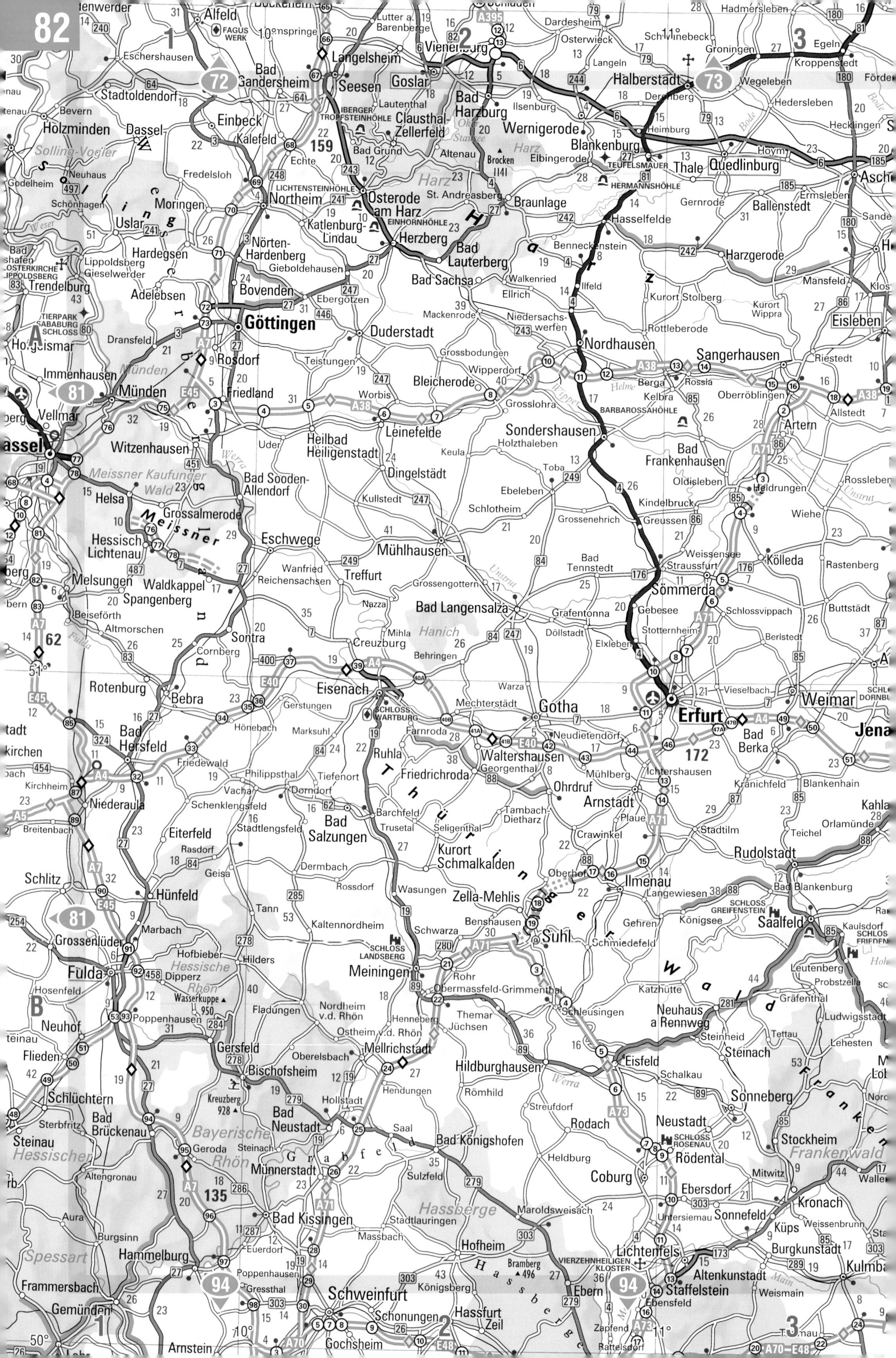
Alfeld
FAGUS WERK
Eschershausen
Bad Gandersheim
Stadtoldendorf
Bevern
Holzminden
Dassel
Einbeck
Kalefeld
Solling-Vogler
Neuhaus
Godelheim
Schönhagen
Fredelsloh
Moringen
Uslar
Northeim
Langelsheim
Seesen
Goslar
Vienenburg
Bad Harzburg
Lautenthal
IBERGER TROPFSTEINHÖHLE
Clausthal-Zellerfeld
Bad Grund
Echte
Altenau
Brocken 1141
Osterode am Harz
LICHTENSTEINHÖHLE
Katlenburg-Lindau
EINHORNHÖHLE
Herzberg
St. Andreasberg
Braunlage
Bad Lauterberg
Bad Sachsa
Walkenried
Ellrich
Wernigerode
Ilsenburg
Osterwieck
Dardesheim
Langeln
Halberstadt
Derenberg
Heimburg
Blankenburg
Elbingerode
TEUFELSMAUER
Thale
Quedlinburg
HERMANNSHÖHLE
Hasselfelde
Benneckenstein
Ilfeld
Gernrode
Ballenstedt
Ermsleben
Harzgerode
Schwanebeck
Groningen
Kroppenstedt
Egeln
Wegeleben
Hedersleben
Hecklingen
Aschersleben
Mansfeld
Kurort Stolberg
Kurort Wippra
Eisleben
Rottleberode
Nordhausen
Niedersachswerfen
Sangerhausen
Riestedt
Berga
Kelbra
Rossla
Oberröblingen
Allstedt
BARBAROSSAHÖHLE
Artern
Bad Frankenhausen
Oldisleben
Heldrungen
Rossleben
Wiehe
Kindelbruck
Greussen
Weissensee
Kölleda
Rastenberg
Straussfurt
Sömmerda
Schlossvippach
Buttstädt
Gebesee
Stotternheim
Berlstedt
Erfurt
Vieselbach
Weimar
Jena
Bad Berka
Blankenhain
Kranichfeld
Ichtershausen
Arnstadt
Plaue
Stadtilm
Rudolstadt
Orlamünde
Kahla
Teichel
Bad Blankenburg
Saalfeld
SCHLOSS GREIFENSTEIN
Königsee
Kaulsdorf
Leutenberg
Probstzella
Gräfenthal
Ludwigsstadt
Lehesten
Tettau
Steinach
Neuhaus a. Rennweg
Steinheid
Katzhütte
Gehren
Langewiesen
Ilmenau
Oberhof
Zella-Mehlis
Suhl
Schmiedefeld
Benshausen
Schleusingen
Eisfeld
Schalkau
Sonneberg
Neustadt
SCHLOSS ROSENAU
Rödental
Coburg
Ebersdorf
Sonnefeld
Untersiemau
Mitwitz
Stockheim
Kronach
Küps
Weissenbrunn
Burgkunstadt
Kulmbach
Weismain
Altenkunstadt
Lichtenfels
VIERZEHNHEILIGEN KLOSTER
Staffelstein
Ebensfeld
Zapfend
Rattelsdorf
Ebern
Bramberg 496
Hofheim
Maroldsweisach
Hassberge
Haßfurt
Zeil
Königsberg
Schweinfurt
Schonungen
Gochsheim
Arnstein
Gemünden
Frammersbach
Spessart
Hammelburg
Euerdorf
Bad Kissingen
Poppenhausen
Gressthal
Stadtlauringen
Massbach
Sulzfeld
Bad Königshofen
Münnerstadt
Bad Neustadt
Saal
Grabfeld
Hollstadt
Hendungen
Mellrichstadt
Ostheim v.d. Rhön
Nordheim v.d. Rhön
Fladungen
Oberelsbach
Bischofsheim
Kreuzberg 928
Gersfeld
Wasserkuppe 950
Hilders
Tann
Kaltennordheim
SCHLOSS LANDSBERG
Meiningen
Rohr
Obermassfeld-Grimmenthal
Henneberg
Themar
Jüchsen
Römhild
Hildburghausen
Streufdorf
Rodach
Heldburg
Schwarza
Wasungen
Dermbach
Rossdorf
Geisa
Rasdorf
Eiterfeld
Hünfeld
Marbach
Grossenlüder
Fulda
Hofbieber
Dipperz
Poppenhausen
Hessische Rhön
Hosenfeld
Neuhof
Flieden
Schlüchtern
Sterbfritz
Bad Brückenau
Steinau
Hessischer
Altengronau
Bayerische Rhön
Geroda
Aura
Burgsinn
Schlitz
Niederaula
Breitenbach
Kirchheim
Bad Hersfeld
Friedewald
Philippsthal
Vacha
Tiefenort
Dorndorf
Schenklengsfeld
Stadtlengsfeld
Bad Salzungen
Barchfeld
Trusetal
Seligenthal
Kurort Schmalkalden
Tambach-Dietharz
Ohrdruf
Crawinkel
Friedrichroda
Ruhla
Farnroda
Georgenthal
Waltershausen
Mechterstädt
Gotha
Neudietendorf
Mühlberg
Warza
Eisenach
SCHLOSS WARTBURG
Gerstungen
Marksuhl
Hönebach
Bebra
Rotenburg
Cornberg
Sontra
Creuzburg
Mihla
Behringen
Hainich
Bad Langensalza
Grafentonna
Döllstädt
Elxleben
Nazza
Grossengottern
Bad Tennstedt
Treffurt
Wanfried
Reichensachsen
Eschwege
Mühlhausen
Kullstedt
Schlotheim
Ebeleben
Grossenehrich
Toba
Keula
Holzthaleben
Sondershausen
Dingelstädt
Heilbad Heiligenstadt
Leinefelde
Uder
Worbis
Bleicherode
Wipperdorf
Grosslohra
Grossbodungen
Teistungen
Duderstadt
Mackenrode
Gieboldehausen
Ebergötzen
Bovenden
Nörten-Hardenberg
Göttingen
Rosdorf
Friedland
Dransfeld
Adelebsen
Hardegsen
Lippoldsberg
Gieselwerder
Trendelburg
TIERPARK SABABURG SCHLOSS
Hofgeismar
Immenhausen
Münden
Vellmar
Kassel
Witzenhausen
Bad Sooden-Allendorf
Meissner Kaufunger Wald
Helsa
Grossalmerode
Meissner
Hessisch Lichtenau
Waldkappel
Melsungen
Spangenberg
Beiseförth
Altmorschen
Fulda
Erfurt
Weimar
Jena

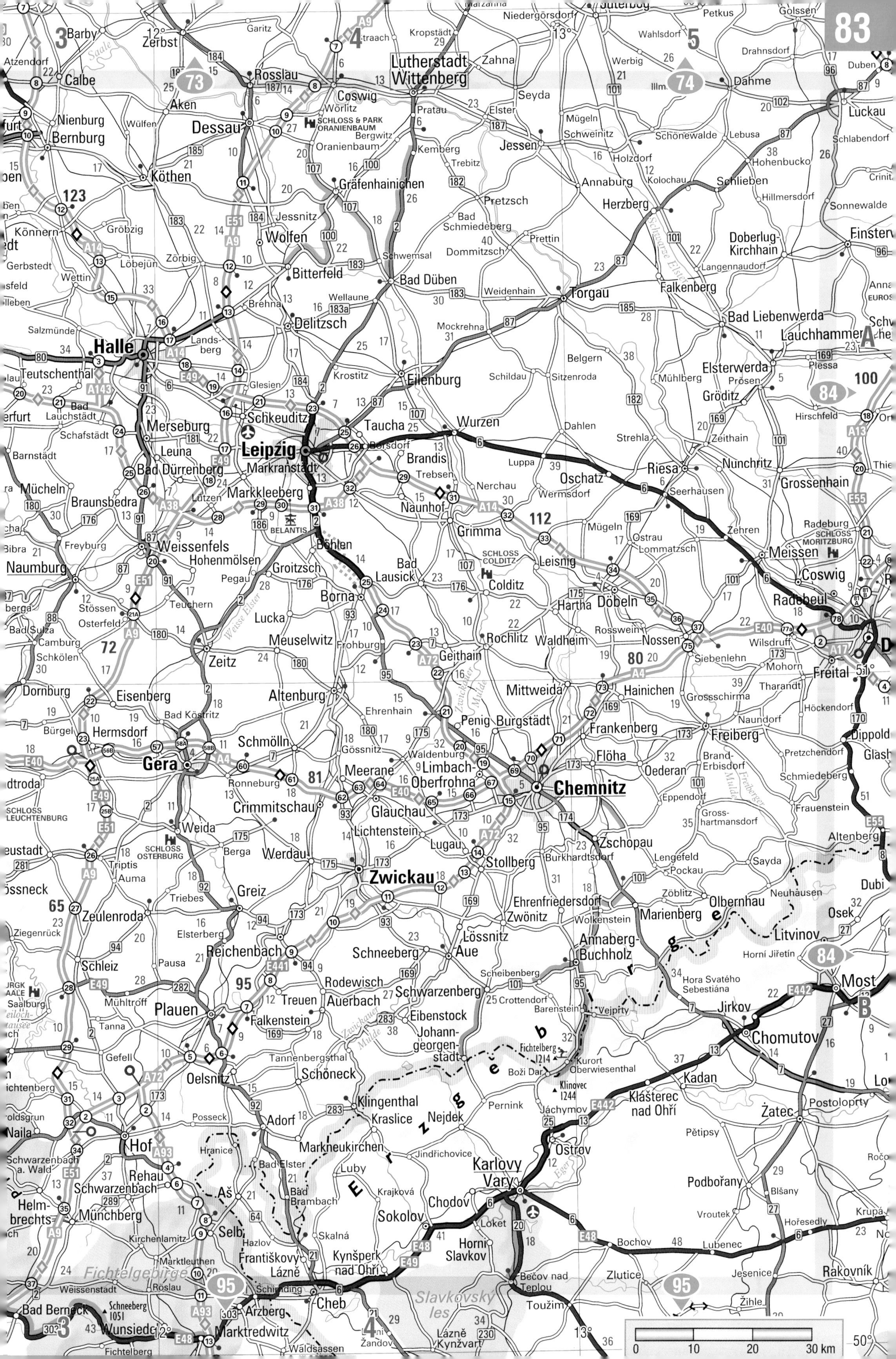

Barby
Zerbst
Garitz
Kropstädt
Niedergörsdorf
Jüterbog
Petkus
Golssen
Wahlsdorf
Atzendorf
Calbe
Rosslau
Lutherstadt Wittenberg
Zahna
Werbig
Drahnsdorf
Dahme
Duben
Coswig
Wörlitz
Pratau
Seyda
Elster
Luckau
Nienburg
Bernburg
Aken
Dessau
Wülfen
SCHLOSS & PARK ORANIENBAUM
Oranienbaum
Bergwitz
Kemberg
Trebitz
Jessen
Mügeln
Schweinitz
Schönewalde
Lebusa
Holzdorf
Schlabendorf
Hohenbucko
Köthen
Gräfenhainichen
Annaburg
Kolochau
Schlieben
Pretzsch
Herzberg
Hillmersdorf
Sonnewalde
Könnern
Gröbzig
Jessnitz
Wolfen
Bad Schmiedeberg
Prettin
Doberlug-Kirchhain
Dommitzsch
Gerbstedt
Löbejün
Zörbig
Schwemsal
Bitterfeld
Langennaudorf
Wettin
Bad Düben
Falkenberg
Brehna
Wellaune
Weidenhain
Torgau
Salzmünde
Delitzsch
Mockrehna
Bad Liebenwerda
Lauchhammer
Halle
Landsberg
Belgern
Elsterwerda
Plessa
Teutschenthal
Krostitz
Eilenburg
Schildau
Sitzenrode
Mühlberg
Prösen
Glesien
Gröditz
Bad Lauchstädt
Schkeuditz
Hirschfeld
Taucha
Wurzen
Dahlen
Schafstädt
Merseburg
Leipzig
Borsdorf
Strehla
Zeithain
Barnstädt
Leuna
Brandis
Luppa
Riesa
Nünchritz
Bad Dürrenberg
Markranstädt
Trebsen
Oschatz
Mücheln
Markkleeberg
Nerchau
Wermsdorf
Seerhausen
Grossenhain
Braunsbedra
Lützen
Naunhof
BELANTIS
Grimma
Mügeln
Zehren
Radeburg
SCHLOSS MORITZBURG
Freyburg
Weissenfels
Böhlen
Ostrau
Lommatzsch
Meissen
Naumburg
Hohenmölsen
Pegau
Groitzsch
Bad Lausick
SCHLOSS COLDITZ
Colditz
Leisnig
Coswig
Stössen
Teuchern
Borna
Hartha
Döbeln
Radebeul
Osterfeld
Lucka
Bad Sulza
Camburg
Schkölen
Meuselwitz
Frohburg
Geithain
Rochlitz
Waldheim
Rosswein
Nossen
Wilsdruff
Zeitz
Siebenlehn
Mohorn
Freital
Dornburg
Eisenberg
Altenburg
Mittweida
Hainichen
Tharandt
Bad Köstritz
Ehrenhain
Penig
Burgstädt
Grossschirma
Höckendorf
Bürgel
Hermsdorf
Frankenberg
Naundorf
Freiberg
Dippoldiswalde
Schmölln
Gössnitz
Waldenburg
Limbach-Oberfrohna
Flöha
Oederan
Pretzschendorf
Gera
Ronneburg
Meerane
Chemnitz
Brand-Erbisdorf
Schmiedeberg
Crimmitschau
Glauchau
Eppendorf
SCHLOSS LEUCHTENBURG
Frauenstein
Weida
Lichtenstein
Gross-hartmansdorf
SCHLOSS OSTERBURG
Berga
Werdau
Lugau
Zschopau
Altenberg
Neustadt
Triptis
Auma
Zwickau
Stollberg
Burkhardtsdorf
Lengefeld
Pockau
Sayda
Pössneck
Greiz
Triebes
Zöblitz
Neuhausen
Dubí
Zeulenroda
Ehrenfriedersdorf
Zwönitz
Marienberg
Olbernhau
Osek
Ziegenrück
Elsterberg
Wolkenstein
Lössnitz
Annaberg-Buchholz
Litvínov
Reichenbach
Schneeberg
Aue
Horní Jiřetín
Schleiz
Pausa
Scheibenberg
Rodewisch
Hora Svatého Sebestiána
Most
Saalburg
Mühltroff
Plauen
Treuen
Auerbach
Schwarzenberg
Crottendorf
Barenstein
Vejprty
Jirkov
Tanna
Falkenstein
Eibenstock
Johanngeorgenstadt
Chomutov
Gefell
Tannenbergsthal
Fichtelberg
Kurort Oberwiesenthal
Boží Dar
Oelsnitz
Schöneck
Klínovec
Kadaň
Lichtenberg
Klingenthal
Kraslice
Nejdek
Pernink
Jáchymov
Klášterec nad Ohří
Postoloprty
Žatec
Posseck
Adorf
Pětipsy
Naila
Hof
Hranice
Markneukirchen
Ostrov
Schwarzenbach a. Wald
Rehau
Bad Elster
Jindřichovice
Karlovy Vary
Podbořany
Schwarzenbach
Aš
Bad Brambach
Luby
Krajková
Chodov
Bìšany
Helmbrechts
Münchberg
Selb
Sokolov
Vroutek
Hořesedly
Kirchenlamitz
Skalná
Loket
Horní Slavkov
Bochov
Lubenec
Hazlov
Marktleuthen
Františkovy Lázně
Kynšperk nad Ohří
Fichtelgebirge
Weissenstadt
Röslau
Schirnding
Cheb
Slavkovský les
Bečov nad Teplou
Žlutice
Jesenice
Rakovník
Bad Berneck
Schneeberg
Arzberg
Toužim
Žihle
Wunsiedel
Marktredwitz
Lázně Kynžvart
Fichtelberg
Waldsassen
Erzgebirge
0 10 20 30 km

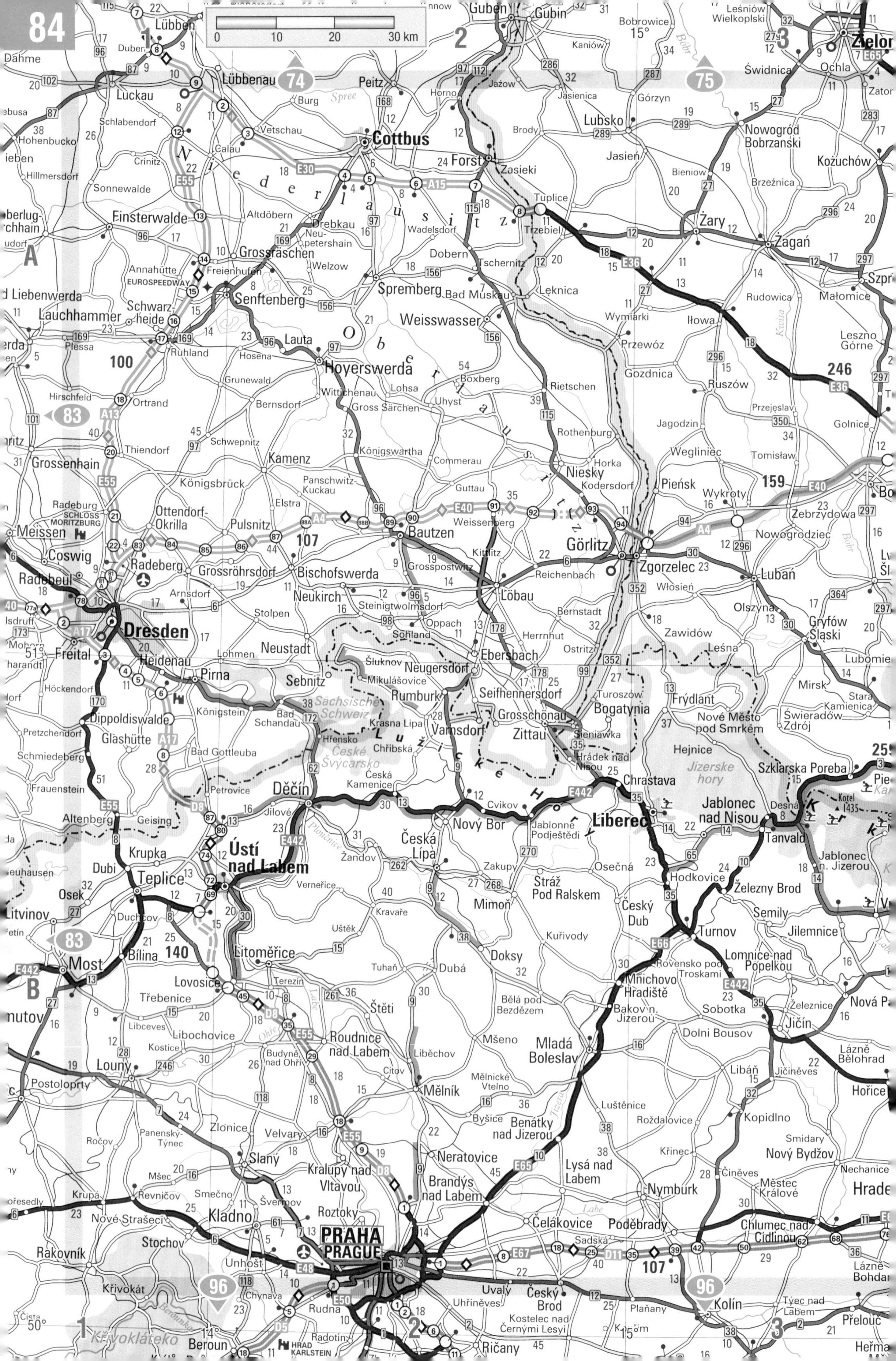

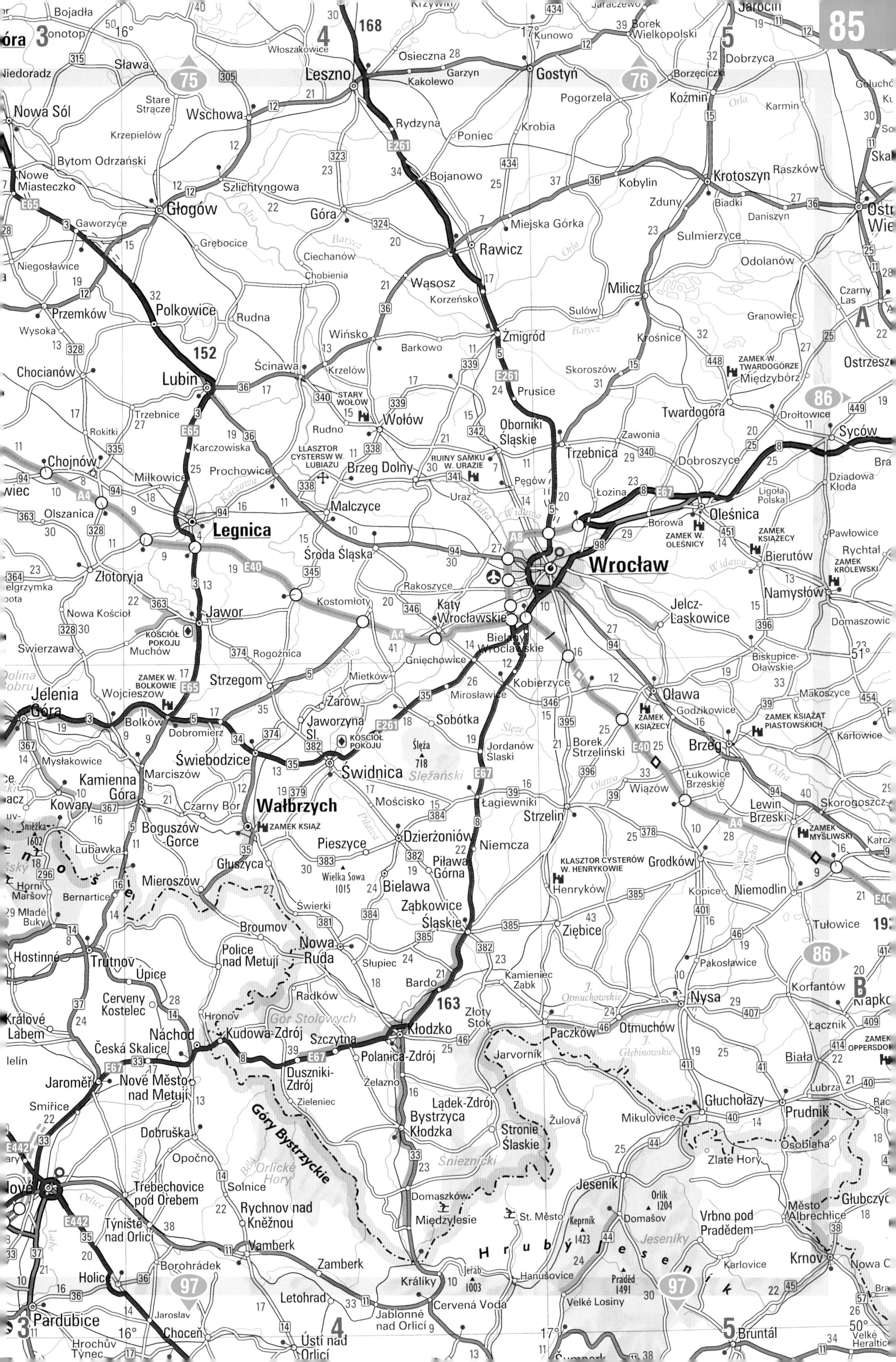
Bojadła
Leszno
Gostyń
Jarocin
Borek Wielkopolski
Dobrzyca
Nowa Sól
Sława
Wschowa
Osieczna
Kakolewo
Garzyn
Krobia
Poniec
Koźmin
Pogorzela
Borzęciczki
Karmin
Rydzyna
Bytom Odrzański
Nowe Miasteczko
Szlichtyngowa
Głogów
Góra
Bojanowo
Krotoszyn
Raszków
Kobylin
Zduny
Biadki
Daniszyn
Miejska Górka
Rawicz
Sulmierzyce
Odolanów
Gaworzyce
Grębocice
Ciechanów
Chobienia
Niegosławice
Wąsosz
Korzeńsko
Milicz
Polkowice
Rudna
Przemków
Wysoka
Żmigród
Sulów
Winsko
Barkowo
Krośnice
Granowiec
Chocianów
Lubin
Ścinawa
Krzelów
Skoroszów
Prusice
Zamek w Twardogórze
Międzybórz
Ostrzeszów
Trzebnice
Rokitki
Stary Wołów
Wołów
Rudno
Oborniki Śląskie
Twardogóra
Drołtowice
Syców
Karczowiska
Klasztor Cystersów w Lubiążu
Brzeg Dolny
Ruiny Zamku w Urazie
Zawonia
Trzebnica
Dobroszyce
Chojnów
Miłkowice
Prochowice
Pęgów
Uraz
Łozina
Oleśnica
Dziadowa Kłoda
Ligota Polska
Olszanica
Legnica
Malczyce
Borowa
Zamek w Oleśnicy
Zamek Książęcy
Pawłowice
Złotoryja
Środa Śląska
Wrocław
Bierutów
Rychtal
Zamek Królewski
Namysłów
Jawor
Nowa Kościół
Kościół Pokoju
Rakoszyce
Kostomłoty
Kąty Wrocławskie
Jelcz-Laskowice
Swierzawa
Muchów
Rogoźnica
Bielany Wrocławskie
Gnięchowice
Domaszowice
Biskupice Oławskie
Zamek w Bolkowie
Strzegom
Mietków
Kobierzyce
Oława
Makoszyce
Jelenia Góra
Wojcieszów
Żarów
Mirosławice
Sobótka
Godzikowice
Zamek Książąt Piastowskich
Bolków
Dobromierz
Jaworzyna Śl.
Ślęża
Jordanów Śląski
Borek Strzeliński
Brzeg
Karłowice
Mysłakowice
Świebodzice
Świdnica
Ślężański
Łukowice Brzeskie
Wiązów
Kamienna Góra
Marciszów
Mościsko
Łagiewniki
Strzelin
Lewin Brzeski
Skorogoszcz
Kowary
Czarny Bór
Wałbrzych
Zamek Książ
Boguszów-Gorce
Pieszyce
Dzierżoniów
Niemcza
Zamek Myśliwski
Śnieżka
Lubawka
Piława Górna
Klasztor Cystersów w Henrykowie
Grodków
Głuszyca
Mieroszów
Wielka Sowa
Bielawa
Henryków
Kopice
Niemodlin
Horní Maršov
Bernartice
Mladé Buky
Świerki
Ząbkowice Śląskie
Ziębice
Tułowice
Broumov
Nowa Ruda
Hostinné
Trutnov
Police nad Metují
Słupiec
Pakosławice
Úpice
Radków
Bardo
Kamieniec Ząbkowicki
Nysa
Korfantów
Červený Kostelec
Gór Stołowych
Złoty Stok
J. Otmuchowskie
Králové Labem
Náchod
Hronov
Kudowa-Zdrój
Szczytna
Kłodzko
Paczków
Otmuchów
Łącznik
Česká Skalice
Polanica-Zdrój
Jarvorník
J. Głębinowskie
Biała
Zamek Oppersdorfów
Jaroměř
Nové Město nad Metují
Duszniki-Zdrój
Żelazno
Lubrza
Smiřice
Zieleniec
Lądek-Zdrój
Głuchołazy
Prudnik
Bystrzyca Kłodzka
Żulová
Mikulovice
Dobruška
Góry Bystrzyckie
Stronie Śląskie
Osoblaha
Opočno
Orlické Hory
Śnieżnicki
Zlaté Hory
Třebechovice pod Orebem
Solnice
Jeseník
Rychnov nad Kněžnou
Domaszków
Międzylesie
St. Město
Praděd
Keprník
Domašov
Vrbno pod Pradědem
Město Albrechtice
Głubczyce
Týniště nad Orlicí
Vamberk
Hrubý Jeseník
Jeseníky
Borohrádek
Zamberk
Králiky
Jeřáb
Hanušovice
Karlovice
Krnov
Nowa Cerekwia
Holice
Letohrad
Červená Voda
Velké Losiny
Pardubice
Jaroslav
Jablonné nad Orlicí
Bruntál
Velké Heraltice
Choceň
Ústí nad Orlicí
Hrochův Týnec
Šumperk
Labe
Odra
Barycz
Orla
Widawa
Bystrzyca
Kaczawa
Ślęza
Oława
Nysa Kłodzka
Bóbr

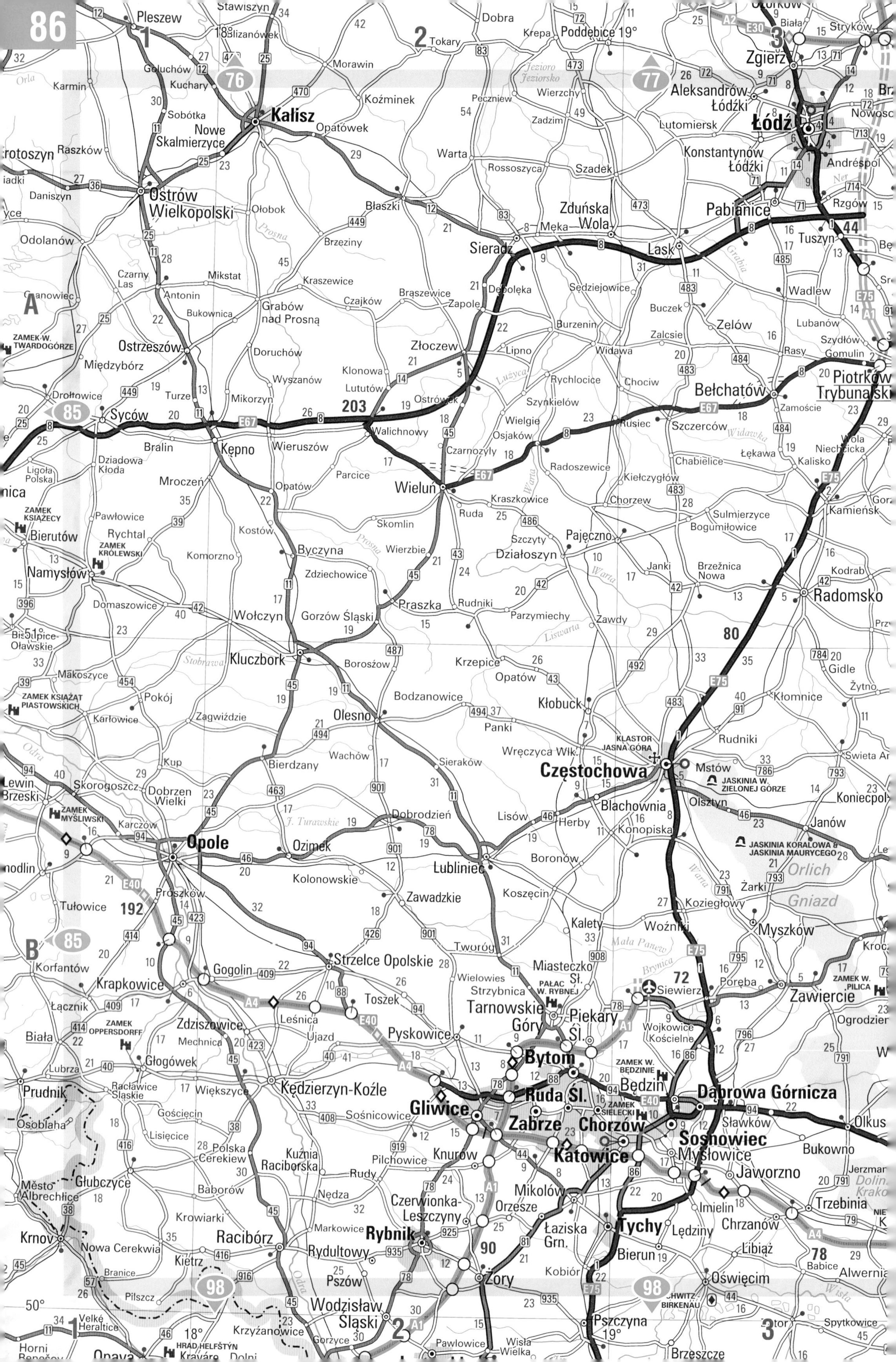

Pleszew
Stawiszyn
Blizanówek
Dobra
Tokary
Krępa
Poddębice
Stryków
Zgierz
Gołuchów
Kuchary
Karmin
Morawin
Jezioro Jeziorsko
Wierzchy
Aleksandrów Łódzki
Łódź
Kalisz
Koźminek
Pęczniew
Zadzim
Lutomiersk
Sobótka
Nowe Skalmierzyce
Opatówek
Warta
Konstantynów Łódzki
Andrespol
Krotoszyn
Raszków
Daniszyn
Ostrów Wielkopolski
Rossoszyca
Szadek
Odolanów
Ołobok
Błaszki
Brzeziny
Zduńska Wola
Męka
Pabianice
Rzgów
Tuszyn
Sieradz
Łask
Czarny Las
Antonin
Mikstat
Kraszewice
Dębołęka
Sędziejowice
Granowiec
Bukownica
Grabów nad Prosną
Czajków
Brąszewice
Zapole
Buczek
Wadlew
Zelów
Lubanów
ZAMEK W. TWARDOGÓRZE
Ostrzeszów
Międzybórz
Doruchów
Złoczew
Burzenin
Lipno
Widawa
Zalcsie
Rasy
Szydłów
Gomulin
Klonowa
Lututów
Rychłocice
Chociw
Piotrków Trybunalski
Drołtowice
Wyszanów
Mikorzyn
Turze
Ostrówek
Szynkielów
Bełchatów
Syców
Wielgie
Osjaków
Rusiec
Szczerców
Zamoście
Bralin
Kępno
Wieruszów
Walichnowy
Dziadowa Kłoda
Ligota Polska
Czarnożyły
Radoszewice
Chabielice
Łękawa
Wola Niechcicka
Kalisko
Mroczeń
Opatów
Parcice
Wieluń
Kiełczygłów
ZAMEK KSIĄŻĘCY
Pawłowice
Kostów
Skomlin
Ruda
Kraszkowice
Chorzew
Sulmierzyce
Bogumiłowice
Kamieńsk
Bierutów
Rychtal
ZAMEK KRÓLEWSKI
Komorzno
Byczyna
Wierzbie
Szczyty
Działoszyn
Pajęczno
Janki
Brzeźnica Nowa
Kodrab
Namysłów
Zdziechowice
Radomsko
Domaszowice
Wołczyn
Gorzów Śląski
Praszka
Rudniki
Parzymiechy
Zawady
Bisku pice Oławskie
Kluczbork
Boroszów
Krzepice
Opatów
Gidle
Makoszyce
ZAMEK KSIĄŻĄT PIASTOWSKICH
Pokój
Bodzanowice
Kłobuck
Kłomnice
Karłowice
Zagwiździe
Olesno
Panki
Rudniki
Wachów
Wręczyca Wlk.
KLASTOR JASNA GÓRA
Kup
Bierdzany
Sieraków
Częstochowa
Mstów
Święta Anna
Lewin Brzeski
Skorogoszcz
Dobrzeń Wielki
JASKINIA W. ZIELONEJ GÓRZE
ZAMEK MYŚLIWSKI
Blachownia
Olsztyn
Koniecpol
Karczów
J. Turawskie
Dobrodzień
Lisów
Herby
Konopiska
Janów
Opole
Ozimek
Lubliniec
JASKINIA KORALOWA & JASKINIA MAURYCEGO
Niemodlin
Kolonowskie
Boronów
Orlich
Proszków
Zawadzkie
Koszęcin
Żarki
Tułowice
Gniazd
Koziegłowy
Kalety
Woźniki
Myszków
Mała Panew
Korfantów
Strzelce Opolskie
Tworóg
Gogolin
Wielowies
Miasteczko Śl.
Brynica
Poręba
ZAMEK W. PILICA
Krapkowice
Toszek
Strzybnica
PAŁAC W. RYBNEJ
Siewierz
Zawiercie
Łącznik
Leśnica
Tarnowskie Góry
Piekary Śl.
Wojkowice Kościelne
Ogrodzieniec
ZAMEK OPPERSDORFF
Zdzieszowice
Ujazd
Pyskowice
Biała
Mechnica
Bytom
Głogówek
ZAMEK W. BĘDZINIE
Lubrza
Będzin
Prudnik
Racławice Śląskie
Większyce
Kędzierzyn-Koźle
Gliwice
Ruda Śl.
Dąbrowa Górnicza
Osoblaha
Gościęcin
Sośnicowice
ZAMEK SIELECKI
Zabrze
Chorzów
Sławków
Olkusz
Lisięcice
Sosnowiec
Polska Cerekiew
Kuźnia Raciborska
Pilchowice
Knurów
Katowice
Mysłowice
Bukowno
Město Albrechtice
Głubczyce
Baborów
Rudy
Jaworzno
Jerzmanowice
Nędza
Czerwionka-Leszczyny
Mikołów
Orzesze
Imielin
Trzebinia
Krowiarki
Markowice
Rybnik
Łaziska Grn.
Tychy
Lędziny
Chrzanów
Krnov
Nowa Cerekwia
Racibórz
Rydułtowy
Bieruń
Libiąż
Kietrz
Branice
Pszów
Żory
Kobiór
Oświęcim
Babice
Alwernia
Pilszcz
Wodzisław Śląski
AUSCHWITZ-BIRKENAU
Wisła
Velké Heraltice
Krzyżanowice
Gorzyce
Pawłowice
Pszczyna
Spytkowice
Horní Benešov
Opava
HRAD HELFŠTÝN
Kravaře
Dolní
Wisła Wielka
Brzeszcze
Odra
Prosna
Warta
Liswarta
Stobrawa
Widawka
Grabia
Ner
Luciąża
Orla
203
80
192
90
72
44
78
A
B
1
2
3
76
77
85
98
50°
18°
19°
E67
E75
E40
A1
A2
A4
E30

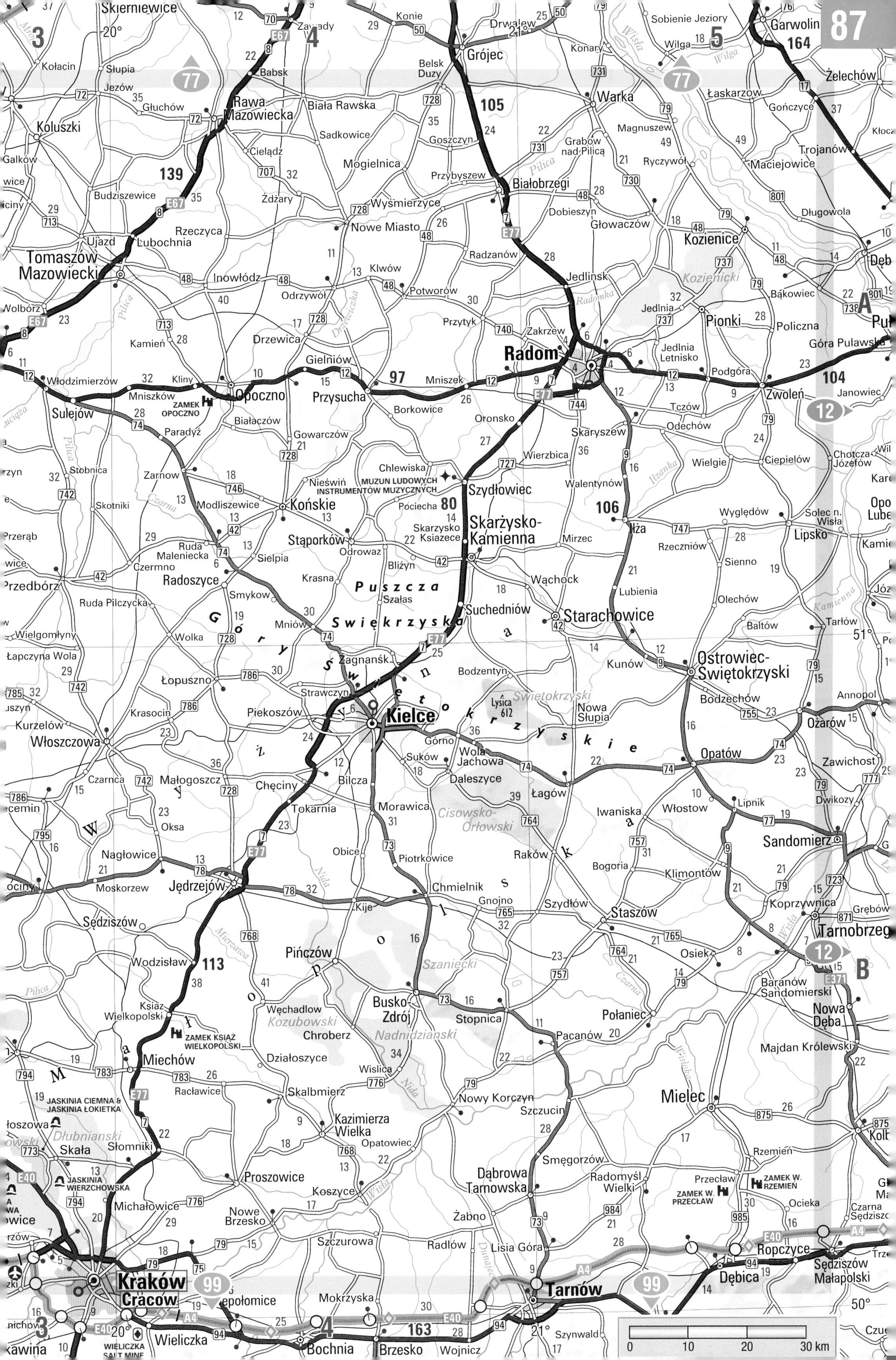
Skierniewice
Grójec
Garwolin
Żelechów
Rawa Mazowiecka
Koluszki
Warka
Białobrzegi
Tomaszów Mazowiecki
Kozienice
Radom
Pionki
Zwoleń
Opoczno
Przysucha
Sulejów
Końskie
Szydłowiec
Skarżysko-Kamienna
Starachowice
Ostrowiec-Świętokrzyski
Lipsko
Puszcza Swiękrzyska
Góry Świętokrzyskie
Kielce
Lysica 612
Opatów
Sandomierz
Włoszczowa
Jędrzejów
Chmielnik
Staszów
Tarnobrzeg
Pińczów
Busko-Zdrój
Połaniec
Miechów
Mielec
Dąbrowa Tarnowska
Kraków
Cracow
Tarnów
Dębica
Ropczyce
Sędziszów Małapolski
Wieliczka
Bochnia
Brzesko
ZAMEK OPOCZNO
MUZUN LUDOWYCH INSTRUMENTÓW MUZYCZNYCH
ZAMEK KSIĄŻ WIELKOPOLSKI
JASKINIA CIEMNA & JASKINIA ŁOKIETKA
JASKINIA WIERZCHOWSKA
ZAMEK W. PRZECŁAW
ZAMEK W. RZEMIEŃ
WIELICZKA SALT MINE
Wisła
Pilica
0 10 20 30 km

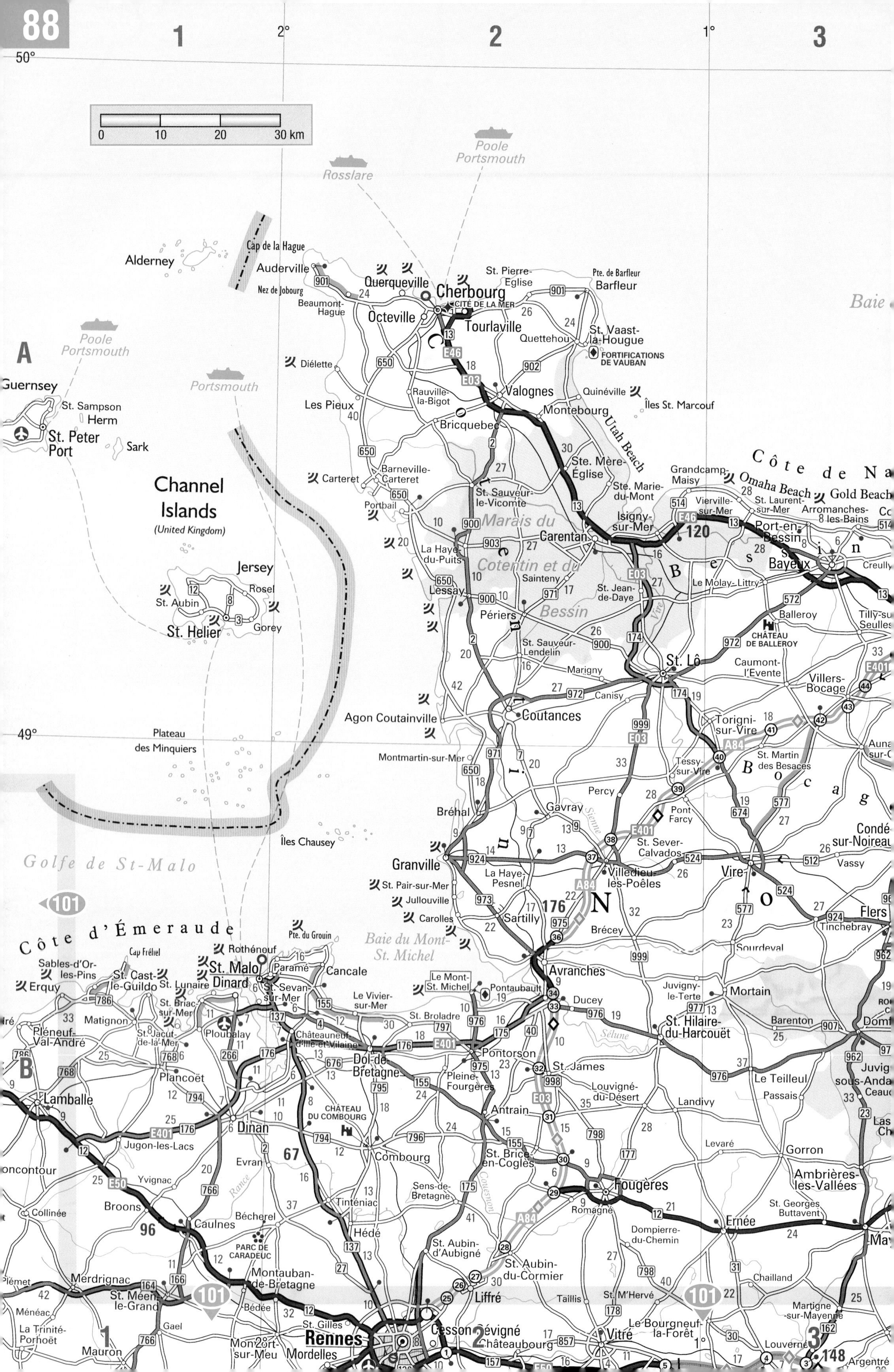

1
2
3
2°
1°
50°
49°
A
B
0 10 20 30 km
Poole
Portsmouth
Rosslare
Channel
Islands
(United Kingdom)
Alderney
Guernsey
St. Sampson
Herm
St. Peter
Port
Sark
Jersey
Rosel
St. Aubin
St. Helier
Gorey
Plateau
des Minquiers
Îles Chausey
Golfe de St-Malo
Côte d'Émeraude
Cap de la Hague
Auderville
Nez de Jobourg
Beaumont-
Hague
Querqueville
Cherbourg
CITÉ DE LA MER
Octeville
Tourlaville
St. Pierre-
Eglise
Pte. de Barfleur
Barfleur
Quettehou
St. Vaast-
la-Hougue
FORTIFICATIONS
DE VAUBAN
Diélette
Rauville-
la-Bigot
Valognes
Quinéville
Îles St. Marcouf
Les Pieux
Montebourg
Utah Beach
Bricquebec
Ste. Mère-
Église
Barneville-
Carteret
Carteret
Portbail
St. Sauveur-
le-Vicomte
Ste. Marie-
du-Mont
Grandcamp-
Maisy
Omaha Beach
Côte de Na
Gold Beach
Vierville-
sur-Mer
St. Laurent-
sur-Mer
Arromanches-
les-Bains
Port-en-
Bessin
Bayeux
Creully
Marais du
Cotentin et du
Bessin
Isigny-
sur-Mer
Carentan
La Haye-
du-Puits
Sainteny
Lessay
St. Jean-
de-Daye
Le Molay-Littry
Périers
Balleroy
CHÂTEAU
DE BALLEROY
Tilly-su
Seulles
St. Sauveur-
Lendelin
Marigny
St. Lô
Caumont-
l'Evente
Villers-
Bocage
Canisy
Coutances
Agon Coutainville
Torigni-
sur-Vire
Montmartin-sur-Mer
Tessy-
sur-Vire
St. Martin
des Besaces
Percy
Gavray
Bréhal
Pont
Farcy
Condé-
sur-Noireau
St. Sever-
Calvados
Granville
La Haye-
Pesnel
Villedieu-
les-Poêles
Vire
Vassy
St. Pair-sur-Mer
Jullouville
Carolles
Sartilly
Brécey
Tinchebray
Flers
Pte. du Grouin
Baie du Mont-
St. Michel
Sourdeval
Cancale
Avranches
Le Mont-
St. Michel
Pontaubault
Cap Fréhel
Sables-d'Or-
les-Pins
Erquy
St. Cast-
le-Guildo
Rothéneuf
St. Malo
Paramé
Dinard
St. Lunaire
St. Servan-
sur-Mer
Le Vivier-
sur-Mer
Ducey
Juvigny-
le-Terte
Mortain
St. Briac-
sur-Mer
Matignon
Pléneuf-
Val-André
St. Jacut-
de-la-Mer
Ploubalay
St. Broladre
St. Hilaire-
du-Harcouët
Barenton
Château-neuf-
d'Ille-et-Vilaine
Dol-de-
Bretagne
Pontorson
St. James
Plancoët
Pleine-
Fougères
Louvigné-
du-Désert
Le Teilleul
Passais
Lamballe
Antrain
Landivy
CHÂTEAU
DU COMBOURG
Dinan
Jugon-les-Lacs
Evran
Combourg
Levaré
Gorron
St. Brice-
en-Coglès
Ambrières-
les-Vallées
Yvignac
Sens-de-
Bretagne
Fougères
Broons
Tinténiac
Romagné
St. Georges-
Buttavent
Collinée
Caulnes
Bécherel
Ernée
Dompierre-
du-Chemin
PARC DE
CARADEUC
Hédé
St. Aubin-
d'Aubigné
St. Aubin-
du-Cormier
Merdrignac
Montauban-
de-Bretagne
Chailland
St. Méen-
le-Grand
Liffré
Taillis
St. M'Hervé
Martigne
-sur-Mayenne
Ménéac
Bédée
La Trinité-
Porhoët
Gael
St. Gilles
Rennes
Cesson-Sévigné
Châteaubourg
Vitré
Le Bourgneuf-
la-Forêt
Mauron
Montfort-
sur-Meu
Mordelles
Louverné
Argentré
101

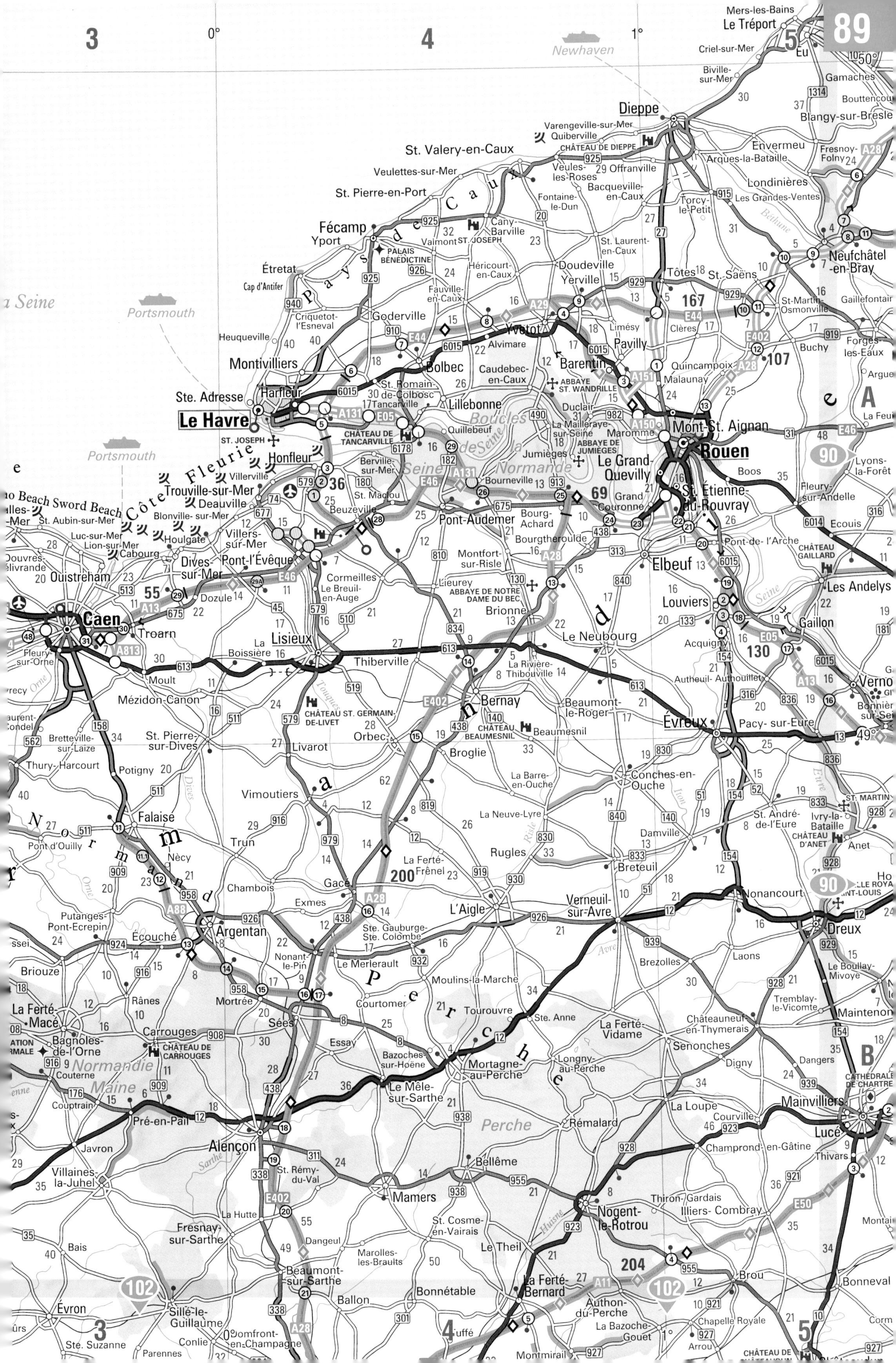
3
0°
4
1°
5
Newhaven
Portsmouth
Mers-les-Bains
Le Tréport
Eu
Criel-sur-Mer
Biville-sur-Mer
Gamaches
Blangy-sur-Bresle
Dieppe
Varengeville-sur-Mer
Quiberville
CHÂTEAU DE DIEPPE
St. Valery-en-Caux
Envermeu
Arques-la-Bataille
Veulettes-sur-Mer
Veules-les-Roses
Offranville
Londinières
Les Grandes-Ventes
St. Pierre-en-Port
Bacqueville-en-Caux
Fontaine-le-Dun
Torcy-le-Petit
Neufchâtel-en-Bray
Fécamp
Yport
Pays de Caux
Cany-Barville
Valmont
ST. JOSEPH
PALAIS BÉNÉDICTINE
St. Laurent-en-Caux
Étretat
Cap d'Antifer
Héricourt-en-Caux
Doudeville
Yerville
Tôtes
St. Saëns
Fauville-en-Caux
Criquetot-l'Esneval
Goderville
Yvetot
Limésy
Clères
St-Martin-Osmonville
Gaillefontaine
Heuqueville
Alvimare
Pavilly
Buchy
Forges-les-Eaux
Montivilliers
Bolbec
Caudebec-en-Caux
Barentin
Quincampoix
ABBAYE ST. WANDRILLE
Malaunay
Ste. Adresse
Harfleur
St. Romain-de-Colbosc
Tancarville
Lillebonne
Duclair
Le Havre
CHÂTEAU DE TANCARVILLE
Boucles de la Seine Normande
Quillebeuf
La Mailleraye-sur-Seine
ABBAYE DE JUMIÈGES
Maromme
Mont-St. Aignan
Rouen
ST. JOSEPH
Honfleur
Berville-sur-Mer
Jumièges
Le Grand-Quevilly
Boos
Lyons-la-Forêt
Côte Fleurie
Villerville
Trouville-sur-Mer
Deauville
St. Maclou
Bourneville
Grand Couronne
St. Étienne-du-Rouvray
Fleury-sur-Andelle
Sword Beach
St. Aubin-sur-Mer
Blonville-sur-Mer
Beuzeville
Pont-Audemer
Bourg-Achard
Ecouis
Luc-sur-Mer
Lion-sur-Mer
Houlgate
Villers-sur-Mer
Bourgtheroulde
Pont-de-l'Arche
CHÂTEAU GAILLARD
Ouistreham
Cabourg
Dives-sur-Mer
Pont-l'Évêque
Montfort-sur-Risle
Elbeuf
Les Andelys
Cormeilles
Le Breuil-en-Auge
Lieurey
ABBAYE DE NOTRE DAME DU BEC
Louviers
Dozulé
Brionne
Caen
Troarn
Lisieux
La Boissière
Le Neubourg
Acquigny
Gaillon
Fleury-sur-Orne
Thiberville
La Rivière-Thibouville
Autheuil-Authouillet
Vernon
Moult
Mézidon-Canon
Bernay
Beaumont-le-Roger
Évreux
Pacy-sur-Eure
Bonnières-sur-Seine
CHÂTEAU ST. GERMAIN-DE-LIVET
CHÂTEAU BEAUMESNIL
Beaumesnil
Bretteville-sur-Laize
St. Pierre-sur-Dives
Orbec
Livarot
Broglie
Thury-Harcourt
Potigny
Conches-en-Ouche
La Barre-en-Ouche
Vimoutiers
Falaise
La Neuve-Lyre
St. André-de-l'Eure
Ivry-la-Bataille
CHÂTEAU D'ANET
Anet
Pont d'Ouilly
Trun
Damville
Nècy
La Ferté-Frênel
Rugles
Breteuil
Chambois
Gacé
Exmes
L'Aigle
Verneuil-sur-Avre
Nonancourt
Putanges-Pont-Ecrepin
Dreux
Écouché
Argentan
Ste. Gauburge-Ste. Colombe
Nonant-le-Pin
Le Merlerault
Laons
Briouze
Brezolles
Le Boullay-Mivoye
Rânes
Moulins-la-Marche
Tremblay-le-Vicomte
La Ferté-Macé
Mortrée
Courtomer
Tourouvre
Maintenon
Sées
Ste. Anne
La Ferté-Vidame
Châteauneuf-en-Thymerais
Bagnoles-de-l'Orne
Carrouges
CHÂTEAU DE CARROUGES
Essay
Bazoches-sur-Hoëne
Senonches
Normandie
Mortagne-au-Perche
Longny-au-Perche
Digny
Dangers
Couterne
Maine
Le Mêle-sur-Sarthe
CATHÉDRALE DE CHARTRES
Couptrain
Pré-en-Pail
La Loupe
Mainvilliers
Perche
Rémalard
Courville
Lucé
Javron
Alençon
Champrond-en-Gâtine
Thivars
Villaines-la-Juhel
St. Rémy-du-Val
Bellême
Mamers
Thiron-Gardais
Illiers-Combray
La Hutte
Nogent-le-Rotrou
Fresnay-sur-Sarthe
St. Cosme-en-Vairais
Bais
Dangeul
Marolles-les-Braults
Le Theil
Beaumont-sur-Sarthe
Brou
Bonneval
Bonnétable
La Ferté-Bernard
Authon-du-Perche
Évron
Ballon
Sillé-le-Guillaume
Tuffé
Chapelle Royale
Domfront-en-Champagne
La Bazoche-Gouet
Ste. Suzanne
Conlie
Parennes
Montmirail
Arrou
CHÂTEAU DE
90
102
A
B

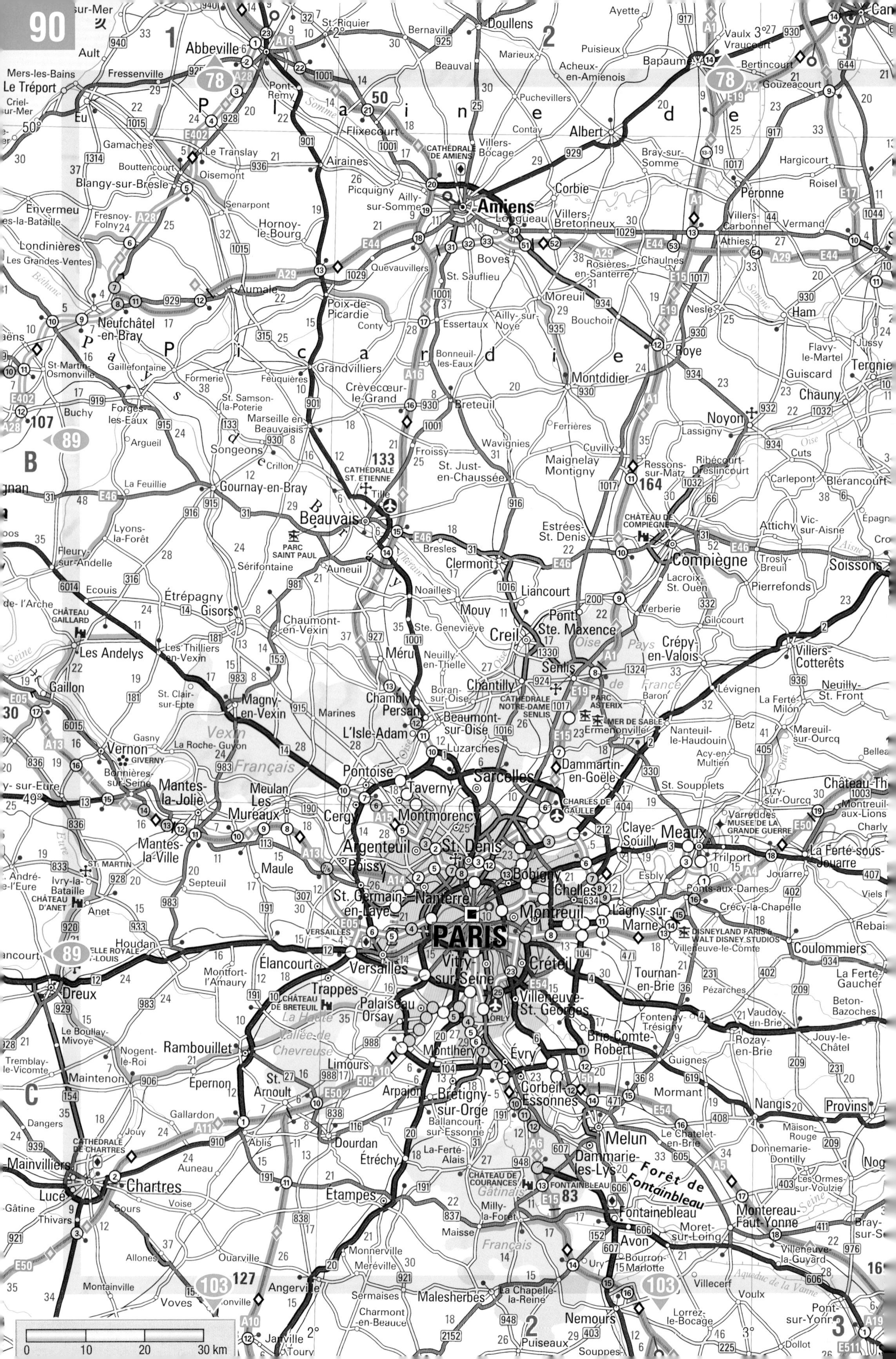
Abbeville
St. Riquier
Bernaville
Doullens
Ayette
Vaulx
Vraucourt
Bapaume
Bertincourt
Gouzeaucourt
Mers-les-Bains
Le Tréport
Criel-sur-Mer
Fressenville
Ault
Eu
Pont-Remy
Flixecourt
Beauval
Marieux
Puisieux
Acheux-en-Amienois
Puchevillers
Contay
Albert
Gamaches
Le Translay
Bouttencourt
Oisemont
Blangy-sur-Bresle
Airaines
Picquigny
Ailly-sur-Somme
CATHÉDRALE DE AMIENS
Villers-Bocage
Amiens
Longueau
Corbie
Villers-Bretonneux
Bray-sur-Somme
Péronne
Hargicourt
Roisel
Villers-Carbonnel
Vermand
Athies
Envermeu
Fresnoy-Folny
Senarpont
Hornoy-le-Bourg
Londinières
Les Grandes-Ventes
Quevauvillers
Boves
St. Sauflieu
Rosières-en-Santerre
Chaulnes
Aumale
Poix-de-Picardie
Conty
Moreuil
Ailly-sur-Noye
Bouchoir
Nesle
Ham
Neufchâtel-en-Bray
St-Martin-Osmonville
Gaillefontaine
Formerie
Feuquières
Grandvilliers
Essertaux
Bonneuil-les-Eaux
Montdidier
Roye
Flavy-le-Martel
Jussy
Tergnier
Guiscard
Chauny
Buchy
Forges-les-Eaux
St. Samson-la-Poterie
Crèvecœur-le-Grand
Breteuil
Noyon
Lassigny
Argueil
Marseille en Beauvaisis
Songeons
Crillon
Froissy
Wavignies
Ferrières
Cuvilly
Ressons-sur-Matz
Ribécourt-Dreslincourt
Cuts
Carlepont
Blérancourt
CATHÉDRALE ST. ETIENNE
Tillé
St. Just-en-Chaussée
Maignelay Montigny
La Feuillie
Gournay-en-Bray
Beauvais
Lyons-la-Forêt
PARC ST PAUL
Estrées-St. Denis
CHÂTEAU DE COMPIÈGNE
Attichy
Vic-sur-Aisne
Compiègne
Fleury-sur-Andelle
Sérifontaine
Auneuil
Bresles
Clermont
Trosly-Breuil
Soissons
Ecouis
Lacroix-St. Ouen
Pierrefonds
Étrépagny
Gisors
Noailles
Liancourt
Verberie
CHÂTEAU GAILLARD
Chaumont-en-Vexin
Mouy
Pont Ste. Maxence
Gilocourt
Les Andelys
Les Thilliers en-Vexin
Ste. Geneviève
Creil
Crépy-en-Valois
Villers-Cotterêts
Méru
Neuilly-en-Thelle
Senlis
Gaillon
St. Clair-sur-Epte
Magny-en-Vexin
Chambly
Persan
Chantilly
CATHÉDRALE NOTRE-DAME SENLIS
Boran-sur-Oise
PARC ASTERIX
Lévignen
La Ferté-Milon
Neuilly-St. Front
Marines
Beaumont-sur-Oise
MER DE SABLE
Ermenonville
Nanteuil-le-Haudouin
Betz
Mareuil-sur-Ourcq
Gasny
Vernon
GIVERNY
La Roche-Guyon
Vexin Français
L'Isle-Adam
Luzarches
Acy-en-Multien
Bonnières-sur-Seine
Mantes-la-Jolie
Pontoise
Sarcelles
Dammartin-en-Goële
St. Soupplets
Lizy-sur-Ourcq
Château-Thierry
Meulan
Les Mureaux
Cergy
Taverny
Montmorency
CHARLES DE GAULLE
Claye-Souilly
Meaux
Varreddes
MUSEE DE LA GRANDE GUERRE
Montreuil-aux-Lions
Charly
Mantes-la-Ville
Argenteuil
St. Denis
Trilport
La Ferté-sous-Jouarre
Ivry-la-Bataille
ST. MARTIN
Maule
Poissy
Bobigny
Esbly
Jouarre
CHÂTEAU D'ANET
Anet
Septeuil
St. Germain-en-Laye
Nanterre
Chelles
Ponts-aux-Dames
Montreuil
Lagny-sur-Marne
Crécy-la-Chapelle
Houdan
Versailles
PARIS
DISNEYLAND PARIS & WALT DISNEY STUDIOS
Villeneuve-le-Comte
Coulommiers
Dreux
Montfort-l'Amaury
Élancourt
Vitry-sur-Seine
Créteil
Tournan-en-Brie
Pézarches
La Ferté-Gaucher
Trappes
CHÂTEAU DE BRETEUIL
Palaiseau
Orsay
Villeneuve-St. Georges
Orly
Fontenay-Trésigny
Vaudoy-en-Brie
Beton-Bazoches
Le Boulay-Mivoye
Tremblay-le-Vicomte
Nogent-le-Roi
Rambouillet
La Haute Vallée de Chevreuse
Montlhéry
Évry
Brie-Comte-Robert
Rozay-en-Brie
Jouy-le-Châtel
Maintenon
Epernon
Limours
St. Arnoult
Arpajon
Brétigny-sur-Orge
Corbeil-Essonnes
Guignes
Mormant
Nangis
Provins
Gallardon
Dangers
Jouy
Ablis
Dourdan
Étréchy
Ballancourt-sur-Essonne
Melun
Le Châtelet-en-Brie
Maison-Rouge
Donnemarie-Dontilly
CATHÉDRALE DE CHARTRES
Mainvilliers
Chartres
Auneau
Lucé
La-Ferté-Alais
CHÂTEAU DE COURANCES
Gâtinais Français
Dammarie-les-Lys
FONTAINEBLEAU
Forêt de Fontainbleau
Les Ormes-sur-Voulzie
Sours
Thivars
Voise
Étampes
Milly-la-Forêt
Fontainebleau
Montereau-Fault-Yonne
Bray-sur-Seine
Maisse
Moret-sur-Loing
Avon
Allonnes
Ouarville
Monnerville
Méréville
Bourron-Marlotte
Villeneuve-la-Guyard
Montainville
Voves
Angerville
Sermaises
Malesherbes
La Chapelle-la-Reine
Villecerf
Voulx
Charmont-en-Beauce
Nemours
Lorrez-le-Bocage
Pont-sur-Yonne
Janville
Toury
Puiseaux
Souppes
Dollot
P i c a r d i e
P i c a r d i e
Pays de Bray
Pays de France
Somme
Oise
Seine
0 10 20 30 km

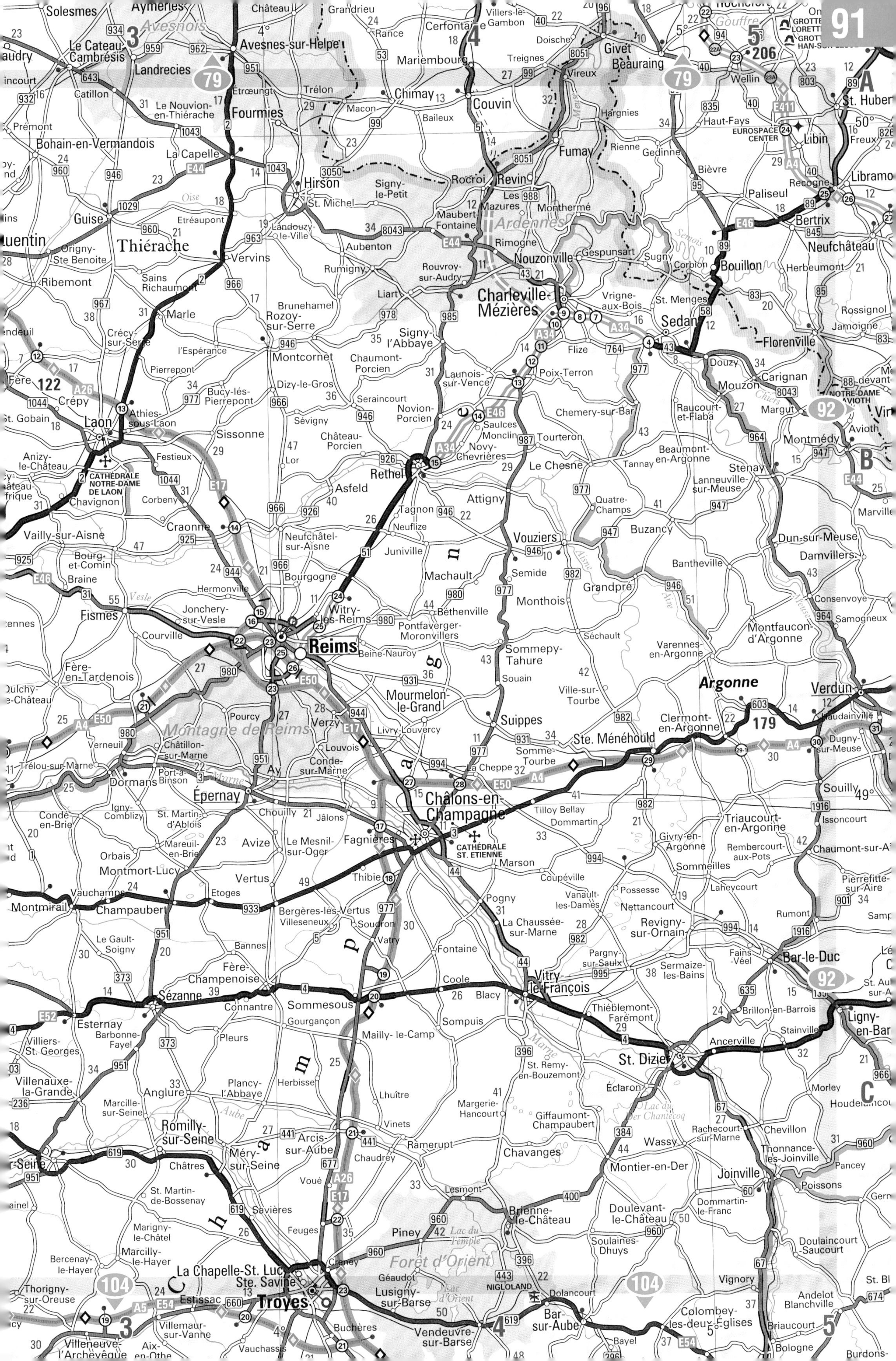
Solesmes
Aymeries
Château
Grandrieu
Villers-le-Gambon
Givet
Rochefort
Gouffre
Grottes Lorette
Grottes Han-sur-Lesse
Avesnois
Avesnes-sur-Helpe
Rance
Cerfontaine
Doische
Beauraing
Le Cateau-Cambrésis
Landrecies
Mariembourg
Treignes
Vireux
Wellin
St. Hubert
Catillon
Trélon
Chimay
Couvin
Hargnies
Etrœungt
Le Nouvion-en-Thiérache
Fourmies
Macon
Baileux
Haut-Fays
Eurospace Center
Libin
Prémont
Bohain-en-Vermandois
La Capelle
Fumay
Rienne
Gedinne
Freux
Bièvre
Libramont
Hirson
Signy-le-Petit
Rocroi
Revin
St. Michel
Les Mazures
Monthermé
Paliseul
Recogne
Oise
Guise
Etréaupont
Maubert-Fontaine
Ardennes
Bertrix
Landouzy-la-Ville
Semois
Neufchâteau
Thiérache
Origny-Ste Benoite
Vervins
Aubenton
Rimogne
Nouzonville
Gespunsart
Sugny
Corbion
Bouillon
Herbeumont
Rumigny
Rouvroy-sur-Audry
Ribemont
Sains-Richaumont
Liart
Charleville-Mézières
Vrigne-aux-Bois
St. Menges
Brunehamel
Rossignol
Marle
Rozoy-sur-Serre
Sedan
Jamoigne
Crécy-sur-Serre
Signy-l'Abbaye
Florenville
L'Espérance
Montcornet
Chaumont-Porcien
Flize
Douzy
Carignan
Pierrepont
Launois-sur-Vence
Poix-Terron
Mouzon
Dizy-le-Gros
Bucy-lès-Pierrepont
Seraincourt
Novion-Porcien
Chemery-sur-Bar
Raucourt-et-Flaba
Margut
Notre-Dame Avioth
Crépy
Laon
Athies-sous-Laon
Sévigny
Saulces Monclin
Tourteron
Avioth
St. Gobain
Sissonne
Château-Porcien
Novy-Chevrières
Beaumont-en-Argonne
Montmédy
Anizy-le-Château
Festieux
Lor
Rethel
Le Chesne
Tannay
Stenay
Cathédrale Notre-Dame de Laon
Asfeld
Lanneuville-sur-Meuse
Chavignon
Corbeny
Attigny
Quatre-Champs
Marville
Tagnon
Buzancy
Neuflize
Craonne
Vailly-sur-Aisne
Neufchâtel-sur-Aisne
Vouziers
Dun-sur-Meuse
Juniville
Damvillers
Bourg-et-Comin
Bantheville
Braine
Semide
Grandpré
Machault
Hermonville
Bourgogne
Monthois
Consenvoye
Béthenville
Fismes
Jonchery-sur-Vesle
Witry-lès-Reims
Samogneux
Montfaucon-d'Argonne
Vesle
Pontfaverger-Moronvillers
Courville
Séchault
Reims
Beine-Nauroy
Sommepy-Tahure
Varennes-en-Argonne
Aisne
Aire
Meuse
Fère-en-Tardenois
Souain
Argonne
Verdun
Oulchy-le-Château
Mourmelon-le-Grand
Ville-sur-Tourbe
Haudainville
Pourcy
Clermont-en-Argonne
Suippes
Dugny-sur-Meuse
Montagne de Reims
Verzy
Livry-Louvercy
Verneuil
Châtillon-sur-Marne
Louvois
Somme-Tourbe
Ste. Ménehould
Trélou-sur-Marne
Conde-sur-Marne
La Cheppe
Ay
Port-à-Binson
Marne
Dormans
Épernay
Châlons-en-Champagne
Souilly
Condé-en-Brie
Igny-Comblizy
Chouilly
Jâlons
Tilloy Bellay
Dommartin
Triaucourt-en-Argonne
Issoncourt
St. Martin-d'Ablois
Givry-en-Argonne
Mareuil-en-Brie
Avize
Le Mesnil-sur-Oger
Fagnières
Cathédrale St. Etienne
Rembercourt-aux-Pots
Chaumont-sur-Aire
Orbais
Marson
Sommeilles
Montmort-Lucy
Vertus
Thibie
Coupéville
Pierrefitte-sur-Aire
Vauchamps
Etoges
Pogny
Possesse
Laheycourt
Montmirail
Champaubert
Bergères-lès-Vertus
Vanault-les-Dames
Nettancourt
Rumont
Villeseneux
Soudron
La Chaussée-sur-Marne
Revigny-sur-Ornain
Le Gault-Soigny
Vatry
Fontaine
Bannes
Pargny-sur-Saulx
Fains-Véel
Bar-le-Duc
Fère-Champenoise
Coole
Sermaize-les-Bains
Sézanne
Connantre
Sommesous
Blacy
Vitry-le-François
Esternay
Gourgançon
Sompuis
Thiéblemont-Farémont
Brillon-en-Barrois
Ligny-en-Barrois
Barbonne-Fayel
Villiers-St. Georges
Pleurs
Mailly-le-Camp
Stainville
Ancerville
St. Dizier
St. Remy-en-Bouzemont
Villenauxe-la-Grande
Plancy-l'Abbaye
Herbisse
Eclaron
Anglure
Lac du Der Chantecoq
Morley
Houdelaincourt
Marcille-sur-Seine
Aube
Lhuître
Margerie-Hancourt
Giffaumont-Champaubert
Romilly-sur-Seine
Arcis-sur-Aube
Vinets
Rachecourt-sur-Marne
Chevillon
Méry-sur-Seine
Ramerupt
Wassy
Thonnance-les-Joinville
Châtres
Chaudrey
Chavanges
Pancey
Montier-en-Der
Joinville
Poissons
Voué
St. Martin-de-Bossenay
Lesmont
Dommartin-le-Franc
Savières
Brienne-le-Château
Doulevant-le-Château
Marigny-le-Châtel
Feuges
Piney
Lac du Temple
Soulaines-Dhuys
Doulaincourt-Saucourt
Marcilly-le-Hayer
Bercenay-le-Hayer
La Chapelle-St. Luc
Creney
Forêt d'Orient
Ste. Savine
Géaudot
Vignory
Thorigny-sur-Oreuse
Troyes
Lusigny-sur-Barse
Lac d'Orient
Nigloland
Dolancourt
Andelot Blanchville
Estissac
Bar-sur-Aube
Colombey-les-deux-Églises
Briaucourt
Villemaur-sur-Vanne
Buchères
Vendeuvre-sur-Barse
Villeneuve-l'Archevêque
Aix-en-Othe
Vauchassis
Bayel
Bologne
Burdons
Champagne
Gemeaux
A
B
C
79
92
104
122
179
206

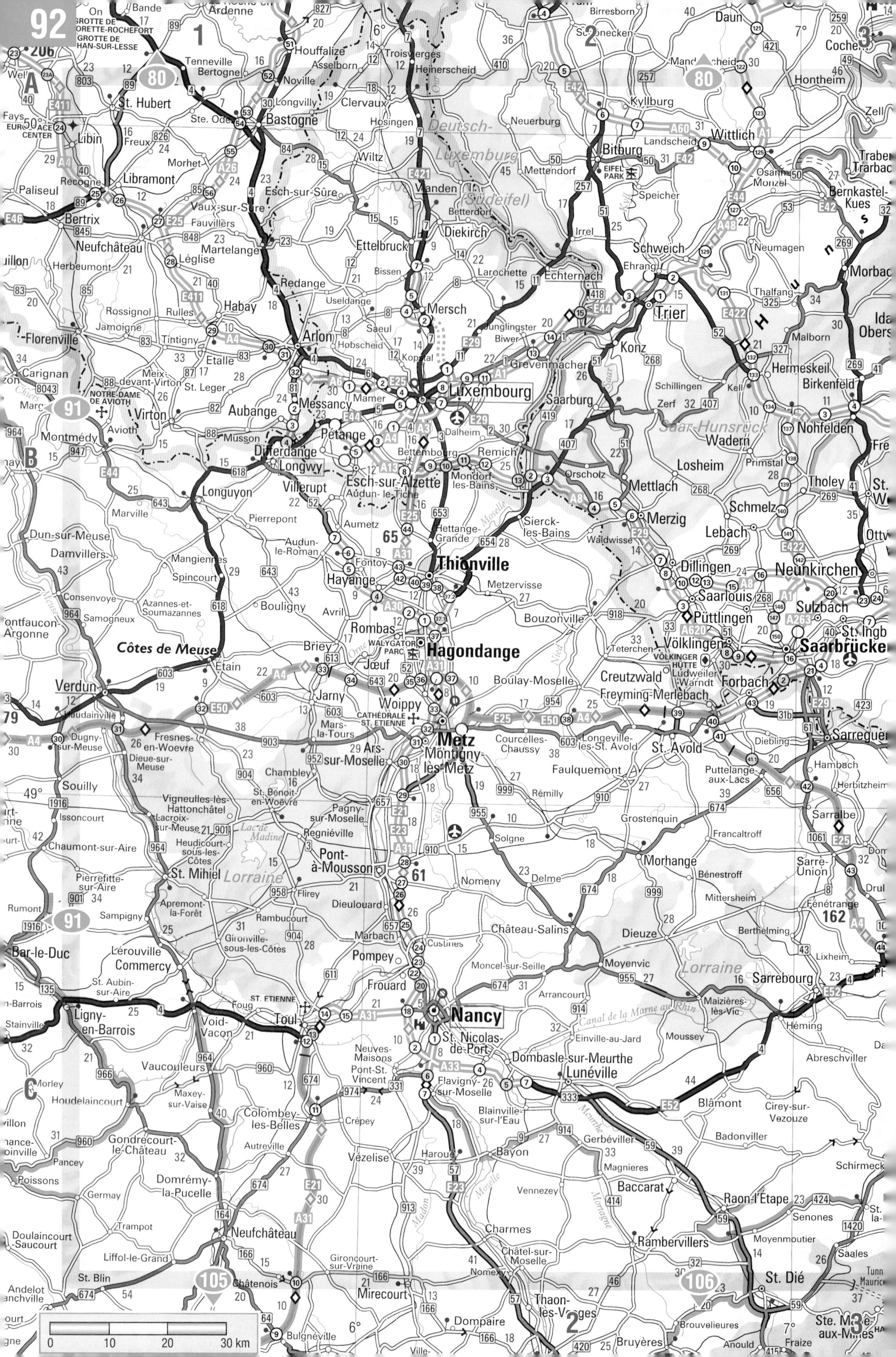

Grotte de Rochefort
Grotte de Han-sur-Lesse
Bande
Ardenne
Houffalize
Tenneville
Bertogne
Noville
St. Hubert
Ste. Ode
Bastogne
Libin
Freux
Morhet
Libramont
Recogne
Paliseul
Bertrix
Euro Space Center
Vaux-sur-Sûre
Fauvillers
Neufchâteau
Martelange
Herbeumont
Léglise
Habay
Rossignol
Rulles
Jamoigne
Tintigny
Florenville
Carignan
Etalle
Meix-devant-Virton
St. Leger
Notre-Dame de Avioth
Virton
Avioth
Aubange
Montmédy
Musson
Differdange
Longwy
Longuyon
Villerupt
Marville
Pierrepont
Dun-sur-Meuse
Damvillers
Mangiennes
Spincourt
Audun-le-Roman
Consenvoye
Azannes-et-Soumazannes
Samogneux
Bouligny
Montfaucon-Argonne
Côtes de Meuse
Etain
Verdun
Haudainville
Dugny-sur-Meuse
Fresnes-en-Woevre
Dieue-sur-Meuse
Souilly
Vigneulles-lès-Hattonchâtel
Lacroix-sur-Meuse
Heudicourt-sous-les-Côtes
Lac de Madine
Issoncourt
Chaumont-sur-Aire
Pierrefitte-sur-Aire
St. Mihiel
Lorraine
Apremont-la-Forêt
Rumont
Sampigny
Girouville-sous-les-Côtes
Rambucourt
Bar-le-Duc
Lérouville
Commercy
St. Aubin-sur-Aire
Ligny-en-Barrois
Stainville
Void-Vacon
Vaucouleurs
Maxey-sur-Vaise
Houdelaincourt
Morley
Gondrecourt-le-Château
Pancey
Poissons
Domrémy-la-Pucelle
Germay
Trampot
Doulaincourt-Saucourt
Liffol-le-Grand
Neufchâteau
St. Blin
Andelot
Châtenois
Bulgnéville
Wiltz
Esch-sur-Sûre
Clervaux
Hosingen
Troisvierges
Asselborn
Heinerscheid
Longvilly
Redange
Arlon
Ettelbruck
Bissen
Mersch
Useldange
Saeul
Hobscheid
Kopstal
Mamer
Messancy
Pétange
Luxembourg
Dalheim
Bettembourg
Esch-sur-Alzette
Audun-le-Tiche
Mondorf-les-Bains
Remich
Aumetz
Hettange-Grande
Sierck-les-Bains
Thionville
Fontoy
Hayange
Metzervisse
Avril
Rombas
Briey
Walygator Parc
Hagondange
Jœuf
Jarny
Woippy
Cathédrale St. Etienne
Mars-la-Tours
Metz
Ars-sur-Moselle
Montigny-lès-Metz
Chambley
St. Benoit-en-Woëvre
Pagny-sur-Moselle
Regniéville
Pont-à-Mousson
Flirey
Dieulouard
Marbach
Pompey
Custines
Frouard
Nancy
Toul
Foug
St. Etienne
St. Nicolas-de-Port
Neuves-Maisons
Pont-St. Vincent
Flavigny-sur-Moselle
Colombey-les-Belles
Crépey
Autreville
Vézelise
Haroué
Blainville-sur-l'Eau
Bayon
Charmes
Vennezey
Gironcourt-sur-Vraine
Mirecourt
Nomexy
Thaon-les-Vosges
Dompaire
Vianden
Deutsch-Luxemburg (Südeifel)
Diekirch
Betterdorf
Larochette
Echternach
Junglinster
Biwer
Grevenmacher
Daun
Birresbuch
Schönecken
Manderscheid
Kyllburg
Neuerburg
Bitburg
Eifel Park
Mettendorf
Landscheid
Wittlich
Speicher
Irrel
Ehrang
Schweich
Trier
Konz
Saarburg
Schillingen
Zerf
Kell
Saar-Hunsrück
Wadern
Losheim
Mettlach
Orscholz
Merzig
Waldwisse
Dillingen
Saarlouis
Püttlingen
Völklingen
Völkinger Hütte
Ludweiler Warndt
Forbach
Bouzonville
Teterchen
Boulay-Moselle
Creutzwald
Freyming-Merlebach
Courcelles-Chaussy
Longeville-lès-St. Avold
St. Avold
Faulquemont
Rémilly
Diebling
Puttelange-aux-Lacs
Grostenquin
Solgne
Nomeny
Delme
Morhange
Francaltroff
Bénestroff
Château-Salins
Moncel-sur-Seille
Dieuze
Moyenvic
Arrancourt
Mittersheim
Berthelming
Canal de la Marne au Rhin
Einville-au-Jard
Maizières-lès-Vic
Moussey
Sarrebourg
Héming
Dombasle-sur-Meurthe
Lunéville
Blâmont
Cirey-sur-Vezouze
Abreschviller
Badonviller
Gerbéviller
Magnieres
Baccarat
Rambervillers
Raon-l'Etape
Senones
Moyenmoutier
St. Dié
Saales
Brouvelieures
Bruyères
Fraize
Ste. Marie-aux-Mines
Cochem
Hontheim
Zell
Traben-Trarbach
Osann-Monzel
Bernkastel-Kues
Neumagen
Thalfang
Hunsrück
Morbach
Malborn
Hermeskeil
Birkenfeld
Nohfelden
Primstal
Tholey
Schmelz
Lebach
Neunkirchen
Sulzbach
Saarbrücken
Hambach
Sarreguemines
Sarralbe
Sarre-Union
Fénétrange
Lixheim
Lorraine
Mosel
Saar
Meuse
Moselle
Meurthe
Mortagne
Madon
Orne
Nied
Seille
0 10 20 30 km

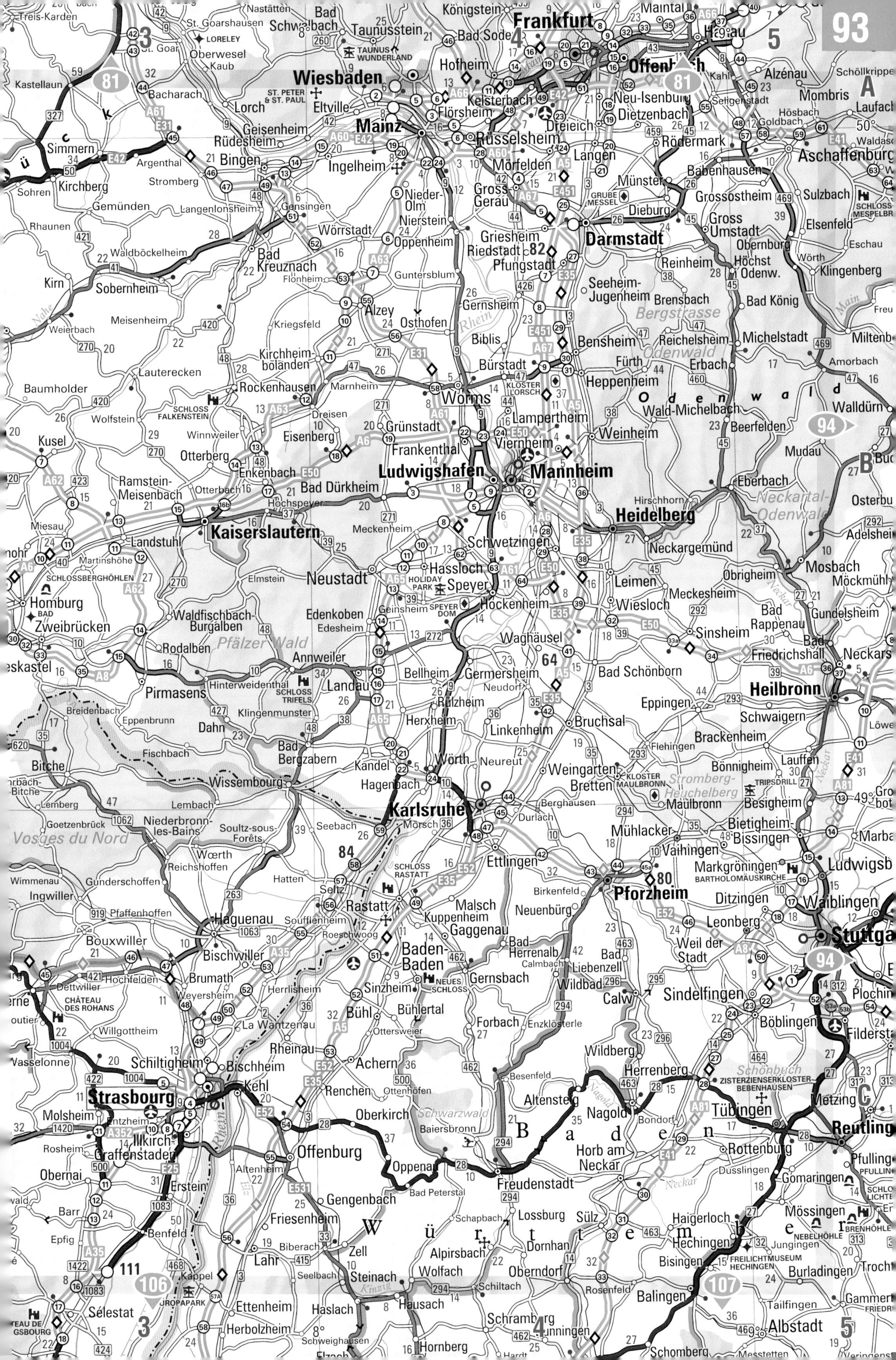

Frankfurt
Wiesbaden
Mainz
Offenbach
Darmstadt
Heidelberg
Mannheim
Ludwigshafen
Kaiserslautern
Karlsruhe
Pforzheim
Stuttgart
Heilbronn
Strasbourg
Offenburg
Tübingen
Reutlingen
Aschaffenburg
Worms
Speyer
Neustadt
Landau
Pirmasens
Baden-Baden
Rastatt
Freudenstadt
Bad Kreuznach
Bingen
Rüsselsheim
Dieburg
Bensheim
Weinheim
Viernheim
Schwetzingen
Hockenheim
Bruchsal
Bretten
Ettlingen
Sindelfingen
Böblingen
Leonberg
Ludwigsburg
Waiblingen
Haguenau
Wissembourg
Sélestat
Lahr
Kehl
Bühl
Achern
Calw
Nagold
Horb am Neckar
Rottenburg
Hechingen
Balingen
Albstadt
Oberndorf
Schramberg
Hausach
Haslach
Wolfach
Alzey
Frankenthal
Bad Dürkheim
Grünstadt
Homburg
Zweibrücken
Landstuhl
Kusel
Simmern
Kirchberg
Kirn
Sobernheim
Eberbach
Mosbach
Sinsheim
Wiesloch
Leimen
Neckargemünd
Michelstadt
Erbach
Walldürn
Mühlacker
Vaihingen
Bietigheim-Bissingen
Besigheim
Pfälzer Wald
Odenwald
Bergstrasse
Schwarzwald
Schönbuch
Vosges du Nord
Baden
Württemberg
Rhein
Neckar
Main
81
94
106
107
3
4
5
A
B
C

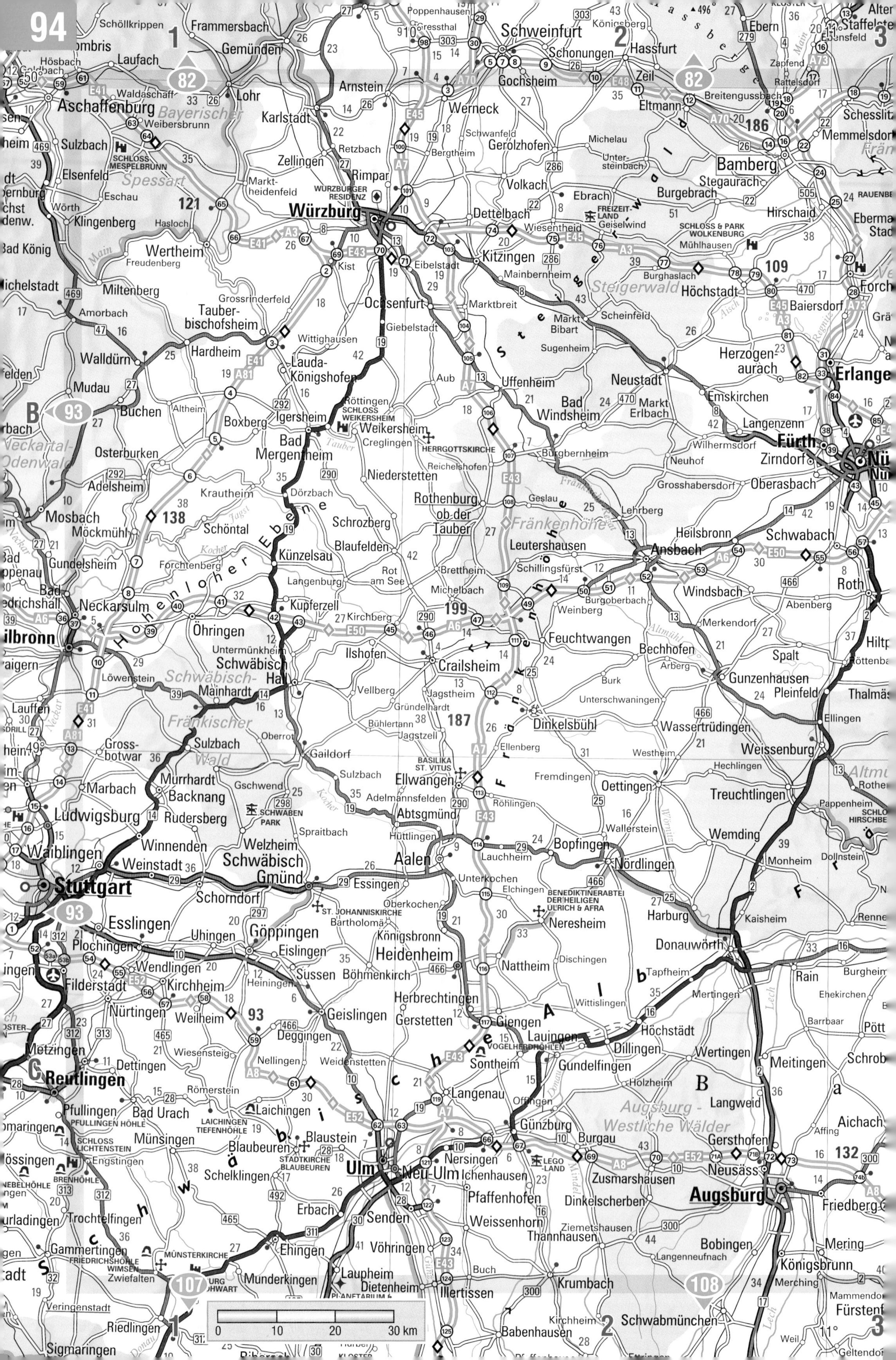
Schöllkrippen
Frammersbach
Gemünden
Hösbach
Laufach
Aschaffenburg
Bayerischer
Weibersbrunn
Lohr
Karlstadt
Arnstein
Poppenhausen
Schweinfurt
Königsberg
Schonungen
Hassfurt
Ebern
Staffelstein
Gochsheim
Zeil
Eltmann
Breitengussbach
Werneck
Schwanfeld
Gerolzhofen
Bergtheim
Retzbach
Zellingen
Rimpar
Sulzbach
Schloss Mespelbrunn
Elsenfeld
Spessart
Eschau
Marktheidenfeld
Würzburger Residenz
Würzburg
Wörth
Klingenberg
Hasloch
Volkach
Dettelbach
Ebrach
Freizeit-Land Geiselwind
Wiesentheid
Michelau
Untersteinbach
Bamberg
Stegaurach
Burgebrach
Hirschaid
Schloss & Park Wolkenburg
Mühlhausen
Bad König
Wertheim
Freudenberg
Kist
Eibelstadt
Kitzingen
Mainbernheim
Burghaslach
Steigerwald
Höchstadt
Baiersdorf
Michelstadt
Miltenberg
Amorbach
Grossrinderfeld
Tauberbischofsheim
Ochsenfurt
Giebelstadt
Marktbreit
Markt Bibart
Scheinfeld
Sugenheim
Herzogenaurach
Erlangen
Walldürn
Hardheim
Wittighausen
Lauda-Königshofen
Aub
Uffenheim
Neustadt
Bad Windsheim
Markt Erlbach
Emskirchen
Langenzenn
Mudau
Buchen
Altheim
Boxberg
Igersheim
Röttingen
Schloss Weikersheim
Weikersheim
Creglingen
Herrgottskirche
Burgbernheim
Wilhermsdorf
Fürth
Zirndorf
Neckartal-Odenwald
Osterburken
Bad Mergentheim
Adelsheim
Krautheim
Niederstetten
Reichelshofen
Neuhof
Grosshabersdorf
Oberasbach
Mosbach
Möckmühl
Schöntal
Dörzbach
Rothenburg ob der Tauber
Geslau
Frankenhöhe
Lehrberg
Heilsbronn
Schwabach
Schrozberg
Blaufelden
Leutershausen
Ansbach
Gundelsheim
Forchtenberg
Künzelsau
Langenburg
Rot am See
Brettheim
Schillingsfürst
Windsbach
Roth
Bad Friedrichshall
Neckarsulm
Hohenloher Ebene
Kupferzell
Kirchberg
Michelbach
Burgoberbach
Weinberg
Abenberg
Heilbronn
Öhringen
Untermünkheim
Ilshofen
Crailsheim
Feuchtwangen
Bechhofen
Merkendorf
Spalt
Arberg
Schwäbisch Hall
Löwenstein
Schwäbisch-
Mainhardt
Vellberg
Jagstheim
Gründelhardt
Burk
Unterschwaningen
Gunzenhausen
Pleinfeld
Lauffen
Fränkischer Wald
Oberrot
Bühlertann
Jagstzell
Dinkelsbühl
Wassertrüdingen
Ellingen
Sulzbach
Gaildorf
Ellenberg
Westheim
Weissenburg
Grossbottwar
Marbach
Murrhardt
Gschwend
Basilika St. Vitus
Ellwangen
Fremdingen
Hechlingen
Oettingen
Treuchtlingen
Backnang
Rudersberg
Schwaben Park
Adelmannsfelden
Abtsgmünd
Röhlingen
Pappenheim
Ludwigsburg
Winnenden
Welzheim
Spraitbach
Hüttlingen
Wallerstein
Wemding
Waiblingen
Weinstadt
Schwäbisch Gmünd
Aalen
Lauchheim
Bopfingen
Nördlingen
Monheim
Dollnstein
Stuttgart
Schorndorf
Essingen
Unterkochen
Elchingen
Benediktinerabtei der Heiligen Ulrich & Afra
Neresheim
Harburg
Kaisheim
Esslingen
St. Johanniskirche
Oberkochen
Bartholomä
Uhingen
Göppingen
Königsbronn
Plochingen
Eislingen
Heidenheim
Nattheim
Dischingen
Donauwörth
Rain
Wendlingen
Süssen
Böhmenkirch
Tapfheim
Filderstadt
Kirchheim
Heiningen
Herbrechtingen
Wittislingen
Mertingen
Nürtingen
Weilheim
Deggingen
Geislingen
Gerstetten
Giengen
Höchstädt
Metzingen
Wiesensteig
Lauingen
Vogelherdhöhlen
Dillingen
Wertingen
Meitingen
Dettingen
Nellingen
Weidenstetten
Sontheim
Gundelfingen
Reutlingen
Römerstein
Holzheim
Langweid
Pfullingen
Pfullingen Höhle
Bad Urach
Laichingen
Laichinger Tiefenhöhle
Langenau
Offingen
Augsburg - Westliche Wälder
Aichach
Schloss Lichtenstein
Münsingen
Blaustein
Blaubeuren
Stadtkirche Blaubeuren
Günzburg
Burgau
Gersthofen
Affing
Engstingen
Bärenhöhle
Nebelhöhle
Schelklingen
Ulm
Neu-Ulm
Nersingen
Lego-Land
Zusmarshausen
Neusäss
Ichenhausen
Pfaffenhofen
Dinkelscherben
Augsburg
Friedberg
Trochtelfingen
Erbach
Senden
Weissenhorn
Thannhausen
Ziemetshausen
Gammertingen
Friedrichshöhle Wimsen
Zwiefalten
Münsterkirche
Ehingen
Vöhringen
Bobingen
Langenneufnach
Mering
Königsbrunn
Munderkingen
Laupheim
Dietenheim
Planetarium
Illertissen
Buch
Krumbach
Merching
Veringenstadt
Riedlingen
Sigmaringen
Kirchheim
Schwabmünchen
Babenhausen
Fürstenfeld
Weil
Schwäbische Alb
Frankenhöhe
Steigerwald
0
10
20
30 km

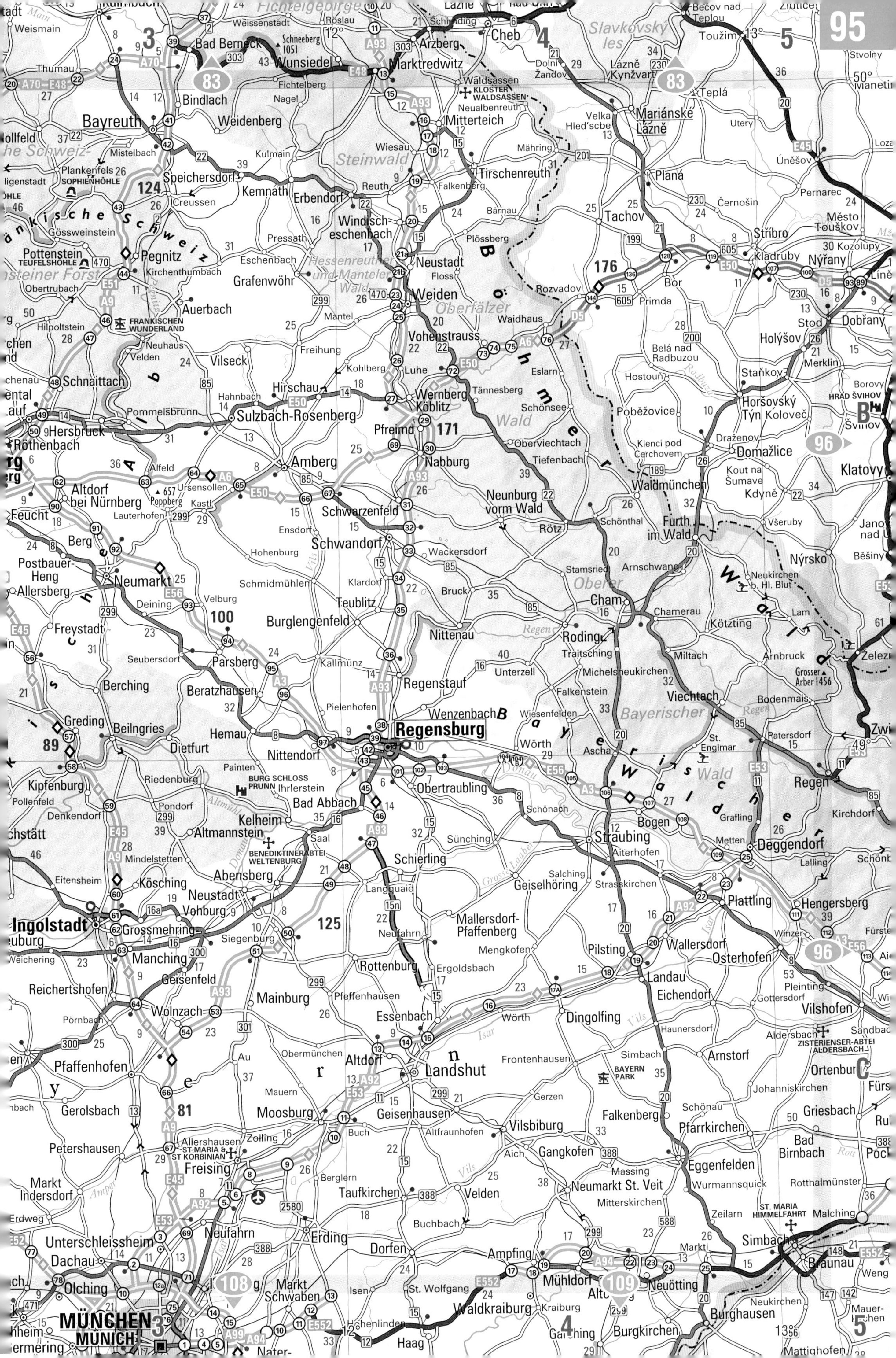
Kulmbach
Weismain
Fichtelgebirge
Weissenstadt
Röslau
Schneeberg 1051
Bad Berneck
Wunsiedel
Arzberg
Marktredwitz
Schirnding
Cheb
Slavkovský les
Bečov nad Teplou
Toužim
Thurnau
Bindlach
Fichtelberg
Nagel
Dolní Žandov
Waldsassen
KLOSTER WALDSASSEN
Lázně Kynžvart
Teplá
Stvolny
Manetín
Bayreuth
Weidenberg
Mitterteich
Neualbenreuth
Velká Hleďscbe
Mariánské Lázně
Utery
Hollfeld
Mistelbach
Kulmbach
Steinwald
Wiesau
Mähring
Tirschenreuth
Plana
Úněšov
Plankenfels
SOPHIENHÖHLE
Speichersdorf
Kemnath
Erbendorf
Reuth
Falkenberg
Creussen
Windischeschenbach
Bärnau
Tachov
Černošin
Pernarec
Město Touškov
Stříbro
Kozolupy
Gössweinstein
Pottenstein
TEUFELSHÖHLE
Pegnitz
Pressath
Eschenbach
Hessenreuther und Manteler Wald
Neustadt
Plössberg
Floss
Kladruby
Nýřany
Bor
Kirchenthumbach
Grafenwöhr
Obertrubach
Weiden
Rozvadov
Primda
Auerbach
FRÄNKISCHEN WUNDERLAND
Hilpoltstein
Mantel
Oberpfälzer Wald
Waidhaus
Stod
Dobřany
Holýšov
Neuhaus
Velden
Vilseck
Freihung
Vohenstrauss
Bělá nad Radbuzou
Merklín
Kohlberg
Luhe
Eslarn
Hostouň
Staňkov
Borovy
Schnaittach
Hirschau
Tännesberg
Hahnbach
Wernberg Köblitz
Schönsee
Poběžovice
Horšovský Týn
Koloveč
HRAD ŠVIHOV
Švihov
Pommelsbrunn
Sulzbach-Rosenberg
Pfreimd
Wald
Hersbruck
Röthenbach
Oberviechtach
Klenčí pod Čerchovem
Draženov
Domažlice
Nabburg
Amberg
Tiefenbach
Klatovy
Kout na Šumave
Alfeld
Ursensollen
657 Poppberg
Altdorf bei Nürnberg
Kastl
Lauterhofen
Schwarzenfeld
Neunburg vorm Wald
Waldmünchen
Kdyně
Feucht
Ensdorf
Rötz
Schönthal
Furth im Wald
Všeruby
Janov nad Úhlavou
Berg
Schwandorf
Wackersdorf
Stamsried
Arnschwang
Nýrsko
Běšiny
Postbauer-Heng
Hohenburg
Neumarkt
Schmidmühlen
Klardorf
Neukirchen b. Hl. Blut
Allersberg
Deining
Velburg
Teublitz
Bruck
Oberer
Cham
Chamerau
Lam
Freystadt
Burglengenfeld
Nittenau
Roding
Kötzting
Traitsching
Miltach
Arnbruck
Seubersdorf
Parsberg
Kallmünz
Unterzell
Michelsneukirchen
Grosser Arber 1456
Zelezná Ruda
Berching
Beratzhausen
Regenstauf
Falkenstein
Viechtach
Bodenmais
Pielenhofen
Wenzenbach
Wiesenfelden
Bayerischer Wald
Greding
Beilngries
Hemau
Regensburg
Wörth
Ascha
St. Englmar
Patersdorf
Zwiesel
Dietfurt
Nittendorf
Painten
BURG SCHLOSS PRUNN
Ihrlerstein
Kipfenburg
Riedenburg
Obertraubling
Regen
Pollenfeld
Pondorf
Altmühl
Bad Abbach
Kelheim
Schönach
Grafling
Kirchdorf
Denkendorf
Altmannstein
Saal
Sünching
Straubing
Bogen
Deggendorf
Eichstätt
BENEDIKTINERABTEI WELTENBURG
Mindelstetten
Schierling
Aiterhofen
Metten
Lalling
Eitensheim
Kösching
Abensberg
Salching
Geiselhöring
Strasskirchen
Plattling
Neustadt
Vohburg
Langquaid
Hengersberg
Ingolstadt
Grossmehring
Mallersdorf-Pfaffenberg
Neufahrn
Siegenburg
Pilsting
Wallersdorf
Osterhofen
Winzer
Manching
Mengkofen
Weichering
Geisenfeld
Rottenburg
Ergoldsbach
Landau
Eichendorf
Pleinting
Reichertshofen
Mainburg
Pfeffenhausen
Dingolfing
Gottersdorf
Vilshofen
Wolnzach
Essenbach
Wörth
Isar
Haunersdorf
Aldersbach
ZISTERIENSER-ABTEI ALDERSBACH
Sandbach
Pörnbach
Obermünchen
Altdorf
Simbach
Arnstorf
Au
Pfaffenhofen
Landshut
Frontenhausen
BAYERN PARK
Ortenburg
Mauern
Johanniskirchen
Gerzen
Schönau
Griesbach
Gerolsbach
Moosburg
Geisenhausen
Vilsbiburg
Falkenberg
Pfarrkirchen
Bad Birnbach
Allershausen
ST.MARIA & ST KORBINIAN
Zolling
Buch
Altfraunhofen
Gangkofen
Eggenfelden
Petershausen
Freising
Aich
Massing
Markt Indersdorf
Amper
Berglern
Taufkirchen
Velden
Neumarkt St. Veit
Wurmannsquick
Rotthalmünster
Mitterskirchen
ST. MARIA HIMMELFAHRT
Malching
Erdweg
Neufahrn
Zeilarn
Unterschleissheim
Erding
Buchbach
Simbach
Dachau
Dorfen
Ampfing
Marktl
Braunau
Mühldorf
Altötting
Neuötting
Weng
Olching
Markt Schwaben
Isen
St. Wolfgang
Waldkraiburg
Kraiburg
Neukirchen
Mauerkirchen
MÜNCHEN
MUNICH
Haag
Garching
Burgkirchen
Burghausen
Mattighofen
Schmiding
Fränkische Schweiz
Böhmer Wald
Frankische Alb
Bayerischer Wald
Donau
Regen
Vils
Rott
Holledau

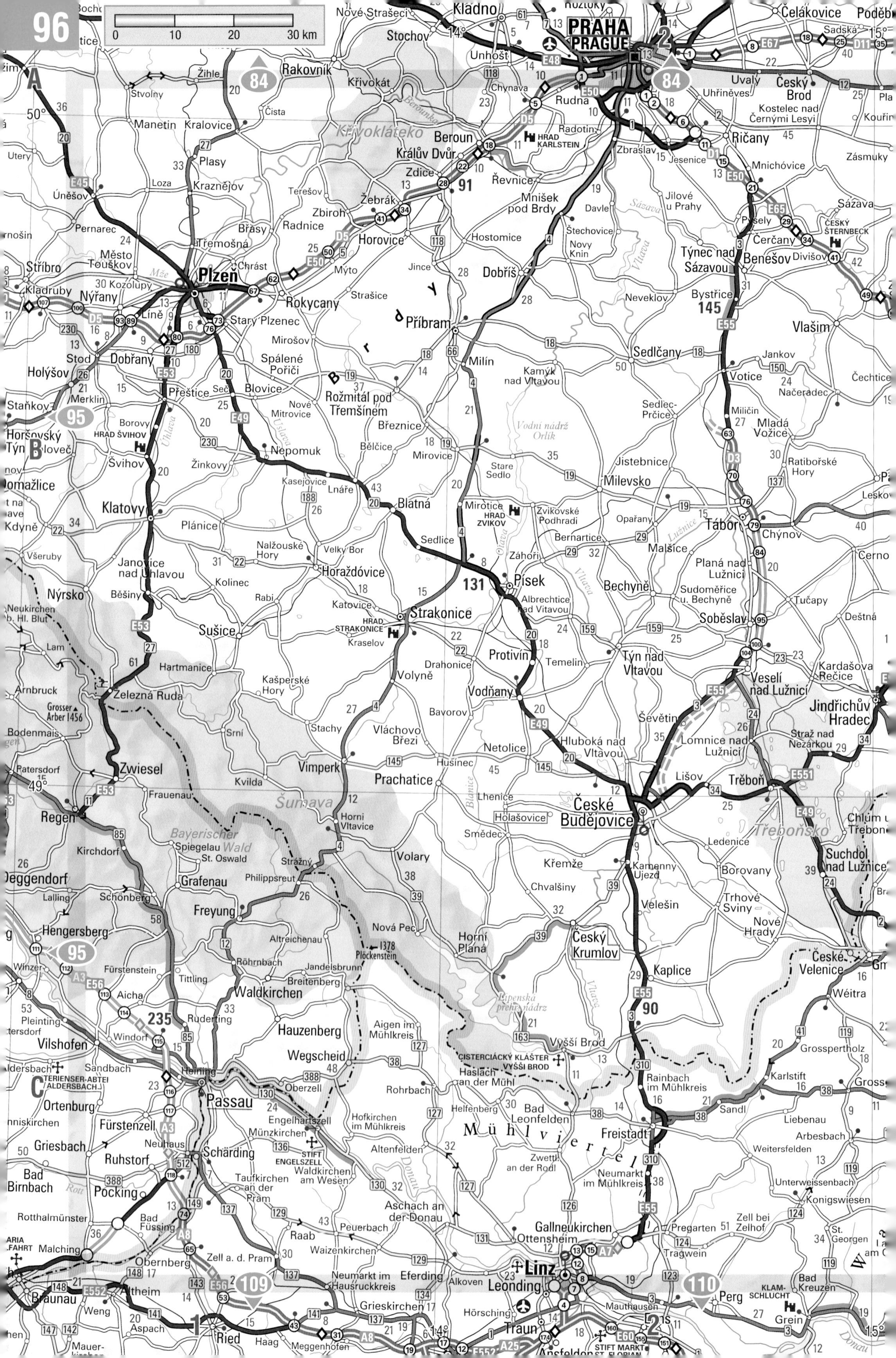
0 10 20 30 km
84
PRAHA
PRAGUE
Kladno
Nové Strašecí
Stochov
Unhošť
Rakovník
Křivoklát
Křivoklátsko
Beroun
Králův Dvůr
Zdice
Řevnice
Mnišek pod Brdy
Radotín
HRAD KARLSTEIN
Rudna
Chynava
Zbraslav
Jesenice
Říčany
Uhříněves
Uvaly
Český Brod
Kostelec nad Černými Lesy
Čelákovice
Mnichóvice
Zásmuky
Sázava
Jílové u Prahy
Davle
Štěchovice
Nový Knín
Týnec nad Sázavou
Benešov
Čerčany
Pyšely
ČESKÝ ŠTERNBECK
Divišov
Vlašim
Bystřice
Neveklov
Sedlčany
Dobříš
Hostomice
Příbram
Milín
Kamýk nad Vltavou
Plzeň
Stříbro
Město Touškov
Nýřany
Kladruby
Kozolupy
Chrást
Třemošná
Plasy
Kralovice
Manetín
Kraznějov
Břasy
Radnice
Zbiroh
Žebrák
Hořovice
Mýto
Rokycany
Strašice
Jince
Starý Plzenec
Líně
Dobřany
Stod
Holýšov
Staňkov
Horšovský Týn
Přeštice
Blovice
Spálené Poříčí
Mirošov
Rožmitál pod Třemšínem
Březnice
Nové Mitrovice
Nepomuk
HRAD ŠVIHOV
Švihov
Klatovy
Domažlice
Kdyně
Všeruby
Nýrsko
Janovice nad Úhlavou
Běšiny
Sušice
Hartmanice
Železná Ruda
Grosser Arber 1456
Bodenmais
Zwiesel
Regen
Frauenau
Deggendorf
Kirchdorf
Grafenau
Spiegelau
St. Oswald
Bayerischer Wald
Šumava
Kvilda
Srní
Kašperské Hory
Vimperk
Stachy
Horažďovice
Kolinec
Rabí
Velký Bor
Nalžovské Hory
Plánice
Žinkovy
Kasejovice
Lnáře
Bělčice
Mirovice
Blatná
Sedlice
Katovice
Strakonice
HRAD STRAKONICE
Kraselov
Volyně
Drahonice
Bavorov
Vodňany
Protivín
Písek
HRAD ZVÍKOV
Zvíkovské Podhradí
Mirotice
Záhoří
Albrechtice nad Vltavou
Temelín
Týn nad Vltavou
Bechyně
Milevsko
Jistebnice
Opařany
Bernartice
Malšice
Tábor
Chýnov
Planá nad Lužnicí
Sudoměřice u. Bechyně
Soběslav
Tučapy
Veselí nad Lužnicí
Jindřichův Hradec
Vodní nádrž Orlík
Stare Sedlo
Votice
Načeradec
Miličín
Mladá Vožice
Sedlec-Prčice
Ratibořské Hory
Čechtice
Ševeřín
Hluboká nad Vltavou
Netolice
Lhenice
Holašovice
Prachatice
Husinec
Vlachovo Březí
Horní Vltavice
Volary
Stražný
Philippsreut
Freyung
České Budějovice
Lomnice nad Lužnicí
Lišov
Třeboň
Stráž nad Nežárkou
Třeboňsko
Ledenice
Borovany
Trhové Sviny
Nové Hrady
Suchdol nad Lužnicí
Chlum u Třeboně
České Velenice
Kamenný Újezd
Křemže
Chvalšiny
Velešin
Český Krumlov
Kaplice
Horní Planá
Nová Pec
Plöckenstein 1378
Lipenská přehr. nádrž
Vyšší Brod
CISTERCIÁCKÝ KLÁŠTER VYŠŠÍ BROD
Haslach an der Mühl
Rainbach im Mühlkreis
Freistadt
Sandl
Liebenau
Weitra
Karlstift
Grosspertholz
Arbesbach
Weitersfelden
Unterweissenbach
Königswiesen
Zell bei Zelhof
Pregarten
St. Georgen
Bad Kreuzen
KLAM-SCHLUCHT
Perg
Grein
Mauthausen
Gallneukirchen
Ottensheim
Linz
Leonding
Traun
Hörsching
Ansfelden
STIFT ST. FLORIAN
Mühlviertel
Bad Leonfelden
Zwettl an der Rodl
Neumarkt im Mühlkreis
Helfenberg
Rohrbach
Aigen im Mühlkreis
Hofkirchen im Mühlkreis
Altenfelden
Aschach an der Donau
Peuerbach
Waizenkirchen
Eferding
Alkoven
Neumarkt im Hausruckkreis
Grieskirchen
Meggenhofen
Haag
Ried
Aspach
Weng
Altheim
Braunau
Obernberg
Zell a. d. Pram
Raab
Taufkirchen an der Pram
Schärding
Neuhaus
STIFT ENGELSZELL
Engelhartszell
Münzkirchen
Waldkirchen am Wesen
Wegscheid
Hauzenberg
Oberzell
Breitenberg
Jandelsbrunn
Waldkirchen
Röhrnbach
Altreichenau
Tittling
Fürstenstein
Aicha
Ruderting
Passau
Heining
Vilshofen
Windorf
Pleinting
Hengersberg
Schönberg
Lalling
Winzer
Sandbach
TERIENSER-ABTEI ALDERSBACH
Ortenburg
Fürstenzell
Griesbach
Ruhstorf
Bad Birnbach
Pocking
Rotthalmünster
Bad Füssing
Malching
Merklín
Borovy
Lam
Neukirchen b. Hl. Blut
Arnbruck
Patersdorf
Stvolny
Žihle
Čista
Loza
Úněšov
Pernarec
Terešov
Chotěšov
Chlum
Holašovice
Smědeč
Drahonice
Hořice
95
109
110
131
145
235
90
91
A
B
C
50°
49°
Vltava
Lužnice
Otava
Blanice
Donau
Úhlava
Úslava
Mže
Berounka
Sázava
Rott

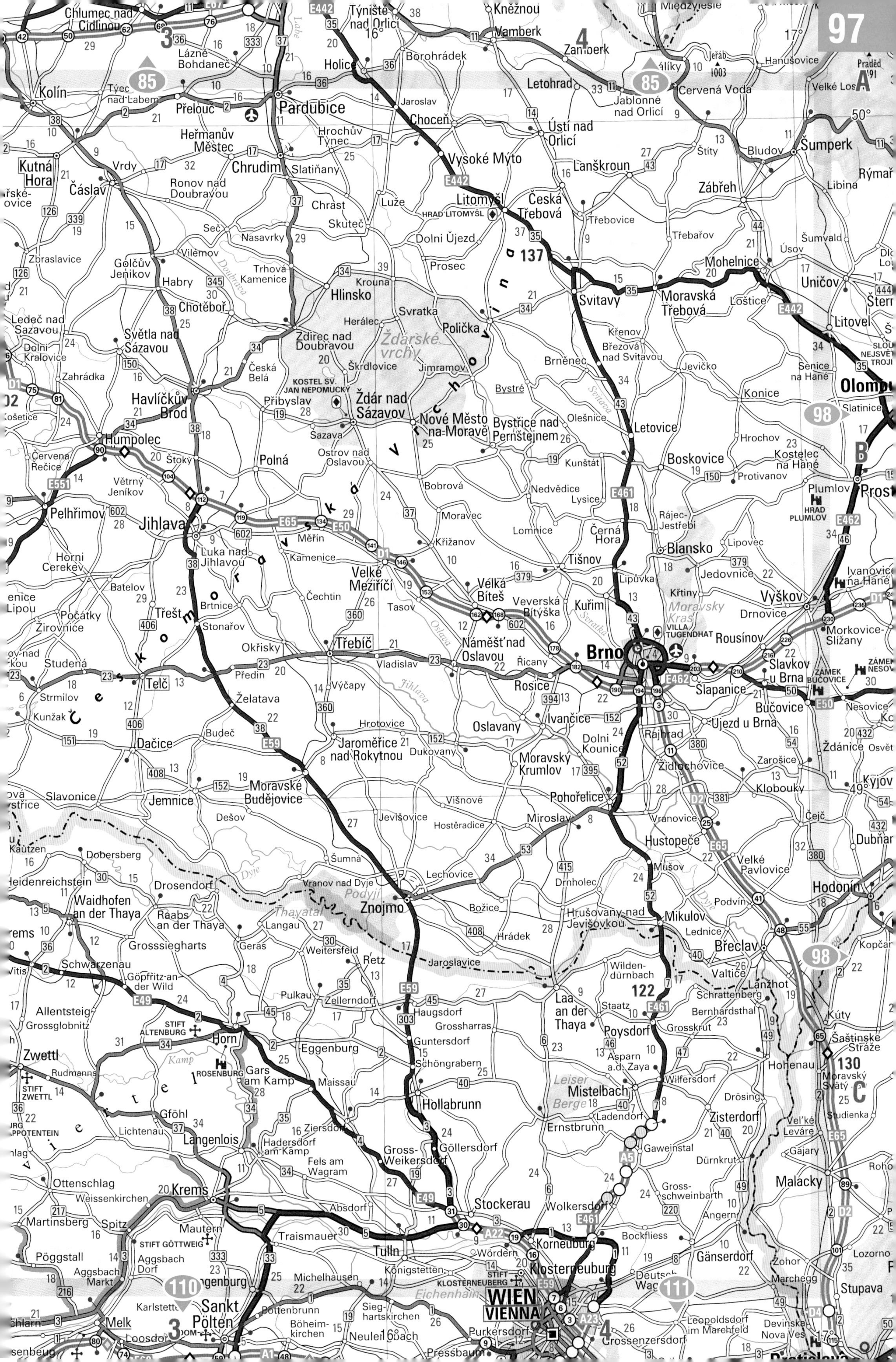
Chlumec nad Cidlinou
Týniště nad Orlicí
Kněžnou
Vamberk
Žamberk
Lázně Bohdaneč
Holice
Borohrádek
Letohrad
Jablonné nad Orlicí
Červená Voda
Hanušovice
Praděd 1491
Velké Losiny
Kolín
Týnec nad Labem
Přelouč
Pardubice
Jaroslav
Choceň
Ústí nad Orlicí
Šumperk
Heřmanův Městec
Hrochův Týnec
Vysoké Mýto
Lanškroun
Štíty
Bludov
Rýmařov
Kutná Hora
Čáslav
Vrdy
Chrudim
Slatiňany
Ronov nad Doubravou
Zábřeh
Libina
Chrast
Luže
Litomyšl
HRAD LITOMYŠL
Česká Třebová
Skuteč
Třebovice
Třebařov
Šumvald
Seč
Nasavrky
Dolní Újezd
Úsov
Zbraslavice
Vilémov
Trhová Kamenice
Prosec
Mohelnice
Uničov
Golčův Jeníkov
Habry
Krouna
Hlinsko
Svitavy
Moravská Třebová
Loštice
Chotěboř
Heralec
Svratka
Polička
Litovel
Ledeč nad Sázavou
Světlá nad Sázavou
Zdírec nad Doubravou
Žďárské vrchy
Křenov
Březová nad Svitavou
Dolní Kralovice
Česká Bělá
Škrdlovice
Jimramov
Brněnec
Jevíčko
Senice na Hané
Zahrádka
KOSTEL SV. JAN NEPOMUCKÝ
Žďár nad Sázavou
Bystré
Konice
Olomouc
Havlíčkův Brod
Přibyslav
Nové Město na Moravě
Bystřice nad Pernštejnem
Olešnice
Slatinice
Košetice
Sazava
Letovice
Humpolec
Červená Řečice
Štoky
Polná
Ostrov nad Oslavou
Kunštát
Boskovice
Hrochov
Kostelec na Hané
Větrný Jeníkov
Bobrová
Nedvědice
Protivanov
Plumlov
HRAD PLUMLOV
Prostějov
Pelhřimov
Jihlava
Lysice
Moravec
Rájec-Jestřebí
Měřín
Lomnice
Černá Hora
Křižanov
Blansko
Lipovec
Horní Cerekev
Luka nad Jihlavou
Kamenice
Tišnov
Jedovnice
Ivanovice na Hané
Velké Meziříčí
Velká Bíteš
Lipůvka
Křtiny
Batelov
Čechtín
Vyškov
Počátky
Třešť
Brtnice
Tasov
Veverská Bítýška
Kuřim
Moravský Kras
Drnovice
Žirovnice
Stonařov
Náměšť nad Oslavou
VILLA TUGENDHAT
Rousínov
Morkovice-Slížany
Okříšky
Třebíč
Vladislav
Řícany
Brno
Slavkov u Brna
ZÁMEK BUČOVICE
Studená
Telč
Předín
Rosice
Šlapanice
Strmilov
Želatava
Výčapy
Bučovice
Nesovice
Kunžak
Oslavany
Ivančice
Újezd u Brna
Hrotovice
Rajhrad
Dačice
Budeč
Jaroměřice nad Rokytnou
Dukovany
Dolní Kounice
Ždánice
Moravský Krumlov
Židlochovice
Zarošice
Kyjov
Slavonice
Jemnice
Moravské Budějovice
Višňové
Pohořelice
Klobouky
Dešov
Jevišovice
Hostěradice
Miroslav
Vranovice
Čejč
Kautzen
Dobersberg
Šumná
Hustopeče
Dubňany
Heidenreichstein
Drosendorf
Lechovice
Drnholec
Mušov
Velké Pavlovice
Vranov nad Dyjí
Podyjí
Hodonín
Waidhofen an der Thaya
Raabs an der Thaya
Znojmo
Božice
Hrušovany nad Jevišovkou
Mikulov
Podivín
Thayatal
Langau
Lednice
Krems
Grosssiegharts
Geras
Hrádek
Břeclav
Kopčany
Weitersfeld
Retz
Jaroslavice
Wildendürnbach
Valtice
Vitis
Schwarzenau
Göpfritz an der Wild
Laa an der Thaya
Lanžhot
Schrattenberg
Allentsteig
Grossglobnitz
Pulkau
Zellerndorf
Haugsdorf
Grossharras
Staatz
Bernhardsthal
Kúty
STIFT ALTENBURG
Horn
Guntersdorf
Poysdorf
Grosskrut
Šaštínske Stráže
Zwettl
Rudmanns
ROSENBURG
Gars am Kamp
Eggenburg
Schöngrabern
Asparn a.d. Zaya
Hohenau
Moravský Svätý Ján
STIFT ZWETTL
Maissau
Leiser Berge
Mistelbach
Wilfersdorf
Hollabrunn
Ladendorf
Drösing
Zisterdorf
Studienka
Gföhl
Lichtenau
Langenlois
Ziersdorf
Ernstbrunn
Veľké Leváre
Gaweinstal
Hadersdorf am Kamp
Göllersdorf
Gajary
Gross-Weikersdorf
Fels am Wagram
Dürnkrut
Ottenschlag
Weissenkirchen
Krems
Stockerau
Gross-schweinbarth
Malacky
Martinsberg
Spitz
Absdorf
Wolkersdorf
Angern
Mautern
STIFT GÖTTWEIG
Traismauer
Tulln
Korneuburg
Bockfliess
Pöggstall
Aggsbach Dorf
Aggsbach Markt
Herzogenburg
Wördern
Königstetten
Klosterneuburg
STIFT KLOSTERNEUBURG
Gänserdorf
Zohor
Lozorno
Michelhausen
Deutsch Wagram
Marchegg
Stupava
Melk
Karlstetten
Sankt Pölten
Pottenbrunn
Sieghartskirchen
Eichenhain
WIEN
VIENNA
Leopoldsdorf im Marchfeld
Devínska Nová Ves
Loosdorf
Böheimkirchen
Neulengbach
Purkersdorf
Pressbaum
Grossenzersdorf
Českomoravská vrchovina
Waldviertel

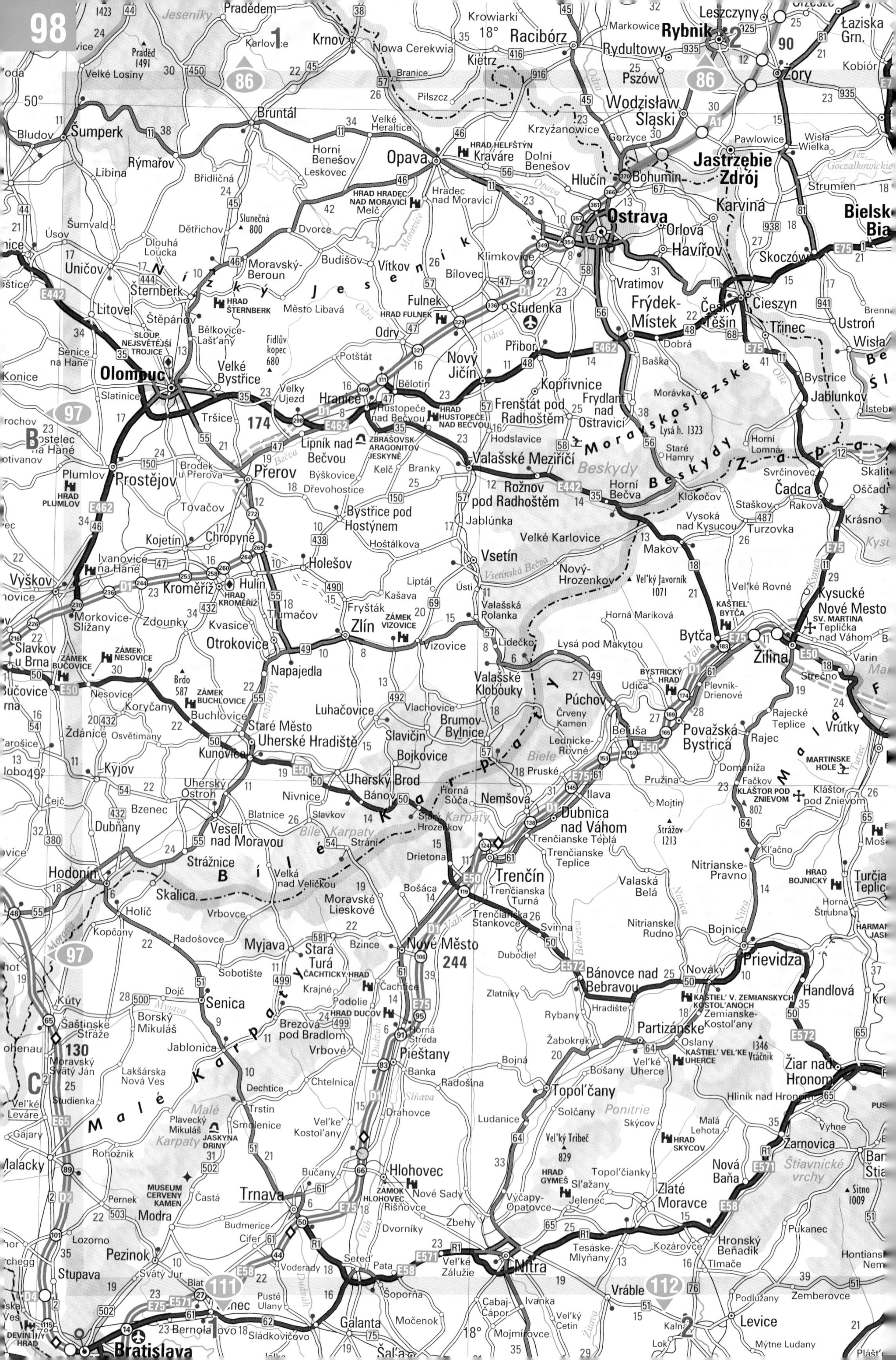

Praděd 1491
Velké Losiny
Šumperk
Bruntál
Krnov
Racibórz
Rybnik
Žory
Wodzisław Śląski
Jastrzębie Zdrój
Opava
Kravaře
Hlučín
Bohumín
Ostrava
Karviná
Orlová
Havířov
Bielsko-Biała
Rýmařov
Šternberk
Uničov
Litovel
Olomouc
Moravský Beroun
Vítkov
Bílovec
Fulnek
Studénka
Odry
Příbor
Nový Jičín
Frýdek-Místek
Český Těšín
Cieszyn
Třinec
Ustroń
Wisła
Jablunkov
Nízký Jeseník
Moravskoslezské Beskydy
Prostějov
Přerov
Hranice
Lipník nad Bečvou
Valašské Meziříčí
Rožnov pod Radhoštěm
Frenštát pod Radhoštěm
Frýdlant nad Ostravicí
Lysá h. 1323
Čadca
Bystřice pod Hostýnem
Holešov
Kroměříž
Hulín
Chropyně
Kojetín
Vyškov
Slavkov u Brna
Bučovice
Zlín
Otrokovice
Vsetín
Velké Karlovice
Nový Hrozenkov
Veľký Javorník 1071
Kysucké Nové Mesto
Bytča
Žilina
Vrútky
Napajedla
Luhačovice
Vizovice
Valašské Klobouky
Púchov
Považská Bystrica
Staré Město
Uherské Hradiště
Kunovice
Uherský Brod
Bojkovice
Slavičín
Brumov-Bylnice
Nemšová
Dubnica nad Váhom
Ilava
Trenčín
Trenčianske Teplice
Kyjov
Veselí nad Moravou
Strážnice
Hodonín
Skalica
Holíč
Bílé Karpaty
Myjava
Stará Turá
Nové Mesto nad Váhom
Bánovce nad Bebravou
Prievidza
Handlová
Nováky
Partizánske
Topoľčany
Žiar nad Hronom
Senica
Piešťany
Hlohovec
Trnava
Malé Karpaty
Malacky
Pezinok
Modra
Stupava
Bratislava
Senec
Galanta
Sereď
Nitra
Zlaté Moravce
Vráble
Levice
Žarnovica
Nová Baňa
Štiavnické vrchy

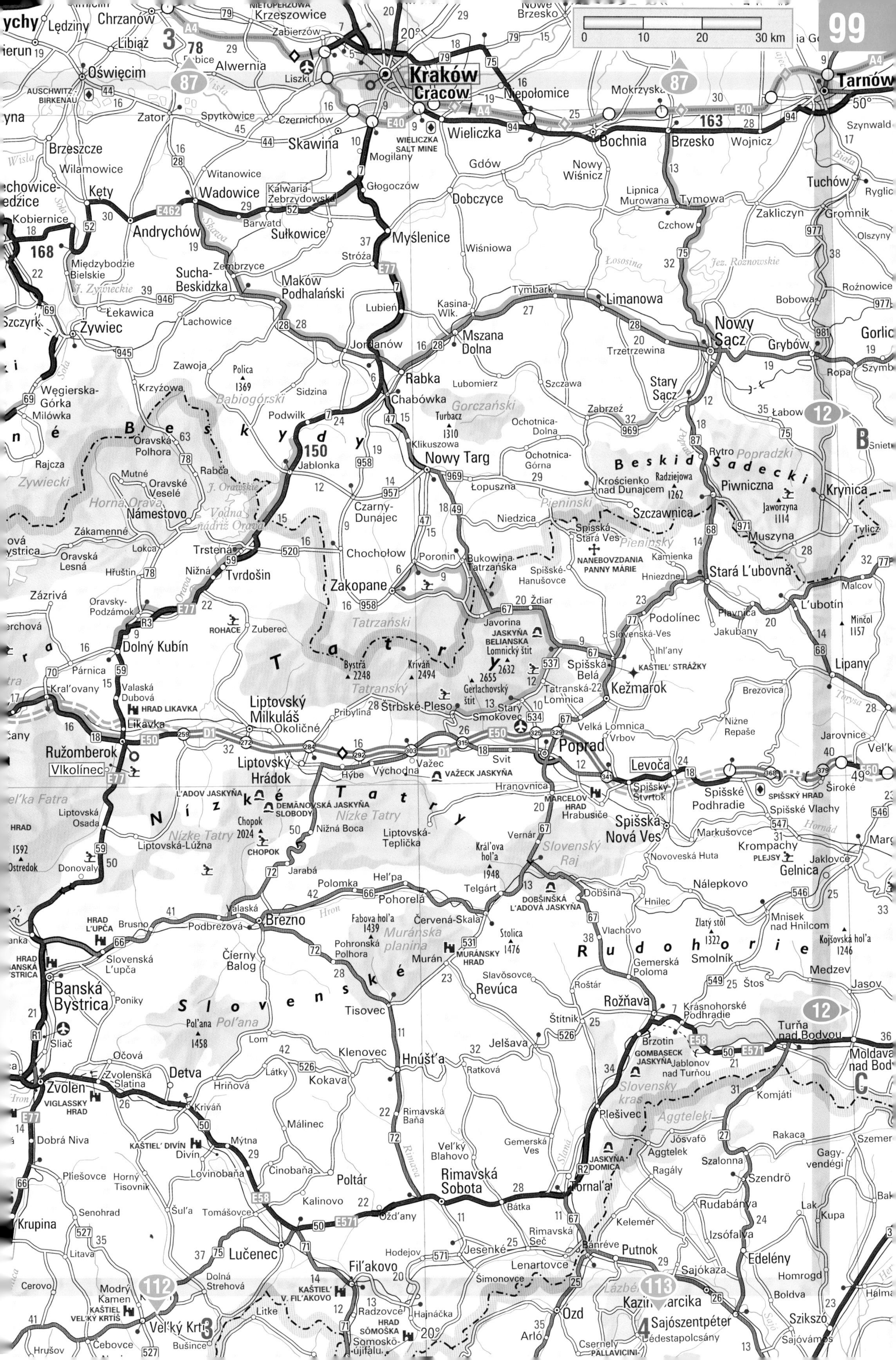

Kraków
Cracow
Tarnów
Oświęcim
AUSCHWITZ-BIRKENAU
Chrzanów
Lędziny
Libiąż
Krzeszowice
Zabierzów
Alwernia
Liszki
Skawina
Zator
Spytkowice
Czernichów
Wieliczka
WIELICZKA SALT MINE
Niepołomice
Bochnia
Brzesko
Wojnicz
Mokrzyska
Szynwałd
Tuchów
Ryglice
Brzeszcze
Wilamowice
Kęty
Kobiernice
Andrychów
Wadowice
Witanowice
Kalwaria-Zebrzydowska
Barwałd
Mogilany
Głogoczów
Gdów
Nowy Wiśnicz
Dobczyce
Lipnica Murowana
Tymowa
Czchów
Zakliczyn
Gromnik
Olszyny
Sułkowice
Myślenice
Stróża
Wiśniowa
Międzybrodzie Bielskie
J. Żywieckie
Sucha-Beskidzka
Zembrzyce
Maków Podhalański
Łekawica
Żywiec
Lachowice
Szczyrk
Lubień
Kasina-Wlk.
Tymbark
Limanowa
Jez. Rożnowskie
Rożnowice
Bobowa
Nowy Sącz
Gorlice
Grybów
Jordanów
Mszana Dolna
Trzetrzewina
Stary Sącz
Ropa
Zawoja
Polica 1369
Sidzina
Rabka
Chabówka
Lubomierz
Szczawa
Krzyżowa
Babiogórski
Gorczański
Turbacz 1310
Ochotnica-Dolna
Zabrzeż
Łabow
Węgierska-Górka
Milówka
Oravská Polhora
Podwilk
Jabłonka
Klikuszowa
Nowy Targ
Ochotnica-Górna
Łopuszna
Beskid Sądecki
Rytro
Popradzki
Piwniczna
Krynica
Rajcza
Żywiecki
Rabča
Mutné
Oravské Veselé
Horná Orava
Námestovo
Vodná nádrž Orava
J. Oravskie
Czarny-Dunajec
Krościenko nad Dunajcem
Radziejowa 1262
Jaworzyna 1114
Niedzica
Pieniński
Szczawnica
Muszyna
Tylicz
Zákamenné
Oravská Lesná
Lokca
Trstená
Tvrdošín
Nižná
Chochołów
Poronin
Bukowina Tatrzańska
Spišská Stará Ves
Pieninský
NANEBOVZDANIA PANNY MÁRIE
Kamienka
Hniezdne
Stará Ľubovňa
Spišské-Hanušovce
Zázrivá
Oravsky-Podzámok
Hruštín
Zakopane
Ždiar
Podolínec
Plavnica
Ľubotín
Malcov
Minčol 1157
Jakubany
ROHACE
Zuberec
Tatrzański
Javorina
JASKYŇA BELIANSKA
Lomnický štít
Slovenská-Ves
Ihľany
KAŠTIEĽ STRÁŽKY
Lipany
Dolný Kubín
Pārnica
Kraľovany
Valaská Dubová
HRAD LIKAVKA
Bystrá 2248
Kriváň 2494
Tatranský
Gerlachovský štít 2655
Spišská Belá
Kežmarok
Tatranská Lomnica
Starý Smokovec
Štrbské Pleso
Pribylina
Liptovský Milkuláš
Okoličné
Likavka
Ružomberok
Vlkolínec
Liptovský Hrádok
Hýbe
Východna
Važec
VAŽECK JASKYŇA
Svit
Poprad
Veľká Lomnica
Vrbov
Nižné Repaše
Brezovica
Torysa
Jarovnice
Levoča
Spišský Štvrtok
Spišské Podhradie
SPIŠSKÝ HRAD
Spišské Vlachy
Široké
Veľká Fatra
Liptovská Osada
ĽADOV JASKYŇA
DEMÄNOVSKÁ JASKYŇA SLOBODY
Nízke Tatry
Chopok 2024
CHOPOK
Nižná Boca
Liptovská-Teplička
Hranovnica
MARCELOV HRAD
Hrabušice
Spišská Nová Ves
Markušovce
Krompachy
PLEJSY
Hornád
Ostredok 1592
Liptovská-Lúžna
Donovaly
Jarabá
Vernár
Slovenský Raj
Kráľova hoľa 1948
Novoveská Huta
Jaklovce
Gelnica
Polomka
Heľpa
Pohorelá
Telgárt
Dobšiná
DOBŠINSKÁ ĽADOVÁ JASKYŇA
Hnilec
Nálepkovo
Mnisek nad Hnilcom
HRAD ĽUPČA
Brusno
Podbrezová
Valaská
Brezno
Hron
Fabova hoľa 1439
Červená-Skala
Muránska planina
Stolica 1476
Vlachovo
Zlatý stôl 1322
Kojšovská hoľa 1246
Slovenská Ľupča
HRAD BANSKÁ BYSTRICA
Banská Bystrica
Poniky
Čierny Balog
Pohronská Polhora
Murán
MURÁNSKY HRAD
Slavošovce
Revúca
Gemerská Poloma
Smolník
Rudohorie
Medzev
Štós
Jasov
Roštár
Rožňava
Krásnohorské Podhradie
Turňa nad Bodvou
Moldava nad Bodvou
Sliač
Poľana 1458
Lom
Tisovec
Klenovec
Hnúšťa
Jelšava
Štítnik
Brzotín
GOMBASECK JASKYŇA
Jablonov nad Turňou
Slovenský kras
Komjáti
Očová
Zvolenská Slatina
Zvolen
VIGLASSKY HRAD
Detva
Hriňová
Látky
Kokava
Ratková
Plešivec
Aggtelek
Jósvafő
Rakaca
Szemere
Kriváň
Dobrá Niva
KAŠTIEĽ DIVÍN
Divín
Mýtna
Málinec
Rimavská Baňa
Veľký Blahovo
Gemerská Ves
JASKYŇA DOMICA
Ragály
Szalonna
Gagy-vendégi
Pliešovce
Horný Tisovník
Lovinobaňa
Cinobaňa
Poltár
Rimavská Sobota
Tornaľa
Szendrő
Krupina
Senohrad
Šuľa
Tomášovce
Kalinovo
Ožďany
Bátka
Rudabánya
Lak
Kupa
Litava
Lučenec
Rimavská Seč
Kelemér
Izsófalva
Hodejov
Jesenké
Bánréve
Putnok
Edelény
Cerovo
Modrý Kameň
KAŠTIEĽ VEĽKÝ KRTÍŠ
Dolná Strehová
KAŠTIEĽ V. FIĽAKOVO
Fiľakovo
Lenartovce
Šimonovce
Sajókaza
Homrogd
Boldva
Radzovce
Hajnáčka
HRAD SOMOŠKA
Somoskő-újfalu
Kazincbarcika
Sajószentpéter
Szikszó
Sajóvámos
Halmaj
Veľký Krtíš
Litke
Hrušov
Cebovce
Bušince
Ožd
Arló
Csernely
Lédestapolcsány
PALLAVICINI
0 10 20 30 km

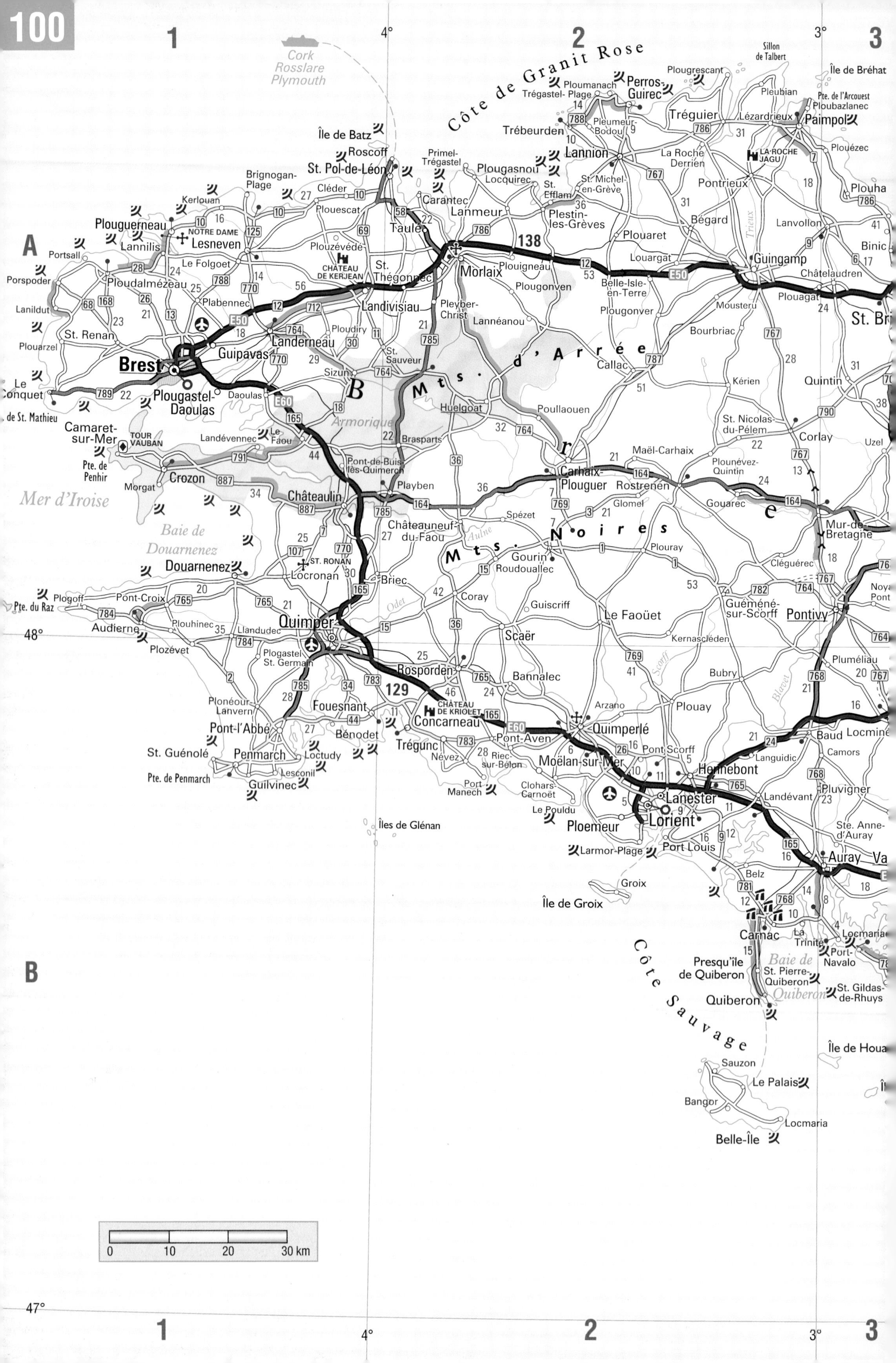
Cork
Rosslare
Plymouth
Côte de Granit Rose
Île de Batz
Roscoff
St. Pol-de-Léon
Brest
Quimper
Morlaix
Lannion
Perros-Guirec
Tréguier
Paimpol
Guingamp
Landerneau
Landivisiau
Lesneven
Plougastel-Daoulas
Camaret-sur-Mer
Crozon
Morgat
Châteaulin
Douarnenez
Mer d'Iroise
Baie de Douarnenez
Pte. du Raz
Audierne
Pont-l'Abbé
Penmarch
Guilvinec
Fouesnant
Bénodet
Concarneau
Rosporden
Pont-Aven
Quimperlé
Lorient
Lanester
Hennebont
Ploemeur
Port Louis
Île de Groix
Carnac
Presqu'île de Quiberon
Quiberon
Baie de Quiberon
Auray
Côte Sauvage
Belle-Île
Le Palais
Pontivy
Carhaix-Plouguer
Rostrenen
Mts. d'Arrée
Mts. Noires
Gourin
Le Faouët
Huelgoat
Callac
Mur-de-Bretagne
Loudéac
Corlay
Quintin
St. Brieuc
Île de Bréhat
Îles de Glénan
47°
48°
4°
3°
0 10 20 30 km

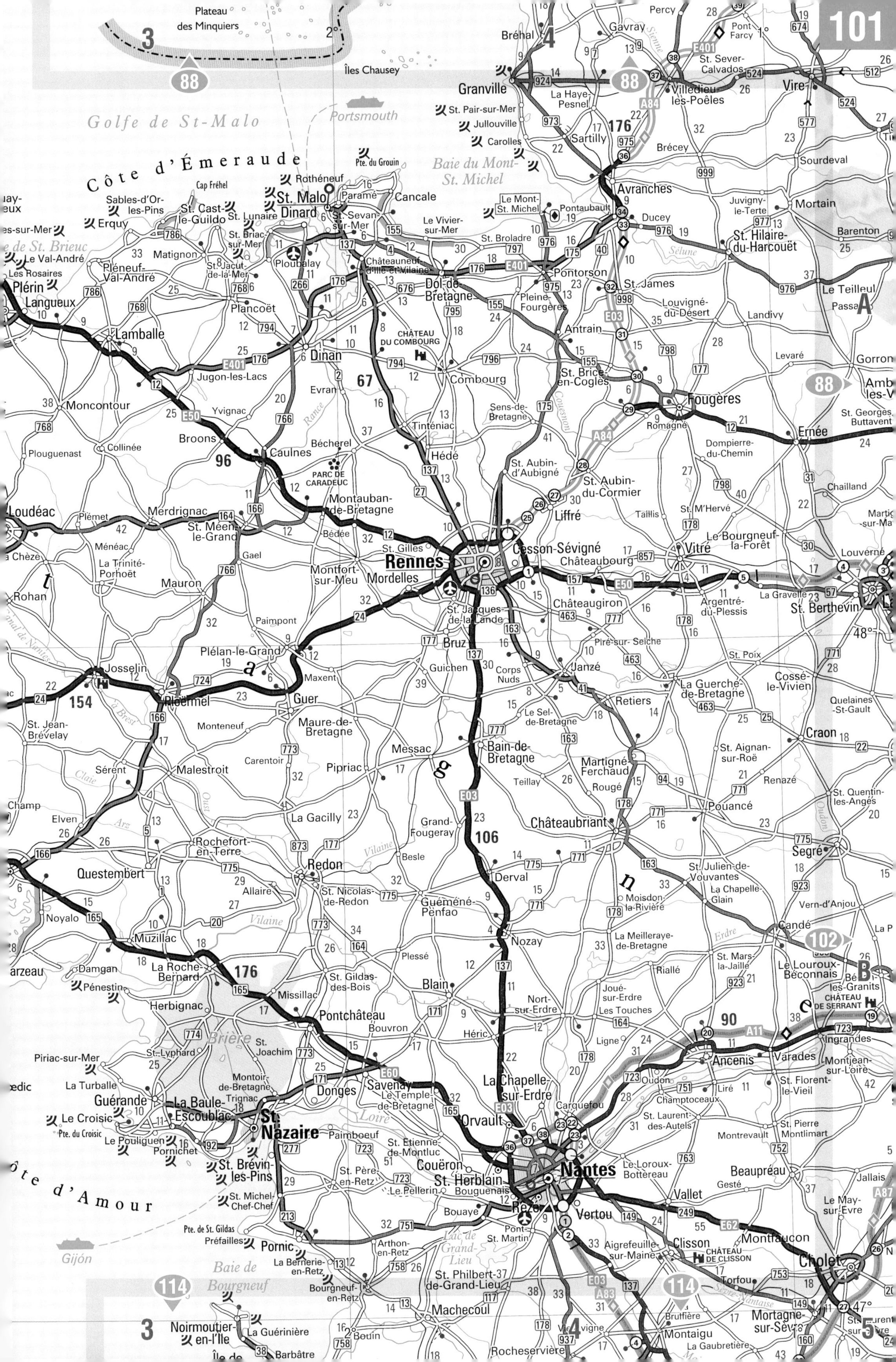

101
Plateau des Minquiers
Îles Chausey
Portsmouth
Golfe de St-Malo
Côte d'Émeraude
Cap Fréhel
Pte. du Grouin
Baie du Mont-St. Michel
Bréhal
Percy
Gavray
Pont Farcy
St. Sever-Calvados
Granville
La Haye-Pesnel
Villedieu-les-Poêles
Vire
St. Pair-sur-Mer
Jullouville
Carolles
Sartilly
Brécey
Sourdeval
Rothéneuf
St. Malo
Paramé
Cancale
Dinard
St. Lunaire
St. Cast-le-Guildo
Sables-d'Or-les-Pins
Erquy
St. Briac-sur-Mer
St. Servan-sur-Mer
Le Vivier-sur-Mer
Le Mont-St. Michel
Pontaubault
Avranches
Juvigny-le-Tertre
Mortain
Ducey
St. Hilaire-du-Harcouët
Barenton
Le Val-André
Les Rosaires
Pléneuf-Val-André
Matignon
St. Jacut-de-la-Mer
Ploubalay
Châteauneuf-d'Ille-et-Vilaine
St. Broladre
Pontorson
St. James
Le Teilleul
Plérin
Langueux
Plancoët
Dol-de-Bretagne
Pleine-Fougères
Louvigné-du-Désert
Landivy
Lamballe
Château du Combourg
Antrain
Jugon-les-Lacs
Dinan
Combourg
St. Brice-en-Coglès
Levaré
Gorron
Moncontour
Evran
Fougères
Yvignac
Broons
Sens-de-Bretagne
Romagné
Tinténiac
St. Georges-Buttavent
Ernée
Plouguenast
Collinée
Caulnes
Bécherel
Parc de Caradeuc
Hédé
Dompierre-du-Chemin
St. Aubin-d'Aubigné
St. Aubin-du-Cormier
Chailland
Loudéac
Plémet
Merdrignac
St. Méen-le-Grand
Montauban-de-Bretagne
Liffré
Taillis
St. M'Hervé
Ménéac
Bédée
Cesson-Sévigné
Le Bourgneuf-la-Forêt
La Trinité-Porhoët
Gael
St. Gilles
Rennes
Châteaubourg
Vitré
Louverné
La Chèze
Rohan
Montfort-sur-Meu
Mordelles
Mauron
Paimpont
St. Jacques-de-la-Lande
Châteaugiron
Argentré-du-Plessis
La Gravelle
St. Berthevin
Plélan-le-Grand
Bruz
Piré-sur-Seiche
St. Poix
Josselin
Guichen
Corps Nuds
Janzé
Maxent
La Guerche-de-Bretagne
Cossé-le-Vivien
Ploërmel
Guer
Retiers
Quelaines-St-Gault
St. Jean-Brévelay
Monteneuf
Le Sel-de-Bretagne
Maure-de-Bretagne
Craon
Messac
Bain-de-Bretagne
St. Aignan-sur-Roë
Sérent
Malestroit
Carentoir
Pipriac
Martigné-Ferchaud
Teillay
Rougé
Renazé
St. Quentin-les-Anges
Champ
Elven
La Gacilly
Grand-Fougeray
Châteaubriant
Pouancé
Rochefort-en-Terre
Segré
Questembert
Redon
Besle
Allaire
St. Nicolas-de-Redon
Derval
St. Julien-de-Vouvantes
La Chapelle-Glain
Noyalo
Guémené-Penfao
Moisdon-la-Rivière
Vern-d'Anjou
Muzillac
Candé
Nozay
La Meilleraye-de-Bretagne
Sarzeau
Damgan
La Roche-Bernard
Plessé
St. Gildas-des-Bois
Riallé
St. Mars-la-Jaille
Le Louroux-Béconnais
Pénestin
Blain
Herbignac
Missillac
Pontchâteau
Nort-sur-Erdre
Joué-sur-Erdre
Les Touches
Château de Serrant
Bouvron
Héric
Brière
St. Joachim
St.-Lyphard
Ligne
Ingrandes
Piriac-sur-Mer
Montoir-de-Bretagne
Ancenis
Varades
Montjean-sur-Loire
La Turballe
Trignac
Savenay
Donges
La Chapelle-sur-Erdre
Oudon
Liré
St. Florent-le-Vieil
Guérande
La Baule-Escoublac
St. Nazaire
Le Temple-de-Bretagne
Carquefou
Champtoceaux
Le Croisic
Pte. du Croisic
Le Pouliguen
Pornichet
Orvault
St. Laurent-des-Autels
St. Pierre Montlimart
Montrevault
Paimboeuf
St. Etienne-de-Montluc
St. Brévin-les-Pins
St. Père-en-Retz
Couëron
Nantes
Le Loroux-Bottereau
Beaupréau
Jallais
St. Herblain
Le Pellerin
Bouguenais
Geste
Côte d'Amour
St. Michel-Chef-Chef
Vallet
Rezé
Vertou
Le May-sur-Evre
Bouaye
Pte. de St. Gildas
Préfailles
Pornic
Arthon-en-Retz
Lac de Grand-Lieu
Pont-St. Martin
Aigrefeuille-sur-Maine
Clisson
Château de Clisson
Montfaucon
Gijón
Baie de Bourgneuf
La Bernerie-en-Retz
St. Philbert-de-Grand-Lieu
Cholet
Bourgneuf-en-Retz
Torfou
Machecoul
Noirmoutier-en-l'Île
La Guérinière
Barbâtre
Bouin
Rocheservière
Vieillevigne
Montaigu
La Gaubretière
Mortagne-sur-Sèvre
Vilaine
Loire
Erdre
Rance
Couesnon
Sélune
Oust
Arz
Claie

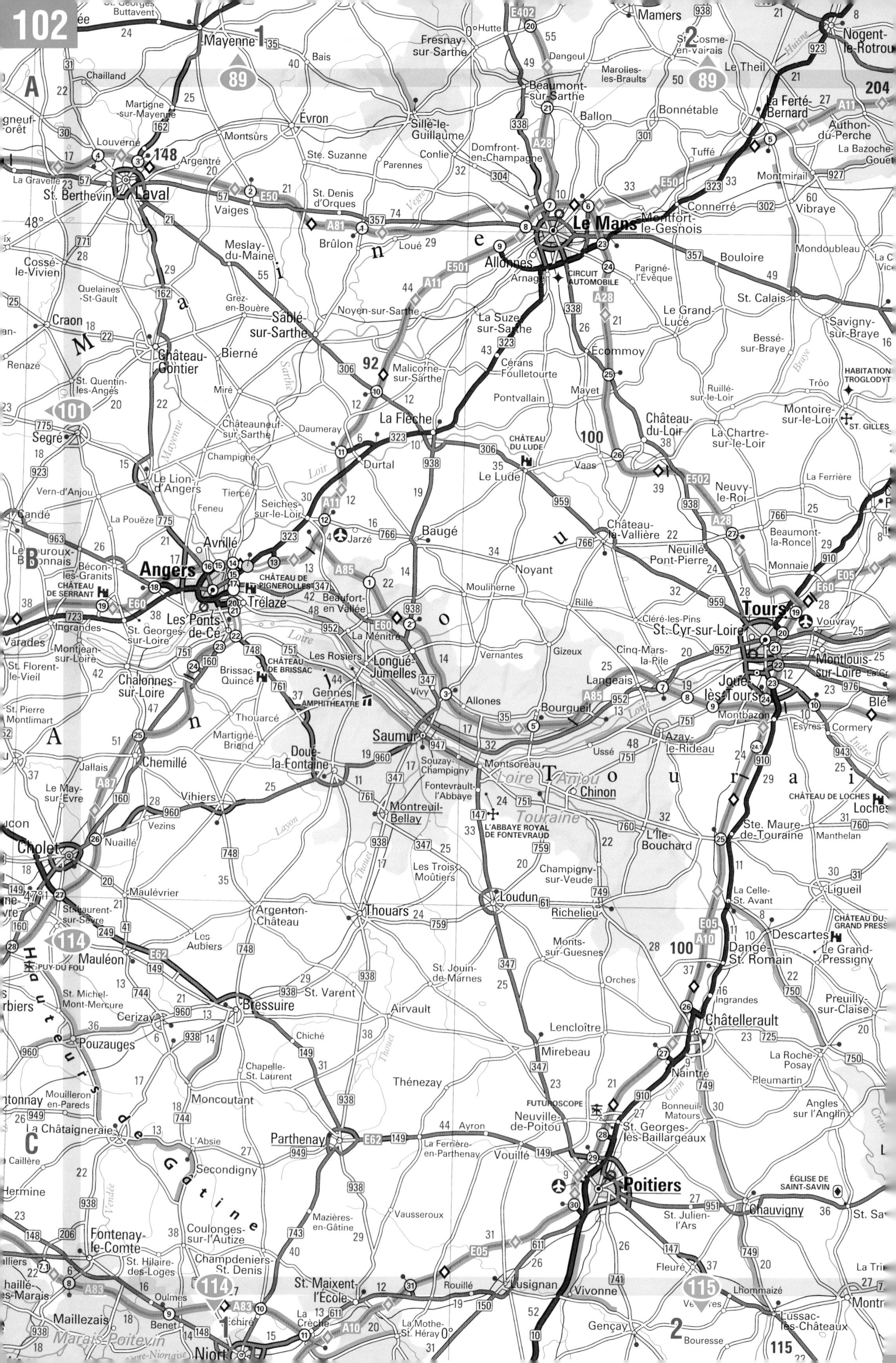
Mayenne
Fresnay-sur-Sarthe
Mamers
St. Cosme-en-Vairais
Nogent-le-Rotrou
Chailland
Martigné-sur-Mayenne
Évron
Sillé-le-Guillaume
Beaumont-sur-Sarthe
Marolles-les-Braults
Bonnétable
La Ferté-Bernard
Authon-du-Perche
Louverné
Montsûrs
Argentré
Ste. Suzanne
Conlie
Domfront-en-Champagne
Ballon
Tuffé
La Bazoche-Gouet
La Gravelle
St. Berthevin
Laval
Vaiges
St. Denis d'Orques
Parennes
Montmirail
Connerré
Montfort-le-Gesnois
Vibraye
Brûlon
Loué
Le Mans
Allonnes
Arnage
CIRCUIT AUTOMOBILE
Parigné-l'Évêque
Bouloire
Mondoubleau
Cossé-le-Vivien
Meslay-du-Maine
Quelaines-St-Gault
Grez-en-Bouère
Sablé-sur-Sarthe
Noyen-sur-Sarthe
La Suze-sur-Sarthe
St. Calais
Le Grand-Lucé
Savigny-sur-Braye
Craon
Château-Gontier
Bierné
Malicorne-sur-Sarthe
Cérans Foulletourte
Écommoy
Bessé-sur-Braye
Renazé
St. Quentin-les-Anges
Miré
Pontvallain
Mayet
Ruillé-sur-le-Loir
Trôo
HABITATION TROGLODYTE
Segré
Châteauneuf-sur-Sarthe
Daumeray
La Flèche
CHÂTEAU DU LUDE
Château-du-Loir
La Chartre-sur-le-Loir
Montoire-sur-le-Loir
ST. GILLES
Champigné
Durtal
Le Lude
Vaas
Vern-d'Anjou
Le Lion-d'Angers
Tiercé
Seiches-sur-le-Loir
Neuvy-le-Roi
La Ferrière
Candé
La Pouëze
Feneu
Baugé
Jarzé
Château-la-Vallière
Beaumont-la-Ronce
Avrillé
Angers
Bécon-les-Granits
CHÂTEAU DE SERRANT
CHÂTEAU DE PIGNEROLLES
Noyant
Neuillé-Pont-Pierre
Monnaie
Trélazé
Beaufort-en-Vallée
Mouliherne
Rillé
Tours
Vouvray
Varades
Ingrandes
Les Ponts-de-Cé
St. Georges-sur-Loire
La Ménitré
Cléré-les-Pins
St. Cyr-sur-Loire
Montjean-sur-Loire
St. Florent-le-Vieil
CHÂTEAU DE BRISSAC
Brissac-Quincé
Les Rosiers
Longué-Jumelles
Vernantes
Gizeux
Cinq-Mars-la-Pile
Montlouis-sur-Loire
Chalonnes-sur-Loire
Gennes
AMPHITHÉÂTRE
Vivy
Allonnes
Langeais
Joué-lès-Tours
St. Pierre Montlimart
Thouarcé
Bourgueil
Montbazon
Esvres
Cormery
Martigné-Briand
Saumur
Azay-le-Rideau
Ussé
Doué-la-Fontaine
Souzay-Champigny
Montsoreau
Jallais
Chemillé
Fontevrault-l'Abbaye
Chinon
Le May-sur-Èvre
Vihiers
Montreuil-Bellay
L'ABBAYE ROYAL DE FONTEVRAUD
CHÂTEAU DE LOCHES
Loches
Vezins
Cholet
Nuaillé
Ste. Maure-de-Touraine
L'Île-Bouchard
Manthelan
Les Trois Moûtiers
Champigny-sur-Veude
Maulévrier
Loudun
Richelieu
La Celle-St. Avant
Ligueil
St. Laurent-sur-Sèvre
Argenton-Château
Thouars
CHÂTEAU DU GRAND PRESSIGNY
Les Aubiers
Monts-sur-Guesnes
Descartes
Le Grand-Pressigny
Mauléon
PUY-DU FOU
Dangé-St. Romain
St. Jouin-de-Marnes
Orches
St. Michel-Mont-Mercure
St. Varent
Airvault
Ingrandes
Preuilly-sur-Claise
Cerizay
Bressuire
Châtellerault
Pouzauges
Lencloître
Chiché
Mirebeau
La Roche-Posay
Chapelle-St. Laurent
Naintré
Pleumartin
Thénezay
Mouilleron en-Pareds
Moncoutant
FUTUROSCOPE
Bonneuil-Matours
Angles sur l'Anglin
La Châtaigneraie
Neuville-de-Poitou
Ayron
St. Georges-lès-Baillargeaux
L'Absie
Parthenay
La Ferrière-en-Parthenay
Vouillé
Secondigny
Poitiers
ÉGLISE DE SAINT-SAVIN
Chauvigny
Mazières-en-Gâtine
Vausseroux
St. Julien-l'Ars
Fontenay-le-Comte
Coulonges-sur-l'Autize
St. Hilaire-des-Loges
Champdeniers-St. Denis
Fleuré
Lussac-les-Châteaux
St. Maixent-l'École
Rouillé
Lusignan
Vivonne
Lhommaizé
Oulmes
Maillezais
Benet
La Crèche
La Mothe-St. Héray
Gençay
Bouresse
Marais Poitevin
Niort
Maine
Anjou
Touraine
Loire Anjou Touraine
Hauteurs de Gâtine
Loire
Sarthe
Mayenne
Loir
Vègre
Layon
Thouet
Vendée
Clain
Braye
Indre
Huisne

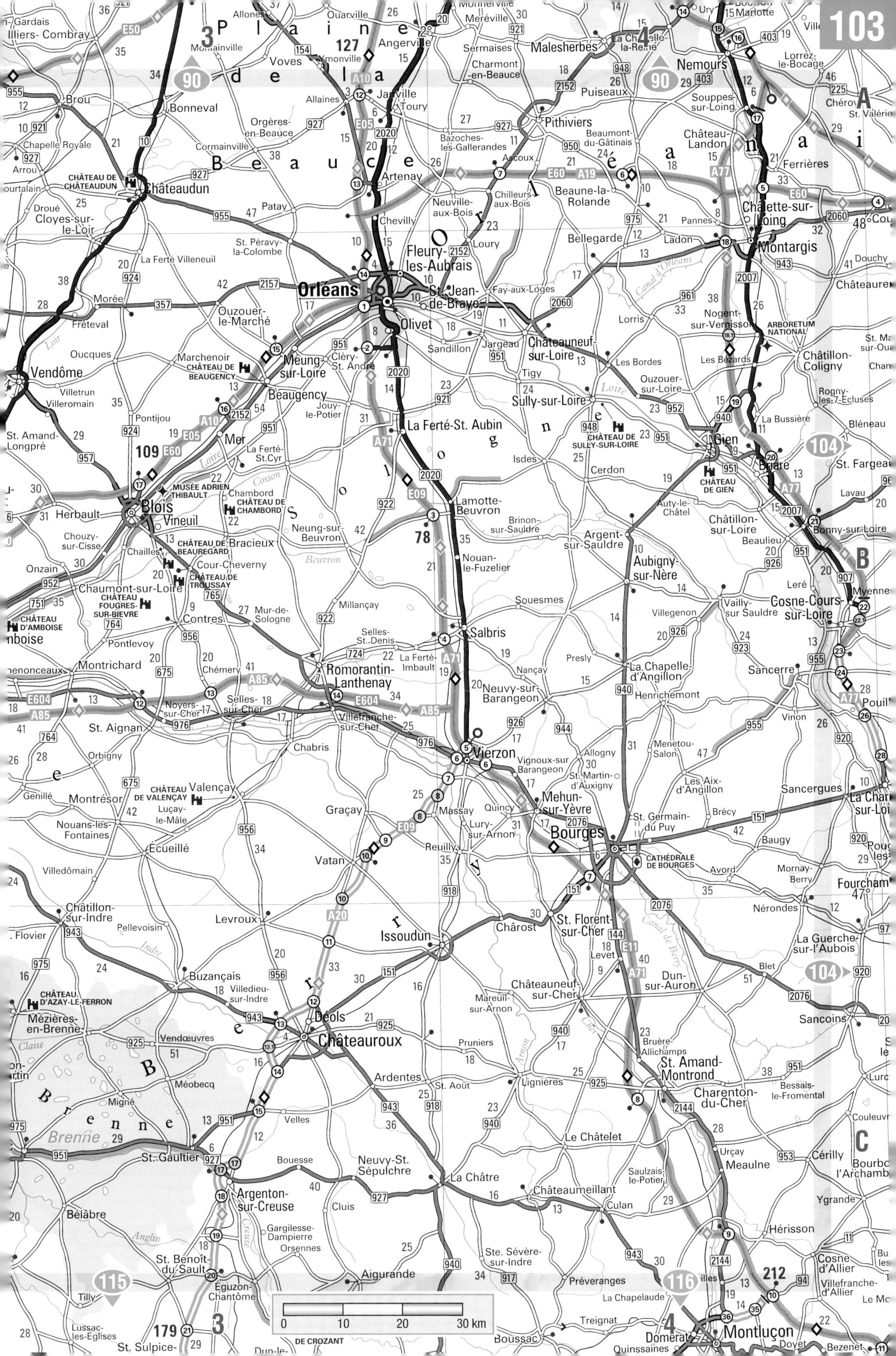
Plaine de la Beauce
Orléanais
Sologne
Berry
Brenne
Gardais
Illiers-Combray
Brou
Bonneval
Chapelle Royale
Arrou
Châteaudun
CHÂTEAU DE CHÂTEAUDUN
Droué
Cloyes-sur-le-Loir
Montainville
Voves
Ymonville
Allonnes
Ouarville
Angerville
Méréville
Sermaises
Malesherbes
La Chapelle-la-Reine
Nemours
Ury
Marlotte
Lorrez-le-Bocage
Chéroy
St. Valérie
Charmont-en-Beauce
Puiseaux
Souppes-sur-Loing
Château-Landon
Ferrières
Orgères-en-Beauce
Cormainville
Allaines
Janville
Toury
Bazoches-les-Gallerandes
Ascoux
Pithiviers
Beaumont-du-Gâtinais
Artenay
Patay
Neuville-aux-Bois
Chilleurs-aux-Bois
Beaune-la-Rolande
Pannes
Châlette-sur-Loing
Montargis
Chevilly
St. Péravy-la-Colombe
La Ferté Villeneuil
Fleury-les-Aubrais
Loury
Bellegarde
Ladon
Orléans
St. Jean-de-Braye
Fay-aux-Loges
Douchy
Châteaurenard
Morée
Fréteval
Ouzouer-le-Marché
Olivet
Sandillon
Jargeau
Châteauneuf-sur-Loire
Lorris
Nogent-sur-Vernisson
ARBORETUM NATIONAL
Les Bordes
Les Bézards
Châtillon-Coligny
Canal d'Orléans
Vendôme
Oucques
Marchenoir
CHÂTEAU DE BEAUGENCY
Meung-sur-Loire
Cléry-St. André
Tigy
Sully-sur-Loire
Ouzouer-sur-Loire
Rogny-les-7-Écluses
Villetrun
Villeromain
Beaugency
Jouy-le-Potier
La Ferté-St. Aubin
CHÂTEAU DE SULLY-SUR-LOIRE
La Bussière
Bléneau
St. Amand-Longpré
Pontijou
Mer
La Ferté-St.Cyr
Isdes
Gien
Briare
St. Fargeau
MUSÉE ADRIEN THIBAULT
Chambord
CHÂTEAU DE CHAMBORD
Cosson
Lamotte-Beuvron
Cerdon
CHÂTEAU DE GIEN
Lavau
Herbault
Blois
Vineuil
Neung-sur-Beuvron
Brinon-sur-Sauldre
Auty-le-Châtel
Châtillon-sur-Loire
Bonny-sur-Loire
Chouzy-sur-Cisse
Chailles
CHÂTEAU DE BEAUREGARD
Bracieux
Beuvron
Nouan-le-Fuzelier
Argent-sur-Sauldre
Aubigny-sur-Nère
Beaulieu
Onzain
Cour-Cheverny
CHÂTEAU DE TROUSSAY
Chaumont-sur-Loire
CHÂTEAU FOUGRES-SUR-BIEVRE
CHÂTEAU D'AMBOISE
Amboise
Mur-de-Sologne
Millançay
Souesmes
Villegenon
Vailly-sur Sauldre
Cosne-Cours-sur-Loire
Léré
Myennes
Contres
Pontlevoy
Selles-St.-Denis
Salbris
Presly
Chenonceaux
Montrichard
Chémery
Romorantin-Lanthenay
La Ferté-Imbault
Nançay
La Chapelle-d'Angillon
Sancerre
Pouilly
Noyers-sur-Cher
Selles-sur-Cher
Neuvy-sur-Barangeon
Henrichemont
St. Aignan
Villefranche-sur-Cher
Vinon
Chabris
Vierzon
Allogny
Menetou-Salon
Orbigny
Vignoux-sur-Barangeon
St. Martin-d'Auxigny
Les Aix-d'Angillon
Genillé
Montrésor
CHÂTEAU DE VALENÇAY
Valençay
Luçay-le-Mâle
Graçay
Massay
Quincy
Mehun-sur-Yèvre
Sancergues
La Charité-sur-Loire
Nouans-les-Fontaines
Écueillé
Lury-sur-Arnon
St. Germain-du-Puy
Brécy
Reuilly
Bourges
Baugy
Vatan
CATHÉDRALE DE BOURGES
Avord
Mornay-Berry
Fourchambault
Villedômain
Châtillon-sur-Indre
Levroux
Issoudun
Chârost
St. Florent-sur-Cher
Nérondes
Pellevoisin
La Guerche-sur-l'Aubois
Indre
Buzançais
Levet
Canal de Berry
Dun-sur-Auron
Blet
CHÂTEAU D'AZAY-LE-FERRON
Villedieu-sur-Indre
Mareuil-sur-Arnon
Châteauneuf-sur-Cher
Mézières-en-Brenne
Déols
Châteauroux
Sancoins
Claise
Vendœuvres
Pruniers
Bruère-Allichamps
Méobecq
Arnon
Cher
St. Amand-Montrond
Ardentes
St. Août
Lignières
Migné
Charenton-du-Cher
Bessais-le-Fromental
Couleuvre
Velles
Le Châtelet
Urçay
Cérilly
St.-Gaultier
Bouesse
Neuvy-St. Sépulchre
Meaulne
La Châtre
Saulzais-le-Potier
Bourbon-l'Archambault
Argenton-sur-Creuse
Cluis
Châteaumeillant
Culan
Ygrande
Bélâbre
Gargilesse-Dampierre
Creuse
Orsennes
Anglin
Hérisson
Ste. Sévère-sur-Indre
Cosne-d'Allier
St. Benoît-du-Sault
Aigurande
Préveranges
Villefranche-d'Allier
Éguzon-Chantôme
La Chapelaude
Tilly
Lussac-les-Églises
St. Sulpice-
Treignat
Boussac
Domérat
Montluçon
Quinssaines
Doyet
Bezenet
DE CROZANT
0 10 20 30 km

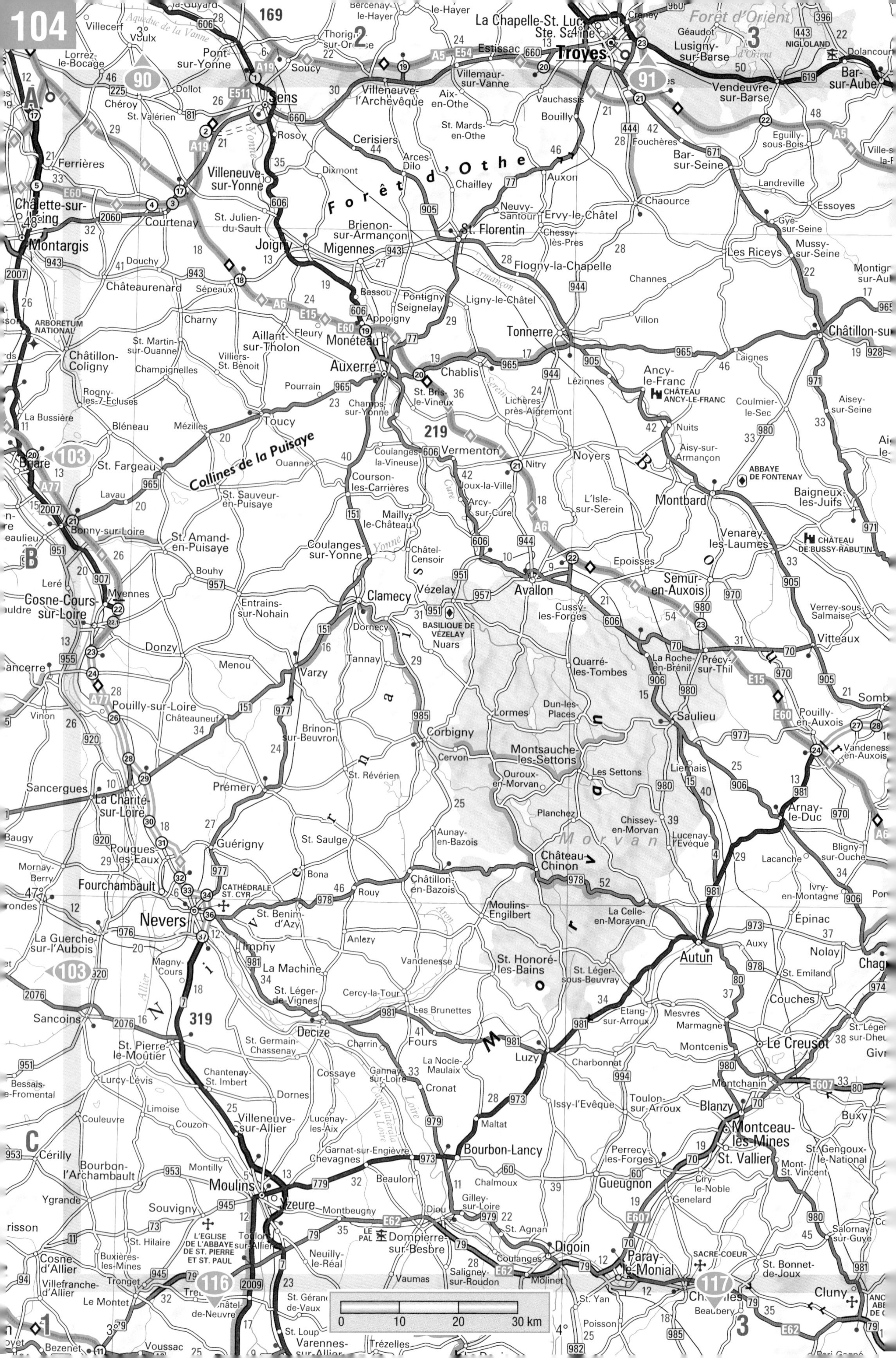
169
Bercenay-le-Hayer
La Chapelle-St. Luc
Ste. Savine
Creney
Forêt d'Orient
396
443
NIGLOLAND
Dolancourt
Villecerf
Aqueduc de la Vanne
3°
Voulx
606
Thorigny-sur-Oreuse
2
24
Estissac
660
Troyes
Géraudot
Lusigny-sur-Barse
3
22
Lorrez-le-Bocage
90
Pont-sur-Yonne
6
22
Soucy
19
A5
E54
Villemaur-sur-Vanne
20
23
91
50
619
Bar-sur-Aube
46
225
Dollot
E511
Sens
30
Villeneuve-l'Archevêque
Aix-en-Othe
Vauchassis
21
Vendeuvre-sur-Barse
Chéroy
St. Valérien
81
26
660
Bouilly
St. Mards-en-Othe
48
29
2
A19
21
Rosoy
Yonne
Cerisiers
44
444
42
Fouchères
22
Eguilly-sous-Bois
A5
21
Ferrières
35
Arces-Dilo
46
28
Bar-sur-Seine
671
Forêt d'Othe
Dixmont
Auxon
33
5
Villeneuve-sur-Yonne
Chailley
77
Landreville
E60
17
Châlette-sur-Loing
4
3
606
905
Neuvy-Sautour
Chaource
Essoyes
48
2060
Courtenay
St. Julien-du-Sault
Brienon-sur-Armançon
Ervy-le-Châtel
Gyé-sur-Seine
32
Montargis
18
Joigny
Migennes
943
St. Florentin
Chessy-lès-Pres
28
Les Riceys
Mussy-sur-Seine
943
Douchy
13
27
28
Flogny-la-Chapelle
22
2007
41
943
18
19
Bassou
Armançon
Channes
Châteaurenard
Sépeaux
A6
24
Pontigny
Seignelay
Ligny-le-Châtel
944
17
26
E15
606
Appoigny
29
Charny
E60
19
Tonnerre
Villon
ARBORETUM NATIONAL
Aillant-sur-Tholon
Fleury
Monéteau
77
Châtillon-sur-Seine
St. Martin-sur-Ouanne
Villiers-St. Benoit
Auxerre
19
17
965
905
965
Laignes
46
19
928
Châtillon-Coligny
Champignelles
20
Chablis
Serein
Lézinnes
Ancy-le-Franc
CHÂTEAU ANCY-LE-FRANC
Pourrain
965
St. Bris-le-Vineux
36
944
24
971
Rogny-les-7-Ecluses
23
Champs-sur-Yonne
Lichères-près-Aigremont
Coulmier-le-Sec
Aisey-sur-Seine
La Bussière
11
Bléneau
Mézilles
Toucy
219
42
Nuits
33
980
33
20
Aisy-sur-Armançon
20
103
Collines de la Puisaye
40
Coulanges-la-Vineuse
606
Vermenton
21
Nitry
Noyers
ABBAYE DE FONTENAY
Briare
13
St. Fargeau
Ouanne
A77
Courson-les-Carrières
42
Joux-la-Ville
Cure
Baigneux-les-Juifs
Lavau
965
St. Sauveur-en-Puisaye
Arcy-sur-Cure
18
L'Isle-sur-Serein
Montbard
15
2007
20
151
Mailly-le-Château
21
Bonny-sur-Loire
St. Amand-en-Puisaye
606
944
A6
Venarey-les-Laumes
CHÂTEAU DE BUSSY-RABUTIN
971
B
951
26
Coulanges-sur-Yonne
Yonne
Châtel-Censoir
10
22
Epoisses
33
20
Bouhy
951
9
Semur-en-Auxois
905
907
957
Vézelay
957
Avallon
Léré
Myennes
Clamecy
951
Cussy-les-Forges
21
980
970
Cosne-Cours-sur-Loire
22
Entrains-sur-Nohain
31
BASILIQUE DE VÉZELAY
54
23
Verrey-sous-Salmaise
22.1
Dornecy
606
13
151
Nuars
Quarré-les-Tombes
70
31
70
Vitteaux
955
23
Donzy
16
La Roche-en-Brénil
Précy-sous-Thil
Sancerre
Menou
Varzy
Tannay
29
906
980
970
24
E15
905
28
15
21
Sombernon
Pouilly-sur-Loire
151
977
985
Lormes
Dun-les-Places
Saulieu
E60
Pouilly-en-Auxois
Vinon
26
Châteauneuf
34
Brinon-sur-Beuvron
Corbigny
977
27
920
24
Montsauche-les-Settons
Liernais
25
Vandenesse-en-Auxois
Cervon
28
29
St. Révérien
Ouroux-en-Morvan
Les Settons
15
906
13
24
Sancergues
10
Prémery
980
40
981
La Charité-sur-Loire
25
Planchez
Arnay-le-Duc
970
30
18
27
Aunay-en-Bazois
Chissey-en-Morvan
39
Lucenay-l'Evêque
A6
Baugy
920
Guérigny
St. Saulge
Morvan
31
Pougues-les-Eaux
Château-Chinon
4
29
Lacanche
Bligny-sur-Ouche
Mornay-Berry
977
Bona
29
32
Châtillon-en-Bazois
978
52
34
47°
Fourchambault
6
33
CATHÉDRALE ST. CYR
46
Rouy
Ivry-en-Montagne
Pon
12
34
978
981
906
Nevers
36
St. Benin-d'Azy
Aron
Moulins-Engilbert
La Celle-en-Moravan
973
Epinac
La Guerche-sur-l'Aubois
976
37
12
Anlezy
Autun
37
Nolay
20
Imphy
Magny-Cours
981
La Machine
Vandenesse
St. Honoré-les-Bains
St. Léger-sous-Beuvray
978
St. Emiland
Chagny
103
920
34
Allier
18
St. Léger-de-Vignes
80
974
2076
Cercy-la-Tour
37
Couches
34
Etang-sur-Arroux
Mesvres
Marmagne
St. Léger-sur-Dheune
Sancoins
2076
16
319
981
Les Brunettes
Decize
41
981
981
Le Creusot
38
St. Pierre-le-Moûtier
St. Germain-Chassenay
Charrin
Fours
Luzy
Montcenis
Givry
951
Chantenay-St. Imbert
Gannay-sur-Loire
La Nocle-Maulaix
33
Charbonnat
994
980
Bessais-le-Fromental
Lurcy-Lévis
Cossaye
Cronat
Montchanin
E607
33
80
Dornes
28
973
Issy-l'Evêque
Toulon-sur-Arroux
Blanzy
70
25
Limoise
Canal latéral à la Loire
Loire
Couleuvre
Villeneuve-sur-Allier
Couzon
Lucenay-les-Aix
979
Maltat
Buxy
C
Montceau-les-Mines
953
Cérilly
Garnat-sur-Engièvre
Chevagnes
973
Bourbon-Lancy
Perrecy-les-Forges
19
70
St. Vallier
St. Gengoux-le-National
Bourbon-l'Archambault
Montilly
953
13
60
Mont-St. Vincent
779
32
Beaulon
11
Chalmoux
39
Gueugnon
Ciry-le-Noble
Ygrande
Moulins
Yzeure
Gilley-sur-Loire
19
Genelard
Souvigny
945
12
Montbeugny
E62
Diou
979
22
980
Salornay-sur-Guye
E607
Bourbon-l'Archambault
73
L'EGLISE DE L'ABBAYE DE ST. PIERRE ET ST. PAUL
Toulon-sur-Allier
79
35
LE PAL
Dompierre-sur-Besbre
St. Agnan
45
11
St. Hilaire
79
Digoin
70
SACRÉ-COEUR
Cosne-d'Allier
Buxières-les-Mines
7
Neuilly-le-Réal
28
Coulanges
12
Paray-le-Monial
St. Bonnet-de-Joux
981
945
Tronget
79
Vaumas
Saligney-sur-Roudon
E62
Molinet
79
12
94
116
2009
23
117
Villefranche-d'Allier
Le Montet
32
Tréteau
Châtel-de-Neuvre
St. Gérand-de-Vaux
0
10
20
30 km
St. Yan
Charolles
Beaubery
79
35
Cluny
1
3
79
17
St. Loup
Varennes-sur-Allier
Trézelles
4°
Poisson
25
982
18
985
3
E62
79
Bezenet
11
Voussac
25

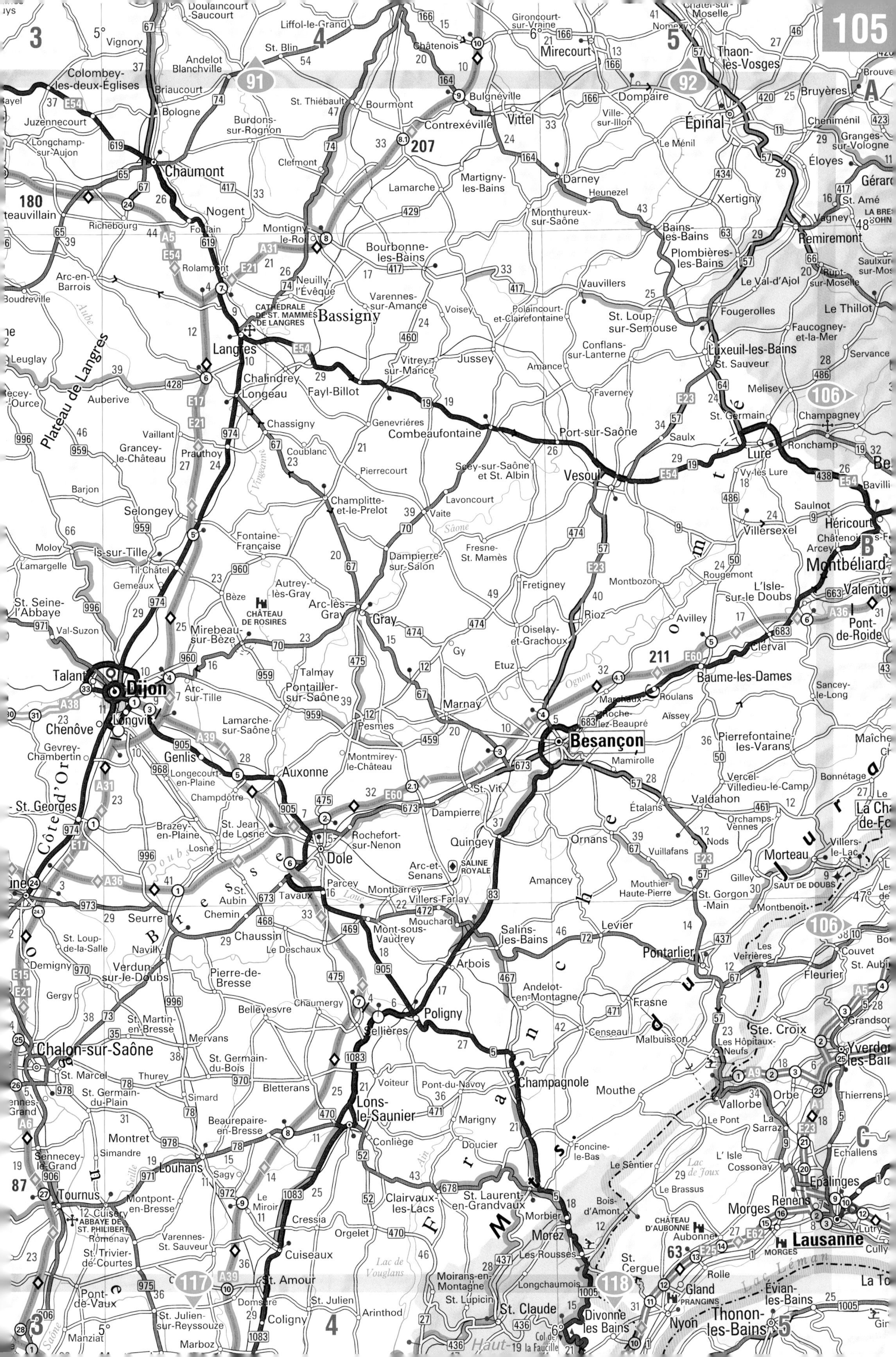
Doulaincourt
Saucourt
Liffol-le-Grand
Vignory
St. Blin
Andelot
Blanchville
Colombey-les-deux-Églises
Briaucourt
Bologne
Juzennecourt
Longchamp-sur-Aujon
Chaumont
Burdons-sur-Rognon
St. Thiébault
Bourmont
Clefmont
Nogent
Richebourg
Foulain
Rolampont
Arc-en-Barrois
Boudreville
Montigny-le-Roi
Neuilly-l'Évêque
CATHÉDRALE DE ST. MAMMÈS DE LANGRES
Bassigny
Langres
Plateau de Langres
Leuglay
Chalindrey
Longeau
Auberive
Recey-s-Ource
Vaillant
Grancey-le-Château
Prauthoy
Chassigny
Barjon
Selongey
Moloy
Is-sur-Tille
Lamargelle
Til-Châtel
Gemeaux
St. Seine-l'Abbaye
Val-Suzon
Mirebeau-sur-Bèze
Bèze
CHÂTEAU DE ROSIRES
Fontaine-Française
Talant
Dijon
Arc-sur-Tille
Chenôve
Longvic
Gevrey-Chambertin
Genlis
Longecourt-en-Plaine
Champdôtre
Auxonne
St. Georges
Côte d'Or
Brazey-en-Plaine
St. Jean de Losne
Losne
Doubs
Seurre
St. Aubin
Chemin
Chaussin
St. Loup-de-la-Salle
Navilly
Demigny
Verdun-sur-le-Doubs
Gergy
Pierre-de-Bresse
St. Martin-en-Bresse
Mervans
Bellevesvre
Chalon-sur-Saône
St. Marcel
St. Germain-du-Plain
St. Germain-du-Bois
Thurey
Simard
Montret
Simandre
Beaurepaire-en-Bresse
Sennecey-le-Grand
Louhans
Sagy
Tournus
Cuisery
ABBAYE DE ST. PHILIBERT
Montpont-en-Bresse
Romenay
Varennes-St. Sauveur
St. Trivier-de-Courtes
Pont-de-Vaux
St. Julien-sur-Reyssouze
Manziat
Marboz
Domsure
Coligny
St. Amour
Cuiseaux
Le Miroir
Cressia
Orgelet
Lac de Vouglans
Arinthod
St. Julien
Bresse
Mirecourt
Gironcourt-sur-Vraine
Châtenois
Bulgnéville
Contrexéville
Vittel
Lamarche
Martigny-les-Bains
Darney
Bourbonne-les-Bains
Varennes-sur-Amance
Voisey
Fayl-Billot
Vitrey-sur-Mance
Jussey
Genevriéres
Combeaufontaine
Coublanc
Pierrecourt
Champlitte-et-le-Prelot
Autrey-lès-Gray
Arc-lès-Gray
Gray
Dampierre-sur-Salon
Fresne-St. Mamès
Saône
Vaite
Lavoncourt
Scey-sur-Saône et St. Albin
Talmay
Pontailler-sur-Saône
Lamarche-sur-Saône
Pesmes
Montmirey-le-Château
Marnay
Gy
Etuz
Dole
Rochefort-sur-Nenon
Parcey
Tavaux
Montbarrey
Loue
Mont-sous-Vaudrey
Le Deschaux
Chaumergy
Sellières
Poligny
Arbois
Villers-Farlay
Mouchard
Arc-et-Senans
SALINE ROYALE
Quingey
Dampierre
St. Vit
Voiteur
Pont-du-Navoy
Lons-le-Saunier
Conliège
Marigny
Doucier
Clairvaux-les-Lacs
Ain
St. Laurent-en-Grandvaux
Morbier
Morez
Les Rousses
Moirans-en-Montagne
St. Lupicin
St. Claude
Longchaumois
Col de la Faucille
Haut-Jura
Epinal
Thaon-les-Vosges
Nomexy
Châtel-sur-Moselle
Dompaire
Ville-sur-Illon
Le Ménil
Heunezel
Monthureux-sur-Saône
Xertigny
Bains-les-Bains
Plombières-les-Bains
Vauvillers
Polaincourt-et-Clairefontaine
St. Loup-sur-Semouse
Conflans-sur-Lanterne
Amance
Faverney
Port-sur-Saône
Vesoul
Luxeuil-les-Bains
St. Sauveur
Fougerolles
Le Val-d'Ajol
Remiremont
Vagney
St. Amé
Bruyères
Cheniménil
Granges-sur-Vologne
Éloyes
Rupt-sur-Moselle
Saulxures-sur-Moselotte
Le Thillot
Faucogney-et-la-Mer
Servance
Melisey
Champagney
Ronchamp
St. Germain
Saulx
Lure
Vy-lès Lure
Saulnot
Villersexel
Héricourt
Montbéliard
Arcey
Rougemont
Montbozon
L'Isle-sur-le-Doubs
Valentigney
Pont-de-Roide
Avilley
Clerval
Baume-les-Dames
Roulans
Marchaux
Roche-lez-Beaupré
Aïssey
Besançon
Mamirolle
Fretigney
Rioz
Oiselay-et-Grachoux
Ognon
Pierrefontaine-les-Varans
Vercel-Villedieu-le-Camp
Valdahon
Étalans
Orchamps-Vennes
Nods
Ornans
Vuillafans
Mouthier-Haute-Pierre
Amancey
Levier
Salins-les-Bains
Andelot-en-Montagne
Champagnole
Censeau
Frasne
Malbuisson
Pontarlier
Les Verrières
St. Gorgon-Main
Montbenoit
Gilley
Morteau
Villers-le-Lac
SAUT DE DOUBS
Sancey-le-Long
Maîche
Bonnétage
Mouthe
Foncine-le-Bas
Le Sentier
Lac de Joux
Le Brassus
Bois-d'Amont
L'Isle
Cossonay
Vallorbe
Le Pont
La Sarraz
Orbe
Ste. Croix
Les Hôpitaux-Neufs
Yverdon-les-Bains
Grandson
Fleurier
Couvet
Thierrens
Echallens
Epalinges
Renens
Morges
Lausanne
Lutry
Cully
CHÂTEAU D'AUBONNE
Aubonne
St. Cergue
Rolle
Gland
PRANGINS
Nyon
Divonne les Bains
Thonon-les-Bains
Évian-les-Bains
Lac Léman
Franche-Comté
Monts du Jura
Jura
MORGES
91
92
105
106
117
118
207
211

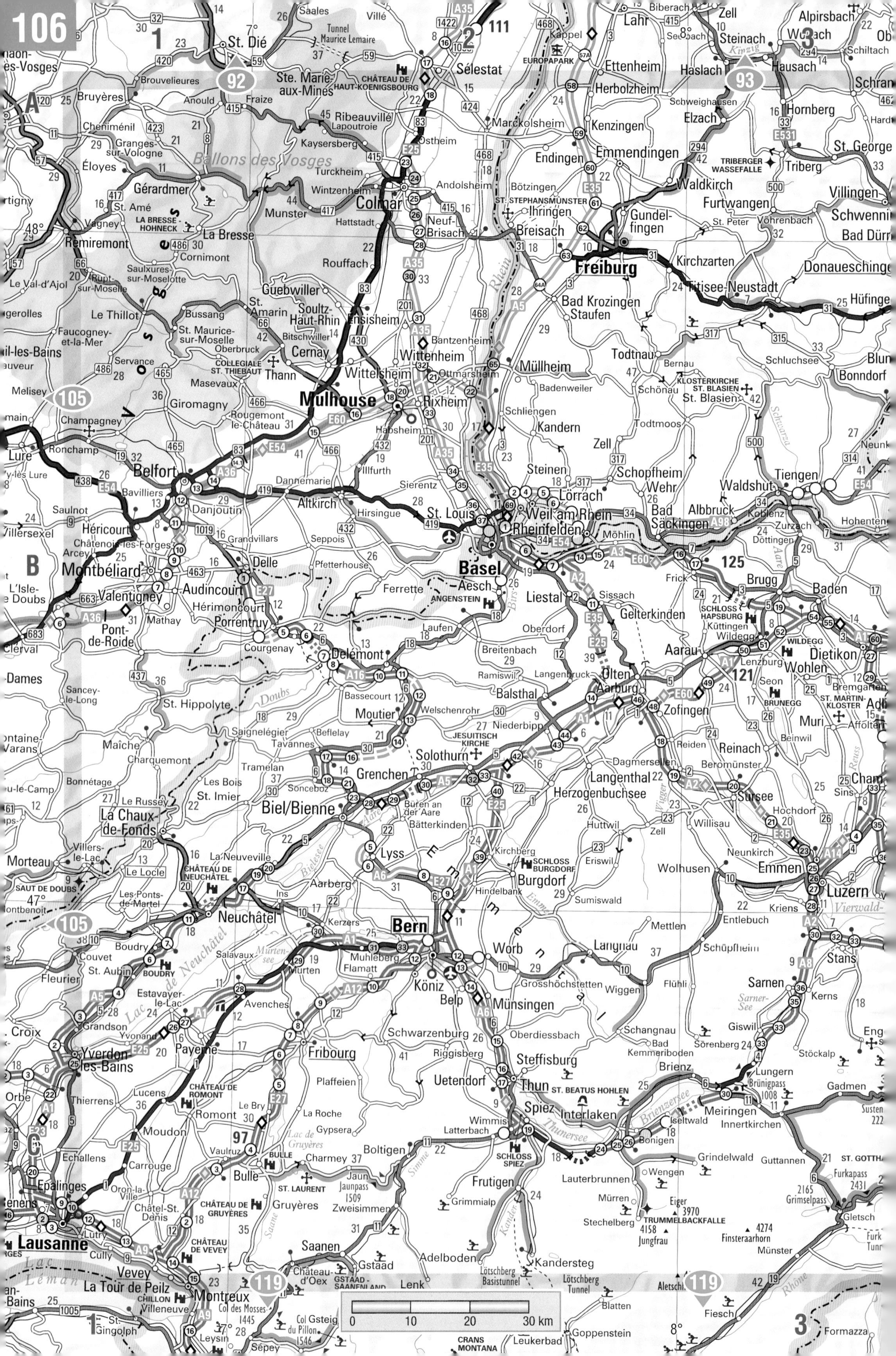
St. Dié
Saales
Villé
Tunnel Maurice Lemaire
Sélestat
Lahr
Biberach
Zell
Alpirsbach
Kappel
EUROPAPARK
Ettenheim
Haslach
Hausach
Steinach
Schiltach
Brouvelieures
Ste. Marie-aux-Mines
CHÂTEAU DE HAUT-KOENIGSBOURG
Herbolzheim
Bruyères
Fraize
Ribeauvillé
Lapoutroie
Marckolsheim
Kenzingen
Elzach
Hornberg
Cheniménil
Kaysersberg
Ostheim
Endingen
Emmendingen
TRIBERGER WASSERFALLE
Triberg
St. Georgen
Granges-sur-Vologne
Ballons des Vosges
Turckheim
Waldkirch
Éloyes
Gérardmer
Wintzenheim
Colmar
Andolsheim
Bötzingen
ST. STEPHANSMÜNSTER
Ihringen
Gundelfingen
Furtwangen
Villingen
St. Amé
Vagney
LA BRESSE-HOHNECK
Munster
Hattstadt
Neuf-Brisach
Breisach
St. Peter
Vöhrenbach
Schwenningen
Remiremont
La Bresse
Cornimont
Rouffach
Freiburg
Kirchzarten
Bad Dürrheim
Donaueschingen
Saulxures-sur-Moselotte
Le Val-d'Ajol
Rupt-sur-Moselle
Guebwiller
Titisee-Neustadt
Hüfingen
Le Thillot
Bussang
St. Amarin
Soultz-Haut-Rhin
Ensisheim
Bad Krozingen
Staufen
Faucogney-et-la-Mer
St. Maurice-sur-Moselle
Oberbruck
Bitschwiller
Cernay
Bantzenheim
Rhein
Todtnau
Bernau
Schluchsee
Bonndorf
Servance
COLLEGIALE ST. THIEBAUT
Thann
Wittenheim
Müllheim
KLOSTERKIRCHE ST. BLASIEN
Schönau
St. Blasien
Melisey
Masevaux
Wittelsheim
Ottmarsheim
Badenweiler
Giromagny
Mulhouse
Rixheim
Schliengen
Champagney
Rougemont-le-Château
Habsheim
Kandern
Todtmoos
Lure
Ronchamp
Zell
Belfort
Illfurth
Steinen
Schopfheim
Tiengen
Bavilliers
Dannemarie
Sierentz
Lörrach
Wehr
Waldshut
Danjoutin
Altkirch
St. Louis
Weil am Rhein
Bad Säckingen
Albbruck
Koblenz
Hohentengen
Saulnot
Héricourt
Hirsingue
Rheinfelden
Möhlin
Zurzach
Villersexel
Châtenois-les-Forges
Grandvillars
Seppois
Döttingen
Arcey
Delle
Pfetterhouse
Basel
Frick
Brugg
Montbéliard
Audincourt
Ferrette
Aesch
Liestal
Sissach
Baden
L'Isle-sur-le-Doubs
Valentigney
Hérimoncourt
ANGENSTEIN
Gelterkinden
SCHLOSS HAPSBURG
Küttingen
Wildegg
Mathay
Pont-de-Roide
Porrentruy
Laufen
Oberdorf
Aarau
WILDEGG
Dietikon
Clerval
Courgenay
Delémont
Breitenbach
Lenzburg
Wohlen
Dames
Ramiswil
Langenbruck
Olten
Aarburg
Seon
BRUNEGG
Bremgarten
Sancey-le-Long
St. Hippolyte
Doubs
Bassecourt
Balsthal
Zofingen
ST. MARTIN-KLOSTER
Muri
Affoltern
Moutier
Welschenrohr
Niederbipp
Beinwil
Maîche
Saignelégier
Beflelay
Tavannes
JESUITISCH KIRCHE
Solothurn
Reiden
Reinach
Charquemont
Tramelan
Dagmersellen
Beromünster
Bonnétage
Les Bois
St. Imier
Sonceboz
Grenchen
Langenthal
Herzogenbuchsee
Wigger
Sursee
Sins
Le Russey
La Chaux-de-Fonds
Biel/Bienne
Büren an der Aare
Bätterkinden
Huttwil
Zell
Willisau
Hochdorf
Villers-le-Lac
Le Locle
Morteau
La Neuveville
Lyss
Kirchberg
SCHLOSS BURGDORF
Eriswil
Neunkirch
Emmen
Wolhusen
SAUT DE DOUBS
CHÂTEAU DE NEUCHÂTEL
Les Ponts-de-Martel
Ins
Aarberg
Burgdorf
Hindelbank
Sumiswald
Luzern
Kriens
Vierwald-
Neuchâtel
Kerzers
Bern
Entlebuch
Mettlen
Boudry
Couvet
St. Aubin
BOUDRY
Salavaux
Murtensee
Murten
Muhleberg
Flamatt
Köniz
Worb
Langnau
Schüpfheim
Stans
Fleurier
Estavayer-le-Lac
Avenches
Belp
Grosshöchstetten
Wiggen
Flühli
Sarnen
Kerns
Sarner-See
Grandson
Yvonand
Payerne
Schwarzenburg
Münsingen
Oberdiessbach
Schangnau
Giswil
Croix
Yverdon-les-Bains
Fribourg
Riggisberg
Steffisburg
Kemmeriboden Bad
Sörenberg
Stöckalp
Engelberg
Orbe
Thierrens
Lucens
CHÂTEAU DE ROMONT
Plaffeien
Uetendorf
Thun
ST. BEATUS HOHLEN
Brienz
Lungern
Brünigpass
Gadmen
Romont
Le Bry
La Roche
Wimmis
Spiez
Interlaken
Brienzersee
Meiringen
Innertkirchen
Susten
Moudon
Lac de Gruyères
Gypsera
Latterbach
Thunersee
Iseltwald
Bönigen
Echallens
Carrouge
Vaulruz
BULLE
Charmey
Boltigen
Simme
SCHLOSS SPIEZ
Grindelwald
Guttannen
ST. GOTTHARD
Epalinges
Bulle
Jaun
Jaunpass
Oron-la-Ville
ST. LAURENT
Frutigen
Lauterbrunnen
Wengen
Furkapass
Grimselpass
Renens
Châtel-St.-Denis
CHÂTEAU DE GRUYÈRES
Gruyères
Zweisimmen
Grimmialp
Mürren
Eiger
TRUMMELBACKFALLE
Gletsch
Lausanne
Lutry
CHÂTEAU DE VEVEY
Saanen
Kander
Stechelberg
Jungfrau
Finsteraarhorn
Münster
Cully
Gstaad
Adelboden
Kandersteg
Lac Léman
Vevey
Château-d'Oex
GSTAAD-SAANENLAND
Lötschberg Basistunnel
Lötschberg Tunnel
La Tour de Peilz
Lenk
Aletsch
Rhône
Evian-les-Bains
CHILLON
Montreux
Villeneuve
Col des Mosses
Blatten
Fiesch
St-Gingolph
Col Gsteig du Pillon
Leysin
Sépey
CRANS MONTANA
Leukerbad
Goppenstein
Formazza
0 10 20 30 km

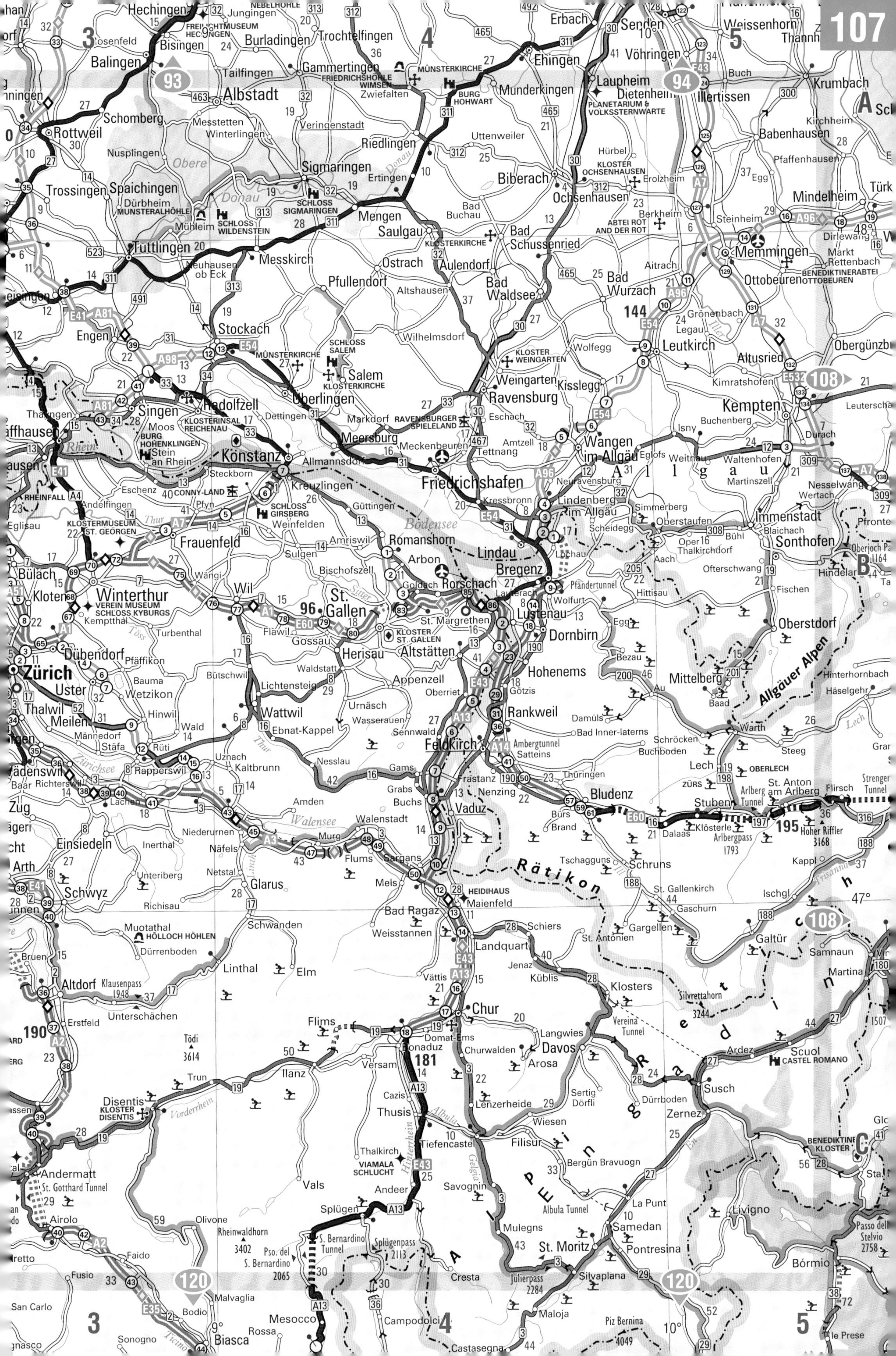

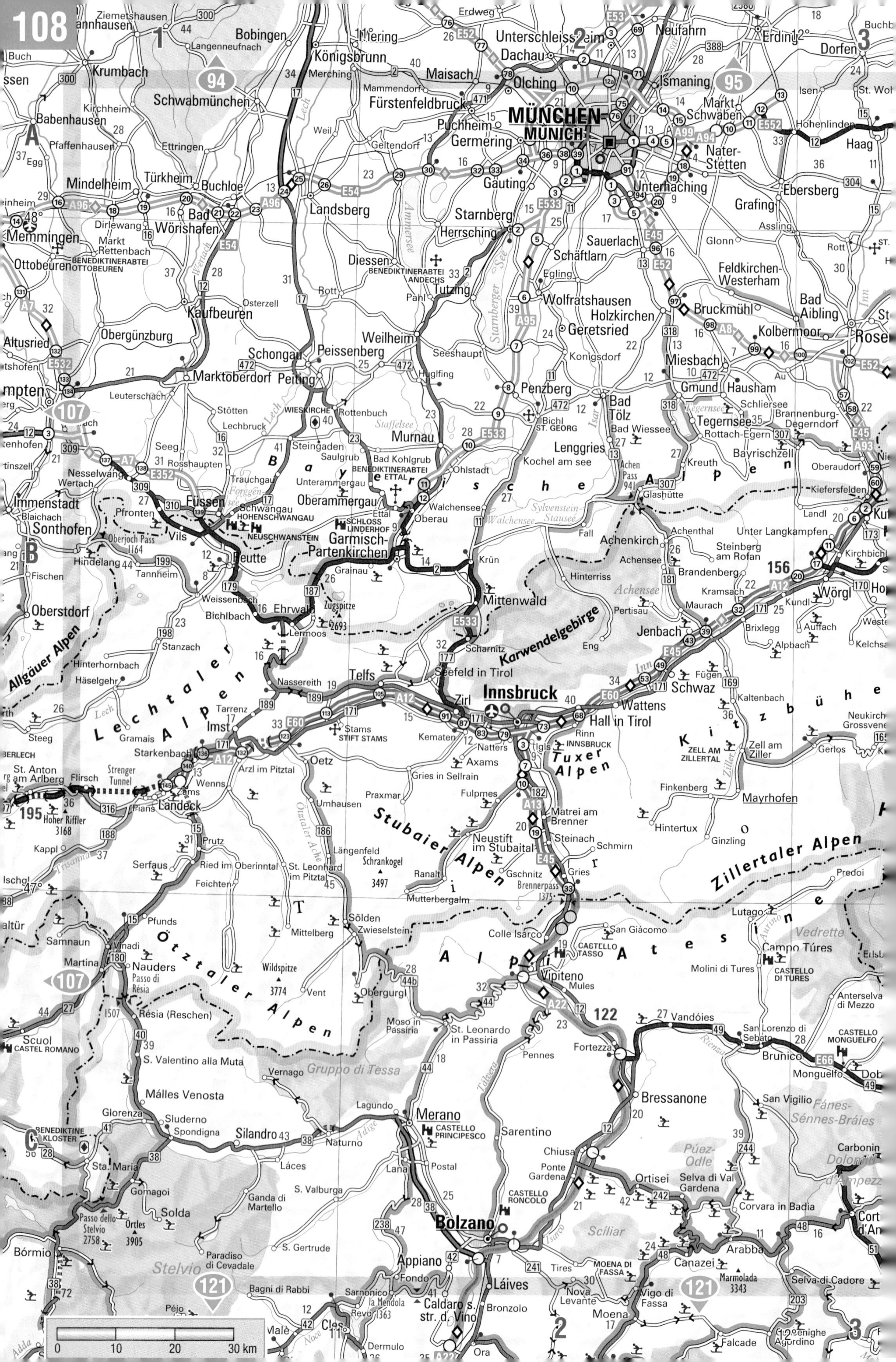
Ziemetshausen
Bobingen
Mering
Königsbrunn
Merching
Erdweg
Unterschleissheim
Neufahrn
Erding
Dorfen
Krumbach
Dachau
Maisach
Olching
Ismaning
Schwabmünchen
Mammendorf
Fürstenfeldbruck
MÜNCHEN-MUNICH
Markt Schwaben
Hohenlinden
Haag
Babenhausen
Kirchheim
Pfaffenhausen
Ettringen
Weil
Geltendorf
Puchheim
Germering
Nater-Stetten
Mindelheim
Türkheim
Buchloe
Landsberg
Gauting
Unterhaching
Ebersberg
Grafing
Bad Wörishofen
Dirlewang
Memmingen
Markt Rettenbach
Starnberg
Herrsching
Sauerlach
Assling
Glonn
Ottobeuren
BENEDIKTINERABTEI OTTOBEUREN
Diessen
BENEDIKTINERABTEI ANDECHS
Tutzing
Schäftlarn
Egling
Rott
Feldkirchen-Westerham
Kaufbeuren
Osterzell
Pähl
Wolfratshausen
Holzkirchen
Bruckmühl
Bad Aibling
Obergünzburg
Weilheim
Geretsried
Kolbermoor
Altusried
Schongau
Peissenberg
Seeshaupt
Königsdorf
Miesbach
Marktoberdorf
Peiting
Hugfling
Penzberg
Gmund
Hausham
Kempten
Leuterschach
Stötten
WIESKIRCHE
Rottenbuch
Staffelsee
Bad Tölz
Schliersee
Lechbruck
Murnau
Bichl
ST. GEORG
Tegernsee
Bad Wiessee
Brannenburg-Degerndorf
Seeg
Steingaden
Saulgrub
Bad Kohlgrub
Lenggries
Rottach-Egern
Bayrischzell
Rosshaupten
BENEDIKTINERABTEI ETTAL
Ohlstadt
Kochel am see
Kreuth
Oberaudorf
Nesselwang
Wertach
Trauchgau
Unterammergau
Achen Pass
Glashütte
Kiefersfelden
Immenstadt
Blaichach
Pfronten
Füssen
Schwangau
HOHENSCHWANGAU
Oberammergau
Walchensee
Sylvenstein-Stausee
Landl
Sonthofen
Vils
NEUSCHWANSTEIN
SCHLOSS LINDERHOF
Ettal
Oberau
Fall
Achenkirch
Achenthal
Unter Langkampfen
Oberjoch Pass
Garmisch-Partenkirchen
Steinberg am Rofan
Kirchbichl
Hindelang
Tannheim
Reutte
Grainau
Krün
Achensee
Hinterriss
Brandenberg
Fischen
Weissenbach
Ehrwald
Zugspitze
Mittenwald
Kramsach
Wörgl
Oberstdorf
Bichlbach
Lermoos
Karwendelgebirge
Pertisau
Maurach
Kundl
Allgäuer Alpen
Stanzach
Scharnitz
Jenbach
Brixlegg
Auffach
Hinterhornbach
Eng
Alpbach
Häselgehr
Seefeld in Tirol
Telfs
Nassereith
Fügen
Schwaz
Zirl
Innsbruck
Wattens
Hall in Tirol
Kaltenbach
Steeg
Lechtaler Alpen
Tarrenz
Imst
Stams
STIFT STAMS
Kematen
Natters
Rinn
INNSBRUCK
Igls
ZELL AM ZILLERTAL
Zell am Ziller
Gerlos
Gramais
Starkenbach
Arzl im Pitztal
Oetz
Axams
Tuxer Alpen
St. Anton am Arlberg
Flirsch
Strenger Tunnel
Wenns
Zams
Landeck
Pians
Gries in Sellrain
Praxmar
Fulpmes
Finkenberg
Mayrhofen
Hoher Riffler
Umhausen
Matrei am Brenner
Stubaier Alpen
Hintertux
Kappl
Prutz
Längenfeld
Schrankogel
Neustift im Stubaital
Steinach
Schmirn
Ginzling
Zillertaler Alpen
Ischgl
Serfaus
Ried im Oberinntal
St. Leonhard im Pitztal
Ranalt
Gschnitz
Brennerpass
Gries
Predoi
Feichten
Mutterbergalm
Galtür
Pfunds
Sölden
Zwieselstein
Mittelberg
Lutago
Colle Isarco
San Giácomo
Vedrette
Samnaun
Vinadi
Martina
Nauders
Passo di Résia
Ötztaler Alpen
Wildspitze
Vent
Obergurgl
CASTELLO TASSO
Vipiteno
Mules
Alpi Atesine
Campo Túres
CASTELLO DI TURES
Molini di Tures
Anterselva di Mezzo
Résia (Reschen)
Moso in Passíria
St. Leonardo in Passiria
Vandóies
San Lorenzo di Sebato
CASTELLO MONGUELFO
Scuol
CASTEL ROMANO
S. Valentino alla Muta
Pennes
Fortezza
Brunico
Monguelfo
Vernago
Gruppo di Tessa
Málles Venosta
Bressanone
San Vigilio
Fánes-Sénnes-Bráies
Glorenza
BENEDIKTINE KLOSTER
Sluderno
Spondigna
Silandro
Naturno
Lagundo
Merano
CASTELLO PRINCIPESCO
Sarentino
Carbonin
Sta. Maria
Láces
Lana
Postal
Chiusa
Púez-Odle
Ponte Gardena
Ortisei
Selva di Val Gardena
Gomagoi
Solda
Ganda di Martello
S. Valburga
CASTELLO RONCOLO
Corvara in Badia
Passo dello Stelvio
Ortles
Bolzano
Sciliar
Cortina d'Ampezzo
Bórmio
Paradiso di Cevadale
S. Gertrude
Appiano
Arabba
Canazei
Tires
Stelvio
Fondo
MOENA DI FASSA
Marmolada
Selva di Cadore
Bagni di Rabbi
Sarnonico
la Mendola
Caldaro s. str. d. Vino
Láives
Nova Levante
Vigo di Fassa
Péjo
Revò
Bronzolo
Moena
Malè
Cles
Dermulo
Ora
Falcade
Agordino
0 10 20 30 km

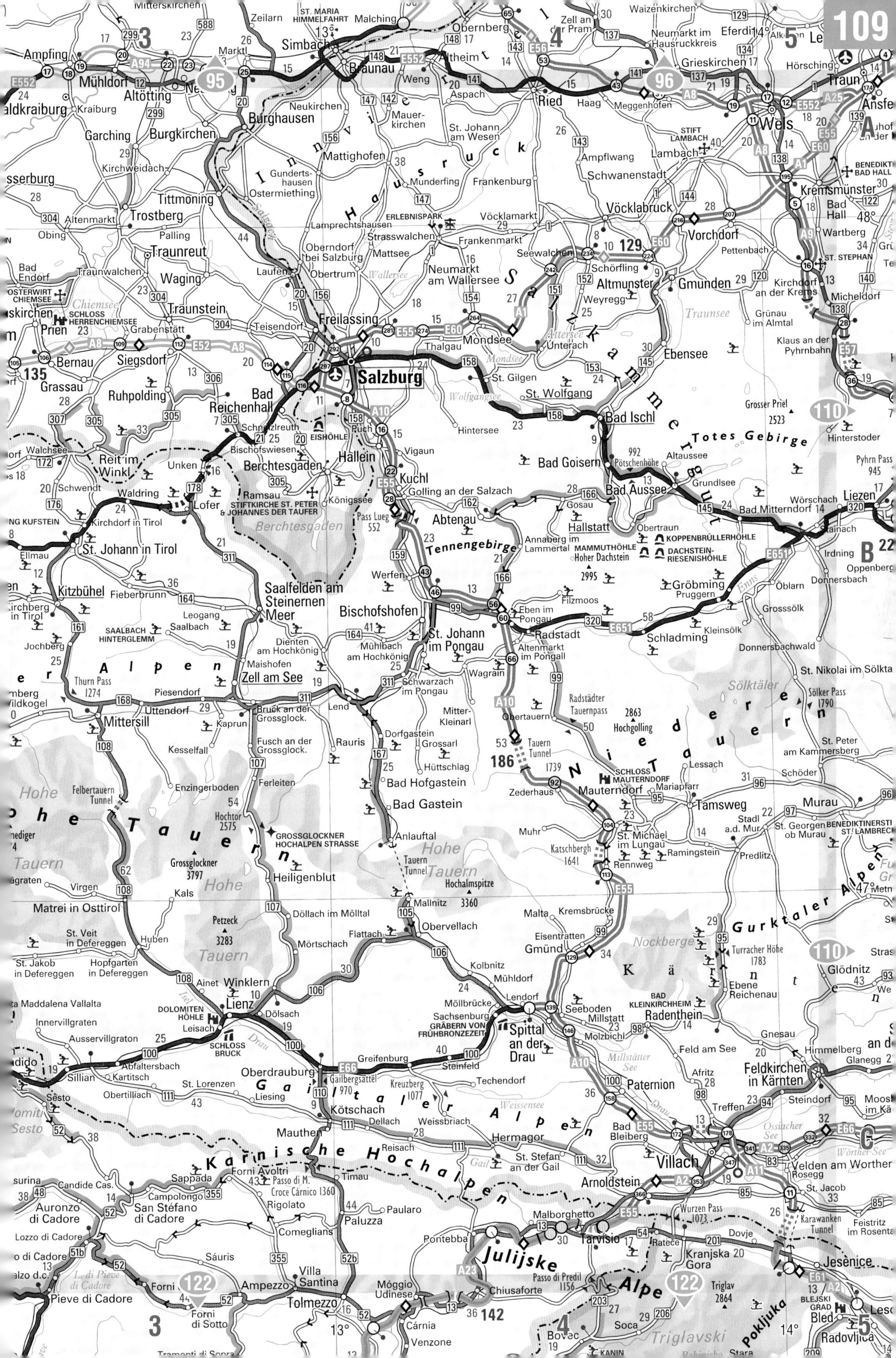
Zeilarn
St. Maria Himmelfahrt
Malching
Obernberg
Zell an der Pram
Waizenkirchen
Neumarkt im Hausruckkreis
Eferding
Ampfing
Mühldorf
Altötting
Marktl
Simbach
Braunau
Altheim
Weng
Aspach
Ried
Haag
Meggenhofen
Grieskirchen
Hörsching
Traun
Ansfelden
Wels
Kraiburg
Neukirchen
Burghausen
Mauerkirchen
St. Johann am Wesen
Stift Lambach
Lambach
Garching
Burgkirchen
Mattighofen
Ampflwang
Schwanenstadt
Kremsmünster
Benedikt. Bad Hall
Bad Hall
Kirchweidach
Gundertshausen
Ostermiething
Munderfing
Frankenburg
Wasserburg
Tittmoning
Innviertel
Hausruck
Altenmarkt
Trostberg
Lamprechtshausen
Erlebnispark
Vöcklamarkt
Vöcklabruck
Vorchdorf
Wartberg
Obing
Palling
Strasswalchen
Frankenmarkt
Pettenbach
St. Stephan
Traunreut
Oberndorf bei Salzburg
Mattsee
Seewalchen
Schörfling
Bad Endorf
Traunwalchen
Laufen
Obertrum
Wallersee
Neumarkt am Wallersee
Altmunster
Gmunden
Kirchdorf an der Krems
Micheldorf
Waging
Weyregg
Osterwirt Chiemsee
Chiemsee
Schloss Herrenchiemsee
Traunstein
Traunsee
Grünau im Almtal
Prien
Grabenstätt
Teisendorf
Freilassing
Salzkammergut
Klaus an der Pyhrnbahn
Bernau
Siegsdorf
Thalgau
Mondsee
Attersee
Unterach
Ebensee
Grassau
Ruhpolding
Bad Reichenhall
Salzburg
St. Gilgen
St. Wolfgang
Wolfgangsee
Grosser Priel
Hintersee
Bad Ischl
Hinterstoder
Schneizlreuth
Eishöhle
Puch
Totes Gebirge
Walchsee
Reit im Winkl
Unken
Bischofswiesen
Hallein
Vigaun
Bad Goisern
Pötschenhöhe
Altaussee
Pyhrn Pass
Berchtesgaden
Kuchl
Grundlsee
Schwendt
Ramsau
Stiftkirche St. Peter & Johannes der Taufer
Königssee
Golling an der Salzach
Gosau
Bad Aussee
Wörschach
Liezen
Waldring
Lofer
Kufstein
Kirchdorf in Tirol
Pass Lueg
Abtenau
Hallstatt
Obertraun
Koppenbrüllerhöhle
Bad Mitterndorf
Stainach
St. Johann in Tirol
Tennengebirge
Annaberg im Lammertal
Mammuthöhle
Hoher Dachstein
Dachstein-Riesenhöhle
Irdning
Ellmau
Oppenberg
Werfen
Gröbming
Pruggern
Öblarn
Donnersbach
Kitzbühel
Fieberbrunn
Saalfelden am Steinernen Meer
Filzmoos
Kirchberg in Tirol
Leogang
Bischofshofen
Eben im Pongau
Grosssölk
Saalbach Hinterglemm
Saalbach
Dienten am Hochkönig
Mühlbach am Hochkönig
St. Johann im Pongau
Radstadt
Schladming
Kleinsölk
Jochberg
Maishofen
Altenmarkt im Pongau
Donnersbachwald
Kitzbüheler Alpen
Zell am See
Wagrain
St. Nikolai im Sölktal
Thurn Pass
Sölktäler
Sölker Pass
Piesendorf
Schwarzach im Pongau
Radstädter Tauernpass
Mittersill
Uttendorf
Bruck an der Grossglock.
Lend
Mitter-Kleinarl
Obertauern
Hochgolling
Kaprun
Dorfgastein
St. Peter am Kammersberg
Kesselfall
Fusch an der Grossglock.
Rauris
Grossarl
Tauern Tunnel
Niedere Tauern
Schöder
Hüttschlag
Schloss Mauterndorf
Lessach
Ferleiten
Bad Hofgastein
Mariapfarr
Zederhaus
Mauterndorf
Tamsweg
Murau
Enzingerboden
Felbertauern Tunnel
Bad Gastein
Stadl a.d. Mur
St. Georgen ob Murau
Hochtor
Grossglockner Hochalpen Strasse
Muhr
St. Michael im Lungau
Benediktinerstift St. Lambrecht
Hohe Tauern
Anlauftal
Katschbergh
Ramingstein
Grossglockner
Heiligenblut
Rennweg
Predlitz
Tauern Tunnel
Hochalmspitze
Virgen
Kals
Gurktaler Alpen
Matrei in Osttirol
Mallnitz
Malta
Kremsbrücke
Petzeck
Döllach im Mölltal
St. Veit in Defereggen
Huben
Flattach
Obervellach
Eisentratten
Nockberge
Turracher Höhe
Mörtschach
Gmünd
St. Jakob in Defereggen
Hopfgarten in Defereggen
Kolbnitz
Glödnitz
Mühldorf
Ebene Reichenau
Kärnten
Ainet
Winklern
Lendorf
Santa Maddalena Vallalta
Dolomiten Höhle
Lienz
Dölsach
Möllbrücke
Seeboden
Bad Kleinkirchheim
Leisach
Sachsenburg
Gräbern von Frühbronzezeit
Millstatt
Radenthein
Innervillgraten
Ausservillgraton
Schloss Bruck
Spittal an der Drau
Molzbichl
Gnesau
Himmelberg
Drau
Abfaltersbach
Greifenburg
Feld am See
Glanegg
Sillian
Kartitsch
Oberdrauburg
Steinfeld
Millstätter See
Afritz
Feldkirchen in Kärnten
St. Lorenzen
Gailbergsattel
Kreuzberg
Techendorf
Paternion
Obertilliach
Liesing
Gailtaler Alpen
Treffen
Steindorf
Moosburg im Kärnten
Sesto
Kötschach
Dellach
Weissbriach
Weissensee
Bad Bleiberg
Ossiacher See
Mauthen
Hermagor
Wörther See
Reisach
St. Stefan an der Gail
Villach
Velden am Worther See
Karnische Hochalpen
Sappada
Forni Avoltri
Passo di M. Croce Cárnico
Timau
Arnoldstein
Rosegg
Candide Cas.
Campolongo
St. Jacob
Auronzo di Cadore
San Stéfano di Cadore
Rigolato
Paularo
Malborghetto
Wurzen Pass
Karawanken Tunnel
Feistritz im Rosental
Lozzo di Cadore
Comeglians
Paluzza
Pontebba
Tarvisio
Ratece
Dovje
Sáuris
Kranjska Gora
Jesenice
Julijske Alpe
Villa Santina
Passo di Predil
Triglav
Forni
Ampezzo
Moggio Udinese
Chiusaforte
Pieve di Cadore
Forni di Sotto
Tolmezzo
Blejski Grad
Bled
Pokljuka
Cárnia
Soca
Bovec
Triglavski
Stara
Radovljica
Venzone
Kanin
Tramonti di Sopra

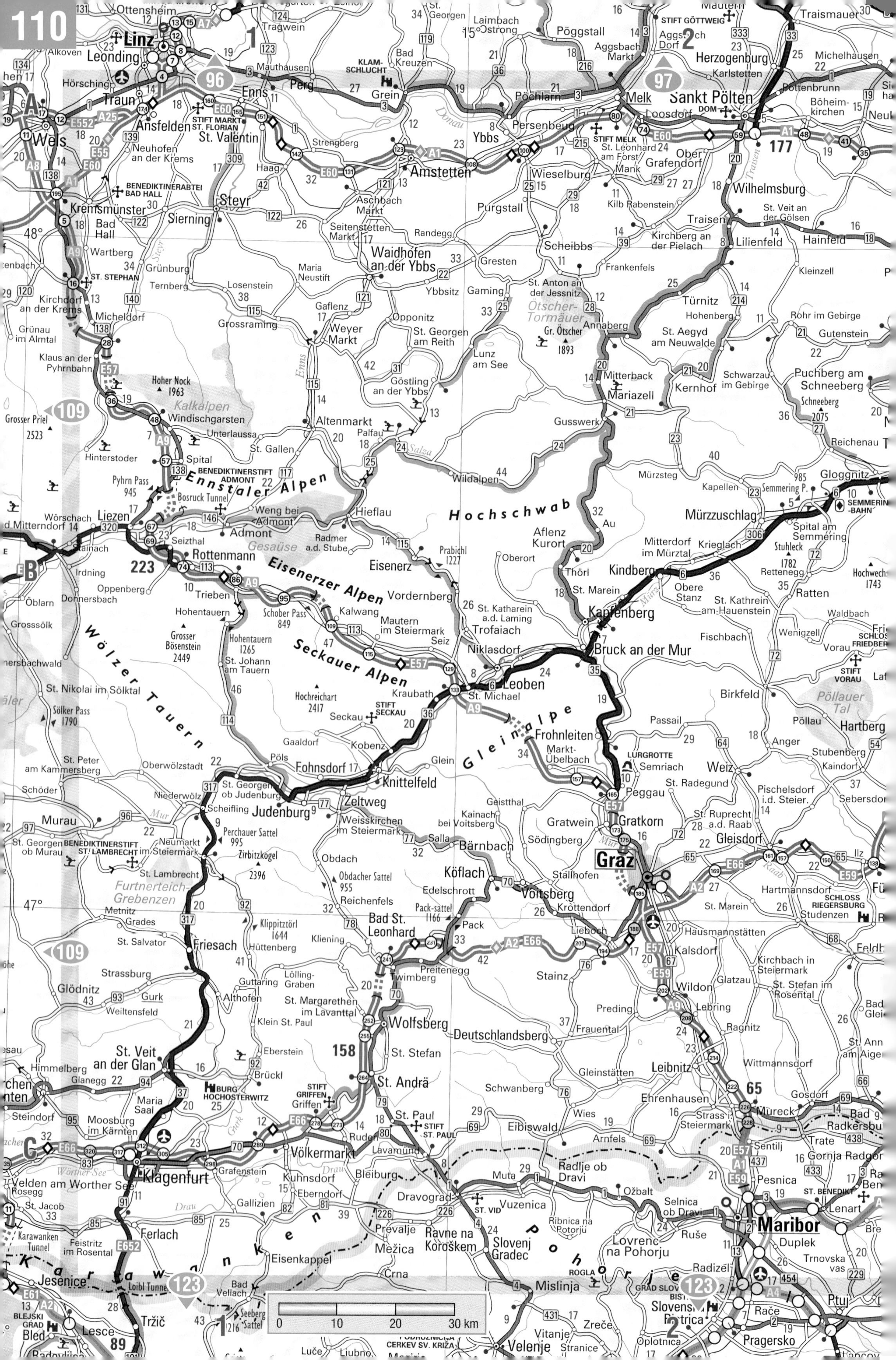

Ottensheim
Linz
Leonding
Alkoven
Hörsching
Traun
Ansfelden
Wels
Tragwein
Mauthausen
Perg
Enns
STIFT MARKT ST. FLORIAN
St. Valentin
Neuhofen an der Krems
Haag
Strengberg
Amstetten
St. Georgen
Laimbach
Ostrong
Pöggstall
Aggsbach Markt
Aggsbach Dorf
STIFT GÖTTWEIG
Traismauer
Herzogenburg
Michelhausen
Karlstetten
Bad Kreuzen
KLAM-SCHLUCHT
Grein
Donau
Persenbeug
Pöchlarn
Ybbs
Melk
Loosdorf
Sankt Pölten
DOM
Pottenbrunn
Böheim-kirchen
STIFT MELK
St. Leonhard am Forst
Mank
Ober Grafendorf
Wieselburg
Purgstall
Kilb
Rabenstein
Wilhelmsburg
Traisen
St. Veit an der Gölsen
Hainfeld
Lilienfeld
Kirchberg an der Pielach
Scheibbs
Frankenfels
Kremsmünster
BENEDIKTINERABTEI BAD HALL
Bad Hall
Steyr
Sierning
Aschbach Markt
Seitenstetten Markt
Randegg
Waidhofen an der Ybbs
Gresten
Wartberg
Grünburg
ST. STEPHAN
Ternberg
Losenstein
Maria Neustift
Ybbsitz
Gaming
St. Anton an der Jessnitz
Ötscher-Tormäuer
Gr. Ötscher 1893
Annaberg
Türnitz
Hohenberg
Kleinzell
Rohr im Gebirge
Gutenstein
Kirchdorf an der Krems
Micheldorf
Grünau im Almtal
Grossraming
Weyer Markt
Opponitz
St. Georgen am Reith
Gaflenz
Lunz am See
Göstling an der Ybbs
Mitterbach
Mariazell
St. Aegyd am Neuwalde
Kernhof
Schwarzau im Gebirge
Puchberg am Schneeberg
Schneeberg 2075
Klaus an der Pyhrnbahn
Hoher Nock 1963
Kalkalpen
Windischgarsten
Grosser Priel 2523
Unterlaussa
Altenmarkt
Palfau
St. Gallen
Gusswerk
Salza
Wildalpen
Mürzsteg
Kapellen
Semmering P. 985
Gloggnitz
Reichenau
Hinterstoder
Spital
BENEDIKTINERSTIFT ADMONT
Pyhrn Pass 945
Bosruck Tunnel
Ennstaler Alpen
Hieflau
Hochschwab
Aflenz Kurort
Au
Mürzzuschlag
SEMMERING-BAHN
Spital am Semmering
Wörschach
Liezen
Mitterndorf
Weng bei Admont
Admont
Gesäuse
Radmer a.d. Stube
Prabichl 1227
Oberort
Mitterdorf im Mürztal
Krieglach
Stuhleck 1782
Rettenegg
Hochwechsel 1743
Stainach
Irdning
Seizthal
Rottenmann
Eisenerz
Eisenerzer Alpen
Vordernberg
Thörl
Kindberg
St. Marein
Obere Stanz
Ratten
Öblarn
Donnersbach
Oppenberg
Trieben
Kalwang
Mautern im Steiermark
Seiz
St. Katharein a.d. Laming
Trofaiach
Kapfenberg
St. Kathrein am Hauenstein
Waldbach
Grosssölk
Hohentauern
Schober Pass 849
Niklasdorf
Bruck an der Mur
Mürz
Fischbach
Wenigzell
Vorau
STIFT VORAU
Wölzer Tauern
Grosser Bösenstein 2449
Hohentauern 1265
St. Johann am Tauern
Seckauer Alpen
Leoben
St. Michael
Kraubath
Birkfeld
Pöllauer Tal
St. Nikolai im Sölktal
Sölker Pass 1790
Hochreichart 2417
Seckau
STIFT SECKAU
Gleinalpe
Frohnleiten
Passail
Pöllau
Hartberg
Gaaldorf
Kobenz
Markt-Übelbach
LURGROTTE
Semriach
Weiz
Anger
Stubenberg
Kaindorf
St. Peter am Kammersberg
Oberwölzstadt
Pöls
Fohnsdorf
Knittelfeld
Glein
Peggau
St. Radegund
Pischelsdorf i.d. Steier.
Sebersdorf
Schöder
St. Georgen ob Judenburg
Niederwölz
Judenburg
Zeltweg
Geistthal
Scheifling
Murau
Weisskirchen im Steiermark
Kainach bei Voitsberg
Gratwein
Gratkorn
St. Ruprecht a.d. Raab
Gleisdorf
St. Georgen ob Murau
BENEDIKTINERSTIFT ST. LAMBRECHT
Neumarkt im Steiermark
Perchauer Sattel 995
Salla
Bärnbach
Södingberg
Graz
Zirbitzkogel 2396
Obdach
Obdacher Sattel 955
Köflach
Stallhofen
Voitsberg
Edelschrott
St. Lambrecht
Furtnerteich-Grebenzen
Reichenfels
Krottendorf
Hartmannsdorf
SCHLOSS RIEGERSBURG
St. Marein
Studenzen
Metnitz
Grades
Pack-sattel 1166
Pack
Bad St. Leonhard
Klippitztörl 1644
Hüttenberg
Kliening
Lieboch
Hausmannstätten
Kalsdorf
St. Salvator
Friesach
Preitenegg
Twimberg
Stainz
Kirchbach in Steiermark
Strassburg
Lölling-Graben
Guttaring
Glatzau
St. Stefan im Rosental
Glödnitz
Gurk
Weitensfeld
Althofen
St. Margarethen im Lavanttal
Wolfsberg
Preding
Wildon
Lebring
Klein St. Paul
Deutschlandsberg
Frauental
Ragnitz
St. Veit an der Glan
Eberstein
St. Stefan
Leibnitz
Wittmannsdorf
Himmelberg
Glanegg
Brückl
St. Andrä
Gleinstätten
Maria Saal
BURG HOCHOSTERWITZ
STIFT GRIFFEN
Griffen
Schwanberg
Ehrenhausen
Gosdorf
Steindorf
Moosburg im Kärnten
St. Paul
STIFT ST. PAUL
Eibiswald
Wies
Strass i. Steiermark
Mureck
Bad Radkersburg
Ruden
Lavamünd
Arnfels
Trate
Gornja Radgona
Wörther See
Klagenfurt
Grafenstein
Völkermarkt
Velden am Worther See
Rosegg
Kühnsdorf
Eberndorf
Bleiburg
Dravograd
Muta
Radlje ob Dravi
Sentilj
Pesnica
Lenart
ST. BENEDIKT
St. Jacob
Drau
Gallizien
Prevalje
Ravne na Koroškem
ST. VID
Vuzenica
Ožbalt
Selnica ob Dravi
Maribor
Ferlach
Feistritz im Rosental
Karawanken Tunnel
Karawanken
Eisenkappel
Mežica
Slovenj Gradec
Pohorje
Ribnica na Pohorju
Lovrenc na Pohorju
Ruše
Duplek
Trnovska vas
Jesenice
Loibl Tunnel
Bad Vellach
Črna
ROGLA
Mislinja
GRAD SLOV. BIST.
Slovenska Bistrica
Radizel
Ptuj
Rače
Pragersko
BLEJSKI GRAD
Bled
Lesce
Tržič
Seeberg Sattel
Zreče
Vitanje
Stranice
Velenje
Oplotnica
Luče
Ljubno
CERKEV SV. KRIŽA
0 10 20 30 km

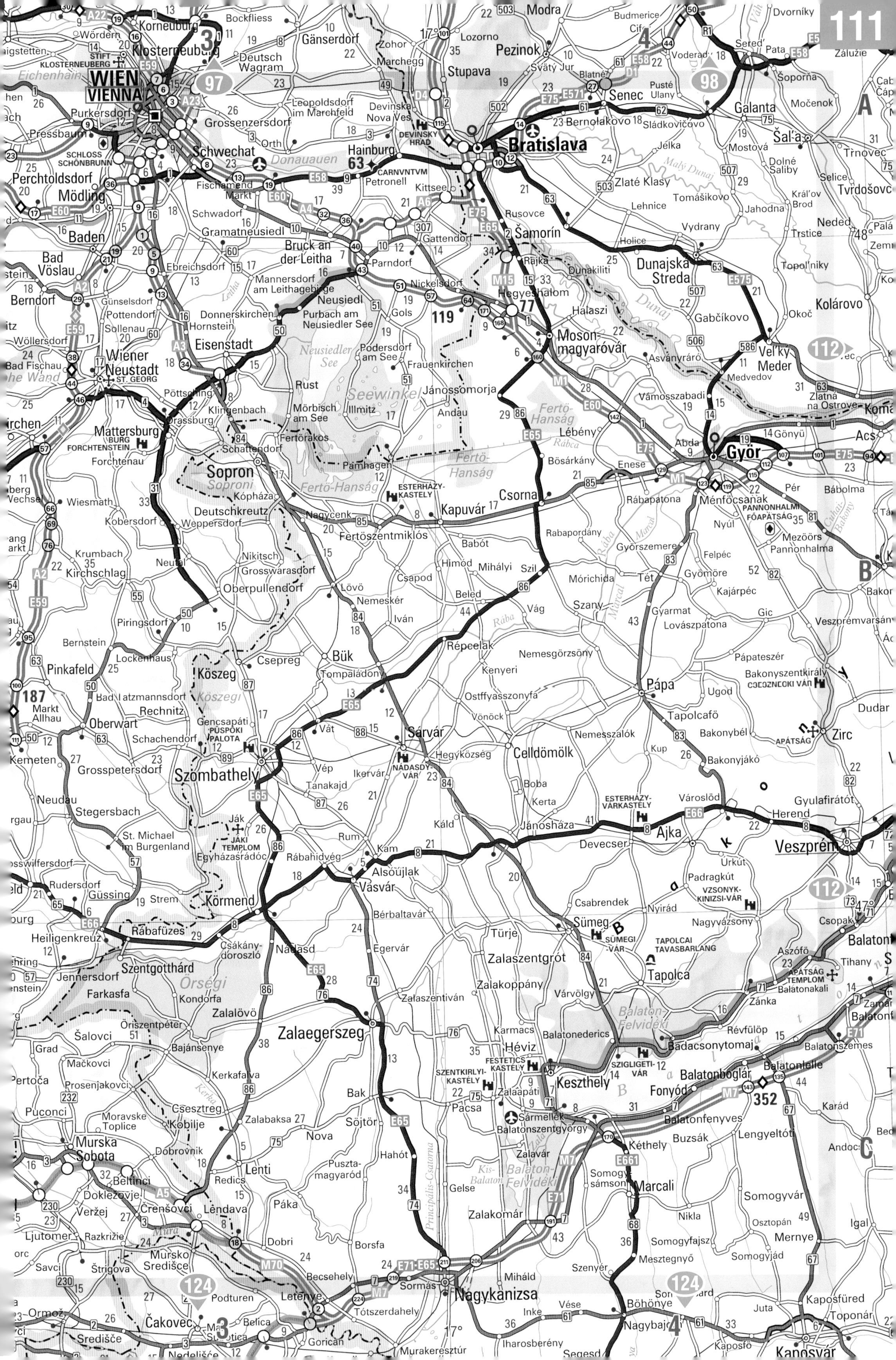

111
Korneuburg
Klosterneuburg
Wördern
Stift Klosterneuburg
Bockfliess
Gänserdorf
Deutsch Wagram
Wien
Vienna
Eichenhain
Purkersdorf
Pressbaum
Schloss Schönbrunn
Perchtoldsdorf
Mödling
Baden
Bad Vöslau
Berndorf
Grossenzersdorf
Orth
Schwechat
Donauauen
Fischamend Markt
Schwadorf
Gramatneusiedl
Ebreichsdorf
Günselsdorf
Pottendorf
Sollenau
Wöllersdorf
Bad Fischau
Wiener Neustadt
St. Georg
Hohe Wand
Leopoldsdorf im Marchfeld
Marchegg
Zohor
Devinská Nová Ves
Devínsky Hrad
Hainburg
Carnuntum
Petronell
Kittsee
Bruck an der Leitha
Parndorf
Mannersdorf am Leithagebirge
Neusiedl
Purbach am Neusiedler See
Donnerskirchen
Hornstein
Eisenstadt
Pöttsching
Klingenbach
Drassburg
Mattersburg
Burg Forchtenstein
Forchtenau
Neusiedler See
Seewinkel
Podersdorf am See
Frauenkirchen
Gols
Nickelsdorf
Rust
Mörbisch am See
Illmitz
Jánossomorja
Andau
Fertörákos
Pamhagen
Schattendorf
Sopron
Soproni
Kópháza
Fertő-Hanság
Deutschkreutz
Weppersdorf
Nagycenk
Fertőszentmiklós
Esterházy-Kastély
Kapuvár
Csorna
Wiesmath
Kobersdorf
Krumbach
Kirchschlag
Neutal
Nikitsch
Grosswarasdorf
Oberpullendorf
Lövö
Nemeskér
Piringsdorf
Bernstein
Lockenhaus
Pinkafeld
Köszeg
Kőszegi
Csepreg
Bük
Tompaládony
Markt Allhau
Bad Tatzmannsdorf
Rechnitz
Oberwart
Gencsapáti Püspöki Palota
Schachendorf
Kemeten
Grosspetersdorf
Szombathely
Neudau
Stegersbach
St. Michael im Burgenland
Ják
Jáki Templom
Egyházasrádóc
Rudersdorf
Güssing
Strem
Körmend
Heiligenkreuz
Rábafüzes
Jennersdorf
Szentgotthárd
Őrségi
Farkasfa
Kondorfa
Zalalövő
Őriszentpéter
Šalovci
Grad
Mačkovci
Petrovci
Prosenjakovci
Puconci
Moravske Toplice
Kobilje
Murska Sobota
Beltinci
Dokležovje
Veržej
Ljutomer
Razkrižje
Črenšovci
Lendava
Mursko Središće
Štrigova
Čakovec
Podturen
Ormož
Središće
Nedelišće
Modra
Budmerice
Dvorníky
Pezinok
Svätý Jur
Stupava
Lozorno
Senec
Blatné
Voderady
Sereď
Pata
Záluzie
Galanta
Sládkovičovo
Bernolákovo
Šaľa
Močenok
Pusté Úlany
Bratislava
Jelka
Mostová
Dolné Saliby
Trnovec
Selice
Tvrdošovce
Zlaté Klasy
Tomášikovo
Jahodná
Kráľov Brod
Lehnice
Malý Dunaj
Rusovce
Šamorín
Gattendorf
Vydrany
Holice
Neded
Trstice
Topoľníky
Rajka
Dunakiliti
Dunajská Streda
Hegyeshalom
Gabčíkovo
Kolárovo
Okoč
Halászi
Mosonmagyaróvár
Ásványráró
Vel'ký Meder
Medvedov
Zlatná na Ostrove
Komárno
Vámosszabadi
Lébény
Fertő-Hanság
Bösárkány
Abda
Enese
Győr
Gönyü
Ács
Ménfőcsanak
Pannonhalmi Főapátság
Pér
Bábolna
Rábapatona
Rabapordány
Nyúl
Mezőörs
Pannonhalma
Győrszemere
Felpéc
Gyömöre
Tét
Mórichida
Szany
Kajárpéc
Gyarmat
Lovászpatona
Gic
Veszprémvarsány
Babót
Himód
Mihályi
Szil
Csapod
Beled
Iván
Vág
Rába
Répcelak
Nemesgörzsöny
Kenyeri
Pápateszér
Bakonyszentkirály
Cseszneki Vár
Pápa
Ugod
Dudar
Ostffyasszonyfa
Vönöck
Tapolcafő
Bakonybél
Zirc
Apátság
Vát
Sárvár
Hegyközség
Nádasdy-Vár
Nemesszalók
Kup
Celldömölk
Bakonyjákó
Vép
Ikervár
Tanakajd
Boba
Kerta
Városlöd
Esterházy-Várkastély
Gyulafirátót
Herend
Veszprém
Ajka
Kald
Jánosháza
Devecser
Rum
Kám
Rábahidvég
Alsóújlak
Vasvár
Úrkút
Padragkút
Vzsonyk-Kinizsi-Vár
Csabrendek
Nyirád
Bérbaltavár
Sümeg
Sümegi Vár
Tapolcai Tavasbarlang
Nagyvázsony
Csopak
Balaton
Türje
Csákánydoroszló
Nádasd
Egervár
Zalaszentgrót
Tapolca
Aszófő
Tihany
Apátság Templom
Balatonakali
Zánka
Zalakoppány
Várvölgy
Zalaszentiván
Zalaegerszeg
Balaton-Felvidéki
Révfülöp
Balatonederics
Karmacs
Badacsonytomaj
Balatonszemes
Hévíz
Festetics Kastély
Szigligeti-Vár
Keszthely
Balatonboglár
Balatonlelle
Szentkirlyi-Kastély
Zalaapáti
Fonyód
Kerkafalva
Bak
Pacsa
Sármellék
Balatonszentgyörgy
Balatonfenyves
Buzsák
Lengyeltóti
Karád
Cseszterg
Zalabaksa
Söjtör
Nova
Kéthely
Zalavár
Kis-Balaton
Lenti
Redics
Hahót
Pusztamagyaród
Gelse
Somogysámson
Marcali
Somogyvár
Andocs
Páka
Zalakomár
Nikla
Osztopán
Mernye
Igal
Dobri
Borsfa
Principális-Csatorna
Somogyfajsz
Mesztegnyő
Somogyjád
Becsehely
Szenyér
Miháld
Sormás
Letenye
Nagykanizsa
Tótszerdahely
Böhönye
Kaposfüred
Toponár
Juta
Inke
Vése
Nagybajom
Kaposvár
Goričan
Iharosberény
Segesd
Murakeresztúr
Kaposfő
97
98
112
124
187
119
352
Mura
Kerka
Dunaj
Leitha

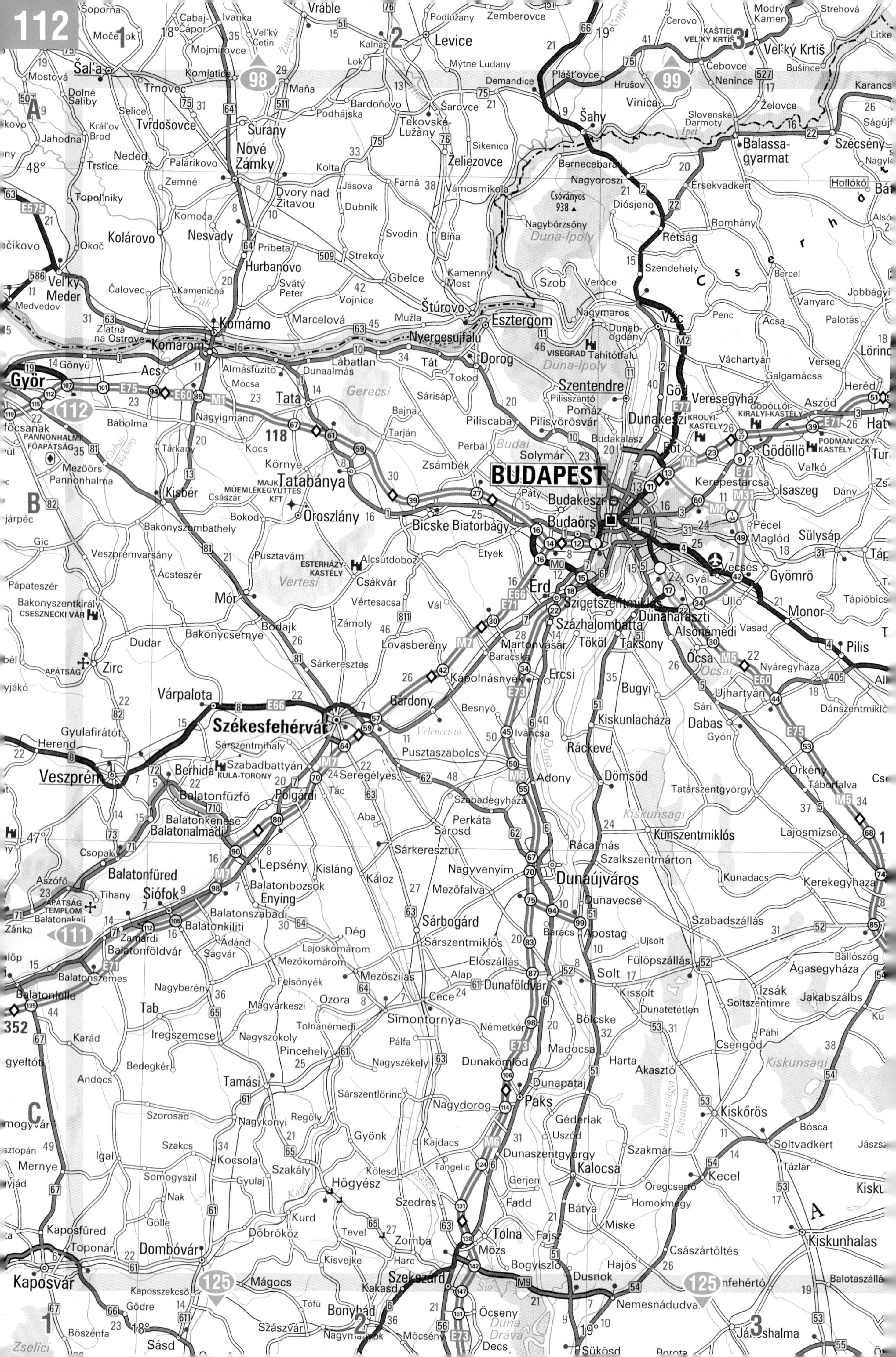
Šoporňa
Cabaj-Čápor
Ivanka
Vráble
Podlužany
Zemberovce
Modrý Kameň
Strehová
Litke
Močenok
Veľký Cetín
Mojmírovce
Kalná
Levice
Cerovo
Kaštieľ Veľký Krtíš
Veľký Krtíš
Šaľa
Komjatice
Mýtne Ludany
Demandice
Plášťovce
Cebovce
Nenince
Bušince
Karancs
Mostová
Trnovec
Maňa
Hrušov
Vinica
Dolné Saliby
Selice
Bardoňovo
Šarovce
Želovce
Tvrdošovce
Šurany
Podhájska
Tekovské Lužany
Šahy
Slovenské Darmoty
Ipeľ
Ságújfalu
Kráľov Brod
Jahodna
Nové Zámky
Sikenica
Balassagyarmat
Szécsény
Neded
Palárikovo
Kolta
Želiezovce
Trstice
Bernecebaráti
Nagyoroszi
Hollókő
Zemné
Jásova
Farná
Vámosmikola
Érsekvadkert
Topoľníky
Dvory nad Žitavou
Csóványos 938
Diósjenő
Komoča
Dubník
Nagybörzsöny
Duna-Ipoly
Romhány
Kolárovo
Nesvady
Svodín
Bíňa
Rétság
Okoč
Pribeta
Strekov
Cserhát
Hurbanovo
Szendehely
Bercel
Veľký Meder
Kamenný Most
Čalovec
Kameničná
Svätý Peter
Gbelce
Szob
Verőce
Vanyarc
Jobbágyi
Medvedov
Vojnice
Štúrovo
Nagymaros
Vác
Penc
Acsa
Palotás
Zlatná na Ostrove
Komárno
Marcelová
Mužla
Esztergom
Dunabogdány
Komárom
Nyergesújfalu
Visegrád
Tahitótfalu
Lőrinci
Gönyű
Ács
Lábatlan
Tát
Dorog
Váchartyán
Verseg
Győr
Almásfüzitő
Dunaalmás
Tokod
Szentendre
Galgamácsa
Heréd
Mocsa
Tata
Gerecsei
Sárisáp
Pilisszántó
Göd
Veresegyház
Aszód
Pomáz
Dunakeszi
Királyi-kastély
Gödöllői Királyi-Kastély
Hatvan
Bábolna
Nagyigmánd
Bajna
Piliscaba
Pilisvörösvár
Fót
Gödöllő
Podmaniczky-kastély
Pannonhalmi Főapátság
Tárkány
Kocs
Tarján
Perbál
Budai
Budakalász
Mezőörs
Pannonhalma
Környe
Solymár
Tura
Tatabánya
Zsámbék
BUDAPEST
Kerepestarcsa
Valkó
Majk Műemlékegyüttes Kft
Kisbér
Császár
Páty
Budakeszi
Isaszeg
Dány
Oroszlány
Bokod
Bicske
Biatorbágy
Budaörs
Pécel
Bakonyszombathely
Maglód
Sülysáp
Gic
Veszprémvarsány
Pusztavám
Etyek
Tápió
Ácsteszér
Esterházy-kastély
Alcsútdoboz
Vecsés
Gyömrő
Pápateszér
Vértesi
Csákvár
Érd
Gyál
Bakonyszentkirály
Cseszneki vár
Mór
Vértesacsa
Vál
Szigetszentmiklós
Üllő
Monor
Tápióbicske
Zámoly
Százhalombatta
Dunaharaszti
Bodajk
Bakonycsernye
Lovasberény
Martonvásár
Tököl
Taksony
Alsónémedi
Vasad
Pilis
Dudar
Sárkeresztes
Baracska
Ócsa
Ócsai
Nyáregyháza
Zirc
Apátság
Kápolnásnyék
Ercsi
Bugyi
Újhartyán
Várpalota
Gárdony
Besnyő
Sári
Dánszentmiklós
Gyulafirátót
Székesfehérvár
Velencei-tó
Kiskunlacháza
Dabas
Gyón
Herend
Sárszentmihály
Iváncsa
Veszprém
Berhida
Szabadbattyán
Kula-torony
Pusztaszabolcs
Ráckeve
Örkény
Táborfalva
Seregélyes
Adony
Dömsöd
Balatonfűzfő
Polgárdi
Tác
Szabadegyháza
Tatárszentgyörgy
Balatonkenese
Balatonalmádi
Aba
Perkáta
Sárosd
Kiskunsági
Lajosmizse
Csopak
Sárkeresztúr
Rácalmás
Kunszentmiklós
Lepsény
Kisláng
Szalkszentmárton
Balatonfüred
Káloz
Nagyvenyim
Dunaújváros
Kunadacs
Kerekegyháza
Aszófő
Tihany
Siófok
Balatonbozsok
Enying
Mezőfalva
Dunavecse
Apátsági Templom
Balatonakali
Balatonszabadi
Sárbogárd
Szabadszállás
Zánka
Balatonkiliti
Dég
Baracs
Apostag
Zamárdi
Ádánd
Lajoskomárom
Sárszentmiklós
Újsolt
Ballószög
Balatonföldvár
Ságvár
Mezőkomárom
Előszállás
Fülöpszállás
Ágasegyháza
Balatonszemes
Mezőszilas
Alap
Solt
Nagyberény
Felsőnyék
Dunaföldvár
Kissolt
Izsák
Balatonlelle
Ozora
Cece
Soltszentimre
Jakabszállás
Tab
Magyarkeszi
Simontornya
Dunatetétlen
Karád
Iregszemcse
Nagyszokoly
Tolnanémedi
Németkér
Bölcske
Páhi
Pálfa
Madocsa
Csengőd
Bedegkér
Pincehely
Nagyszékely
Dunakömlőd
Harta
Akasztó
Kiskunsági
Andocs
Tamási
Dunapataj
Sárszentlőrinc
Paks
Kiskőrös
Szorosad
Nagykonyi
Regöly
Nagydorog
Gédérlak
Bócsa
Uszód
Duna-völgyi-főcsatorna
Szakcs
Gyönk
Kajdacs
Soltvadkert
Igal
Kocsola
Szakály
Dunaszentgyörgy
Szakmár
Tázlár
Mernye
Somogyszil
Gyulaj
Kölesd
Tengelic
Kalocsa
Kecel
Höggyész
Gerjen
Öregcsertő
Nak
Szedres
Fadd
Homokmégy
Gölle
Kurd
Bátya
Miske
Kaposfüred
Döbrököz
Tevel
Tolna
Fajsz
Kiskunhalas
Toponár
Dombóvár
Zomba
Mözs
Császártöltés
Kisvejke
Harc
Bogyiszló
Hajós
Kaposvár
Mágocs
Szekszárd
Dusnok
Kiskunfélegyháza
Balotaszállás
Kaposszekcső
Kakasd
Sió
Nemesnádudvar
Gödre
Tófű
Bonyhád
Őcsény
Böszénfa
Szászvár
Duna-Dráva
Nagymányok
Mőcsény
Decs
Sükösd
Jánoshalma
Sásd
Zselici
Borota

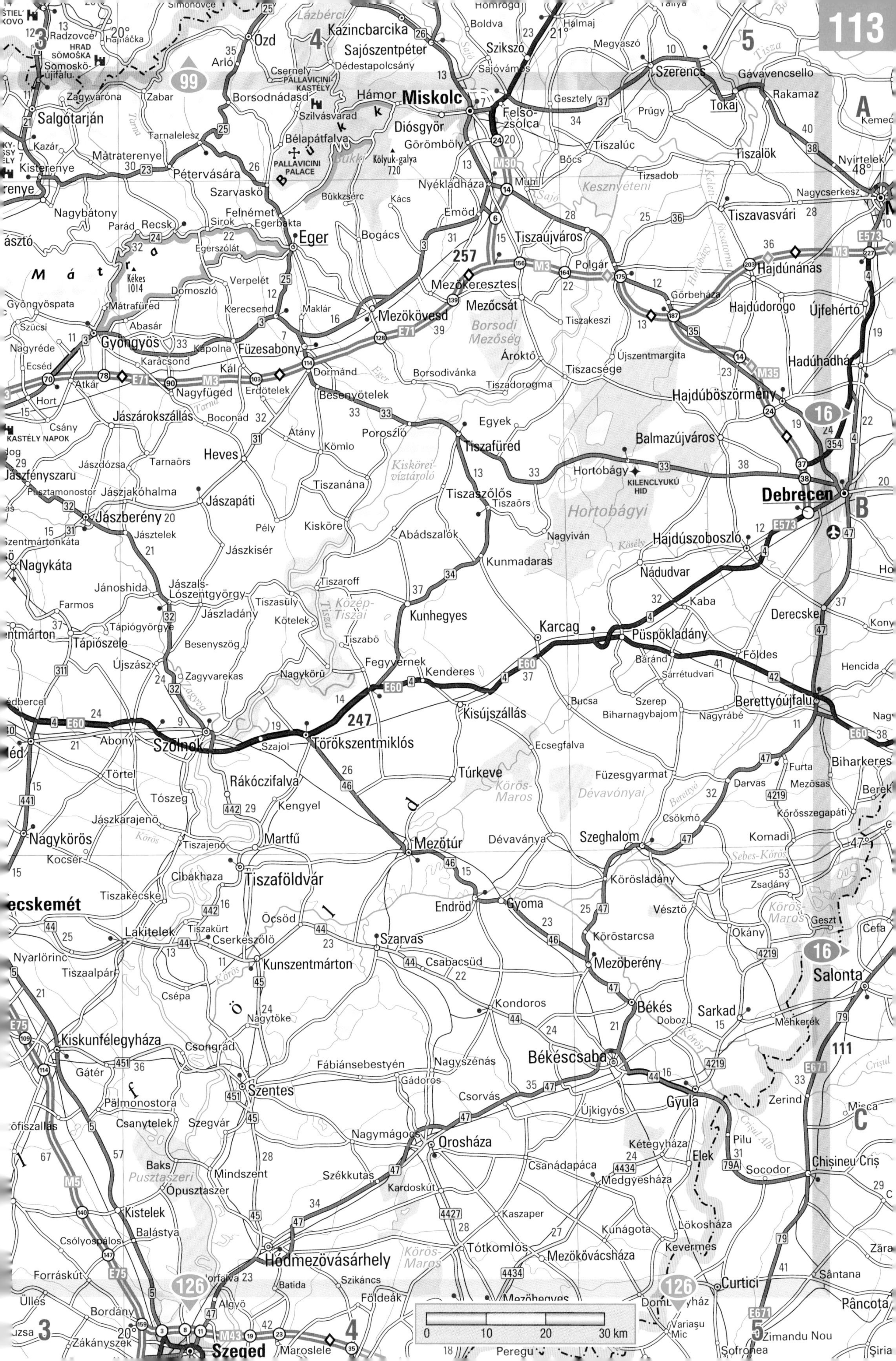
Ózd
Kazincbarcika
Sajószentpéter
Dédestapolcsány
Lázbérci
Boldva
Halmaj
Megyaszó
Szikszó
Sajóvámos
Szerencs
Gávavencsello
Rakamaz
Tokaj
Prügy
Gesztely
Felsőzsolca
Miskolc
Hámor
Diósgyőr
Görömböly
Szilvásvárad
Bélapátfalva
PALLAVICINI PALACE
PALLAVICINI-KASTÉLY
Kölyuk-galya 720
Bükkszérc
Kács
Nyékládháza
Emőd
Muhi
Tiszalúc
Bőcs
Tiszadob
Tiszalök
Nyírtelek
Nagycserkesz
Tiszavasvári
Kesznyéteni
Salgótarján
Radzovce
Hajnáčka
HRAD SOMOŠKA
Somoskőújfalu
Zagyvaróna
Zabar
Borsodnádasd
Arló
Csernely
Kazár
Mátraterenye
Kisterenye
Pétervására
Tarnalelesz
Szarvaskő
Nagybátony
Parád
Recsk
Sirok
Felnémet
Egerbakta
Eger
Egerszólát
Bogács
Tiszaújváros
Polgár
Hajdúnánás
Mezőkeresztes
Mezőcsát
Görbeháza
Hajdúdorog
Újfehértó
Kékes 1014
Verpelét
Domoszló
Mátrafüred
Kerecsend
Maklár
Mezőkövesd
Gyöngyöspata
Abasár
Gyöngyös
Szűcsi
Nagyréde
Ecsed
Kápolna
Karácsond
Füzesabony
Kál
Dormánd
Borsodivánka
Tiszakeszi
Borsodi Mezőség
Árokto
Újszentmargita
Tiszacsege
Tiszadorogma
Hadúhadház
Hajdúböszörmény
Atkár
Hort
Nagyfüged
Erdőtelek
Besenyőtelek
Jászárokszállás
Boconád
Egyek
Poroszló
Átány
Kömlő
Tiszafüred
Balmazújváros
Csány
KASTÉLY NAPOK
Heves
Tarnaörs
Jászdózsa
Jászfényszaru
Pusztamonostor
Jászjákóhalma
Jászapáti
Kiskörei-víztároló
Tiszanána
Tiszaszőlős
Tiszaörs
Hortobágy
KILENCLYUKÚ HÍD
Hortobágyi
Debrecen
Jászberény
Jásztelek
Pély
Kisköre
Abádszalók
Nagyiván
Hajdúszoboszló
Kösély
Nagykáta
Jászkisér
Kunmadaras
Nádudvar
Jánoshida
Jászalsószentgyörgy
Tiszaroff
Farmos
Tiszasüly
Jászladány
Közép-Tiszai
Kunhegyes
Kaba
Derecske
Tápiógyörgye
Tápiószele
Kötelek
Besenyszög
Tiszabő
Karcag
Püspökladány
Földes
Újszász
Zagyvarékas
Nagykörű
Fegyvernek
Kenderes
Bárand
Sárrétudvari
Hencida
Bucsa
Szerep
Biharnagybajom
Nagyrábé
Berettyóújfalu
Abony
Szolnok
Szajol
Törökszentmiklós
Kisújszállás
Ecsegfalva
Törtel
Rákóczifalva
Túrkeve
Füzesgyarmat
Dévaványai
Darvas
Furta
Mezősas
Biharkeresztes
Tószeg
Kengyel
Csökmő
Kőrösszegapáti
Jászkarajenő
Nagykőrös
Tiszajenő
Martfű
Mezőtúr
Dévaványa
Szeghalom
Komadi
Kocsér
Cibakháza
Tiszaföldvár
Endrőd
Gyoma
Körösladány
Sebes-Körös
Zsadány
Kecskemét
Tiszakécske
Öcsöd
Vésztő
Geszt
Lakitelek
Tiszakürt
Cserkeszőlő
Szarvas
Köröstarcsa
Okány
Nyarlőrinc
Tiszaalpár
Kunszentmárton
Csabacsüd
Mezőberény
Salonta
Csépa
Kondoros
Békés
Sarkad
Nagytőke
Doboz
Méhkerék
Kiskunfélegyháza
Csongrád
Gátér
Fábiánsebestyén
Nagyszénás
Békéscsaba
Gádoros
Szentes
Pálmonostora
Csorvás
Újkígyós
Gyula
Zerind
Mișca
Csanytelek
Szegvár
Orosháza
Nagymágocs
Kétegyháza
Elek
Pilu
Baks
Mindszent
Pusztaszeri
Ópusztaszer
Székkutas
Csanádapáca
Medgyesháza
Socodor
Chișineu Criș
Kardoskút
Kistelek
Balástya
Kaszaper
Kunágota
Lőkösháza
Csólyospálos
Tótkomlós
Kevermes
Mezőkovácsháza
Hódmezővásárhely
Zăra
Forráskút
Batida
Szikáncs
Curtici
Sântana
Üllés
Algyő
Földeák
Mezőhegyes
Dombegyház
Pâncota
Bordány
Zákányszék
Szeged
Maroslele
Variașu Mic
Zimandu Nou
Peregu
Sofronea
Sîria
E71
M3
M30
E573
E60
M35
M43
M5
E75
E671
257
247
99
16
126
111
A
B
C
3
4
5
0 10 20 30 km

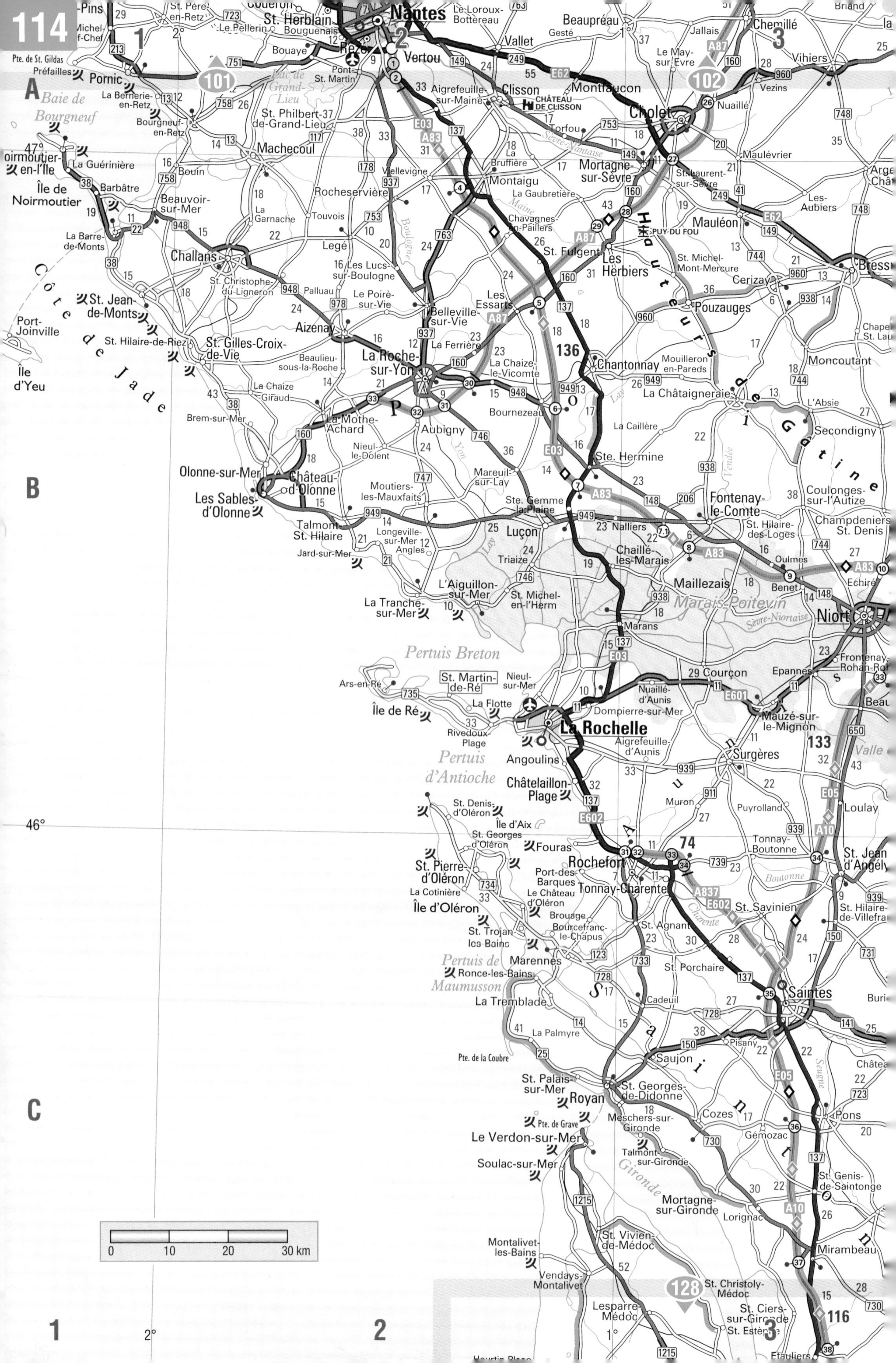
Nantes
St. Herblain
Rezé
Vertou
Clisson
Montaigu
Cholet
Pornic
Machecoul
Challans
Île de Noirmoutier
Noirmoutier-en-l'Île
Côte de Jade
St. Jean-de-Monts
St. Gilles-Croix-de-Vie
Île d'Yeu
La Roche-sur-Yon
Les Herbiers
Mortagne-sur-Sèvre
Mauléon
Pouzauges
Chantonnay
Hauteurs de la Gâtine
Les Sables-d'Olonne
Luçon
Fontenay-le-Comte
Marais Poitevin
Niort
Pertuis Breton
Île de Ré
La Rochelle
Pertuis d'Antioche
Rochefort
Île d'Oléron
Surgères
St. Jean-d'Angély
Saintes
Marennes
La Tremblade
Royan
Saintonge
Gironde
Pons
Mirambeau
Le Verdon-sur-Mer
Soulac-sur-Mer
Lesparre-Médoc
Baie de Bourgneuf
47°
46°
0 10 20 30 km

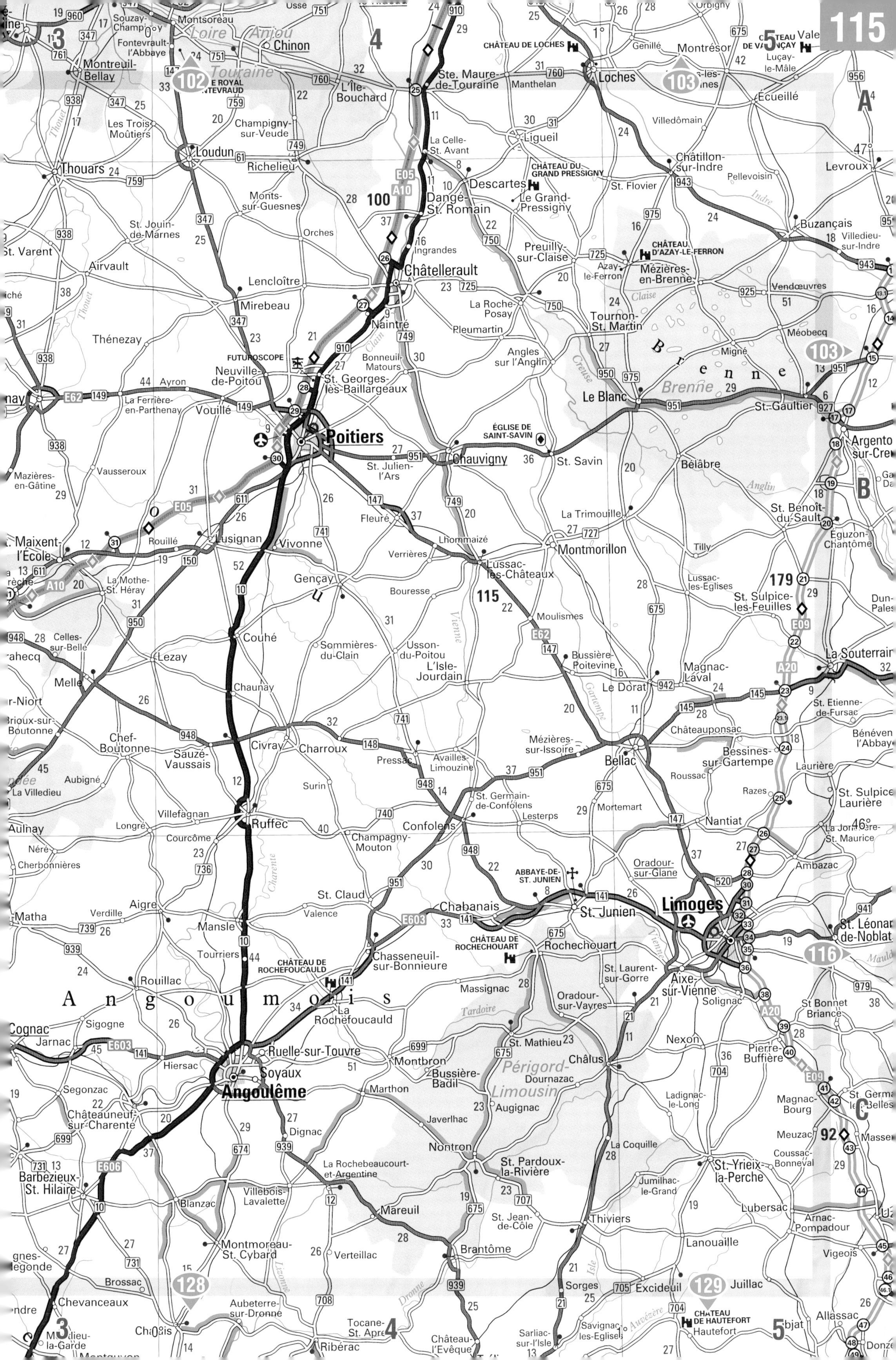
Montsoreau
Souzay-Champigny
Fontevrault-l'Abbaye
Loire
Anjou
Chinon
Usse
Touraine
Montreuil-Bellay
Ste. Maure-de-Touraine
L'Île-Bouchard
Manthelan
Château de Loches
Loches
Genillé
Montrésor
Orbigny
Château de Valençay
Luçay-le-Mâle
Écueillé
Villedômain
Champigny-sur-Veude
Les Trois-Moûtiers
Loudun
Richelieu
Thouars
Monts-sur-Guesnes
La Celle-St. Avant
Ligueil
Château du Grand Pressigny
Descartes
Le Grand-Pressigny
Châtillon-sur-Indre
Pellevoisin
Levroux
St. Flovier
Dangé-St. Romain
St. Jouin-de-Marnes
Orches
Ingrandes
Buzançais
Villedieu-sur-Indre
St. Varent
Airvault
Lencloître
Châtellerault
Preuilly-sur-Claise
Azay-le-Ferron
Château d'Azay-le-Ferron
Mézières-en-Brenne
Vendœuvres
Mirebeau
La Roche-Posay
Naintré
Tournon-St. Martin
Claise
Méobecq
Thénezay
Pleumartin
Futuroscope
Neuville-de-Poitou
Bonneuil-Matours
St. Georges-lès-Baillargeaux
Angles sur l'Anglin
Brenne
Migné
Creuse
Le Blanc
St. Gaultier
Ayron
La Ferrière-en-Parthenay
Vouillé
Poitiers
Église de Saint-Savin
Chauvigny
St. Savin
St. Julien-l'Ars
Argenton-sur-Creuse
Bélâbre
Anglin
Mazières-en-Gâtine
Vausseroux
St. Benoît-du-Sault
La Trimouille
Fleuré
Éguzon-Chantôme
St. Maixent-l'École
Rouillé
Lusignan
Vivonne
Lhommaizé
Verrières
Montmorillon
Tilly
La Mothe-St. Héray
Gençay
Lussac-les-Châteaux
Bouresse
Lussac-les-Églises
St. Sulpice-les-Feuilles
Celles-sur-Belle
Couhé
Sommières-du-Clain
Moulismes
Usson-du-Poitou
L'Isle-Jourdain
Vienne
Lezay
Bussière-Poitevine
Le Dorat
Magnac-Laval
La Souterraine
Melle
Chaunay
Gartempe
St. Étienne-de-Fursac
Brioux-sur-Boutonne
Chef-Boutonne
Sauzé-Vaussais
Civray
Charroux
Pressac
Availles-Limouzine
Mézières-sur-Issoire
Bellac
Châteauponsac
Bessines-sur-Gartempe
Bénévent-l'Abbaye
Laurière
Aubigné
La Villedieu
Surin
St. Germain-de-Confolens
Lesterps
Mortemart
Roussac
Razes
St. Sulpice-Laurière
Villefagnan
Ruffec
Longré
Confolens
Nantiat
La Jonchère-St. Maurice
Aulnay
Néré
Courcôme
Champagny-Mouton
Charente
Abbaye-de-St. Junien
Oradour-sur-Glane
Ambazac
Cherbonnières
Aigre
St. Claud
Chabanais
St. Junien
Limoges
Matha
Verdille
Valence
Mansle
Château de Rochechouart
Rochechouart
St. Léonard-de-Noblat
Tourriers
Chasseneuil-sur-Bonnieure
Château de Rochefoucauld
Rouillac
Massignac
St. Laurent-sur-Gorre
Aixe-sur-Vienne
Solignac
St Bonnet Briance
Angoumois
Tardoire
Oradour-sur-Vayres
Cognac
Sigogne
La Rochefoucauld
Jarnac
Hiersac
Ruelle-sur-Touvre
Montbron
St. Mathieu
Châlus
Nexon
Pierre-Buffière
Soyaux
Angoulême
Bussière-Badil
Périgord-Limousin
Dournazac
Segonzac
Châteauneuf-sur-Charente
Marthon
Augignac
Ladignac-le-Long
Magnac-Bourg
Javerlhac
Dignac
Meuzac
Nontron
La Coquille
Coussac-Bonneval
Barbezieux-St. Hilaire
La Rochebeaucourt-et-Argentine
St. Pardoux-la-Rivière
St-Yrieix-la-Perche
Jumilhac-le-Grand
Villebois-Lavalette
Blanzac
Mareuil
St. Jean-de-Côle
Thiviers
Lubersac
Arnac-Pompadour
Montmoreau-St. Cybard
Verteillac
Brantôme
Lanouaille
Vigeois
Brossac
Lizonne
Dronne
Sorges
Excideuil
Juillac
Chevanceaux
Aubeterre-sur-Dronne
Isle
Auvézère
Tocane-St. Apre
Château de Hautefort
Hautefort
Allassac
Montguyon
Ribérac
Château-l'Évêque
Sarliac-sur-l'Isle
Savignac-les-Églises
Chalais
Montlieu-la-Garde
A10
E05
E62
E603
E606
E09
A20
102
103
116
128
129

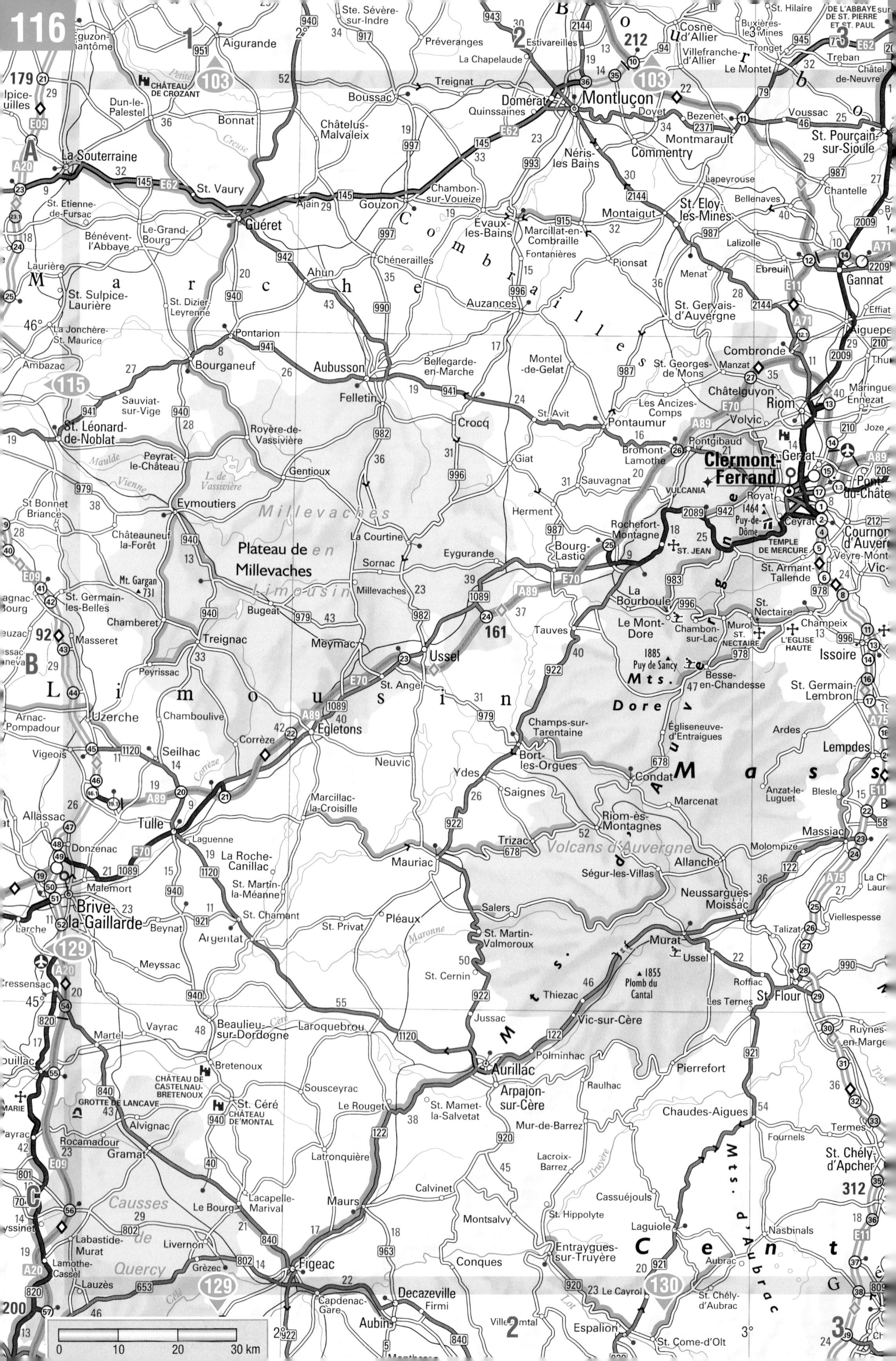
Eguzon-Chantôme
Aigurande
Ste. Sévère-sur-Indre
Préveranges
La Chapelaude
Estivareilles
Cosne d'Allier
Buxières-les-Mines
Villefranche-d'Allier
Le Montet
Tronget
St. Hilaire
DE L'ABBAYE DE ST. PIERRE ET ST. PAUL
Treban
Châtel-de-Neuvre
CHÂTEAU DE CROZANT
Dun-le-Palestel
Bonnat
Boussac
Treignat
Domérat
Montluçon
Quinssaines
Doyet
Bezenet
Montmarault
Voussac
St. Pourçain-sur-Sioule
Châtelus-Malvaleix
Commentry
Néris-les Bains
La Souterraine
St. Vaury
Chambon-sur-Voueize
Lapeyrouse
Chantelle
St. Etienne-de-Fursac
Guéret
Ajain
Gouzon
Evaux-les-Bains
Marcillat-en-Combraille
Montaigut
St. Eloy-les-Mines
Bellenaves
Bénévent-l'Abbaye
Le-Grand-Bourg
Fontanières
Lalizolle
Ebreuil
Gannat
Laurière
Chénerailles
Ahun
Pionsat
Menat
St. Sulpice-Laurière
St. Dizier-Leyrenne
Auzances
St. Gervais-d'Auvergne
Effiat
La Jonchère-St. Maurice
Pontarion
Aigueperse
Ambazac
Bourganeuf
Aubusson
Bellegarde-en-Marche
Montel-de-Gelat
St. Georges-de Mons
Manzat
Combronde
Maringues
Ennezat
Sauviat-sur-Vige
Felletin
Les Ancizes-Comps
Châtelguyon
Riom
St. Léonard-de-Noblat
Royère-de-Vassivière
Crocq
St. Avit
Pontaumur
Volvic
Joze
Maulde
Peyrat-le-Château
L. de Vassivière
Gentioux
Giat
Bromont-Lamothe
Pontgibaud
Clermont-Ferrand
Gerzat
Pont-du-Château
Vienne
Sauvagnat
VULCANIA
Royat
St Bonnet Briance
Eymoutiers
Millevaches
Herment
Puy-de-Dôme
Ceyrat
Châteauneuf la-Forêt
La Courtine
Rochefort-Montagne
ST. JEAN
TEMPLE DE MERCURE
Cournon d'Auvergne
Veyre-Monton
Vic-le-Comte
Plateau de Millevaches
Sornac
Eygurande
Bourg-Lastic
St. Armant-Tallende
Mt. Gargan 731
Limousin
Millevaches
La Bourboule
St. Germain-les-Belles
Bugeat
Le Mont-Dore
Chambon-sur-Lac
Murol
ST. NECTAIRE
St. Nectaire
Champeix
L'EGLISE HAUTE
Chamberet
Masseret
Treignac
Meymac
Tauves
Issoire
Ussel
1885 Puy de Sancy
Mts. Dore
Besse-en-Chandesse
Peyrissac
St. Angel
St. Germain-Lembron
Limousin
Uzerche
Arnac-Pompadour
Chamboulive
Egletons
Champs-sur-Tarentaine
Eglisenneuve-d'Entraigues
Ardes
Vigeois
Seilhac
Corrèze
Neuvic
Bort-les-Orgues
Lempdes
Ydes
Condat
Monts du Cantal
Anzat-le-Luguet
Blesle
Allassac
Tulle
Marcillac-la-Croisille
Saignes
Marcenat
Riom-ès-Montagnes
Massiac
Donzenac
Laguenne
La Roche-Canillac
Trizac
Volcans d'Auvergne
Molompize
Allanche
Mauriac
Ségur-les-Villas
Malemort
St. Martin-la-Méanne
Brive-la-Gaillarde
Neussargues-Moissac
Larche
Beynat
St. Chamant
St. Privat
Pléaux
Salers
Talizat
Viellespesse
Argentat
Maronne
St. Martin-Valmeroux
Murat
Ussel
Meyssac
St. Cernin
1855 Plomb du Cantal
Cressensac
Thiezac
Roffiac
Les Ternes
St. Flour
Beaulieu-sur-Dordogne
Vayrac
Martel
Laroquebrou
Jussac
Vic-sur-Cère
Ruynes-en-Margeride
Souillac
Bretenoux
Aurillac
Polminhac
Pierrefort
CHÂTEAU DE CASTELNAU-BRETENOUX
GROTTE DE LANCAVE
St. Céré
CHÂTEAU DE MONTAL
Sousceyrac
Le Rouget
St. Mamet-la-Salvetat
Arpajon-sur-Cère
Raulhac
Chaudes-Aigues
Alvignac
Rocamadour
Gramat
Latronquière
Mur-de-Barrez
Lacroix-Barrez
Fournels
Termes
St. Chély-d'Apcher
Causses de Quercy
Le Bourg
Lacapelle-Marival
Maurs
Calvinet
Montsalvy
Cassuéjouls
St. Hippolyte
Laguiole
Nasbinals
Labastide-Murat
Livernon
Entraygues-sur-Truyère
Conques
Mts. d'Aubrac
Lamothe-Cassel
Grèzec
Figeac
Aubrac
Lauzès
Capdenac-Gare
Decazeville
Firmi
Le Cayrol
St. Chély-d'Aubrac
Aubin
Villecomtal
Espalion
St. Come-d'Olt
Marche
Combrailles
Limousin
Bourbonnais
Massif Central
0 10 20 30 km

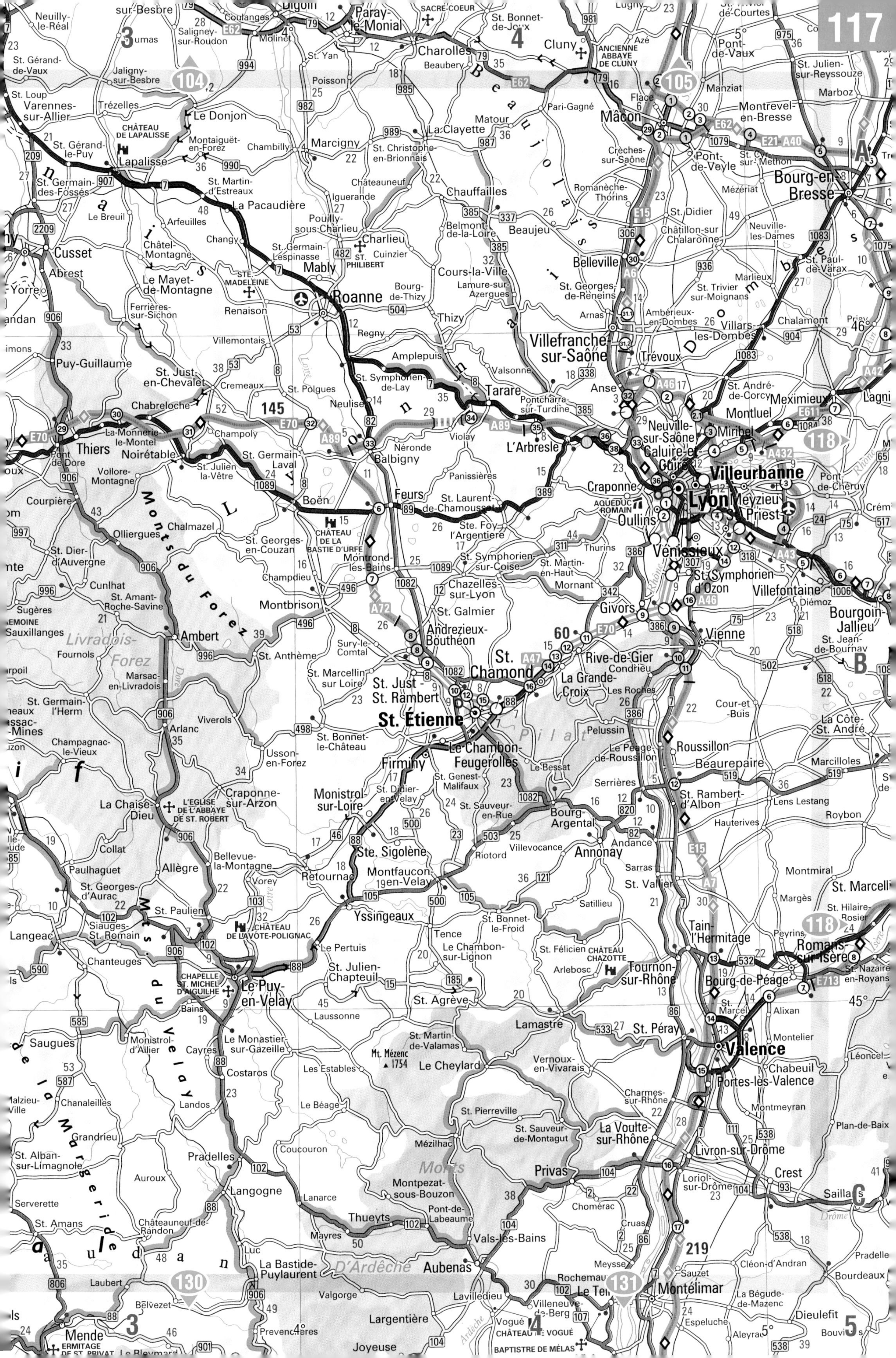
Neuilly-le-Réal
sur-Besbre
Coulanges
Digoin
Paray-le-Monial
SACRÉ-COEUR
St. Bonnet-de-Joux
Cluny
ANCIENNE ABBAYE DE CLUNY
Lugny
Azé
Pont-de-Vaux
Saligney-sur-Roudon
Molinet
St. Yan
Charolles
Beaubery
St. Julien-sur-Reyssouze
St. Gérand-de-Vaux
Jaligny-sur-Besbre
Poisson
Manziat
Marboz
St. Loup
Varennes-sur-Allier
Trézelles
Le Donjon
Matour
Pari-Gagné
Mâcon
Montrevel-en-Bresse
CHÂTEAU DE LAPALISSE
Montaiguët-en-Forez
Chambilly
Marcigny
La Clayette
St. Christophe-en-Brionnais
Crêches-sur-Saône
Pont-de-Veyle
St. Cyr-sur-Menthon
St. Gérand-le-Puy
Lapalisse
Bourg-en-Bresse
St. Germain-des-Fossés
St. Martin-d'Estreaux
Châteauneuf
Chauffailles
Romanèche-Thorins
Mézériat
Le Breuil
Arfeuilles
La Pacaudière
Iguerande
Pouilly-sous-Charlieu
Belmont-de-la-Loire
Beaujeu
St. Didier
Neuville-les-Dames
Cusset
Changy
Charlieu
Châtillon-sur-Chalaronne
Abrest
Châtel-Montagne
St. Germain-Lespinasse
Cuinzier
Belleville
St. Paul-de-Varax
Mably
ST. PHILIBERT
Cours-la-Ville
Marlieux
Le Mayet-de-Montagne
STE. MADELEINE
Roanne
Bourg-de-Thizy
Lamure-sur-Azergues
St. Georges-de-Reneins
St. Trivier-sur-Moignans
Ferrières-sur-Sichon
Renaison
Thizy
Arnas
Ambérieux-en-Dombes
Chalamont
Regny
Villars-les-Dombes
Villemontais
Villefranche-sur-Saône
Trévoux
Puy-Guillaume
Amplepuis
St. Just-en-Chevalet
Valsonne
St. André-de-Corcy
Cremeaux
St. Polgues
St. Symphorien-de-Lay
Tarare
Anse
Meximieux
Chabreloche
Neulise
Pontcharra-sur-Turdine
Montluel
La Monnerie-le-Montel
Thiers
Champoly
Balbigny
Néronde
Violay
L'Arbresle
Neuville-sur-Saône
Miribel
Noirétable
Pont de Dore
St. Julien-la-Vêtre
St. Germain-Laval
Caluire-et-Cuire
Villeurbanne
Vollore-Montagne
Panissières
Craponne
Courpière
Boën
Feurs
St. Laurent-de-Chamousset
AQUEDUC ROMAIN
Lyon
Meyzieu
Pont-de-Chéruy
Chalmazel
Ste. Foy-l'Argentière
Oullins
St. Priest
Olliergues
St. Georges-en-Couzan
CHÂTEAU DE LA BASTIE D'URFÉ
Thurins
Vénissieux
St. Dier-d'Auvergne
Montrond-les-Bains
St. Symphorien-sur-Coise
St. Martin-en-Haut
St. Symphorien d'Ozon
Villefontaine
Champdieu
Chazelles-sur-Lyon
Mornant
Cunlhat
St. Amant-Roche-Savine
Montbrison
St. Galmier
Givors
Diémoz
Sugères
Bourgoin-Jallieu
Sauxillanges
Livradois-Forez
Ambert
Andrézieux-Bouthéon
Rive-de-Gier
Vienne
St. Jean-de-Bournay
Fournols
St. Anthème
Sury-le-Comtal
St. Chamond
Condrieu
Marsac-en-Livradois
St. Marcellin sur Loire
St. Just-St. Rambert
La Grande-Croix
Les Roches
St. Germain-l'Herm
Cour-et-Buis
Viverols
St. Étienne
Arlanc
St. Bonnet-le-Château
Pelussin
La Côte-St. André
Champagnac-le-Vieux
Usson-en-Forez
Le Chambon-Feugerolles
Firminy
Pilat
Le Péage-de-Roussillon
Roussillon
Beaurepaire
Marcilloles
St. Genest-Malifaux
Le Bessat
Serrières
Craponne-sur-Arzon
Monistrol-sur-Loire
St. Didier-en-Velay
La Chaise-Dieu
L'EGLISE DE L'ABBAYE DE ST. ROBERT
St. Sauveur-en-Rue
Bourg-Argental
St. Rambert-d'Albon
Lens Lestang
Roybon
Hauterives
Ste. Sigolène
Villevocance
Andance
Collat
Riotord
Annonay
Paulhaguet
Allègre
Bellevue-la-Montagne
Retournac
Montfaucon-en-Velay
Sarras
Montmiral
St. Georges-d'Aurac
Vorey
St. Vallier
St. Marcellin
Satillieu
Margès
St. Paulien
Yssingeaux
St. Bonnet-le-Froid
St. Hilaire-du-Rosier
Siaugues-St. Romain
CHÂTEAU DE LAVOÛTE-POLIGNAC
Tain-l'Hermitage
Langeac
Le Pertuis
Tence
Peyrins
Romans-sur-Isère
Chanteuges
Le Chambon-sur-Lignon
St. Félicien
CHÂTEAU CHAZOTTE
St. Nazaire-en-Royans
CHAPELLE ST. MICHEL D'AIGUILHE
Le Puy-en-Velay
St. Julien-Chapteuil
Arlebosc
Tournon-sur-Rhône
Bourg-de-Péage
St. Agrève
Bains
Laussonne
St. Marcel
Alixan
Saugues
Monistrol-d'Allier
Le Monastier-sur-Gazeille
Lamastre
St. Péray
Cayres
St. Martin-de-Valamas
Montelier
Mt. Mézenc 1754
Valence
Léoncel
Costaros
Les Estables
Le Cheylard
Vernoux-en-Vivarais
Chabeuil
Portes-les-Valence
Malzieu-Ville
Chanaleilles
Landos
Charmes-sur-Rhône
Montmeyran
Le Béage
St. Pierreville
Plan-de-Baix
Grandrieu
St. Sauveur-de-Montagut
La Voulte-sur-Rhône
St. Alban-sur-Limagnole
Pradelles
Mézilhac
Coucouron
Livron-sur-Drôme
Monts
Privas
Crest
Auroux
Montpezat-sous-Bouzon
Loriol-sur-Drôme
Langogne
Serverette
Lanarce
Chomérac
Saillans
St. Amans
Châteauneuf-de-Randon
Pont-de-Labeaume
Thueyts
Mayres
Vals-les-Bains
Cruas
Luc
La Bastide-Puylaurent
D'Ardèche
Aubenas
Meysse
Sauzet
Cléon-d'Andran
Pradelle
Bourdeaux
Laubert
Rochemaure
Le Teil
Montélimar
La Bégude-de-Mazenc
Valgorge
Lavilledieu
Villeneuve-de-Berg
Belvezet
Dieulefit
Largentière
Vogüé
Espeluche
Mende
Prevenchères
CHÂTEAU DE VOGÜÉ
Aleyrac
Bouvières
ERMITAGE DE ST. PRIVAT
Le Bleymard
Joyeuse
BAPTISTRE DE MÉLAS
Beaujolais
Roannais
Lyonnais
Monts du Forez
Dombes
Monts du Velay
Monts de la Margeride
Gévaudan
Loire
Rhône
Isère
Drôme
Ardèche
Dore
45°
46°
5°
4°
104
105
118
130
131
3
4
5
A
B
C
145
60
219

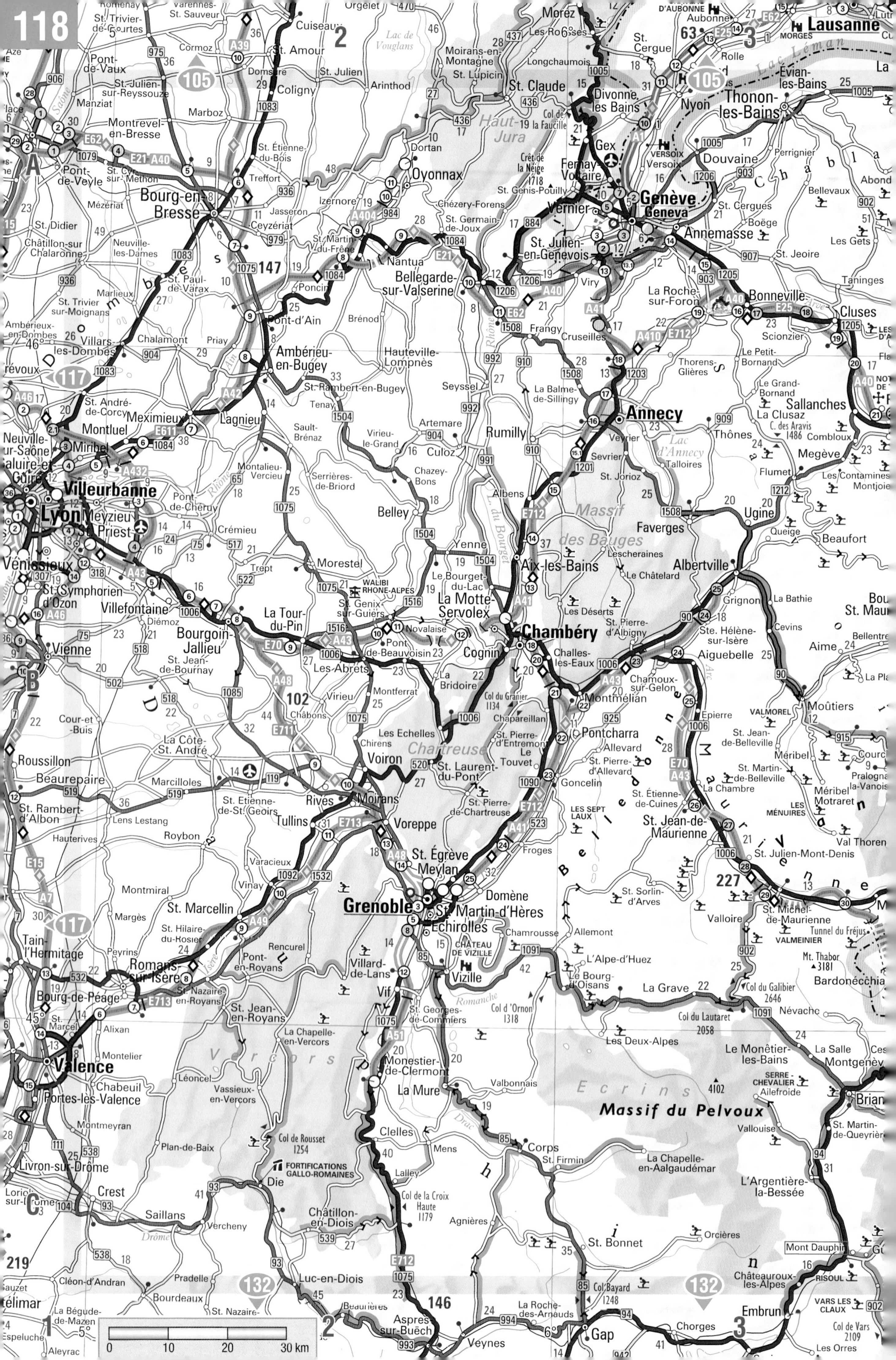
St. Trivier-de-Courtes
Cuiseaux
St. Amour
Lac de Vouglans
Moirans-en-Montagne
St. Lupicin
Morez
Les Rousses
Longchaumois
D'AUBONNE
Aubonne
Lausanne
MORGES
St. Cergue
Rolle
Lac Léman
Évian-les-Bains
Thonon-les-Bains
Pont-de-Vaux
Cormoz
Domsure
St. Julien
Coligny
Arinthod
St. Julien-sur-Reyssouze
Manziat
Marboz
St. Claude
Divonne-les-Bains
Nyon
Col de la Faucille
Haut-Jura
Montrevel-en-Bresse
St. Étienne-du-Bois
Dortan
Oyonnax
Gex
Ferney-Voltaire
VERSOIX
Versoix
Douvaine
Perrignier
Chablais
Crêt de la Neige 1718
Pont-de-Veyle
St. Cyr-sur-Menthon
Treffort
Bourg-en-Bresse
Mézériat
Jasseron
Izernore
Chézery-Forens
St. Genis-Pouilly
Vernier
Genève
Geneva
St. Cergues
Boëge
Bellevaux
Abond
St. Didier
Châtillon-sur-Chalaronne
Neuville-les-Dames
Ceyzériat
St. Martin-du-Frêne
St. Germain-de-Joux
St. Julien-en-Genevois
Annemasse
Les Gets
St. Jeoire
Nantua
Bellegarde-sur-Valserine
St. Paul-de-Varax
Marlieux
Poncin
Viry
La Roche-sur-Foron
Bonneville
Taninges
Cluses
St. Trivier-sur-Moignans
Dombes
Ambérieux-en-Dombes
Villars-les-Dombes
Chalamont
Priay
Pont-d'Ain
Brénod
Frangy
Cruseilles
Scionzier
Trévoux
Ambérieu-en-Bugey
Hauteville-Lompnès
Thorens-Glières
Le Petit-Bornand
St. Rambert-en-Bugey
Seyssel
La Balme-de-Sillingy
Le Grand-Bornand
St. André-de-Corcy
Meximieux
Lagnieu
Tenay
Annecy
La Clusaz
Sallanches
C. des Aravis 1486
Combloux
Neuville-sur-Saône
Montluel
Miribel
Sault-Brénaz
Virieu-le-Grand
Artemare
Rumilly
Veyrier
Lac d'Annecy
Thônes
Megève
Caluire-et-Cuire
Montalieu-Vercieu
Culoz
Sevrier
Talloires
Flumet
Les Contamines-Montjoie
Villeurbanne
Serrières-de-Briord
Chazey-Bons
St. Jorioz
Lyon
Meyzieu
St. Priest
Pont-de-Chéruy
Albens
Massif des Bauges
Faverges
Ugine
Belley
Crémieu
L. du Bourget
Queige
Beaufort
Vénissieux
Trept
Yenne
Lescheraines
Albertville
Morestel
Aix-les-Bains
Le Châtelard
St. Symphorien-d'Ozon
WALIBI RHONE-ALPES
Le Bourget-du-Lac
Villefontaine
St. Genix-sur-Guiers
La Motte-Servolex
Grignon
La Bathie
Diémoz
La Tour-du-Pin
Les Déserts
St. Pierre-d'Albigny
Bourgoin-Jallieu
Novalaise
Chambéry
Cevins
Vienne
Pont-de-Beauvoisin
Cognin
Challes-les-Eaux
Ste. Hélène-sur-Isère
Aime
Bellentre
St. Jean-de-Bournay
Les Abrets
Aiguebelle
La Bridoire
Chamoux-sur-Gelon
Montmélian
Montferrat
Col du Granier 1134
Virieu
Moûtiers
Chabons
Chapareillan
VALMOREL
Epierre
Cour-et-Buis
St. Pierre-d'Entremont
Pontcharra
St. Jean-de-Belleville
La Côte-St. André
Les Echelles
Chirens
Chartreuse
Allevard
Méribel
Roussillon
Voiron
St. Laurent-du-Pont
Le Touvet
St. Pierre-d'Allevard
St. Martin-de-Belleville
Pralognan-la-Vanoise
Beaurepaire
Marcilloles
Goncelin
La Chambre
Méribel Motraret
St. Rambert-d'Albon
Lens Lestang
St. Etienne-de-St. Geoirs
Rives
Moirans
St. Pierre-de-Chartreuse
St. Étienne-de-Cuines
LES MÉNUIRES
Hauterives
Roybon
Tullins
Voreppe
LES SEPT LAUX
St. Jean-de-Maurienne
Belledonne
Maurienne
Val Thorens
St. Julien-Mont-Denis
Varacieux
St. Égrève
Meylan
Froges
Vanoise
Montmiral
Vinay
Domène
St. Sorlin-d'Arves
St. Marcellin
Grenoble
St. Martin-d'Hères
Margès
Echirolles
Valloire
St. Michel-de-Maurienne
St. Hilaire-du-Rosier
Chamrousse
Allemont
Tunnel du Fréjus
VALMEINIER
Tain-l'Hermitage
Peyrins
Rencurel
CHATEAU DE VIZILLE
L'Alpe-d'Huez
Mt. Thabor 3181
Romans-sur-Isère
Pont-en-Royans
Villard-de-Lans
Vizille
Le Bourg-d'Oisans
Bardonécchia
Bourg-de-Péage
St. Nazaire-en-Royans
Vif
La Grave
Col du Galibier 2646
St. Marcel
Alixan
St. Jean-en-Royans
Romanche
St. Georges-de-Commiers
Col d'Ornon 1318
Névache
Col du Lautaret 2058
Montelier
La Chapelle-en-Vercors
Les Deux-Alpes
La Salle
Valence
Vercors
Monestier-de-Clermont
Le Monêtier-les-Bains
Montgenèvre
Chabeuil
Léoncel
Valbonnais
Ecrins
SERRE-CHEVALIER
Portes-lès-Valence
Vassieux-en-Vercors
La Mure
Massif du Pelvoux
Ailefroide
Briançon
Montmeyran
Vallouise
St. Martin-de-Queyrières
Plan-de-Baix
Col de Rousset 1254
Clelles
Mens
Corps
Livron-sur-Drôme
FORTIFICATIONS GALLO-ROMAINES
St. Firmin
La Chapelle-en-Aalgaudémar
L'Argentière-la-Bessée
Loriol-sur-Drôme
Crest
Die
Lalley
Col de la Croix Haute 1179
Saillans
Vercheny
Châtillon-en-Diois
Agnières
Drôme
St. Bonnet
Orcières
Mont Dauphin
Pradelle
Luc-en-Diois
Col Bayard 1248
Châteauroux-les-Alpes
RISOUL
Montélimar
Cléon-d'Andran
Bourdeaux
La Bégude-de-Mazenc
St. Nazaire-le-Désert
Beaurières
Aspres-sur-Buëch
La Roche-des-Arnauds
Gap
Chorges
Embrun
VARS LES CLAUX
Col de Vars 2109
Espeluche
Aleyrac
Veynes
Les Orres
0
10
20
30 km

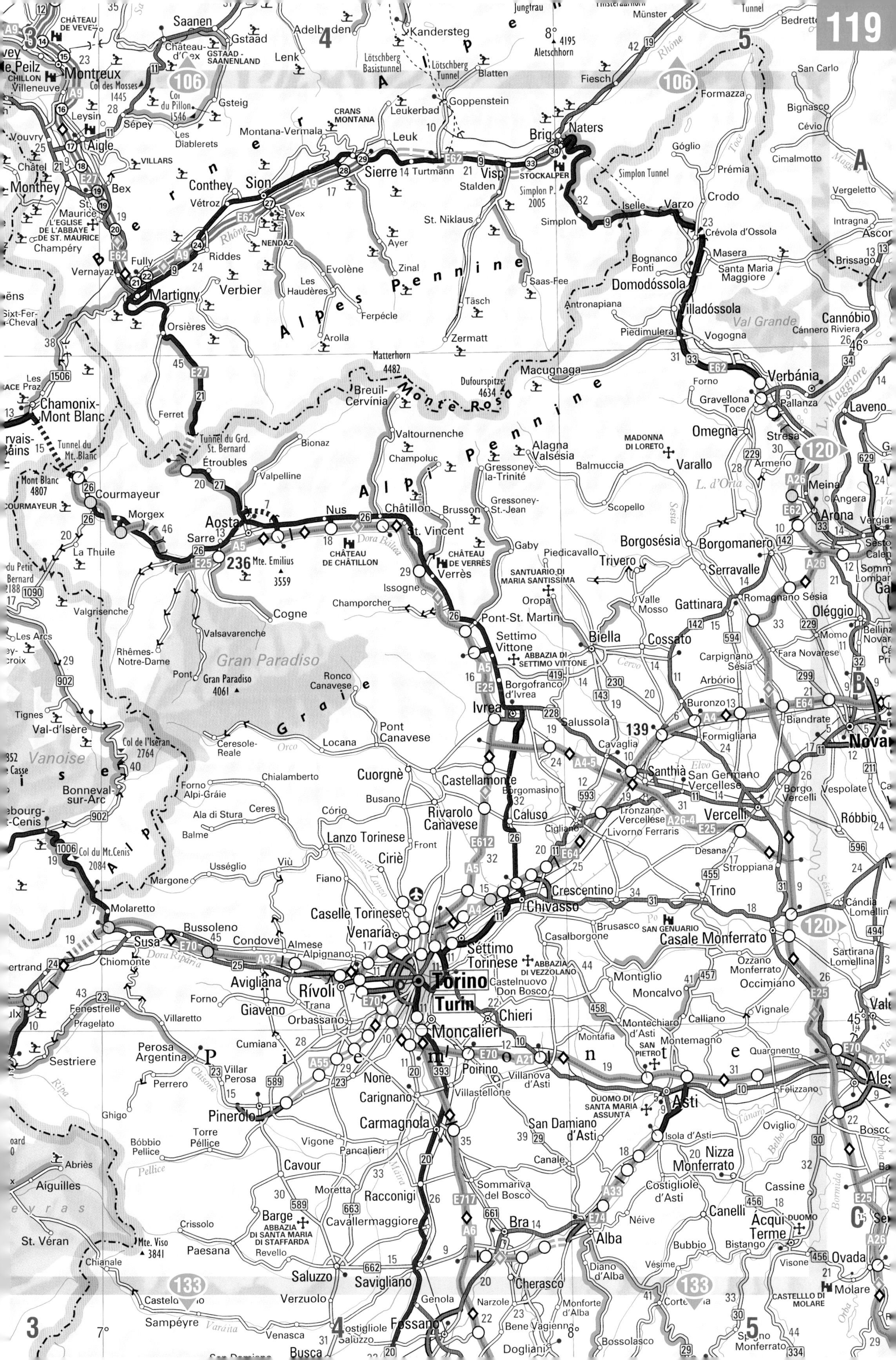
Saanen
Gstaad
Château-d'Œx
GSTAAD - SAANENLAND
Adelboden
Kandersteg
Lenk
Lötschberg Basistunnel
Lötschberg Tunnel
Blatten
Jungfrau
4195 Aletschhorn
Münster
Fiesch
Bedretto
Montreux
CHILLON
Villeneuve
Col des Mosses 1445
Col du Pillon 1546
Gsteig
Leysin
Sépey
Les Diablerets
Aigle
Vouvry
Châtel
VILLARS
Monthey
Bex
St. Maurice
L'EGLISE DE L'ABBAYE DE ST. MAURICE
Champéry
Conthey
Sion
Vétroz
Riddes
Fully
Vernayaz
Martigny
Verbier
Orsières
NENDAZ
Vex
Evolène
Les Haudères
Arolla
Ferpècle
Zinal
Ayer
Sierre
Turtmann
Leuk
Leukerbad
Goppenstein
CRANS MONTANA
Montana-Vermala
Visp
STOCKALPER
Stalden
St. Niklaus
Täsch
Zermatt
Saas-Fee
Brig
Naters
Simplon P. 2005
Simplon
Simplon Tunnel
Iselle
Varzo
Crodo
Formazza
Góglio
Prémia
Crévola d'Ossola
Masera
Santa Maria Maggiore
Bognanco Fonti
Domodóssola
Villadóssola
Antronapiana
Piedimulera
Vogogna
Val Grande
Cannóbio
Cánnero Riviera
San Carlo
Bignasco
Cévio
Cimalmotto
Vergeletto
Intragna
Ascona
Brissago
Alpes Pennine
Alpi Pennine
Matterhorn 4482
Monte Rosa
Dufourspitze 4634
Macugnaga
Breuil-Cervínia
Valtournenche
Champoluc
Bionaz
Valpelline
Tunnel du Grd. St. Bernard
Étroubles
Ferret
Chamonix-Mont Blanc
Tunnel du Mt. Blanc
Mont Blanc 4807
Courmayeur
COURMAYEUR
Morgex
La Thuile
Aosta
Sarre
Nus
Châtillon
CHÂTEAU DE CHÂTILLON
Dora Baltea
St. Vincent
Brusson
CHÂTEAU DE VERRÈS
Verrès
Issogne
Champorcher
236 Mte. Emilius 3559
Cogne
Valsavarenche
Rhêmes-Notre-Dame
Valgrisenche
Gran Paradiso
Gran Paradiso 4061
Ronco Canavese
Graie
Pont-St. Martin
Settimo Vittone
ABBAZIA DI SETTIMO VITTONE
Borgofranco d'Ivrea
Ivrea
Gressoney-la-Trinité
Gressoney-St.-Jean
Gaby
Alagna Valsésia
Balmuccia
Piedicavallo
SANTUARIO DI MARIA SANTISSIMA
Oropa
Biella
Cossato
Valle Mosso
Trivero
MADONNA DI LORETO
Varallo
Scopello
Borgosésia
Borgomanero
Serravalle
Gattinara
Romagnano Sésia
Carpignano Sésia
Fara Novarese
Arbório
Verbánia
Pallanza
Forno
Gravellona Toce
Omegna
Stresa
Armeno
L. d'Orta
Meina
Angera
Arona
Laveno
L. Maggiore
Oléggio
Novara
Biandrate
Buronzo
Formigliana
Salussola
Cavaglia
Santhià
San Germano Vercellese
Tronzano-Vercellese
Livorno Ferraris
Vercelli
Borgo Vercelli
Vespolate
Róbbio
Desana
Stroppiana
Trino
Crescentino
Chivasso
Cigliano
Borgomasino
Caluso
Castellamonte
Cuorgnè
Pont Canavese
Locana
Ceresole-Reale
Orco
Col de l'Iseran 2764
Val-d'Isère
Tignes
Les Arcs
Vanoise
Bonneval-sur-Arc
Col du Mt.Cenis 2084
Chialamberto
Forno Alpi-Gráie
Ala di Stura
Ceres
Balme
Usséglio
Viù
Margone
Cório
Busano
Rivarolo Canavese
Lanzo Torinese
Front
Ciriè
Fiano
Caselle Torinese
Venaría
Settimo Torinese
ABBAZIA DI VEZZOLANO
Castelnuovo Don Bosco
Brusasco
SAN GENUARIO
Casalborgone
Casale Monferrato
Ozzano Monferrato
Occimiano
Sartirana Lomellina
Cándia Lomellina
Montiglio
Moncalvo
Calliano
Vignale
Montechiaro d'Asti
Montafia
Montemagno
Quargnento
SAN PIETRO
Molaretto
Bussoleno
Susa
Condove
Almese
Alpignano
Dora Riparia
Chiomonte
Avigliana
Rívoli
Trana
Giaveno
Forno
Orbassano
Torino
Turin
Moncalieri
Chieri
Fenestrelle
Pragelato
Villaretto
Cumiana
Perosa Argentina
Villar Perosa
Sestriere
Perrero
Chisone
Pinerolo
None
Carignano
Poirino
Villanova d'Asti
Villastellone
Carmagnola
San Damiano d'Asti
DUOMO DI SANTA MARIA ASSUNTA
Asti
Isola d'Asti
Nizza Monferrato
Felizzano
Oviglio
Torre Péllice
Bóbbio Péllice
Ghigo
Vigone
Pancalieri
Cavour
Moretta
Racconigi
Sommariva del Bosco
Canale
Costigliole d'Asti
Canelli
Acqui Terme
DUOMO
Cassine
Bistagno
Bubbio
Néive
Alba
Bra
Cherasco
Diano d'Alba
Vésime
Barge
ABBAZIA DI SANTA MARIA DI STAFFARDA
Cavallermaggiore
Crissolo
Paesana
Revello
Mte. Viso 3841
Saluzzo
Savigliano
Abriès
Aiguilles
St. Véran
Chianale
Castelmagno
Verzuolo
Genola
Narzole
Monforte d'Alba
Bene Vagienna
Dogliani
Sampéyre
Varaita
Venasca
Costigliole Saluzzo
Fossano
Busca
Bossolasco
Cortemilia
Spigno Monferrato
Visone
Ovada
Molare
CASTELLO DI MOLARE
Alessandria
Bosco
106
120
133
139
3
4
5
A
B
C
7°
8°
46°
45°

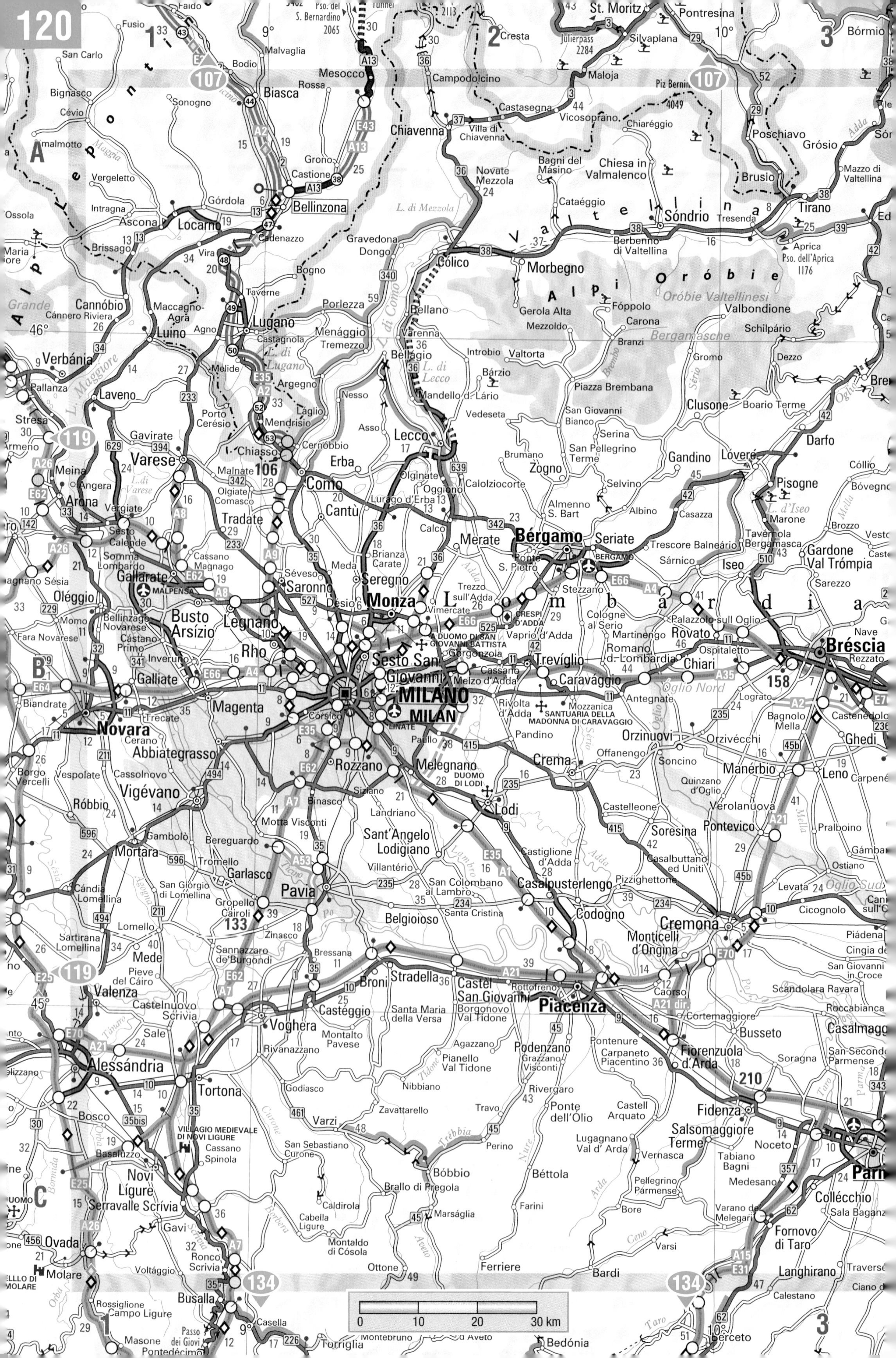

St. Moritz
Pontresina
Bórmio
Cresta
Julierpass
2284
Silvaplana
Maloja
Piz Bernina
4049
Psо. del S. Bernardino
2065
Mesocco
Rossa
Malvaglia
Fusio
Faido
San Carlo
Bodio
Biasca
Campodolcino
Castasegna
Vicosoprano
Chiareggio
Sonogno
Bignasco
Cévio
Chiavenna
Villa di Chiavenna
Poschiavo
Grósio
Chiesa in Valmalenco
Bagni del Másino
Brusio
Mazzo di Valtellina
Tirano
Tresenda
Maggia
Vergeletto
Grono
Castione
Bellinzona
Novate Mezzola
Cataéggio
Sóndrio
Intragna
Górdola
Ascona
Locarno
Cadenazzo
L. di Mezzola
Valtellina
Berbenno di Valtellina
Aprica
Pso. dell'Aprica
1176
Brissago
Vira
Gravedona
Dongo
Colico
Morbegno
Alpi Oróbie
Oróbie Valtellinesi
Bogno
Taverne
Porlezza
Fóppolo
Gerola Alta
Valbondione
Cannóbio
Cánnero Riviera
Maccagno-Agra
Lugano
Bellano
Carona
Mezzoldo
Schilpário
Luino
Agno
Castagnola
Ménaggio
Varenna
Branzi
Tremezzo
Bergamasche
Verbánia
L. di Lugano
Melide
Argegno
Bellágio
L. di Lecco
Introbio
Valtorta
Gromo
Dezzo
Pallanza
L. Maggiore
Bárzio
Piazza Brembana
Laveno
Porto Cerésio
Mandello d. Lário
Nesso
Láglio
Mendrísio
Vedeseta
San Giovanni Bianco
Clusone
Boario Terme
Stresa
Armeno
Gavirate
Cernóbbio
Asso
Lecco
Serina
Darfo
Varese
Chiasso
Malnate
Erba
Brumano
San Pellegrino Terme
Gandino
Lóvere
Meina
L. di Varese
Olgiate Comasco
Como
Olginate
Oggiono
Calolziocorte
Zogno
Selvino
Pisogne
Cóllio
Angera
Arona
Vergiate
Cantù
Lurago d'Erba
Almenno S. Bart
Albino
Casazza
Marone
L. d'Iseo
Bóvegno
Tradate
Calco
Merate
Bérgamo
Seriate
Trescore Balneário
Tavernola Bergamasca
Brozzo
Sesto Calende
Somma Lombardo
Cassano Magnago
Brianza Carate
Meda
Ponte S. Pietro
Sárnico
Iseo
Gardone Val Trómpia
Gallarate
Malpensa
Séveso
Seregno
Trezzo sull'Adda
Stezzano
Sarezzo
Agnano Sésia
Oléggio
Saronno
Monza
Vimercate
Lombardia
Crespi d'Adda
Cologne al Serio
Palazzolo sull'Oglio
Momo
Bellinzago Novarese
Busto Arsízio
Legnano
Désio
Duomo di San Giovanni Battista
Vaprio d'Adda
Martinengo
Rovato
Nave
Fara Novarese
Castano Primo
Rho
Sesto San Giovanni
Gorgonzola
Romano d. Lombardia
Ospitaletto
Bréscia
Rezzato
Inveruno
Cassano
Treviglio
Chiari
Galliate
Magenta
Milano
Milan
Melzo d'Adda
Caravággio
Antegnate
Oglio Nord
Lograto
Biandrate
Novara
Trecate
Córsico
Linate
Rivolta d'Adda
Santuario della Madonna di Caravaggio
Mozzanica
Bagnolo Mella
Castenedolo
Cerano
Abbiategrasso
Paullo
Pandino
Orzinuovi
Orzivécchi
Ghedi
Borgo Vercelli
Vespolate
Cassolnovo
Rozzano
Melegnano
Duomo di Lodi
Crema
Offanengo
Soncino
Manérbio
Leno
Carpenè
Vigévano
Siziano
Quinzano d'Oglio
Róbbio
Binasco
Landriano
Lodi
Castelleone
Verolanuova
Motta Visconti
Sant'Angelo Lodigiano
Soresina
Pontevico
Pralboino
Gambolò
Bereguardo
Mortara
Tromello
Garlasco
Villantério
Castiglione d'Adda
Casalbuttano ed Uniti
Ostiano
Gámbara
Cándia Lomellina
San Giorgio di Lomellina
Pavia
San Colombano al Lambro
Casalpusterlengo
Pizzighettone
Levata
Oglio Sud
Gropello Cairoli
Santa Cristina
Codogno
Cremona
Cicognolo
Lomello
Zinasco
Belgioioso
Monticelli d'Ongina
Piádena
Sartirana Lomellina
Mede
Sannazzaro de'Burgondi
Bressana
Cingia de
Pieve del Cáiro
Broni
Stradella
Castel San Giovanni
Rottofreno
Piacenza
Caorso
San Giovanni in Croce
Scandolara Ravara
Valenza
Castelnuovo Scrivia
Voghera
Casteggio
Santa Maria della Versa
Borgonovo Val Tidone
Cortemaggiore
Roccabianca
Sale
Montalto Pavese
Busseto
Casalmaggiore
Alessándria
Rivanazzano
Pianello Val Tidone
Agazzano
Podenzano
Grazzano Visconti
Pontenure
Carpaneto Piacentino
Fiorenzuola d'Arda
San Secondo Parmense
Soragna
Tortona
Godiasco
Nibbiano
Rivergaro
Bosco
Zavattarello
Travo
Ponte dell'Ólio
Castell Arquato
Fidenza
Varzi
Villaggio medievale di Novi Ligure
Trébbia
Salsomaggiore Terme
Noceto
Basaluzzo
Cassano Spinola
San Sebastiano Curone
Perino
Lugagnano Val d'Arda
Vernasca
Tabiano Bagni
Novi Lígure
Bóbbio
Béttola
Medesano
Parma
Serravalle Scrívia
Caldirola
Brallo di Pregola
Pellegrino Parmense
Colléchio
Gavi
Cabella Ligure
Marságlia
Farini
Bore
Varano de' Melegari
Sala Baganza
Fornovo di Taro
Ovada
Ronco Scrivia
Montaldo di Cósola
Varsi
Molare
Voltággio
Ottone
Ferriere
Bardi
Langhirano
Traversetolo
Castello di Molare
Busalla
Calestano
Rossiglione
Campo Ligure
Passo dei Giovi
Casella
Masone
Pontedécimo
Torriglia
Montebruno
Bedónia
Berceto
Ciano d'
0
10
20
30 km

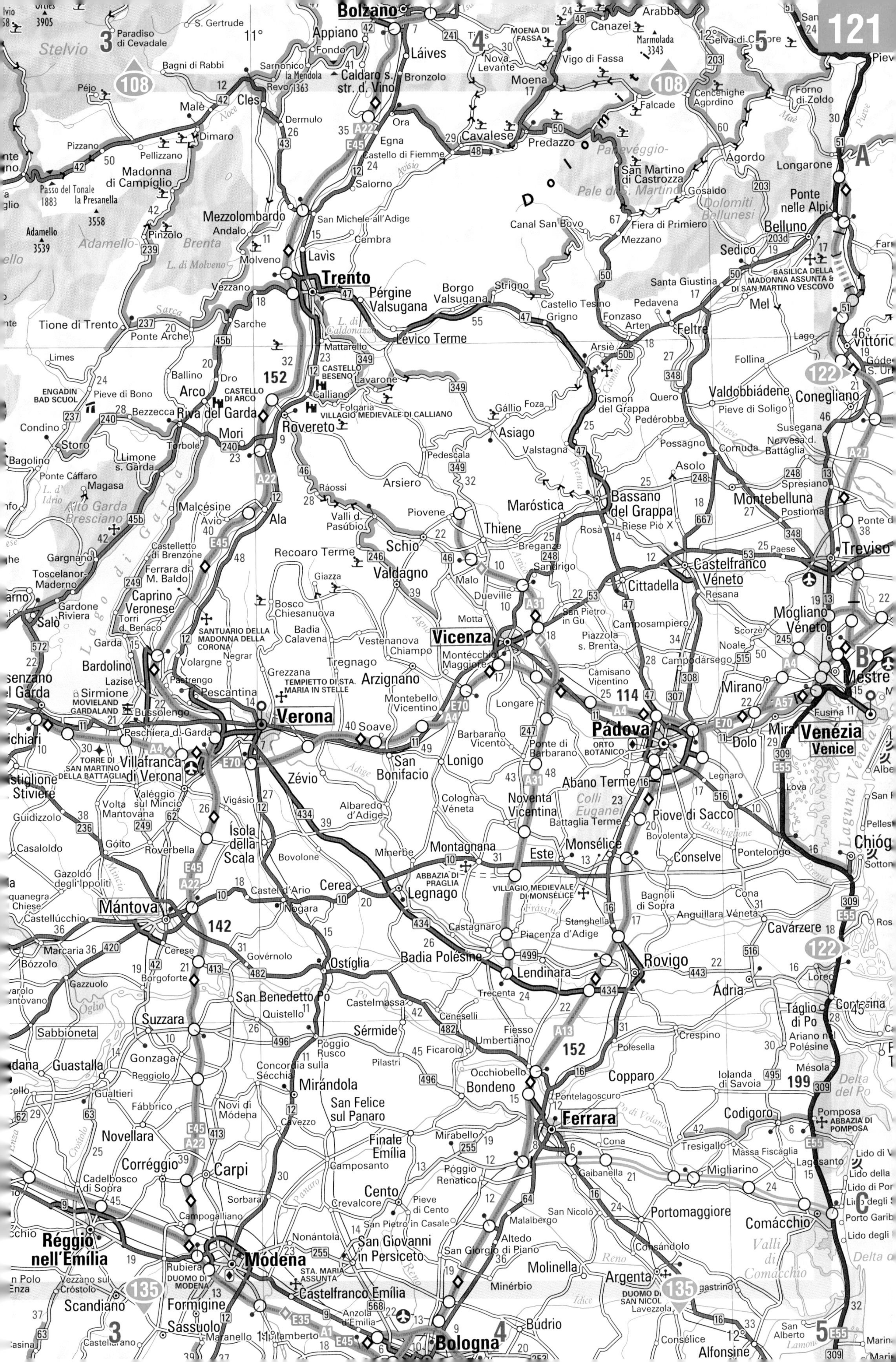

Bolzano
Appiano
Paradiso di Cevadale
S. Gertrude
Stelvio
Láives
Fondo
Sarnonico
la Mendola 1363
Revò
Caldaro s. str. d. Vino
Bronzolo
Bagni di Rabbi
Péio
Cles
Malè
Dimaro
Dermulo
Ora
Egna
Castello di Fiemme
Cavalese
Predazzo
Moena
MOENA DI FASSA
Nova Levante
Canazei
Arabba
Marmolada 3343
Selva di Cadore
Vigo di Fassa
Cencenighe Agordino
Falcade
Forno di Zoldo
Agordo
Longarone
Dolomiti
Paneveggio-Pale di S. Martino
San Martino di Castrozza
Gosaldo
Dolomiti Bellunesi
Ponte nelle Alpi
Belluno
Sedico
BASILICA DELLA MADONNA ASSUNTA & DI SAN MARTINO VESCOVO
Fiera di Primiero
Mezzano
Canal San Bovo
Pizzano
Pellizzano
Madonna di Campíglio
Passo del Tonale 1883
la Presanella 3558
Adamello 3539
Adamello
Brenta
Pinzolo
Mezzolombardo
Andalo
Molveno
L. di Molveno
San Michele all'Adige
Cembra
Lavis
Trento
Pérgine Valsugana
Borgo Valsugana
Strigno
Castello Tesino
Grigno
Santa Giustina
Pedavena
Mel
Fonzaso
Arten
Feltre
Vezzano
Sarche
Tione di Trento
Ponte Arche
Sarca
L. di Caldonazzo
Levico Terme
Mattarello
CASTELLO BESENO
Lavarone
Limes
Ballino
Dro
Arco
CASTELLO DI ARCO
Riva del Garda
ENGADIN BAD SCUOL
Pieve di Bono
Bezzecca
Condino
Storo
Bagolino
Mori
Torbole
Roveretto
Calliano
Folgaria
VILLAGGIO MEDIEVALE DI CALLIANO
Gállio
Foza
Asiago
Arsiè
Cismon del Grappa
Quero
Valdobbiádene
Pieve di Soligo
Conegliano
Follina
Lago
Vittório
Pedérobba
Susegana
Nervesa d. Battáglia
Possagno
Cornuda
Asolo
Valstagna
Limone s. Garda
Ponte Cáffaro
L. d'Idro
Magasa
Alto Garda Bresciano
Lago di Garda
Malcésine
Avio
Ala
Ráossi
Valli d. Pasúbio
Arsiero
Pedescala
Piovene
Thiene
Maróstica
Bassano del Grappa
Montebelluna
Spresiano
Postioma
Riese Pio X
Rosà
Breganze
Treviso
Paese
Castelfranco Véneto
Cittadella
Resana
Gargnano
Toscolano-Maderno
Castelletto di Brenzone
Ferrara di M. Baldo
Caprino Veronese
Recoaro Terme
Schio
Valdagno
Malo
Sandrigo
Dueville
Gardone Riviera
Salò
Torri d. Benaco
Garda
SANTUARIO DELLA MADONNA DELLA CORONA
Bosco Chiesanuova
Giazza
Badia Calavena
Vestenanova
Chiampo
Vicenza
Motta
San Pietro in Gu
Piazzola s. Brenta
Camposampiero
Mogliano Véneto
Scorzè
Noale
Campodársego
Mirano
Mestre
Bardolino
Lazise
Sirmione
MOVIELAND GARDALAND
Pastrengo
Pescantina
Volargne
Negrar
Grezzana
Tregnago
TEMPIETTO DI STA. MARIA IN STELLE
Arzignano
Montebello Vicentino
Montécchio Maggiore
Camisano Vicentino
Longare
Padova
ORTO BOTANICO
Venézia
Venice
Fusina
Mira
Dolo
Desenzano del Garda
Peschiera d. Garda
Bussolengo
Verona
Soave
San Bonifacio
Barbarano Vicento
Ponte di Barbarano
Lonigo
TORRE DI SAN MARTINO DELLA BATTAGLIA
Villafranca di Verona
Castiglione delle Stiviere
Valéggio sul Mincio
Zévio
Vigásio
Volta Mantovana
Guidizzolo
Cologna Véneta
Albaredo d'Adige
Noventa Vicentina
Abano Terme
Colli Euganei
Battaglia Terme
Piove di Sacco
Bovolenta
Legnaro
Lova
Laguna Véneta
Chióggia
Sottomarina
Casaloldo
Góito
Roverbella
Ísola della Scala
Bovolone
Minerbe
Montagnana
Este
Monsélice
Conselve
Pontelongo
ABBAZIA DI PRAGLIA
VILLAGGIO MEDIEVALE DI MONSELICE
Gazoldo degli Ippoliti
Acquanegra s. Chiese
Mántova
Castel d'Ario
Nogara
Cerea
Legnago
Bagnoli di Sopra
Cona
Anguillara Véneta
Cavárzere
Castellúcchio
Marcaria
Cerese
Castagnaro
Piacenza d'Adige
Stanghella
Bozzolo
Borgoforte
Govérnolo
Ostíglia
Badia Polésine
Lendinara
Rovigo
Ádria
Gazzuolo
San Benedetto Po
Quistello
Castelmassa
Ceneselli
Trecenta
Fiesso Umbertiano
Táglio di Po
Contarina
Ariano nel Polésine
Suzzara
Sabbioneta
Gonzaga
Póggio Rusco
Sérmide
Ficarolo
Crespino
Polesella
Guastalla
Reggiolo
Concordia sulla Sécchia
Pilastri
Occhiobello
Bondeno
Copparo
Iolanda di Savoia
Mésola
Delta del Po
Gualtieri
Fábbrico
Novi di Módena
Mirándola
San Felice sul Panaro
Cavezzo
Pontelagoscuro
Ferrara
Codigoro
Pomposa
ABBAZIA DI POMPOSA
Novellara
Finale Emília
Mirabello
Tresigallo
Massa Fiscáglia
Correggio
Carpi
Cadelbosco di Sopra
Camposanto
Póggio Renatico
Gaibanella
Migliarino
Lagosanto
Lido di Volano
Lido delle Nazioni
Lido di Pomposa
Lido degli Scacchi
Porto Garibaldi
Lido degli Estensi
Sorbara
Cento
Pieve di Cento
Crevalcore
Campogalliano
San Nicolò
Portomaggiore
Comácchio
Valli di Comácchio
Réggio nell'Emília
Módena
Nonántola
San Pietro in Casale
San Giovanni in Persiceto
Malalbergo
Altedo
Consándolo
Rubiera
DUOMO DI MODENA
STA. MARIA ASSUNTA
San Giorgio di Piano
Molinella
Argenta
DUOMO DI SAN NICOLÒ
Vezzano sul Cróstolo
Scandiano
Formigine
Castelfranco Emília
Minérbio
Lavezzola
Sassuolo
Anzola d'Emília
Maranello
Spilamberto
Bologna
Búdrio
Consélice
Alfonsine
San Alberto
Lamone
Dolomiti

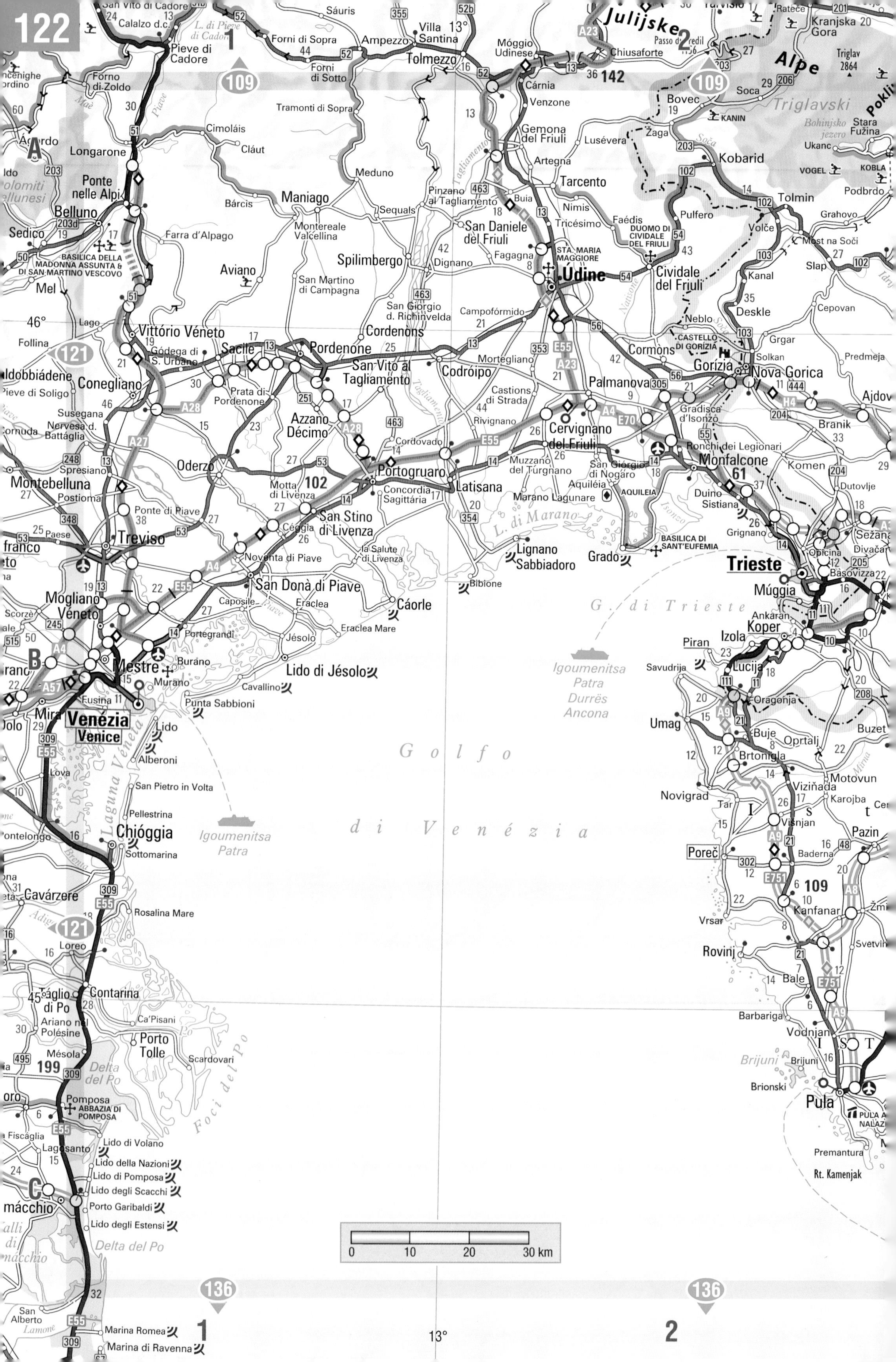
Venézia
Venice
Mestre
Trieste
Údine
Pordenone
Treviso
Belluno
Gorízia
Nova Gorica
Koper
Pula
Poreč
Rovinj
Chióggia
Golfo di Venézia
G. di Trieste
Igoumenitsa
Patra
Durrës
Ancona
0
10
20
30 km
1
2
13°

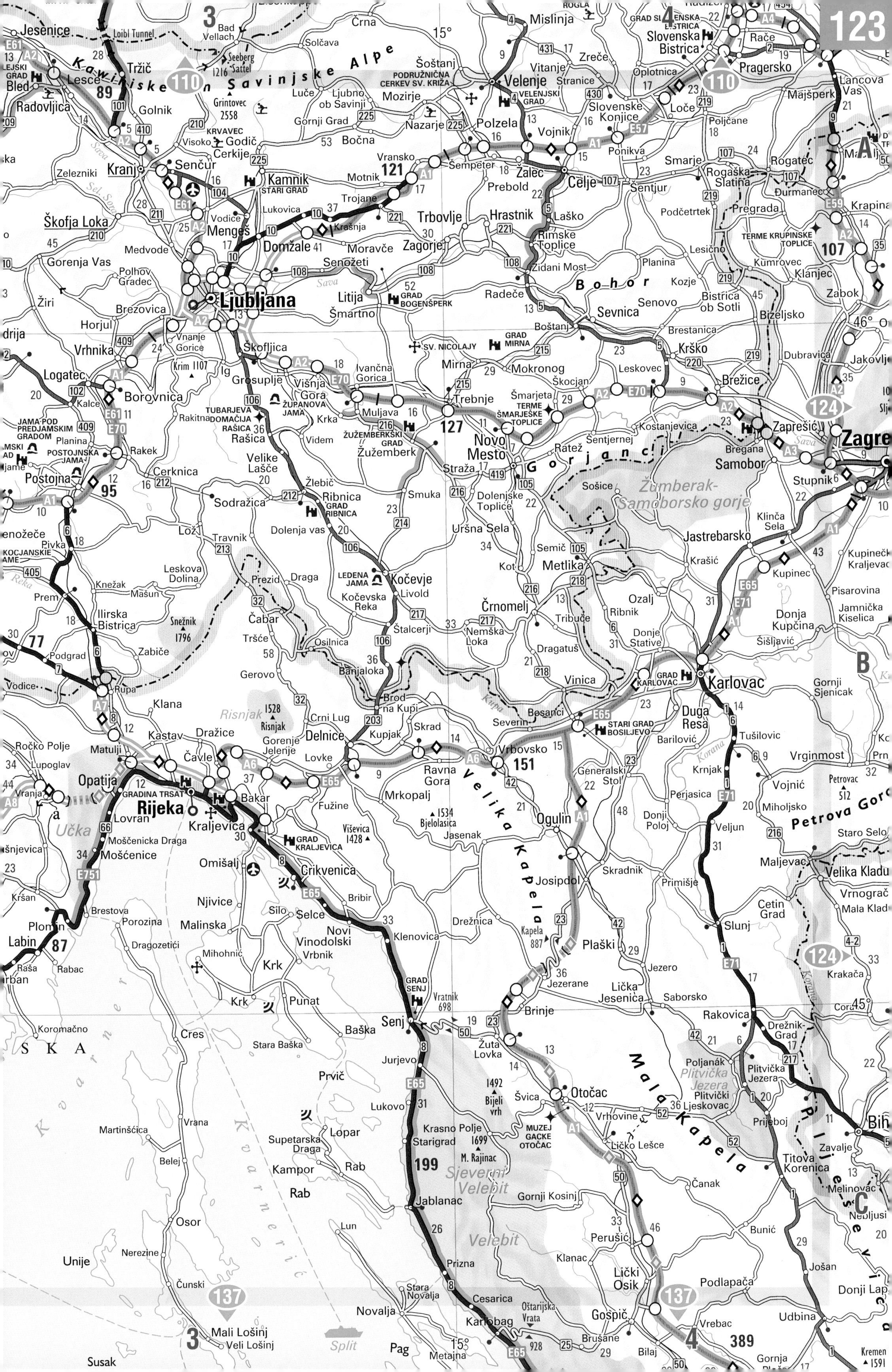

Jesenice
Loibl Tunnel
Bad Vellach
Seeberg Sattel
Črna
Solčava
Kawinske
Savinjske Alpe
Mislinja
Slovenska Bistrica
Rače
Pragersko
Lesce
Bled
Radovljica
Tržič
Golnik
Grintovec 2558
Luče
Ljubno ob Savinji
Mozirje
Šoštanj
Velenje
Vitanje
Zreče
Oplotnica
Loče
Poljčane
Majšperk
Lancova Vas
Gornji Grad
Nazarje
Polzela
Vojnik
Slovenske Konjice
Kranj
Visoko
Godič
Cerkije
Bočna
Vransko
Šempeter
Žalec
Celje
Ponikva
Smarje
Rogatec
Zelezniki
Senčur
Kamnik
Motnik
Prebold
Šentjur
Rogaška Slatina
Đurmanec
Škofja Loka
Vodice
Mengeš
Lukovica
Trojane
Trbovlje
Hrastnik
Laško
Podčetrtek
Pregrada
Krapina
Medvode
Domžale
Moravče
Zagorje
Rimske Toplice
Lesično
Terme Krupinske Toplice
Gorenja Vas
Polhov Gradec
Senožeti
Zidani Most
Planina
Kumrovec
Klanjec
Ljubljana
Litija
Šmartno
Grad Bogenšperk
Radeče
Bohor
Kozje
Bistrica ob Sotli
Zabok
Žiri
Horjul
Brezovica
Vnanje Gorice
Sevnica
Senovo
Bizeljsko
Vrhnika
Škofljica
Boštanj
Brestanica
Krško
Dubravica
Jakovlje
Logatec
Krim 1107
Ig
Grosuplje
Višnja Gora
Ivančna Gorica
Sv. Nicolajy
Grad Mirna
Mirna
Mokronog
Leskovec
Brežice
Borovnica
Kalce
Županova Jama
Trebnje
Šmarjeta
Škocjan
Terme Šmarješke Toplice
Kostanjevica
Zaprešić
Zagreb
Jama pod Predjamskim Gradom
Rakitna
Tubarjeva Domačija
Rašica
Muljava
Krka
Videm
Žužemberški Grad
Žužemberk
Novo Mesto
Šentjernej
Bregana
Samobor
Stupnik
Postojnska Jama
Rakek
Velike Lašče
Straža
Ratež
Gorjanci
Žumberak-Samoborsko gorje
Sošice
Postojna
Cerknica
Ribnica
Grad Ribnica
Smuka
Dolenjske Toplice
Klinča Sela
Sodražica
Žlebič
Dolenja vas
Uršna Sela
Jastrebarsko
Ložd
Travnik
Semič
Krašić
Kupinečki Kraljevac
Pivka
Leskova Dolina
Prezid
Draga
Ledena Jama
Kočevje
Livold
Kot
Metlika
Kupinec
Knežak
Mašun
Kočevska Reka
Črnomelj
Ozalj
Pisarovina
Prem
Ilirska Bistrica
Snežnik 1796
Čabar
Štalcerji
Nemška Loka
Tribuče
Ribnik
Donja Kupčina
Jamnička Kiselica
Tršće
Osilnica
Dragatuš
Donje Stative
Šišljavić
Podgrad
Zabiče
Gerovo
Banjaloka
Brod na Kupi
Vinica
Karlovac
Grad Karlovac
Gornji Sjenicak
Vodice
Rupa
Klana
Risnjak 1528
Crni Lug
Skrad
Kupa
Bosanci
Severin
Duga Resa
Stari Grad Bosiljevo
Tušilovic
Rročko Polje
Kastav
Dražice
Gorenje Jelenje
Delnice
Kupjak
Lovke
Vrbovsko
Barilović
Vrginmost
Lupoglav
Matulji
Čavle
Ravna Gora
Generalski Stol
Krnjak
Vojnić
Petrovac 512
Opatija
Vranja
Gradina Trsat
Rijeka
Bakar
Fužine
Mrkopalj
Perjasica
Miholjsko
Petrova Gora
Lovran
Kraljevica
Učka
Grad Kraljevica
Viševica 1428
1534 Bjelolasica
Jasenak
Ogulin
Donji Poloj
Veljun
Staro Selo
Mošćenička Draga
Mošćenice
Omišalj
Crikvenica
Josipdol
Skradnik
Primišje
Maljevac
Velika Kladuša
Velika Kapela
Njivice
Bribir
Cetin Grad
Vrnograč
Mala Kladuša
Kršan
Brestova
Silo
Selce
Drežnica
Malinska
Novi Vinodolski
Klenovica
Slunj
Plomin
Porozina
Kapela 887
Plaški
Labin
Dragozetići
Mihohnić
Vrbnik
Krk
Jezero
Krakača
Raša
Rabac
Jezerane
Lička Jesenica
Saborsko
Punat
Grad Senj
Vratnik 698
Brinje
Rakovica
Koromačno
Cres
Baška
Senj
Žuta Lovka
Drežnik-Grad
Stara Baška
Jurjevo
Mala Kapela
Poljanák
Plitvička Jezera
Plitvički Ljeskovac
Prvič
1492 Bijeli vrh
Švica
Otočac
Lukovo
Vrhovine
Muzej Gacke Otočac
Prijeboj
Martinšćica
Vrana
Krasno Polje
Starigrad
1699 M. Rajinac
Ličko Lešce
Supetarska Draga
Lopar
Zavalje
Bihać
Belej
Kampor
Rab
Sjeverni Velebit
Titova Korenica
Melinovac
Čanak
Gornji Kosinj
Nebljusi
Osor
Lun
Velebit
Perušić
Bunić
Plješevica
Unije
Nerezine
Prizna
Klanac
Lički Osik
Jošan
Čunski
Stara Novalja
Cesarica
Podlapača
Donji Lapac
Novalja
Oštarijska Vrata
Gospić
Vrebac
Udbina
Mali Lošinj
Veli Lošinj
Split
Pag
Karlobag
Metajna
Brušane
Bilaj
Susak
Kremen 1591
Kvarner
Kvarnerić
Reka
Sava

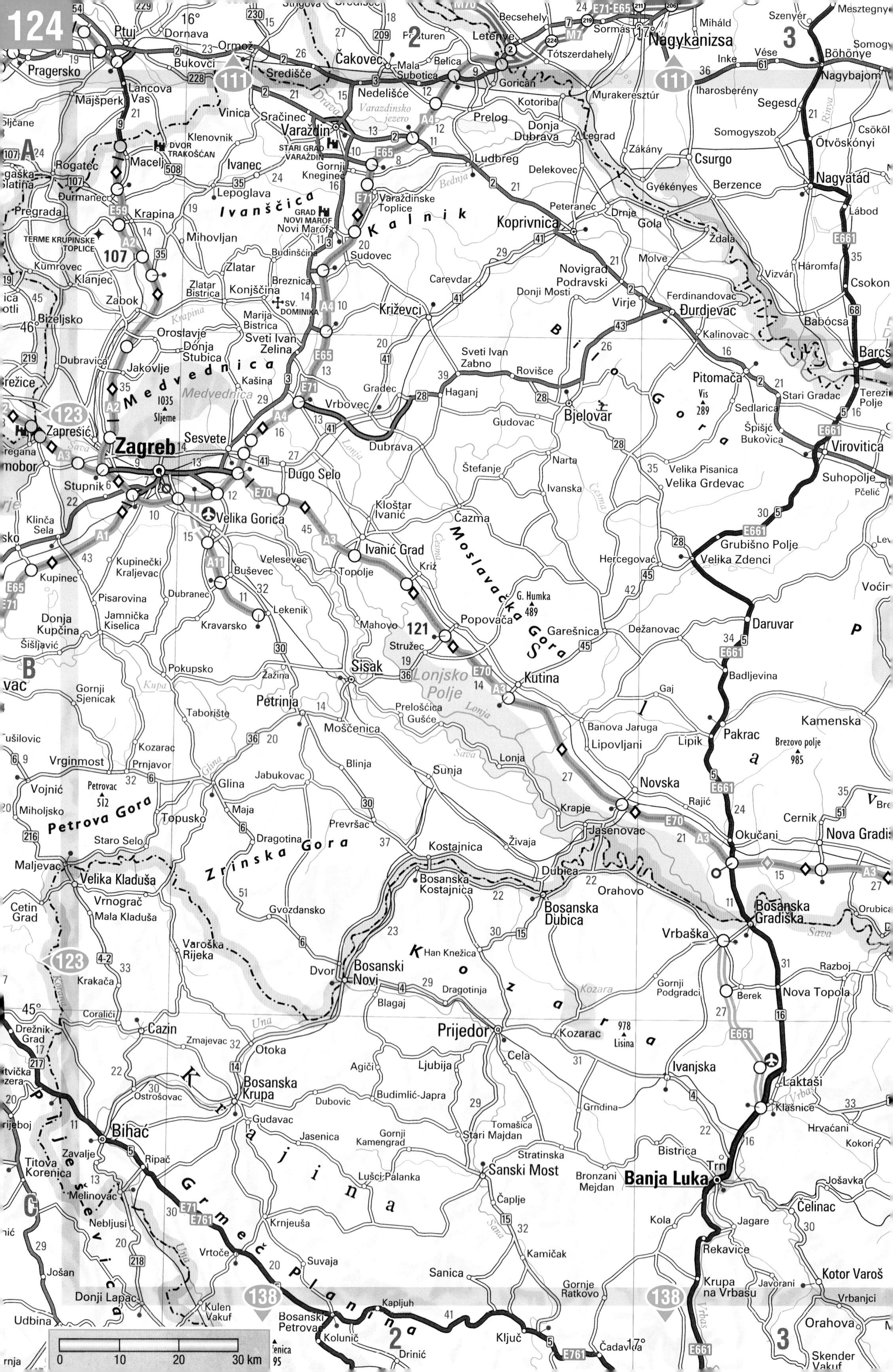

Ptuj
Dornava
Pragersko
Ormož
Bukovci
Središče
Čakovec
Mala Subotica
Belica
Letenye
Becsehely
Sormás
Nagykanizsa
Mihálď
Tótszerdahely
Szenyér
Mesztegnyő
Somogy
Böhönye
Nagybajom
Inke
Vése
Iharosberény
Segesd
Somogyszob
Csökölÿ
Ötvöskónyi
Murakeresztúr
Goričan
Nedelišće
Kotoriba
Prelog
Donja Dubrava
Legrad
Zákány
Csurgo
Lancova Vas
Majšperk
Vinica
Sračinec
Varaždin
Varazdinsko jezero
Drava
Klenovnik
DVOR TRAKOŠĆAN
STARI GRAD VARAŽDIN
Macelj
Rogatec
Đurmanec
Ivanec
Lepoglava
Gornji Kneginec
Ludbreg
Delekovec
Gyékényes
Berzence
Nagyatád
Lábod
Pregrada
Krapina
Ivanšćica
GRAD NOVI MAROF
Novi Marof
Varaždinske Toplice
Kalnik
Bednja
Koprivnica
Peteranec
Drnje
Gola
Ždala
TERME KRUPINSKE TOPLICE
Mihovljan
Budinšćina
Sudovec
Molve
Háromfa
Vizvár
Csokon
Kumrovec
Klanjec
Zlatar
Zlatar Bistrica
Konjščina
Breznica
Carevdar
Novigrad Podravski
Donji Mosti
Virje
Ferdinandovac
Đurđevac
Babócsa
Zabok
SV. DOMINIKA
Križevci
Kalinovac
Bizeljsko
Krapina
Marija Bistrica
Oroslavje
Donja Stubica
Sveti Ivan Zelina
Sveti Ivan Zabno
Bilo Gora
Pitomača
Barcs
Dubravica
Jakovlje
Medvednica
Kašina
Rovišce
Haganj
Gradec
Stari Gradac
Terezino Polje
Brežice
Sljeme
Vrbovec
Bjelovar
Vis
Sedlarica
Zaprešić
Zagreb
Sesvete
Gudovac
Dubrava
Lonja
Špišić Bukovica
Virovitica
Samobor
Stupnik
Dugo Selo
Štefanje
Narta
Velika Pisanica
Velika Grdevac
Suhopolje
Pčelić
Klinča Sela
Velika Gorica
Ivanska
Česma
Kloštar Ivanić
Čazma
Moslavačka Gora
Ivanić Grad
Križ
Grubišno Polje
Velika Zdenci
Hercegovac
Kupinečki Kraljevac
Velesevec
Topolje
Kupinec
Bušečec
Pisarovina
Dubranec
Lekenik
G. Humka
Popovača
Garešnica
Dežanovac
Daruvar
Voćin
Donja Kupčina
Jamnička Kiselica
Kravarsko
Mahovo
Stružec
Šišljavić
Pokupsko
Žažina
Sisak
Lonjsko Polje
Kutina
Badljevina
Gornji Sjenicak
Kupa
Taborište
Petrinja
Prelošćica
Gušće
Gaj
Kamenska
Banova Jaruga
Lipovljani
Lipik
Pakrac
Brezovo polje
Tušilović
Kozarac
Vrginmost
Prnjavor
Moščenica
Blinja
Sava
Lonja
Vojnić
Petrovac
Glina
Jabukovac
Sunja
Novska
Rajić
Cernik
Miholjsko
Petrova Gora
Topusko
Maja
Krapje
Okučani
Nova Gradiška
Prevršac
Jasenovac
Staro Selo
Dragotina
Zrinska Gora
Živaja
Maljevac
Velika Kladuša
Kostajnica
Dubica
Orahovo
Bosanska Kostajnica
Bosanska Dubica
Bosanska Gradiška
Orubica
Cetin Grad
Vrnograč
Mala Kladuša
Gvozdansko
Vrbaška
Varoška Rijeka
Han Knežica
Kozara
Razboj
Bosanski Novi
Krakača
Dvor
Dragotinja
Gornji Podgradci
Berek
Nova Topola
Blagaj
Coralići
Una
Drežnik-Grad
Cazin
Prijedor
Kozarac
Lisina
Zmajevac
Otoka
Cela
Ivanjska
Agići
Ljubija
Laktaši
Plitvička Jezera
Bosanska Krupa
Ostrožac
Budimlić-Japra
Dubovic
Grmdina
Klašnice
Hrvaćani
Gudavac
Bihać
Jasenica
Gornji Kamengrad
Tomašica
Stari Majdan
Kokori
Zavalje
Ripač
Stratinska
Bistrica
Titova Korenica
Sanski Most
Lušci Palanka
Bronzani Mejdan
Banja Luka
Trn
Jošavka
Melinovac
Krajina
Čaplje
Čelinac
Nebljusi
Grmeč Planina
Krnjeuška
Kola
Jagare
Sana
Vrtoče
Kamičak
Rekavice
Jošan
Suvaja
Plješevica
Sanica
Gornje Ratkovo
Krupa na Vrbasu
Javorani
Kotor Varoš
Vrbanjci
Donji Lapac
Kulen Vakuf
Kapljuh
Orahova
Udbina
Bosanski Petrovac
Kolunič
Drinić
Ključ
Čadavica
Skender Vakuf
Vrbas
0
10
20
30 km

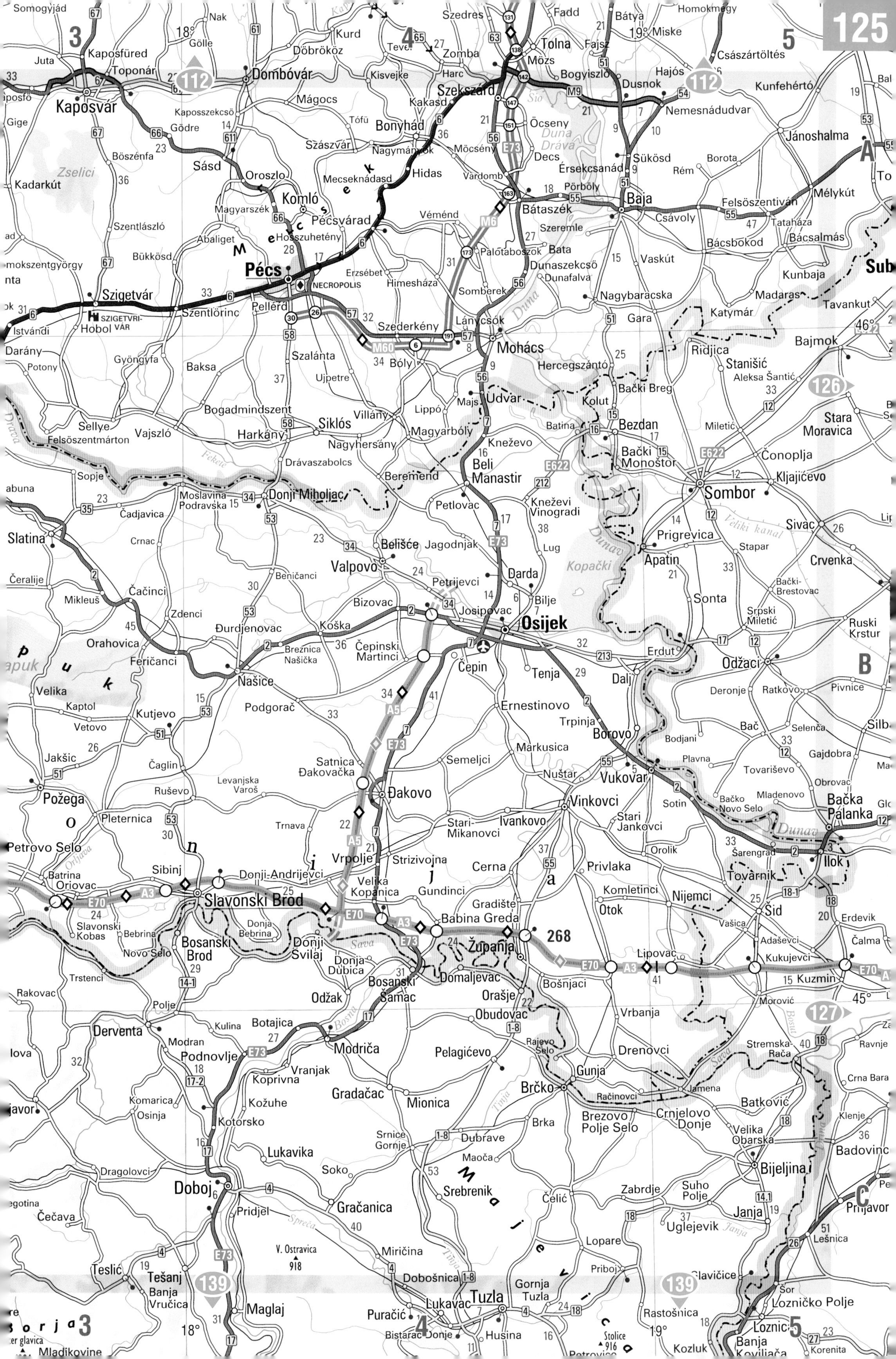
Somogyjád
Kaposfüred
Toponár
Kaposvár
Juta
Gige
Dombóvár
Gölle
Nak
Kurd
Döbrököz
Tevel
Zomba
Szedres
Fadd
Bátya
Miske
Homokmégy
Tolna
Mözs
Fajsz
Bogyiszló
Dusnok
Hajós
Császártöltés
Kunfehértó
Nemesnádudvar
Szekszárd
Harc
Kisvejke
Kakasd
Mágocs
Kaposszekcső
Gödre
Tófű
Bonyhád
Szászvár
Nagymányok
Mőcsény
Öcseny
Decs
Duna
Dráva
Sükösd
Érsekcsanád
Borota
Rém
Jánoshalma
Mélykút
Bőszénfa
Zselici
Kadarkút
Sásd
Oroszló
Komló
Magyarszék
Mecseknádasd
Hidas
Várdomb
Pörböly
Baja
Bátaszék
Csávoly
Felsőszentiván
Tataháza
Bácsalmás
Bácsbokod
Szentlászló
Abaliget
Pécsvárad
Hosszúhetény
Véménd
Szeremle
Palotabozsok
Bata
Dunaszekcső
Dunafalva
Vaskút
Kunbaja
Bükkösd
Pécs
Erzsébet
Himesháza
NECROPOLIS
Szigetvár
SZIGETVÁRI VÁR
Szentlőrinc
Pellérd
Somberek
Nagybaracska
Madaras
Tavankut
Hobol
Istvándi
Szederkény
Lánycsók
Gara
Katymár
Mohács
Bajmok
Darány
Potony
Gyöngyfa
Baksa
Szalánta
Bóly
Hercegszántó
Ridjica
Stanišić
Aleksa Šantić
Újpetre
Majs
Udvar
Kolut
Bački Breg
Bogadmindszent
Lippó
Stara Moravica
Sellye
Felsőszentmárton
Vajszló
Harkány
Siklós
Villány
Nagyharsány
Magyarbóly
Batina
Bezdan
Miletić
Kneževo
Bački Monoštor
Čonoplja
Drávaszabolcs
Beremend
Beli Manastir
Kljajićevo
Sopje
Moslavina Podravska
Donji Miholjac
Petlovac
Kneževi Vinogradi
Sombor
Slatina
Čadjavica
Crnac
Prigrevica
Sivac
Čeralije
Belišće
Jagodnjak
Lug
Apatin
Stapar
Crvenka
Valpovo
Beničanci
Darda
Kopački
Mikleuš
Čačinci
Bizovac
Petrijevci
Bilje
Sonta
Bački-Brestovac
Zdenci
Josipovac
Osijek
Srpski Miletić
Ruski Krstur
Orahovica
Đurdjenovac
Koška
Breznica Našička
Čepinski Martinci
Čepin
Tenja
Erdut
Odžaci
Feričanci
Našice
Dalj
Deronje
Ratkovo
Pivnice
Velika
Kaptol
Podgorač
Ernestinovo
Trpinja
Borovo
Bodjani
Bač
Selenča
Vetovo
Kutjevo
Markusica
Plavna
Gajdobra
Jakšic
Čaglin
Satnica Đakovačka
Semeljci
Tovariševo
Požega
Levanjska Varoš
Ruševo
Đakovo
Nuštar
Vukovar
Obrovac
Mladenovo
Pleternica
Trnava
Stari Mikanovci
Ivankovo
Vinkovci
Stari Jankovci
Sotin
Bačko Novo Selo
Bačka Palanka
Petrovo Selo
Vrpolje
Strizivojna
Cerna
Privlaka
Orolik
Šarengrad
Dunav
Ilok
Batrina
Oriovac
Sibinj
Donji Andrijevci
Velika Kopanica
Gundinci
Komletinci
Nijemci
Tovarnik
Šid
Slavonski Brod
Gradište
Otok
Erdevik
Slavonski Kobas
Bebrina
Bosanski Brod
Donja Bebrina
Donji Svilaj
Babina Greda
Županja
268
Vašica
Adaševci
Čalma
Novo Selo
Donja Dubica
Lipovac
Kukujevci
Kuzmin
Trstenci
Domaljevac
Bošnjaci
Odžak
Bosanski Šamac
Orašje
Morović
Rakovac
Polje
Obudovac
Vrbanja
Derventa
Kulina
Botajica
Modran
Podnovlje
Modriča
Pelagićevo
Rajevo Selo
Drenovci
Stremska-Rača
Ravnje
Vranjak
Koprivna
Gunja
Crna Bara
Komarica
Kožuhe
Gradačac
Mionica
Brčko
Račinovci
Jamena
Batković
Osinja
Kotorsko
Brka
Brezovo Polje Selo
Crnjelovo Donje
Velika Obarska
Klenje
Badovinci
Srnice Gornje
Dubrave
Lukavika
Maoča
Dragolovci
Soko
Bijeljina
Doboj
Srebrenik
Čelić
Zabrdje
Suho Polje
Prnjavor
Pridjel
Gračanica
Janja
Čečava
Uglejevik
Lešnica
Spreča
V. Ostravica
918
Miričina
Lopare
Teslić
Tešanj
Banja Vručica
Dobošnica
Priboj
Slavičice
Gornja Tuzla
Tuzla
Sor
Lozničko Polje
Maglaj
Puračić
Lukavac
Rastošnica
Loznica
Bistarac Donje
Husina
Stolice
916
Kozluk
Banja Koviljača
Korenita
Mladikovine
Majevica
Papuk
Dilj
Mecsek
Dráva
Sava
Bosna
Tinja
Sió
Veliki kanal
Fekete
Orljava
Jamija
Drina
E73
E70
E622
M6
M60
M9
A3
A5
3
4
5
A
B
C
112
126
127
139
18°
19°
45°
46°
NECROPOLIS

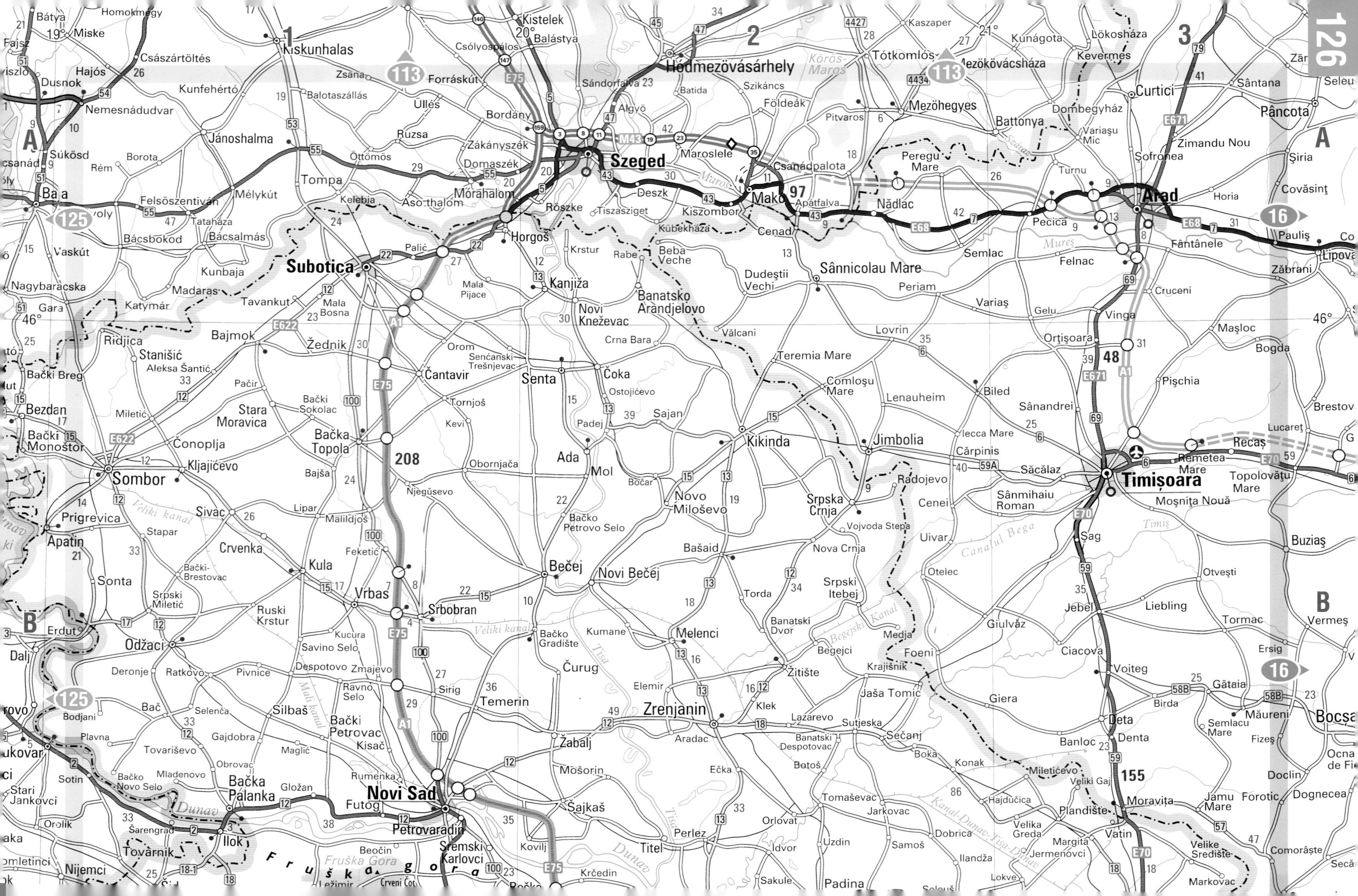

A
B
1
2
3
16
113
125
46°
20°
21°
97
48
155
208
Kiskunhalas
Hódmezővásárhely
Szeged
Makó
Mezőkovácsháza
Mezőhegyes
Battonya
Tótkomlós
Kaszaper
Kunágota
Lőkösháza
Kevermes
Dombegyház
Kistelek
Balástya
Sándorfalva
Algyő
Batida
Maroslele
Földeák
Szikáncs
Pitvaros
Csanádpalota
Apátfalva
Kiszombor
Kübekháza
Deszk
Tiszasziget
Röszke
Mórahalom
Domaszék
Zákányszék
Bordány
Forráskút
Üllés
Ruzsa
Öttömös
Ásotthalom
Zsana
Balotaszállás
Tompa
Kelebia
Mélykút
Jánoshalma
Kunfehértó
Császártöltés
Nemesnádudvar
Hajós
Miske
Homokmégy
Dusnok
Sükösd
Vaskút
Nagybaracska
Bácsbokod
Bácsalmás
Tataháza
Felsőszentiván
Borota
Rém
Kunbaja
Madaras
Katymár
Csólyospálos
Arad
Curtici
Pâncota
Sântana
Zimandu Nou
Şiria
Covăsinţ
Pauliş
Zăbrani
Şofronea
Variaşu Mic
Turnu
Pecica
Semlac
Felnac
Fântânele
Horia
Cruceni
Vinga
Orţişoara
Maşloc
Bogda
Pişchia
Recaş
Lucareţ
Remetea Mare
Topolovăţu Mare
Timişoara
Moşniţa Nouă
Buziaş
Vermeş
Ocna de Fier
Dognecea
Doclin
Comorâşte
Tormac
Ersig
Măureni
Fizeş
Gătaia
Semlacu Mare
Otveşti
Liebling
Jamu Mare
Forotic
Voiteg
Birda
Deta
Denta
Jebel
Şag
Ciacova
Banloc
Moraviţa
Vatin
Sânandrei
Biled
Sânmihaiu Roman
Săcălaz
Cărpiniş
Iecea Mare
Jimbolia
Cenei
Uivar
Otelec
Giulvăz
Giera
Foeni
Variaş
Periam
Sânnicolau Mare
Nădlac
Peregu Mare
Lovrin
Lenauheim
Comloşu Mare
Teremia Mare
Dudeştii Vechi
Cenad
Vălcani
Beba Veche
Kikinda
Banatsko Arandjelovo
Novi Kneževac
Rabe
Krstur
Kanjiža
Horgoš
Palić
Mala Pijace
Subotica
Čoka
Senta
Ada
Mol
Padej
Sajan
Ostojićevo
Crna Bara
Bočar
Novo Miloševo
Bašaid
Melenci
Zrenjanin
Elemir
Aradac
Ečka
Perlez
Titel
Žabalj
Čurug
Mošorin
Šajkaš
Kovilj
Bečej
Novi Bečej
Bačko Petrovo Selo
Bačko Gradište
Kumane
Srbobran
Temerin
Sirig
Novi Sad
Petrovaradin
Sremski Karlovci
Futog
Rumenka
Kisač
Bački Petrovac
Ravno Selo
Zmajevo
Vrbas
Kula
Crvenka
Feketić
Mali Iđoš
Bačka Topola
Čantavir
Orom
Senćanski Trešnjevac
Tornjoš
Kevi
Obornjača
Njegoševo
Žednik
Mala Bosna
Tavankut
Bajmok
Stara Moravica
Bački Sokolac
Pačir
Čonoplja
Kljajićevo
Stanišić
Aleksa Šantić
Riđica
Miletić
Sombor
Bački Monoštor
Bezdan
Bački Breg
Gara
Apatin
Prigrevica
Sonta
Stapar
Sivac
Srpski Miletić
Odžaci
Deronje
Bođani
Bač
Plavna
Bačka Palanka
Ilok
Silbaš
Despotovo
Savino Selo
Kucura
Lipar
Bajša
Ruski Krstur
Bački Brestovac
Pivnice
Ratkovo
Selenča
Gajdobra
Obrovac
Maglić
Tovariševo
Mladenovo
Bačko Novo Selo
Gložan
Šarengrad
Tovarnik
Sotin
Erdut
Dalj
Stari Jankovci
Orolik
Nijemci
Beočin
Srpska Crnja
Vojvoda Stepa
Radojevo
Nova Crnja
Srpski Itebej
Međa
Krajišnik
Jaša Tomić
Sečanj
Begejci
Žitište
Banatski Dvor
Torda
Lazarevo
Klek
Banatski Despotovac
Sutjeska
Boka
Konak
Hajdučica
Miletićevo
Veliki Gaj
Plandište
Margita
Jermenovci
Velika Greda
Ilandža
Dobrica
Samoš
Jarkovac
Tomaševac
Botoš
Orlovat
Idvor
Uzdin
Padina
Sakule
Velike Središte
Markovac
Lokve
Krčedin
Fruška Gora
Fruška gora
Tisa
Dunav
Maroš
Mureş
Timiş
Canalul Bega
Begejski Kanal
Veliki kanal
Mali kanal
Kanal Dunav-Tisa-Dunav
Körös-Maros
E75
E68
E70
E671
E622
A1
M43

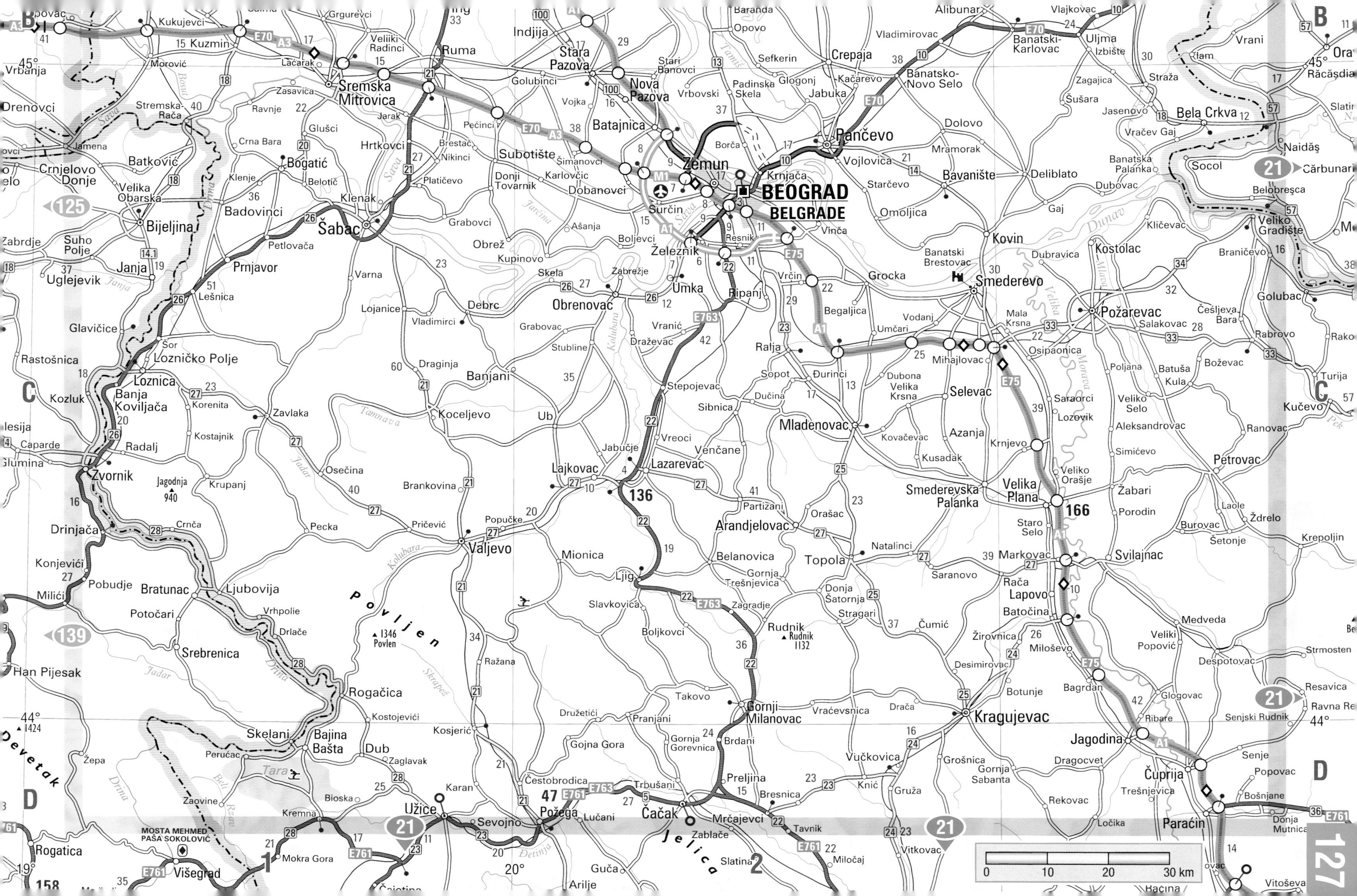
BEOGRAD
BELGRADE
Zemun
Pančevo
Smederevo
Požarevac
Kragujevac
Jagodina
Ćuprija
Paraćin
Čačak
Užice
Požega
Valjevo
Šabac
Loznica
Zvornik
Bijeljina
Sremska Mitrovica
Ruma
Indjija
Stara Pazova
Nova Pazova
Batajnica
Obrenovac
Lazarevac
Mladenovac
Arandjelovac
Topola
Gornji Milanovac
Ljig
Lajkovac
Ub
Koceljevo
Banjani
Smederevska Palanka
Velika Plana
Svilajnac
Markovac
Lapovo
Batočina
Kovin
Bela Crkva
Kostolac
Veliko Gradište
Golubac
Kučevo
Petrovac
Crepaja
Vršac
Kovin
Bavanište
Deliblato
Dolovo
Banatski Karlovac
Alibunar
Vladimirovac
Uljma
Vlajkovac
Grocka
Ripanj
Sopot
Ralja
Železnik
Surčin
Dobanovci
Subotište
Pećinci
Prnjavor
Lešnica
Bogatić
Badovinci
Janja
Uglejevik
Ljubovija
Bratunac
Srebrenica
Bajina Bašta
Rogačica
Skelani
Višegrad
Rogatica
Drinjača
Milići
Han Pijesak
Kosjerić
Mionica
Povljen
1346 Povlen
Jelica
Rudnik
Rudnik 1132
Jagodnja 940
Devetak
1424
MOSTA MEHMED PAŠA SOKOLOVIĆ
Sava
Drina
Dunav
Morava
Velika
Mlava
Kolubara
Tamnava
Jadar
Tara
Pek
Detinja
E70
E75
E763
E761
A1
A3
M1
21
125
139
136
166
47
158
45°
44°
20°
19°
0
10
20
30 km
B
C
D
1
2

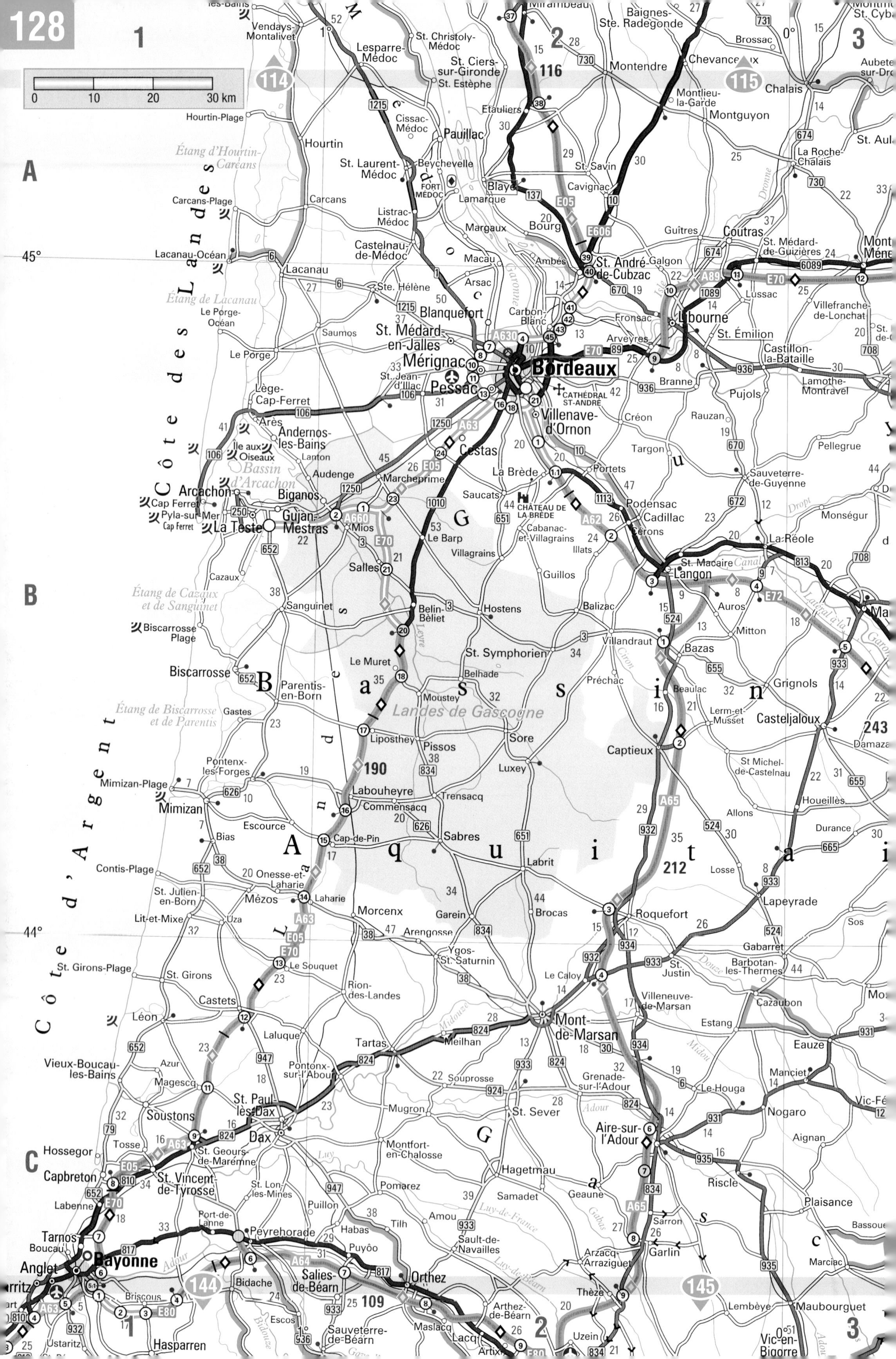
1
2
3
A
B
C
0
10
20
30 km
114
115
116
144
145
45°
44°
0°
Bordeaux
Mérignac
Pessac
St. Médard-en-Jalles
Blanquefort
Villenave-d'Ornon
Cestas
La Brède
Libourne
St. Émilion
St. André-de-Cubzac
Blaye
Bourg
Pauillac
St. Laurent-Médoc
Lesparre-Médoc
Castelnau-de-Médoc
Lacanau
Lacanau-Océan
Hourtin
Carcans
Arcachon
La Teste
Gujan-Mestras
Biganos
Andernos-les-Bains
Cap Ferret
Pyla-sur-Mer
Langon
Bazas
Cadillac
Podensac
Créon
Branne
Coutras
Montendre
Chalais
Montguyon
Castillon-la-Bataille
Sauveterre-de-Guyenne
La Réole
Casteljaloux
Captieux
Belin-Bèliet
Hostens
St. Symphorien
Biscarrosse
Parentis-en-Born
Sanguinet
Mimizan
Mimizan-Plage
Pissos
Sabres
Labouheyre
Morcenx
Roquefort
Mont-de-Marsan
Tartas
Castets
Dax
St. Paul-lès-Dax
Soustons
Hossegor
Capbreton
St. Vincent-de-Tyrosse
Bayonne
Anglet
Tarnos
Peyrehorade
Orthez
Salies-de-Béarn
St. Sever
Hagetmau
Aire-sur-l'Adour
Grenade-sur-l'Adour
Villeneuve-de-Marsan
Gabarret
Eauze
Nogaro
Riscle
Plaisance
Maubourguet
Vic-en-Bigorre
Garlin
Arzacq-Arraziguet
Sauveterre-de-Béarn
Hasparren
Côte des Landes
Côte d'Argent
Landes de Gascogne
Bassin d'Arcachon
Étang de Lacanau
Étang de Cazaux et de Sanguinet
Étang de Biscarrosse et de Parentis
Étang d'Hourtin-Carcans
CATHÉDRAL ST-ANDRÉ
CHÂTEAU DE LA BRÈDE
FORT MÉDOC
A63
A62
A65
A64
A89
A630
A660
E05
E70
E72
E80
E606
190
212
243
109

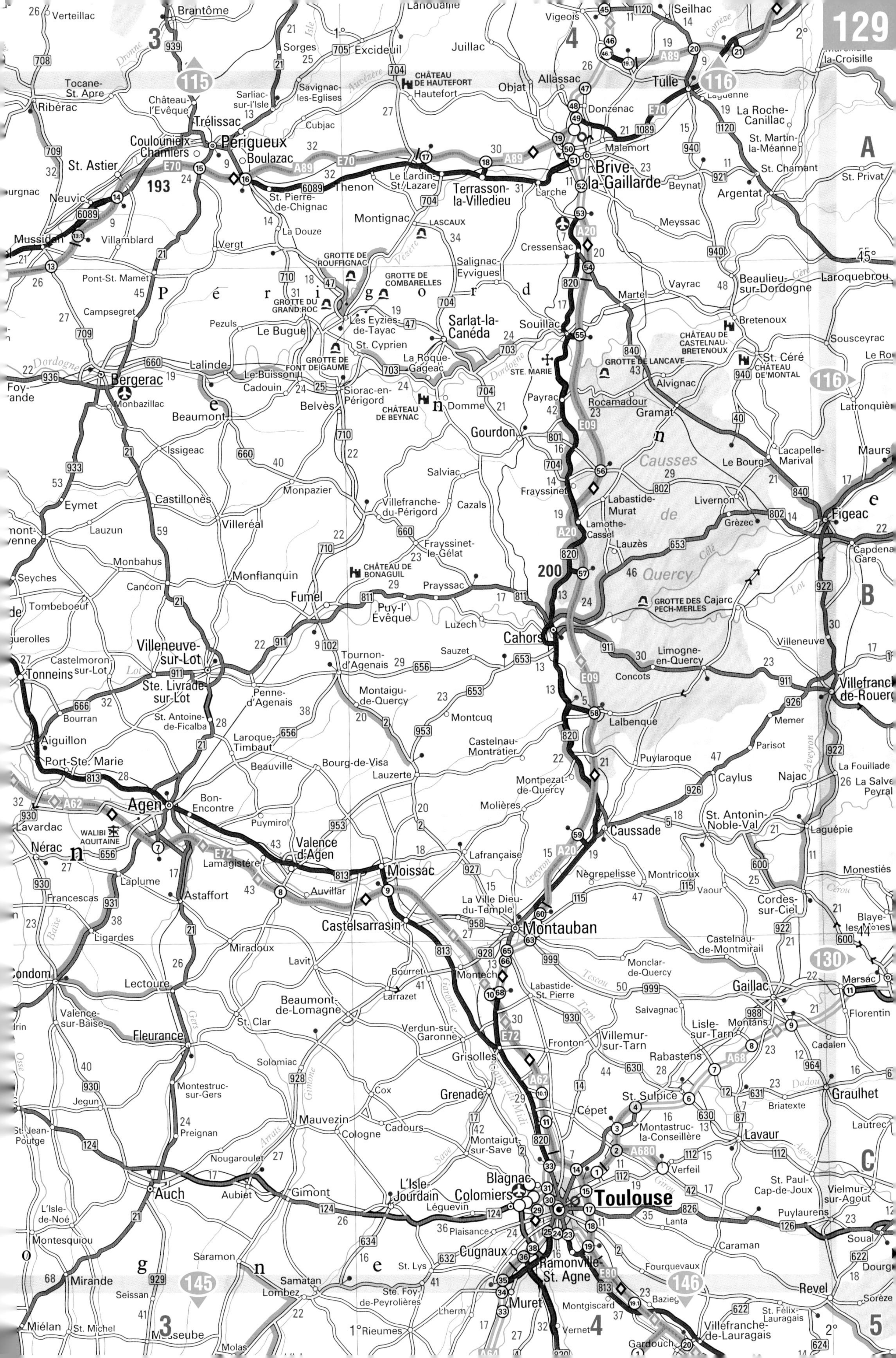

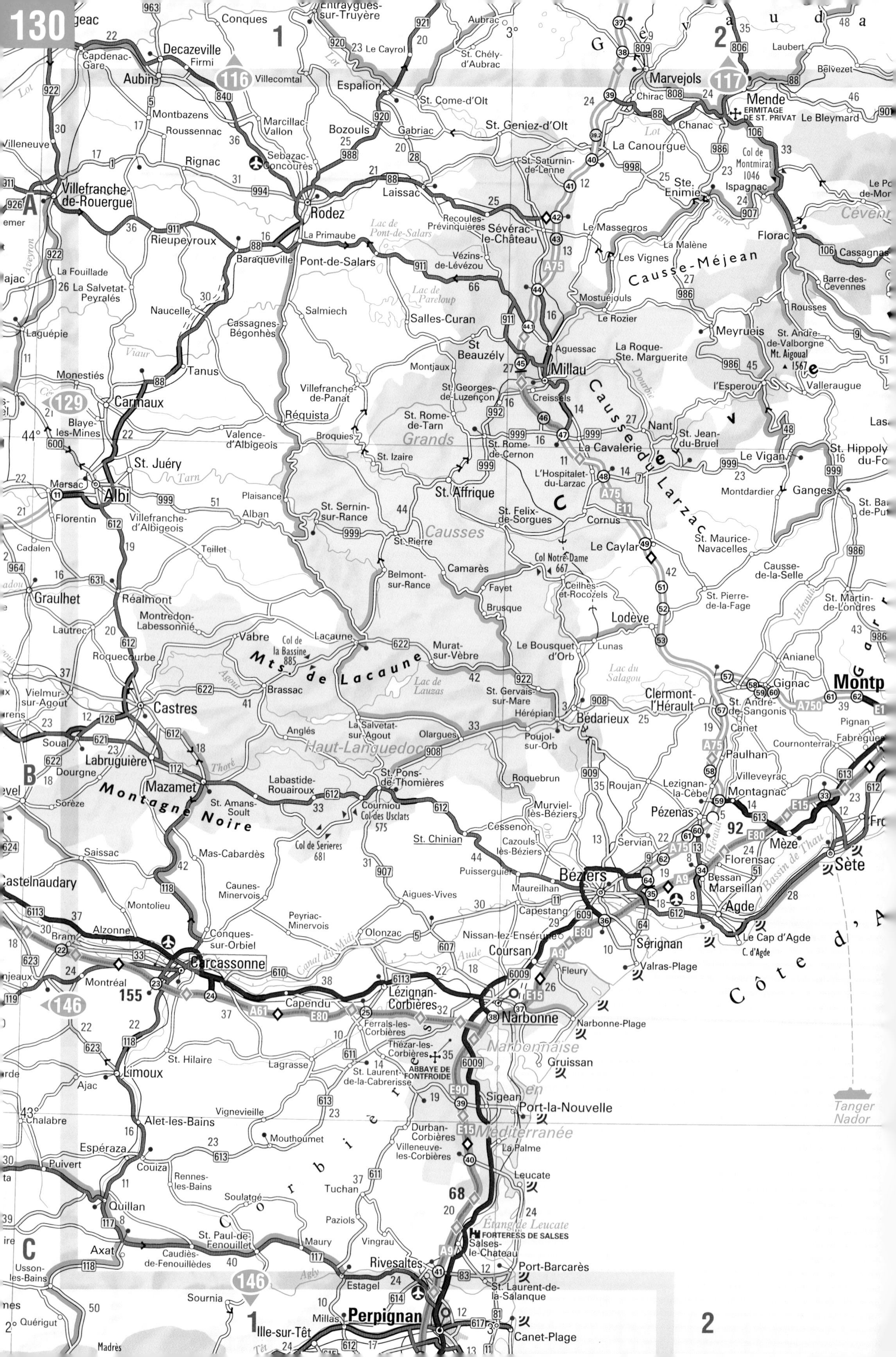
1
2
A
B
C
116
117
129
146
Conques
Entraygues-sur-Truyère
Aubrac
Decazeville
Firmi
Capdenac-Gare
Aubin
Villecomtal
Le Cayrol
St. Chély-d'Aubrac
Marvejols
Mende
Laubert
Belvezet
Espalion
St. Come-d'Olt
Chirac
ERMITAGE DE ST. PRIVAT
Le Bleymard
Montbazens
Roussennac
Marcillac-Vallon
Bozouls
Gabriac
St. Geniez-d'Olt
Chanac
La Canourgue
Col de Montmirat 1046
Villeneuve
Rignac
Sebazac-Concourès
St. Saturnin-de-Lenne
Ste. Enimie
Ispagnac
Villefranche-de-Rouergue
Rodez
Laissac
Le Pont-de-Monvert
Recoules-Prévinquières
Sévérac-le-Château
Le Massegros
Florac
Cévennes
Rieupeyroux
La Primaube
Lac de Pont-de-Salars
La Malène
Cassagnas
Baraqueville
Pont-de-Salars
Vézins-de-Lévézou
Les Vignes
Causse-Méjean
La Fouillade
La Salvetat-Peyralès
Lac de Pareloup
Barre-des-Cevennes
Naucelle
Salmiech
Mostuéjouls
Cassagnes-Bégonhès
Salles-Curan
Le Rozier
Rousses
Laguépie
Meyrueis
St. Andre-de-Valborgne
Viaur
St Beauzély
Aguessac
La Roque-Ste. Marguerite
Mt. Aigoual 1567
Tanus
Montjaux
Millau
Monestiés
Villefranche-de-Panat
St. Georges-de-Luzençon
Creissels
Causse du Larzac
Dourbie
l'Esperou
Valleraugue
Carmaux
Réquista
St. Rome-de-Tarn
Nant
St. Jean-du-Bruel
Blaye-les-Mines
Valence-d'Albigeois
Broquies
Grands Causses
St. Rome-de-Cernon
La Cavalerie
St. Hippolyte-du-Fort
St. Juéry
Tarn
St. Izaire
L'Hospitalet-du-Larzac
Le Vigan
Marsac
Albi
Plaisance
St. Affrique
Montdardier
Ganges
Florentin
Villefranche-d'Albigeois
Alban
St. Sernin-sur-Rance
St. Felix-de-Sorgues
Cornus
St. Pierre
Causses
Le Caylar
St. Maurice-Navacelles
Cadalen
Teillet
Col Notre-Dame 667
Belmont-sur-Rance
Camarès
Causse-de-la-Selle
Graulhet
Réalmont
Fayet
Ceilhes-et-Rocozels
St. Pierre-de-la-Fage
St. Martin-de-Londres
Montredon-Labessonnié
Brusque
Lodève
Hérault
Lautrec
Vabre
Col de la Bassine 885
Lacaune
Murat-sur-Vèbre
Le Bousquet d'Orb
Lunas
Aniane
Roquecourbe
Mts. de Lacaune
Lac du Salagou
Gignac
Montpellier
Vielmur-sur-Agout
Brassac
Lac de Laouzas
St. Gervais-sur-Mare
Clermont-l'Hérault
St. André-de-Sangonis
Castres
Agout
Hérépian
Bédarieux
Pignan
Anglès
La Salvetat-sur-Agout
Olargues
Poujol-sur-Orb
Canet
Fabrègues
Soual
Labruguière
Haut-Languedoc
Cournonterral
Dourgne
Thoré
St. Pons-de-Thomières
Paulhan
Mazamet
Labastide-Rouairoux
Roquebrun
Villeveyrac
Sorèze
Montagne Noire
St. Amans-Soult
Courniou
Col des Usclats 575
Roujan
Lezignan-la-Cèbe
Montagnac
Murviel-lès-Béziers
Pézenas
Col de Serieres 681
Cessenon
St. Chinian
Cazouls-lès-Béziers
Servian
Mèze
Saissac
Mas-Cabardès
Florensac
Sète
Bassin de Thau
Castelnaudary
Puisserguier
Béziers
Bessan
Marseillan
Caunes-Minervois
Maureilhan
Aigues-Vives
Agde
Montolieu
Capestang
Peyriac-Minervois
Alzonne
Bram
Conques-sur-Orbiel
Olonzac
Nissan-lez-Enserune
Sérignan
Le Cap d'Agde
C. d'Agde
Côte d'Azur
Canal du Midi
Carcassonne
Aude
Coursan
Valras-Plage
Montréal
Fleury
Capendu
Lézignan-Corbières
Narbonne
Narbonne-Plage
Ferrals-les-Corbières
Thézan-les-Corbières
ABBAYE DE FONTFROIDE
Narbonnaise en Méditerranée
Gruissan
St. Hilaire
Lagrasse
St. Laurent-de-la-Cabrerisse
Limoux
Ajac
Sigean
Port-la-Nouvelle
Tanger
Nador
Chalabre
Alet-les-Bains
Vignevieille
Durban-Corbières
Espéraza
Mouthoumet
Villeneuve-les-Corbières
La Palme
Puivert
Couiza
Rennes-les-Bains
Leucate
Tuchan
Corbières
Quillan
Soulatgé
Paziols
Étang de Leucate
FORTERESS DE SALSES
Salses-le-Chateau
St. Paul-de-Fenouillet
Maury
Vingrau
Axat
Caudiès-de-Fenouillèdes
Rivesaltes
Port-Barcarès
Usson-les-Bains
Agly
Estagel
St. Laurent-de-la-Salanque
Sournia
Quérigut
Millas
Perpignan
Ille-sur-Têt
Canet-Plage
Madrès
Têt

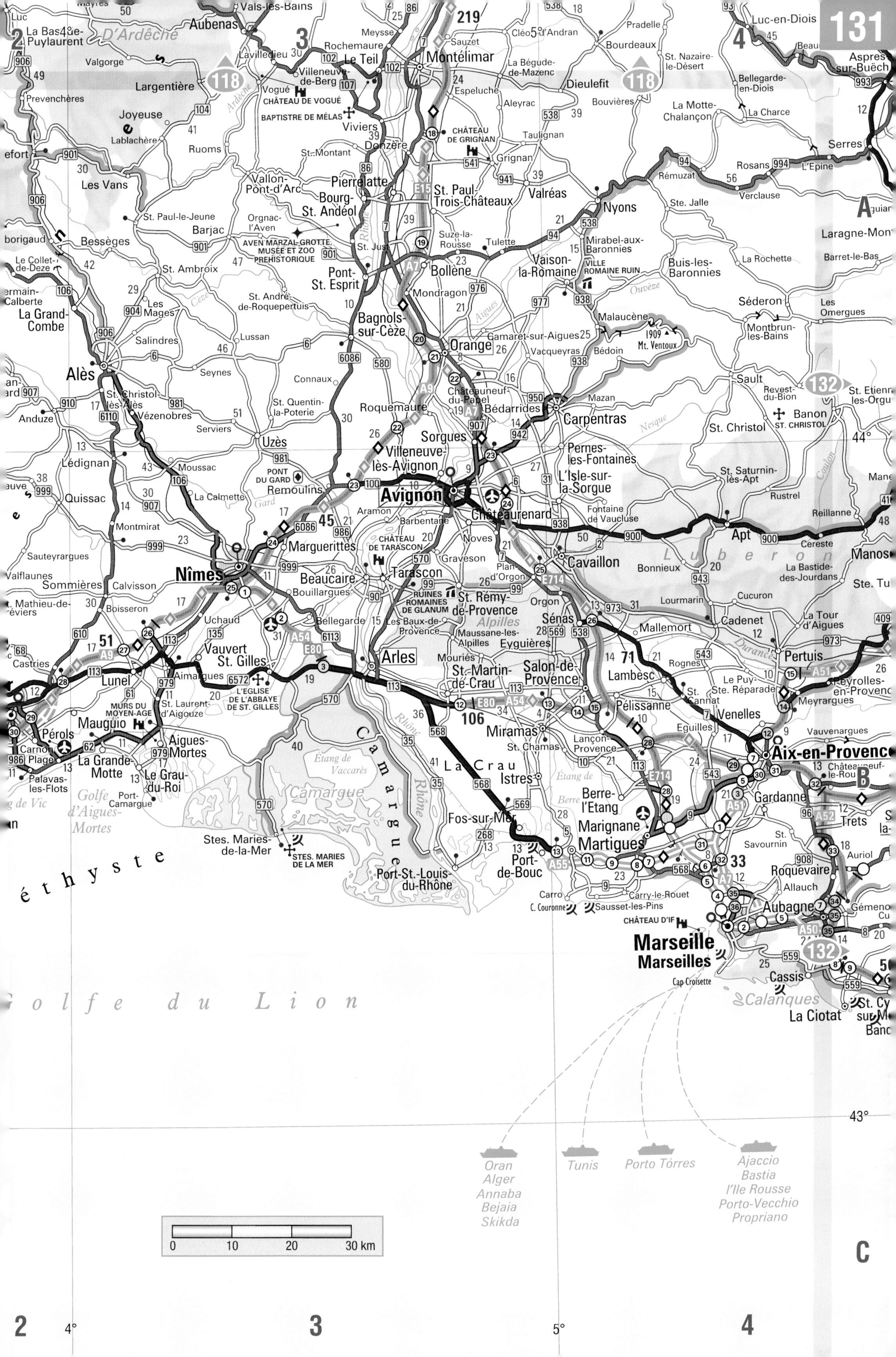

Aubenas
Vals-les-Bains
Montélimar
Le Teil
Viviers
Donzère
Largentière
Joyeuse
Ruoms
Les Vans
Vallon-Pont-d'Arc
Pierrelatte
Bourg-St. Andéol
St. Paul-Trois-Châteaux
Valréas
Grignan
Dieulefit
Nyons
Vaison-la-Romaine
Bollène
Pont-St. Esprit
Bagnols-sur-Cèze
Orange
Carpentras
Alès
Uzès
Avignon
Villeneuve-lès-Avignon
Sorgues
Châteauneuf-du-Pape
Remoulins
Nîmes
Beaucaire
Tarascon
Arles
St. Rémy-de-Provence
Cavaillon
L'Isle-sur-la-Sorgue
Apt
Pertuis
Salon-de-Provence
Lunel
St. Gilles
Vauvert
Aigues-Mortes
Le Grau-du-Roi
La Grande-Motte
Stes. Maries-de-la-Mer
Camargue
Istres
Miramas
Fos-sur-Mer
Martigues
Marignane
Aix-en-Provence
Gardanne
Aubagne
Marseille
Marseilles
Cassis
La Ciotat
Luberon
Mt. Ventoux
Golfe du Lion
Oran
Alger
Annaba
Bejaia
Skikda
Tunis
Porto Tórres
Ajaccio
Bastia
l'Ile Rousse
Porto-Vecchio
Propriano
0
10
20
30 km

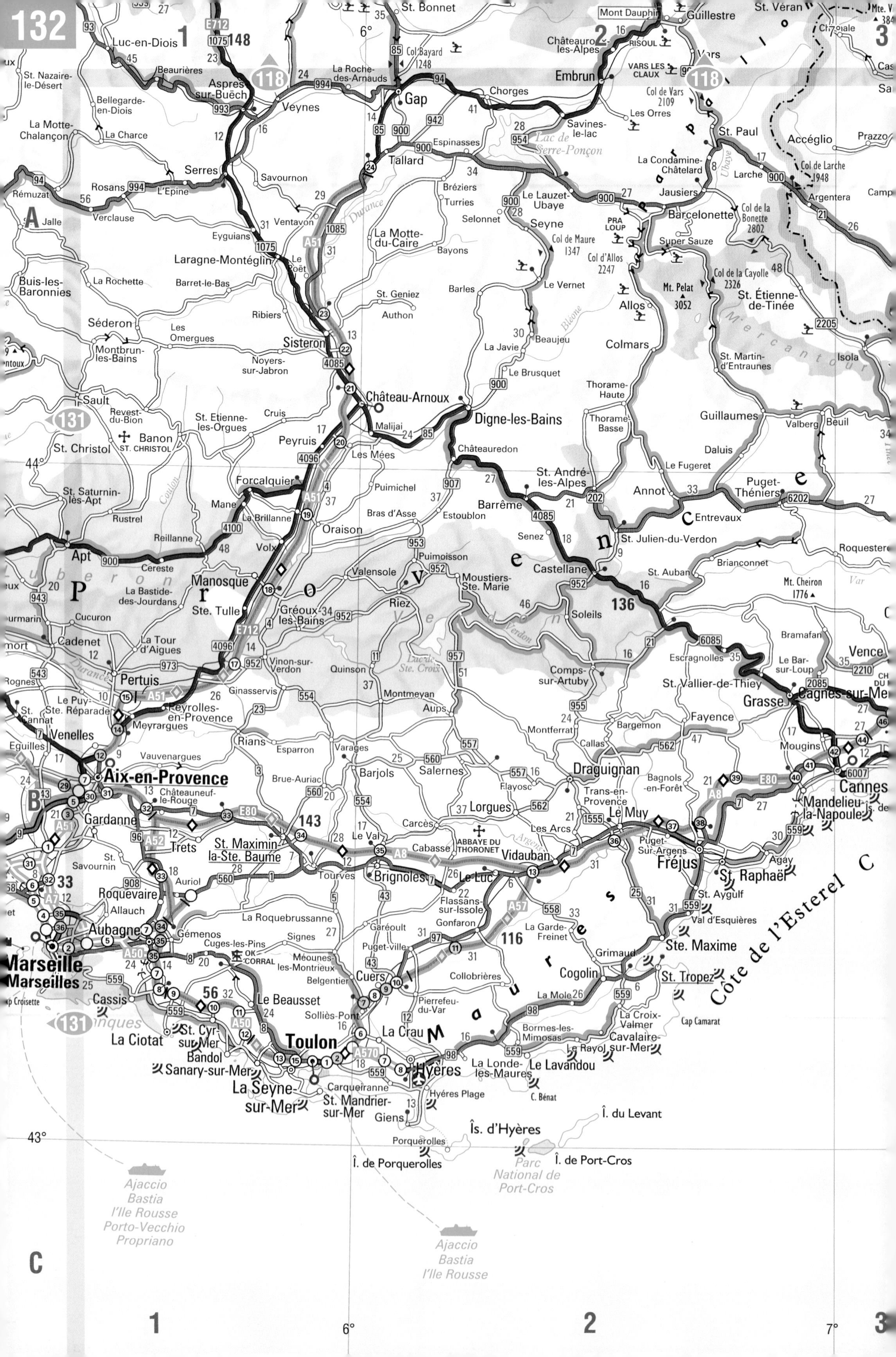

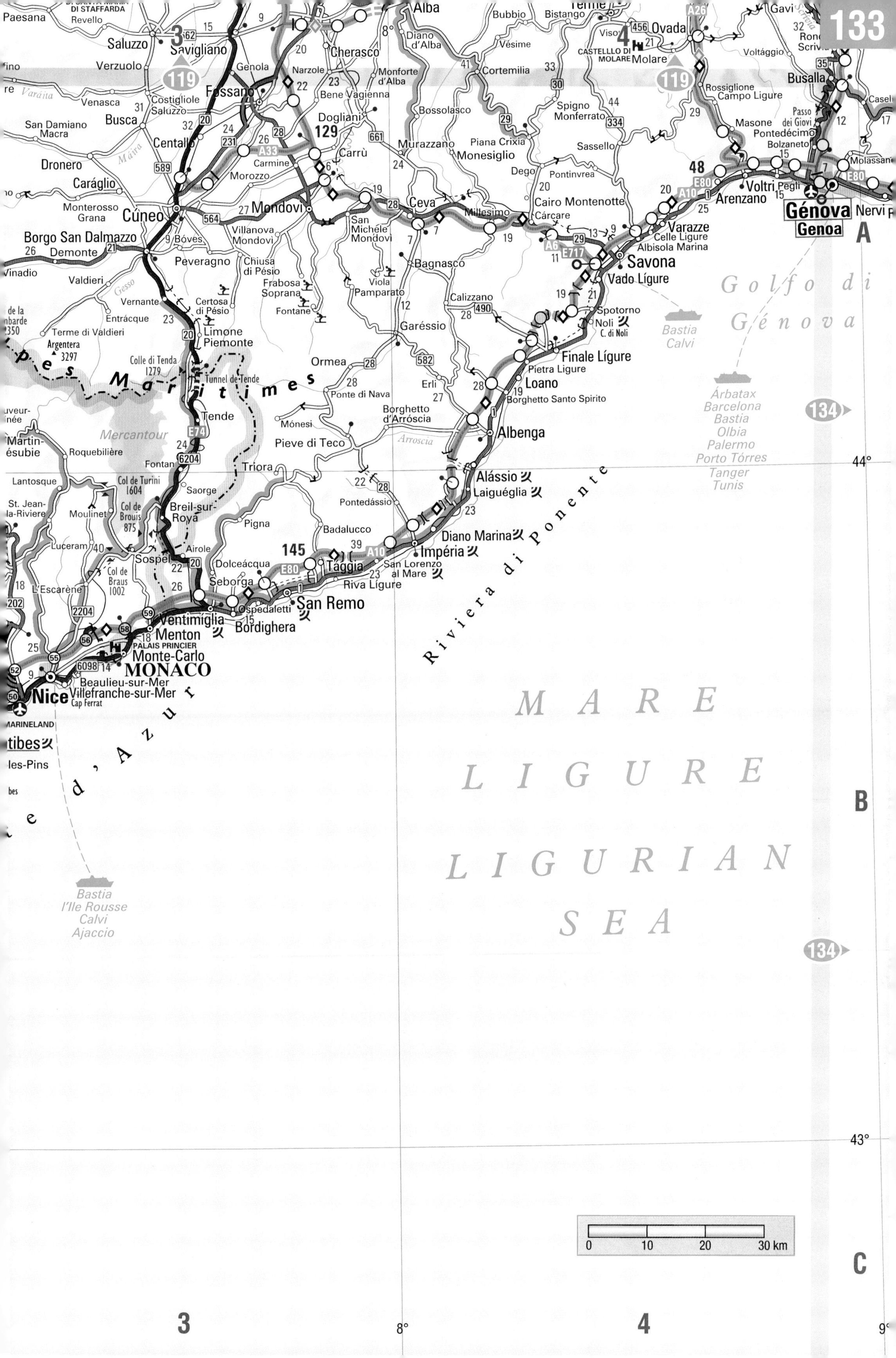
Paesana
Revello
Saluzzo
Savigliano
Verzuolo
Genola
Cherasco
Alba
Diano d'Alba
Narzole
Monforte d'Alba
Bene Vagienna
Venasca
Costigliole Saluzzo
Fossano
Busca
San Damiano Macra
Centallo
Dogliani
Dronero
Carmine
Carrù
Morozzo
Caráglio
Monterosso Grana
Cúneo
Mondovì
Villanova Mondovì
Borgo San Dalmazzo
Demonte
Bóves
Peveragno
Chiusa di Pésio
Valdieri
Vernante
Entrácque
Certosa di Pésio
Frabosa Soprana
Fontane
Terme di Valdieri
Argentera 3297
Limone Piemonte
Colle di Tenda 1279
Tunnel de Tende
Alpes Maritimes
Tende
Mercantour
Roquebilière
Fontan
Lantosque
Col de Turini 1604
Saorge
St. Jean-la-Riviere
Moulinet
Col de Brouis 875
Breil-sur-Roya
Luceram
Sospel
Col de Braus 1002
Airole
L'Escarène
Ventimiglia
Menton
PALAIS PRINCIER
Monte-Carlo
MONACO
Beaulieu-sur-Mer
Villefranche-sur-Mer
Cap Ferrat
Nice
MARINELAND
Côte d'Azur
Bubbio
Bistagno
Vésime
Cortemilia
Bossolasco
Murazzano
Piana Crixia
Monesiglio
Ceva
San Michele Mondovì
Millesimo
Bagnasco
Viola
Pamparato
Calizzano
Garéssio
Ormea
Ponte di Nava
Erli
Borghetto d'Arróscia
Mónesi
Pieve di Teco
Triora
Pontedássio
Pigna
Badalucco
Dolceácqua
Tággia
Seborga
Ospedaletti
San Remo
Bordighera
Riva Ligure
San Lorenzo al Mare
Impéria
Diano Marina
Laiguéglia
Alássio
Albenga
Borghetto Santo Spirito
Loano
Pietra Ligure
Finale Lígure
Noli
C. di Noli
Spotorno
Vado Lígure
Savona
Albisola Marina
Celle Ligure
Varazze
Arenzano
Cairo Montenotte
Cárcare
Dego
Pontinvrea
Sassello
Spigno Monferrato
Ovada
Viso
CASTELLO DI MOLARE
Molare
Rossiglione
Campo Ligure
Masone
Passo dei Giovi
Pontedécimo
Bolzaneto
Busalla
Voltággio
Gavi
Voltri
Pegli
Génova
Genoa
Nervi
Golfo di Génova
Bastia
Calvi
Árbatax
Barcelona
Bastia
Olbia
Palermo
Porto Tórres
Tanger
Tunis
Riviera di Ponente
MARE LIGURE
LIGURIAN SEA
Bastia
l'Ile Rousse
Calvi
Ajaccio
44°
43°
8°
9°
0
10
20
30 km
A
B
C
3
4

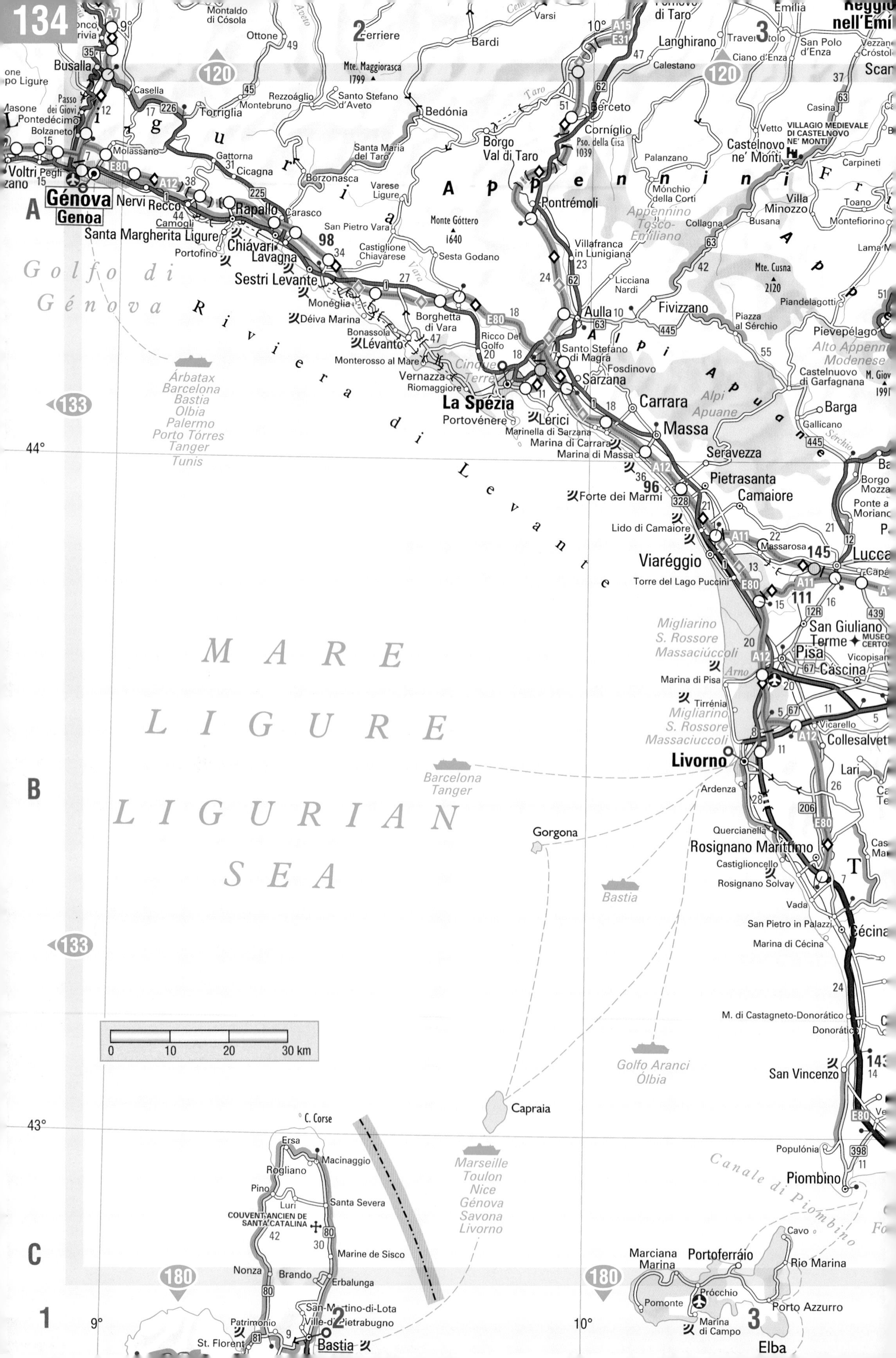

Génova
Genoa
Golfo di Génova
Riviera di Levante
Liguria
Appennini
Alpi Apuane
MARE LIGURE
LIGURIAN SEA
La Spézia
Livorno
Pisa
Lucca
Viaréggio
Massa
Carrara
Sarzana
Pontrémoli
Aulla
Rapallo
Chiávari
Lavagna
Sestri Levante
Santa Margherita Ligure
Portofino
Camogli
Recco
Nervi
Busalla
Casella
Torriglia
Bedónia
Borgo Val di Taro
Berceto
Langhirano
Castelnovo ne' Monti
Fivizzano
Cinque Terre
Monterosso al Mare
Vernazza
Riomaggiore
Portovénere
Lérici
Forte dei Marmi
Pietrasanta
Camaiore
Seravezza
Barga
Rosignano Maríttimo
Cécina
San Vincenzo
Piombino
Canale di Piombino
Portoferráio
Rio Marina
Porto Azzurro
Marina di Campo
Elba
Capraia
Gorgona
Bastia
C. Corse
Macinaggio
Rogliano
Ersa
Santa Severa
Marine de Sisco
Erbalunga
Brando
Nonza
Patrimonio
St. Florent
COUVENT ANCIEN DE SANTA CATALINA
Árbatax
Barcelona
Bastia
Olbia
Palermo
Porto Tórres
Tanger
Tunis
Barcelona
Tanger
Golfo Aranci
Ólbia
Marseille
Toulon
Nice
Génova
Savona
Livorno
Mte. Maggiorasca 1799
Monte Góttero 1640
Pso. della Cisa 1039
Mte. Cusna 2120
Migliarino S. Rossore Massaciúccoli
VILLAGIO MEDIEVALE DI CASTELNOVO NE' MONTI
Pso. della Cisa
0 10 20 30 km
44°
43°
9°
10°
A
B
C
1
2
3
120
133
180

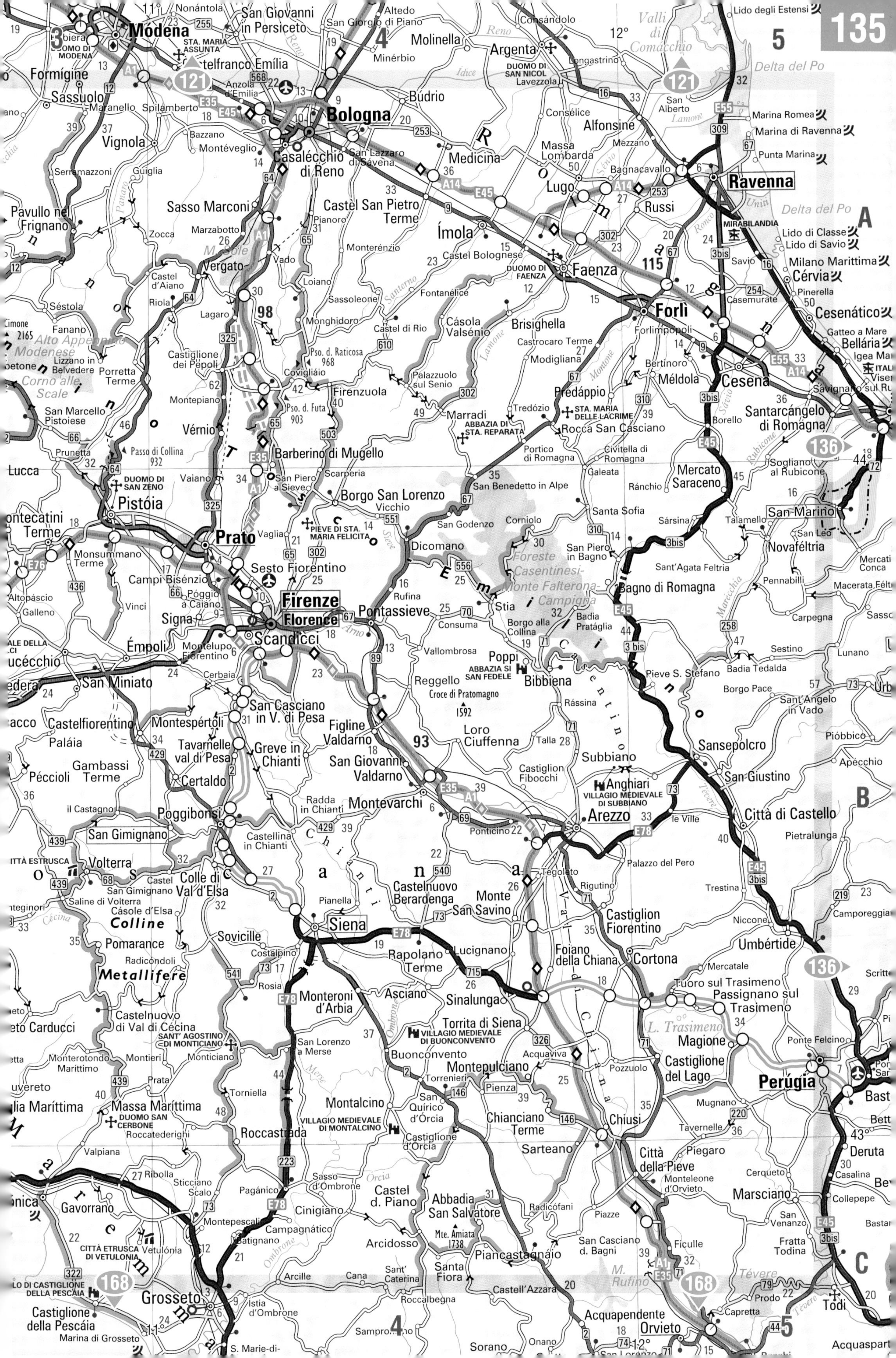

Módena
Nonántola
San Giovanni in Persiceto
San Giorgio di Piano
Altedo
Molinella
Argenta
Consándolo
Valli di Comácchio
Lido degli Estensi
Delta del Po
DUOMO DI MODENA
STA. MARIA ASSUNTA
Castelfranco Emília
Minérbio
Formígine
Sassuolo
Maranello
Spilamberto
Anzola d'Emília
Bologna
Búdrio
DUOMO DI SAN NICOL
Lavezzola
Longastrino
San Alberto
Marina Romea
Marina di Ravenna
Punta Marina
Vignola
Bazzano
Montéveglio
Casalécchio di Reno
San Lazzaro di Sávena
Medicina
Conselice
Alfonsine
Massa Lombarda
Mezzano
Bagnacavallo
Ravenna
Serramazzoni
Guíglia
Castel San Pietro Terme
Lugo
Russi
Pavullo nel Frignano
Sasso Marconi
Marzabotto
Zocca
Pianoro
Ímola
MIRABILANDIA
Lido di Classe
Lido di Savio
Monterénzio
Castel Bolognese
Faenza
DUOMO DI FAENZA
Savio
Milano Maríttima
Cérvia
Vergato
Castel d'Aiano
Riola
Vado
Loiano
Sassoleone
Fontanélice
Forlì
Casemurate
Pinerella
Cesenático
Sèstola
Lagaro
Monghidoro
Castel di Rio
Cásola Valsénio
Brisighella
Forlimpópoli
Gatteo a Mare
Bellária
Igea Marina
Cimone 2165
Fanano
Alto Appennino Modenese
Lizzano in Belvedere
Castiglione dei Pépoli
Pso. d. Raticosa 968
Covigliáio
Castrocaro Terme
Modigliana
Bertinoro
Méldola
Cesena
Savignano sul Rubicone
Corno alle Scale
Porretta Terme
Firenzuola
Palazzuolo sul Senio
Predáppio
Santarcángelo di Romagna
Montepiano
Pso. d. Futa 903
Marradi
Tredózio
STA. MARIA DELLE LACRIME
Rocca San Casciano
Borello
San Marcello Pistoiese
ABBAZIA DI STA. REPARATA
Vérnio
Portico di Romagna
Civitella di Romagna
Prunetta
Passo di Collina 932
Barberino di Mugello
Sogliano al Rubicone
Lucca
DUOMO DI SAN ZENO
Vaiano
San Piero a Sieve
Scarperia
San Benedetto in Alpe
Galeata
Mercato Saraceno
Ránchio
Pistóia
Borgo San Lorenzo
Vicchio
Santa Sofia
Sársina
Talamello
San Marino
Montecatini Terme
Prato
Vaglia
PIEVE DI STA. MARIA FELICITA
San Godenzo
Corniolo
San Leo
Monsummano Terme
Campi Bisénzio
Sesto Fiorentino
Dicomano
Foreste Casentinesi-Monte Falterona-Campigna
San Piero in Bagno
Novafeltria
Sant'Agata Feltria
Mercatino Conca
Altopáscio
Galleno
Vinci
Póggio a Caiano
Firenze
Florence
Rufina
Pontassieve
Stia
Bagno di Romagna
Pennabilli
Macerata Feltria
Signa
Consuma
Borgo alla Collina
Badia Pratáglia
Carpegna
Émpoli
Montelupo Fiorentino
Scandicci
Vallombrosa
Poppi
ABBAZIA SI SAN FEDELE
Bibbiena
Sestino
Lunano
Fucécchio
San Miniato
Cerbaia
Reggello
Croce di Pratomagno 1592
Pieve S. Stefano
Badia Tedalda
Borgo Pace
Sant'Angelo in Vado
San Casciano in V. di Pesa
Rássina
Castelfiorentino
Montespértoli
Figline Valdarno
Loro Ciuffenna
Talla
Palaia
Tavarnelle val di Pesa
Greve in Chianti
San Giovanni Valdarno
Subbiano
Sansepolcro
Piobbico
Gambassi Terme
Péccioli
Certaldo
Castiglion Fibocchi
Anghiari
VILLAGGIO MEDIEVALE DI SUBBIANO
San Giustino
Apécchio
il Castagno
Poggibonsi
Radda in Chianti
Montevarchi
Arezzo
le Ville
Città di Castello
San Gimignano
Castellina in Chianti
Ponticino
Pietralunga
CITTÀ ETRUSCA
Volterra
Castel San Gimignano
Colle di Val d'Elsa
Palazzo del Pero
Saline di Volterra
Cásole d'Elsa
Pianella
Castelnuovo Berardenga
Monte San Savino
Rigutino
Tegoleto
Trestina
Colline
Siena
Castiglion Fiorentino
Niccone
Camporeggiano
Pomarance
Sovicille
Costalpino
Rapolano Terme
Lucignano
Foiano della Chiana
Cortona
Umbértide
Radicóndoli
Metallifere
Rosia
Monteroni d'Arbia
Asciano
Sinalunga
Mercatale
Tuoro sul Trasimeno
Passignano sul Trasimeno
Castelnuovo di Val di Cécina
SANT' AGOSTINO DI MONTICIANO
Torrita di Siena
VILLAGIO MEDIEVALE DI BUONCONVENTO
L. Trasimeno
Magione
Monterotondo Maríttimo
Montieri
Monticiano
San Lorenzo a Merse
Buonconvento
Acquaviva
Pozzuolo
Castiglione del Lago
Ponte Felcino
Montepulciano
Perúgia
Massa Maríttima
DUOMO SAN CERBONE
Prata
Torniella
Torrenieri
Pienza
Montalcino
San Quírico d'Órcia
Chianciano Terme
Chiusi
Mugnano
Roccatederighi
Roccastrada
VILLAGIO MEDIEVALE DI MONTALCINO
Castiglione d'Orcia
Sarteano
Tavernelle
Piegaro
Città della Pieve
Deruta
Valpiana
Ribolla
Sticciano
Scalo
Pagánico
Sasso d'Ombrone
Castel d. Piano
Abbadia San Salvatore
Radicófani
Monteleone d'Orvieto
Cerqueto
Marsciano
Casalina
Gavorrano
Cinigiano
Piazze
Collepepe
Montepescali
Campagnático
Mte. Amiata 1738
San Casciano d. Bagni
San Venanzo
Batignano
Arcidosso
Piancastagnáio
Ficulle
Fratta Todina
CITTÀ ETRUSCA DI VETULONIA
Vetulónia
Arcille
Cana
Sant' Caterina
Santa Fiora
M. Rufino
Castell'Azzara
Prodo
Todi
Grosseto
Roccalbegna
Capretta
Castiglione della Pescáia
Ístia d'Ombrone
Acquapendente
Orvieto
Marina di Grosseto
Samprugnano
Sorano
Onano
Acquasparta
S. Marie-di-
Maremma
Chianti
Casentino
Val di Chiana

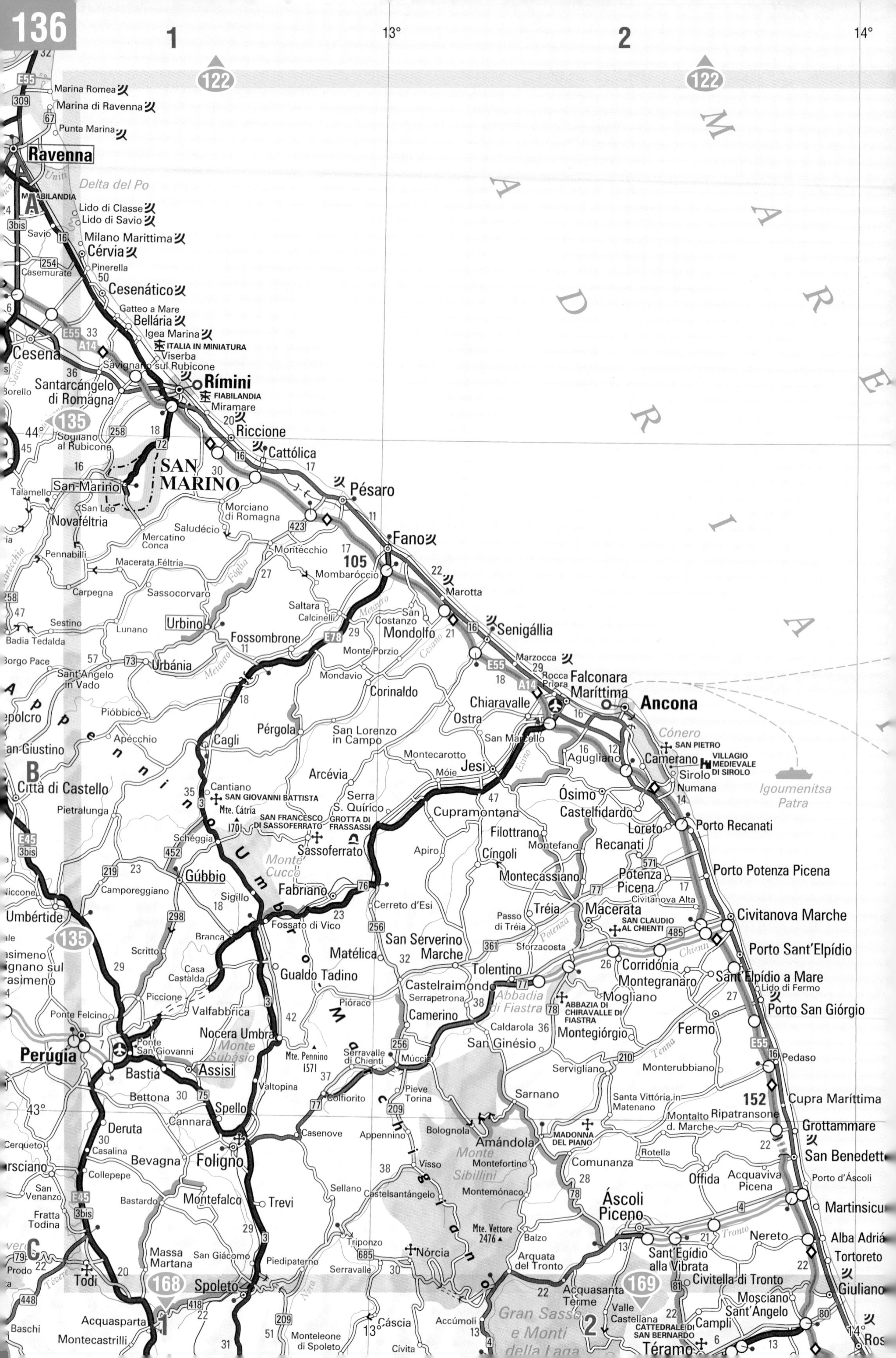

Marina Romea
Marina di Ravenna
Punta Marina
Ravenna
Delta del Po
MIRABILANDIA
Lido di Classe
Lido di Savio
Milano Marittima
Cérvia
Pinerella
Casemurate
Cesenático
Gatteo a Mare
Bellária
Igea Marina
ITALIA IN MINIATURA
Viserba
Cesena
Savignano sul Rubicone
Rímini
Santarcángelo di Romagna
FIABILANDIA
Miramare
Riccione
Cattólica
Sogliano al Rubicone
SAN MARINO
San Marino
Pésaro
Talamello
San Leo
Novaféltria
Morciano di Romagna
Saludécio
Mercatino Conca
Pennabilli
Macerata Féltria
Montécchio
Fano
Mombaróccio
Carpegna
Sassocorvaro
Marotta
Urbino
Sestino
Lunano
Saltara
Calcinelli
San Costanzo
Mondolfo
Senigállia
Badia Tedalda
Fossombrone
Monte Porzio
Borgo Pace
Sant'Angelo in Vado
Urbánia
Mondavio
Marzocca
Rocca Priora
Falconara Maríttima
Ancona
Corinaldo
Chiaravalle
Ostra
Piòbbico
Apécchio
Cagli
Pérgola
San Lorenzo in Campo
San Marcello
Cònero
SAN PIETRO
Camerano
VILLAGIO MEDIEVALE DI SIROLO
Sirolo
Numana
Igoumenitsa
Patra
Montecarotto
Móie
Jesi
Agugliano
Arcévia
Cantiano
SAN GIOVANNI BATTISTA
Mte. Cátria
Serra S. Quírico
Città di Castello
Pietralunga
SAN FRANCESCO DI SASSOFERRATO
GROTTA DI FRASSASSI
Cupramontana
Ósimo
Castelfidardo
Loreto
Porto Recanati
Filottrano
Montefano
Recanati
Schéggia
Sassoferrato
Apiro
Cíngoli
Monte Cucco
Gúbbio
Montecassiano
Potenza Picena
Porto Potenza Picena
Camporeggiano
Fabriano
Civitanova Alta
Umbértide
Sigillo
Cerreto d'Esi
Passo di Tréia
Tréia
Macerata
SAN CLAUDIO AL CHIENTI
Civitanova Marche
Fossato di Vico
Branca
San Severino Marche
Porto Sant'Elpídio
Scritto
Matélica
Sforzacosta
Corridónia
Sant'Elpídio a Mare
Lido di Fermo
Casa Castalda
Gualdo Tadino
Tolentino
Montegranaro
Castelraimondo
Serrapetrona
Piccione
Pióraco
Abbadia di Fiastra
ABBAZIA DI CHIARAVALLE DI FIASTRA
Mogliano
Porto San Giórgio
Ponte Felcino
Valfabbrica
Camerino
Caldarola
Montegiórgio
Fermo
Nocera Umbra
Perúgia
Ponte San Giovanni
Bastia
Assisi
Monte Subásio
Mte. Pennino 1571
Serravalle di Chienti
Múccia
San Ginésio
Pedaso
Servigliano
Monterubbiano
Valtopina
Bettona
Spello
Colfiorito
Pieve Torina
Sarnano
Santa Vittória in Matenano
Cupra Maríttima
Cannara
Montalto d. Marche
Ripatransone
Deruta
Casenove
Appennino
Bologna
MADONNA DEL PIANO
Grottammare
Casalina
Bevagna
Foligno
Amándola
Monte Sibillini
Montefortino
Rotella
San Benedetto
Cerqueto
Collepepe
Visso
Comunanza
San Venanzo
Sellano
Montemónaco
Offida
Acquaviva Picena
Porto d'Ascoli
Bastardo
Montefalco
Trevi
Castelsantángelo
Áscoli Piceno
Martinsicuro
Fratta Todina
Mte. Vettore 2476
Balzo
Nereto
Alba Adriática
Massa Martana
San Giácomo
Tripónzo
Nórcia
Arquata del Tronto
Sant'Egídio alla Vibrata
Tortoreto
Prodo
Todi
Piedipaterno
Serravalle
Civitella di Tronto
Giuliano
Spoleto
Acquasanta Terme
Mosciano Sant'Angelo
Gran Sasso e Monti della Laga
Valle Castellana
Campli
CATTEDRALE DI SAN BERNARDO
Baschi
Acquasparta
Montecastrilli
Monteleone di Spoleto
Cáscia
Accúmoli
Civita
Téramo
MARE ADRIATICO
Appennino Umbro Marchigiano

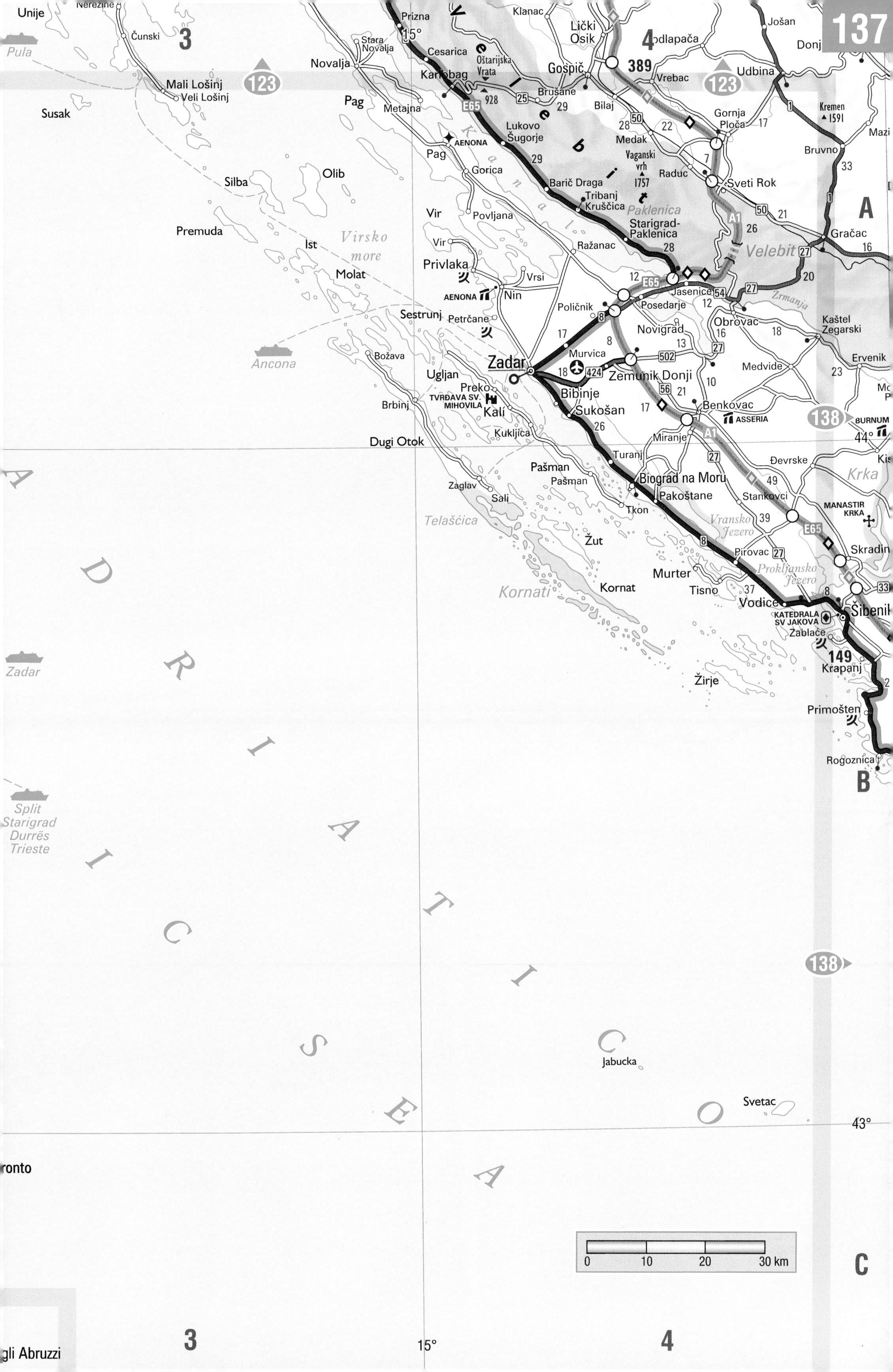
Unije
Čunski
Pula
Mali Lošinj
Veli Lošinj
Susak
Novalja
Stara Novalja
Pag
Metajna
Prizna
Cesarica
Karlobag
Klanac
Lički Osik
Gospić
Podlapača
Udbina
Jošan
Vrebac
Brušane
Bilaj
Lukovo Šugorje
Gornja Ploča
Kremen
Medak
Vaganski vrh 1757
Raduč
Sveti Rok
Bruvno
Baric Draga
Tribanj Kruščica
Paklenica
Starigrad-Paklenica
Velebit
Gračac
Silba
Olib
Premuda
Ist
Molat
Virsko more
Vir
Povljana
Ražanac
Privlaka
Vrsi
Nin
Jasenice
Posedarje
Obrovac
Kaštel Žegarski
Zrmanja
Sestrunj
Petrčane
Poličnik
Novigrad
Ervenik
Ancona
Božava
Zadar
Murvica
Zemunik Donji
Medvide
Ugljan
Preko
Bibinje
Benkovac
ASSERIA
BURNUM
Brbinj
Kali
Sukošan
Kukljica
Dugi Otok
Miranje
Turanj
Pašman
Đevrske
Krka
Biograd na Moru
Pakoštane
Stankovci
Zaglav
Sali
Tkon
MANASTIR KRKA
Telašćica
Vransko Jezero
Žut
Pirovac
Skradin
Murter
Prokljansko Jezero
Kornati
Kornat
Tisno
Vodice
Šibenik
KATEDRALA SV JAKOVA
Zablaće
Krapanj
Žirje
Primošten
Rogoznica
Split Starigrad Durrës Trieste
ADRIATICO
SEA
Jabucka
Svetac
43°
44°
15°
0 10 20 30 km

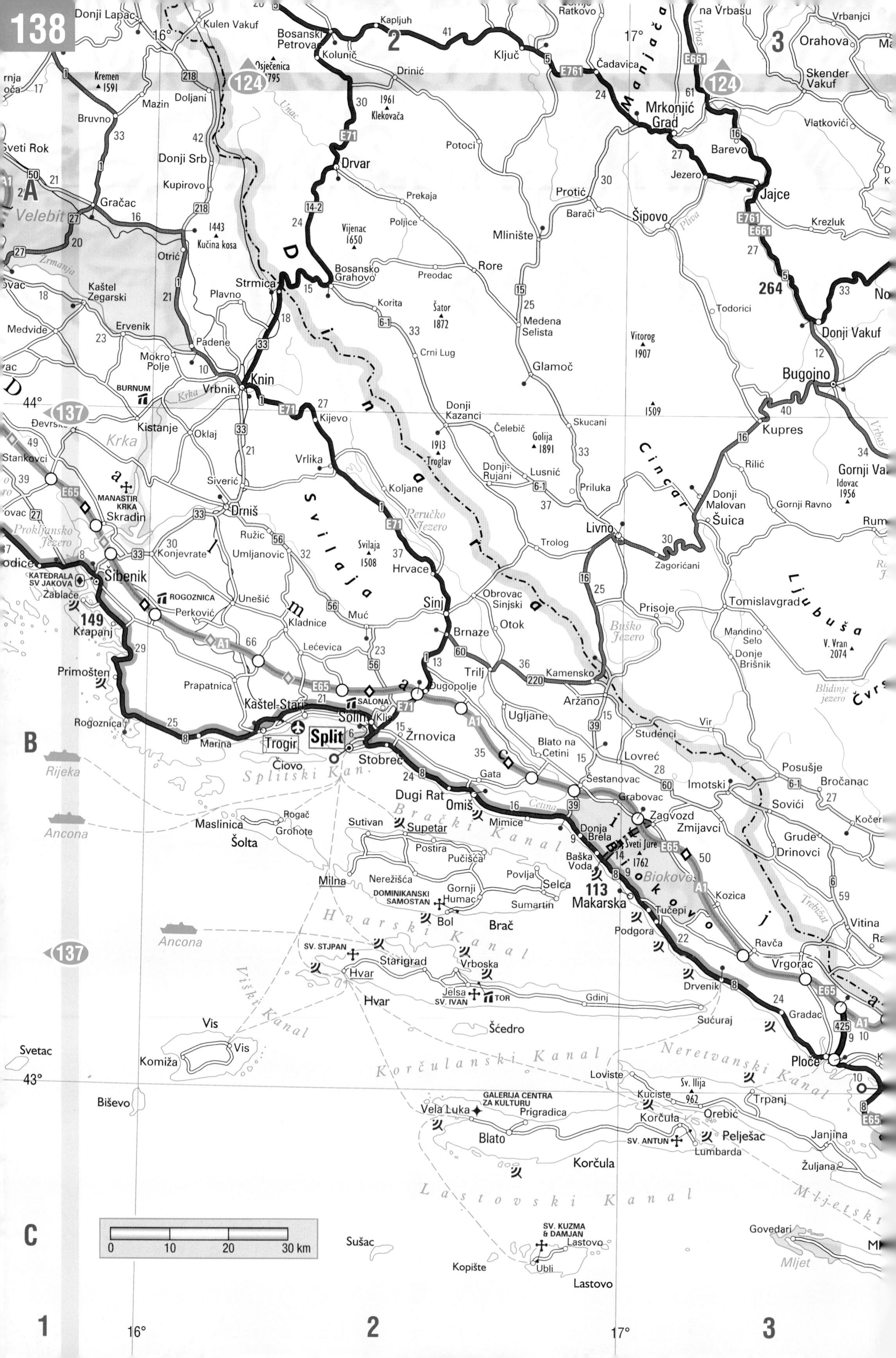
Donji Lapac
Kulen Vakuf
Bosanski Petrovac
Kapljuh
Kolunič
Drinić
Ključ
Čadavica
Mrkonjić Grad
Manjača
na Vrbasu
Vrbanjci
Orahova
Skender Vakuf
Vlatkovići
Kremen 1591
Osječenica 1795
Mazin
Doljani
Bruvno
Sveti Rok
Donji Srb
Kupirovo
Gračac
Velebit
Zrmanja
1443 Kučina kosa
Otrić
Unac
1961 Klekovača
Drvar
Potoci
Barevo
Jezero
Jajce
Protić
Barači
Šipovo
Pliva
Krezluk
Prekaja
Vijenac 1650
Poljice
Mliništa
Rore
Bosansko Grahovo
Preodac
Strmica
Plavno
Kaštel Zegarski
Ervenik
Medvide
Padene
Mokro Polje
Burnum
Krka
Vrbnik
Knin
Korita
Šator 1872
Crni Lug
Medena Selista
Vitorog 1907
Glamoč
Todorici
Donji Vakuf
Bugojno
Kupres
Dinara
44°
Đevrske
Kistanje
Oklaj
Kijevo
Donji Kazanci
Čelebić
Golija 1891
Skucani
1509
Vrlika
1913 Troglav
Donji Rujani
Lusnić
Priluka
Cincar
Rilić
Gornji Vakuf
Idovac 1956
Stankovci
Manastir Krka
Skradin
Siverić
Drniš
Koljane
Peručko Jezero
Svilaja
Donji Malovan
Gornji Ravno
Šuica
Livno
Trolog
Zagoričani
Prokljansko Jezero
Konjevrate
Ružić
Umljanović
Svilaja 1508
Hrvace
Katedrala Sv Jakova
Šibenik
Zablaće
Rogoznica
Unešić
Perković
Kladnice
Muć
Sinj
Obrovac Sinjski
Otok
Brnaze
Buško Jezero
Prisoje
Tomislavgrad
Ljubuša
Mandino Selo
Donje Brišnik
V. Vran 2074
Krapanj
Primošten
Lećevica
Prapatnica
Dugopolje
Trilj
Kamensko
Aržano
Blidinje jezero
Kaštel-Stari
Salona
Solin
Klis
Split
Trogir
Marina
Žrnovica
Ugljane
Studenci
Vir
Blato na Cetini
Lovreć
Posušje
Bročanac
Čiovo
Stobreč
Splitski Kan.
Gata
Šestanovac
Imotski
Grabovac
Sovići
Rijeka
Ancona
Dugi Rat
Omiš
Cetina
Mimice
Zagvozd
Zmijavci
Kočerin
Rogač
Maslinica
Grohote
Šolta
Sutivan
Supetar
Brački Kanal
Postira
Pučišća
Donja Brela
Baška Voda
Sveti Jure 1762
Biokovo
Grude
Drinovci
Milna
Nerežišća
Povlja
Selca
Dominikanski Samostan
Gornji Humac
Sumartin
Makarska
Kozica
Tučepi
Bol
Brač
Podgora
Hvarski Kanal
Ravča
Vitina
Trebižat
Sv. Stjpan
Starigrad
Vrboska
Vrgorac
Hvar
Jelsa
Sv. Ivan
Tor
Gdinj
Drvenik
Gradac
Viški Kanal
Šćedro
Sućuraj
Vis
Komiža
Svetac
Korčulanski Kanal
Neretvanski Kanal
Ploče
43°
Loviste
Sv. Ilija 962
Biševo
Kuciste
Trpanj
Galerija Centra za Kulturu
Vela Luka
Prigradica
Korčula
Orebić
Blato
Sv. Antun
Pelješac
Lumbarda
Janjina
Žuljana
Lastovski Kanal
Mljetski
Sušac
Sv. Kuzma & Damjan
Lastovo
Ubli
Kopište
Govedari
Mljet
0 10 20 30 km
16°
17°
1
2
3
A
B
C
137
124
264
149
113
E65
E71
E761
E661
A1

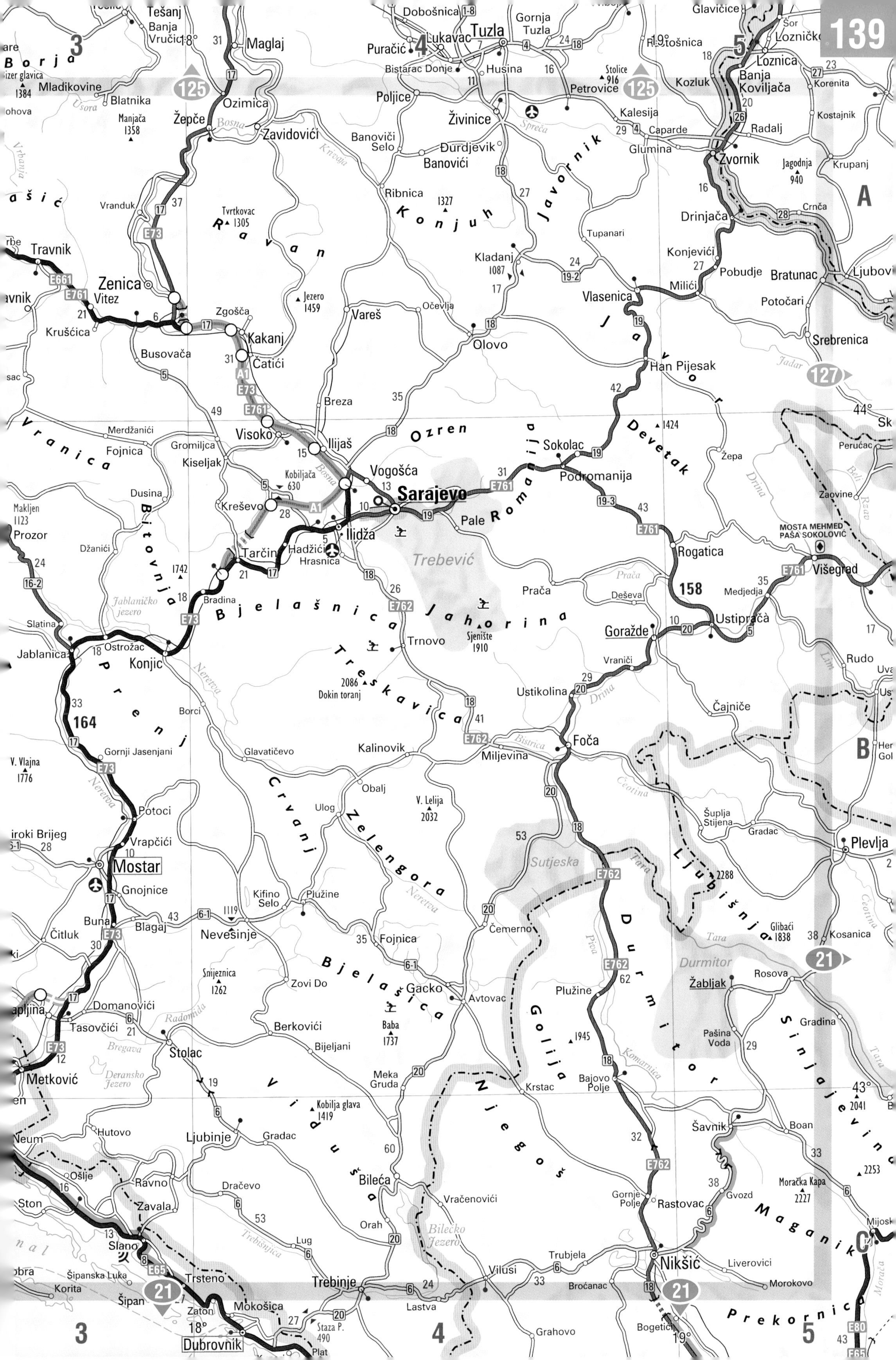
Tešanj
Banja Vrućica
Maglaj
Dobošnica
Lukavac
Tuzla
Gornja Tuzla
Puračić
Bistarac Donje
Husina
Glavičice
Šor
Lozničko
Loznica
Banja Koviljača
Korenita
Kostajnik
Mladikovine
Blatnika
Manjača 1358
Ozimica
Žepče
Zavidovići
Poljice
Živinice
Stolice 916
Petrovice
Kalesija
Caparde
Kozluk
Radalj
Zvornik
Glumina
Jagodnja 940
Krupanj
Banovići Selo
Đurđevik
Banovići
Ribnica
Konjuh
Javornik
Vranduk
Tvrtkovac 1305
Ravan
Drinjača
Crnča
Travnik
Zenica
Vitez
Kruščica
Zgošča
Kakanj
Čatići
Busovača
Jezero 1459
Vareš
Očevlja
Kladanj 1087
Tupanari
Konjevići
Pobudje
Bratunac
Milići
Vlasenica
Potočari
Srebrenica
Ljubovija
Olovo
Han Pijesak
Javor
Breza
Ozren
Devetak 1424
Merdžanići
Fojnica
Gromiljca
Kiseljak
Visoko
Ilijaš
Vranica
Kobiljača 630
Vogošća
Sarajevo
Sokolac
Podromanija
Romanija
Žepa
Perućac
Zaovine
Dusina
Kreševo
Ilidža
Hadžići
Hrasnica
Tarčin
Pale
Trebević
Rogatica
Most Mehmed Paša Sokolović
Višegrad
Makljen 1123
Prozor
Džanići
Bitovnja 1742
Jablaničko jezero
Bradina
Bjelašnica
Jahorina
Prača
Deševa
Goražde
Ustiprača
Medjedja
Slatina
Jablanica
Ostrožac
Konjic
Trnovo
Sjenište 1910
Treskavica
2086 Dokin toranj
Vraniči
Ustikolina
Rudo
Prenj
Borci
Čajniče
Foča
Miljevina
Kalinovik
Glavatičevo
Gornji Jasenjani
V. Vlajna 1776
Obalj
Ulog
V. Lelija 2032
Crvanj
Zelengora
Šuplja Stijena
Gradac
Pljevlja
Potoci
Vrapčići
Široki Brijeg
Mostar
Gnojnice
Sutjeska
Ljubišnja
2288
Kifino Selo
Plužine
Buna
Blagaj
Nevesinje
Čitluk
Fojnica
Čemerno
Glibači 1838
Kosanica
Bjelašica
Snijeznica 1262
Zovi Do
Gacko
Avtovac
Durmitor
Žabljak
Rosova
Plužine
Domanovići
Čapljina
Tasovčići
Berkovići
Baba 1737
Golija
1945
Sinjajevina
Gradina
Pašina Voda
Metković
Deransko Jezero
Stolac
Bijeljani
Meka Gruda
Krstac
Bajovo Polje
Vidusa
Njegoš
Kobilja glava 1419
Hutovo
Neum
Ljubinje
Gradac
Šavnik
Boan
Ošlje
Ravno
Dračevo
Bileća
Vračenovići
Bilećko Jezero
Gornje Polje
Rastovac
Gvozd
Moračka Kapa 2227
2253
Maganik
Ston
Zavala
Orah
Slano
Lug
Trebišnjica
Nikšić
Liverovici
Morokovo
Šipanska Luka
Korita
Šipan
Trsteno
Trebinje
Vilusi
Trubjela
Broćanac
Lastva
Zaton
Mokošica
Dubrovnik
Staza P. 490
Plat
Grahovo
Bogetići
Prekornica
Mijoska
Rudo
Drina
Neretva
Bosna
Spreča
Tara
Lim
Piva
Komarnica
Ćeotina
Bistrica
Jadar
Krivaja
Usora
Radomida
Bregava
158
164
125
127
21

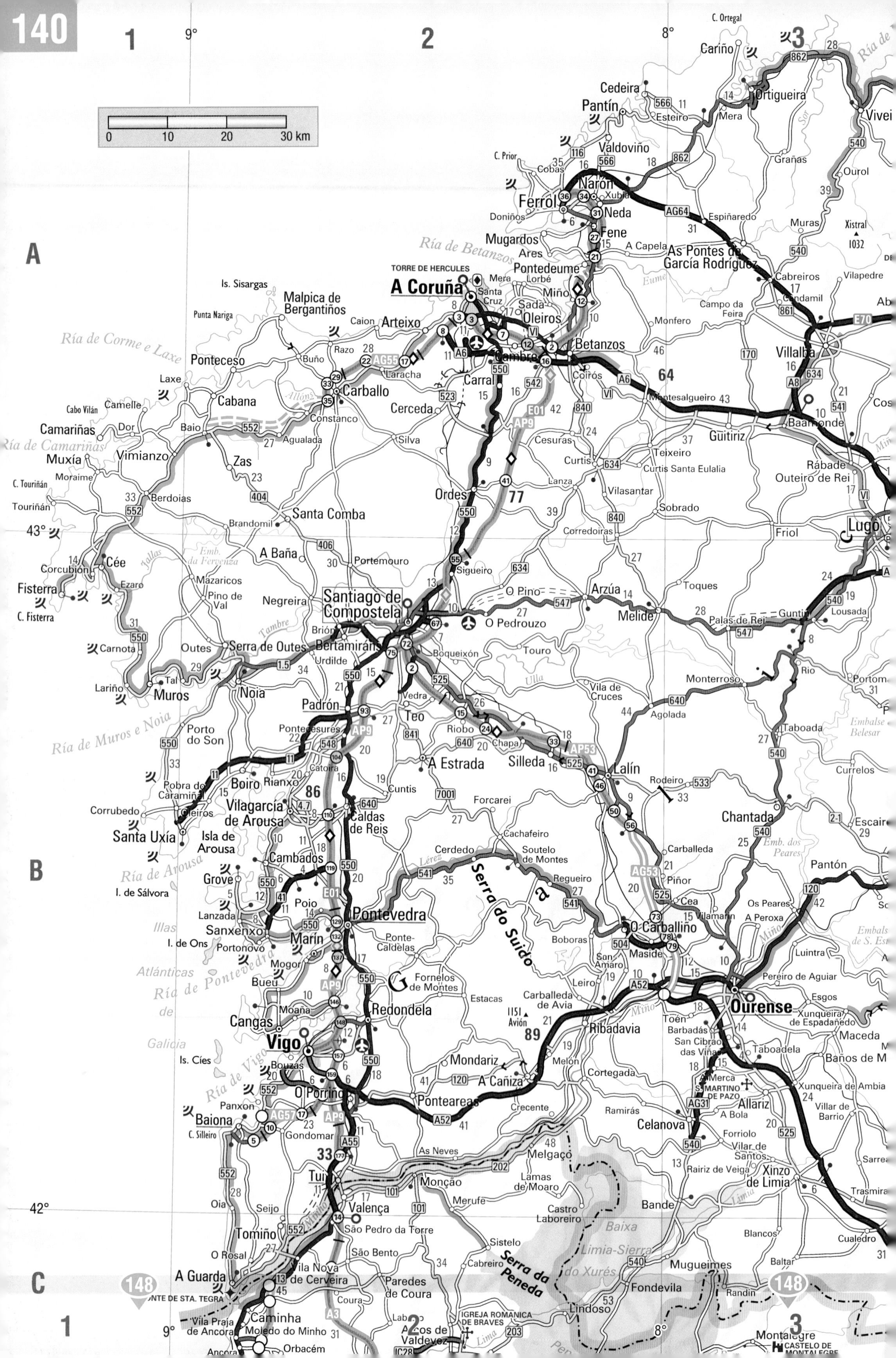
0
10
20
30 km
A
B
C
1
2
3
9°
8°
43°
42°
C. Ortegal
Cariño
Ortigueira
Cedeira
Pantín
Esteiro
Mera
Vivei
Valdoviño
C. Prior
Cobas
Grañas
Narón
Ourol
Xubia
Ferrol
Neda
Doniños
Espiñaredo
Fene
Muras
Xistral
1032
Mugardos
Ares
A Capela
As Pontes de García Rodríguez
Ría de Betanzos
TORRE DE HERCULES
Pontedeume
Cabreiros
Vilapedre
A Coruña
Mera
Lorbé
Is. Sisargas
Miño
Santa Cruz
Candamil
Malpica de Bergantiños
Sada
Oleiros
Campo da Feira
Punta Nariga
Caion
Arteixo
Monfero
Villalba
Ría de Corme e Laxe
Razo
Betanzos
Ponteceso
Buño
Cambre
Laracha
Coirós
Laxe
Carral
Carballo
Montesalgueiro
Cabo Vilán
Camelle
Cabana
Constanco
Cerceda
Baamonde
Camariñas
Dor
Baio
Agualada
Silva
Cesuras
Ría de Camariñas
Guitiriz
Muxía
Vimianzo
Zas
Teixeiro
Curtis
Curtis Santa Eulalia
Moraime
Rábade
Outeiro de Rei
C. Touriñán
Lanza
Vilasantar
Touriñán
Berdoias
Ordes
Sobrado
Santa Comba
Brandomil
Corredoiras
Friol
Lugo
A Baña
Emb. da Fervenza
Corcubión
Cée
Portemouro
Sigueiro
Ezaro
Mazaricos
Toques
Fisterra
Pino de Val
O Pino
Arzúa
Negreira
Santiago de Compostela
Melide
Lousada
C. Fisterra
O Pedrouzo
Palas de Rei
Guntín
Brión
Carnota
Outes
Serra de Outes
Bertamiráns
Boqueixón
Touro
Urdilde
Rio
Portom
Lariño
Tal
Muros
Noia
Vila de Cruces
Monterroso
Padrón
Vedra
Teo
Agolada
Ría de Muros e Noia
Porto do Son
Pontecesures
Riobo
Chapa
Taboada
Emblase Belesar
Silleda
Lalín
Catoira
A Estrada
Pobra do Caramiñal
Boiro
Rianxo
Rodeiro
Currelos
Cuntis
Corrubedo
Vilagarcía de Arousa
Oleiros
Forcarei
Caldas de Reis
Santa Uxía
Isla de Arousa
Cachafeiro
Chantada
Escair
Cerdedo
Souteio de Montes
Carballeda
Ría de Arousa
Cambados
Emb. dos Peares
Grove
Regueiro
Piñor
Pantón
I. de Sálvora
Serra do Suido
Cea
Lanzada
Poio
Os Peares
Illas
Sanxenxo
Pontevedra
Vilamarín
A Peroxa
I. de Ons
Marín
O Carballiño
Portonovo
Ponte-Caldelas
Boboras
Maside
Luintra
Atlánticas
Mogor
San Amaro
Ría de Pontevedra
Bueu
Fornelos de Montes
Leiro
Pereiro de Aguiar
Estacas
Carballeda de Avia
Esgos
Ourense
Moaña
Redondela
Cangas
Avión
Ribadavia
Xunqueira de Espadañedo
Vigo
Toén
Barbadás
Maceda
Galicia
San Cibrao das Viñas
Is. Cíes
Melón
Taboadela
Mondariz
Baños de M
Bouzas
Cortegada
A Merca
Ría de Vigo
A Cañiza
S. MARTINO DE PAZO
Xunqueira de Ambia
O Porriño
Panxon
Ponteareas
Allariz
Crecente
Ramirás
Villar de Barrio
Baiona
C. Silleiro
Gondomar
A Bola
Celanova
Forriolo
Vilar de Santos
As Neves
Melgaço
Sarrea
Rairiz de Veiga
Tui
Monção
Xinzo de Limia
Lamas de Moaro
Trasmira
Oia
Merufe
Bande
Valença
Castro Laboreiro
Seijo
Baixa Limia-Sierra do Xurés
São Pedro da Torre
Blancos
Tomiño
Cualedro
Sistelo
O Rosal
São Bento
Mugueimes
Baltar
Vila Nova de Cerveira
Cabreiro
A Guarda
Paredes de Coura
Serra da Peneda
Fondevila
Randín
Coura
Lindoso
Caminha
Vila Praja de Ancora
Moledo do Minho
IGREJA ROMANICA DE BRAVES
Arcos de Valdevez
Montalegre
CASTELO DE MONTALEGRE
Orbacém
Ancora
148
148

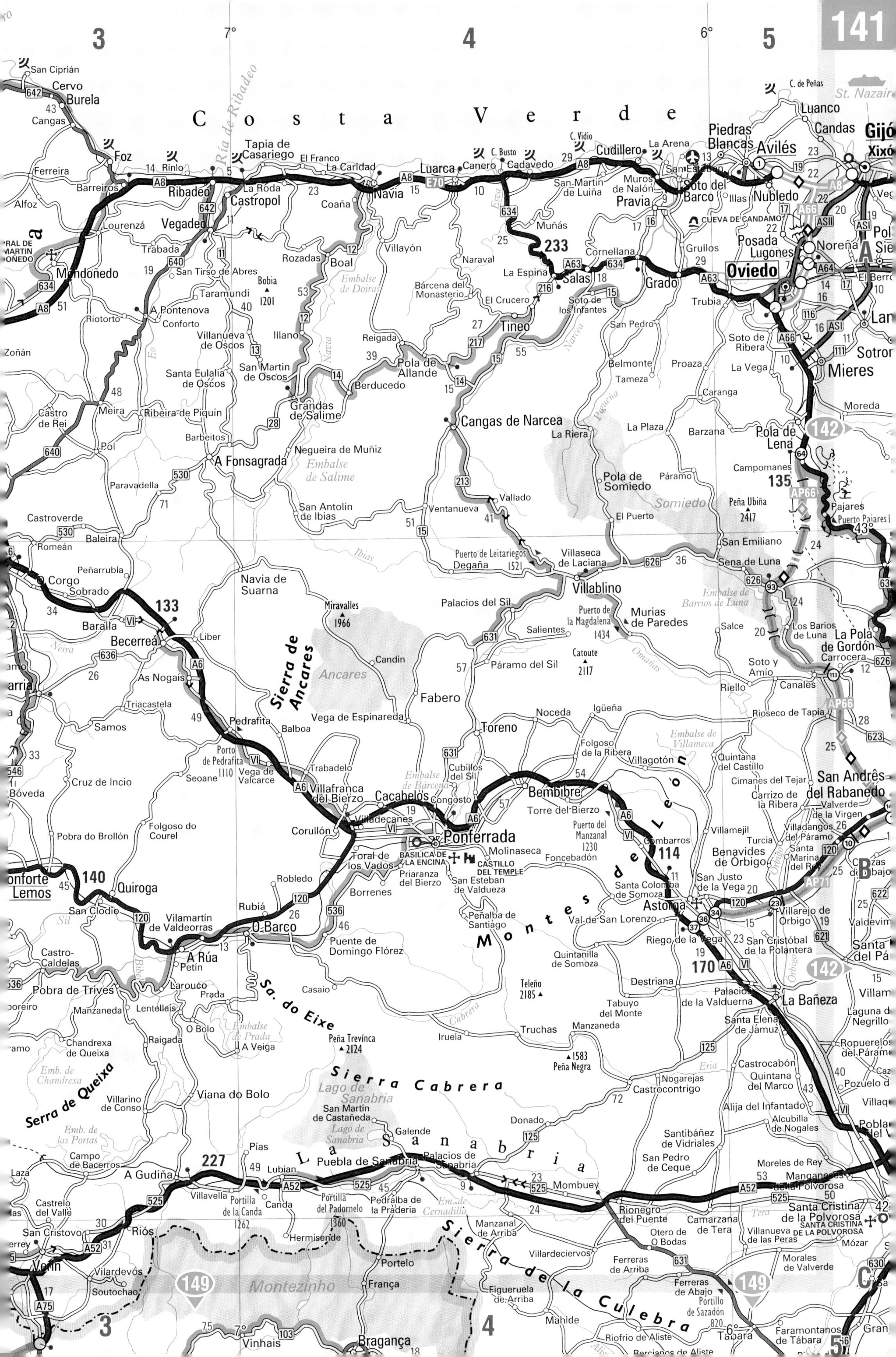
3
4
5
7°
6°
Costa Verde
San Ciprián
Cervo
Burela
Cangas
Foz
Ferreira
Barreiros
Alfoz
Lourenzá
Mondoñedo
Rinlo
Ribadeo
Vegadeo
Trabada
Ría de Ribadeo
Tapia de Casariego
El Franco
La Caridad
La Roda
Castropol
Coaña
Navia
Luarca
Canero
C. Busto
Cadavedo
C. Vidio
Cudillero
La Arena
Muros de Nalón
San Martín de Luiña
Pravia
Piedras Blancas
San Esteban
Soto del Barco
Avilés
Illas
Nubledo
C. de Peñas
Luanco
Candas
Gijón
St. Nazaire
Cueva de Candamo
Posada
Lugones
Noreña
Oviedo
Grullos
Trubia
Grado
Cornellana
Salas
La Espina
Muñás
Naraval
Villayón
Boal
Rozadas
San Tirso de Abres
Bobia 1201
Taramundi
A Pontenova
Conforto
Riotorto
Villanueva de Oscos
Illano
Embalse de Doiras
Bárcena del Monasterio
El Crucero
Tineo
Soto de los Infantes
San Pedro
Reigada
Pola de Allande
Berducedo
Santa Eulalia de Oscos
San Martín de Oscos
Grandas de Salime
Castro de Rei
Meira
Ribeira de Piquín
Barbeitos
A Fonsagrada
Negueira de Muñiz
Embalse de Salime
Pol
Paravadella
Castroverde
Baleira
Romeán
Peñarrubla
O Corgo
Sobrado
Baralla
Becerreá
Liber
Navia de Suarna
Miravalles 1966
Sierra de Ancares
Ancares
Candin
Cangas de Narcea
La Riera
La Plaza
Barzana
Pola de Lena
Belmonte
Tameza
Proaza
Soto de Ribera
La Vega
Caranga
Mieres
Moreda
Campomanes
Peña Ubiña 2417
Pajares
Puerto Pajares
Pola de Somiedo
Somiedo
Páramo
El Puerto
San Emiliano
Sena de Luna
Embalse de Barrios de Luna
Vallado
Ventanueva
San Antolín de Ibias
Ibias
Puerto de Leitariegos 1521
Degaña
Villaseca de Laciana
Villablino
Palacios del Sil
Puerto de la Magdalena 1434
Murias de Paredes
Salientes
Catoute 2117
Omañas
Páramo del Sil
Fabero
Vega de Espinareda
Toreno
Noceda
Igüeña
Los Barios de Luna
La Pola de Gordón
Carrocera
Salce
Soto y Amío
Riello
Canales
Rioseco de Tapia
Embalse de Villameca
Folgoso de la Ribera
Villagotón
Quintana del Castillo
Cimanes del Tejar
Carrizo de la Ribera
San Andrés del Rabanedo
Valverde de la Virgen
Villadangos del Páramo
Villamejil
Turcia
Benavides de Orbigo
Santa Marina del Rey
Neira
As Nogais
Triacastela
Samos
Pedrafita
Balboa
Porto de Pedrafita 1110
Vega de Valcarce
Seoane
Trabadelo
Villafranca del Bierzo
Cacabelos
Embalse de Bárcena
Cubillos del Sil
Congosto
Bembibre
Torre del Bierzo
Puerto del Manzanal 1230
Combarros
Montes de León
Villadecanes
Corullón
Ponferrada
Molinaseca
Basílica de la Encina
Castillo del Temple
Toral de los Vados
Priaranza del Bierzo
Fonsebadón
San Esteban de Valdueza
Santa Colomba de Somoza
Astorga
San Justo de la Vega
Villarejo de Órbigo
Cruz de Incio
Bóveda
Pobra do Brollón
Folgoso do Courel
Monforte de Lemos
Quiroga
San Clodio
Sil
Vilamartín de Valdeorras
Rubiá
Robledo
Borrenes
O Barco
Puente de Domingo Flórez
Peñalba de Santiago
Val de San Lorenzo
Riego de la Vega
San Cristóbal de la Polantera
Castro-Caldelas
A Rúa
Petín
Larouco
Pobra de Trives
Manzaneda
Lentellais
Prada
Casaio
Sa. do Eixe
Quintanilla de Somoza
Teleño 2185
Destriana
Tabuyo del Monte
Palacios de la Valduerna
La Bañeza
Santa Elena de Jamuz
Truchas
Manzaneda
Cabrera
Iruela
O Bolo
Embalse de Prada
A Veiga
Raigada
Chandrexa de Queixa
Emb. de Chandrexa
Peña Trevinca 2124
1583 Peña Negra
Sierra Cabrera
Lago de Sanabria
Serra de Queixa
Villarino de Conso
Viana do Bolo
San Martín de Castañeda
Galende
Donado
Nogarejas
Castrocontrigo
Castrocabón
Quintana del Marco
Alija del Infantado
Alcubilla de Nogales
Laguna de Negrillos
Ropuerelos del Páramo
Pozuelo de
Emb. de las Portas
Campo de Bacerros
A Gudiña
Pías
Lubián
La Sanabria
Puebla de Sanabria
Palacios de Sanabria
Santibáñez de Vidriales
San Pedro de Ceque
Moreles de Rey
Manganeses de la Polvorosa
Santa Cristina de la Polvorosa
Villavella
Portilla de la Canda 1262
Canda
Portilla del Padornelo 1360
Pedralba de la Pradería
Em. de Cernadilla
Mombuey
Rionegro del Puente
Camarzana de Tera
Otero de O Bodas
Villanueva de las Peras
Tera
Mózar
Castrelo del Valle
San Cristovo
Ríos
Hermisende
Manzanal de Arriba
Sierra de la Culebra
Villardeciervos
Ferreras de Arriba
Ferreras de Abajo
Portillo de Sazadón 820
Morales de Valverde
Verín
Vilardevós
Soutochao
Montezinho
Portelo
França
Figueruela de Arriba
Mahide
Vinhais
Bragança
Riofrío de Aliste
Tábara
Faramontanos de Tábara
Laza

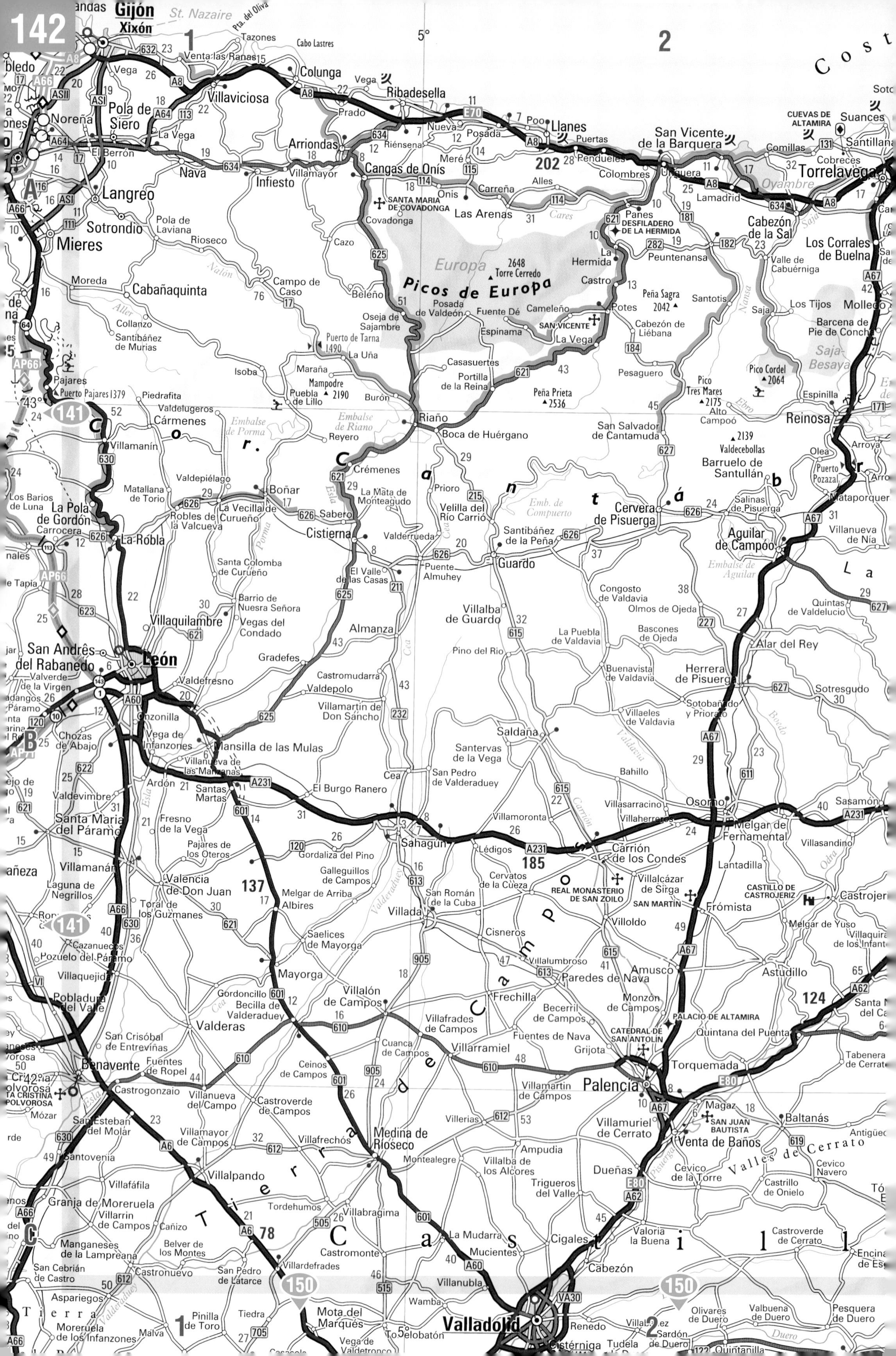
Gijón
Xixón
St. Nazaire
Pta. del Oliva
Tazones
Cabo Lastres
Venta las Ranas
Colunga
Vega
Villaviciosa
Ribadesella
Pola de Siero
Noreña
La Vega
Prado
Nueva
Posada
Poo
Llanes
Arriondas
Riénsena
El Berrón
Nava
Infiesto
Villamayor
Cangas de Onís
Mere
Puertas
Pendueles
San Vicente de la Barquera
Colombres
Unquera
Comillas
Cobreces
Torrelavega
Suances
Santillana
CUEVAS DE ALTAMIRA
Langreo
Sotrondio
Mieres
Pola de Laviana
Rioseco
Onís
Carreña
Alles
SANTA MARIA DE COVADONGA
Covadonga
Las Arenas
Cares
Panes
DESFILADERO DE LA HERMIDA
Lamadrid
Cabezón de la Sal
Los Corrales de Buelna
Oyambre
Saja
Cazo
Europa
Picos de Europa
2648 Torre Cerredo
La Hermida
Peuntenansa
Valle de Cabuérniga
Moreda
Cabañaquinta
Nalón
Campo de Caso
Beleño
Castro
Peña Sagra 2042
Santotis
Nansa
Los Tijos
Molledo
Aller
Collanzo
Santibáñez de Murias
Oseja de Sajambre
Posada de Valdeón
Fuente Dé
Cameleño
Potes
SAN VICENTE
Cabezón de Liébana
Barcena de Pie de Concha
Puerto de Tarna 1490
La Uña
Espinama
La Vega
Casasuertes
Portilla de la Reina
Pesaguero
Pico Cordel 2064
Saja-Besaya
Pajares
Puerto Pajares 1379
Isoba
Maraña
Mampodre 2190
Puebla de Lillo
Burón
Peña Prieta 2536
Pico Tres Mares 2175
Alto Campoó
Ebro
Espinilla
Reinosa
Piedrafita
Valdelugeros
Cármenes
Embalse de Porma
Embalse de Riano
Riaño
Reyero
Boca de Huérgano
San Salvador de Cantamuda
2139 Valdecebollas
Barruelo de Santullán
Olea
Arroyo
Puerto Pozazal
Mataporquera
Villamanín
Cordillera Cantábrica
Crémenes
Valdepiélago
Matallana de Torio
Boñar
La Mata de Monteagudo
Prioro
Emb. de Compuerto
Cervera de Pisuerga
Salinas de Pisuerga
Aguilar de Campóo
Villanueva de Nía
Los Barios de Luna
La Pola de Gordón
Carrocera
La Robla
La Vecilla de Curueño
Robles de la Valcueva
Sabero
Cistierna
Velilla del Río Carrió
Santibáñez de la Peña
Valderrueda
Puente Almuhey
Guardo
Embalse de Aguilar
Santa Colomba de Curueño
El Valle de las Casas
Congosto de Valdavia
Olmos de Ojeda
Quintas de Valdelucio
Barrio de Nuesra Señora
Vegas del Condado
Villaquilambre
Almanza
Villalba de Guardo
La Puebla de Valdavia
Bascones de Ojeda
Alar del Rey
San Andrés del Rabanedo
León
Valverde de la Virgen
Gradefes
Pino del Rio
Buenavista de Valdavia
Herrera de Pisuerga
Sotresgudo
Valdefresno
Castromudarra
Valdepolo
Villamartín de Don Sancho
Villaeles de Valdavia
Sotobañado y Priorato
Onzonilla
Chozas de Abajo
Vega de Infanzones
Mansilla de las Mulas
Saldaña
Santervas de la Vega
Valdavia
Villanueva de las Manzanas
Cea
San Pedro de Valderaduey
Bahillo
Ardón
Santas Martas
El Burgo Ranero
Villasarracino
Osorno
Sasamón
Valdevimbre
Villaherreros
Melgar de Fernamental
Santa María del Páramo
Fresno de la Vega
Villamoronta
Villasandino
Pajares de los Oteros
Sahagún
Ledigos
Carrión de los Condes
Gordaliza del Pino
Villamanán
Galleguillos de Campos
Cervatos de la Cueza
REAL MONASTERIO DE SAN ZOILO
Villalcázar de Sirga
Lantadilla
Laguna de Negrillos
Valencia de Don Juan
Melgar de Arriba
San Román de la Cuba
SAN MARTÍN
Frómista
CASTILLO DE CASTROJERIZ
Castrojeriz
Toral de los Guzmanes
Albires
Villada
Villoldo
Melgar de Yuso
Cazanuecos
Pozuelo del Páramo
Saelices de Mayorga
Cisneros
Villaquirán de los Infantes
Villaquejida
Mayorga
Villalumbroso
Paredes de Nava
Amusco
Astudillo
Tierra de Campos
Pobladura del Valle
Gordoncillo
Becilla de Valderaduey
Villalón de Campos
Frechilla
Monzón de Campos
Valderas
Villafrades de Campos
Becerril de Campos
PALACIO DE ALTAMIRA
Quintana del Puente
San Crisóbal de Entreviñas
Cuanca de Campos
Fuentes de Nava
CATEDRAL DE SAN ANTOLÍN
Villarramiel
Grijota
Tabenera de Cerrato
Benavente
Fuentes de Ropel
Ceinos de Campos
Torquemada
Palencia
Castrogonzaio
Villanueva del Campo
Castroverde de Campos
Villamartín de Campos
Magaz
Mózar
San Esteban del Molar
Villerias
Villamuriel de Cerrato
SAN JUAN BAUTISTA
Baltanás
Villamayor de Campos
Villafrechós
Medina de Ríoseco
Ampudia
Venta de Baños
Valles de Cerrato
Santovenia
Montealegre
Villalba de los Alcores
Pisuerga
Cevico de la Torre
Cevico Navero
Villafáfila
Villalpando
Trigueros del Valle
Dueñas
Castrillo de Oniela
Granja de Moreruela
Villarrin de Campos
Tordehumos
Villabragima
Cañizo
Manganeses de la Lampreana
Belver de los Montes
Castromonte
La Mudarra
Mucientes
Cigales
Valoria la Buena
Castroverde de Cerrato
Castilla
San Cebrián de Castro
Castronuevo
San Pedro de Latarce
Villardefrades
Cabezón
Villanubla
Aspariegos
Wamba
Tierra
Moreruela de los Infanzones
Pinilla de Toro
Tiedra
Mota del Marqués
Valladolid
Renedo
Olivares de Duero
Valbuena de Duero
Pesquera de Duero
Duero
Malva
Vega de Valdetronco
Toro
Zelobatón
Cistérniga
Tudela de Duero
Sardón de Duero
Quintanilla

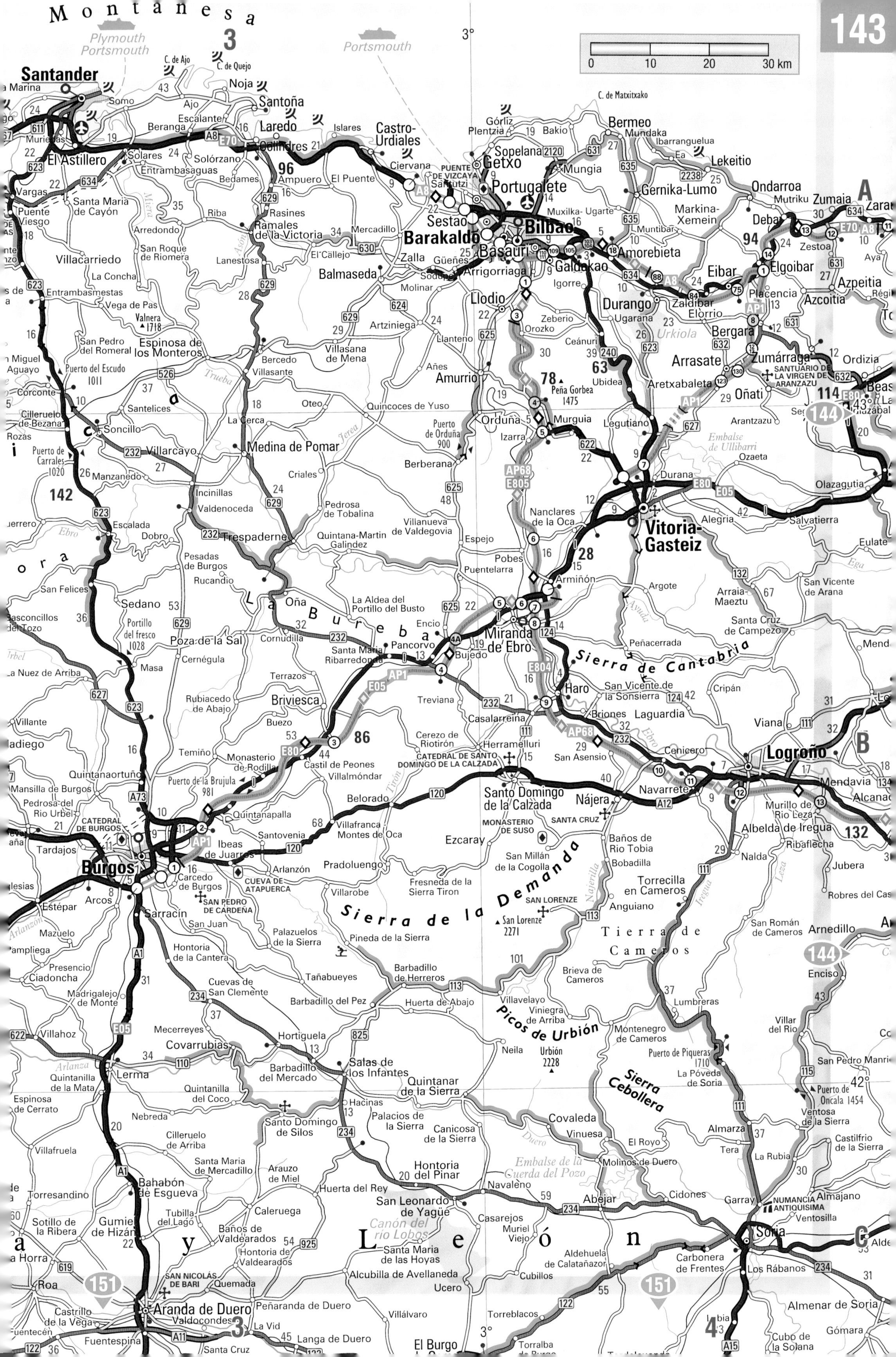
Montanesa
Plymouth
Portsmouth
Portsmouth
3°
0
10
20
30 km
Santander
C. de Ajo
C. de Quejo
Noja
Santoña
Somo
Ajo
Escalante
Beranga
Laredo
Islares
Castro-Urdiales
C. de Matxitxako
Bermeo
Mundaka
Ibarranguelua
Lekeitio
Górliz
Plentzia
Bakio
Sopelana
Getxo
Mungia
Portugalete
Sestao
Barakaldo
Bilbao
Basauri
Galdakao
Amorebieta
Gernika-Lumo
Ondarroa
Mutriku
Zumaia
Deba
Markina-Xemein
Muxilka-Ugarte
Muntibar
Zestoa
Eibar
Elgoibar
Azpeitia
Azcoitia
Placencia
Zaldibar
Elorrio
Durango
Ugarana
Urkiola
Bergara
Arrasate
Zumárraga
Ordizia
SANTUARIO DE LA VIRGEN DE ARANZAZU
Oñati
Aretxabaleta
Arantzazu
Embalse de Ullibarri
Ozaeta
Olazagutia
Salvatierra
Alegria
Vitoria-Gasteiz
Durana
Legutiano
Ubidea
Ceánuri
Zeberio
Orozko
Igorre
Llodio
Arrigorriaga
Güeñes
Zalla
Sodupe
Balmaseda
Molinar
Artziniega
Llanteno
Amurrio
Añes
Villasana de Mena
Quincoces de Yuso
Orduña
Puerto de Orduña 900
Berberana
78 Peña Gorbea 1475
Murguia
Izarra
Nanclares de la Oca
Pobes
Puentelarra
Espejo
Villanueva de Valdegovia
Armiñón
Argote
Arraia-Maeztu
San Vicente de Arana
Eulate
Santa Cruz de Campezo
Peñacerrada
Sierra de Cantabria
Miranda de Ebro
Bujedo
Haro
San Vicente de la Sonsierra
Briones
Laguardia
Cripán
Viana
Logroño
Cenicero
Navarrete
San Asensio
Casalarreina
Herramelluri
Santo Domingo de la Calzada
CATEDRAL DE SANTO DOMINGO DE LA CALZADA
Nájera
SANTA CRUZ
MONASTERIO DE SUSO
San Millán de la Cogolla
Baños de Rio Tobia
Bobadilla
Torrecilla en Cameros
Anguiano
SAN LORENZE
San Lorenze 2271
Sierra de la Demanda
Tierra de Cameros
Ezcaray
Belorado
Villafranca Montes de Oca
Pradoluengo
Fresneda de la Sierra Tiron
Villarobe
Pineda de la Sierra
Palazuelos de la Sierra
Barbadillo de Herreros
Barbadillo del Pez
Huerta de Abajo
Villavelayo
Viniegra de Arriba
Picos de Urbión
Neila
Urbión 2228
Brieva de Cameros
Montenegro de Cameros
Lumbreras
Puerto de Piqueras 1710
La Póveda de Soria
Sierra Cebollera
Covaleda
Vinuesa
El Royo
Molinos de Duero
Embalse de la Cuerda del Pozo
Almarza
Tera
La Rubia
Cidones
Garray
NUMANCIA ANTIQUISIMA
Almajano
Ventosilla
Soria
Los Rábanos
Carbonera de Frentes
Almenar de Soria
Gómara
Cubo de la Solana
Mendavia
Murillo de Rio Leza
Albelda de Iregua
Ribaflecha
Nalda
Jubera
Robres del Castillo
San Román de Cameros
Arnedillo
Enciso
Villar del Rio
San Pedro Manrique
Puerto de Oncala 1454
Ventosa de la Sierra
Castilfrío de la Sierra
Alcanadre
El Astillero
Muriedas
Solares
Entrambasaguas
Solórzano
Colindres
Ampuero
El Puente
Ciervana
PUENTE DE VIZCAYA
Santurtzi
Bedames
Vargas
Santa María de Cayón
Puente Viesgo
Riba
Rasines
Ramales de la Victoria
Mercadillo
El Callejo
Arredondo
San Roque de Riomera
Lanestosa
Villacarriedo
La Concha
Entrambasmestas
Vega de Pas
Valnera 1718
San Pedro del Romeral
Espinosa de los Monteros
Bercedo
Villasante
Puerto del Escudo 1011
Corconte
Cilleruelo de Bezana
Santelices
Soncillo
Oteo
La Cerca
Medina de Pomar
Villarcayo
Puerto de Carrales 1020
Manzanedo
Criales
Pedrosa de Tobalina
Incinillas
Valdenoceda
Quintana-Martin Galindez
Escalada
Dobro
Trespaderne
Pesadas de Burgos
Rucandio
San Felices
Sedano
La Bureba
Oña
La Aldea del Portillo del Busto
Encio
Pancorvo
Santa Maria Ribarredonda
Cornudilla
Poza de la Sal
Portillo del fresco 1028
Basconcillos del Tozo
Masa
Cernégula
Terrazos
Briviesca
Rubiacedo de Abajo
Buezo
Treviana
Cerezo de Riotirón
Temiño
Monasterio de Rodilla
Castil de Peones
Villalmóndar
Puerto de la Brujula 981
Quintanaortuño
Mansilla de Burgos
Pedrosa del Rio Urbel
Quintanapalla
Santovenia
CATEDRAL DE BURGOS
Burgos
Tardajos
Ibeas de Juarros
Arlanzón
Carcedo de Burgos
CUEVA DE ATAPUERCA
SAN PEDRO DE CARDEÑA
Arcos
Estépar
Sarracín
San Juan
Hontoria de la Cantera
Cuevas de San Clemente
Mazuelo
Presencio
Ciadoncha
Madrigalejo de Monte
Mecerreyes
Covarrubias
Hortiguela
Villahoz
Lerma
Quintanilla de la Mata
Barbadillo del Mercado
Salas de los Infantes
Quintanar de la Sierra
Quintanilla del Coco
Espinosa de Cerrato
Nebreda
Hacinas
Santo Domingo de Silos
Palacios de la Sierra
Canicosa de la Sierra
Cilleruelo de Arriba
Villafruela
Santa Maria de Mercadillo
Arauzo de Miel
Hontoria del Pinar
Huerta del Rey
Navaleno
Abejar
Bahabón de Esgueva
Torresandino
Caleruega
San Leonardo de Yagüe
Casarejos
Muriel Viejo
Cañon del rio Lobos
Sotillo de la Ribera
Gumiel de Hizán
Tubilla del Lago
Baños de Valdearados
Hontoria de Valdearados
Santa Maria de las Hoyas
Aldehuela de Calatañazor
Cubillos
La Horra
Roa
SAN NICOLÁS DE BARI
Quemada
Alcubilla de Avellaneda
Ucero
Castrillo de la Vega
Aranda de Duero
Peñaranda de Duero
Valdocondes
Villálvaro
Torreblacos
La Vid
Langa de Duero
Fuentespina
Fuentecén
Santa Cruz
El Burgo
Torralba
Castilla y León
Ebro
Trueba
Jerea
Tirón
Duero
Arlanza
Arlanzón
Ayuda
Ega
Najerilla
Iregua
Leza
Mera
Asón
A
B
C
142
114
144
151
3
4
96
94
63
28
86
132

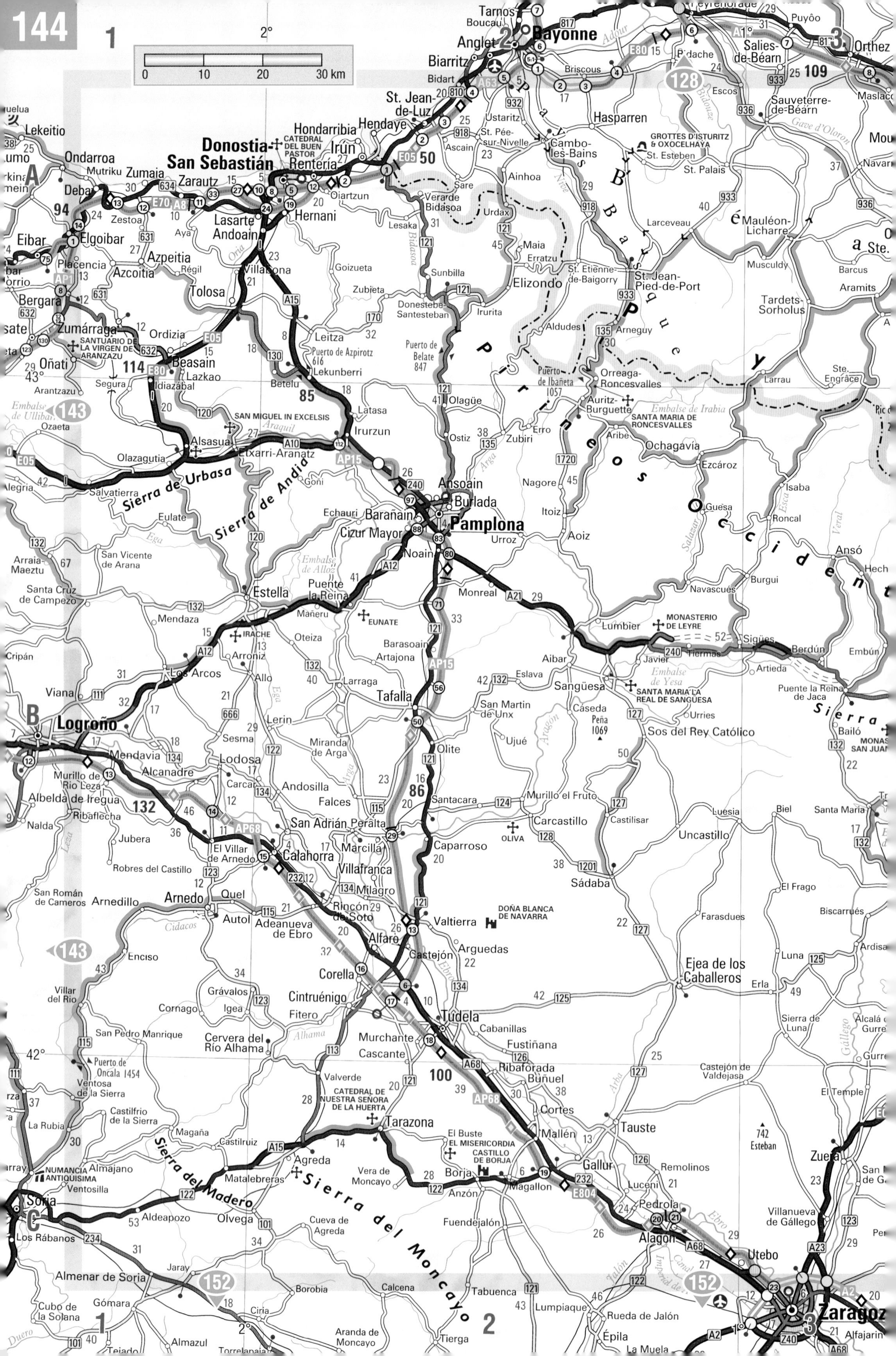
0 10 20 30 km
Bayonne
Anglet
Biarritz
Bidart
Tarnos
Boucau
St. Jean-de-Luz
Hendaye
Irun
Hondarribia
Donostia-San Sebastián
Rentería
Oiartzun
Hernani
Lasarte
Andoain
Zarautz
Zumaia
Mutriku
Deba
Ondarroa
Lekeitio
Eibar
Elgoibar
Zestoa
Azpeitia
Azkoitia
Placencia
Bergara
Zumárraga
Oñati
Ordizia
Beasain
Lazkao
Idiazábal
Segura
Tolosa
Villabona
Aya
Régil
Goizueta
Zubieta
Leitza
Lekunberri
Betelu
Latasa
Irurzun
Alsasua
Olazagutia
Etxarri-Aranatz
Salvatierra
Sierra de Urbasa
Sierra de Andía
Goñi
Echauri
Barañain
Cizur Mayor
Ansoain
Burlada
Pamplona
Noain
Urroz
Aoiz
Itoiz
Nagore
Zubiri
Erro
Ostiz
Olagüe
Orreaga-Roncesvalles
Auritz-Burguette
Ochagavía
Ezcároz
Isaba
Roncal
Ansó
Burgui
Navascués
Lumbier
Monasterio de Leyre
Sigües
Berdún
Embún
Artieda
Javier
Tiermas
Aibar
Sangüesa
Eslava
San Martín de Unx
Ujué
Cáseda
Sos del Rey Católico
Puente la Reina de Jaca
Bailó
Estella
Puente la Reina
Mañeru
Eunate
Monreal
Barasoain
Artajona
Tafalla
Olite
Larraga
Oteiza
Irache
Arroniz
Allo
Los Arcos
Viana
Logroño
Mendavia
Lodosa
Sesma
Lerin
Miranda de Arga
Andosilla
Falces
Carcar
Alcanadre
Murillo de Río Leza
Albelda de Iregua
Ribaflecha
Nalda
Jubera
El Villar de Arnedo
Calahorra
San Adrián
Peralta
Marcilla
Villafranca
Milagro
Caparroso
Santacara
Murillo el Fruto
Carcastillo
Oliva
Castilisar
Uncastillo
Luesia
Biel
Sádaba
El Frago
Biscarrués
Farasdues
Ejea de los Caballeros
Erla
Luna
Rincón de Soto
Valtierra
Doña Blanca de Navarra
Arguedas
Castejón
Alfaro
Corella
Cintruénigo
Fitero
Tudela
Cabanillas
Fustiñana
Murchante
Cascante
Ribaforada
Buñuel
Cortes
Mallén
Tauste
Gallur
Remolinos
Pedrola
Alagón
Utebo
Zaragoza
Arnedo
Quel
Autol
Arnedillo
Adeanueva de Ebro
Enciso
Grávalos
Igea
Cornago
Cervera del Río Alhama
San Pedro Manrique
Valverde
Tarazona
Catedral de Nuestra Señora de la Huerta
El Buste
Borja
Magallon
Agreda
Sierra del Moncayo
Sierra del Madero
Vera de Moncayo
Soria
Numancia
Ventosilla
Aldeapozo
Olvega
Almenar de Soria
Gómara
Borobia
Calcena
Tabuenca
Lumpiaque
Rueda de Jalón
Épila
Fuendejalón
Pirineos Occidentales
Pays Basque
Hasparren
Cambo-les-Bains
Ustaritz
Ainhoa
St. Jean-Pied-de-Port
St. Étienne-de-Baigorry
Elizondo
Mauléon-Licharre
Sauveterre-de-Béarn
Salies-de-Béarn
Orthez
Tardets-Sorholus

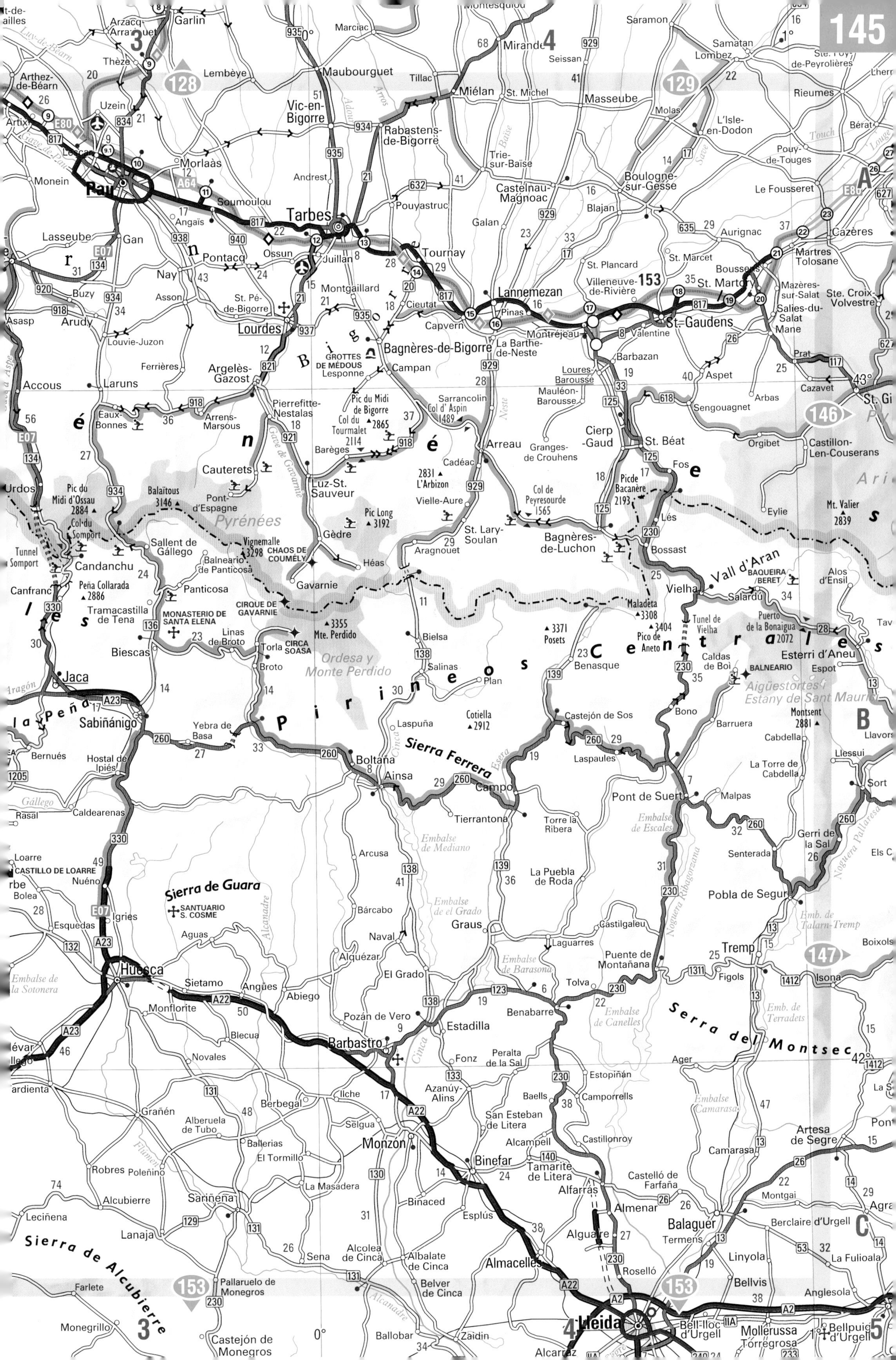

145
Garlin
Marciac
Mirande
Seissan
Saramon
Samatan
Lombez
Ste. Foy-de-Peyrolières
Arzacq-Arraziguet
Thèze
Lembeye
Maubourguet
Tillac
Miélan
St. Michel
Masseube
Arthez-de-Béarn
Artix
Uzein
Vic-en-Bigorre
Rabastens-de-Bigorre
Trie-sur-Baïse
Molas
L'Isle-en-Dodon
Rieumes
Bérat
Pouy-de-Touges
Lescar
Pau
Morlaàs
Andrest
Monein
Soumoulou
Tarbes
Pouyastruc
Castelnau-Magnoac
Boulogne-sur-Gesse
Le Fousseret
Angaïs
Galan
Blajan
Aurignac
Cazères
Lasseube
Gan
Ossun
Juillan
Tournay
Martres Tolosane
Pontacq
Nay
St. Plancard
St. Marcet
Boussens
Buzy
Asson
St. Pé-de-Bigorre
Montgaillard
Villeneuve-de-Rivière
St. Martory
Mazères-sur-Salat
Ste. Croix-Volvestre
Salies-du-Salat
Mane
Arudy
Lourdes
Cieutat
Capvern
Lannemezan
Pinas
Montréjeau
Valentine
St. Gaudens
Asasp
Louvie-Juzon
GROTTES DE MÉDOUS
Lesponne
Bagnères-de-Bigorre
La Barthe-de-Neste
Barbazan
Aspet
Ferrières
Argelès-Gazost
Campan
Loures-Barousse
Mauléon-Barousse
Arbas
Cazavet
Accous
Laruns
Pic du Midi de Bigorre
Sarrancolin
Col d'Aspin 1489
Sengouagnet
Eaux-Bonnes
Arrens-Marsous
Pierrefitte-Nestalas
Col du Tourmalet 2114
2865
Barèges
Arreau
Granges-de Crouhens
Cierp-Gaud
St. Béat
Orgibet
Castillon-Len-Couserans
Cauterets
Cadéac
Fos
Urdos
Pic du Midi d'Ossau 2884
Balaïtous 3146
Pont-d'Espagne
Luz-St. Sauveur
2831 L'Arbizon
Col de Peyresourde 1565
Picde Bacanère 2193
Vielle-Aure
Pic Long 3192
Lés
Eylie
Mt. Valier 2839
Col du Somport
Pyrénées
St. Lary-Soulan
Tunnel Somport
Sallent de Gállego
Vignemalle 3298
CHAOS DE COUMÉLY
Gèdre
Aragnouet
Bagnères-de-Luchon
Bossast
Candanchu
Balneario de Panticosa
Héas
Vall d'Aran
BAQUEIRA /BERET
Alos d'Ensil
Canfranc
Peña Collarada 2886
Panticosa
Gavarnie
Vielha
Salardú
Tramacastilla de Tena
MONASTERIO DE SANTA ELENA
CIRQUE DE GAVARNIE
Maladeta 3308
Tunel de Vielha
Puerto de la Bonaigua 2072
3355 Mte. Perdido
Bielsa
3371 Posets
3404 Pico de Aneto
Linas de Broto
Biescas
Torla
CIRCA SOASA
Salinas
Benasque
Caldas de Boi
BALNEARIO
Esterri d'Aneu
Espot
Broto
Ordesa y Monte Perdido
Plan
Aigüestortes i Estany de Sant Maurici
Jaca
Sabiñánigo
Laspuña
Cotiella 2912
Castejón de Sos
Bono
Barruera
Montsent 2881
Llavorsí
Yebra de Basa
Sierra Ferrera
Laspaules
Cabdella
Bernués
Hostal de Ipiés
Boltaña
Ainsa
Campo
La Torre de Cabdella
Llessui
Sort
Pont de Suert
Malpas
Caldearenas
Tierrantona
Torre la Ribera
Embalse de Escales
Gerri de la Sal
Rasal
Embalse de Mediano
Senterada
Loarre
CASTILLO DE LOARRE
Arcusa
La Puebla de Roda
Nueno
Sierra de Guara
SANTUARIO S. COSME
Bolea
Embalse de el Grado
Pobla de Segur
Bárcabo
Graus
Emb. de Talarn-Tremp
Esquedas
Igries
Aguas
Castilgaleu
Naval
Laguarres
Boixols
Tremp
Embalse de Barasona
Puente de Montañana
Alquézar
El Grado
Figols
Isona
Huesca
Sietamo
Angües
Tolva
Embalse de la Sotonera
Abiego
Benabarre
Monflorite
Pozán de Vero
Estadilla
Embalse de Canelles
Serra del Montsec
Emb. de Terradets
Blecua
Barbastro
Peralta de la Sal
Fonz
Ager
Novales
Estopiñán
Azanúy-Alins
Baells
Camporrells
Berbegal
Iliche
Embalse Camarasa
Grañén
Alberuela de Tubo
Selgua
San Esteban de Litera
Artesa de Segre
Ballerias
Alcampell
Castillonroy
El Tormillo
Monzón
Binefar
Tamarite de Litera
Camarasa
Robres
Poleñino
Castelló de Farfaña
Alfarrás
Montgai
La Masadera
Sariñena
Binaced
Almenar
Alcubierre
Esplús
Leciñena
Berclaire d'Urgell
Balaguer
Lanaja
Alguaire
Termens
Sierra de Alcubierre
Sena
Alcolea de Cinca
Albalate de Cinca
Linyola
La Fulioala
Almacelles
Rosselló
Farlete
Pallaruelo de Monegros
Belver de Cinca
Bellvis
Anglesola
Monegrillo
Castejón de Monegros
Ballobar
Zaidin
Lleida
Bell-lloc d'Urgell
Mollerussa
Torregrosa
Bellpuig d'Urgell
Alcarraz
Sierra de la Peña
128
129
146
147
153

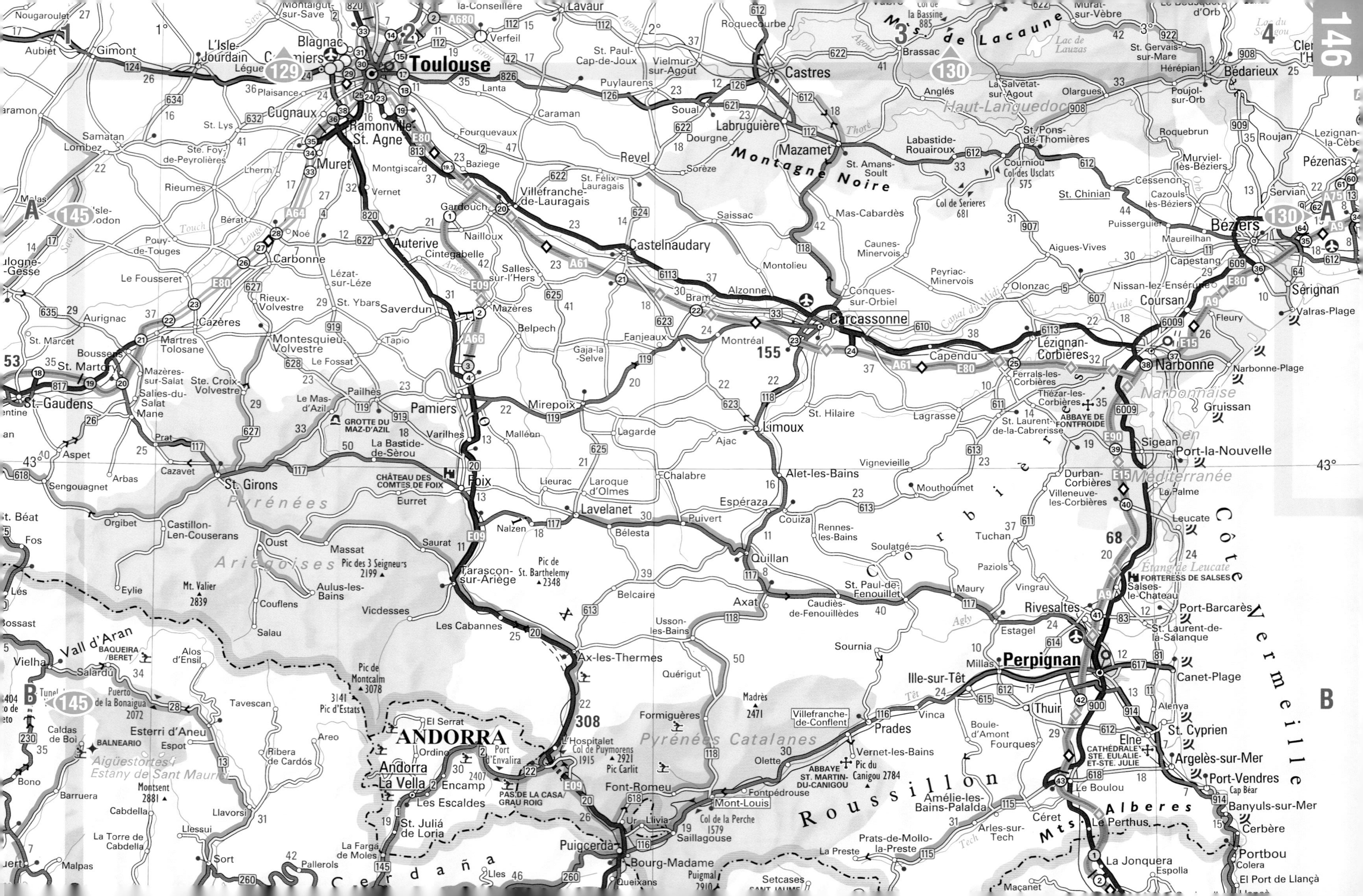
Toulouse
Blagnac
Colomiers
L'Isle-Jourdain
Gimont
Aubiet
Samatan
Lombez
Plaisance
Cugnaux
Ramonville-St. Agne
Muret
St. Lys
Ste. Foy-de-Peyrolières
Rieumes
Lherm
Bérat
Noé
Carbonne
Le Fousseret
Rieux-Volvestre
Cazères
Aurignac
Martres Tolosane
St. Marcet
St. Martory
St.-Gaudens
Mazères-sur-Salat
Salies-du-Salat
Mane
Ste. Croix-Volvestre
Montesquieu-Volvestre
Le Fossat
Lézat-sur-Léze
St. Ybars
Saverdun
Auterive
Cintegabelle
Nailloux
Gardouch
Villefranche-de-Lauragais
Montgiscard
Vernet
Baziege
Fourquevaux
Caraman
Lanta
Verfeil
Puylaurens
St. Paul-Cap-de-Joux
Lavaur
Vielmur-sur-Agout
Revel
Sorèze
St. Félix-Lauragais
Castelnaudary
Salles-sur-l'Hers
Mazères
Belpech
Pamiers
Varilhes
Mirepoix
Fanjeaux
Gaja-la-Selve
Bram
Alzonne
Montréal
Saissac
Montolieu
Carcassonne
Conques-sur-Orbiel
Castres
Roquecourbe
Soual
Labruguière
Dourgne
Mazamet
Montagne Noire
St. Amans-Soult
Mas-Cabardès
Caunes-Minervois
Peyriac-Minervois
Brassac
Anglès
Monts de Lacaune
La Salvetat-sur-Agout
Haut-Languedoc
Labastide-Rouairoux
St. Pons-de-Thomières
Courniou
Col des Usclats 575
Col de Serieres 681
Olargues
St. Chinian
Bédarieux
St. Gervais-sur-Mare
Hérépian
Poujol-sur-Orb
Roquebrun
Roujan
Murviel-lès-Béziers
Cessenon
Cazouls-lès-Béziers
Puisserguier
Pézenas
Servian
Béziers
Maureilhan
Capestang
Nissan-lez-Ensérune
Sérignan
Valras-Plage
Aigues-Vives
Olonzac
Coursan
Fleury
Narbonne
Narbonne-Plage
Gruissan
Lézignan-Corbières
Capendu
Canal du Midi
Ferrals-les-Corbières
Thézan-les-Corbières
ABBAYE DE FONTFROIDE
St. Laurent-de-la-Cabrerisse
Lagrasse
St. Hilaire
Limoux
Ajac
Lagarde
Malléon
Foix
CHÂTEAU DES COMTES DE FOIX
GROTTE DU MAZ-D'AZIL
Le Mas-d'Azil
Pailhès
La Bastide-de-Sèrou
St. Girons
Aspet
Cazavet
Prat
Arbas
Sengouagnet
Orgibet
Castillon-Len-Couserans
Massat
Oust
Aulus-les-Bains
Couflens
Salau
Eylie
Mt. Valier 2839
Pic des 3 Seigneurs 2199
Pyrénées Ariégoises
Eurret
Saurat
Tarascon-sur-Ariège
Nalzen
Lavelanet
Lieurac
Laroque d'Olmes
Bélesta
Chalabre
Puivert
Espéraza
Alet-les-Bains
Couiza
Rennes-les-Bains
Quillan
Axat
Belcaire
Vicdesses
Les Cabannes
Ax-les-Thermes
Pic de St. Barthelemy 2348
Usson-les-Bains
Quérigut
Vignevieille
Mouthoumet
Corbières
Tuchan
Paziols
Soulatgé
St. Paul-de-Fenouillet
Caudiès-de-Fenouillèdes
Maury
Vingrau
Sournia
Durban-Corbières
Villeneuve-les-Corbières
Sigean
Port-la-Nouvelle
Méditerranée
La Palme
Leucate
Étang de Leucate
FORTERESS DE SALSES
Salses-le-Château
Port-Barcarès
St. Laurent-de-la-Salanque
Côte Vermeille
Rivesaltes
Estagel
Perpignan
Millas
Ille-sur-Têt
Canet-Plage
Thuir
Alenya
St. Cyprien
Elne
CATHÉDRALE STE. EULALIE-ET-STE. JULIE
Argelès-sur-Mer
Port-Vendres
Cap Béar
Banyuls-sur-Mer
Cerbère
Portbou
Colera
El Port de Llançà
Le Boulou
Céret
Le Perthus
Mts. Albères
La Jonquera
Espolla
Maçanet
Arles-sur-Tech
Amélie-les-Bains-Palalda
Boule-d'Amont
Fourques
Vinca
Prades
Roussillon
Vernet-les-Bains
Pic du Canigou 2784
ABBAYE ST. MARTIN-DU-CANIGOU
Villefranche-de-Conflent
Olette
Prats-de-Mollo-la-Preste
La Preste
Madrès 2471
Formiguères
Pyrénées Catalanes
Fontpédrouse
Mont-Louis
Col de la Perche 1579
Saillagouse
Font-Romeu
Llivia
Puigcerdà
Bourg-Madame
Puigmal
Setcases
Queixans
L'Hospitalet
Col de Puymorens 1915
Pic Carlit 2921
Port d'Envalira 2407
PAS DE LA CASA/GRAU ROIG
ANDORRA
Andorra La Vella
Encamp
Les Escaldes
Ordino
El Serrat
St. Juliá de Loria
La Farga de Moles
Cerdaña
Lles
Pic de Montcalm 3078
Pic d'Estats 3141
Areo
Ribera de Cardós
Tavescan
Alos d'Ensil
Llavorsi
Llessui
Sort
Pallerols
Esterri d'Aneu
Espot
Puerto de la Bonaigua 2072
Aigüestortes i Estany de Sant Maurici
Montsent 2881
Cabdella
La Torre de Cabdella
Malpas
Barruera
Bono
Caldas de Boi
BALNEARIO
Salardú
BAQUEIRA/BERET
Vall d'Aran
Vielha
St. Béat
Fos
Lés
Bossast
Nougaroulet
43°
1°
2°
3°
155
308
68

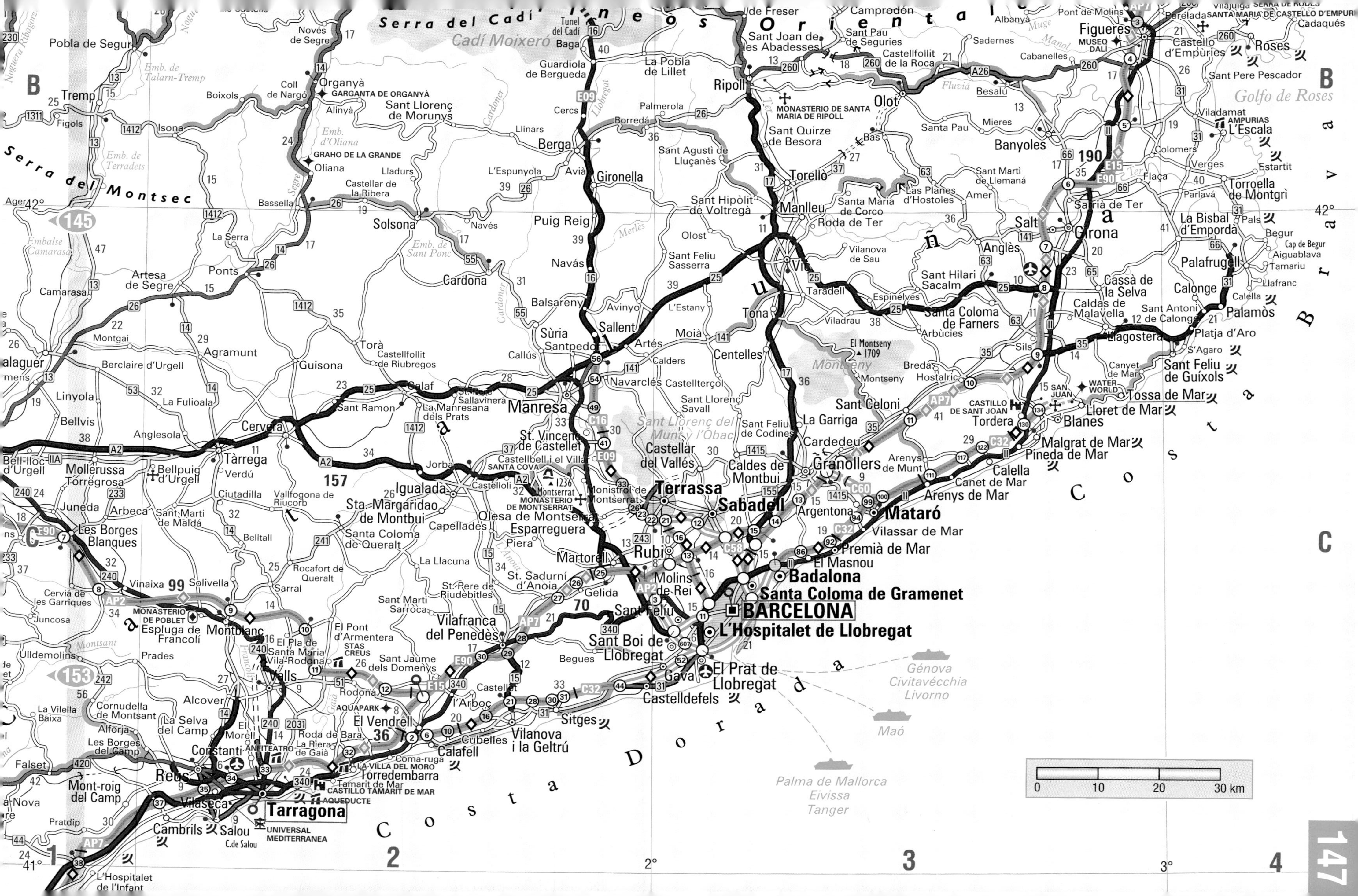

147
Serra del Cadí
Cadí Moixeró
Pirineos Orientales
Serra del Montsec
Costa Brava
Costa Daurada
Golfo de Roses
Pobla de Segur
Tremp
Figols
Isona
Boixols
Coll de Nargó
Organyà
GARGANTA DE ORGANYÀ
Alinyà
Oliana
GRAHO DE LA GRANDE
Noves de Segre
Sant Llorenç de Morunys
Lladurs
Castellar de la Ribera
Bassella
Solsona
Navés
Cardona
Emb. de Sant Ponç
Emb. de Talarn-Tremp
Emb. de Terradets
Emb. d'Oliana
Embalse Camarasa
Ager
La Serra
Ponts
Artesa de Segre
Camarasa
Balaguer
Montgai
Agramunt
Berclaire d'Urgell
Linyola
Bellvis
La Fuliola
Anglesola
Guisona
Torà
Castellfollit de Riubregos
Calaf
Sant Ramon
Cervera
Tàrrega
Verdú
Bell-lloc d'Urgell
Mollerussa
Torregrosa
Bellpuig d'Urgell
Juneda
Arbeca
Sant Martí de Maldà
Ciutadilla
Vallfogona de Riucorb
Les Borges Blanques
Belltall
Cervià de les Garrigues
Juncosa
Vinaixa
Solivella
MONASTERIO DE POBLET
Espluga de Francolí
Montblanc
Sarral
Rocafort de Queralt
Santa Coloma de Queralt
Sta. Margaridao de Montbui
Igualada
Jorba
Ulldemolins
Prades
Alcover
La Vilella Baixa
Cornudella de Montsant
Alforja
La Selva del Camp
Les Borges del Camp
Falset
Mont-roig del Camp
Reus
Constantí
Vilaseca
Cambrils
Salou
C.de Salou
Tarragona
UNIVERSAL MEDITERRANEA
L'Hospitalet de l'Infant
Pratdip
Valls
El Pla de Santa Maria
Vila-Rodona
Rodonyà
El Morell
Roda de Barà
La Riera de Gaià
Torredembarra
Tamarit de Mar
CASTILLO TAMARIT DE MAR
AQUEDUCTE
LA VILLA DEL MORO
Coma-ruga
El Vendrell
AQUAPARK
ANFITEATRO
Calafell
Cubelles
Vilanova i la Geltrú
Sitges
Castellet
l'Arboç
Sant Jaume dels Domenys
STAS CREUS
El Pont d'Armentera
Sant Martí Sarroca
Vilafranca del Penedès
St. Pere de Riudebitlles
La Llacuna
Capellades
Piera
St. Sadurní d'Anoia
Gelida
Esparreguera
Olesa de Montserrat
Martorell
MONASTERIO DE MONTSERRAT
Montserrat 1236
Monistrol de Montserrat
SANTA COVA
Castellolí
Castellbell i el Vilar
St. Vicenç de Castellet
Manresa
Sallavinera
La Manresana dels Prats
Callús
Súria
Sant Pedor
Sallent
Artés
Avinyó
Balsareny
Navás
Puig Reig
Gironella
Avià
Berga
Cercs
Llinars
L'Espunyola
Borredà
Guardiola de Bergueda
Baga
Tunel del Cadí
La Pobla de Lillet
Palmerola
Sant Agustí de Lluçanès
Sant Hipòlit de Voltregà
Olost
Sant Feliu Sasserra
L'Estany
Moià
Calders
Navarclés
Castellterçol
Sant Llorenç Savall
Sant Llorenç del Munt y l'Obac
Castellar del Vallés
Terrassa
Sabadell
Rubí
Molins de Rei
Sant Feliu
Sant Boi de Llobregat
Begues
Gavà
Castelldefels
El Prat de Llobregat
L'Hospitalet de Llobregat
BARCELONA
Santa Coloma de Gramenet
Badalona
El Masnou
Premià de Mar
Vilassar de Mar
Mataró
Argentona
Granollers
Cardedeu
La Garriga
Sant Feliu de Codines
Caldes de Montbui
Centelles
Tona
Vic
Manlleu
Roda de Ter
Torelló
Ripoll
Sant Joan de les Abadesses
Sant Quirze de Besora
MONASTERIO DE SANTA MARIA DE RIPOLL
Camprodon
Sant Pau de Seguries
Castellfollit de la Roca
Olot
Bas
Santa Pau
Besalú
Mieres
Banyoles
Santa Maria de Corco
Las Planes d'Hostoles
Amer
Sant Martí de Llemaná
Vilanova de Sau
Taradell
Viladrau
Espinelves
Sant Hilari Sacalm
Santa Coloma de Farners
Arbúcies
El Montseny 1709
Montseny
Breda
Hostalric
Sant Celoni
Arenys de Munt
Arenys de Mar
Canet de Mar
Calella
Pineda de Mar
Malgrat de Mar
Tordera
CASTILLO DE SANT JOAN
Blanes
Lloret de Mar
WATER WORLD
Tossa de Mar
Canyet de Mar
Sant Feliu de Guíxols
S'Agaro
Platja d'Aro
Llagostera
Sils
Caldas de Malavella
Cassà de la Selva
Anglès
Salt
Girona
Sarrià de Ter
Sant Antoni de Calonge
Calonge
Palamós
Calella
Llafranc
Palafrugell
Tamariu
Aiguablava
Cap de Begur
Begur
Pals
La Bisbal d'Empordà
Parlavà
Torroella de Montgrí
Estartit
Flaça
Verges
Colomers
L'Escala
AMPURIAS
Viladamat
Sant Pere Pescador
Roses
Castello d'Empúries
Cadaqués
SANTA MARIA DE CASTELLO D'EMPURIES
Vilajuiga
Peralada
Figueres
MUSEO DALI
Pont de Molins
Albanya
Sadernes
Cabanelles
Génova
Civitavécchia
Livorno
Maó
Palma de Mallorca
Eivissa
Tanger
0 10 20 30 km

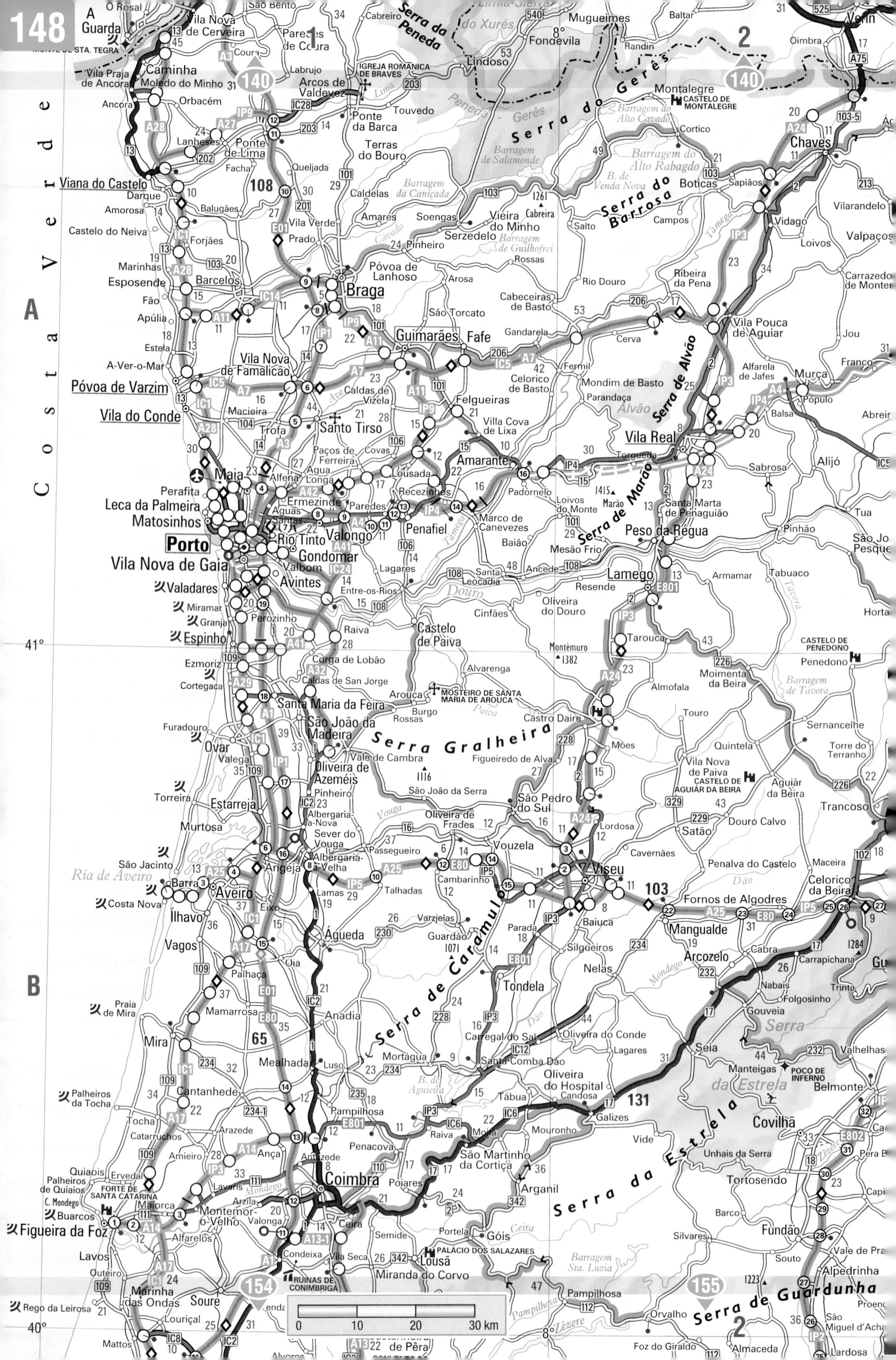
Costa Verde
Serra da Peneda
Serra do Gerês
Serra do Barroso
Serra de Alvão
Serra de Marão
Serra Gralheira
Serra de Caramulo
Serra da Estrela
Serra de Guardunha
Ría de Aveiro
A Guarda
Monte de Sta. Tegra
Vila Nova de Cerveira
Paredes de Coura
Caminha
Moledo do Minho
Vila Praia de Ancora
Ancora
Orbacém
Arcos de Valdevez
Igreja Romanica de Braves
Ponte da Barca
Terras do Bouro
Lindoso
Fondevila
Mugueimes
Montalegre
Castelo de Montalegre
Barragem do Alto Cavado
Barragem de Salamonde
Barragem do Alto Rabagdo
B. de Venda Nova
Cortiço
Chaves
Verín
Oimbra
Randín
Baltar
Lanheses
Ponte de Lima
Viana do Castelo
Darque
Amorosa
Castelo do Neiva
Balugães
Forjães
Marinhas
Esposende
Barcelos
Fão
Apúlia
Estela
A-Ver-o-Mar
Póvoa de Varzim
Vila do Conde
Queljada
Barragem da Caniçada
Caldelas
Amares
Vila Verde
Prado
Soengas
Vieira do Minho
Cabreira
Serzedelo
Barragem de Guilhofrei
Rossas
Pinheiro
Póvoa de Lanhoso
Braga
Arosa
São Torcato
Cabeceiras de Basto
Rio Douro
Salto
Campos
Boticas
Sapiãos
Vidago
Vilarandelo
Valpaços
Loivos
Ribeira da Pena
Vila Pouca de Aguiar
Cerva
Gandarela
Guimarães
Fafe
Vila Nova de Famalicão
Caldas de Vizela
Celorico de Basto
Fermil
Mondim de Basto
Parandaça
Alvão
Alfarela de Jafes
Murça
Pópulo
Jou
Balsa
Abreiro
Vila Real
Torgueda
Sabrosa
Alijó
Macieira
Trofa
Santo Tirso
Felgueiras
Villa Cova de Lixa
Amarante
Padornelo
Loivos do Monte
Marão
Paços de Ferreira
Covas
Agua Longa
Lousada
Recezinhos
Marco de Canevezes
Baião
Mesão Frio
Santa Marta de Penaguião
Peso da Régua
Pinhão
Tua
Maia
Alfena
Perafita
Leca da Palmeira
Matosinhos
Ermezinde
Aguas Santas
Paredes
Rio Tinto
Valongo
Penafiel
Porto
Vila Nova de Gaia
Gondomar
Valbom
Avintes
Lagares
Santa Leocadia
Ancede
Resende
Lamego
Armamar
Tabuaco
Valadares
Miramar
Granja
Espinho
Perozinho
Entre-os-Rios
Douro
Cinfães
Oliveira do Douro
Castelo de Paiva
Raiva
Tarouca
Montemuro
Castelo de Penedono
Penedono
Moimenta da Beira
Barragem de Tavora
Almofala
Ezmoriz
Cortegaça
Corga de Lobão
Caldas de San Jorge
Alvarenga
Arouca
Mosteiro de Santa Maria de Arouca
Burgo
Rossas
Santa Maria da Feira
São João da Madeira
Furadouro
Ovar
Valega
Oliveira de Azeméis
Vale de Cambra
Castro Daire
Touro
Sernancelhe
Quintela
Torre do Terranho
Figueiredo de Alva
Moes
Vila Nova de Paiva
Castelo de Aguiar da Beira
Aguiar da Beira
Torreira
Estarreja
Pinheiro
Albergaria-a-Nova
São João da Serra
São Pedro do Sul
Oliveira de Frades
Trancoso
Murtosa
Sever do Vouga
Vouga
Passegueiro
Vouzela
Lordosa
Satão
Douro Calvo
São Jacinto
Angeja
Albergaria-a-Velha
Cambarinho
Cavernães
Penalva do Castelo
Maceira
Barra
Aveiro
Costa Nova
Ilhavo
Lamas
Talhadas
Eixo
Viseu
Celorico da Beira
Fornos de Algodres
Mangualde
Vagos
Águeda
Varzjelas
Guardão
Parada
Baiuca
Silgueiros
Nelas
Arcozelo
Cabra
Carrapichana
Palhaça
Oia
Tondela
Nabais
Folgosinho
Trinta
Praia de Mira
Mamarrosa
Anadia
Mondego
Gouveia
Mira
Mealhada
Luso
Mortágua
Carregal do Sal
Oliveira do Conde
Lagares
Seia
Valhelhas
Palheiros da Tocha
Cantanhede
B. de Aguieira
Santa Comba Dão
Oliveira do Hospital
Candosa
Manteigas
Poco de Inferno
Belmonte
Tocha
Pampilhosa
Tábua
Galizes
Covilhã
Catarruchos
Arazede
Mouronho
Vide
Unhais da Serra
Amieiro
Anca
Penacova
Raiva
Mota
São Martinho da Cortiça
Quiaois
Palheiros de Quiaois
Erveda
Forte de Santa Catarina
C. Mondego
Antazede
Lavaris
Coimbra
Poiares
Arganil
Tortosendo
Buarcos
Figueira da Foz
Maiorca
Arzila
Montemor-o-Velho
Valonga
Alfarelos
Ceira
Semide
Portela
Góis
Barco
Fundão
Silvares
Lavos
Condeixa
Vila Seca
Lousã
Palácio dos Salazares
Barragem Sta. Luzia
Souto
Alpedrinha
Vale de Prazeres
Outeiro
Ruinas de Conimbriga
Miranda do Corvo
Pampilhosa
Marinha das Ondas
Soure
Rego da Leirosa
Louriçal
Orvalho
São Miguel d'Acha
Mattos
Foz do Giraldo
Almaceda
Lardosa
Castanheira de Pêra
Zêzere
Pedrógão
0
10
20
30 km
41°
40°
8°
A
B
1
2
140
154
155
108
65
103
131

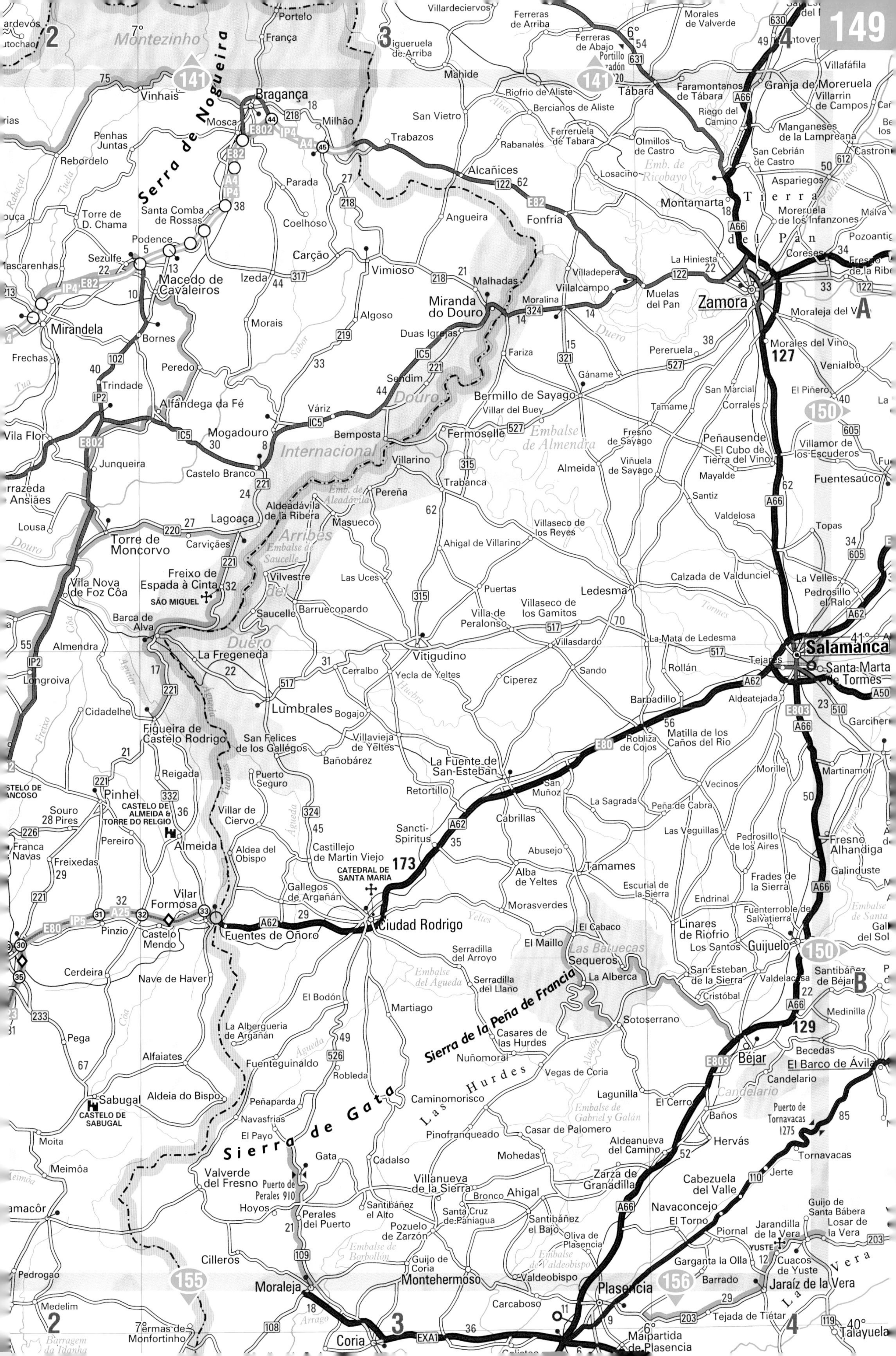

Montezinho
Portelo
França
Vinhais
Serra de Nogueira
Bragança
Mosca
Milhão
Penhas Juntas
Rebordelo
Trabazos
Parada
Torre de D. Chama
Santa Comba de Rossas
Coelhoso
Podence
Sezulfe
Carção
Macedo de Cavaleiros
Izeda
Vimioso
Mirandela
Bornes
Morais
Algoso
Frechas
Peredo
Trindade
Alfândega da Fé
Mogadouro
Váriz
Vila Flor
Junqueira
Castelo Branco
Carrazeda de Ansiães
Lousa
Lagoaça
Torre de Moncorvo
Carviçães
Freixo de Espada à Cinta
São Miguel
Vila Nova de Foz Côa
Barca de Alva
Almendra
Longroiva
Cidadelhe
Figueira de Castelo Rodrigo
Reigada
Pinhel
Castelo de Almeida & Torre do Relgio
Souro Pires
Pereiro
Almeida
Freixedas
Vilar Formosa
Pinzio
Castelo Mendo
Cerdeira
Nave de Haver
Pega
Alfaiates
Sabugal
Castelo de Sabugal
Aldeia do Bispo
Moita
Meimôa
Penamacôr
Pedrogão
Medelim
Termas de Monfortinho
Villardeciervos
Figueruela de Arriba
Mahíde
San Vietro
Alcañices
Angueira
Miranda do Douro
Duas Igrejas
Sendim
Douro Internacional
Bemposta
Villarino
Pereña
Aldeadávila de la Ribera
Masueco
Arribes del Duero
Vilvestre
Las Uces
Saucelle
Barruecopardo
La Fregeneda
Cerralbo
Lumbrales
Bogajo
San Felices de los Gallegos
Villavieja de Yeltes
Bañobárez
Puerto Seguro
Villar de Ciervo
Aldea del Obispo
Castillejo de Martin Viejo
Catedral de Santa Maria
Gallegos de Argañán
Fuentes de Oñoro
Ciudad Rodrigo
Serradilla del Arroyo
Serradilla del Llano
Embalse del Águeda
El Bodón
Martiago
La Alberguería de Argañán
Fuenteguinaldo
Robleda
Peñaparda
Navasfrias
El Payo
Sierra de Gata
Gata
Cadalso
Valverde del Fresno
Puerto de Perales 910
Hoyos
Perales del Puerto
Cilleros
Moraleja
Coria
Ferreras de Arriba
Ferreras de Abajo
Portillo Tazadón
Tábara
Riofrio de Aliste
Bercianos de Aliste
Ferreruela de Tabara
Rabanales
Fonfría
Villadepera
Villalcampo
Moralina
Fariza
Bermillo de Sayago
Villar del Buey
Fermoselle
Embalse de Almendra
Trabanca
Ahigal de Villarino
Puertas
Villa de Peralonso
Vitigudino
Yecla de Yeltes
Ciperez
La Fuente de San-Esteban
Retortillo
Sancti-Spiritus
Cabrillas
Abusejo
Alba de Yeltes
Morasverdes
El Maíllo
Las Batuecas
Sequeros
La Alberca
Sierra de la Peña de Francia
Casares de las Hurdes
Nuñomoral
Las Hurdes
Caminomorisco
Pinofranqueado
Villanueva de la Sierra
Santibáñez el Alto
Santa Cruz de Paniagua
Pozuelo de Zarzón
Embalse de Borbollón
Guijo de Coria
Montehermoso
Carcaboso
Morales de Valverde
Faramontanos de Tábara
Riego del Camino
Olmillos de Castro
Losacino
Emb. de Ricobayo
Montamarta
Tierra del Pan
La Hiniesta
Muelas del Pan
Zamora
Pereruela
Gáname
Tamame
Fresno de Sayago
Viñuela de Sayago
Almeida
Villaseco de los Reyes
Ledesma
Villaseco de los Gamitos
Villasdardo
Sando
La Mata de Ledesma
Rollán
Barbadillo
Matilla de los Caños del Rio
Robliza de Cojos
San Muñoz
La Sagrada
Peña de Cabra
Vecinos
Las Veguillas
Tamames
Escurial de la Sierra
El Cabaco
Endrinal
Linares de Riofrio
Los Santos
San Esteban de la Sierra
Cristóbal
Sotoserrano
Vegas de Coria
Lagunilla
Embalse de Gabriel y Galán
Casar de Palomero
Mohedas
Aldeanueva del Camino
Zarza de Granadilla
Ahigal
Bronco
Santibáñez el Bajo
Oliva de Plasencia
Embalse de Valdeobispo
Valdeobispo
Plasencia
Malpartida de Plasencia
Granja de Moreruela
Villarrín de Campos
Villafáfila
Manganeses de la Lampreana
San Cebrián de Castro
Aspariegos
Moreruela de los Infanzones
Coreses
Fresno de la Ribera
Moraleja del Vino
Morales del Vino
Venialbo
El Piñero
San Marcial
Corrales
Peñausende
El Cubo de Tierra del Vino
Villamor de los Escuderos
Mayalde
Fuentesaúco
Santiz
Valdelosa
Topas
Calzada de Valdunciel
La Velles
Pedrosillo el Ralo
Salamanca
Tejares
Santa Marta de Tormes
Aldeatejada
Garcihernández
Martinamor
Morille
Pedrosillo de los Aires
Fresno Alhandiga
Galinduste
Frades de la Sierra
Fuenterroble de Salvatierra
Guijuelo
Valdelacasa
Santibáñez de Béjar
Medinilla
Béjar
Becedas
El Barco de Ávila
Candelario
El Cerro
Baños
Hervás
Puerto de Tornavacas 1275
Tornavacas
Jerte
Cabezuela del Valle
Navaconcejo
El Torno
Piornal
Jarandilla de la Vera
Guijo de Santa Bárbara
Losar de la Vera
Yuste
Cuacos de Yuste
Garganta la Olla
Barrado
Jaraíz de la Vera
Tejada de Tiétar
Talayuela
La Vera

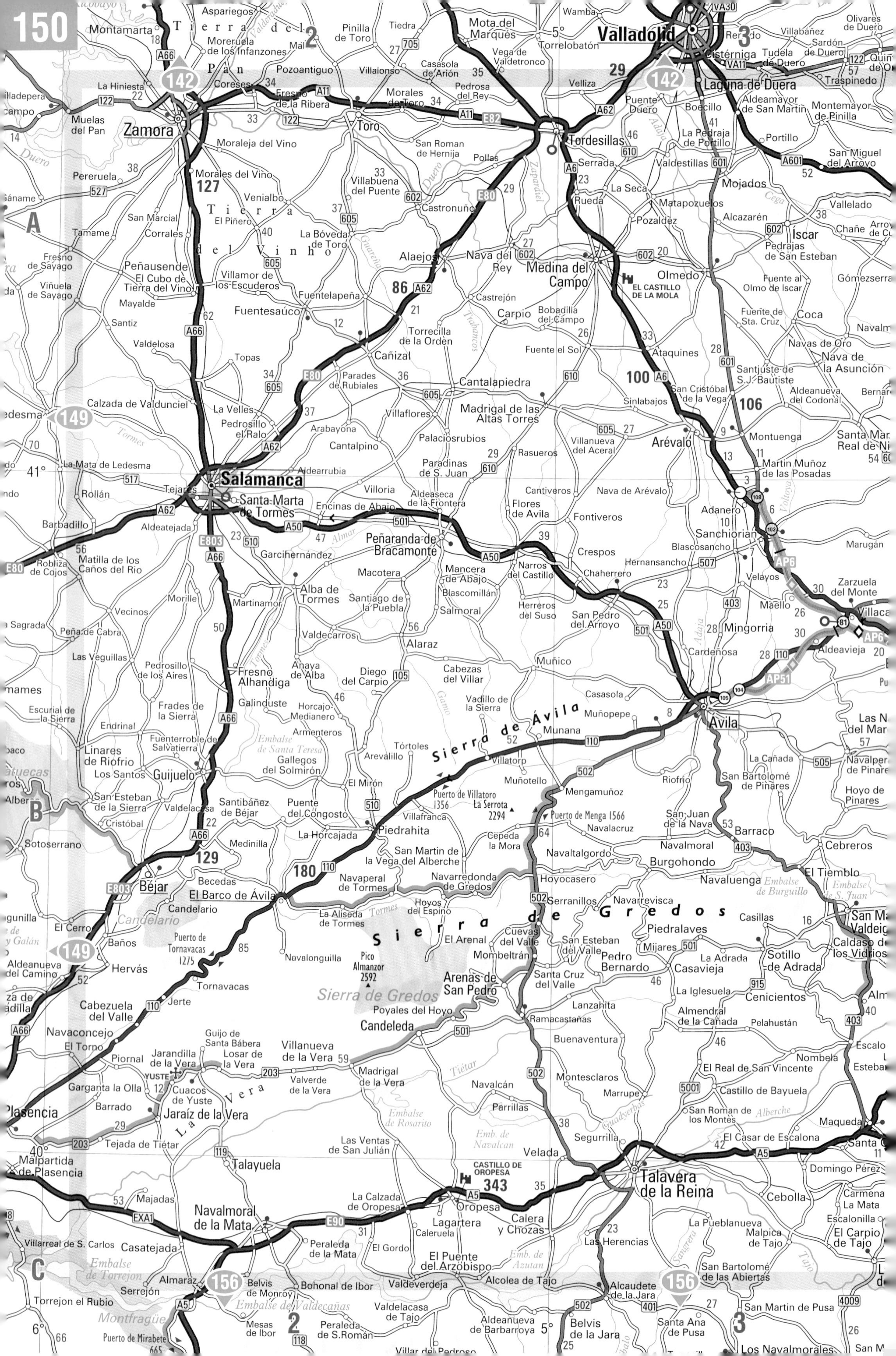

Montamarta
Aspariegos
Tierra del Pan
Moreruela de los Infanzones
Pinilla de Toro
Tiedra
Mota del Marqués
Wamba
Valladolid
Olivares de Duero
Villabáñez
Sardón de Duero
Tudela de Duero
Cistérniga
Renedo
Vega de Valdetronco
Torrelobatón
Casasola de Arión
Villalonso
Pozoantiguo
La Hiniesta
Coreses
Fresno de la Ribera
Morales de Toro
Pedrosa del Rey
Velliza
Laguna de Duera
Traspinedo
Zamora
Muelas del Pan
Toro
Tordesillas
Puente Duero
Boecillo
Aldeamayor de San Martín
Montemayor de Pinilla
Moraleja del Vino
San Roman de Hernija
Pollas
La Pedraja de Portillo
Portillo
San Miguel del Arroyo
Pereruela
Morales del Vino
Villabuena del Puente
Serrada
Valdestillas
Mojados
Tierra del Vinho
Venialbo
Castronuño
La Seca
Rueda
Matapozuelos
Vallelado
San Marcial
El Piñero
Corrales
Pozaldez
Alcazarén
Íscar
Chañe
Tamame
La Bóveda de Toro
Alaejos
Nava del Rey
Medina del Campo
Pedrajas de San Esteban
Fresno de Sayago
Peñausende
El Cubo de Tierra del Vino
Olmedo
Fuente al Olmo de Iscar
Gómezserracín
Viñuela de Sayago
Villamor de los Escuderos
EL CASTILLO DE LA MOLA
Mayalde
Fuentelapeña
Castrejón
Fuentesaúco
Carpio
Bobadilla del Campo
Fuente de Sta. Cruz
Coca
Santiz
Torrecilla de la Orden
Navas de Oro
Valdelosa
Cañizal
Fuente el Sol
Ataquines
Nava de la Asunción
Topas
Parades de Rubiales
Cantalapiedra
Santiuste de S.J. Bautiste
San Cristóbal de la Vega
Aldeanueva del Codonal
Calzada de Valdunciel
La Velles
Villaflores
Madrigal de las Altas Torres
Sinlabajos
Pedrosillo el Ralo
Arabayona
Cantalpino
Palaciosrubios
Villanueva del Aceral
Arévalo
Montuenga
Santa María Real de Nieva
La Mata de Ledesma
Aldearrubia
Paradinas de S. Juan
Rasueros
Martín Muñoz de las Posadas
Salamanca
Rollán
Tejares
Villoria
Aldeaseca de la Frontera
Cantiveros
Nava de Arévalo
Santa Marta de Tormes
Encinas de Abajo
Flores de Avila
Adanero
Barbadillo
Aldeatejada
Peñaranda de Bracamonte
Fontiveros
Sanchiorian
Marugán
Matilla de los Caños del Rio
Robliza de Cojos
Garcihernández
Crespos
Blascosancho
Macotera
Mancera de Abajo
Narros del Castillo
Chaherrero
Hernansancho
Velayos
Zarzuela del Monte
Alba de Tormes
Santiago de la Puebla
Blascomillán
Herreros del Suso
San Pedro del Arroyo
Maello
Morille
Martinamor
Salmoral
Mingorria
Vecinos
Sagrada
Peña de Cabra
Valdecarros
Alaraz
Cardeñosa
Aldeavieja
Las Veguillas
Pedrosillo de los Aires
Fresno Alhandiga
Anaya de Alba
Diego del Carpio
Cabezas del Villar
Muñico
Galinduste
Frades de la Sierra
Horcajo-Medianero
Vadillo de la Sierra
Casasola
Escurial de la Sierra
Endrinal
Armenteros
Sierra de Ávila
Muñopepe
Ávila
Las Navas del Marqués
Fuenterroble de Salvatierra
Embalse de Santa Teresa
Tórtoles
Munana
Linares de Riofrío
Gallegos del Solmirón
Arevalillo
Villatoro
La Cañada
Navalperal de Pinares
Los Santos
Guijuelo
El Mirón
Muñotello
Riofrío
San Bartolomé de Pinares
Hoyo de Pinares
San Esteban de la Sierra
Santibáñez de Béjar
Puente del Congosto
Puerto de Villatoro 1356
La Serrota 2294
Mengamuñoz
Valdelacasa
Cristóbal
Villafranca
Puerto de Menga 1566
Navalacruz
San Juan de la Nava
Sotoserrano
Medinilla
La Horcajada
Piedrahita
Cepeda la Mora
Barraco
Navalmoral
Cebreros
Navaltalgordo
San Martín de la Vega del Alberche
Burgohondo
Béjar
Becedas
Navaperal de Tormes
Navarredonda de Gredos
Hoyocasero
Navaluenga
Embalse de Burguillo
El Tiemblo
Embalse de S. Juan
El Barco de Ávila
Candelario
Hoyos del Espino
La Aliseda de Tormes
Serranillos
Navarrevisca
Sierra de Gredos
Casillas
San Martín de Valdeiglesias
El Cerro
Puerto de Tornavacas 1275
Cuevas del Valle
El Arenal
San Esteban del Valle
Piedralaves
Mijares
Baños
Navalonguilla
Pico Almanzor 2592
Mombeltrán
Pedro Bernardo
La Adrada
Sotillo de Adrada
Caldaso de los Vidrios
Aldeanueva del Camino
Hervás
Arenas de San Pedro
Santa Cruz del Valle
Casavieja
Tornavacas
La Iglesuela
Cenicientos
Cabezuela del Valle
Jerte
Poyales del Hoyo
Lanzahita
Almendral de la Cañada
Pelahustán
Navaconcejo
Candeleda
Ramacastañas
El Torno
Guijo de Santa Bábera
Villanueva de la Vera
Buenaventura
Escalona
Piornal
Jarandilla de la Vera
Losar de la Vera
Madrigal de la Vera
Nombela
YUSTE
Valverde de la Vera
Navalcán
El Real de San Vincente
Garganta la Olla
Cuacos de Yuste
Montesclaros
Marrupe
Castillo de Bayuela
Barrado
La Vera
Parrillas
Plasencia
Jaraíz de la Vera
Embalse de Rosarito
Segurrilla
San Roman de los Montes
Maqueda
Emb. de Navalcán
Tejada de Tiétar
Las Ventas de San Julián
Velada
El Casar de Escalona
Santa Olalla
Malpartida de Plasencia
Talayuela
CASTILLO DE OROPESA
Talavera de la Reina
Domingo Pérez
Majadas
La Calzada de Oropesa
Oropesa
Calera y Chozas
Cebolla
Carmena
La Mata
Navalmoral de la Mata
Lagartera
Las Herencias
La Pueblanueva
Malpica de Tajo
Escalonilla
El Carpio de Tajo
Villarreal de S. Carlos
Casatejada
Peraleda de la Mata
El Gordo
El Puente del Arzobispo
Emb. de Azutan
San Bartolomé de las Abiertas
Embalse de Torrejón
Almaraz
Belvis de Monroy
Bohonal de Ibor
Valdeverdeja
Alcolea de Tajo
Alcaudete de la Jara
Serrejón
Torrejón el Rubio
Embalse de Valdecañas
Valdelacasa de Tajo
San Martín de Pusa
Montfragüe
Mesas de Ibor
Peraleda de San Román
Aldeanueva de Barbarroya
Belvis de la Jara
Santa Ana de Pusa
Puerto de Mirabete
Villar del Pedroso
Los Navalmorales
Duero
Tormes
Adaja
Cega
Voltoya
Zapardiel
Trabancos
Guareña
Almar
Gamo
Tiétar
Alberche
Tajo
Sangrera
Guadyerbas
A
B
C
2
3
41°
40°
6°
5°
142
149
156
A66
A11
E82
A62
A6
A601
E80
A50
E803
AP6
AP51
A5
E90
EXA1

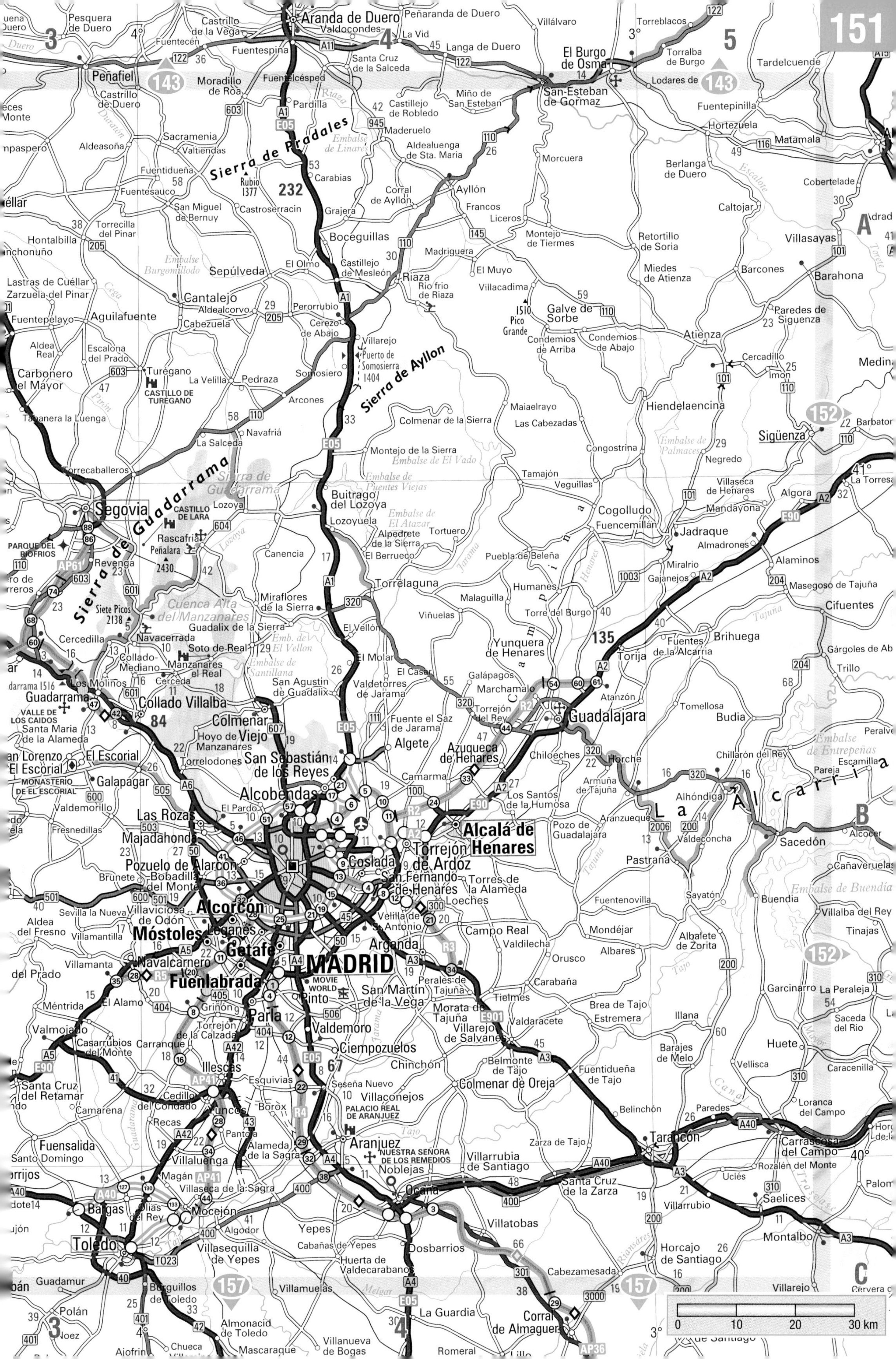

Pesquera de Duero
Castrillo de la Vega
Aranda de Duero
Peñaranda de Duero
Villálvaro
Torreblacos
Valdocondes
La Vid
Fuentecén
Fuentespina
Langa de Duero
El Burgo de Osma
Torralba de Burgo
Tardelcuende
Peñafiel
143
Moradillo de Roa
Fuentelcésped
Santa Cruz de la Salceda
Miño de San Esteban
San Esteban de Gormaz
Lodares de
Castrillo de Duero
Pardilla
Castillejo de Robledo
Fuentepinilla
Maderuelo
Hortezuela
Sierra de Pradales
Embalse de Linares
Aldealuenga de Sta. Maria
Matamala
Aldeasoña
Sacramenia
Valtiendas
Morcuera
Berlanga de Duero
Fuentidueña
Rubio 1377
Carabias
Cobertelade
Fuentesauco
232
Corral de Ayllón
Ayllón
San Miguel de Bernuy
Castroserracin
Grajera
Francos
Caltojar
Torrecilla del Pinar
Liceros
Hontalbilla
Boceguillas
Montejo de Tiermes
Retortillo de Soria
Villasayas
Madriguera
Embalse Burgomillodo
Sepúlveda
El Olmo
Castillejo de Mesleón
El Muyo
Miedes de Atienza
Barcones
Lastras de Cuéllar
Riaza
Barahona
Zarzuela del Pinar
Rio frio de Riaza
Villacadima
Cantalejo
Galve de Sorbe
Aldealcorvo
Perorrubio
Pico Grande 1510
Paredes de Siguenza
Fuentepelayo
Aguilafuente
Cabezuela
Cerezo de Abajo
Condemios de Arriba
Condemios de Abajo
Atienza
Aldea Real
Escalona del Prado
Villarejo
Puerto de Somosierra 1404
Cercadillo
Imon
Medina
Carbonero el Mayor
Turégano
La Velilla
Pedraza
Somosierra
Castillo de Turegano
Sierra de Ayllon
Arcones
Hiendelaencina
Tabanera la Luenga
Maiaelrayo
Colmenar de la Sierra
Las Cabezadas
Sigüenza
Barbatona
Navafriá
La Salceda
Montejo de la Sierra
Embalse de El Vado
Congostrina
Embalse de Palmaces
Negredo
Torrecaballeros
Sierra de Guadarrama
Embalse de Puentes Viejas
Tamajón
Veguillas
Villaseca de Henares
Algora
La Torresa
Segovia
Castillo de Lara
Lozoya
Buitrago del Lozoya
Cogolludo
Mandayona
Lozoyuela
Embalse de El Atazar
Fuencemillán
Jadraque
Rascafría
Alpedrete de la Sierra
Tortuero
Almadrones
Parque del Biofrios
Peñalara 2430
Canencia
El Berrueco
Puebla de Beleña
Miralrio
Alaminos
Revenga
Gajanejos
Masegoso de Tajuña
Torrelaguna
Humanes
Cifuentes
Cuenca Alta del Manzanares
Miraflores de la Sierra
Malaguilla
Siete Picos 2138
Viñuelas
Torre del Burgo
Navacerrada
Guadalix de la Sierra
El Vellón
Brihuega
Cercedilla
Emb. de El Vellon
Soto de Real
Fuentes de la Alcarria
Gárgoles de Abajo
Collado-Mediano
Manzanares el Real
El Molar
Yunquera de Henares
Torija
Embalse de Santillana
El Casar
Trillo
Los Molinos
Cerceda
San Agustin de Guadalix
Valdetorres de Jarama
Galápagos
Marchamalo
Atanzón
Guadarrama
Collado Villalba
Torrejón del Rey
Guadalajara
Tomellosa
Budia
Valle de los Caidos
Colmenar Viejo
Fuente el Saz de Jarama
Santa Maria de la Alameda
Hoyo de Manzanares
Algete
Azuqueca de Henares
Chiloeches
Horche
Chillarón del Rey
Embalse de Entrepeñas
San Lorenzo El Escorial
El Escorial
Torrelodones
San Sebastián de los Reyes
Escamilla
Pareja
Monasterio de El Escorial
Galapagar
Camarma
Armuña de Tajuña
Alcobendas
Los Santos de la Humosa
Alhóndiga
La Alcarria
Valdemorillo
El Pardo
Las Rozas
Alcalá de Henares
Pozo de Guadalajara
Aranzueque
Sacedón
Alcocer
Fresnedillas
Majadahonda
Torrejón de Ardoz
Valdeconcha
Pozuelo de Alarcón
Coslada
Pastrana
Cañaveruelas
Brunete
Bobadilla del Monte
San Fernando de Henares
Torres de la Alameda
Embalse de Buendía
Sevilla la Nueva
Villaviciosa de Odón
Alcorcón
Loeches
Fuentenovilla
Sayatón
Buendia
Villalba del Rey
Aldea del Fresno
Villamantilla
Móstoles
Leganés
Velilla de S. Antonio
Campo Real
Mondéjar
Albalete de Zorita
Tinajas
Valdilecha
Getafe
Arganda
Orusco
Albares
Navalcarnero
MADRID
Villamanta
Fuenlabrada
Movie World
Perales de Tajuña
Carabaña
del Prado
San Martín de la Vega
Garcinarro
La Peraleja
El Alamo
Pinto
Tielmes
Méntrida
Griñón
Morata de Tajuña
Brea de Tajo
Parla
Valdaracete
Estremera
Illana
Saceda del Rio
Valmojado
Torrejón de la Calzada
Valdemoro
Villarejo de Salvanés
Huete
Casarrubios del Monte
Carranque
Ciempozuelos
Barajes de Melo
Illescas
Chinchón
Belmonte de Tajo
Fuentidueña de Tajo
Vellisca
Caracenilla
Santa Cruz del Retamar
Esquivias
Colmenar de Oreja
Seseña Nuevo
Cedillo del Condado
Villaconejos
Belinchón
Lorenca del Campo
Camarena
Borox
Palacio Real de Aranjuez
Yuncos
Paredes
Recas
Pantoja
Tarancón
Carrascosa del Campo
Fuensalida
Alameda de la Sagra
Aranjuez
Zarza de Tajo
Santo Domingo
Villaluenga
Nuestra Señora de los Remedios
Villarrubia de Santiago
Rozalén del Monte
Magán
Noblejas
Uclés
Villaseca de la Sagra
Ocaña
Santa Cruz de la Zarza
Saelices
Bargas
Olias del Rey
Mocejón
Villarrubio
Algodor
Villatobas
Toledo
Yepes
Montalbo
Villasequilla de Yepes
Cabañas de Yepes
Dosbarrios
Horcajo de Santiago
Huerta de Valdecarabanos
Cabezamesada
Guadamur
Burguillos de Toledo
Villamuelas
Villarejo
Cervera
Polán
La Guardia
Corral de Almaguer
Almonacid de Toledo
Chueca
Villanueva de Bogas
Ajofrín
Mascaraque
Romeral
157
152
0
10
20
30 km

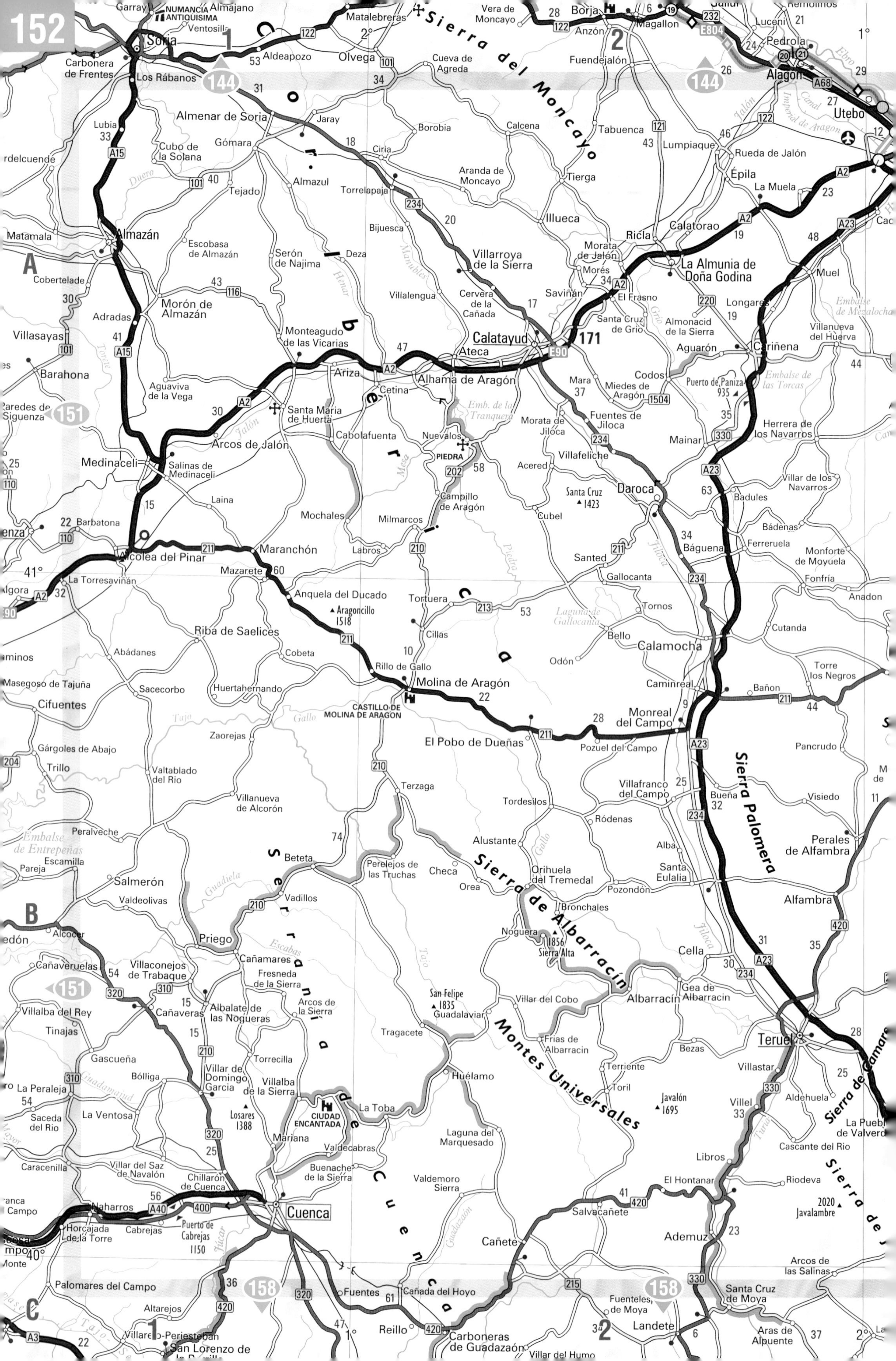
Garray
NUMANCIA ANTIQUISIMA
Almajano
Ventosilla
Soria
Carbonera de Frentes
Los Rábanos
Aldeapozo
Olvega
Matalebreras
Sierra del Moncayo
Vera de Moncayo
Borja
Anzón
Magallon
Fuendejalón
Luceni
Pedrola
Alagón
Utebo
Ebro
Remolinos
Cueva de Agreda
Almenar de Soria
Jaray
Borobia
Calcena
Tabuenca
Lumpiaque
Rueda de Jalón
Épila
La Muela
Lubia
Cubo de la Solana
Gómara
Ciria
Aranda de Moncayo
Tierga
Almazul
Torrelapaja
Tejado
rdelcuende
Duero
Bijuesca
Illueca
Ricla
Calatorao
Matamala
Almazán
Escobasa de Almazán
Serón de Najima
Deza
Villarroya de la Sierra
Morata de Jalón
Morés
La Almunia de Doña Godina
Muel
Cobertelade
Villalengua
Cervera de la Cañada
Savinán
El Frasno
Almonacid de la Sierra
Longares
Embalse de Mezalocha
Adradas
Morón de Almazán
Monteagudo de las Vicarias
Calatayud
Ateca
Santa Cruz de Grío
Aguarón
Cariñena
Villanueva del Huerva
Villasayas
Barahona
Ariza
Cetina
Alhama de Aragón
Mara
Miedes de Aragón
Codos
Puerto de Paniza 935
Embalse de las Torcas
Aguaviva de la Vega
Emb. de la Tranquera
Morata de Jiloca
Fuentes de Jiloca
Herrera de los Navarros
Paredes de Siguenza
Santa María de Huerta
Arcos de Jalón
Jalón
Cabolafuenta
Nuevalos
PIEDRA
Mainar
Medinaceli
Salinas de Medinaceli
Acered
Villafeliche
Daroca
Villar de los Navarros
Campillo de Aragón
Santa Cruz 1423
Badules
Laina
Mochales
Milmarcos
Cubel
Bádenas
Barbatona
Báguena
Ferreruela
Alcolea del Pinar
Maranchón
Labros
Santed
Monforte de Moyuela
Mazarete
Gallocanta
Fonfría
La Torresavinán
Anquela del Ducado
Aragoncillo 1518
Tortuera
Tornos
Anadon
Riba de Saelices
Cillas
Laguna de Gallocanta
Bello
Cutanda
Abádanes
Cobeta
Calamocha
Odón
Torre los Negros
Masegoso de Tajuña
Sacecorbo
Huertahernando
Rillo de Gallo
Molina de Aragón
Caminreal
Bañon
Cifuentes
CASTILLO DE MOLINA DE ARAGON
Monreal del Campo
Tajo
Gallo
Zaorejas
El Pobo de Dueñas
Pozuel del Campo
Sierra Palomera
Gárgoles de Abajo
Pancrudo
Trillo
Valtablado del Rio
Terzaga
Villafranco del Campo
Tordesilos
Buena
Visiedo
Villanueva de Alcorón
Ródenas
Embalse de Entrepeñas
Peralveche
Alustante
Perales de Alfambra
Escamilla
Alba
Pareja
Beteta
Perelejos de las Truchas
Checa
Sierra de Albarracín
Orihuela del Tremedal
Santa Eulalia
Salmerón
Orea
Pozondón
Alfambra
Valdeolivas
Vadillos
Serranía de Cuenca
Bronchales
Alcocer
Priego
Noguera
1856 Sierra Alta
Cella
Escabas
Cañaveruelas
Villaconejos de Trabaque
Cañamares
Fresneda de la Sierra
Gea de Albarracín
Albarracín
San Felipe 1835
Guadalaviar
Villar del Cobo
Villalba del Rey
Cañaveras
Albalate de las Nogueras
Arcos de la Sierra
Tinajas
Tragacete
Montes Universales
Frias de Albarracin
Teruel
Gascueña
Torrecilla
Bezas
Terriente
Villastar
Bólliga
Villar de Domingo Garcia
Villalba de la Sierra
Huélamo
Toril
Javalón 1695
Aldehuela
La Peraleja
Losares 1388
CIUDAD ENCANTADA
La Toba
Villel
Sierra de Camarena
Saceda del Rio
La Ventosa
Mariana
Laguna del Marquesado
Cascante del Rio
La Puebla de Valverde
Valdecabras
Caracenilla
Villar del Saz de Navalón
Chillarón de Cuenca
Buenache de la Sierra
Valdemoro Sierra
Libros
Riodeva
El Hontanar
Naharros
Cuenca
Salvacañete
2020 Javalambre
Horcajada de la Torre
Cabrejas
Puerto de Cabrejas 1150
Júcar
Cañete
Ademuz
Sierra de Javalambre
Palomares del Campo
Fuentes
Cañada del Hoyo
Fuenteles de Moya
Santa Cruz de Moya
Arcos de las Salinas
Altarejos
Reillo
Carboneras de Guadazaón
Landete
Villarejo-Periesteban
San Lorenzo de la Parrilla
Villar del Humo
Aras de Alpuente
A2
A15
A23
A40
A3
A68
E90
E804
101
110
116
122
121
144
151
158
171
202
204
210
211
213
215
220
232
234
310
320
330
400
420
1504
A
B
C
1
2
1°
2°
40°
41°

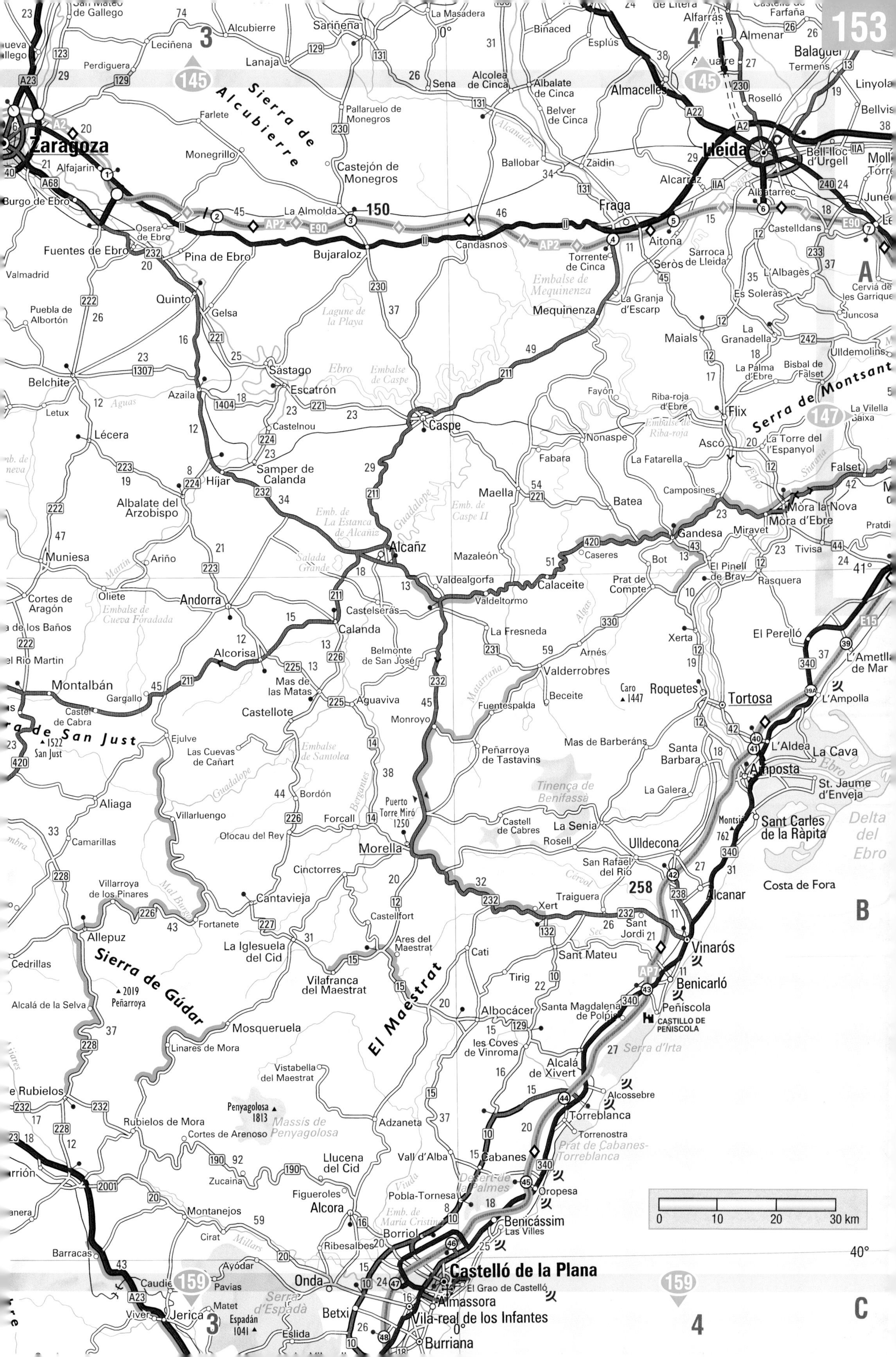

Zaragoza
Alfajarín
Burgo de Ebro
Fuentes de Ebro
Osera de Ebro
Pina de Ebro
Valmadrid
Puebla de Albortón
Quinto
Gelsa
Belchite
Letux
Lécera
Azaila
Sástago
Escatrón
Castelnou
Samper de Calanda
Híjar
Albalate del Arzobispo
Muniesa
Ariño
Andorra
Oliete
Cortes de Aragón
Embalse de Cueva Foradada
Alcorisa
Montalbán
Gargallo
Castel de Cabra
Ejulve
San Just
Sierra de San Just
Las Cuevas de Cañart
Aliaga
Villarluengo
Camarillas
Villarroya de los Pinares
Allepuz
Cedrillas
Alcalá de la Selva
Peñarroya
Sierra de Gúdar
Linares de Mora
Rubielos de Mora
Cortes de Arenoso
Mosqueruela
Vistabella del Maestrat
Penyagolosa
Massís de Penyagolosa
Zucaina
Montanejos
Cirat
Barracas
Caudiel
Pavias
Jerica
Viver
Matet
Espadán
Serra d'Espadà
Ayódar
Onda
Betxi
Eslida
Alcora
Figueroles
Ribesalbes
Llucena del Cid
Adzaneta
Vall d'Alba
Pobla-Tornesa
Borriol
Castelló de la Plana
El Grao de Castelló
Almassora
Vila-real de los Infantes
Burriana
Benicàssim
Las Villes
Oropesa
Cabanes
Desert de les Palmes
Emb. de María Cristina
Torreblanca
Torrenostra
Prat de Cabanes-Torreblanca
Alcossebre
Alcalà de Xivert
les Coves de Vinromà
Albocàsser
Santa Magdalena de Polpís
Peñíscola
CASTILLO DE PEÑISCOLA
Serra d'Irta
Benicarló
Vinarós
Sant Jordi
Sant Mateu
Tirig
Catí
Xert
Traiguera
San Rafael del Río
Ulldecona
Alcanar
Costa de Fora
Sant Carles de la Ràpita
Montsià
Delta del Ebro
St. Jaume d'Enveja
Amposta
La Cava
L'Aldea
L'Ampolla
L'Ametlla de Mar
El Perelló
Tortosa
Roquetes
Xerta
Caro
Santa Barbara
La Galera
Mas de Barberáns
La Senia
Rosell
Castell de Cabres
Tinença de Benifassà
Peñarroya de Tastavins
Fuentespalda
Beceite
Valderrobres
Arnés
La Fresneda
Valdeltormo
Calaceite
Valdealgorfa
Castelserás
Caseres
Prat de Compte
Bot
El Pinell de Bray
Rasquera
Gandesa
Batea
Miravet
Tivisa
Mora d'Ebre
Mora la Nova
Falset
Pratdip
Camposines
La Fatarella
Ascó
La Torre del l'Espanyol
Flix
Riba-roja d'Ebre
Embalse de Riba-roja
Nonaspe
Fabara
Maella
Emb. de Caspe II
Mazaleón
Fayón
Caspe
Embalse de Caspe
Alcañiz
Emb. de La Estanca de Alcañiz
Salada Grande
Calanda
Belmonte de San José
Mas de las Matas
Aguaviva
Castellote
Embalse de Santolea
Monroyo
Bordón
Forcall
Puerto Torre Miró
Morella
Cinctorres
Cantavieja
Fortanete
La Iglesuela del Cid
Castellfort
Ares del Maestrat
Vilafranca del Maestrat
El Maestrat
Sierra de Alcubierre
Alcubierre
Leciñena
Perdiguera
Farlete
Monegrillo
Lanaja
Sariñena
Castejón de Monegros
Pallaruelo de Monegros
La Almolda
Bujaraloz
Candasnos
Sena
Alcolea de Cinca
La Masadera
Binaced
Albalate de Cinca
Belver de Cinca
Ballobar
Zaidín
Esplús
Almacelles
Fraga
Torrente de Cinca
Embalse de Mequinenza
Mequinenza
La Granja d'Escarp
Lagune de la Playa
Aitona
Seròs
Sarroca de Lleida
Alcarràz
Lleida
Alfarràs
Almenar
Alguaire
Roselló
Balaguer
Termens
Linyola
Bellvís
Bell-lloc d'Urgell
Mollerussa
Albatàrrec
Castelldans
L'Albagès
Cervià de les Garrigues
Juncosa
Es Solerás
Maials
La Granadella
La Palma d'Ebre
Bisbal de Falset
Ulldemolins
Serra de Montsant
La Vilella Baixa
Ebro
Martín
Guadalope
Matarraña
Algas
Cérvol
Millars
Mal Burgo
Bergantes
San Mateo de Gallego
0°
40°
41°
0 10 20 30 km

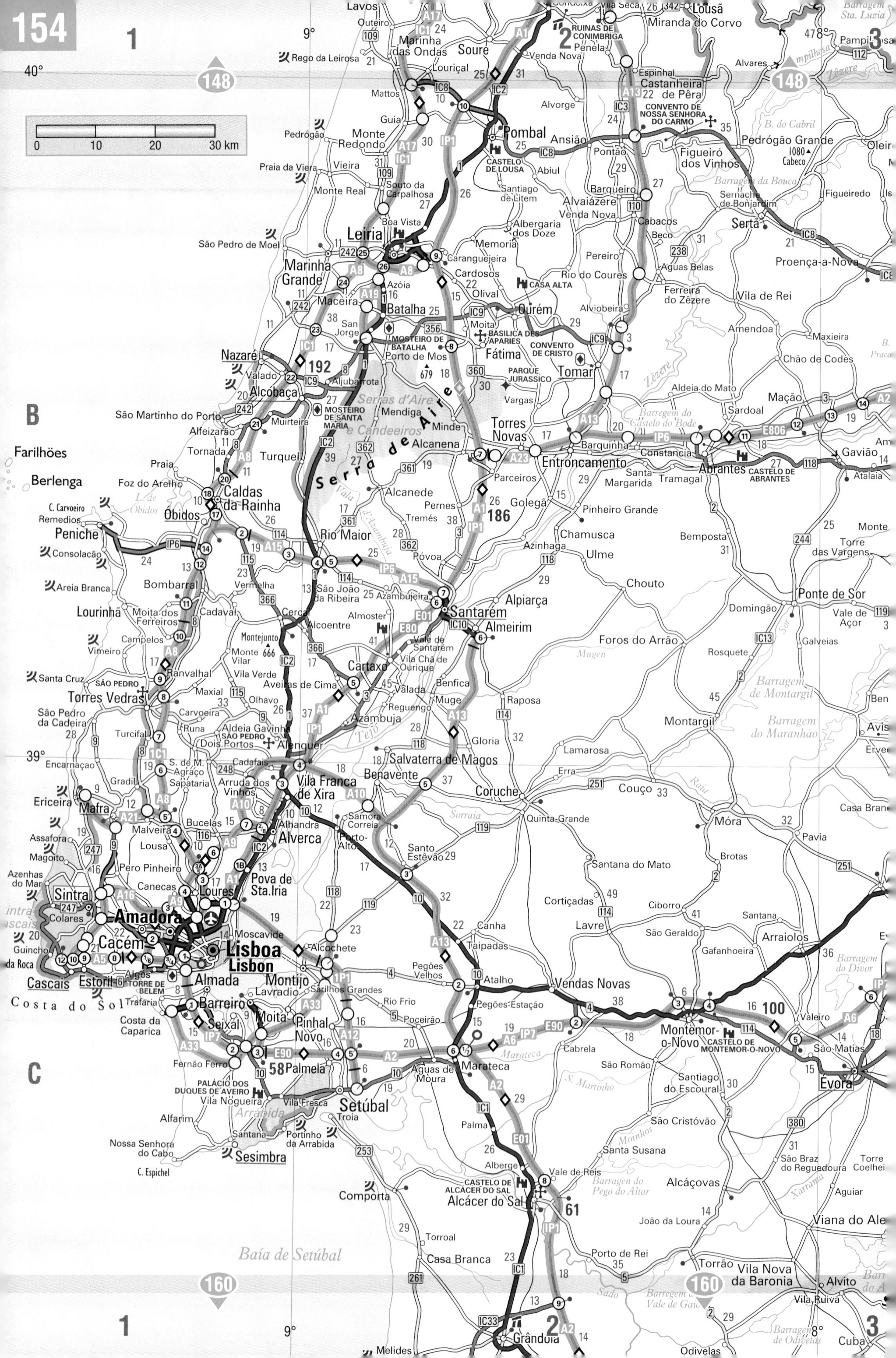

154
1
2
3
B
C
40°
39°
9°
8°
148
160
0
10
20
30 km
Lisboa
Lisbon
Amadora
Cacém
Sintra
Colares
Cascais
Estoril
Costa do Sol
Almada
Barreiro
Seixal
Moita
Montijo
Alcochete
Pinhal Novo
Palmela
Setúbal
Sesimbra
Troia
Vila Fresca
Vila Nogueira
Arrabida
Portinho da Arrabida
Nossa Senhora do Cabo
C. Espichel
Costa da Caparica
Trafaria
Fernão Ferro
PALÁCIO DOS DUQUES DE AVEIRO
TORRE DE BELEM
Algés
Guincho
Cabo da Roca
Loures
Pova de Sta.Iria
Moscavide
Alverca
Alhandra
Vila Franca de Xira
Mafra
Ericeira
Malveira
Bucelas
Lousa
Pero Pinheiro
Canecas
Torres Vedras
SÃO PEDRO
Alenquer
Azambuja
Cartaxo
Santarém
Almeirim
Alpiarça
Benavente
Samora Correia
Salvaterra de Magos
Coruche
Porto Alto
Santo Estêvão
Pegões Velhos
Pegões Estação
Canha
Taipadas
Atalho
Vendas Novas
Marateca
Águas de Moura
Alcácer do Sal
CASTELO DE ALCÁCER DO SAL
Comporta
Palma
Alberge
Torroal
Casa Branca
Baía de Setúbal
Grândola
Melides
Montemor-o-Novo
CASTELO DE MONTEMOR-O-NOVO
Évora
Arraiolos
Mora
Pavia
Montargil
Ponte de Sor
Abrantes
CASTELO DE ABRANTES
Constancia
Entroncamento
Torres Novas
Tomar
CONVENTO DE CRISTO
Fátima
BASILICA DES APARIES
Ourém
Batalha
MOSTEIRO DE BATALHA
Porto de Mos
Leiria
Marinha Grande
Nazaré
Alcobaça
MOSTEIRO DE SANTA MARIA
Caldas da Rainha
Óbidos
Peniche
Berlenga
Farilhões
Lourinhã
Bombarral
Cadaval
Rio Maior
Serra de Aire
Serras d'Aire e Candeeiros
Alcanena
Minde
Golegã
Chamusca
Pombal
CASTELO DE LOUSA
Soure
Penela
RUINAS DE CONIMBRIGA
Miranda do Corvo
Lousã
Ansião
Castanheira de Pêra
Pedrógão Grande
Figueiró dos Vinhos
CONVENTO DE NOSSA SENHORA DO CARMO
Sertã
Proença-a-Nova
Vila de Rei
Sardoal
Mação
Gavião
Alcáçovas
Viana do Alentejo
Alvito
Vila Nova da Baronia
Torrão
Santiago do Escoural
São Cristóvão
Santa Susana
Ciborro
Lavre
Corticadas
Couço
Ulme
Chouto
Foros do Arrão
Galveias
Cabeço
1080
Montejunto
666
PARQUE JURASSICO
CASA ALTA
192
186
100
61
58

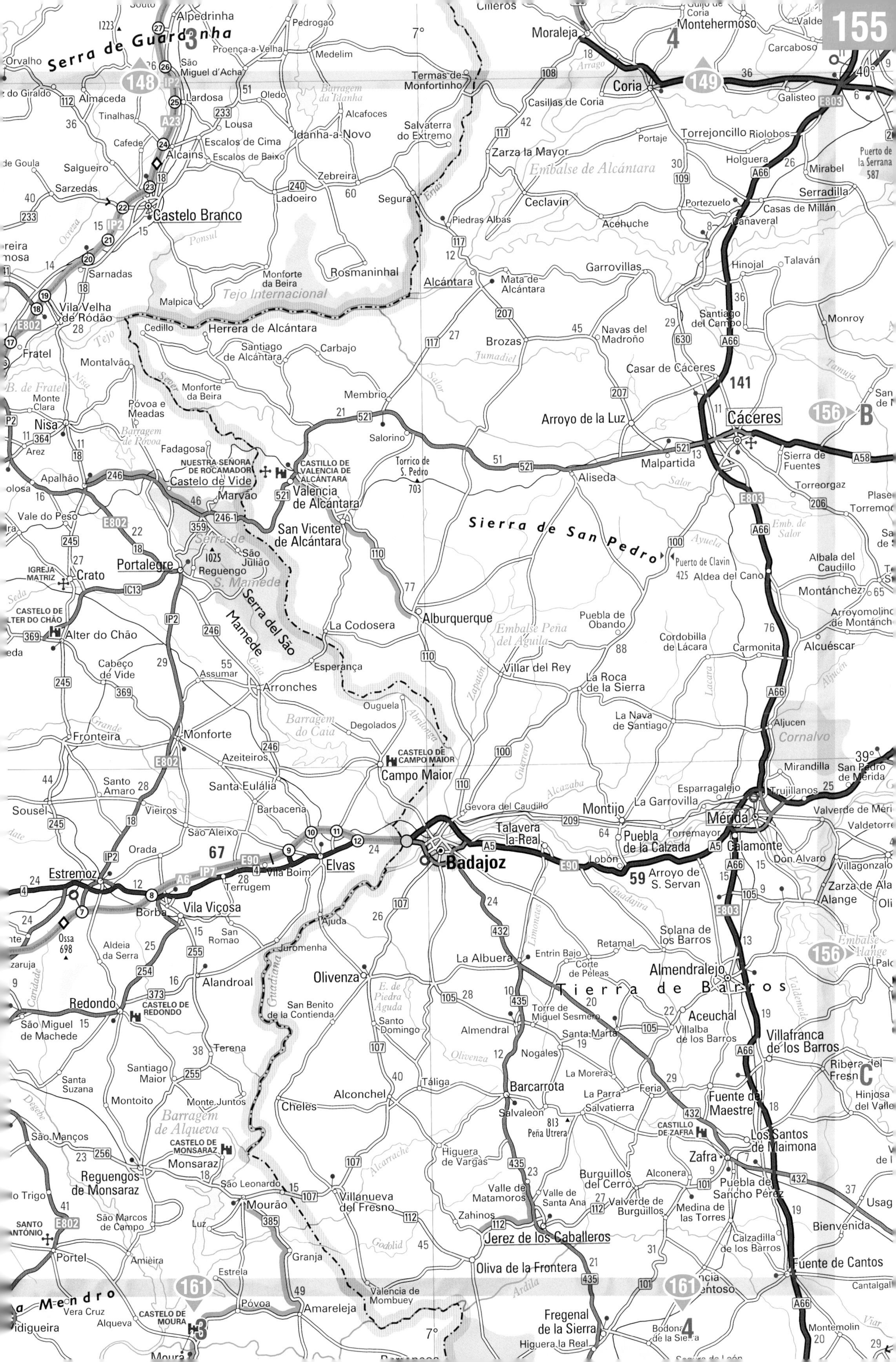

Serra de Guardunha
Alpedrinha
Pedrogão
Proença-a-Velha
São Miguel d'Acha
Orvalho
Medelim
Termas de Monfortinho
Barragem da Idanha
Alcafoces
Oledo
Lardosa
Almaceda
Tinalhas
Lousa
Cafede
Escalos de Cima
Escalos de Baixo
Alcains
Idanha-a-Novo
Salvaterra do Extremo
Salgueiro
Sarzedas
Zebreira
Ladoeiro
Segura
Castelo Branco
Ponsul
Ocreza
Rosmaninhal
Sarnadas
Monforte da Beira
Malpica
Tejo Internacional
Vila Velha de Ródão
Fratel
Cedillo
Herrera de Alcántara
Santiago de Alcántara
Carbajo
Montalvão
Nisa
Monte Clara
B. de Fratel
Póvoa e Meadas
Barragem de Póvoa
Arez
Fadagosa
Apalhão
Nuestra Señora de Rocamador
Castelo de Vide
Marvão
Castillo de Valencia de Alcántara
Valencia de Alcántara
San Vicente de Alcántara
Vale do Peso
Portalegre
Crato
Igreja Matriz
São Julião
Reguengo
Serra de S. Mamede
Serra del São Mamede
Castelo de Alter do Chão
Alter do Chão
Cabeço de Vide
Assumar
Arronches
Esperança
La Codosera
Ouguela
Degolados
Barragem do Caia
Fronteira
Monforte
Azeiteiros
Santo Amaro
Santa Eulália
Castelo de Campo Maior
Campo Maior
Sousel
Vieiros
Barbacena
São Aleixo
Orada
Estremoz
Elvas
Vila Boim
Terrugem
Borba
Vila Viçosa
Ossa 698
Aldeia da Serra
San Romao
Ajuda
Juromenha
Alandroal
Redondo
Castelo de Redondo
São Miguel de Machede
Olivenza
E. de Piedra Aguda
San Benito de la Contienda
Santo Domingo
Terena
Santiago Maior
Santa Suzana
Montoito
Monte Juntos
Barragem de Alqueva
Cheles
Alconchel
Táliga
São Manços
Castelo de Monsaraz
Monsaraz
Reguengos de Monsaraz
São Leonardo
Mourão
Villanueva del Fresno
São Marcos de Campo
Luz
Santo António
Portel
Amieira
Granja
Estrela
Póvoa
Amareleja
Valencia de Mombuey
Vera Cruz
Alqueva
Castelo de Moura
Vidigueira
Moura
Cilleros
Moraleja
Gata de Coria
Montehermoso
Valdelacasa
Carcaboso
Coria
Casillas de Coria
Galisteo
Arrago
Zarza la Mayor
Embalse de Alcántara
Portaje
Torrejoncillo
Riolobos
Holguera
Mirabel
Puerto de la Serrana 587
Ceclavín
Portezuelo
Serradilla
Casas de Millán
Cañaveral
Piedras Albas
Acehuche
Alcántara
Mata de Alcántara
Garrovillas
Hinojal
Talaván
Santiago del Campo
Monroy
Brozas
Navas del Madroño
Jumadiel
Casar de Cáceres
Tamuja
Membrio
Salor
Arroyo de la Luz
Cáceres
Salorino
Torrico de S. Pedro 703
Malpartida
Aliseda
Sierra de Fuentes
Torreorgaz
Sierra de San Pedro
Ayuela
Puerto de Clavin 425
Aldea del Cano
Albala del Caudillo
Montánchez
Arroyomolinos de Montánchez
Alburquerque
Embalse Peña del Águila
Puebla de Obando
Cordobilla de Lácara
Carmonita
Alcuéscar
Villar del Rey
La Roca de la Sierra
Zapatón
Lácara
La Nava de Santiago
Aljucén
Cornalvo
Mirandilla
San Pedro de Mérida
Trujillanos
Guerrero
Alcazaba
Esparragalejo
La Garrovilla
Mérida
Gevora del Caudillo
Montijo
Talavera la Real
Puebla de la Calzada
Torremayor
Calamonte
Valverde de Mérida
Valdetorres
Badajoz
Lobón
Arroyo de S. Servan
Don Álvaro
Villagonzalo
Zarza de Alange
Alange
Guadajira
Solana de los Barros
Retamal
La Albuera
Entrín Bajo
Corte de Peleas
Limonetes
Almendralejo
Tierra de Barros
Torre de Miguel Sesmero
Aceuchal
Villalba de los Barros
Almendral
Santa Marta
Villafranca de los Barros
Nogales
Olivenza
La Morera
Barcarrota
La Parra
Feria
Fuente del Maestre
Ribera del Fresno
Hinojosa del Valle
Salvaleón
813 Peña Utrera
Salvatierra
Castillo de Zafra
Los Santos de Maimona
Zafra
Higuera de Vargas
Burguillos del Cerro
Alconera
Puebla de Sancho Pérez
Valle de Matamoros
Valle de Santa Ana
Valverde de Burguillos
Medina de las Torres
Zahinos
Jerez de los Caballeros
Calzadilla de los Barros
Bienvenida
Oliva de la Frontera
Fuente de Cantos
Fregenal de la Sierra
Bodonal de la Sierra
Higuera la Real
Montemolín
Cantalgallo
Ardila
Godolid
Alcarrache
Viar
Mendro

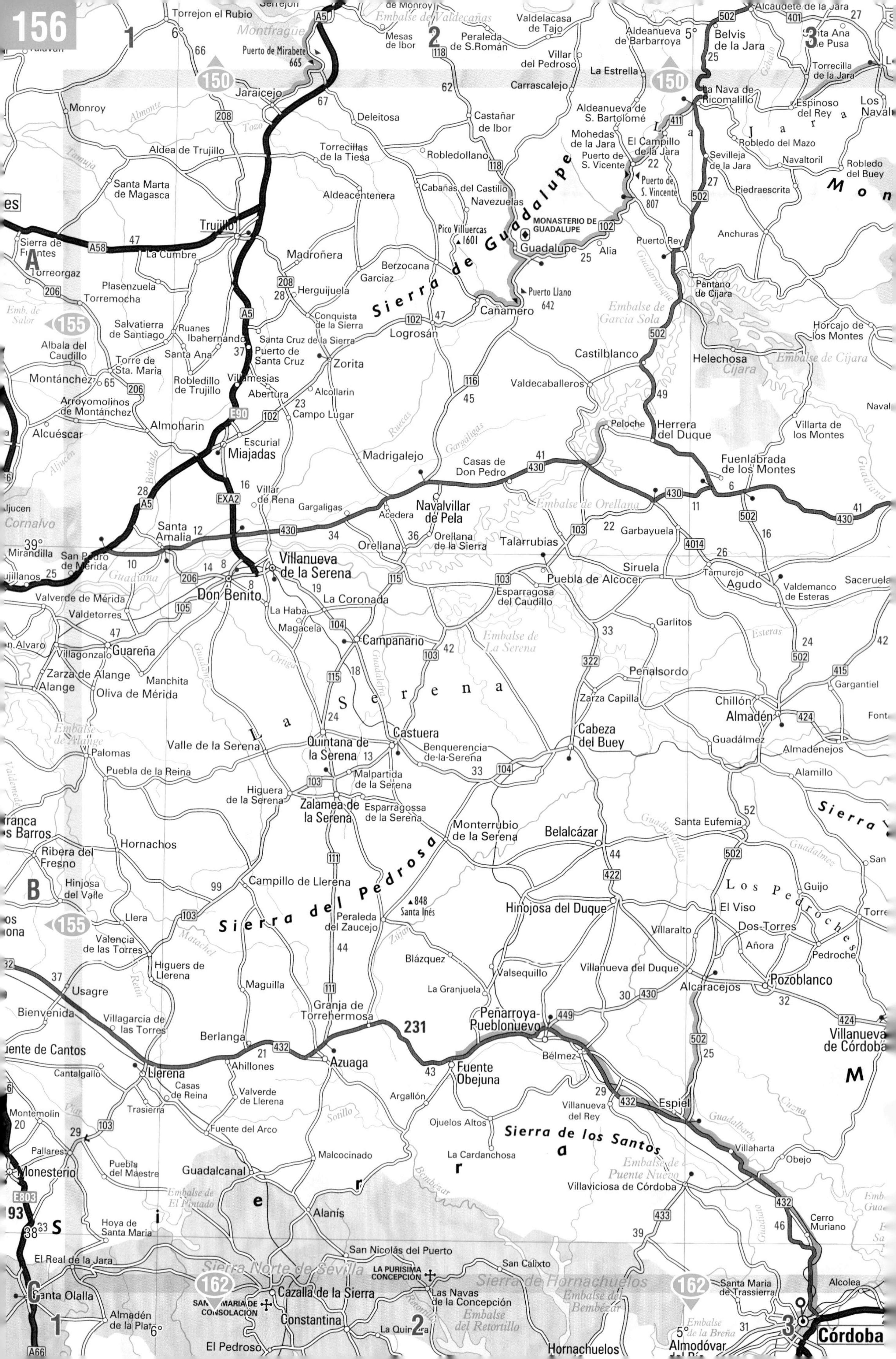

Torrejon el Rubio
Montfragüe
Puerto de Mirabete 665
Embalse de Valdecañas
Mesas de Ibor
Peraleda de S.Román
Valdelacasa de Tajo
Aldeanueva de Barbarroya
Belvis de la Jara
Alcaudete de la Jara
Santa Ana de Pusa
Villar del Pedroso
La Estrella
Torrecilla de la Jara
Jaraicejo
Carrascalejo
La Nava de Ricomalillo
Espinoso del Rey
Los Navalmorales
Monroy
Deleitosa
Castañar de Ibor
Aldeanueva de S. Bartolomé
La Jara
Robledo del Mazo
Aldea de Trujillo
Torrecillas de la Tiesa
Robledollano
Mohedas de la Jara
El Campillo de la Jara
Puerto de S. Vicente
Sevilleja de la Jara
Navaltoril
Robledo del Buey
Santa Marta de Magasca
Aldeacentenera
Cabañas del Castillo
Navezuelas
Puerto de S. Vincente 807
Piedraescrita
Montes
Trujillo
Sierra de Fuentes
Pico Villuercas 1601
MONASTERIO DE GUADALUPE
Guadalupe
Alía
Puerto Rey
Anchuras
La Cumbre
Madroñera
Sierra de Guadalupe
Torreorgaz
Plasenzuela
Berzocana
Garciaz
Herguijuela
Pantano de Cíjara
Torremocha
Puerto Llano 642
Cañamero
Embalse de García Sola
Emb. de Salor
Salvatierra de Santiago
Ruanes
Ibahernando
Conquista de la Sierra
Logrosán
Horcajo de los Montes
Albala del Caudillo
Santa Cruz de la Sierra
Puerto de Santa Cruz
Zorita
Castilblanco
Helechosa
Embalse de Cíjara
Torre de Sta. María
Santa Ana
Montánchez
Robledillo de Trujillo
Villamesías
Valdecaballeros
Abertura
Alcollarín
Arroyomolinos de Montánchez
Campo Lugar
Peloche
Herrera del Duque
Villarta de los Montes
Almoharín
Alcuéscar
Escurial
Miajadas
Madrigalejo
Casas de Don Pedro
Fuenlabrada de los Montes
Villar de Rena
Gargáligas
Navalvillar de Pela
Embalse de Orellana
Aljucén
Cornalvo
Santa Amalia
Acedera
Orellana
Orellana de la Sierra
Talarrubias
Garbayuela
Mirandilla
San Pedro de Mérida
Villanueva de la Serena
Siruela
Tamurejo
Agudo
Valdemanco de Esteras
Saceruela
Guadiana
Don Benito
La Coronada
Esparragosa del Caudillo
Puebla de Alcocer
Valverde de Mérida
Valdetorres
La Haba
Magacela
Garlitos
Embalse de La Serena
Campanario
Guareña
Villagonzalo
Zarza de Alange
Alange
Manchita
Oliva de Mérida
Peñalsordo
Zarza Capilla
Chillón
Almadén
Gargantiel
La Serena
Castuera
Cabeza del Buey
Embalse de Alange
Palomas
Valle de la Serena
Quintana de la Serena
Benquerencia de la Serena
Guadálmez
Almadenejos
Puebla de la Reina
Malpartida de la Serena
Alamillo
Higuera de la Serena
Zalamea de la Serena
Esparragossa de la Serena
Monterrubio de la Serena
Belalcázar
Santa Eufemia
Sierra Madrona
Hornachos
Ribera del Fresno
Hinjosa del Valle
Campillo de Llerena
Sierra del Pedrosa
Los Pedroches
Guijo
848 Santa Inés
Peraleda del Zaucejo
Hinojosa del Duque
El Viso
Llera
Villaralto
Dos-Torres
Añora
Valencia de las Torres
Blázquez
Pedroche
Higuers de Llerena
Valsequillo
Villanueva del Duque
Maguilla
La Granjuela
Alcaracejos
Pozoblanco
Usagre
Bienvenida
Granja de Torrehermosa
Villagarcia de las Torres
Peñarroya-Pueblonuevo
Villanueva de Córdoba
Berlanga
Fuente de Cantos
Ahillones
Azuaga
Bélmez
Cantalgallo
Llerena
Casas de Reina
Fuente Obejuna
Valverde de Llerena
Argallón
Villanueva del Rey
Espiel
Montemolín
Trasierra
Ojuelos Altos
Sierra de los Santos
Fuente del Arco
Villaharta
Obejo
Pallares
Malcocinado
La Cardanchosa
Puebla del Maestre
Guadalcanal
Embalse de Puente Nuevo
Monesterio
Villaviciosa de Córdoba
Embalse de El Pintado
Sierra
Alanís
Hoya de Santa María
Cerro Muriano
El Real de la Jara
San Nicolás del Puerto
Sierra Norte de Sevilla
San Calixto
LA PURÍSIMA CONCEPCIÓN
Sierra de Hornachuelos
Santa Olalla
SANTA MARÍA DE CONSOLACIÓN
Cazalla de la Sierra
Las Navas de la Concepción
Embalse del Bembézar
Santa María de Trassierra
Alcolea
Almadén de la Plata
Constantina
Embalse del Retortillo
Embalse de la Breña
La Quintera
El Pedroso
Hornachuelos
Almodóvar del Río
Córdoba

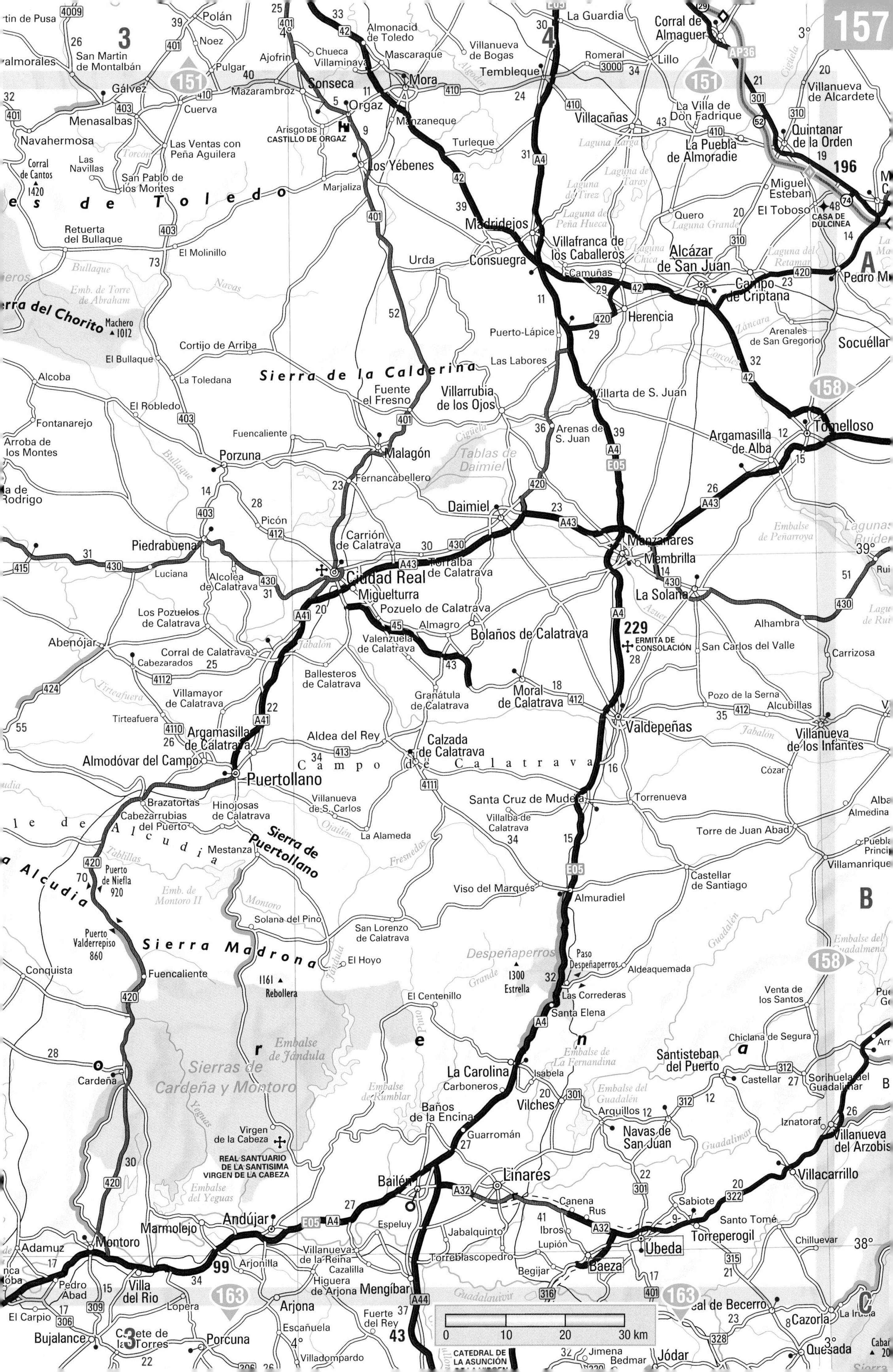
Polán
Almonacid de Toledo
La Guardia
Corral de Almaguer
Noez
Chueca
Villaminaya
Mascaraque
Villanueva de Bogas
Romeral
Lillo
San Martin de Montalbán
Pulgar
Ajofrín
Mora
Tembleque
Villanueva de Alcardete
Gálvez
Mazarambroz
Sonseca
Orgaz
Cuerva
Menasalbas
Manzaneque
Villacañas
La Villa de Don Fadrique
Quintanar de la Orden
Arisgotas
CASTILLO DE ORGAZ
Navahermosa
Las Ventas con Peña Aguilera
Turleque
La Puebla de Almoradie
Los Yébenes
San Pablo de los Montes
Marjaliza
Miguel Esteban
El Toboso
CASA DE DULCINEA
Madridejos
Quero
Villafranca de los Caballeros
Alcázar de San Juan
Retuerta del Bullaque
El Molinillo
Urda
Consuegra
Camuñas
Campo de Criptana
Pedro Muñoz
Herencia
Machero 1012
Puerto-Lápice
Arenales de San Gregorio
Socuéllar
Cortijo de Arriba
El Bullaque
Las Labores
Sierra de la Calderina
Alcoba
La Toledana
Fuente el Fresno
Villarrubia de los Ojos
Villarta de S. Juan
El Robledo
Fontanarejo
Fuencaliente
Arenas de S. Juan
Argamasilla de Alba
Tomelloso
Arroba de los Montes
Porzuna
Malagón
Tablas de Daimiel
Fernancabellero
Daimiel
Picón
Carrión de Calatrava
Manzanares
Piedrabuena
Membrilla
Luciana
Ciudad Real
Torralba de Calatrava
Alcolea de Calatrava
Miguelturra
La Solana
Pozuelo de Calatrava
Los Pozuelos de Calatrava
Almagro
Alhambra
Abenójar
Bolaños de Calatrava
Valenzuela de Calatrava
ERMITA DE CONSOLACIÓN
San Carlos del Valle
Carrizosa
Corral de Calatrava
Cabezarados
Ballesteros de Calatrava
Granátula de Calatrava
Moral de Calatrava
Pozo de la Serna
Alcubillas
Villamayor de Calatrava
Tirteafuera
Valdepeñas
Villanueva de los Infantes
Argamasilla de Calatrava
Aldea del Rey
Calzada de Calatrava
Almodóvar del Campo
Puertollano
Campo de Calatrava
Cózar
Brazatortas
Hinojosas de Calatrava
Villanueva de S. Carlos
Santa Cruz de Mudela
Torrenueva
Cabezarrubias del Puerto
Villalba de Calatrava
Almedina
La Alameda
Torre de Juan Abad
Sierra de Puertollano
Mestanza
Valle de Alcudia
Puerto de Niefla 920
Castellar de Santiago
Villamanrique
Viso del Marqués
Almuradiel
Puerto Valderrepiso 860
Solana del Pino
San Lorenzo de Calatrava
Sierra Madrona
Conquista
El Hoyo
Despeñaperros
Paso Despeñaperros
Aldeaquemada
Fuencaliente
1161 Rebollera
1300 Estrella
Las Correderas
El Centenillo
Venta de los Santos
Santa Elena
Embalse de Jándula
Chiclana de Segura
Cardeña
Sierras de Cardeña y Montoro
La Carolina
Santisteban del Puerto
Isabela
Carboneros
Castellar
Sorihuela del Guadalimar
Vilches
Baños de la Encina
Arquillos
Navas de San Juan
Iznatoraf
Villanueva del Arzobispo
Virgen de la Cabeza
REAL SANTUARIO DE LA SANTISIMA VIRGEN DE LA CABEZA
Guarromán
Villacarrillo
Bailén
Linares
Embalse del Yeguas
Canena
Rus
Sabiote
Marmolejo
Andújar
Espeluy
Jabalquinto
Ibros
Santo Tomé
Torreperogil
Chilluevar
Montoro
Adamuz
Villanueva de la Reina
Lupión
Úbeda
Torreblascopedro
Arjonilla
Cazalilla
Begíjar
Baeza
Pedro Abad
Villa del Río
Higuera de Arjona
Mengíbar
Real de Becerro
Cazorla
La Iruela
El Carpio
Lopera
Arjona
Fuente del Rey
Bujalance
Cañete de las Torres
Escañuela
Porcuna
Quesada
Villadompardo
Jimena
Bedmar
Jódar
CATEDRAL DE LA ASUNCIÓN
0 10 20 30 km

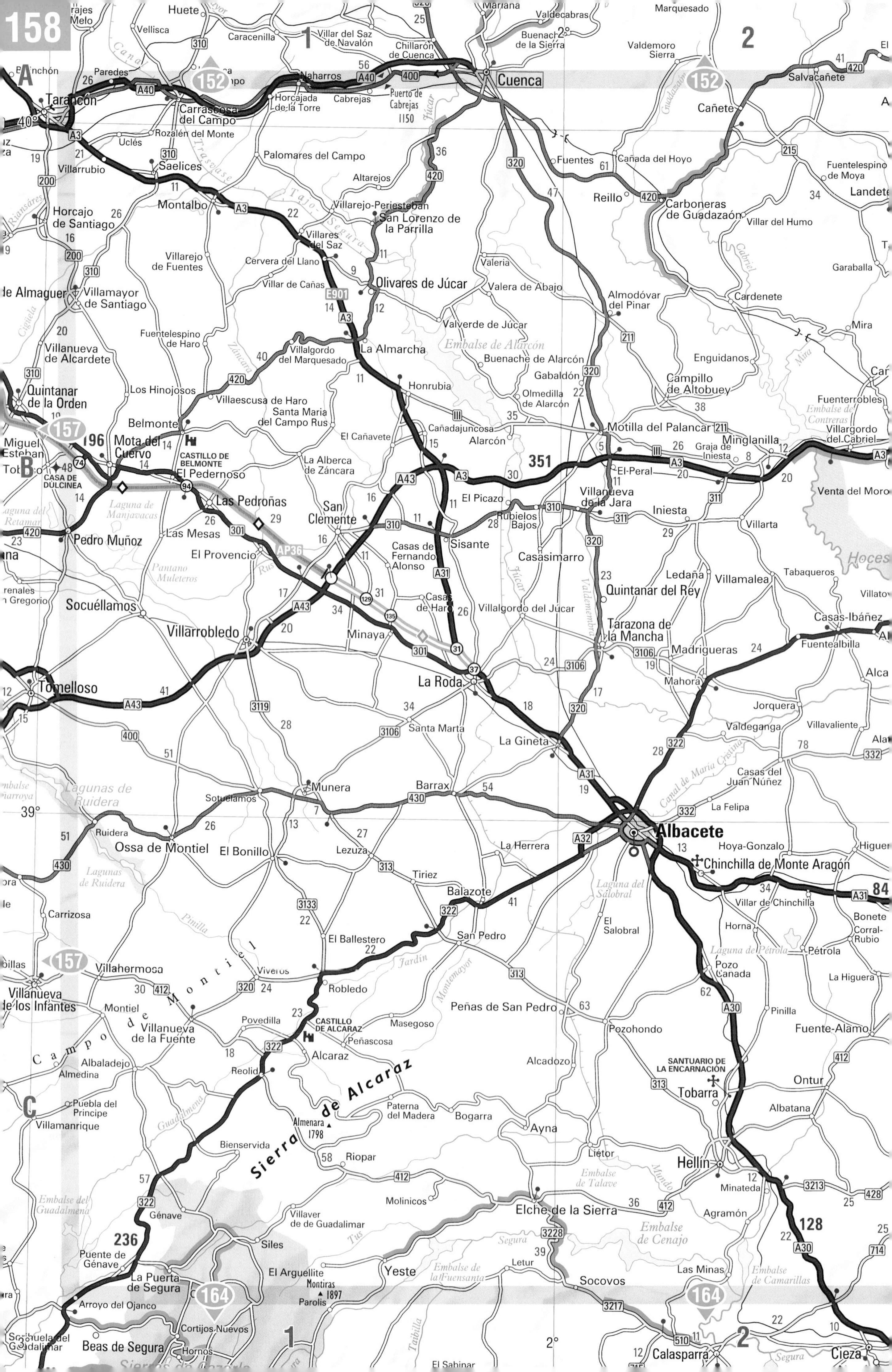
Huete
Vellisca
Caracenilla
Villar del Saz de Navalón
Chillarón de Cuenca
Mariana
Valdecabras
Buenache de la Sierra
Marquesado
Valdemoro Sierra
Salvacañete
Cuenca
Tarancón
Paredes
Carrascosa del Campo
Naharros
Horcajada de la Torre
Cabrejas
Puerto de Cabrejas 1150
Júcar
Cañete
Uclés
Rozalén del Monte
Palomares del Campo
Saelices
Villarrubio
Fuentes
Cañada del Hoyo
Fuentelespino de Moya
Reillo
Carboneras de Guadazaón
Villar del Humo
Landete
Altarejos
Montalbo
Horcajo de Santiago
Villarejo-Periesteban
San Lorenzo de la Parrilla
Villares del Saz
Villarejo de Fuentes
Cervera del Llano
Villar de Cañas
Olivares de Júcar
Valeria
Valera de Abajo
Garaballa
Almodóvar del Pinar
Cardenete
Villamayor de Santiago
Valverde de Júcar
Mira
Fuentelespino de Haro
Villanueva de Alcardete
Villalgordo del Marquesado
La Almarcha
Embalse de Alarcón
Buenache de Alarcón
Enguídanos
Gabaldón
Quintanar de la Orden
Los Hinojosos
Villaescusa de Haro
Santa María del Campo Rus
Honrubia
Olmedilla de Alarcón
Campillo de Altobuey
Fuenterrobles
Embalse de Contreras
Belmonte
Mota del Cuervo
Castillo de Belmonte
El Cañavete
Cañadajuncosa
Alarcón
Motilla del Palancar
Minglanilla
Villargordo del Cabriel
Graja de Iniesta
El Toboso
Casa de Dulcinea
El Pedernoso
La Alberca de Záncara
El Peral
Venta del Moro
Villanueva de la Jara
Laguna de Manjavacas
Las Pedroñas
San Clemente
El Picazo
Rubielos Bajos
Iniesta
Pedro Muñoz
Las Mesas
Sisante
Villarta
Casas de Fernando Alonso
Casasimarro
El Provencio
Pantano Muleteros
Ledaña
Villamalea
Tabaqueros
Hoces
Quintanar del Rey
Socuéllamos
Casas de Haro
Villalgordo del Júcar
Casas-Ibáñez
Villarrobledo
Minaya
Tarazona de la Mancha
Madrigueras
Fuentealbilla
Mahora
Tomelloso
La Roda
Alcalá
Jorquera
Santa Marta
La Gineta
Valdeganga
Villavaliente
Canal de María Cristina
Casas del Juan Núñez
Lagunas de Ruidera
Munera
Barrax
Sotuélamos
La Felipa
Ruidera
Albacete
Ossa de Montiel
El Bonillo
Lezuza
La Herrera
Hoya-Gonzalo
Chinchilla de Monte Aragón
Lagunas de Ruidera
Tiriez
Balazote
Laguna del Salobral
Villar de Chinchilla
Bonete
Carrizosa
El Salobral
Horna
Corral-Rubio
San Pedro
Pinilla
El Ballestero
Laguna de Pétrola
Pétrola
Villahermosa
Viveros
Jardín
Pozo Cañada
La Higuera
Villanueva de los Infantes
Montiel
Robledo
Villanueva de la Fuente
Campo de Montiel
Peñas de San Pedro
Pinilla
Povedilla
Castillo de Alcaraz
Masegoso
Pozohondo
Fuente-Álamo
Peñascosa
Albaladejo
Alcaraz
Alcadozo
Almedina
Reolid
Santuario de la Encarnación
Sierra de Alcaraz
Tobarra
Ontur
Puebla del Príncipe
Paterna del Madera
Bogarra
Almenara 1798
Ayna
Albatana
Villamanrique
Bienservida
Riopar
Liétor
Hellín
Embalse de Talave
Minateda
Molinicos
Elche de la Sierra
Agramón
Embalse del Guadalmena
Génave
Villaver de Guadalimar
Embalse de Cenajo
Siles
Puente de Génave
Yeste
Letur
Las Minas
El Arguellite
Montiras 1897
Embalse de la Fuensanta
Embalse de Camarillas
La Puerta de Segura
Parolis
Socovos
Arroyo del Ojanco
Cortijos Nuevos
Beas de Segura
Hornos
Calasparra
Cieza
El Sabinar
Segura
Mundo
Taibilla
Tus
Guadalmena
Cabriel
Záncara
39°
2°
A3
A31
A32
A30
A40
A43
AP36
E901
152
157
164
84
128
196
236
351

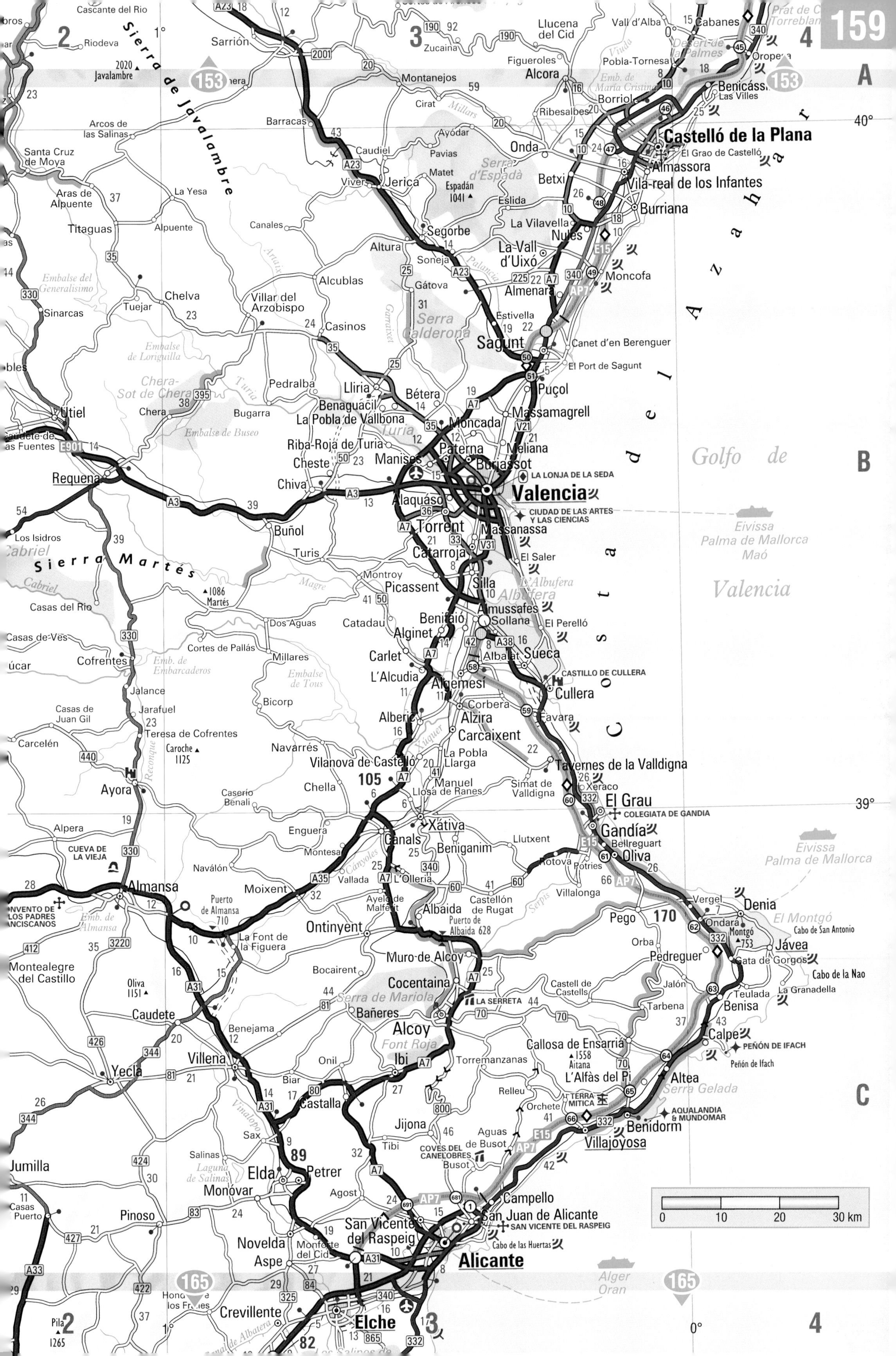
Sierra de Javalambre
Javalambre
Sarrión
Montanejos
Llucena del Cid
Vall d'Alba
Cabanes
Alcora
Oropesa
Benicàssim
Borriol
Castelló de la Plana
El Grao de Castelló
Almassora
Vila-real de los Infantes
Burriana
Onda
Betxi
Serra d'Espadà
Espadán 1041
Jerica
Segorbe
Nules
La Vall d'Uixó
Moncofa
Almenara
Serra Calderona
Sagunt
Canet d'en Berenguer
El Port de Sagunt
Puçol
Massamagrell
Costa del Azahar
Golfo de Valencia
Utiel
Requena
Chelva
Titaguas
Alpuente
Santa Cruz de Moya
Aras de Alpuente
Villar del Arzobispo
Casinos
Alcublas
Lliria
Bétera
Benaguacil
La Pobla de Vallbona
Riba-Roja de Turia
Cheste
Chiva
Manises
Paterna
Moncada
Burjassot
Valencia
LA LONJA DE LA SEDA
CIUDAD DE LAS ARTES Y LAS CIENCIAS
Eivissa
Palma de Mallorca
Maó
Alaquàs
Torrent
Massanassa
Catarroja
El Saler
Buñol
Turis
Sierra Martés
Martés 1086
Picassent
Silla
L'Albufera
Almussafes
Sollana
El Perelló
Benifaió
Alginet
Sueca
Carlet
L'Alcudia
Algemesí
CASTILLO DE CULLERA
Cullera
Alzira
Carcaixent
Favara
Alberic
Navarrés
Vilanova de Castelló
La Pobla Llarga
Tavernes de la Valldigna
Ayora
Cofrentes
Teresa de Cofrentes
Caroche 1125
Chella
Xàtiva
Canals
Enguera
El Grau
COLEGIATA DE GANDIA
Gandía
Oliva
Almansa
CUEVA DE LA VIEJA
Ontinyent
Albaida
Puerto de Almansa 710
Dénia
El Montgó
Cabo de San Antonio
Jávea
Cabo de la Nao
Pego
Pedreguer
Muro de Alcoy
Cocentaina
Serra de Mariola
LA SERRETA
Benisa
Calpe
PEÑÓN DE IFACH
Alcoy
Font Roja
Callosa de Ensarriá
Aitana 1558
Caudete
Villena
Yecla
Ibi
Castalla
Altea
L'Alfàs del Pi
TERRA MITICA
AQUALANDIA & MUNDOMAR
Benidorm
Villajoyosa
Jijona
Elda
Petrer
Monóvar
Jumilla
Pinoso
Campello
San Juan de Alicante
San Vicente del Raspeig
Alicante
Cabo de las Huertas
Novelda
Aspe
Crevillente
Elche
Alger
Oran
0 10 20 30 km
A
B
C
2
3
4

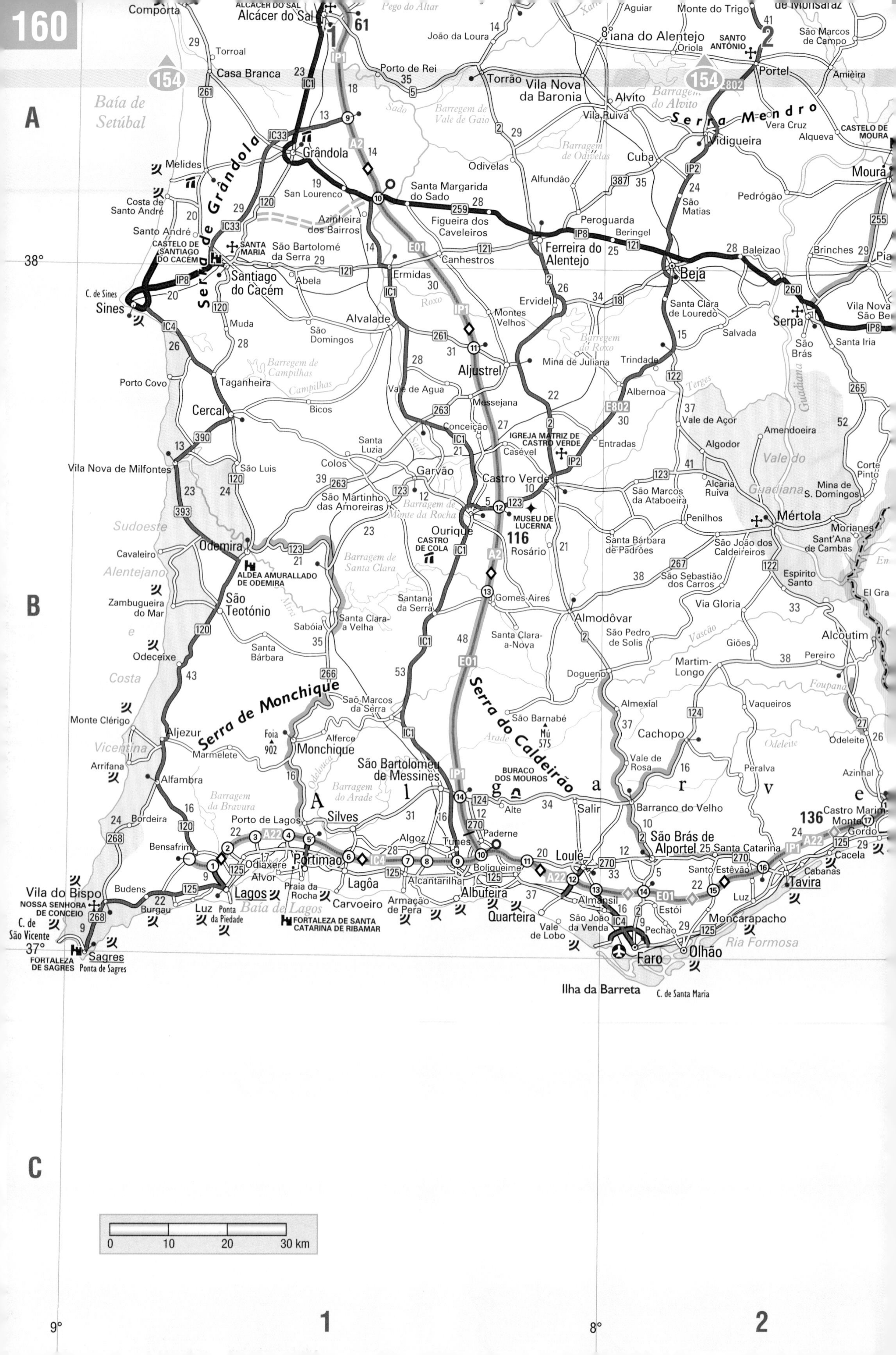
A
B
C
1
2
9°
8°
38°
37°
154
136
116
61
Baía de Setúbal
Comporta
Alcácer do Sal
Pego do Altar
Aguiar
Monte do Trigo
São Marcos de Campo
João da Loura
Viana do Alentejo
Oriola
Santo António
Torroal
Casa Branca
Porto de Rei
Torrão
Vila Nova da Baronia
Alvito
Barragem do Alvito
Portel
Amièira
Barregem de Vale de Gaio
Sado
Vila Ruiva
Serra Mendro
Vera Cruz
Castelo de Moura
Vidigueira
Alqueva
Grândola
Melides
Serra de Grândola
Barragem de Odivelas
Cuba
Moura
Odivelas
Alfundão
Santa Margarida do Sado
São Matias
Pedrógão
San Lourenco
Costa de Santo André
Azinheira dos Bairros
Figueira dos Caveleiros
Peroguarda
Beringel
Santo André
Castelo de Santiago do Cacém
Santa Maria
São Bartolomé da Serra
Canhestros
Ferreira do Alentejo
Baleizao
Brinches
Santiago do Cacém
Abela
Ermidas
Beja
C. de Sines
Sines
Erviedel
Santa Clara de Louredo
Serpa
Vila Nova São Be
Muda
São Domingos
Alvalade
Roxo
Montes Velhos
Barregem do Roxo
Salvada
Santa Iria
São Brás
Porto Covo
Barregem de Campilhas
Campilhas
Taganheira
Aljustrel
Mina de Juliana
Trindade
Vale de Agua
Albernoa
Terges
Cercal
Bicos
Messejana
Conceição
Vale de Açor
Amendoeira
Guadiana
Igreja Matriz de Castro Verde
Entradas
Algodor
Vale do Guadiana
Santa Luzia
Casével
Vila Nova de Milfontes
São Luis
Colos
Garvão
Castro Verde
Alcaria Ruiva
Corte Pinto
Mina de S. Domingos
São Martinho das Amoreiras
Barragem de Monte da Rocha
Museu de Lucerna
São Marcos da Ataboeira
Penilhos
Mértola
Sudoeste Alentejano e Costa Vicentina
Ourique
Castro de Cola
Rosário
Santa Bárbara de Padrões
São João dos Caldeireiros
Moriones
Sant'Ana de Cambas
Cavaleiro
Odemira
Aldea Amurallado de Odemira
Barragem de Santa Clara
São Sebastião dos Carros
Espirito Santo
Zambugueira do Mar
São Teotónio
Mira
Santana da Serra
Gomes Aires
Via Gloria
El Gra
Sabóia
Santa Clara-a-Velha
Almodôvar
São Pedro de Solis
Vascão
Alcoutim
Odeceixe
Santa Bárbara
Santa Clara-a-Nova
Gióes
Pereiro
Martim-Longo
Dogueno
Foupana
Serra de Monchique
São Marcos da Serra
Serra do Caldeirão
Almexial
Vaqueiros
Monte Clérigo
Aljezur
Foia 902
Alferce
São Barnabé
Mú 575
Cachopo
Odeleite
Arrifana
Marmelete
Monchique
São Bartolomeu de Messines
Arade
Vale de Rosa
Peralva
Azinhal
Alfambra
Barragem do Arade
Buraco dos Mouros
Algarve
Barragem da Bravura
Odelouca
Silves
Alte
Salir
Barranco do Velho
Castro Marim
Monte Gordo
Bordeira
Porto de Lagos
Paderne
São Brás de Alportel
Santa Catarina
Bensafrim
Algoz
Tunes
Loulé
Cacela
Odiaxere
Portimao
Boliqueime
Santo Estêvão
Cabanas
Alvor
Alcantarilha
Tavira
Vila do Bispo
Budens
Lagos
Praia da Rocha
Lagôa
Albufeira
Almansil
Luz
Nossa Senhora de Conceio
Burgau
Luz
Ponta da Piedade
Baía de Lagos
Carvoeiro
Armação de Pera
Quarteira
Estói
Moncarapacho
C. de São Vicente
Fortaleza de Santa Catarina de Ribamar
Vale de Lobo
São João da Venda
Pechão
Ria Formosa
Fortaleza de Sagres
Sagres
Ponta de Sagres
Faro
Olhão
Ilha da Barreta
C. de Santa Maria
0
10
20
30 km

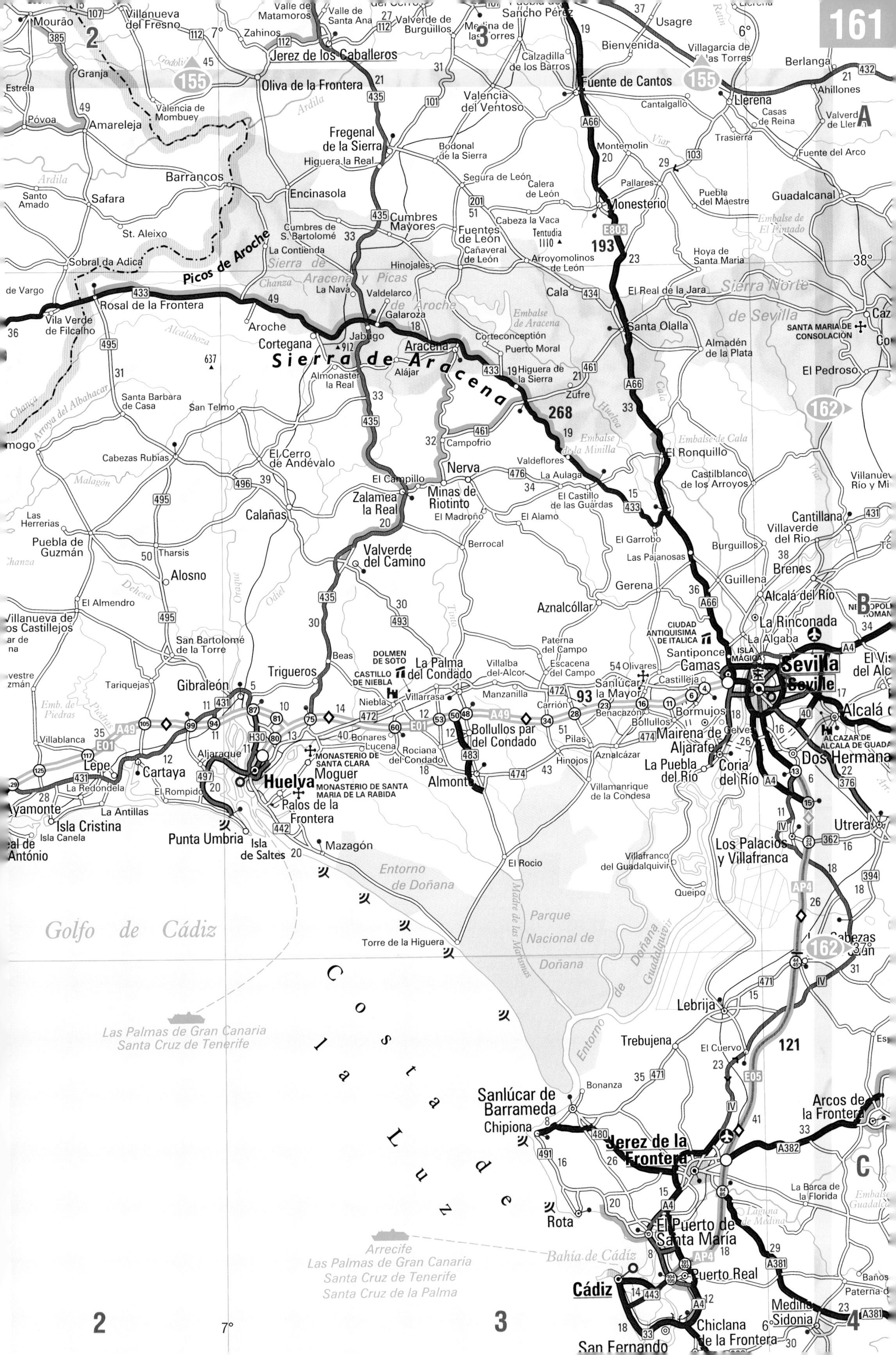
Mourão
Villanueva del Fresno
Valle de Matamoros
Valle de Santa Ana
Valverde de Burguillos
Medina de las Torres
Sancho Pérez
Usagre
Bienvenida
Villagarcia de las Torres
Berlanga
Zahinos
Jerez de los Caballeros
Granja
Estrela
Oliva de la Frontera
Calzadilla de los Barros
Fuente de Cantos
Ahillones
Llerena
Valencia de Mombuey
Amareleja
Póvoa
Valencia del Ventoso
Cantalgallo
Casas de Reina
Valverde de Llerena
Fregenal de la Sierra
Bodonal de la Sierra
Montemolín
Trasierra
Fuente del Arco
Higuera la Real
Barrancos
Segura de León
Calera de León
Pallares
Puebla del Maestre
Guadalcanal
Santo Amado
Safara
Encinasola
Monesterio
Cumbres Mayores
Cumbres de S. Bartolomé
Fuentes de León
Cabeza la Vaca
Tentudía
Embalse de El Pintado
St. Aleixo
Picos de Aroche
La Contienda
Cañaveral de León
Hoya de Santa María
Sobral da Adica
Sierra de Aracena y Picas de Aroche
Hinojales
Arroyomolinos de León
38°
La Nava
Valdelarco
Cala
El Real de la Jara
Sierra Norte de Sevilla
de Vargo
Rosal de la Frontera
Galaroza
Vila Verde de Filcalho
Aroche
Jabugo
Embalse de Aracena
Corteconcepción
Santa Olalla
Santa María de Consolación
Cortegana
Aracena
Puerto Moral
Almadén de la Plata
Sierra de Aracena
Almonaster la Real
Alájar
Higuera de la Sierra
El Pedroso
Santa Barbara de Casa
San Telmo
Zufre
Campofrío
Embalse de la Minilla
Embalse de Cala
El Ronquillo
Cabezas Rubias
El Cerro de Andévalo
Valdeflores
La Aulaga
Castilblanco de los Arroyos
Villanueva del Río y Minas
El Campillo
Nerva
Minas de Riotinto
Zalamea la Real
El Castillo de las Guardas
Las Herrerias
Calañas
El Madroño
El Alamo
Cantillana
Villaverde del Río
Puebla de Guzmán
Tharsis
Berrocal
El Garrobo
Burguillos
Valverde del Camino
Las Pajanosas
Brenes
Alosno
Gerena
Guillena
Alcalá del Río
El Almendro
Aznalcóllar
La Rinconada
Villanueva de los Castillejos
Ciudad Antiquísima de Italica
Paterna del Campo
La Algaba
San Bartolomé de la Torre
Santiponce
Isla Mágica
Sevilla
Seville
Dolmen de Soto
Castillo de Niebla
La Palma del Condado
Villalba del Alcor
Escacena del Campo
Olivares
Camas
Tariquejas
Trigueros
Beas
Gibraleón
Niebla
Villarrasa
Manzanilla
Carrión
Sanlúcar la Mayor
Castilleja
Bormujos
Alcalá
Emb. de Piedras
Benacazón
Bollullos
Villablanca
Bonares
Lucena
Bollullos par del Condado
Pilas
Mairena de Aljarafe
Gelves
Alcazar de Alcala de Guadaira
Dos Hermanas
Lepe
Cartaya
Aljaraque
Monasterio de Santa Clara
Rociana del Condado
Aznalcázar
Hinojos
La Puebla del Río
Coria del Río
La Redondela
El Rompido
Huelva
Moguer
Monasterio de Santa Maria de la Rabida
Almonte
Villamanrique de la Condesa
Ayamonte
La Antillas
Palos de la Frontera
Utrera
Isla Cristina
Isla Canela
Punta Umbria
Isla de Saltes
Mazagón
Los Palacios y Villafranca
Villafranco del Guadalquivir
El Rocio
Entorno de Doñana
Queipo
Golfo de Cádiz
Parque Nacional de Doñana
Torre de la Higuera
Las Cabezas de San Juan
37°
Costa de la Luz
Lebrija
Las Palmas de Gran Canaria
Santa Cruz de Tenerife
Trebujena
El Cuervo
Bonanza
Sanlúcar de Barrameda
Arcos de la Frontera
Chipiona
Jerez de la Frontera
La Barca de la Florida
Rota
El Puerto de Santa María
Arrecife
Santa Cruz de la Palma
Bahía de Cádiz
Puerto Real
Cádiz
Paterna de Rivera
Medina Sidonia
Chiclana de la Frontera
San Fernando
Baños
2
3
4
7°
6°
A
B
C
155
162
193
268
93
121

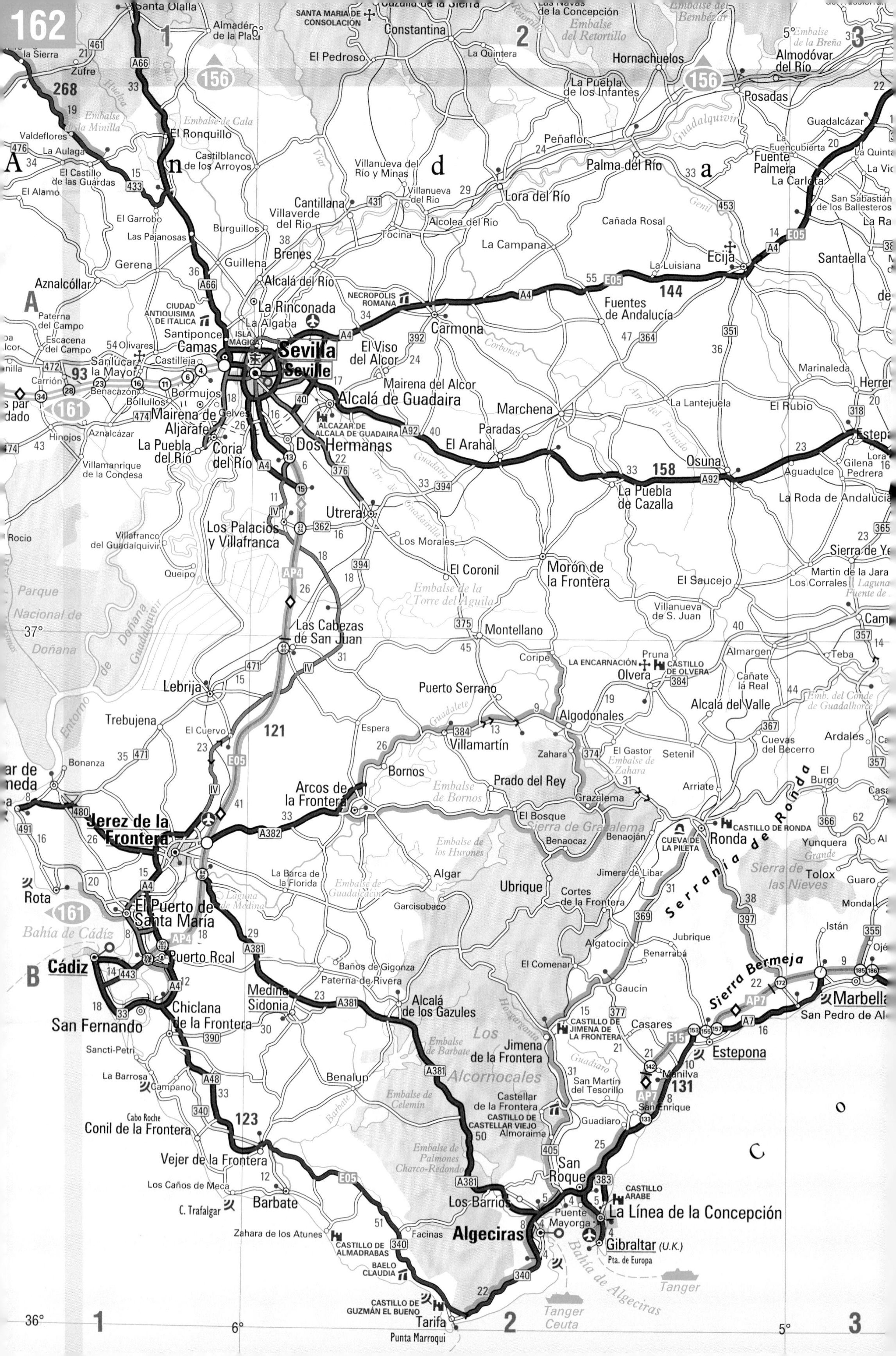

Santa Olalla
Almadén de la Plata
Constantina
El Pedroso
La Puebla de los Infantes
Hornachuelos
Almodóvar del Río
Posadas
Zufre
Valdeflores
El Ronquillo
Castilblanco de los Arroyos
Villanueva del Río y Minas
Peñaflor
Palma del Río
Fuente Palmera
La Carlota
Guadalcázar
El Castillo de las Guardas
Cantillana
Villaverde del Río
Lora del Río
Alcolea del Río
Tocina
Cañada Rosal
El Garrobo
Las Pajanosas
Burguillos
Brenes
La Campana
Écija
La Luisiana
Gerena
Guillena
Alcalá del Río
Aznalcóllar
La Rinconada
Fuentes de Andalucía
Carmona
Santaella
Camas
Sevilla
Seville
El Viso del Alcor
Mairena del Alcor
Alcalá de Guadaira
Marchena
Paradas
El Arahal
Sanlúcar la Mayor
Olivares
Castilleja
Bormujos
Mairena de Aljarafe
Gelves
La Puebla del Río
Coria del Río
Dos Hermanas
Osuna
La Puebla de Cazalla
Estepa
Marinaleda
Herrera
El Rubio
La Lantejuela
Utrera
Los Palacios y Villafranca
Los Morales
El Coronil
Morón de la Frontera
El Saucejo
Villanueva de S. Juan
La Roda de Andalucía
Aguadulce
Gilena
Pedrera
Sierra de Yeguas
Martín de la Jara
Los Corrales
Las Cabezas de San Juan
Montellano
Coripe
Pruna
Olvera
Almargen
Teba
Cañete la Real
Lebrija
Puerto Serrano
Algodonales
Alcalá del Valle
Trebujena
El Cuervo
Espera
Villamartín
Zahara
El Gastor
Setenil
Ardales
Cuevas del Becerro
Bonanza
Bornos
Arcos de la Frontera
Prado del Rey
Grazalema
Arriate
El Burgo
Jerez de la Frontera
El Bosque
Benaocaz
Benaoján
Ronda
Yunquera
Sierra de Grazalema
Serranía de Ronda
Rota
La Barca de la Florida
Algar
Ubrique
Jimera de Libar
Cortes de la Frontera
Tolox
Guaro
Monda
El Puerto de Santa María
Garcisobaco
Sierra de las Nieves
Bahía de Cádiz
Cádiz
Puerto Real
Baños de Gigonza
Paterna de Rivera
Algatocín
Benarrabá
Jubrique
Istán
El Comenar
Gaucín
Sierra Bermeja
Marbella
San Pedro de Alcántara
Medina Sidonia
Alcalá de los Gazules
Chiclana de la Frontera
San Fernando
Casares
Estepona
Sancti-Petri
Jimena de la Frontera
Los Alcornocales
Manilva
La Barrosa
Campano
Benalup
San Martín del Tesorillo
San Enrique
Castellar de la Frontera
Almoraima
Guadiaro
Cabo Roche
Conil de la Frontera
Vejer de la Frontera
San Roque
Los Caños de Meca
Barbate
Los Barrios
La Línea de la Concepción
C. Trafalgar
Puente Mayorga
Algeciras
Gibraltar (U.K.)
Pta. de Europa
Zahara de los Atunes
Facinas
Bahía de Algeciras
Tanger
Ceuta
Tarifa
Punta Marroquí

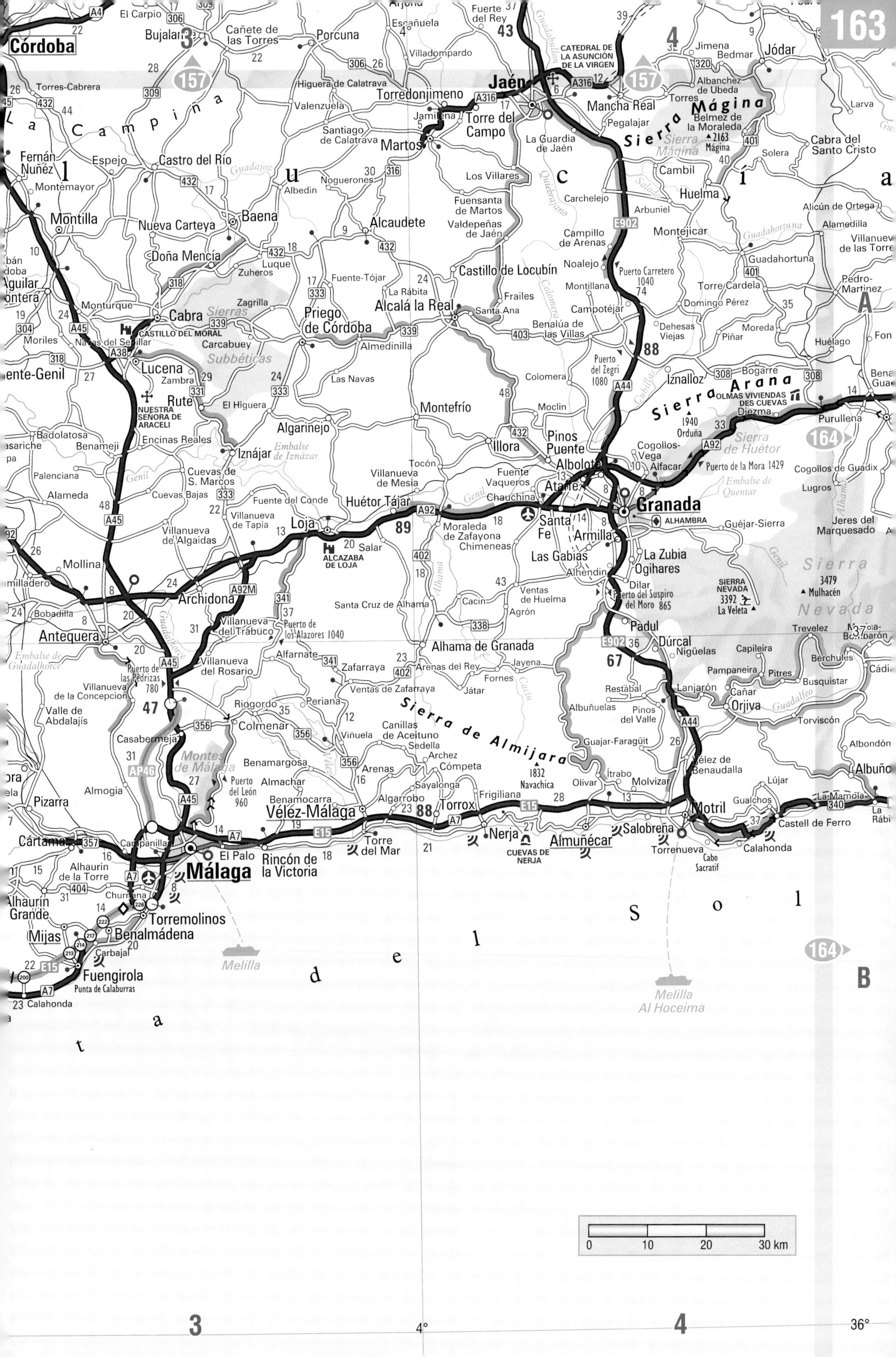
Córdoba
El Carpio
Bujalance
Cañete de las Torres
Porcuna
Arjona
Escañuela
Villardompardo
Fuerte del Rey
Jaén
CATEDRAL DE LA ASUNCIÓN DE LA VIRGEN
Jimena
Bedmar
Jódar
Torres-Cabrera
La Campiña
Higuera de Calatrava
Torredonjimeno
Valenzuela
Jamilena
Torre del Campo
Mancha Real
Albanchez de Ubeda
Torres
Pegalajar
Sierra Mágina
Belmez de la Moraleda
Mágina 2163
Larva
Cabra del Santo Cristo
Santiago de Calatrava
Martos
La Guardia de Jaén
Solera
Fernán Núñez
Espejo
Castro del Río
Guadajoz
Noguerones
Albedín
Los Villares
Cambil
Huelma
Montemayor
Carchelejo
Arbuniel
Alicún de Ortega
Montilla
Nueva Carteya
Baena
Fuensanta de Martos
Alcaudete
Valdepeñas de Jaén
Campillo de Arenas
Montejícar
Alamedilla
Villanueva de las Torres
Doña Mencía
Luque
Zuheros
Castillo de Locubín
Noalejo
Puerto Carretero 1040
Guadahortuna
Aguilar de la Frontera
Fuente-Tójar
La Rábita
Montillana
Torre Cardela
Pedro-Martínez
Monturque
Cabra
Zagrilla
Sierras Subbéticas
Priego de Córdoba
Alcalá la Real
Frailes
Santa Ana
Campotéjar
Domingo Pérez
CASTILLO DEL MORAL
Benalúa de las Villas
Dehesas Viejas
Moreda
Piñar
Huélago
Moriles
Nava del Sellar
Carcabuey
Almedinilla
Puerto del Zegri 1080
Lucena
Zambra
Las Navas
Colomera
Iznalloz
Bogarre
Puente-Genil
Rute
El Higuera
Sierra Arana
OLMAS VIVIENDAS DES CUEVAS
Diezma
Purullena
NUESTRA SEÑORA DE ARACELI
Montefrío
Moclín
1940 Orduña
Badolatosa
Benamejí
Algarinejo
Encinas Reales
Illora
Pinos Puente
Cogollos-Vega
Sierra de Huétor
Iznájar
Embalse de Iznájar
Albolote
Alfacar
Puerto de la Mora 1429
Cogollos de Guadix
Palenciana
Cuevas de S. Marcos
Tocón
Villanueva de Mesía
Fuente Vaqueros
Atarfe
Embalse de Quentar
Lugros
Alameda
Cuevas Bajas
Fuente del Conde
Huétor Tájar
Chauchina
Granada
ALHAMBRA
Villanueva de Tapia
Loja
Moraleda de Zafayona
Chimeneas
Santa Fe
Armilla
Güéjar-Sierra
Jeres del Marquesado
Villanueva de Algaidas
Salar
ALCAZABA DE LOJA
Las Gabias
La Zubia
Ogíjares
Sierra Nevada
Mollina
Alhama
Alhendín
Dílar
SIERRA NEVADA
3392 La Veleta
3479 Mulhacén
Archidona
Santa Cruz de Alhama
Cacín
Ventas de Huelma
Puerto del Suspiro del Moro 865
Bobadilla
Agrón
Padul
Antequera
Villanueva del Trabuco
Puerto de los Alazores 1040
Dúrcal
Nigüelas
Capileira
Trevelez
Bérchules
Embalse de Guadalhorce
Alfarnate
Alhama de Granada
Jayena
Pampaneira
Pitres
Busquistar
Cádiar
Puerto de las Pedrizas 780
Villanueva del Rosario
Zafarraya
Arenas del Rey
Fornes
Villanueva de la Concepción
Ventas de Zafarraya
Játar
Restábal
Lanjarón
Cañar
Órgiva
Valle de Abdalajís
Riogordo
Periana
Sierra de Almijara
Pinos del Valle
Albuñuelas
Torviscón
Colmenar
Canillas de Aceituno
Viñuela
Sedella
Guajar-Faragüit
Casabermeja
Montes de Málaga
Benamargosa
Archez
Cómpeta
Vélez de Benaudalla
Albondón
Arenas
Almachar
Puerto del León 960
Sayalonga
1832 Navachica
Ítrabo
Olivar
Molvízar
Lújar
Albuñol
Almogia
Benamocarra
Frigiliana
La Mamola
Pizarra
Vélez-Málaga
Algarrobo
Torrox
Motril
Gualchos
Castell de Ferro
Cártama
Campanillas
Torre del Mar
Nerja
CUEVAS DE NERJA
Almuñécar
Salobreña
Torrenueva
Cabo Sacratif
Calahonda
El Palo
Rincón de la Victoria
Málaga
Alhaurín de la Torre
Churriana
Alhaurín Grande
Torremolinos
Benalmádena
Mijas
Carbajal
Fuengirola
Punta de Calaburras
Calahonda
Melilla
Melilla Al Hoceima
Costa del Sol
0 10 20 30 km
3
4
A
B
157
164
36°
4°

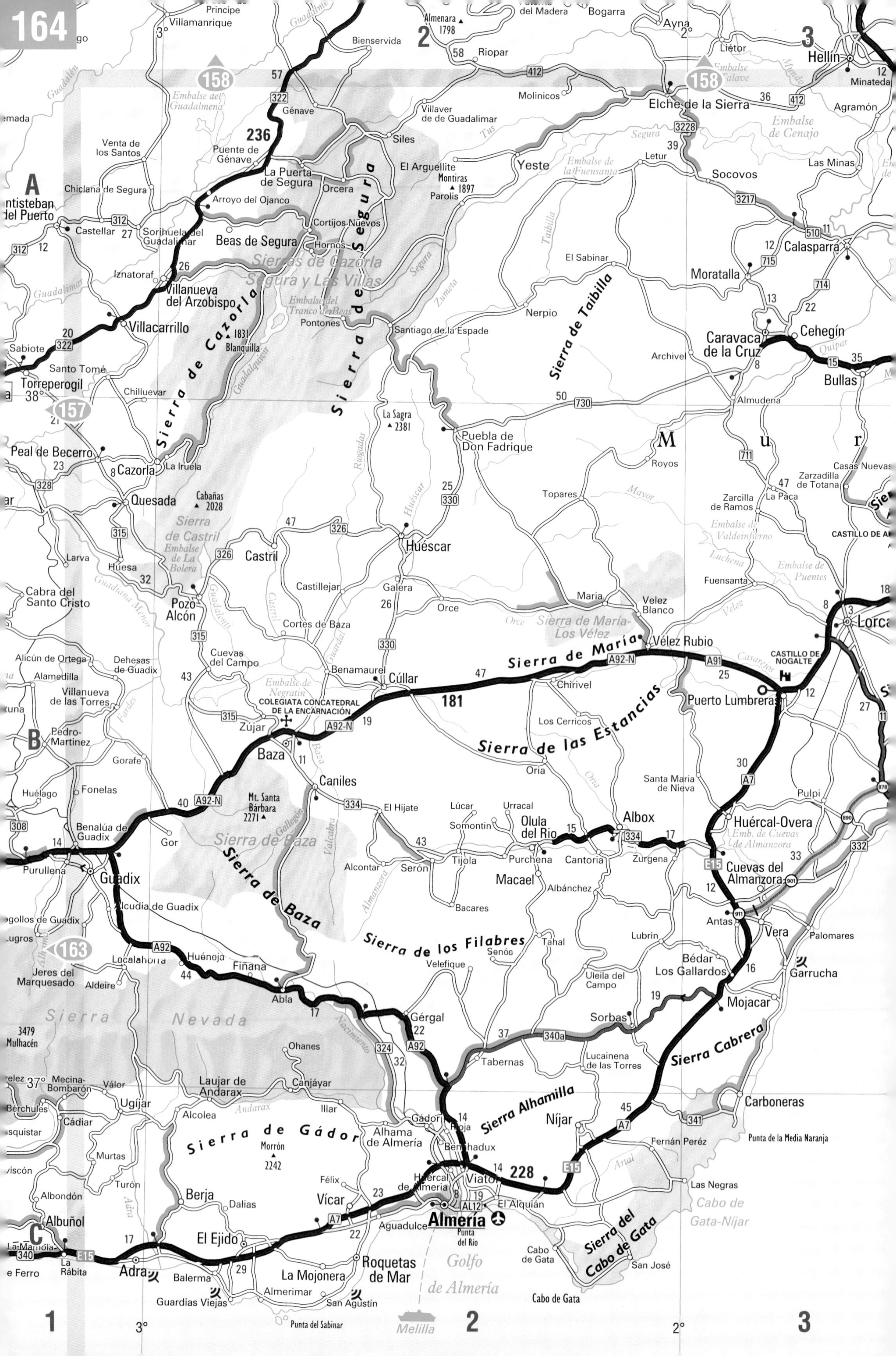

Principe
Villamanrique
Almenara
1798
del Madera
Bogarra
Ayna
Liétor
Hellín
Minateda
Bienservida
Riopar
Molinicos
Elche de la Sierra
Agramón
Embalse del Guadalmena
Génave
Villaver de de Guadalimar
Embalse de Cenajo
Venta de los Santos
Puente de Génave
Siles
Yeste
Letur
Embalse de la Fuensanta
La Puerta de Segura
El Arguellite
Montiras
1897
Parolis
Socovos
Las Minas
Chiclana de Segura
Orcera
Arroyo del Ojanco
Santisteban del Puerto
Castellar
Sorihuela del Guadalimar
Cortijos Nuevos
Beas de Segura
Hornos
Sierras de Cazorla Segura y Las Villas
Calasparra
El Sabinar
Moratalla
Iznatoraf
Villanueva del Arzobispo
Embalse del Tranco de Beas
Pontones
Nerpio
Sierra de Taibilla
Villacarrillo
Santiago de la Espade
Caravaca de la Cruz
Cehegín
Archivel
Sabiote
Santo Tomé
Torreperogil
Blanquilla
1831
Sierra de Cazorla
Sierra de Segura
Bullas
Chilluevar
La Sagra
2381
Almudena
Puebla de Don Fadrique
Murcia
Peal de Becerro
Cazorla
La Iruela
Royos
Casas Nuevas
Zarzadilla de Totana
Quesada
Cabañas
2028
Topares
Zarcilla de Ramos
La Paca
Sierra de Castril
Embalse de La Bolera
Embalse de Valdeinfierno
CASTILLO DE AL
Castril
Huéscar
Larva
Huesa
Embalse de Puentes
Fuensanta
Cabra del Santo Cristo
Castillejar
Galera
Pozo Alcón
Orce
Maria
Velez Blanco
Sierra de María-Los Vélez
Lorca
Cortes de Baza
Vélez Rubio
Alicún de Ortega
Dehesas de Guadix
Cuevas del Campo
Sierra de María
CASTILLO DE NOGALTE
Alamedilla
Villanueva de las Torres
Benamaurel
Cúllar
Chirivel
Embalse de Negratín
Puerto Lumbreras
COLEGIATA CONCATEDRAL DE LA ENCARNACIÓN
Zújar
Los Cerricos
Sierra de las Estancias
Pedro-Martinez
Baza
Gorafe
Oria
Caniles
Santa Maria de Nieva
Huélago
Fonelas
Mt. Santa Bárbara
2271
El Hijate
Lúcar
Urracal
Pulpi
Somontin
Olula del Rio
Albox
Huércal-Overa
Benalúa de Guadix
Gor
Sierra de Baza
Emb. de Cuevas de Almanzora
Purullena
Guadix
Alcontar
Serón
Tíjola
Purchena
Cantoria
Zurgena
Cuevas del Almanzora
Macael
Albánchez
Alcudia de Guadix
Bacares
Antas
Vera
Palomares
Jerez del Marquesado
Aldeire
La Calahorra
Huénoja
Fiñana
Sierra de los Filabres
Senés
Tahal
Lubrin
Bédar
Los Gallardos
Garrucha
Velefique
Uleila del Campo
Abla
Gérgal
Sorbas
Mojacar
Sierra Nevada
3479
Mulhacén
Ohanes
Lucainena de las Torres
Sierra Cabrera
Tabernas
Mecina-Bombarón
Válor
Laujar de Andarax
Canjáyar
Carboneras
Bérchules
Ugíjar
Cádiar
Alcolea
Illar
Gádor
Rioja
Sierra Alhamilla
Níjar
Alhama de Almería
Benahadux
Sierra de Gádor
Morrón
2242
Fernán Peréz
Punta de la Media Naranja
Murtas
Turón
Félix
Viator
Huércal de Almería
Las Negras
Albondón
Berja
Dalias
Vícar
El Alquián
Cabo de Gata-Níjar
Albuñol
Aguadulce
Almería
Punta del Río
Sierra del Cabo de Gata
El Ejido
Cabo de Gata
La Rábita
Adra
Roquetas de Mar
Golfo de Almería
San José
Balerma
La Mojonera
Almerimar
Guardias Viejas
San Agustín
Cabo de Gata
Punta del Sabinar
Melilla

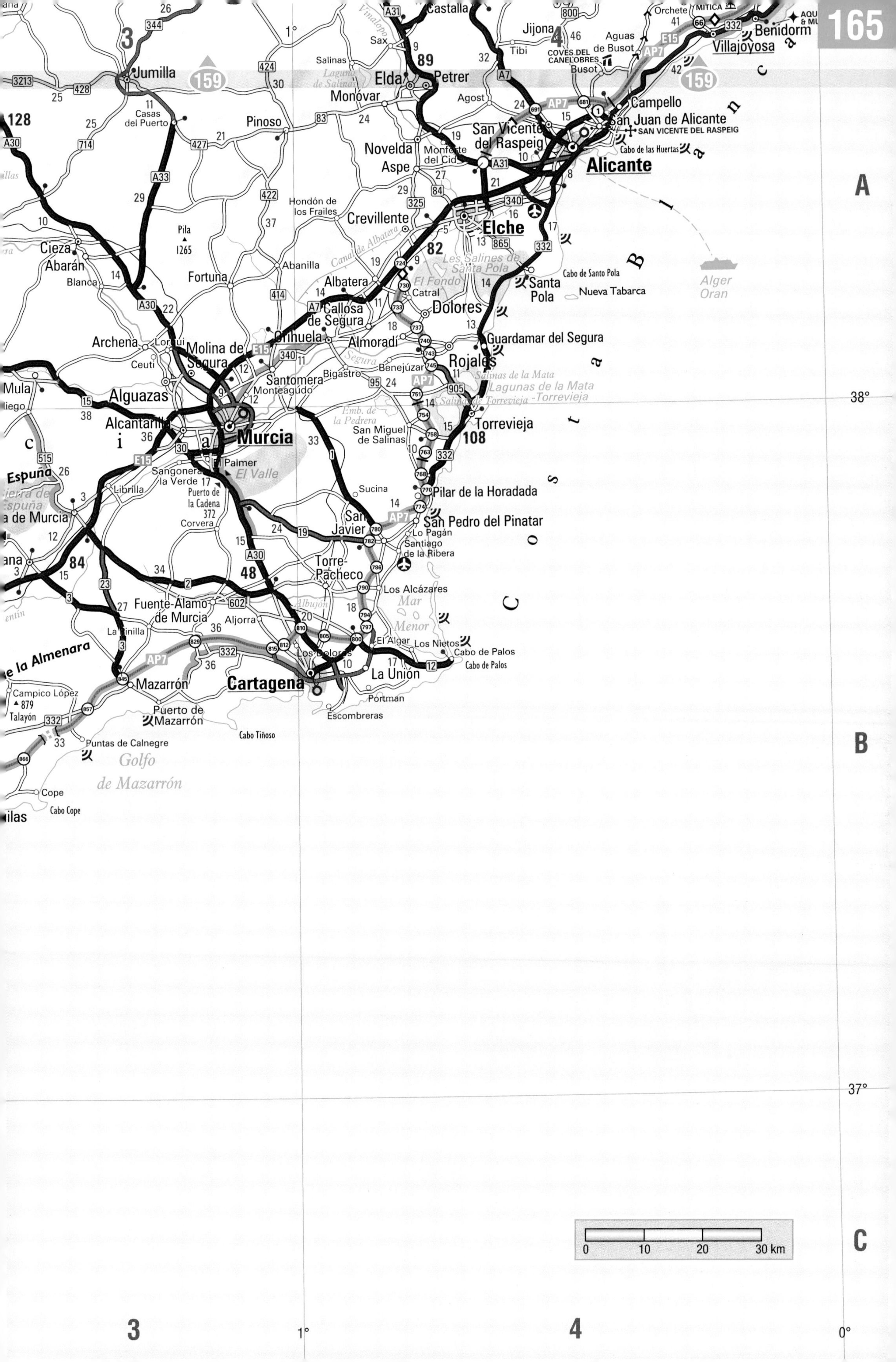

Jumilla
Casas del Puerto
Pinoso
Salinas
Laguna de Salinas
Monóvar
Elda
Petrer
Sax
Castalla
Jijona
Tibi
Agost
Coves del Canelobres
Aguas de Busot
Busot
Orcheta
Benidorm
Villajoyosa
Campello
San Juan de Alicante
San Vicente del Raspeig
Cabo de las Huertas
Alicante
Novelda
Monforte del Cid
Aspe
Hondón de los Frailes
Crevillente
Elche
Canal de Albatera
Les Salines de Santa Pola
El Fondo
Santa Pola
Cabo de Santo Pola
Nueva Tabarca
Alger
Oran
Pila
1265
Cieza
Abarán
Blanca
Fortuna
Abanilla
Albatera
Catral
Callosa de Segura
Dolores
Guardamar del Segura
Archena
Lorquí
Ceutí
Molina de Segura
Orihuela
Almoradí
Segura
Benejúzar
Rojales
Salinas de la Mata
Lagunas de la Mata -Torrevieja
Salinas de Torrevieja
Torrevieja
Mula
Alguazas
Alcantarilla
Santomera
Bigastro
Monteagudo
Murcia
Emb. de la Pedrera
San Miguel de Salinas
Palmer
El Valle
Sangonera la Verde
Puerto de la Cadena
372
Corvera
Librilla
Sierra de Espuña
Espuña
Sucina
San Javier
Pilar de la Horadada
San Pedro del Pinatar
Lo Pagán
Santiago de la Ribera
Torre-Pacheco
Los Alcázares
Mar Menor
Fuente-Álamo de Murcia
Aljorra
Albujón
La Pinilla
El Algar
Los Nietos
Cabo de Palos
Los Dolores
La Unión
Cartagena
Portman
Escombreras
Cabo Tiñoso
Mazarrón
Puerto de Mazarrón
Campico López
879
Talayón
Puntas de Calnegre
Golfo de Mazarrón
Cope
Cabo Cope
Costa Blanca
38°
37°
1°
0°
A
B
C
3
4
0
10
20
30 km

A

40°

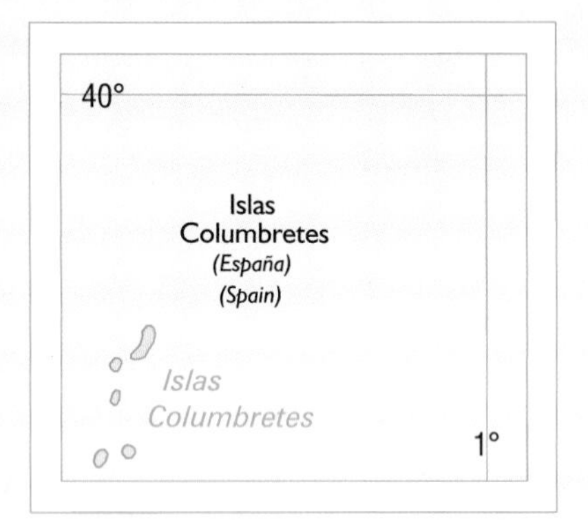

40°

Islas
Columbretes
(España)
(Spain)

Islas
Columbretes

1°

B

# ISLAS BALEARES

## BALEARIC ISLANDS

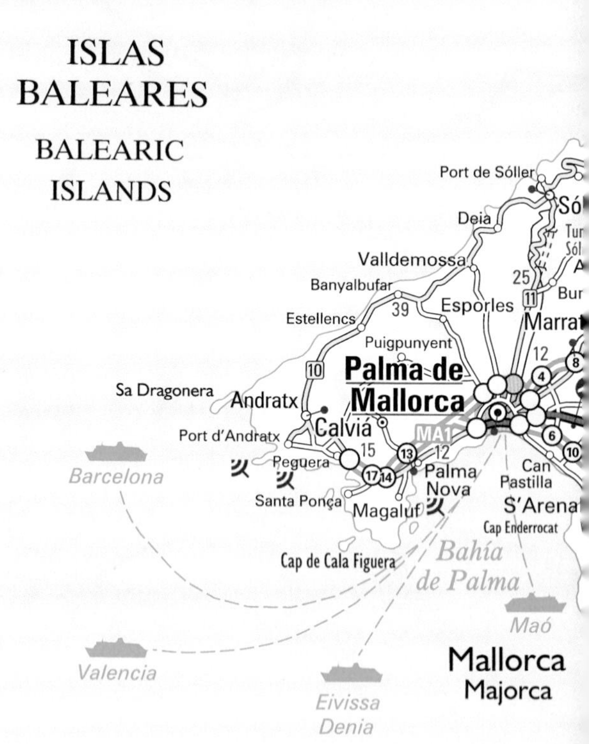

Port de Sóller
Só
Deià
Tur
Sól
Valldemossa
25
Banyalbufar
Bur
Esporles
11
Estellencs
39
Marra
Puigpunyent
12
10
8
Sa Dragonera
**Palma de Mallorca**
4
Andratx
MA
6
Calvià
Port d'Andratx
15
10
Peguera
13
12
Can
17 14
Palma
Pastilla
Nova
Santa Ponça
S'Arena
Magaluf
Cap Enderrocat

*Barcelona*

Cap de Cala Figuera
*Bahía de Palma*

*Maó*

*Valencia*

## Mallorca
Majorca

*Eivissa
Denia*

C

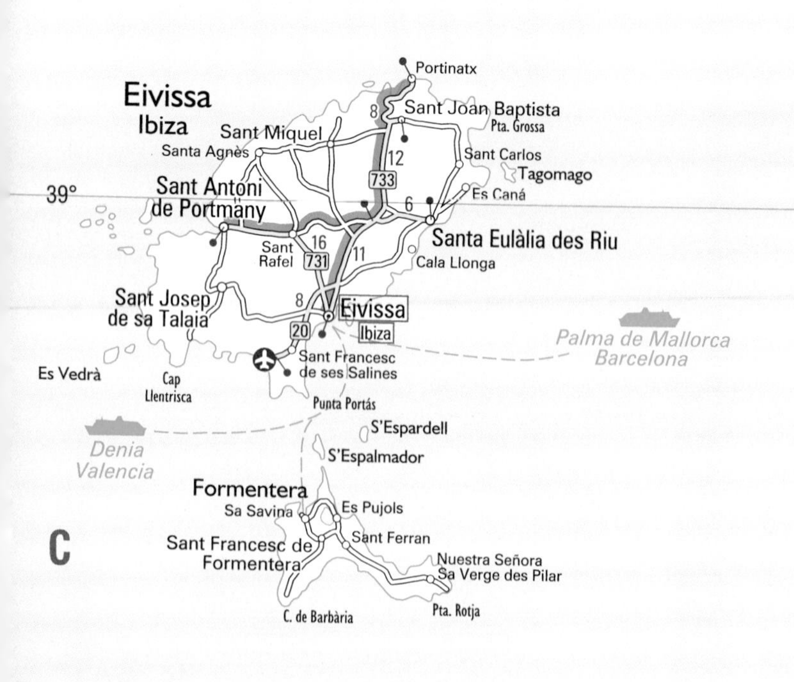

# Eivissa
## Ibiza

Portinatx
8
Sant Joan Baptista
Sant Miquel
Pta. Grossa
Santa Agnès
12
Sant Carlos
733
Tagomago
Es Caná
**Sant Antoni**
**de Portmany**
6
39°
16
Santa Eulàlia des Riu
Sant
731
11
Rafel
Cala Llonga
**Sant Josep**
**de sa Talaia**
8
**Eivissa**
Ibiza
20
Es Vedrà
Sant Francesc
Cap
de ses Salines
*Palma de Mallorca*
Llentrisca
*Barcelona*
Punta Portás
S'Espardell
*Denia*
S'Espalmador
*Valencia*
# Formentera
Sa Savina
Es Pujols
Sant Ferran
**Sant Francesc de**
**Formentera**
Nuestra Señora
Sa Verge des Pilar
C. de Barbària
Pta. Rotja

1
2°
2

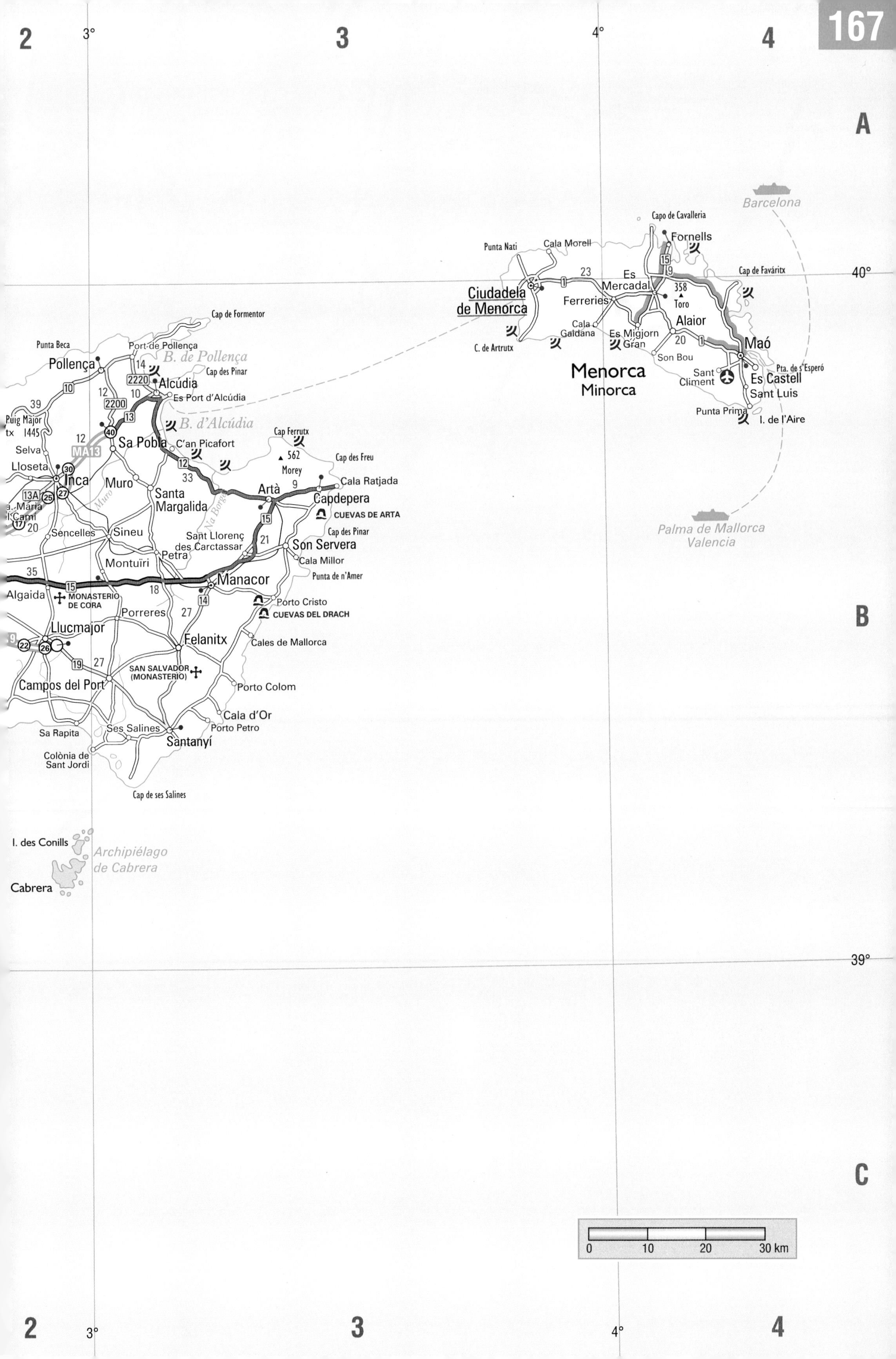

2
3
4
3°
4°
A
B
C
40°
39°
Barcelona
Capo de Cavalleria
Fornells
Punta Nati
Cala Morell
Cap de Favàritx
23
Es
Mercadal
358
Toro
Ciudadela
de Menorca
Ferreries
Cala
Galdana
Alaior
Es Migjorn
Gran
20
Son Bou
Maó
C. de Artrutx
Menorca
Minorca
Sant
Climent
Es Castell
Sant Luis
Pta. de s'Esperó
Punta Prima
I. de l'Aire
Palma de Mallorca
Valencia
Cap de Formentor
Punta Beca
Port de Pollença
B. de Pollença
Pollença
Cap des Pinar
Alcúdia
Es Port d'Alcúdia
B. d'Alcúdia
Puig Major
1445
Selva
Sa Pobla
C'an Picafort
Cap Ferrutx
562
Morey
Cap des Freu
Lloseta
Inca
Muro
Santa
Margalida
Artà
Cala Ratjada
Capdepera
CUEVAS DE ARTA
Cap des Pinar
Sencelles
Sineu
Sant Llorenç
des Carctassar
Petra
Son Servera
Cala Millor
Montuïri
Punta de n'Amer
Algaida
MONASTERIO
DE CORA
Manacor
Porto Cristo
CUEVAS DEL DRACH
Porreres
Llucmajor
Felanitx
Cales de Mallorca
SAN SALVADOR
(MONASTERIO)
Campos del Port
Porto Colom
Cala d'Or
Porto Petro
Sa Rapita
Ses Salines
Santanyí
Colònia de
Sant Jordi
Cap de ses Salines
I. des Conills
Archipiélago
de Cabrera
Cabrera
0
10
20
30 km

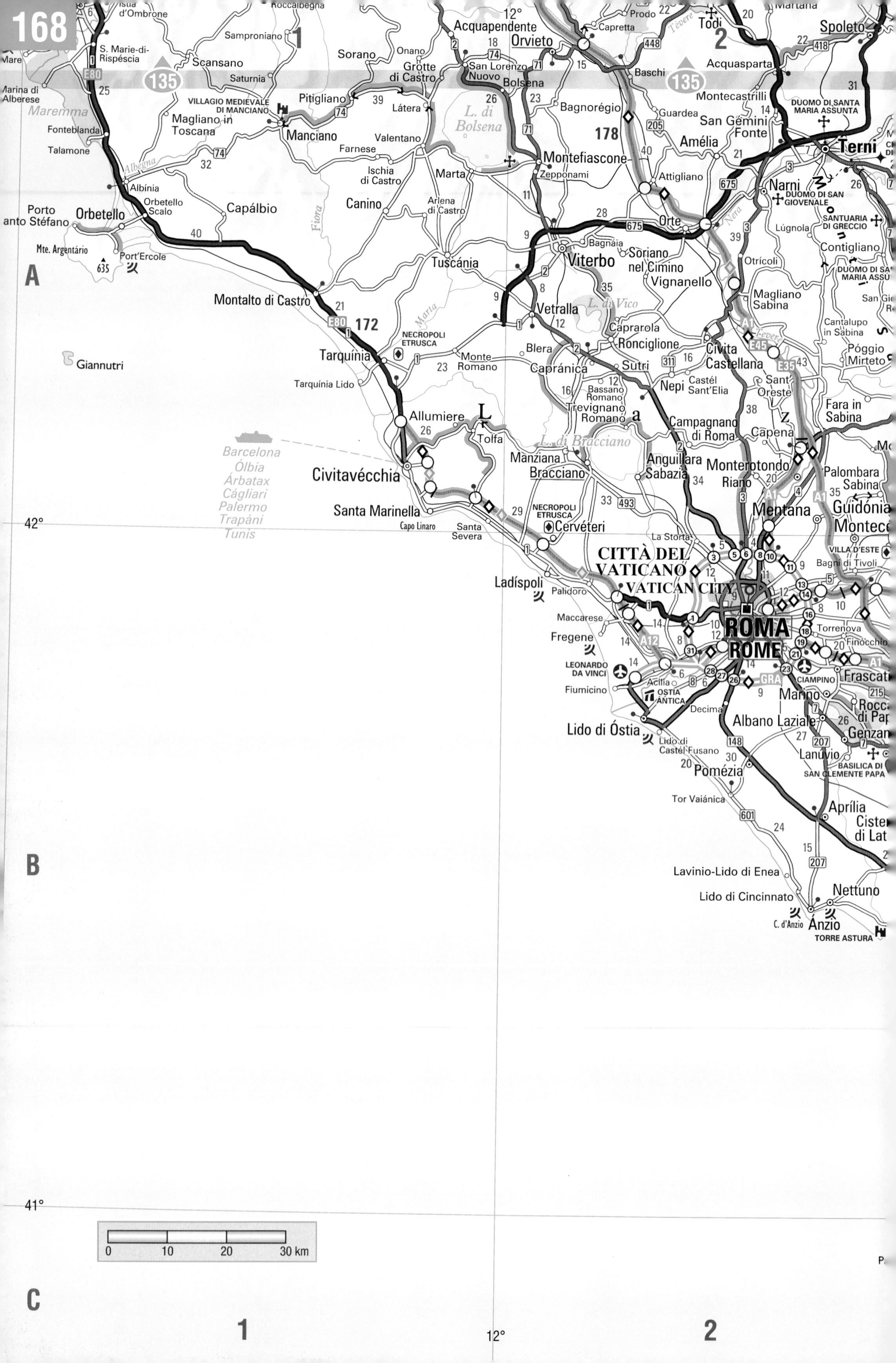

Acquapendente
Orvieto
Todi
Spoleto
Sampronianо
Scansano
Sorano
Onano
Grotte di Castro
San Lorenzo Nuovo
Bolsena
Capretta
Prodo
Baschi
Acquasparta
Montecastrilli
S. Marie-di-Rispéscia
Marina di Alberese
Maremma
Saturnia
Pitigliano
Látera
L. di Bolsena
Bagnorégio
Guardea
San Gémini Fonte
DUOMO DI SANTA MARIA ASSUNTA
Terni
VILLAGIO MEDIEVALE DI MANCIANO
Magliano in Toscana
Manciano
Valentano
Fonteblanda
Talamone
Farnese
Montefiascone
Zepponami
Amélia
Attigliano
Albegna
Ischia di Castro
Marta
Albínia
Orbetello Scalo
Porto Santo Stéfano
Orbetello
Capálbio
Canino
Arlena di Castro
Fiora
Orte
Narni
DUOMO DI SAN GIOVENALE
SANTUARIA DI GRECCIO
Lúgnola
Mte. Argentário
Port'Ercole
Tuscánia
Viterbo
Bagnáia
Soriano nel Cimino
Vignanello
Otrícoli
Contigliano
DUOMO DI SANTA MARIA ASSUNTA
Montalto di Castro
Vetralla
L. di Vico
Magliano Sabina
Caprarola
Ronciglione
Cantalupo in Sabina
Póggio Mirteto
NECROPOLI ETRUSCA
Tarquínia
Giannutri
Monte Romano
Blera
Caprаnica
Sutri
Civita Castellana
Nepi
Castél Sant'Elia
Sant'Oreste
Tarquínia Lido
Bassano Romano
Trevignano Romano
Fara in Sabina
Allumiere
Tolfa
L. di Bracciano
Campagnano di Roma
Capena
Barcelona
Ólbia
Árbatax
Cágliari
Palermo
Trapáni
Tunis
Civitavécchia
Manziana
Bracciano
Anguillara Sabazia
Monterotondo
Riano
Palombara Sabina
Santa Marinella
Capo Linaro
Santa Severa
NECROPOLI ETRUSCA
Cervéteri
Mentana
Guidónia
La Storta
CITTÀ DEL VATICANO
VATICAN CITY
VILLA D'ESTE
Bagni di Tivoli
Ladíspoli
Palidoro
Maccarese
Fregene
ROMA
ROME
Torrenova
Finocchio
LEONARDO DA VINCI
Fiumicino
Acilia
OSTIA ANTICA
CIAMPINO
Frascati
Marino
Decima
Albano Laziale
Lido di Óstia
Lido di Castél Fusano
Pomézia
Lanúvio
BASILICA DI SAN CLEMENTE PAPA
Tor Vaiánica
Aprília
Lavinio-Lido di Enea
Lido di Cincinnato
Nettuno
C. d'Anzio
Anzio
TORRE ASTURA
42°
41°
12°
0 10 20 30 km
A
B
C
1
2

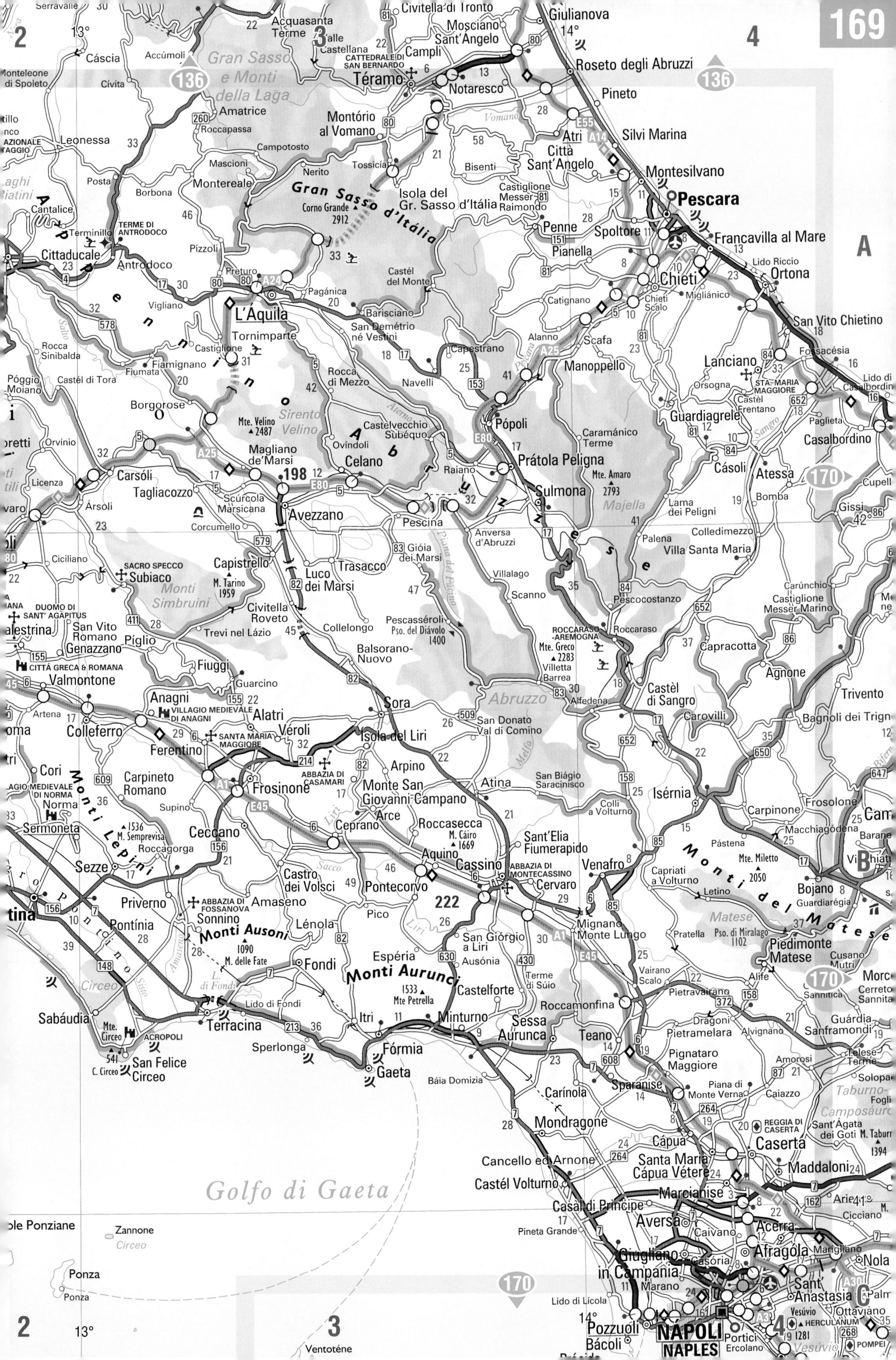
Gran Sasso e Monti della Laga
Gran Sasso d'Itália
Corno Grande 2912
Téramo
Giulianova
Roseto degli Abruzzi
Pineto
Silvi Marina
Atri
Città Sant'Angelo
Montesilvano
Pescara
Francavilla al Mare
Chieti
Ortona
San Vito Chietino
Lanciano
Fossacésia
Guardiagrele
Casalbordino
Atessa
Vasto
Amatrice
Leonessa
Campotosto
Montório al Vomano
Notaresco
Campli
Civitella di Tronto
Acquasanta Terme
Cáscia
Accúmoli
Montereale
Posta
Borbona
Cittaducale
Antrodoco
Terme di Antrodoco
Terminillo
Cantalice
L'Aquila
Tornimparte
Castiglione
Fiamignano
Borgorose
Mte. Velino 2487
Sirente Velino
Celano
Magliano de'Marsi
Avezzano
Carsóli
Tagliacozzo
Scúrcola Marsicana
Capistrello
Subiaco
Sacro Speco
Monti Simbruini
M. Tarino 1959
Luco dei Marsi
Trasacco
Pescina
Castelvecchio Subequo
Pópoli
Prátola Peligna
Sulmona
Raiano
Mte. Amaro 2793
Majella
Caramánico Terme
Manoppello
Scafa
Penne
Pianella
Spoltore
Capestrano
Navelli
Anversa d'Abruzzi
Scanno
Villalago
Pescasséroli
Pso. del Diávolo 1400
Roccaraso
Pescocostanzo
Castèl di Sangro
Capracotta
Agnone
Isérnia
Venafro
Sora
Isola del Liri
Arpino
Frosinone
Ferentino
Alatri
Anagni
Fiuggi
Colleferro
Valmontone
Palestrina
Genazzano
Ceccano
Ceprano
Pontecorvo
Aquino
Cassino
Abbazia di Montecassino
Monti Lepini
Sezze
Latina
Priverno
Pontínia
Sonnino
Monti Ausoni
Fondi
Terracina
Sabáudia
San Felice Circeo
Sperlonga
Gaeta
Fórmia
Monti Aurunci
Minturno
Sessa Aurunca
Teano
Mondragone
Cápua
Caserta
Maddaloni
Santa Maria Cápua Vétere
Marcianise
Aversa
Acerra
Afrágola
Giugliano in Campania
Nola
Pozzuoli
Bácoli
Nápoli
Naples
Portici
Ercolano
Vesúvio
Ottaviano
Sant'Anastasia
Piedimonte Matese
Monti del Matese
Bojano
Golfo di Gaeta
Isole Ponziane
Zannone
Ponza
Ventoténe
Abruzzo
Appennino Abruzzese

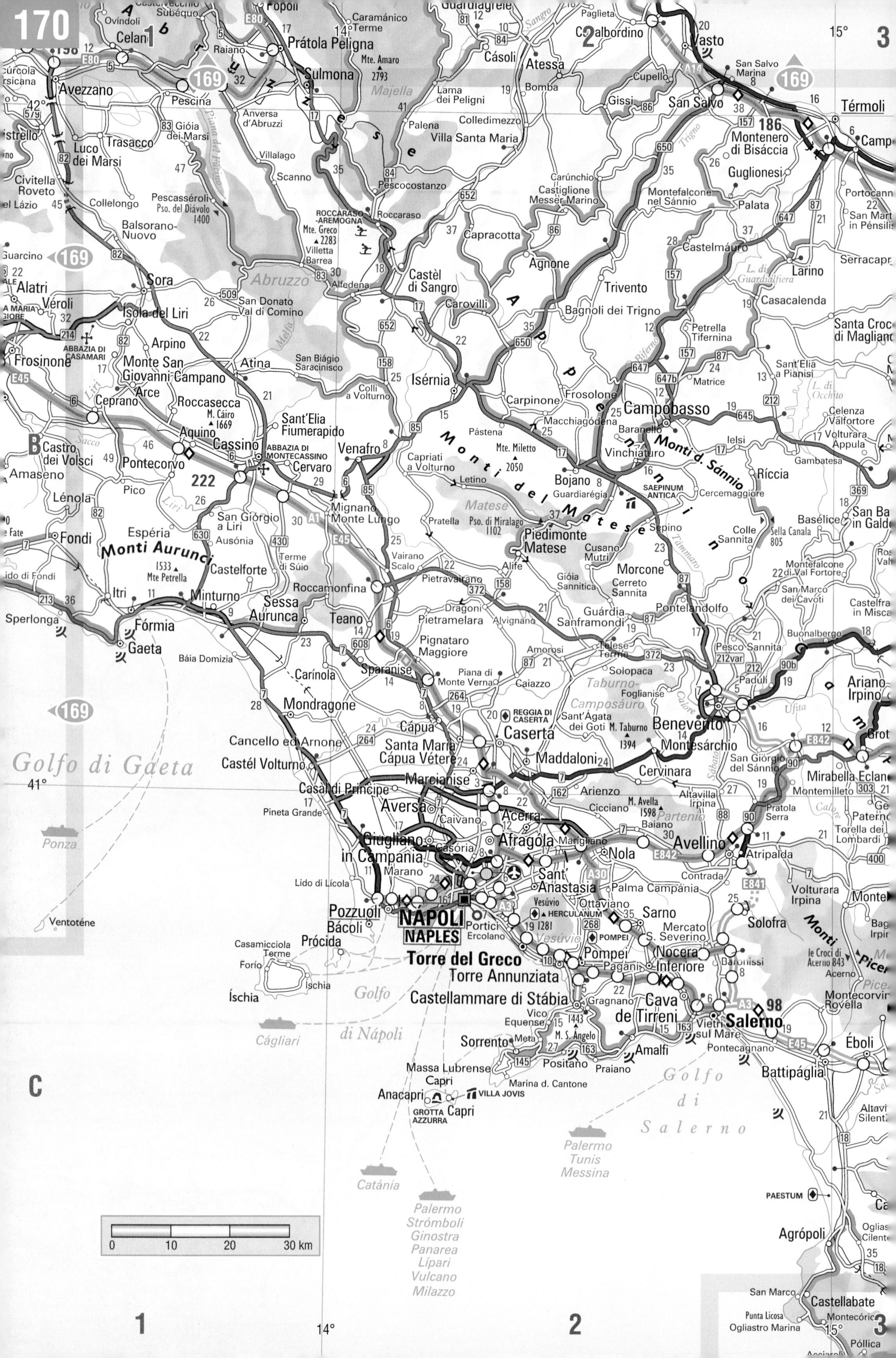

Ovíndoli
Celano
Pratola Peligna
Caramánico Terme
Raiano
Sulmona
Mte. Amaro 2793
Majella
Avezzano
Pescina
Anversa d'Abruzzo
Gióia dei Marsi
Luco dei Marsi
Trasacco
Villalago
Scanno
Civitella Roveto
Collelongo
Pescasséroli
Pso. del Diávolo 1400
Balsorano-Nuovo
Roccaraso
Mte. Greco 2283
Villetta Barrea
Alfedena
Pescocostanzo
Palena
Villa Santa Maria
Colledimezzo
Lama dei Peligni
Cásoli
Atessa
Bomba
Casalbordino
Vasto
San Salvo Marina
San Salvo
Cupello
Gissi
Térmoli
Montenero di Bisáccia
Guglionesi
Montefalcone nel Sánnio
Palata
Carúnchio
Castiglione Messer Marino
Capracotta
Agnone
Castelmáuro
Larino
Trivento
Casacalenda
Santa Croce di Magliano
Castèl di Sangro
Carovilli
Bagnoli dei Trigno
Petrella Tifernina
Sant'Elia a Pianisi
Abruzzo
Sora
Alatri
Véroli
Ísola del Liri
San Donato Val di Comino
Arpino
Frosinone
Abbazia di Casamari
Monte San Giovanni Campano
Atina
San Biágio Saracinisco
Arce
Ceprano
Roccasecca
M. Cáiro 1669
Aquino
Cassino
Abbazia di Montecassino
Cervaro
Pontecorvo
Castro dei Volsci
Amaseno
Pico
Lénola
Fondi
Espéria
San Giórgio a Liri
Ausónia
Monti Aurunci
Mte Petrella 1533
Castelforte
Terme di Súio
Itri
Minturno
Sperlonga
Fórmia
Gaeta
Báia Domizia
Sessa Aurunca
Roccamonfina
Teano
Colli a Volturno
Isérnia
Venafro
Mignano Monte Lungo
Vairano Scalo
Pietravairano
Capriati a Volturno
Letino
Monti del Matese
Mte. Miletto 2050
Matese
Pso. di Miralago 1102
Pratella
Piedimonte Matese
Alife
Carpinone
Frosolone
Macchiagódena
Campobasso
Baranello
Vinchiaturo
Monti d. Sánnio
Bojano
Guardiarégia
Saepinum Antica
Sepino
Cercemaggiore
Ríccia
Gambatesa
Colle Sannita
Morcone
Cusano Mutri
Cerreto Sannita
Gióia Sannitica
Guárdia Sanframondi
Pontelandolfo
Pesco Sannita
Dragoni
Pietramelara
Pignataro Maggiore
Sparanise
Carínola
Mondragone
Cancello ed Arnone
Castél Volturno
Piana di Monte Verna
Caiazzo
Cápua
Santa Maria Cápua Vétere
Reggia di Caserta
Caserta
Maddaloni
Marcianise
Casal di Príncipe
Aversa
Acerra
Afragola
Giugliano in Campania
Marano
Caivano
Casória
Marigliano
Nola
Sant'Anastasia
Palma Campania
Telese Terme
Solopaca
Taburno-Camposáuro
Sant'Ágata dei Goti
M. Taburno 1394
Benevento
Montesárchio
Cervinara
Arienzo
Cicciano
M. Avella 1598
Baiano
Avellino
Atripalda
Ariano Irpino
Mirabella Eclano
Golfo di Gaeta
Ponza
Ventoténe
Lido di Lícola
Pozzuoli
Bácoli
Prócida
Casamicciola Terme
Forío
Íschia
NÁPOLI
NAPLES
Pórtici
Ercolano
Vesúvio 1281
Herculanum
Pompei
Ottaviano
Sarno
Torre del Greco
Torre Annunziata
Castellammare di Stábia
Nocera Inferiore
Cava de' Tirreni
Salerno
Vietri sul Mare
Golfo di Nápoli
Vico Equense
Sorrento
Positano
Amalfi
Praiano
Massa Lubrense
Capri
Anacapri
Grotta Azzurra
Villa Jovis
Marina d. Cantone
Cágliari
Catánia
Palermo Tunis Messina
Palermo Strómboli Ginostra Panarea Lípari Vulcano Milazzo
Golfo di Salerno
Solofra
Pontecagnano
Battipáglia
Éboli
Paestum
Agrópoli
Castellabate
San Marco
Punta Licosa
Ogliastro Marina
0 10 20 30 km
41°
14°
15°
1
2
3
B
C

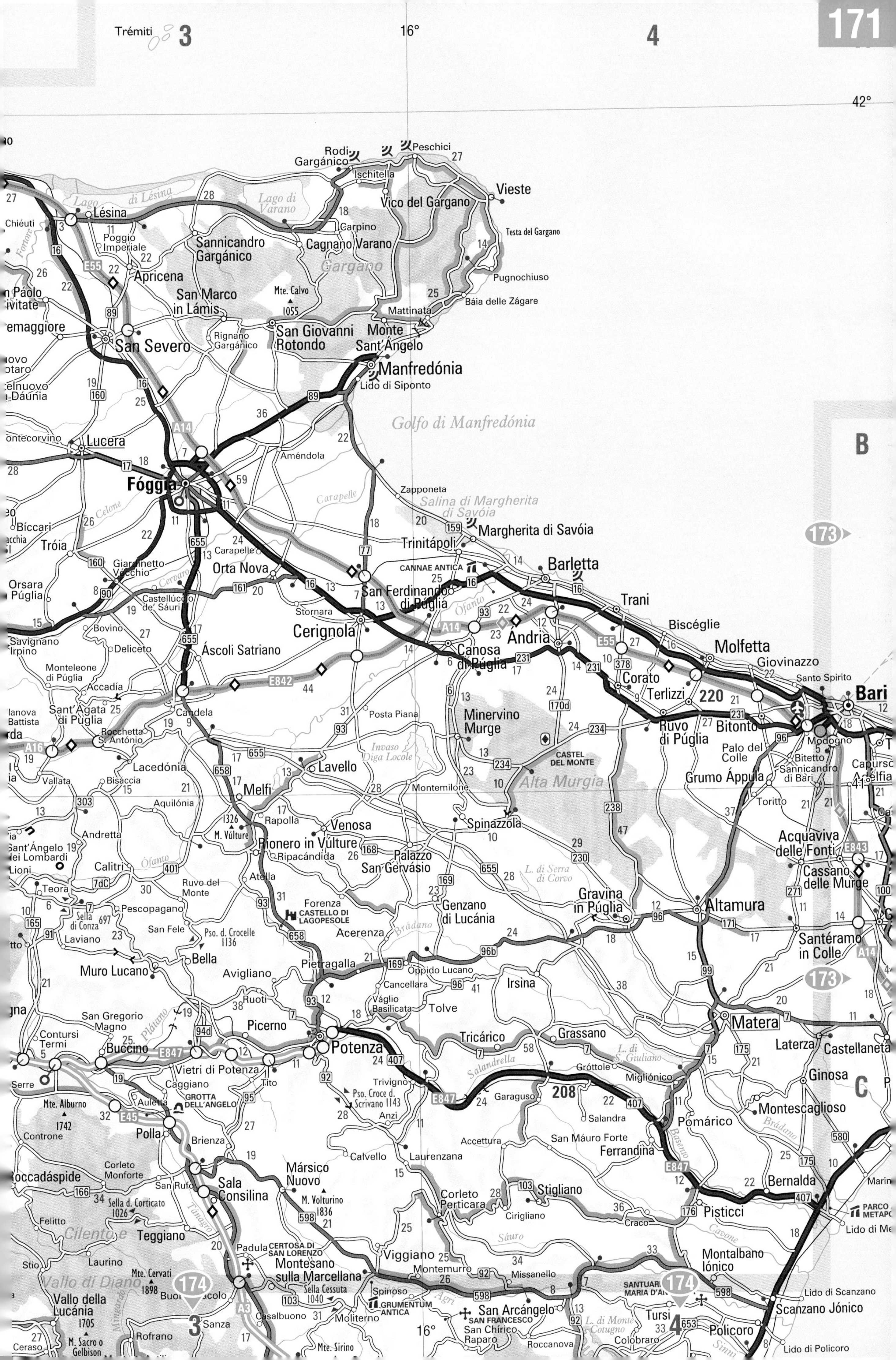
Trémiti
3
16°
4
42°
Rodi Gargánico
Peschici
Ischitella
Vieste
Lago di Lésina
Lago di Varano
Vico del Gargano
Lésina
Carpino
Testa del Gargano
Chiéuti
Poggio Imperiale
Sannicandro Gargánico
Cagnano Varano
Gargano
Apricena
Pugnochiuso
San Paolo di Civitate
San Marco in Lámis
Mte. Calvo 1055
Báia delle Zágare
Mattinata
San Giovanni Rotondo
Monte Sant'Ángelo
Rignano Gargánico
San Severo
Manfredónia
Lido di Siponto
Golfo di Manfredónia
Lucera
Fóggia
Améndola
B
Zapponeta
Salina di Margherita di Savóia
Bíccari
Tróia
Margherita di Savóia
Trinitápoli
Carapelle
Giardinetto Vecchio
Orta Nova
CANNAE ANTICA
Barletta
Orsara di Púglia
San Ferdinando di Púglia
Trani
Castelluccio de' Sáuri
Stornara
Biscéglie
Cerignola
Ándria
Bovino
Molfetta
Savignano Irpino
Deliceto
Áscoli Satriano
Canosa di Púglia
Giovinazzo
Monteleone di Púglia
Corato
Santo Spirito
Accadía
Terlizzi
Bari
Sant'Ágata di Púglia
Candela
Posta Piana
Minervino Murge
Ruvo di Púglia
Bitonto
Rocchetta S. António
Modugno
Palo del Colle
Bitetto
Lacedónia
Lavello
Invaso Diga Locone
CASTEL DEL MONTE
Sannicandro di Bari
Vallata
Bisáccia
Melfi
Montemilone
Alta Murgia
Grumo Áppula
Aquilónia
Toritto
Rapolla
Spinazzola
Andretta
M. Vúlture
Venosa
Sant'Ángelo dei Lombardi
Rionero in Vúlture
Acquaviva delle Fonti
Calitri
Ripacándida
Palazzo San Gervásio
Lioni
Cassano delle Murge
Ruvo del Monte
Atella
L. di Serra di Corvo
Teora
Forenza
Gravina in Púglia
Altamura
Pescopagano
CASTELLO DI LAGOPESOLE
Genzano di Lucánia
Sella di Conza
Acerenza
Laviano
San Fele
Pso. d. Crocelle 1136
Santéramo in Colle
Bella
Muro Lucano
Avigliano
Pietragalla
Oppido Lucano
Irsina
Cancellara
Ruoti
Váglio Basilicata
Tolve
San Gregorio Magno
Matera
Contursi Terme
Picerno
Tricárico
Grassano
Laterza
Castellaneta
Buccino
Vietri di Potenza
Potenza
L. di S. Giuliano
Serre
Tito
Gróttole
Migliónico
Ginosa
Caggiano
Trivigno
C
Mte. Alburno 1742
Auletta
GROTTA DELL'ANGELO
Pso. Croce d. Scrivano 1143
Garaguso
Montescaglioso
Anzi
Salandra
Pomárico
Polla
Controne
Brienza
Accettura
San Máuro Forte
Ferrandina
Calvello
Laurenzana
Corleto Monforte
Roccadáspide
Sala Consilina
Bernalda
San Rufo
Mársico Nuovo
Stigliano
Sella d. Corticato 1026
M. Volturino 1836
Corleto Perticara
Pisticci
PARCO METAPONTO
Felitto
Cirigliano
Cilento e
Teggiano
Craco
Lido di Metaponto
Padula
CERTOSA DI SAN LORENZO
Montesano sulla Marcellana
Viggiano
Montalbano Iónico
Stio
Laurino
Vallo di Diano
Mte. Cervati 1898
Montemurro
Missanello
SANTUARIO MARIA D'ANGLONA
Vallo della Lucánia
Sella Cessuta 1040
Spinoso
Lido di Scanzano
GRUMENTUM ANTICA
San Arcángelo
SAN FRANCESCO
Scanzano Jónico
Sanza
Casalbuono
Moliterno
San Chírico Raparo
L. di Monte Cotugno
Tursi
Policoro
Rofrano
M. Sacro o Gelbison
Mte. Sirino
Roccanova
Colobraro
Lido di Policoro
Ceraso
173
174

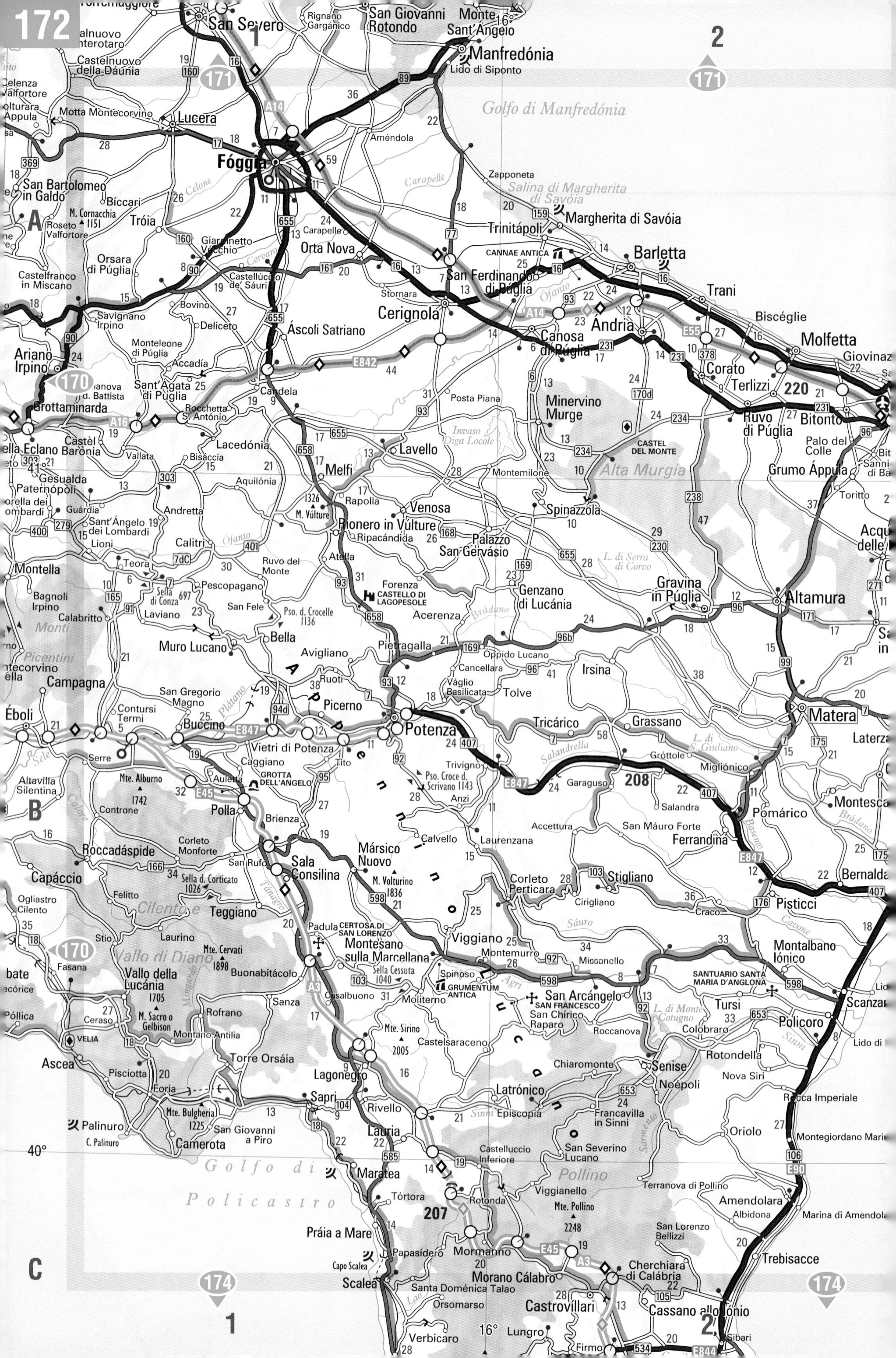

San Severo
Rignano Gargánico
San Giovanni Rotondo
Monte Sant'Angelo
Manfredónia
Lido di Siponto
Castelnuovo della Dáunia
Celenza Valfortore
Volturara Appula
Motta Montecorvino
Lucera
Fóggia
Golfo di Manfredónia
Améndola
Zapponeta
Salina di Margherita di Savóia
Margherita di Savóia
Trinitápoli
San Bartolomeo in Galdo
Bíccari
M. Cornacchia 1151
Roseto Valfortore
Tróia
Giardinetto Vecchio
Orsara di Púglia
Carapelle
Orta Nova
CANNAE ANTICA
Barletta
Castelfranco in Miscano
Castelluccio de' Sauri
San Ferdinando di Púglia
Stornara
Cerignola
Trani
Bisceglie
Molfetta
Giovinazzo
Savignano Irpino
Bovino
Deliceto
Áscoli Satriano
Canosa di Púglia
Ándria
Corato
Terlizzi
Ariano Irpino
Monteleone di Púglia
Accadía
Sant'Ágata di Puglia
Candela
Posta Piana
Minervino Murge
Ruvo di Púglia
Bitonto
Grottaminarda
Rocchetta S. António
Invaso Diga Locone
CASTEL DEL MONTE
Palo del Colle
Mirabella Eclano
Castèl Baronia
Vallata
Bisáccia
Lacedónia
Lavello
Montemilone
Alta Murgia
Grumo Áppula
Gesualdo
Paternópoli
Aquilónia
Melfi
Rapolla
Venosa
Spinazzola
Guárdia Lombardi
Andretta
M. Vúlture 1326
Toritto
Sant'Ángelo dei Lombardi
Lioni
Calitri
Rionero in Vúlture
Ripacándida
Palazzo San Gervásio
Montella
Teora
Ruvo del Monte
Atella
L. di Serra di Corvo
Bagnoli Irpino
Sella di Conza 697
Pescopagano
Forenza
CASTELLO DI LAGOPESOLE
Genzano di Lucánia
Gravina in Púglia
Altamura
Calabritto
Laviano
San Fele
Pso. d. Crocelle 1136
Acerenza
Monti Picentini
Muro Lucano
Bella
Avigliano
Pietragalla
Oppido Lucano
Irsina
Montecorvino Rovella
Campagna
Ruoti
Cancellara
Váglio Basilicata
Tolve
Matera
San Gregorio Magno
Picerno
Contursi Terme
Éboli
Buccino
Potenza
Tricárico
Grassano
Vietri di Potenza
L. di S. Giuliano
Laterza
Serre
Caggiano
Tito
Trivigno
Grottole
Miglionico
Altavilla Silentina
Auletta
GROTTA DELL'ANGELO
Pso. Croce d. Scrivano 1143
Garaguso
Mte. Alburno 1742
Anzi
Salandra
Controne
Polla
Brienza
Accettura
San Máuro Forte
Pomárico
Montescaglioso
Ferrandina
Roccadáspide
Corleto Monforte
Calvello
Laurenzana
San Rufo
Sala Consilina
Mársico Nuovo
Capáccio
Sella d. Corticato 1026
M. Volturino 1836
Corleto Perticara
Stigliano
Bernalda
Ogliastro Cilento
Felitto
Teggiano
Cirigliano
Pisticci
Cilento e Vallo di Diano
Craco
Padula
CERTOSA DI SAN LORENZO
Viggiano
Stio
Laurino
Montesano sulla Marcellana
Montemurro
Montalbano Iónico
Mte. Cervati 1898
Missanello
Fasana
Vallo della Lucánia
Buonabitácolo
Sella Cessuta 1040
Spinoso
GRUMENTUM ANTICA
SANTUARIO SANTA MARIA D'ANGLONA
Mte. Sacro o Gelbison 1705
Casalbuono
Moliterno
San Arcángelo
SAN FRANCESCO
San Chírico Raparo
Tursi
Scanzano
Ceraso
Sanza
Rofrano
L. di Monte Cotugno
Colobraro
Policoro
VELIA
Montano Antilia
Mte. Sirino 2005
Castelsaraceno
Roccanova
Ascea
Torre Orsáia
Rotondella
Lido di Policoro
Pisciotta
Lagonegro
Chiaromonte
Senise
Nóepoli
Nova Siri
Foria
Latrónico
Rocca Imperiale
Palinuro
Mte. Bulgheria 1225
Sapri
Rivello
Episcopia
Francavilla in Sinni
C. Palinuro
San Giovanni a Piro
Camerota
Lauria
Oriolo
Montegiordano Marina
Castelluccio Inferiore
San Severino Lucano
Golfo di Policastro
Maratea
Pollino
Terranova di Pollino
Tórtora
Rotonda
Viggianello
Amendolara
Albidona
Mte. Pollino 2248
Marina di Amendolara
Práia a Mare
San Lorenzo Bellizzi
Papasídero
Mormanno
Trebisacce
Capo Scalea
Morano Cálabro
Cerchiara di Calábria
Scalea
Santa Doménica Talao
Orsomarso
Castrovillari
Cassano allo Iónio
Verbicaro
Lungro
Firmo
Sibari
Appennino Lucano
40°
16°

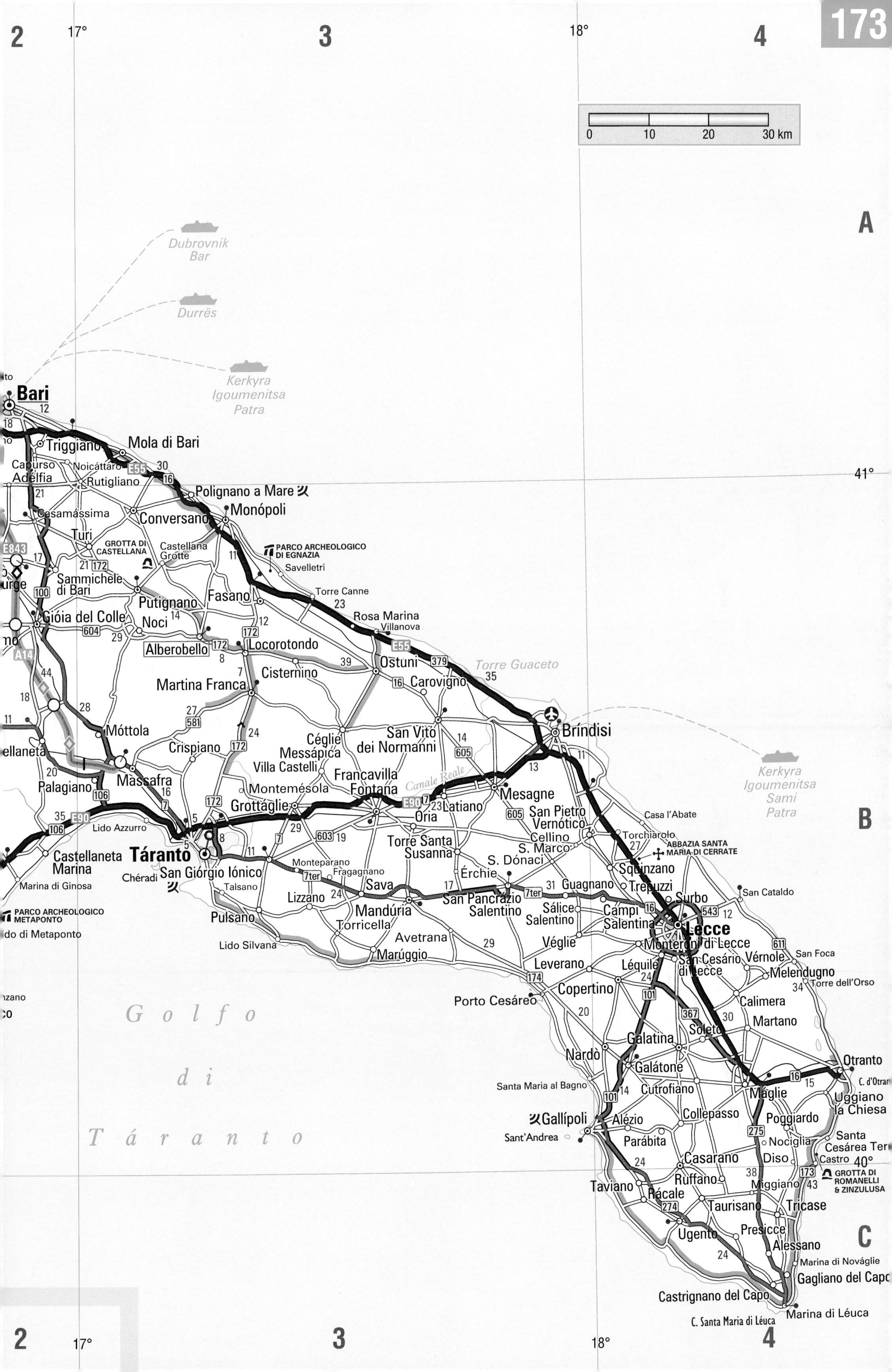
2
17°
3
18°
4
0
10
20
30 km
A
B
C
41°
40°
Dubrovnik
Bar
Durrës
Kerkyra
Igoumenitsa
Patra
Bari
Triggiano
Mola di Bari
Capurso
Noicáttaro
Adélfia
Rutigliano
Polignano a Mare
Monópoli
Casamássima
Conversano
Turi
GROTTA DI CASTELLANA
Castellana Grotte
PARCO ARCHEOLOGICO DI EGNAZIA
Savelletri
Sammichele di Bari
Fasano
Torre Canne
Putignano
Gióia del Colle
Noci
Rosa Marina
Villanova
Alberobello
Locorotondo
Ostuni
Cisternino
Carovigno
Torre Guaceto
Martina Franca
Bríndisi
Móttola
Crispiano
Céglie Messápica
San Vito dei Normanni
Villa Castelli
Francavilla Fontana
Canale Reale
Massafra
Palagiano
Montemésola
Grottáglie
Mesagne
Latiano
Oria
San Pietro Vernótico
Lido Azzurro
Castellaneta Marina
Táranto
Marina di Ginosa
Chéradi
San Giórgio Iónico
Talsano
Monteparano
Fragagnano
Torre Santa Susanna
Cellino
S. Marco
S. Dónaci
Casa l'Abate
Torchiarolo
ABBAZIA SANTA MARIA DI CERRATE
Squinzano
Trepuzzi
Érchie
Guagnano
Sava
Lizzano
Mandúria
San Pancrazio Salentino
Sálice Salentino
Campi Salentina
Surbo
San Cataldo
Lecce
PARCO ARCHEOLOGICO METAPONTO
Lido di Metaponto
Pulsano
Torricella
Avetrana
Marúggio
Lido Silvana
Véglie
Monteroni di Lecce
Leverano
Léquile
San Cesário di Lecce
Vérnole
San Foca
Melendugno
Torre dell'Orso
Porto Cesáreo
Copertino
Calimera
Martano
Golfo di Táranto
Galatina
Soleto
Nardò
Galátone
Otranto
C. d'Otranto
Santa Maria al Bagno
Cutrofiano
Máglie
Uggiano la Chiesa
Gallípoli
Alézio
Collepasso
Poggiardo
Sant'Andrea
Parábita
Nociglia
Santa Cesárea Terme
Casarano
Diso
Castro
GROTTA DI ROMANELLI & ZINZULUSA
Taviano
Ruffano
Miggiano
Rácale
Taurisano
Tricase
Ugento
Presicce
Alessano
Marina di Nováglie
Gagliano del Capo
Castrignano del Capo
C. Santa Maria di Léuca
Marina di Léuca
E55
E90
E843
A14
16
100
172
604
581
106
7
7ter
603
605
379
543
611
174
101
367
275
101
173
274
2
17°
3
18°
4

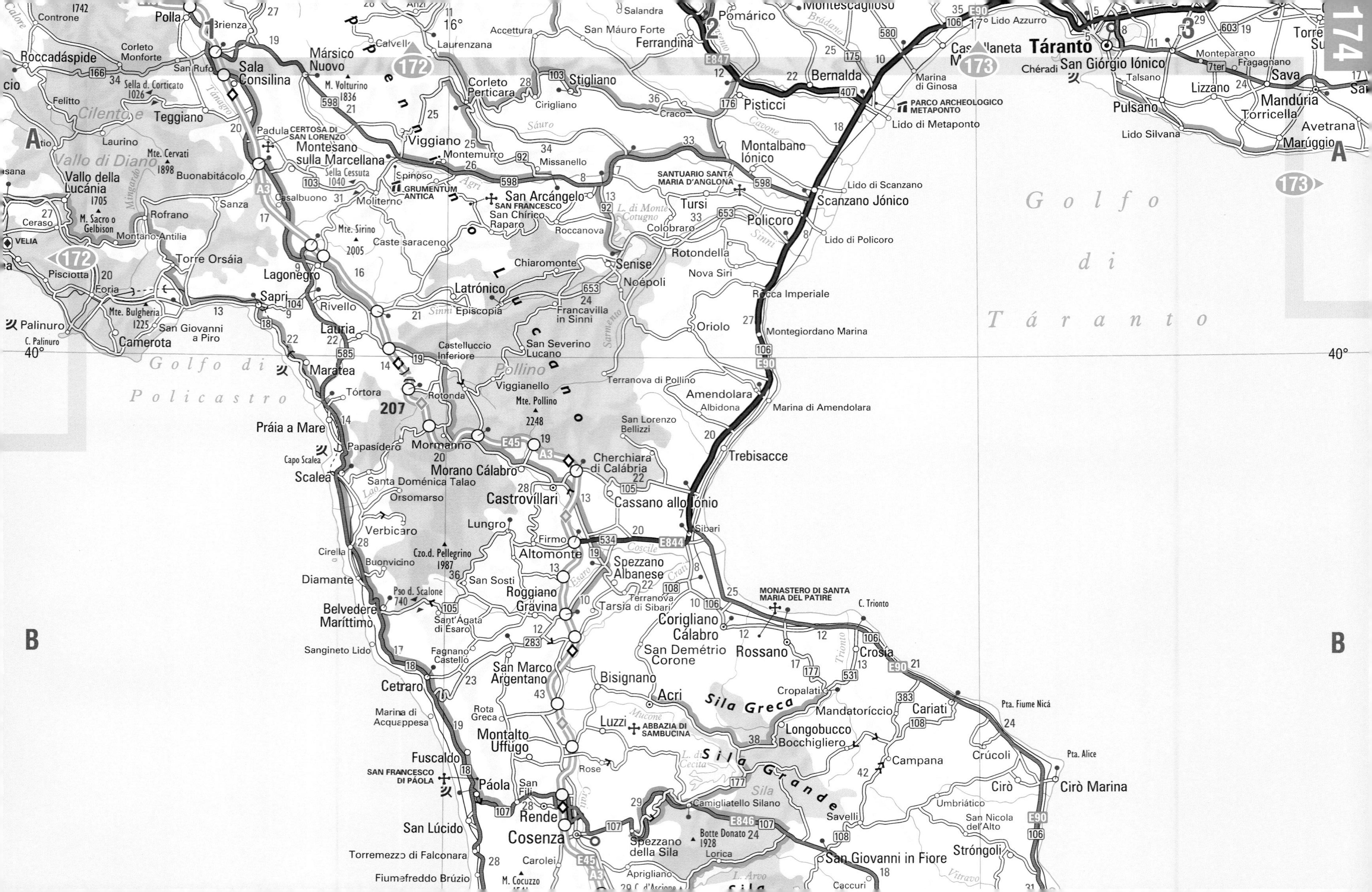

Golfo di Táranto
Golfo di Policastro
Táranto
San Giórgio Iónico
Pulsano
Lizzano
Sava
Mandúria
Torricella
Avetrana
Marúggio
Lido Silvana
Castellaneta
Marina di Ginosa
Bernalda
Pisticci
PARCO ARCHEOLOGICO METAPONTO
Lido di Metaponto
Pomárico
Ferrandina
Salandra
San Máuro Forte
Accettura
Stigliano
Cirigliano
Craco
Montalbano Iónico
Scanzano Jónico
Lido di Scanzano
Policoro
Lido di Policoro
Tursi
SANTUARIO SANTA MARIA D'ANGLONA
Colobraro
Rotondella
Nova Siri
Rocca Imperiale
Oriolo
Montegiordano Marina
Amendolara
Albidona
Marina di Amendolara
Trebisacce
Senise
Noépoli
Chiaromonte
Latrónico
Episcopia
Francavilla in Sinni
San Severino Lucano
Terranova di Pollino
San Lorenzo Bellizzi
Pollino
Mte. Pollino 2248
Viggianello
Rotonda
Castelluccio Inferiore
Cerchiara di Calábria
Cassano allo Iónio
Sibari
Castrovillari
Morano Cálabro
Mormanno
Laurenzana
Corleto Perticara
Viggiano
Montemurro
Missanello
San Arcángelo
SAN FRANCESCO
San Chírico Raparo
Roccanova
Castelsaraceno
Moliterno
GRUMENTUM ANTICA
Spinoso
Mte. Sirino 2005
Lagonegro
Rivello
Lauria
Maratea
Tórtora
Práia a Mare
Papasídero
Capo Scalea
Scalea
Santa Doménica Talao
Orsomarso
Verbicaro
Cirella
Diamante
Buonvicino
Czo.d. Pellegrino 1987
Lungro
Firmo
Altomonte
San Sosti
Pso d. Scalone 740
Belvedere Maríttimo
Sant'Ágata di Esaro
Roggiano Gravina
Spezzano Albanese
Terranova da Sibari
Tarsia
Corigliano Cálabro
San Demétrio Corone
Rossano
MONASTERO DI SANTA MARIA DEL PATIRE
C. Trionto
Crosia
Cropalati
Mandatoríccio
Cariati
Pta. Fiume Nicá
Longobucco
Bocchigliero
Campana
Crúcoli
Pta. Alice
Cirò
Cirò Marina
Umbriático
San Nicola dell'Alto
Stróngoli
Savelli
San Giovanni in Fiore
Caccuri
Sila Greca
Sila Grande
Acri
Bisignano
Luzzi
ABBAZIA DI SAMBUCINA
San Marco Argentano
Fagnano Castello
Sangineto Lido
Cetraro
Marina di Acquappesa
Rota Greca
Montalto Uffugo
Rose
Fuscaldo
SAN FRANCESCO DI PÁOLA
Páola
San Fili
Rende
Cosenza
San Lúcido
Torremezzo di Falconara
Fiumefreddo Brúzio
Carolei
M. Cocuzzo
Camigliatello Silano
Botte Donato 1928
Lorica
Spezzano della Sila
Aprigliano
Polla
Brienza
Sala Consilina
Mársico Nuovo
M. Volturino 1836
Calvello
Padula
CERTOSA DI SAN LORENZO
Montesano sulla Marcellana
Sella Cessuta 1040
Casalbuono
Sanza
Buonabitácolo
Mte. Cervati 1898
Teggiano
San Rufo
Sella d. Corticato 1026
Corleto Monforte
Roccadáspide
Controne
Felitto
Laurino
Cilento e Vallo di Diano
Vallo della Lucánia
M. Sacro o Gelbison 1705
Rofrano
Montano Antilia
Torre Orsáia
Ceraso
VELIA
Pisciotta
Foria
Mte. Bulgheria 1225
San Giovanni a Piro
Camerota
Palinuro
C. Palinuro
Sapri
40°
16°
17°

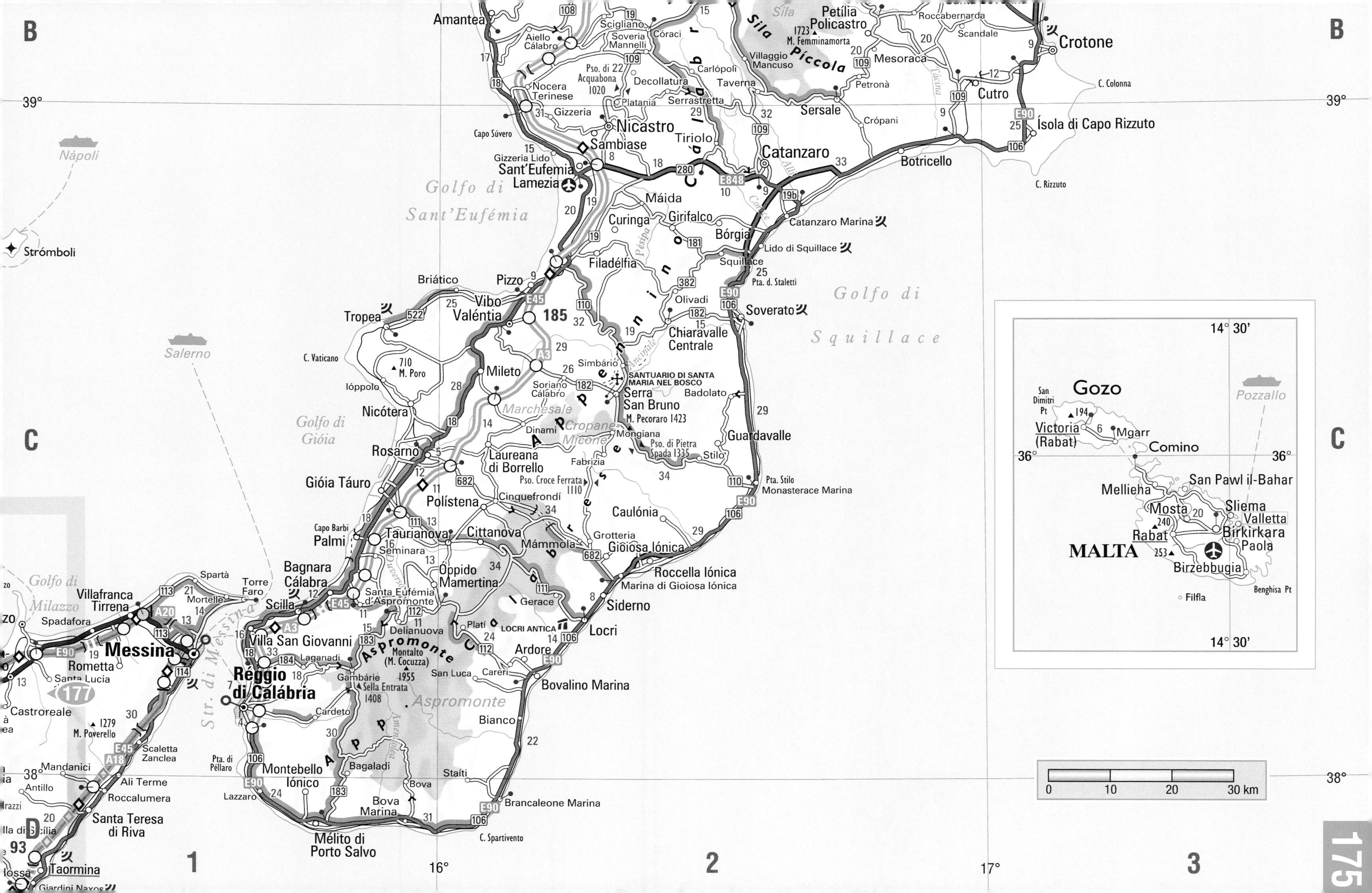

B B

39°

C

C

38°

**GOZO**

San Dimitri Pt

Victoria (Rabat)
194
6 Mgarr

Comino

Mellieħa

San Pawl il-Baħar
Mosta
20
Rabat 253
240
Sliema
Valletta
Birkirkara
Paola
Birżebbuġia

Benghia Pt

Filfla

**MALTA**

14° 30'

14° 30'

36°

36°

17°

30 km

20

10

0

3

Crotone
C. Colonna
9

Ísola di Capo Rizzuto
25
106
E90

C. Rizzuto

Roccabernarda
Scandale
20
12
9
Cutro

Petilia
Policastro
1723 M. femminamorta
109
Mesoraca
Petronà
20
109
L'ácina

Sila Piccola

Villaggio Mancuso

Sersale

Sila

Botricello

Crópani

Golfo di

Catanzaro Marina

Squillace

Golfo di Squillace

Lido di Squillace
25
Pta. d. Staletti

Carlópoli
Taverna
32
109
Soverato

Serrastretta
Decollatura
29
Tiriolo
Girifalco
181
Borgia
Squillace
E90
106

Coraci
Soveria Mannelli

Pso. di 22
Aquabona
1020
Platanía
Gizzeria
18
Máida
382
Olivadi
182
Chiaravalle Centrale
Badolato
29
Guadavalle

Pta. Stilo

Monasterace Marina

Scigliano
19
109
Nicastro
Sambiase
8
Filadélfia
19
15
Curinga
Serra San Bruno
M. Pecoraro 1423
Pso. di Pietra
Spada 1331
Stilo
110
E90
106

108
Nocera Terinese
31
Sant'Eufémia Lamezia
19
Soriano Cálabro
26
Dinami
Mongiana
M. Crocco
1110
Fabrizia
34
Caulónia

Aiello Cálabro
18
Gizzeria Lido
15
185
29
Simbário
182
Laureana di Borrello
Pso. Croce Ferrata
34
Grotteria
Roccella Iónica

Amantea
17
Capo Súvero
Golfo di Sant'Eufémia
Pizzo
9
E45
A3
Mileto
14
682
Cinquefrondi
Gioiosa Iónica
Marina di Gioiosa Iónica

Briático
Vibo Valéntia
Polistena
111
Cittanova
Mámmola
682
Siderno

Tropea
522
25
Nicótera
28
18
Rosarno
682
Óppido Mamertina
34
111
Gerace
8
Locri

C. Vaticano
710 M. Poro
Ióppolo
Gioia Táuro
11
Taurianova
13
Delianuova
112
Montalto (M. Cocuzza) 1955
Platí
24
Careri
Ardore
E90
106
Bovalino Marina

Golfo di Gioia
Capo Barbi
Palmi
12
Seminara
Santa Eufémia d'Aspromonte
Santa Cristina
San Luca
Staiti
22
Brancaleone Marina

Bagnara Cálabra
Scilla
A3
18
Gambárie 1408
Sella Entrata
183
Bova
31
C. Spartivento

Villa San Giovanni
33
184
LOCRI ANTICA
Cardeto
Bagaladi
Bova Marina
E90
106

Torre Faro
Spartà
21
Réggio di Calábria
16
Montebello Iónico
24
Mélito di Porto Salvo

Messina
113
A20
Villafranca Tirrena
Rometta
114
Pta. di Péllaro
Lazzaro

Strómboli

Nápoli

Salerno

Messina
E90
A18
Villafranca Tirrena
Spadafora
1279 M. Poverello
Castroreale
Rometta
Santa Lucia
Mandanici
Antillo
20
Ali Terme
Roccalumera
Santa Teresa di Riva
30
Scaletta Zanclea
Taormina
Giardini Naxos
38°
177
93

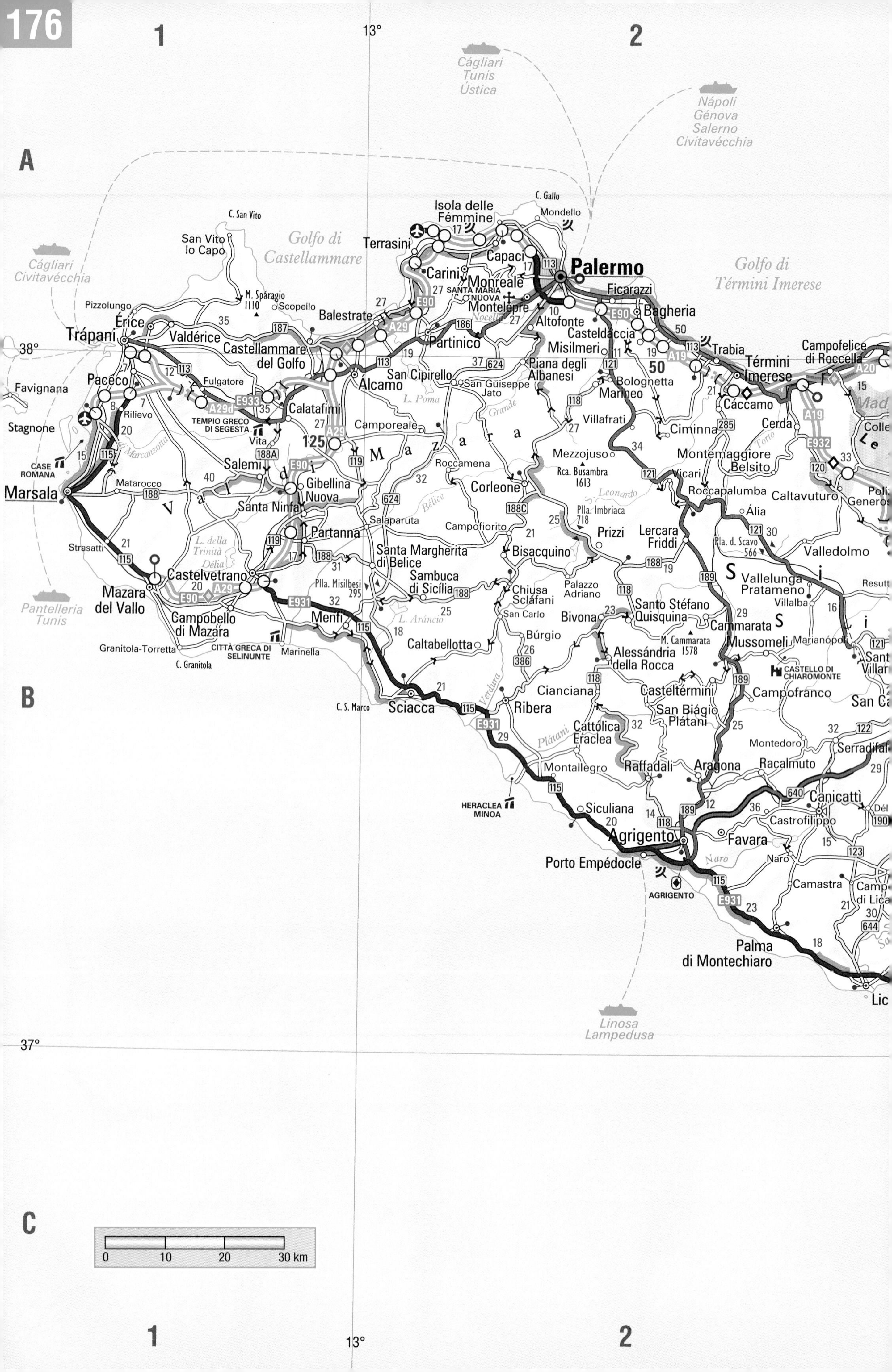
Cágliari
Tunis
Ústica
Nápoli
Génova
Salerno
Civitavécchia
Golfo di Castellammare
Golfo di Términi Imerese
Palermo
Trápani
Marsala
Agrigento
Mazara del Vallo
Castelvetrano
Sciacca
Alcamo
Partinico
Monreale
Bagheria
Términi Imerese
Corleone
Ribera
Canicattì
Favara
Licata
Palma di Montechiaro
Porto Empédocle
Érice
Paceco
Favignana
Stagnone
Salemi
Calatafimi
Castellammare del Golfo
San Vito lo Capo
Terrasini
Carini
Capaci
Isola delle Fémmine
Mondello
Misilmeri
Piana degli Albanesi
Lercara Friddi
Prizzi
Bisacquino
Menfi
Sambuca di Sicília
Santa Margherita di Belice
Partanna
Gibellina Nuova
Santa Ninfa
Caltabellotta
Bivona
Santo Stéfano Quisquina
Cammarata
Mussomeli
Casteltérmini
Raffadali
Aragona
Siculiana
Cattólica Eraclea
Montallegro
Campobello di Mazara
Linosa
Lampedusa
Pantelleria
Tunis
0 10 20 30 km

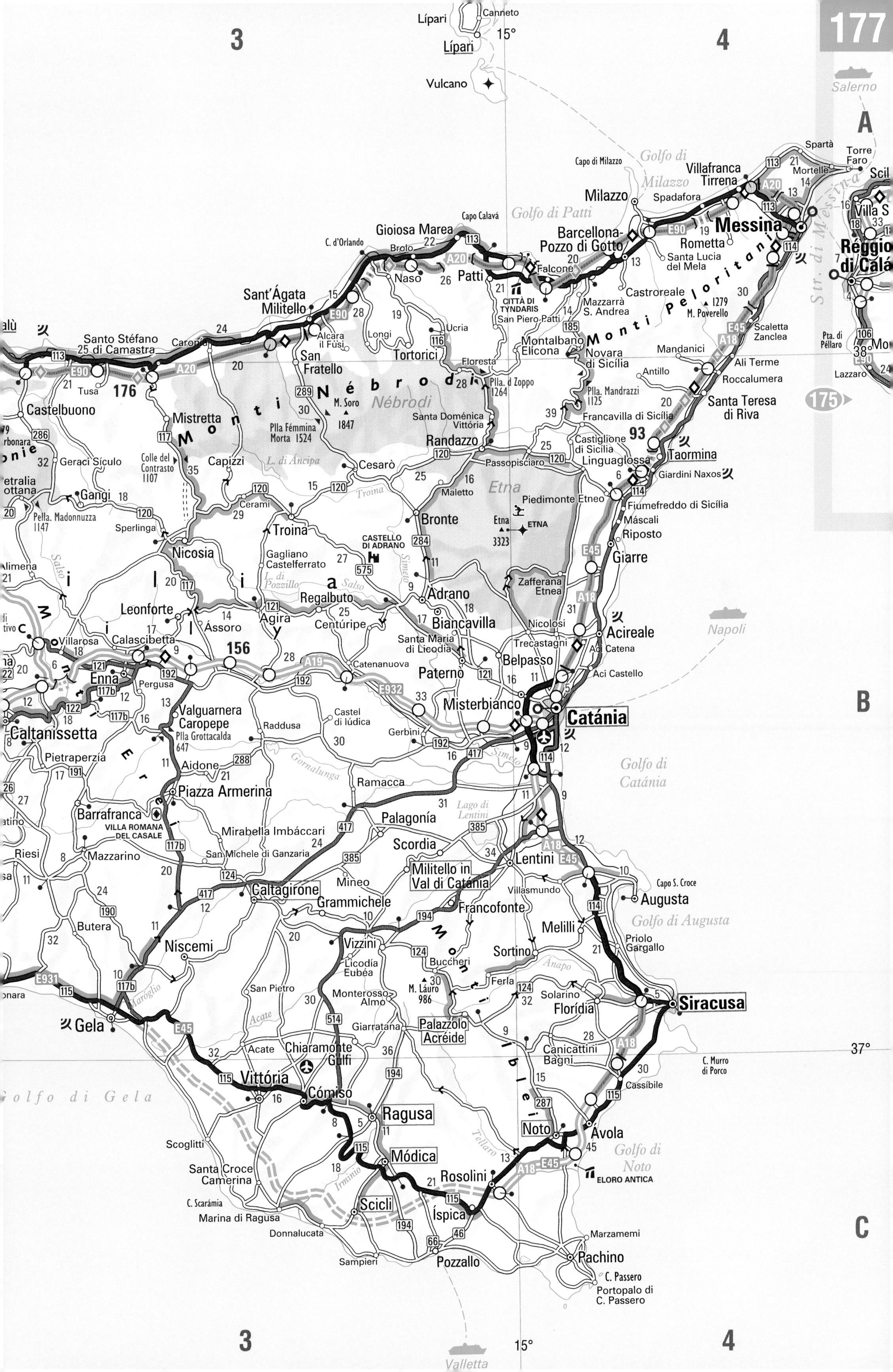

Lípari
Canneto
Vulcano
Salerno
Golfo di Milazzo
Capo di Milazzo
Villafranca Tirrena
Spartà
Torre Faro
Mortelle
Milazzo
Spadafora
Messina
Golfo di Patti
Capo Calavá
Gioiosa Marea
Barcellona-Pozzo di Gotto
Rometta
Santa Lucia del Mela
Réggio di Calábria
C. d'Orlando
Brolo
Naso
Patti
Falcone
Castroreale
Monti Peloritani
M. Poverello
Sant'Ágata Militello
Città di Tyndaris
San Piero Patti
Mazzarrà S. Andrea
Scaletta Zanclea
Santo Stéfano di Camastra
Caronia
Alcara li Fusi
Longi
Ucria
Tortorici
Montalbano Elicona
Novara di Sicília
Mandanici
Pta. di Péllaro
Lazzaro
San Fratello
Floresta
Ali Terme
Antillo
Roccalumera
Tusa
Monti Nébrodi
Nébrodi
M. Soro
Plla. d Zoppo
Plla. Mandrazzi
Santa Teresa di Riva
Castelbuono
Mistretta
Plla Fémmina Morta
Santa Doménica Vittória
Francavilla di Sicília
Randazzo
Castiglione di Sicília
Taormina
Colle del Contrasto
Geraci Sículo
Capizzi
L. di Áncipa
Cesarò
Passopisciaro
Linguaglossa
Giardini Naxos
Petralia Sottana
Gangi
Pella. Madonnuzza
Maletto
Etna
Piedimonte Etneo
Fiumefreddo di Sicília
Sperlinga
Cerami
Troina
Bronte
Máscali
Riposto
Castello di Adrano
Nicosia
Gagliano Castelferrato
Giarre
L. di Pozzillo
Regalbuto
Adrano
Zafferana Etnea
Leonforte
Agira
Centúripe
Biancavilla
Nicolosi
Acireale
Ássoro
Villarosa
Calascibetta
Santa Maria di Licodia
Trecastagni
Aci Catena
Napoli
Enna
Pergusa
Catenanuova
Paterno
Belpasso
Aci Castello
Caltanissetta
Valguarnera Caropepe
Plla Grottacalda
Raddusa
Castel di Iúdica
Misterbianco
Catánia
Gerbini
Pietraperzia
Aidone
Golfo di Catánia
Piazza Armerina
Ramacca
Barrafranca
Villa Romana del Casale
Palagonía
Lago di Lentini
Mirabella Imbáccari
Riesi
Mazzarino
San Michele di Ganzaria
Scordia
Lentini
Militello in Val di Catánia
Capo S. Croce
Caltagirone
Mineo
Villasmundo
Augusta
Grammichele
Francofonte
Golfo di Augusta
Butera
Melilli
Priolo Gargallo
Niscemi
Vizzini
Sortino
Licodía Eubéa
Buccheri
M. Láuro
Ferla
Siracusa
Gela
San Pietro
Monterosso Almo
Solarino
Florídia
Giarratana
Palazzolo Acréide
Canicattini Bagni
Acate
Chiaramonte Gulfi
Monti Iblei
C. Murro di Porco
Vittória
Cássibile
Golfo di Gela
Cómiso
Ragusa
Noto
Avola
Scoglitti
Módica
Golfo di Noto
Santa Croce Camerina
Rosolini
Eloro Antica
C. Scarámia
Scicli
Íspica
Marina di Ragusa
Donnalucata
Marzamemi
Pachino
Sampieri
Pozzallo
C. Passero
Portopalo di C. Passero
Valletta
15°
37°
A
B
C
3
4

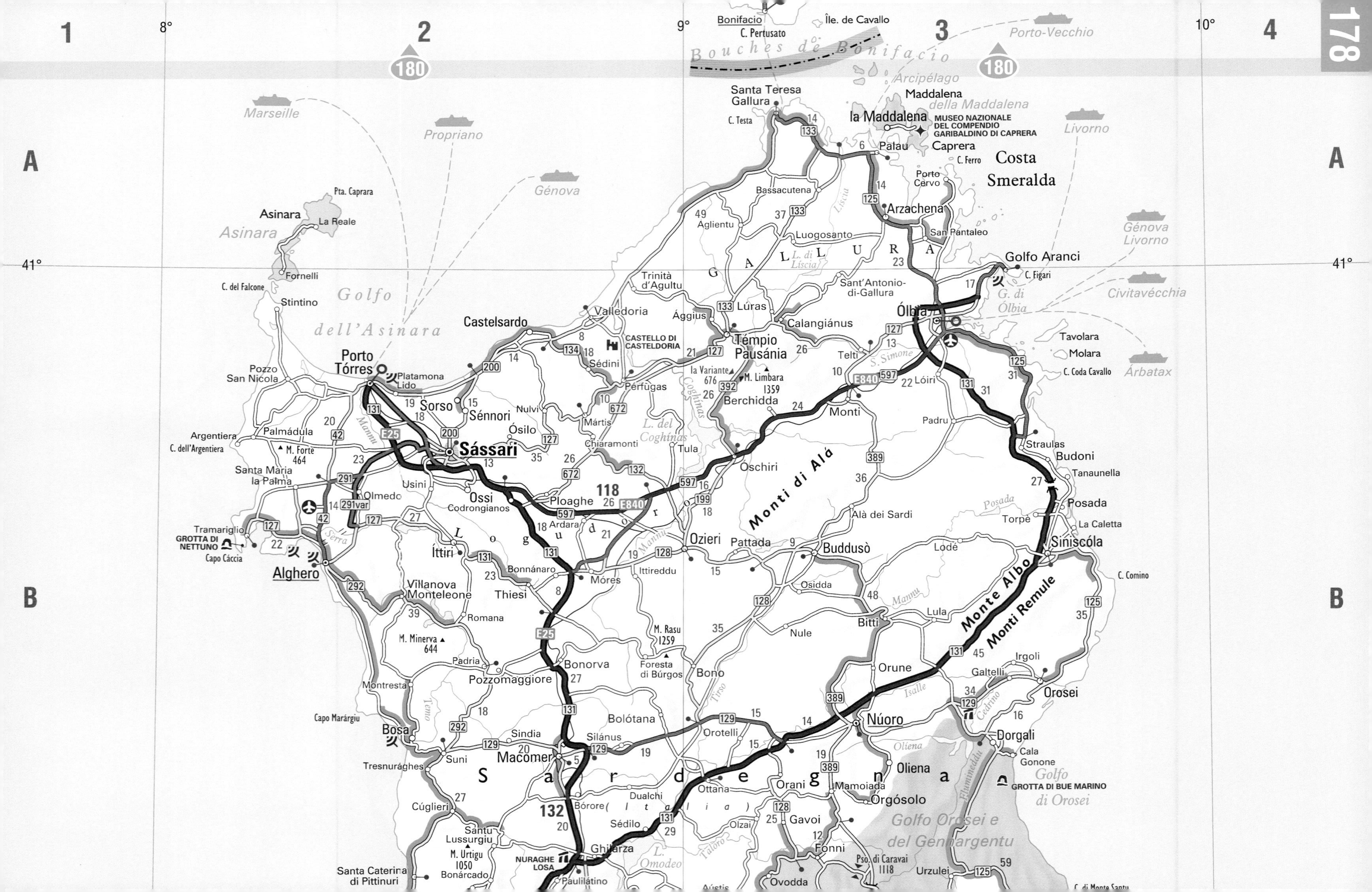

1
2
3
4
A
B
8°
9°
10°
41°
180
Bonifacio
C. Pertusato
Île. de Cavallo
Bouches de Bonifacio
Porto-Vecchio
Arcipélago
Maddalena
della Maddalena
la Maddalena
MUSEO NAZIONALE DEL COMPENDIO GARIBALDINO DI CAPRERA
Caprera
C. Ferro
Costa Smeralda
Porto Cervo
Livorno
Génova Livorno
Civitavécchia
Árbatax
Marseille
Propriano
Génova
Santa Teresa Gallura
C. Testa
Palau
Arzachena
San Pantaleo
Golfo Aranci
C. Figari
G. di Ólbia
Ólbia
Tavolara
Molara
C. Coda Cavallo
Asinara
Pta. Caprara
La Reale
Fornelli
C. del Falcone
Stintino
Golfo dell'Asinara
Bassacutena
Aglientu
Luogosanto
L. di Liscia
Liscia
GALLURA
Trinità d'Agultu
Valledoria
Aggius
Lúras
Sant'Antonio-di-Gallura
Calangiánus
Castelsardo
CASTELLO DI CASTELDORIA
Témpio Pausánia
Telti
S. Simone
Sédini
Pérfugas
la Variante 676
M. Limbara 1359
Berchidda
Lóiri
Porto Tórres
Platamona Lido
Pozzo San Nicola
Sorso
Sénnori
Nulvi
Ósilo
Mártis
Chiaramonti
L. del Coghinas
Coghinas
Tula
Monti
Padru
Argentiera
C. dell'Argentiera
Palmádula
M. Forte 464
Sássari
Óschiri
Straulas
Budoni
Tananunella
Santa Maria la Palma
Usini
Ossi
Codrongianos
Ploaghe
Olmedo
Monti di Alá
Alà dei Sardi
Posada
Torpè
La Caletta
Tramariglio
GROTTA DI NETTUNO
Capo Cáccia
Alghero
Serra
Íttiri
Ardara
Logudoro
Mannu
Ozieri
Pattada
Buddusò
Lodè
Siniscóla
C. Comino
Bonnánaro
Mores
Ittireddu
Osidda
Villanova Monteleone
Thiesi
Romana
M. Minerva 644
Padria
Pozzomaggiore
Bonorva
M. Rasu 1259
Foresta di Búrgos
Bono
Tirso
Nule
Bitti
Lula
Monte Albo
Monti Remule
Orune
Irgoli
Galtellì
Orosei
Isalle
Cedrino
Montresta
Temo
Capo Marárgiu
Bosa
Sindia
Bolótana
Silánus
Orotelli
Núoro
Dorgali
Cala Gonone
Golfo di Orosei
GROTTA DI BUE MARINO
Flumineddu
Tresnurághes
Suni
Macomer
Sardegna
Ottana
Orani
Mamoiada
Oliena
Orgósolo
Golfo Orosei e del Gennargentu
Cúglieri
Santu Lussurgiu
M. Urtigu 1050
Bonárcado
Bórore
Dualchi
Sédilo
Italia
Olzai
Gavoi
Fonni
Pso. di Caravai 1118
Urzulei
Taloro
L. Omodeo
Ghilarza
NURAGHE LOSA
Paulilátino
Santa Caterina di Pittinuri
Ovodda
Áustis
C. di Monte Santu
E25
E840
118
131
132
133
125
127
134
200
291
291var
292
42
392
597
672
199
128
129
389

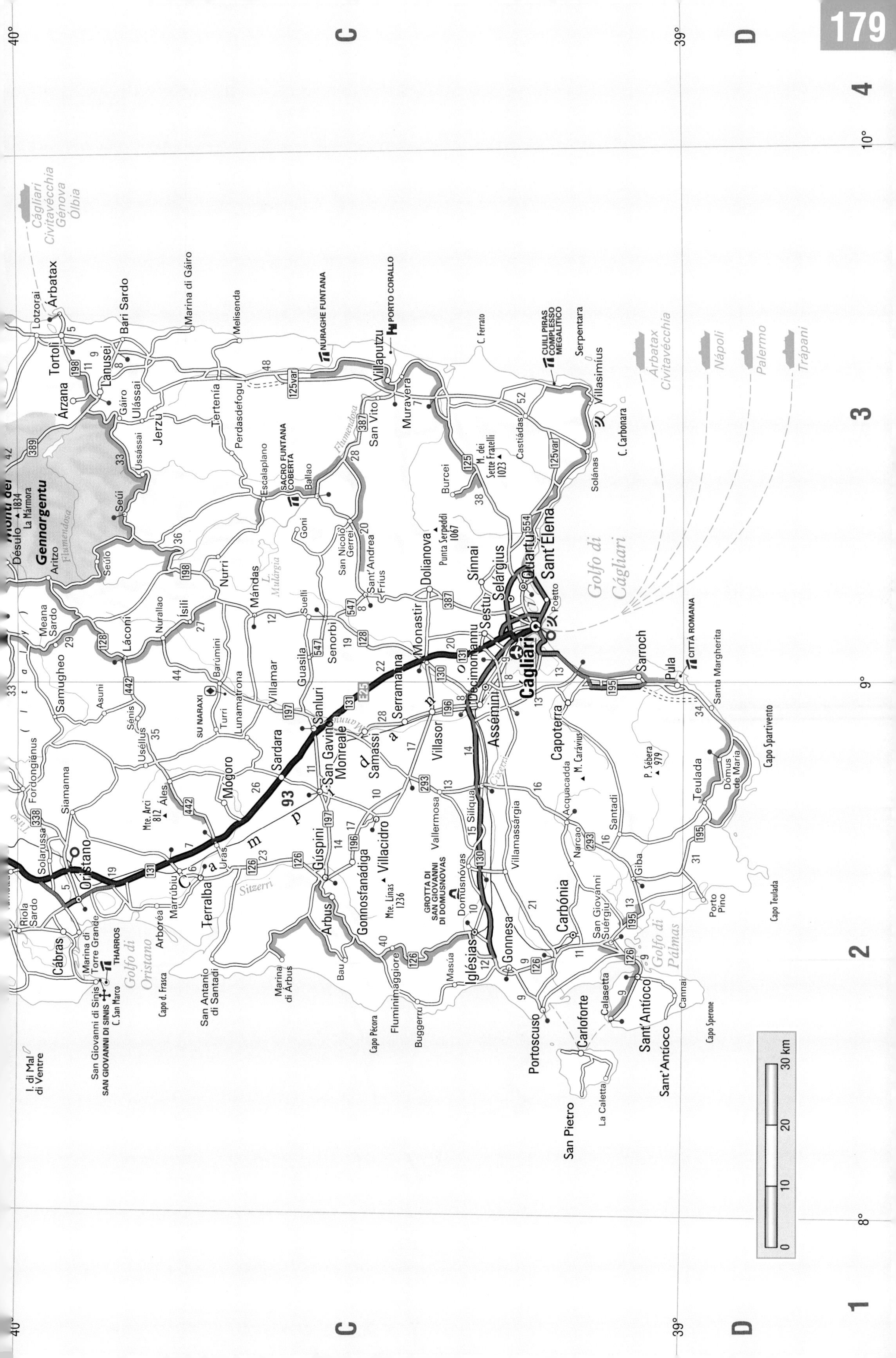

Monti dei

Gennargentu
Désulo ▲1834
La Mármora
Aritzo

Cágliari
Civitavécchia
Génova
Ólbia

Lotzorai
Tortolì
Árbatax
Arzana
Lanusei
Bari Sardo
Marina di Gáiro
Marina di Gáiro
Melisenda

Meana Sardo
Séui
Ussássai
Ulássai
Jerzu
Gáiro
Tertenia
Perdasdefogu

NURAGHE FUNTANA
Villaputzu
PORTO CORALLO

Samugheo
Fordongiánus
Siamanna
Asuni
Láconi
Nurallao
Isili
Nurri
Mándas
Escalaplano

SACRO FUNTANA COBERTA
Ballao
San Vito
San Nicoló Gerrei
Goni
Sant'Andrea Frius

Muravera
C. Ferrato

CUILI PIRAS
COMPLESSO MEGALITICO
Serpentara
Villasímius
C. Carbonara

Sénis
Uséllus
Barúmini
Suelli
Guasila
Senorbì
Villamar
Turri
Lunamatrona

SU NARAXI
Mógoro
Sardara
San Gavino Monreale
Samassi
Serramanna

Monastir
Dolianova
Sínnai
Selárgius
Sestu

M. dei Sette Fratelli 1023
Burcei
Castiádas
Solánas

Uras
 Áles
Mte. Arci 812
Guspini
Villacidro
Villasor
Assémini
Decimomannu

Cágliari
Quartu Sant'Elena
Poetto
Golfo di Cágliari

Oristano
Solarussa
Terralba
Gonnosfanádiga
Mte. Linas 1236
Vallermosa
Villaspeciosa
Siliqua
Villamassárgia

GROTTA DI SAN GIOVANNI DI DOMUSNÓVAS
Domusnóvas
Narcao
Santadi

Capoterra
M. Carávius
P. Sébera 979
Teulada
Domus de Maria
Capo Spartivento

Sarroch
Pula
Santa Margherita
CITTÀ ROMANA
Santa Margherita

Riola Sardo
Cábras
Marina di Torre Grande
SAN GIOVANNI DI SINIS
THARROS
C. San Marco
San Giovanni di Sinis
Golfo di Oristano

Capo d. Frasca
Arboréa
Marrúbiu
San Antonio di Santadi
Marina di Árbus
Capo Pécora
Buggerru
Fluminimaggiore

Iglésias
Gonnesa
Carbónia
San Giovanni Suérgiu
Giba
Narcao

Portoscuso
Carloforte
Calasetta
Sant'Antíoco
Cannai
Golfo di Pálmas

San Pietro
La Caletta
Sant'Antíoco
Capo Sperone
Capo Teulada
Porto Pino

I. di Mal di Ventre

Árbatax
Civitavécchia
Nápoli
Palermo
Trápani

Golfo di Cágliari
Città Romana

30 km
0   10   20   30 km

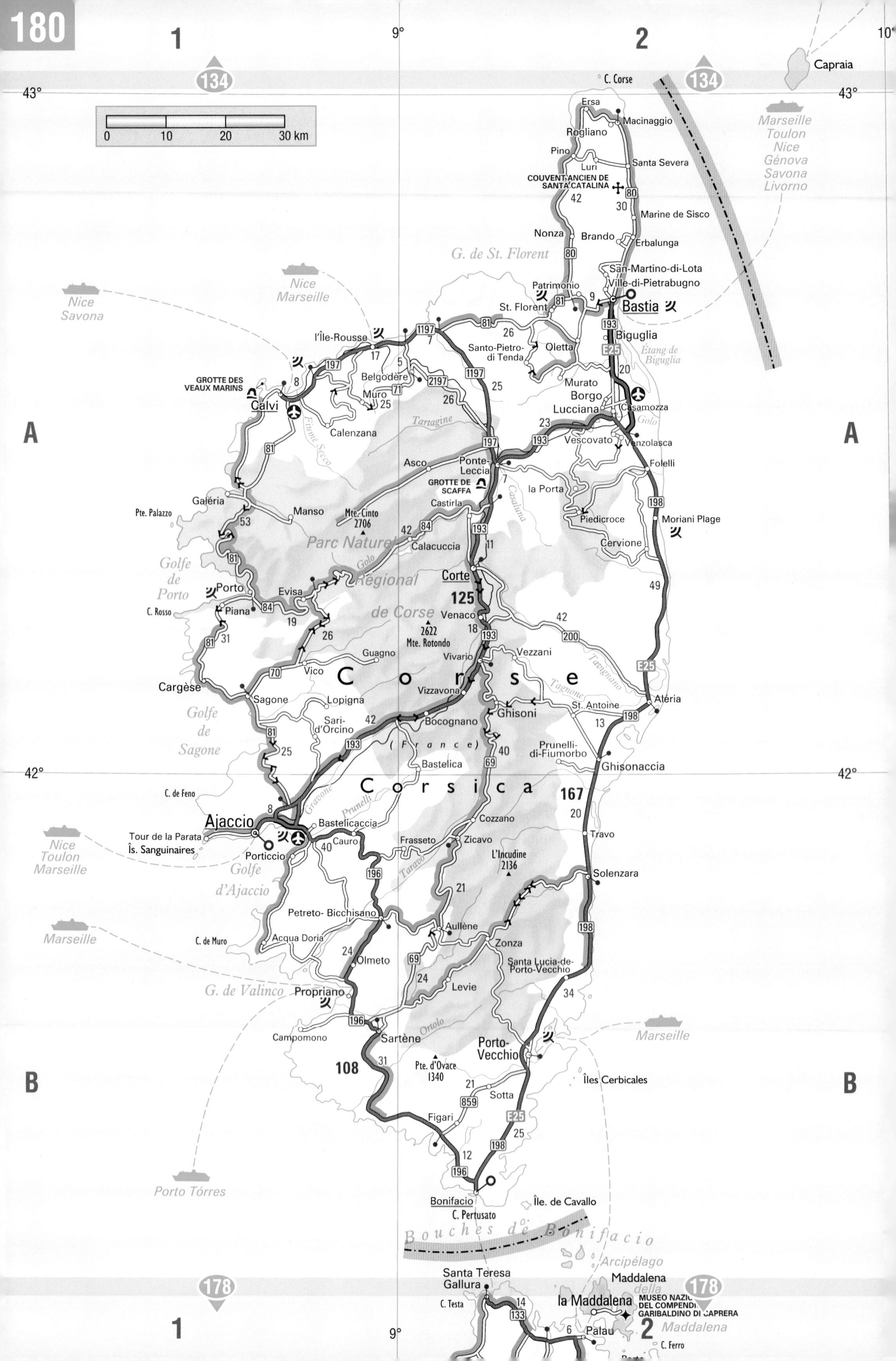
1
2
9°
10°
134
C. Corse
Capraia
43°
0 10 20 30 km
Ersa
Macinaggio
Rogliano
Pino
Luri
Santa Severa
COUVENT ANCIEN DE SANTA CATALINA
Marseille
Toulon
Nice
Génova
Savona
Livorno
Marine de Sisco
Nonza
Brando
Erbalunga
G. de St. Florent
San-Martino-di-Lota
Ville-di-Pietrabugno
Patrimonio
Bastia
St. Florent
Nice
Savona
Nice
Marseille
l'Île-Rousse
Santo-Pietro-di Tenda
Oletta
Biguglia
Étang de Biguglia
GROTTE DES VEAUX MARINS
Belgodère
Muro
Murato
Borgo
Lucciana
Casamozza
Calvi
Calenzana
Tartagine
Golo
Vescovato
Venzolasca
A
Fiume Secco
Asco
Ponte-Leccia
Folelli
GROTTE DE SCAFFA
la Porta
Galéria
Castirla
Pte. Palazzo
Manso
Mte. Cinto 2706
Piedicroce
Moriani Plage
Parc Naturel
Calacuccia
Cervione
Golfe de Porto
Régional
Corte
Porto
Evisa
de Corse
C. Rosso
Piana
Venaco
2622 Mte. Rotondo
Vezzani
Guagno
Vivario
Tavignano
Cargèse
Vico
Corse
Vizzavona
Tagnone
Aléria
Sagone
Lopigna
St. Antoine
Golfe de Sagone
Sari-d'Orcino
Bocognano
Ghisoni
(France)
Prunelli-di-Fiumorbo
Bastelica
Ghisonaccia
42°
C. de Feno
Corsica
Gravone
Prunelli
Cozzano
Ajaccio
Bastelicaccia
Travo
Tour de la Parata
Îs. Sanguinaires
Porticcio
Cauro
Frasseto
Zicavo
Nice
Toulon
Marseille
Golfe d'Ajaccio
Taravo
L'Incudine 2136
Solenzara
Petreto- Bicchisano
Marseille
C. de Muro
Acqua Doria
Aullène
Zonza
Olmeto
Santa Lucia-de-Porto-Vecchio
G. de Valinco
Propriano
Levie
Campomono
Sartène
Ortolo
Marseille
Porto-Vecchio
Pte. d'Ovace 1340
Îles Cerbicales
B
Sotta
Figari
Porto Tórres
Bonifacio
C. Pertusato
Île. de Cavallo
Bouches de Bonifacio
Arcipélago
Santa Teresa Gallura
Maddalena
della
Maddalena
178
C. Testa
la Maddalena
Palau
C. Ferro

# CYPRUS

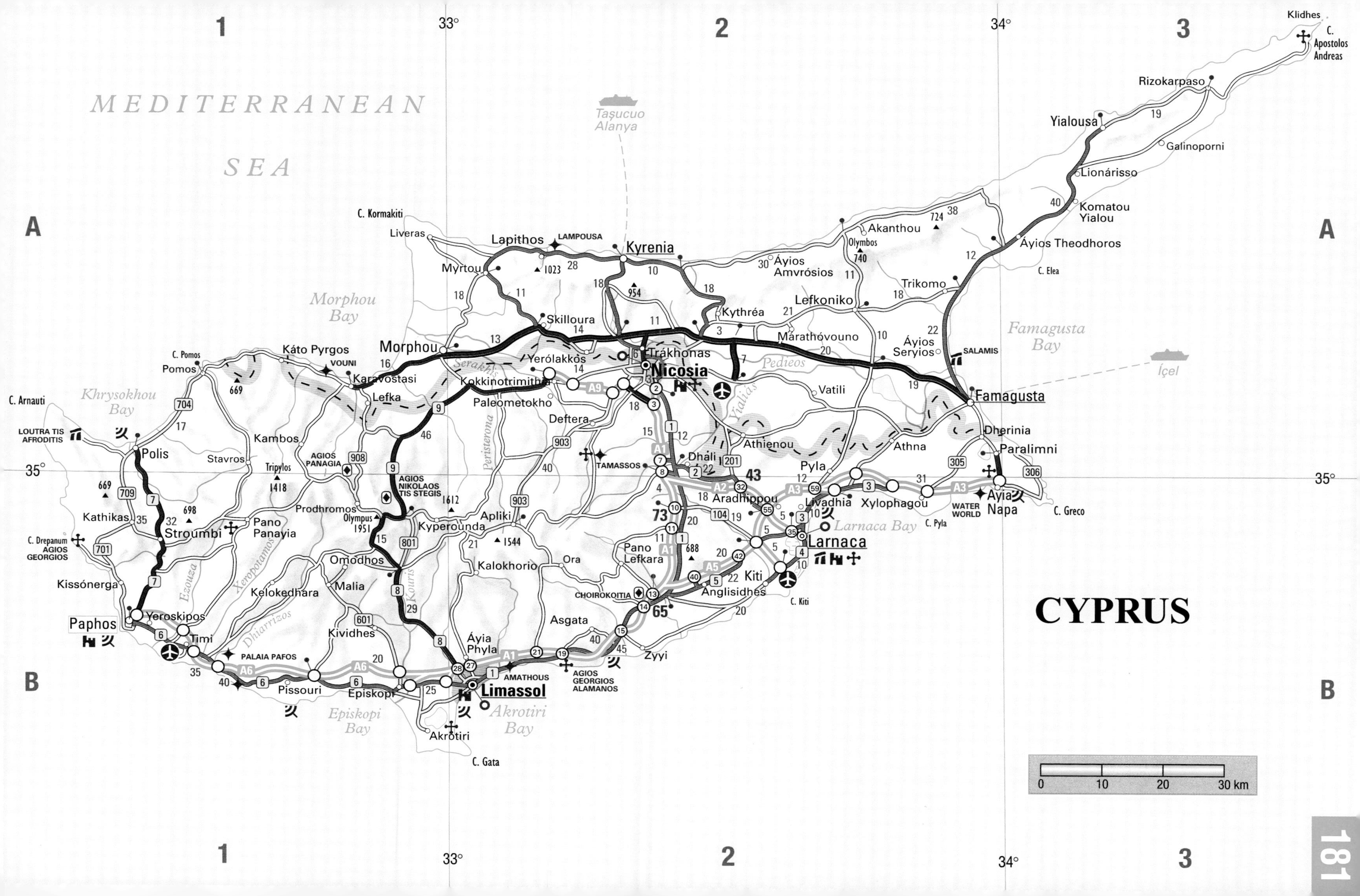
MEDITERRANEAN
SEA
CYPRUS
Nicosia
Famagusta
Kyrenia
Larnaca
Limassol
Paphos
Morphou
Lapithos
LAMPOUSA
Myrtou
Liveras
C. Kormakiti
Skilloura
Yerólakkos
Trákhonas
Kokkinotrimithia
Paleometokho
Deftera
Kythréa
Lefkoniko
Marathóvouno
Vatili
Athienou
Dhali
Pyla
Athna
Dherinia
Paralimni
Ayia Napa
WATER WORLD
C. Greco
C. Pyla
Xylophagou
Livadhia
Aradhippou
Kiti
C. Kiti
Anglisidhes
Pano Lefkara
CHOIROKOITIA
Ora
Kalokhorio
Asgata
Zyyi
AGIOS GEORGIOS ALAMANOS
AMATHOUS
Áyia Phyla
Akrotiri
C. Gata
Akrotiri Bay
Episkopi
Episkopi Bay
Pissouri
Kividhes
Malia
Omodhos
Kelokedhara
PALAIA PAFOS
Timi
Yeroskipos
Kissónerga
C. Drepanum
AGIOS GEORGIOS
Kathikas
Stroumbi
Pano Panayia
Polis
Khrysokhou Bay
LOUTRA TIS AFRODITIS
C. Arnauti
Pomos
C. Pomos
Káto Pyrgos
VOUNI
Karavostasi
Lefka
Kambos
Stavros
Tripylos
AGIOS PANAGIA
AGIOS NIKOLAOS TIS STEGIS
Olympus
Prodhromos
Kyperounda
Apliki
TAMASSOS
Morphou Bay
Akanthou
Olymbos
Áyios Amvrósios
Trikomo
Áyios Seryios
SALAMIS
Famagusta Bay
C. Elea
Áyios Theodhoros
Komatou Yialou
Lionárisso
Galinoporni
Yialousa
Rizokarpaso
Klidhes
C. Apostolos Andreas
Taşucuo Alanya
İçel
Larnaca Bay
Serakhis
Pedieos
Yialias
Peristerona
Kouris
Xeropotamos
Ezouza
Dhiarrizos
0 10 20 30 km
33°
34°
35°
1
2
3
A
B

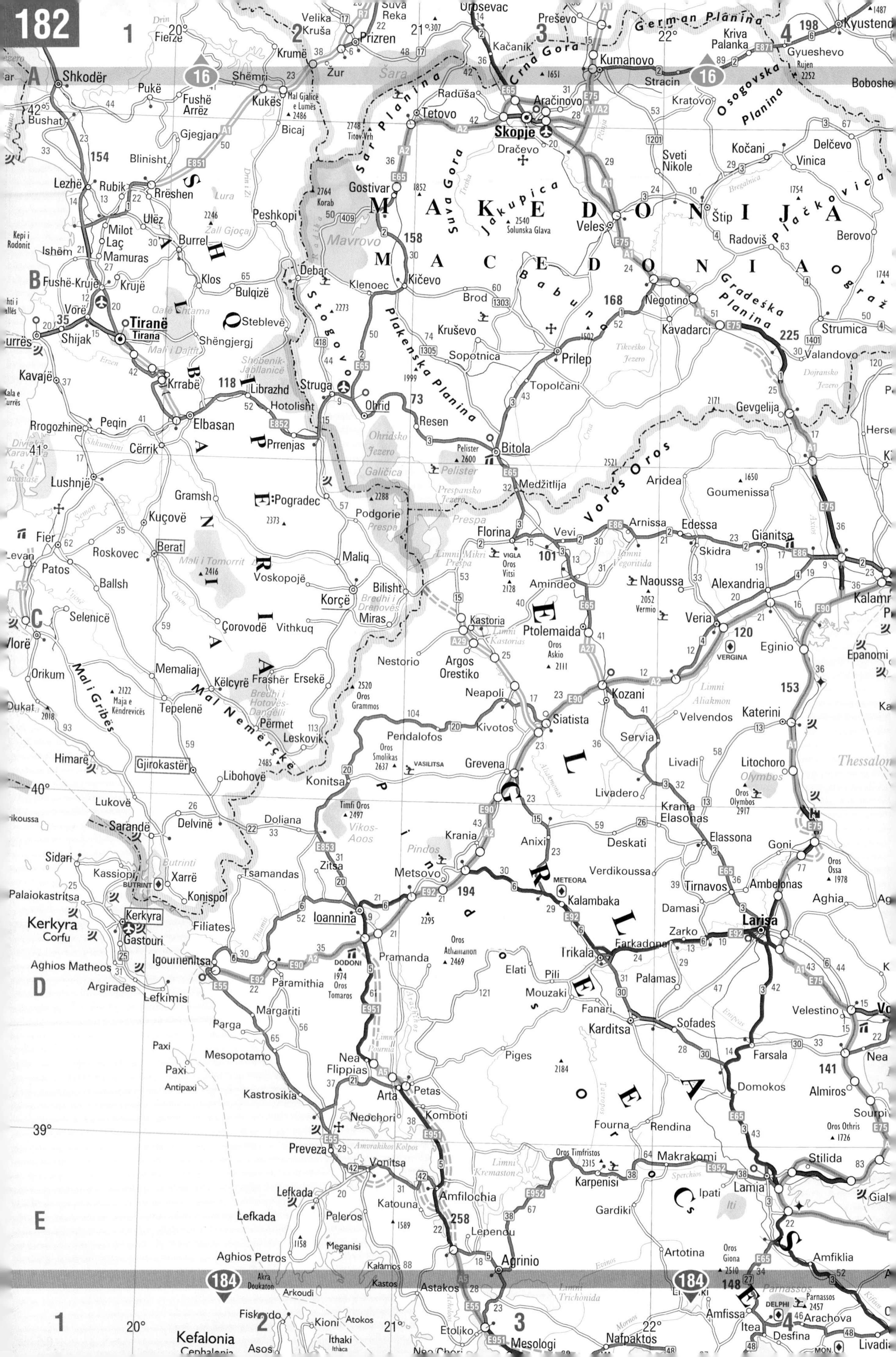

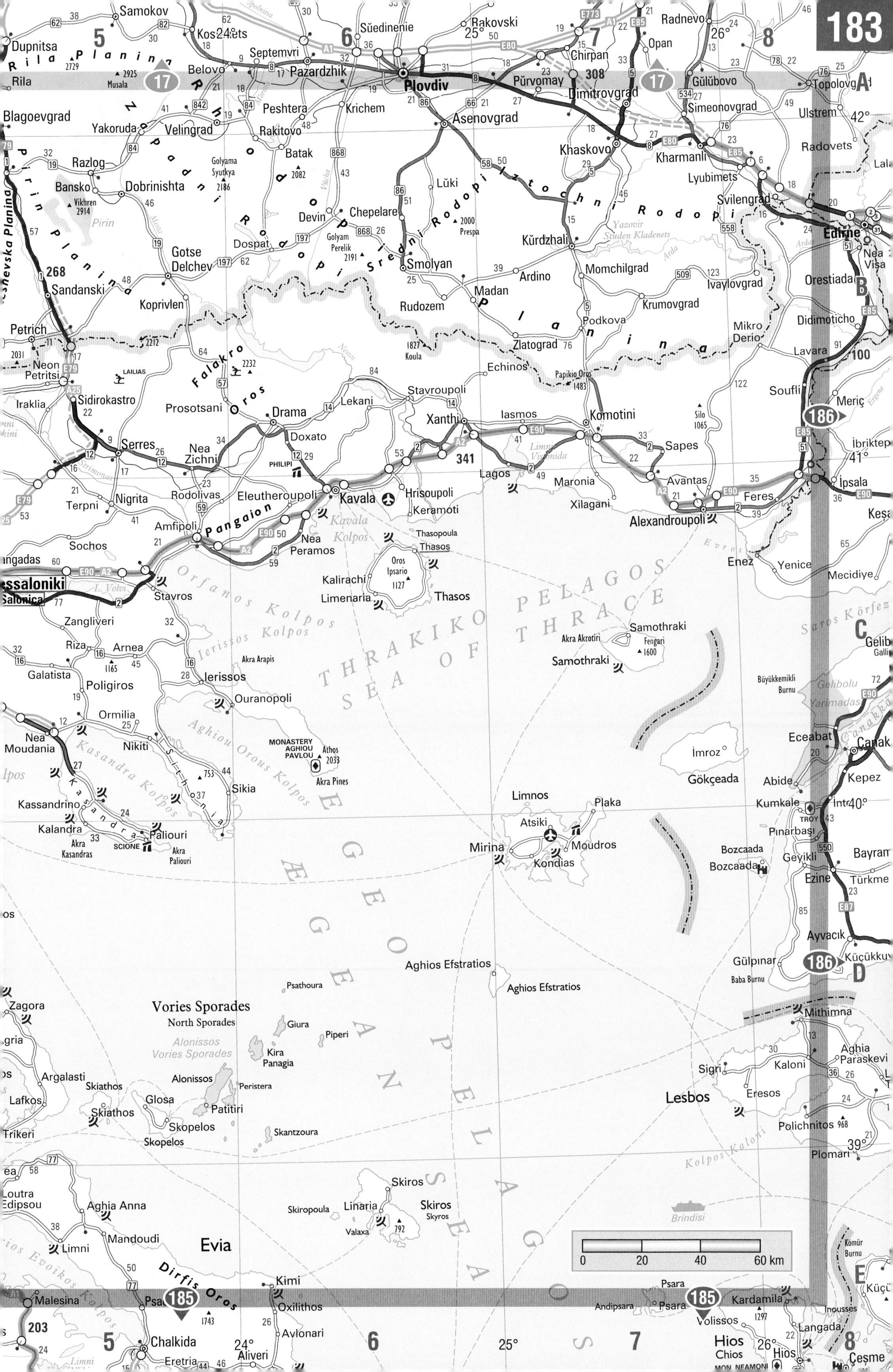
Samokov
Dupnitsa
Rila Planina
Rila
Musala
Belovo
Septemvri
Pazardzhik
Sŭedinenie
Plovdiv
Rakovski
Chirpan
Radnevo
Opan
Gŭlŭbovo
Topolovgrad
Dimitrovgrad
Pŭrvomay
Blagoevgrad
Yakoruda
Velingrad
Peshtera
Rakitovo
Krichem
Asenovgrad
Simeonovgrad
Ulstrem
Khaskovo
Kharmanli
Radovets
Lyubimets
Razlog
Batak
Bansko
Dobrinishta
Golyama Syutkya
Vikhren
Pirin
Lŭki
Chepelare
Devin
Svilengrad
Edirne
Gotse Delchev
Dospat
Golyam Perelik
Smolyan
Prespa
Kŭrdzhali
Momchilgrad
Ivaylovgrad
Orestiada
Sandanski
Koprivlen
Ardino
Madan
Rudozem
Krumovgrad
Didimoticho
Petrich
Podkova
Mikro Derio
Zlatograd
Koula
Neon Petritsi
Lavara
Echinos
Papikio Oros
Iraklia
Sidirokastro
Prosotsani
Falakro Oros
Drama
Lekani
Stavroupoli
Soufli
Xanthi
Iasmos
Komotini
Meriç
Doxato
Serres
Nea Zichni
Philipi
Lagos
Sapes
İbriktepe
Maroni
Avantas
İpsala
Rodolivas
Eleutheroupoli
Kavala
Hrisoupoli
Keramoti
Xilagani
Feres
Nigrita
Terpni
Amfipoli
Pangaion
Alexandroupoli
Keşan
Sochos
Nea Peramos
Thasopoula
Thasos
Enez
Yenice
Mecidiye
Thessaloniki
Salonica
Stavros
Orfanos Kolpos
Kalirachi
Limenaria
Oros Ipsario
Thasos
Zangliveri
Thrakiko Pelagos
Sea of Thrace
Samothraki
Akra Akrotiri
Fengari
Saros Körfezi
Riza
Arnea
Ierissos Kolpos
Akra Arapis
Galatista
Poligiros
Ierissos
Ouranopoli
Büyükkemikli Burnu
Gelibolu Yarımadası
Ormilia
Nea Moudania
Nikiti
Aghiou Orous Kolpos
Monastery Aghiou Pavlou
Athos
Akra Pines
İmroz
Gökçeada
Eceabat
Çanakkale
Abide
Kepez
Sithonia
Sikia
Kassandrino
Kasandra Kolpos
Kasandra
Limnos
Plaka
Kumkale
Troy
Kalandra
Paliouri
Akra Kasandras
Scione
Akra Paliouri
Atsiki
Mirina
Moudros
Kondias
Pınarbaşı
Bozcaada
Geyikli
Ezine
Bayramiç
Türkmen
Aegean Sea
Aigaio Pelagos
Ayvacık
Aghios Efstratios
Gülpınar
Küçükkuyu
Baba Burnu
Psathoura
Vories Sporades
North Sporades
Zagora
Giura
Piperi
Mithimna
Alonissos
Kira Panagia
Aghia Paraskevi
Argalasti
Skiathos
Peristera
Patitiri
Sigri
Kaloni
Lafkos
Glosa
Eresos
Lesbos
Skopelos
Trikeri
Skantzoura
Polichnitos
Kolpos Kaloni
Plomari
Loutra Edipsou
Skiros
Aghia Anna
Skiropoula
Linaria
Valaxa
Brindisi
Mandoudi
Limni
Evia
Kömür Burnu
Dirfis Oros
Kimi
Psara
Malesina
Oxilithos
Andipsara
Kardamila
Inousses
Volissos
Chalkida
Avlonari
Langada
Hios
Chios
Eretria
Aliveri
Çeşme
0 20 40 60 km

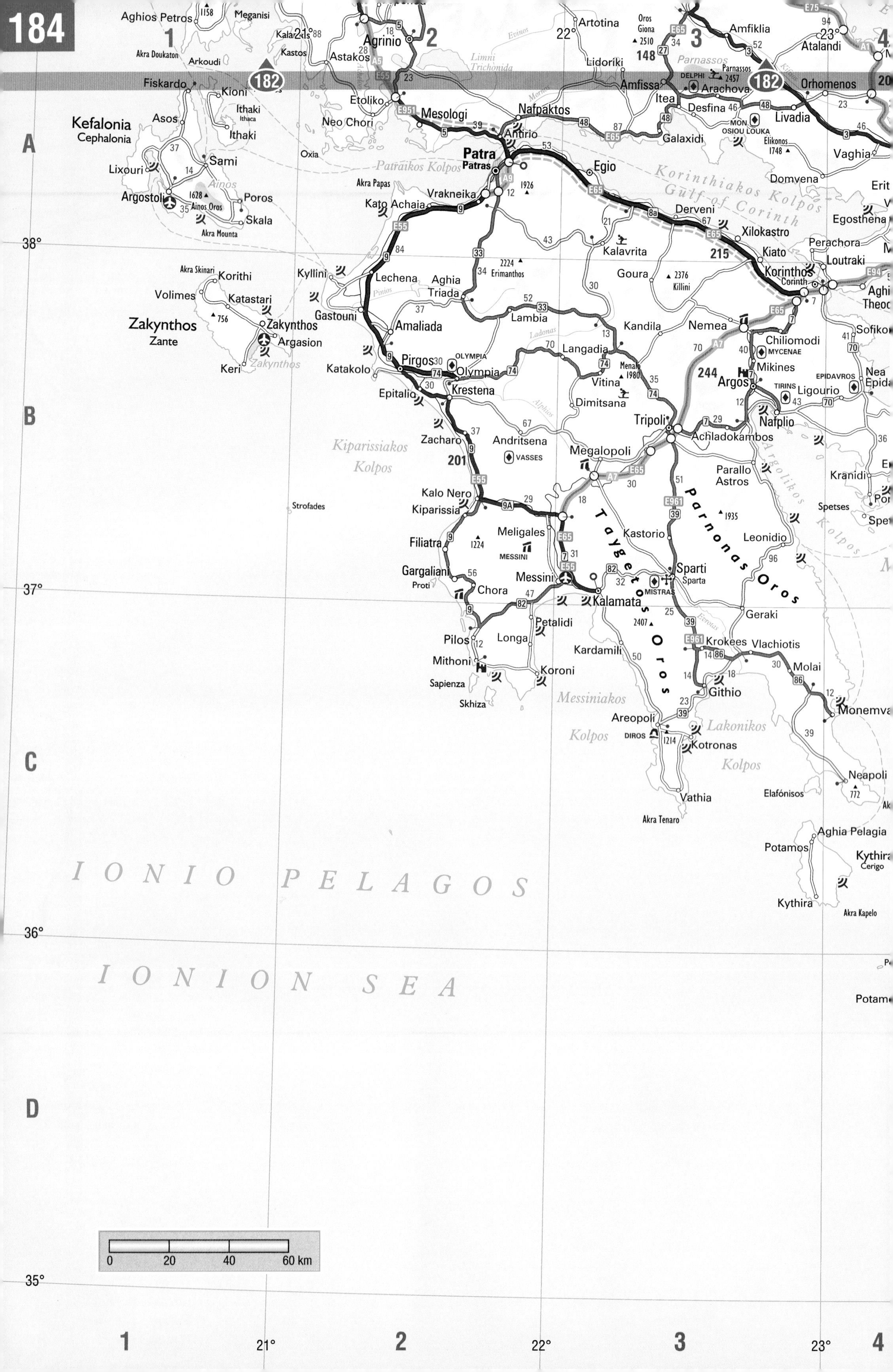
Kefalonia
Cephalonia
Argostoli
Lixouri
Sami
Poros
Skala
Fiskardo
Asos
Ithaki
Ithaca
Zakynthos
Zante
Keri
Argasion
Patra
Patras
Patraikos Kolpos
Korinthiakos Kolpos
Gulf of Corinth
Mesologi
Nafpaktos
Antirio
Egio
Amfissa
Delphi
Itea
Galaxidi
Livadia
Orhomenos
Korinthos
Corinth
Loutraki
Kiato
Xilokastro
Kalavrita
Pirgos
Olympia
Krestena
Amaliada
Gastouni
Kyllini
Katakolo
Zacharo
Kiparissia
Filiatra
Gargaliani
Chora
Pilos
Mithoni
Methoni
Koroni
Kalamata
Messini
Megalopoli
Tripoli
Argos
Mycenae
Mikines
Nafplio
Tirins
Epidavros
Ligourio
Sparti
Sparta
Mistras
Githio
Areopoli
Vathia
Monemvasia
Neapoli
Kythira
Cerigo
Parnonas Oros
Taygetos Oros
Kiparissiakos Kolpos
Messiniakos Kolpos
Lakonikos Kolpos
Argolikos Kolpos
Strofades
IONIO PELAGOS
IONION SEA
0 20 40 60 km
35°
36°
37°
38°
21°
22°
23°
1 2 3 4
A B C D

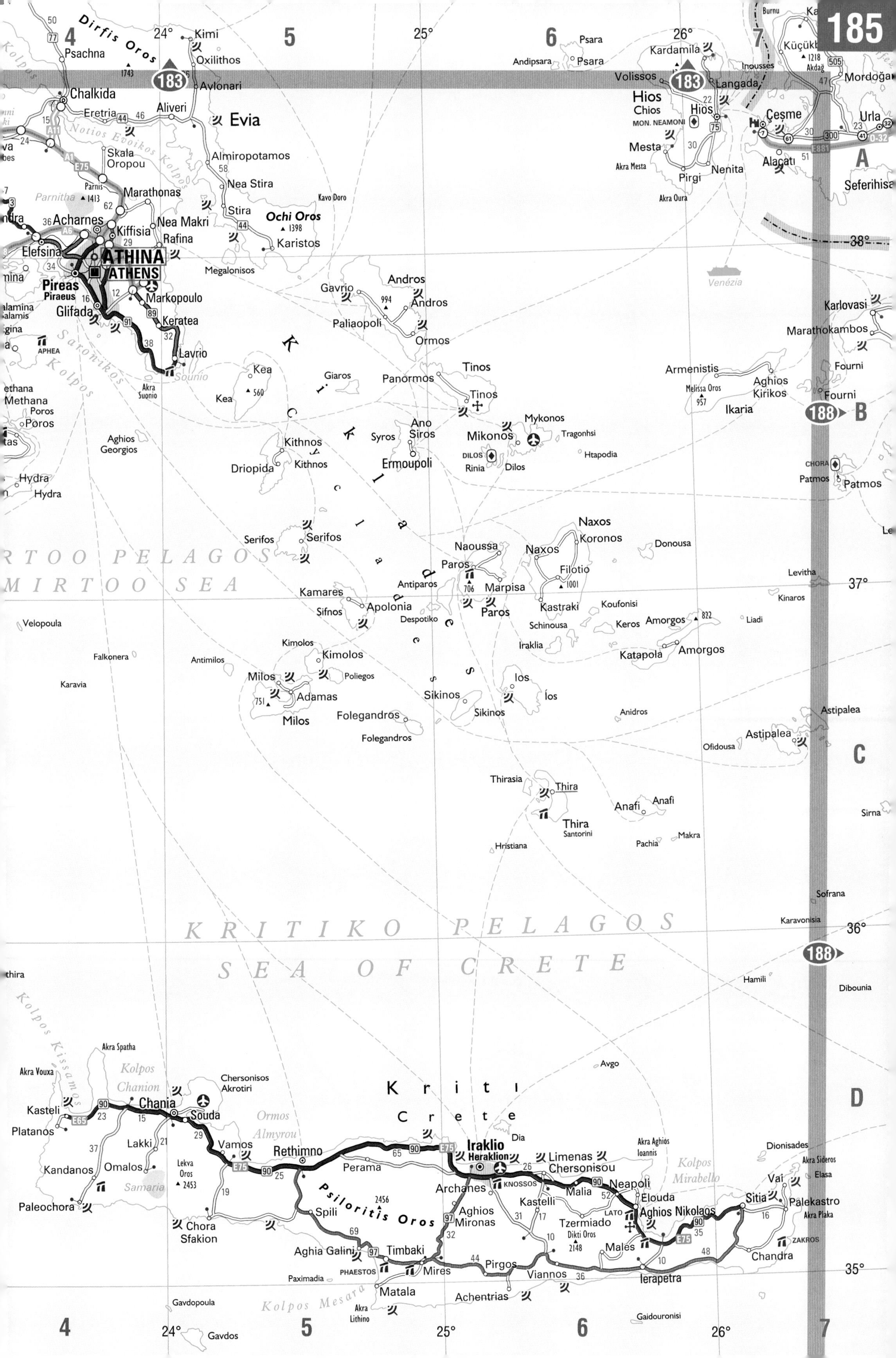
4
5
6
7
24°
25°
26°
Dirfis Oros
Psachna
1743
Kimi
Oxilithos
Avlonari
183
Chalkida
Eretria
Aliveri
Evia
Notios Evoikos Kolpos
Skala Oropou
Almiropotamos
Nea Stira
Stira
Parnitha 1413
Marathonas
Acharnes
Kiffisia
Nea Makri
Rafina
Ochi Oros
1398
Karistos
Kavo Doro
Elefsina
ATHINA
ATHENS
Pireas
Piraeus
Glifada
Markopoulo
Keratea
Lavrio
Sounio
Akra Suonio
Megalonisos
Saronikos Kolpos
Salamina
Salamis
APHEA
Methana
Poros
Hydra
Aghios Georgios
Kea
560
Kithnos
Driopida
Giaros
Andros
Gavrio
994
Paliaopoli
Ormos
Tinos
Panormos
Syros
Ano Siros
Ermoupoli
Mykonos
Mikonos
Tragonhsi
Htapodia
DILOS
Rinia
Dilos
Kiklades
Cyclades
Serifos
Sifnos
Kamares
Apolonia
Antiparos
Despotiko
Paros
Naoussa
Marpisa
706
Naxos
Koronos
Filotio
1001
Kastraki
Donousa
Koufonisi
Schinousa
Keros
Iraklia
Amorgos
822
Katapola
Levitha
Kinaros
Liadi
MIRTOO PELAGOS
MIRTOO SEA
Velopoula
Falkonera
Karavia
Antimilos
Kimolos
Poliegos
Milos
Adamas
751
Folegandros
Sikinos
Ios
Anidros
Astipalea
Ofidousa
Thirasia
Thira
Santorini
Anafi
Pachia
Makra
Hristiana
Sirna
Sofrana
Karavonisia
36°
37°
38°
35°
KRITIKO PELAGOS
SEA OF CRETE
188
Hamili
Dibounia
Psara
Andipsara
Kardamila
Volissos
Langada
Hios
Chios
MON. NEAMONI
Mesta
Akra Mesta
Pirgi
Nenita
Akra Oura
Inousses
Burnu
Küçükbahçe
1218 Akdağ
Mordoğan
Çeşme
Urla
Alaçatı
Seferihisar
Venézia
Karlovasi
Marathokambos
Fourni
Armenistis
Melissa Oros
957
Aghios Kirikos
Ikaria
CHORA
Patmos
A
B
C
D
Kriti
Crete
Akra Spatha
Akra Vouxa
Kolpos Kissamos
Kolpos Chanion
Chersonisos Akrotiri
Kasteli
Platanos
Chania
Souda
Kolpos Almyrou
Lakki
Omalos
Kandanos
Lekva Oros 2453
Samaria
Paleochora
Chora Sfakion
Vamos
Rethimno
Perama
Psiloritis Oros
2456
Spili
Aghia Galini
Timbaki
PHAESTOS
Mires
Paximadia
Matala
Kolpos Mesara
Akra Lithino
Gavdopoula
Gavdos
Iraklio
Heraklion
Dia
KNOSSOS
Archanes
Aghios Mironas
Limenas Chersonisou
Malia
Kastelli
Tzermiado
Dikti Oros
2148
Pirgos
Viannos
Achentrias
Avgo
Akra Aghios Ioannis
Kolpos Mirabello
Neapoli
Elouda
LATO
Aghios Nikolaos
Males
Ierapetra
Gaidouronisi
Sitia
Dionisades
Akra Sideros
Elasa
Vai
Palekastro
Akra Plaka
ZAKROS
Chandra
E75
90
97

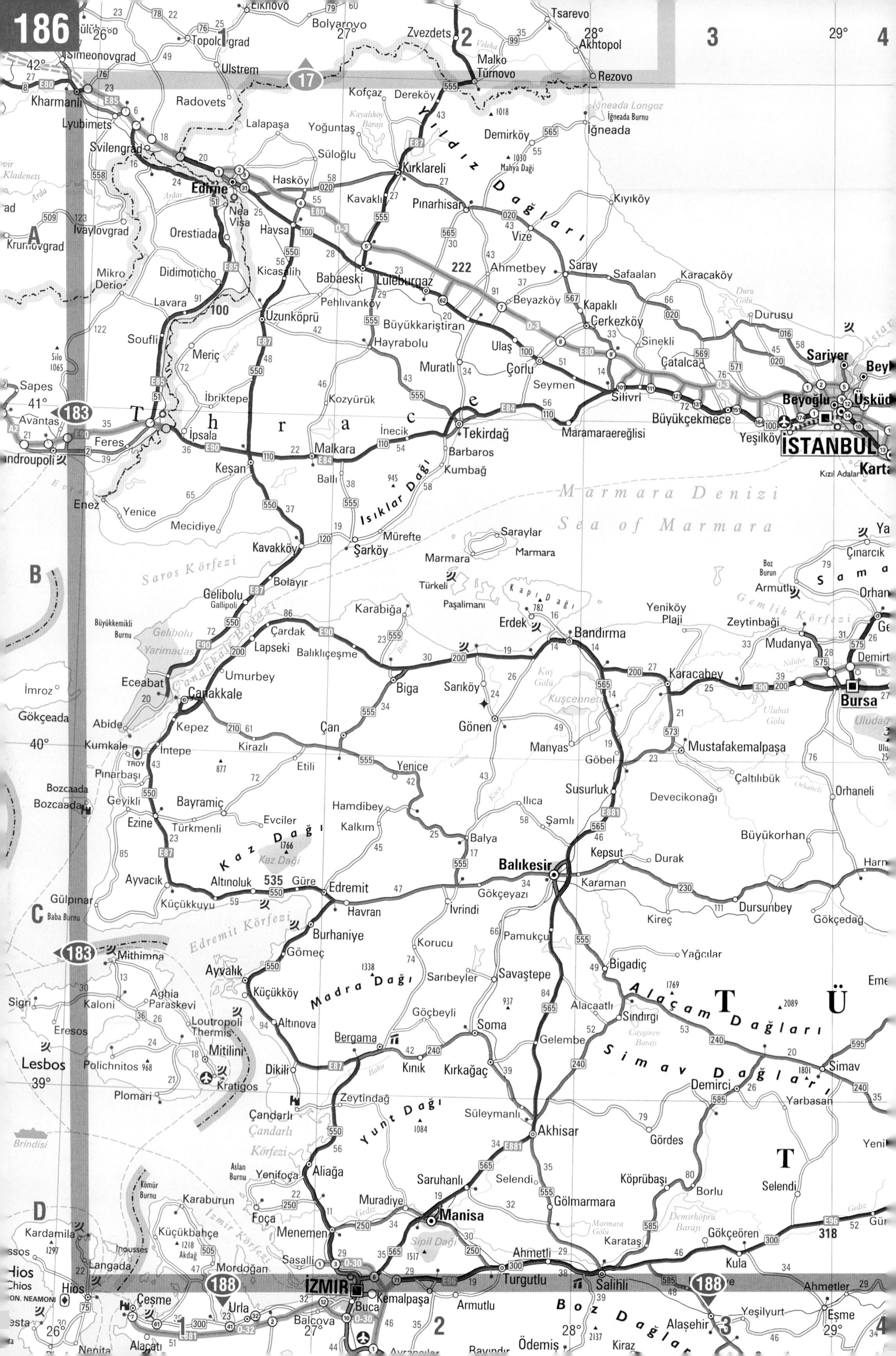

Edirne
Kırklareli
Tekirdağ
İSTANBUL
Beyoğlu
Üsküdar
Marmara Denizi
Sea of Marmara
Saros Körfezi
Gelibolu
Çanakkale
Bandırma
Bursa
Balıkesir
Edremit
Ayvalık
Bergama
Manisa
İZMIR
Akhisar
Salihli
Lesbos
Mitilini
Hios
Yıldız Dağları
Kaz Dağı
Madra Dağı
Yunt Dağı
Simav Dağları
Alaçam Dağları
Boz Dağlar
Thrace
Kharmanli
Svilengrad
Alexandroupoli
Keşan
Uzunköprü
Lüleburgaz
Çorlu
Silivri
Büyükçekmece
Sarıyer
Karacabey
Mudanya
Gönen
Biga
Ezine
Ayvacık
Dikili
Çandarlı
Foça
Aliağa
Menemen
Turgutlu
Kemalpaşa
Çeşme
Urla
Soma
Kırkağaç
Bigadiç
Sındırgı
Simav
Demirci
Gördes
Kula
Alaşehir
Ödemiş

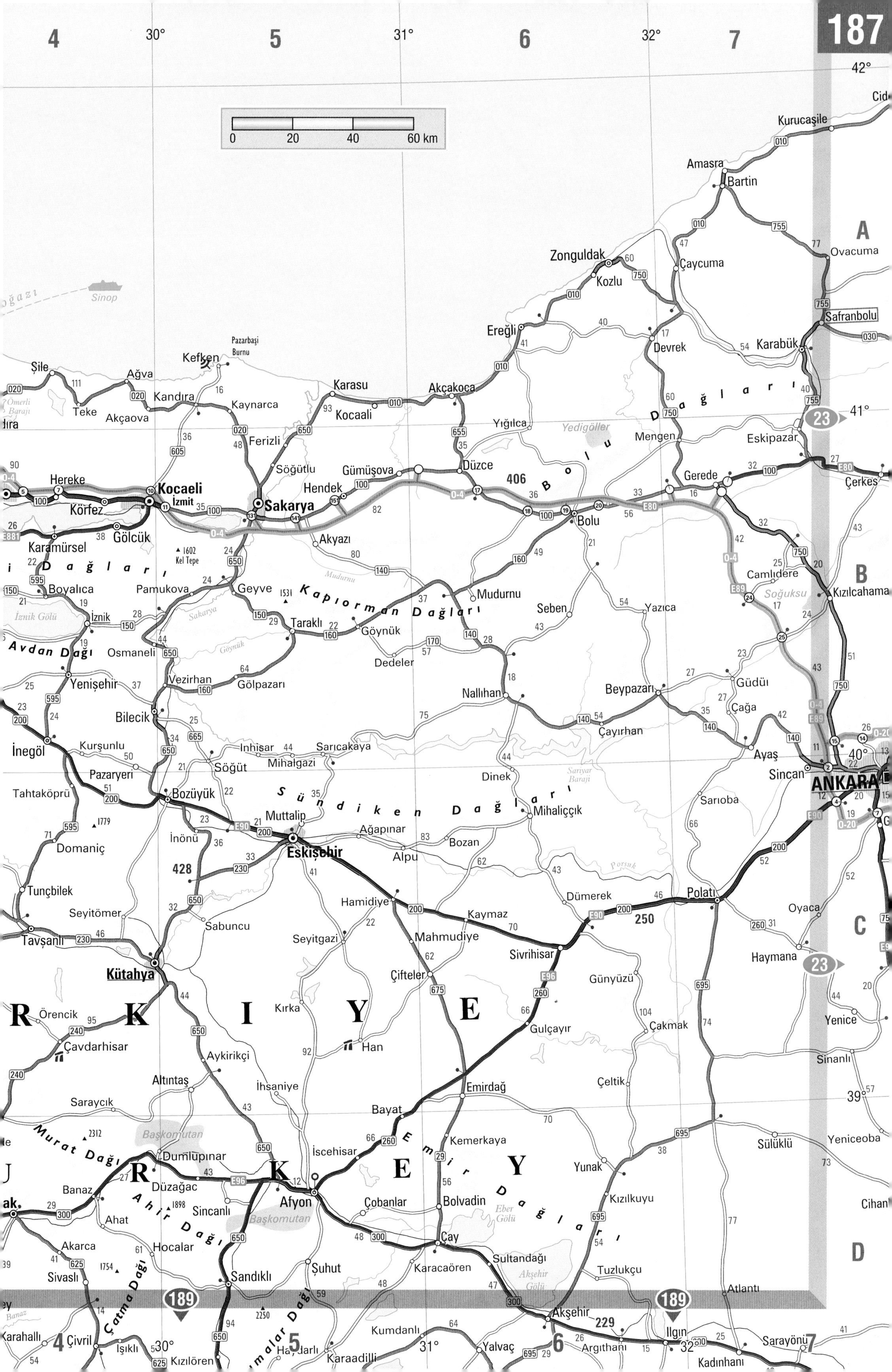
0 20 40 60 km
Zonguldak
Bartin
Amasra
Kurucaşile
Ovacuma
Çaycuma
Kozlu
Ereğli
Devrek
Karabük
Safranbolu
Şile
Ağva
Kefken
Pazarbaşi Burnu
Kandıra
Kaynarca
Karasu
Kocaali
Akçakoca
Yığılca
Yedigöller
Mengen
Eskipazar
Ferizli
Söğütlu
Gümüşova
Düzce
Hendek
Bolu Dağları
Gerede
Çerkeş
Hereke
Kocaeli
İzmit
Körfez
Sakarya
Bolu
Gölcük
Karamürsel
Kel Tepe
Akyazı
Mudurnu
Camlıdere
Soğuksu
Kızılcahamam
Yalova
Boyalıca
Pamukova
Geyve
Kapıorman Dağları
Seben
Yazıca
İznik
İznik Gölü
Taraklı
Göynük
Avdan Dağı
Osmaneli
Dedeler
Güdül
Vezirhan
Gölpazarı
Nallıhan
Beypazarı
Çağa
Yenişehir
Bilecik
Çayırhan
Ayaş
İnegöl
Kurşunlu
Inhisar
Sarıcakaya
Söğüt
Mihalgazi
Sincan
ANKARA
Pazaryeri
Dinek
Sarıyar Barajı
Tahtaköprü
Bozüyük
Sündiken Dağları
Mihalıççık
Sarıoba
Muttalip
Ağapınar
Domaniç
İnönü
Eskişehir
Alpu
Bozan
Porsuk
Tunçbilek
Hamidiye
Dümerek
Polatlı
Seyitömer
Sabuncu
Kaymaz
Oyaca
Tavşanlı
Seyitgazi
Mahmudiye
Sivrihisar
Haymana
Kütahya
Çifteler
Günyüzü
TÜRKIYE
Örencik
Kırka
Gulçayır
Çakmak
Yenice
Çavdarhisar
Han
Aykirikçi
Sinanlı
Altıntaş
İhsaniye
Emirdağ
Çeltik
Saraycık
Bayat
Murat Dağı
Başkomutan
Emir Dağları
Kemerkaya
Sülüklü
Yeniceoba
Dumlupınar
İscehisar
Yunak
Banaz
Düzağac
Afyon
Bolvadin
Kızılkuyu
Cihan
Uşak
Sincanlı
Çobanlar
Eber Gölü
Ahat
Ahır Dağı
Akarca
Hocalar
Çay
Sivaslı
Sandıklı
Şuhut
Sultandağı
Karacaören
Tuzlukçu
Çatma Dağı
Akşehir Gölü
Atlantı
Akşehir
Karahallı
Çivril
Işıklı
Kızılören
Haydarlı
Kumdanlı
Karaadilli
Yalvaç
Argıthanı
Ilgın
Kadınhanı
Sarayönü
Sinop
Boğazı
Ömerli Barajı
Teke
Akçaova
E80
E90
E96
E89
E881
O-4
O-20
23
189

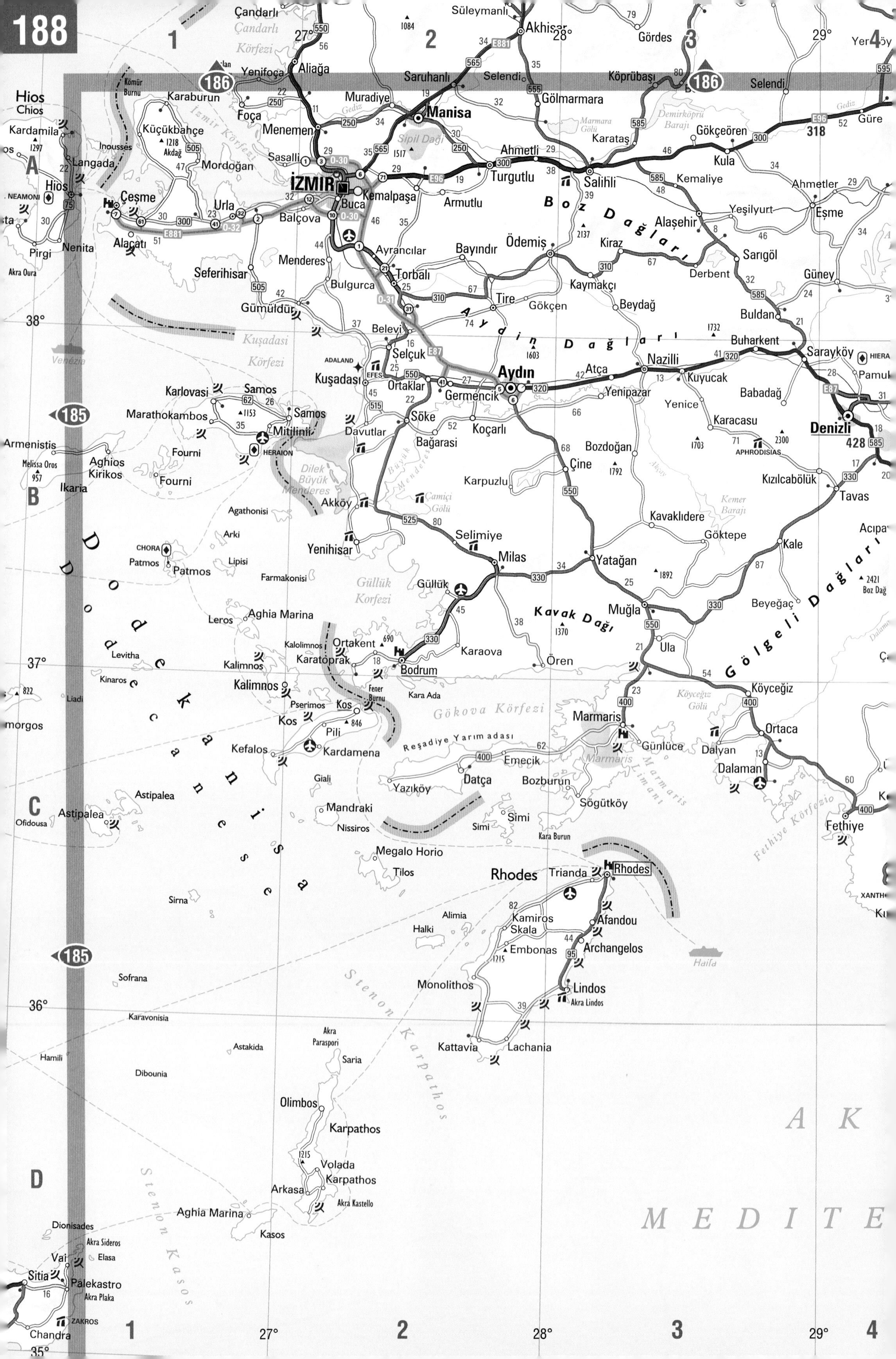
Çandarlı
Çandarlı Körfezi
Aliağa
Yenifoça
Foça
Karaburun
Küçükbahçe
Menemen
Muradiye
Manisa
Saruhanlı
Akhisar
Gördes
Selendi
Köprübaşı
Gölmarmara
Gökçeören
Kula
Güre
Salihli
Turgutlu
Ahmetli
Sasalli
İZMIR
Kemalpaşa
Buca
Balçova
Urla
Çeşme
Alaçatı
Mordoğan
Hios
Chios
Kardamila
Langada
Inousses
Pirgi
Nenita
Seferihisar
Menderes
Torbalı
Bayındır
Ödemiş
Boz Dağları
Alaşehir
Kiraz
Derbent
Sarıgöl
Eşme
Ahmetler
Yeşilyurt
Kemaliye
Güney
Buldan
Beydağ
Kaymakçı
Tire
Gökçen
Aydın Dağları
Gümüldür
Bulgurca
Kuşadası Körfezi
Belevi
Selçuk
Kuşadası
Ortaklar
Germencik
Aydın
Atça
Nazilli
Buharkent
Sarayköy
Kuyucak
Yenipazar
Babadağ
Denizli
Pamuk
Yenice
Karacasu
Aphrodisias
Tavas
Kızılcabölük
Söke
Koçarlı
Bağarasi
Davutlar
Samos
Karlovasi
Marathokambos
Mitilinii
Heraion
Fourni
Aghios Kirikos
Ikaria
Armenistis
Akköy
Bozdoğan
Çine
Karpuzlu
Kavaklıdere
Göktepe
Kale
Acıpayam
Selimiye
Milas
Yatağan
Muğla
Beyeğaç
Gölgeli Dağları
Boz Dağ
Yenihisar
Agathonisi
Arki
Lipisi
Patmos
Chora
Farmakonisi
Güllük Körfezi
Güllük
Kavak Dağı
Ören
Karaova
Leros
Aghia Marina
Ortakent
Karatoprak
Bodrum
Kalimnos
Kos
Pserimos
Kardamena
Pili
Kefalos
Gökova Körfezi
Reşadiye Yarımadası
Datça
Emecik
Bozburun
Marmaris
Günlüce
Köyceğiz
Ortaca
Dalyan
Dalaman
Fethiye
Fethiye Körfezi
Ula
Dodecanese
Astipalea
Levitha
Kinaros
Amorgos
Giali
Nissiros
Mandraki
Yazıköy
Simi
Megalo Horio
Tilos
Rhodes
Trianda
Kamiros Skala
Afandou
Archangelos
Embonas
Lindos
Akra Lindos
Monolithos
Kattavia
Lachania
Alimia
Halki
Sirna
Sofrana
Karavonisia
Astakida
Hamili
Dibounia
Akra Paraspori
Saria
Olimbos
Karpathos
Volada
Arkasa
Akra Kastello
Stenon Karpathos
Stenon Kasos
Aghia Marina
Kasos
Dionisades
Akra Sideros
Elasa
Vai
Sitia
Palekastro
Akra Plaka
Zakros
Chandra
Venézia
Haifa
MEDITE
AK
38°
37°
36°
35°
27°
28°
29°
1
2
3
4
A
B
C
D
186
185

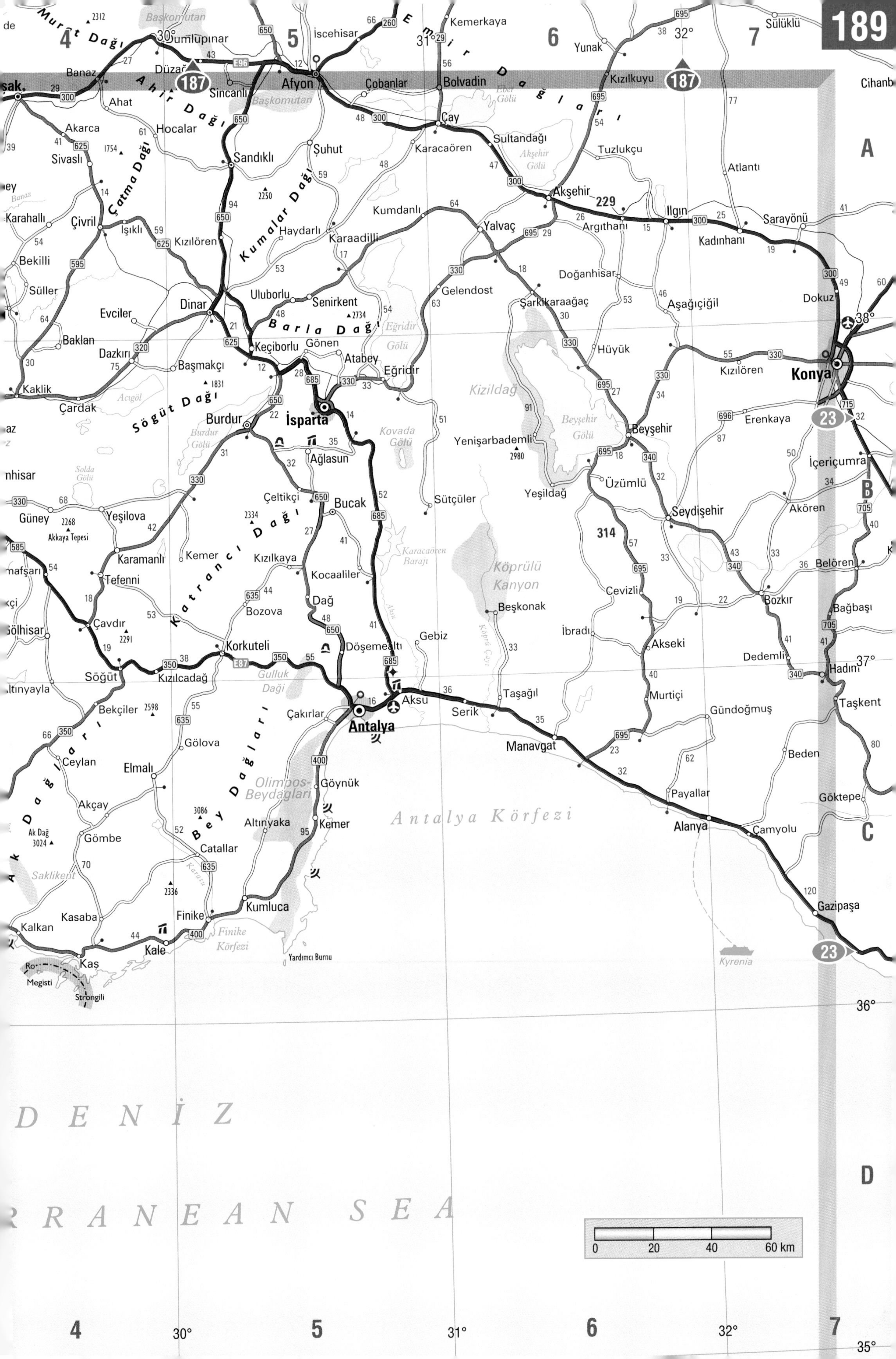
Afyon
Bolvadin
Çay
Akşehir
Ilgın
Konya
Sandıklı
Dinar
Isparta
Burdur
Eğridir
Beyşehir
Seydişehir
Antalya
Manavgat
Alanya
Gazipaşa
Kemer
Kumluca
Finike
Kaş
Kale
Elmalı
Korkuteli
Serik
Aksu
Bucak
Akseki
Bozkır
Hadım
Taşkent
Antalya Körfezi
Finike Körfezi
Beyşehir Gölü
Eğridir Gölü
Burdur Gölü
Akşehir Gölü
Köprülü Kanyon
Olimpos-Beydağları
Bey Dağları
Katrancı Dağı
Barla Dağı
Söğüt Dağı
Kumalar Dağı
Çatma Dağı
Ahır Dağı
Emir Dağları
Murat Dağı
Ak Dağları
Ak Dağ 3024
Megisti
Strongili
Kyrenia
Yardımcı Burnu
D E N İ Z
RANEAN SEA
0 20 40 60 km
30°
31°
32°
36°
35°
37°
38°
4
5
6
7
A
B
C
D

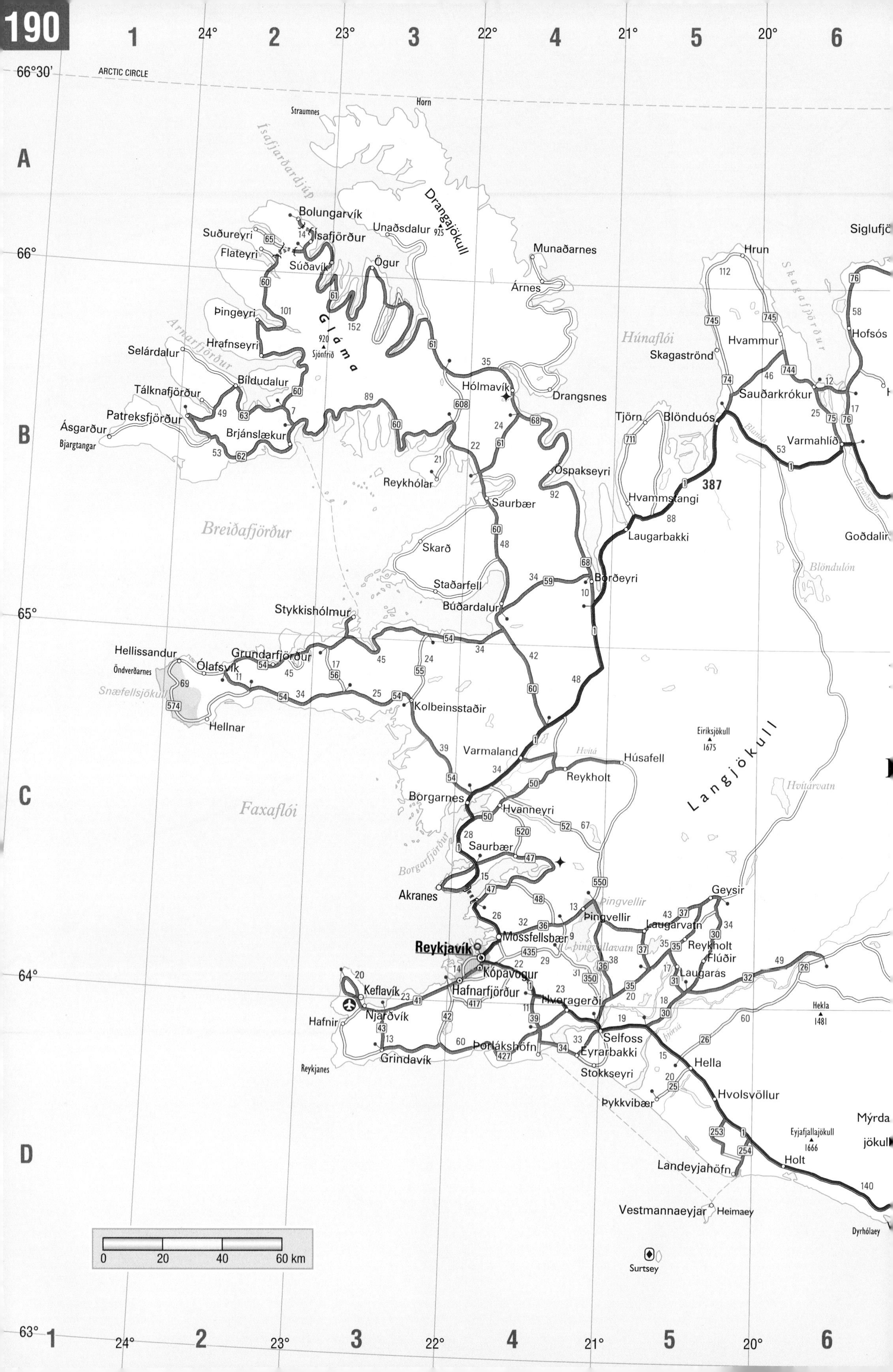

ARCTIC CIRCLE
Horn
Straumnes
Ísafjarðardjúp
Drangajökull
Bolungarvík
Ísafjörður
Unaðsdalur
Suðureyri
Flateyri
Súðavík
Ögur
Munaðarnes
Árnes
Hrun
Siglufjö
Þingeyri
Glámа
Sjónfríð
Hrafnseyri
Selárdalur
Arnarfjörður
Bíldudalur
Tálknafjörður
Patreksfjörður
Ásgarður
Bjargtangar
Brjánslækur
Hólmavík
Drangsnes
Húnaflói
Skagaströnd
Hvammur
Skagafjörður
Hofsós
Sauðarkrókur
Tjörn
Blönduós
Varmahlíð
Reykhólar
Ospakseyri
Hvammstangi
Saurbær
Laugarbakki
Goðdalir
Breiðafjörður
Skarð
Staðarfell
Borðeyri
Búðardalur
Blöndulón
Stykkishólmur
Hellissandur
Öndverðarnes
Ólafsvík
Grundarfjörður
Snæfellsjökull
Kolbeinsstaðir
Hellnar
Eiríksjökull
Varmaland
Hvítá
Húsafell
Reykholt
Langjökull
Hvítárvatn
Borgarnes
Faxaflói
Hvanneyri
Borgarfjörður
Akranes
Geysir
Þingvellir
Laugarvatn
Mossfellsbær
Þingvallavatn
Reykjavík
Flúðir
Kópavogur
Laugarás
Keflavík
Hafnarfjörður
Hveragerði
Hekla
Njarðvík
Hafnir
Selfoss
Þjórsá
Reykjanes
Grindavík
Þorlákshöfn
Eyrarbakki
Stokkseyri
Hella
Hvolsvöllur
Þykkvibær
Mýrda
jökull
Eyjafjallajökull
Landeyjahöfn
Holt
Vestmannaeyjar
Heimaey
Dyrhólaey
Surtsey
0 20 40 60 km

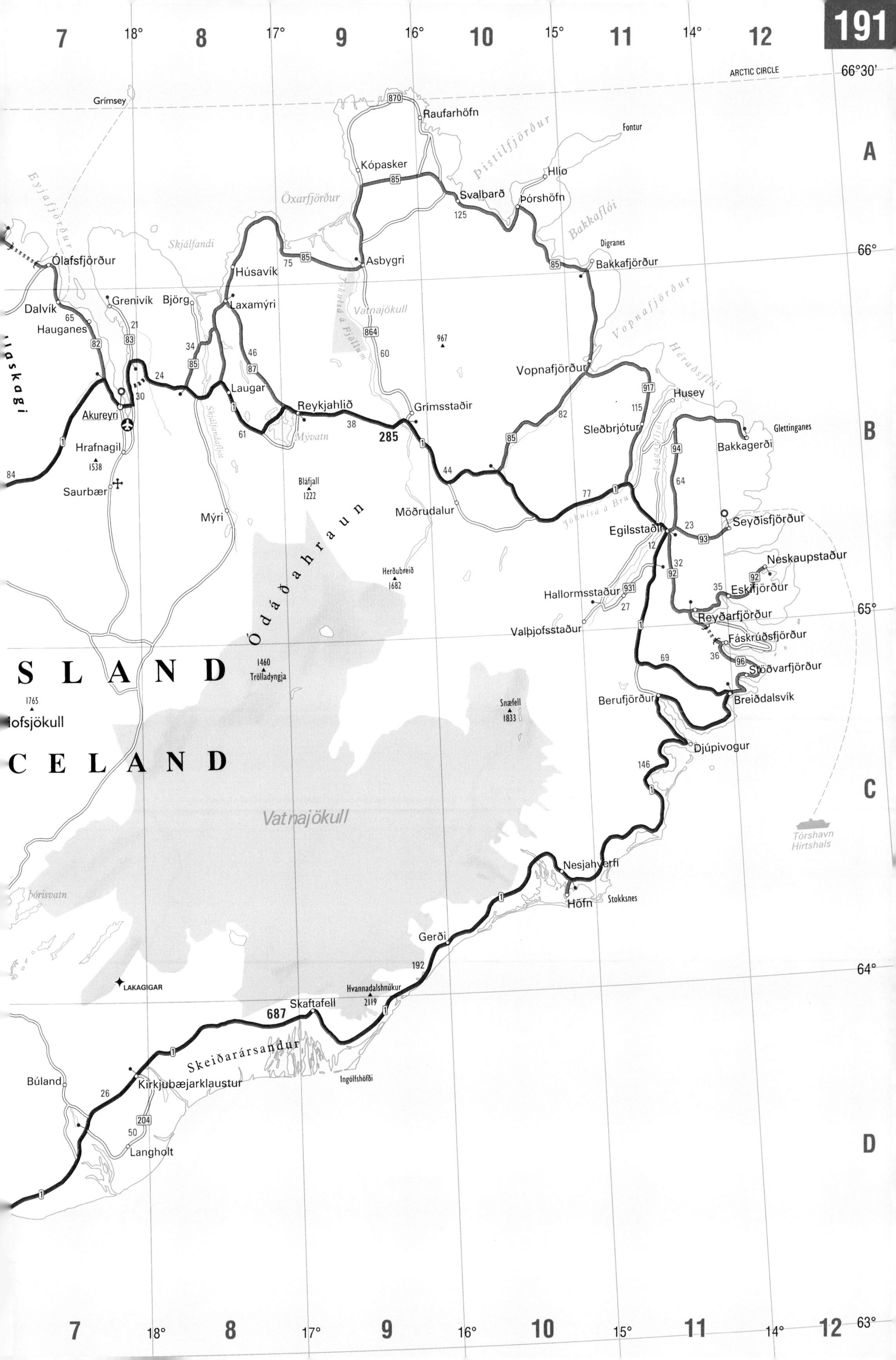
ARCTIC CIRCLE
Grímsey
Raufarhöfn
Fontur
Kópasker
Hlíð
Svalbarð
Þórshöfn
Öxarfjörður
Pistilfjörður
Bakkaflói
Skjálfandi
Eyjafjörður
Ólafsfjörður
Húsavík
Ásbygri
Digranes
Bakkafjörður
Dalvík
Hauganes
Grenivík
Björg
Laxamýri
Vatnajökull
Vopnafjörður
Héraðsflói
Laugar
Reykjahlíð
Mývatn
Grímsstaðir
Husey
Akureyri
Hrafnagil
1538
Saurbær
Sleðbrjótur
Glettinganes
Bakkagerði
Bláfjall
1222
Möðrudalur
Mýri
Ódáðahraun
Egilsstaðir
Seyðisfjörður
Herðubreið
1682
Neskaupstaður
Eskifjörður
Hallormsstaður
Valþjofsstaður
Reyðarfjörður
Fáskrúðsfjörður
Stöðvarfjörður
SLAND
ICELAND
1460
Trölladyngja
1765
Hofsjökull
Snæfell
1833
Berufjörður
Breiðdalsvík
Djúpivogur
Vatnajökull
Tórshavn
Hirtshals
Nesjahverfi
Höfn
Stokksnes
Þórisvatn
Gerði
LAKAGIGAR
Hvannadalshnúkur
2119
Skaftafell
Skeiðarársandur
Ingólfshöfði
Búland
Kirkjubæjarklaustur
Langholt
7
8
9
10
11
12
18°
17°
16°
15°
14°
66°30'
66°
65°
64°
63°
A
B
C
D

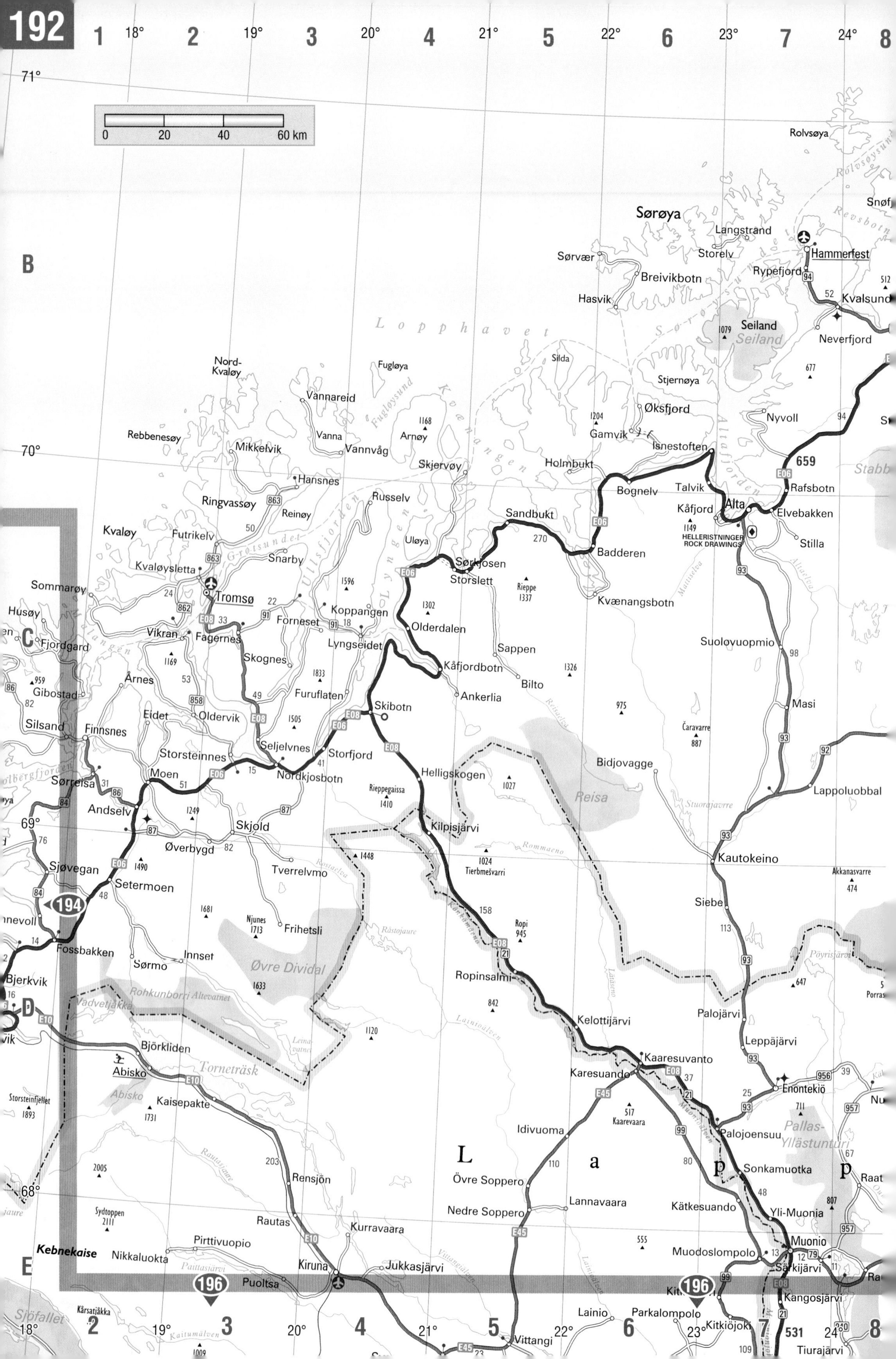
0 20 40 60 km
Sørøya
Langstrand
Storelv
Hammerfest
Rypefjord
Sørvær
Breivikbotn
Hasvik
Kvalsund
Seiland
Neverfjord
Rolvsøya
Lopphavet
Silda
Stjernøya
Nord-Kvaløy
Fugløya
Vannareid
Øksfjord
Nyvoll
Rebbenesøy
Vanna
Vannvåg
Arnøy
Gamvik
Isnestoften
Mikkelvik
Skjervøy
Holmbukt
Hansnes
Bognelv
Talvik
Rafsbotn
Ringvassøy
Reinøy
Russelv
Kåfjord
Alta
Elvebakken
Kvaløy
Futrikelv
Sandbukt
HELLERISTNINGER ROCK DRAWINGS
Stilla
Uløya
Kvaløysletta
Snarby
Badderen
Sommarøy
Tromsø
Sørkjosen
Storslett
Riеppe 1337
Kvænangsbotn
Husøy
Koppangen
Forneset
Vikran
Fagernes
Lyngseidet
Olderdalen
Fjordgard
Skognes
Sappen
Suolovuopmio
Gibostad
Årnes
Kåfjordbotn
Bilto
Furuflaten
Ankerlia
Masi
Skibotn
Silsand
Finnsnes
Eidet
Oldervik
Čaravarre 887
Seljelvnes
Storfjord
Storsteinnes
Bidjovagge
Sørreisa
Moen
Helligskogen
Nordkjosbotn
Reisa
Rieppegaissa 1410
Lappoluobbal
Andselv
Skjold
Kilpisjärvi
Øverbygd
Kautokeino
Sjøvegan
Tverrelvmo
Tierbmešvarri
Akkanasvarre 474
Setermoen
Siebe
Fossbakken
Njunes 1713
Frihetsli
Ropi 945
Bjerkvik
Sørmo
Innset
Øvre Dividal
Ropinsalmi
Vadvetjåkka
Rohkunborri
Altevatnet
Palojärvi
Kelottijärvi
Björkliden
Leppäjärvi
Abisko
Torneträsk
Kaaresuvanto
Karesuando
Enontekiö
Kaisepakte
Kaarevaara
Storsteinfjellet 1893
Palojoensuu
Idivuoma
Pallas-Yllästunturi
Rensjön
L a p p
Sonkamuotka
Övre Soppero
Lannavaara
Nedre Soppero
Kätkesuando
Yli-Muonio
Sydtoppen 2111
Rautas
Kurravaara
Pirttivuopio
Muodoslompolo
Muonio
Kebnekaise
Nikkaluokta
Kiruna
Jukkasjärvi
Särkijärvi
Puoltsa
Kangosjärvi
Kårsatjäkka
Lainio
Parkalompolo
Kitkiöjoki
Sjöfallet
Vittangi
Tiurajärvi
194
196
196

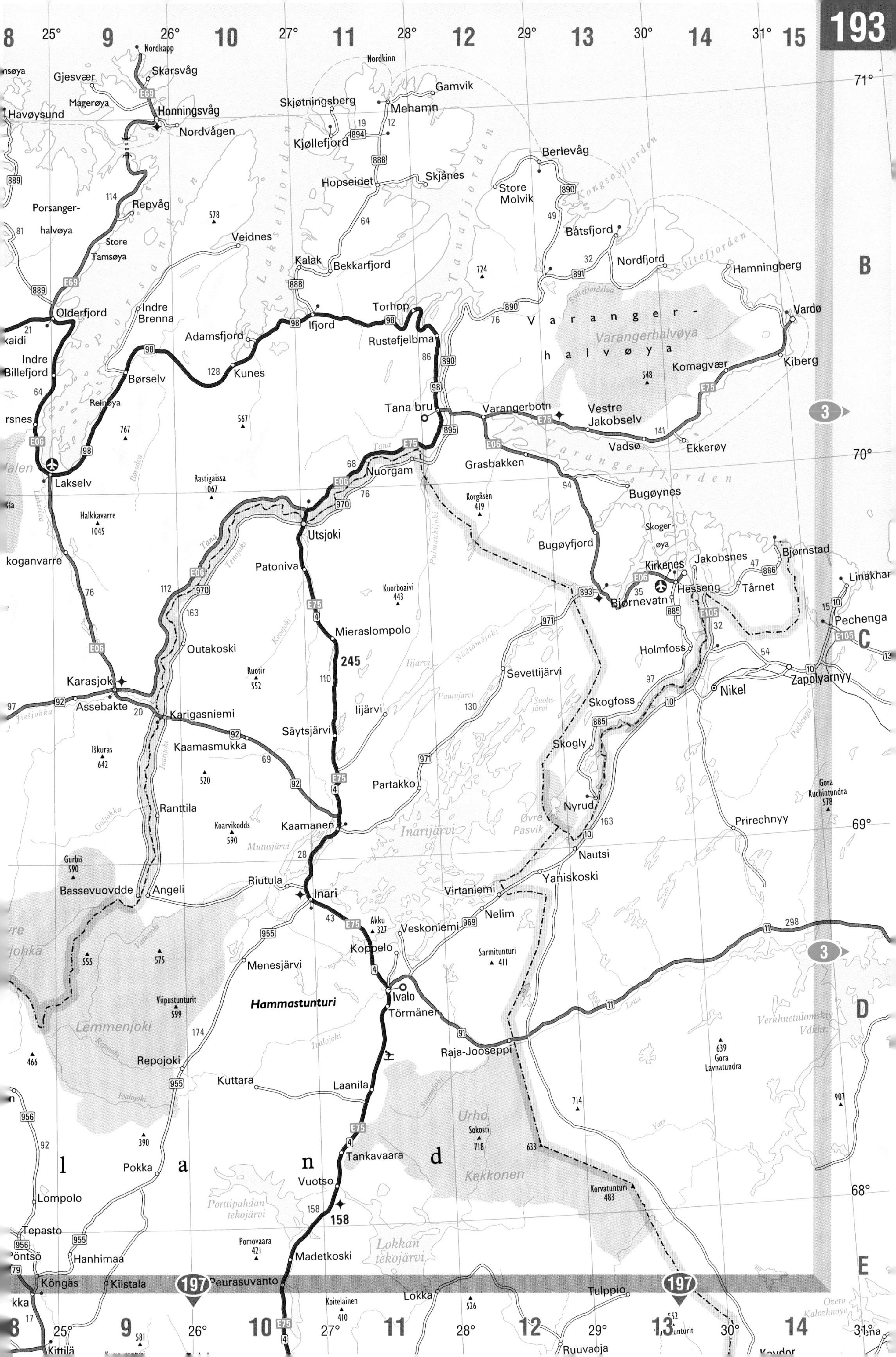
Nordkapp
Skarsvåg
Gjesvær
Magerøya
Honningsvåg
Havøysund
Nordvågen
Nordkinn
Gamvik
Skjøtningsberg
Mehamn
Kjøllefjord
Hopseidet
Skjånes
Berlevåg
Store Molvik
Kongsøyfjorden
Repvåg
Porsanger-
halvøya
Store Tamsøya
Veidnes
Porsangen
Laksefjorden
Tanafjorden
Båtsfjord
Nordfjord
Syltefjorden
Hamningberg
Kalak
Bekkarfjord
Olderfjord
Indre Brenna
Torhop
Ifjord
Adamsfjord
Rustefjelbma
Vardø
Varanger-
halvøya
Varangerhalvøya
Komagvær
Kiberg
Indre Billefjord
Børselv
Kunes
Reinøya
Tana bru
Varangerbotn
Vestre Jakobselv
Vadsø
Ekkerøy
Varangerfjorden
Grasbakken
Lakselv
Nuorgam
Rastigaissa 1067
Bugøynes
Halkkavarre 1045
Korgåsen 419
Utsjoki
Skoger-
øya
Bugøyfjord
Bjørnstad
koganvarre
Patoniva
Kuorboaivi 443
Kirkenes
Jakobsnes
Hesseng
Tårnet
Linakhar
Bjørnevatn
Pechenga
Mieraslompolo
Outakoski
Holmfoss
Karasjok
Ruotir 552
Sevettijärvi
Nikel
Zapolyarnyy
Assebakte
Karigasniemi
Iijärvi
Skogfoss
Säytsjärvi
Kaamasmukka
Skogly
Iškuras 642
Partakko
Gora Kuchintundra 578
Ranttila
Nyrud
Koarvikodds 590
Kaamanen
Øvre Pasvik
Inarijärvi
Prirechnyy
Nautsi
Gurbiš 590
Yaniskoski
Bassevuovdde
Angeli
Riutula
Inari
Virtaniemi
Nelim
Akku 327
Veskoniemi
Koppelo
Sarmitunturi 411
Menesjärvi
Ivalo
Hammastunturi
Viipustunturit 599
Törmänen
Lemmenjoki
Raja-Jooseppi
Verkhnetulomskiy Vdkhr.
Repojoki
Gora Lavnatundra 639
Kuttara
Laanila
Urho
Sokosti 718
Tankavaara
Pokka
Vuotso
Kekkonen
Korvatunturi 483
Lompolo
Porttipahdan tekojärvi
Tepasto
Pomovaara 421
Madetkoski
Lokkan tekojärvi
Pöntsö
Hanhimaa
Köngäs
Kiistala
Peurasuvanto
Lokka
Tulppio
Koitelainen 410
Kittilä
Ruuvaoja
Kovdor
197
3
B
C
D
E
71°
70°
69°
68°
25°
26°
27°
28°
29°
30°
31°
8
9
10
11
12
13
14
15

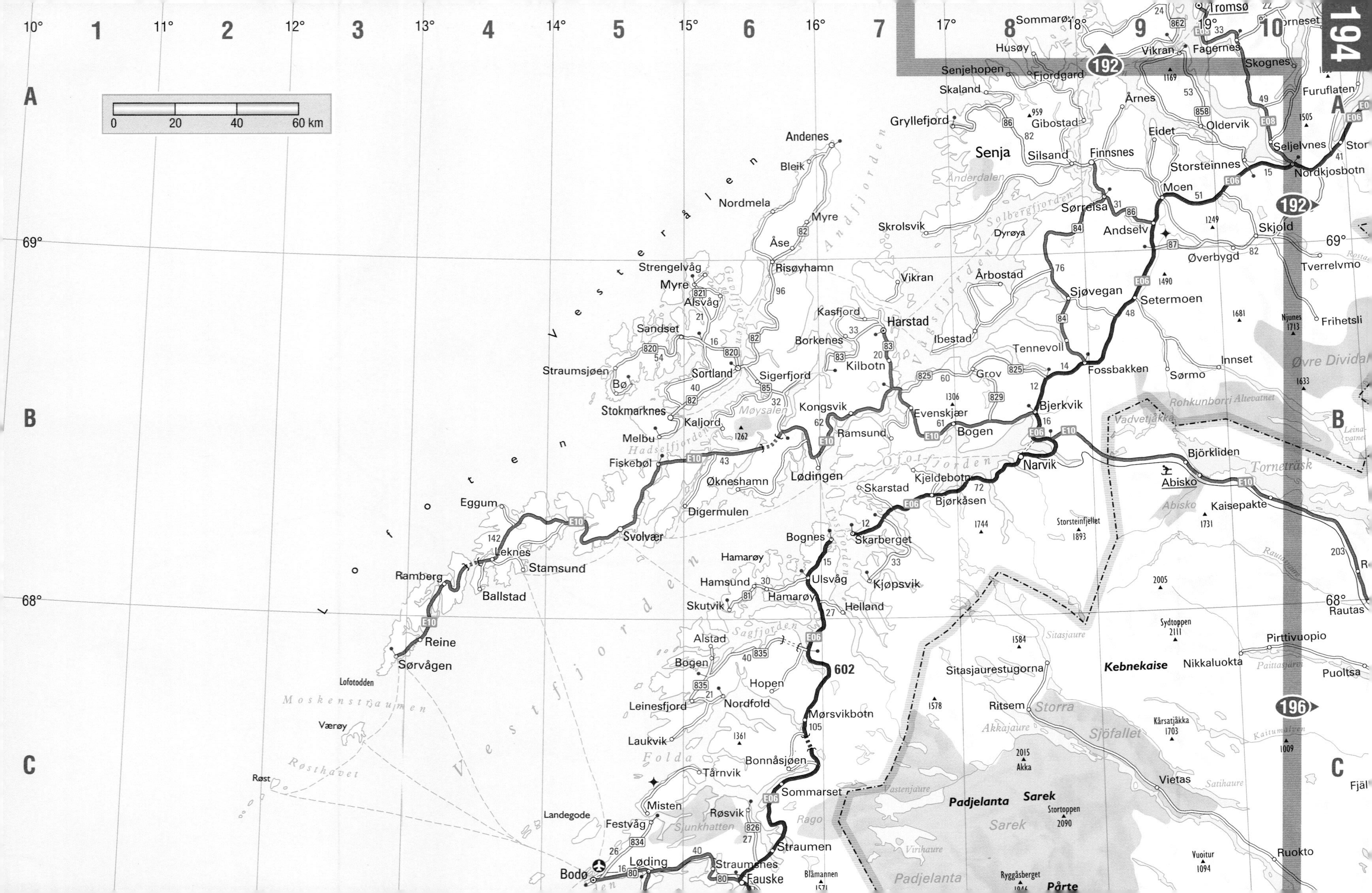

192
196
Tromsø
Fagernes
Skognes
Vikran
Nordkjosbotn
Seljelvnes
Furuflaten
Storsteinnes
Oldervik
Eidet
Årnes
Moen
Skjold
Tverrelvmo
Frihetsli
Øverbygd
Andselv
Setermoen
Sørmo
Innset
Finnsnes
Sørreisa
Sjøvegan
Fossbakken
Silsand
Gibostad
Fjordgard
Husøy
Sommarøy
Senjehopen
Skaland
Senja
Dyrøya
Gryllefjord
Skrolsvik
Årbostad
Tennevoll
Bjerkvik
Narvik
Björkliden
Abisko
Kaisepakte
Grov
Bogen
Evenskjær
Ibestad
Vikran
Harstad
Kilbotn
Kasfjord
Borkenes
Ramsund
Kongsvik
Kjeldebotn
Bjørkåsen
Skarstad
Skarberget
Kjøpsvik
Bognes
Ulsvåg
Helland
Tysfjorden
Ofotfjorden
602
Mørsvikbotn
Andenes
Bleik
Myre
Åse
Risøyhamn
Nordmela
Sigerfjord
Sortland
Lødingen
Gavlfjorden
Møysalen
Kaljord
Øksneshamn
Digermulen
Hamarøy
Hamsund
Skutvik
Sagfjorden
Alstad
Bogen
Nordfold
Hopen
Bonnåsjøen
Sommarset
Straumen
Fauske
Straumsnes
Røsvik
Tårnvik
Laukvik
Leinesfjord
Misten
Festvåg
Løding
Bodø
Landegode
Folda
Strengelvåg
Myre
Alsvåg
Sandset
Stokmarknes
Melbu
Straumsjøen
Bø
Fiskebøl
Svolvær
Stamsund
Leknes
Ballstad
Eggum
Ramberg
Reine
Sørvågen
Lofotodden
Værøy
Røst
Vestfjorden
Vesterålen
Lofoten
Moskenstraumen
Røsthavet
Kebnekaise
Nikkaluokta
Pirttivuopio
Puoltsa
Rautas
Ruokto
Vietas
Ritsem
Sitasjaurestugorna
Sarek
Padjelanta
Pårte
Storra Sjöfallet
Torneträsk
Øvre Dividal
Sydtoppen 2111
Kårsatjåkka 1703
Akka 2015
Stortoppen 2090
Vuoitur 1094
Blåmannen
60 km
0
20
40
10°
11°
12°
13°
14°
15°
16°
17°
18°
19°
68°
69°
1
2
3
4
5
6
7
8
9
10
A
B
C

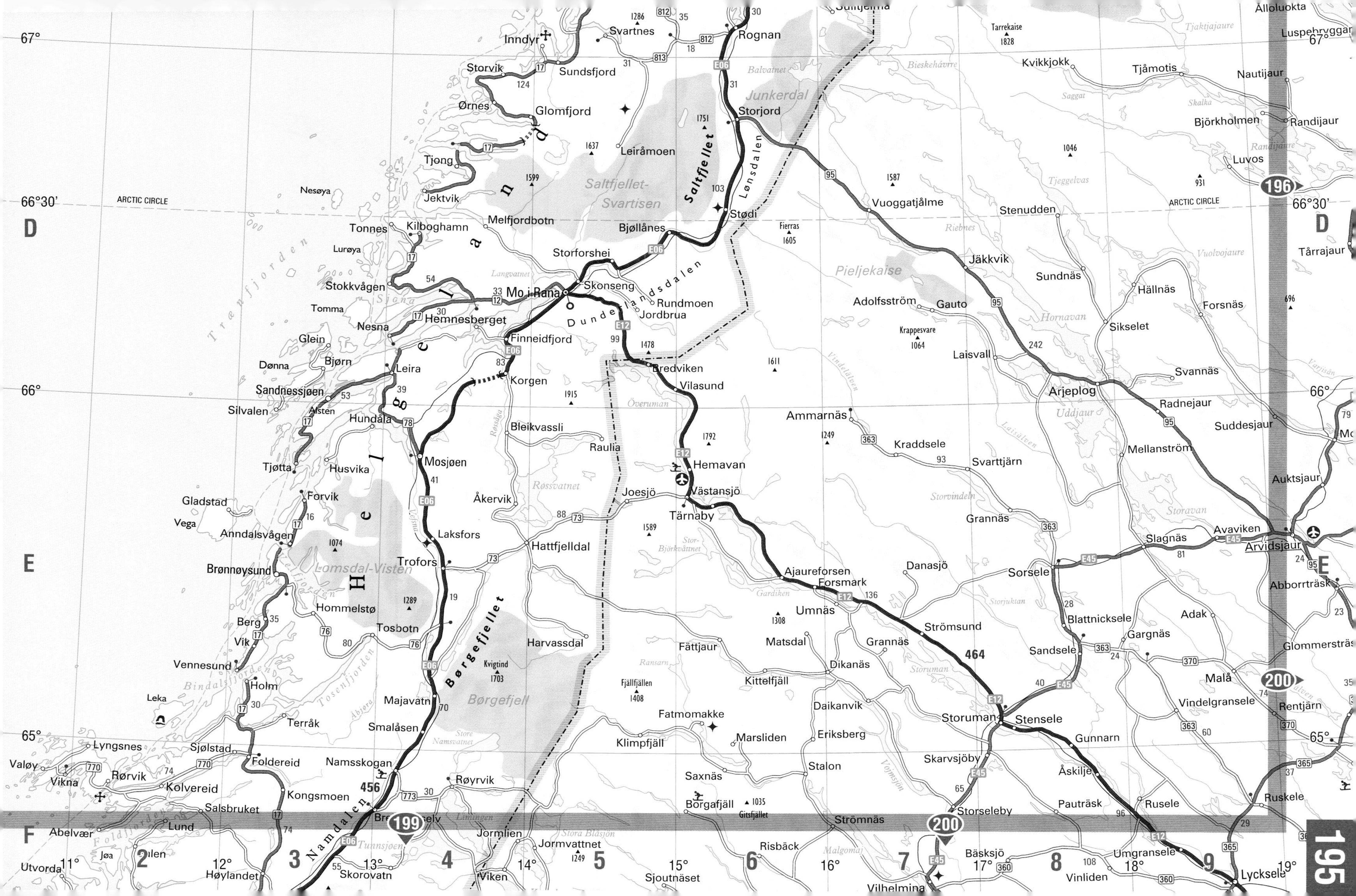

Rognan
Svartnes
Inndyr
Storvik
Sundsfjord
Ørnes
Glomfjord
Leiråmoen
Tjong
Jektvik
Nesøya
ARCTIC CIRCLE
Tonnes
Kilboghamn
Melfjordbotn
Saltfjellet-Svartisen
Saltfjellet
Storjord
Junkerdal
Lønsdalen
Stødi
Bjøllånes
Storforshei
Lurøya
Stokkvågen
Mo i Rana
Skonseng
Dunderlandsdalen
Rundmoen
Jordbrua
Tomma
Hemnesberget
Nesna
Finneidfjord
Glein
Bjørn
Dønna
Leira
Korgen
Sandnessjøen
Alsten
Silvalen
Hundåla
Bleikvassli
Raulia
Mosjøen
Tjøtta
Husvika
Forvik
Gladstad
Vega
Åkervik
Laksfors
Anndalsvågen
Lomsdal-Visten
Trofors
Hattfjelldal
Brønnøysund
Helgeland
Hommelstø
Tosbotn
Berg
Vik
Børgefjellet
Harvassdal
Vennesund
Holm
Leka
Terråk
Majavatn
Smalåsen
Børgefjell
Lyngsnes
Sjølstad
Foldereid
Namsskogan
Valøy
Vikna
Rørvik
Kolvereid
Kongsmoen
Røyrvik
Salsbruket
Abelvær
Lund
Namdalen
Jormlien
Jormvattnet
Utvorda
Høylandet
Skorovatn
Viken
Sjoutnäset
Bredviken
Vilasund
Hemavan
Västansjö
Joesjö
Tärnaby
Ajaureforsen
Forsmark
Umnäs
Matsdal
Fättjaur
Grannäs
Dikanäs
Kittelfjäll
Daikanvik
Fatmomakke
Marsliden
Eriksberg
Klimpfjäll
Stalon
Saxnäs
Borgafjäll
Strömnäs
Risbäck
Vilhelmina
Ammarnäs
Kraddsele
Svarttjärn
Danasjö
Strömsund
Storuman
Stensele
Gunnarn
Skarvsjöby
Åskilje
Storseleby
Pauträsk
Bäsksjö
Umgransele
Vinliden
Lycksele
Pieljekaise
Adolfsström
Gauto
Laisvall
Vuoggatjålme
Jäkkvik
Arjeplog
Stenudden
Sundnäs
Sikselet
Hällnäs
Forsnäs
Svannäs
Radnejaur
Suddesjaur
Mellanström
Auktsjaur
Slagnäs
Avaviken
Arvidsjaur
Sorsele
Blattnicksele
Gargnäs
Adak
Sandsele
Abborrträsk
Glommersträsk
Malå
Vindelgransele
Rentjärn
Rusele
Ruskele
Kvikkjokk
Tjåmotis
Nautijaur
Björkholmen
Randijaur
Luvos
Tårrajaur
Alloluokta

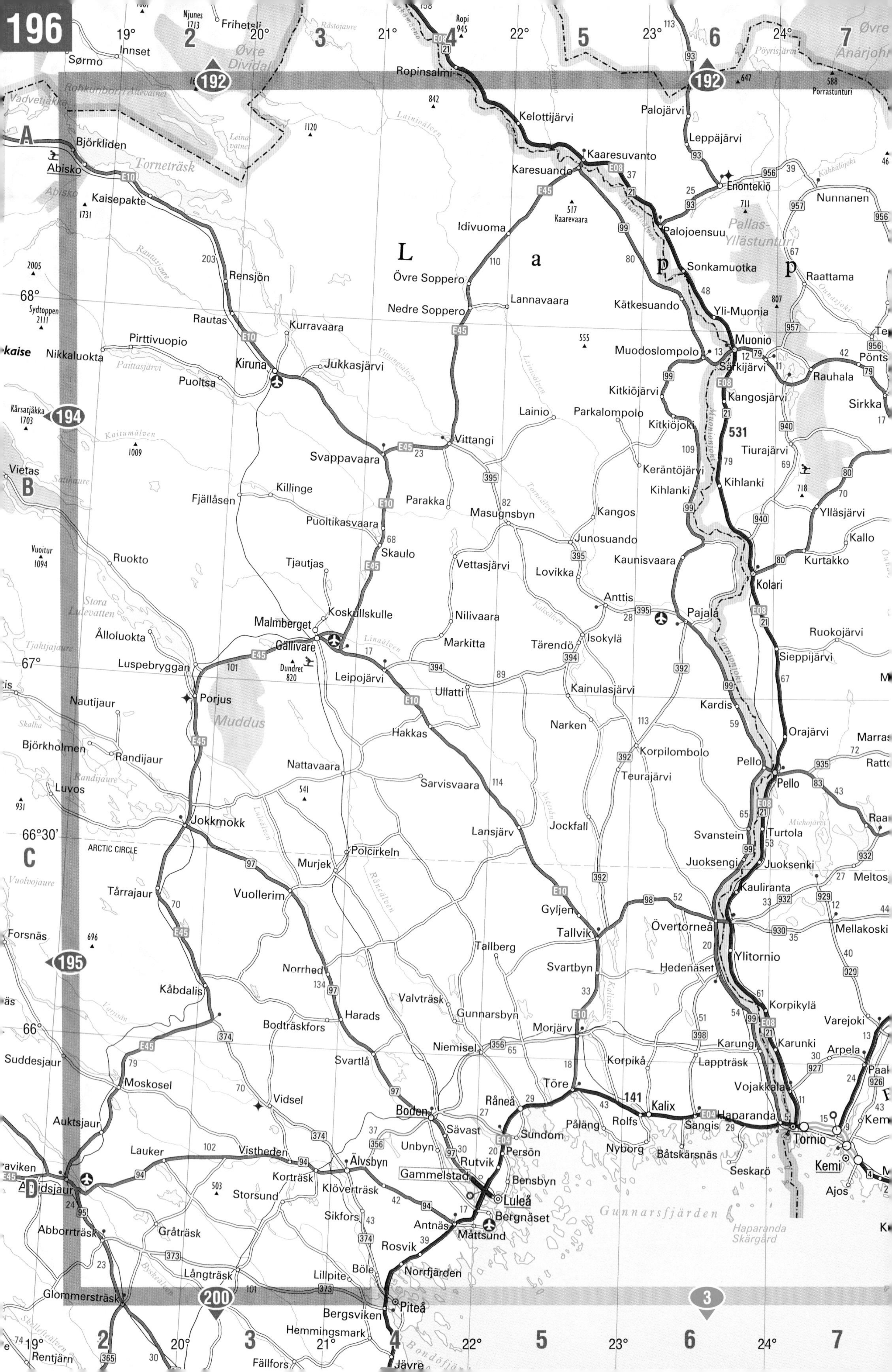
Lapp
Kiruna
Gällivare
Jokkmokk
Arvidsjaur
Boden
Luleå
Piteå
Kalix
Haparanda
Tornio
Kemi
Pajala
Kolari
Muonio
Pello
Övertorneå
Ylitornio
Abisko
Björkliden
Torneträsk
Karesuando
Kaaresuvanto
Enontekiö
Vittangi
Svappavaara
Porjus
Moskosel
Älvsbyn
Gunnarsfjärden
Haparanda Skärgård
ARCTIC CIRCLE
66°30'
67°
68°
66°

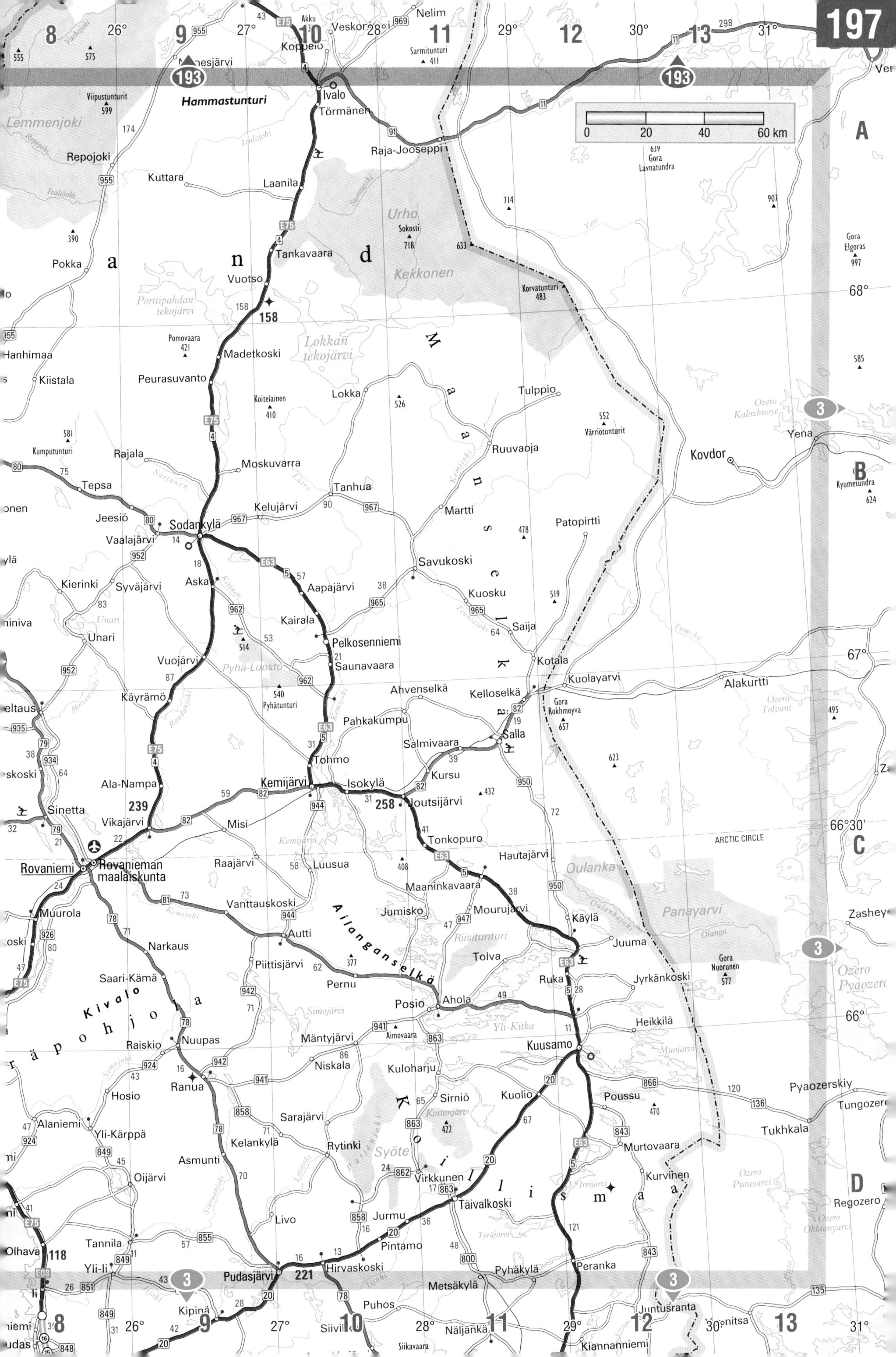
Hammastunturi
Lemmenjoki
Repojoki
Kuttara
Laanila
Ivalo
Törmänen
Koppelo
Akku
Veskoniemi
Nelim
Sarmitunturi
Raja-Jooseppi
Urho
Kekkonen
Sokosti
718
Tankavaara
Vuotso
158
Pokka
Porttipahdan tekojärvi
Lokkan tekojärvi
Pomovaara
421
Madetkoski
Peurasuvanto
Hanhimaa
Kiistala
Korvatunturi
483
Koitelainen
410
Lokka
Tulppio
Ruuvaoja
Värriötunturit
552
Kovdor
Yena
Kumputunturi
581
Rajala
Moskuvarra
Tepsa
Jeesiö
Sodankylä
Vaalajärvi
Kelujärvi
Tanhua
Martti
Patopirtti
Savukoski
Kuosku
Saija
Kotala
Kuolayarvi
Alakurtti
Kelloselkä
Salla
Kierinki
Syväjärvi
Aska
Aapajärvi
Kairala
Pelkosenniemi
Saunavaara
Unari
Vuojärvi
Pyhä-Luosto
Pyhätunturi
540
Käyrämö
Ahvenselkä
Pahkakumpu
Salmivaara
Kursu
Tohmo
Kemijärvi
Isokylä
Joutsijärvi
258
Ala-Nampa
239
Sinetta
Vikajärvi
Misi
Tonkopuro
Hautajärvi
Rovaniemi
Rovaniemen maalaiskunta
Raajärvi
Luusua
Maaninkavaara
Muurola
Vanttauskoski
Autti
Jumisko
Mourujärvi
Käylä
Juuma
Oulanka
Panayarvi
Riisitunturi
Tolva
Ruka
Jyrkänkoski
Narkaus
Piittisjärvi
Ailangan selkä
Pernu
Posio
Ahola
Saari-Kämä
Kivalo
Nuupas
Raiskio
Mäntyjärvi
Aimovaara
Kuusamo
Heikkilä
Yli-Kitka
Niskala
Kuloharju
Ranua
Hosio
Sirniö
Kuolio
Poussu
Pyaozerskiy
Tungozero
Alaniemi
Yli-Kärppä
Sarajärvi
Kelankylä
Rytinki
Syöte
Tukhkala
Murtovaara
Asmunti
Oijärvi
Virkkunen
Taivalkoski
Kurvinen
Livo
Jurmu
Pintamo
Regozero
Olhava
118
Tannila
Yli-Ii
Pudasjärvi
221
Hirvaskoski
Metsäkylä
Pyhäkylä
Peranka
Kipinä
Puhos
Juntusranta
Siivikko
Näljänkä
Siikavaara
Kiannanniemi
ARCTIC CIRCLE
Gora Lavnatundra
Gora Elgoras
997
Gora Rokhmoyva
657
Gora Nuorunen
577
Kyumetundra
624
Zashey
Ozero Pyaozero
0 20 40 60 km
68°
67°
66°30'
66°
A
B
C
D
8 9 10 11 12 13
26° 27° 28° 29° 30° 31°
M a a n s e l k ä
K o i l l i s m a a
Kivalo
r ä p o h j o l a
l a n d

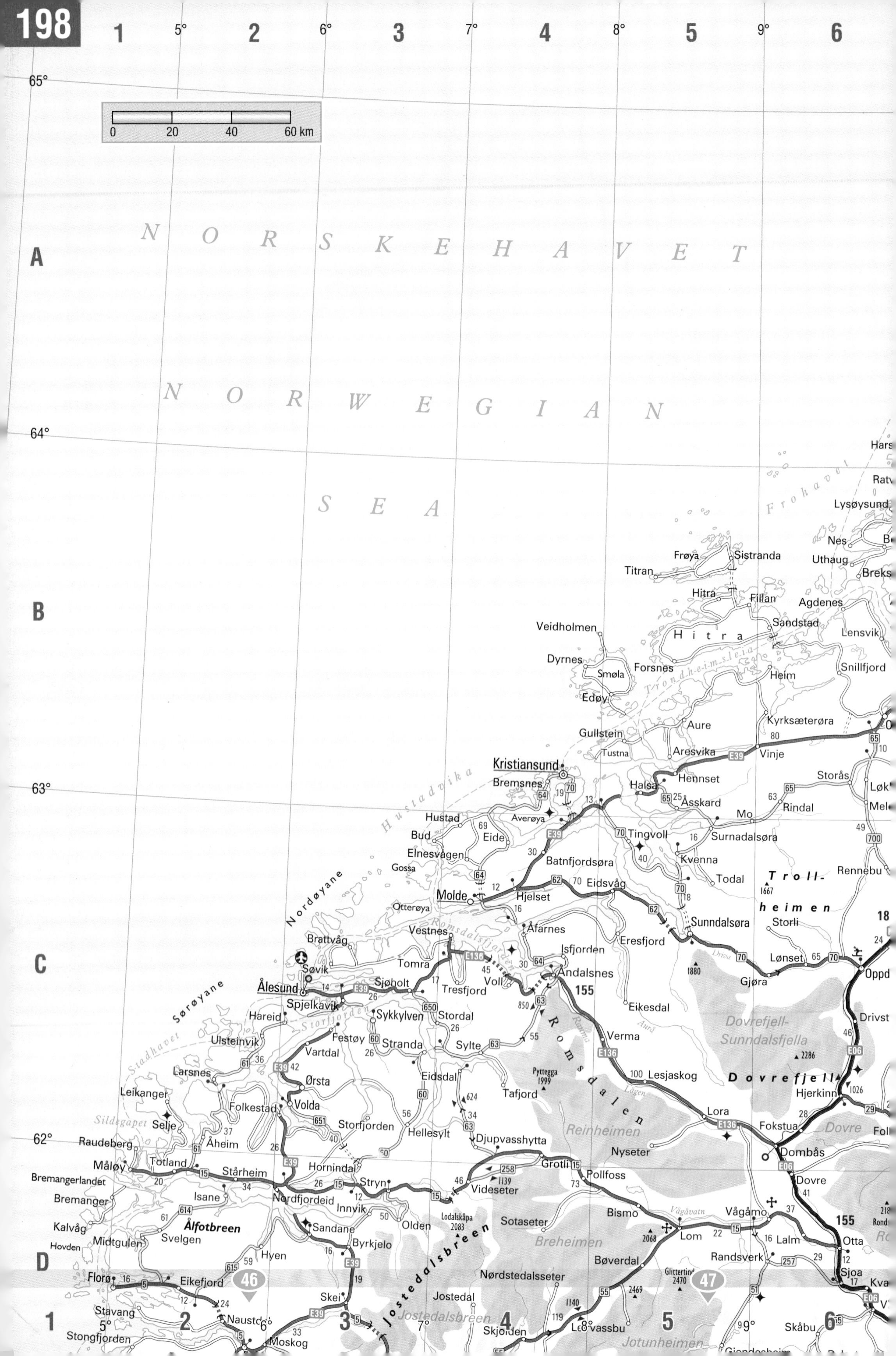

0
20
40
60 km
N O R S K E H A V E T
N O R W E G I A N
S E A
Frohavet
Hitra
Trondheimsleia
Hustadvika
Nordøyane
Sørøyane
Stadhavet
Sildegapet
Romsdalsfjorden
Storfjorden
Frøya
Sistranda
Titran
Hitra
Fillan
Agdenes
Sandstad
Lensvik
Veidholmen
Dyrnes
Smøla
Forsnes
Edøy
Heim
Snillfjord
Kyrksæterøra
Aure
Gullstein
Tustna
Aresvika
Vinje
Kristiansund
Bremsnes
Halsa
Hennset
Storås
Åsskard
Rindal
Mo
Hustad
Averøya
Tingvoll
Surnadalsøra
Bud
Eide
Elnesvågen
Batnfjordsøra
Kvenna
Rennebu
Gossa
Todal
Trollheimen
Molde
Hjelset
Eidsvåg
Otterøya
Sunndalsøra
Storli
Vestnes
Åfarnes
Brattvåg
Eresfjord
Isfjorden
Lønset
Oppdal
Tomra
Søvik
Åndalsnes
Gjøra
Ålesund
Sjøholt
Tresfjord
Voll
Spjelkavik
Eikesdal
Hareid
Sykkylven
Stordal
Drivstua
Ulsteinvik
Festøy
Stranda
Sylte
Verma
Dovrefjell-Sunndalsfjella
Vartdal
Romsdalen
Larsnes
Eidsdal
Pyttegga 1999
Lesjaskog
Dovrefjell
Ørsta
Tafjord
Hjerkinn
Leikanger
Volda
Folkestad
Lora
Selje
Storfjorden
Hellesylt
Reinheimen
Fokstua
Dovre
Raudeberg
Åheim
Djupvasshytta
Dombås
Måløy
Totland
Stårheim
Hornindal
Grotli
Nyseter
Bremangerlandet
Stryn
Pollfoss
Dovre
Bremanger
Isane
Nordfjordeid
Videseter
Innvik
Bismo
Vågåmo
Kalvåg
Ålfotbreen
Sandane
Olden
Lodalskåpa 2083
Sotaseter
Lom
Lalm
Otta
Hovden
Midtgulen
Svelgen
Byrkjelo
Jostedalsbreen
Breheimen
Randsverk
Hyen
Bøverdal
Sjoa
Florø
Eikefjord
Nordstedalsseter
Glittertind 2470
Jostedal
Skei
Stavang
Naustdal
Stongfjorden
Moskog
Jostedalsbreen
Skjolden
Leirvassbu
Jotunheimen
Skåbu
Gjendesheim
Harstad
Ratvika
Lysøysund
Nes
Uthaug
Brekstad
Drivstua
Løkken
Meldal

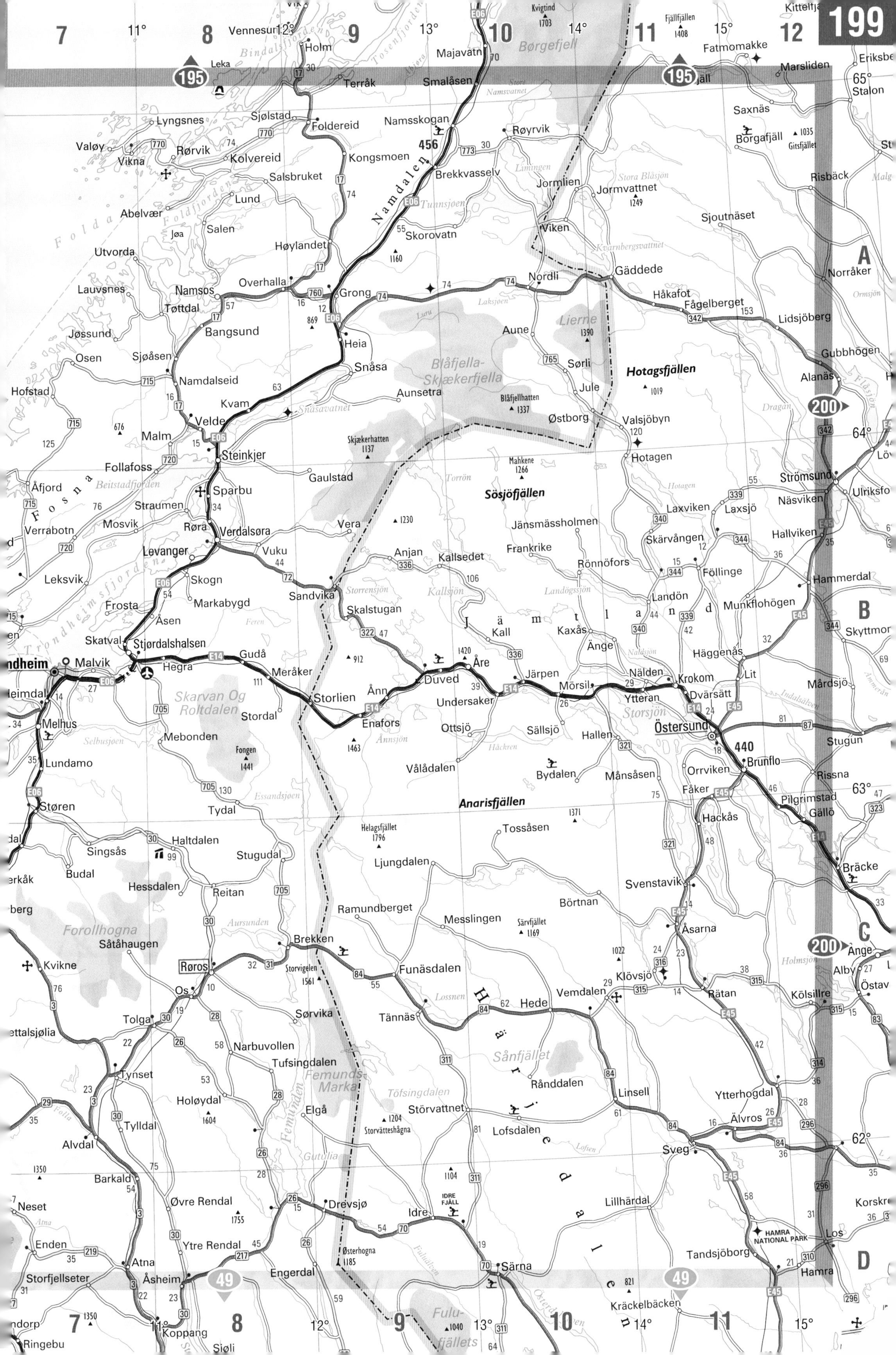

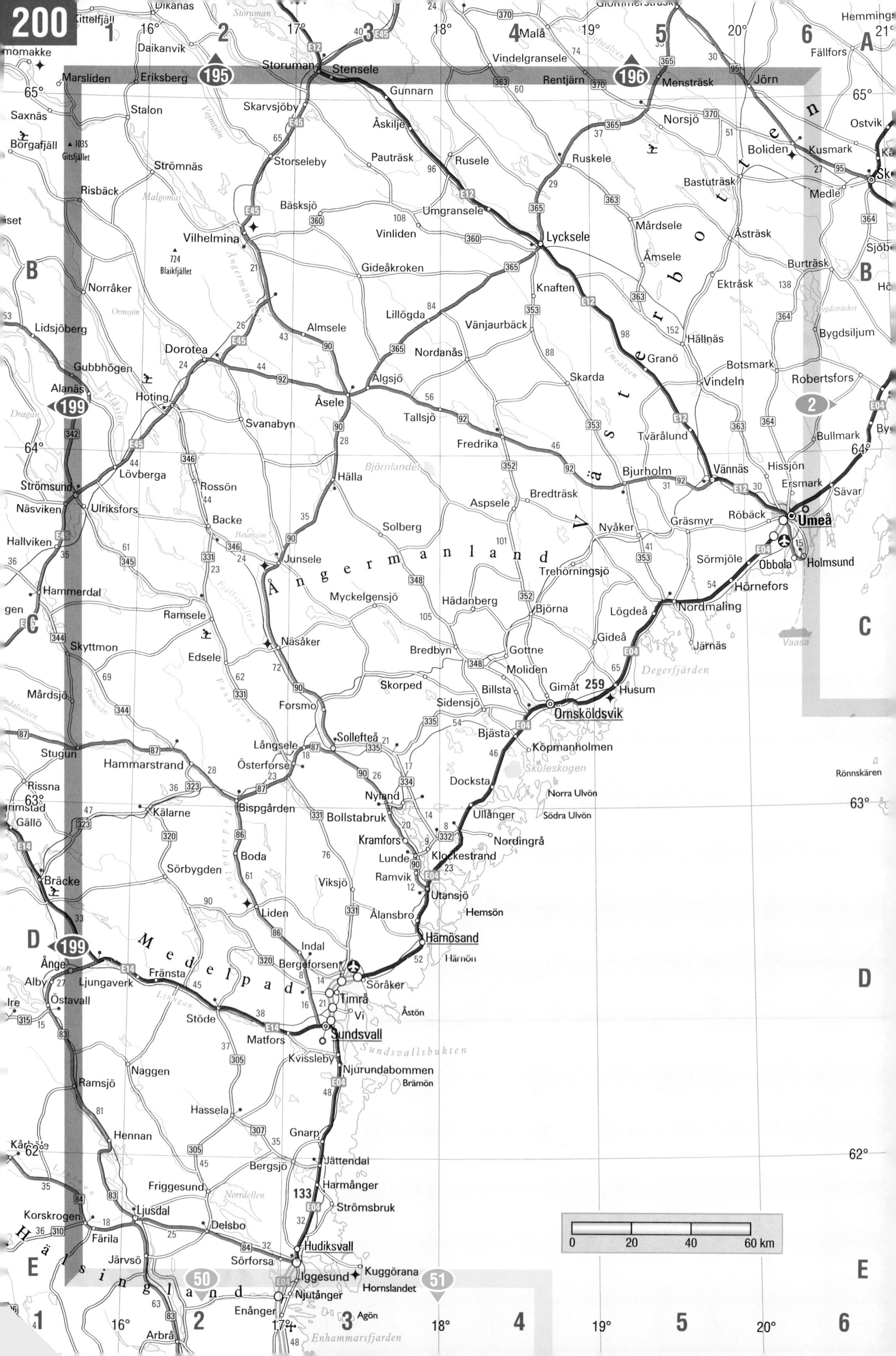
Storuman
Stensele
Malå
Vindelgranselle
Rentjärn
Jörn
Mensträsk
Fällfors
Marsliden
Eriksberg
Daikanvik
Gunnarn
Stalon
Skarvsjöby
Åskilje
Norsjö
Boliden
Kusmark
Ostvik
Saxnäs
Borgafjäll
Gitsfjället
Strömnäs
Storseleby
Pauträsk
Rusele
Ruskele
Bastuträsk
Medle
Risbäck
Malgomaj
Bäsksjö
Umgransele
Vinliden
Lycksele
Mårdsele
Åsträsk
Åmsele
Vilhelmina
Blaikfjället
Gideåkroken
Knaften
Burträsk
Ekträsk
Norråker
Ormsjön
Lillögda
Vänjaurbäck
Hällnäs
Bygdsiljum
Lidsjöberg
Almsele
Nordanås
Granö
Botsmark
Dorotea
Gubbhögen
Skarda
Vindeln
Robertsfors
Alanäs
Hoting
Ålgsjö
Åsele
Tallsjö
Bullmark
Svanabyn
Fredrika
Tvärålund
Lövberga
Hälla
Björnlandet
Bjurholm
Vännäs
Hissjön
Strömsund
Rossön
Ersmark
Sävar
Näsviken
Ulriksfors
Bredträsk
Aspsele
Backe
Solberg
Gräsmyr
Röbäck
Umeå
Hallviken
Nyåker
Junsele
Sörmjöle
Obbola
Holmsund
Trehörningsjö
Hammerdal
Ångermanland
Västerbotten
Myckelgensjö
Hädanberg
Lögdeå
Hörnefors
Nordmaling
Ramsele
Björna
Gideå
Järnäs
Skyttmon
Näsåker
Edsele
Bredbyn
Gottne
Moliden
Vaasa
Degerfjärden
Husum
Mårdsjö
Skorped
Billsta
Gimåt
Forsmo
Sidensjö
Örnsköldsvik
Bjästa
Köpmanholmen
Stugun
Solleftеå
Långsele
Hammarstrand
Österforse
Skuleskogen
Rissna
Docksta
Rönnskären
Nyland
Norra Ulvön
Södra Ulvön
Kälarne
Bispgården
Bollstabruk
Ullånger
Gällö
Kramfors
Nordingrå
Boda
Lunde
Klockestrand
Sörbygden
Ramvik
Bräcke
Viksjö
Utansjö
Hemsön
Liden
Ålansbro
Härnösand
Indal
Härnön
Ånge
Bergeforsen
Fränsta
Medelpad
Söråker
Alby
Ljungaverk
Östavall
Timrå
Vi
Åstön
Stöde
Matfors
Sundsvall
Sundsvallsbukten
Kvissleby
Njurundabommen
Naggen
Brämön
Ramsjö
Hassela
Gnarp
Hennan
Jättendal
Bergsjö
Harmånger
Friggesund
Norrdellen
Strömsbruk
Ljusdal
Korskrogen
Färila
Delsbo
Hudiksvall
Järvsö
Sörforsa
Iggesund
Kuggörana
Hornslandet
Hälsingland
Njutånger
Enånger
Agön
Arbrå
Enhammarsfjärden
0 20 40 60 km

## City plans • Plans de villes
## Stadtpläne • Piante di città

| | | | |
|---|---|---|---|
| Motorway | Autoroute | Autobahn | Autostrada |
| Major through route | Route principale majeur | Hauptstrecke | Strada di grande communicazione |
| Through route | Route principale | Schnellstrasse | Strada d'importanza regionale |
| Secondary road | Route secondaire | Nebenstrasse | Strada d'interesse locale |
| Dual carriageway | Chaussées séparées | Zweispurig Schnellstrasse | Strada a carreggiate doppie |
| Other road | Autre route | Nebenstrecke | Altra strada |
| Tunnel | Tunnel | Tunnel | Galleria stradale |
| Limited access / pedestrian road | Rue réglementée / rue piétonne | Beschränkter Zugang/ Fussgängerzone | Strada pedonale / a accesso limitato |
| One-way street | Sens unique | Einbahnstrasse | Senso unico |
| Parking | Parc de stationnement | Parkplatz | Parcheggio |
| Motorway number A7 | Numéro d'autoroute | Autobahnnummer A7 | Numero di autostrada |
| National road number 447 | Numéro de route nationale | Nationalstrassen- nummer 447 | Numero di strada nazionale |
| European road number E45 | Numéro de route européenne | Europäische Strassennummer E45 | Numero di strada europea |
| Destination GENT | Destination | Ziel GENT | Destinazione |
| Car ferry | Bac passant les autos | Autofähre | Traghetto automobili |
| Railway | Chemin de fer | Eisenbahn | Ferrovia |
| Rail/bus station | Gare/gare routière | Bahnhof/ Busstation | Stazione ferrovia / pullman |
| Underground, metro station | Station de métro | U-Bahnstation | Metropolitano |
| Cable car | Téléférique | Drahtseilbahn | Funivia |
| Abbey, cathedral | Abbaye, cathédrale | Abtei, Kloster, Kathedrale | Abbazia, duomo |
| Church of interest | Église intéressante | Interessante Kirche | Chiesa da vedere |
| Synagogue | Synagogue | Synagoge | Sinagoga |
| Hospital | Hôpital | Krankenhaus | Ospedale |
| Police station | Police | Polizeiwache | Polizia |
| Post office | Bureau de poste | Postamt | Ufficio postale |
| Tourist information | Office de tourisme | Informationsbüro | Ufficio informazioni turistiche |
| Place of interest Theatre | Autre curiosité | Sonstige Sehenswürdigkeit Theatre | Luogo da vedere |

## Approach maps • Agglomérations
## Carte régionale • Regionalkarte

| | | | |
|---|---|---|---|
| Toll motorway – with motorway number A10 | Autoroute à péage – avec numéro d'autoroute | Gebührenpflichtige Autobahn – mit Autobahnnummer A10 | Autostrada a pedaggio – con numero |
| Toll-free motorway – with European road number E51 | Autoroute – avec numéro de route européenne | Gebührenfreie Autobahn – Europäische Strassennummer E51 | Autostrada – con numero di strada europea |
| Pre-pay motorway – vignette required | Autoroute – 'vignette' | Autobahn – 'vignette' | Autostrada – 'vignette' |
| Motorway services | Aire de service | Autobahnservice | Area di servizio autostradale |
| Motorway junction full access, restricted access 24 | Échangeur d'autoroute – accès libre, accès reglementé | Autobahnkreuz – voller/begrenzter Zugang 24 | Raccordi autostradali – completo/parziali |
| Under construction | En construction | Im Bau | In construzione |
| Tunnel | Tunnel | Tunnel | Galleria stradale |
| Major route dual carriageway 14 single carriageway 14 | Route principale chausées séparées chausée sans séparation | Hauptstrecke – zweispurige 14 Schnellstrasse 14 | Strada di grande communicazione carreggiata doppia carreggiata unica |
| Secondary route dual carriageway 96 single carriageway 96 | Route secondaire chausées séparées chausée sans séparation | Nebenstrasse – zweispurige 96 Schnellstrasse 96 | Strada d'interesse locale – carreggiata doppia carreggiata unica |
| Other road | Autre route | Nebenstrecke | Altra strada |
| Car ferry | Bac passant les autos | Autofähre | Traghetto automobili |
| Destination GIRONA | Destination | Ziel GIRONA | Destinazione |
| Railway | Chemin de fer | Eisenbahn | Ferrovia |
| Railway station Estación Central | Gare | Hauptbahnhof Estación Central | Stazione ferrovia |
| Height – in metres 234 | Altitude – en mètres | Höhe – über dem Meeresspiegel 234 | Altezza in metri |
| Airport | Aéroport principal | Flughafen | Aeroporto |
| Airfield | Autre aéroport | Flugplatz | Aerodromo/ campo d'aviazione |
| City plan coverage area | Région de plan de ville | Vom Stadtplan abgedecktes Gebiet | Area della pianta della città |

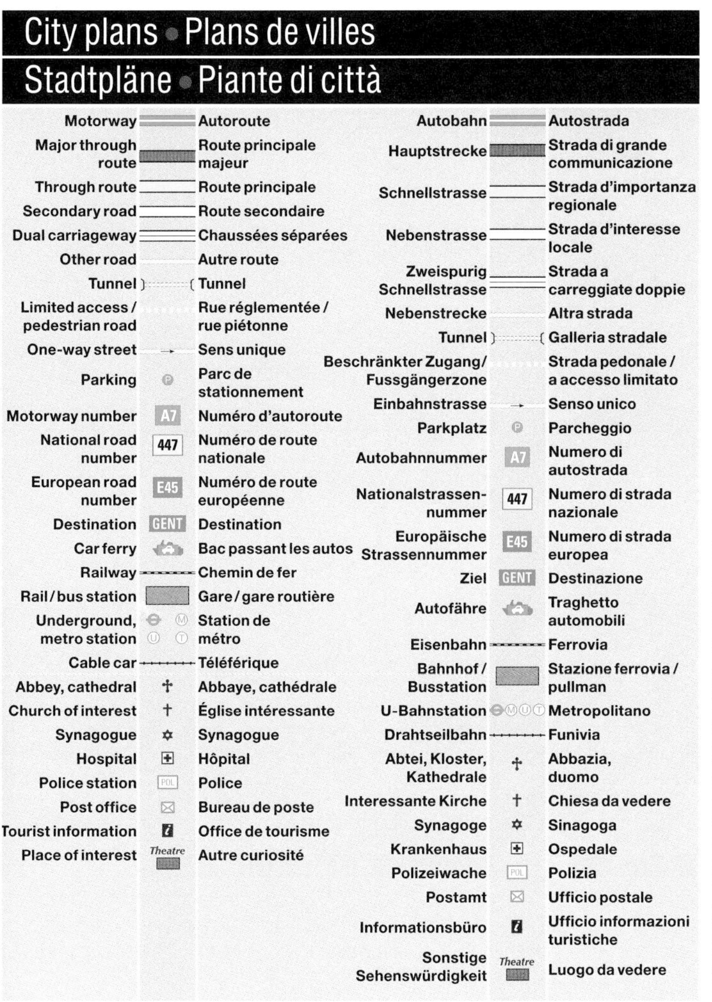
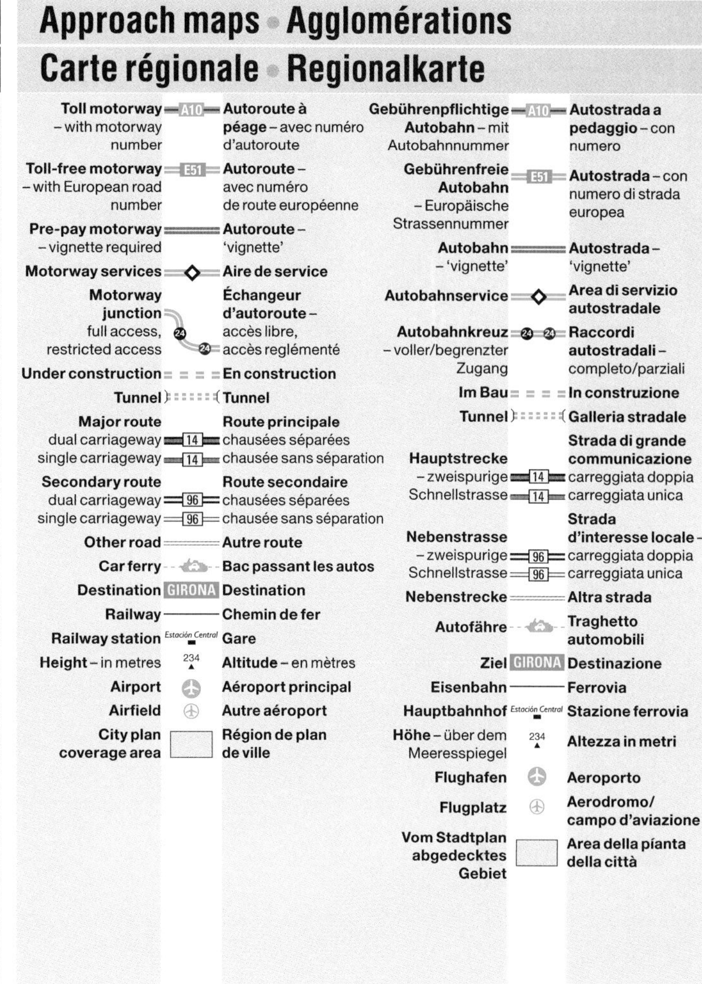
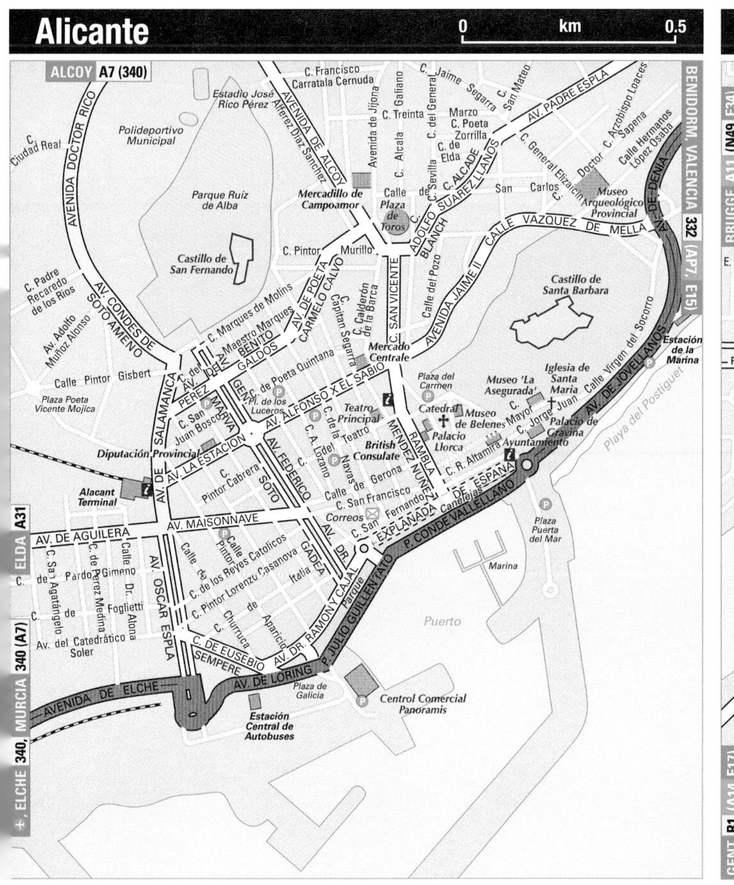
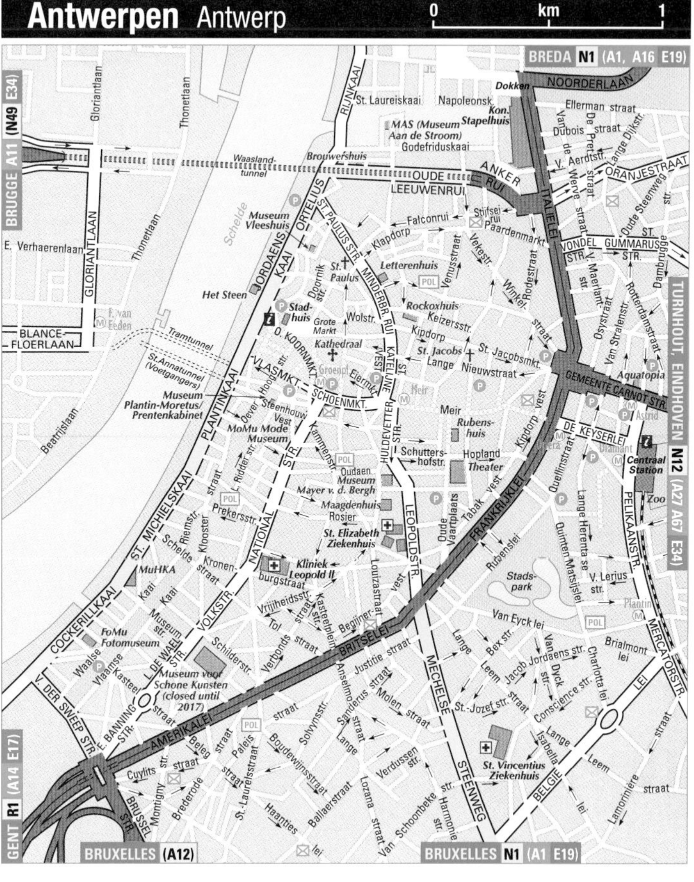

## Amsterdam

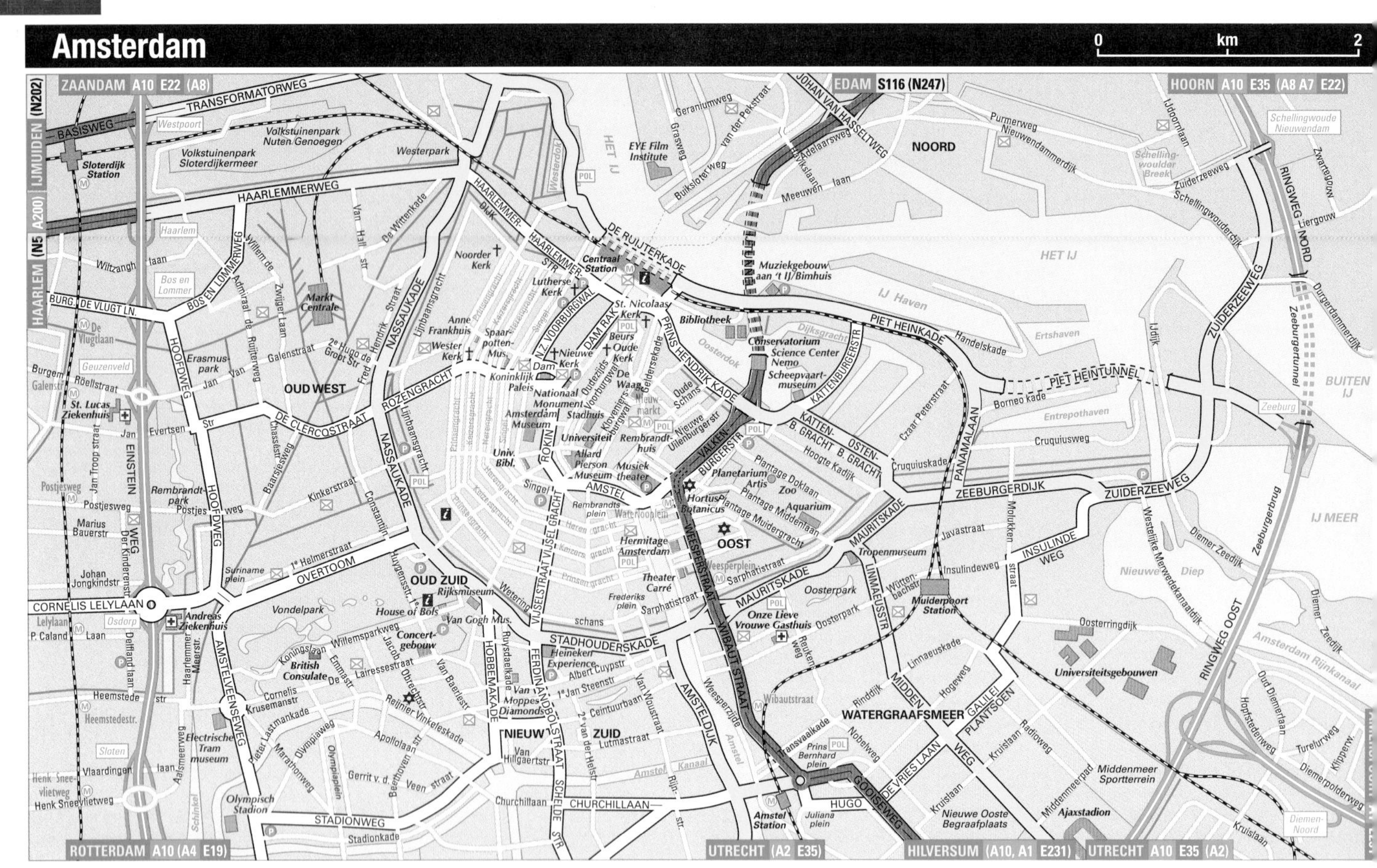
0 km 2
ZAANDAM A10 E22 (A8)
EDAM S116 (N247)
HOORN A10 E35 (A8 A7 E22)
IJMUIDEN (N202)
HAARLEM (N5 A200)
ROTTERDAM A10 (A4 E19)
UTRECHT (A2 E35)
HILVERSUM (A10, A1 E231)
UTRECHT A10 E35 (A2)
TRANSFORMATORWEG
BASISWEG
HAARLEMMERWEG
Sloterdijk Station
Volkstuinenpark Nuten Genoegen
Volkstuinenpark Sloterdijkermeer
Westerpark
EYE Film Institute
HET IJ
NOORD
JOHAN VAN HASSELTWEG
DE RUIJTERKADE
Centraal Station
Noorder Kerk
Lutherse Kerk
St. Nicolaas Kerk
Muziekgebouw aan 't IJ/Bimhuis
Bibliotheek
Conservatorium
Science Center Nemo
Scheepvaart-museum
PIET HEINKADE
PIET HEINTUNNEL
Markt Centrale
Anne Frankhuis
Wester Kerk
Nieuwe Kerk
Dam
Koninklijk Paleis
Nationaal Monument
Oude Kerk
Beurs
De Waag
Amsterdam Museum
Universiteit
Rembrandt-huis
Muziek theater
Allard Pierson Museum
Univ. Bibl.
Hortus Botanicus
Planetarium
Artis Zoo
Aquarium
OUD WEST
DE CLERCQSTRAAT
ROZENGRACHT
NASSAUKADE
HOOFDWEG
EINSTEIN WEG
St. Lucas Ziekenhuis
Erasmus-park
Rembrandt-park
OVERTOOM
Vondelpark
Rijksmuseum
House of Bols
OUD ZUID
Concert-gebouw
Van Gogh Mus.
Heineken Experience
Van Moppes Diamonds
Hermitage Amsterdam
Theater Carré
STADHOUDERSKADE
OOST
Tropenmuseum
Muiderpoort Station
Onze Lieve Vrouwe Gasthuis
Oosterpark
WATERGRAAFSMEER
Universiteitsgebouwen
ZEEBURGERDIJK
ZUIDERZEEWEG
RINGWEG NOORD
RINGWEG OOST
IJ MEER
BUITEN IJ
CORNELIS LELYLAAN
Andreas Ziekenhuis
British Consulate
Electrische Tram museum
Olympisch Stadion
STADIONWEG
CHURCHILLAAN
NIEUW ZUID
AMSTELDIJK
Amstel Station
HUGO DE VRIES LAAN
GOOISEWEG
Nieuwe Ooste Begraafplaats
Middenmeer Sportterrein
Ajaxstadion

## Amsterdam

## Athina Athens

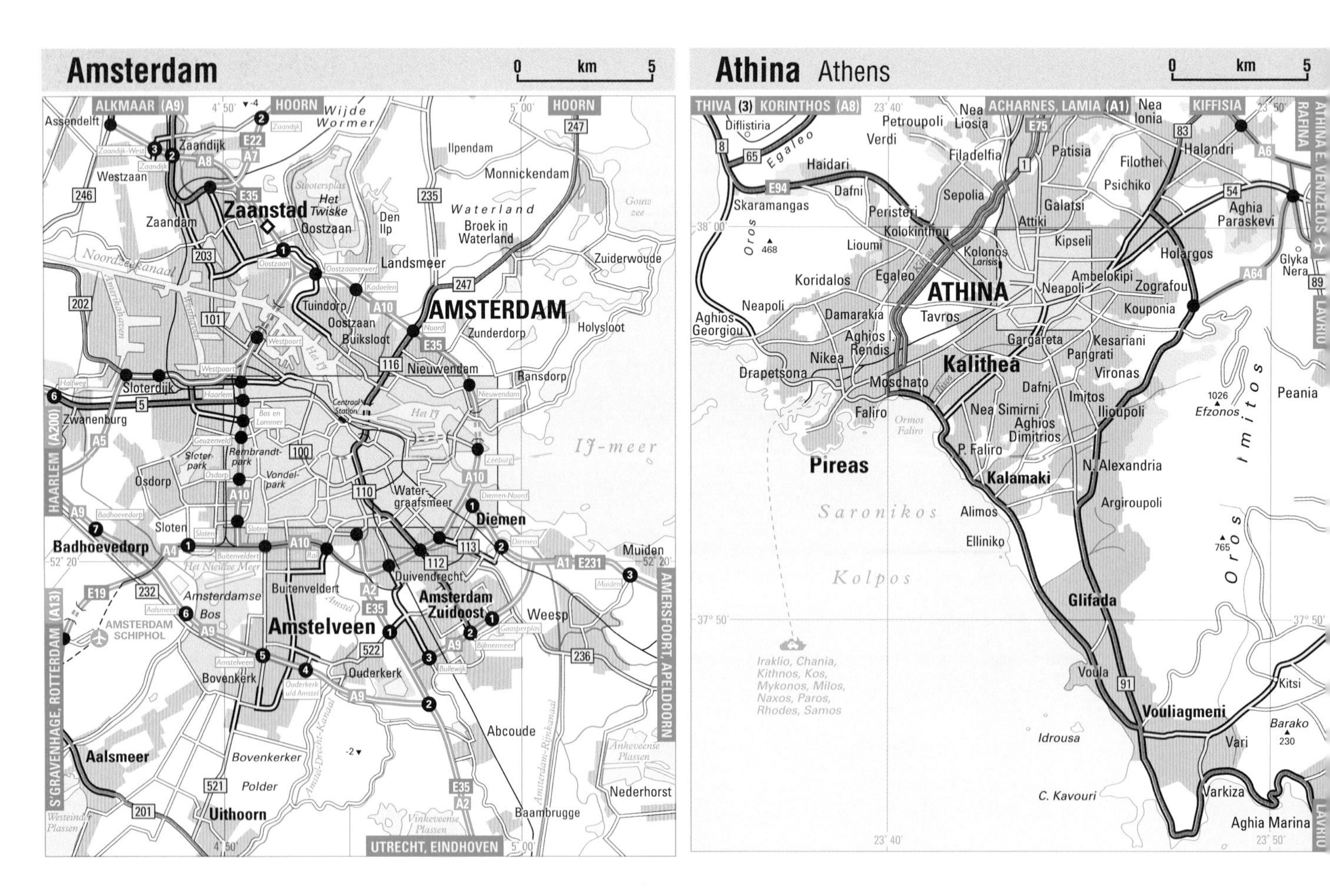
0 km 5
ALKMAAR (A9)
HOORN
HAARLEM (A200)
S'GRAVENHAGE, ROTTERDAM (A13)
UTRECHT, EINDHOVEN
AMERSFOORT, APELDOORN
Assendelft
Zaandijk
Westzaan
Zaanstad
Zaandam
Wijde Wormer
Ilpendam
Monnickendam
Het Twiske
Oostzaan
Den Ilp
Waterland
Broek in Waterland
Landsmeer
Zuiderwoude
Tuindorp Oostzaan
Buiksloot
AMSTERDAM
Zunderdorp
Holysloot
Nieuwendam
Ransdorp
Sloterdijk
Zwanenburg
IJ-meer
Osdorp
Sloter park
Rembrandt-park
Vondel-park
Water-graafsmeer
Diemen
Sloten
Badhoevedorp
Muiden
Buitenveldert
Duivendrecht
Amsterdam Zuidoost
Amsterdamse Bos
AMSTERDAM SCHIPHOL
Amstelveen
Weesp
Bovenkerk
Ouderkerk
Abcoude
Aalsmeer
Bovenkerker Polder
Uithoorn
Nederhorst
Baambrugge
THIVA (3) KORINTHOS (A8)
ACHARNES, LAMIA (A1)
KIFFISIA
ATHINA E. VENIZELOS
RAFINA
LAVRIO
Diflistiria
Petroupoli
Nea Liosia
Nea Ionia
Verdi
Filadelfia
Patisia
Filothei
Halandri
Haidari
Dafni
Sepolia
Psichiko
Skaramangas
Peristeri
Galatsi
Aghia Paraskevi
Kolokinthou
Attiki
Liouni
Kolonos
Kipseli
Holargos
Glyka Nera
Koridalos
Egaleo
Ambelokipi
Zografou
Neapoli
ATHINA
Kouponia
Aghios Georgiou
Damarakia
Tavros
Aghios I. Rendis
Gargareta
Kesariani
Pangrati
Nikea
Kalithea
Drapetsona
Viron as
Moschato
Dafni
Imitos
Peania
Faliro
Nea Smirni
Ilioupoli
Aghios Dimitrios
Efzonos
Pireas
P. Faliro
N. Alexandria
Kalamaki
Saronikos Kolpos
Alimos
Argiroupoli
Elliniko
Oros Imitos
Glifada
Iraklio, Chania, Kithnos, Kos, Mykonos, Milos, Naxos, Paros, Rhodes, Samos
Voula
Kitsi
Vouliagmeni
Barako
Idrousa
Vari
C. Kavouri
Varkiza
Aghia Marina

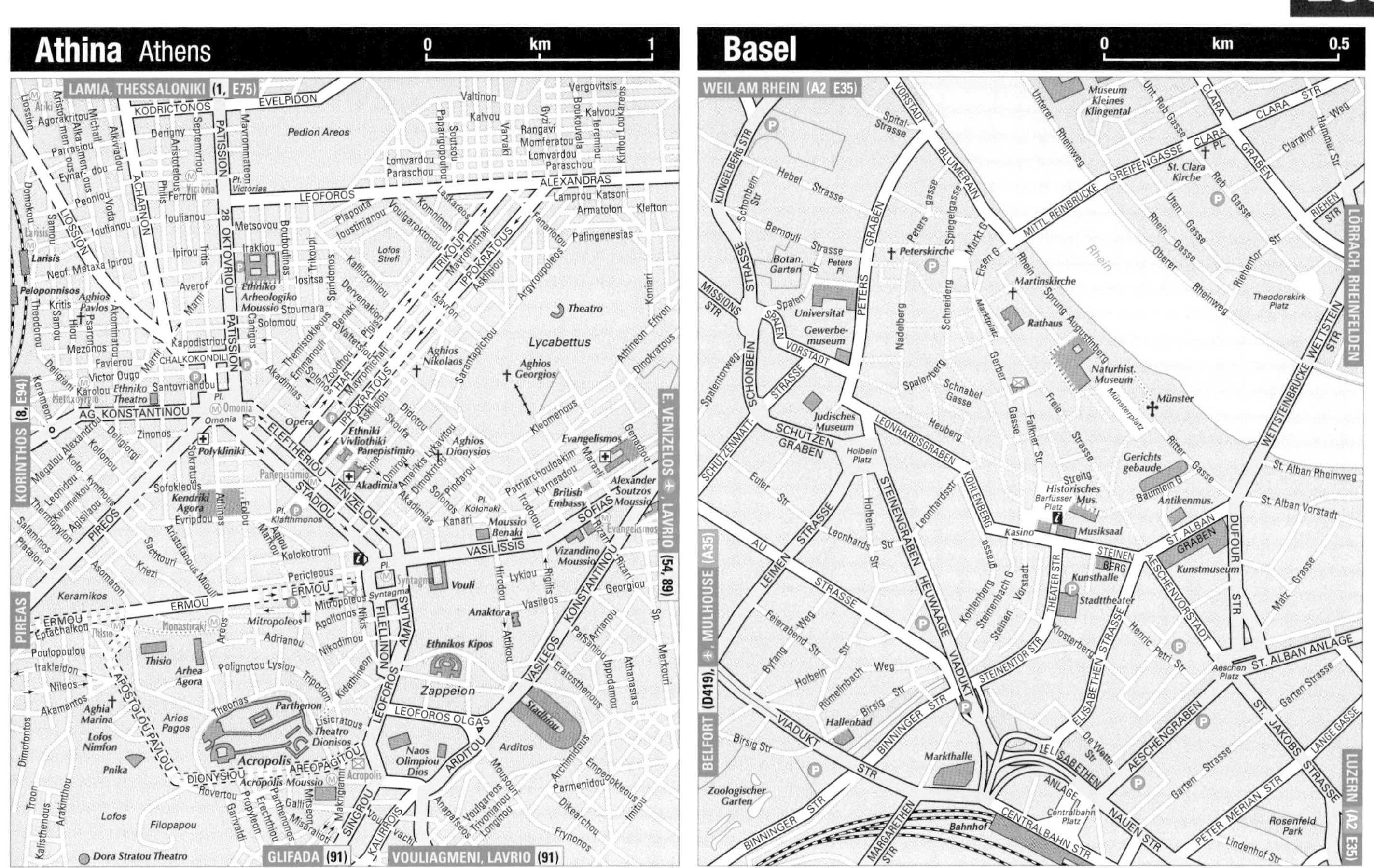
Athina Athens
0 km 1
LAMIA, THESSALONIKI (1, E75)
KORINTHOS (8, E94)
PIREAS
E. VENIZELOS ✈ LAVRIO (54, 89)
GLIFADA (91)
VOULIAGMENI, LAVRIO (91)
Pedion Areos
Lycabettus
Omonia
Syntagma
Akropolis
Zappeion
Ethnikos Kipos
Thisio
Filopapou
Dora Stratou Theatro
Basel
0 km 0.5
WEIL AM RHEIN (A2 E35)
LÖRRACH, RHEINFELDEN
BELFORT (D419), ✈ MULHOUSE (A35)
LUZERN (A2 E35)
Rhein
Münster
Rathaus
Universität
Kunstmuseum
Bahnhof
Zoologischer Garten
Rosenfeld Park

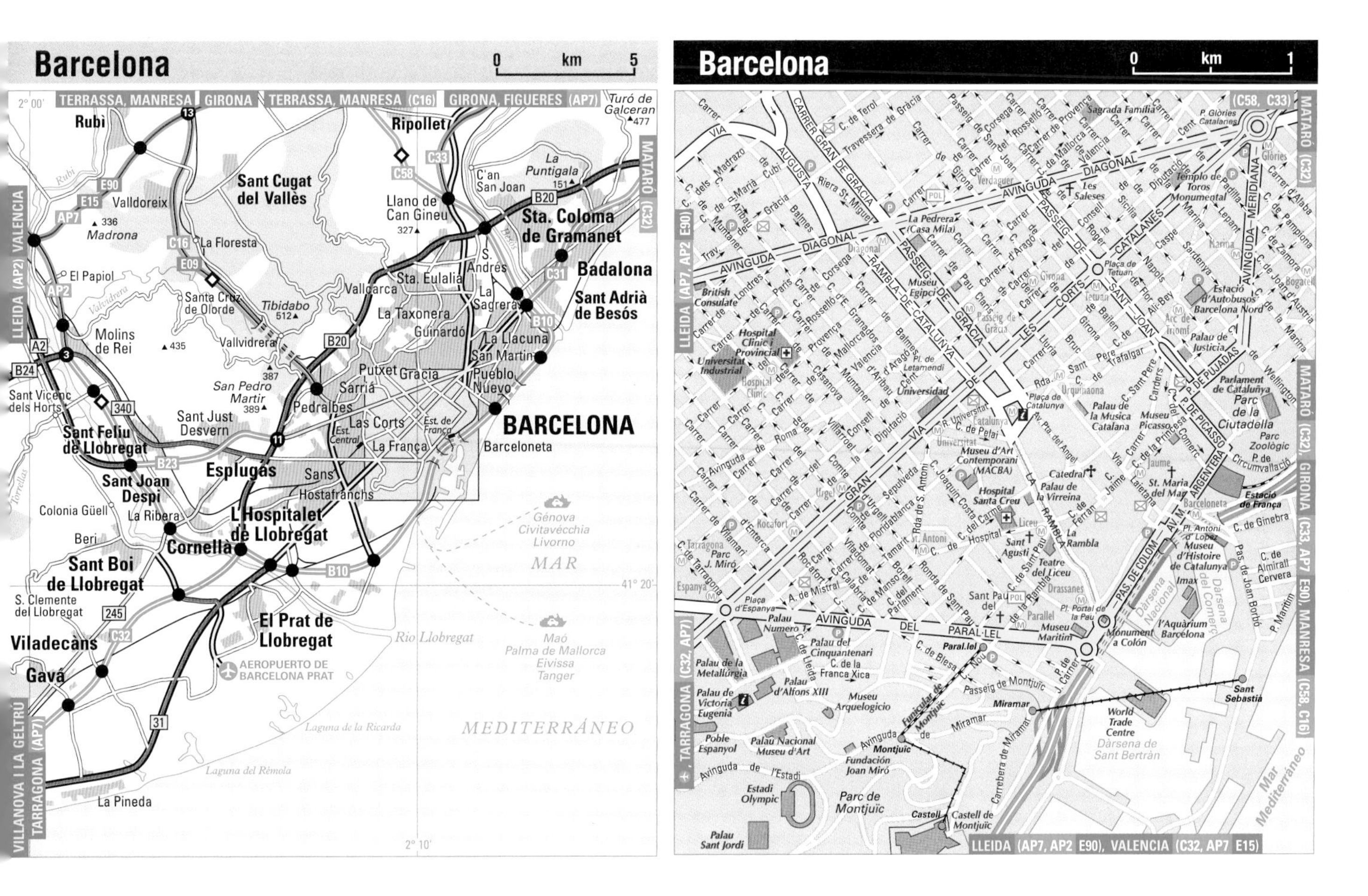
Barcelona
0 km 5
TERRASSA, MANRESA
GIRONA
TERRASSA, MANRESA (C16)
GIRONA, FIGUERES (AP7)
MATARÓ (C32)
LLEIDA (AP2) VALENCIA
VILLANOVA I LA GELTRU TARRAGONA (AP7)
BARCELONA
Sabadell
Rubí
Sant Cugat del Vallès
Ripollet
Sta. Coloma de Gramanet
Badalona
Sant Adrià de Besós
Tibidabo
L'Hospitalet de Llobregat
Cornellà
Sant Boi de Llobregat
El Prat de Llobregat
Viladecans
Gavà
AEROPUERTO DE BARCELONA PRAT
MAR MEDITERRÁNEO
Barcelona
0 km 1
MATARÓ (C32)
LLEIDA (AP7, AP2 E90)
TARRAGONA (C32, AP7)
MATARÓ (C32), GIRONA (C33, AP7 E90), MANRESA (C58, C16)
LLEIDA (AP7, AP2 E90), VALENCIA (C32, AP7 E15)
AVINGUDA DIAGONAL
GRAN VIA DE LES CORTS CATALANES
Sagrada Família
Parc de la Ciutadella
La Rambla
Catedral
Parc de Montjuïc
Estadi Olympic
Castell de Montjuïc
World Trade Centre
Monument a Colón

## Berlin

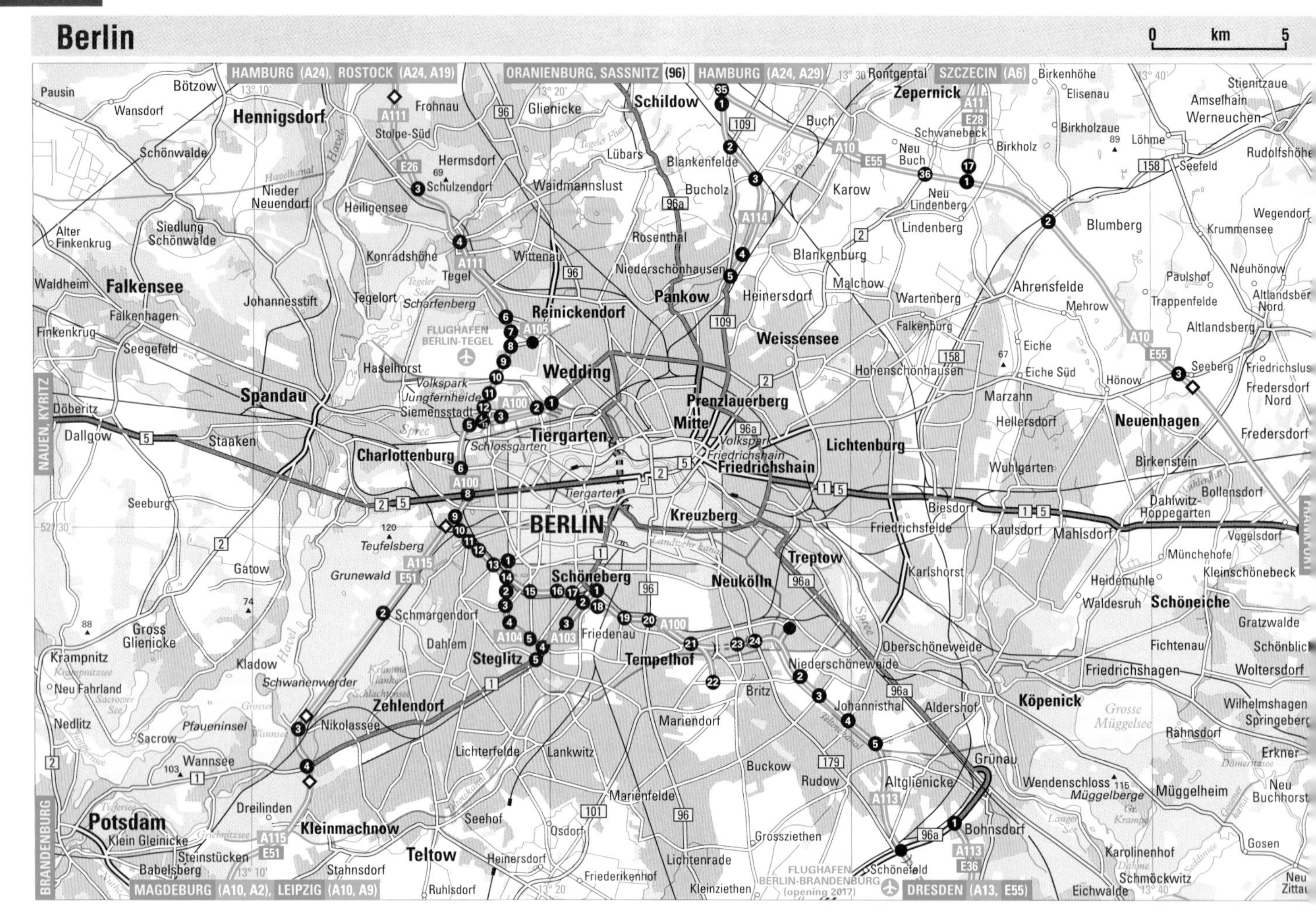
0 km 5
HAMBURG (A24), ROSTOCK (A24, A19)
ORANIENBURG, SASSNITZ (96)
HAMBURG (A24, A29)
SZCZECIN (A6)
Pausin
Bötzow
Wansdorf
Hennigsdorf
Frohnau
Stolpe-Süd
Glienicke
Schildow
Zepernick
Birkenhöhe
Elisenau
Stienitzaue
Amselhain
Werneuchen
Schönwalde
Hermsdorf
Schulzendorf
Lübars
Blankenfelde
Buch
Schwanebeck
Neu Buch
Birkholzaue
Birkholz
Löhme
Rudolfshöhe
Seefeld
Nieder Neuendorf
Heiligensee
Waidmannslust
Bucholz
Karow
Neu Lindenberg
Lindenberg
Blumberg
Wegendorf
Krummensee
Alter Finkenkrug
Siedlung Schönwalde
Konradshöhe
Tegel
Wittenau
Rosenthal
Niederschönhausen
Blankenburg
Malchow
Ahrensfelde
Mehrow
Paulshof
Neuhönow
Trappenfelde
Altlandsberg Nord
Altlandsberg
Waldheim
Falkensee
Johannesstift
Tegelort
Scharfenberg
Reinickendorf
Pankow
Heinersdorf
Wartenberg
Falkenhagen
Finkenkrug
Seegefeld
FLUGHAFEN BERLIN-TEGEL
Weissensee
Falkenburg
Eiche
Eiche Süd
Seeberg
Friedrichsluste
Fredersdorf Nord
Haselhorst
Volkspark Jungfernheide
Siemensstadt
Wedding
Hohenschönhausen
Hönow
Spandau
Prenzlauerberg
Mitte
Marzahn
Hellersdorf
Neuenhagen
Fredersdorf
Döberitz
Dallgow
Staaken
Charlottenburg
Schlossgarten
Tiergarten
Volkspark Friedrichshain
Friedrichshain
Lichtenberg
Wuhlgarten
Birkenstein
NAUEN, KYRITZ
Seeburg
Teufelsberg
BERLIN
Kreuzberg
Biesdorf
Friedrichsfelde
Kaulsdorf
Mahlsdorf
Dahlwitz-Hoppegarten
Bollensdorf
Vogelsdorf
Gatow
Grunewald
Schöneberg
Neukölln
Treptow
Karlshorst
Münchehofe
Heidemühle
Kleinschönebeck
Waldesruh
Schöneiche
Gross Glienicke
Schmargendorf
Dahlem
Friedenau
Tempelhof
Oberschöneweide
Gratzwalde
Schönblick
Fichtenau
Krampnitz
Kladow
Steglitz
Niederschöneweide
Friedrichshagen
Woltersdorf
Neu Fahrland
Schwanenwerder
Zehlendorf
Britz
Johannisthal
Aldershof
Köpenick
Grosse Müggelsee
Wilhelmshagen
Springeberg
Nedlitz
Pfaueninsel
Sacrow
Nikolassee
Mariendorf
Rahnsdorf
Wannsee
Lichterfelde
Lankwitz
Buckow
Grünau
Erkner
Rudow
Altglienicke
Wendenschloss
Müggelberge
Müggelheim
Neu Buchhorst
Dreilinden
Marienfelde
Potsdam
Klein Gleinicke
Kleinmachnow
Seehof
Osdorf
Grossziethen
Bohnsdorf
Gosen
Teltow
Karolinenhof
Steinstücken
Babelsberg
Stahnsdorf
Heinersdorf
Lichtenrade
Schönefeld
Schmöckwitz
Ruhlsdorf
Friederikenhof
Kleinziethen
FLUGHAFEN BERLIN-BRANDENBURG (opening 2017)
Eichwalde
Neu Zittau
BRANDENBURG
MAGDEBURG (A10, A2), LEIPZIG (A10, A9)
DRESDEN (A13, E55)

## Berlin

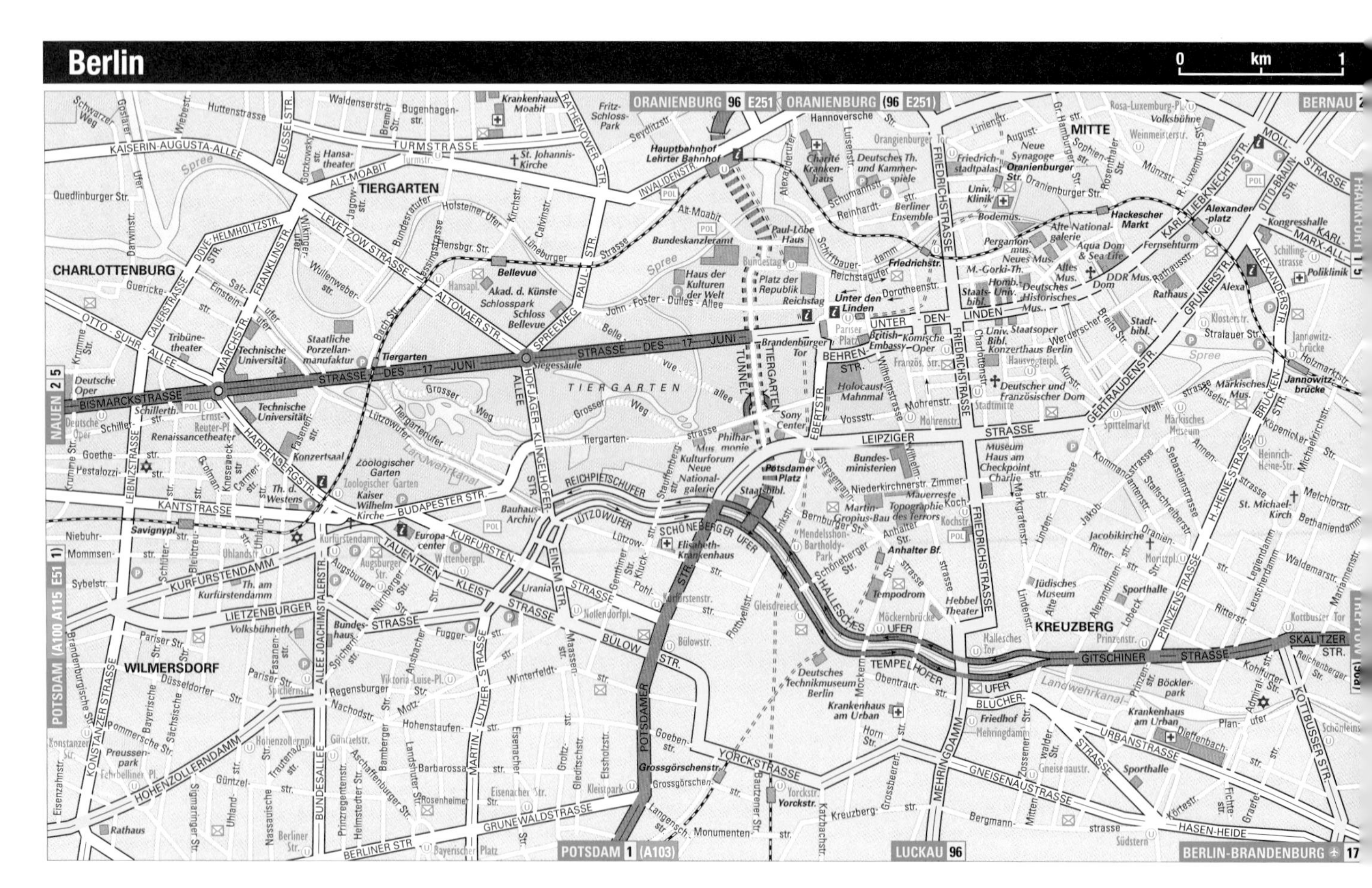
0 km 1
ORANIENBURG 96 E251
ORANIENBURG (96 E251)
BERNAU
Huttenstrasse
Waldenserstr.
Bugenhagen-str.
Krankenhaus Moabit
Fritz-Schloss-Park
KAISERIN-AUGUSTA-ALLEE
TURMSTRASSE
ALT-MOABIT
TIERGARTEN
St. Johannis-Kirche
Hauptbahnhof Lehrter Bahnhof
INVALIDENSTR.
Charité Krankenhaus
Deutsches Th. und Kammerspiele
MITTE
Neue Synagoge
Oranienburger Str.
Volksbühne
Quedlinburger Str.
Hansa-theater
Holsteiner Ufer
Bundeskanzleramt
Paul-Löbe Haus
Reinhardt-str.
Berliner Ensemble
Bodemus.
Hackescher Markt
Alexanderplatz
Fernsehturm
Kongresshalle
CHARLOTTENBURG
Guericke-str.
Bellevue
Akad. d. Künste
Schlosspark
Schloss Bellevue
Haus der Kulturen der Welt
Platz der Republik
Reichstag
Friedrichstr.
Alte National-gal.
Pergamon mus.
Neues Mus.
Altes Mus.
Aqua Dom & Sea Life
Dom
DDR Mus.
Rathaus
Alexa
Poliklinik
OTTO-SUHR-ALLEE
Tribüne-theater
Technische Universität
Staatliche Porzellan-manufaktur
Tiergarten
Siegessäule
John-Foster-Dulles-Allee
Unter den Linden
Dorotheenstr.
M.-Gorki-Th.
Staats-bibl.
Humb.-Univ.
Deutsches Historisches Mus.
LINDEN
Stadtbibl.
Klosterstr.
Stralauer Str.
Deutsche Oper
BISMARCKSTRASSE
STRASSE DES 17. JUNI
TIERGARTEN
Brandenburger Tor
British Embassy
Komische Oper
Univ. Bibl.
Staatsoper
Konzerthaus Berlin
Hausvogteipl.
Jannowitz-brücke
Schillerth.
Renaissancetheater
Technische Universität
Grosser Weg
Holocaust Mahnmal
Deutscher und Französischer Dom
Märkisches Mus.
NAUEN 2 5
Goethe-str.
Pestalozzi-str.
Konzertsaal
Zoologischer Garten
Sony Center
Philharmonie
Kulturforum
Neue Nationalgalerie
Potsdamer Platz
Staatsbibl.
LEIPZIGER STRASSE
Bundes-ministerien
Museum Haus am Checkpoint Charlie
Spittelmarkt
Märkisches Museum
Heinrich-Heine-Str.
KANTSTRASSE
Kaiser Wilhelm Kirche
BUDAPESTER STR.
Th. d. Westens
REICHPIETSCHUFER
Bauhaus Archiv
Martin-Gropius-Bau
Topographie des Terrors
Jacobikirche
St. Michael-Kirch
Savignypl.
Europa-center
KURFÜRSTENSTR.
LÜTZOWUFER
SCHÖNEBERGER UFER
Elisabeth-Krankenhaus
Anhalter Bf.
Niebuhr-str.
Mommsen-str.
KURFÜRSTENDAMM
TAUENTZIEN
Wittenbergpl.
KLEISTSTRASSE
Urania
Tempodrom
Jüdisches Museum
Sporthalle
Sybelstr.
Th. am Kurfürstendamm
LIETZENBURGER STRASSE
Volksbühneth.
Bundes-haus
Gleisdreieck
HALLESCHES UFER
Hebbel Theater
KREUZBERG
Hallesches Tor
SKALITZER STR.
POTSDAM (A100 A115 E51 1)
WILMERSDORF
Pariser Str.
Düsseldorfer Str.
Bülowstr.
BÜLOW STR.
TEMPELHOFER UFER
GITSCHINER STRASSE
Deutsches Technikmuseum Berlin
Krankenhaus am Urban
Böckler-park
Viktoria-Luise-Pl.
Nachodstr.
Hohenstaufen-str.
Winterfeldt-str.
POTSDAMER STR.
BLÜCHERSTR.
Friedhof
URBANSTRASSE
Dieffenbach
Sporthalle
HOHENZOLLERNDAMM
Preussen-park
Barbarossa-str.
Goeben-str.
Grossgörschenstr.
YORCKSTRASSE
MEHRINGDAMM
GNEISENAUSTRASSE
Kottbusser Str.
Rathaus
BUNDESALLEE
GRUNEWALDSTRASSE
Yorckstr.
Kreuzberg-str.
Bergmann-str.
HASEN-HEIDE
Südstern
BERLINER STR.
Bayerischer Platz
Monumenten-str.
Katzbachstr.
POTSDAM 1 (A103)
LUCKAU 96
BERLIN-BRANDENBURG 17

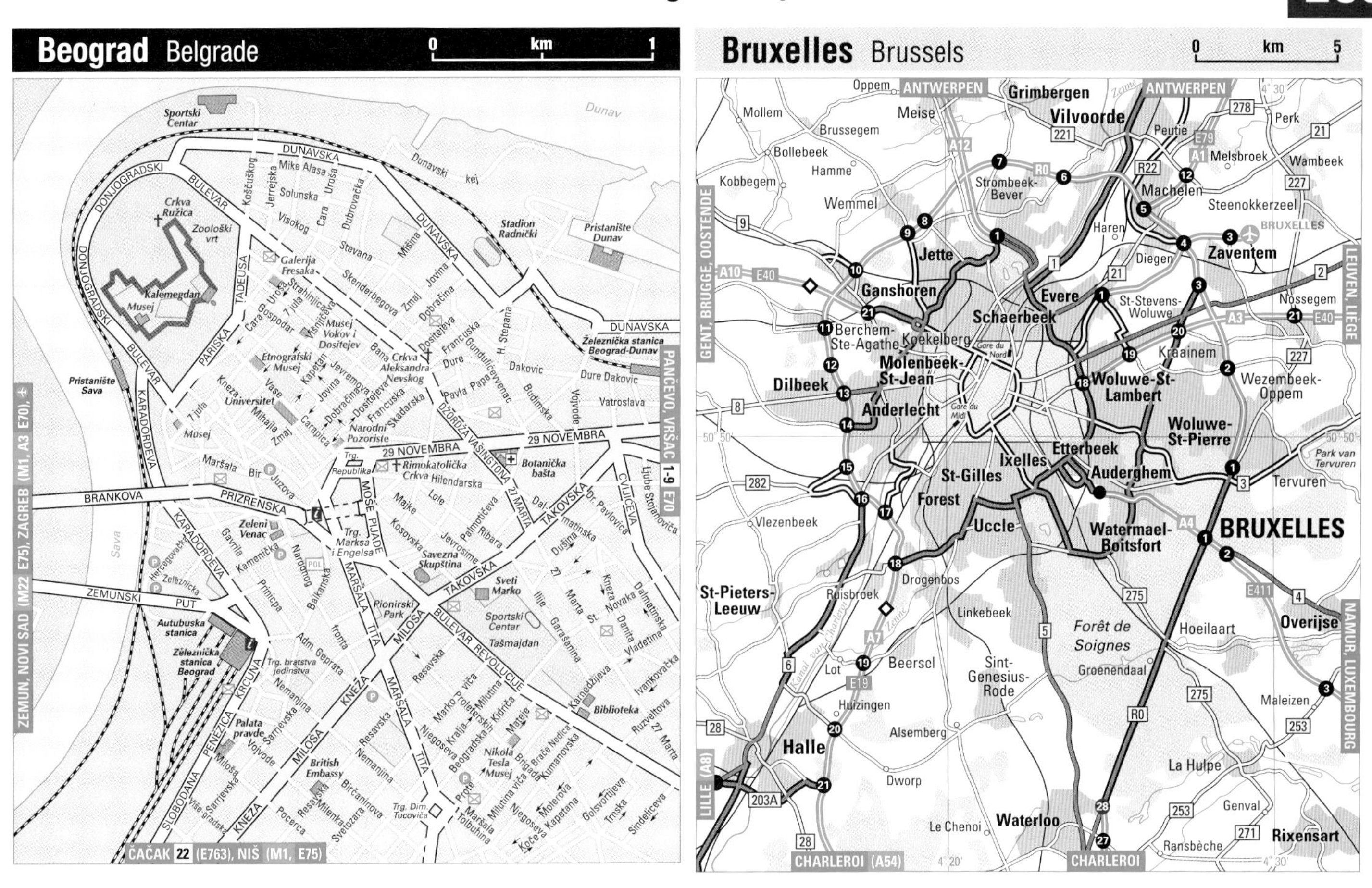
Beograd Belgrade
0 km 1
Sportski Centar
Dunav
DUNAVSKA
DONJOGRADSKI BULEVAR
Crkva Ružica
Zoološki vrt
Kalemegdan
Musej
Stadion Radnički
Pristanište Dunav
Galerija Fresaka
Skenderbegova
Musej Vokov i Dositejev
Etnografski Musej
Univerzitet
Narodni Pozorište
Železnička stanica Beograd-Dunav
Pristanište Sava
KARAĐORĐEVA
29 NOVEMBRA
Rimokatolička Crkva
Botanička bašta
BRANKOVA
PRIZRENSKA
Zeleni Venac
ZEMUNSKI PUT
Autubuska stanica
Železnička stanica Beograd
Trg. Marksa i Engelsa
Savezna Skupština
Sveti Marko
Sportski Centar
Tašmajdan
Pionirski Park
TAKOVSKA
BULEVAR REVOLUCIJE
Biblioteka
Palata pravde
British Embassy
Trg. Dim. Tucovića
Sava
ZEMUN, NOVI SAD (M22 E75), ZAGREB (M1, A3 E70)
PANČEVO, VRŠAC 1-9 E70
ČAČAK 22 (E763), NIŠ (M1, E75)
Bruxelles Brussels
0 km 5
ANTWERPEN
Grimbergen
Vilvoorde
Meise
Mollem
Brussegem
Bollebeek
Hamme
Kobbegem
Wemmel
Strombeek-Bever
Peutie
Perk
Melsbroek
Wambeek
Machelen
Steenokkerzeel
Haren
Diegem
Zaventem
BRUXELLES
Jette
Ganshoren
Evere
Schaerbeek
Berchem-Ste-Agathe
Koekelberg
St-Stevens-Woluwe
Nossegem
Kraainem
Dilbeek
Molenbeek-St-Jean
Woluwe-St-Lambert
Wezembeek-Oppem
Anderlecht
Woluwe-St-Pierre
Ixelles
Etterbeek
Auderghem
St-Gilles
Forest
Tervuren
Park van Tervuren
Vlezenbeek
Uccle
Watermael-Boitsfort
BRUXELLES
St-Pieters-Leeuw
Drogenbos
Ruisbroek
Linkebeek
Forêt de Soignes
Hoeilaart
Overijse
Groenendaal
Lot
Beersel
Sint-Genesius-Rode
Huizingen
Maleizen
Alsemberg
Halle
La Hulpe
Dworp
Genval
Le Chenoi
Waterloo
Ransbèche
Rixensart
GENT, BRUGGE, OOSTENDE
LEUVEN, LIÈGE
NAMUR, LUXEMBOURG
LILLE (A8)
CHARLEROI (A54)
CHARLEROI

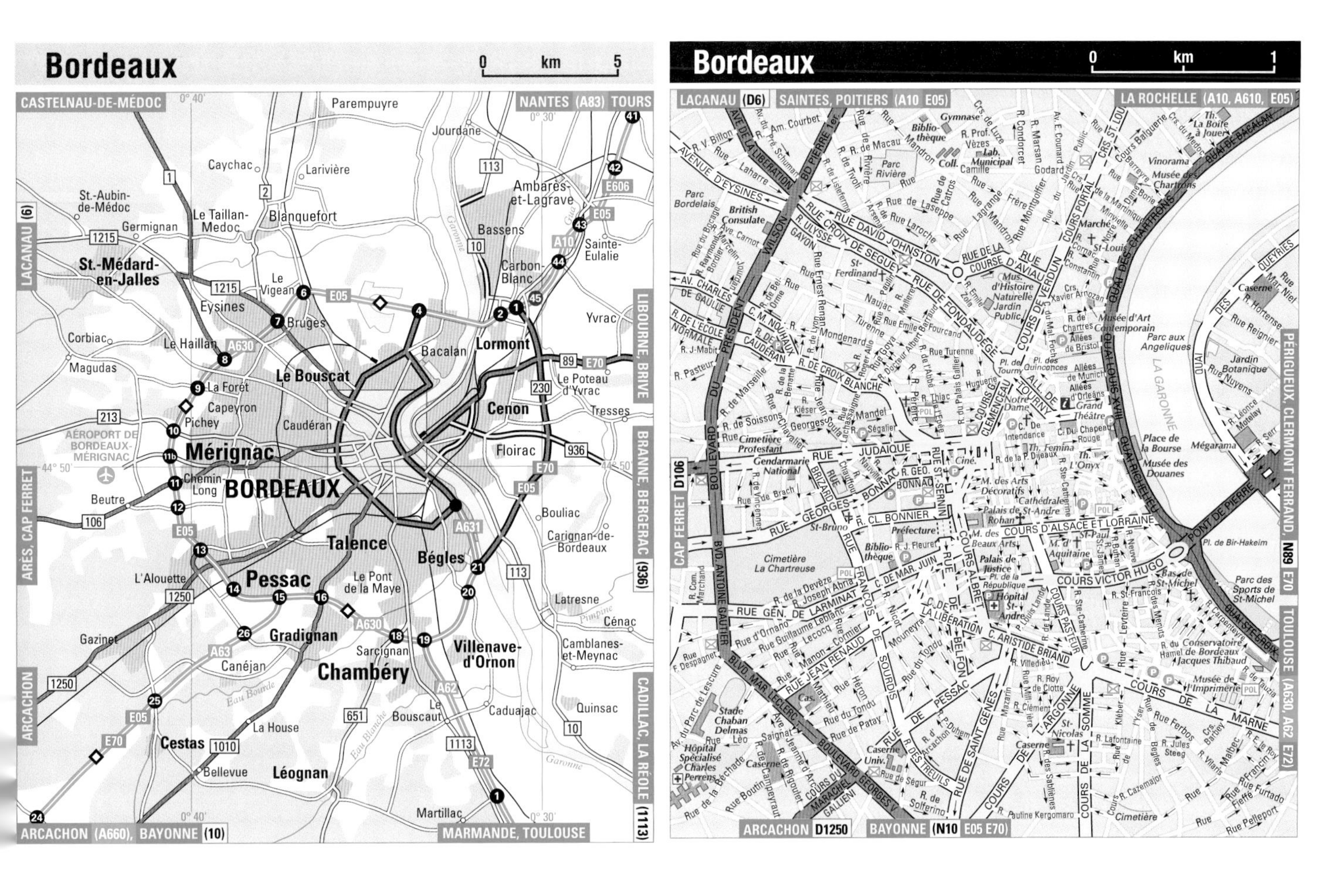
Bordeaux
0 km 5
CASTELNAU-DE-MÉDOC
NANTES (A83) TOURS
Parempuyre
Jourdane
Caychac
Larivière
Ambarès-et-Lagrave
St.-Aubin-de-Médoc
Le Taillan-Medoc
Blanquefort
Germignan
Bassens
Sainte-Eulalie
St.-Médard-en-Jalles
Le Vigean
Carbon-Blanc
Eysines
Bruges
Yvrac
Corbiac
Le Haillan
Lormont
Magudas
Bacalan
Le Bouscat
Le Poteau d'Yvrac
La Forêt
Capeyron
Cenon
Tresses
Pichey
Caudéran
AÉROPORT DE BORDEAUX-MÉRIGNAC
Mérignac
Floirac
Chemin Long
BORDEAUX
Beutre
Bouliac
Carignan-de-Bordeaux
Talence
Bégles
L'Alouette
Pessac
Le Pont de la Maye
Latresne
Cénac
Gazinet
Gradignan
Villenave-d'Ornon
Camblanes-et-Meynac
Canéjan
Sarcignan
Chambéry
Le Bouscaut
Caduajac
Quinsac
Cestas
La House
Bellevue
Léognan
Martillac
LACANAU (6)
LIBOURNE, BRIVE
BRANNE, BERGERAC (936)
ARÈS, CAP FERRET
ARCACHON
CADILLAC, LA RÉOLE (1113)
ARCACHON (A660), BAYONNE (10)
MARMANDE, TOULOUSE
Bordeaux
0 km 1
LACANAU (D6)
SAINTES, POITIERS (A10 E05)
LA ROCHELLE (A10, A610, E05)
Parc Bordelais
British Consulate
AVENUE D'ESYINES
RUE DAVID JOHNSTON
RUE CROIX DE SEGUEY
COURS DE VERDUN
QUAI DES CHARTRONS
Vinorama
Musée des Chartrons
Mus. d'Histoire Naturelle
Jardin Public
Musée d'Art Contemporain
Parc aux Angeliques
Jardin Botanique
LA GARONNE
Cimetière Protestant
Gendarmerie National
Grand Théâtre
Place de la Bourse
Musée des Douanes
Cathédrale
Palais de St-André
Préfecture
M. des Beaux Arts
Palais de Justice
Cimetière La Chartreuse
Hôpital St-André
COURS VICTOR HUGO
PONT DE PIERRE
Pl. de Bir-Hakeim
Parc des Sports de St-Michel
Stade Chaban Delmas
Hôpital Specialisé Charles Perrens
Musée de l'Imprimerie
COURS DE LA MARNE
PÉRIGUEUX, CLERMONT FERRAND N89 E70
TOULOUSE (A630, A62, E72)
CAP FERRET D106
ARCACHON D1250
BAYONNE (N10 E05 E70)

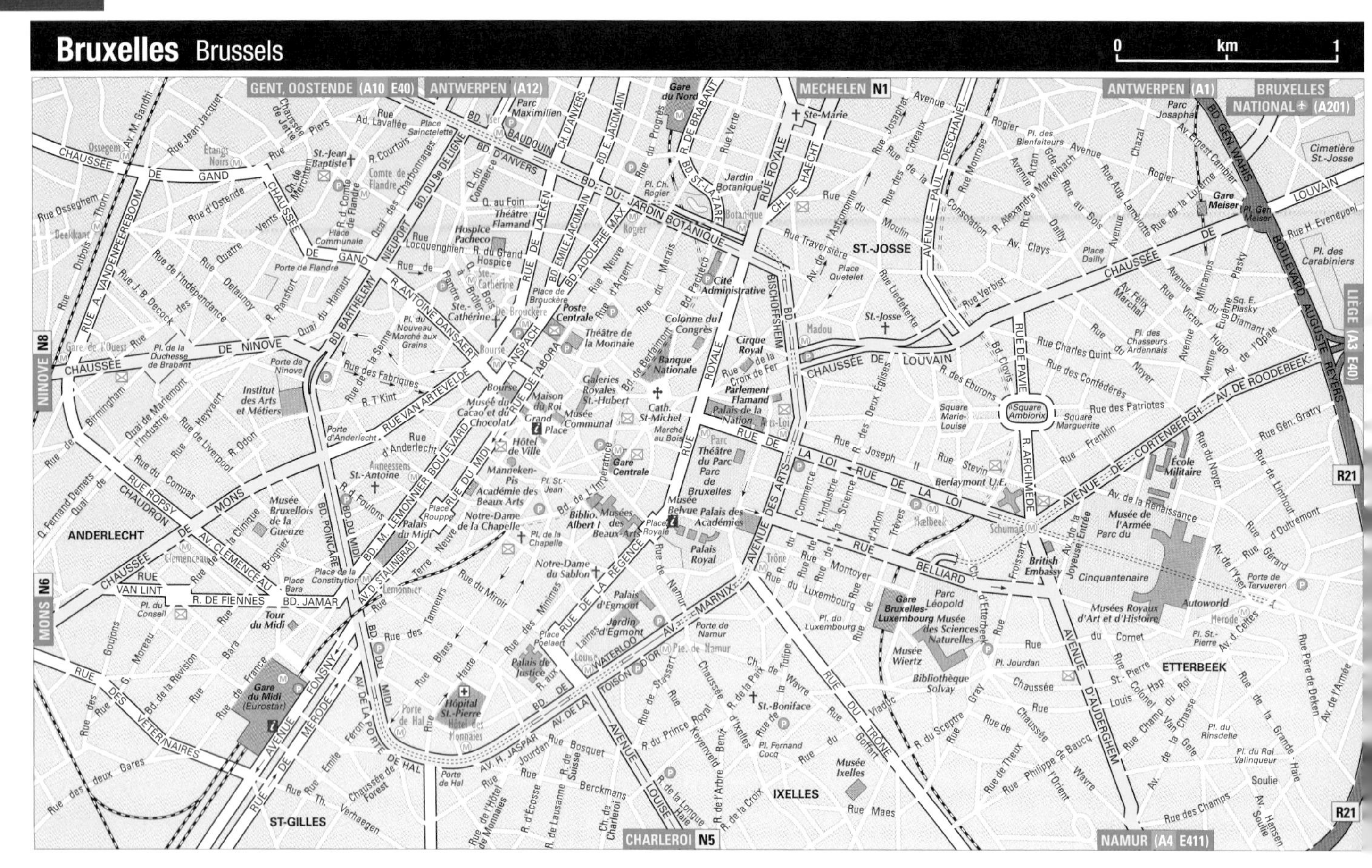
Bruxelles Brussels
0 km 1
GENT, OOSTENDE (A10 E40)
ANTWERPEN (A12)
MECHELEN N1
ANTWERPEN (A1)
BRUXELLES NATIONAL (A201)
LIÈGE (A3 E40)
R21
NAMUR (A4 E411)
CHARLEROI N5
MONS N6
NINOVE N8
Gare du Nord
ST.-JOSSE
ANDERLECHT
ETTERBEEK
IXELLES
ST-GILLES
Gare du Midi (Eurostar)
Gare Centrale
Musée de l'Armée
Parc du Cinquantenaire
Parc de Bruxelles
Gare Bruxelles-Luxembourg
Hôtel de Ville
Manneken-Pis
Grand Place
Palais Royal
Palais de Justice
Square Ambiorix
British Embassy
Autoworld
Cimetière St.-Josse

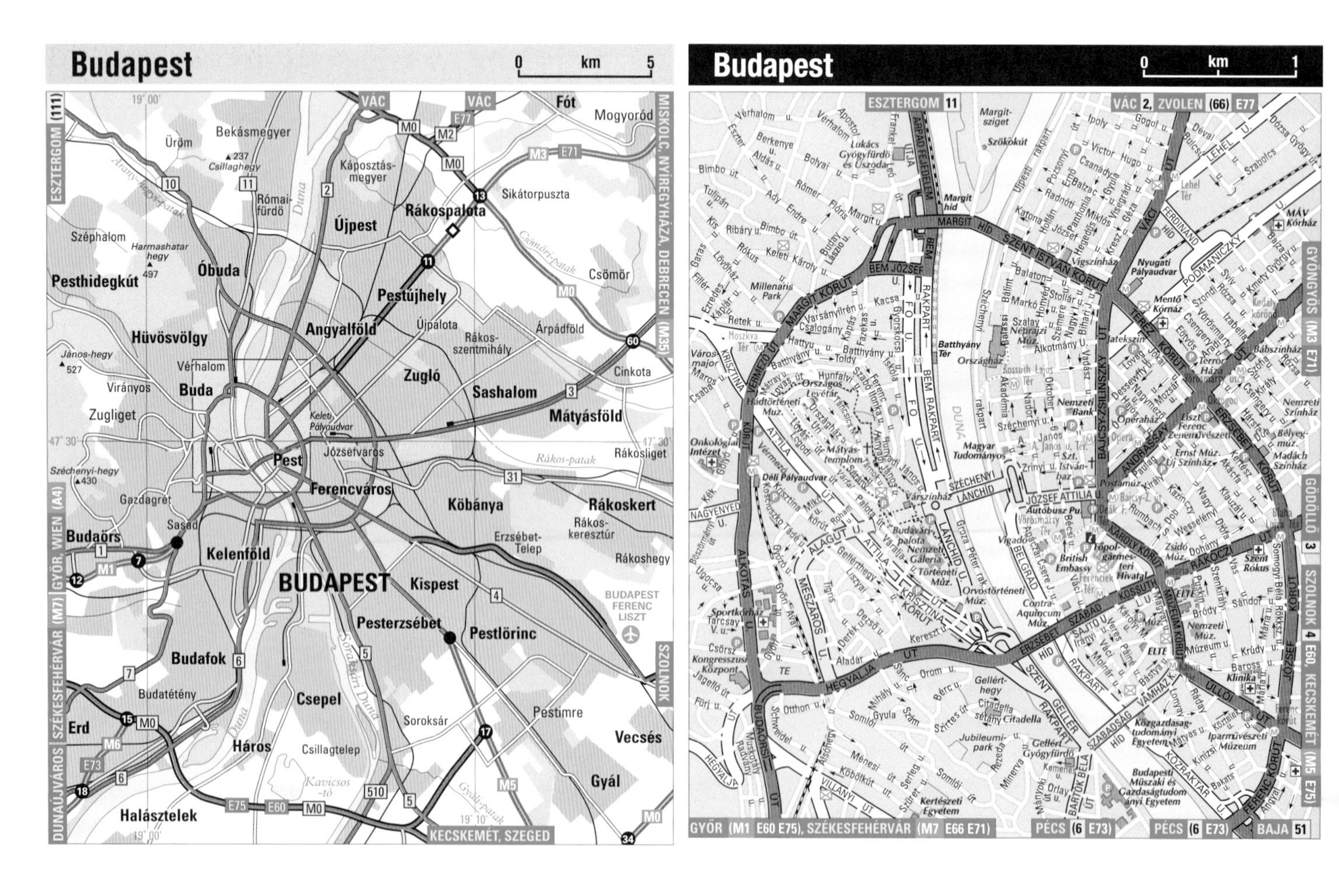
Budapest
0 km 5
VÁC
Fót
Mogyoród
Üröm
Békásmegyer
Káposztásmegyer
Újpest
Rákospalota
Sikátorpuszta
Óbuda
Pesthidegkút
Pestújhely
Csömör
Angyalföld
Újpalota
Árpádföld
Hüvösvölgy
Zugló
Cinkota
Buda
Sashalom
Mátyásföld
Zugliget
Pest
Józsefváros
Rákosliget
Ferencváros
Kőbánya
Rákoskert
Budaörs
Kelenföld
BUDAPEST
Kispest
Pesterzsébet
Pestlőrinc
Budafok
Csepel
Soroksár
Pestimre
Vecsés
Erd
Háros
Csillagtelep
Gyál
Halásztelek
BUDAPEST FERENC LISZT
ESZTERGOM (111)
MISKOLC, NYÍREGYHÁZA, DEBRECEN (M35)
GYŐR WIEN (A4)
DUNAÚJVÁROS SZÉKESFEHÉRVÁR (M7)
SZOLNOK
KECSKEMÉT, SZEGED
Budapest
0 km 1
ESZTERGOM 11
VÁC 2, ZVOLEN (66) E77
Margit-sziget
MARGIT HÍD
SZENT ISTVÁN KÖRÚT
Nyugati Pályaudvar
Batthyány Tér
Országház
Mátyás-templom
Budavári-palota
LÁNCHÍD
Déli Pályaudvar
Magyar Tudományos Akadémia
ERZSÉBET HÍD
SZABADSÁG HÍD
Gellért-hegy
Citadella
Gellért Gyógyfürdő
British Embassy
Nemzeti Múz.
Keleti Pályaudvar
GÖDÖLLŐ 3
SZOLNOK 4 E60 KECSKEMÉT (M5 E75)
GYÖNGYÖS (M3 E71)
GYŐR (M1 E60 E75), SZÉKESFEHÉRVÁR (M7 E66 E71)
PÉCS (6 E73)
BAJA 51

## Dublin

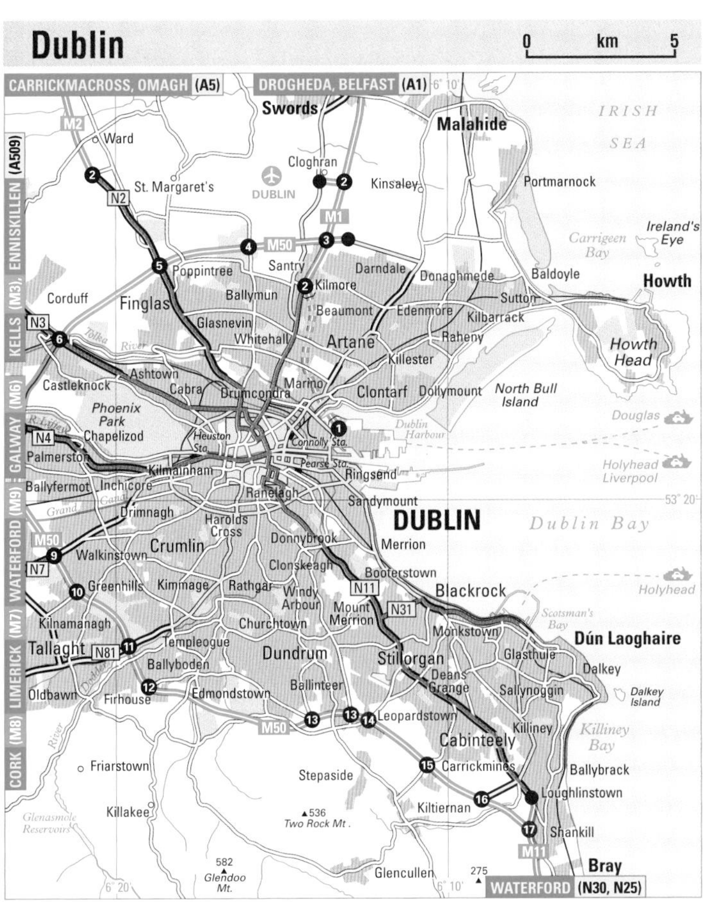

## Dublin

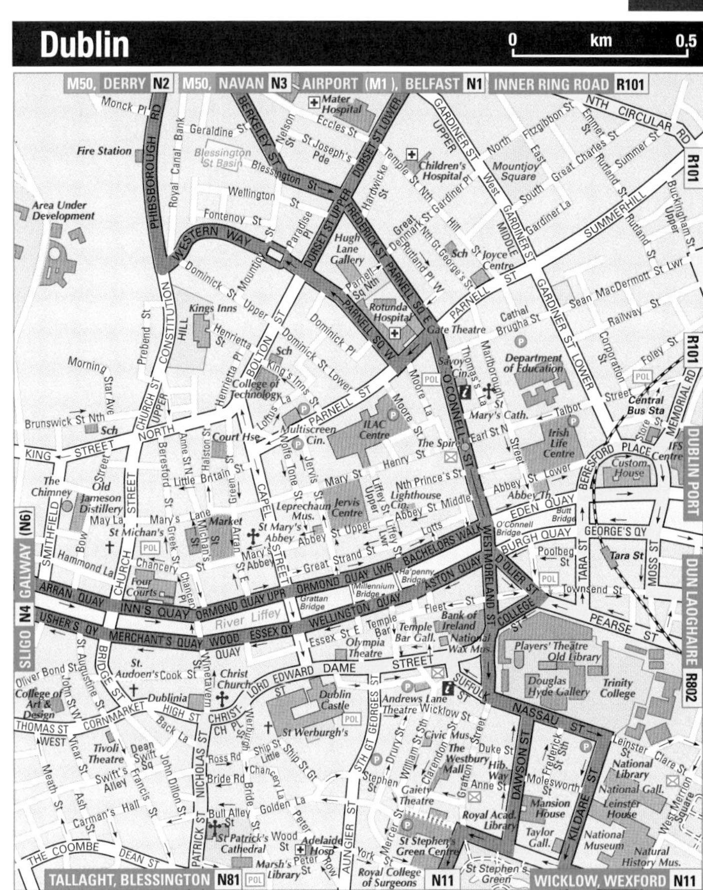

## Düsseldorf

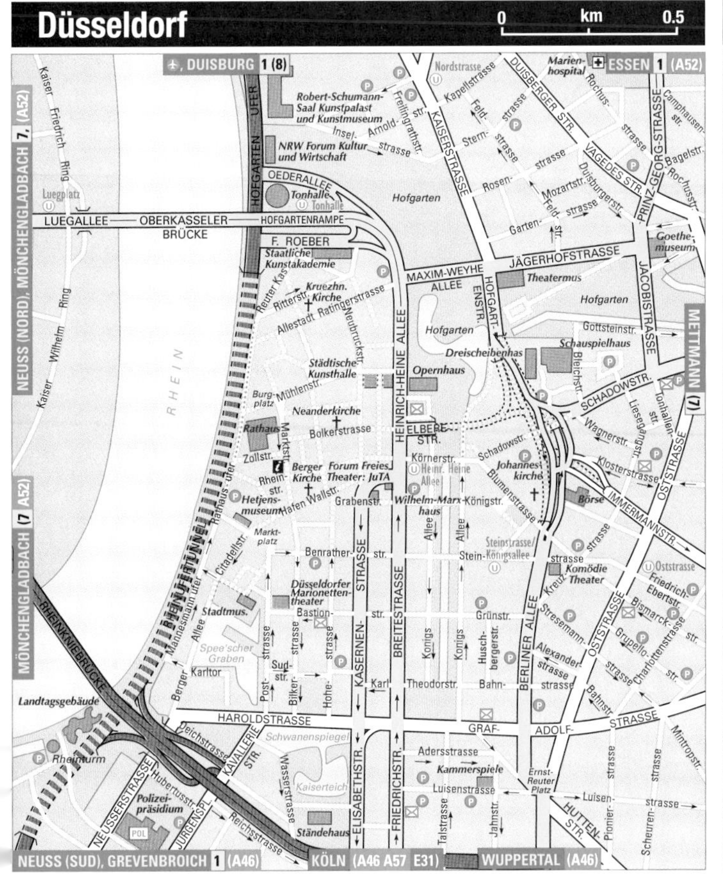

## Edinburgh

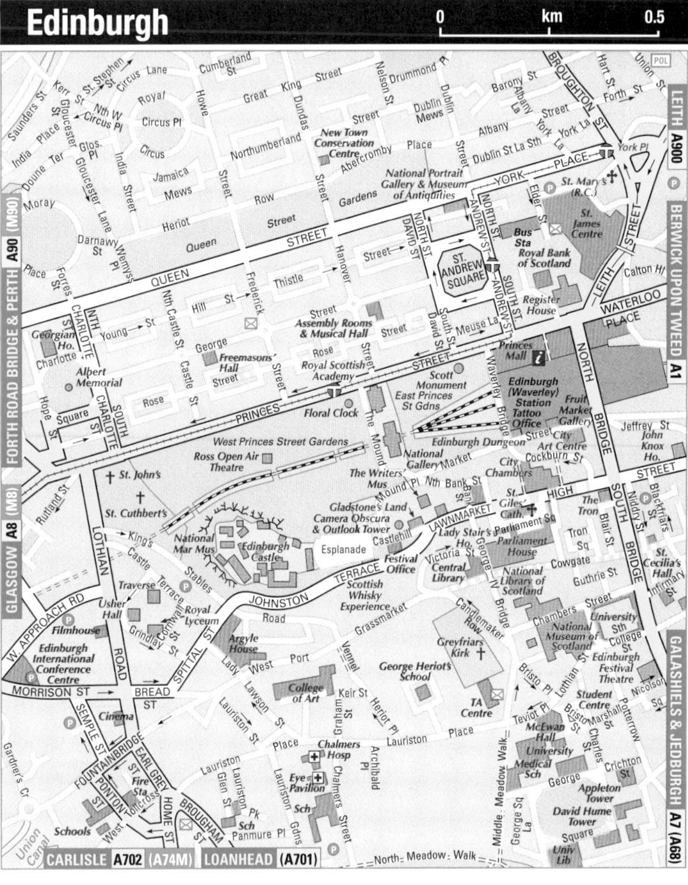

For **Cologne** see page 212
For **Copenhagen** see page 212

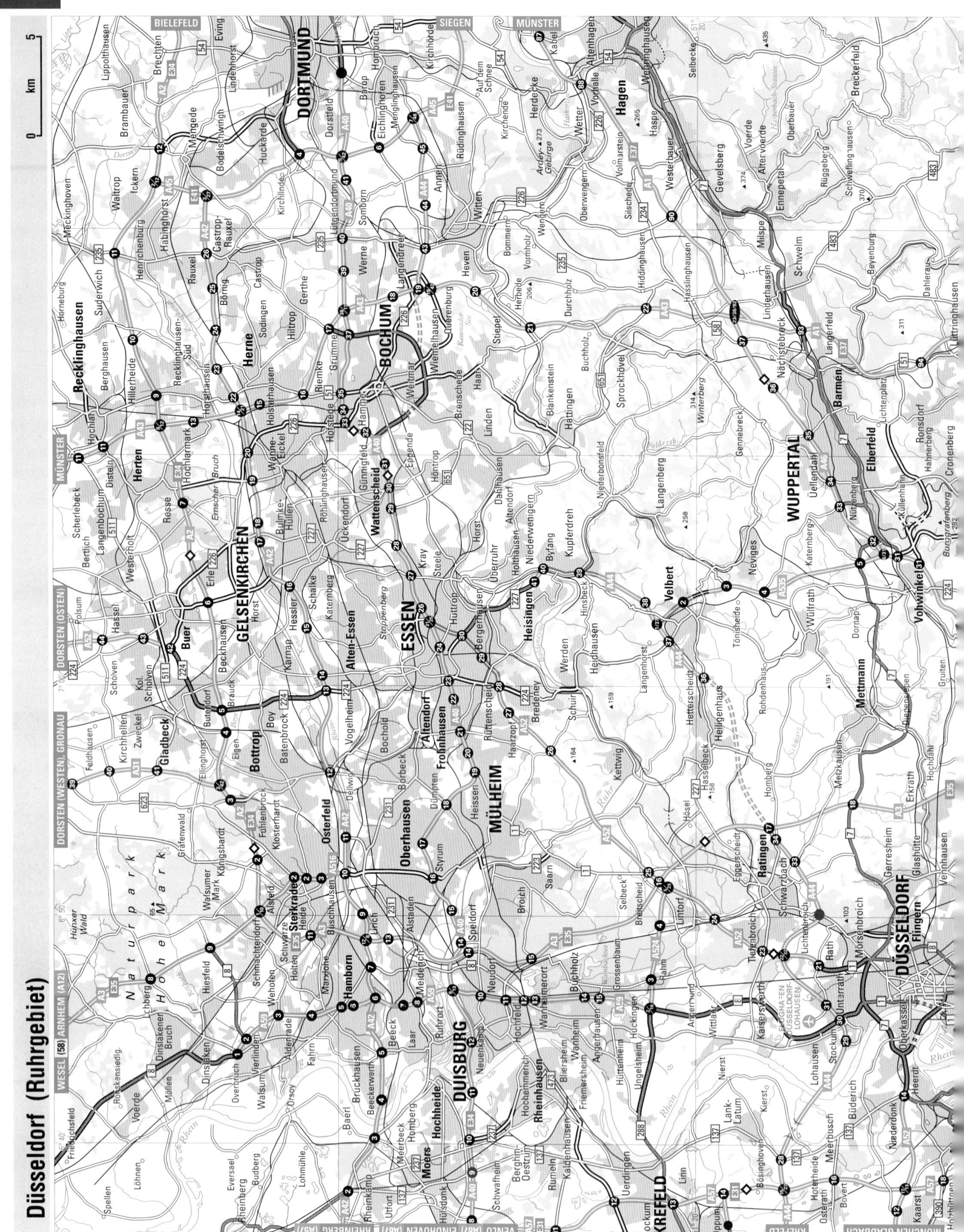

Düsseldorf (Ruhrgebiet)
km
0
5
DORTMUND
BOCHUM
Recklinghausen
Herne
Herten
GELSENKIRCHEN
Buer
Gladbeck
Bottrop
ESSEN
Alten-Essen
Wattenscheid
Oberhausen
Osterfeld
MÜLHEIM
DUISBURG
Hamborn
Moers
Rheinhausen
KREFELD
Ratingen
DÜSSELDORF
Mettmann
WUPPERTAL
Barmen
Elberfeld
Velbert
Heisingen
Hagen
Vohwinkel
BIELEFELD
SIEGEN
MÜNSTER
DORSTEN (OSTEN)
DORSTEN (WESTEN), GRONAU
WESEL
ARNHEM (A12)
RHEINBERG (A57)
EINDHOVEN (A67)
VENLO (A67)
KREFELD
MÖNCHEN GLADBACH

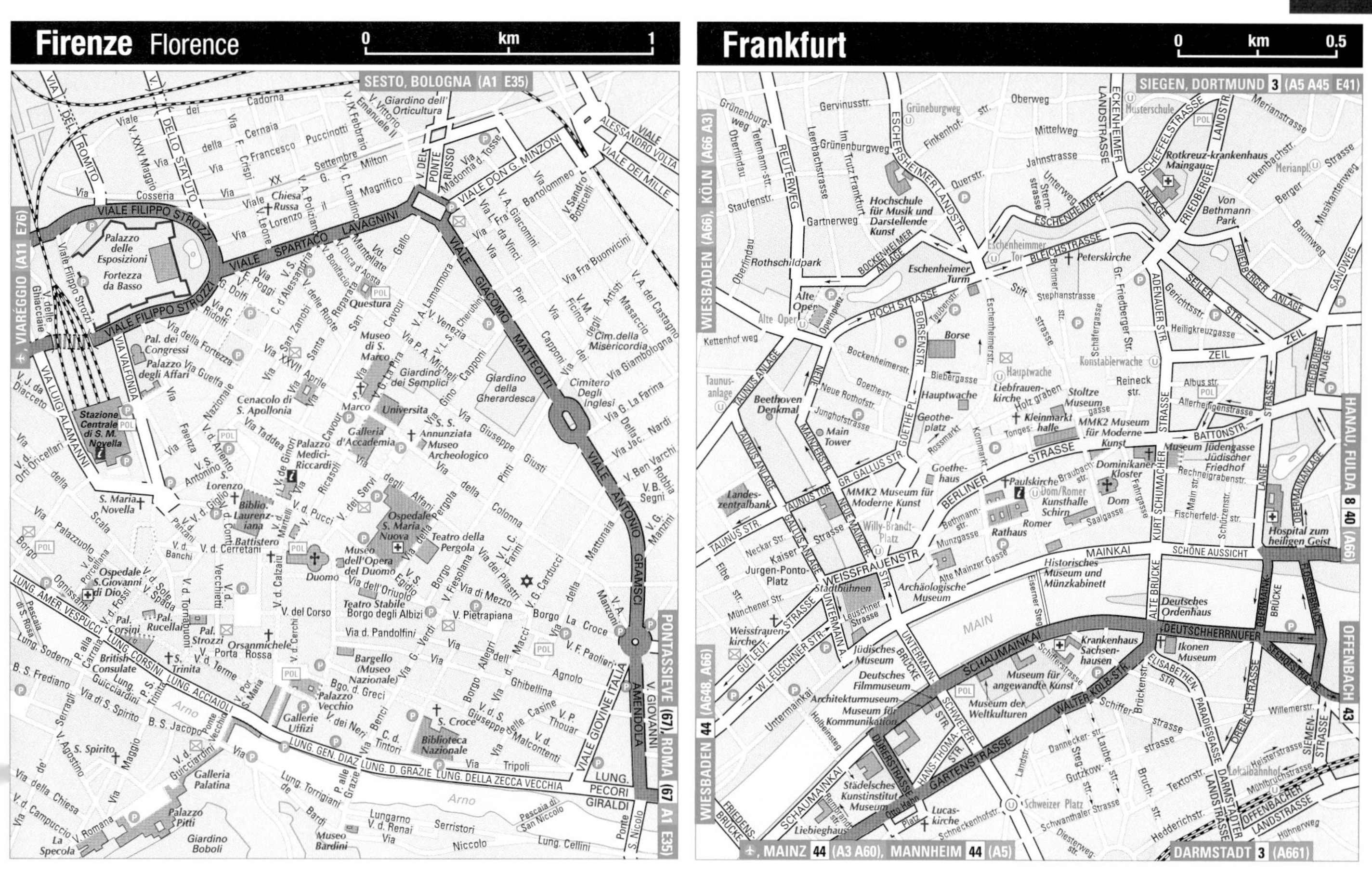
Firenze Florence
0 km 1
SESTO, BOLOGNA (A1 E35)
VIAREGGIO (A11 E76)
PONTASSIEVE (67), ROMA (67 A1 E35)
VIALE FILIPPO STROZZI
VIALE SPARTACO LAVAGNINI
VIALE GIACOMO MATTEOTTI
VIALE ANTONIO GRAMSCI
VIALE DON G. MINZONI
VIALE GIOVINE ITALIA
Palazzo delle Esposizioni
Fortezza da Basso
Pal. dei Congressi
Palazzo degli Affari
Stazione Centrale di S. M. Novella
Cenacolo di S. Apollonia
Giardino dei Semplici
Museo di S. Marco
Galleria d'Accademia
Museo Archeologico
Palazzo Medici-Riccardi
Biblio. Laurenziana
Battistero
Duomo
Museo dell'Opera del Duomo
Ospedale S. Maria Nuova
Teatro della Pergola
Teatro Stabile
Giardino della Gherardesca
Cimitero Degli Inglesi
Cim. della Misericordia
S. Maria Novella
Ospedale S. Giovanni di Dio
Orsanmichele
Bargello (Museo Nazionale)
Palazzo Vecchio
Gallerie Uffizi
S. Croce
Biblioteca Nazionale
British Consulate
Galleria Palatina
Palazzo Pitti
Giardino Boboli
Museo Bardini
LUNG. AMER. VESPUCCI
LUNG. CORSINI
LUNG. ACCIAIOLI
LUNG. GEN. DIAZ
LUNG. DELLA ZECCA VECCHIA
Arno
Frankfurt
0 km 0,5
SIEGEN, DORTMUND 3 (A5 A45 E41)
WIESBADEN (A66), KÖLN (A66 A3)
HANAU, FULDA 8 40 (A66)
OFFENBACH 43
WIESBADEN 44 (A648, A66)
MAINZ 44 (A3 A60), MANNHEIM 44 (A5)
DARMSTADT 3 (A661)
Grüneburgweg
Rothschildpark
Hochschule für Musik und Darstellende Kunst
Eschenheimer Turm
Alte Oper
Rotkreuz-krankenhaus Maingau
Von Bethmann Park
Peterskirche
Börse
Beethoven Denkmal
Main Tower
Hauptwache
Liebfrauen-kirche
Kleinmarkt halle
MMK2 Museum für Moderne Kunst
Stoltze Museum
Goethe-haus
Paulskirche
Dom/Römer
Kunsthalle Schirn
Dom
Dominikaner-Kloster
Rathaus
Römer
Museum Jüdengasse
Jüdischer Friedhof
Hospital zum heiligen Geist
Landes-zentralbank
Willy-Brandt-Platz
Archäologische Museum
Historisches Museum und Münzkabinett
Deutsches Ordenhaus
Ikonen Museum
Jüdisches Museum
Deutsches Filmmuseum
Architekturmuseum
Museum für Kommunikation
Museum für angewandte Kunst
Museum der Weltkulturen
Krankenhaus Sachsen-hausen
Städelsches Kunstinstitut Museum
Liebieghaus
MAIN
SCHAUMAINKAI
DEUTSCHHERRNUFER
MAINKAI
SCHÖNE AUSSICHT
GARTENSTRASSE
ZEIL
BERLINER STRASSE
WEISSFRAUENSTR

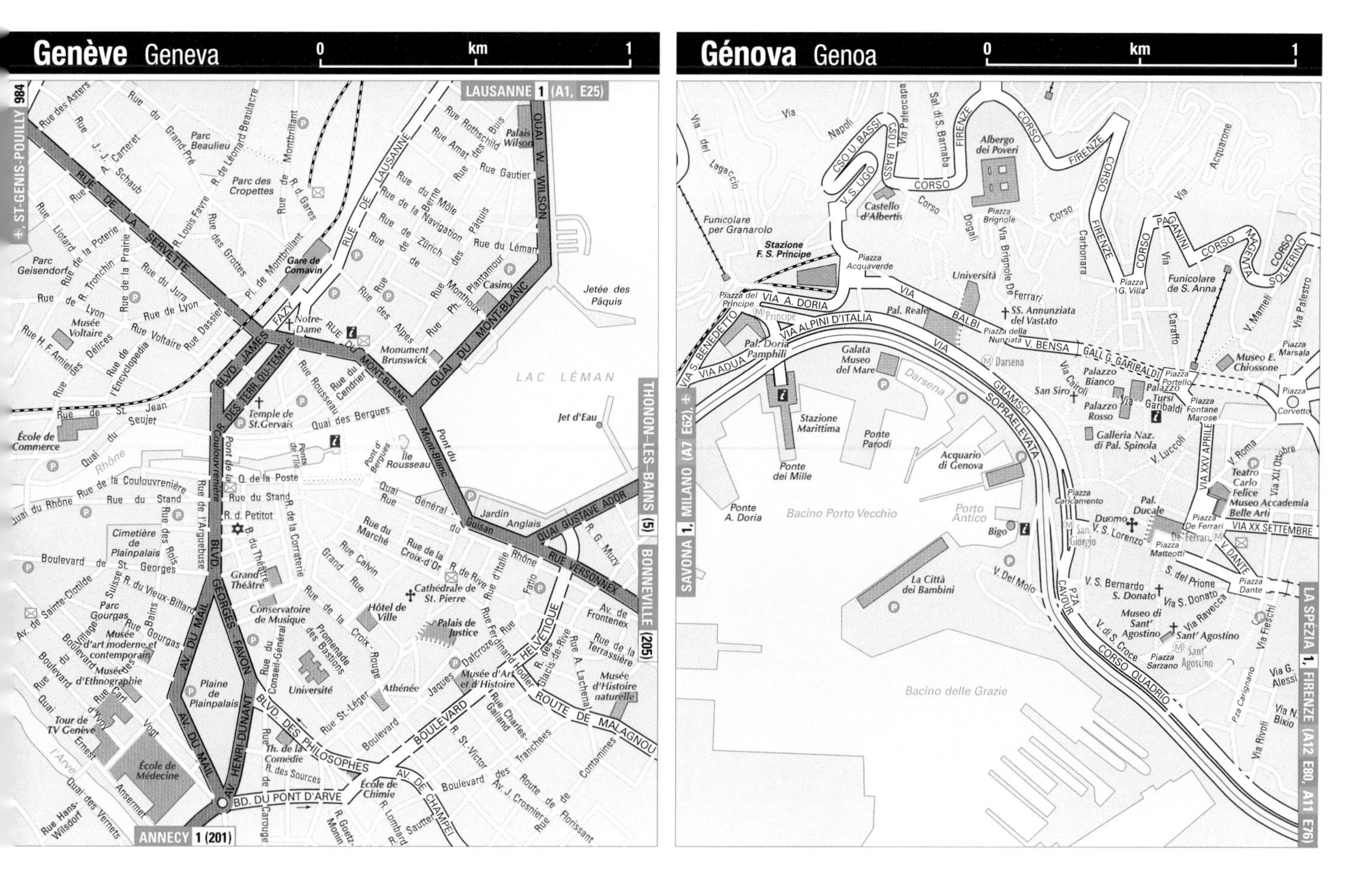
Genève Geneva
0 km 1
LAUSANNE 1 (A1, E25)
ST-GENIS-POUILLY 984
THONON-LES-BAINS (5) BONNEVILLE (205)
ANNECY 1 (201)
RUE DE LA SERVETTE
QUAI W. WILSON
QUAI DU MONT-BLANC
RUE DU MONT-BLANC
QUAI GUSTAVE ADOR
RUE VERSONNEX
BLVD. GEORGES-FAVON
AV. DU MAIL
AV. HENRI-DUNANT
BLVD. DES PHILOSOPHES
BD. DU PONT D'ARVE
ROUTE DE MALAGNOU
BOULEVARD HELVÉTIQUE
Parc Beaulieu
Parc des Cropettes
Gare de Cornavin
Palais Wilson
Casino
Notre-Dame
Monument Brunswick
Temple de St.Gervais
Ile Rousseau
Pont du Mont-Blanc
Jet d'Eau
LAC LÉMAN
Jetée des Pâquis
Jardin Anglais
Cathédrale de St. Pierre
Hôtel de Ville
Palais de Justice
Musée d'Art et d'Histoire
Musée d'Histoire naturelle
Grand Théâtre
Conservatoire de Musique
Promenade des Bastions
Université
Plaine de Plainpalais
Cimetière de Plainpalais
Musée d'art moderne et contemporain
Musée d'Ethnographie
Tour de TV Genève
École de Médecine
École de Commerce
Parc Geisendorf
Musée Voltaire
Rhône
l'Arve
Génova Genoa
0 km 1
SAVONA 1, MILANO (A7 E62)
LA SPEZIA 1, FIRENZE (A12 E80, A11 E76)
Albergo dei Poveri
Castello d'Albertis
Funicolare per Granarolo
Stazione F. S. Principe
Università
SS. Annunziata del Vastato
Pal. Reale
Pal. Doria Pamphili
Galata Museo del Mare
Stazione Marittima
Ponte Parodi
Ponte dei Mille
Ponte A. Doria
Acquario di Genova
Porto Antico
Bigo
Bacino Porto Vecchio
La Città dei Bambini
Bacino delle Grazie
Palazzo Bianco
Palazzo Tursi
Palazzo Rosso
Galleria Naz. di Pal. Spinola
Pal. Ducale
Duomo
Teatro Carlo Felice
Museo Accademia Belle Arti
Museo E. Chiossone
Funicolare de S. Anna
S. Donato
Museo di Sant' Agostino
Sant' Agostino
VIA GRAMSCI SOPRAELEVATA
CORSO QUADRIO
VIA XX SETTEMBRE
VIA XXV APRILE
VIA BALBI
VIA A. DORIA

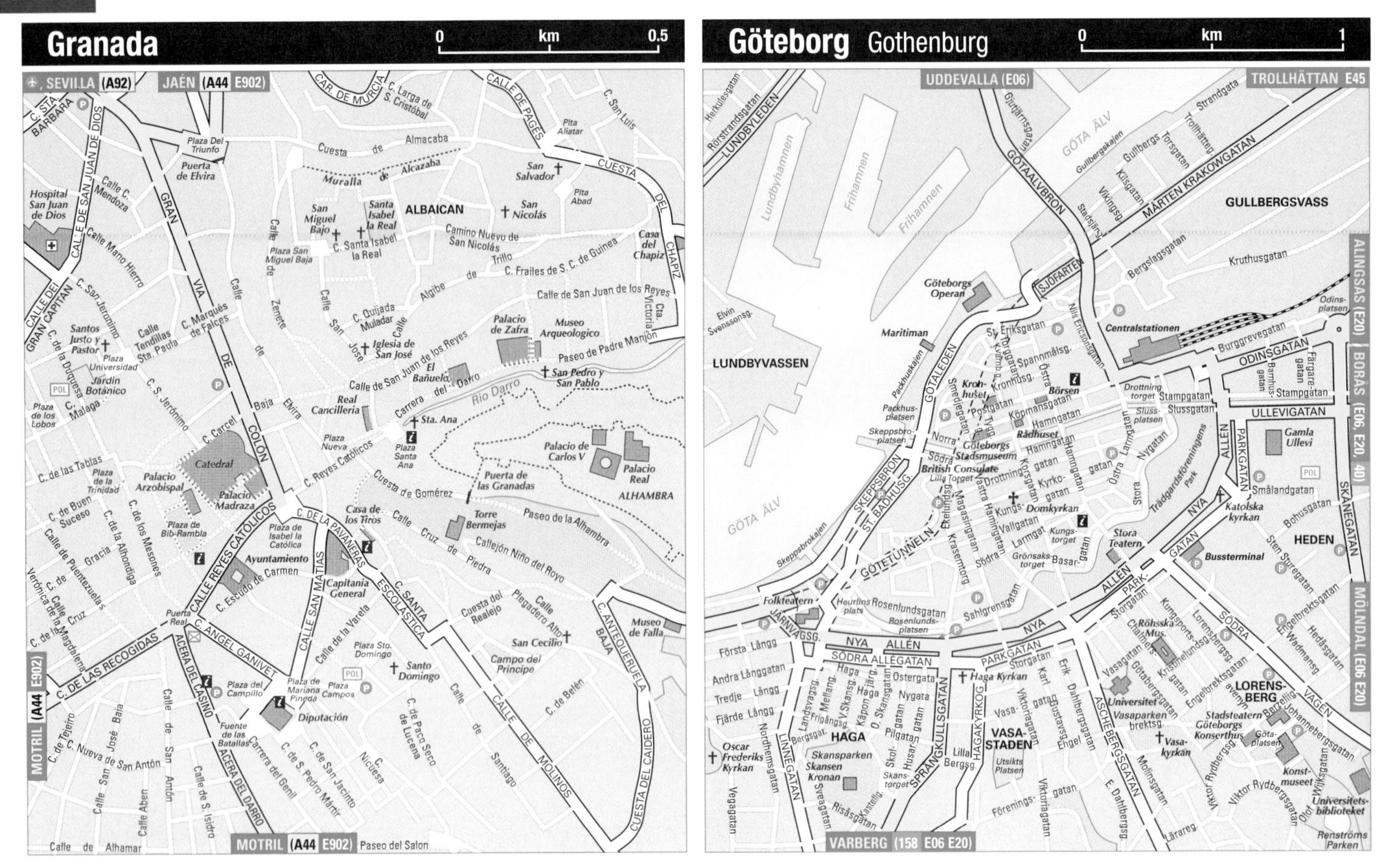

Granada
0 km 0.5
SEVILLA (A92)
JAÉN (A44 E902)
MOTRIL (A44 E902)
MOTRIL (A44 E902) Paseo del Salon
ALBAICAN
San Nicolás
San Salvador
Cuesta de Almacaba
Muralla de Alcazaba
Hospital San Juan de Dios
GRAN VIA DE COLON
Catedral
Palacio Arzobispal
Palacio Madraza
Ayuntamiento
Capitania General
CALLE REYES CATÓLICOS
Plaza Nueva
Real Cancillería
Santa Ana
Palacio de Carlos V
Palacio Real
ALHAMBRA
Puerta de las Granadas
Torre Bermejas
Casa de los Tiros
Paseo de la Alhambra
Paseo de Padre Manjón
Río Darro
Palacio de Zafra
Museo Arqueologico
San Pedro y San Pablo
El Bañuelo
Santo Domingo
Campo del Principe
San Cecilio
Museo de Falla
Diputación
CALLE DE MOLINOS
CUESTA DEL CAIDERO
C. DE LAS RECOGIDAS
ACERA DEL CASINO
CALLE SAN MATIAS
C. SANTA ESCOLASTICA
Göteborg Gothenburg
0 km 1
UDDEVALLA (E06)
TROLLHÄTTAN E45
ALINGSÅS (E20)
BORÅS (E06, E20, 40)
MÖLNDAL (E06 E20)
VARBERG (158 E06 E20)
GULLBERGSVASS
MÅRTEN KRAKOWGATAN
Göteborgs Operan
Maritiman
LUNDBYVASSEN
Lundbyhamnen
Frihamnen
GÖTA ÄLV
Centralstationen
Börsen
Rådhuset
Stadsmuseum
British Consulate
Domkyrkan
Stora Teatern
Bussterminal
Katolska kyrkan
HEDEN
ULLEVIGATAN
Gamla Ullevi
Feskekörka
NYA ALLÉN
SÖDRA ALLÉGATAN
HAGA
Haga Kyrkan
Oscar Frederiks Kyrkan
Skansparken Skansen Kronan
VASA-STADEN
Universitet
LORENSBERG
Stadsteatern
Konstmuseet
Universitetsbiblioteket
Renströms Parken
Röhsska Mus.
ODINSGATAN

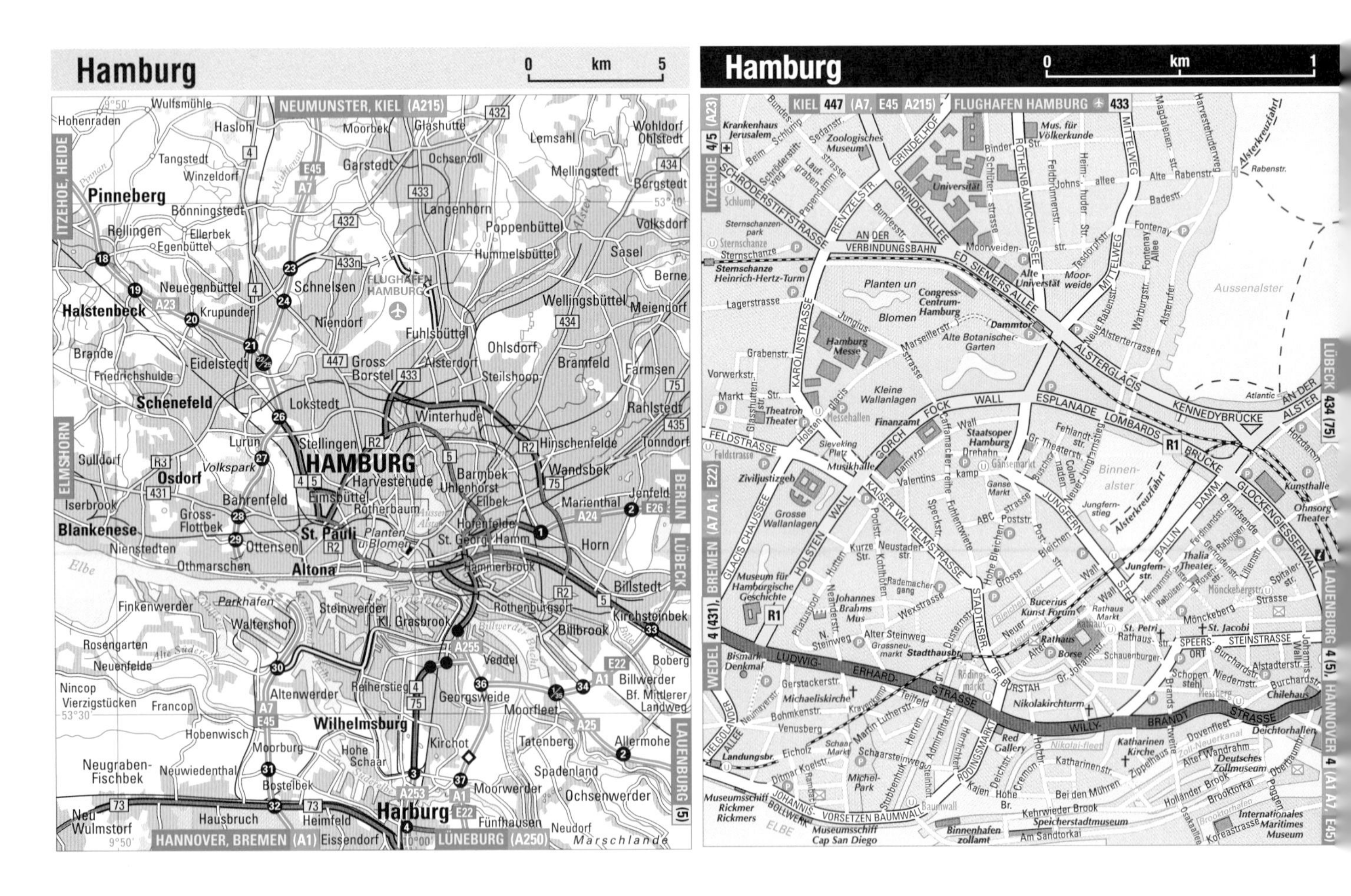

Hamburg
0 km 5
NEUMÜNSTER, KIEL (A215)
ITZEHOE, HEIDE
ELMSHORN
BERLIN
LÜBECK
LAUENBURG (5)
HANNOVER, BREMEN (A1)
LÜNEBURG (A250)
Pinneberg
Halstenbeck
Schenefeld
Osdorf
Blankenese
HAMBURG
Altona
St. Pauli
Harburg
Wilhelmsburg
Norderstedt
Langenhorn
Poppenbüttel
Fuhlsbüttel
FLUGHAFEN HAMBURG
Wandsbek
Barmbek
Eimsbüttel
Wellingsbüttel
Bramfeld
Rahlstedt
Billstedt
Bergedorf
Neugraben-Fischbek
Finkenwerder
Elbe
Hamburg
0 km 1
KIEL 447 (A7, E45 A215)
FLUGHAFEN HAMBURG 433
ITZEHOE 4/5
WEDEL 4 (431), BREMEN (A7 A1, E22)
LÜBECK 434 (75)
LAUENBURG 4 (5), HANNOVER 4 (A1 A7, E45)
Universität
Planten un Blomen
Congress-Centrum-Hamburg
Dammtor
Hamburg Messe
Aussenalster
Binnenalster
KENNEDYBRÜCKE
LOMBARDSBRÜCKE
Staatsoper Hamburg
Museum für Hamburgische Geschichte
Michaeliskirche
Rathaus
Börse
St. Petri
St. Jacobi
Kunsthalle
LUDWIG-ERHARD-STRASSE
WILLY-BRANDT-STRASSE
Deutsches Zollmuseum
Internationales Maritimes Museum
Speicherstadtmuseum
Museumsschiff Rickmer Rickmers
Museumsschiff Cap San Diego
ELBE

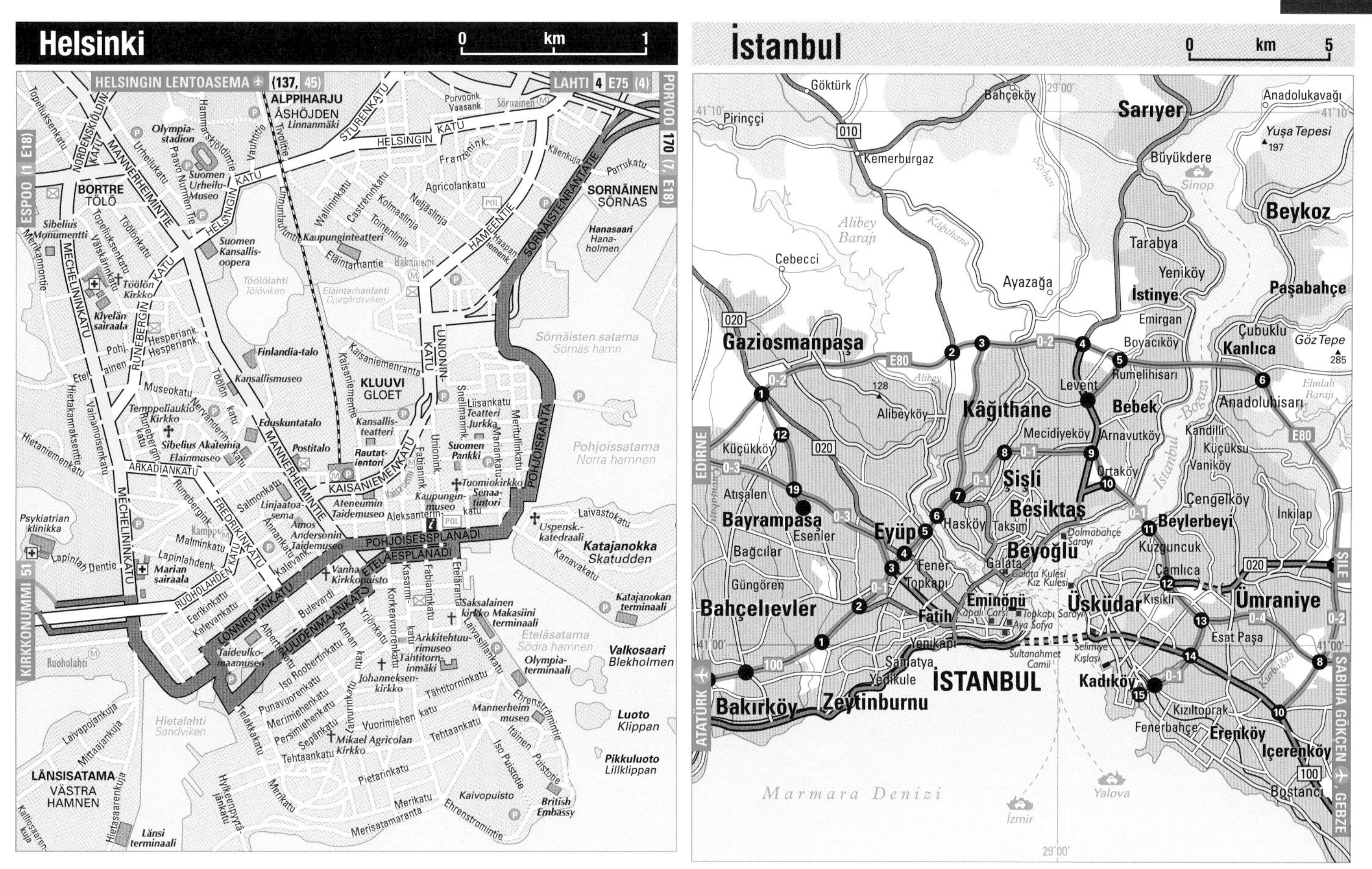
Helsinki
0 km 1
HELSINGIN LENTOASEMA (137, 45)
LAHTI 4 E75 (4)
PORVOO 170 (7, E18)
ESPOO (1 E18)
KIRKKONUMMI 51
ALPPIHARJU
ÅSHÖJDEN
Linnanmäki
Olympia-stadion
Suomen Urheilu-museo
BORTRE TÖÖLÖ
MANNERHEIMINTIE
Sibelius Monumentti
Töölön Kirkko
Kiyelän sairaala
Suomen Kansallis-oopera
Töölönlahti Tölöviken
Finlandia-talo
Kansallismuseo
Temppeliaukion Kirkko
Sibelius Akatemia
Eduskuntatalo
KLUUVI GLOET
Kansallis-teatteri
Rautat-ientori
KAISANIEMI
Postitalo
Ateneumin Taidemuseo
Tuomiokirkko
Senaa-tintori
Uspensk-katedraali
Katajanokka Skatudden
Katajanokan terminaali
POHJOISESPLANADI
ETELÄESPLANADI
Amos Andersonin Taidemuseo
Vanha Kirkko
Marian sairaala
Psykiatrian klinikka
Ruoholahti
LÖNNROTINKATU
BULEVARDI
Taideulko-maamuseo
Arkkitehtuu-rimuseo
Johanneksen-kirkko
Mikael Agricolan Kirkko
Mannerheim museo
Saksalainen kirkko
Makasiini terminaali
Eteläsatama Södra hamnen
Olympia-terminaali
Valkosaari Blekholmen
Luoto Klippan
Pikkuluoto Lillklippan
British Embassy
Kaivopuisto
Hietalahti Sandviken
LÄNSISATAMA VÄSTRA HAMNEN
Länsi terminaali
SÖRNÄINEN SÖRNÄS
Hanasaari Hana-holmen
Sörnäisten satama Sörnäs hamn
Pohjoissatama Norra hamnen
İstanbul
0 km 5
Göktürk
Bahçeköy
Sarıyer
Anadolukavağı
Yuşa Tepesi 197
Pirinççi
Kemerburgaz
Büyükdere
Sinop
Beykoz
Alibey Barajı
Cebecci
Tarabya
Yeniköy
İstinye
Paşabahçe
Ayazağa
Emirgan
Boyacıköy
Çubuklu
Kanlıca
Göz Tepe 285
Gaziosmanpaşa
Rumelihisarı
Levent
Bebek
Anadoluhisarı
Alibeyköy
Kâğıthane
Mecidiyeköy
Arnavutköy
Kandilli
Küçüksu
Vaniköy
Küçükköy
Şişli
Ortaköy
Çengelköy
İnkilap
Atışalen
Bayrampaşa
Esenler
Eyüp
Hasköy
Taksim
Beşiktaş
Dolmabahçe Sarayı
Beylerbeyi
Bağcılar
Fener
Beyoğlu
Kuzguncuk
Güngören
Topkapı
Galata
Galata Kulesi
Kız Kulesi
Çamlıca
Bahçelievler
Eminönü
Üsküdar
Kısıklı
Ümraniye
Fatih
Kapalı Çarşı
Topkapı Sarayı
Aya Sofya
Esat Paşa
Yenikapı
Sultanahmet Camii
Selimiye Kışlası
Samatya
Yedikule
İSTANBUL
Kadıköy
Bakırköy
Zeytinburnu
Kızıltoprak
Fenerbahçe
Erenköy
İçerenköy
Bostancı
Marmara Denizi
Yalova
İzmir
EDİRNE
ATATÜRK
ŞİLE
SABIHA GÖKÇEN
GEBZE

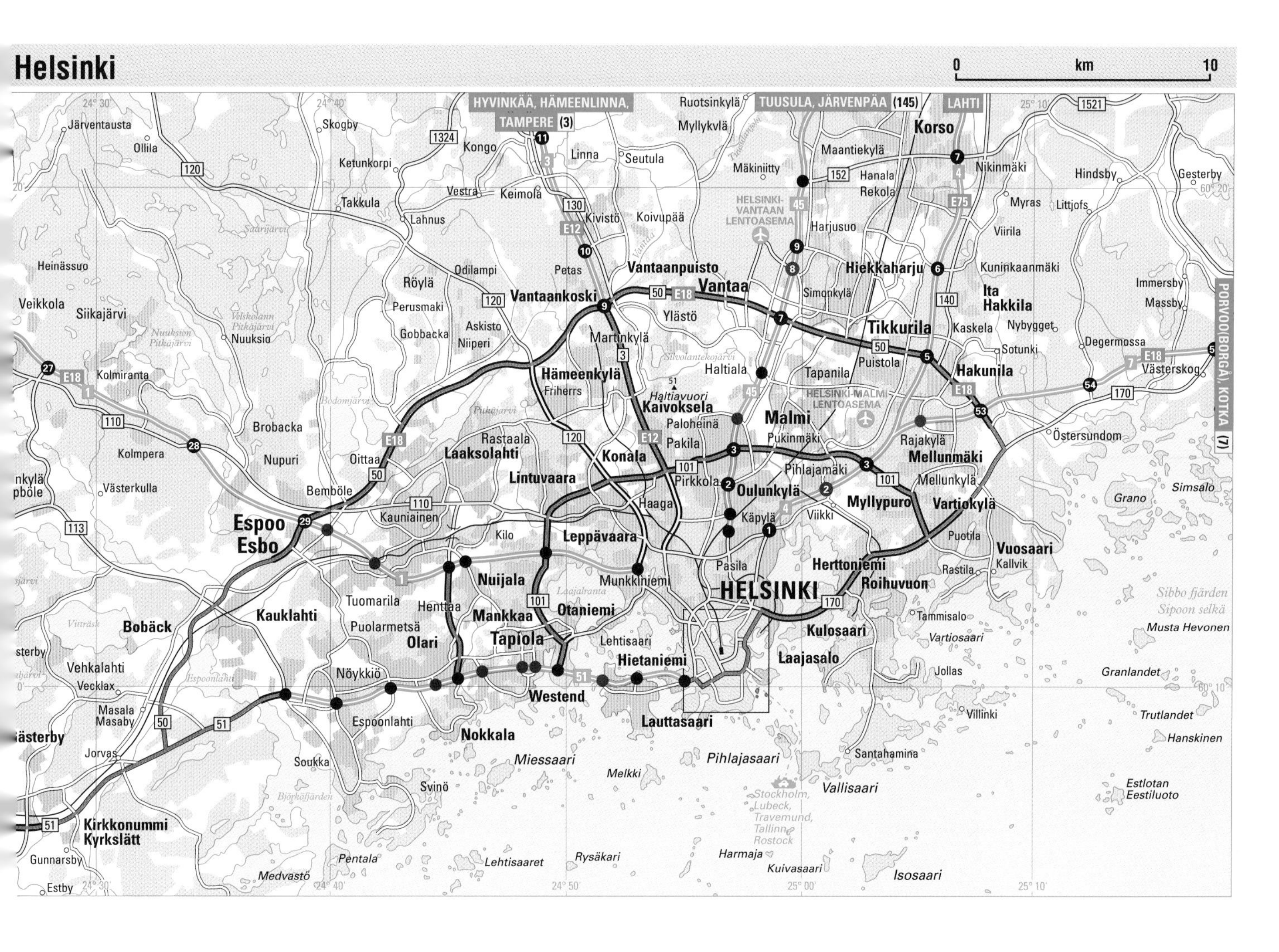
Helsinki
0 km 10
HYVINKÄÄ, HÄMEENLINNA, TAMPERE (3)
TUUSULA, JÄRVENPÄÄ (145)
LAHTI
PORVOO/BORGÅ, KOTKA (7)
Järventausta
Ollila
Skogby
Ketunkorpi
Kongo
Linna
Seutula
Ruotsinkylä
Myllykylä
Korso
Mäntiekylä
Nikinmäki
Hindsby
Gesterby
Mäkiniitty
Hanala
Rekola
Myras
Littjofs
Takkula
Lahnus
Keimola
Kivistö
Koivupää
HELSINKI-VANTAAN LENTOASEMA
Harjusuo
Viirila
Heinässuo
Odilampi
Petas
Vantaanpuisto
Hiekkaharju
Kuninkaanmäki
Veikkola
Siikajärvi
Röylä
Vantaankoski
Vantaa
Simonkylä
Ita Hakkila
Immersby
Massby
Perusmaki
Ylästö
Nuuksio
Gobbacka
Askisto
Niipéri
Martinkylä
Tikkurila
Kaskela
Nybygget
Degermossa
Sotunki
Puistola
Hakunila
Västerskog
Kolmiranta
Hämeenkylä
Friherrs
Haltiala
Tapanila
HELSINKI-MALMI LENTOASEMA
Haltiavuori
Kaivoksela
Malmi
Brobacka
Paloheinä
Pukinmäki
Rajakylä
Östersundom
Rastaala
Pakila
Kolmpera
Nupuri
Oittaa
Laaksolahti
Konala
Mellunmäki
Lintuvaara
Pirkkola
Pihlajamäki
Västerkulla
Bemböle
Oulunkylä
Myllypuro
Mellunkylä
Vartiokylä
Grano
Simsalö
Haaga
Kauniainen
Käpylä
Viikki
Espoo Esbo
Kilo
Leppävaara
Puotila
Vuosaari
Pasila
Herttoniemi
Rastila
Kallvik
Nuijala
Munkkiniemi
HELSINKI
Roihuvuori
Sibbo fjärden Sipoon selkä
Tuomarila
Henttaa
Kauklahti
Mankkaa
Otaniemi
Tammisalo
Bobäck
Puolarmetsä
Olari
Tapiola
Lehtisaari
Kulosaari
Musta Hevonen
Vartiosaari
Vehkalahti
Hietaniemi
Laajasalo
Vecklax
Nöykkiö
Jollas
Granlandet
Westend
Masala Masaby
Espoonlahti
Lauttasaari
Villinki
Trutlandet
Västerby
Nokkala
Jorvas
Santahamina
Hanskinen
Soukka
Miessaari
Pihlajasaari
Melkki
Vallisaari
Estlotan Eestiluoto
Svinö
Stockholm, Lubeck, Travemünd, Tallinn, Rostock
Kirkkonummi Kyrkslätt
Gunnarsby
Pentala
Lehtisaaret
Rysäkari
Harmaja
Kuivasaari
Isosaari
Medvastö
Estby

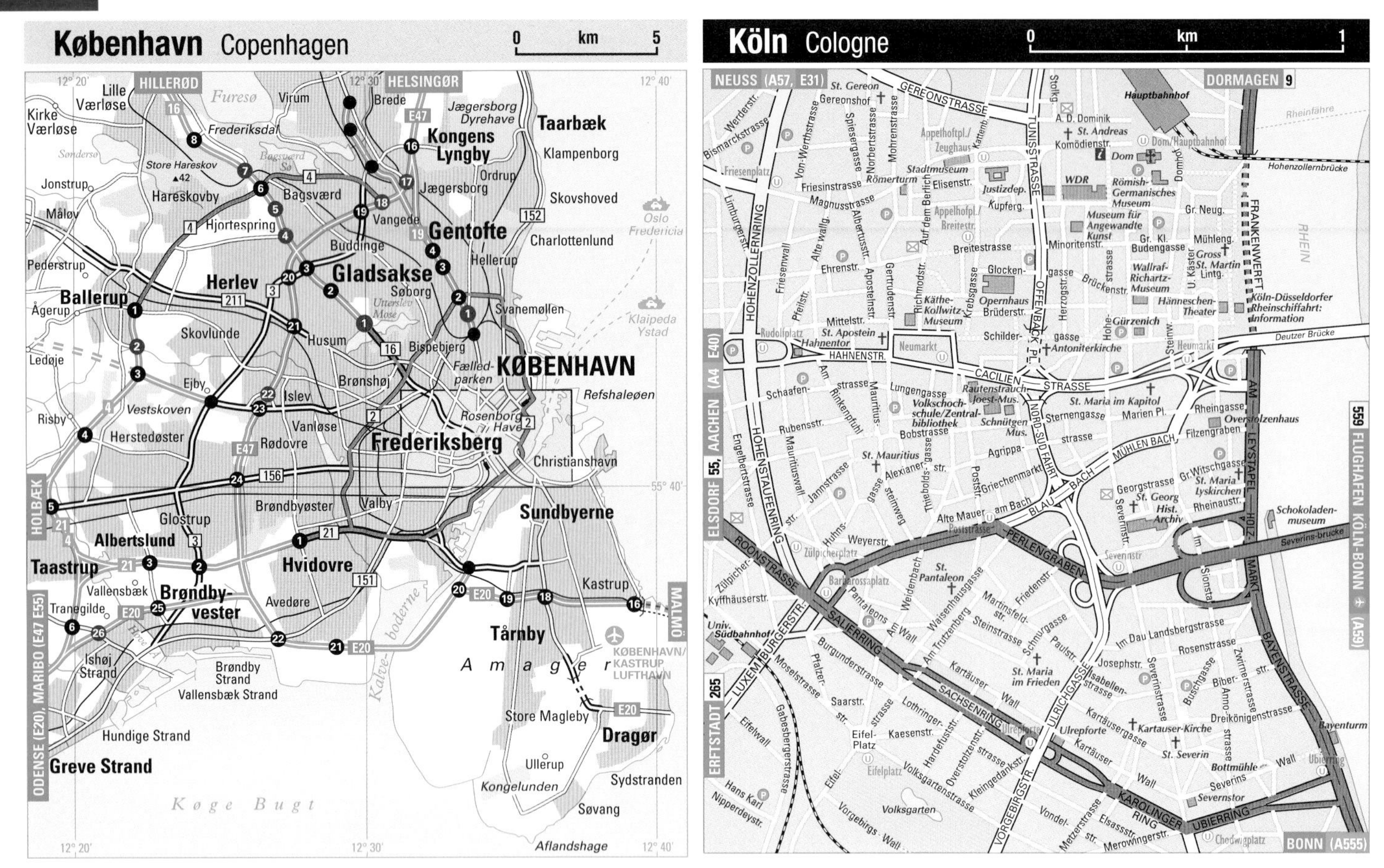
København Copenhagen
0 km 5
HILLERØD
HELSINGØR
Furesø
Virum
Brede
Lille Værløse
Kirke Værløse
Frederiksdal
Jægersborg Dyrehave
Kongens Lyngby
Taarbæk
Klampenborg
Store Hareskov
Jonstrup
Hareskovby
Bagsværd
Ordrup
Jægersborg
Skovshoved
Måløv
Hjortespring
Vangede
Gentofte
Charlottenlund
Oslo Fredericia
Pederstrup
Buddinge
Hellerup
Herlev
Gladsakse
Ballerup
Søborg
Ågerup
Skovlunde
Husum
Svanemøllen
Klaipeda Ystad
Ledøje
Bispebjerg
Fælled-parken
KØBENHAVN
Ejby
Brønshøj
Refshaleøen
Risby
Vestskoven
Islev
Rosenborg Have
Herstedøster
Vanløse
Rødovre
Frederiksberg
Christianshavn
HOLBÆK
Brøndbyøster
Valby
Glostrup
Sundbyerne
Albertslund
Taastrup
Hvidovre
Vallensbæk
Brøndby-vester
Kastrup
Tranegilde
Avedøre
MALMÖ
Ishøj Strand
Brøndby Strand
Tårnby
Vallensbæk Strand
Amager
KØBENHAVN/KASTRUP LUFTHAVN
Kalvebod Fælled
Store Magleby
Hundige Strand
Dragør
Greve Strand
Ullerup
Kongelunden
Sydstranden
Køge Bugt
Søvang
Aflandshage
ODENSE (E20), MARIBO (E47 E55)
Köln Cologne
0 km 1
NEUSS (A57, E31)
DORMAGEN 9
Hauptbahnhof
St. Gereon
Gereonshof
Gereonstrasse
A. D. Dominik
St. Andreas
Komödienstr.
Dom
Friesenplatz
Stadtmuseum
Römerturm
Elisenstr.
Justizdep.
WDR
Römisch-Germanisches Museum
Hohenzollernbrücke
Friesinstrasse
Magnusstrasse
Kupferg.
Museum für Angewandte Kunst
Gr. Neug.
Minoritenstr.
Budengasse
Mühleng.
Gross St. Martin
Breitestrasse
Glocken-gasse
Wallraf-Richartz-Museum
Ehrenstr.
Hänneschen-Theater
Käthe-Kollwitz-Museum
Opernhaus
Brüderstr.
Köln-Düsseldorfer Rheinschiffahrt: Information
Gürzenich
Mittelstr.
St. Aposteln
Hahnentor
Rudolfplatz
Schilder-gasse
Antoniterkirche
HAHNENSTR.
Neumarkt
Heumarkt
Deutzer Brücke
CÄCILIEN STRASSE
Schaafen-strasse
Rautenstrauch-Joest-Mus.
Volkshochschule/Zentral-bibliothek
Schnütgen Mus.
St. Maria im Kapitol
Rheingasse
Overstolzenhaus
Rubensstr.
Sternengasse
Marien Pl.
Filzengraben
ELSDORF 55, AACHEN (A4 E40)
559 FLUGHAFEN KÖLN-BONN (A59)
St. Mauritius
Agrippa-
Mühlenbach
Georgstrasse
Gr. Witschgasse
St. Maria Lyskirchen
St. Georg
Rheinaustr.
Hist. Archiv
Schokoladen-museum
Alte Mauer am Bach
Weyerstr.
Perlengraben
Severinsbrücke
Zülpicher Platz
Barbarossaplatz
St. Pantaleon
Kyffhäuserstr.
Univ. Südbahnhof
Salierring
Im Dau
Landsbergstrasse
Rosenstrasse
Luxemburger Str.
Sachsenring
Josephstr.
St. Maria im Frieden
Kartäuser Wall
Ulrichgasse
Ulrepforte
Kartäuser-Kirche
Dreikönigenstrasse
Bayenturm
ERFTSTADT 265
St. Severin
Eifelplatz
Bottmühle
Severinstor
Karolinger Ring
Ubierring
Volksgarten
Merowingerstr.
Chlodwigplatz
BONN (A555)
Hohenzollernring
Hohenstaufenring
Am Leystapel
Holzmarkt
Bayenstrasse

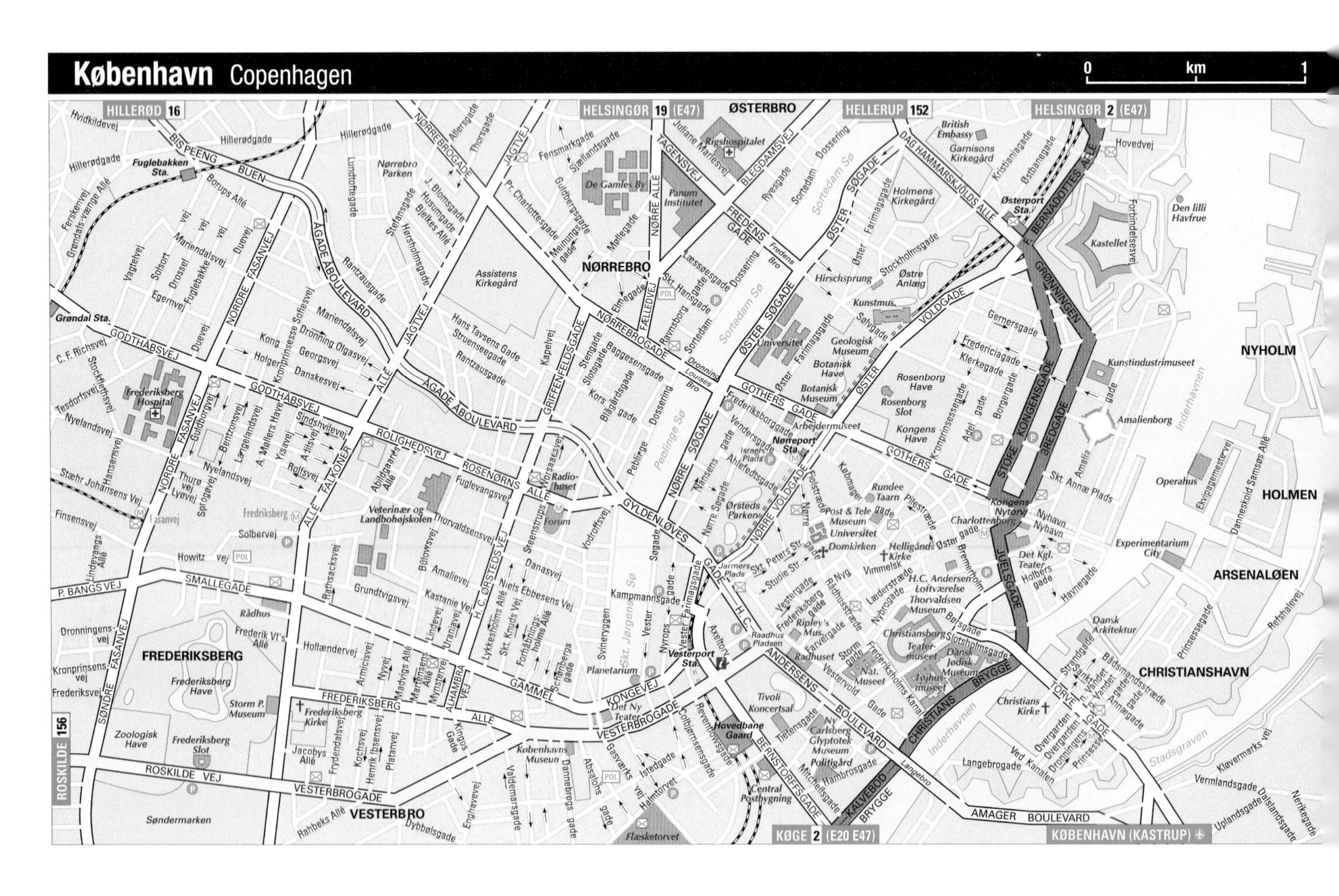
København Copenhagen
0 km 1
HILLERØD 16
HELSINGØR 19 (E47)
ØSTERBRO
HELLERUP 152
HELSINGØR 2 (E47)
Fuglebakken Sta.
Bispeengbuen
Nørrebro Parken
Rigshospitalet
Panum Institutet
British Embassy
Garnisons Kirkegård
De Gamles By
Holmens Kirkegård
Østerport Sta.
Kastellet
Den lille Havfrue
Assistens Kirkegård
NØRREBRO
Hirschsprung
Østre Anlæg
Kunstmus.
Grøndal Sta.
Godthåbsvej
Universitet
Geologisk Museum
Botanisk Have
Botanisk Museum
Kunstindustrimuseet
NYHOLM
Frederiksberg Hospital
Rosenborg Have
Rosenborg Slot
Amalienborg
Arbejdermuseet
Kongens Have
Nørreport Sta.
Radio-huset
Veterinær og Landbohøjskolen
Forum
Operahus
HOLMEN
Ørsteds Parken
Post & Tele Museum
Universitet
Domkirken
Helligånds Kirke
Charlottenborg
Kongens Nytorv
Det Kgl. Teater
Experimentarium City
ARSENALØEN
Rådhus
Ripley's Mus.
H.C. Andersen Loftværelse
Thorvaldsen Museum
Christiansborg Slot
Raadhus Pladsen
Dansk Arkitektur
FREDERIKSBERG
Frederiksberg Have
Storm P. Museum
Vesterport Sta.
Planetarium
Teater-museet
Dansk Jødisk Museum
Tøjhus-museet
Nat. Museet
Christians Kirke
CHRISTIANSHAVN
Tivoli Koncertsal
Ny Carlsberg Glyptotek
Politigård
Frederiksberg Kirke
Zoologisk Have
Frederiksberg Slot
Hovedbane Gaard
Københavns Museum
Central Postbygning
Langebrogade
ROSKILDE 156
VESTERBRO
Søndermarken
Flæsketorvet
KØGE 2 (E20 E47)
KØBENHAVN (KASTRUP)
Amager Boulevard
Kalvebod Brygge
Christians Brygge
Store Kongensgade
Bredgade
Gothersgade
Nørre Søgade
Peblinge Sø
Sortedam Sø
Vesterbrogade
Gammel Kongevej
H.C. Andersens Boulevard
Åboulevard
Smallegade
Roskilde Vej

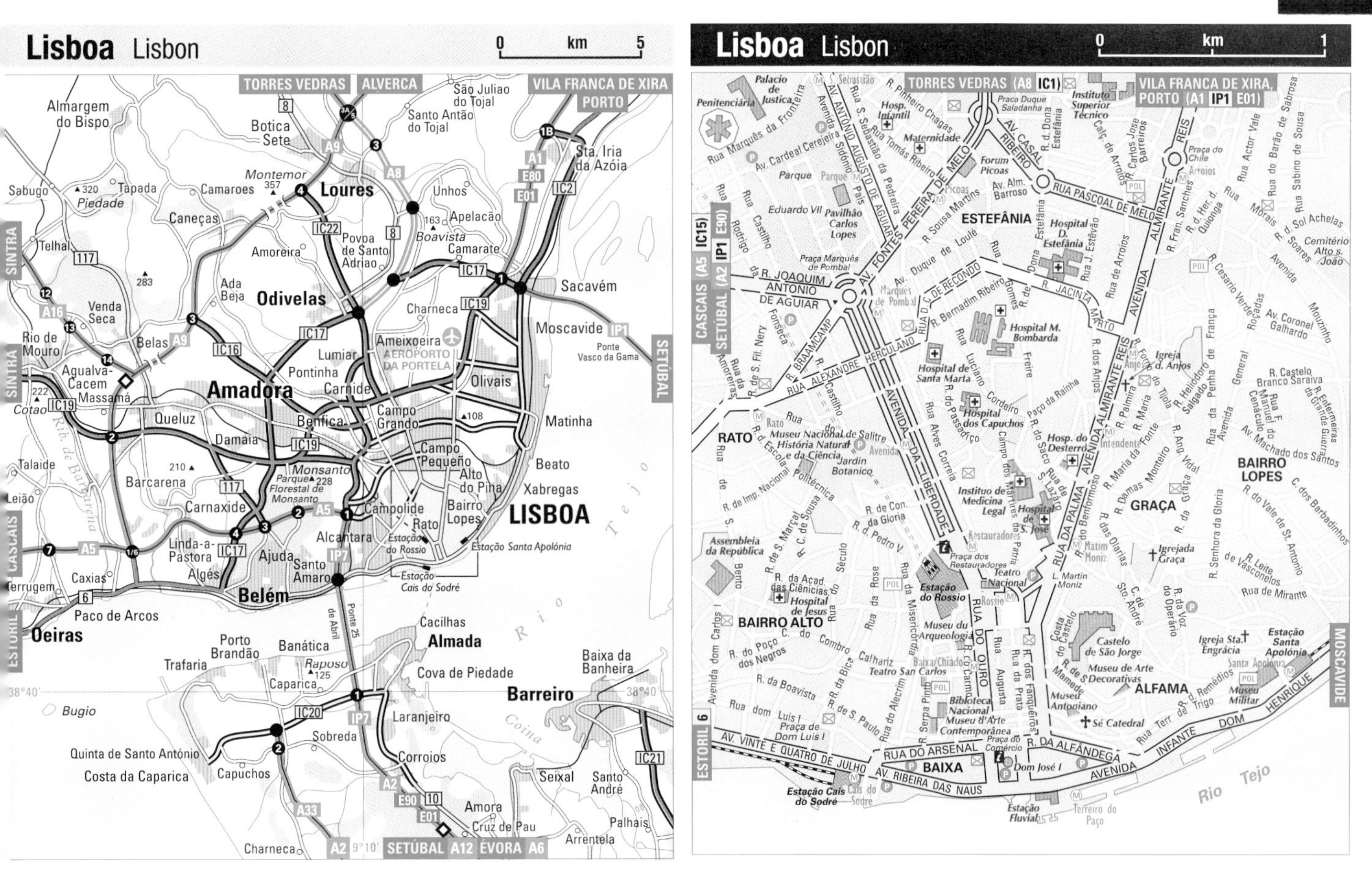
Lisboa Lisbon
0 km 5
TORRES VEDRAS
ALVERCA
VILA FRANCA DE XIRA
PORTO
SINTRA
CASCAIS
ESTORIL
SETÚBAL
ÉVORA
Almargem do Bispo
Botica Sete
São Julião do Tojal
Santo Antão do Tojal
Sta. Iria da Azóia
Sabugo
Tapada
Piedade
Camarões
Montemor
Loures
Unhos
Apelação
Caneças
Póvoa de Santo Adrião
Boavista
Camarate
Telhal
Amoreira
Sacavém
Ada Beja
Odivelas
Charneca
Venda Seca
Moscavide
Rio de Mouro
Belas
Ameixoeira
AEROPORTO DA PORTELA
Ponte Vasco da Gama
Lumiar
Agualva-Cacém
Pontinha
Olivais
Massamá
Amadora
Carnide
Cotão
Queluz
Benfica
Campo Grande
Matinha
Damaia
Talaide
Campo Pequeno
Beato
Barcarena
Monsanto
Parque Florestal de Monsanto
Alto do Pina
Xabregas
Leião
Carnaxide
Campolide
Bairro Lopes
LISBOA
Rato
Estação do Rossio
Linda-a-Pastora
Ajuda
Alcântara
Estação Santa Apolónia
Caxias
Algés
Santo Amaro
Estação Cais do Sodré
Ferrugem
Belém
Paço de Arcos
Oeiras
Ponte 25 de Abril
Cacilhas
Rio Tejo
Almada
Porto Brandão
Banática
Trafaria
Raposo
Caparica
Cova de Piedade
Baixa da Banheira
Barreiro
Bugio
Laranjeiro
Sobreda
Quinta de Santo António
Costa da Caparica
Corroios
Capuchos
Seixal
Santo André
Amora
Palhais
Cruz de Pau
Charneca
Arrentela
Lisboa Lisbon
0 km 1
TORRES VEDRAS (A8 IC1)
VILA FRANCA DE XIRA, PORTO (A1 IP1 E01)
CASCAIS (A5 IC15)
SETÚBAL (A2 IP1 E90)
ESTORIL 6
MOSCAVIDE
Palácio de Justiça
Penitenciária
Parque Eduardo VII
Pavilhão Carlos Lopes
Hosp. Infantil
Maternidade
Forum Picoas
Instituto Superior Técnico
Praça Duque Saldanha
ESTEFÂNIA
Hospital D. Estefânia
Praça Marquês de Pombal
R. JOAQUIM ANTÓNIO DE AGUIAR
AV. FONTES PEREIRA DE MELO
AV. DA REPÚBLICA
AVENIDA ALMIRANTE REIS
Hospital M. Bombarda
Hospital de Santa Marta
Hospital dos Capuchos
AVENIDA DA LIBERDADE
RATO
Museu Nacional de História Natural e da Ciência
Jardim Botânico
Instituto de Medicina Legal
Hospital de S. José
Hosp. do Desterro
Igreja d. Anjos
BAIRRO LOPES
GRAÇA
Assembleia da República
Hospital de Jesus
Estação do Rossio
Praça dos Restauradores
Teatro Nacional
Igrejada Graça
BAIRRO ALTO
Museu do Arqueologia
Castelo de São Jorge
Museu de Arte Decorativas
Igreja Sta. Engrácia
Estação Santa Apolónia
Museu Militar
Teatro San Carlos
Biblioteca Nacional
Museu d'Arte Contemporânea
ALFAMA
Museu Antoniano
Sé Catedral
AV. VINTE E QUATRO DE JULHO
RUA DO ARSENAL
BAIXA
R. DA ALFÂNDEGA
AVENIDA INFANTE DOM HENRIQUE
Estação Cais do Sodré
Estação Fluvial
Terreiro do Paço
Rio Tejo

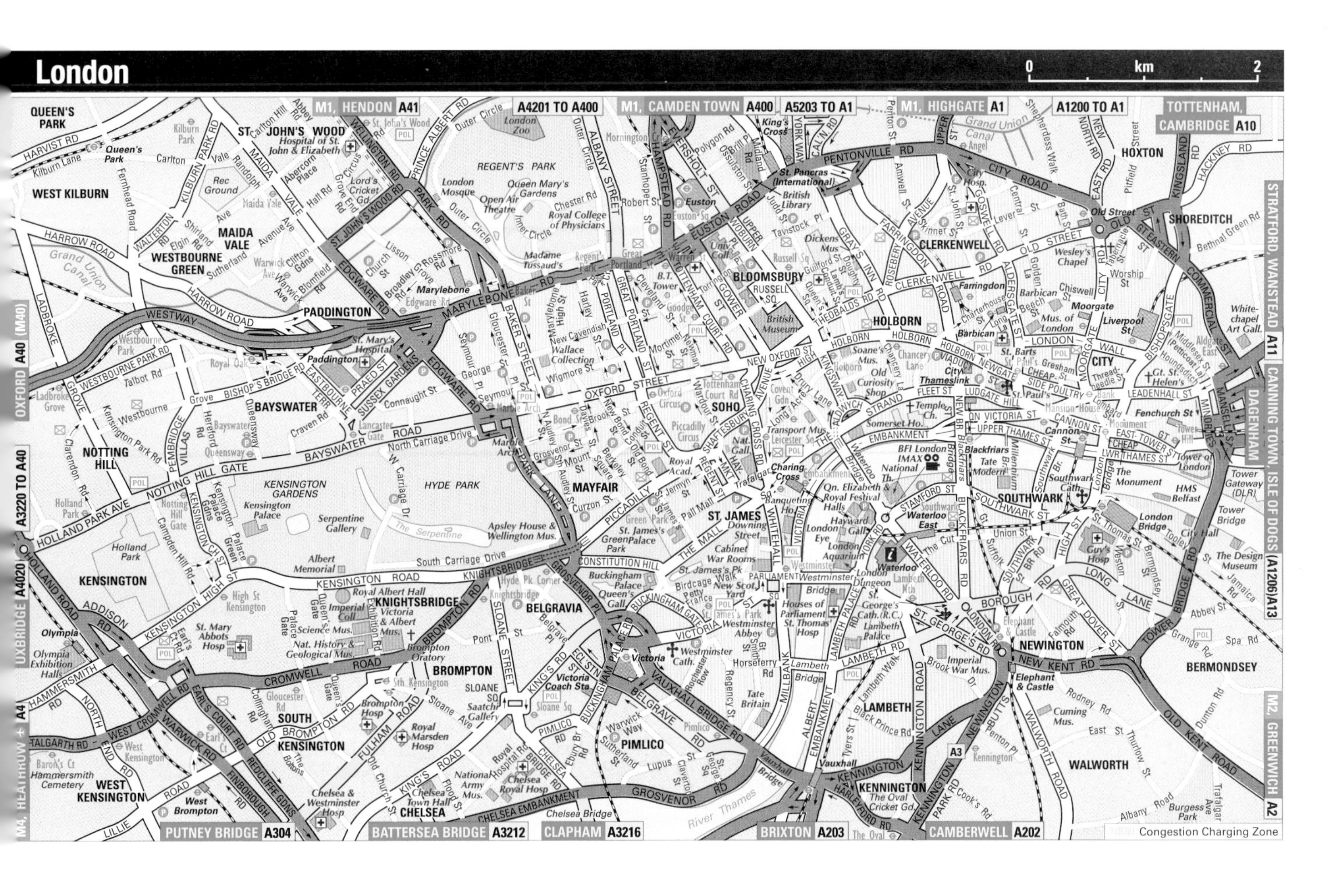
London
0 km 2
M1, HENDON A41
A4201 TO A400
M1, CAMDEN TOWN A400
A5203 TO A1
M1, HIGHGATE A1
A1200 TO A1
TOTTENHAM, CAMBRIDGE A10
STRATFORD, WANSTEAD A11
CANNING TOWN, ISLE OF DOGS (A1206) A13
DAGENHAM
M2, GREENWICH A2
OXFORD A40 (M40)
A3220 TO A40
UXBRIDGE A4020
M4, HEATHROW + A4
PUTNEY BRIDGE A304
BATTERSEA BRIDGE A3212
CLAPHAM A3216
BRIXTON A203
CAMBERWELL A202
QUEEN'S PARK
ST. JOHN'S WOOD
Hospital of St. John & Elizabeth
REGENT'S PARK
London Zoo
King's Cross
St. Pancras (International)
British Library
HOXTON
WEST KILBURN
Lord's Cricket Ground
MAIDA VALE
WESTBOURNE GREEN
London Mosque
Queen Mary's Gardens
Open Air Theatre
Royal College of Physicians
Euston
BLOOMSBURY
CLERKENWELL
SHOREDITCH
Madame Tussaud's
Marylebone
B.T. Tower
British Museum
PADDINGTON
St. Mary's Hospital
Wallace Collection
HOLBORN
Barbican
Farringdon
Moorgate
Liverpool St
Whitechapel Art Gall.
BAYSWATER
Sir John Soane's Mus.
Old Curiosity Shop
City Thameslink
St. Paul's
CITY
NOTTING HILL
SOHO
Covent Garden
Fenchurch St
Marble Arch
Somerset Ho.
Blackfriars
Tate Modern
Cannon St
Monument
Tower of London
KENSINGTON GARDENS
HYDE PARK
MAYFAIR
Piccadilly Circus
Trafalgar Sq.
Nat. Gall.
Charing Cross
BFI London IMAX
Royal Festival Halls
SOUTHWARK
Tower Bridge
HMS Belfast
Kensington Palace
Serpentine Gallery
Apsley House & Wellington Mus.
ST. JAMES
Green Park
St. James's Park
London Eye
London Aquarium
Waterloo
London Bridge
Guy's Hosp
The Design Museum
Holland Park
Albert Memorial
Buckingham Palace
Cabinet War Rooms
Houses of Parliament
Westminster Abbey
St. Thomas' Hosp
KENSINGTON
Royal Albert Hall
KNIGHTSBRIDGE
Victoria & Albert Mus.
BELGRAVIA
Lambeth Palace
Imperial War Mus.
Elephant & Castle
NEWINGTON
BERMONDSEY
Olympia
Olympia Exhibition Halls
Science Mus.
Nat. History & Geological Mus.
Brompton Oratory
BROMPTON
Victoria
Westminster Cath.
Victoria Coach Sta
Saatchi Gallery
Tate Britain
LAMBETH
Cuming Mus.
SOUTH KENSINGTON
Royal Marsden Hosp
PIMLICO
WALWORTH
Hammersmith Cemetery
WEST KENSINGTON
Chelsea & Westminster Hosp
CHELSEA
National Army Mus.
Chelsea Royal Hosp
KENNINGTON
The Oval Cricket Gd.
Chelsea Bridge
Vauxhall
River Thames
Congestion Charging Zone

## London

0 km 10

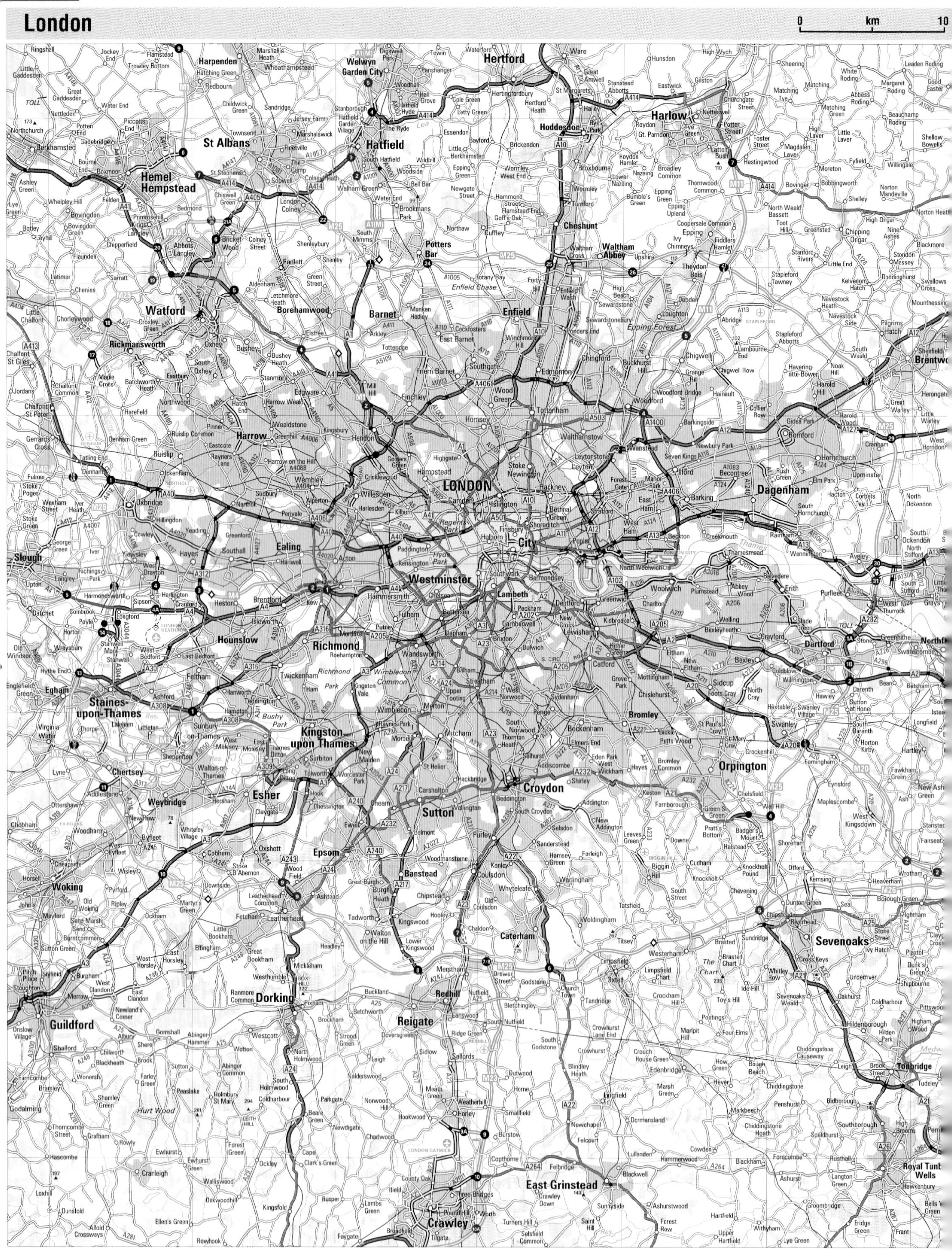
Hertford
Welwyn Garden City
Harpenden
Harlow
Hoddesdon
St Albans
Hatfield
Hemel Hempstead
Cheshunt
Waltham Abbey
Potters Bar
Watford
Borehamwood
Barnet
Enfield
Rickmansworth
Brentwood
Harrow
LONDON
Romford
Dagenham
Ealing
Slough
City
Westminster
Lambeth
Hounslow
Richmond
Dartford
Staines-upon-Thames
Kingston upon Thames
Bromley
Orpington
Chertsey
Weybridge
Esher
Croydon
Sutton
Epsom
Banstead
Woking
Caterham
Sevenoaks
Dorking
Redhill
Reigate
Guildford
Tonbridge
East Grinstead
Crawley
Royal Tunbridge Wells

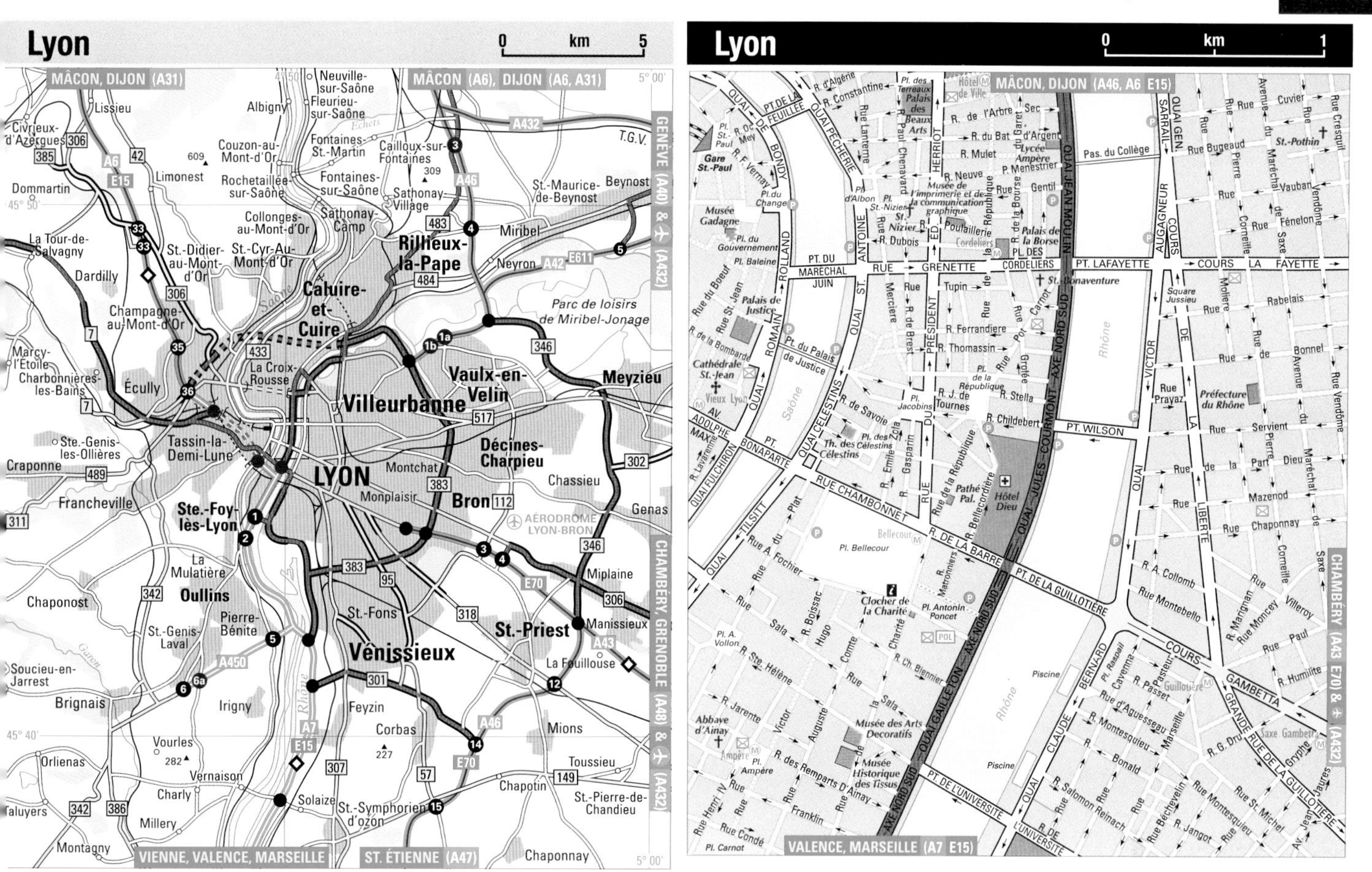
Lyon
0 km 5
MÂCON, DIJON (A31)
MÂCON (A6), DIJON (A6, A31)
GENÈVE (A40) & ✈ (A432)
CHAMBÉRY, GRENOBLE (A48) & ✈ (A432)
VIENNE, VALENCE, MARSEILLE
ST. ÉTIENNE (A47)
Lissieu
Civrieux-d'Azergues
Dommartin
La Tour-de-Salvagny
Dardilly
Champagne-au-Mont-d'Or
Marcy-l'Étoile
Charbonnières-les-Bains
Écully
Ste.-Genis-les-Ollières
Craponne
Francheville
Tassin-la-Demi-Lune
Ste.-Foy-lès-Lyon
La Mulatière
Oullins
Chaponost
St.-Genis-Laval
Pierre-Bénite
Soucieu-en-Jarrest
Brignais
Irigny
Vourles
Orlienas
Vernaison
Charly
Millery
Montagny
Taluyers
Albigny
Neuville-sur-Saône
Fleurieu-sur-Saône
Couzon-au-Mont-d'Or
Limonest
Rochetaillée-sur-Saône
Fontaines-St.-Martin
Fontaines-sur-Saône
Cailloux-sur-Fontaines
Collonges-au-Mont-d'Or
St.-Didier-au-Mont-d'Or
St.-Cyr-Au-Mont-d'Or
Sathonay-Camp
Sathonay-Village
Rillieux-la-Pape
Caluire-et-Cuire
La Croix-Rousse
Villeurbanne
LYON
Montchat
Monplaisir
Vaulx-en-Velin
Décines-Charpieu
Bron
Chassieu
AÉRODROME LYON-BRON
Genas
Meyzieu
Miribel
Neyron
St.-Maurice-de-Beynost
Beynost
Parc de loisirs de Miribel-Jonage
St.-Fons
Vénissieux
St.-Priest
Manissieux
Miplaine
La Fouillouse
Feyzin
Corbas
Mions
Solaize
St.-Symphorien-d'ozon
Toussieu
Chapotin
St.-Pierre-de-Chandieu
Chaponnay
T.G.V.
Lyon
0 km 1
MÂCON, DIJON (A46, A6 E15)
VALENCE, MARSEILLE (A7 E15)
CHAMBÉRY (A43 E70 & ✈ (A432)
Gare St.-Paul
Musée Gadagne
Pl. du Gouvernement
Palais de Justice
Cathédrale St.-Jean
Pl. du Change
QUAI PÊCHERIE
R. Constantine
Hôtel de Ville
Palais des Beaux Arts
Musée de l'imprimerie et de la communication graphique
Pl. des Terreaux
St. Nizier
Palais de la Borse
RUE GRENETTE
PT. DU MARÉCHAL JUIN
St. Bonaventure
Pl. des Célestins
Th. des Célestins
Pl. Bellecour
Pathé Pal.
Hôtel Dieu
Clocher de la Charité
Pl. Antonin Poncet
Musée des Arts Decoratifs
Musée Historique des Tissus
Abbaye d'Ainay
Pl. Ampère
Pl. Carnot
RUE CHAMBONNET
PT. DE LA GUILLOTIÈRE
PT. DE L'UNIVERSITÉ
PT. LAFAYETTE
PT. WILSON
Rhône
Saône
Piscine
Pas. du Collège
QUAI SARRAIL
QUAI GEN.
COURS LA FAYETTE
Square Jussieu
Préfecture du Rhône
COURS GAMBETTA
GRANDE RUE DE LA GUILLOTIÈRE
QUAI VICTOR AUGAGNEUR
COURS DE LA LIBERTÉ
QUAI CLAUDE BERNARD
QUAI JULES COURMONT
QUAI GAILLETON
QUAI DR. GAILLETON
AXE NORD SUD

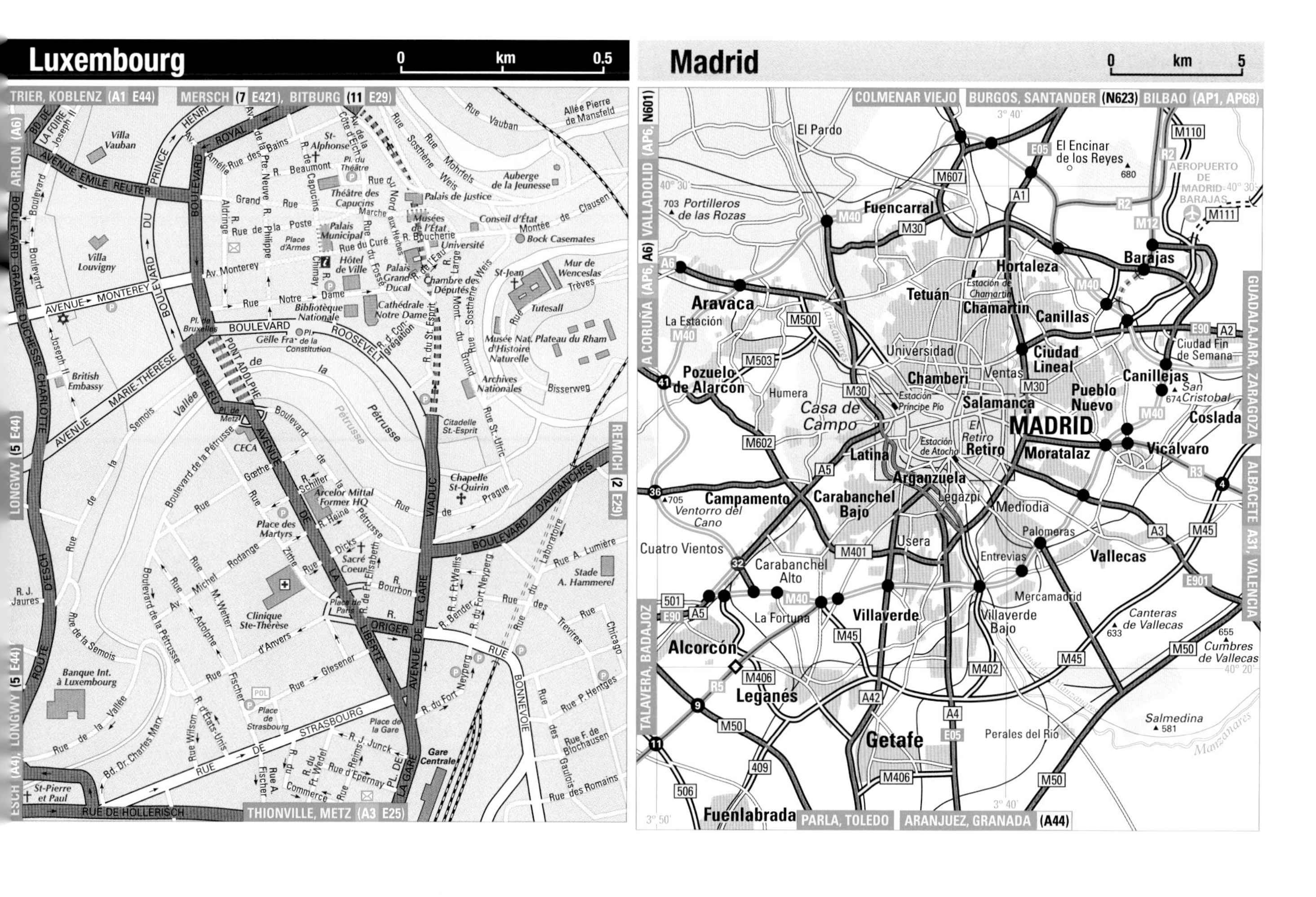
Luxembourg
0 km 0.5
TRIER, KOBLENZ (A1 E44)
MERSCH (7 E421), BITBURG (11 E29)
ARLON (A6)
LONGWY (5 E44)
REMICH (2 E29)
THIONVILLE, METZ (A3 E25)
Villa Vauban
AVENUE EMILE REUTER
Villa Louvigny
AVENUE MONTEREY
AVENUE MARIE-THÉRÈSE
BOULEVARD GRANDE DUCHESSE CHARLOTTE
British Embassy
BOULEVARD ROYAL
BOULEVARD DU PRINCE HENRI
Théâtre des Capucins
Palais Municipal
Place d'Armes
Hôtel de Ville
Palais Grand Ducal
Palais de Justice
Musées de l'État
Conseil d'État
Bock Casemates
Université
Chambre des Députés
Cathédrale Notre Dame
Bibliothèque Nationale
St-Jean
Mur de Wenceslas
Tutesall
Musée Nat. d'Histoire Naturelle
Plateau du Rham
Archives Nationales
Auberge de la Jeunesse
BOULEVARD ROOSEVELT
PONT ADOLPHE
Pétrusse
Citadelle St.-Esprit
Chapelle St-Quirin
CECA
Arcelor Mittal Former HQ
Place des Martyrs
Sacré Coeur
Clinique Ste-Thérèse
Banque Int. à Luxembourg
BOULEVARD D'AVRANCHES
AVENUE DE LA GARE
AVENUE DE LA LIBERTÉ
Gare Centrale
RUE DE STRASBOURG
RUE DE HOLLERISCH
St-Pierre et Paul
Stade A. Hammerel
Allée Pierre de Mansfeld
Madrid
0 km 5
COLMENAR VIEJO
BURGOS, SANTANDER (N623)
BILBAO (AP1, AP68)
VALLADOLID (AP6, N601)
A CORUÑA (AP6, A6)
GUADALAJARA, ZARAGOZA
ALBACETE A31, VALENCIA
TALAVERA, BADAJOZ
PARLA, TOLEDO
ARANJUEZ, GRANADA (A44)
El Pardo
703 Portilleros de las Rozas
Fuencarral
El Encinar de los Reyes
AEROPUERTO DE MADRID-BARAJAS
Barajas
Hortaleza
Tetuán
Chamartín
Canillas
Aravaca
La Estación
Pozuelo de Alarcón
Humera
Casa de Campo
Universidad
Chamberí
Ventas
Ciudad Lineal
Pueblo Nuevo
Canillejas
San Cristobal
Ciudad Fin de Semana
Coslada
Vicálvaro
Salamanca
MADRID
Retiro
Moratalaz
Latina
Arganzuela
Legazpi
Mediodia
Campamento
705 Ventorro del Cano
Carabanchel Bajo
Carabanchel Alto
Cuatro Vientos
Usera
Palomeras
Entrevias
Vallecas
Mercamadrid
La Fortuna
Villaverde
Villaverde Bajo
Canteras de Vallecas
Cumbres de Vallecas
Alcorcón
Leganés
Getafe
Perales del Río
Salmedina
Manzanares
Fuenlabrada

# Madrid

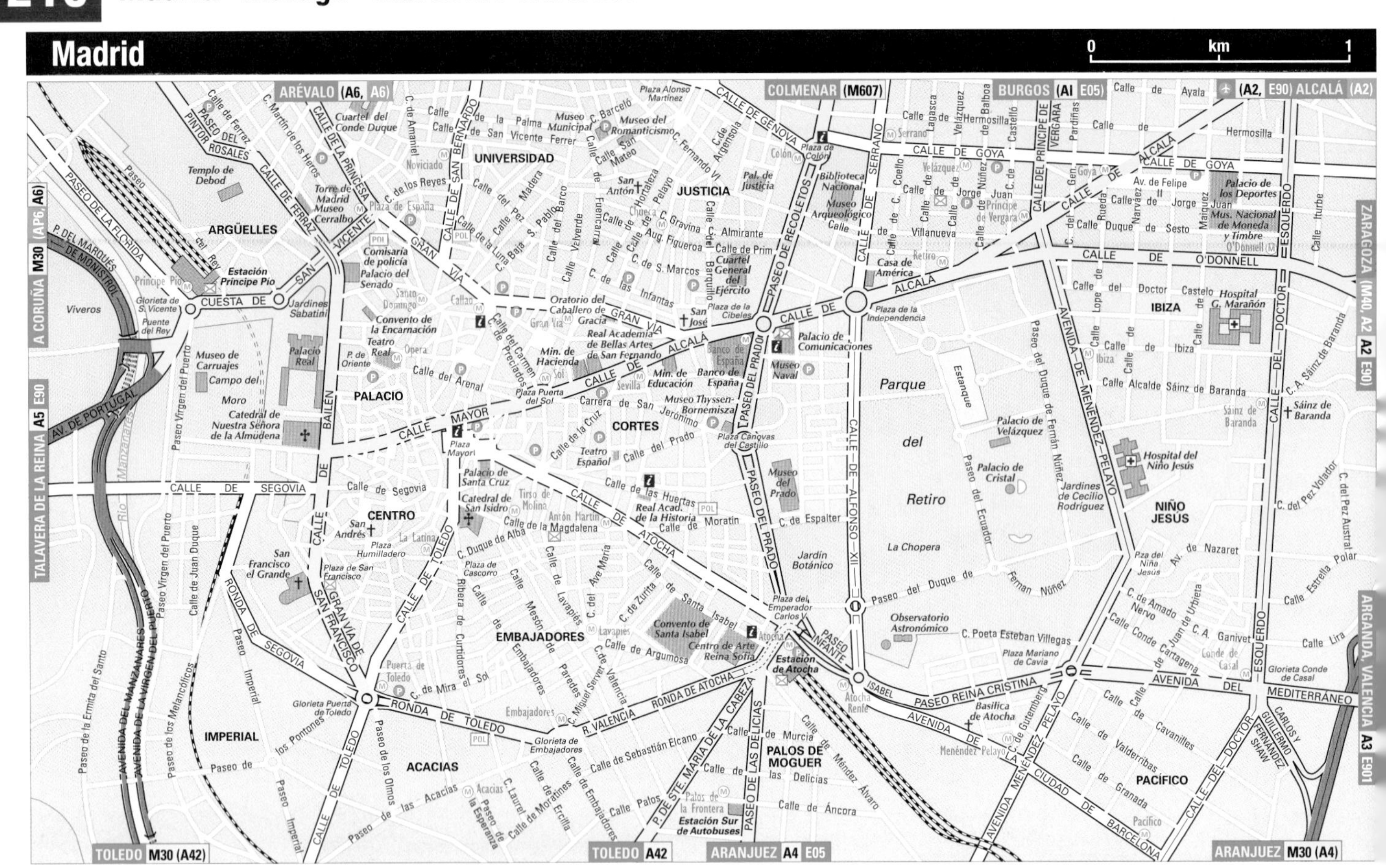

0 ————— km ————— 1

# Málaga

0 ——— km ——— 0.5

# Marseille Marseilles

0 ——— km ——— 0.5

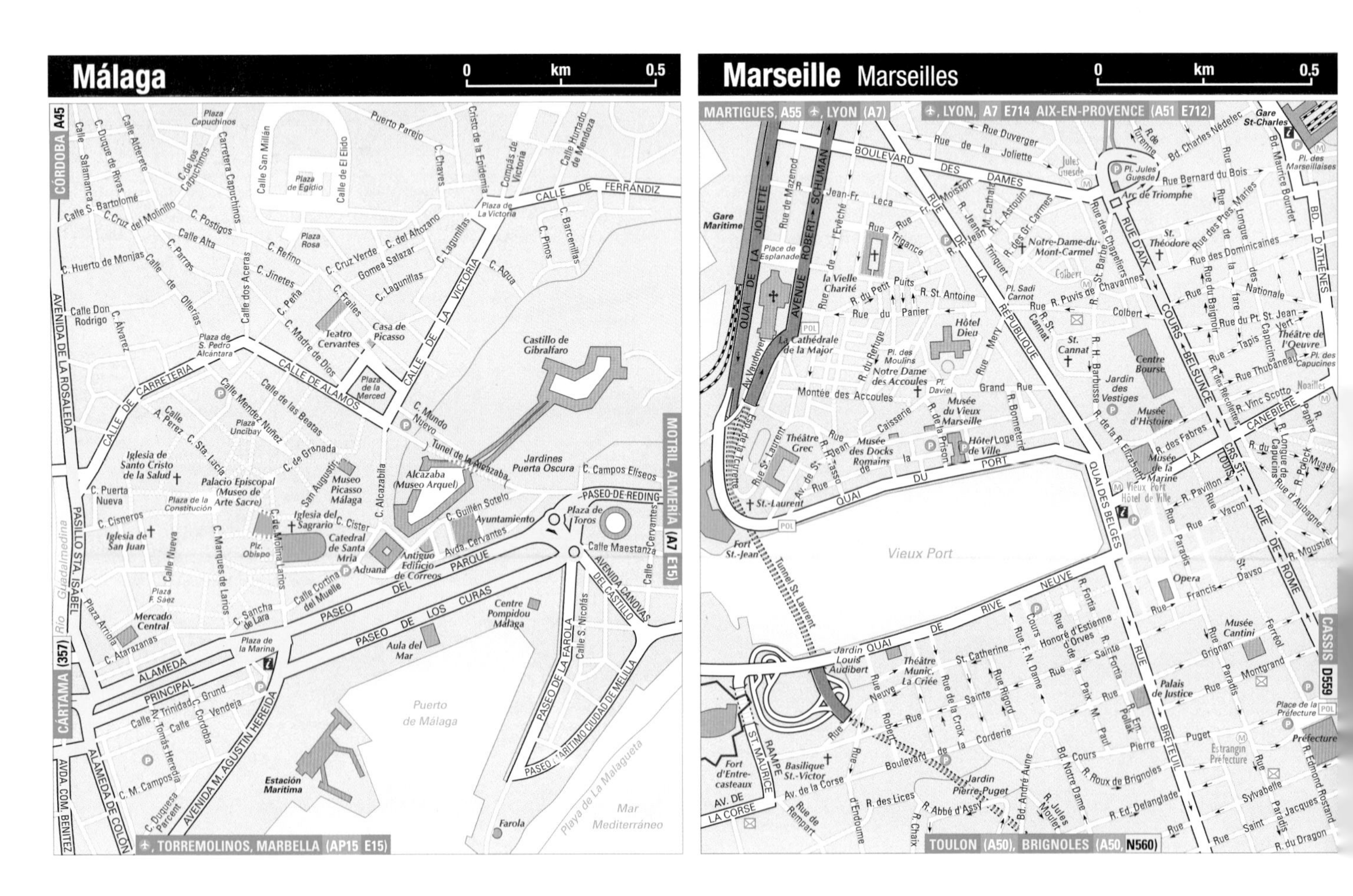

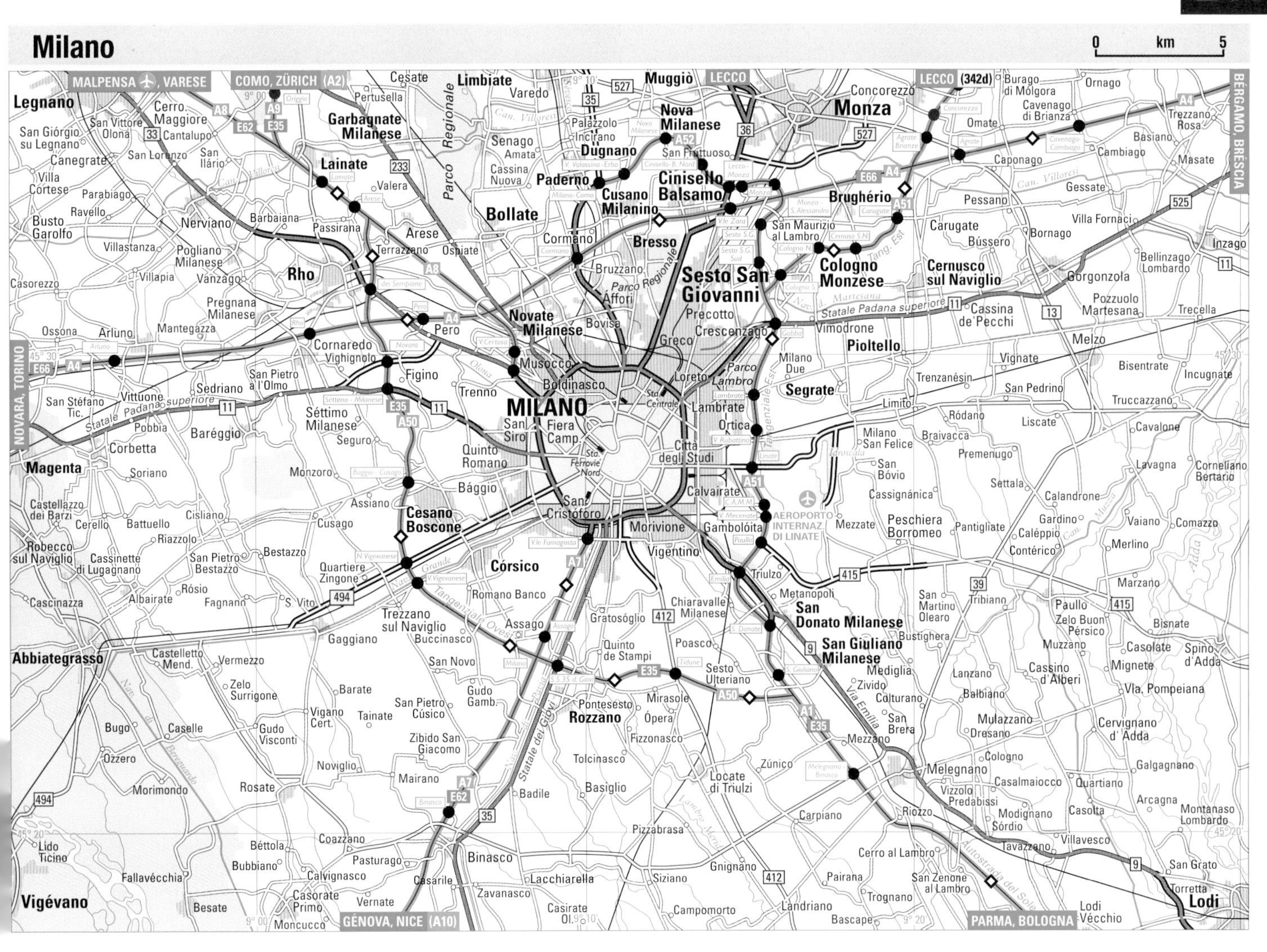
Milano
0 km 5
MALPENSA, VARESE
COMO, ZÜRICH (A2)
LECCO
LECCO (342d)
BÉRGAMO, BRÉSCIA
NOVARA, TORINO
GÉNOVA, NICE (A10)
PARMA, BOLOGNA
MILANO
Legnano
Monza
Rho
Bollate
Sesto San Giovanni
Cinisello Balsamo
Cusano Milanino
Paderno Dugnano
Nova Milanese
Muggiò
Limbiate
Lainate
Garbagnate Milanese
Bresso
Cologno Monzese
Brughério
Cernusco sul Naviglio
Pioltello
Segrate
San Donato Milanese
San Giuliano Milanese
Peschiera Borromeo
Melegnano
Lodi
Rozzano
Corsico
Cesano Boscone
Trezzano sul Naviglio
Magenta
Abbiategrasso
Vigévano
Binasco
Assago
Novate Milanese
Sedriano
Cornaredo
Pero
Nerviano
Busto Garolfo
AEROPORTO INTERNAZ. DI LINATE
Statale Padana superiore

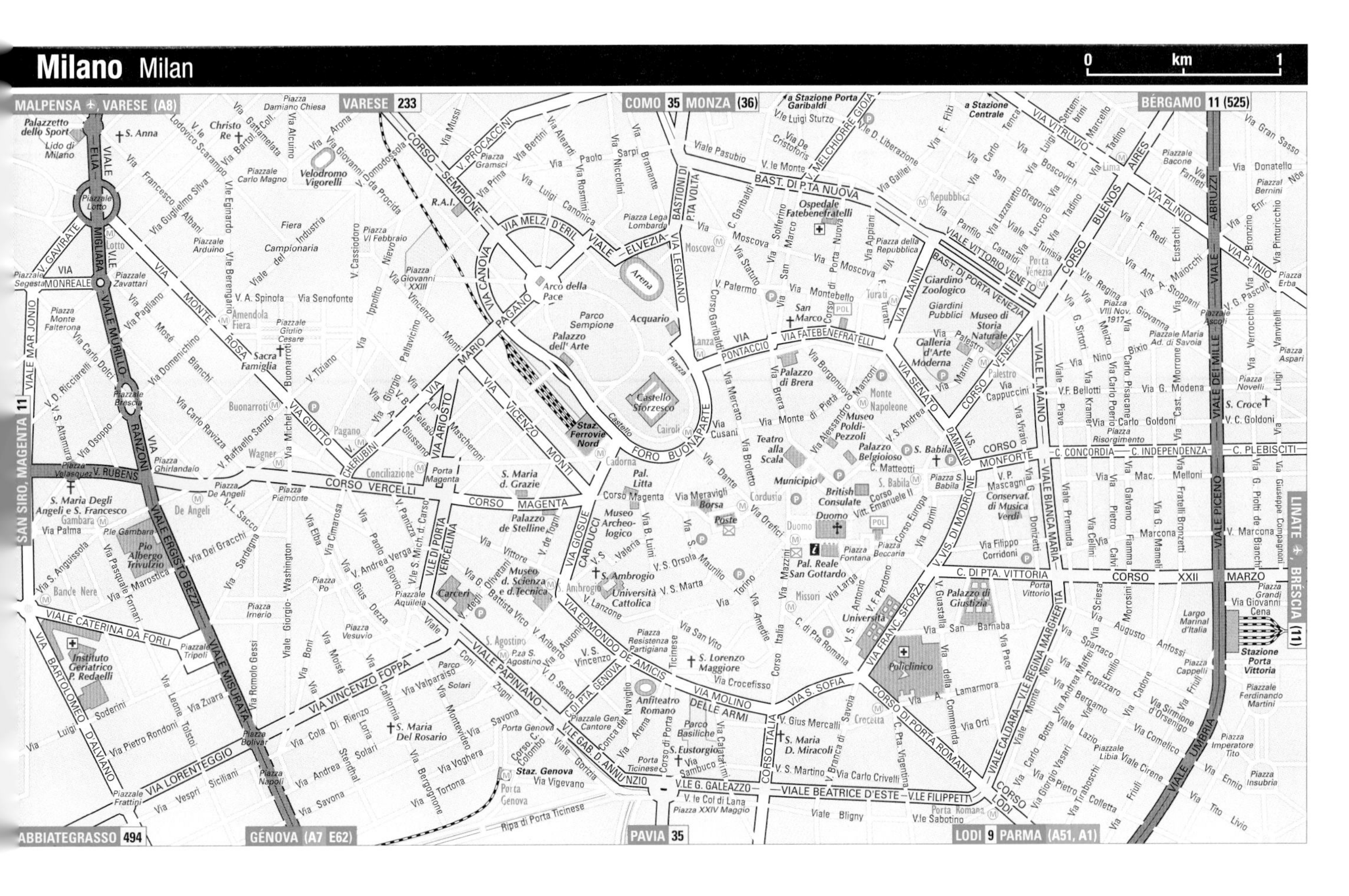
Milano Milan
0 km 1
MALPENSA, VARESE (A8)
VARESE 233
COMO 35 MONZA (36)
BÉRGAMO 11 (525)
SAN SIRO, MAGENTA 11
LINATE, BRÉSCIA (11)
ABBIATEGRASSO 494
GÉNOVA (A7 E62)
PAVIA 35
LODI 9 PARMA (A51, A1)
Castello Sforzesco
Parco Sempione
Arco della Pace
Arena
Staz. Ferrovie Nord
Duomo
Teatro alla Scala
Palazzo di Brera
Museo Poldi-Pezzoli
Giardini Pubblici
Università Cattolica
S. Ambrogio
S. Maria delle Grazie
Stazione Porta Vittoria
Staz. Genova
Policlinico
Palazzo di Giustizia
CORSO MAGENTA
CORSO VERCELLI
CORSO SEMPIONE
CORSO BUENOS AIRES
VIALE ABRUZZI
VIALE UMBRIA
CORSO XXII MARZO
CORSO DI PORTA ROMANA
CORSO ITALIA
CORSO VENEZIA
FORO BUONAPARTE

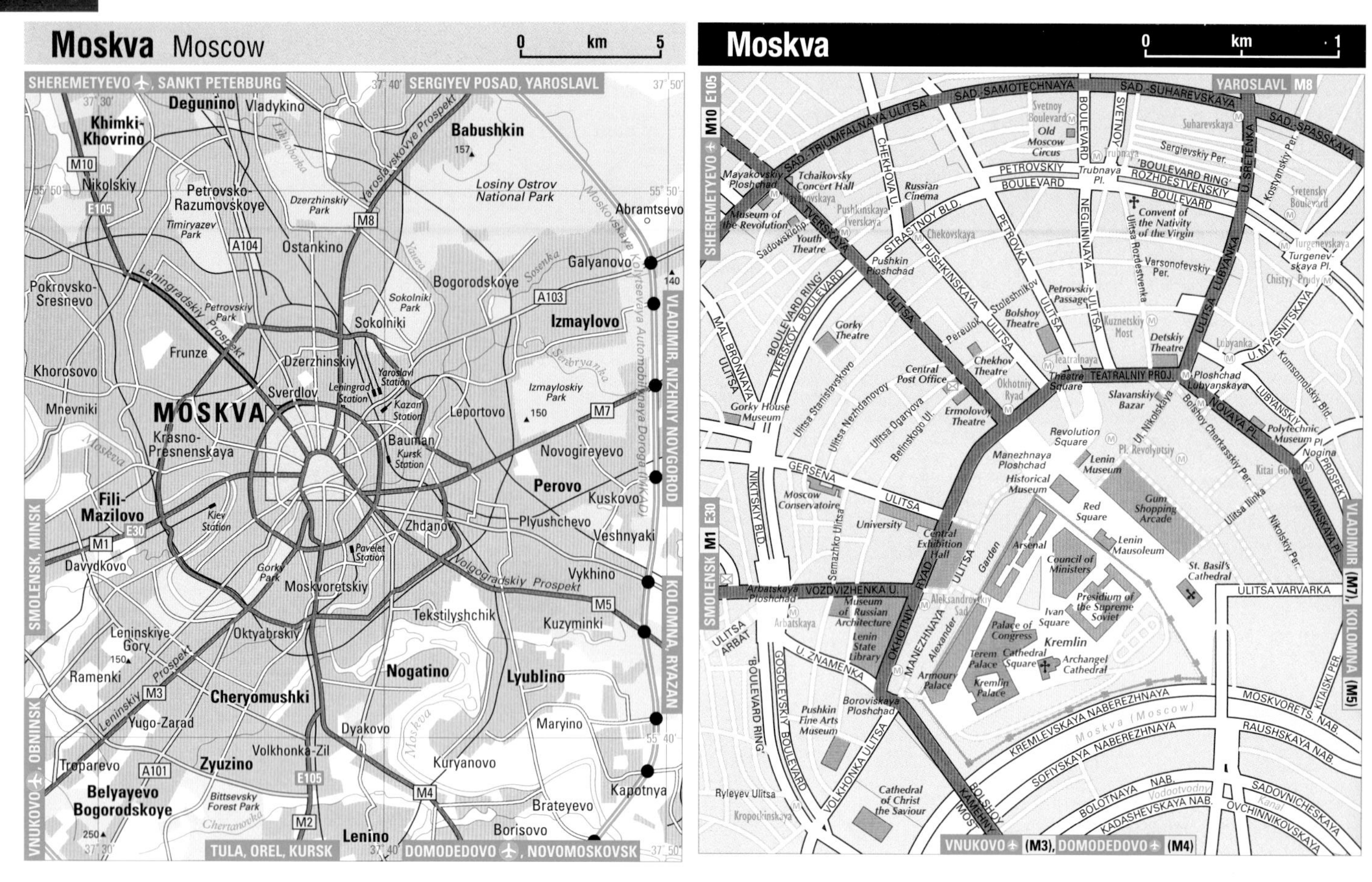
Moskva Moscow
0 km 5
SHEREMETYEVO, SANKT PETERBURG
SERGIYEV POSAD, YAROSLAVL
Degunino
Vladykino
Khimki-Khovrino
Babushkin
Losiny Ostrov National Park
Nikolskiy
Petrovsko-Razumovskoye
Dzerzhinskiy Park
Abramtsevo
Timiryazev Park
Ostankino
Galyanovo
Pokrovsko-Sresnevo
Bogorodskoye
Sokolniki Park
Sokolniki
Izmaylovo
Petrovskiy Park
Leningradskiy Prospekt
Frunze
Dzerzhinskiy
Khorosovo
Izmayloskiy Park
Sverdlov
Mnevniki
MOSKVA
Leningrad Station
Yaroslavl Station
Kazan Station
Leportovo
Krasno-Presnenskaya
Bauman
Kursk Station
Novogireyevo
Fili-Mazilovo
Perovo
Kuskovo
Kiev Station
Plyushchevo
Zhdanov
Veshnyaki
Davydkovo
Paveletz Station
Gorky Park
Moskvoretskiy
Volgogradskiy Prospekt
Vykhino
Tekstilyshchik
Leninskiye Gory
Oktyabrskiy
Kuzyminki
Ramenki
Nogatino
Lyublino
Cheryomushki
Yugo-Zarad
Dyakovo
Maryino
Volkhonka-Zil
Troparevo
Zyuzino
Kuryanovo
Belyayevo Bogorodskoye
Bittsevsky Forest Park
Kapotnya
Brateyevo
Lenino
Borisovo
TULA, OREL, KURSK
DOMODEDOVO, NOVOMOSKOVSK
VNUKOVO, OBNINSK
SMOLENSK, MINSK
VLADIMIR, NIZHNIY NOVGOROD
KOLOMNA, RYAZAN
Moskva
0 km 1
YAROSLAVL M8
SHEREMETYEVO M10 E105
SAD.-SAMOTECHNAYA
SAD.-SUHAREVSKAYA
SAD.-SPASSKAYA
SAD.-TRIUMFALNAYA ULITSA
Svetnoy Boulevard
Old Moscow Circus
Suharevskaya
Sergievskiy Per.
Mayakovskiy Ploshchad
Tchaikovsky Concert Hall
Russian Cinema
PETROVSKIY BOULEVARD
Trubnaya Pl.
ROZHDESTVENSKIY BOULEVARD
Museum of the Revolution
Convent of the Nativity of the Virgin
Youth Theatre
Pushkin Ploshchad
Varsonofevskiy Per.
Turgenevskaya Pl.
Petrovskiy Passage
Bolshoy Theatre
Kuznetskiy Most
Gorky Theatre
Detskiy Theatre
Chekhov Theatre
TEATRALNIY PROJ.
Theatre Square
Ploshchad Lubyanskaya
Central Post Office
Slavanskiy Bazar
Polytechnic Museum
Gorky House Museum
Ermolova Theatre
Revolution Square
Pl. Revolyutsiy
Manezhnaya Ploshchad
Lenin Museum
Historical Museum
Moscow Conservatoire
Red Square
Gum Shopping Arcade
University
Central Exhibition Hall
Arsenal
Lenin Mausoleum
Council of Ministers
St. Basil's Cathedral
ULITSA VARVARKA
VOZDVIZHENKA U.
Museum of Russian Architecture
Presidium of the Supreme Soviet
Ivan Square
Palace of Congress
Kremlin
Lenin State Library
Terem Palace
Cathedral Square
Archangel Cathedral
Armoury Palace
Kremlin Palace
MOSKVORETS. NAB.
RAUSHSKAYA NAB.
Pushkin Fine Arts Museum
Borovitskaya Ploshchad
KREMLEVSKAYA NABEREZHNAYA
SOFIYSKAYA NABEREZHNAYA
SADOVNICHESKAYA
Cathedral of Christ the Saviour
BOLOTNAYA NAB.
KADASHEVSKAYA NAB.
OVCHINNIKOVSKAYA
VNUKOVO (M3), DOMODEDOVO (M4)
SMOLENSK M1 E30
VLADIMIR (M7), KOLOMNA (M5)

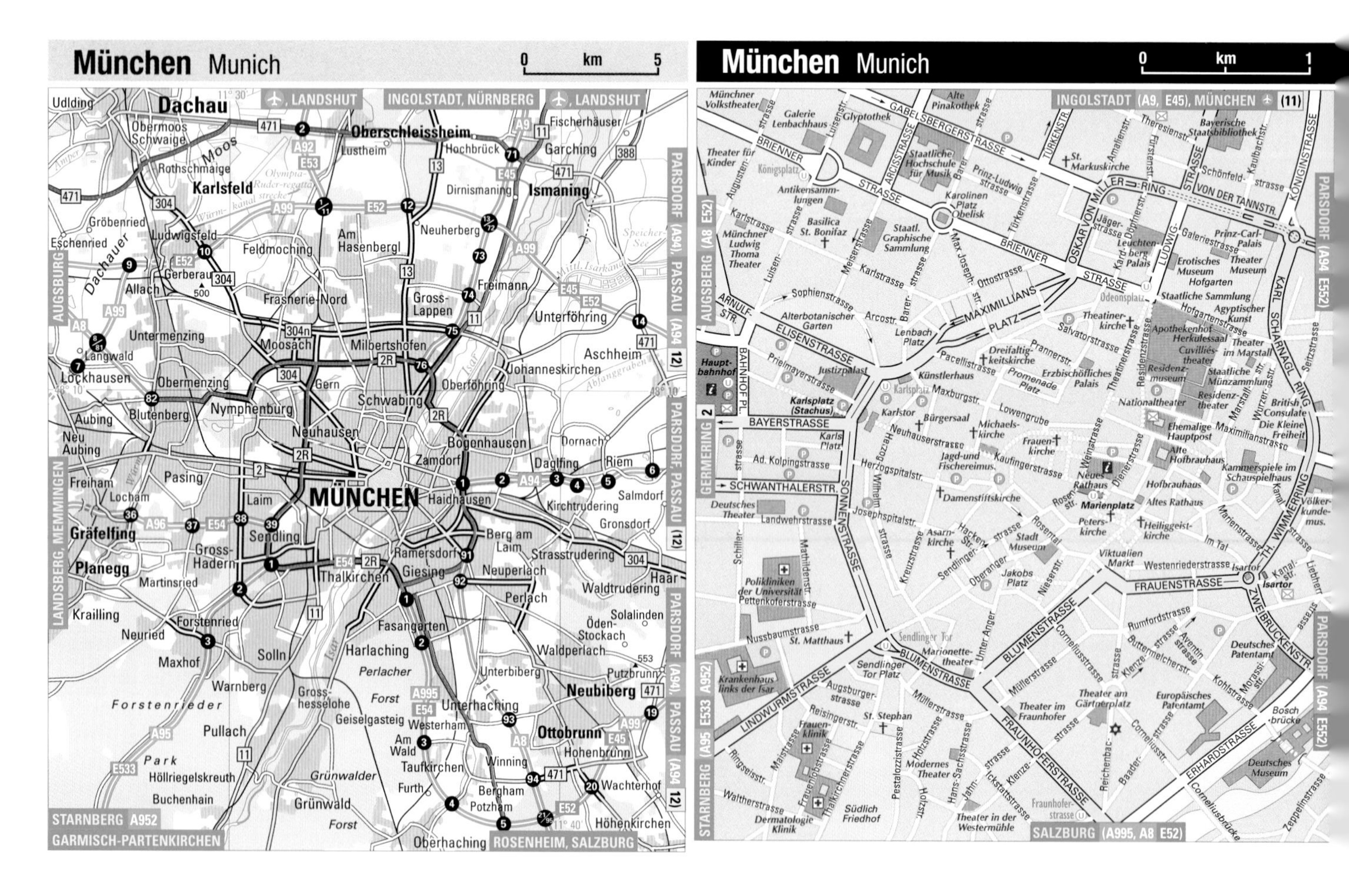
München Munich
0 km 5
LANDSHUT
INGOLSTADT, NÜRNBERG
Udlding
Dachau
Obermoos Schwaige
Oberschleissheim
Fischerhäuser
Lustheim
Hochbrück
Garching
Rothschmaige
Karlsfeld
Dirnismaning
Ismaning
Gröbenried
Ludwigsfeld
Am Hasenbergl
Neuherberg
Eschenried
Feldmoching
Allach
Gerberau
Freimann
Frasnerie-Nord
Gross-Lappen
Unterföhring
Untermenzing
Langwald
Milbertshofen
Aschheim
Lochhausen
Johanneskirchen
Obermenzing
Oberföhring
Aubing
Blutenberg
Nymphenburg
Schwabing
Neu Aubing
Neuhausen
Bogenhausen
Dornach
Zamdorf
Daglfing
Riem
Freiham
Pasing
Laim
MÜNCHEN
Haidhausen
Salmdorf
Lochham
Kirchtrudering
Gräfelfing
Sendling
Gronsdorf
Berg am Laim
Planegg
Gross-Hadern
Ramersdorf
Strasstrudering
Martinsried
Thalkirchen
Giesing
Neuperlach
Haar
Waldtrudering
Perlach
Krailling
Solalinden
Forstenried
Fasangarten
Öden-Stockach
Neuried
Harlaching
Waldperlach
Maxhof
Solln
Perlacher Forst
Putzbrunn
Unterbiberg
Warnberg
Neubiberg
Forstenrieder Park
Gross-hesselohe
Unterhaching
Geiselgasteig
Westerham
Ottobrunn
Pullach
Am Wald
Hohenbrunn
Winning
Taufkirchen
Höllriegelskreuth
Grünwalder Forst
Wachterhof
Buchenhain
Furth
Bergham
Grünwald
Potzham
Höhenkirchen
Oberhaching
STARNBERG A952
GARMISCH-PARTENKIRCHEN
ROSENHEIM, SALZBURG
AUGSBURG
LANDSBERG, MEMMINGEN
PARSDORF (A94), PASSAU (A94)
München Munich
0 km 1
INGOLSTADT (A9, E45), MÜNCHEN (11)
Münchner Volkstheater
Alte Pinakothek
Galerie Lenbachhaus
Glyptothek
Theresienstr.
Bayerische Staatsbibliothek
Theater für Kinder
BRIENNER
Staatliche Hochschule für Musik
St. Markuskirche
Königsplatz
Prinz-Ludwig strasse
Schönfeld-strasse
Antikensammlungen
Karolinen Platz Obelisk
VON DER TANNSTR.
Basilica St. Bonifaz
Staatl. Graphische Sammlung
Münchner Ludwig Thoma Theater
Prinz-Carl-Palais
Leuchtenberg Palais
Erotisches Museum
Theater Museum
Hofgarten
Staatliche Sammlung Ägyptischer Kunst
Alterbotanischer Garten
MAXIMILIANS PLATZ
Lenbach Platz
Theatinerkirche
Apothekenhof
Herkulessaal
Cuvilliés-theater
ELISENSTRASSE
Dreifaltigkeitskirche
Hauptbahnhof
Justizpalast
Künstlerhaus
Erzbischöfliches Palais
Residenz-museum
Staatliche Münzsammlung
Karlsplatz (Stachus)
Maxburgstr.
Nationaltheater
Residenz-theater
British Consulate
Bürgersaal
Ehemalige Hauptpost
Die Kleine Freiheit
BAYERSTRASSE
Michaelskirche
Frauenkirche
Alte Hofbraühaus
Jagd-und Fischereimus.
Neues Rathaus
Kammerspiele im Schauspielhaus
Ad. Kolpingstrasse
Hofbrauhaus
SCHWANTHALERSTR.
Damenstiftskirche
Marienplatz
Altes Rathaus
Deutsches Theater
Landwehrstrasse
Peterskirche
Heiliggeistkirche
Stadt Museum
Viktualien Markt
Westenriederstrasse
Isartor
Asamkirche
FRAUENSTRASSE
Polikliniken der Universität Pettenkoferstrasse
Jakobs Platz
Nussbaumstrasse
St. Matthaus
Sendlinger Tor
Marionettetheater
BLUMENSTRASSE
Deutsches Patentamt
Sendlinger Tor Platz
Krankenhaus links der Isar
LINDWURMSTRASSE
St. Stephan
Theater im Fraunhofer
Theater am Gärtnerplatz
Europäisches Patentamt
Bosch-brücke
Frauenklinik
Modernes Theater
FRAUNHOFERSTRASSE
ERHARDTSTRASSE
Deutsches Museum
Südlich Friedhof
Dermatologie Klinik
Theater in der Westermühle
SALZBURG (A995, A8 E52)
AUGSBURG (A8 E52)
GERMERING 2
STARNBERG (A95 E533 A952)
PARSDORF (A94 E552)

## Nápoli Naples

## Nápoli Naples

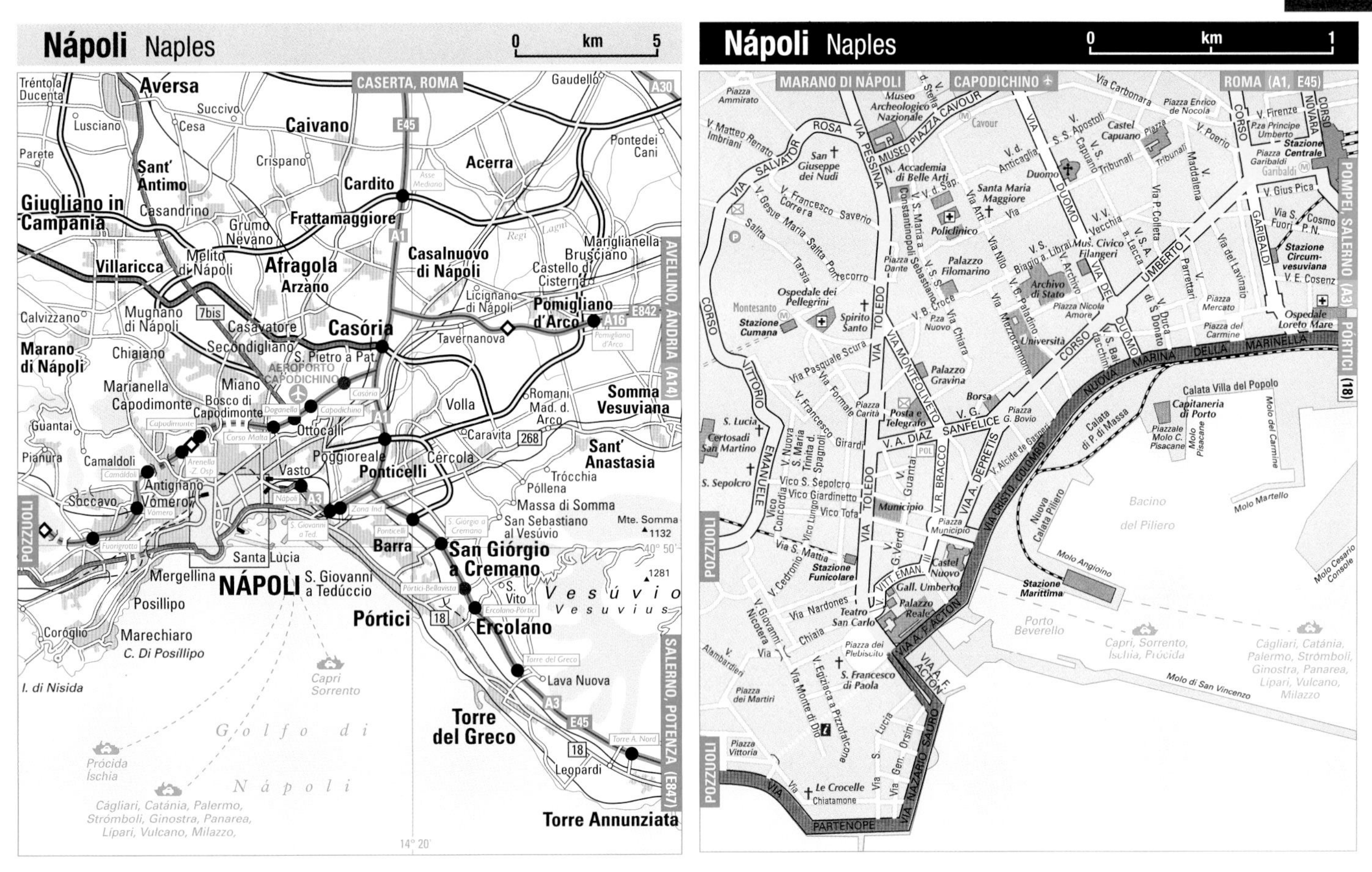
0 km 5
0 km 1
CASERTA, ROMA
Aversa
Caivano
Acerra
Cardito
Frattamaggiore
Giugliano in Campania
Sant' Antimo
Afragola
Casalnuovo di Nápoli
Villaricca
Pomigliano d'Arco
Casória
Marano di Nápoli
AEROPORTO CAPODICHINO
Somma Vesuviana
Sant' Anastasia
Ponticelli
Vomero
NÁPOLI
San Giórgio a Cremano
Pórtici
Ercolano
Vesúvio Vesuvius
Torre del Greco
Torre Annunziata
Golfo di Nápoli
POZZUOLI
AVELLINO, ÁNDRIA (A14)
SALERNO, POTENZA (E847)
MARANO DI NÁPOLI
CAPODICHINO
ROMA (A1, E45)
POMPEI, SALERNO (A3)
PÓRTICI (18)
Stazione Centrale
Stazione Marittima
Molo Angioino
Bacino del Piliero
Capri, Sorrento, Ischia, Prócida
Cágliari, Catánia, Palermo, Strómboli, Ginostra, Panarea, Lipari, Vulcano, Milazzo

## Oslo

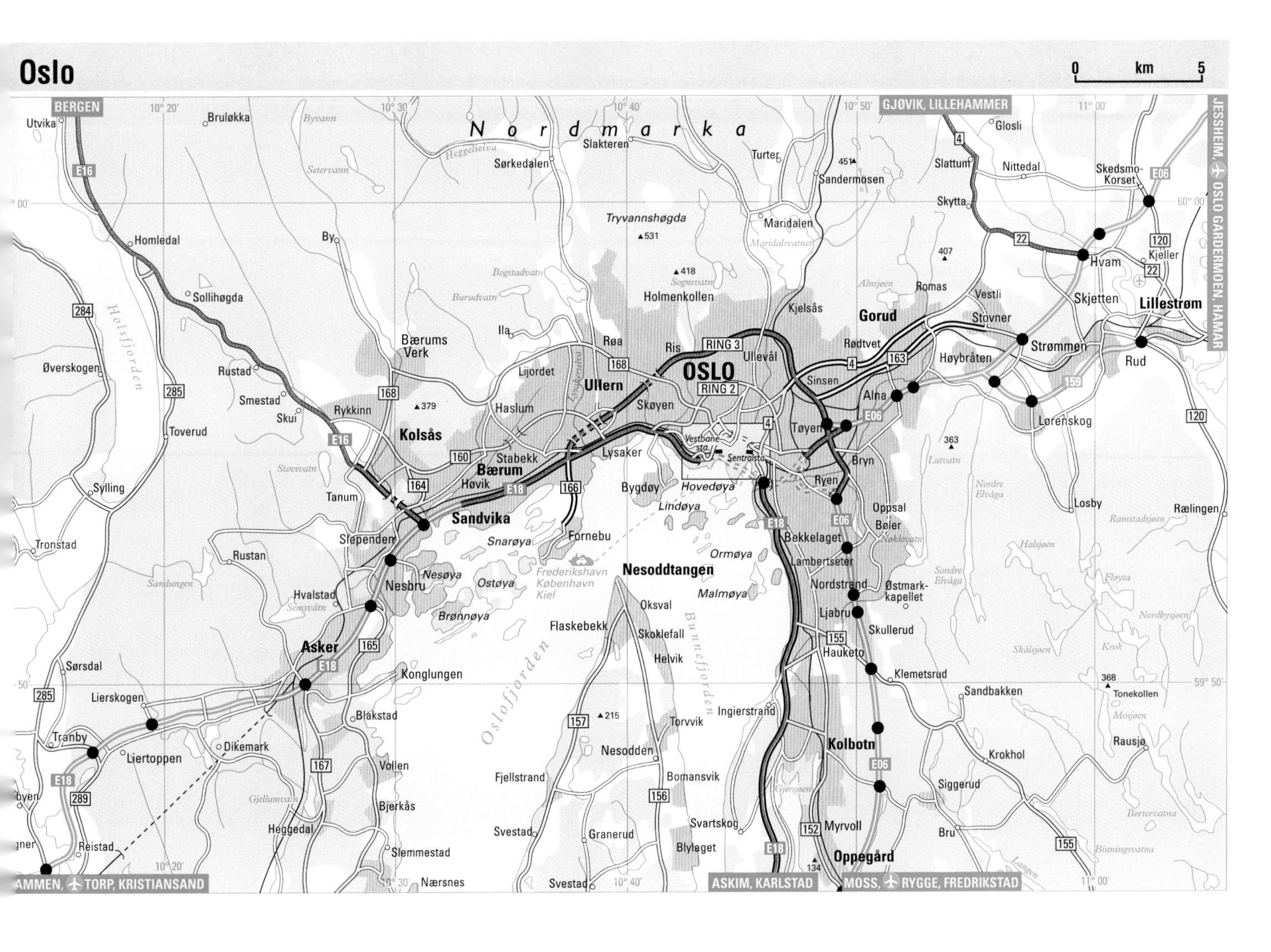
0 km 5
BERGEN
GJØVIK, LILLEHAMMER
JESSHEIM, OSLO GARDERMOEN, HAMAR
Nordmarka
OSLO
RING 3
RING 2
Ullern
Kolsås
Bærum
Sandvika
Asker
Nesbru
Nesoddtangen
Lillestrøm
Gorud
Kolbotn
Oppegård
Holsfjorden
Oslofjorden
Bunnefjorden
Frederikshavn København Kiel
ASKIM, KARLSTAD
MOSS, RYGGE, FREDRIKSTAD
AMMEN, TORP, KRISTIANSAND

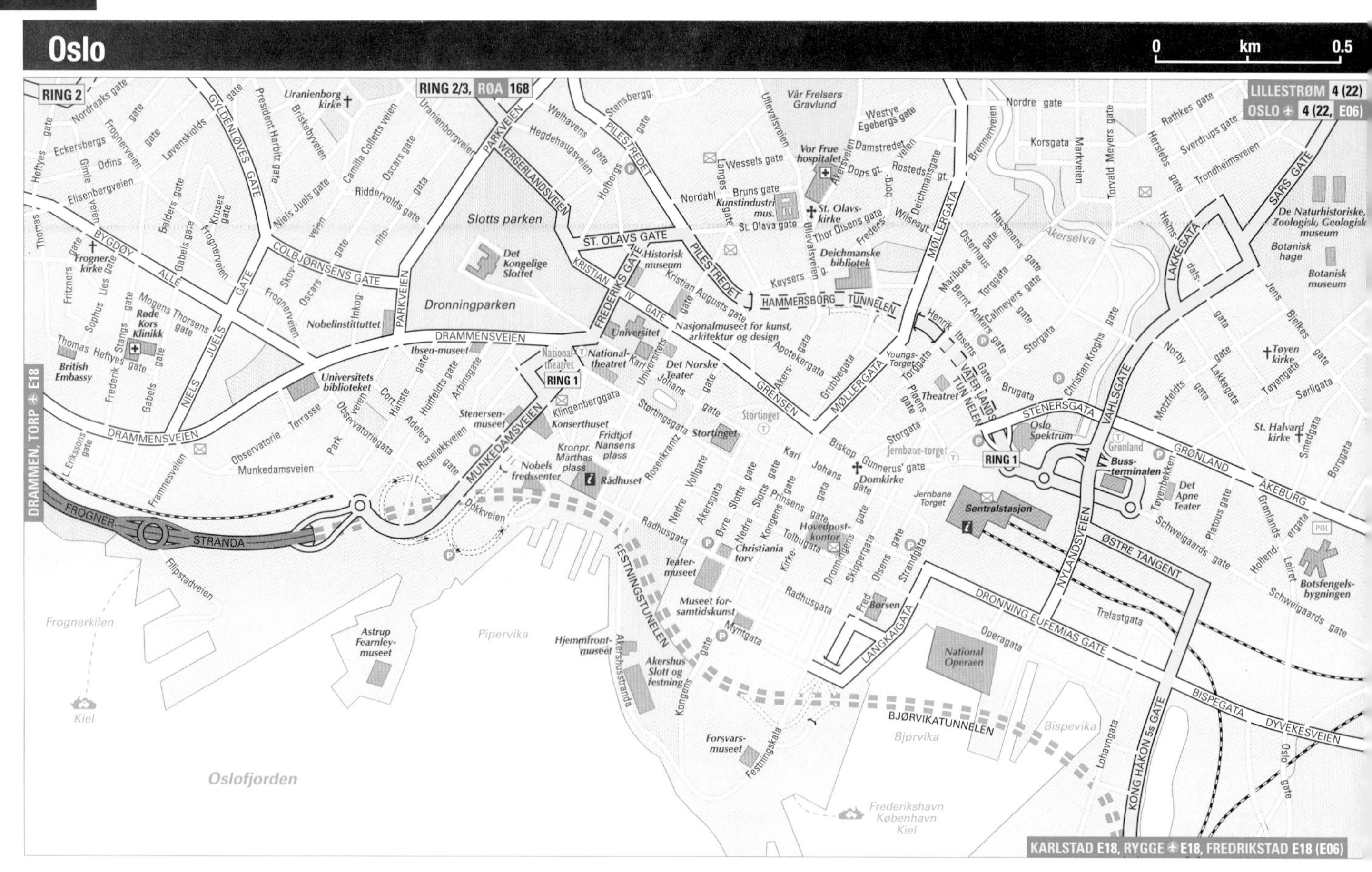
Oslo
0 km 0.5
RING 2
RING 2/3, RØA 168
LILLESTRØM 4 (22)
OSLO 4 (22, E06)
DRAMMEN, TORP E18
KARLSTAD E18, RYGGE E18, FREDRIKSTAD E18 (E06)
Uranienborg kirke
Vår Frelsers Gravlund
Slotts parken
Det Kongelige Slottet
Dronningparken
Frogner kirke
Røde Kors Klinikk
British Embassy
Nobelinstituttet
Universitets biblioteket
Ibsen-museet
Nationaltheatret
RING 1
Stenersen-museet
Konserthuset
Nobels fredssenter
Rådhuset
Kunstindustri mus.
Vor Frue hospital
St. Olavs kirke
Deichmanske bibliotek
Historisk museum
Nasjonalmuseet for kunst, arkitektur og design
Universitetet
Det Norske Teater
Stortinget
Domkirke
Theatret
Oslo Spektrum
Buss-terminalen
Sentralstasjon
Jernbanetorget
Teater-museet
Christiania torv
Museet for samtidskunst
Børsen
Akershus Slott og festning
Forsvars-museet
National Operaen
Astrup Fearnley-museet
Hjemmefront-museet
Det Apne Teater
Tøyen kirke
St. Halvard kirke
Botsfengels-bygningen
De Naturhistoriske, Zoologisk, Geologisk museum
Botanisk hage
Botanisk museum
Frognerkilen
Pipervika
Oslofjorden
Bjørvika
Bispevika
Akerselva
Kiel
Frederikshavn København Kiel
DRAMMENSVEIEN
FROGNER
STRANDA
MUNKEDAMSVEIEN
HAMMERSBORG TUNNELEN
FESTNINGSTUNELEN
BJØRVIKATUNNELEN
GRØNLAND
ÅKEBURG
ØSTRE TANGENT
DRONNING EUFEMIAS GATE
BISPEGATA
DYVEKESVEIEN
KONG HÅKON 5s GATE
NYLANDSVEIEN
VAHLSGATE
STENERSGATA
MØLLERGATA
GRENSEN
PILESTREDET
ST. OLAVS GATE
PARKVEIEN
COLBJØRNSENS GATE
BYGDØY ALLE
NIELS JUELS
GYLDENLØVES GATE
LAKKEGATA
SARS GATE
LANGKAIGATA

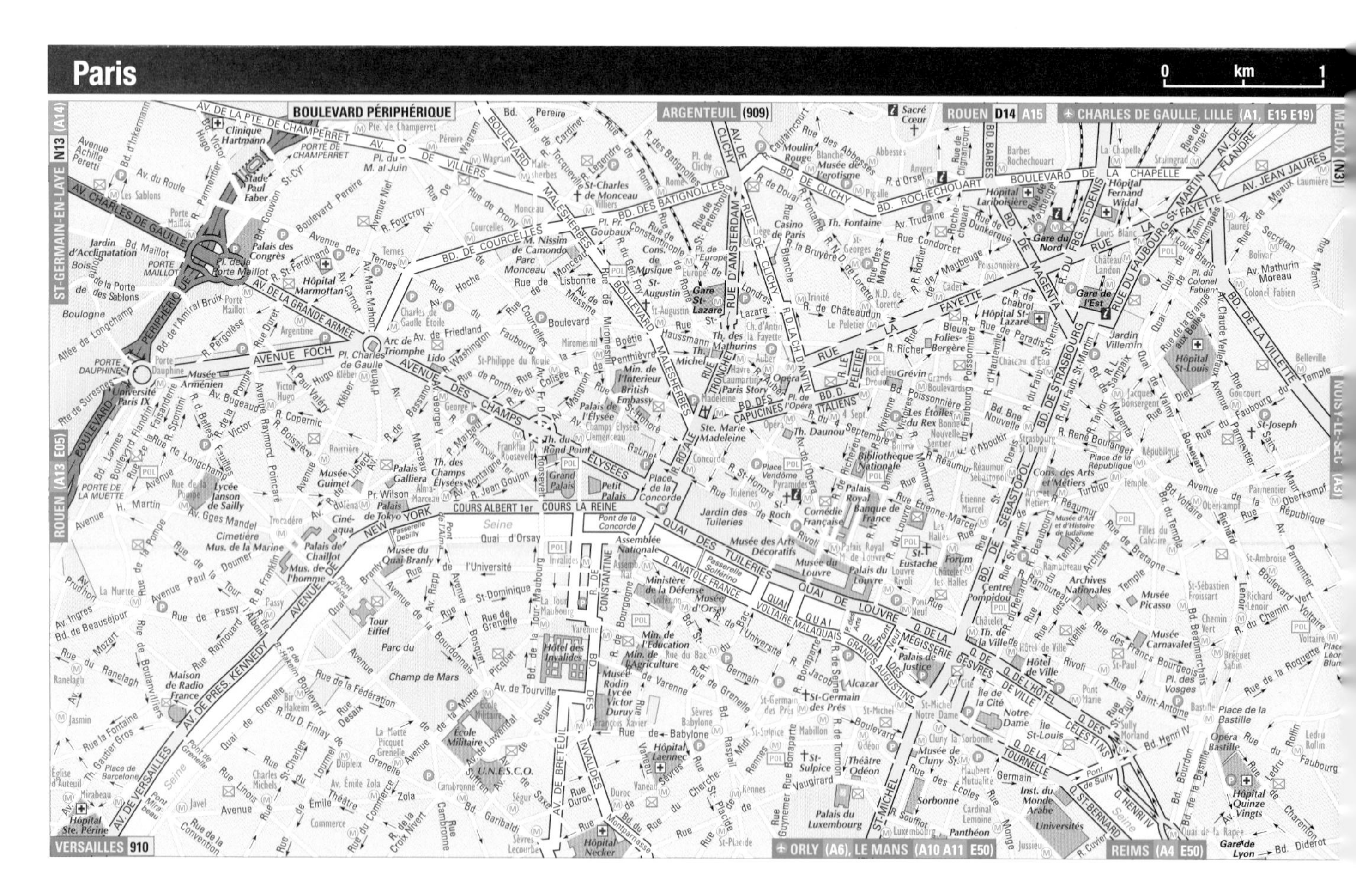
Paris
0 km 1
BOULEVARD PÉRIPHÉRIQUE
ARGENTEUIL (909)
ROUEN D14 A15
CHARLES DE GAULLE, LILLE (A1, E15 E19)
MEAUX (N3)
ST-GERMAIN-EN-LAYE N13 (A14)
ROUEN (A13 E05)
VERSAILLES 910
ORLY (A6), LE MANS (A10 A11 E50)
REIMS (A4 E50)
Sacré Cœur
Moulin Rouge
Musée de l'erotisme
Hôpital Lariboisière
Gare du Nord
Gare de l'Est
Hôpital Fernand Widal
Hôpital St-Louis
Jardin Villemin
Stade Paul Faber
Palais des Congrès
Hôpital Marmottan
Jardin d'Acclimatation
Bois de Boulogne
Arc de Triomphe
Pl. Charles de Gaulle
Université Paris IX
Musée Arménien
Musée Guimet
Palais de Tokyo
Palais de Chaillot
Mus. de l'homme
Palais Galliera
Tour Eiffel
Champ de Mars
Maison de Radio France
Ecole Militaire
U.N.E.S.C.O.
Hôtel des Invalides
Musée Rodin
Grand Palais
Petit Palais
Place de la Concorde
Assemblée Nationale
Musée d'Orsay
Jardin des Tuileries
Musée des Arts Décoratifs
Musée du Louvre
Palais du Louvre
Palais Royal
Banque de France
Bibliothèque Nationale
Opéra
Ste. Marie Madeleine
Gare St. Lazare
Parc Monceau
Forum des Halles
St. Eustache
Centre Pompidou
Musée Picasso
Archives Nationales
Hôtel de Ville
Palais de Justice
Notre Dame
Ile de la Cité
Ile St-Louis
Sorbonne
Panthéon
Palais du Luxembourg
Inst. du Monde Arabe
Opéra Bastille
Place de la Bastille
Pl. des Vosges
Hôpital Necker
Hôpital Laennec
Hôpital Ste. Périne
Gare de Lyon
Seine
AV. CHARLES DE GAULLE
AVENUE FOCH
AV. DE LA GRANDE ARMÉE
AVENUE DES CHAMPS ELYSÉES
COURS LA REINE
COURS ALBERT 1er
AV. DE NEW YORK
QUAI DES TUILERIES
QUAI DU LOUVRE
AV. DE PRES. KENNEDY
AV. DE VERSAILLES
BD. DE COURCELLES
BD. DES BATIGNOLLES
BD. DE CLICHY
BD. ROCHECHOUART
BOULEVARD DE LA CHAPELLE
AV. JEAN JAURES
BD. DE MAGENTA
BD. DE STRASBOURG
BD. DE SEBASTOPOL
RUE LA FAYETTE
BD. DES CAPUCINES
BD. DES ITALIENS
BD. ST-MICHEL
BD. DE LA VILLETTE

# Paris

0 km 5

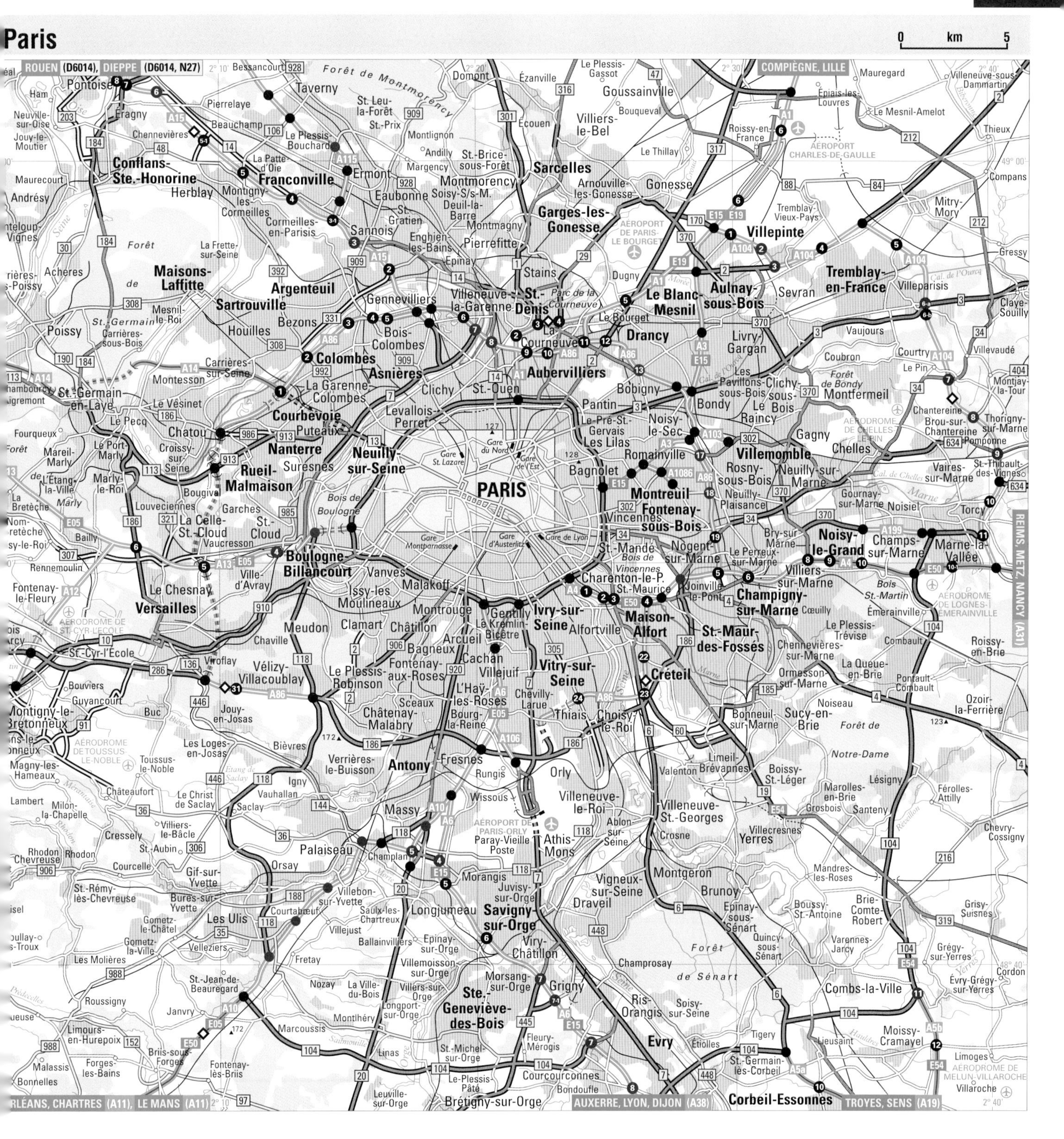
ROUEN (D6014), DIEPPE (D6014, N27)
COMPIÈGNE, LILLE
REIMS, METZ, NANCY (A31)
ORLÉANS, CHARTRES (A11), LE MANS (A11)
AUXERRE, LYON, DIJON (A38)
TROYES, SENS (A19)
PARIS
Versailles
Nanterre
Créteil
Evry
Corbeil-Essonnes

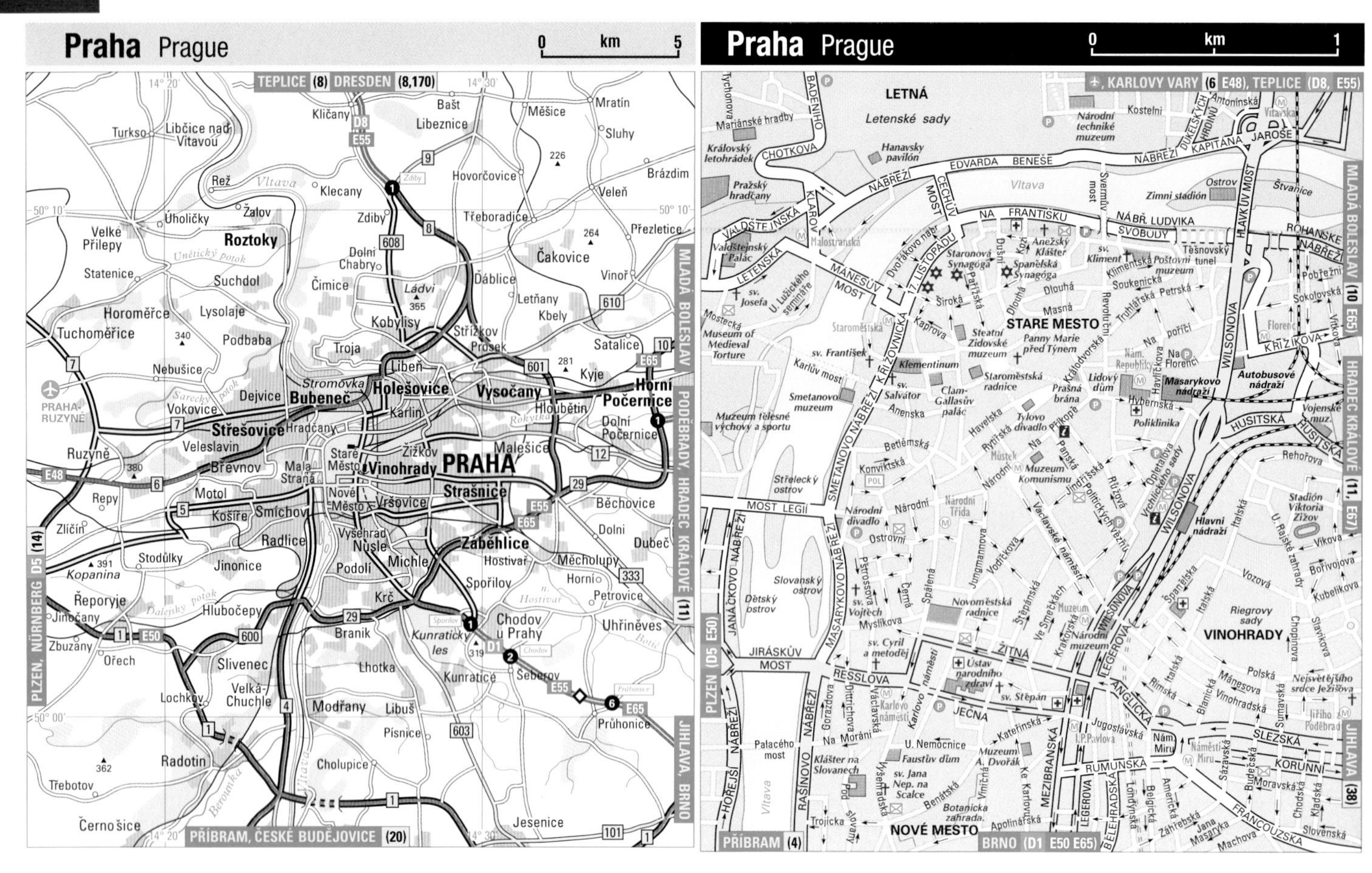

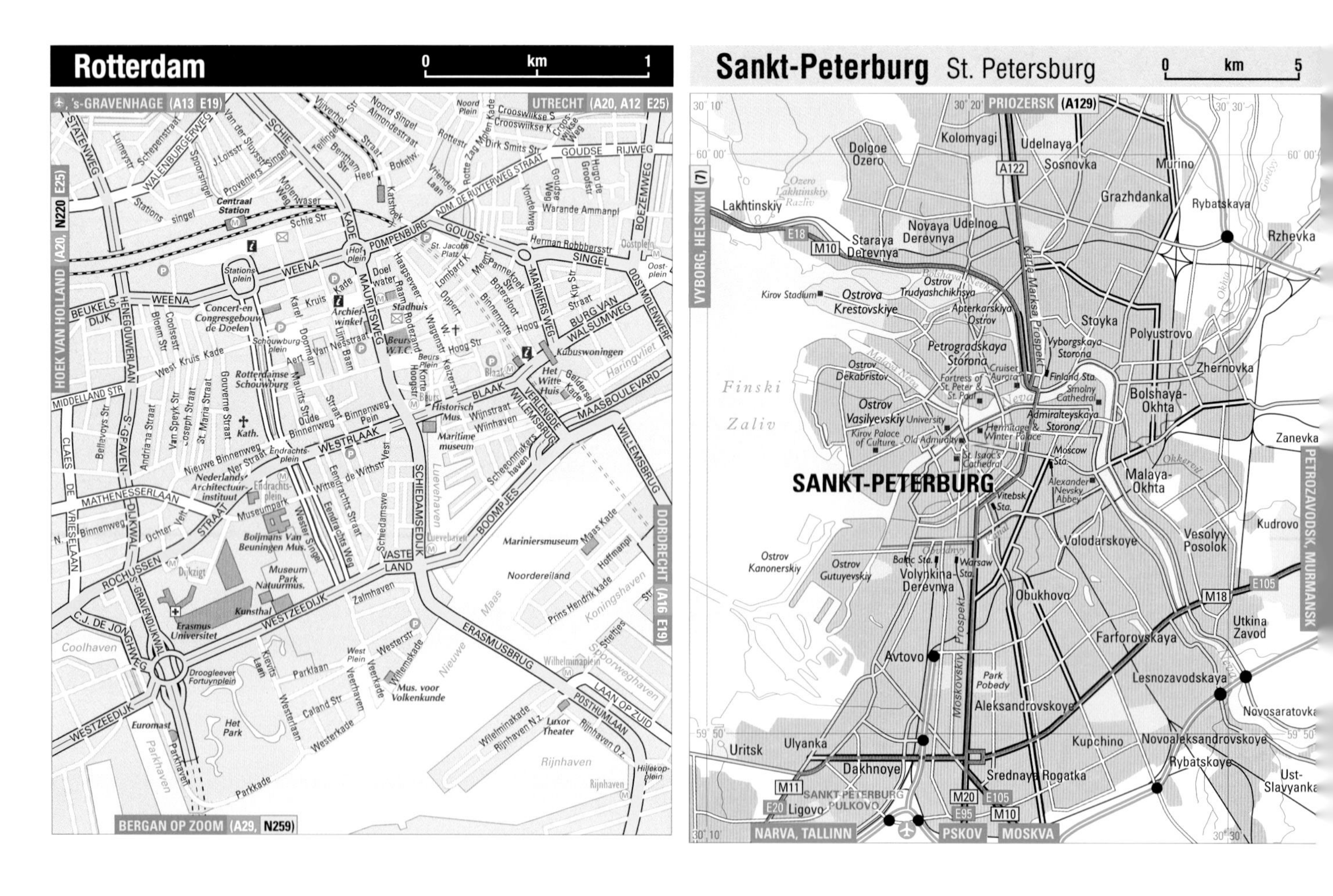

## Roma Rome

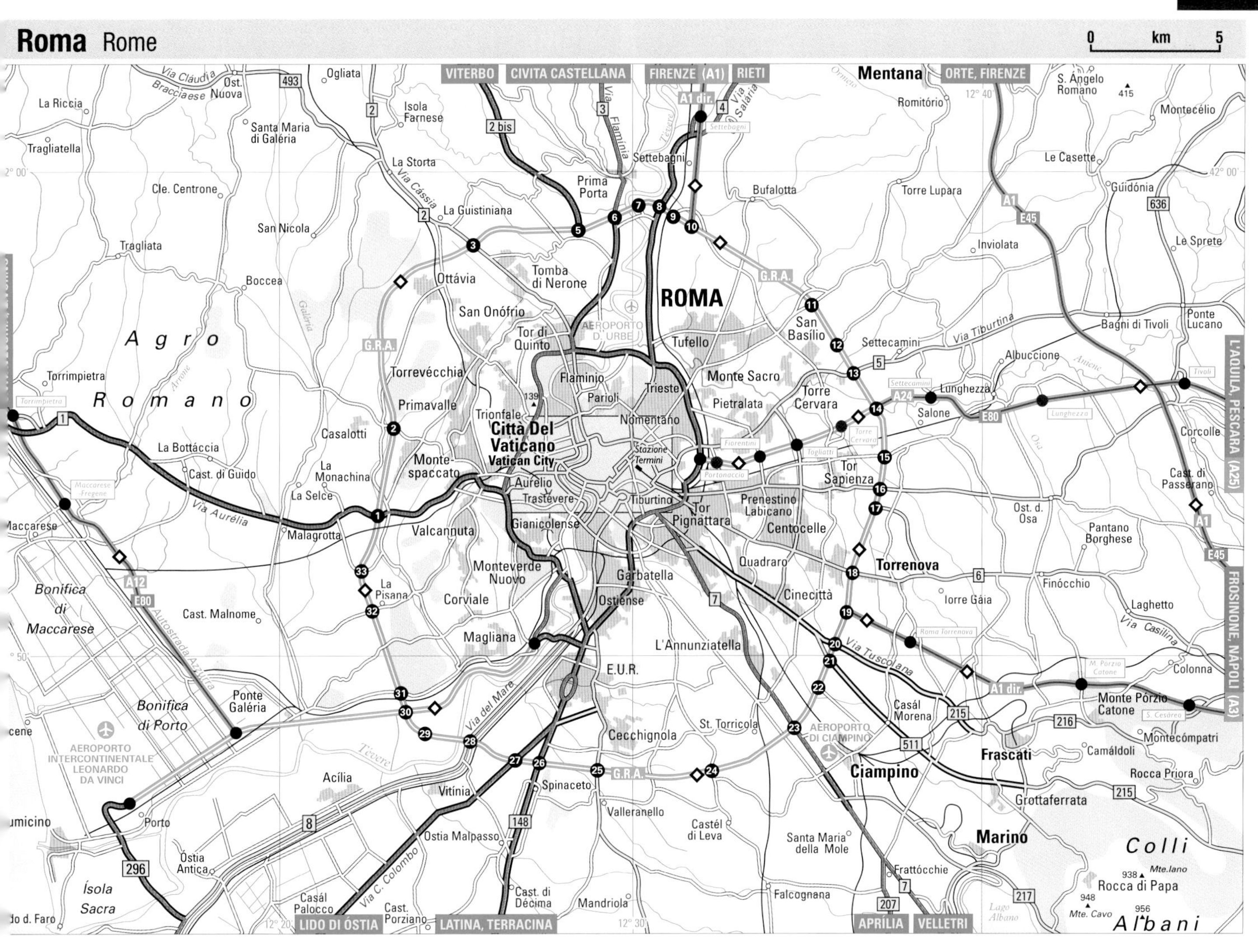
0 km 5
VITERBO
CIVITA CASTELLANA
FIRENZE (A1)
RIETI
ORTE, FIRENZE
Mentana
S. Angelo Romano
Montecélio
Romitório
La Riccia
Ogliata
Isola Farnese
Santa Maria di Galéria
Tragliatella
La Storta
Settebagni
Bufalotta
Torre Lupara
Le Casette
Guidónia
Cle. Centrone
Prima Porta
La Guistiniana
San Nicola
Inviolata
Lé Sprete
Tragliata
Boccea
Ottávia
Tomba di Nerone
ROMA
San Basílio
Bagni di Tivoli
Ponte Lucano
San Onófrio
AEROPORTO D. URBE
Tor di Quinto
Tufello
Settecamini
Via Tiburtina
Albuccione
Agro Romano
Torrimpietra
Torrevécchia
Flaminio
Parioli
Trieste
Monte Sacro
Torre Cervara
Lunghezza
Primavalle
Nomentano
Pietralata
Salone
Trionfale
Città Del Vaticano
Vatican City
Casalotti
La Bottáccia
Corcolle
Monte-spaccato
Stazione Termini
Tor Sapienza
Cast. di Guido
La Monachina
Aurelio
Trastevere
Tiburtino
Tor Pignattara
Prenestino Labicano
Cast. di Passerano
Via Aurélia
La Selce
Centocelle
Ost. d. Osa
Maccarese
Malagrotta
Valcannuta
Gianicolense
Pantano Borghese
Monteverde Nuovo
Garbatella
Quadraro
Torrenova
Bonifica di Maccarese
La Pisana
Corviale
Ostiense
Cinecittà
Finócchio
Iorre Gáia
Laghetto
Via Casilina
Cast. Malnome
Magliana
L'Annunziatella
Via Tuscolana
Colonna
E.U.R.
Monte Pórzio Catone
Bonifica di Porto
Ponte Galéria
Via del Mare
Casál Morena
Montecómpatri
AEROPORTO INTERCONTINENTALE LEONARDO DA VINCI
Cecchignola
St. Torricola
AEROPORTO DI CIAMPINO
Camáldoli
Frascati
Ciampino
Rocca Priora
Acília
Spinaceto
Vitinia
Grottaferrata
Porto
Valleranello
Castél di Leva
Santa Maria della Mole
Marino
Ostia Malpasso
Colli Albani
Óstia Antica
Frattócchie
Ísola Sacra
Mte. Iano
Rocca di Papa
Casál Palocco
Cast. di Décima
Mandriola
Falcognana
Mte. Cavo
Cast. Porziano
Via C. Colombo
LIDO DI ÓSTIA
LATINA, TERRACINA
APRÍLIA
VELLETRI
L'AQUILA, PESCARA (A25)
FROSINONE, NÁPOLI (A3)
G.R.A.
Tevere
Fiumicino

## Roma Rome

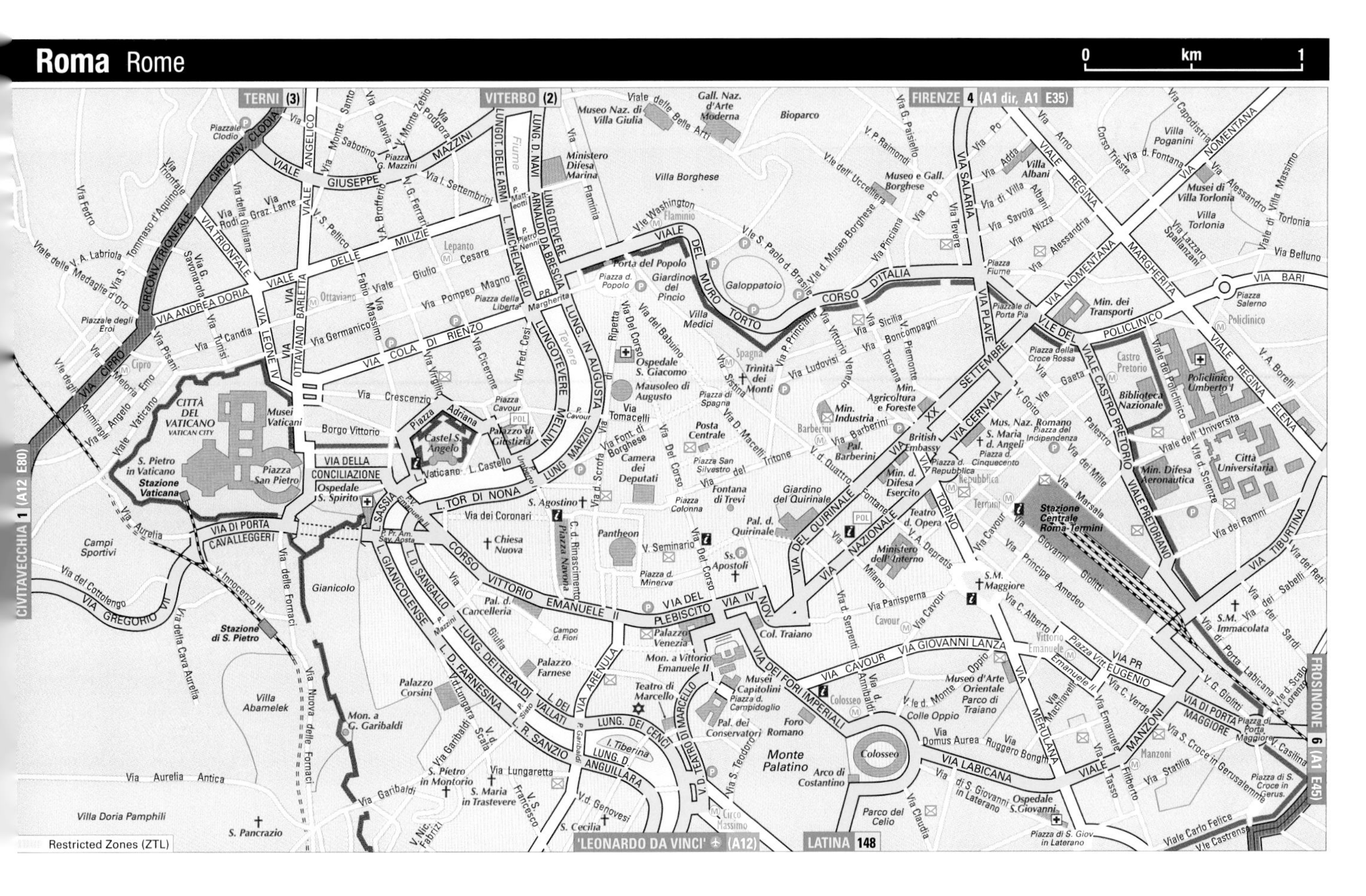
0 km 1
TERNI (3)
VITERBO (2)
FIRENZE 4 (A1 dir, A1 E35)
Museo Naz. di Villa Giulia
Gall. Naz. d'Arte Moderna
Bioparco
Ministero Difesa Marina
Villa Borghese
Museo e Gall. Borghese
Villa Albani
Villa Poganini
Musei di Villa Torlonia
Villa Torlonia
Piazza Mazzini
VIALE GIUSEPPE MAZZINI
VIA DELLE MILIZIE
Lepanto
Porta del Popolo
Piazza d. Popolo
Giardino del Pincio
Galoppatoio
Villa Medici
CORSO D'ITALIA
Piazzale di Porta Pia
Min. dei Trasporti
VIA NOMENTANA
VIALE REGINA MARGHERITA
VIA BARI
Piazza Salerno
Policlinico
Ottaviano
Via Cola di Rienzo
VIA ANDREA DORIA
Piazza Cavour
Castel S. Angelo
Palazzo di Giustizia
Ospedale S. Giacomo
Mausoleo di Augusto
Spagna
Trinità dei Monti
Piazza di Spagna
Min. Agricoltura e Foreste
Castro Pretorio
Policlinico Umberto I
CITTÀ DEL VATICANO
VATICAN CITY
Musei Vaticani
S. Pietro in Vaticano
Stazione Vaticana
Piazza San Pietro
Borgo Vittorio
VIA DELLA CONCILIAZIONE
Ospedale S. Spirito
Barberini
Min. Industria
British Embassy
Mus. Naz. Romano
S. Maria d. Angeli
Piazza della Repubblica
Città Universitaria
Min. Difesa Aeronautica
Viale dell' Università
Posta Centrale
Camera dei Deputati
Fontana di Trevi
Pal. Barberini
Min. d. Difesa Esercito
Giardino del Quirinale
Teatro d. Opera
Stazione Centrale Roma-Termini
Campi Sportivi
VIA DI PORTA CAVALLEGGERI
S. Agostino
Pantheon
Chiesa Nuova
Piazza Navona
Pal. d. Quirinale
Ministero dell' Interno
S.M. Maggiore
VIA TIBURTINA
S.M. Immacolata
Gianicolo
Stazione di S. Pietro
CORSO VITTORIO EMANUELE II
Pal. d. Cancelleria
Campo d. Fiori
Palazzo Venezia
Col. Traiano
Via Cavour
VIA GIOVANNI LANZA
Vittorio Emanuele
Palazzo Farnese
Palazzo Corsini
Mon. a Vittorio Emanuele II
Teatro di Marcello
Musei Capitolini
Piazza d. Campidoglio
Pal. dei Conservatori
Foro Romano
VIA DEI FORI IMPERIALI
Colosseo
Museo d'Arte Orientale
Parco di Traiano
Colle Oppio
Domus Aurea
VIA MERULANA
VIALE MANZONI
Villa Abamelek
Mon. a G. Garibaldi
Via Aurelia Antica
S. Pietro in Montorio
S. Maria in Trastevere
Monte Palatino
Arco di Costantino
VIA LABICANA
Ospedale S. Giovanni
Piazza di S. Croce in Gerus.
Villa Doria Pamphili
S. Pancrazio
S. Cecilia
Circo Massimo
Parco del Celio
Piazza di S. Giov. in Laterano
Viale Carlo Felice
Restricted Zones (ZTL)
'LEONARDO DA VINCI' (A12)
LATINA 148
CIVITAVECCHIA 1 (A12 E80)
FROSINONE 6 (A1 E45)

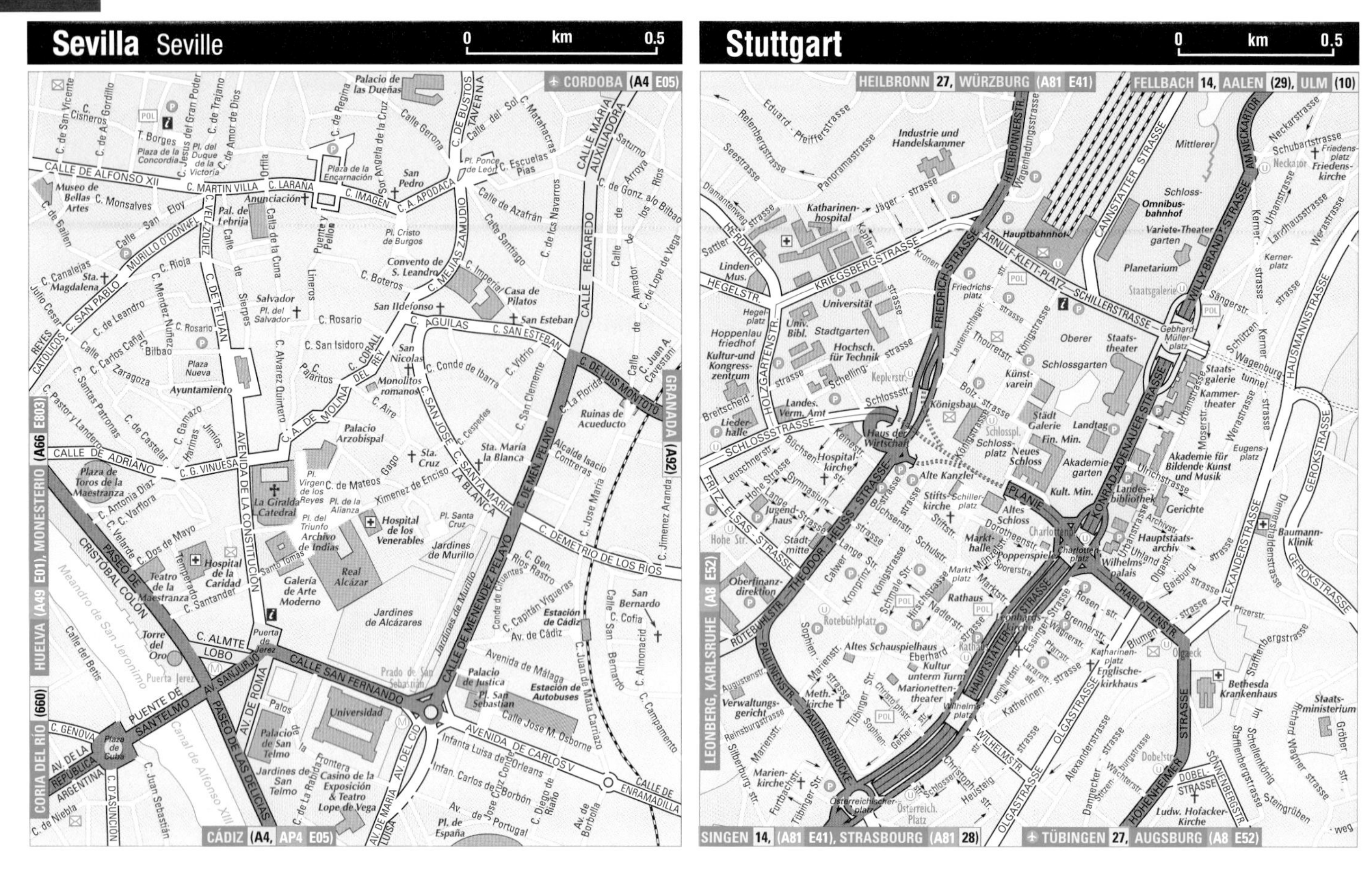
Sevilla Seville
0 km 0.5
CORDOBA (A4 E05)
GRANADA (A92)
CÁDIZ (A4, AP4 E05)
CORIA DEL RÍO (660)
HUELVA (A49 E01), MONESTERIO (A66 E803)
Palacio de las Dueñas
Museo de Bellas Artes
Pal. de Lebrija
Salvador
Convento de S. Leandro
Casa de Pilatos
San Esteban
Ayuntamiento
Palacio Arzobispal
La Giralda Catedral
Archivo de Indias
Real Alcázar
Hospital de los Venerables
Jardines de Murillo
Jardines de Alcázares
Plaza de Toros de la Maestranza
Hospital de la Caridad
Teatro de la Maestranza
Torre del Oro
Universidad
Palacio de San Telmo
Casino de la Exposición & Teatro Lope de Vega
Palacio de Justicia
Estación de Autobuses
Estación de Cádiz
Ruinas de Acueducto
Stuttgart
0 km 0.5
HEILBRONN 27, WÜRZBURG (A81 E41)
FELLBACH 14, AALEN (29), ULM (10)
LEONBERG, KARLSRUHE (A8 E52)
SINGEN 14, (A81 E41), STRASBOURG (A81 28)
TÜBINGEN 27, AUGSBURG (A8 E52)
Industrie und Handelskammer
Katharinen-hospital
Hauptbahnhof
Universität
Planetarium
Schlossgarten
Staats-theater
Neues Schloss
Altes Schloss
Landes-bibliothek
Akademie für Bildende Kunst und Musik
Rathaus
Altes Schauspielhaus
Marionetten-theater
Bethesda Krankenhaus
Staats-ministerium
Baumann-Klinik

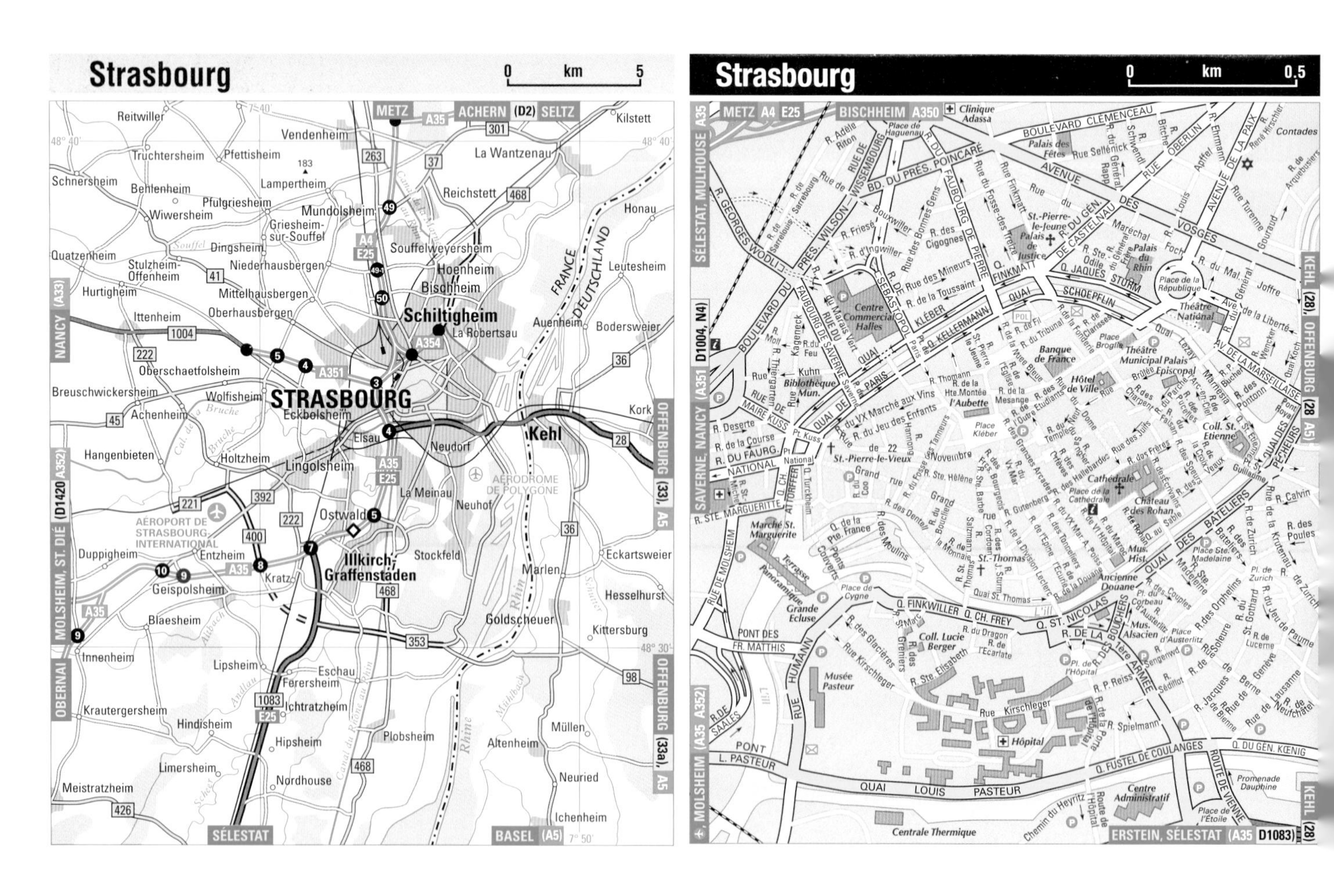
Strasbourg
0 km 5
METZ
ACHERN (D2) SELTZ
NANCY (A33)
OFFENBURG (33), A5
OFFENBURG (33a), A5
MOLSHEIM, ST. DIÉ (D1420 A352)
OBERNAI
SÉLESTAT
BASEL (A5)
STRASBOURG
Schiltigheim
Kehl
Illkirch-Graffenstaden
AÉROPORT DE STRASBOURG-INTERNATIONAL
AÉRODROME DE POLYGONE
FRANCE
DEUTSCHLAND
Strasbourg
0 km 0.5
METZ A4 E25
BISCHHEIM A350
SELESTAT, MULHOUSE A35
SAVERNE, NANCY (A351 D1004 N4)
MOLSHEIM (A35 A352)
KEHL (28), OFFENBURG (28 A5)
ERSTEIN, SÉLESTAT (A35 D1083)
Palais des Fêtes
Centre Commercial Halles
Bibliothèque Mun.
Banque de France
Hôtel de Ville
Cathédrale
Château des Rohan
Théâtre National
Théâtre Municipal
Palais du Rhin
Musée Pasteur
Hôpital
Centre Administratif
Centrale Thermique
Ancienne Douane

## Stockholm

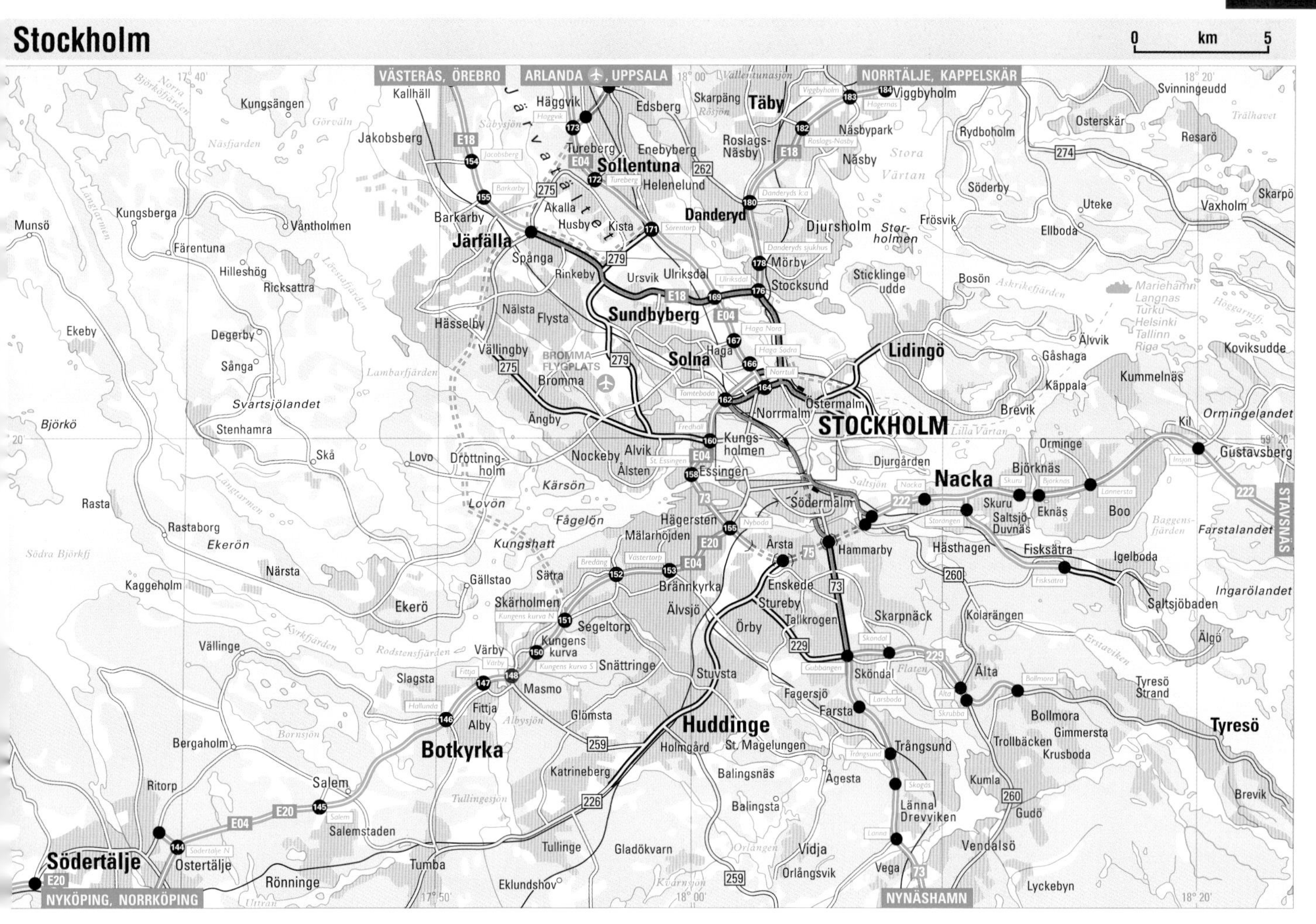

0 km 5
VÄSTERÅS, ÖREBRO
ARLANDA, UPPSALA
NORRTÄLJE, KAPPELSKÄR
STAVSNÄS
NYKÖPING, NORRKÖPING
NYNÄSHAMN
STOCKHOLM
Kungsängen
Kallhäll
Jakobsberg
Häggvik
Edsberg
Skarpäng
Täby
Viggbyholm
Svinningeudd
Tureberg
Enebyberg
Sollentuna
Helenelund
Roslags-Näsby
Näsbypark
Näsby
Rydboholm
Österskär
Resarö
Järvafältet
Barkarby
Akalla
Husby
Kista
Danderyd
Djursholm
Stora Värtan
Söderby
Frösvik
Ellboda
Uteke
Vaxholm
Skarpö
Munsö
Kungsberga
Vänthomen
Färentuna
Hilleshög
Ricksattra
Järfälla
Spånga
Rinkeby
Ursvik
Ulriksdal
Mörby
Stocksund
Sticklinge udde
Bosön
Stora Värtan
Ekeby
Degerby
Sånga
Hässelby
Nälsta
Flysta
Sundbyberg
Solna
Haga
Lidingö
Älvvik
Gåshaga
Koviksudde
Vällingby
Bromma Flygplats
Bromma
Käppala
Kummelnäs
Svartsjölandet
Stenhamra
Ängby
Norrmalm
Östermalm
Brevik
Ormingelandet
Björkö
Skå
Lovö
Drottningholm
Nockeby
Alvik
Ålsten
Kungsholmen
Djurgården
Gustavsberg
Kil
Orminge
Björknäs
Nacka
Essingen
Kärsön
Rasta
Rastaborg
Ekerön
Lovön
Fågelön
Södermalm
Skuru
Saltsjö-Duvnäs
Eknäs
Boo
Farstalandet
Kungshatt
Hägersten
Mälarhöjden
Årsta
Hammarby
Hästhagen
Fisksätra
Igelboda
Närsta
Gällstao
Sätra
Bredäng
Enskede
Saltsjöbaden
Ingarölandet
Kaggeholm
Skärholmen
Brännkyrka
Älvsjö
Stureby
Talkrogen
Ekerö
Örby
Skarpnäck
Kolarängen
Vällinge
Segeltorp
Kungens kurva
Värby
Snättringe
Stuvsta
Sköndal
Älta
Älgö
Slagsta
Masmo
Fagersjö
Farsta
Tyresö Strand
Fittja
Alby
Glömsta
Huddinge
Bollmora
Gimmersta
Tyresö
Bergaholm
Botkyrka
Holmgård
St. Magelungen
Trångsund
Trollbäcken
Krusboda
Balingsnäs
Ritorp
Salem
Katrineberg
Ågesta
Kumla
Brevik
Balingsta
Länna
Drevviken
Gudö
Salemstaden
Södertälje
Östertälje
Tumba
Tullinge
Gladökvarn
Vidja
Vendalsö
Rönninge
Eklundshov
Orlångsvik
Vega
Lyckebyn
Tullingesjön
E18
E04
E20
279
275
262
274
73
75
229
259
260
226
222

## Stockholm

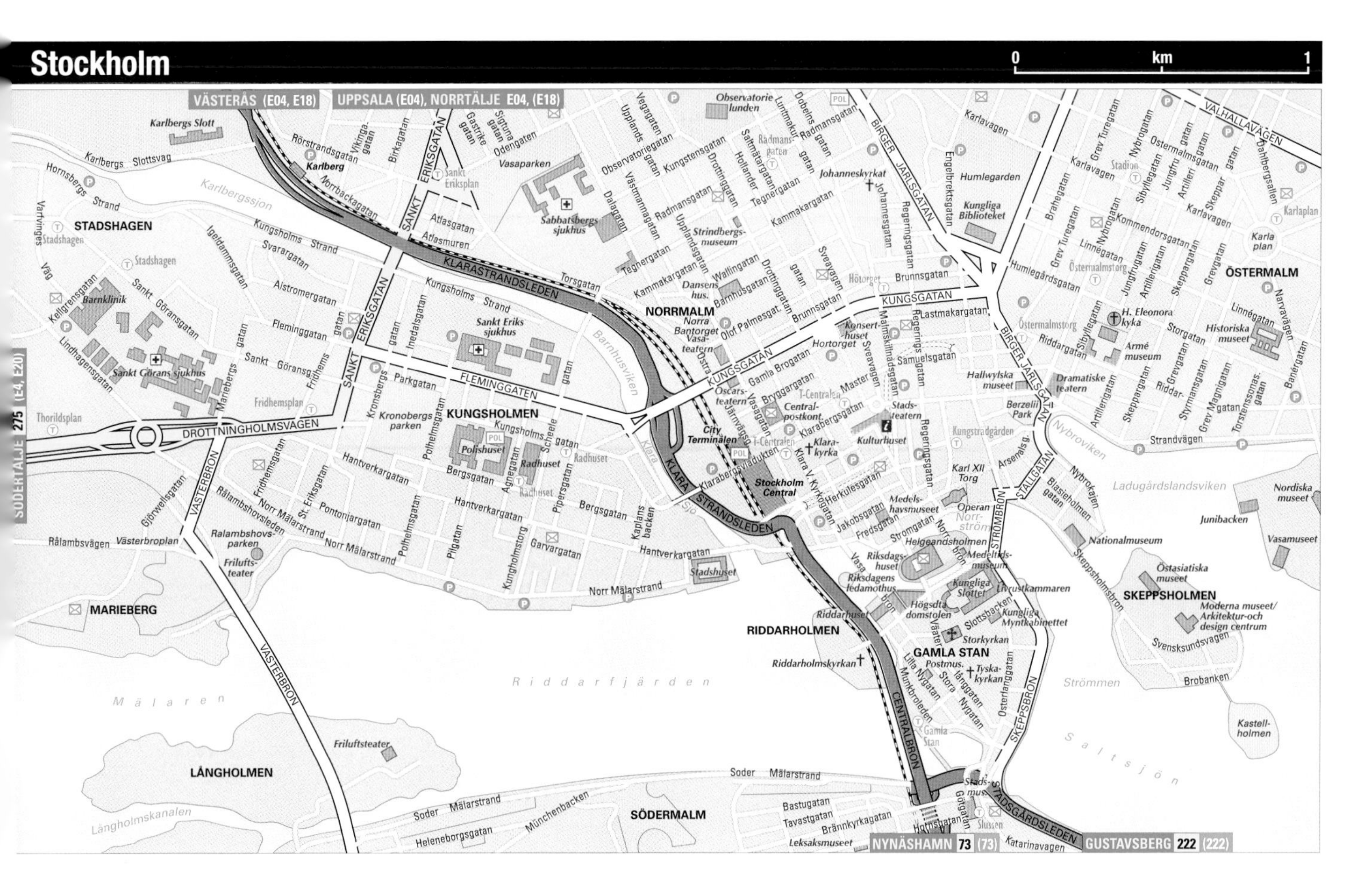

0 km 1
VÄSTERÅS (E04, E18)
UPPSALA (E04), NORRTÄLJE E04, (E18)
SÖDERTÄLJE 275 (E4, E20)
NYNÄSHAMN 73 (73)
GUSTAVSBERG 222 (222)
Karlbergs Slott
Karlberg
Karlbergssjön
STADSHAGEN
Observatorie lunden
Vasaparken
Sabbatsbergs sjukhus
Humlegården
Kungliga Biblioteket
Johanneskyrkan
Strindbergs-museum
NORRMALM
KLARASTRANDSLEDEN
Barnklinik
Sankt Görans sjukhus
Sankt Eriks sjukhus
KUNGSHOLMEN
Kronobergs parken
Polishuset
Rådhuset
DROTTNINGHOLMSVÄGEN
FLEMINGGATAN
KUNGSGATAN
Hötorget
Konserthuset
Kulturhuset
City Terminalen
Stockholm Central
Centralpostkont
Stadsteatern
Berzelii Park
Dramatiska teatern
Hallwylska museet
Historiska museet
Armé museum
ÖSTERMALM
Karlaplan
Ladugårdslandsviken
Nordiska museet
Junibacken
Vasamuseet
Nationalmuseum
Östasiatiska museet
SKEPPSHOLMEN
Moderna museet/ Arkitektur-och design centrum
Kungliga Slottet
Storkyrkan
GAMLA STAN
Riddarholmskyrkan
RIDDARHOLMEN
Riksdagshuset
Medelhavsmuseet
Stadshuset
Riddarfjärden
Mälaren
MARIEBERG
LÅNGHOLMEN
Friluftsteater
SÖDERMALM
Långholmskanalen
Strömmen
Saltsjön
Kastellholmen
Brobanken
Västerbron
Centralbron
Slussen
Skeppsbron
Strömbron
Kungsträdgården
STADSGÅRDSLEDEN
Katarinavägen
Leksaksmuseet

## Torino Turin

0 km 5

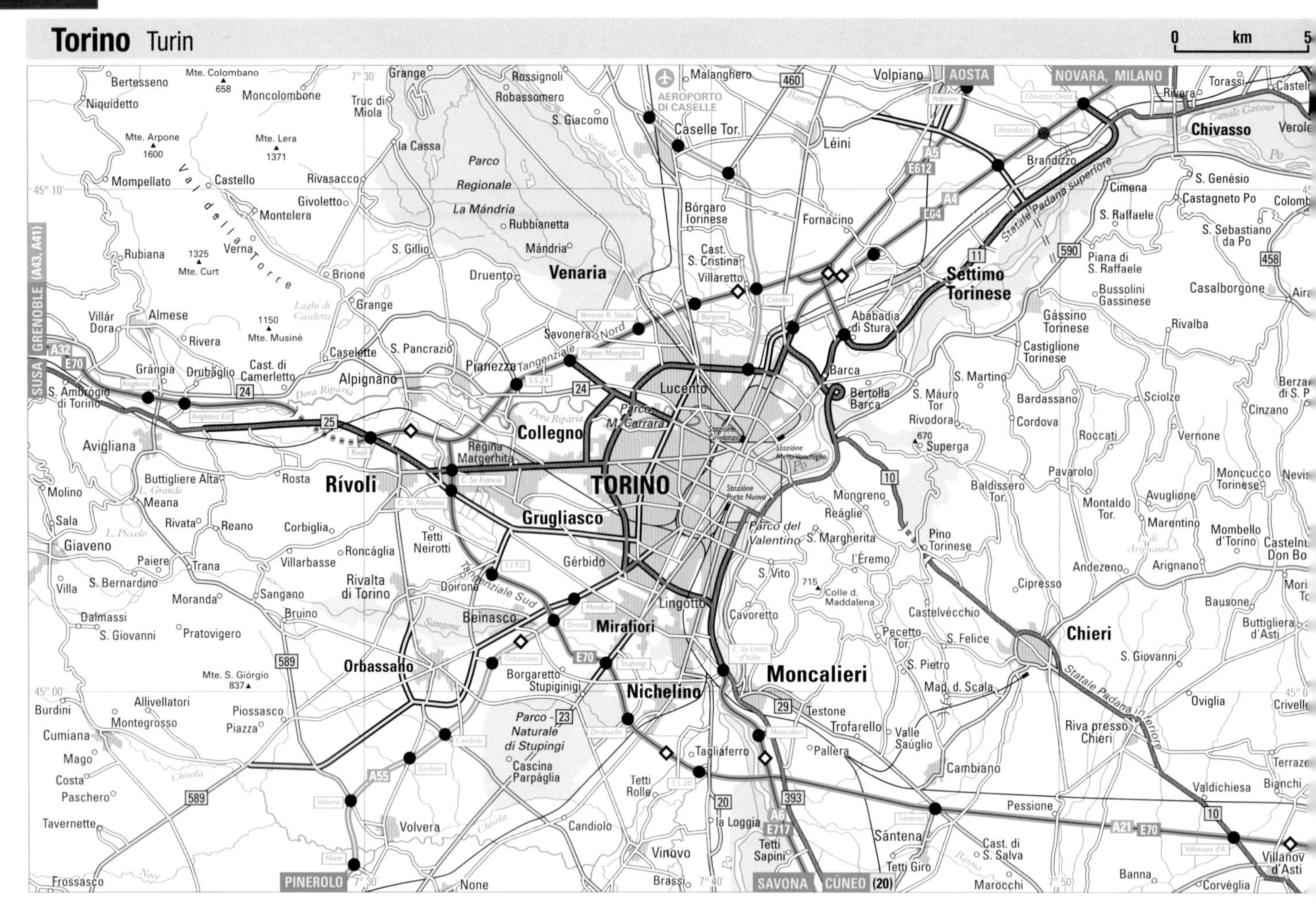
Bertesseno
Mte. Colombano 658
Moncolombone
Niquidetto
Truc di Miola
Grange
Rossignoli
Robassomero
Malanghero
AEROPORTO DI CASELLE
460
Volpiano
AOSTA
NOVARA, MILANO
Torassi
Chivasso
Mte. Arpone 1600
Mte. Lera 1371
la Cassa
S. Giacomo
Caselle Tor.
Léini
Brandizzo
Mompellato
Castello
Rivasacco
Parco Regionale La Mándria
Cimena
S. Genésio
Castagneto Po
Givoletto
Montelera
Rubbianetta
Bórgaro Torinese
Fornacino
S. Raffaele
S. Sebastiano da Po
Rubiana
1325 Mte. Curt
Verna
Val della Torre
S. Gillio
Mándria
Venaria
Cast. S. Cristina
Villaretto
Settimo Torinese
Piana di S. Raffaele
Bussolini Gassinese
Casalborgone
Brione
Druento
Villár Dora
Almese
Grange
1150 Mte. Musinè
Rivera
Savonera
Tangenziale Nord
Abbadia di Stura
Gássino Torinese
Rivalba
Castiglione Torinese
S. Pancrazio
Caselette
Grángia
Drubáglio
Cast. di Camerletto
Alpignano
Pianezza
Lucento
Barca
Bertolla Barca
S. Martino
S. Máuro Tor
Bardassano
Sciolze
Cinzano
SUSA GRENOBLE (A43, A41)
S. Ambrógio di Torino
Avigliana
Collegno
Parco M. Carrara
Rivodora
Cordova
670 Superga
Roccati
Vernone
Regina Margherita
TORINO
Pavarolo
Moncucco Torinese
Molino
Buttigliere Alta
Meana
Rosta
Rívoli
Mongreno
Reáglie
Baldissero Tor.
Montaldo Tor.
Avuglione
Sala
Giaveno
Rivata
Reano
Corbiglia
Grugliasco
Parco del Valentino
S. Margherita
Pino Torinese
Marentino
Mombello d'Torino
Paiere
Trana
Roncáglia
Villarbasse
Tetti Neirotti
Gérbido
l'Éremo
Andezeno
Arignano
Villa
S. Bernardino
Moranda
Sangano
Rivalta di Torino
Doirone
Tangenziale Sud
S. Vito
715 Colle d. Maddalena
Cipresso
Bausone
Dalmassi
S. Giovanni
Pratovigero
Bruino
Beinasco
Mirafiori
Lingotto
Cavoretto
Castelvécchio
Pecetto Tor.
S. Felice
Chieri
Buttigliera d'Asti
Mte. S. Giórgio 837
Orbassano
Borgaretto
Stupinigi
Nichelino
Moncalieri
S. Pietro
Mad. d. Scala
S. Giovanni
Burdini
Allivellatori
Montegrosso
Piossasco
Piazza
Parco Naturale di Stupinigi
Testone
Trofarello
Valle Sauglio
Statale Padana inferiore
Oviglia
Riva presso Chieri
Cumiana
Mago
Costa
Paschero
Cascina Parpáglia
Tagliaferro
Pallera
Cambiano
Terraze
Valdichiesa
Bianchi
Tetti Rolle
la Loggia
Pessione
Tavernette
Volvera
Candiolo
Tetti Sapini
Sántena
Cast. di S. Salva
Villanova d'Asti
Frossasco
Vinovo
Brassi
Tetti Giro
Marocchi
Banna
Corvéglia
PINEROLO
None
SAVONA
CÚNEO (20)
A32
E70
A55
A6
E717
A21
A5
E612
A4
E64
24
25
589
23
20
393
10
11
590
458

## Venézia Venice

0 km 0.5

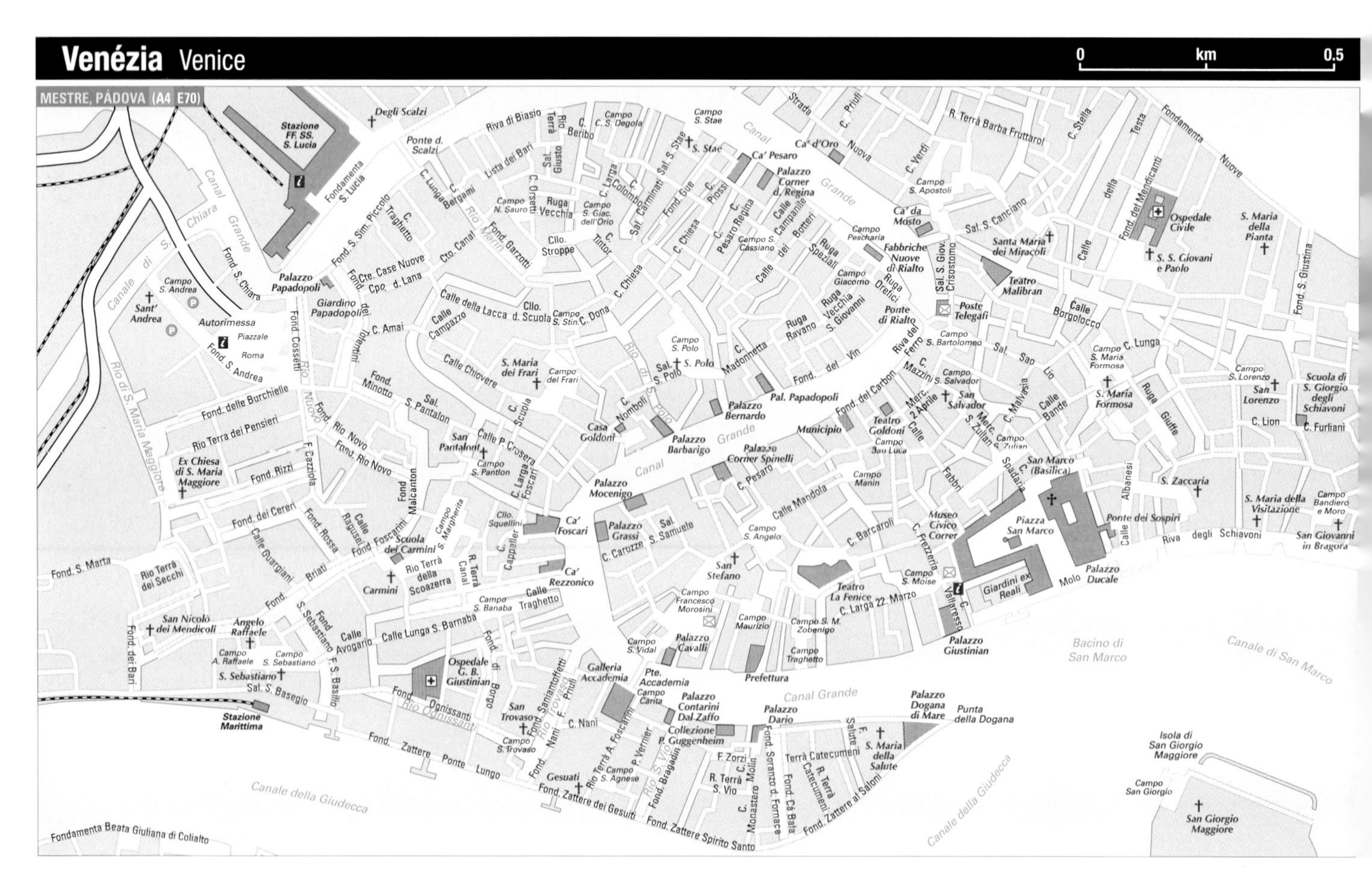
MESTRE, PÁDOVA (A4 E70)
Stazione FF. SS. S. Lucia
Degli Scalzi
Ponte d. Scalzi
Riva di Biasio
Campo S. Stae
Canal Grande
Ca' d'Oro
Strada Nuova
R. Terrà Barba Fruttarol
Fondamenta Nuove
Ca' Pesaro
Palazzo Corner d. Regina
Campo S. Apostoli
Ca' da Mosto
Sal. S. Canciano
Santa Maria dei Miracoli
Ospedale Civile
S. S. Giovani e Paolo
S. Maria della Pianta
Fond. S. Giustina
Teatro Malibran
Fabbriche Nuove di Rialto
Campo Pescaria
Ponte di Rialto
Poste Telegrafi
Campo S. Bartolomeo
Palazzo Papadopoli
Giardino Papadopoli
Campo S. Andrea
Sant' Andrea
Autorimessa
Piazzale Roma
Fond. S. Andrea
Fond. S. Chiara
Fond. delle Burchielle
Rio Terra dei Pensieri
Ex Chiesa di S. Maria Maggiore
Fond. Rizzi
Fond. dei Cereri
Campo S. Polo
S. Polo
S. Maria dei Frari
Campo dei Frari
Casa Goldoni
Palazzo Bernardo
Pal. Papadopoli
Municipio
Teatro Goldoni
Campo S. Luca
Campo S. Salvador
San Salvador
Campo S. Maria Formosa
S. Maria Formosa
Campo S. Lorenzo
San Lorenzo
Scuola di S. Giorgio degli Schiavoni
C. Lion
C. Furlani
San Pantalon
Campo S. Pantalon
Palazzo Barbarigo
Palazzo Corner Spinelli
Campo Manin
San Marco (Basilica)
S. Zaccaria
S. Maria della Visitazione
Campo Bandiera e Moro
San Giovanni in Bragora
Palazzo Mocenigo
Ca' Foscari
Palazzo Grassi
Campo S. Samuele
Campo S. Angelo
Museo Civico Correr
Piazza San Marco
Ponte dei Sospiri
Riva degli Schiavoni
Palazzo Ducale
Molo
Giardini ex Reali
Fond. S. Marta
Rio Terrà dei Secchi
Carmini
Scuola dei Carmini
Rio Terrà della Scoazzera
Ca' Rezzonico
Campo S. Barnaba
San Stefano
Campo Francesco Morosini
Teatro La Fenice
Campo S. Moisè
C. Larga 22. Marzo
Palazzo Giustinian
Bacino di San Marco
Canale di San Marco
San Nicolò dei Mendicoli
Angelo Raffaele
Campo A. Raffaele
Campo S. Sebastiano
S. Sebastiano
Ospedale G. B. Giustinian
Galleria Accademia
Pte. Accademia
Campo Carità
Palazzo Cavalli
Campo S. Vidal
Campo Maurizio
Campo S. M. Zobenigo
Campo Traghetto
Prefettura
Sal. S. Basegio
Stazione Marittima
Fond. dei Bari
Rio Onissanti
San Trovaso
Campo S. Trovaso
Palazzo Contarini Dal Zaffo
Collezione P. Guggenheim
Palazzo Dario
Canal Grande
Palazzo Dogana di Mare
Punta della Dogana
S. Maria della Salute
Terrà Catecumeni
Isola di San Giorgio Maggiore
Campo San Giorgio
San Giorgio Maggiore
Fond. Zattere Ponte Lungo
Gesuati
Campo S. Agnese
Fond. Zattere dei Gesuiti
Fond. Zattere Spirito Santo
Fond. Zattere al Saloni
Canale della Giudecca
Fondamenta Beata Giuliana di Colialto

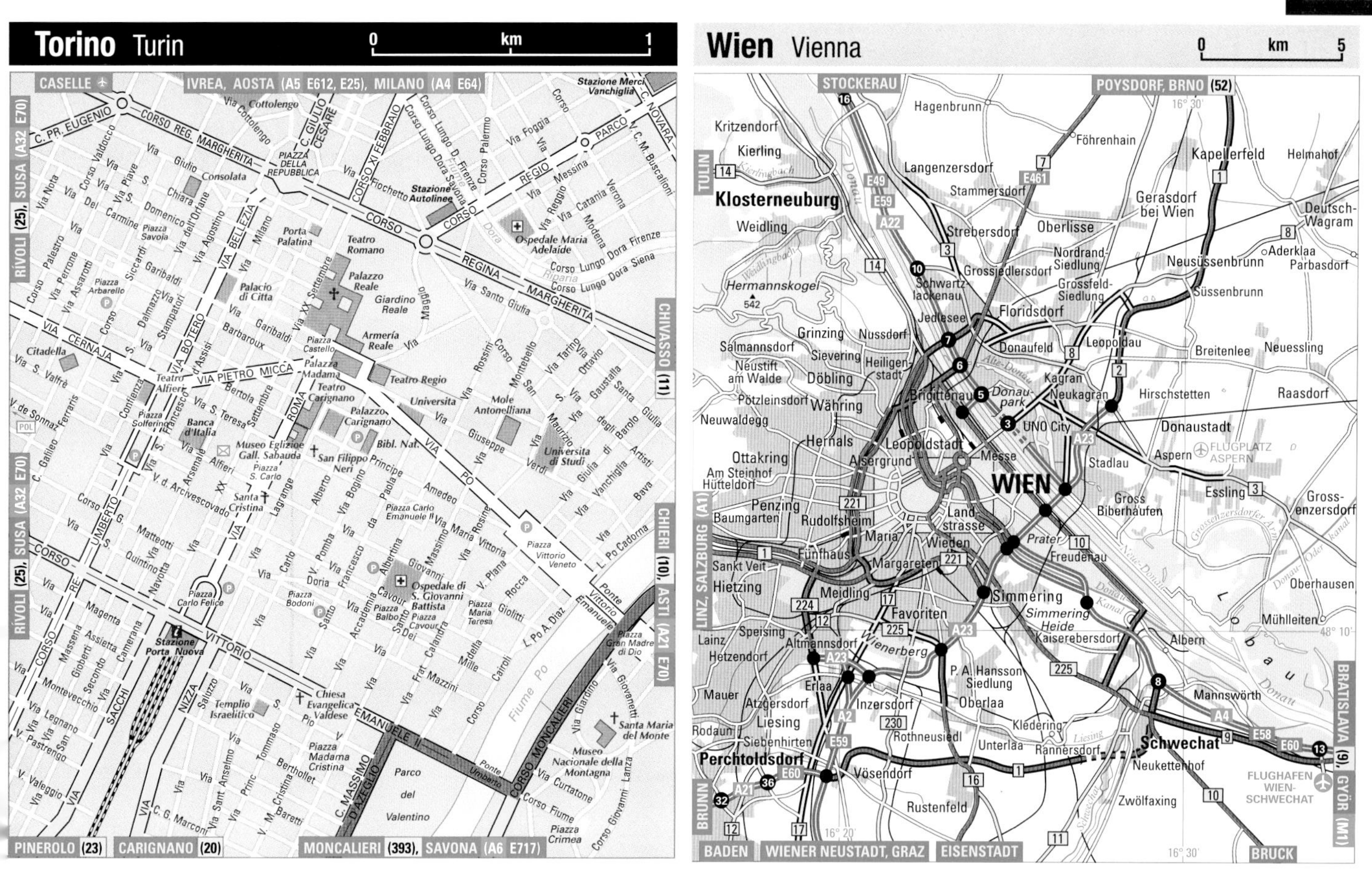
Torino Turin
0 km 1
CASELLE
IVREA, AOSTA (A5 E612, E25), MILANO (A4 E64)
RIVOLI (25), SUSA (A32 E70)
CHIVASSO (11)
CHIERI (10), ASTI (A21 E70)
PINEROLO (23)
CARIGNANO (20)
MONCALIERI (393), SAVONA (A6 E717)
Stazione Merci Vanchiglia
Corso Regina Margherita
Piazza della Repubblica
Consolata
Porta Palatina
Teatro Romano
Palazzo Reale
Giardino Reale
Armeria Reale
Palazzo di Città
Citadella
Teatro Regio
Teatro Carignano
Palazzo Carignano
Università
Mole Antonelliana
Università di Studi
Bibl. Naz.
Museo Egizio e Gall. Sabauda
San Filippo Neri
Banca d'Italia
Santa Cristina
Piazza Carlo Emanuele II
Piazza Vittorio Veneto
Ospedale Maria Adelaide
Ospedale di S. Giovanni Battista
Stazione Porta Nuova
Piazza Carlo Felice
Tempio Israelitico
Chiesa Evangelica Valdese
Piazza Madama Cristina
Corso Vittorio Emanuele II
Fiume Po
Parco del Valentino
Museo Nazionale della Montagna
Santa Maria del Monte
Piazza Crimea
Ponte Umberto I
Ponte Vittorio Emanuele I
Piazza Gran Madre di Dio
Corso Moncalieri
Corso Massimo d'Azeglio
Wien Vienna
0 km 5
STOCKERAU
POYSDORF, BRNO (52)
TULLN
LINZ, SALZBURG (A1)
BRNN
BADEN
WIENER NEUSTADT, GRAZ
EISENSTADT
BRUCK
BRATISLAVA (9), GYÖR (M1)
Hagenbrunn
Kritzendorf
Kierling
Klosterneuburg
Weidling
Föhrenhain
Langenzersdorf
Stammersdorf
Kapellerfeld
Helmahof
Gerasdorf bei Wien
Deutsch-Wagram
Strebersdorf
Oberlisse
Aderklaa
Parbasdorf
Neusüssenbrunn
Süssenbrunn
Hermannskogel
Schwarzlackenau
Grossjedlersdorf
Nordrand-Siedlung
Grossfeld-Siedlung
Floridsdorf
Jedlesee
Grinzing
Nussdorf
Salmannsdorf
Sievering
Heiligenstadt
Donaufeld
Leopoldau
Breitenlee
Neuessling
Neustift am Walde
Döbling
Kagran
Neukagran
Hirschstetten
Raasdorf
Pötzleinsdorf
Währing
Brigittenau
Donaupark
UNO City
Neuwaldegg
Hernals
Leopoldstadt
Donaustadt
Ottakring
Alsergrund
Messe
Stadlau
Aspern
FLUGPLATZ ASPERN
Am Steinhof
Hütteldorf
WIEN
Gross Biberhaufen
Essling
Gross-Enzersdorf
Penzing
Baumgarten
Rudolfsheim
Landstrasse
Prater
Fünfhaus
Mariahilf
Wieden
Margareten
Freudenau
Sankt Veit
Hietzing
Meidling
Favoriten
Simmering
Simmeringer Heide
Kaiserebersdorf
Oberhausen
Mühlleiten
Lainz
Speising
Hetzendorf
Altmannsdorf
Wienerberg
Albern
Lobau
Donau
Mauer
Erlaa
P. A. Hansson Siedlung
Mannswörth
Atzgersdorf
Inzersdorf
Oberlaa
Liesing
Rodaun
Siebenhirten
Rothneusiedl
Kledering
Unterlaa
Rannersdorf
Schwechat
Perchtoldsdorf
Vösendorf
Neukettenhof
FLUGHAFEN WIEN-SCHWECHAT
Zwölfaxing
Rustenfeld

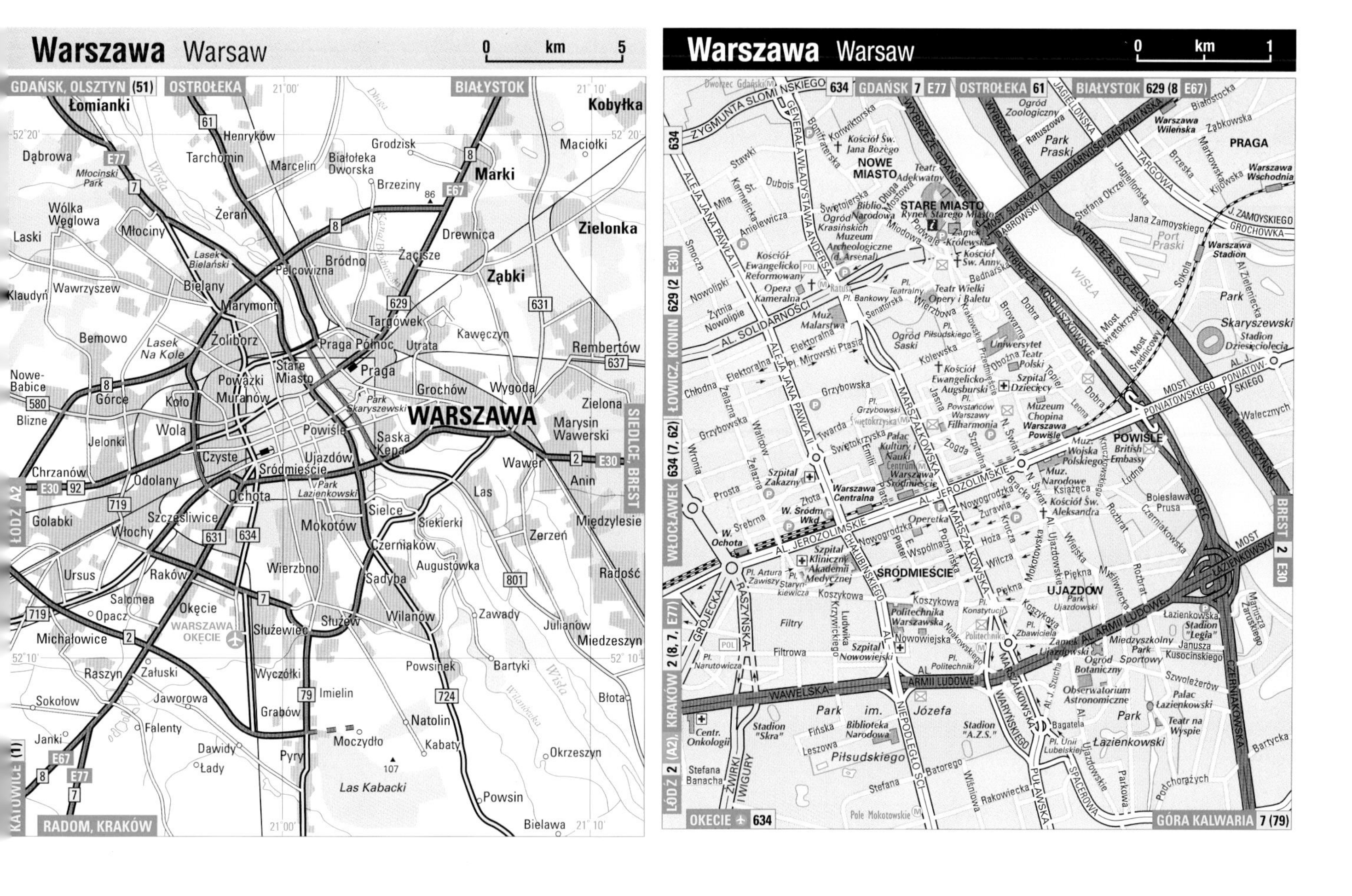
Warszawa Warsaw
0 km 5
GDAŃSK, OLSZTYN (51)
OSTROŁĘKA
BIAŁYSTOK
SIEDLCE, BREST
ŁÓDŹ A2
KATOWICE (1)
RADOM, KRAKÓW
Łomianki
Kobyłka
Henryków
Dąbrowa
Tarchomin
Grodzisk
Marcelin
Białołęka Dworska
Maciołki
Marki
Brzeziny
Młociński Park
Wólka Węglowa
Żerań
Drewnica
Zielonka
Laski
Młociny
Lasek Bielański
Pelcowizna
Bródno
Zacisze
Ząbki
Wawrzyszew
Bielany
Kaweczyn
Klaudyń
Marymont
Targówek
Rembertów
Bemowo
Lasek Na Kole
Żoliborz
Praga Północ
Utrata
Nowe-Babice
Stare Miasto
Praga
Grochów
Wygoda
Górce
Powązki
Muranów
Koło
Park Skaryszewski
WARSZAWA
Zielona
Marysin Wawerski
Blizne
Jelonki
Wola
Powiśle
Saska Kępa
Czyste
Śródmieście
Ujazdów
Wawer
Chrzanów
Odolany
Park Łazienkowski
Anin
Ochota
Las
Golabki
Szczęśliwice
Sielce
Włochy
Siekierki
Międzylesie
Mokotów
Zerzeń
Czerniaków
Ursus
Raków
Augustówka
Radość
Wierzbno
Sadyba
Salomea
Okęcie
Opacz
WARSZAWA OKĘCIE
Służewiec
Służew
Wilanów
Zawady
Julianów
Michałowice
Miedzeszyn
Powsinek
Bartyki
Raszyn
Załuski
Wyczółki
Imielin
Błota
Sokołów
Jaworowa
Grabów
Natolin
Falenty
Moczydło
Janki
Dawidy
Kabaty
Pyry
Okrzeszyn
Łady
Las Kabacki
Powsin
Bielawa
Wisła
Warszawa Warsaw
0 km 1
GDAŃSK 7 E77
OSTROŁĘKA 61
BIAŁYSTOK 629 (8 E67)
WŁOCŁAWEK 634 (7, 62)
ŁOWICZ, KONIN 629 (2 E30)
KRAKÓW 2 (8, 7, E77)
ŁÓDŹ 2 (A2)
OKĘCIE 634
GÓRA KALWARIA 7 (79)
BREST 2 E30
Dworzec Gdański
Ogród Zoologiczny
Park Praski
Warszawa Wileńska
PRAGA
Kościół Św. Jana Bożego
NOWE MIASTO
Teatr Adekwatny
STARE MIASTO
Rynek Starego Miasta
Zamek Królewski
Warszawa Wschodnia
Ogród Krasińskich
Muzeum Archeologiczne (d. Arsenał)
Port Praski
Warszawa Stadion
Kościół Ewangelicko Reformowany
Opera Kameralna
Teatr Wielki Opery i Baletu
Kościół Św. Anny
Pl. Bankowy
Pl. Teatralny
Muz. Malarstwa
Ogród Saski
Pl. Piłsudskiego
Uniwersytet
Teatr Polski
Park Skaryszewski
Stadion Dziesięciolecia
Most Świętokrzyski
Most Średnicowy
Most Poniatowskiego
Pl. Mirowski
Kościół Ewangelicko Augsburski
Szpital Dziecięcy
Muzeum Chopina
Filharmonia
Muzeum Warszawa Powiśle
POWIŚLE
British Embassy
Pałac Kultury i Nauki
Centrum Warszawa Śródmieście
Warszawa Centralna
Muz. Wojska Polskiego
Muz. Narodowe
Książęca
Kościół Św. Aleksandra
W. Śródm. Wkd
W. Ochota
Szpital Zakaźny
Szpital Kliniczny Akademii Medycznej
ŚRÓDMIEŚCIE
UJAZDÓW
Park Ujazdowski
Politechnika Warszawska
Pl. Konstytucji
Pl. Zbawiciela
Szpital Nowowiejski
Pl. Politechniki
Pl. Unii Lubelskiej
Stadion "Legia"
Miedzyszkolny Park Sportowy
Ogród Botaniczny
Obserwatorium Astronomiczne
Pałac Łazienkowski
Teatr na Wyspie
Park Łazienkowski
Centr. Onkologii
Stadion "Skra"
Biblioteka Narodowa
Park im. Józefa Piłsudskiego
Stadion "A.Z.S."
Pole Mokotowskie
Pl. Narutowicza
Wisła

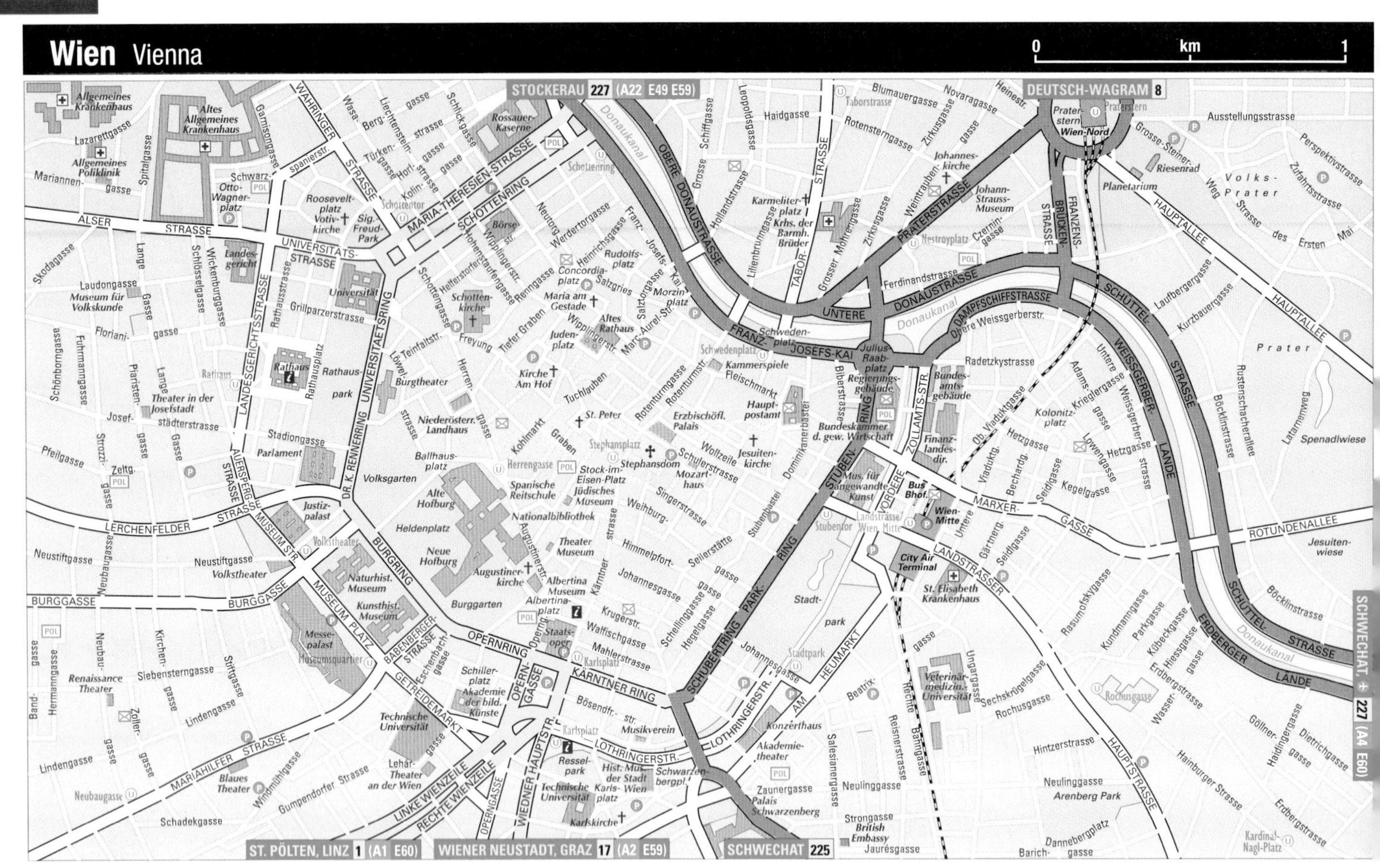
Wien Vienna
0 km 1
STOCKERAU 227 (A22 E49 E59)
DEUTSCH-WAGRAM 8
ST. PÖLTEN, LINZ 1 (A1 E60)
WIENER NEUSTADT, GRAZ 17 (A2 E59)
SCHWECHAT 225
SCHWECHAT ✈ 227 (A4 E60)
Allgemeines Krankenhaus
Altes Allgemeines Krankenhaus
Allgemeines Poliklinik
Rossauer-Kaserne
Donaukanal
OBERE DONAUSTRASSE
Praterstern
Wien-Nord
Riesenrad
Planetarium
Volks-Prater
Prater
HAUPTALLEE
Ausstellungsstrasse
ALSER STRASSE
UNIVERSITÄTSSTRASSE
Votivkirche
Sig.-Freud-Park
MARIA-THERESIEN-STRASSE
SCHOTTENRING
Börse
Landesgericht
Universität
Rathaus
Rathauspark
Burgtheater
Parlament
Volksgarten
Justizpalast
Schottenkirche
Ruprechtskirche
Morzinplatz
Altes Rathaus
Am Hof
Hoher Markt
Judenplatz
Freyung
Graben
Stephansplatz
Stephansdom
Kohlmarkt
Spanische Reitschule
Alte Hofburg
Heldenplatz
Neue Hofburg
Nationalbibliothek
Augustinerkirche
Albertina Museum
Burggarten
Naturhist. Museum
Kunsthist. Museum
Messepalast
Museumsquartier
Volkstheater
BURGRING
OPERNRING
KÄRNTNER RING
Staatsoper
Karlsplatz
Karlskirche
Technische Universität
Akademie der bild. Künste
Musikverein
Konzerthaus
Akademietheater
Schwarzenbergplatz
Palais Schwarzenberg
Stadtpark
SCHUBERTRING
PARKRING
STUBENRING
Postsparkasse
Regierungsgebäude
Mus. für angewandte Kunst
Wien-Mitte
City Air Terminal
St. Elisabeth Krankenhaus
Veterinärmedizin. Universität
Rochusgasse
UNTERE DONAUSTRASSE
FRANZ-JOSEFS-KAI
Schwedenplatz
Julius-Raab-platz
Bundesamtsgebäude
Finanzlandesdir.
Radetzkystrasse
Kolonitzplatz
Hetzgasse
MARXERGASSE
LANDSTRASSER HAUPTSTRASSE
ROTUNDENALLEE
Jesuitenwiese
SCHÜTTELSTRASSE
WEISSGERBERLÄNDE
ERDBERGER LÄNDE
Rennweg
Neulinggasse
Arenberg Park
British Embassy
Jaurèsgasse
LERCHENFELDER STRASSE
BURGGASSE
MARIAHILFER STRASSE
LINKE WIENZEILE
RECHTE WIENZEILE
WIEDNER HAUPTSTR.
LOTHRINGERSTR.
Secession
Theater an der Wien
Technische Universität
Kirchengasse
Stiftgasse
Neubaugasse
Raimund Theater
Schadekgasse
Gumpendorfer Strasse
Theater in der Josefstadt
Laudongasse
Museum für Volkskunde
Florianigasse
Josefstädter Strasse
Lange Gasse
Piaristengasse
Landesgerichtsstrasse
Neustiftgasse
Siebensterngasse
Dr. K. Renner Ring
Universitätsring
Heinestr.
Taborstrasse
Karmeliterplatz
Krhs. der Barmh. Brüder
Johann-Strauss-Museum
PRATERSTRASSE
Nestroyplatz
Leopoldsgasse
Haidgasse
Gross Schiffgasse
Kammerspiele
Fleischmarkt
Hauptpostamt
Erzbischöfl. Palais
Jesuitenkirche
Bundeskammer d. gew. Wirtschaft
Dominikanerbastei
Singerstrasse
Weihburggasse
Himmelpfortgasse
Johannesgasse
Seilerstätte
Annagasse
Krugerstr.
Walfischgasse
Mozarthaus
Herrengasse
Minoritenplatz
Ballhausplatz
Niederösterr. Landhaus
Tuchlauben
Wipplingerstr.
Renngasse
Concordiaplatz
Rudolfsplatz
Salztorgasse
Schwedenbrücke

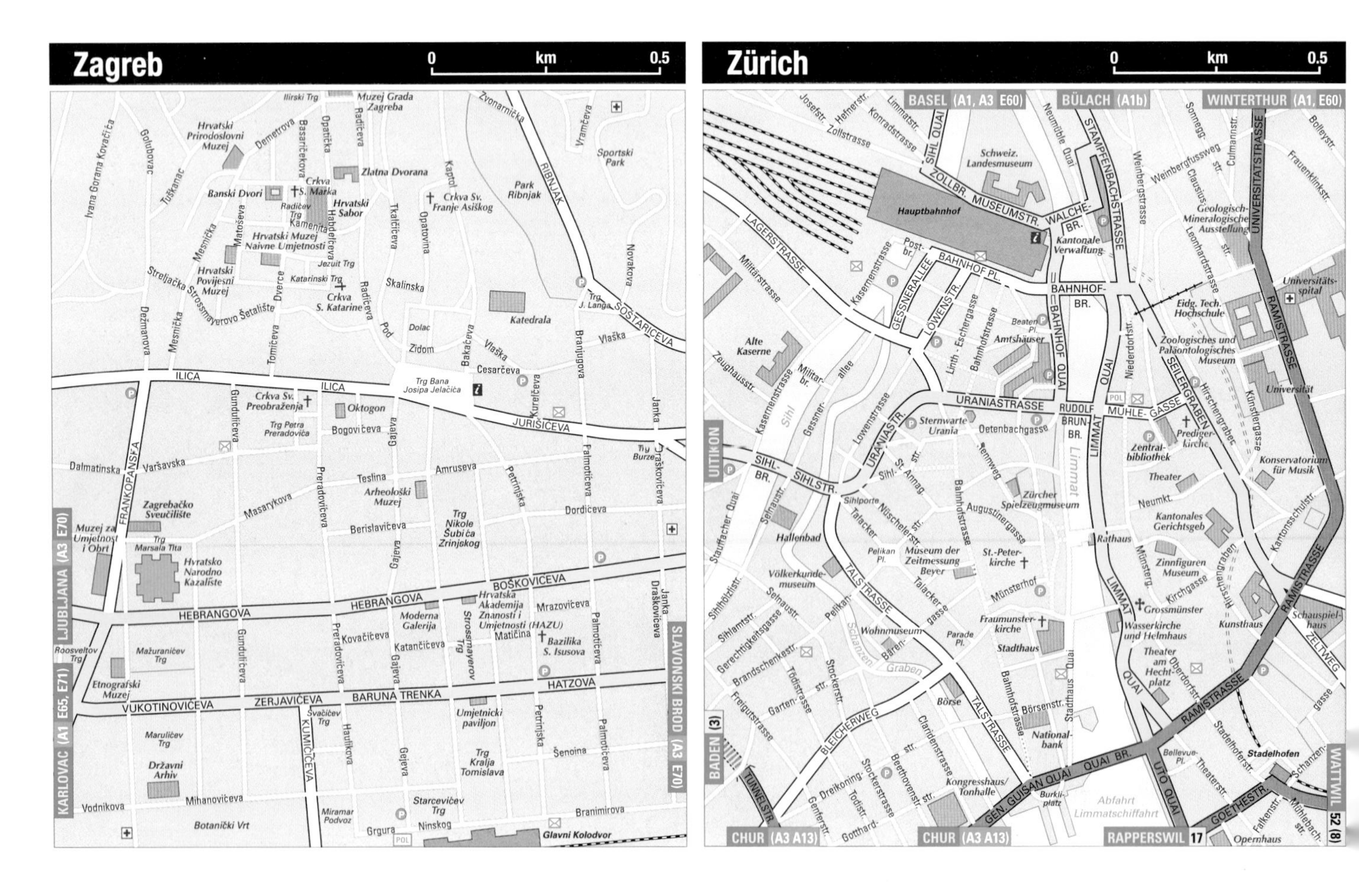
Zagreb
0 km 0.5
LJUBLJANA (A3 E70)
KARLOVAC (A1 E65, E71)
SLAVONSKI BROD (A3 E70)
Muzej Grada Zagreba
Hrvatski Prirodoslovni Muzej
Zlatna Dvorana
Banski Dvori
Crkva S. Marka
Hrvatski Sabor
Crkva Sv. Franje Asiškog
Park Ribnjak
Sportski Park
Hrvatski Muzej Naivne Umjetnosti
Hrvatski Povijesni Muzej
Crkva S. Katarine
Katedrala
Dolac
Trg Bana Josipa Jelačića
ILICA
JURIŠIĆEVA
Crkva Sv. Preobraženja
Oktogon
Trg Petra Preradovića
Bogovićeva
Arheološki Muzej
Amruševa
Trg Nikole Šubića Zrinjskog
Zagrebačko Sveučilište
Muzej za Umjetnost i Obrt
Trg Maršala Tita
Hrvatsko Narodno Kazalište
HEBRANGOVA
BOŠKOVIĆEVA
Moderna Galerija
Hrvatska Akademija Znanosti i Umjetnosti (HAZU)
Bazilika S. Isusova
Mažuranićev Trg
Etnografski Muzej
VUKOTINOVIĆEVA
ZERJAVIĆEVA
BARUNA TRENKA
HATZOVA
Umjetnički paviljon
Trg Kralja Tomislava
Maruličev Trg
Državni Arhiv
Botanički Vrt
Mihanovićeva
Starčevićev Trg
Branimirova
Glavni Kolodvor
FRANKOPANSKA
Masarykova
Teslina
Gundulićeva
Preradovićeva
Praška
Draškovićeva
Palmotićeva
Petrinjska
Vlaška
Kaptol
Opatovina
Tkalčićeva
Radićeva
Mesnička
Vodnikova
Dalmatinska

Zürich
0 km 0.5
BASEL (A1, A3 E60)
BÜLACH (A1b)
WINTERTHUR (A1, E60)
UITIKON
BADEN (3)
CHUR (A3 A13)
RAPPERSWIL 17
WATTWIL 52 (8)
Schweiz. Landesmuseum
Hauptbahnhof
ZOLLBR.
MUSEUMSTR.
WALCHEBR.
Kantonale Verwaltung
BAHNHOFPL.
BAHNHOFBR.
LAGERSTRASSE
STAMPFENBACHSTRASSE
UNIVERSITÄTSTRASSE
RÄMISTRASSE
Universitätsspital
Eidg. Tech. Hochschule
Geologisch-Mineralogische Ausstellung
Zoologisches und Paläontologisches Museum
Universität
Konservatorium für Musik
Alte Kaserne
Sihl
Limmat
URANIASTRASSE
Sternwarte Urania
RUDOLF BRUN-BR.
MÜHLEGASSE
SEILERGRABEN
Zentralbibliothek
Predigerkirche
Theater
Neumarkt
Kantonales Gerichtsgeb.
Rathaus
Zinnfiguren Museum
Zürcher Spielzeugmuseum
Hallenbad
Völkerkundemuseum
Museum der Zeitmessung Beyer
St.-Peterkirche
Wohnmuseum
Fraumünsterkirche
Stadthaus
Grossmünster
Wasserkirche und Helmhaus
Theater am Hechtplatz
Kunsthaus
Schauspielhaus
ZELTWEG
Börse
National-bank
Kongresshaus/Tonhalle
GEN. GUISAN QUAI
QUAI BR.
UTO QUAI
Bürkliplatz
Abfahrt Limmatschiffahrt
Stadelhofen
Opernhaus
GOETHESTR.
TALSTRASSE
BLEICHERWEG
SIHLBR.
SIHLSTR.
LIMMAT QUAI
Bahnhofstrasse
Löwenstrasse
Gessnerallee
Kasernenstrasse
Militärstrasse
Zeughausstr.
Stauffacher Quai
Selnaustr.
Stockerstr.
Dreikönigstr.
Beethovenstr.
Claridenstrasse
Tödistr.
Gotthardstr.
Schanzengraben
Paradeplatz
Münsterhof
Pelikanstr.
Niederdorfstr.
Hirschengraben
Künstlergasse
Kantonsschulstr.
Heimplatz
Bellevueplatz
Theaterstr.
Falkenstr.
Mühlebachstr.

| Code | English | French | German | Italian |
|---|---|---|---|---|
| A | Austria | Autriche | Österreich | Austria |
| AL | Albania | Albanie | Albanien | Albania |
| AND | Andorra | Andorre | Andorra | Andorra |
| B | Belgium | Belgique | Belgien | Belgio |
| BG | Bulgaria | Bulgarie | Bulgarien | Bulgaria |
| BIH | Bosnia-Herzegovin | Bosnia-Herzegovine | Bosnien-Herzegowina | Bosnia-Herzogovina |
| BY | Belarus | Belarus | Weissrussland | Bielorussia |
| CH | Switzerland | Suisse | Schweiz | Svizzera |
| CY | Cyprus | Chypre | Zypern | Cipro |
| CZ | Czech Republic | République Tchèque | Tschechische Republik | Repubblica Ceca |
| D | Germany | Allemagne | Deutschland | Germania |
| DK | Denmark | Danemark | Dänemark | Danimarca |
| E | Spain | Espagne | Spanien | Spagna |
| EST | Estonia | Estonie | Estland | Estonia |
| F | France | France | Frankreich | Francia |
| FIN | Finland | Finlande | Finnland | Finlandia |
| FL | Liechtenstein | Liechtenstein | Liechtenstein | Liechtenstein |
| FO | Faeroe Islands | Îles Féroé | Färoër-Inseln | Isole Faroe |
| GB | United Kingdom | Royaume Uni | Grossbritannien und Nordirland | Regno Unito |
| GBZ | Gibraltar | Gibraltar | Gibraltar | Gibilterra |
| GR | Greece | Grèce | Greichenland | Grecia |
| H | Hungary | Hongrie | Ungarn | Ungheria |
| HR | Croatia | Croatie | Kroatien | Croazia |

| Code | English | French | German | Italian |
|---|---|---|---|---|
| I | Italy | Italie | Italien | Italia |
| IRL | Ireland | Irlande | Irland | Irlanda |
| IS | Iceland | Islande | Island | Islanda |
| KOS | Kosovo | Kosovo | Kosovo | Kosovo |
| L | Luxembourg | Luxembourg | Luxemburg | Lussemburgo |
| LT | Lithuania | Lituanie | Litauen | Lituania |
| LV | Latvia | Lettonie | Lettland | Lettonia |
| M | Malta | Malte | Malta | Malta |
| MC | Monaco | Monaco | Monaco | Monaco |
| MD | Moldova | Moldavie | Moldawien | Moldavia |
| MK | Macedonia | Macédoine | Makedonien | Macedonia |
| MNE | Montenegro | Monténégro | Montenegro | Montenegro |
| N | Norway | Norvège | Norwegen | Norvegia |
| NL | Netherlands | Pays-Bas | Niederlande | Paesi Bassi |
| P | Portugal | Portugal | Portugal | Portogallo |
| PL | Poland | Pologne | Polen | Polonia |
| RO | Romania | Roumanie | Rumanien | Romania |
| RSM | San Marino | Saint-Marin | San Marino | San Marino |
| RUS | Russia | Russie | Russland | Russia |
| S | Sweden | Suède | Schweden | Svezia |
| SK | Slovak Republic | République Slovaque | Slowak Republik | Repubblica Slovacca |
| SLO | Slovenia | Slovénie | Slowenien | Slovenia |
| SRB | Serbia | Serbie | Serbien | Serbia |
| TR | Turkey | Turquie | Türkei | Turchia |
| UA | Ukraine | Ukraine | Ukraine | Ucraina |

## A

**Aabenraa** DK 64 A2
**Aabybro** DK 58 A2
**Aach** D 107 B4
**Aachen** D 80 B2
**Aalborg** DK 58 A2
**Aalen** D 94 C2
**Aalestrup** DK 58 B2
**Aalsmeer** NL 70 B1
**Aalst** B 79 B4
**Aalten** NL 71 C3
**Aalter** B 79 A3
**Äänekoski** FIN 8 A4
**Aapajärvi** FIN 197 B10
**Ağapınar** TR 187 C5
**Aarau** CH 106 B3
**Aarberg** CH 106 B2
**Aarburg** CH 106 B2
**Aardenburg** NL 79 A3
**Aars** DK 58 B2
**Aarschot** B 79 B4
**Aarup** DK 59 C3
**Aba** H 112 B2
**Abádanes** E 152 B1
**Abades** E 151 B3
**Abadin** E 141 A3
**Abádszalók** H 113 B4
**Abaliget** H 125 A4
**Abana** TR 23 A8
**A Baña** E 140 B2
**Abanilla** E 165 A3
**Abano Terme** I 121 B4
**Abarán** E 165 A3
**Abasár** H 113 B4
**Abbadia San Salvatore** I 135 C4
**Abbaue** D 74 A2
**Abbehausen** D 72 A1
**Abbekäs** S 66 A2
**Abbeville** F 90 A1
**Abbey** IRL 28 A3
**Abbeydorney** IRL 29 B2
**Abbeyfeale** IRL 29 B2
**Abbeyleix** IRL 30 B1
**Abbey Town** GB 36 B3
**Abbiategrasso** I 120 B1
**Abborrträsk** S 196 D2
**Abbots Bromley** GB 40 C2
**Abbotsbury** GB 43 B4
**Abda** H 111 B4
**Abejar** E 143 C4
**Abela** P 160 B1
**Abelvær** N 199 A8
**Abenberg** D 94 B2
**Abenójar** E 157 B3
**Abensberg** D 95 C3
**Aberaeron** GB 39 B2
**Abercarn** GB 39 C3
**Aberchirder** GB 33 D4
**Aberdare** GB 39 C3
**Aberdaron** GB 38 B2
**Aberdeen** GB 33 D4
**Aberdulais** GB 39 C3
**Aberdyfi** GB 39 B2
**Aberfeldy** GB 35 B4
**Aberffraw** GB 38 A2
**Aberfoyle** GB 34 B3
**Abergavenny** GB 39 C3
**Abergele** GB 38 A3
**Abergynolwyn** GB 38 B3
**Aberporth** GB 39 B2
**Abersoch** GB 38 B2
**Abertillery** GB 39 C3
**Abertura** E 156 A2
**Aberystwyth** GB 39 B2
**Abetone** I 135 A3
**Abfaltersbach** A 109 C3
**Abide**
*Çanakkale* TR 186 B1
*Kütahya* TR 187 D4
**Abiego** E 145 B3
**Abild** DK 64 B1
**Abingdon-on-Thames** GB 44 B2
**Abington** GB 36 A3
**Abisko** S 194 B9
**Abiul** P 154 B2
**Abla** E 164 B2
**Ablis** F 90 C1
**A Bola** E 140 B3
**Abondance** F 118 A3
**Abony** H 113 B4
**Aboyne** GB 33 D4
**Abrantes** P 154 B2
**Abreiro** P 148 A2
**Abreschviller** F 92 C3
**Abrest** F 117 A3
**Abriès** F 119 C3
**Abrud** RO 17 B5
**Absdorf** A 97 C3
**Abtenau** A 109 B4
**Abtsgmünd** D 94 C1
**Abusejo** E 149 B3
**Åby**
*Kronoberg* S 62 A2
*Östergötland* S 56 B2
**Åbyggeby** S 51 B4
**Åbytorp** S 55 A6
**A Cañiza** E 140 B2
**A Capela** E 140 A2
**Acate** I 177 B3
**Accadia** I 171 B3
**Accéglio** I 132 A2
**Accettura** I 172 B2
**Acciaroli** I 170 C3
**Accous** F 145 A3
**Accrington** GB 40 B1
**Accúmoli** I 169 A3
**Acedera** E 156 A2
**Acehuche** E 155 B4
**Acered** E 152 A2
**Acerenza** I 172 B1
**Acerno** I 170 C3
**Acerra** I 170 C2
**Aceuchal** E 155 C4
**Acharacle** GB 34 B2
**Acharnes** GR 185 A4
**Achavanich** GB 32 C3
**Achene** B 79 B5
**Achenkirch** A 108 B2
**Achensee** A 108 B2
**Achenthal** A 108 B2
**Achentrias** GR 185 E6
**Achern** D 93 C4
**Acheux-en-Amienois** F 90 A2
**Achiltibuie** GB 32 C1
**Achim** D 72 A2
**Achladokambos** GR 184 B3
**Achnasheen** GB 32 D1
**Achnashellach** GB 32 D1
**Achosnich** GB 34 B1
**Aci Castello** I 177 B4
**Aci Catena** I 177 B4
**Acilia** I 168 B2
**Acıpayam** TR 189 B4
**Acireale** I 177 B4
**Acle** GB 41 C5
**A Coruña** E 140 A2
**Acquacadda** I 179 C2
**Acqua Doria** F 180 B1
**Acquanegra sul Chiese** I 121 B3
**Acquapendente** I 168 A1
**Acquasanta Terme** I 136 C2
**Acquasparta** I 168 A2
**Acquaviva** I 135 B4
**Acquaviva delle Fonti** I 171 C4
**Acquaviva Picena** I 136 C2
**Acquigny** F 89 A5
**Ácqui Terme** I 119 C5
**Acri** I 174 B2
**Acs** H 112 B2
**Acsa** H 112 B3
**Ácsteszér** H 112 B1
**Acy-en-Multien** F 90 B2
**Ada** SRB 126 B2
**Adak** S 195 E9
**Ådalsbruk** N 48 B3
**Adamas** GR 185 C5
**Adamsfjord** N 193 B10
**Adamuz** E 157 B3
**Adana** TR 23 C8
**Ádánd** H 112 C2
**Adanero** E 150 B3
**Adare** IRL 29 B3
**Adaševci** SRB 125 B5
**Adeanueva de Ebro** E 144 B2
**Adelboden** CH 106 C2
**Adelebsen** D 82 A1
**Adélfia** I 173 A2
**Adelmannsfelden** D 94 C2
**Adelsheim** D 94 B1
**Adelsö** S 57 A3
**Ademuz** E 152 B2
**Adenau** D 80 B2
**Adendorf** D 72 A3
**Adinkerke** B 78 A2
**Adjud** RO 17 B7
**Adliswil** CH 107 B3
**Admont** A 110 B1
**Ådneram** N 52 A2
**Adolfsström** S 195 D7
**Adony** H 112 B2
**Adorf**
*Hessen* D 81 A4
*Sachsen* D 83 B4
**Adra** E 164 C1
**Adradas** E 152 A1
**Adrall** E 147 B2
**Adrano** I 177 B3
**Ádria** I 121 B5
**Adrigole** IRL 29 C2
**Adwick le Street** GB 40 B2
**Adzaneta** E 153 B3
**Aesch** CH 106 B2
**A Estrada** E 140 B2
**Afandou** GR 188 C3
**Åfarnes** N 198 C4
**Affing** D 94 C2
**Affoltern** CH 106 B3
**Affric Lodge** GB 32 D1
**Åfjord** N 199 B7
**Aflenz Kurort** A 110 B2
**A Fonsagrada** E 141 A3
**Afragóla** I 170 C2
**Afritz** A 109 C4
**Afyon** TR 187 D5
**Ágasegyháza** H 112 C3
**Agay** F 132 B2
**Agazzano** I 120 C2
**Agde** F 130 B2
**Agdenes** N 198 B6
**Agen** F 129 B3
**Ager** E 145 C4
**Agerbæk** DK 59 C1
**Agerskov** DK 64 A2
**Agger** DK 58 B1
**Aggersund** DK 58 A2
**Ággius** I 178 B3
**Aggsbach Dorf** A 97 C3
**Aggsbach Markt** A 97 C3
**Aggtelek** H 99 C4
**Aghalee** GB 27 B4
**Aghia** GR 182 D4
**Aghia Anna** GR 183 E5
**Aghia Galini** GR 185 D5
**Aghia Marina** GR 188 D1
**Aghia Paraskevi** GR 186 C1
**Aghia Pelagia** GR 184 C3
**Aghia Triada** GR 184 B2
**Aghiokambos** GR 182 D4
**Aghios Efstratios** GR 183 D6
**Aghios Kirikos** GR 185 B7
**Aghios Matheos** GR 182 D1
**Aghios Mironas** GR 185 D6
**Aghios Nikolaos** GR 185 D6
**Aghios Petros** GR 182 E2
**Aghio Theodori** GR 184 B4
**Agiči** BIH 124 C2
**Agira** I 177 B3
**Aglientu** I 178 A3
**Agnières** F 118 C2
**Agno** CH 120 B1
**Agnone** I 170 B2
**Agolada** E 140 B2
**Agon Coutainville** F 88 A2
**Ágordo** I 121 A5
**Agost** E 165 A4
**Agramón** E 158 C2
**Agramunt** E 147 C2
**Agreda** E 144 C2
**Agria** GR 183 D5
**Agrigento** I 176 B2
**Agrinio** GR 182 E3
**Agrón** E 163 A4
**Agrópoli** I 170 C2
**Aguadulce**
*Almería* E 164 C2
*Sevilla* E 162 A3
**Agualada** E 140 A2
**Agua Longa** P 148 A1
**A Guarda** E 140 C2
**Aguarón** E 152 A2
**Aguas** E 145 B3
**Aguas Belas** P 154 B2
**Aguas de Busot** E 159 C3
**Aguas de Moura** P 154 C2
**Águas Frias** P 148 A2
**Aguas Santas** P 148 A1
**Aguaviva** E 153 B3
**Aguaviva de la Vega** E 152 A1
**A Gudiña** E 141 B3
**Agudo** E 156 B3
**Águeda** P 148 B1
**Aguessac** F 130 A2
**Agugliano** I 136 B2
**Aguiar** P 154 C3
**Aguiàr da Beira** P 148 B2
**Aguilafuente** E 151 A3

**Aguilar de Campóo** E 142 B2
**Aguilar de la Frontera** E 163 A3
**Aguilas** E 164 B3
**Agunnaryd** S 60 C4
**Ahat** TR 187 D4
**Ahaus** D 71 B3
**Åheim** N 198 C2
**Ahigal** E 149 B3
**Ahigal de Villarino** E 149 A3
**Ahillones** E 156 B2
**Ahlbeck**
*Mecklenburg-Vorpommern* D 66 C3
*Mecklenburg-Vorpommern* D 74 A3
**Ahlen** D 81 A3
**Ahlhorn** D 71 B5
**Ahmetbey** TR 186 A2
**Ahmetler** TR 188 A4
**Ahmetli** TR 188 A2
**Ahoghill** GB 27 B4
**Ahola** FIN 197 C11
**Ahrensbök** D 65 B3
**Ahrensburg** D 72 A3
**Ahrenshoop** D 66 B1
**Ahun** F 116 A2
**Åhus** S 63 C2
**Ahvenselkä** FIN 197 C11
**Aibar** E 144 B2
**Aich** D 95 C4
**Aicha** D 96 C1
**Aichach** D 94 C3
**Aidone** I 177 B3
**Aiello Cálabro** I 175 B2
**Aigen im Mühlkreis** A 96 C1
**Aigle** CH 119 A3
**Aignan** F 128 C3
**Aignay-le-Duc** F 104 B3
**Aigre** F 115 C4
**Aigrefeuille-d'Aunis** F 114 B3
**Aigrefeuille-sur-Maine** F 101 B4
**Aiguablava** E 147 C4
**Aiguebelle** F 118 B3
**Aigueperse** F 116 A3
**Aigues-Mortes** F 131 B3
**Aigues-Vives** F 130 B1
**Aiguilles** F 119 C3
**Aiguillon** F 129 B3
**Aigurande** F 103 C3
**Ailefroide** F 118 C3
**Aillant-sur-Tholon** F 104 B2

Ailly-sur-Noye F 90 B2
Ailly-sur-Somme F 90 B2
Aimargues F 131 B3
Aime F 118 B3
Ainaži LV 8 D4
Ainet A 109 C3
Ainhoa F 144 A2
Ainsa E 145 B4
Airaines F 90 B1
Aird GB 34 B2
Aird Asaig Tairbeart
GB 31 B2
Airdrie GB 35 C4
Aire-sur-l'Adour F 128 C2
Aire-sur-la-Lys F 78 B2
Airole I 133 B3
Airolo CH 107 C3
Airvault F 102 C1
Aisey-sur-Seine F 104 B3
Aïssey F 105 B5
Aisy-sur-Armançon
F 104 B3
Aiterhofen D 95 C4
Aith
*Orkney* GB 33 B4
*Shetland* GB 33 A5
Aitona E 153 A4
Aitrach D 107 B5
Aiud RO 17 B5
Aix-en-Othe F 104 A2
Aix-en-Provence F 131 B4
Aixe-sur-Vienne F 115 C5
Aix-les-Bains F 118 B2
Aizenay F 114 B2
Aizkraukle LV 8 D4
Aizpute LV 8 D2
Ajac F 146 A3
Ajaccio F 180 B1
Ajain F 116 A1
Ajaureforsen S 195 E6
Ajdovščina SLO 122 B2
Ajka H 111 B4
Ajo E 143 A3
Ajofrín E 157 A4
Ajos FIN 196 D7
Ajuda P 155 C3
Akanthou CY 181 A2
Akarca TR 189 A4
Akasztó H 112 C3
Akçakoca TR 187 A6
Akçaova TR 187 A4
Akçay TR 189 C4
Aken D 83 A4
Åkerby S 51 B4
Åkernes N 52 B3
Åkersberga S 57 A4
Åkers styckebruk S 56 A3
Åkervik N 195 E4
Akhisar TR 186 D2
Åkirkeby DK 67 A3
Akköy TR 188 B2
Akkrum NL 70 A2
Akören TR 189 B7
Åkra N 52 A2
Akranes IS 190 C3
Åkrehamn N 52 A1
Akrotiri CY 181 B1
Aksaray TR 23 B8
Akşehir TR 189 A6
Akseki TR 189 B6
Aksla N 46 A3
Aksu TR 189 C5
Aktsyabrski BY 13 B8
Akureyri IS 191 B7
Åkvåg N 53 B5
Akyazı TR 187 B5
Ål N 47 B5
Ala I 121 B4
Alaca TR 23 A8
Alacaatlı TR 186 C3
Alaçam TR 23 A8
Alaçatı TR 188 A1
Alàdei Sardi I 178 B3
Ala di Stura I 119 B4
Alaejos E 150 A2
Alagna Valsésia I 119 B4
Alagón E 144 C2
Alaior E 167 B4
Alájar E 161 B3
Alakurtti RUS 197 C13
Alakylä FIN 196 B7
Alameda E 163 A3
Alameda de la Sagra
E 151 B4
Alamedilla E 163 A4
Alamillo E 156 B3
Alaminos E 151 B5
Ala-Nampa FIN 197 C9
Alanäs S 199 A12
Alandroal P 155 C3
Alange E 156 B1
Alaniemi FIN 197 D8
Alanís E 156 B2
Alanno I 169 A3
Ålansbro S 200 D3
Alanya TR 189 C7
Alap H 112 C2
Alaquáso E 159 B3
Alaraz E 150 B2
Alarcón E 158 B1
Alar del Rey E 142 B2
Alaró E 167 B2
Alaşehir TR 188 A3
Alássio I 133 A4
Ağlasun TR 189 B5
Alatoz E 158 B2
Alatri I 169 B3
Alavus FIN 8 A3
Alba
E 152 B2
I 119 C5
Alba Adriática I 136 C2
Albacete E 158 C2
Alba de Tormes E 150 B2
Alba de Yeltes E 149 B3
Albaida E 159 C3
Alba-Iulia RO 17 B5
Albæk DK 58 A3
Albaladejo E 158 C1
Albala del Caudillo
E 156 A1
Albalat E 159 B3
Albalate de Cinca
E 145 C4
Albalate del Arzobispo
E 153 A3
Albalate de las
Nogueras E 152 B1
Albalete de Zorita
E 151 B5
Alban F 130 B1
Albánchez E 164 B2
Albanchez de Ubeda
E 163 A4
Albano Laziale I 168 B2
Albanyà E 147 B3
Albaredo d'Adige I 121 B4
Albares E 151 B4
Albarracín E 152 B2
Albatana E 158 C2
Albatarrec E 153 A4
Albatera E 165 A4
Albbruck D 106 B3
Albedin E 163 A3
Albelda de Iregua
E 143 B4
Albenga I 133 A4
Albens F 118 B2
Ålberga
*Södermanland* S 56 A2
*Södermanland* S 56 B2
Albergaria-a-Nova
P 148 B1
Albergaria-a-Velha
P 148 B1
Albergaria dos Doze
P 154 B2
Alberge P 154 C2
Alberic E 159 B3
Albernoa P 160 B2
Alberobello I 173 B3
Alberoni I 122 B1
Albersdorf D 64 B2
Albersloh D 81 A3
Albert F 90 A2
Albertirsa H 112 B3
Albertville F 118 B3
Alberuela de Tubo
E 145 C3
Albi F 130 B1
Albidona I 174 B2
Albínia I 168 A1
Albino I 120 B2
Albinshof D 66 C2
Albires E 142 B1
Albisola Marina I 133 A4
Albocácer E 153 B4
Albolote E 163 A4
Albondón E 164 C1
Alborea E 158 B2
Albox E 164 B2
Albrechtice nad Vitavou
CZ 96 B2
Albstadt D 107 A4
Albufeira P 160 B1
Albuñol E 164 C1
Albuñuelas E 163 B4
Alburquerque E 155 B3
Alby
*Öland* S 63 B4
*Västernorrland* S 200 D1
Alcácer do Sal P 154 C2
Alcáçovas P 154 C2
Alcadozo E 158 C2
Alcafoces P 155 B3
Alcains P 155 B3
Alcaláde Guadaira
E 162 A2
Alcaláde Gurrea E 144 B3
Alcaláde Henares
E 151 B4
Alcaláde la Selva
E 153 B3
Alcaládel Júcar E 158 B2
Alcaláde los Gazules
E 162 B2
Alcaládel Río E 162 A2
Alcaládel Valle E 162 B2
Alcaláde Xivert E 153 B4
Alcalála Real E 163 A4
Álcamo I 176 B1
Alcampell E 145 C4
Alcanadre E 144 B1
Alcanar E 153 B4
Alcanede P 154 B2
Alcanena P 154 B2
Alcañices E 149 A3
Alcántara E 155 B4
Alcantarilha P 160 B1
Alcantarilla E 165 B3
Alcañiz E 153 A3
Alcaracejos E 156 B3
Alcara il Fusi I 177 A3
Alcaraz E 158 C1
Alcaria Ruiva P 160 B2
Alcarraz E 153 A4
Alcaudete E 163 A3
Alcaudete de la Jara
E 150 C3
Alcázar de San Juan
E 157 A4
Alcazarén E 150 A3
Alcester GB 44 A2
Alcoba E 157 A3
Alcobaça P 154 B1
Alcobendas E 151 B4
Alcocer E 151 B5
Alcochete P 154 C2
Alcoentre P 154 B2
Alcolea
*Almería* E 164 C2
*Córdoba* E 156 C3
Alcolea de Calatrava
E 157 B3
Alcolea de Cinca E 145 C4
Alcolea del Pinar E 152 A1
Alcolea del Rio E 162 A2
Alcolea de Tajo E 150 C2
Alcollarin E 156 A2
Alconchel E 155 C3
Alconera E 155 C4
Alcontar E 164 B2
Alcora E 153 B3
Alcorcón E 151 B4
Alcorisa E 153 B3
Alcossebre E 153 B4
Alcoutim P 160 B2
Alcover E 147 C2
Alcoy E 159 C3
Alcsútdoboz H 112 B2
Alcubierre E 145 C3
Alcubilla de Avellaneda
E 143 C3
Alcubilla de Nogales
E 141 B5
Alcubillas E 157 B4
Alcublas E 159 B3
Alcúdia E 167 B3
Alcudia de Guadix
E 164 B1
Alcuéscar E 155 B4
Aldbrough GB 41 B3
Aldeacentenera E 156 A2
Aldeadávila de la Ribera
E 149 A3
Aldea del Cano E 155 B4
Aldea del Fresno E 151 B3
Aldea del Obispo
E 149 B3
Aldea del Rey E 157 B4
Aldea de Trujillo E 156 A2
Aldealcorvo E 151 A4
Aldealuenga de Santa
Maria E 151 A4
Aldeamayor de San
Martin E 150 A3
Aldeanueva de
Barbarroya E 150 C2
Aldeanueva del Camino
E 149 B4
Aldeanueva del Codonal
E 150 A3
Aldeanueva de San
Bartolomé E 156 A2
Aldeapozo E 144 C1
Aldeaquemada E 157 B4
Aldea Real E 151 A3
Aldearrubia E 150 A2
Aldeaseca de la
Frontera E 150 B2
Aldeasoña E 151 A3
Aldeatejada E 150 B2
Aldeavieja E 150 B3
Aldeburgh GB 45 A5
Aldehuela E 152 B2
Aldehuela de
Calatañazor E 143 C4
Aldeia da Serra P 155 C3
Aldeia do Bispo P 149 B3
Aldeia do Mato P 154 B2
Aldeia Gavinha P 154 B1
Aldeire E 164 B1
Aldenhoven D 80 B2
Aldersbach D 95 C5
Aldershot GB 44 B3
Aldudes F 144 A2
Åled S 60 C2
Aledo E 165 B3
Alegria E 143 B4
Aleksandrovac
SRB 127 C3
Aleksandrów Kujawski
PL 76 B3
Aleksandrów Łódźki
PL 86 A3
Aleksa Šantić SRB 126 B1
Ålem S 62 B4
Alençon F 89 B4
Alenquer P 154 B1
Alenya F 146 B3
Aléria F 180 A2
Alès F 131 A3
Áles I 179 C2
Alessándria I 120 C1
Alessándria della Rocca
I 176 B2
Alessano I 173 C4
Ålesund N 198 C3
Alet-les-Bains F 146 B3
Alexandria
GB 34 C3
Alexandria *continued*
GR 182 C4
RO 17 D6
Alexandroupoli
GR 183 C7
Aleyrac F 131 A3
Alézio I 173 B4
Alfacar E 163 A4
Alfaiates P 149 B3
Alfajarin E 153 A3
Alfambra
E 152 B2
P 160 B1
Alfândega da Fé P 149 A3
Alfarela de Jafes P 148 A2
Alfarelos P 148 B1
Alfarim P 154 C1
Alfarnate E 163 B3
Alfaro E 144 B2
Alfarrás E 145 C4
Alfaz del Pi E 159 C3
Alfedena I 169 B4
Alfeizarão P 154 B1
Alfeld
*Bayern* D 95 B3
*Niedersachsen* D 72 C2
Alfena P 148 A1
Alferce P 160 B1
Alfhausen D 71 B4
Alfonsine I 135 A5
Alford
*Aberdeenshire*
GB 33 D4
*Lincolnshire* GB 41 B4
Alforja E 147 C1
Alfoz E 141 A3
Alfreton GB 40 B2
Alfta S 50 A3
Alfundão P 160 A1
Algaida E 167 B2
Algar E 162 B2
Älgarås S 55 B5
Ålgård N 52 B1
Algarinejo E 163 A3
Algarrobo E 163 B3
Algatocin E 162 B2
Algeciras E 162 B2
Algemesí E 159 B3
Algés P 154 C1
Algete E 151 B4
Alghero I 178 B2
Älghult S 62 A3
Alginet E 159 B3
Algodonales E 162 B2
Algodor
E 151 C4
P 160 B2
Algora E 151 B5
Algoso P 149 A3
Algoz P 160 B1
Älgsjö S 200 B3
Alguaire E 145 C4
Alguazas E 165 A3
Algutsrum S 63 B4
Algyő H 126 A2
Alhama de Almería
E 164 C2
Alhama de Aragón
E 152 A2
Alhama de Granada
E 163 B4
Alhama de Murcia
E 165 B3
Alhambra E 157 B4
Alhandra P 154 C1
Alhaurin de la Torre
E 163 B3
Alhaurín el Grande
E 163 B3
Alhendín E 163 A4
Alhóndiga E 151 B5
Alia E 156 A2
Ália I 176 B2
Aliağa TR 186 D1
Aliaga E 153 B3
Alibunar SRB 127 B2
Alicante E 165 A4
Alicún de Ortega E 164 B1
Alife I 170 B2
Alija del Infantado
E 141 B5
Alijó P 148 A2
Alimena I 177 B3
Alingsås S 60 B2
Alinyà E 147 B2
Aliseda E 155 B4
Ali Terme I 177 A4
Aliveri GR 185 A5
Alixan F 117 C5
Aljaraque E 161 B2
Aljezur P 160 B1
Aljorra E 165 B3
Aljubarrota P 154 B2
Aljucen E 155 B4
Aljustrel P 160 B1
Alken B 79 B5
Alkmaar NL 70 B1
Alkoven A 96 C2
Allaines F 103 A3
Allaire F 101 B3
Allanche F 116 B2
Alland A 111 A3
Allariz E 140 B3
Allassac F 129 A4
Allauch F 131 B4
Alleen N 52 B3
Allègre F 117 B3
Allemont F 118 B3
Allendale Town GB 37 B4
Allendorf D 81 B4
Allentsteig A 97 C3
Allepuz E 153 B3
Allersberg D 95 B3
Allershausen D 95 C3
Alles E 142 A2
Allevard F 118 B3
Allgunnen S 62 A3
Allihies IRL 29 C1
Allingåbro DK 58 B3
Allmannsdorf D 107 B4
Allo E 144 B1
Alloa GB 35 B4
Allogny F 103 B4
Ålloluokta S 196 B2
Allones
*Eure et Loire* F 90 C1
*Maine-et-Loire* F 102 B2
Allonnes F 102 B2
Allons F 128 B2
Allos F 132 A2
Allstedt D 82 A3
Alltwalis GB 39 C2
Allumiere I 168 A1
Almaceda P 155 B3
Almacelles E 145 C4
Almachar E 163 B3
Almada P 154 C1
Almadén E 156 B3
Almadén de la Plata
E 161 B3
Almadenejos E 156 B3
Almadrones E 151 B5
Almagro E 157 B4
Almajano E 144 C1
Almansa E 159 C2
Almansil P 160 B1
Almanza E 142 B1
Almaraz E 150 C2
Almargen E 162 B2
Almarza E 143 C4
Almásfüzitő H 112 B2
Almassora E 159 B3
Almazán E 152 A1
Almazul E 152 A1
Alme D 81 A4
Almedina E 158 C1
Almedinilla E 163 A3
Almeida
E 149 A3
P 149 B3
Almeirim P 154 B2
Almelo NL 71 B3
Almenar E 145 C4
Almenara E 159 B3
Almenar de Soria
E 152 A1
Almendra P 149 B2
Almendral E 155 C4
Almendral de la Cañada
E 150 B3
Almendralejo E 155 C4
Almenno San
Bartolomeo I 120 B2
Almere NL 70 B2
Almería E 164 C2
Almerimar E 164 C2
Almese I 119 B4
Almexial P 160 B2
Älmhult S 63 B2
Almiropotamos
GR 185 A5
Almiros GR 182 D4
Almodôvar P 160 B1
Almodóvar del Campo
E 157 B3
Almodóvar del Pinar
E 158 B2
Almodóvar del Río
E 162 A2
Almofala P 148 B2
Almogia E 163 B3
Almoharin E 156 A1
Almonacid de la Sierra
E 152 A2
Almonacid de Toledo
E 157 A4
Almonaster la Real
E 161 B3
Almondsbury GB 43 A4
Almonte E 161 B3
Almoradí E 165 A4
Almoraima E 162 B2
Almorox E 150 B3
Almoster P 154 B2
Almsele S 200 B3
Älmsta S 51 C5
Almudena E 164 A3
Almudévar E 145 B3
Almuñécar E 163 B4
Almunge S 51 C5
Almuradiel E 157 B4
Almussafes E 159 B3
Almvik S 62 A4
Alness GB 32 D2
Alnmouth GB 37 A5
Alnwick GB 37 A5
Åloppe S 51 C4
Álora E 163 B3
Alos d'Ensil E 146 B2
Alosno E 161 B2
Alozaina E 162 B3
Alpbach A 108 B2
Alpedrete de la Sierra
E 151 B4
Alpedrinha P 148 B2
Alpen D 80 A2
Alpera E 159 C2
Alphen aan de Rijn
NL 70 B1
Alpiarça P 154 B2
Alpignano I 119 B4
Alpirsbach D 93 C4
Alpu TR 187 C5
Alpuente E 159 B2
Alqueva P 160 A2
Alquézar E 145 B4
Als DK 58 B3
Alsasua E 144 B1
Alsdorf D 80 B2
Alselv DK 59 C1
Alsfeld D 81 B5
Alsike S 57 A3
Alskog S 57 C4
Alsleben D 83 A3
Alsónémedi H 112 B3
Alsótold H 112 B3
Alsóújlak H 111 B3
Alstad N 194 C6
Alstätte D 71 B3
Alsterbro S 62 B3
Alstermo S 62 B3
Alston GB 37 B4
Alsvåg N 194 B6
Alsvik N 194 C5
Alta N 192 C7
Älta S 57 A4
Altamura I 172 B2
Altarejos E 158 B1
Altaussee A 109 B4
Altavilla Irpina I 170 B2
Altavilla Silentina I 170 C3
Altdöbern D 84 A2
Altdorf
CH 107 C3
D 95 C4
Altdorf bei Nürnberg
D 95 B3
Alte P 160 B1
Altea E 159 C3
Altedo I 121 C4
Altena D 81 A3
Altenau D 82 A2
Altenberg D 84 B1
Altenberge D 71 B4
Altenbruch D 64 C1
Altenburg D 83 B4
Altenfelden A 96 C1
Altengronau D 82 B1
Altenheim D 93 C3
Altenhundem D 81 A4
Altenkirchen
*Mecklenburg-*
*Vorpommern* D 66 B2
*Radom* D 81 B3
Altenkunstadt D 82 B3
Altenmarkt
A 110 B1
D 109 A3
Altenmarkt im Pongall
A 109 B4
Altensteig D 93 C4
Altentreptow D 74 A2
Altenwalde D 64 C1
Alten-weddingen D 73 B4
Alter do Chão P 155 B3
Altfraunhofen D 95 C4
Altheim
A 109 A4
D 94 B1
Althofen A 110 C1
Altınoluk TR 186 C1
Altınova TR 186 C1
Altıntaş TR 187 C5
Altınyaka TR 189 C5
Altınyayla TR 189 B4
Altkirch F 106 B2
Altlandsberg D 74 B2
Altlewin D 74 B3
Altmannstein D 95 C3
Altmorschen D 82 A1
Altmunster A 109 B4
Altnaharra GB 32 C2
Alto Campoó E 142 A2
Altofonte I 176 A2
Altomonte I 174 B2
Alton
*Hampshire* GB 44 B3
*Staffordshire* GB 40 C2
Altopáscio I 135 B3
Altötting D 109 A3
Altreichenau D 96 C1
Alt Ruppin D 74 B1
Altshausen D 107 B4
Altstätten CH 107 B4
Altura E 159 B3
Altusried D 107 B5
Alūksne LV 8 D5
Alunda S 51 B5
Alustante E 152 B2
Alva GB 35 B4
Alvaiázere P 154 B2
Alvalade P 160 B1
Älvängen S 60 B2
Alvarenga P 148 B1
Alvares P 154 A2
Alvdal N 199 C7
Älvdalen S 49 A6
Alverca P 154 C1
Alversund N 46 B2
Alvesta S 62 B2
Alvignac F 129 B4
Alvignano I 170 B2
Ålvik N 46 B3
Alvik S 50 B1

Alvimare F 89 A4
Alviobeira P 154 B2
Alvito P 160 A2
Älvkarleby S 51 B4
Älvkarleöbruk S 51 B4
Alvor P 160 B1
Alvorge P 154 B2
Alvøy N 46 B2
Älvros S 199 C11
Alvsbacka S 55 A4
Älvsbyn S 196 D4
Älvsered S 60 B2
Alwernia PL 86 B3
Alwinton GB 37 A4
Alyth GB 35 B4
Alytus LT 13 A6
Alzénau D 93 A5
Alzey D 93 B4
Alzira E 159 B3
Alzonne F 146 A3
Amadora P 154 C1
Åmål S 55 A3
Amalfi I 170 C2
Amaliada GR 184 B2
Amance F 105 B5
Amancey F 105 B5
Amándola I 136 C2
Amantea I 175 B2
Amarante P 148 A1
Amareleja P 161 A2
Amares P 148 A1
Amaseno I 169 B3
Amasra TR 187 A7
Amatrice I 169 A3
Amay B 79 B5
Ambarnyy RUS 3 D13
Ambazac F 115 C5
Ambelonas GR 182 D4
Amberg D 95 B3
Ambérieu-en-Bugey
F 118 B2
Ambérieux-en-Dombes
F 117 A4
Ambert F 117 B3
Ambés F 128 A2
Ambjörby S 49 B5
Ambjörnarp S 60 B3
Amble GB 37 A5
Ambleside GB 36 B4
Ambleteuse F 78 B1
Amboise F 102 B2
Ambrières-les-Vallées
F 88 B3
Amden CH 107 B4
Amel B 80 B2
Amélia I 168 A2
Amélie-les-Bains-
Palalda F 146 B3
Amelinghausen D 72 A3
Amendoa P 154 B2
Amendoeira P 160 B2
Améndola I 171 B3
Amendolara I 174 B2
Amer E 147 B3
A Merca E 140 B3
Amerongen NL 70 B2
Amersfoort NL 70 B2
Amersham GB 44 B3
Amesbury GB 44 B2
Amfiklia GR 182 E4
Amfilochia GR 182 E3
Amfipoli GR 183 C5
Amfissa GR 184 A3
Amièira P 155 C3
Amieira P 154 B3
Amieiro P 148 B1
Amiens F 90 B2
Amindeo GR 182 C3
Åminne S 60 B3
Åmli N 53 B4
Amlwch GB 38 A2
Ammanford GB 39 C3
Ammarnäs S 195 E7
Åmmeberg S 55 B5
Amorbach D 94 B1
Amorebieta E 143 A4
Amorgos GR 185 C6
Amorosa P 148 A1
Amorosi I 170 B2
Åmot
Buskerud N 48 C1
Telemark N 53 A3
S 50 B3
Åmotfors S 54 A3
Åmotsdal N 53 A4
Amou F 128 C2
Ampezzo I 122 A1
Ampfing D 95 C4
Ampflwang A 109 A4
Amplepuis F 117 B4
Amposta E 153 B4
Ampthill GB 44 A3
Ampudia E 142 C2
Ampuero E 143 A3
Amriswil CH 107 B4
Åmsele S 200 B5
Amstelveen NL 70 B1
Amsterdam NL 70 B1
Amstetten A 110 A1
Amtzell D 107 B4
Amulree GB 35 B4
Amurrio E 143 A4
Amusco E 142 B2
Anacapri I 170 C2
Anadia P 148 B1
Anadon E 152 B2
Anafi GR 185 C6
Anagni I 169 B3
Anamur TR 23 C7
Ananyiv UA 17 B8
Anascaul IRL 29 B1
Ånäset S 2 D7
Åna-Sira N 52 B2
Anastaźewo PL 76 B3
Anaya de Alba E 150 B2
Ança P 148 B1
Ancaster GB 40 C3
Ancede P 148 A1
Ancenis F 101 B4
Ancerville F 91 C5
Anchuras E 156 A3
Ancona I 136 B2
Ancora P 148 A1
Ancrum GB 35 C5
Ancy-le-Franc F 104 B3
Andalo I 121 A3
Åndalsnes N 198 C4
Andance F 117 B4
Andau A 111 B4
Andebu N 53 A6
Andeer CH 107 C4
Andelfingen CH 107 B3
Andelot-Blanchville
F 105 A4
Andelot-en-Montagne
F 105 C4
Andenes N 194 A7
Andenne B 79 B5
Anderlues B 79 B4
Andermatt CH 107 C3
Andernach D 80 B3
Andernos-les-Bains
F 128 B1
Anderslöv S 66 A2
Anderstorp S 60 B3
Andijk NL 70 B2
Andoain E 144 A1
Andocs H 112 C1
Andolsheim F 106 A2
Andorra E 153 B3
Andorra La Vella
AND 146 B2
Andosilla E 144 B2
Andover GB 44 B2
Andratx E 166 B2
Andreapol RUS 9 D8
Andreas GB 36 B2
Andréspol PL 86 A3
Andrest F 145 A4
Andretta I 172 B1
Andrezieux-Bouthéon
F 117 B4
Ándria I 171 B4
Andrijevica MNE 16 D3
Andritsena GR 184 B2
Andros GR 185 B5
Andrychów PL 99 B3
Andselv N 194 A9
Andújar E 157 B3
Anduze F 131 A2
Åneby N 48 B2
Aneby S 62 A2
Añes E 143 A3
Anet F 90 C1
Anfo I 121 B3
Ang S 62 A2
Anga S 57 C4
Angaïs F 145 A3
Ånge S 199 B11
Ånge S 200 D1
Angeja P 148 B1
Ängelholm S 61 C2
Angeli FIN 193 D9
Ängelsberg S 50 C3
Anger A 110 B2
Angera I 120 B1
Angermünde D 74 A3
Angern A 97 C4
Angers F 102 B1
Angerville F 90 C2
Anghiari I 135 B5
Angle GB 39 C1
Anglès E 147 C3
Anglés F 130 B1
Angles F 114 B2
Anglesola E 147 C2
Angles sur l'Anglin
F 115 B4
Anglet F 128 C1
Anglisidhes CY 181 B2
Anglure F 91 C3
Angoulême F 115 C4
Angoulins F 114 B2
Angsö S 56 A2
Angueira P 149 A3
Angües E 145 B3
Anguiano E 143 B4
Anguillara Sabazia
I 168 A2
Anguillara Véneta
I 121 B4
Anhée B 79 B4
Anholt DK 60 C1
Aniane F 130 B2
Aniche F 78 B3
Ånimskog S 54 B3
Anina RO 16 C4
Anixi GR 182 D3
Anizy-le-Château F 91 B3
Anjalankoski FIN 8 B5
Anjan S 199 B9
Ankara TR 187 C7
Ankaran SLO 122 B2
Ankarsrum S 62 A4
Ankerlia N 192 C4
Anklam D 66 C2
Ankum D 71 B4
Anlauftal A 109 B4
Anlezy F 104 C2
Ånn S 199 B9
Annaberg A 110 B2
Annaberg-Buchholz
D 83 B5
Annaberg im Lammertal
A 109 B4
Annaburg D 83 A5
Annahütte D 84 A1
Annalong GB 27 B5
Annan GB 36 B3
Anndalsvågen N 195 E3
Anneberg
Halland S 60 B2
Jönköping S 62 A2
Annecy F 118 B3
Annelund S 60 B3
Annemasse F 118 A3
Annenskiy Most
RUS 9 B10
Annerstad S 60 C3
Annestown IRL 30 B1
Annevoie-Rouillon
B 79 B4
Annonay F 117 B4
Annot F 132 B2
Annweiler D 93 B3
Ano Poroia GR 183 B5
Añora E 156 B3
Ano Siros GR 185 B5
Anould F 106 A1
Anquela del Ducado
E 152 B1
Anröchte D 81 A4
Ans DK 59 B2
Ansager DK 59 C1
Ansbach D 94 B2
Anse F 117 B4
Anseroeul B 79 B3
Ansfelden A 110 A1
Ansião P 154 B2
Ansó E 144 B3
Ansoain E 144 B2
Anstruther GB 35 B5
Antalya TR 189 C5
Antas E 164 B3
Antegnate I 120 B2
Antequera E 163 A3
Anterselva di Mezzo
I 108 C3
Antibes F 132 B3
Antigüedad E 142 C2
Antillo I 177 B4
Antirio GR 184 A2
Antnäs S 196 D4
An t-Ob GB 31 B1
Antoing B 79 B3
Antonin PL 86 A1
Antrain F 88 B2
Antrim GB 27 B4
Antrodoco I 169 A3
Antronapiana I 119 A5
Anttis S 196 B5
Antuzede P 148 B1
Antwerp = Antwerpen
B 79 A4
Antwerpen = Antwerp
B 79 A4
Anversa d'Abruzzi
I 169 B3
Anvin F 78 B2
Anzat-le-Luguet F 116 B3
Anzi I 172 B1
Ánzio I 168 B2
Anzola d'Emilia I 135 A4
Anzón E 144 C2
Aoiz E 144 B2
Aosta I 119 B4
Apalhão P 155 B3
Apátfalva H 126 A2
Apatin SRB 125 B5
Apatity RUS 3 C13
Apc H 112 B3
Apécchio I 136 B1
Apeldoorn NL 70 B2
Apen D 71 A4
Apenburg D 73 B4
Apensen D 72 A2
A Peroxa E 140 B3
Apiro I 136 B2
Apliki CY 181 B2
Apolda D 82 A3
Apolonia GR 185 C5
A Pontenova E 141 A3
Apostag H 112 C2
Äppelbo S 49 B6
Appennino I 136 C2
Appenzell CH 107 B4
Appiano I 108 C2
Appingedam NL 71 A3
Appleby-in-
Westmorland GB 37 B4
Applecross GB 31 B3
Appledore GB 42 A2
Appoigny F 104 B2
Apremont-la-Forêt
F 92 C1
Aprica I 120 A3
Apricena I 171 B3
Aprigliano I 174 B2
Aprília I 168 B2
Apt F 131 B4
Apúlia P 148 A1
Aquiléia I 122 B2
Aquilónia I 172 B1
Aquino I 169 B3
Ar S 57 C4
Arabayona E 150 A2
Arabba I 108 C2
Araç TR 23 A7
Aracena E 161 B3
Arachova GR 184 A3
Aračinovo MK 182 A3
Arad RO 126 A3
Aradac SRB 126 B2
Aradhippou CY 181 B2
Aragnouet F 145 B4
Aragona I 176 B2
Aramits F 144 A3
Aramon F 131 B3
Aranda de Duero E 143 C3
Aranda de Moncayo
E 152 A2
Arandjelovac SRB 127 C2
Aranjuez E 151 B4
Arantzazu E 143 B4
Aranzueque E 151 B4
Aras de Alpuente
E 159 B2
Arauzo de Miel E 143 C3
Arazede P 148 B1
Arbas F 145 B4
Árbatax I 179 C3
Arbeca E 147 C1
Arberg D 94 B2
Arbesbach A 96 C2
Arboga S 56 A1
Arbois F 105 C4
Arbon CH 107 B4
Arboréa I 179 C2
Arbório I 119 B5
Årbostad N 194 B8
Arbrå S 50 A3
Arbroath GB 35 B5
Arbùcies E 147 C3
Arbuniel E 163 A4
Arbus I 179 C2
Arcachon F 128 B1
Arce I 169 B3
Arcen NL 80 A2
Arc-en-Barrois F 105 B3
Arces-Dilo F 104 A2
Arc-et-Senans F 105 B4
Arcévia I 136 B1
Arcey F 106 B1
Archanes GR 185 D6
Archangelos GR 188 C3
Archena E 165 A3
Archez E 163 B4
Archiac F 115 C3
Archidona E 163 A3
Archiestown GB 32 D3
Archivel E 164 A3
Arcidosso I 135 C4
Arcille I 135 C4
Arcis-sur-Aube F 91 C4
Arc-lès-Gray F 105 B4
Arco I 121 B3
Arcones E 151 A4
Arcos E 143 B3
Arcos de Jalón E 152 A1
Arcos de la Frontera
E 162 B2
Arcos de la Sierra
E 152 B1
Arcos de las Salinas
E 159 B2
Arcos de Valdevez
P 148 A1
Arcozelo P 148 B2
Arc-sur-Tille F 105 B4
Arcusa E 145 B4
Arcy-sur-Cure F 104 B2
Ardagh IRL 29 B2
Årdal N 52 A2
Ardala S 55 B4
Ardales E 162 B3
Årdalstangen N 47 A4
Ardara
I 178 B2
IRL 26 B2
Ardarroch GB 31 B3
Ardbeg GB 34 C1
Ardcharnich GB 32 D1
Ardchyle GB 34 B3
Ardee IRL 27 C4
Arden DK 58 B2
Ardentes F 103 C3
Ardenza I 134 B3
Ardersier GB 32 D2
Ardes F 116 B3
Ardessie GB 32 D1
Ardez CH 107 C5
Ardfert IRL 29 B2
Ardgay GB 32 D2
Ardglass GB 27 B5
Ardgroom IRL 29 C2
Ardhasig GB 31 B2
Ardino BG 183 B7
Ardisa E 144 B3
Ardkearagh IRL 29 C1
Ardlui GB 34 B3
Ardlussa GB 34 B2
Ardón E 142 B1
Ardooie B 78 B3
Ardore I 175 C2
Ardre S 57 C4
Ardres F 78 B1
Ardrishaig GB 34 B2
Ardrossan GB 34 C3
Are N 52 A1
Åre S 199 B10
Areia Branca P 154 B1
Aremark N 54 A2
Arenales de San
Gregorio E 157 A4
Arenas E 163 B3
Arenas de Iguña E 142 A2
Arenas del Rey E 163 B4
Arenas de San Juan
E 157 A4
Arenas de San Pedro
E 150 B2
Arendal N 53 B4
Arendonk B 79 A5
Arengosse F 128 B2
Arentorp S 55 B3
Arenys de Mar E 147 C3
Arenys de Munt E 147 C3
Arenzano I 133 A4
Areo E 146 B2
Areopoli GR 184 C3
Ares E 140 A2
Arès F 128 B1
Ares del Maestrat
E 153 B3
Aresvika N 198 B5
Arette F 144 A3
Aretxabaleta E 143 A4
Arevalillo E 150 B2
Arévalo E 150 A3
Arez P 155 B3
Arezzo I 135 B4
Arfeuilles F 117 A3
Argalasti GR 183 D5
Argallón E 156 B2
Argamasilla de Alba
E 157 A4
Argamasilla de
Calatrava E 157 B3
Arganda E 151 B4
Arganil P 148 B1
Argasion GR 184 B1
Argegno I 120 B2
Argelès-Gazost F 145 A3
Argelès-sur-Mer F 146 B4
Argenta I 121 C4
Argentan F 89 B3
Argentat F 116 B1
Argentera I 132 A2
Argenteuil F 90 C2
Argenthal D 93 B3
Argentiera I 178 B2
Argentona E 147 C3
Argenton-Château
F 102 C1
Argenton-sur-Creuse
F 103 C3
Argentré F 102 A1
Argentré-du-Plessis
F 101 A4
Argent-sur-Sauldre
F 103 B4
Argirades GR 182 D1
Argithanı TR 189 A6
Argos GR 184 B3
Argos Orestiko GR 182 C3
Argostoli GR 184 A1
Argote E 143 B4
Arguedas E 144 B2
Argueil F 90 B1
Arholma S 51 C6
Århus DK 59 B3
Ariano Irpino I 170 B3
Ariano nel Polésine
I 121 C5
Aribe E 144 B2
Aridea GR 182 C4
Arienzo I 170 B2
Arild S 61 C2
Arileod GB 34 B1
Arinagour GB 34 B1
Ariño E 153 A3
Arinthod F 118 A2
Arisaig GB 34 B2
Arisgotas E 157 A4
Aritzo I 179 C3
Ariza E 152 A1
Årjäng S 54 A3
Arjeplog S 195 D8
Arjona E 157 C3
Arjonilla E 157 C3
Arkasa GR 188 D2
Arkelstorp S 63 B2
Arklow IRL 30 B2
Arkösund S 56 B2
Ärla S 56 A2
Arlanc F 117 B3
Arlanzón E 143 B3
Arlebosc F 117 B4
Arlena di Castro I 168 A1
Arles F 131 B3
Arles-sur-Tech F 146 B3
Arló H 113 A4
Arlon B 92 B1
Armação de Pera
P 160 B1
Armadale
Highland GB 31 B3
West Lothian GB 35 C4
Armagh GB 27 B4
Armamar P 148 A2
Armenistis GR 185 B7
Armeno I 119 B5
Armenteros E 150 B2
Armentières F 78 B2
Armilla E 163 A4
Armiñón E 143 B4
Armoy GB 27 A4
Armuña de Tajuña
E 151 B4
Armutlu
Bursa TR 186 B3
İzmir TR 188 A2
Arnac-Pompadour
F 115 C5
Arnafjord N 46 A3
Arnage F 102 B2
Arnas F 117 A4
Årnäs S 55 B4
Arnay-le-Duc F 104 B3
Arnborg DK 59 B2
Arnbruck D 95 B4
Arnea GR 183 C5
Arneberg
Hedmark N 48 A2
Hedmark N 49 B4
Arneburg D 73 B5
Arnedillo E 144 B1
Arnedo E 144 B1
Arneguy F 144 A2
Arnés E 153 B4
Årnes IS 190 A4
Årnes
Akershus N 48 B3
Troms N 194 A9
Arnfels A 110 C2
Arnhem NL 70 C2
Arnissa GR 182 C3
Arno S 56 B3
Arnold GB 40 B2
Arnoldstein A 109 C4
Arnsberg D 81 A4
Arnschwang D 95 B4
Arnsdorf D 84 A1
Årnset N 198 B6
Arnside GB 37 B4
Arnstadt D 82 B2
Arnstein D 94 B1
Arnstorf D 95 C4
Arnum DK 59 C1
Aroche E 161 B3
Ároktő H 113 B4
Arolla CH 119 A4
Arolsen D 81 A5
Arona I 119 B5
Åros N 54 A1
Arosa
CH 107 C4
P 148 A1
Ærøskøbing DK 65 B3
Arøsund DK 59 C2
Arouca P 148 B1
Årøysund N 54 A1
Arpajon F 90 C2
Arpajon-sur-Cère
F 116 C2
Arpela FIN 196 C7
Arpino I 169 B3
Arquata del Tronto
I 136 C2
Arques F 78 B2
Arques-la-Bataille F 89 A5
Arquillos E 157 B4
Arraia-Maeztu E 143 B4
Arraiolos P 154 C2
Arrancourt F 92 C2
Arras F 78 B2
Arrasate E 143 A4
Årre DK 59 C1
Arreau F 145 B4
Arredondo E 143 A3
Arrens-Marsous F 145 B3
Arriate E 162 B2
Arrifana P 160 B1
Arrigorriaga E 143 A4
Arriondas E 142 A1
Arroba de los Montes
E 157 A3
Arrochar GB 34 B3
Arromanches-les-Bains
F 88 A3
Arronches P 155 B3
Arroniz E 144 B1
Arrou F 103 A3
Arroya E 142 B2
Arroya de Cuéllar
E 150 A3
Arroyal E 142 B2
Arroyo de la Luz E 155 B4
Arroyo del Ojanco
E 164 A2
Arroyo de San Servan
E 155 C4
Arroyomolinos de León
E 161 A3
Arroyomolinos de
Montánchez E 156 A1
Arruda dos Vinhos
P 154 C1
Arsac F 128 B2
Ars-en-Ré F 114 B2
Arsiè I 121 B4
Arsiero I 121 B4
Årslev DK 59 C3
Ársoli I 169 A3
Ars-sur-Moselle F 92 B2
Årsunda S 50 B3
Artà E 167 B3
Arta GR 182 D3
Artajona E 144 B2
Artegna I 122 A2
Arteixo E 140 A2
Artemare F 118 B2
Arten I 121 A4
Artena I 169 B2

Artenay F 103 A3
Artern D 82 A3
Artés E 147 C2
Artesa de Segre E 147 C2
Arth CH 107 B3
Arthez-de-Béarn F 145 A3
Arthon-en-Retz F 101 B4
Arthurstown IRL 30 B2
Artieda E 144 B3
Artix F 145 A3
Artotina GR 182 E4
Artsyz UA 17 B8
Artziniega E 143 A3
A Rúa E 141 B3
Arudy F 145 A3
Arundel GB 44 C3
Arveyres F 128 B2
Arvidsjaur S 196 D2
Arvieux F 118 C3
Arvika S 54 A3
Åryd
*Blekinge* S 63 B3
*Kronoberg* S 62 B2
Arzachena I 178 A3
Arzacq-Arraziguet F 128 C2
Árzana I 179 C3
Arzano F 100 B2
Aržano HR 138 B2
Arzberg D 95 A4
Arzignano I 121 B4
Arzila P 148 B1
Arzl im Pitztal A 108 B1
Arzúa E 140 B2
As B 80 A1
Aš CZ 83 B4
Ås N 54 A1
Åsa S 60 B2
Asaa DK 58 A3
Aşağıçiğil TR 189 A6
Ašanja SRB 127 C2
Åsarna S 199 C11
Åsarøy N 52 A2
Åsarp S 55 B4
Asasp F 145 A3
Åsbro S 55 A6
Åsby S 60 B2
Åsby S 62 A3
Asbygri IS 191 A9
Ascain F 144 A2
Ascea I 172 B1
Ascha D 95 B4
Aschach an der Donau A 96 C2
Aschaffenburg D 93 B5
Aschbach Markt A 110 A1
Ascheberg
*Nordrhein-Westfalen* D 81 A3
*Schleswig-Holstein* D 65 B3
Aschendorf D 71 A4
Aschersleben D 82 A3
Asciano I 135 B4
Ascó E 153 A4
Asco F 180 A2
Áscoli Piceno I 136 C2
Áscoli Satriano I 171 B3
Ascona CH 120 A1
Ascot GB 44 B3
Ascoux F 103 A4
Åse N 194 A6
Åseda S 62 A3
Åsele S 200 B3
Åsen
N 199 B8
S 49 A5
Asendorf D 72 B2
Asenovgrad BG 183 A6
Åsensbruk S 54 B3
Åseral N 52 B3
Asfeld F 91 B4
Åsgårdstrand N 54 A1
Ásgarður IS 190 D1
Asgate CY 181 B2
Ash
*Kent* GB 45 B5
*Surrey* GB 44 B3
Åshammar S 50 B3
Ashbourne
GB 40 B2
IRL 30 A2
Ashburton GB 43 B3
Ashby-de-la-Zouch GB 40 C2
Ashchurch GB 44 B1
Åsheim N 199 D8
Ashford GB 45 B4
Ashington GB 37 A5
Ashley GB 38 B4
Ashmyany BY 13 A6
Ashton Under Lyne GB 40 B1
Ashwell GB 44 A3
Asiago I 121 B4
Asipovichy BY 13 B8
Aska FIN 197 B9
Askam-in-Furness GB 36 B3
Askeaton IRL 29 B3
Asker N 48 C2
Askersund S 55 B5
Åskilje S 200 B3
Askim N 54 A2
Askland N 53 B4
Äsköping S 56 A2
Askvoll N 46 A2
Åsljunga S 61 C3
Asmunti FIN 197 D9
Asnæs DK 61 D1
As Neves E 140 B2
As Nogaís E 141 B3
Ásola I 120 B3
Asolo I 121 B4
Asos GR 184 A1
Asotthalom H 126 A1
Aspach A 109 A4
Aspang Markt A 111 B3
Aspariegos E 149 A4
Asparn an der Zaya A 97 C4
Aspatria GB 36 B3
Aspberg S 55 A4
Aspe E 165 A4
Aspet F 145 A4
Äspö S 63 B3
As Pontes de García Rodríguez E 140 A3
Aspres-sur-Buëch F 132 A1
Aspsele S 200 C4
Assafora P 154 C1
Asse B 79 B4
Assebakte N 193 C9
Assel D 72 A2
Asselborn L 92 A1
Assémini I 179 C2
Assen NL 71 B3
Assenede B 79 A3
Assens
*Aarhus Amt.* DK 58 B3
*Fyns Amt.* DK 59 C2
Assesse B 79 B5
Assisi I 136 B1
Åsskard N 198 B5
Assling D 108 B3
Asso I 120 B2
Asson F 145 A3
Ássoro I 177 B3
Assumar P 155 B3
Åsta N 48 A3
Astaffort F 129 B3
Astakos GR 184 A2
Asten NL 80 A1
Asti I 119 C5
Astipalea GR 188 C1
Astorga E 141 B4
Åstorp S 61 C2
Åsträsk S 200 B5
Astudillo E 142 B2
Asuni I 179 C2
Asványráró H 111 B4
Aszód H 112 B3
Aszófő H 111 C4
Atabey TR 189 B5
Atalaia P 154 B3
Atalandi GR 182 E4
Atalho P 154 C2
Átány H 113 B4
Atanzón E 151 B4
Ataquines E 150 A3
Atarfe E 163 A4
Atça TR 188 B3
Ateca E 152 A2
A Teixeira E 141 B3
Atella I 172 B1
Atessa I 169 A4
Ath B 79 B3
Athboy IRL 30 A2
Athea IRL 29 B2
Athenry IRL 28 A3
Athens = Athina GR 185 B4
Atherstone GB 40 C2
Athienou CY 181 A2
Athies F 90 B2
Athies-sous-Laon F 91 B3
Athina = Athens GR 185 B4
Athleague IRL 28 A3
Athlone IRL 28 A4
Athna CY 181 A2
Athy IRL 30 B2
Atienza E 151 A5
Atina I 169 B3
Atkár H 113 B3
Atlantı TR 189 A7
Atna N 199 D7
Åtorp S 55 A5
Atrå N 47 C5
Ätran S 60 B2
Atri I 169 A3
Atripalda I 170 C2
Atsiki GR 183 D7
Attendorn D 81 A3
Attichy F 90 B3
Attigliano I 168 A2
Attigny F 91 B4
Attleborough GB 41 C5
Åtvidaberg S 56 B1
Atzendorf D 73 C4
Au
*Steiermark* A 110 B2
*Vorarlberg* A 107 B4
*Bayern* D 95 C3
*Bayern* D 108 B2
Aub D 94 B2
Aubagne F 132 B1
Aubange B 92 B1
Aubel B 80 B1
Aubenas F 117 C4
Aubenton F 91 B4
Auberive F 105 B4
Aubeterre-sur-Dronne F 128 A3
Aubiet F 129 C3
Aubigné F 115 B3
Aubigny F 114 B2
Aubigny-au-Bac F 78 B3
Aubigny-en-Artois F 78 B2
Aubigny-sur-Nère F 103 B4
Aubin F 130 A1
Aubonne CH 105 C5
Aubrac F 116 C2
Aubusson F 116 B2
Auch F 129 C3
Auchencairn GB 36 B3
Auchinleck GB 36 A2
Auchterarder GB 35 B4
Auchtermuchty GB 35 B4
Auchtertyre GB 31 B3
Auchy-au-Bois F 78 B2
Audenge F 128 B1
Auderville F 88 A2
Audierne F 100 A1
Audincourt F 106 B1
Audlem GB 38 B4
Audruicq F 78 B2
Audun-le-Roman F 92 B1
Audun-le-Tiche F 92 B1
Aue
*Nordrhein-Westfalen* D 81 A4
*Sachsen* D 83 B4
Auerbach
*Bayern* D 95 B3
*Sachsen* D 83 B4
Auffach A 108 B3
Augher GB 27 B3
Aughnacloy GB 27 B4
Aughrim IRL 30 B2
Augignac F 115 C4
Augsburg D 94 C2
Augusta I 177 B4
Augusten-borg DK 64 B2
Augustfehn D 71 A4
Augustów PL 12 B5
Aukrug D 64 B2
Auktsjaur S 196 D2
Auldearn GB 32 D3
Aulendorf D 107 B4
Auletta I 172 B1
Aulla I 134 A2
Aullène F 180 B2
Aulnay F 115 B3
Aulnoye-Aymeries F 79 B3
Ault F 90 A1
Aultbea GB 31 B3
Aulum DK 59 B1
Aulus-les-Bains F 146 B2
Auma D 83 B3
Aumale F 90 B1
Aumetz F 92 B1
Aumont-Aubrac F 116 C3
Aunay-en-Bazois F 104 B2
Aunay-sur-Odon F 88 A3
Aune N 199 A10
Auneau F 90 C1
Auneuil F 90 B1
Auning DK 58 B3
Aunsetra N 199 A9
Aups F 132 B2
Aura D 82 B1
Auray F 100 B3
Aurdal N 47 B6
Aure N 198 B5
Aurich D 71 A4
Aurignac F 145 A4
Aurillac F 116 C2
Auriol F 132 B1
Auritz-Burguette E 144 B2
Aurlandsvangen N 47 B4
Auronzo di Cadore I 109 C3
Auros F 128 B2
Auroux F 117 C3
Aurskog N 48 C3
Aursmoen N 48 C3
Ausónia I 169 B3
Ausservillgraton A 109 C3
Austad N 52 B3
Austbygda N 47 B5
Aústis I 178 B3
Austmarka N 49 B4
Austre Moland N 53 B4
Austre Vikebygd N 52 A1
Austrheim N 46 B1
Auterive F 146 A2
Autheuil-Authouillet F 89 A5
Authon F 132 A2
Authon-du-Perche F 102 A2
Autol E 144 B2
Autreville F 92 C1
Autrey-lès-Gray F 105 B4
Autti FIN 197 C10
Autun F 104 C3
Auty-le-Châtel F 103 B4
Auvelais B 79 B4
Auvillar F 129 B3
Auxerre F 104 B2
Auxi-le-Château F 78 B2
Auxon F 104 A2
Auxonne F 105 B4
Auxy F 104 C3
Auzances F 116 A2
Auzon F 117 B3
Ağva TR 187 A4
Availles-Limouzine F 115 B4
Avaldsnes N 52 A1
Avallon F 104 B2
Avantas GR 183 C7
Avaviken S 195 E9
Avebury GB 44 B2
A Veiga E 141 B3
Aveiras de Cima P 154 B2
Aveiro P 148 B1
Avelgem B 79 B3
Avellino I 170 C2
Avenches CH 106 C2
A-Ver-o-Mar P 148 A1
Aversa I 170 C2
Avesnes-le-Comte F 78 B2
Avesnes-sur-Helpe F 91 A3
Avesta S 50 B3
Avetrana I 173 B3
Avezzano I 169 A3
Avià E 147 B2
Aviano I 122 A1
Aviemore GB 32 D3
Avigliana I 119 B4
Avigliano I 172 B1
Avignon F 131 B3
Ávila E 150 B3
Avilés E 141 A5
Avilley F 105 B5
Avintes P 148 A1
Avinyo E 147 C2
Àvio I 121 B3
Avioth F 92 B1
Avis P 154 B3
Avize F 91 C4
Avlonari GR 185 A5
Ávola I 177 C4
Avon F 90 C2
Avonmouth GB 43 A4
Avord F 103 B4
Avranches F 88 B2
Avril F 92 B1
Avrillé F 102 B1
Avtovac BIH 139 B4
Awans B 79 B5
Axams A 108 B2
Axat F 146 B3
Axbridge GB 43 A4
Axel NL 79 A3
Ax-les-Thermes F 146 B2
Axmarby S 51 B4
Axmarsbruk S 51 A4
Axminster GB 43 B3
Axvall S 55 B4
Ay F 91 B4
Aya E 144 A1
Ayamonte E 161 B2
Ayancık TR 23 A8
Ayaş TR 187 B7
Aydın TR 188 B2
Ayelo de Malferit E 159 C3
Ayer CH 119 A4
Ayerbe E 144 B3
Ayette F 78 B2
Ayia Napa CY 181 B2
Áyia Phyla CY 181 B2
Áyios Amvrósios CY 181 A2
Áyios Seryios CY 181 A2
Áyios Theodhoros CY 181 A3
Aykirikçi TR 187 C5
Aylesbury GB 44 B3
Ayllón E 151 A4
Aylsham GB 41 C5
Ayna E 158 C1
Ayódar E 159 B3
Ayora E 159 B2
Ayr GB 36 A2
Ayrancı TR 23 C7
Ayrancılar TR 188 A2
Ayron F 115 B4
Aysgarth GB 37 B4
Ayton GB 35 C5
Aytos BG 17 D7
Ayvacık TR 186 C1
Ayvalık TR 186 C1
Aywaille B 80 B1
Azaila E 153 A3
Azambuja P 154 B2
Azambujeira P 154 B2
Azanja SRB 127 C2
Azannes-et-Soumazannes F 92 B1
Azanúy-Alins E 145 C4
Azaruja P 155 C3
Azay-le-Ferron F 115 B5
Azay-le-Rideau F 102 B2
Azcoitia E 143 A4
Azé F 117 A4
Azeiteiros P 155 B3
Azenhas do Mar P 154 C1
Azinhaga P 154 B2
Azinhal P 160 B2
Azinheira dos Bairros P 160 A1
Aznalcázar E 161 B3
Aznalcóllar E 161 B3
Azóia P 154 B2
Azpeitia E 144 A1
Azuaga E 156 B2
Azuara E 153 A3
Azuqueca de Henares E 151 B4
Azur F 128 C1
Azzano Décimo I 122 B1


## B


Baad A 107 B5
Baamonde E 140 A3
Baar CH 107 B3
Bağarasi TR 188 B2
Baarle-Nassau B 79 A4
Baarn NL 70 B2
Babadağ TR 188 B3
Babadag RO 17 C8
Babaeski TR 186 A2
Babayevo RUS 9 C9
Babenhausen
*Bayern* D 107 A5
*Hessen* D 93 B4
Babiak PL 76 B3
Babice PL 86 B3
Babigoszcz PL 75 A3
Babimost PL 75 B4
Babina Greda HR 125 B4
Babócsa H 124 A3
Bábolma H 112 B1
Baborów PL 86 B1
Baboszewo PL 77 B5
Babót H 111 B4
Babruysk BY 13 B8
Babsk PL 87 A4
Bac GB 31 A2
Bač SRB 125 B5
Bacares E 164 B2
Bacău RO 17 B7
Baccarat F 92 C2
Bacharach D 93 A3
Backa S 50 B2
Bačka Palanka SRB 126 B1
Backaryd S 63 B3
Bačka Topola SRB 126 B1
Backe S 200 C2
Bäckebo S 62 B4
Bäckefors S 54 B3
Bäckhammar S 55 A5
Bački Breg SRB 125 B4
Bački-Brestovac SRB 126 B1
Bački Monoštor SRB 125 B4
Bački Petrovac SRB 126 B1
Bački Sokolac SRB 126 B1
Backnang D 94 C1
Bačko Gradište SRB 126 B2
Bačko Novo Selo SRB 125 B5
Bačko Petrovo Selo SRB 126 B2
Bácoli I 170 C2
Bacqueville-en-Caux F 89 A5
Bácsalmás H 126 A1
Bácsbokod H 125 A5
Bad Abbach D 95 C4
Badacsonytomaj H 111 C4
Bad Aibling D 108 B3
Badajoz E 155 C4
Badalona E 147 C3
Badalucco I 133 B3
Bad Aussee A 109 B4
Bad Bederkesa D 72 A1
Bad Bentheim D 71 B4
Bad Bergzabern D 93 B3
Bad Berka D 82 B3
Bad Berleburg D 81 A4
Bad Berneck D 95 A3
Bad Bevensen D 73 A3
Bad Bibra D 82 A3
Bad Birnbach D 95 C5
Bad Blankenburg D 82 B3
Bad Bleiberg A 109 C4
Bad Brambach D 83 B4
Bad Bramstedt D 64 C2
Bad Breisig D 80 B3
Bad Brückenau D 82 B1
Bad Buchau D 107 A4
Bad Camberg D 81 B4
Badderen N 192 C6
Bad Doberan D 65 B4
Bad Driburg D 81 A5
Bad Düben D 83 A4
Bad Dürkheim D 93 B4
Bad Dürrenberg D 83 A4
Bad Dürrheim D 107 A3
Bad Elster D 83 B4
Bad Ems D 81 B3
Baden
A 111 A3
CH 106 B3
Bádenas E 152 A2
Baden-Baden D 93 C4
Bad Endorf D 109 B3
Badenweiler D 106 B2
Baderna HR 122 B2
Bad Essen D 71 B5
Bad Fischau A 111 B3
Bad Frankenhausen D 82 A3
Bad Freienwalde D 74 B3
Bad Friedrichshall D 93 B5
Bad Füssing D 96 C1
Bad Gandersheim D 82 A2
Bad Gastein A 109 B4
Bad Gleichenberg A 110 C2
Bad Goisern A 109 B4
Bad Gottleuba D 84 B1
Bad Grund D 82 A2
Bad Hall A 110 A1
Bad Harzburg D 82 A2
Bad Herrenalb D 93 C4
Bad Hersfeld D 82 B1
Bad Hofgastein A 109 B4
Bad Homburg D 81 B4
Bad Honnef D 80 B3
Bad Hönningen D 80 B3
Badia Calavena I 121 B4
Badia Polésine I 121 B4
Badia Pratáglia I 135 B4
Badia Tedalda I 135 B5
Bad Iburg D 71 B5
Bad Innerlaterns A 107 B4
Bad Ischl A 109 B4
Bad Karlshafen D 81 A5
Bad Kemmeriboden CH 106 C2
Bądki PL 69 B3
Bad Kissingen D 82 B2
Bad Kleinen D 65 C4
Bad Kohlgrub D 108 B2
Bad König D 93 B5
Bad Königshofen D 82 B2
Bad Köstritz D 83 B4
Badkowo PL 76 B3
Bad Kreuzen A 110 A1
Bad Kreuznach D 93 B3
Bad Krozingen D 106 B2
Bad Laasphe D 81 B4
Bad Langensalza D 82 A2
Bad Lauchstädt D 83 A3
Bad Lausick D 83 A4
Bad Lauterberg D 82 A2
Bad Leonfelden A 96 C2
Bad Liebenwerda D 83 A5
Bad Liebenzell D 93 C4
Bad Lippspringe D 81 A4
Badljevina HR 124 B3
Bad Meinberg D 81 A4
Bad Mergentheim D 94 B1
Bad Mitterndorf A 109 B4
Bad Münder D 72 B2
Bad Münstereifel D 80 B2
Bad Muskau D 84 A2
Bad Nauheim D 81 B4
Bad Nenndorf D 72 B2
Bad Neuenahr-Ahrweiler D 80 B3
Bad Neustadt D 82 B2
Bad Oeynhausen D 72 B1
Badolato I 175 C2
Badolatosa E 163 A3
Bad Oldesloe D 65 C3
Badonviller F 92 C2
Bad Orb D 81 B5
Badovinci SRB 127 C1
Bad Peterstal D 93 C4
Bad Pyrmont D 72 C2
Bad Radkersburg A 110 C2
Bad Ragaz CH 107 C4
Bad Rappenau D 93 B5
Bad Reichenhall D 109 B3
Bad Saarow-Pieskow D 74 B3
Bad Sachsa D 82 A2
Bad Säckingen D 106 B2
Bad Salzdetfurth D 72 B3
Bad Salzig D 81 B3
Bad Salzuflen D 72 B1
Bad Salzungen D 82 B2
Bad Sankt Leonhard A 110 C1
Bad Sassendorf D 81 A4
Bad Schandau D 84 B2
Bad Schmiedeberg D 83 A4
Bad Schönborn D 93 B4
Bad Schussenried D 107 A4
Bad Schwalbach D 81 B4
Bad Schwartau D 65 C3
Bad Segeberg D 64 C3
Bad Soden D 81 B4
Bad Soden-Salmünster D 81 B5
Bad Sooden-Allendorf D 82 A1
Bad Sulza D 83 A3
Bad Sülze D 66 B1
Bad Tatzmannsdorf A 111 B3
Bad Tennstedt D 82 A2
Bad Tölz D 108 B2
Badules E 152 A2
Bad Urach D 94 C1
Bad Vellach A 110 C1
Bad Vilbel D 81 B4
Bad Vöslau A 111 B3
Bad Waldsee D 107 B4
Bad Wiessee D 108 B2
Bad Wildungen D 81 A5
Bad Wilsnack D 73 B4
Bad Windsheim D 94 B2
Bad Wörishofen D 108 A1
Bad Wurzach D 107 B4
Bad Zwesten D 81 A5
Bad Zwischenahn D 71 A5
Baells E 145 C4
Baena E 163 A3
Baesweiler D 80 B2
Baeza E 157 C4
Baflo NL 71 A3
Baga E 147 B2
Bagaladi I 175 C1

Bagenkop DK 65 B3
Baggetorp S 56 A2
Bagh a Chaisteil GB 31 C1
Bagheria I 176 A2
Bagn N 47 B6
Bagnacavallo I 135 A4
Bagnáia I 168 A2
Bagnara Cálabra I 175 C1
Bagnasco I 133 A4
Bagnères-de-Bigorre
F 145 A4
Bagnères-de-Luchon
F 145 B4
Bagni del Másino I 120 A2
Bagni di Lucca I 134 A3
Bagni di Rabbi I 121 A3
Bagni di Tivoli I 168 B2
Bagno di Romagna
I 135 B4
Bagnoles-de-l'Orne
F 89 B3
Bagnoli dei Trigno
I 170 B2
Bagnoli di Sopra I 121 B4
Bagnoli Irpino I 170 C3
Bagnolo Mella I 120 B3
Bagnols-en-Forêt
F 132 B2
Bagnols-sur-Cèze
F 131 A3
Bagnorégio I 168 A2
Bagolino I 121 B3
Bagrationovsk RUS 12 A4
Bagrdan SRB 127 C3
Báguena E 152 A2
Bahabón de Esgueva
E 143 C3
Bahillo E 142 B2
Báia delle Zágare
I 171 B4
Báia Domizia I 169 B3
Baia Mare RO 17 B5
Baiano I 170 C2
Baião P 148 A1
Baiersbronn D 93 C4
Baiersdorf D 94 B3
Baignes-Ste Radegonde
F 115 C3
Baigneux-les-Juifs
F 104 B3
Baildon GB 40 B2
Bailén E 157 B4
Băileşti RO 17 C5
Baileux B 91 A4
Bailieborough IRL 27 C4
Bailleul F 78 B2
Baillonville B 79 B5
Bailó E 144 B3
Bain-de-Bretagne
F 101 B4
Bains F 117 B3
Bains-les-Bains F 105 A5
Bainton GB 40 B3
Baio E 140 A2
Baiona E 140 B2
Bais F 89 B3
Baiso I 134 A3
Baiuca P 148 B2
Baja H 125 A4
Bajánsenye H 111 C3
Bajina Bašta SRB 127 D1
Bajmok SRB 126 B1
Bajna H 112 B2
Bajovo Polje MNE 139 B4
Bajša SRB 126 B1
Bak H 111 C3
Bakar HR 123 B3
Bakewell GB 40 B2
Bakio E 143 A4
Bakka N 47 C6
Bakkafjörður IS 191 A11
Bakkagerði IS 191 B12
Bække DK 59 C2
Bakken N 48 B3
Baklan TR 189 B4
Bækmarksbro DK 58 B1
Bakonybél H 111 B4
Bakonycsernye H 112 B2
Bakonyjákó H 111 B4
Bakonyszentkirály
H 111 B4
Bakonyszombathely
H 112 B1
Bakov nad Jizerou
CZ 84 B2
Bąkowiec PL 87 A5
Baks H 113 C4
Baksa H 125 B4
Bakum D 71 B5
Bala GB 38 B3
Bâlâ TR 23 B7
Balaguer E 145 C4
Balassagyarmat H 112 A3
Balástya H 113 C4
Balatonakali H 111 C4
Balatonalmádi H 112 B2
Balatonboglár H 111 C4
Balatonbozsok H 112 C2
Balatonederics H 111 C4
Balatonfenyves H 111 C4
Balatonföldvár H 112 C1
Balatonfüred H 112 C1
Balatonfüzfő H 112 B2
Balatonkenese H 112 B2
Balatonkiliti H 112 C2
Balatonlelle H 111 C4
Balatonszabadi H 112 C2
Balatonszemes H 111 C4
Balatonszentgyörgy
H 111 C4
Balazote E 158 C1
Balbeggie GB 35 B4
Balbigny F 117 B4
Balboa E 141 B4
Balbriggan IRL 30 A2
Balchik BG 17 D8
Balçova TR 188 A2
Baldock GB 44 B3
Bale HR 122 B2
Baleira E 141 A3
Baleizao P 160 A2
Balen B 79 A5
Balerma E 164 C2
Balestrand N 46 A3
Balestrate I 176 A2
Balfour GB 33 B4
Bälganet S 63 B3
Balıkesir TR 186 C2
Balıklıçeşme TR 186 B2
Bälinge S 51 C4
Balingen D 107 A3
Balingsta S 56 A3
Balintore GB 32 D3
Balizac F 128 B2
Balk NL 70 B2
Balkbrug NL 71 B3
Balla IRL 28 A2
Ballachulish GB 34 B2
Ballaghaderreen
IRL 26 C2
Ballancourt-sur-
Essonne F 90 C2
Ballantrae GB 36 A2
Ballao I 179 C3
Ballasalla GB 36 B2
Ballater GB 32 D3
Ballen DK 59 C3
Ballenstedt D 82 A3
Ballerias E 145 C3
Balleroy F 88 A3
Ballerup DK 61 D2
Ballesteros de Calatrava
E 157 B4
Ballı TR 186 B2
Ballina IRL 26 B1
Ballinalack IRL 30 A1
Ballinamore IRL 26 B3
Ballinascarty IRL 29 C3
Ballinasloe IRL 28 A3
Ballindine IRL 28 A3
Balling DK 58 B1
Ballingarry
*Limerick* IRL 29 B3
*Tipperary* IRL 30 B1
Ballingeary IRL 29 C2
Ballinhassig IRL 29 C3
Ballinluig GB 35 B4
Ballino I 121 B3
Ballinrobe IRL 28 A2
Ballinskelligs IRL 29 C1
Ballinspittle IRL 29 C3
Ballintra IRL 26 B2
Ballivor IRL 30 A2
Ballobar E 153 A4
Ballon
F 102 A2
IRL 30 B2
Ballószög H 112 C3
Ballsh AL 182 C1
Ballstad N 194 B4
Ballum DK 64 A1
Ballybay IRL 27 B4
Ballybofey IRL 26 B3
Ballybunion IRL 29 B2
Ballycanew IRL 30 B2
Ballycarry GB 27 B5
Ballycastle
GB 27 A4
IRL 26 B1
Ballyclare GB 27 B5
Ballyconneely IRL 28 A1
Ballycotton IRL 29 C3
Ballycroy IRL 26 B1
Ballydehob IRL 29 C2
Ballyferriter IRL 29 B1
Ballygawley GB 27 B3
Ballygowan GB 27 B5
Ballyhaunis IRL 28 A3
Ballyheige IRL 29 B2
Ballyjamesduff IRL 27 C3
Ballylanders IRL 29 B3
Ballylynan IRL 30 B1
Ballymahon IRL 28 A4
Ballymena GB 27 B4
Ballymoe IRL 28 A3
Ballymoney GB 27 A4
Ballymore IRL 28 A4
Ballymote IRL 26 B2
Ballynacorra IRL 29 C3
Ballynagore IRL 30 A1
Ballynahinch GB 27 B5
Ballynure GB 27 B5
Ballyragget IRL 30 B1
Ballysadare IRL 26 B2
Ballyshannon IRL 26 B2
Ballyvaughan IRL 28 A2
Ballyvourney IRL 29 C2
Ballywalter GB 27 B5
Balmaclellan GB 36 A2
Balmaseda E 143 A3
Balmazújváros H 113 B5
Balme I 119 B4
Balmedie GB 33 D4
Balmuccia I 119 B5
Balna-paling GB 32 D2
Balneario de Panticosa
E 145 B3
Balotaszállás H 126 A1
Balsa P 148 A2
Balsareny E 147 C2
Balsorano-Nuovo I 169 B3
Bålsta S 57 A3
Balsthal CH 106 B2
Balta UA 17 A8
Baltanás E 142 C2
Baltar E 140 C3
Baltasound GB 33 A6
Bălţi MD 17 B7
Baltimore IRL 29 C2
Baltinglass IRL 30 B2
Baltiysk RUS 69 A4
Baltów PL 87 A5
Balugães P 148 A1
Bælum DK 58 B3
Balve D 81 A3
Balvi LV 8 D5
Balvicar GB 34 B2
Balya TR 186 C2
Balzo I 136 C2
Bamberg D 94 B2
Bamburgh GB 37 A5
Banatska Palanka
SRB 127 C3
Banatski Brestovac
SRB 127 C2
Banatski Despotovac
SRB 126 B2
Banatski Dvor SRB 126 B2
Banatski-Karlovac
SRB 127 B3
Banatsko Arandjelovo
SRB 126 A2
Banatsko-Novo Selo
SRB 127 C2
Banaz TR 187 D4
Banbridge GB 27 B4
Banbury GB 44 A2
Banchory GB 33 D4
Bande
B 79 B5
E 140 B3
Bandholm DK 65 B4
Bandırma TR 186 B2
Bandol F 132 B1
Bandon IRL 29 C3
Bañeres E 159 C3
Banff GB 33 D4
Bangor
F 100 B2
*Down* GB 27 B5
*Gwynedd* GB 38 A2
IRL 26 B1
Bangsund N 199 A8
Banie PL 74 A3
Banja Koviljača
SRB 127 C1
Banjaloka SLO 123 B3
Banja Luka BIH 124 C3
Banjani SRB 127 C1
Banja Vručica BIH 125 C3
Banka SK 98 C1
Bankekind S 56 B1
Bankend GB 36 A3
Bankeryd S 62 A2
Bankfoot GB 35 B4
Banloc RO 126 B3
Bannalec F 100 B2
Bannes F 91 C3
Bannockburn GB 35 B4
Bañobárez E 149 B3
Bañon E 152 B2
Banon F 132 A1
Baños E 149 B4
Baños de Gigonza
E 162 B2
Baños de la Encina
E 157 B4
Baños de Molgas
E 140 B3
Baños de Rio Tobia
E 143 B4
Baños de Valdearados
E 143 C3
Bánov CZ 98 C1
Banova Jaruga HR 124 B2
Bánovce nad Bebravou
SK 98 C2
Banovići BIH 139 A4
Banovići Selo BIH 139 A4
Bánréve H 99 C4
Bansin D 66 C3
Banská Belá SK 98 C2
Banská Bystrica SK 99 C3
Banská Štiavnica
SK 98 C2
Bansko BG 183 B5
Banstead GB 44 B3
Banteer IRL 29 B3
Bantheville F 91 B5
Bantry IRL 29 C2
Bantzenheim F 106 B2
Banyalbufar E 166 B2
Banyoles E 147 B3
Banyuls-sur-Mer F 146 B4
Bapaume F 90 A2
Bar
MNE 16 D3
UA 13 D7
Barabhas GB 31 A2
Barači BIH 138 A2
Baracs H 112 C2
Baracska H 112 B2
Barahona E 151 A5
Barajes de Melo E 151 B5
Barakaldo E 143 A4
Baralla E 141 B3
Barañain E 144 B2
Baranavichy BY 13 B7
Báránd H 113 B5
Baranda SRB 127 B2
Baranello I 170 B2
Baranów Sandomierski
PL 87 B5
Baraqueville F 130 A1
Barasoain E 144 B2
Barbacena P 155 C3
Barbadás E 140 B3
Barbadillo E 149 B4
Barbadillo de Herreros
E 143 B3
Barbadillo del Mercado
E 143 B3
Barbadillo del Pez
E 143 B3
Barban HR 123 B3
Barbarano Vicento
I 121 B4
Barbariga HR 122 C2
Barbaros TR 186 B2
Barbastro E 145 B4
Barbate E 162 B2
Barbatona E 152 A1
Barbâtre F 114 B1
Barbazan F 145 A4
Barbeitos E 141 A3
Barbentane F 131 B3
Barberino di Mugello
I 135 A4
Barbezieux-St Hilaire
F 115 C3
Barbonne-Fayel F 91 C3
Barbotan-les-Thermes
F 128 C2
Barby D 73 C4
Bárcabo E 145 B4
Barca de Alva P 149 A3
Barcarrota E 155 C4
Barcellona-Pozzo di
Gotto I 177 A4
Barcelona E 147 C3
Barcelonette F 132 A2
Barcelos P 148 A1
Bárcena del Monasterio
E 141 A4
Barcena de Pie de
Concha E 142 A2
Barchfeld D 82 B2
Barcin PL 76 B2
Barcino PL 68 A1
Bárcis I 122 A1
Barco P 148 B2
Barcones E 151 A5
Barcs H 124 B3
Barcus F 144 A3
Bardejov SK 12 D4
Bårdesø DK 59 C3
Bardi I 120 C2
Bardney GB 40 B3
Bardo PL 85 B4
Bardolino I 121 B3
Bardonécchia I 118 B3
Bardoňovo SK 112 A2
Barèges F 145 B4
Barenstein D 83 B5
Barentin F 89 A4
Barenton F 88 B3
Barevo BIH 138 A3
Barfleur F 88 A2
Barga I 134 A3
Bargas E 151 C3
Barge I 119 C4
Bargemon F 132 B2
Barghe I 120 B3
Bargoed GB 39 C3
Bargrennan GB 36 A2
Bargteheide D 64 C3
Barham GB 45 B5
Bari I 173 A2
Barič Draga HR 137 A4
Barilović HR 123 B4
Bari Sardo I 179 C3
Barisciano I 169 A3
Barjac F 131 A3
Barjols F 132 B1
Barjon F 105 B3
Bårkåker N 54 A1
Barkald N 199 D7
Barkowo
*Dolnośląskie* PL 85 A4
*Pomorskie* PL 68 B2
Bârlad RO 17 B7
Bar-le-Duc F 91 C5
Barles F 132 A2
Barletta I 171 B4
Barlinek PL 75 B4
Barmouth GB 38 B2
Barmstedt D 64 C2
Barnard Castle GB 37 B5
Barnarp S 62 A2
Bärnau D 95 B4
Bärnbach A 110 B2
Barneberg D 73 B4
Barnenitz D 74 B1
Barnet GB 44 B3
Barnetby le Wold
GB 40 B3
Barneveld NL 70 B2
Barneville-Carteret
F 88 A2
Barnoldswick GB 40 B1
Barnowko PL 75 B3
Barnsley GB 40 B2
Barnstädt D 83 A3
Barnstaple GB 42 A2
Barnstorf D 72 B1
Barntrup D 72 C2
Baron F 90 B2
Baronissi I 170 C2
Barqueiro P 154 B2
Barquinha P 154 B2
Barr
F 93 C3
GB 36 A2
Barra P 148 B1
Barracas E 159 A3
Barraco E 150 B3
Barrado E 150 B2
Barrafranca I 177 B3
Barranco do Velho
P 160 B2
Barrancos P 161 A3
Barrax E 158 B1
Barrbaar D 94 C2
Barre-des-Cevennes
F 130 A2
Barreiro P 154 C1
Barreiros E 141 A3
Barrême F 132 B2
Barret-le-Bas F 132 A1
Barrhead GB 34 C3
Barrhill GB 36 A2
Barrio de Nuesra
Señora E 142 B1
Barrowford GB 40 B1
Barrow-in-Furness
GB 36 B3
Barrow upon Humber
GB 40 B3
Barruecopardo E 149 A3
Barruelo de Santullán
E 142 B2
Barruera E 145 B4
Barry GB 39 C3
Bårse DK 65 A4
Barsinghausen D 72 B2
Barssel D 71 A4
Bar-sur-Aube F 104 A3
Bar-sur-Seine F 104 A3
Barth D 66 B1
Bartholomä D 94 C1
Bartin TR 187 A7
Barton upon Humber
GB 40 B3
Barúmini I 179 C2
Baruth D 74 B2
Barvaux B 80 B1
Barver D 72 B1
Barwatd PL 99 B3
Barwice PL 68 B1
Barysaw BY 13 A8
Barzana E 141 A5
Bârzava RO 16 B4
Bárzio I 120 B2
Bas E 147 B3
Bašaid SRB 126 B2
Basaluzzo I 120 C1
Basarabeasca MD 17 B8
Basauri E 143 A4
Baschi I 168 A2
Baschurch GB 38 B4
Basconcillos del Tozo
E 143 B3
Bascones de Ojeda
E 142 B2
Basécles B 79 B3
Basel CH 106 B2
Basélice I 170 B2
Basildon GB 45 B4
Basingstoke GB 44 B2
Baška
CZ 98 B2
HR 123 C3
Baška Voda HR 138 B2
Bäsksjö S 200 B3
Baslow GB 40 B2
Başmakçı TR 189 B5
Basovizza I 122 B2
Bassacutena I 178 A3
Bassano del Grappa
I 121 B4
Bassano Romano I 168 A2
Bassecourt CH 106 B2
Bassella E 147 B2
Bassevuovdde N 193 D9
Bassou F 104 B2
Bassoues F 128 C3
Bassum D 72 B1
Båstad S 61 C2
Bastardo I 136 C1
Bastelica F 180 A2
Bastelicaccia F 180 B1
Bastia
F 180 A2
I 136 B1
Bastogne B 92 A1
Baston GB 40 C3
Bastuträsk S 200 B6
Bata H 125 A4
Batajnica SRB 127 C2
Batak BG 183 B6
Batalha P 154 B2
Bátaszék H 125 A4
Batea E 153 A4
Batelov CZ 97 B3
Bath GB 43 A4
Bathgate GB 35 C4
Batida H 126 A2
Batignano I 135 C4
Batina HR 125 B4
Bátka SK 99 C4
Batković BIH 125 C5
Batley GB 40 B2
Batnfjordsøra N 198 C4
Batočina SRB 127 C3
Bátonyterenye H 113 B3
Batrina HR 125 B3
Båtsfjord N 193 B13
Båtskärsnäs S 196 D6
Battaglia Terme I 121 B4
Bätterkinden CH 106 B2
Battice B 80 B1
Battipáglia I 170 C2
Battle GB 45 C4
Battonya H 126 A3
Batuša SRB 127 C3
Bátya H 112 C2
Bau I 179 C2
Baud F 100 B2
Baudour B 79 B3
Baugé F 102 B1
Baugy F 103 B4
Bauma CH 107 B3
Baume-les-Dames
F 105 B5
Baumholder D 93 B3
Baunatal D 81 A5
Baunei I 178 B3
Bauska LV 8 D4
Bautzen D 84 A2
Bavanište SRB 127 C2
Bavay F 79 B3
Bavilliers F 106 B1
Bavorov CZ 96 B2
Bawdsey GB 45 A5
Bawinkel D 71 B4
Bawtry GB 40 B2
Bayat TR 187 D5
Bayel F 105 A3
Bayeux F 88 A3
Bayındır TR 188 A2
Bayon F 92 C2
Bayonne F 128 C1
Bayons F 132 A2
Bayramiç TR 186 C1
Bayreuth D 95 B3
Bayrischzell D 108 B3
Baza E 164 B2
Bazas F 128 B2
Baziege F 146 A2
Bazoches-les-
Gallerandes F 103 A4
Bazoches-sur-Hoëne
F 89 B4
Bazzano I 135 A4
Beaconsfield GB 44 B3
Beade E 140 B2
Beadnell GB 37 A5
Beaminster GB 43 B4
Bearsden GB 34 C3
Beas E 161 B3
Beasain E 144 A1
Beas de Segura E 164 A2
Beattock GB 36 A3
Beaubery F 117 A4
Beaucaire F 131 B3
Beaufort
F 118 B3
IRL 29 B2
Beaufort-en Vallée
F 102 B1
Beaugency F 103 B3
Beaujeu
*Alpes-de-Haute-Provence* F 132 A2
*Rhône* F 117 A4
Beaulac F 128 B2
Beaulieu
F 103 B4
GB 44 C2
Beaulieu-sous-la-Roche
F 114 B2
Beaulieu-sur-Dordogne
F 129 B4
Beaulieu-sur-Mer F 133 B3
Beaulon F 104 C2
Beauly GB 32 D2
Beaumaris GB 38 A2
Beaumesnil F 89 A4
Beaumetz-lès-Loges
F 78 B2
Beaumont
B 79 B4
F 129 B3
Beaumont-de-Lomagne
F 129 C3
Beaumont-du-Gâtinais
F 103 A4
Beaumont-en-Argonne
F 91 B5
Beaumont-Hague F 88 A2
Beaumont-la-Ronce
F 102 B2
Beaumont-le-Roger
F 89 A4
Beaumont-sur-Oise
F 90 B2
Beaumont-sur-Sarthe
F 102 A2
Beaune F 105 B3
Beaune-la-Rolande
F 103 A4
Beaupréau F 101 B5
Beauraing B 91 A4
Beaurepaire F 117 B5

Beaurepaire-en-Bresse F 105 C4
Beaurières F 132 A1
Beauvais F 90 B2
Beauval F 90 A2
Beauville F 129 B3
Beauvoir-sur-Mer F 114 B1
Beauvoir-sur-Niort F 114 B3
Beba Veche RO 126 A2
Bebertal D 73 B4
Bebington GB 38 A3
Bebra D 82 B1
Bebrina HR 125 B3
Beccles GB 45 A5
Becedas E 150 B2
Beceite E 153 B4
Bečej SRB 126 B2
Becerreá E 141 B3
Becerril de Campos E 142 B2
Bécherel F 101 A4
Bechhofen D 94 B2
Bechyně CZ 96 B2
Becilla de Valderaduey E 142 B1
Beckfoot GB 36 B3
Beckingham GB 40 B3
Beckum D 81 A4
Beco P 154 B2
Bécon-les-Granits F 102 B1
Bečov nad Teplou CZ 83 B4
Becsehely H 111 C3
Bedale GB 37 B5
Bedames E 143 A3
Bédar E 164 B3
Bédarieux F 130 B2
Bédarrides F 131 A3
Bedburg D 80 B2
Beddgelert GB 38 A2
Beddingestrand S 66 A2
Bédée F 101 A4
Bedegkér H 112 C2
Beden TR 189 C7
Bedford GB 44 A3
Będków PL 87 A3
Bedlington GB 37 A5
Bedlno PL 77 B4
Bedmar E 163 A4
Bédoin F 131 A4
Bedónia I 134 A2
Bedretto CH 107 C3
Bedsted DK 58 B1
Bedum NL 71 A3
Bedwas GB 39 C3
Bedworth GB 40 C2
Będzin PL 86 B3
Beekbergen NL 70 B2
Beek en Donk NL 80 A1
Beelen D 71 C5
Beelitz D 74 B1
Beer GB 43 B3
Beerfelde D 74 B3
Beerfelden D 93 B4
Beernem B 78 A3
Beeskow D 74 B3
Beetsterzwaag NL 70 A3
Beetzendorf D 73 B4
Beflelay CH 106 B2
Begaljica SRB 127 C2
Bégard F 100 A2
Begejci SRB 126 B2
Begijar E 157 C4
Begijnendijk B 79 A4
Begndal N 48 B1
Begues E 147 C2
Beguildy GB 39 B3
Begur E 147 C4
Beho B 80 B1
Behringen D 82 A2
Beilen NL 71 B3
Beilngries D 95 B3
Beine-Nauroy F 91 B4
Beinwil CH 106 B3
Beiseförth D 82 A1
Beith GB 34 C3
Beitostølen N 47 A5
Beiuş RO 16 B5
Beja P 160 A2
Béjar E 149 B4
Bekçiler TR 189 C4
Békés H 113 C5
Békéscsaba H 113 C5
Bekilli TR 189 A4
Bekkarfjord N 193 B11
Bela SK 98 B2
Bélâbre F 115 B5
Bela Crkva SRB 127 C3
Belalcázar E 156 B2
Belánad Radbuzou CZ 95 B4
Belanovica SRB 127 C2
Bélapátfalva H 113 A4
Bělápod Bezdězem CZ 84 B2
Belcaire F 146 B2
Bełchatów PL 86 A3
Belchite E 153 A3
Bělčice CZ 96 B1
Belcoo GB 26 B3
Belecke D 81 A4
Beled H 111 B4
Belej HR 123 C3
Beleño E 142 A1
Bélesta F 146 B2
Belevi TR 188 A2
Belfast GB 27 B5
Belford GB 37 A5
Belfort F 106 B1
Belgentier F 132 B1
Belgern D 83 A5
Belgioioso I 120 B2
Belgodère F 180 A2
Belgooly IRL 29 C3
Belgrade = Beograd SRB 127 C2
Belhade F 128 B2
Belica HR 124 A2
Beli Manastir HR 125 B4
Belin-Bèliet F 128 B2
Belinchón E 151 B4
Belišće HR 125 B4
Bělkovice-Lašťany CZ 98 B1
Bella I 172 B1
Bellac F 115 B5
Bellágio I 120 B2
Bellananagh IRL 27 C3
Bellano I 120 A2
Bellária I 136 A1
Bellavary IRL 26 C1
Belleau F 90 B3
Belleek GB 26 B2
Bellegarde
*Gard* F 131 B3
*Loiret* F 103 B4
Bellegarde-en-Diois F 132 A1
Bellegarde-en-Marche F 116 B2
Bellegarde-sur-Valserine F 118 A2
Belle-Isle-en-Terre F 100 A2
Bellême F 89 B4
Bellenaves F 116 A3
Bellentre F 118 B3
Bellevaux F 118 A3
Bellevesvre F 105 C4
Belleville F 117 A4
Belleville-sur-Vie F 114 B2
Bellevue-la-Montagne F 117 B3
Belley F 118 B2
Bellheim D 93 B4
Bellinge DK 59 C3
Bellingham GB 37 A4
Bellinzago Novarese I 120 B1
Bellinzona CH 120 A2
Bell-lloc d'Urgell E 153 A4
Bello E 152 B2
Bellpuig d'Urgell E 147 C2
Bellreguart E 159 C3
Bellsbank GB 36 A2
Belltall E 147 C2
Belluno I 121 A5
Bellver de Cerdanya E 146 B2
Bellvis E 147 C1
Bélmez E 156 B2
Belmez de la Moraleda E 163 A4
Belmont GB 33 A6
Belmont-de-la-Loire F 117 A4
Belmonte
*Asturias* E 141 A4
*Cuenca* E 158 B1
P 148 B2
Belmonte de San José E 153 B3
Belmonte de Tajo E 151 B4
Belmont-sur-Rance F 130 B1
Belmullet IRL 26 B1
Belobreşca RO 127 C3
Beloeil B 79 B3
Belogradchik BG 16 D5
Belokorovichi UA 13 C8
Belorado E 143 B3
Belotič SRB 127 C1
Bělotin CZ 98 B1
Belovo BG 183 A6
Belozersk RUS 9 C10
Belp CH 106 C2
Belpasso I 177 B3
Belpech F 146 A2
Belper GB 40 B2
Belsay GB 37 A5
Belsk Duzy PL 87 A4
Beltinci SLO 111 C3
Beltra IRL 26 C1
Belturbet IRL 27 B3
Beluša SK 98 B2
Belvedere Maríttimo I 174 B1
Belver de Cinca E 153 A4
Belver de los Montes E 142 C1
Belvès F 129 B3
Belvezet F 130 A2
Belvis de la Jara E 150 C3
Belvis de Monroy E 150 C2
Belyy RUS 9 E8
Belz F 100 B2
Bełżec PL 13 C5
Belzig D 73 B5
Bembibre E 141 B4
Bembridge GB 44 C2
Bemmel NL 80 A1
Bemposta
*Bragança* P 149 A3
*Santarém* P 154 B2
Benabarre E 145 B4
Benacazón E 161 B3
Benaguacil E 159 B3
Benahadux E 164 C2
Benalmádena E 163 B3
Benalúa de Guadix E 164 B1
Benalúa de las Villas E 163 A4
Benalup E 162 B2
Benamargosa E 163 B3
Benamaurel E 164 B2
Benameji E 163 A3
Benamocarra E 163 B3
Benaocaz E 162 B2
Benaoján E 162 B2
Benarrabá E 162 B2
Benasque E 145 B4
Benátky nad Jizerou CZ 84 B2
Benavente
E 142 B1
P 154 C2
Benavides de Órbigo E 141 B5
Benavila P 154 B3
Bendorf D 81 B3
Benedikt SLO 110 C2
Benejama E 159 C3
Benejúzar E 165 A4
Benešov CZ 96 B2
Bénestroff F 92 C2
Benet F 114 B3
Bene Vagienna I 133 A3
Bénévent-l'Abbaye F 116 A1
Benevento I 170 B2
Benfeld F 93 C3
Benfica P 154 B2
Bengtsfors S 54 A3
Bengtsheden S 50 B2
Beničanci HR 125 B4
Benicarló E 153 B4
Benicássim E 153 B4
Benidorm E 159 C3
Benifaió E 159 B3
Beniganim E 159 C3
Benington GB 41 B4
Benisa E 159 C4
Benkovac HR 137 A4
Benllech GB 38 A2
Benneckenstein D 82 A2
Bénodet F 100 B1
Benquerencia de la Serena E 156 B2
Bensafrim P 160 B1
Bensbyn S 196 D5
Bensdorf D 73 B5
Benshausen D 82 B2
Bensheim D 93 B4
Bentley GB 44 B3
Bentwisch D 65 B5
Beočin SRB 126 B1
Beograd = Belgrade SRB 127 C2
Beragh GB 27 B3
Beranga E 143 A3
Berat AL 182 C1
Bérat F 146 A2
Beratzhausen D 95 B3
Bérbaltavár H 111 B3
Berbegal E 145 C3
Berbenno di Valtellina I 120 A2
Berberana E 143 B3
Bercedo E 143 A3
Bercel H 112 B3
Bercenay-le-Hayer F 91 C3
Berceto I 134 A2
Berchem B 79 B3
Berchidda I 178 B3
Berching D 95 B3
Berchtesgaden D 109 B4
Bérchules E 163 B4
Bercianos de Aliste E 149 A3
Berck F 78 B1
Berclaire d'Urgell E 147 C1
Berdoias E 140 A1
Berducedo E 141 A4
Berdún E 144 B3
Berdychiv UA 13 D8
Bere Alston GB 42 B2
Bereguardo I 120 B2
Berehommen N 53 A3
Berehove UA 16 A5
Berek BIH 124 B3
Beremend H 125 B4
Bere Regis GB 43 B4
Berestechko UA 13 C6
Berettyóújfalu H 113 B5
Berezhany UA 13 D6
Berezivka UA 17 B9
Berezna UA 13 C9
Berg
D 95 B3
N 195 E3
S 56 B2
Berga
*Sachsen-Anhalt* D 82 A3
Berga *continued*
*Thüringen* D 83 B4
E 147 B2
S 62 A4
Bergama TR 186 C2
Bérgamo I 120 B2
Bergara E 143 A4
Bergby S 51 B4
Berge
*Brandenburg* D 74 B1
*Niedersachsen* D 71 B4
*Telemark* N 53 A4
*Telemark* N 53 A4
Bergeforsen S 200 D3
Bergen
*Mecklenburg-Vorpommern* D 66 B2
*Niedersachsen* D 72 B2
*Niedersachsen* D 73 B3
N 46 B2
NL 70 B1
Bergen op Zoom NL 79 A4
Bergerac F 129 B3
Bergères-lés-Vertus F 91 C4
Bergeyk NL 79 A5
Berghausen D 93 C4
Bergheim D 80 B2
Berghem S 60 B2
Berg im Gau D 95 C3
Bergisch Gladbach D 80 B3
Bergkamen D 81 A3
Bergkvara S 63 B4
Berglern D 95 C3
Bergnäset S 196 D5
Bergneustadt D 81 A3
Bergsäng S 49 B5
Bergshamra S 57 A4
Bergsjö S 200 E3
Bergs slussar S 56 B1
Bergsviken S 196 D4
Bergtheim D 94 B2
Bergues F 78 B2
Bergum NL 70 A2
Bergün Bravuogn CH 107 C4
Bergwitz D 83 A4
Berhida H 112 B2
Beringel P 160 A2
Beringen B 79 A5
Berja E 164 C2
Berkåk N 199 C7
Berkeley GB 43 A4
Berkenthin D 65 C3
Berkhamsted GB 44 B3
Berkheim D 107 A5
Berkhof D 72 B2
Berkovići BIH 139 B4
Berkovitsa BG 17 D5
Berlanga E 156 B2
Berlanga de Duero E 151 A5
Berlevåg N 193 B13
Berlikum NL 70 A2
Berlin D 74 B2
Berlstedt D 82 A3
Bermeo E 143 A4
Bermillo de Sayago E 149 A3
Bern CH 106 C2
Bernalda I 174 A2
Bernardos E 150 A3
Bernartice
*Jihočeský* CZ 96 B2
*Vychodočeský* CZ 85 B3
Bernau
*Baden-Württemberg* D 106 B3
*Bayern* D 109 B3
*Brandenburg* D 74 B2
Bernaville F 90 A2
Bernay F 89 A4
Bernburg D 83 A3
Berndorf A 111 B3
Berne D 72 A1
Bernecebarati H 112 A2
Bernhardsthal A 97 C4
Bernkastel-Kues D 92 B3
Bernolakovo SK 111 A4
Bernsdorf D 84 A2
Bernstadt D 84 A2
Bernstein A 111 B3
Bernués E 145 B3
Beromünster CH 106 B3
Beroun CZ 96 B2
Berovo MK 182 B4
Berre-l'Etang F 131 B4
Berriedale GB 32 C3
Berriew GB 39 B3
Berrocal E 161 B3
Bersenbrück D 71 B4
Bershad' UA 13 D8
Bertamiráns E 140 B2
Berthåga S 51 C4
Berthelming F 92 C2
Bertincourt F 90 A2
Bertinoro I 135 A5
Bertogne B 92 A1
Bertrix B 91 B5
Berufjörður IS 191 C11
Berville-sur-Mer F 89 A4
Berwick-upon-Tweed GB 37 A4
Berzasca RO 16 C4
Berzence H 124 A3
Berzocana E 156 A2
Besalú E 147 B3
Besançon F 105 B5
Besenfeld D 93 C4
Besenyötelek H 113 B4
Besenyszög H 113 B4
Beshenkovichi BY 13 A8
Besigheim D 93 C5
Běšiny CZ 96 B1
Beška SRB 126 B2
Beşkonak TR 189 B6
Besle F 101 B4
Besnyö H 112 B2
Bessais-le-Fromental F 103 C4
Bessan F 130 B2
Besse-en-Chandesse F 116 B2
Bessèges F 131 A3
Bessé-sur-Braye F 102 B2
Bessines-sur-Gartempe F 115 B5
Best NL 79 A5
Bestorp S 56 B1
Betanzos E 140 A2
Betelu E 144 A2
Bétera E 159 B3
Beteta E 152 B1
Béthenville F 91 B4
Bethesda GB 38 A2
Béthune F 78 B2
Beton-Bazoches F 90 C3
Bettembourg L 92 B2
Betterdorf L 92 B2
Bettna S 56 B2
Béttola I 120 C2
Bettona I 136 B1
Bettyhill GB 32 C2
Betws-y-Coed GB 38 A3
Betxi E 159 B3
Betz F 90 B2
Betzdorf D 81 B3
Beuil F 132 A2
Beulah GB 39 B3
Beuzeville F 89 A4
Bevagna I 136 C1
Bevens-bruk S 56 A1
Beveren B 79 A4
Beverley GB 40 B3
Bevern D 81 A5
Beverstedt D 72 A1
Beverungen D 81 A5
Beverwijk NL 70 B1
Bex CH 119 A4
Bexhill GB 45 C4
Beyazköy TR 186 A2
Beychevelle F 128 A2
Beydağ TR 188 A3
Beyeğaç TR 188 B3
Beykoz TR 186 A4
Beynat F 129 A4
Beyoğlu TR 186 A4
Beypazarı TR 187 B6
Beyşehir TR 189 B6
Bezas E 152 B2
Bezau A 107 B4
Bezdan SRB 125 B4
Bèze F 105 B4
Bezenet F 116 A2
Bezhetsk RUS 9 D10
Béziers F 130 B2
Bezzecca I 121 B3
Biadki PL 85 A5
Biała
*Łódzkie* PL 77 C4
*Opolskie* PL 85 B5
Białaczów PL 87 A4
Biała Podlaska PL 13 B5
Biała Rawska PL 87 A4
Biale Błota PL 76 A2
Białobłoty PL 76 B2
Białobrzegi PL 87 A4
Białogard PL 67 C4
Białośliwie PL 76 A2
Białowąs PL 68 B1
Biały Bór PL 68 B1
Białystok PL 13 B5
Biancavilla I 177 B3
Bianco I 175 C2
Biandrate I 119 B5
Biar E 159 C3
Biarritz F 144 A2
Bias F 128 B1
Biasca CH 120 A1
Biatorbágy H 112 B2
Bibbiena I 135 B4
Bibbona I 134 B3
Biberach
*Baden-Württemberg* D 93 C4
*Baden-Württemberg* D 107 A4
Bibinje HR 137 A4
Bibione I 122 B2
Biblis D 93 B4
Bibury GB 44 B2
Bicaj AL 182 B2
Biccari I 171 B3
Bicester GB 44 B2
Bichl D 108 B2
Bichlbach A 108 B1
Bicorp E 159 B3
Bicos P 160 B1
Bicske H 112 B2
Bidache F 128 C1
Bidart F 144 A2
Biddinghuizen NL 70 B2
Biddulph GB 40 B1
Bideford GB 42 A2
Bidford-on-Avon GB 44 A2
Bidjovagge N 192 C6
Bie S 56 A2
Bieber D 81 B5
Biebersdorf D 74 C2
Biedenkopf D 81 B4
Biel E 144 B3
Bielany Wroclawskie PL 85 A4
Bielawa PL 85 B4
Bielawy PL 77 B4
Biel/Bienne CH 106 B2
Bielefeld D 72 B1
Biella I 119 B5
Bielsa E 145 B4
Bielsk PL 77 B4
Bielsko-Biała PL 99 B3
Bielsk Podlaski PL 13 B5
Bienenbuttel D 72 A3
Bieniow PL 84 A3
Bienservida E 158 C1
Bienvenida E 156 B1
Bierdzany PL 86 B2
Bierné F 102 B1
Biersted DK 58 A2
Bierun PL 86 B3
Bierutów PL 85 A5
Bierwart B 79 B5
Bierzwina PL 75 A4
Bierzwnik PL 75 A4
Biescas E 145 B3
Biesenthal D 74 B2
Biesiekierz PL 67 B5
Bietigheim-Bissingen D 93 C5
Bièvre B 91 B5
Bieżuń PL 77 B4
Biga TR 186 B2
Bigadiç TR 186 C3
Biganos F 128 B2
Bigas P 148 B2
Bigastro E 165 A4
Bigbury GB 42 B3
Biggar GB 36 A3
Biggin Hill GB 45 B4
Biggleswade GB 44 A3
Bignasco CH 119 A5
Biguglia F 180 A2
Bihać BIH 124 C1
Biharnagybajom H 113 B5
Bijeljani BIH 139 B4
Bijeljina BIH 125 C5
Bijuesca E 152 A2
Bilaj HR 137 A4
Bila Tserkva UA 13 D9
Bilbao E 143 A4
Bilcza PL 87 B4
Bildudalur IS 190 B2
Bileća BIH 139 C4
Bilecik TR 187 B4
Biled RO 126 B2
Biłgoraj PL 12 C5
Bilhorod-Dnistrovskyy UA 17 B9
Bilina CZ 84 B1
Bilisht AL 182 C2
Bilje HR 125 B4
Billdal S 60 B1
Billerbeck D 71 C4
Billericay GB 45 B4
Billesholm S 61 C2
Billingborough GB 40 C3
Billinge S 61 D3
Billingham GB 37 B5
Billinghay GB 41 B3
Billingsfors S 54 B3
Billingshurst GB 44 B3
Billom F 116 B3
Billsta S 200 C4
Billund DK 59 C2
Bílovec CZ 98 B2
Bilstein D 81 A4
Bilthoven NL 70 B2
Bilto N 192 C5
Bilzen B 80 B1
Bíňa SK 112 B2
Binaced E 145 C4
Binasco I 120 B2
Binbrook GB 41 B3
Binche B 79 B4
Bindlach D 95 B3
Bindslev DK 58 A3
Binefar E 145 C4
Bingen D 93 B3
Bingham GB 40 C3
Bingley GB 40 B2
Bingsjö S 50 A2
Binic F 100 A3
Binz D 66 B2
Biograd na Moru HR 137 B4
Bionaz I 119 B4
Bioska SRB 127 D1
Birda RO 126 B3
Birdlip GB 44 B1
Biri N 48 B2
Birkeland N 53 B4
Birkenfeld
*Baden-Württemberg* D 93 C4
*Rheinland-Pfalz* D 92 B3
Birkenhead GB 38 A3
Birkerød DK 61 D2
Birkfeld A 110 B2
Birkirkara M 175 C3
Birmingham GB 40 C2
Birr IRL 28 A4

Birresborn D 80 B2
Birstein D 81 B5
Biržai LT 8 D4
Birzebbugia M 175 C3
Bisáccia I 172 A1
Bisacquino I 176 B2
Bisbal de Falset E 153 A4
Biscarosse F 128 B1
Biscarosse Plage
F 128 B1
Biscarrués E 144 B3
Biscéglie I 171 B4
Bischheim F 93 C3
Bischofsheim D 82 B1
Bischofshofen A 109 B4
Bischofswerda D 84 A2
Bischofswiesen D 109 B3
Bischofszell CH 107 B4
Bischwiller F 93 C3
Bisenti I 169 A3
Bishop Auckland
GB 37 B5
Bishop's Castle GB 39 B4
Bishops Lydeard
GB 43 A3
Bishop's Stortford
GB 45 B4
Bishop's Waltham
GB 44 C2
Bisignano I 174 B2
Bisingen D 93 C4
Biskupice-Oławskie
PL 85 A5
Biskupiec PL 69 B4
Bismark D 73 B4
Bismo N 198 D5
Bispgården S 200 C2
Bispingen D 72 A2
Bissen L 92 B2
Bissendorf D 71 B5
Bisserup DK 65 A4
Bistango I 119 C5
Bistarac Donje BIH 139 A4
Bistrica BIH 124 C3
Bistrica ob Sotli
SLO 123 A4
Bistriţa RO 17 B6
Bitburg D 92 B2
Bitche F 93 B3
Bitetto I 171 B4
Bitola MK 182 B3
Bitonto I 171 B4
Bitschwiller F 106 B2
Bitterfeld D 83 A4
Bitti I 178 B3
Biville-sur-Mer F 89 A5
Bivona I 176 B2
Biwer L 92 B2
Bizeljsko SLO 123 A4
Bizovac HR 125 B4
Bjåen N 52 A3
Bjärnum S 61 C3
Bjärred S 61 D3
Bjästa S 200 C4
Bjelland
*Vest-Agder* N 52 B2
*Vest-Agder* N 52 B3
Bjelovar HR 124 B2
Bjerkreim N 52 B2
Bjerkvik N 194 B8
Bjerreby DK 65 B3
Bjerregrav DK 58 B2
Bjerringbro DK 59 B2
Bjøberg N 47 B5
Bjøllånes N 195 D5
Björbo S 50 B1
Bjordal N 46 A2
Björg IS 191 B8
Bjørkåsen N 194 B7
Björke
*Gävleborg* S 51 B4
*Östergötland* S 56 B1
Bjørkelangen N 48 C3
Björketorp S 60 B2
Björkholmen S 196 C2
Björkliden S 194 B9
Björklinge S 51 B4
Björko S 51 C6
Björkö S 60 B1
Björköby S 62 A2
Björkvik S 56 B2
Bjørn N 195 D3
Björna S 200 C4
Björneborg S 55 A5
Bjørnerod S 54 A2
Bjørnevatn N 193 C13
Björnlunda S 56 A3
Bjørnstad N 193 C14
Björsäter S 56 B2
Bjurberget S 49 B4
Bjurholm S 200 C5
Bjursås S 50 B2
Bjurtjärn S 55 A5
Bjuv S 61 C2
Blachownia PL 86 B2
Blackburn GB 38 A4
Blackpool GB 38 A3
Blackstad S 62 A4
Blackwater IRL 30 B2
Blackwaterfoot GB 34 C2
Blacy F 91 C4
Bladåker S 51 B5
Blaenau Ffestiniog
GB 38 B3
Blaenavon GB 39 C3
Blaengarw GB 39 C3
Blagaj
BIH 124 B2
Blagaj *continued*
BIH 139 B3
Blagdon GB 43 A4
Blagnac F 129 C4
Blagoevgrad BG 183 A5
Blaichach D 107 B5
Blain F 101 B4
Blainville-sur-l'Eau
F 92 C2
Blair Atholl GB 35 B4
Blairgowrie GB 35 B4
Blajan F 145 A4
Blakeney GB 39 C4
Blakstad N 53 B4
Blâmont F 92 C2
Blanca E 165 A3
Blancos E 140 C3
Blandford Forum
GB 43 B4
Blanes E 147 C3
Blangy-sur-Bresle F 90 B1
Blankaholm S 62 A4
Blankenberge B 78 A3
Blankenburg D 82 A2
Blankenfelde D 74 B2
Blankenhain D 82 B3
Blankenheim D 80 B2
Blanquefort F 128 B2
Blansko CZ 97 B4
Blanzac F 115 C4
Blanzy F 104 C3
Blaricum NL 70 B2
Blarney IRL 29 C3
Blascomillán E 150 B2
Blascosancho E 150 B3
Błaszki PL 86 A2
Blatná CZ 96 B1
Blatné SK 111 A4
Blatnice CZ 98 C1
Blatnika BIH 139 A3
Blato HR 138 C2
Blato na Cetini HR 138 B2
Blatten CH 119 A4
Blattnicksele S 195 E8
Blatzheim D 80 B2
Blaubeuren D 94 C1
Blaufelden D 94 B1
Blaustein D 94 C1
Blaydon GB 37 B5
Blaye F 128 A2
Blaye-les-Mines F 130 A1
Blázquez E 156 B2
Bleckede D 73 A3
Blecua E 145 B3
Bled SLO 123 A3
Bleiburg A 110 C1
Bleichenbach D 81 B5
Bleicherode D 82 A2
Bleik N 194 A6
Bleikvassli N 195 E4
Bléneau F 104 B1
Blentarp S 61 D3
Blera I 168 A2
Blérancourt F 90 B3
Bléré F 102 B2
Blesle F 116 B3
Blessington IRL 30 A2
Blet F 103 C4
Bletchley GB 44 B3
Bletterans F 105 C4
Blidö S 57 A4
Blidsberg S 60 B3
Blieskastel D 92 B3
Bligny-sur-Ouche
F 104 B3
Blikstorp S 55 B5
Blinisht AL 182 B1
Blinja HR 124 B2
Blizanówek PL 76 C3
Bliżyn PL 87 A4
Blois F 103 B3
Blokhus DK 58 A2
Blokzijl NL 70 B2
Blombacka S 55 A4
Blomberg D 72 C2
Blomskog S 54 A3
Blomstermåla S 62 B4
Blomvåg N 46 B1
Blönduós IS 190 B5
Błonie PL 77 B5
Blonville-sur-Mer F 89 A4
Blötberget S 50 B2
Blovice CZ 96 B1
Bloxham GB 44 A2
Blšany CZ 83 B5
Bludenz A 107 B4
Bludov CZ 97 B4
Blumberg D 107 B3
Blyberg S 49 A6
Blyth
*Northumberland*
GB 37 A5
*Nottinghamshire*
GB 40 B2
Blyth Bridge GB 35 C4
Blythburgh GB 45 A5
Blythe Bridge GB 40 C1
Bø
*Nordland* N 194 B5
*Telemark* N 53 A5
Boal E 141 A4
Boan MNE 139 C5
Boario Terme I 120 B3
Boat of Garten GB 32 D3
Boa Vista P 154 B2
Boğazkale TR 23 A8
Boğazlıyan TR 23 B8
Boba H 111 B4
Bobadilla
*Logroño* E 143 B4
*Málaga* E 163 A3
Bobadilla del Campo
E 150 A2
Bobadilla del Monte
E 151 B4
Bóbbio I 120 C2
Bóbbio Pellice I 119 C4
Bobigny F 90 C2
Bobingen D 94 C2
Böblingen D 93 C5
Bobolice PL 68 B1
Boboras E 140 B2
Boboshevo BG 182 A4
Bobowa PL 99 B4
Bobrová CZ 97 B4
Bobrovitsa UA 13 C9
Bobrowice PL 75 C4
Bobrówko PL 75 B4
Boca de Huérgano
E 142 B2
Bocairent E 159 C3
Bočar SRB 126 B2
Bocchigliero I 174 B2
Boceguillas E 151 A4
Bochnia PL 99 B4
Bocholt
B 80 A1
D 80 A2
Bochov CZ 83 B5
Bochum D 80 A3
Bockara S 62 A4
Bockenem D 72 B3
Bockfliess A 97 C4
Bockhorn D 71 A5
Bočna SLO 123 A3
Bocognano F 180 A2
Boconád H 113 B4
Bőcs H 113 A4
Boczów PL 75 B3
Boda S 50 A2
Böda S 62 A5
Boda
*Stockholm* S 51 B5
*Värmland* S 55 A4
*Västernorrland* S 200 D2
Bodafors S 62 A2
Boda Glasbruk S 63 B3
Bodajk H 112 B2
Boddam
*Aberdeenshire*
GB 33 D5
*Shetland* GB 33 B5
Boddin D 73 A4
Bödefeld-Freiheit D 81 A4
Boden S 196 D4
Bodenmais D 95 B5
Bodenteich D 73 B3
Bodenwerder D 72 C2
Bodiam GB 45 B4
Bodinnick GB 42 B2
Bodio CH 120 A1
Bodjani SRB 125 B5
Bodmin GB 42 B2
Bodø N 194 C5
Bodonal de la Sierra
E 161 A3
Bodrum TR 188 B2
Bodstedt D 66 B1
Bodträskfors S 196 C3
Bodzanów PL 77 B5
Bodzanowice PL 86 B2
Bodzechów PL 87 B5
Bodzentyn PL 87 B4
Boecillo E 150 A3
Boëge F 118 A3
Boën F 117 B3
Bogács H 113 B4
Bogadmindszent H 125 B4
Bogajo E 149 B3
Bogarra E 158 C1
Bogarre E 163 A4
Bogatić SRB 127 C1
Bogatynia PL 84 B2
Bogda RO 126 B3
Bogdaniec PL 75 B4
Boge S 57 C4
Bogen
D 95 C4
*Nordland* N 194 B7
*Nordland* N 194 C6
S 49 B4
Bogense DK 59 C3
Bognanco Fonti I 119 A5
Bognelv N 192 B6
Bognes N 194 B7
Bogno CH 120 A2
Bognor Regis GB 44 C3
Bogoria PL 87 B5
Bograngen S 49 B4
Boguchwaly PL 69 B5
Bogumiłowice PL 86 A3
Boguslav UA 13 D9
Boguszów-Gorce
PL 85 B4
Bogyiszló H 112 C2
Bohain-en-Vermandois
F 91 B3
Böheimkirchen A 110 A2
Bohinjska Bistrica
SLO 122 A2
Böhlen D 83 A4
Böhmenkirch D 94 C1
Bohmte D 71 B5
Bohonal de Ibor E 150 C2
Böhönye H 124 A3
Bohumin CZ 98 B2
Boiro E 140 B2
Bois-d'Amont F 105 C5
Boisseron F 131 B3
Boitzenburg D 74 A2
Boixols E 147 B2
Boizenburg D 73 A3
Bojadła PL 75 C4
Bojano I 170 B2
Bojanowo PL 85 A4
Bøjden DK 64 A3
Bojkovice CZ 98 B1
Bojná SK 98 C2
Bojnice SK 98 C2
Boka SRB 126 B2
Böklund D 64 B2
Bokod H 112 B2
Böksholm S 62 A2
Boksitogorsk RUS 9 C8
Bol HR 138 B2
Bolaños de Calatrava
E 157 B4
Bolayır TR 186 B1
Bolbec F 89 A4
Bölcske H 112 C2
Bolderslev DK 64 B2
Boldog H 112 B3
Boldva H 113 A4
Böle S 196 D4
Bolea E 145 B3
Bolekhiv UA 13 D5
Bolesławiec PL 84 A3
Boleszkowice PL 74 B3
Bolewice PL 75 B5
Bólgheri I 134 B3
Bolhrad UA 17 C8
Boliden S 200 B6
Bolimów PL 77 B5
Boliqueime P 160 B1
Boljevci SRB 127 C2
Boljkovci SRB 127 C2
Bolków PL 85 B4
Bollebygd S 60 B2
Bollène F 131 A3
Bólliga E 152 B1
Bollnäs S 50 A3
Bollstabruk S 200 D3
Bollullos E 161 B3
Bollullos par del
Condado E 161 B3
Bologna I 135 A4
Bologne F 105 A4
Bolognetta I 176 B2
Bolognola I 136 C2
Bologoye RUS 9 D9
Bolótana I 178 B2
Bolsena I 168 A1
Bolshaya Vradiyevka
UA 17 B9
Bolsover GB 40 B2
Bolstad S 54 B3
Bolsward NL 70 A2
Boltaña E 145 B4
Boltenhagen D 65 C4
Boltigen CH 106 C2
Bolton GB 38 A4
Bolu TR 187 B6
Bolungarvík IS 190 A2
Bolvadin TR 187 D6
Bóly H 125 B4
Bolzaneto I 133 A4
Bolzano I 108 C2
Bomba I 169 A4
Bombarral P 154 B1
Bömenzien D 73 B4
Bomlitz D 72 B2
Bømlo N 52 A1
Bøn N 48 B3
Bona F 104 B2
Bonaduz CH 107 C4
Bonanza E 161 C3
Boñar E 142 B1
Bonarbridge GB 32 D2
Bonárcado I 178 B2
Bonares E 161 B3
Bonäs S 50 A1
Bonassola I 134 A2
Bonawe GB 34 B2
Bondal N 53 A4
Bondeno I 121 C4
Bondorf D 93 C4
Bondstorp S 60 B3
Bon-Encontre F 129 B3
Bo'ness GB 35 B4
Bonete E 158 C2
Bonifacio F 180 B2
Bonigen CH 106 C2
Bonin PL 67 B5
Bonn D 80 B3
Bonnánaro I 178 B2
Bonnåsjøen N 194 C6
Bonnat F 116 A1
Bonndorf D 106 B3
Bonnétable F 102 A2
Bonnétage F 106 B1
Bonneuil-les-Eaux F 90 B2
Bonneuil-Matours
F 115 B4
Bonneval F 103 A3
Bonneval-sur-Arc
F 119 B4
Bonneville F 118 A3
Bonnières-sur-Seine
F 90 B1
Bonnieux F 131 B4
Bönnigheim D 93 B5
Bonnyrigg GB 35 C4
Bonny-sur-Loire F 103 B4
Bono
E 145 B4
I 178 B3
Bonorva I 178 B2
Bønsnes N 48 B2
Bonyhád H 125 A4
Boom B 79 A4
Boos F 89 A5
Boostedt D 64 B3
Bootle
*Cumbria* GB 36 B3
*Merseyside* GB 38 A3
Bopfingen D 94 C2
Boppard D 81 B3
Boqueixón E 140 B2
Bor
CZ 95 B4
S 62 A2
SRB 16 C5
TR 23 C8
Boran-sur-Oise F 90 B2
Borås S 60 B2
Borba P 155 C3
Borbona I 169 A3
Borča SRB 127 C2
Borci BIH 139 B4
Borculo NL 71 B3
Bordány H 126 A1
Bordeaux F 128 B2
Bordeira P 160 B1
Bordesholm D 64 B3
Borðeyri IS 190 B4
Bordighera I 133 B3
Bording DK 59 B2
Bordón E 153 B3
Bore I 120 C2
Borehamwood GB 44 B3
Borek Strzeliński PL 85 B5
Borek Wielkopolski
PL 76 C2
Boreland GB 36 A3
Borello I 135 A5
Borensberg S 56 B1
Borgafjäll S 199 A12
Borgarnes IS 190 C4
Borgentreich D 81 A5
Börger D 71 B4
Borger NL 71 B3
Borggård S 56 B1
Borghamn S 55 B5
Borghetta di Vara I 134 A2
Borghetto d'Arróscia
I 133 A3
Borghetto Santo Spirito
I 133 A4
Borgholm S 62 B4
Borghorst D 71 B4
Bórgia I 175 C2
Borgloon B 79 B5
Børglum DK 58 A2
Borgo F 180 A2
Borgo alla Collina I 135 B4
Borgo a Mozzano I 134 B3
Borgoforte I 121 B3
Borgofranco d'Ivrea
I 119 B4
Borgomanero I 119 B5
Borgomasino I 119 B4
Borgonovo Val Tidone
I 120 B2
Borgo Pace I 135 B5
Borgorose I 169 A3
Borgo San Dalmazzo
I 133 A3
Borgo San Lorenzo
I 135 B4
Borgosésia I 119 B5
Borgo Val di Taro I 134 A2
Borgo Valsugana I 121 A4
Borgo Vercelli I 119 B5
Borgstena S 60 B3
Borgue GB 36 B2
Borgund N 47 A4
Borgvik S 55 A3
Borja E 144 C2
Bork D 80 A3
Borken D 80 A2
Borkenes N 194 B7
Børkop DK 59 C2
Borkowice PL 87 A4
Borkowo PL 77 B5
Borkum D 71 A3
Borlänge S 50 B2
Borlu TR 186 D3
Bormes-les-Mimosas
F 132 B2
Bórmio I 107 C5
Bormujos E 161 B3
Borna D 83 A4
Borne NL 71 B3
Bornes P 149 A2
Borne Sulinowo PL 68 B1
Bornheim D 80 B2
Bornhöved D 64 B3
Börnicke D 74 B1
Bornos E 162 B2
Borobia E 152 A2
Borodino RUS 9 E9
Borohrádek CZ 85 B4
Boronów PL 86 B2
Bórore I 178 B2
Borosźow PL 86 B2
Borota H 126 A1
Boroughbridge GB 40 A2
Borovany CZ 96 C2
Borovichi RUS 9 C8
Borovnica SLO 123 B3
Borovo HR 125 B4
Borovsk RUS 9 E10
Borovy CZ 96 B1
Borowa PL 85 A5
Borox E 151 B4
Borrby S 66 A3
Borre
DK 65 B5
N 54 A1
Borredá E 147 B2
Borrenes E 141 B4
Borriol E 159 A3
Borris
DK 59 C1
IRL 30 B2
Borris-in-Ossory
IRL 28 B4
Borrisokane IRL 28 B3
Borrisoleigh IRL 28 B4
Borrowdale GB 36 B3
Børrud N 49 C4
Borşa RO 17 B6
Borsdorf D 83 A4
Børselv N 193 B9
Borsfa H 111 C3
Borský Mikuláš SK 98 C1
Borsodivánka H 113 B4
Borsodnádasd H 113 A4
Börte N 53 A3
Borth GB 39 B2
Bort-les-Orgues F 116 B2
Börtnan S 199 C10
Børtnes N 47 B6
Borup DK 61 D1
Boryslav UA 13 D5
Boryspil UA 13 C9
Boryszyn PL 75 B4
Borzęciczki PL 85 A5
Borzęcin PL 77 B5
Borzonasca I 134 A2
Borzyszkowy PL 68 A2
Borzytuchom PL 68 A2
Bosa I 178 B2
Bošáca SK 98 C1
Bosanci HR 123 B4
Bosanska Dubica
BIH 124 B2
Bosanska Gradiška
BIH 124 B3
Bosanska Kostajnica
BIH 124 B2
Bosanska Krupa
BIH 124 C2
Bosanski Brod BIH 125 B3
Bosanski Novi BIH 124 B2
Bosanski Petrovac
BIH 124 C2
Bosanski Šamac
BIH 125 B4
Bosansko Grahovo
BIH 138 A2
Bošany SK 98 C2
Bösárkány H 111 B4
Bosau D 65 B3
Bósca H 112 C3
Boscastle GB 42 B2
Bosco I 120 C1
Bosco Chiesanuova
I 121 B4
Bösdorf D 65 B3
Bösel D 71 A4
Bosham GB 44 C3
Bösingfeld D 72 B2
Bosjön S 49 C5
Boskoop NL 70 B1
Boskovice CZ 97 B4
Bošnjaci HR 125 B4
Bošnjane SRB 127 D3
Bossast E 145 B4
Bossolasco I 133 A4
Boštanj SLO 123 A4
Boston GB 41 C3
Bostrak N 53 A4
Böszénfa H 125 A3
Bot E 153 A4
Botajica BIH 125 C4
Bøte By DK 65 B4
Bothel GB 36 B3
Boticas P 148 A2
Botilsäter S 55 A4
Botngård N 198 B6
Botoš SRB 126 B2
Botoşani RO 17 B7
Botricello I 175 C2
Botsmark S 200 B6
Bottendorf D 81 A4
Bottesford GB 40 C3
Bottnaryd S 60 B3
Bottrop D 80 A2
Botunje SRB 127 C3
Bötzingen D 106 A2
Bouaye F 101 B4
Bouça P 149 A2
Boucau F 128 C1
Bouchain F 78 B3
Bouchoir F 90 B2
Boudreville F 105 B3
Boudry CH 106 C1
Bouesse F 103 C3
Bouguenais F 101 B4
Bouhy F 104 B2
Bouillargues F 131 B3
Bouillon B 91 B5
Bouilly F 104 A2
Bouin F 114 B2
Boulay-Moselle F 92 B2

Boulazac F 129 A3
Boule-d'Amont F 146 B3
Bouligny F 92 B1
Boulogne-sur-Gesse F 145 A4
Boulogne-sur-Mer F 78 B1
Bouloire F 102 B2
Bouquemaison F 78 B2
Bourbon-Lancy F 104 C2
Bourbon-l'Archambault F 104 C2
Bourbonne-les-Bains F 105 B4
Bourbourg F 78 B2
Bourbriac F 100 A2
Bourcefranc-le-Chapus F 114 C2
Bourdeaux F 131 A4
Bouresse F 115 B4
Bourg F 128 A2
Bourg-Achard F 89 A4
Bourganeuf F 116 B1
Bourg-Argental F 117 B4
Bourg-de-Péage F 117 B5
Bourg-de-Thizy F 117 A4
Bourg-de-Visa F 129 B3
Bourg-en-Bresse F 118 A2
Bourges F 103 B4
Bourg-et-Comin F 91 B3
Bourg-Lastic F 116 B2
Bourg-Madame F 146 B2
Bourgneuf-en-Retz F 114 A2
Bourgogne F 91 B4
Bourgoin-Jallieu F 118 B2
Bourg-St Andéol F 131 A3
Bourg-St Maurice F 119 B3
Bourgtheroulde F 89 A4
Bourgueil F 102 B2
Bourmont F 105 A4
Bourne GB 40 C3
Bournemouth GB 43 B5
Bourneville F 89 A4
Bournezeau F 114 B2
Bourran F 129 B3
Bourret F 129 C4
Bourron-Marlotte F 90 C2
Bourton-on-The-Water GB 44 B2
Boussac F 116 A2
Boussens F 145 A4
Boutersem B 79 B4
Bouttencourt F 90 B1
Bouvières F 131 A4
Bouvron F 101 B4
Bouxwiller F 93 C3
Bouzas E 140 B2
Bouzonville F 92 B2
Bova I 175 D1
Bovalino Marina I 175 C2
Bovallstrand S 54 B2
Bova Marina I 175 D1
Bovec SLO 122 A2
Bóveda E 141 B3
Bóvegno I 120 B3
Bovenau D 64 B2
Bovenden D 82 A1
Bøverdal N 198 D5
Boves F 90 B2
Bôves I 133 A3
Bovey Tracey GB 43 B3
Bovino I 171 B3
Bøvlingbjerg DK 58 B1
Bovolenta I 121 B4
Bovolone I 121 B4
Bowes GB 37 B5
Bowmore GB 34 C1
Bowness-on-Windermere GB 36 B4
Box GB 43 A4
Boxberg
*Baden-Württemberg* D 94 B1
*Sachsen* D 84 A2
Boxholm S 55 B6
Boxmeer NL 80 A1
Boxtel NL 79 A5
Boyabat TR 23 A8
Boyalıca TR 187 B4
Boyle IRL 26 C2
Bozan TR 187 C6
Božava HR 137 A3
Bozburun TR 188 C3
Bozcaada TR 186 C1
Bozdoğan TR 188 B3
Bożepole Wielkie PL 68 A2
Boževac SRB 127 C3
Božice CZ 97 C4
Boži Dar CZ 83 B4
Bozkır TR 189 B7
Bozouls F 130 A1
Bozova TR 189 B5
Bozüyük TR 187 C5
Bózzolo I 121 B3
Bra I 119 C4
Braås S 62 A3
Brabrand DK 59 B3
Bracadale GB 31 B2
Bracciano I 168 A2
Bracieux F 103 B3
Bräcke S 199 C12
Brackenheim D 93 B5
Brackley GB 44 A2
Bracklin IRL 27 C4
Bracknell GB 44 B3
Brackwede D 72 C1
Braco GB 35 B4
Brad RO 16 B5
Bradford GB 40 B2
Bradford on Avon GB 43 A4
Bradina BIH 139 B4
Brådland N 52 B2
Brædstrup DK 59 C2
Brae GB 33 A5
Braemar GB 32 D3
Braemore GB 32 D1
Braga P 148 A1
Bragança P 149 A3
Brăila RO 17 C7
Braine F 91 B3
Braine-le-Comte B 79 B4
Braintree GB 45 B4
Braives B 79 B5
Brake D 72 A1
Brakel
B 79 B3
D 81 A5
Bräkne-Hoby S 63 B3
Brålanda S 54 B3
Bralin PL 86 A1
Brallo di Pregola I 120 C2
Bram F 146 A3
Bramafan F 132 B2
Bramberg am Wildkogel A 109 B3
Bramdrupdam DK 59 C2
Bramming DK 59 C1
Brampton GB 37 B4
Bramsche D 71 B4
Branca I 136 B1
Brancaleone Marina I 175 D2
Brancaster GB 41 C4
Brand
*Nieder Östereich* A 96 C3
*Vorarlberg* A 107 B4
Brandbu N 48 B2
Brande DK 59 C2
Brande-Hornerkirchen D 64 C2
Brandenberg A 108 B2
Brandenburg D 73 B5
Brand-Erbisdorf D 83 B5
Brandis D 83 A4
Brando F 180 A2
Brandomil E 140 A2
Brandon GB 45 A4
Brandshagen D 66 B2
Brandval N 49 B4
Brandýs nad Labem CZ 84 B2
Branice PL 98 A1
Braničevo SRB 127 C3
Braniewo PL 69 A4
Branik SLO 122 B2
Brankovina SRB 127 C1
Branky CZ 98 B1
Branne F 128 B2
Brannenburg-Degerndorf D 108 B3
Brantôme F 115 C4
Branzi I 120 A2
Bras d'Asse F 132 B2
Braskereidfoss N 48 B3
Braslaw BY 13 A7
Braşov RO 17 C6
Brasparts F 100 A2
Brassac F 130 B1
Brassac-les-Mines F 116 B3
Brasschaat B 79 A4
Brastad S 54 B2
Břasy CZ 96 B1
Brąszewice PL 86 A2
Bratislava SK 111 A4
Brattfors S 55 A5
Brattvåg N 198 C3
Bratunac BIH 127 C1
Braubach D 81 B3
Braunau A 95 C5
Braunfels D 81 B4
Braunlage D 82 A2
Braunsbedra D 83 A3
Braunschweig D 73 B3
Bray IRL 30 A2
Bray Dunes F 78 A2
Bray-sur-Seine F 90 C3
Bray-sur-Somme F 90 B2
Brazatortas E 157 B3
Brazey-en-Plaine F 105 B4
Brbinj HR 137 A4
Brčko BIH 125 C4
Brdani SRB 127 D2
Brdów PL 76 B3
Brea de Tajo E 151 B4
Brécey F 88 B2
Brechen D 81 B4
Brechin GB 35 B5
Brecht B 79 A4
Brecketfeld D 80 A3
Břeclav CZ 97 C4
Brecon GB 39 C3
Brécy F 103 B4
Breda
E 147 C3
NL 79 A4
Bredaryd S 60 B3
Bredbyn S 200 C4
Breddin D 73 B5
Bredebro DK 64 A1
Bredelar D 81 A4
Bredenfelde D 74 A2
Bredsjö S 50 C1
Bredstedt D 64 B1
Bredsten DK 59 C2
Bredträsk S 200 C4
Bredviken S 195 D5
Bree B 80 A1
Bregana HR 123 B4
Breganze I 121 B4
Bregenz A 107 B4
Bréhal F 88 B2
Brehna D 83 A4
Breiðdalsvík IS 191 C11
Breidenbach F 93 B3
Breil-sur-Roya F 133 B3
Breisach D 106 A2
Breitenbach
CH 106 B2
D 81 B5
Breitenberg D 96 C1
Breitenfelde D 73 A3
Breitengussbach D 94 B2
Breivikbotn N 192 B6
Brejning DK 59 C2
Brekke N 46 A2
Brekken N 199 C8
Brekkestø N 53 B4
Brekkvasselv N 199 A10
Brekstad N 198 B6
Breland N 53 B3
Bremanger N 198 D1
Bremen D 72 A1
Bremerhaven D 72 A1
Bremervörde D 72 A2
Bremgarten CH 106 B3
Bremsnes N 198 B4
Brem-sur-Mer F 114 B2
Brenderup DK 59 C2
Brenes E 162 A2
Brengova SLO 110 C2
Brenna PL 98 B2
Breno I 120 B3
Brénod F 118 A2
Brensbach D 93 B4
Brentwood GB 45 B4
Brescello I 121 C3
Bréscia I 120 B3
Breskens NL 79 A3
Bresles F 90 B2
Bresnica SRB 127 D2
Bressana I 120 B2
Bressanone I 108 C2
Bressuire F 102 C1
Brest
BY 13 B5
F 100 A1
HR 122 B2
Brestač SRB 127 C1
Brestanica SLO 123 A4
Brestova HR 123 B3
Brestovac HR 125 B3
Bretenoux F 129 B4
Breteuil
*Eure* F 89 B4
*Oise* F 90 B2
Brétigny-sur-Orge F 90 C2
Bretten D 93 B4
Bretteville-sur-Laize F 89 A3
Brettheim D 94 B2
Breuil-Cervinia I 119 B4
Breukelen NL 70 B2
Brevik
N 53 A5
*Stockholm* S 57 A4
*Västra Götaland* S 55 B5
Breza BIH 139 A4
Brežice SLO 123 B4
Bréziers F 132 A2
Breznica HR 124 A2
Breznica Našička HR 125 B4
Březnice CZ 96 B1
Brezno SK 99 C3
Brezolles F 89 B5
Březovánad Svitavou CZ 97 B4
Brezovápod Bradlom SK 98 C1
Brezovica
SK 99 B4
SLO 123 A3
Brezovo Polje Selo BIH 125 C4
Briançon F 118 C3
Brianconnet F 132 B2
Briare F 103 B4
Briatexte F 129 C4
Briático I 175 C2
Briaucourt F 105 A4
Bribir HR 123 B3
Bricquebec F 88 A2
Bridgend
*Argyll & Bute* GB 34 C1
*Bridgend* GB 39 C3
Bridge of Cally GB 35 B4
Bridge of Don GB 33 D4
Bridge of Earn GB 35 B4
Bridge of Orchy GB 34 B3
Bridgnorth GB 39 B4
Bridgwater GB 43 A4
Břidličná CZ 98 B1
Bridlington GB 41 A3
Bridport GB 43 B4
Briec F 100 A1
Brie-Comte-Robert F 90 C2
Brienne-le-Château F 91 C4
Brienon-sur-Armançon F 104 B2
Brienz CH 106 C3
Brienza I 172 B1
Briesen D 74 B3
Brieskow Finkenheerd D 74 B3
Brietlingen D 72 A3
Brieva de Cameros E 143 B4
Briey F 92 B1
Brig CH 119 A5
Brigg GB 40 B3
Brighouse GB 40 B2
Brightlingsea GB 45 B5
Brighton GB 44 C3
Brignogan-Plage F 100 A1
Brignoles F 132 B2
Brigstock GB 40 C3
Brihuega E 151 B5
Brijuni HR 122 C2
Brillon-en-Barrois F 91 C5
Brilon D 81 A4
Brimnes N 46 B3
Brinches P 160 A2
Bríndisi I 173 B3
Brinje HR 123 B4
Brinon-sur-Beuvron F 104 B2
Brinon-sur-Sauldre F 103 B4
Brinyan GB 33 B3
Brión E 140 B2
Briones E 143 B4
Brionne F 89 A4
Brioude F 117 B3
Brioux-sur-Boutonne F 115 B3
Briouze F 89 B3
Briscous F 144 A2
Brisighella I 135 A4
Brissac-Quincé F 102 B1
Brissago CH 120 A1
Bristol GB 43 A4
Brive-la-Gaillarde F 129 A4
Briviesca E 143 B3
Brixham GB 43 B3
Brixlegg A 108 B2
Brjánslækur IS 190 B2
Brka BIH 125 C4
Brnaze HR 138 B2
Brněnec CZ 97 B4
Brno CZ 97 B4
Bro S 57 A3
Broadclyst GB 43 B3
Broadford
GB 31 B3
IRL 28 B3
Broad Haven GB 39 C1
Broadstairs GB 45 B5
Broadstone GB 43 B4
Broadway GB 44 A2
Broager DK 64 B2
Broaryd S 60 B3
Broby S 61 C4
Brobyværk DK 59 C3
Bročanac BIH 138 B3
Brocas F 128 B2
Brock D 71 B4
Brockel D 72 A2
Brockenhurst GB 44 C2
Broczyno PL 75 A5
Brod MK 182 B3
Brodalen S 54 B2
Broddbo S 50 C3
Brodek u Přerova CZ 98 B1
Broden-bach D 80 B3
Brodick GB 34 C2
Brod na Kupi HR 123 B3
Brodnica PL 69 B4
Brodnica Graniczna PL 68 A3
Brodowe Łąki PL 77 A6
Brody
*Lubuskie* PL 75 B4
*Lubuskie* PL 84 A2
*Mazowieckie* PL 77 B5
UA 13 C6
Broglie F 89 B4
Brójce PL 75 B4
Brokind S 56 B1
Brolo I 177 A3
Brome D 73 B3
Bromley GB 45 B4
Bromölla S 63 B2
Bromont-Lamothe F 116 B2
Brömsebro S 63 B3
Bromsgrove GB 44 A1
Bromyard GB 39 B4
Bronchales E 152 B2
Bronco E 149 B3
Brønderslev DK 58 A2
Broni I 120 B2
Brønnøysund N 195 E3
Brøns DK 59 C1
Bronte I 177 B3
Bronzani Mejdan BIH 124 C2
Bronzolo I 121 A4
Broons F 101 A3
Broquies F 130 A1
Brora GB 32 C3
Brørup DK 59 C2
Brösarp S 63 C2
Brossac F 115 C3
Brostrud N 47 B5
Brotas P 154 C2
Brötjärna S 50 B2
Broto E 145 B3
Brottby S 57 A4
Brøttum N 48 A2
Brou F 103 A3
Brouage F 114 C2
Brough GB 37 B4
Broughshane GB 27 B4
Broughton GB 35 C4
Broughton-in-Furness GB 36 B3
Broumov CZ 85 B4
Broût-Vernet F 116 A3
Brouvelieures F 106 A1
Brouwershaven NL 79 A3
Brovary UA 13 C9
Brovst DK 58 A2
Brownhills GB 40 C2
Brozas E 155 B4
Brozzo I 120 B3
Brtnice CZ 97 B3
Brtonigla HR 122 B2
Bruay-la-Buissière F 78 B2
Bruchhausen-Vilsen D 72 B2
Bruchsal D 93 B4
Bruck D 95 B4
Brück D 74 B1
Bruck an der Grossglocknerstrasse A 109 B3
Bruck an der Leitha A 111 A3
Bruck an der Mur A 110 B2
Brückl A 110 C1
Bruckmühl D 108 B2
Brue-Auriac F 132 B1
Brüel D 65 C4
Bruen CH 107 C3
Bruère-Allichamps F 103 C4
Bruff IRL 29 B3
Bruflat N 47 B6
Brugg CH 106 B3
Brugge B 78 A3
Brüggen D 80 A2
Brühl D 80 B2
Bruinisse NL 79 A4
Brûlon F 102 B1
Brumano I 120 B2
Brumath F 93 C3
Brummen NL 70 B3
Brumov-Bylnice CZ 98 B2
Brumunddal N 48 B2
Brunau D 73 B4
Brunehamel F 91 B4
Brünen D 80 A2
Brunete E 151 B3
Brunflo S 199 B11
Brunico I 108 C2
Brunkeberg N 53 A4
Brunn D 74 A2
Brunnen CH 107 C3
Brunsbüttel D 64 C2
Brunssum NL 80 B1
Bruntál CZ 98 B1
Brušane HR 137 A4
Brusasco I 119 B5
Brusio CH 120 A3
Brusno SK 99 C3
Brusque F 130 B1
Brussels = Bruxelles B 79 B4
Brusson I 119 B4
Brüssow D 74 A3
Brusy PL 68 B2
Bruton GB 43 A4
Bruvno HR 138 A1
Bruvoll N 48 B3
Bruxelles = Brussels B 79 B4
Bruyères F 106 A1
Bruz F 101 A4
Bruzaholm S 62 A3
Brwinów PL 77 B5
Brynamman GB 39 C3
Bryncrug GB 39 B2
Bryne N 52 B1
Brynmawr GB 39 C3
Bryrup DK 59 B2
Brzeg PL 85 B5
Brzeg Dolny PL 85 A4
Brześć Kujawski PL 76 B3
Brzesko PL 99 B4
Brzeszcze PL 99 B3
Brzezie PL 68 B1
Brzeziny
*Łódzkie* PL 87 A3
*Wielkopolskie* PL 86 A2
Brzeźnica PL 84 A3
Brzeźnica Nowa PL 86 A3
Brzeżno PL 75 A4
Brzotin SK 99 C4
Brzozie Lubawskie PL 69 B4
Bua S 60 B2
Buarcos P 148 B1
Buaveg N 52 A1
Bubbio I 119 C5
Bubry F 100 B2
Buca TR 188 A2
Bucak TR 189 B5
Bučany SK 98 C1
Buccheri I 177 B3
Buccino I 172 B1
Bucelas P 154 C1
Buch
*Bayern* D 94 C2
*Bayern* D 95 C4
Buchach UA 13 D6
Bucharest = Bucureşti RO 17 C7
Buchbach D 95 C4
Buchboden A 107 B4
Buchen D 94 B1
Büchen D 73 A3
Buchenberg D 107 B5
Buchères F 104 A3
Buchholz D 72 A2
Buchloe D 108 A1
Buchlovice CZ 98 B1
Buchlyvie GB 34 B3
Bucholz D 73 A5
Buchs CH 107 B4
Buchy F 89 A5
Bückeburg D 72 B2
Buckfastleigh GB 42 B3
Buckhaven GB 35 B4
Buckie GB 33 D4
Buckingham GB 44 A3
Buckley GB 38 A3
Bückwitz D 73 B5
Bučovice CZ 97 B5
Bucsa H 113 B5
Bucureşti = Bucharest RO 17 C7
Bucy-lés-Pierreport F 91 B3
Buczek PL 86 A3
Bud N 198 C3
Budakalasz H 112 B3
Budakeszi H 112 B2
Budal N 199 C7
Budaörs H 112 B2
Budapest H 112 B3
Búðardalur IS 190 B4
Budča SK 99 C3
Buddusò I 178 B3
Bude GB 42 B2
Budeč CZ 97 B3
Büdelsdorf D 64 B2
Budens P 160 B1
Budia E 151 B5
Budimlić-Japra BIH 124 C2
Büdingen D 81 B5
Budinšćina HR 124 A2
Budišov CZ 98 B1
Budleigh Salterton GB 43 B3
Budmerice SK 98 C1
Budoni I 178 B3
Búdrio I 135 A4
Budva MNE 16 D3
Budyněnad Ohří CZ 84 B2
Budziszewice PL 87 A3
Budzyń PL 76 B1
Bue N 52 B1
Bueña E 152 B2
Buenache de Alarcón E 158 B1
Buenache de la Sierra E 152 B2
Buenaventura E 150 B3
Buenavista de Valdavia E 142 B2
Buendia E 151 B5
Bueu E 140 B2
Buezo E 143 B3
Bugac H 112 C3
Bugarra E 159 B3
Bugeat F 116 B1
Buggerru I 179 C2
Bugojno BIH 138 A3
Bugøyfjord N 193 C13
Bugøynes N 193 C13
Bugyi H 112 B3
Buharkent TR 188 B3
Bühl
*Baden-Württemberg* D 93 C4
*Bayern* D 107 B5
Bühlertal D 93 C4
Bühlertann D 94 B1
Buia I 122 A2
Builth Wells GB 39 B3
Buin N 47 B6
Buis-les-Baronnies F 131 A4
Buitenpost NL 70 A3
Buitrago del Lozoya E 151 B4
Bujalance E 157 C3
Bujaraloz E 153 A3
Buje HR 122 B2
Bujedo E 143 B3
Bük H 111 B3
Buk PL 75 B5
Bükkösd H 125 A3
Bükkzsérc H 113 B4
Bukovci SLO 124 A1
Bukowiec PL 75 B5
Bukowina Tatrzańska PL 99 B4
Bukownica PL 86 A2
Bukowno PL 86 B3
Bülach CH 107 B3
Búland IS 191 D7

Buldan TR 188 A3
Bulgari BG 17 D7
Bulgnéville F 105 A4
Bulgurca TR 188 A2
Bülkau D 64 C1
Bulken N 46 B3
Bulkowo PL 77 B5
Bullas E 164 A3
Bulle CH 106 C2
Büllingen B 80 B2
Bullmark S 200 B6
Bulqizë AL 182 B2
Buna BIH 139 B3
Bunahowen IRL 26 B1
Bunbeg IRL 26 A2
Bunclody IRL 30 B2
Buncrana IRL 27 A3
Bunde D 71 A4
Bünde D 72 B1
Bundoran IRL 26 B2
Bunessan GB 34 B1
Bungay GB 45 A5
Bunge S 57 C5
Bunić HR 123 C4
Bunmahon IRL 30 B1
Bunnyconnellan IRL 26 B1
Buño E 140 A2
Buñol E 159 B3
Bunratty IRL 29 B3
Bunsbeek B 79 B4
Buñuel E 144 C2
Bunyola E 166 B2
Buonabitácolo I 172 B1
Buonalbergo I 170 B2
Buonconvento I 135 B4
Buonvicino I 174 B1
Burano I 122 B1
Burbach D 81 B4
Burcei I 179 C3
Burdons-sur-Rognon
F 105 A4
Burdur TR 189 B5
Bureå S 2 D7
Burela E 141 A3
Büren D 81 A4
Büren an der Aare
CH 106 B2
Burford GB 44 B2
Burg
*Cottbus* D 84 A2
*Magdeburg* D 73 B4
*Schleswig-Holstein*
D 64 C2
Burgas BG 17 D7
Burgau
A 111 B3
D 94 C2
P 160 B1
Burg auf Fehmarn D 65 B4
Burgbernheim D 94 B2
Burgdorf
CH 106 B2
D 72 B3
Burgebrach D 94 B2
Bürgel D 83 B3
Burgess Hill GB 44 C3
Burghaslach D 94 B2
Burghausen D 109 A3
Burghead GB 32 D3
Burgheim D 94 C3
Burgh le Marsh GB 41 B4
Búrgio I 176 B2
Burgkirchen D 109 A3
Burgkunstadt D 82 B3
Burglengenfeld D 95 B4
Burgo P 148 B1
Burgoberbach D 94 B2
Burgohondo E 150 B3
Burgos E 143 B3
Burgsinn D 82 B1
Burgstädt D 83 B4
Burgstall D 73 B4
Burg Stargard D 74 A2
Burgsvik S 57 C4
Burgui E 144 B3
Burguillos E 162 A2
Burguillos del Cerro
E 155 C4
Burguillos de Toledo
E 151 C4
Burhaniye TR 186 C1
Burhave D 71 A5
Burie F 114 C3
Burjassot E 159 B3
Burk D 94 B2
Burkhardtsdorf D 83 B4
Burlada E 144 B2
Burladingen D 107 A4
Burlage D 71 A4
Burness GB 33 B4
Burnham GB 44 B3
Burnham Market
GB 41 C4
Burnham-on-Crouch
GB 45 B4
Burnham-on-Sea
GB 43 A4
Burniston GB 40 A3
Burnley GB 40 B1
Burntisland GB 35 B4
Burón E 142 A1
Buronzo I 119 B5
Burovac SRB 127 C3
Burow D 74 A2
Burravoe GB 33 A5
Burrel AL 182 B2
Burret F 146 B2
Burriana E 159 B3
Burry Port GB 39 C2
Bürs A 107 B4
Bursa TR 186 B4
Burseryd S 60 B3
Bürstadt D 93 B4
Burton GB 37 B4
Burton Agnes GB 41 A3
Burton Bradstock
GB 43 B4
Burton Latimer GB 44 A3
Burton upon Stather
GB 40 B3
Burton upon Trent
GB 40 C2
Burträsk S 200 B6
Burujón E 151 C3
Burwell GB 45 A4
Burwick GB 33 C4
Bury GB 40 B1
Bury St Edmunds
GB 45 A4
Burzenin PL 86 A2
Busachi I 179 B2
Busalla I 134 A1
Busana I 134 A3
Busano I 119 B4
Busca I 133 A3
Busch D 73 B4
Buševec HR 124 B2
Bushat AL 182 B1
Bushey GB 44 B3
Bushmills GB 27 A4
Bušince SK 112 A3
Buskhyttan S 56 B2
Busko-Zdrój PL 87 B4
Busot E 159 C3
Busovača BIH 139 A3
Busquistar E 163 B4
Bussang F 106 B1
Busseto I 120 C3
Bussière-Badil F 115 C4
Bussière-Poitevine
F 115 B4
Bussolengo I 121 B3
Bussoleno I 119 B4
Bussum NL 70 B2
Busto Arsízio I 120 B1
Büsum D 64 B1
Butera I 177 B3
Butgenbach B 80 B2
Butler's Bridge IRL 27 B3
Butryny PL 77 A5
Bütschwil CH 107 B4
Buttermere GB 36 B3
Buttevant IRL 29 B3
Buttle S 57 C4
Buttstädt D 82 A3
Butzbach D 81 B4
Bützfleth D 72 A2
Bützow D 65 C4
Buxières-les-Mines
F 104 C1
Buxtehude D 72 A2
Buxton GB 40 B2
Buxy F 104 C3
Büyükçekmece
TR 186 A3
Büyükkariştiran
TR 186 A2
Büyükorhan TR 186 C3
Buzançais F 103 C3
Buzancy F 91 B4
Buzău RO 17 C7
Buzet HR 122 B2
Buziaş RO 126 B3
Buzsák H 111 C4
Buzy F 145 A3
By S 50 B3
Byala BG 17 D6
Byaroza BY 13 B6
Byczyna PL 86 A2
Bydalen S 199 B10
Bydgoszcz PL 76 A3
Bygdin N 47 A5
Bygdsiljum S 200 B6
Bygland N 53 B3
Byglandsfjord N 53 B3
Bygstad N 46 A2
Bykhaw BY 13 B9
Bykle N 52 A3
Bylderup-Bov DK 64 B2
Byrkjedal N 52 B2
Byrkjelo N 198 D3
Byrum DK 58 A3
Byšice CZ 84 B2
Byske S 2 D7
Býškovice CZ 98 B1
Bysław PL 76 A2
Bystré CZ 97 B4
Bystřice CZ 96 B2
Bystrice CZ 98 B2
Bystřice nad
Pernštejnem CZ 97 B4
Bystřice pod Hostýnem
CZ 98 B1
Bystrzyca Kłodzka
PL 85 B4
Bytča SK 98 B2
Bytnica PL 75 B4
Bytom PL 86 B2
Bytom Odrzański
PL 85 A3
Bytów PL 68 A2
Byxelkrok S 62 A5
Bzenec CZ 98 C1
Bzince SK 98 C1

## C

Çağa TR 187 B7
Cabacos P 154 B2
Cabaj-Čápor SK 98 C2
Cabana E 140 A2
Cabanac-et-Villagrains
F 128 B2
Cabañaquinta E 142 A1
Cabanas P 160 B2
Cabañas del Castillo
E 156 A2
Cabañas de Yepes
E 151 C4
Cabanelles E 147 B3
Cabanes E 153 B4
Cabanillas E 144 B2
Čabar HR 123 B3
Cabasse F 132 B2
Cabdella E 146 B2
Cabeceiras de Basto
P 148 A1
Cabeço de Vide P 155 B3
Cabella Ligure I 120 C2
Cabeza del Buey E 156 B2
Cabeza la Vaca E 161 A3
Cabezamesada E 151 C4
Cabezarados E 157 B3
Cabezarrubias del
Puerto E 157 B3
Cabezas del Villar
E 150 B2
Cabezas Rubias E 161 B2
Cabezón E 142 C2
Cabezón de la Sal
E 142 A2
Cabezón de Liébana
E 142 A2
Cabezuela E 151 A4
Cabezuela del Valle
E 149 B4
Cabo de Gata E 164 C2
Cabo de Palos E 165 B4
Cabolafuenta E 152 A1
Cabourg F 89 A3
Cabra
E 163 A3
P 148 B2
Cabrach GB 32 D3
Cabra del Santo Cristo
E 163 A4
Cábras I 179 C2
Cabreiro P 140 C2
Cabreiros E 140 A3
Cabrejas E 152 B1
Cabrela P 154 C2
Cabrillas E 149 B3
Cabuna HR 125 B3
Cacabelos E 141 B4
Čačak SRB 127 D2
Cáccamo I 176 B2
Caccuri I 174 B2
Cacela P 160 B2
Cacém P 154 C1
Cáceres E 155 B4
Cachafeiro E 140 B2
Cachopo P 160 B2
Čachtice SK 98 C1
Cacin E 163 A4
Čačinci HR 125 B3
Cadafais P 154 C1
Cadalen F 129 C5
Cadalso E 149 B3
Cadaqués E 147 B4
Cadaval P 154 B1
Cadavedo E 141 A4
Čadavica BIH 138 A2
Čadca SK 98 B2
Cadéac F 145 B4
Cadelbosco di Sopra
I 121 C3
Cadenazzo CH 120 A1
Cadenberge D 64 C2
Cadenet F 131 B4
Cadeuil F 114 C3
Cádiar E 164 C1
Cadillac F 128 B2
Cádiz E 162 B1
Čadjavica HR 125 B3
Cadouin F 129 B3
Cadours F 129 C4
Cadrete E 152 A3
Caen F 89 A3
Caerleon GB 39 C4
Caernarfon GB 38 A2
Caerphilly GB 39 C3
Caersws GB 39 B3
Cafede P 155 B3
Caggiano I 172 B1
Cagli I 136 B1
Cágliari I 179 C3
Čaglin HR 125 B3
Cagnano Varano I 171 B3
Cagnes-sur-Mer F 132 B3
Caher IRL 29 B4
Caherciveen IRL 29 C1
Caherdaniel IRL 29 C1
Cahors F 129 B4
Cahul MD 17 C8
Caiazzo I 170 B2
Caion E 140 A2
Cairndow GB 34 B3
Cairnryan GB 36 B1
Cairo Montenotte I 133 A4
Caister-on-Sea GB 41 C5
Caistor GB 41 B3
Caivano I 170 C2
Cajarc F 129 B4
Čajniče BIH 139 B5
Çakırlar TR 189 C5
Çakmak TR 187 C6
Čakovec HR 124 A2
Çal TR 189 A4
Cala E 161 B3
Calabritto I 172 B1
Calaceite E 153 B4
Calacuccia F 180 A2
Cala d'Or E 167 B3
Calaf E 147 C2
Calafat RO 17 C5
Calafell E 147 C2
Cala Galdana E 167 B3
Cala Gonone I 178 B3
Calahonda
*Granada* E 163 B4
*Málaga* E 163 B3
Calahorra E 144 B2
Calais F 78 B1
Cala Llonga E 166 C1
Calalzo di Cadore I 109 C3
Cala Millor E 167 B3
Calamocha E 152 B2
Calamonte E 155 C4
Cala Morell E 167 A3
Calanais GB 31 A2
Calañas E 161 B3
Calanda E 153 B3
Calangiánus I 178 B3
Călăraşi RO 17 C7
Cala Ratjada E 167 B3
Calascibetta I 177 B3
Calasetta I 179 C2
Calasparra E 164 A3
Calatafimi I 176 B1
Calatayud E 152 A2
Calatorao E 152 A2
Calau D 84 A1
Calbe D 73 C4
Calcena E 152 A2
Calcinelli I 136 B1
Calco I 120 B2
Caldarola I 136 B2
Caldaro sulla strada del
Vino I 121 A4
Caldas da Rainha
P 154 B1
Caldas de Bo i E 145 B4
Caldas de Malavella
E 147 C3
Caldas de Reis E 140 B2
Caldas de San Jorge
P 148 B1
Caldas de Vizela P 148 A1
Caldaso de los Vidrios
E 150 B3
Caldbeck GB 36 B3
Caldearenas E 145 B3
Caldelas P 148 A1
Calders E 147 C2
Caldes de Montbui
E 147 C3
Caldicot GB 39 C4
Caldirola I 120 C2
Caledon GB 27 B4
Calella
*Barcelona* E 147 C3
*Girona* E 147 C4
Calenzana F 180 A1
Calera de León E 161 A3
Calera y Chozas E 150 C3
Caleruega E 143 C3
Caleruela E 150 C2
Cales de Mallorca
E 167 B3
Calestano I 134 A3
Calfsound GB 33 B4
Calgary GB 34 B1
Calimera I 173 B4
Calitri I 172 B1
Calizzano I 133 A4
Callac F 100 A2
Callan IRL 30 B1
Callander GB 35 B3
Callas F 132 B2
Calliano
*Piemonte* I 119 B5
*Trentino Alto Adige*
I 121 B4
Callington GB 42 B2
Callosa de Ensarriá
E 159 C3
Callosa de Segura
E 165 A4
Callús E 147 C2
Čalma SRB 127 B1
Calmbach D 93 C4
Calne GB 43 A5
Calolziocorte I 120 B2
Calonge E 147 C4
Čalovec SK 112 B1
Calpe E 159 C4
Caltabellotta I 176 B2
Caltagirone I 177 B3
Caltanissetta I 177 B3
Caltavuturo I 176 B2
Çaltılıbük TR 186 C3
Caltojar E 151 A5
Caluire-et-Cuire F 117 B4
Caluso I 119 B4
Calvello I 172 B1
Calvi F 180 A1
Calviá E 166 B2
Calvinet F 116 C2
Calvisson F 131 B3
Calvörde D 73 B4
Calw D 93 C4
Calzada de Calatrava
E 157 B4
Calzada de Valdunciel
E 150 A2
Calzadilla de los Barros
E 155 C4
Cam GB 43 A4
Camaiore I 134 B3
Camarasa E 145 C4
Camarena E 151 B3
Camarès F 130 B1
Camaret-sur-Aigues
F 131 A3
Camaret-sur-Mer F 100 A1
Camarillas E 153 B3
Camariñas E 140 A1
Camarma E 151 B4
Camarzana de Tera
E 141 B4
Camas E 162 A1
Camastra I 176 B2
Cambados E 140 B2
Cambarinho P 148 B1
Camberley GB 44 B3
Cambil E 163 A4
Cambligeu F 78 B2
Cambo-les-Bains F 144 A2
Camborne GB 42 B1
Cambrai F 78 B3
Cambre E 140 A2
Cambridge GB 45 A4
Cambrils E 147 C2
Cambs D 65 C4
Camburg D 83 A3
Camden GB 44 B3
Cameleño E 142 A2
Camelford GB 42 B2
Çameli TR 189 B4
Camelle E 140 A1
Camerano I 136 B2
Camerino I 136 B2
Camerota I 172 B1
Camigliatello Silano
I 174 B2
Caminha P 148 A1
Caminomorisco E 149 B3
Caminreal E 152 B2
Camisano Vicentino
I 121 B4
Camlıdere TR 187 B7
Cammarata I 176 B2
Camogli I 134 A2
Camors F 100 B3
Camp IRL 29 B2
Campagna I 172 B1
Campagnano di Roma
I 168 A2
Campagnático I 135 C4
Campan F 145 A4
Campana I 174 B2
Campanario E 156 B2
Campanillas E 163 B3
Campano E 162 B1
Campaspero E 151 A3
Campbeltown GB 34 C2
Campello E 165 A4
Campelos P 154 B1
Campi Bisénzio I 135 B4
Campico López E 165 B3
Campíglia Maríttima
I 134 B3
Campillo de Altobuey
E 158 B2
Campillo de Aragón
E 152 A2
Campillo de Arenas
E 163 A4
Campillo de Llerena
E 156 B2
Campillos E 162 A3
Câmpina RO 17 C6
Campi Salentina I 173 B4
Campli I 136 C2
Campo E 145 B4
Campobasso I 170 B2
Campobello di Licata
I 176 B2
Campobello di Mazara
I 176 B1
Campo da Feira E 140 A3
Campodársego I 121 B4
Campo de Bacerros
E 141 B3
Campo de Caso E 142 A1
Campo de Criptana
E 157 A4
Campodolcino I 120 A2
Campofelice di Roccella
I 176 B2
Campofiorito I 176 B2
Campofórmido I 122 A2
Campofranco I 176 B2
Campofrio E 161 B3
Campogalliano I 121 C3
Campo Ligure I 133 A4
Campolongo I 109 C3
Campo Lugar E 156 A2
Campo Maior P 155 B3
Campomanes E 141 A5
Campomarino I 170 B3
Campo Molino I 133 A3
Campomono F 180 B1
Campo Real E 151 B4
Camporeale I 176 B2
Camporeggiano I 136 B1
Camporrells E 145 C4
Camporrobles E 158 B2
Campos P 148 A2
Camposa P 148 A1
Camposampiero I 121 B4
Camposanto I 121 C4
Campos del Port E 167 B3
Camposines E 153 A4
Campotéjar E 163 A4
Campotosto I 169 A3
Campo Túres I 108 C2
Camprodón E 147 B3
Campsegret F 129 B3
Camrose GB 39 C1
Camuñas E 157 A4
Çamyolu TR 189 C7
Çan TR 186 B2
Cana I 135 C4
Cañada del Hoyo
E 158 B2
Cañadajuncosa E 158 B1
Cañada Rosal E 162 A2
Čanak HR 123 C4
Çanakkale TR 186 B1
Canale I 119 C4
Canales
*Asturias* E 141 B5
*Castellón de la Plana*
E 159 B3
Canals E 159 C3
Canal San Bovo I 121 A4
Cañamares E 152 B1
Cañamero E 156 A2
Cañar E 163 B4
Cañate la Real E 162 B2
Cañaveral E 155 B4
Cañaveral de León
E 161 A3
Cañaveras E 152 B1
Cañaveruelas E 151 B5
Canazei I 108 C2
Cancale F 88 B2
Cancellara I 172 B1
Cancello ed Arnone
I 170 B2
Cancon F 129 B3
Canda E 141 B4
Candamil E 140 A3
Candanchu E 145 B3
Çandarlı TR 186 D1
Candas E 141 A5
Candasnos E 153 A4
Candé F 101 B4
Candela I 172 A1
Candelario E 150 B2
Candeleda E 150 B2
Cándia Lomellina I 120 B1
Candide Casamazzagno
I 109 C3
Candin E 141 B4
Candosa P 148 B2
Canecas P 154 C1
Canelli I 119 C5
Canena E 157 B4
Canencia E 151 B4
Canero E 141 A4
Canet F 130 B2
Canet de Mar E 147 C3
Canet d'en Berenguer
E 159 B3
Cañete E 158 A2
Cañete de las Torres
E 163 A3
Canet-Plage F 146 B4
Canfranc E 145 B3
Cangas
*Lugo* E 141 A3
*Pontevedra* E 140 B2
Cangas de Narcea
E 141 A4
Cangas de Onís E 142 A1
Canha P 154 C2
Canhestros P 160 A1
Canicattì I 176 B2
Canicattini Bagni I 177 B4
Canicosa de la Sierra
E 143 C3
Caniles E 164 B2
Canillas de Aceituno
E 163 B3
Canino I 168 A1
Canisy F 88 A2
Cañizal E 150 A2
Cañizo E 142 C1
Canjáyar E 164 C2
Çankırı TR 23 A7
Cannai I 179 C2
Cannara I 136 B1
Cánnero Riviera I 120 A1
Cannes F 132 B3
Canneto
*Sicilia* I 177 A3
*Toscana* I 135 B3
Canneto sull'Oglio
I 120 B3
Cannich GB 32 D2
Cannóbio I 120 A1
Cannock GB 40 C1
Canonbie GB 36 A4
Canosa di Púglia I 171 B4
Can Pastilla E 166 B2
C'an Picafort E 167 B3
Cantalapiedra E 150 A2
Cantalejo E 151 A4
Cantalgallo E 161 A3
Cantalice I 169 A2
Cantalpino E 150 A2

Cantalupo in Sabina I 168 A2
Cantanhede P 148 B1
Cantavieja E 153 B3
Čantavir SRB 126 B1
Canterbury GB 45 B5
Cantiano I 136 B1
Cantillana E 162 A2
Cantiveros E 150 B3
Cantoria E 164 B2
Cantù I 120 B2
Canvey GB 45 B4
Cany-Barville F 89 A4
Canyet de Mar E 147 C3
Caol GB 34 B2
Cáorle I 122 B1
Caorso I 120 B2
Capáccio I 172 B1
Capaci I 176 A2
Capálbio I 168 A1
Capánnori I 134 B3
Caparde BIH 139 A4
Caparroso E 144 B2
Capbreton F 128 C1
Capdenac-Gare F 116 C2
Capdepera E 167 B3
Cap-de-Pin F 128 B2
Capel Curig GB 38 A3
Capellades E 147 C2
Capena I 168 A2
Capendu F 146 A3
Capestang F 130 B2
Capestrano I 169 A3
Cap Ferret F 128 B1
Capileira E 163 B4
Capinha P 148 B2
Ca'Pisani I 122 C1
Capistrello I 169 B3
Capizzi I 177 B3
Čaplje BIH 124 C2
Čapljina BIH 139 B3
Capo di Ponte I 120 A3
Caposile I 122 B1
Capoterra I 179 C2
Cappamore IRL 29 B3
Cappeln D 71 B5
Cappoquin IRL 29 B4
Capracotta I 169 B4
Capránica I 168 A2
Caprarola I 168 A2
Capretta I 135 C5
Capri I 170 C2
Capriati a Volturno I 170 B2
Caprino Veronese I 121 B3
Captieux F 128 B2
Cápua I 170 B2
Capurso I 173 A2
Capvern F 145 A4
Carabaña E 151 B4
Carabias E 151 A4
Caracal RO 17 C6
Caracenilla E 152 B1
Caráglio I 133 A3
Caraman F 146 A2
Caramánico Terme I 169 A4
Caranga E 141 A4
Caranguejeira P 154 B2
Caransebeş RO 16 C5
Carantec F 100 A2
Carapelle I 171 B3
Carasco I 134 A2
Carate Brianza I 120 B2
Caravaca de la Cruz E 164 A3
Caravággio I 120 B2
Carbajal E 163 B3
Carbajo E 155 B3
Carballeda E 140 B3
Carballeda de Avia E 140 B2
Carballo E 140 A2
Carbis Bay GB 42 B1
Carbon-Blanc F 128 B2
Carbonera de Frentes E 143 C4
Carboneras E 164 C3
Carboneras de Guadazaón E 158 B2
Carbonero el Mayor E 151 A3
Carboneros E 157 B4
Carbónia I 179 C2
Carbonin I 108 C3
Carbonne F 146 A2
Carbost
*Highland* GB 31 B2
*Highland* GB 31 B2
Carcaboso E 149 B3
Carcabuey E 163 A3
Carcaixent E 159 B3
Carcans F 128 A1
Carcans-Plage F 128 A1
Carção P 149 A3
Carcar E 144 B2
Cárcare I 133 A4
Carcassonne F 146 A3
Carcastillo E 144 B2
Carcedo de Burgos E 143 B3
Carcelén E 159 B2
Carcès F 132 B2
Carchelejo E 163 A4
Çardak
*Çanakkale* TR 186 B1
*Denizli* TR 189 B4
Cardedeu E 147 C3
Cardeña E 157 B3
Cardenete E 158 B2
Cardeñosa E 150 B3
Cardeto I 175 C1
Cardiff GB 39 C3
Cardigan GB 39 B2
Cardona E 147 C2
Cardosos P 154 B2
Carei RO 16 B5
Carentan F 88 A2
Carentoir F 101 B3
Careri I 175 C2
Carevdar HR 124 A2
Cargèse F 180 A1
Carhaix-Plouguer F 100 A2
Caria P 148 B2
Cariati I 174 B2
Carignan F 91 B5
Carignano I 119 C4
Cariñena E 152 A2
Carini I 176 A2
Cariño E 140 A3
Carínola I 170 B1
Carisbrooke GB 44 C2
Carlabhagh GB 31 A2
Carlepont F 90 B3
Carlet E 159 B3
Carlingford IRL 27 B4
Carlisle GB 36 B4
Carloforte I 179 C2
Carlópoli I 175 B2
Carlow
D 65 C3
IRL 30 B2
Carlton GB 40 C2
Carluke GB 35 C4
Carmagnola I 119 C4
Carmarthen GB 39 C2
Carmaux F 130 A1
Carmena E 150 C3
Cármenes E 142 B1
Carmine I 133 A3
Carmona E 162 A2
Carmonita E 155 B4
Carmyllie GB 35 B5
Carnac F 100 B2
Carndonagh IRL 27 A3
Carnew IRL 30 B2
Carnforth GB 37 B4
Cárnia I 122 A2
Carnlough GB 27 B5
Carno GB 39 B3
Carnon Plage F 131 B2
Carnota E 140 B1
Carnoustie GB 35 B5
Carnwath GB 35 C4
Carolei I 174 B2
Carolinensiel D 71 A4
Carolles F 88 B2
Carona I 120 A2
Caronía I 177 A3
Carovigno I 173 B3
Carovilli I 170 B2
Carpaneto Piacentino I 120 C2
Carpegna I 135 B5
Carpenédolo I 121 B3
Carpentras F 131 A4
Carpi I 121 C3
Carpignano Sésia I 119 B5
Carpineti I 134 A3
Carpineto Romano I 169 B3
Cărpiniş RO 126 B2
Carpino I 171 B3
Carpinone I 170 B2
Carpio E 150 A2
Carquefou F 101 B4
Carqueiranne F 132 B2
Carral E 140 A2
Carranque E 151 B4
Carrapichana P 148 B2
Carrara I 134 A3
Carraroe IRL 28 A2
Carrascalejo E 156 A2
Carrascosa del Campo E 151 B5
Carratraca E 162 B3
Carrazeda de Ansiães P 148 A2
Carrazedo de Montenegro P 148 A2
Carrbridge GB 32 D3
Carregal do Sal P 148 B1
Carreña E 142 A2
Carrick IRL 26 B2
Carrickart IRL 26 A3
Carrickfergus GB 27 B5
Carrickmacross IRL 27 C4
Carrick-on-Shannon IRL 26 C2
Carrick-on-Suir IRL 30 B1
Carrigallen IRL 27 C3
Carrión E 161 B3
Carrión de Calatrava E 157 A4
Carrión de los Condes E 142 B2
Carrizo de la Ribera E 141 B5
Carrizosa E 157 B5
Carro F 131 B4
Carrocera E 142 B1
Carros F 133 B3
Carrouge CH 106 C1
Carrouges F 89 B3
Carrù I 133 A3
Carryduff GB 27 B5
Carry-le-Rouet F 131 B4
Carsóli I 169 A3
Carsphairn GB 36 A2
Cartagena E 165 B4
Cártama E 163 B3
Cartaxo P 154 B2
Cartaya E 161 B2
Carteret F 88 A2
Cartes E 142 A2
Carúnchio I 170 B2
Carviçães P 149 A3
Carvin F 78 B2
Carvoeira P 154 B1
Carvoeiro P 160 B1
Casabermeja E 163 B3
Casa Branca
*Portalegre* P 154 C3
*Setúbal* P 154 C2
Casacalenda I 170 B2
Casa Castalda I 136 B1
Casaio E 141 B4
Casa l'Abate I 173 B4
Casalarreina E 143 B4
Casalbordino I 169 A4
Casalborgone I 119 B4
Casalbuono I 174 A1
Casalbuttano ed Uniti I 120 B2
Casàl di Principe I 170 B2
Casalécchio di Reno I 135 A4
Casale Monferrato I 119 B5
Casalina I 136 C1
Casalmaggiore I 121 C3
Casalnuovo Monterotaro I 170 B3
Casaloldo I 121 B3
Casalpusterlengo I 120 B2
Casamássima I 173 B2
Casamicciola Terme I 170 C1
Casamozza F 180 A2
Casarabonela E 162 B3
Casarano I 173 B4
Casar de Cáceres E 155 B4
Casar de Palomero E 149 B3
Casarejos E 143 C3
Casares E 162 B2
Casares de las Hurdes E 149 B3
Casariche E 163 A3
Casarrubios del Monte E 151 B3
Casas de Don Pedro E 156 A2
Casas de Fernando Alonso E 158 B1
Casas de Haro E 158 B1
Casas de Juan Gil E 159 B2
Casas del Juan Núñez E 158 B2
Casas del Puerto E 159 C2
Casas del Rio E 159 B2
Casas de Millán E 155 B4
Casas de Reina E 156 B2
Casas de Ves E 159 B2
Casas-Ibáñez E 158 B2
Casasimarro E 158 B1
Casas Nuevas E 164 B3
Casasola E 150 B3
Casasola de Arión E 150 A2
Casasuertes E 142 A2
Casatejada E 150 C2
Casavieja E 150 B3
Casazza I 120 B2
Cascais P 154 C1
Cascante E 144 C2
Cascante del Rio E 152 B2
Cáscia I 169 A3
Casciana Terme I 134 B3
Cáscina I 134 B3
Cáseda E 144 B2
Casekow D 74 A3
Casella I 134 A2
Caselle Torinese I 119 B4
Casemurate I 135 A5
Casenove I 136 C1
Caseres E 153 A4
Caserío Benali E 159 B3
Caserta I 170 B2
Casével P 160 B1
Cashel IRL 29 B4
Casillas E 150 B3
Casillas de Coria E 155 B4
Casina I 134 A3
Casinos E 159 B3
Čáslav CZ 97 B3
Cásola Valsénio I 135 A4
Cásole d'Elsa I 135 B4
Cásoli I 169 A4
Casória I 170 C2
Caspe E 153 A3
Cassàde la Selva E 147 C3
Cassagnas F 130 A2
Cassagnes-Bégonhès F 130 A1
Cassano allo Iónio I 174 B2
Cassano d'Adda I 120 B2
Cassano delle Murge I 171 C4
Cassano Magnago I 120 B1
Cassano Spinola I 120 C1
Cassel F 78 B2
Cassíbile I 177 C4
Cassine I 119 C5
Cassino I 169 B3
Cassis F 132 B1
Cassolnovo I 120 B1
Cassuéjouls F 116 C2
Častá SK 98 C1
Castagnaro I 121 B4
Castagneto Carducci I 134 B3
Castagnola CH 120 A1
Castalla E 159 C3
Castañar de Ibor E 156 A2
Castanheira de Pêra P 154 A2
Cástano Primo I 120 B1
Castasegna CH 120 A2
Castéggio I 120 B2
Casteição P 148 B2
Castejón E 144 B2
Castejón de Monegros E 153 A3
Castejón de Sos E 145 B4
Castejón de Valdejasa E 144 C3
Castèl Baronia I 172 A1
Castel Bolognese I 135 A4
Castelbuono I 177 B3
Casteldáccia I 176 A2
Castel d'Aiano I 135 A3
Castel d'Ario I 121 B3
Castel de Cabra E 153 B3
Casteldelfino I 132 A3
Castél del Monte I 169 A3
Castel del Piano I 135 C4
Castel di Iúdica I 177 B3
Castel di Rio I 135 A4
Castèl di Sangro I 169 B4
Castél di Tora I 169 A2
Castelfidardo I 136 B2
Castelfiorentino I 135 B3
Castelforte I 169 B3
Castelfranco Emília I 121 C4
Castelfranco in Miscano I 170 B3
Castelfranco Véneto I 121 B4
Castèl Frentano I 169 A4
Casteljaloux F 128 B3
Castellabate I 170 C2
Castellammare del Golfo I 176 A1
Castellammare di Stábia I 170 C2
Castellamonte I 119 B4
Castellana Grotte I 173 B3
Castellane F 132 B2
Castellaneta I 173 B2
Castellaneta Marina I 173 B2
Castellar E 157 B4
Castellarano I 135 A3
Castellar de la Frontera E 162 B2
Castellar de la Ribera E 147 B2
Castellar del Vallés E 147 C3
Castellar de Santiago E 157 B4
Castell Arquato I 120 C2
Castell'Azzara I 135 C4
Castellbell i Villar E 147 C2
Castelldans E 153 A4
Castell de Cabres E 153 B4
Castell de Castells E 159 C3
Castelldefels E 147 C2
Castell de Ferro E 163 B4
Castelleone I 120 B2
Castellet E 147 C2
Castelletto di Brenzone I 121 B3
Castellfollit de la Roca E 147 B3
Castellfollit de Riubregos E 147 C2
Castellfort E 153 B3
Castellina in Chianti I 135 B4
Castellina Marittima I 134 B3
Castellóde Farfaña E 145 C4
Castellóde la Plana E 159 B3
Castello d'Empùries E 147 B4
Castello di Fiemme I 121 A4
Castelloli E 147 C2
Castellón de Rugat E 159 C3
Castellote E 153 B3
Castello Tesino I 121 A4
Castellterçol E 147 C3
Castellúcchio I 121 B3
Castellúccio de'Sáuri I 171 B3
Castelluccio Inferiore I 174 B1
Castelmassa I 121 B4
Castelmáuro I 170 B2
Castelmoron-sur-Lot F 129 B3
Castelnaudary F 146 A2
Castelnau-de-Médoc F 128 A2
Castelnau-de-Montmirail F 129 C4
Castelnau-Magnoac F 145 A4
Castelnau-Montratier F 129 B4
Castelnou E 153 A3
Castelnovo ne'Monti I 134 A3
Castelnuovo Berardenga I 135 B4
Castelnuovo della Dáunia I 170 B3
Castelnuovo di Garfagnana I 134 A3
Castelnuovo di Val di Cécina I 135 B3
Castelnuovo Don Bosco I 119 B4
Castelnuovo Scrivia I 120 C1
Castelo Branco
*Bragança* P 149 A3
*Castelo Branco* P 155 B3
Castelo de Paiva P 148 A1
Castelo de Vide P 155 B3
Castelo do Neiva P 148 A1
Castelo Mendo P 149 B3
Castelraimondo I 136 B2
Castel San Gimignano I 135 B4
Castèl San Giovanni I 120 B2
Castèl San Pietro Terme I 135 A4
Castelsantángelo I 136 C2
Castél Sant'Elia I 168 A2
Castelsaraceno I 174 A1
Castelsardo I 178 B2
Castelsarrasin F 129 B4
Castelserás E 153 B3
Casteltérmini I 176 B2
Castelvecchio Subéquo I 169 A3
Castelvetrano I 176 B1
Castél Volturno I 170 B1
Castenédolo I 120 B3
Castets F 128 C1
Castiádas I 179 C3
Castiglioncello I 134 B3
Castiglione I 169 A3
Castiglione Chiavarese I 134 A2
Castiglione d'Adda I 120 B2
Castiglione dei Pepoli I 135 A4
Castiglione del Lago I 135 B5
Castiglione della Pescáia I 135 C3
Castiglione delle Stiviere I 121 B3
Castiglione di Sicília I 177 B4
Castiglione d'Órcia I 135 B4
Castiglione Messer Marino I 170 B2
Castiglione Messer Raimondo I 169 A3
Castiglion Fibocchi I 135 B4
Castiglion Fiorentino I 135 B4
Castilblanco E 156 A2
Castilblanco de los Arroyos E 161 B4
Castil de Peones E 143 B3
Castilfrío de la Sierra E 144 C1
Castilgaleu E 145 B4
Castilisar E 144 B2
Castilleja E 161 B3
Castillejar E 164 B2
Castillejo de Martin Viejo E 149 B3
Castillejo de Mesleón E 151 A4
Castillejo de Robledo E 151 A4
Castillo de Bayuela E 150 B3
Castillo de Locubín E 163 A4
Castillonès F 129 B3
Castillon-la-Bataille F 128 B2
Castillon-Len-Couserans F 146 B2
Castillonroy E 145 C4
Castilruiz E 144 C1
Castione CH 120 A2
Castions di Strada I 122 B2
Castirla F 180 A2
Castlebar IRL 28 A2
Castlebellingham IRL 27 C4
Castleblaney IRL 27 B4
Castlebridge IRL 30 B2
Castle Cary GB 43 A4
Castlecomer IRL 30 B1
Castlederg GB 27 B3
Castledermot IRL 30 B2
Castle Douglas GB 36 B3
Castleford GB 40 B2
Castleisland IRL 29 B2
Castlemaine IRL 29 B2
Castlemartyr IRL 29 C3
Castlepollard IRL 30 A1
Castlerea IRL 28 A3
Castleton GB 40 B2
Castletown
*Highland* GB 32 C3
*Isle of Man* GB 36 B2
Castletown Bearhaven IRL 29 C2
Castletownroche IRL 29 B3
Castlewellan GB 27 B5
Casto I 120 B3
Castrejón E 150 A2
Castrelo del Valle E 141 B3
Castres F 130 B1
Castricum NL 70 B1
Castries F 131 B2
Castrignano del Capo I 173 C4
Castril E 164 B2
Castrillo de Duero E 151 A4
Castrillo de la Vega E 143 C3
Castrillo de Onielo E 142 C2
Castro
E 142 A2
I 173 B4
Castrocabón E 141 B5
Castro-Caldelas E 141 B3
Castrocaro Terme I 135 A4
Castrocontrigo E 141 B4
Castro Daire P 148 B2
Castro dei Volsci I 169 B3
Castro del Río E 163 A3
Castro de Rey E 141 A3
Castrofilippo I 176 B2
Castrogonzaio E 142 B1
Castrojeriz E 142 B2
Castro Laboreiro P 140 B2
Castro Marim P 160 B2
Castromonte E 142 C1
Castromudarra E 142 B1
Castronuevo E 142 C1
Castronuño E 150 A2
Castropol E 141 A3
Castroreale I 177 A4
Castroserracin E 151 A4
Castro-Urdiales E 143 A3
Castroverde E 141 A3
Castro Verde P 160 B1
Castroverde de Campos E 142 C1
Castroverde de Cerrato E 142 C2
Castrovillari I 174 B2
Castuera E 156 B2
Catadau E 159 B3
Cataéggio I 120 A2
Çatalca TR 186 A3
Catallar TR 189 C5
Çatalzeytin TR 23 A8
Catánia I 177 B4
Catanzaro I 175 C2
Catanzaro Marina I 175 C2
Catarroja E 159 B3
Catarruchos P 148 B1
Catcleugh GB 37 A4
Catenanuova I 177 B3
Caterham GB 44 B3
Cati E 153 B4
Čatići BIH 139 A4
Catignano I 169 A3
Catillon F 91 A3
Catoira E 140 B2
Caton GB 37 B4
Catral E 165 A4
Catterick GB 37 B5
Cattólica I 136 B1
Cattólica Eraclea I 176 B2
Catton GB 37 B4
Caudebec-en-Caux F 89 A4
Caudete E 159 C3
Caudete de las Fuentes E 159 B2
Caudiel E 159 B3
Caudiès-de-Fenouillèdes F 146 B3
Caudry F 91 A3
Caulkerbush GB 36 B3
Caulnes F 101 A3
Caulónia I 175 C2
Caumont-l'Evente F 88 A3
Caunes-Minervois F 146 A3
Cauro F 180 B1
Caussade F 129 B4

Causse-de-la-Selle F 130 B2
Cauterets F 145 B3
Cava de Tirreni I 170 C2
Cavaglia I 119 B5
Cavaillon F 131 B4
Cavalaire-sur-Mer F 132 B2
Cavaleiro P 160 B1
Cavalese I 121 A4
Cavallermaggiore I 119 C4
Cavallino I 122 B1
Cavan IRL 27 C3
Cavárzere I 121 B5
Çavdarhisar TR 187 C4
Çavdır TR 189 B4
Cavernães P 148 B2
Cavezzo I 121 C4
Cavignac F 128 A2
Čavle HR 123 B3
Cavo I 134 C3
Cavour I 119 C4
Cawdor GB 32 D3
Çay TR 187 D6
Çaycuma TR 187 A7
Cayeux-sur-Mer F 78 B1
Cayiralan TR 23 B8
Çayırhan TR 187 B6
Caylus F 129 B4
Cayres F 117 C3
Cazalilla E 157 C4
Cazalla de la Sierra E 156 C2
Cazals F 129 B4
Cazanuecos E 142 B1
Cazaubon F 128 C2
Cazaux F 128 B1
Cazavet F 146 A2
Cazères F 146 A2
Cazin BIH 124 C1
Cazis CH 107 C4
Čazma HR 124 B2
Cazo E 142 A1
Cazorla E 164 B2
Cazouls-lès-Béziers F 130 B2
Cea
*León* E 142 B1
*Orense* E 140 B3
Ceánuri E 143 A4
Ceauce F 88 B3
Cebolla E 150 C3
Čebovce SK 112 A3
Cebreros E 150 B3
Čečava BIH 125 C3
Ceccano I 169 B3
Cece H 112 C2
Cecenowo PL 68 A2
Čechtice CZ 96 B3
Čechtín CZ 97 B3
Cécina I 134 B3
Ceclavín E 155 B4
Cedégolo I 120 A3
Cedeira E 140 A2
Cedillo E 155 B3
Cedillo del Condado E 151 B4
Cedrillas E 153 B3
Cedynia PL 74 B3
Cée E 140 B1
Cefalù I 177 A3
Céggia I 122 B1
Cegléd H 113 B3
Ceglédbercel H 112 B3
Céglie Messápica I 173 B3
Cehegín E 164 A3
Ceilhes-et-Rocozels F 130 B2
Ceinos de Campos E 142 B1
Ceira P 148 B1
Čejč CZ 97 C4
Cekcyn PL 76 A3
Cela BIH 124 C2
Čelákovice CZ 84 B2
Celano I 169 A3
Celanova E 140 B3
Celbridge IRL 30 A2
Čelebič BIH 138 B2
Celenza Valfortore I 170 B2
Čelić BIH 125 C4
Čelinac BIH 124 C3
Celje SLO 123 A4
Cella E 152 B2
Celldömölk H 111 B4
Celle D 72 B3
Celle Ligure I 133 A4
Celles B 79 B4
Celles-sur-Belle F 115 B3
Cellino San Marco I 173 B3
Celorico da Beira P 148 B2
Celorico de Basto P 148 A1
Çeltik TR 187 C6
Çeltikçi TR 189 B5
Cemaes GB 38 A2
Cembra I 121 A4
Čemerno BIH 139 B4
Cenad RO 126 A2
Cencenighe Agordino I 121 A4
Cenei RO 126 B2
Ceneselli I 121 B4
Cenicero E 143 B4
Cenicientos E 150 B3
Censeau F 105 C5
Čenta SRB 126 B2
Centallo I 133 A3
Centelles E 147 C3
Cento I 121 C4
Centúripe I 177 B3
Cepeda la Mora E 150 B2
Cépet F 129 C4
Čepin HR 125 B4
Čepinski Martinci HR 125 B4
Cepovan SLO 122 A2
Ceprano I 169 B3
Čeralije HR 125 B3
Cerami I 177 B3
Cerano I 120 B1
Cérans Foulletourte F 102 B2
Ceraso I 172 B1
Cerbaia I 135 B4
Cerbère F 146 B4
Cercadillo E 151 A5
Cercal
*Lisboa* P 154 B1
*Setúbal* P 160 B1
Čerčany CZ 96 B2
Cerceda E 151 B4
Cercedilla E 151 B3
Cercemaggiore I 170 B2
Cercs E 147 B2
Cercy-la-Tour F 104 C2
Cerda I 176 B2
Cerdedo E 140 B2
Cerdeira P 149 B2
Cerdon F 103 B4
Cerea I 121 B4
Ceres
GB 35 B5
I 119 B4
Cerese I 121 B3
Ceresole-Reale I 119 B4
Cereste F 132 B1
Céret F 146 B3
Cerezo de Abajo E 151 A4
Cerezo de Riotirón E 143 B3
Cerfontaine B 79 B4
Cergy F 90 B2
Cerignola I 171 B3
Cérilly F 103 C4
Cerisiers F 104 A2
Cerizay F 114 B3
Çerkeş TR 23 A7
Çerkezköy TR 186 A3
Cerkije SLO 123 A3
Cerknica SLO 123 B3
Cerkno SLO 122 A2
Cerkwica PL 67 B4
Cerna HR 125 B4
Černá Hora CZ 97 B4
Cernavodă RO 17 C8
Cernay F 106 B2
Cerne Abbas GB 43 B4
Cernégula E 143 B3
Cernik HR 124 B3
Cernóbbio I 120 B2
Černošin CZ 95 B4
Cernovice CZ 96 B2
Cérons F 128 B2
Cerovlje HR 123 B3
Cerovo SK 99 C3
Cerqueto I 135 C5
Cerralbo E 149 B3
Cerreto d'Esi I 136 B1
Cerreto Sannita I 170 B2
Cerrigydrudion GB 38 A3
Cërrik AL 182 B1
Cerro Muriano E 156 B3
Certaldo I 135 B4
Certosa di Pésio I 133 A3
Cerva P 148 A2
Cervaro I 169 B3
Cervatos de la Cueza E 142 B2
Červena Řečice CZ 97 B3
Červená-Skala SK 99 C4
Cervená Voda CZ 97 A4
Cerveny Kostelec CZ 85 B4
Cervera E 147 C2
Cervera de la Cañada E 152 A2
Cervera del Llano E 158 B1
Cervera del Río Alhama E 144 B2
Cervera de Pisuerga E 142 B2
Cervéteri I 168 B2
Cérvia I 135 A5
Cerviáde les Garriques E 147 C1
Cervignano del Friuli I 122 B2
Cervinara I 170 B2
Cervione F 180 A2
Cervo E 141 A3
Cervon F 104 B2
Cesana Torinese I 119 C3
Cesarica HR 137 A4
Cesarò I 177 B3
Cesena I 135 A5
Cesenático I 135 A5
Cēsis LV 8 D4
Česká Belá CZ 97 B3
Česká Kamenice CZ 84 B2
Česká Lípa CZ 84 B2
Česká Skalice CZ 85 B4
Česká Třebová CZ 97 B4
České Budějovice CZ 96 C2
České Velenice CZ 96 C2
Český Brod CZ 96 A2
Český Dub CZ 84 B2
Český Krumlov CZ 96 C2
Český Těšin CZ 98 B2
Čėšljeva Bara SRB 127 C3
Çeşme TR 188 A1
Cessenon F 130 B2
Cesson-Sévigné F 101 A4
Cestas F 128 B2
Čestobrodica SRB 127 D2
Cesuras E 140 A2
Cetina E 152 A2
Cetin Grad HR 123 B4
Cetinje MNE 16 D3
Cetraro I 174 B1
Ceuti E 165 A3
Ceva I 133 A4
Cevico de la Torre E 142 C2
Cevico Navero E 142 C2
Cevins F 118 B3
Cévio CH 119 A5
Cevizli TR 189 B6
Cewice PL 68 A2
Ceylan TR 189 C4
Ceyrat F 116 B3
Ceyzériat F 118 A2
Chaam NL 79 A4
Chabanais F 115 C4
Chabeuil F 117 C5
Chabielice PL 86 A3
Chablis F 104 B2
Châbons F 118 B2
Chabówka PL 99 B3
Chabreloche F 117 B3
Chabris F 103 B3
Chagford GB 42 B3
Chagny F 105 C3
Chagoda RUS 9 C9
Chaherrero E 150 B3
Chailland F 88 B3
Chaillé-les-Marais F 114 B2
Chailles F 103 B3
Chailley F 104 A2
Chalabre F 146 B3
Chalais F 128 A3
Chalamont F 118 B2
Châlette-sur-Loing F 103 A4
Chalindrey F 105 B4
Chalkida GR 185 A4
Challacombe GB 42 A3
Challans F 114 B2
Challes-les-Eaux F 118 B2
Chalmazel F 117 B3
Chalmoux F 104 C2
Chalonnes-sur-Loire F 102 B1
Châlons-en-Champagne F 91 C4
Chalon-sur-Saône F 105 C3
Chalupy PL 69 A3
Châlus F 115 C4
Cham
CH 106 B3
D 95 B4
Chamberet F 116 B1
Chambéry F 118 B2
Chambilly F 117 A4
Chambley F 92 B1
Chambly F 90 B2
Chambois F 89 B4
Chambon-sur-Lac F 116 B2
Chambon-sur-Voueize F 116 A2
Chambord F 103 B3
Chamborigaud F 131 A2
Chamboulive F 116 B1
Chamerau D 95 B4
Chamonix-Mont Blanc F 119 B3
Chamoux-sur-Gelon F 118 B3
Champagnac-le-Vieux F 117 B3
Champagney F 106 B1
Champagnole F 105 C4
Champagny-Mouton F 115 B4
Champaubert F 91 C3
Champdeniers-St Denis F 114 B3
Champdieu F 117 B4
Champdôtre F 105 B4
Champeix F 116 B3
Champéry CH 119 A3
Champigne F 102 B1
Champignelles F 104 B2
Champigny-sur-Veude F 102 B2
Champlitte-et-le-Prelot F 105 B4
Champoluc I 119 B4
Champoly F 117 B3
Champorcher I 119 B4
Champrond-en-Gâtine F 89 B5
Champs-sur-Tarentaine F 116 B2
Champs-sur-Yonne F 104 B2
Champtoceaux F 101 B4
Chamrousse F 118 B2
Chamusca P 154 B2
Chanac F 130 A2
Chanaleilles F 117 C3
Chandler's Ford GB 44 C2
Chandra GR 185 D7
Chandrexa de Queixa E 141 B3
Chañe E 150 A3
Changy F 117 A3
Chania GR 185 D5
Channes F 104 B3
Chantada E 140 B3
Chantelle F 116 A3
Chantenay-St Imbert F 104 C2
Chanteuges F 117 B3
Chantilly F 90 B2
Chantonnay F 114 B2
Chão de Codes P 154 B2
Chaource F 104 A3
Chapa E 140 B2
Chapareillan F 118 B2
Chapel en le Frith GB 40 B2
Chapelle Royale F 103 A3
Chapelle-St Laurent F 102 C1
Charbonnat F 104 C3
Chard GB 43 B4
Charenton-du-Cher F 103 C4
Charlbury GB 44 B2
Charleroi B 79 B4
Charlestown
GB 42 B2
IRL 26 C2
Charlestown of Aberlour GB 32 D3
Charleville IRL 29 B3
Charleville-Mézières F 91 B4
Charlieu F 117 A4
Charlottenberg S 49 C4
Charlton Kings GB 44 B1
Charly F 90 C3
Charmes F 92 C2
Charmes-sur-Rhône F 117 C4
Charmey CH 106 C2
Charminster GB 43 B4
Charmont-en-Beauce F 103 A4
Charny F 104 B2
Charolles F 117 A4
Chârost F 103 C4
Charquemont F 106 B1
Charrin F 104 C2
Charroux F 115 B4
Chartres F 90 C1
Charzykow PL 68 B2
Chasseneuil-sur-Bonnieure F 115 C4
Chassigny F 105 B4
Château-Arnoux F 132 A2
Châteaubernard F 115 C3
Châteaubourg F 101 A4
Châteaubriant F 101 B4
Château-Chinon F 104 B2
Château-d'Oex CH 106 C2
Château-d'Olonne F 114 B2
Château-du-Loir F 102 B2
Châteaudun F 103 A3
Châteaugiron F 101 A4
Château-Gontier F 102 B1
Château-Landon F 103 A4
Château-la-Vallière F 102 B2
Château-l'Evêque F 129 A3
Châteaulin F 100 A1
Châteaumeillant F 103 C4
Châteauneuf
*Nièvre* F 104 B2
*Saône-et-Loire* F 117 A4
Châteauneuf-de-Randon F 117 C3
Châteauneuf-d'Ille-et-Vilaine F 88 B2
Châteauneuf-du-Faou F 100 A2
Châteauneuf-du-Pape F 131 A3
Châteauneuf-en-Thymerais F 89 B5
Châteauneuf la-Forêt F 116 B1
Châteauneuf-le-Rouge F 132 B1
Châteauneuf-sur-Charente F 115 C3
Châteauneuf-sur-Cher F 103 C4
Châteauneuf-sur-Loire F 103 B4
Châteauneuf-sur-Sarthe F 102 B1
Châteauponsac F 115 B5
Château-Porcien F 91 B4
Châteauredon F 132 A2
Châteaurenard
*Bouches du Rhône* F 131 B3
*Loiret* F 104 B1
Château-Renault F 102 B2
Châteauroux F 103 C3
Châteauroux-les-Alpes F 118 C3
Château-Salins F 92 C2
Château-Thierry F 91 B3
Châteauvillain F 105 A3
Châtel F 119 A3
Châtelaillon-Plage F 114 B2
Châtelaudren F 100 A3
Châtel-Censoir F 104 B2
Châtel-de-Neuvre F 116 A3
Châtelet B 79 B4
Châtelguyon F 116 B3
Châtellerault F 115 B4
Châtel-Montagne F 117 A3
Châtel-St Denis CH 106 C1
Châtel-sur-Moselle F 92 C2
Châtelus-Malvaleix F 116 A2
Châtenois F 105 A4
Châtenois-les-Forges F 106 B1
Chatham GB 45 B4
Châtillon I 119 B4
Châtillon-Coligny F 103 B4
Châtillon-en-Bazois F 104 B2
Châtillon-en-Diois F 118 C2
Châtillon-sur Chalaronne F 117 A4
Châtillon-sur-Indre F 103 C3
Châtillon-sur-Loire F 103 B4
Châtillon-sur-Marne F 91 B3
Châtillon-sur-Seine F 104 B3
Châtres F 91 C3
Chatteris GB 45 A4
Chatton GB 37 A5
Chauchina E 163 A4
Chaudes-Aigues F 116 C3
Chaudrey F 91 C4
Chauffailles F 117 A4
Chaulnes F 90 B2
Chaument Gistoux B 79 B4
Chaumergy F 105 C4
Chaumont F 105 A4
Chaumont-en-Vexin F 90 B1
Chaumont-Porcien F 91 B4
Chaumont-sur-Aire F 91 C5
Chaumont-sur-Loire F 103 B3
Chaunay F 115 B4
Chauny F 90 B3
Chaussin F 105 C4
Chauvigny F 115 B4
Chavagnes-en-Paillers F 114 B2
Chavanges F 91 C4
Chaves P 148 A2
Chavignon F 91 B3
Chazelles-sur-Lyon F 117 B4
Chazey-Bons F 118 B2
Cheadle
*Greater Manchester* GB 40 B1
*Staffordshire* GB 40 C2
Cheb CZ 83 B4
Chebsara RUS 9 C11
Checa E 152 B2
Chęciny PL 87 B4
Cheddar GB 43 A4
Cheddleton GB 40 B1
Chef-Boutonne F 115 B3
Cheles E 155 C3
Chella E 159 B3
Chelles F 90 C2
Chełm PL 13 C5
Chełmno
*Kujawsko-Pomorskie* PL 76 A3
*Wielkopolskie* PL 76 B3
Chelmsford GB 45 B4
Chelmuzhi RUS 9 A9
Chelmża PL 76 A3
Cheltenham GB 44 B1
Chelva E 159 B2
Chémery F 103 B3
Chemery-sur-Bar F 91 B4
Chemillé F 102 B1
Chemin F 105 C4
Chemnitz D 83 B4
Chénerailles F 116 A2
Cheniménil F 105 A5
Chenonceaux F 103 B3
Chenôve F 105 B3
Chepelare BG 183 B6
Chepstow GB 39 C4
Chera E 159 B3
Cherasco I 119 C4
Cherbonnières F 115 C3
Cherbourg F 88 A2
Cherchiara di Calábria I 174 B2
Cherepovets RUS 9 C10
Chernihiv UA 13 C9
Chernivtsi UA 17 A6
Chernobyl = Chornobyl UA 13 C9
Chernyakhovsk RUS 12 A4
Chéroy F 104 A1
Cherven BY 13 B8
Chervonohrad UA 13 C6
Cherykaw BY 13 B9
Chesham GB 44 B3
Cheshunt GB 44 B3
Chessy-lès-Pres F 104 A2
Cheste E 159 B3
Chester GB 38 A4
Chesterfield GB 40 B2
Chester-le-Street GB 37 B5
Chevagnes F 104 C2
Chevanceaux F 115 C3
Chevillon F 91 C5
Chevilly F 103 A3
Chew Magna GB 43 A4
Chézery-Forens F 118 A2
Chialamberto I 119 B4
Chiampo I 121 B4
Chianale I 119 C4
Chianciano Terme I 135 B4
Chiaramonte Gulfi I 177 B3
Chiaramonti I 178 B2
Chiaravalle I 136 B2
Chiaravalle Centrale I 175 C2
Chiaréggio I 120 A2
Chiari I 120 B2
Chiaromonte I 174 A2
Chiasso CH 120 B2
Chiávari I 134 A2
Chiavenna I 120 A2
Chiché F 102 C1
Chichester GB 44 C3
Chiclana de la Frontera E 162 B1
Chiclana de Segura E 164 A1
Chiddingfold GB 44 B3
Chieri I 119 B4
Chiesa in Valmalenco I 120 A2
Chieti I 169 A4
Chieti Scalo I 169 A4
Chiéuti I 171 B3
Chigwell GB 45 B4
Chiliomodi GR 184 B3
Chillarón de Cuenca E 152 B1
Chillarón del Rey E 151 B5
Chilleurs-aux-Bois F 103 A4
Chillón E 156 B3
Chilluevar E 164 B1
Chiloeches E 151 B4
Chimay B 91 A4
Chimeneas E 163 A4
Chinchilla de Monte Aragón E 158 C2
Chinchón E 151 B4
Chingford GB 45 B4
Chinon F 102 B2
Chióggia I 122 B1
Chiomonte I 119 B3
Chipiona E 161 C3
Chippenham GB 43 A4
Chipping Campden GB 44 A2
Chipping Norton GB 44 B2
Chipping Ongar GB 45 B4
Chipping Sodbury GB 43 A4
Chirac F 130 A2
Chirbury GB 39 B3
Chirens F 118 B2
Chirivel E 164 B2
Chirk GB 38 B3
Chirnside GB 35 C5
Chişinău = Khisinev MD 17 B8
Chişineu Criş RO 113 C5
Chissey-en-Morvan F 104 B3
Chiusa I 108 C2
Chiusa di Pésio I 133 A3
Chiusaforte I 122 A2
Chiusa Scláfani I 176 B2
Chiusi I 135 B4
Chiva E 159 B3
Chivasso I 119 B4
Chlewiska PL 87 A4
Chludowo PL 75 B5
Chlumec nad Cidlinou CZ 84 B3
Chlum u Třeboně CZ 96 C2
Chmielnik PL 87 B4
Chobienia PL 85 A4
Chobienice PL 75 B4
Choceň CZ 97 A4
Choceń PL 77 B4
Chochołow PL 99 B3

Chocianów PL 85 A3
Chociw PL 86 A3
Chociwel PL 75 A4
Choczewo PL 68 A2
Chodaków PL 77 B5
Chodecz PL 77 B4
Chodov CZ 83 B4
Chodzież PL 75 B5
Chojna PL 74 B3
Chojnice PL 68 B2
Chojno
*Kujawsko-Pomorskie* PL 77 B4
*Wielkopolskie* PL 75 B5
Chojnów PL 85 A3
Cholet F 114 A3
Chomérac F 117 C4
Chomutov CZ 83 B5
Chop UA 12 D5
Chora GR 184 B2
Chora Sfakion GR 185 D5
Chorges F 132 A2
Chorley GB 38 A4
Chornobyl = Chernobyl UA 13 C9
Chortkiv UA 13 D6
Chorzele PL 77 A5
Chorzew PL 86 A2
Chorzów PL 86 B2
Choszczno PL 75 A4
Chotěboř CZ 97 B3
Chouilly F 91 B4
Chouto P 154 B2
Chouzy-sur-Cisse F 103 B3
Chozas de Abajo E 142 B1
Chrast CZ 97 B3
Chrást CZ 96 B1
Chrastava CZ 84 B2
Chřibská CZ 84 B2
Christchurch GB 44 C2
Christiansfeld DK 59 C2
Chroberz PL 87 B4
Chropyně CZ 98 B1
Chrudim CZ 97 B3
Chrzanów PL 86 B3
Chtelnica SK 98 C1
Chudovo RUS 9 C7
Chueca E 157 A4
Chulmleigh GB 42 B3
Chur CH 107 C4
Church Stretton GB 39 B4
Churriana E 163 B3
Churwalden CH 107 C4
Chvalšiny CZ 96 C2
Chwaszczyno PL 69 A3
Chynava CZ 96 A2
Chýnov CZ 96 B2
Ciacova RO 126 B3
Ciadîr-Lunga MD 17 B8
Ciadoncha E 143 B3
Cianciana I 176 B2
Ciano d'Enza I 134 A3
Ciążen PL 76 B2
Cibakhaza H 113 C4
Ciborro P 154 C2
Cicagna I 134 A2
Cicciano I 170 C2
Ciciliano I 169 B2
Cicognolo I 120 B3
Cidadelhe P 149 B2
Cide TR 23 A7
Cidones E 143 C4
Ciechanów
*Dolnośląskie* PL 85 A4
*Mazowieckie* PL 77 B5
Ciechocinek PL 76 B3
Cielądz PL 87 A4
Ciemnik PL 75 A4
Ciempozuelos E 151 B4
Ciepielów PL 87 A5
Čierny Balog SK 99 C3
Cierp-Gaud F 145 B4
Cierpice PL 76 B3
Ciervana E 143 A3
Cierznie PL 68 B2
Cieslé PL 77 B5
Cieszyn PL 98 B2
Cieutat F 145 A4
Cieza E 165 A3
Cifer SK 98 C1
Çifteler TR 187 C6
Cifuentes E 151 B5
Cigales E 142 C2
Cigliano I 119 B5
Cihanbeyli TR 23 B7
Cillas E 152 B2
Cilleros E 149 B3
Cilleruelo de Arriba E 143 C3
Cilleruelo de Bezana E 143 B3
Cimalmotto CH 119 A5
Cimanes del Tejar E 141 B5
Ciminna I 176 B2
Cimişlia MD 17 B8
Cimoláis I 122 A1
Cîmpulung RO 17 C6
Çınarcık TR 186 B4
Cinctorres E 153 B3
Cinderford GB 39 C4
Çine TR 188 B3
Činěves CZ 84 B3
Ciney B 79 B5
Cinfães P 148 A1
Cingia de Botti I 120 B3
Cingoli I 136 B2
Cinigiano I 135 C4
Cinobaňa SK 99 C3
Cinq-Mars-la-Pile F 102 B2
Cinquefrondi I 175 C2
Cintegabelle F 146 A2
Cintruénigo E 144 B2
Ciółkowo PL 77 B4
Ciperez E 149 B3
Cirat E 153 B3
Cirella I 174 B1
Cirencester GB 44 B2
Cirey-sur-Vezouze F 92 C2
Ciria E 152 A2
Ciriè I 119 B4
Cirigliano I 174 A2
Cirò I 174 B3
Cirò Marina I 174 B3
Ciry-le-Noble F 104 C3
Cislău RO 17 C7
Cismon del Grappa I 121 B4
Cisneros E 142 B2
Cissac-Médoc F 128 A2
Čista CZ 96 A1
Cisterna di Latina I 169 B2
Cistérniga E 150 A3
Cisternino I 173 B3
Cistierna E 142 B1
Čitluk BIH 139 B3
Citov CZ 84 B2
Cittadella I 121 B4
Cittàdella Pieve I 135 C5
Cittádel Vaticano = Vatican City I 168 B2
Cittàdi Castello I 135 B5
Cittaducale I 169 A2
Cittanova I 175 C2
Città Sant'Angelo I 169 A4
Ciudadela de Menorca E 167 B3
Ciudad Real E 157 B4
Ciudad Rodrigo E 149 B3
Ciutadilla E 147 C2
Cividale del Friuli I 122 A2
Cívita I 169 A3
Cívita Castellana I 168 A2
Civitanova Alta I 136 B2
Civitanova Marche I 136 B2
Civitavécchia I 168 A1
Civitella di Romagna I 135 A4
Civitella di Tronto I 136 C2
Civitella Roveto I 169 B3
Civray F 115 B4
Çivril TR 189 A4
Cizur Mayor E 144 B2
Clabhach GB 34 B1
Clachan GB 31 B2
Clachan na Luib GB 31 B1
Clacton-on-Sea GB 45 B5
Cladich GB 34 B2
Claggan GB 34 B2
Clairvaux-les-Lacs F 105 C4
Clamecy F 104 B2
Claonaig GB 34 C2
Clarecastle IRL 28 B3
Claregalway IRL 28 A3
Claremorris IRL 28 A2
Clarinbridge IRL 28 A3
Clashmore
GB 32 D2
IRL 29 B4
Claudy GB 27 B3
Clausthal-Zellerfeld D 82 A2
Cláut I 122 A1
Clay Cross GB 40 B2
Claye-Souilly F 90 C2
Cléder F 100 A1
Cleethorpes GB 41 B3
Clefmont F 105 A4
Cléguérec F 100 A2
Clelles F 118 C2
Clenze D 73 B3
Cleobury Mortimer GB 39 B4
Cléon-d'Andran F 117 C4
Cléré-les-Pins F 102 B2
Clères F 89 A5
Clermont F 90 B2
Clermont-en-Argonne F 91 B5
Clermont-Ferrand F 116 B3
Clermont-l'Hérault F 130 B2
Clerval F 105 B5
Clervaux L 92 A2
Clèry-St André F 103 B3
Cles I 121 A4
Clevedon GB 43 A4
Cleveleys GB 38 A3
Cley GB 41 C5
Clifden IRL 28 A1
Clifford GB 39 B3
Clisson F 101 B4
Clitheroe GB 40 B1
Clogh IRL 30 B1
Cloghan
*Donegal* IRL 26 B3
*Offaly* IRL 28 A4
Clogheen IRL 29 B4
Clogher GB 27 B3
Cloghjordan IRL 28 B3
Clohars-Carnoët F 100 B2
Clonakilty IRL 29 C3
Clonaslee IRL 30 A1
Clondalkin IRL 30 A2
Clones IRL 27 B3
Clonmany IRL 27 A3
Clonmel IRL 29 B4
Clonmellon IRL 30 A1
Clonord IRL 30 A1
Clonroche IRL 30 B2
Cloone IRL 26 C3
Cloppenburg D 71 B5
Closeburn GB 36 A3
Clough GB 27 B5
Clova GB 35 B4
Clovelly GB 42 B2
Clowne GB 40 B2
Cloyes-sur-le-Loir F 103 B3
Cloyne IRL 29 C3
Cluis F 103 C3
Cluj-Napoca RO 17 B5
Clun GB 39 B3
Clunes GB 34 B3
Cluny F 117 A4
Cluses F 118 A3
Clusone I 120 B2
Clydach GB 39 C3
Clydebank GB 34 C3
Coachford IRL 29 C3
Coagh GB 27 B4
Coalisland GB 27 B4
Coalville GB 40 C2
Coaña E 141 A4
Çobanlar TR 187 D5
Cobas E 140 A2
Cobertelade E 151 A5
Cobeta E 152 B1
Cóbh IRL 29 C3
Cobreces E 142 A2
Coburg D 82 B2
Coca E 150 A3
Cocentaina E 159 C3
Cochem D 80 B3
Cockburnspath GB 35 C5
Cockermouth GB 36 B3
Codigoro I 121 C5
Codogno I 120 B2
Codos E 152 A2
Codróipo I 122 B1
Codrongianos I 178 B2
Coelhoso P 149 A3
Coesfeld D 71 C4
Coevorden NL 71 B3
Cofrentes E 159 B2
Cogeces del Monte E 150 A3
Coggeshall GB 45 B4
Cognac F 115 C3
Cogne I 119 B4
Cognin F 118 B2
Cogolin F 132 B2
Cogollos de Guadix E 164 B1
Cogollos-Vega E 163 A4
Cogolludo E 151 B4
Coimbra P 148 B1
Coín E 163 B3
Coirós E 140 A2
Čoka SRB 126 B2
Col SLO 123 B3
Colares P 154 C1
Cölbe D 81 B4
Colbitz D 73 B4
Colchester GB 45 B4
Coldingham GB 35 C5
Colditz D 83 A4
Coldstream GB 35 C5
Colebrooke GB 43 B3
Colera E 146 B4
Coleraine GB 27 A4
Colfiorito I 136 B1
Cólico I 120 A2
Coligny F 118 A2
Colindres E 143 A3
Collado-Mediano E 151 B3
Collado Villalba E 151 B4
Collagna I 134 A3
Collanzo E 142 A1
Collat F 117 B3
Coll de Nargó E 147 B2
Collécchio I 120 C3
Colledimezzo I 169 B4
Colle di Val d'Elsa I 135 B4
Colleferro I 169 B3
Colle Isarco I 108 C2
Collelongo I 169 B3
Collepasso I 173 B4
Collepepe I 136 C1
Collesalvetti I 134 B3
Colle Sannita I 170 B2
Collesano I 176 B2
Colli a Volturno I 169 B4
Collin GB 36 A3
Collinée F 101 A3
Collingham
*Nottinghamshire* GB 40 B2
*West Yorkshire* GB 40 B3
Collinghorst D 71 A4
Cóllio I 120 B3
Collobrières F 132 B2
Collon IRL 27 C4
Collooney IRL 26 B2
Colmar F 106 A2
Colmars F 132 A2
Colmenar E 163 B3
Colmenar de la Sierra E 151 A4
Colmenar de Oreja E 151 B4
Colmenar Viejo E 151 B4
Colmonel GB 36 A2
Colne GB 40 B1
Colobraro I 174 A2
Cologna Véneta I 121 B4
Cologne = Köln D 80 B2
Cologne F 129 C3
Cologne al Serio I 120 B2
Colombey-les-Belles F 92 C1
Colombey-les-deux-Églises F 105 A3
Colombres E 142 A2
Colomera E 163 A4
Colomers E 147 B3
Colomiers F 129 C4
Colònia de Sant Jordi E 167 B3
Colorno I 120 C3
Colos P 160 B1
Cölpin D 74 A2
Colpy GB 33 D4
Colsterworth GB 40 C3
Coltishall GB 41 C5
Colunga E 142 A1
Colwell GB 37 A4
Colwyn Bay GB 38 A3
Colyford GB 43 B3
Comácchio I 121 C5
Coma-ruga E 147 C2
Combarros E 141 B4
Combeaufontaine F 105 B4
Comber GB 27 B5
Comblain-au-Pont B 80 B1
Combloux F 118 B3
Combourg F 88 B2
Combronde F 116 B3
Comeglians I 109 C3
Comillas E 142 A2
Comines F 78 B3
Cómiso I 177 C3
Comloşu Mare RO 126 B2
Commensacq F 128 B2
Commentry F 116 A2
Commerau D 84 A2
Commercy F 92 C1
Como I 120 B2
Cómpeta E 163 B4
Compiègne F 90 B2
Comporta P 154 C2
Comps-sur-Artuby F 132 B2
Comrat MD 17 B8
Comrie GB 35 B4
Comunanza I 136 C2
Cona
*Emilia Romagna* I 121 C4
*Veneto* I 121 B5
Concarneau F 100 B2
Conceição P 160 B1
Conches-en-Ouche F 89 B4
Concordia Sagittária I 122 B1
Concordia sulla Sécchia I 121 C3
Concots F 129 B4
Condat F 116 B2
Condé-en-Brie F 91 C3
Condeixa P 148 B1
Condemios de Abajo E 151 A4
Condemios de Arriba E 151 A4
Condé-sur-l'Escaut F 79 B3
Conde-sur-Marne F 91 B4
Condé-sur-Noireau F 88 B3
Condino I 121 B3
Condom F 129 C3
Condove I 119 B4
Condrieu F 117 B4
Conegliano I 122 B1
Conflans-sur-Lanterne F 105 B5
Confolens F 115 B4
Conforto E 141 A3
Cong IRL 28 A2
Congleton GB 40 B1
Congosto E 141 B4
Congosto de Valdavia E 142 B2
Congostrina E 151 A4
Conil de la Frontera E 162 B1
Coningsby GB 41 B3
Coniston GB 36 B3
Conlie F 102 A1
Conliège F 105 C4
Conna IRL 29 B3
Connah's Quay GB 38 A3
Connantre F 91 C3
Connaugh IRL 28 B3
Connaux F 131 A3
Connel GB 34 B2
Connerré F 102 A2
Cononbridge GB 32 D2
Čonoplja SRB 126 B1
Conques F 116 C2
Conques-sur-Orbiel F 146 A3
Conquista E 157 B3
Conquista de la Sierra E 156 A2
Consándolo I 121 C4
Consélice I 135 A4
Conselve I 121 B4
Consenvoye F 91 B5
Consett GB 37 B5
Consolacão P 154 B1
Constancia P 154 B2
Constanco E 140 A2
Constanța RO 17 C8
Constanti E 147 C2
Constantina E 162 A2
Consuegra E 157 A4
Consuma I 135 B4
Contarina I 122 B1
Contay F 90 B2
Conthey CH 119 A4
Contigliano I 168 A2
Contis-Plage F 128 B1
Contrada I 170 C2
Contres F 103 B3
Contrexéville F 105 A4
Controne I 172 B1
Contursi Termi I 172 B1
Conty F 90 B2
Conversano I 173 B3
Conwy GB 38 A3
Cookstown GB 27 B4
Coole F 91 C4
Coolgreany IRL 30 B2
Cooneen GB 27 B3
Cootehill IRL 27 B3
Cope E 165 B3
Copenhagen = København DK 61 D2
Copertino I 173 B4
Copparo I 121 C4
Coppenbrugge D 72 B2
Corabia RO 17 D6
Córaci I 175 B2
Coralići BIH 124 C1
Corato I 171 B4
Coray F 100 A2
Corbeil-Essonnes F 90 C2
Corbeny F 91 B3
Corbera E 159 B3
Corbie F 90 B2
Corbigny F 104 B2
Corbion B 91 B4
Corbridge GB 37 B4
Corby GB 40 C3
Corconte E 143 A3
Corcubión E 140 B1
Corcumello I 169 A3
Cordenòns I 122 B1
Cordes-sur-Ciel F 129 B4
Córdoba E 156 C3
Cordobilla de Lácara E 155 B4
Cordovado I 122 B1
Corella E 144 B2
Coreses E 150 A2
Corfe Castle GB 43 B4
Corga de Lobão P 148 B1
Cori I 169 B2
Coria E 155 B4
Coria del Río E 162 A1
Corigliano Cálabro I 174 B2
Corinaldo I 136 B1
Corinth = Korinthos GR 184 B3
Cório I 119 B4
Coripe E 162 B2
Cork IRL 29 C3
Corlay F 100 A2
Corleone I 176 B2
Corleto Monforte I 172 B1
Corleto Perticara I 174 A2
Çorlu TR 186 A2
Cormainville F 103 A3
Cormatin F 104 C3
Cormeilles F 89 A4
Cormery F 102 B2
Cormòns I 122 B2
Cormoz F 118 A2
Cornago E 144 B1
Cornberg D 82 A1
Cornellana E 141 A4
Cornești MD 17 B8
Corníglio I 134 A3
Cornimont F 106 B1
Corniolo I 135 B4
Cornuda I 121 B5
Cornudella de Montsant E 147 C1
Cornudilla E 143 B3
Cornus F 130 B2
Çorovodë AL 182 C2
Corpach GB 34 B2
Corps F 118 C2
Corps Nuds F 101 B4
Corral de Almaguer E 157 A4
Corral de Ayllon E 151 A4
Corral de Calatrava E 157 B3
Corrales E 149 A4
Corral-Rubio E 158 C2
Corran GB 34 B2
Corredoiras E 140 A2
Corréggio I 121 C3
Corrèze F 116 B1
Corridónia I 136 B2
Corris GB 38 B3
Corrubedo E 140 B1
Córsico I 120 B2
Corsock GB 36 A3
Corte F 180 A2
Corteconcepción E 161 B3
Corte de Peleas E 155 C4
Cortegaca P 148 B1
Cortegada E 140 B2
Cortegana E 161 B3
Cortemaggiore I 120 B2
Cortemilia I 133 A4
Corte Pinto P 160 B2
Cortes E 144 C2
Cortes de Aragón E 153 B3
Cortes de Arenoso E 153 B3
Cortes de Baza E 164 B2
Cortes de la Frontera E 162 B2
Cortes de Pallás E 159 B3
Cortiçadas P 154 C2
Cortico P 148 A2
Cortijo de Arriba E 157 A3
Cortijos Nuevos E 164 A2
Cortina d'Ampezzo I 108 C3
Corton GB 41 C5
Cortona I 135 B4
Coruche P 154 C2
Corullón E 141 B4
Çorum TR 23 A8
Corvara in Badia I 108 C2
Corvera E 165 B3
Corwen GB 38 B3
Cosenza I 174 B2
Cosham GB 44 C2
Coslada E 151 B4
Cosne-Cours-sur-Loire F 104 B1
Cosne d'Allier F 103 C4
Cospeito E 140 A3
Cossato I 119 B5
Cossaye F 104 C2
Cossé-le-Vivien F 101 B5
Cossonay CH 105 C5
Costa da Caparica P 154 C1
Costa de Santo André P 160 A1
Costalpino I 135 B4
Costa Nova P 148 B1
Costaros F 117 C3
Costeşti RO 17 C6
Costigliole d'Asti I 119 C5
Costigliole Saluzzo I 133 A3
Coswig
*Sachsen* D 83 A5
*Sachsen-Anhalt* D 83 A4
Cotherstone GB 37 B5
Cotronei I 175 B2
Cottbus D 84 A2
Cottenham GB 45 A4
Cottingham GB 40 B3
Coublanc F 105 B4
Couches F 104 C3
Couço P 154 C2
Coucouron F 117 C3
Coucy-le-Château-Auffrique F 90 B3
Couëron F 101 B4
Couflens F 146 B2
Couhé F 115 B4
Couiza F 146 B3
Coulags GB 31 B3
Coulanges F 104 C2
Coulanges-la-Vineuse F 104 B2
Coulanges-sur-Yonne F 104 B2
Couleuvre F 104 C1
Coulmier-le-Sec F 104 B3
Coulommiers F 90 C3
Coulonges-sur-l'Autize F 114 B3
Coulounieix-Chamiers F 129 A3
Coulport GB 34 B3
Coupar Angus GB 35 B4
Coupéville F 91 C4
Couptrain F 89 B3
Coura P 140 C2
Courcelles B 79 B4
Courcelles-Chaussy F 92 B2
Courchevel F 118 B3
Cour-Cheverny F 103 B3
Courcôme F 115 C4
Courçon F 114 B3
Cour-et-Buis F 117 B4
Courgenay CH 106 B2
Courmayeur I 119 B3
Courniou F 130 B1
Cournon-d'Auvergne F 116 B3
Cournonterral F 130 B2
Courpière F 117 B3
Coursan F 130 B2
Courseulles-sur-Mer F 89 A3
Cours-la-Ville F 117 A4
Courson-les-Carrières F 104 B2
Courtalain F 103 A3
Courtenay F 104 A2
Courtomer F 89 B4

Courville
*Eure-et-Loire* F 89 B5
*Marne* F 91 B3
Coussac-Bonneval F 115 C5
Coutances F 88 A2
Couterne F 89 B3
Coutras F 128 A2
Couvet CH 106 C1
Couvin B 91 A4
Couzon F 104 C2
Covadonga E 142 A1
Covaleda E 143 C4
Covarrubias E 143 B3
Covas P 148 A1
Cove GB 31 B3
Coventry GB 44 A2
Coverack GB 42 B1
Covigliáio I 135 A4
Covilhã P 148 B2
Cowbridge GB 39 C3
Cowdenbeath GB 35 B4
Cowes GB 44 C2
Cox F 129 C4
Cózar E 157 B4
Cozes F 114 C3
Cozzano F 180 B2
Craco I 174 A2
Cracow = Kraków PL 99 A3
Craibstone GB 33 D4
Craighouse GB 34 C2
Craignure GB 34 B2
Crail GB 35 B5
Crailsheim D 94 B2
Craiova RO 17 C5
Cramlington GB 37 A5
Cranleigh GB 44 B3
Craon F 101 B5
Craonne F 91 B3
Craponne F 117 B4
Craponne-sur-Arzon F 117 B3
Crathie GB 32 D3
Crato P 155 B3
Craughwell IRL 28 A3
Craven Arms GB 39 B4
Crawford GB 36 A3
Crawinkel D 82 B2
Crawley GB 44 B3
Creag Ghoraidh GB 31 B1
Crecente E 140 B2
Crèches-sur-Saône F 117 A4
Crécy-en-Ponthieu F 78 B1
Crécy-la-Chapelle F 90 C2
Crécy-sur-Serre F 91 B3
Crediton GB 43 B3
Creeslough IRL 26 A3
Creetown GB 36 B2
Creeve GB 27 B4
Creglingen D 94 B2
Creil F 90 B2
Creissels F 130 A2
Crema I 120 B2
Cremeaux F 117 B3
Crémenes E 142 B1
Crémieu F 118 B2
Cremlingen D 73 B3
Cremona I 120 B3
Creney F 91 C4
Črenšovci SLO 111 C3
Créon F 128 B2
Crepaja SRB 127 B2
Crépey F 92 C1
Crépy F 91 B3
Crépy-en-Valois F 90 B2
Cres HR 123 C3
Crescentino I 119 B5
Crespino I 121 C4
Crespos E 150 B3
Cressage GB 39 B4
Cressensac F 129 A4
Cressia F 105 C4
Crest F 117 C5
Cresta CH 107 C4
Créteil F 90 C2
Creully F 88 A3
Creussen D 95 B3
Creutzwald F 92 B2
Creuzburg D 82 A2
Crevalcore I 121 C4
Crèvecoeur-le-Grand F 90 B2
Crevillente E 165 A4
Crévola d'Ossola I 119 A5
Crewe GB 38 A4
Crewkerne GB 43 B4
Criales E 143 B3
Crianlarich GB 34 B3
Criccieth GB 38 B2
Crickhowell GB 39 C3
Cricklade GB 44 B2
Crieff GB 35 B4
Criel-sur-Mer F 90 A1
Crikvenica HR 123 B3
Crillon F 90 B1
Crimmitschau D 83 B4
Crimond GB 33 D5
Crinitz D 84 A1
Cripán E 143 B4
Criquetot-l'Esneval F 89 A4
Crispiano I 173 B3
Crissolo I 119 C4
Cristóbal E 149 B4
Crivitz D 73 A4
Črna SLO 110 C1
Crna Bara
*Srbija* SRB 127 C1
*Vojvodina* SRB 126 B2
Crnac HR 125 B3
Crnča SRB 127 C1
Crni Lug
BIH 138 A2
HR 123 B3
Črni Vrh SLO 123 B3
Crnjelovo Donje BIH 125 C5
Črnomelj SLO 123 B4
Crocketford GB 36 A3
Crocq F 116 B2
Crodo I 119 A5
Croglin GB 37 B4
Crolly IRL 26 A2
Cromarty GB 32 D2
Cromer GB 41 C5
Cronat F 104 C2
Crookhaven IRL 29 C2
Crookstown IRL 29 C3
Croom IRL 29 B3
Cropalati I 174 B2
Crópani I 175 C2
Crosbost GB 31 A2
Crosby GB 38 A3
Crosía I 174 B2
Crossakiel IRL 27 C3
Cross-Hands GB 39 C2
Crosshaven IRL 29 C3
Crosshill GB 36 A2
Crossmolina IRL 26 B1
Crotone I 175 B3
Crottendorf D 83 B4
Crouy F 90 B3
Crowborough GB 45 B4
Crowland GB 41 C3
Crowthorne GB 44 B3
Croyde GB 42 A2
Croydon GB 44 B3
Crozon F 100 A1
Cruas F 117 C4
Cruceni RO 126 A3
Crúcoli I 174 B3
Cruden Bay GB 33 D5
Crudgington GB 38 B4
Cruis F 132 A1
Crumlin GB 27 B4
Cruseilles F 118 A3
Crusheen IRL 28 B3
Cruz de Incio E 141 B3
Crvenka SRB 126 B1
Črveny Kamen SK 98 B2
Csabacsüd H 113 C4
Csabrendek H 111 B4
Csákánydoroszló H 111 C3
Csákvár H 112 B2
Csanádapáca H 113 C4
Csanádpalota H 126 A2
Csány H 113 B3
Csanytelek H 113 C4
Csapod H 111 B3
Császár H 112 B2
Császártöltés H 112 C3
Csávoly H 125 A5
Csemö H 113 B3
Csengöd H 112 C3
Csépa H 113 C4
Csepreg H 111 B3
Cserkeszölö H 113 C4
Csernely H 113 A4
Csesztreg H 111 C3
Csökmö H 113 B5
Csököly H 124 A3
Csokonyavisonta H 124 A3
Csólyospálos H 113 C3
Csongrád H 113 C4
Csopak H 112 C1
Csorna H 111 B4
Csorvás H 113 C4
Csurgo H 124 A3
Cuacos de Yuste E 150 B2
Cualedro E 140 C3
Cuanca de Campos E 142 B1
Cuba P 160 A2
Cubel E 152 A2
Cubelles E 147 C2
Cubillos E 143 C4
Cubillos del Sil E 141 B4
Cubjac F 129 A3
Cubo de la Solana E 152 A1
Çubuk TR 23 A7
Cuckfield GB 44 B3
Cucuron F 131 B4
Cudillero E 141 A4
Cuéllar E 151 A3
Cuenca E 152 B1
Cuers F 132 B2
Cuerva E 157 A3
Cueva de Agreda E 144 C2
Cuevas Bajas E 163 A3
Cuevas del Almanzora E 164 B3
Cuevas del Becerro E 162 B2
Cuevas del Campo E 164 B2
Cuevas del Valle E 150 B2
Cuevas de San Clemente E 143 B3
Cuevas de San Marcos E 163 A3
Cuges-les-Pins F 132 B1
Cúglieri I 178 B2
Cugnaux F 129 C4
Cuijk NL 80 A1
Cuinzier F 117 A4
Cuiseaux F 105 C4
Cuisery F 105 C4
Culan F 103 C4
Culemborg NL 79 A5
Cúllar E 164 B2
Cullaville GB 27 B4
Cullera E 159 B3
Cullivoe GB 33 A5
Cullompton GB 43 B3
Cully CH 106 C1
Culoz F 118 B2
Cults GB 33 D4
Cumbernauld GB 35 C4
Cumbres de San Bartolomé E 161 A3
Cumbres Mayores E 161 A3
Cumiana I 119 C4
Čumić SRB 127 C2
Cumnock GB 36 A2
Çumra TR 23 C7
Cúneo I 133 A3
Cunlhat F 117 B3
Čunski HR 123 C3
Cuntis E 140 B2
Cuorgnè I 119 B4
Cupar GB 35 B4
Cupello I 170 A2
Cupra Maríttima I 136 B2
Cupramontana I 136 B2
Ćuprija SRB 127 D3
Curinga I 175 C2
Currelos E 140 B3
Currie GB 35 C4
Curtea de Argeş RO 17 C6
Curtici RO 126 A3
Curtis E 140 A2
Curtis Santa Eulalia E 140 A2
Čurug SRB 126 B2
Cusano Mutri I 170 B2
Cushendall GB 27 A4
Cusset F 117 A3
Cussy-les-Forges F 104 B3
Custines F 92 C2
Cutanda E 152 B2
Cutro I 175 B2
Cutrofiano I 173 B4
Cuts F 90 B3
Cuvilly F 90 B2
Cuxhaven D 64 C1
Cvikov CZ 84 B2
Cwmbran GB 39 C3
Cybinka PL 75 B3
Czacz PL 75 B5
Czajków PL 86 A2
Czaplinek PL 75 A5
Czarlin PL 69 A3
Czarna-Dąbrówka PL 68 A2
Czarna Woda PL 68 B3
Czarnca PL 87 B3
Czarne PL 68 B1
Czarnków PL 75 B5
Czarnowo PL 76 A3
Czarnozyly PL 86 A2
Czarny Bór PL 85 B4
Czarny-Dunajec PL 99 B3
Czarny Las PL 86 A1
Czchow PL 99 B4
Czechowice-Dziedzice PL 98 B2
Czempiń PL 75 B5
Czermno PL 87 A4
Czernichow PL 99 B3
Czerniejewo PL 76 B2
Czernikowo PL 76 B3
Czersk PL 68 B2
Czerwieńsk PL 75 B4
Czerwionka-Leszczyny PL 86 B2
Częstochowa PL 86 B3
Czeszewo PL 76 B2
Człopa PL 75 A5
Człuchów PL 68 B2
Czołpino PL 68 A2

## D

Dağ TR 189 B5
Daaden D 81 B3
Dabas H 112 B3
Dąbie PL 76 B3
Dąbki PL 67 B5
Dabo F 92 C3
Dabrowa PL 76 B2
Dąbrowa Górnicza PL 86 B3
Dąbrowa Tarnowska PL 87 B4
Dąbrowice PL 77 B4
Dabrowno PL 77 A5
Dachau D 108 A2
Dačice CZ 97 B3
Daday TR 23 A7
Dagali N 47 B5
Dägebüll D 64 B1
Dagmersellen CH 106 B2
Dahlen D 83 A4
Dahlenburg D 73 A3
Dahme D 83 A5
Dahn D 93 B3
Dähre D 73 B3
Daikanvik S 195 E7
Dail bho Dheas GB 31 A2
Dailly GB 36 A2
Daimiel E 157 A4
Daingean IRL 30 A1
Đakovica KOS 16 D4
Đakovo HR 125 B4
Dal
*Akershus* N 48 B3
*Telemark* N 47 C5
Dalaas A 107 B5
Dalabrog GB 31 B1
Dala-Floda S 50 B1
Dala-Husby S 50 B2
Dala-Järna S 50 B1
Dalaman TR 188 C3
Dalarö S 57 A4
Dalbeattie GB 36 B3
Dalby
DK 59 C3
*Skåne* S 61 D3
*Uppsala* S 57 A3
*Värmland* S 49 B4
Dale
*Pembrokeshire* GB 39 C1
*Shetland* GB 33 A5
*Hordaland* N 46 B2
*Sogn og Fjordane* N 46 A2
Dalen
*Akershus* N 48 C3
*Telemark* N 53 A4
Daleszyce PL 87 B4
Dalhalvaig GB 32 C3
Dalheim L 92 B2
Dalhem S 57 C4
Dalias E 164 C2
Dalj HR 125 B4
Dalkeith GB 35 C4
Dalkey IRL 30 A2
Dalmally GB 34 B3
Dalmellington GB 36 A2
Dalmose DK 65 A4
Daløy N 46 A1
Dalry
*Dumfries & Galloway* GB 34 C3
*North Ayrshire* GB 36 A2
Dalrymple GB 36 A2
Dalseter N 47 A6
Dalsjöfors S 60 B3
Dalskog S 54 B3
Dals Långed S 54 B3
Dals Rostock S 54 B3
Dalston GB 36 B4
Dalstorp S 60 B3
Dalton-in-Furness GB 36 B3
Daluis F 132 A2
Dalum
D 71 B4
S 60 B3
Dalvík IS 191 B7
Dalwhinnie GB 32 E2
Dalyan TR 188 C3
Damasi GR 182 D4
Damasławek PL 76 B2
Damazan F 129 B3
Damgan F 101 B3
Dammarie-les-Lys F 90 C2
Dammartin-en-Goële F 90 B2
Damme D 71 B5
Damnica PL 68 A2
Dampierre F 105 B4
Dampierre-sur-Salon F 105 B4
Damüls A 107 B4
Damville F 89 B5
Damvillers F 92 B1
Damwoude NL 70 A2
Danasjö S 195 E7
Danbury GB 45 B4
Dångebo S 63 B3
Dangers F 89 B5
Dangé-St Romain F 102 C2
Dangeul F 89 B4
Danilovgrad MNE 16 D3
Danischenhagen D 64 B3
Daniszyn PL 85 A5
Danjoutin F 106 B1
Dannas S 60 B3
Dannemarie F 106 B2
Dannemora S 51 B4
Dannenberg D 73 A4
Dánszentmiklós H 112 B3
Dány H 112 B3
Daoulas F 100 A1
Darabani RO 17 A7
Darány H 125 B3
Darda HR 125 B4
Dardesheim D 73 C3
Darfeld D 71 B4
Darfo I 120 B3
Dargiń PL 68 A1
Dargun D 66 C1
Darlington GB 37 B5
Darłowo PL 68 A1
Darmstadt D 93 B4
Darney F 105 A5
Daroca E 152 A2
Darque P 148 A1
Darragh IRL 28 B2
Dartford GB 45 B4
Dartington GB 43 B3
Dartmouth GB 43 B3
Darton GB 40 B2
Daruvar HR 124 B3
Darvas H 113 B5
Darvel GB 36 A2
Darwen GB 38 A4
Dassel D 82 A1
Dassow D 65 C3
Datça TR 188 C2
Datteln D 80 A3
Dattenfeld D 81 B3
Daugard DK 59 C2
Daugavpils LV 8 E5
Daumeray F 102 B1
Daun D 80 B2
Daventry GB 44 A2
Davle CZ 96 B2
Davor HR 124 B3
Davos CH 107 C4
Davutlar TR 188 B2
Davyd Haradok BY 13 B7
Dawlish GB 43 B3
Dax F 128 C1
Dazkırı TR 189 B4
Deal GB 45 B5
Deauville F 89 A4
Deba E 143 A4
Debar MK 182 B2
Dębe PL 77 B5
Dębica PL 87 B5
Dębnica Kaszubska PL 68 A2
Dębno PL 74 B3
Dębołęka PL 86 A2
Dębowa Łaka PL 69 B4
Debrc SRB 127 C1
Debrecen H 113 B5
Debrznica PL 75 B4
Debrzno PL 68 B2
Debstedt D 72 A1
Decazeville F 130 A1
Dechtice SK 98 C1
Decima I 168 B2
Decimomannu I 179 C2
Děčín CZ 84 B2
Decize F 104 C2
De Cocksdorp NL 70 A1
Decollatura I 175 B2
Decs H 125 A4
Deddington GB 44 B2
Dedeler TR 187 B5
Dedelow D 74 A2
Dedemli TR 189 B7
Dedemsvaart NL 71 B3
Dédestapolcsány H 113 A4
Dedovichi RUS 9 D6
Deeping St Nicholas GB 41 C3
Deftera CY 181 A2
Dég H 112 C2
Degaña E 141 B4
Degeberga S 61 D4
Degerby FIN 51 B7
Degerfors S 55 A5
Degerhamn S 63 B4
Degernes N 54 A2
Deggendorf D 95 C4
Deggingen D 94 C1
Dego I 133 A4
Degolados P 155 B3
De Haan B 78 A3
Dehesas de Guadix E 164 B1
Dehesas Viejas E 163 A4
Deia E 166 B2
Deining D 95 B3
Deinze B 79 B3
Déiva Marina I 134 A2
Dej RO 17 B5
Deje S 55 A4
De Koog NL 70 A1
Delabole GB 42 B2
Delary S 61 C3
Delbrück D 81 A4
Delčevo MK 182 B4
Delden NL 71 B3
Deleitosa E 156 A2
Delekovec HR 124 A2
Delémont CH 106 B2
Delft NL 70 B1
Delfzijl NL 71 A3
Délia I 176 B2
Delianuova I 175 C1
Deliblato SRB 127 C3
Delice TR 23 B7
Deliceto I 171 B3
Delitzsch D 83 A4
Dellach A 109 C4
Delle F 106 B2
Delme F 92 C2
Delmen-horst D 72 A1
Delnice HR 123 B3
Delsbo S 200 E2
Delvin IRL 30 A1
Delvinë AL 182 D2
Demandice SK 112 A2
Demen D 73 A4
Demidov RUS 13 A9
Demigny F 105 C3
Demirci TR 186 C3
Demirköy TR 186 A2
Demirtaş TR 186 B4
Demmin D 66 C2
Demonte I 133 A3
Demyansk RUS 9 D8
Denain F 78 B3
Denbigh GB 38 A3
Den Burg NL 70 A1
Dender-monde B 79 A4
Denekamp NL 71 B4
Den Ham NL 71 B3
Den Helder NL 70 B1
Denholm GB 35 C5
Denia E 159 C4
Denizli TR 188 B4
Denkendorf D 95 C3
Denklingen D 81 B3
Denny GB 35 B4
Den Oever NL 70 B2
Denta RO 126 B3
Déols F 103 C3
De Panne B 78 A2
Derbent TR 188 A3
Derby GB 40 C2
Derecske H 113 B5
Dereköy TR 186 A2
Derenberg D 82 A2
Derinkuyu TR 23 B8
Dermbach D 82 B2
Dermulo I 121 A4
Deronje SRB 125 B5
Derrygonnelly GB 26 B3
Derrylin GB 27 B3
Derry/Londonderry GB 27 B3
Dersingham GB 41 C4
Deruta I 136 C1
Dervaig GB 34 B1
Derval F 101 B4
Derveni GR 184 A3
Derventa BIH 125 C3
Dervock GB 27 A4
Desana I 119 B5
Descartes F 102 C2
Desenzano del Garda I 121 B3
Deset N 48 A3
Deševa BIH 139 B4
Desfina GR 184 A3
Desimirovac SRB 127 C2
Désio I 120 B2
Deskati GR 182 D3
Deskle SLO 122 A2
Desná CZ 84 B3
Dešov CZ 97 C3
Despotovac SRB 127 C3
Despotovo SRB 126 B1
Dessau D 83 A4
Deštná CZ 96 B2
Destriana E 141 B4
Désulo I 179 B3
Desvres F 78 B1
Deszk H 126 A2
Deta RO 126 B3
Detmold D 72 C1
Dětřichov CZ 98 B1
Dettelbach D 94 B2
Dettingen
*Baden-Württemberg* D 94 C1
*Baden-Württemberg* D 107 B4
Dettwiller F 93 C3
Detva SK 99 C3
Deurne NL 80 A1
Deutschkreutz A 111 B3
Deutschlandsberg A 110 C2
Deutsch Wagram A 111 A3
Deva RO 16 C5
Dévaványa H 113 B4
Devecikonağı TR 186 C3
Devecser H 111 B4
Develi TR 23 B8
Deventer NL 70 B3
Devil's Bridge GB 39 B3
Devin BG 183 B6
Devinska Nova Ves SK 111 A3
Devizes GB 43 A5
Devonport GB 42 B2
Devrek TR 187 A6
Devrekâni TR 23 A7
Ðevrske HR 137 B4
De Wijk NL 71 B3
Dewsbury GB 40 B2
Deza E 152 A1
Dežanovac HR 124 B3
Dezzo I 120 B3
Dhali CY 181 A2
Dherinia CY 181 A2
Diamante I 174 B1
Dianalund DK 61 D1
Diano d'Alba I 119 C5
Diano Marina I 133 B4
Dicomano I 135 B4
Didcot GB 44 B2
Didimoticho GR 186 A1
Die F 118 C2
Diebling F 92 B2
Dieburg D 93 B4
Diego del Carpio E 150 B2
Diekirch L 92 B2
Diélette F 88 A2
Diémoz F 118 B2
Dienten am Hochkönig A 109 B3
Diepenbeck B 79 B5

Diepholz D 71 B5
Dieppe F 89 A5
Dierberg D 74 A1
Dierdorf D 81 B3
Dieren NL 70 B3
Dierhagen D 66 B1
Diesdorf D 73 B3
Diessen D 108 B2
Diest B 79 B5
Dietenheim D 94 C2
Dietfurt D 95 B3
Dietikon CH 106 B3
Dietzenbach D 93 A4
Dieue-sur-Meuse F 92 B1
Dieulefit F 131 A4
Dieulouard F 92 C2
Dieuze F 92 C2
Diever NL 71 B3
Diez D 81 B4
Diezma E 163 A4
Differdange L 92 B1
Digermulen N 194 B6
Dignac F 115 C4
Dignano I 122 A1
Digne-les-Bains F 132 A2
Digny F 89 B5
Digoin F 104 C2
Dijon F 105 B4
Dikanäs S 195 E7
Dikili TR 186 C1
Diksmuide B 78 A2
Dilar E 163 A4
Dillenburg D 81 B4
Dillingen
Bayern D 94 C2
Saarland D 92 B2
Dilsen B 80 A1
Dimaro I 121 A3
Dimitrovgrad BG 183 A7
Dimitsana GR 184 B3
Dinami I 175 C2
Dinan F 101 A3
Dinant B 79 B4
Dinar TR 189 A5
Dinard F 101 A3
Dinek TR 187 C6
Dingden D 80 A2
Dingelstädt D 82 A2
Dingle
IRL 29 B1
S 54 B2
Dingolfing D 95 C4
Dingtuna S 56 A2
Dingwall GB 32 D2
Dinkelsbühl D 94 B2
Dinkelscherben D 94 C2
Dinklage D 71 B5
Dinslaken D 80 A2
Dinxperlo NL 80 A2
Diö S 63 B2
Diósgyör H 113 A4
Diósjeno H 112 B3
Diou F 104 C2
Dippen GB 34 C2
Dipperz D 82 B1
Dippoldiswalde D 84 B1
Dirdal N 52 B2
Dirksland NL 79 A4
Dirlewang D 108 B1
Dischingen D 94 C2
Disentis CH 107 C3
Diso I 173 B4
Diss GB 45 A5
Dissen D 71 B5
Distington GB 36 B3
Ditzingen D 93 C5
Ditzum D 71 A4
Divača SLO 122 B2
Dives-sur-Mer F 89 A3
Divín SK 99 C3
Divion F 78 B2
Divišov CZ 96 B2
Divonne les Bains
F 118 A3
Dixmont F 104 A2
Dizy-le-Gros F 91 B4
Djúpivogur IS 191 C11
Djupvasshytta N 198 C4
Djura S 50 B1
Djurås S 50 B2
Djurmo S 50 B2
Djursdala S 62 A3
Dlouhá Loucka CZ 98 B1
Długowola PL 87 A5
Dmitrov RUS 9 D10
Dno RUS 9 D6
Doade E 141 B3
Doğanhisar TR 189 A6
Dobanovci SRB 127 C2
Dobbertin D 73 A5
Dobbiaco I 108 C3
Dobczyce PL 99 B4
Dobele LV 8 D3
Döbeln D 83 A5
Doberlug-Kirchhain
D 83 A5
Dobern D 84 A2
Dobersberg A 97 C3
Dobiegniew PL 75 B4
Dobieszyn PL 87 A5
Doboj BIH 125 C4
Dobošnica BIH 125 C4
Doboz H 113 C5
Dobrá CZ 98 B2
Dobra
Wielkopolskie PL 76 C3
Zachodnio-Pomorskie
PL 74 A3
Zachodnio-Pomorskie
PL 75 A4
Dobrá Niva SK 99 C3
Dobřany CZ 96 B1
Dobre PL 76 B3
Dobre Miasto PL 69 B5
Dobreta-Turnu-Severin
RO 16 C5
Dobri H 111 C3
Dobrica SRB 126 B2
Dobrich BG 17 D7
Dobrinishta BG 183 B5
Dobříš CZ 96 B2
Dobro E 143 B3
Dobrodzień PL 86 B2
Döbrököz H 112 C2
Dobromierz PL 85 B4
Dobrosołowo PL 76 B3
Dobroszyce PL 85 A5
Dobrovnik SLO 111 C3
Dobrush BY 13 B9
Dobruška CZ 85 B4
Dobrzany PL 75 A4
Dobrzen Wielki PL 86 B1
Dobrzyca
Wielkopolskie PL 75 A5
Wielkopolskie PL 85 A5
Zachodnio-Pomorskie
PL 67 B4
Dobrzyńnad Wisłą
PL 77 B4
Dobšiná SK 99 C4
Dobwalls GB 42 B2
Dochamps B 80 B1
Docking GB 41 C4
Docksta S 200 C4
Doddington GB 37 A4
Döderhult S 62 A4
Doesburg NL 70 B3
Doetinchem NL 71 C3
Dogliani I 133 A3
Dogueno P 160 B2
Doische B 91 A4
Dois Portos P 154 B1
Dojč SK 98 C1
Dokka N 48 B2
Dokkedal DK 58 B3
Dokkum NL 70 A2
Dokležovje SLO 111 C3
Doksy CZ 84 B2
Dokuz TR 189 A7
Dolancourt F 104 A3
Dolceácqua I 133 B3
Dol-de-Bretagne F 88 B2
Dole F 105 B4
Dølemo N 53 B4
Dolenja vas SLO 123 B3
Dolenjske Toplice
SLO 123 B4
Dolfor GB 39 B3
Dolgarrog GB 38 A3
Dolgellau GB 38 B3
Doliana GR 182 D2
Dolianova I 179 C3
Dolice PL 75 A4
Doljani HR 138 A2
Döllach im Mölltal
A 109 C3
Dolle D 73 B4
Dollnstein D 94 C3
Dollot F 104 A2
Döllstadt D 82 A2
Dolná Strehová SK 99 C3
Dolné Saliby SK 111 A4
Dolni Benešov CZ 98 B2
Dolni Bousov CZ 84 B3
Dolni Kounice CZ 97 B4
Dolni Kralovice CZ 97 B3
Dolni Ŭjezd CZ 97 B4
Dolni Žandov CZ 95 A4
Dolný Kubín SK 99 B3
Dolo I 121 B5
Dolores E 165 A4
Dolovo SRB 127 C2
Dölsach A 109 C3
Dolsk PL 76 B2
Dolwyddelan GB 38 A3
Domaljevac BIH 125 B4
Domaniç TR 187 C4
Domaniža SK 98 B2
Domanovići BIH 139 B3
Domašov CZ 85 B5
Domaszék H 126 A1
Domaszków PL 85 B4
Domaszowice PL 86 A1
Domat-Ems CH 107 C4
Domažlice CZ 95 B4
Dombås N 198 C6
Dombasle-sur-Meurthe
F 92 C2
Dombegyház H 126 A3
Dombóvár H 112 C2
Domène F 118 B2
Domérat F 116 A2
Domfessel F 92 C3
Domfront F 88 B3
Domfront-en-
Champagne F 102 A2
Domingão P 154 B2
Domingo Pérez
Granada E 163 A4
Toledo E 150 C3
Dömitz D 73 A4
Dommartin F 91 C4
Dommartin-le-Franc
F 91 C4
Domme F 129 B4
Dommitzsch D 83 A4
Domodóssola I 119 A5
Domokos GR 182 D4
Domoszló H 113 B4
Dompaire F 105 A5
Dompierre-du-Chemin
F 88 B2
Dompierre-sur-Besbre
F 104 C2
Dompierre-sur-Mer
F 114 B2
Domrémy-la-Pucelle
F 92 C1
Dömsöd H 112 B3
Domsure F 118 A2
Dómus de Maria I 179 D2
Domusnóvas I 179 C2
Domvena GR 184 A3
Domžale SLO 123 A3
Donado E 141 B4
Donaghadee GB 27 B5
Don Alvaro E 155 C4
Doña Mencía E 163 A3
Donaueschingen D 106 B3
Donauwörth D 94 C2
Don Benito E 156 B2
Doncaster GB 40 B2
Donegal IRL 26 B2
Donestebe-Santesteban
E 144 A2
Donges F 101 B3
Dongo I 120 A2
Donington GB 41 C3
Doniños E 140 A2
Donja Bebrina HR 125 B4
Donja Brela HR 138 B2
Donja Dubica BIH 125 B4
Donja Dubrava HR 124 A2
Donja Kupčina HR 123 B4
Donja Šatornja
SRB 127 C2
Donja Stubica HR 124 B1
Donje Brišnik BIH 138 B3
Donje Stative HR 123 B4
Donji-Andrijevci
HR 125 B4
Donji Kazanci BIH 138 B2
Donji Koričáni BIH 138 A3
Donji Lapac HR 124 C1
Donji Malovan BIH 138 B3
Donji Miholjac HR 125 B4
Donji Mosti HR 124 A2
Donji Poloj HR 123 B4
Donji-Rujani BIH 138 B2
Donji Srb HR 138 A2
Donji Svilaj BIH 125 B4
Donji Tovarnik
SRB 127 C1
Donji Vakuf BIH 138 A3
Donnalucata I 177 C3
Donnemarie-Dontilly
F 90 C3
Donnersbach A 110 B1
Donnersbachwald
A 109 B5
Donnerskirchen A 111 B3
Donorático I 134 B3
Donostia-San Sebastián
E 144 A2
Donovaly SK 99 C3
Donzenac F 129 A4
Donzère F 131 A3
Donzy F 104 B2
Doonbeg IRL 29 B2
Doorn NL 70 B2
Dor E 140 A1
Dorchester GB 43 B4
Dørdal N 53 B5
Dordrecht NL 79 A4
Dörenthe D 71 B4
Dores GB 32 D2
Dorfen D 95 C4
Dorfgastein A 109 B4
Dorfmark D 72 B2
Dorf Mecklenburg D 65 C4
Dorgali I 178 B3
Dorking GB 44 B3
Dormagen D 80 A2
Dormánd H 113 B4
Dormans F 91 B3
Dornava SLO 124 A1
Dornbirn A 107 B4
Dornburg D 83 A3
Dorndorf D 82 B2
Dornecy F 104 B2
Dornes F 104 C2
Dornhan D 93 C4
Dornie GB 31 B3
Dornoch GB 32 D2
Dornum D 71 A4
Dorog H 112 B2
Dorohoi RO 17 B7
Dorotea S 200 B2
Dorotowo PL 69 B5
Dörpen D 71 B4
Dorsten D 80 A2
Dortan F 118 A2
Dortmund D 80 A3
Doruchów PL 86 A2
Dorum D 64 C1
Dörverden D 72 B2
Dörzbach D 94 B1
Dos Aguas E 159 B3
Dosbarrios E 151 C4
Döşemealtı TR 189 B5
Dos Hermanas E 162 A2
Dospat BG 183 B6
Dos-Torres E 156 B3
Dötlingen D 72 B1
Dottignies B 78 B3
Döttingen CH 106 B3
Douai F 78 B3
Douarnenez F 100 A1
Douchy F 104 B2
Douchy-les-Mines F 78 B3
Doucier F 105 C4
Doudeville F 89 A4
Doué-la-Fontaine
F 102 B1
Douglas
Isle of Man GB 36 B2
South Lanarkshire
GB 36 A3
Doulaincourt-Saucourt
F 91 C5
Doulevant-le-Château
F 91 C4
Doullens F 90 A2
Dounby GB 33 B3
Doune GB 35 B3
Dounreay GB 32 C3
Dour B 79 B3
Dourdan F 90 C2
Dourgne F 146 A3
Dournazac F 115 C4
Douro Calvo P 148 B2
Douvaine F 118 A3
Douvres-la-Délivrande
F 89 A3
Douzy F 91 B5
Dover GB 45 B5
Dovje SLO 109 C4
Dovre N 198 D6
Downham Market
GB 41 C4
Downhill GB 27 A4
Downpatrick GB 27 B5
Dowra IRL 26 B2
Doxato GR 183 B6
Doyet F 116 A2
Dozule F 89 A3
Drača SRB 127 C2
Dračevo
BIH 139 C4
MK 182 B3
Drachten NL 70 A3
Draga SLO 123 B3
Drăgăşani RO 17 C6
Dragatuš SLO 123 B4
Dragichyn BY 13 B6
Draginja SRB 127 C1
Dragocvet SRB 127 D3
Dragolovci BIH 125 C3
Dragoni I 170 B2
Dragør DK 61 D2
Dragotina HR 124 B2
Dragotinja BIH 124 B2
Dragozetići HR 123 B3
Draguignan F 132 B2
Drahnsdorf D 74 C2
Drahonice CZ 96 B2
Drahovce SK 98 C1
Drama GR 183 B6
Drammen N 54 A1
Drangedal N 53 A5
Drangsnes IS 190 B4
Dransfeld D 82 A1
Dranske D 66 B2
Draperstown GB 27 B4
Drassburg A 111 B3
Drávaszabolcs H 125 B4
Dravograd SLO 110 C2
Drawno PL 75 A4
Drawsko Pomorskie
PL 75 A4
Drayton GB 41 C5
Drązdżewo PL 77 A6
Draženov CZ 95 B4
Draževac SRB 127 C2
Dražice HR 123 B3
Drebkau D 84 A2
Dreieich D 93 A4
Dreisen D 93 B4
Drenovci HR 125 C4
Drensteinfurt D 81 A3
Dresden D 84 A1
Dretyń PL 68 A1
Dreux F 89 B5
Dřevohostice CZ 98 B1
Drevsjø N 199 D9
Drewitz D 73 B5
Drezdenko PL 75 B4
Drežnica HR 123 B4
Drežnik-Grad HR 123 C4
Drietona SK 98 C1
Driffield GB 40 A3
Drimnin GB 34 B2
Drimoleague IRL 29 C2
Dringenberg D 81 A5
Drinić BIH 138 A2
Drinjača BIH 139 A5
Drinovci BIH 138 B3
Driopida GR 185 B5
Drivstua N 198 C6
Drlače SRB 127 C1
Drnholec CZ 97 C4
Drniš HR 138 B2
Drnje HR 124 A2
Drnovice CZ 97 B4
Dro I 121 B3
Drøbak N 54 A1
Drobin PL 77 B5
Drochia MD 17 A7
Drochtersen D 64 C2
Drogheda IRL 30 A2
Drohobych UA 13 D5
Droitwich Spa GB 44 A1
Drołtowice PL 85 A5
Dromahair IRL 26 B2
Dromcolliher IRL 29 B3
Dromore
Down GB 27 B4
Tyrone GB 27 B3
Dromore West IRL 26 B2
Dronero I 133 A3
Dronfield GB 40 B2
Drongan GB 36 A2
Dronninglund DK 58 A3
Dronrijp NL 70 A2
Dronten NL 70 B2
Drosendorf A 97 C3
Drösing A 97 C4
Drottningholm S 57 A3
Droué F 103 A3
Drulingen F 92 C3
Drumbeg GB 32 C1
Drumcliff IRL 26 B2
Drumgask GB 32 D2
Drumkeeran IRL 26 B2
Drummore GB 36 B2
Drumnadrochit GB 32 D2
Drumquin GB 27 B3
Drumshanbo IRL 26 B2
Drumsna IRL 26 C2
Drunen NL 79 A5
Druskininkai LT 13 A5
Druten NL 80 A1
Druya BY 13 A7
Družetići SRB 127 C2
Drvar BIH 138 A2
Drvenik HR 138 B3
Drwalew PL 77 C6
Drymen GB 34 B3
Drynoch GB 31 B2
Drzewce PL 76 B2
Drzewiany PL 68 B1
Drzewica PL 87 A4
Dualchi I 178 B2
Duas Igrejas P 149 A3
Dub SRB 127 D1
Dubá CZ 84 B2
Dubăsari MD 17 B8
Duben D 74 C2
Dübendorf CH 107 B3
Dubi CZ 84 B1
Dubica HR 124 B2
Dublin IRL 30 A2
Dubna RUS 9 D10
Dubňany CZ 98 C1
Dubnica nad Váhom
SK 98 C2
Dubnik SK 112 B2
Dubno UA 13 C6
Dubodiel SK 98 C2
Dubona SRB 127 C2
Dubovac SRB 127 C3
Dubovic BIH 124 C2
Dubranec HR 124 B1
Dubrava HR 124 B2
Dubrave BIH 125 C4
Dubravica
HR 123 B4
SRB 127 C3
Dubrovnik HR 139 C4
Dubrovytsya UA 13 C7
Ducey F 88 B2
Duchcov CZ 84 B1
Ducherow D 74 A2
Dučina SRB 127 C2
Duclair F 89 A4
Dudar H 112 B1
Duddington GB 40 C3
Duderstadt D 82 A2
Dudeştii Vechi RO 126 A2
Dudley GB 40 C1
Dueñas E 142 C2
Duesund N 46 B2
Dueville I 121 B4
Duffel B 79 A4
Duffield GB 40 C2
Dufftown GB 32 D3
Duga Resa HR 123 B4
Dugi Rat HR 138 B2
Dugny-sur-Meuse F 92 B1
Dugopolje HR 138 B2
Dugo Selo HR 124 B2
Duino I 122 B2
Duisburg D 80 A2
Dukat AL 182 C1
Dukovany CZ 97 B4
Duleek IRL 30 A2
Dülken D 80 A2
Dülmen D 80 A3
Dulovo BG 17 D7
Dulpetorpet N 49 B4
Dulverton GB 43 A3
Dumbarton GB 34 C3
Dümerek TR 187 C6
Dumfries GB 36 A3
Dumlupınar TR 187 D4
Dümpelfeld D 80 B2
Dunaalmás H 112 B2
Dunabogdány H 112 B3
Dunafalva H 125 A4
Dunaföldvár H 112 C2
Dunaharaszti H 112 B3
Dunajská Streda
SK 111 B4
Dunakeszi H 112 B3
Dunakiliti H 111 B4
Dunakömlöd H 112 C2
Dunapataj H 112 C2
Dunaszekcsö H 125 A4
Dunaszentgyorgy
H 112 C2
Dunatetétlen H 112 C3
Dunaújváros H 112 C2
Dunavecse H 112 C2
Dunbar GB 35 B5
Dunbeath GB 32 C3
Dunblane GB 35 B4
Dunboyne IRL 30 A2
Dundalk IRL 27 B4
Dundee GB 35 B5
Dundrennan GB 36 B3
Dundrum GB 27 B5
Dunfanaghy IRL 26 A3
Dunfermline GB 35 B4
Dungannon GB 27 B4
Dungarvan IRL 29 B4
Dungiven GB 27 B4
Dunglow IRL 26 B2
Dungourney IRL 29 C3
Duninowo PL 68 A1
Dunkeld GB 35 B4
Dunker S 56 A2
Dunkerque = Dunkirk
F 78 A2
Dunkineely IRL 26 B2
Dunkirk = Dunkerque
F 78 A2
Dun Laoghaire IRL 30 A2
Dunlavin IRL 30 A2
Dunleer IRL 27 C4
Dun-le-Palestel F 116 A1
Dun-les-Places F 104 B3
Dunlop GB 36 A2
Dunloy GB 27 A4
Dunmanway IRL 29 C2
Dunmore IRL 28 A3
Dunmore East IRL 30 B2
Dunmurry GB 27 B4
Dunnet GB 32 C3
Dunningen D 107 A3
Dunoon GB 34 C3
Duns GB 35 C5
Dunscore GB 36 A3
Dunsford GB 43 B3
Dunshaughlin IRL 30 A2
Dunstable GB 44 B3
Dunster GB 43 A3
Dun-sur-Auron F 103 C4
Dun-sur-Meuse F 91 B5
Dunvegan GB 31 B2
Duplek SLO 110 C2
Dupnitsa BG 17 D5
Durağan TR 23 A8
Durach D 107 B5
Durak TR 186 C3
Durana E 143 B4
Durance F 128 B3
Durango E 143 A4
Durankulak BG 17 D8
Duras F 128 B3
Durban-Corbières
F 146 B3
Dürbheim D 107 A3
Durbuy B 79 B5
Dúrcal E 163 B4
Đurđenovac HR 125 B4
Đurđevac HR 124 A3
Đurđevik BIH 139 A4
Düren D 80 B2
Durham GB 37 B5
Đurinci SRB 127 C2
Durlach D 93 C4
Đurmanec HR 124 A1
Durness GB 32 C2
Dürnkrut A 97 C4
Dürrboden CH 107 C4
Dürrenboden CH 107 C3
Durrës AL 182 B1
Durrow IRL 30 B1
Durrus IRL 29 C2
Dursunbey TR 186 C3
Durtal F 102 B1
Durup DK 58 B1
Durusu TR 186 A3
Dusina BIH 139 B3
Dusnok H 112 C2
Dusocin PL 69 B3
Düsseldorf D 80 A2
Dusslingen D 93 C5
Duszniki PL 75 B5
Duszniki-Zdrój PL 85 B4
Dutovlje SLO 122 B2
Duvebo S 55 B5
Duved S 199 B9
Düzağac TR 187 D5
Düzce TR 187 B6
Dvärsätt S 199 B11
Dvor HR 124 B2
Dvorce CZ 98 B1
Dvorníky SK 98 C1
Dvory nad Žitavou
SK 112 B2
Dvůr Královénad Labem
CZ 85 B3
Dybvad DK 58 A3
Dyce GB 33 D4
Dygowo PL 67 B4
Dykehead GB 35 B4
Dymchurch GB 45 B5
Dymer UA 13 C9
Dyrnes N 198 B4
Dywity PL 69 B5
Džanići BIH 139 B3
Dziadowa Kłoda PL 86 A1
Działdowo PL 77 A5

Działoszyce PL 87 B4
Działoszyn PL 86 A2
Dziemiany PL 68 A2
Dzierząźnia PL 77 B5
Dzierzgoń PL 69 B4
Dzierzgowo PL 77 A5
Dzierżoniów PL 85 B4
Dzisna BY 13 A8
Dziwnów PL 67 B3
Dźwierzuty PL 77 A5
Dzyarzhynsk BY 13 B7
Dzyatlava BY 13 B6

## E

Ea E 143 A4
Eaglesfield GB 36 A3
Ealing GB 44 B3
Eardisley GB 39 B3
Earls Barton GB 44 A3
Earl Shilton GB 40 C2
Earlston GB 35 C5
Easington GB 41 B4
Easky IRL 26 B2
Eastbourne GB 45 C4
East Calder GB 35 C4
East Dereham GB 41 C4
Easter Skeld GB 33 A5
East Grinstead GB 45 B4
East Ilsley GB 44 B2
East Kilbride GB 36 A2
Eastleigh GB 44 C2
East Linton GB 35 C5
East Markham GB 40 B3
Easton GB 43 B4
East Wittering GB 44 C3
Eaton Socon GB 44 A3
Eaux-Bonnes F 145 B3
Eauze F 128 C3
Ebberup DK 59 C2
Ebbs A 108 B3
Ebbw Vale GB 39 C3
Ebeleben D 82 A2
Ebeltoft DK 59 B3
Ebene Reichenau A 109 C4
Eben im Pongau A 109 B4
Ebensee A 109 B4
Ebensfeld D 94 A2
Eberbach D 93 B4
Ebergötzen D 82 A2
Ebermann-Stadt D 94 B3
Ebern D 82 B2
Eberndorf A 110 C1
Ebersbach D 84 A2
Ebersberg D 108 A2
Ebersdorf
*Bayern* D 82 B3
*Niedersachsen* D 72 A2
Eberstein A 110 C1
Eberswalde D 74 B2
Ebnat-Kappel CH 107 B4
Éboli I 170 C3
Ebrach D 94 B2
Ebreichsdorf A 111 B3
Ebreuil F 116 A3
Ebstorf D 72 A3
Ecclefechan GB 36 A3
Eccleshall GB 40 C1
Eceabat TR 186 B1
Echallens CH 106 C1
Echauri E 144 B2
Echinos GR 183 B7
Echiré F 114 B3
Échirolles F 118 B2
Echourgnac F 128 A3
Echt NL 80 A1
Echte D 82 A2
Echternach L 92 B2
Ecija E 162 A2
Ečka SRB 126 B2
Eckartsberga D 82 A3
Eckelshausen D 81 B4
Eckental D 94 B3
Eckernförde D 64 B2
Eckerö FIN 51 B6
Eckington GB 40 B2
Éclaron F 91 C4
Écommoy F 102 B2
Écouché F 89 B3
Ecouis F 90 B1
Ecséd H 113 B3
Ecsegfalva H 113 B4
Écueillé F 103 B3
Ed S 54 B2
Eda S 49 C4
Eda glasbruk S 49 C4
Edam NL 70 B2
Edane S 55 A3
Edderton GB 32 D2
Ede NL 70 B2
Edebäck S 49 B5
Edebo S 51 B5
Edelény H 99 C4
Edelschrott A 110 B2
Edemissen D 72 B3
Edenbridge GB 45 B4
Edenderry IRL 30 A1
Edenkoben D 93 B4
Edesheim D 93 B4
Edessa GR 182 C4
Edewecht D 71 A4
Edgeworthstown IRL 30 A1
Edinburgh GB 35 C4
Edineţ MD 17 A7
Edirne TR 186 A1
Edland N 52 A3
Edolo I 120 A3
Edøy N 198 B5
Edremit TR 186 C2
Edsbro S 51 C5
Edsbruk S 56 B2
Edsbyn S 50 A2
Edsele S 200 C2
Edsleskog S 54 A3
Edsvalla S 55 A4
Eekloo B 79 A3
Eemshaven NL 71 A3
Eerbeek NL 70 B3
Eersel NL 79 A5
Eferding A 96 C2
Effiat F 116 A3
Efteløt N 53 A5
Egeln D 73 C4
Eger H 113 B4
Egerbakta H 113 B4
Egernsund DK 64 B2
Egersund N 52 B2
Egerszólát H 113 B4
Egervár H 111 C3
Egg
A 107 B4
D 107 A5
Eggby S 55 B4
Eggedal N 47 B6
Eggenburg A 97 C3
Eggenfelden D 95 C4
Eggesin D 74 A3
Eggum N 194 B4
Egham GB 44 B3
Éghezée B 79 B4
Egiertowo PL 68 A3
Egilsstaðir IS 191 B11
Egina GR 185 B4
Eginio GR 182 C4
Egio GR 184 A3
Égletons F 116 B2
Egling D 108 B2
Eglinton GB 27 A3
Eglisau CH 107 B3
Égliseneuve-d'Entraigues F 116 B2
Eglofs D 107 B4
Egmond aan Zee NL 70 B1
Egna I 121 A4
Egosthena GR 184 A4
Egremont GB 36 B3
Egtved DK 59 C2
Eguilles F 131 B4
Eguilly-sous-Bois F 104 A3
Éguzon-Chantôme F 103 C3
Egyek H 113 B4
Egyházasrádóc H 111 B3
Ehekirchen D 94 C3
Ehingen D 94 C1
Ehra-Lessien D 73 B3
Ehrang D 92 B2
Ehrenfriedersdorf D 83 B4
Ehrenhain D 83 B4
Ehrenhausen A 110 C2
Ehringshausen D 81 B4
Ehrwald A 108 B1
Eibar E 143 A4
Eibelstadt D 94 B2
Eibenstock D 83 B4
Eibergen NL 71 B3
Eibiswald A 110 C2
Eichenbarleben D 73 B4
Eichendorf D 95 C4
Eichstätt D 95 C3
Eickelborn D 81 A4
Eide
*Hordaland* N 46 B3
*Møre og Romsdal* N 198 C4
Eidet N 194 A9
Eidfjord N 46 B4
Eidsberg N 54 A2
Eidsbugarden N 47 A5
Eidsdal N 198 C4
Eidsfoss N 53 A6
Eidskog N 49 B4
Eidsvåg
*Hordaland* N 46 B2
*Møre og Romsdal* N 198 C5
Eidsvoll N 48 B3
Eikefjord N 46 A2
Eikelandsosen N 46 B2
Eiken N 52 B3
Eikesdal N 198 C5
Eikstrand N 53 A5
Eilenburg D 83 A4
Eilsleben D 73 B4
Eina N 48 B2
Einbeck D 82 A1
Eindhoven NL 79 A5
Einsiedeln CH 107 B3
Einville-au-Jard F 92 C2
Eisenach D 82 B2
Eisenberg
*Rheinland-Pfalz* D 93 B4
*Thüringen* D 83 B3
Eisenerz A 110 B1
Eisenhüttenstadt D 74 B3
Eisenkappel A 110 C1
Eisenstadt A 111 B3
Eisentratten A 109 C4
Eisfeld D 82 B2
Eisleben D 82 A3
Eislingen D 94 C1
Eitensheim D 95 C3
Eiterfeld D 82 B1
Eitorf D 80 B3
Eivindvik N 46 B2
Eivissa = Ibiza E 166 C1
Eixo P 148 B1
Ejby DK 59 C2
Ejea de los Caballeros E 144 B2
Ejstrupholm DK 59 C2
Ejulve E 153 B3
Eke B 79 B3
Ekeby
*Gotland* S 57 C4
*Skåne* S 61 D2
*Uppsala* S 51 B5
Ekeby-Almby S 56 A1
Ekenäs S 55 B4
Ekenässjön S 62 A3
Ekerö S 57 A3
Eket S 61 C3
Eketorp S 63 B4
Ekevik S 56 B2
Ekkerøy N 193 B14
Ekshärad S 49 B5
Eksingedal N 46 B2
Eksjö S 62 A2
Eksta S 57 C4
Ekträsk S 200 B5
El Alamo
*Madrid* E 151 B4
*Sevilla* E 161 B3
El Algar E 165 B4
El Almendro E 161 B2
El Alquián E 164 C2
Élancourt F 90 C1
El Arahal E 162 A2
El Arenal E 150 B2
El Arguellite E 164 A2
Elassona GR 182 D4
El Astillero E 143 A3
Elati GR 182 D3
Żelazno PL 85 B4
El Ballestero E 158 C1
El Barco de Ávila E 150 B2
Elbasan AL 182 B2
El Berrón E 142 A1
El Berrueco E 151 B4
Elbeuf F 89 A4
Elbingerode D 82 A2
Elbląg PL 69 A4
El Bodón E 149 B3
El Bonillo E 158 C1
El Bosque E 162 B2
El Bullaque E 157 A3
Elburg NL 70 B2
El Burgo E 162 B3
El Burgo de Ebro E 153 A3
El Burgo de Osma E 151 A4
El Burgo Ranero E 142 B1
El Buste E 144 C2
El Cabaco E 149 B3
El Callejo E 143 A3
El Campillo E 161 B3
El Campillo de la Jara E 156 A2
El Cañavete E 158 B1
El Carpio E 157 C3
El Carpio de Tajo E 150 C3
El Casar E 151 B4
El Casar de Escalona E 150 B3
El Castillo de las Guardas E 161 B3
El Centenillo E 157 B4
El Cerro E 149 B4
El Cerro de Andévalo E 161 B3
Elche E 165 A4
Elche de la Sierra E 158 C1
Elchingen D 94 C2
El Comenar E 162 B2
El Coronil E 162 A2
El Crucero E 141 A4
El Cubo de Tierra del Vino E 149 A4
El Cuervo E 162 B1
Elda E 159 C3
Eldena D 73 A4
Eldingen D 72 B3
Elefsina GR 185 A4
El Ejido E 164 C2
Elek H 113 C5
Elemir SRB 126 B2
El Escorial E 151 B3
El Espinar E 151 B3
Eleutheroupoli GR 183 C6
El Frago E 144 B3
El Franco E 141 A4
El Frasno E 152 A2
Elgå N 199 C8
El Garrobo E 161 B3
El Gastor E 162 B2
Elgin GB 32 D3
Elgoibar E 143 A4
Elgol GB 31 B2
El Gordo E 150 C2
El Grado E 145 B4
El Granado E 161 B2
El Grao de Castelló E 159 B4
El Grau E 159 C3
Elgshøa N 49 A4
El Higuera E 163 A3
El Hijate E 164 B2
El Hontanar E 152 B2
El Hoyo E 157 B4
Elie GB 35 B5
Elizondo E 144 A2
Ełk PL 12 B5
Elkhovo BG 17 D7
Ellenberg D 94 B2
Ellesmere GB 38 B4
Ellesmere Port GB 38 A4
Ellezelles B 79 B3
Ellingen D 94 B2
Ellmau A 109 B3
Ellon GB 33 D4
Ellös S 54 B2
Ellrich D 82 A2
Ellwangen D 94 C2
Elm
CH 107 C4
D 72 A2
Elmadağ TR 23 B7
El Madroño E 161 B3
El Maillo E 149 B3
Elmalı TR 189 C4
El Masnou E 147 C3
El Mirón E 150 B2
El Molar E 151 B4
El Molinillo E 157 A3
El Morell E 147 C2
Elmshorn D 64 C2
Elmstein D 93 B3
El Muyo E 151 A4
Elne F 146 B3
Elnesvågen N 198 C4
El Olmo E 151 A4
Elorrio E 143 A4
Elöszállás H 112 C2
Elouda GR 185 D6
Éloyes F 105 A5
El Palo E 163 B3
El Pardo E 151 B4
El Payo E 149 B3
El Pedernoso E 158 B1
El Pedroso E 162 A2
El Peral E 158 B2
El Perelló
*Tarragona* E 153 B4
*Valencia* E 159 B3
Elphin GB 32 C1
El Picazo E 158 B1
El Pinell de Bray E 153 A4
El Piñero E 150 A2
El Pla de Santa Maria E 147 C2
El Pobo E 153 B3
El Pobo de Dueñas E 152 B2
El Pont d'Armentera E 147 C2
El Port de la Selva E 147 B4
El Port de Llançà E 146 B4
El Port de Sagunt E 159 B3
El Prat de Llobregat E 147 C3
El Provencio E 158 B1
El Puente E 143 A3
El Puente del Arzobispo E 150 C2
El Puerto E 141 A4
El Puerto de Santa María E 162 B1
El Real de la Jara E 161 B3
El Real de San Vincente E 150 B3
El Robledo E 157 A3
El Rocio E 161 B3
El Rompido E 161 B2
El Ronquillo E 161 B3
El Royo E 143 C4
El Rubio E 162 A3
El Sabinar E 164 A2
El Saler E 159 B3
El Salobral E 158 C2
El Saucejo E 162 A2
Els Castells E 147 B2
Elsdorf D 80 B2
Elsenfeld D 93 B5
El Serrat AND 146 B2
Elsfleth D 72 A1
Elspeet NL 70 B2
Elst NL 70 C2
Elstead GB 44 B3
Elster D 83 A4
Elsterberg D 83 B4
Elsterwerda D 83 A5
Elstra D 84 A2
El Temple E 144 C3
El Tiemblo E 150 B3
Eltmann D 94 B2
El Toboso E 157 A5
El Tormillo E 145 C3
El Torno E 149 B4
Eltville D 93 A4
El Valle de las Casas E 142 B1
Elvas P 155 C3
Elvebakken N 192 C7
El Vellón E 151 B4
Elven F 101 B3
El Vendrell E 147 C2
Elverum N 48 B3
El Villar de Arnedo E 144 B1
Elvington GB 40 B3
El Viso E 156 B3
El Viso del Alcor E 162 A2
Elxleben D 82 A2
Ely GB 45 A4
Elzach D 106 A3
Elze D 72 B2
Emådalen S 50 A1
Embleton GB 37 A5
Embonas GR 188 C2
Embrun F 132 A2
Embún E 144 B3
Emden D 71 A4
Emecik TR 188 C2
Emet TR 186 C4
Emirdağ TR 187 C6
Emlichheim D 71 B3
Emmaboda S 63 B3
Emmaljunga S 61 C3
Emmeloord NL 70 B2
Emmen
CH 106 B3
NL 71 B3
Emmendingen D 106 A2
Emmer-Compascuum NL 71 B4
Emmerich D 80 A2
Emmern D 72 B2
Emöd H 113 B4
Émpoli I 135 B3
Emsbüren D 71 B4
Emsdetten D 71 B4
Emsfors S 62 A4
Emskirchen D 94 B2
Emstek D 71 B5
Emsworth GB 44 C3
Emyvale IRL 27 B4
Enafors S 199 B9
Enånger S 51 A4
Encamp AND 146 B2
Encarnaçao P 154 C1
Encinas de Abajo E 150 B2
Encinas de Esgueva E 142 C2
Encinasola E 161 A3
Encinas Reales E 163 A3
Encio E 143 B3
Enciso E 144 B1
Enden N 199 D7
Endingen D 106 A2
Endrinal E 149 B4
Endröd H 113 C4
Enebakk N 54 A2
Eneryda S 63 B2
Enese H 111 B4
Enez TR 183 C8
Enfield IRL 30 A2
Eng A 108 B2
Engelberg CH 106 C3
Engelhartszell A 96 C1
Engelskirchen D 80 B3
Engen D 107 B3
Enger N 48 B2
Engerdal N 199 D8
Engerneset N 49 A4
Enge-sande D 64 B1
Engesvang DK 59 B2
Enghien B 79 B4
Engstingen D 94 C1
Engter D 71 B5
Enguera E 159 C3
Enguidanos E 158 B2
Enkenbach D 93 B3
Enkhuizen NL 70 B2
Enklinge FIN 51 B7
Enköping S 56 A3
Enna I 177 B3
Ennezat F 116 B3
Ennigerloh D 81 A4
Enningdal N 54 B2
Ennis IRL 28 B3
Enniscorthy IRL 30 B2
Enniskean IRL 29 C3
Enniskillen GB 27 B3
Ennistimon IRL 28 B2
Enns A 110 A1
Eno FIN 9 A7
Enontekiö FIN 196 A6
Ens NL 70 B2
Enschede NL 71 B3
Ensdorf D 95 B3
Ensisheim F 106 B2
Enstaberga S 56 B2
Enstone GB 44 B2
Entlebuch CH 106 B3
Entrácque I 133 A3
Entradas P 160 B1
Entrains-sur-Nohain F 104 B2
Entrambasaguas E 143 A3
Entrambasmestas E 143 A3
Entraygues-sur-Truyère F 116 C2
Entre-os-Rios P 148 A1
Entrevaux F 132 B2
Entrin Bajo E 155 C4
Entroncamento P 154 B2
Entzheim F 93 C3
Envermeu F 89 A5
Enviken S 50 B2
Enying H 112 C2
Enzingerboden A 109 B3
Enzklösterle D 93 C4
Épagny F 90 B3
Epalinges CH 106 C1
Epannes F 114 B3
Epanomi GR 182 C4
Epe
D 71 B4
NL 70 B2
Épernay F 91 B3
Épernon F 90 C1
Epfig F 93 C3
Epierre F 118 B3
Épila E 152 A2
Épinac F 104 C3
Épinal F 105 A5
Episcopia I 174 A2
Episkopi CY 181 B1
Epitalio GR 184 B2
Epoisses F 104 B3
Eppenbrunn D 93 B3
Eppendorf D 83 B5
Epping GB 45 B4
Eppingen D 93 B4
Epsom GB 44 B3
Epworth GB 40 B3
Eraclea I 122 B1
Eraclea Mare I 122 B1
Erba I 120 B2
Erbach
*Baden-Württemberg* D 94 C1
*Hessen* D 93 B4
Erbalunga F 180 A2
Erbendorf D 95 B4
Érchie I 173 B3
Ercolano I 170 C2
Ercsi H 112 B2
Érd H 112 B2
Erdek TR 186 B2
Erdemli TR 23 C8
Erdevik SRB 126 B1
Erding D 95 C3
Erdötelek H 113 B4
Erdut HR 125 B5
Erdweg D 95 C3
Ereğli
*Konya* TR 23 C8
*Zonguldak* TR 187 A6
Erenkaya TR 189 B7
Eresfjord N 198 C5
Eresos GR 183 D7
Eretria GR 185 A4
Erfde D 64 B2
Erfjord N 52 A2
Erfstadt D 80 B2
Erfurt D 82 B3
Ērgli LV 8 D4
Ergoldsbach D 95 C4
Eriboll GB 32 C2
Érice I 176 A1
Ericeira P 154 C1
Eğridir TR 189 B5
Eriksberg S 195 E6
Eriksmåla S 62 B3
Eringsboda S 63 B3
Eriswil CH 106 B2
Erithres GR 185 A4
Erkelenz D 80 A2
Erkner D 74 B2
Erkrath D 80 A2
Erla E 144 B3
Erlangen D 94 B3
Erli I 133 A4
Erlsbach A 109 C3
Ermelo NL 70 B2
Ermenak TR 23 C7
Ermenonville F 90 B2
Ermezinde P 148 A1
Ermidas P 160 A1
Ermioni GR 184 B4
Ermoupoli GR 185 B5
Ermsleben D 82 A3
Erndtebrück D 81 B4
Ernée F 88 B3
Ernestinovo HR 125 B4
Ernstbrunn A 97 C4
Erolzheim D 107 A5
Erquelinnes B 79 B4
Erquy F 101 A3
Erra P 154 C2
Erratzu E 144 A2
Errindlev DK 65 B4
Erro E 144 B2
Ersa F 180 A2
Érsekcsanád H 125 A4
Ersekë AL 182 C2
Érsekvadkert H 112 B3
Ersmark S 200 C6
Erstein F 93 C3
Erstfeld CH 107 C3
Ertebølle DK 58 B2
Ertingen D 107 A4
Ervedal
*Coimbra* P 148 B1
*Portalegre* P 154 B3
Ervenik HR 138 A1
Ervidel P 160 B1
Ervy-le-Châtel F 104 A2
Erwitte D 81 A4
Erxleben D 73 B4
Erzsébet H 125 A4
Esbjerg DK 59 C1
Esbly F 90 C2
Escacena del Campo E 161 B3
Escairón E 140 B3
Escalada E 143 B3
Escalante E 143 A3
Escalaplano I 179 C3
Escalona E 150 B3

Escalona del Prado E 151 A3
Escalonilla E 150 C3
Escalos de Baixo P 155 B3
Escalos de Cima P 155 B3
Escamilla E 152 B1
Es Caná E 166 B1
Escañuela E 157 C3
Es Castell E 167 B4
Escatrón E 153 A3
Eschach D 107 B4
Eschau D 94 B1
Eschede D 72 B3
Eschenau D 95 B3
Eschenbach D 95 B3
Eschenz CH 107 B3
Eschershausen D 72 C2
Esch-sur-Alzette L 92 B1
Esch-sur-Sûre L 92 B1
Eschwege D 82 A2
Eschweiler D 80 B2
Escobasa de Almazán E 152 A1
Escoeuilles F 78 B1
Escombreras E 165 B4
Escos F 144 A2
Escource F 128 B1
Escragnolles F 132 B2
Escrick GB 40 B2
Escurial E 156 A2
Escurial de la Sierra E 149 B4
Esens D 71 A4
Esgos E 140 B3
Esher GB 44 B3
Eskdalemuir GB 36 A3
Eskifjörður IS 191 B12
Eskilhem S 57 C4
Eskilsäter S 55 B4
Eskilstrup DK 65 B4
Eskilstuna S 56 A2
Eskipazar TR 187 B7
Eskişehir TR 187 C5
Eslarn D 95 B4
Eslava E 144 B2
Eslida E 159 B3
Eslohe D 81 A4
Eslöv S 61 D3
Eşme TR 188 A3
Es Mercadal E 167 B4
Es Migjorn Gran E 167 B4
Espa N 48 B3
Espalion F 130 A1
Esparragalejo E 155 C4
Esparragosa del Caudillo E 156 B2
Esparragossa de la Serena E 156 B2
Esparreguera E 147 C2
Esparron F 132 B1
Espe N 46 B3
Espedal N 52 B2
Espejo
*Alava* E 143 B3
*Córdoba* E 163 A3
Espeland N 46 B2
Espelkamp D 72 B1
Espeluche F 131 A3
Espeluy E 157 B4
Espera E 162 B2
Esperança P 155 B3
Espéraza F 146 B3
Espéria I 169 B3
Espevær N 52 A1
Espiel E 156 B2
Espinama E 142 A2
Espiñaredo E 140 A3
Espinasses F 132 A2
Espinelves E 147 C3
Espinhal P 154 A2
Espinho P 148 A1
Espinilla E 142 A2
Espinosa de Cerrato E 143 C3
Espinosa de los Monteros E 143 A3
Espinoso del Rey E 156 A3
Espirito Santo P 160 B2
Espluga de Francolí E 147 C2
Esplús E 145 C4
Espolla E 146 B3
Espoo FIN 8 B4
Esporles E 166 B2
Es Port d'Alcúdia E 167 B3
Esposende P 148 A1
Espot E 146 B2
Es Pujols E 166 C1
Esquedas E 145 B3
Esquivias E 151 B4
Essay F 89 B4
Essen
B 79 A4
*Niedersachsen* D 71 B4
*Nordrhein-Westfalen* D 80 A3
Essenbach D 95 C4
Essertaux F 90 B2
Essingen D 94 C2
Esslingen D 94 C1
Es Soleràs E 153 A4
Essoyes F 104 A3
Estacas E 140 B2
Estadilla E 145 B4
Estagel F 146 B3
Estaires F 78 B2
Estang F 128 C2
Estarreja P 148 B1
Estartit E 147 B4
Estavayer-le-Lac CH 106 C1
Este I 121 B4
Esteiro E 140 A2
Estela P 148 A1
Estella E 144 B1
Estellencs E 166 B2
Estepa E 162 A3
Estépar E 143 B3
Estepona E 162 B2
Esternay F 91 C3
Esterri d'Aneu E 146 B2
Esterwegen D 71 B4
Estissac F 104 A2
Estivadas E 140 B3
Estivareilles F 116 A2
Estivella E 159 B3
Estói P 160 B2
Estopiñán E 145 C4
Estoril P 154 C1
Estoublon F 132 B2
Estrée-Blanche F 78 B2
Estrées-St Denis F 90 B2
Estrela P 155 C3
Estremera E 151 B4
Estremoz P 155 C3
Estuna S 51 C5
Esyres F 102 B2
Esztergom H 112 B2
Etables-sur-Mer F 100 A3
Étain F 92 B1
Étalans F 105 B5
Etalle B 92 B1
Étampes F 90 C2
Etang-sur-Arroux F 104 C3
Étaples F 78 B1
Etauliers F 128 A2
Etili TR 186 C1
Etna N 48 B1
Etne N 52 A1
Etoges F 91 C3
Etoliko GR 184 A2
Eton GB 44 B3
Etréaupont F 91 B3
Étréchy F 90 C2
Étrépagny F 90 B1
Étretat F 89 A4
Étroeungt F 91 A3
Étroubles I 119 B4
Ettal D 108 B2
Ettelbruck L 92 B2
Etten NL 79 A4
Ettenheim D 106 A2
Ettington GB 44 A2
Ettlingen D 93 C4
Ettringen D 108 A1
Etuz F 105 B4
Etxarri-Aranatz E 144 B1
Etyek H 112 B2
Eu F 90 A1
Euerdorf D 82 B2
Eulate E 144 B1
Eupen B 80 B2
Europoort NL 79 A4
Euskirchen D 80 B2
Eutin D 65 B3
Evanger N 46 B3
Évaux-les-Bains F 116 A2
Evciler
*Afyon* TR 189 A4
*Çanakkale* TR 186 C1
Evenskjær N 194 B7
Evenstad N 48 A3
Evercreech GB 43 A4
Evergem B 79 A3
Everöd S 61 D4
Eversberg D 81 A4
Everswinkel D 71 C4
Evertsberg S 49 A5
Evesham GB 44 A2
Évian-les-Bains F 118 A3
Evisa F 180 A1
Evje N 53 B3
Evolène CH 119 A4
Évora P 154 C3
Evoramonte P 155 C3
Evran F 101 A4
Evrecy F 89 A3
Évreux F 89 A5
Évron F 102 A1
Évry F 90 C2
Ewell GB 44 B3
Ewersbach D 81 B4
Excideuil F 115 C5
Exeter GB 43 B3
Exmes F 89 B4
Exminster GB 43 B3
Exmouth GB 43 B3
Eydehamn N 53 B4
Eye
*Peterborough* GB 41 C3
*Suffolk* GB 45 A5
Eyemouth GB 35 C5
Eyguians F 132 A1
Eyguières F 131 B4
Eygurande F 116 B2
Eylie F 145 B4
Eymet F 129 B3
Eymoutiers F 116 B1
Eynsham GB 44 B2
Eyrarbakki IS 190 D4
Eystrup D 72 B2
Ezaro E 140 B1
Ezcaray E 143 B4
Ezcároz E 144 B2
Ezine TR 186 C1
Ezmoriz P 148 B1

## F

Fabara E 153 A4
Fábbrico I 121 C3
Fåberg N 48 A2
Fabero E 141 B4
Fábiánsebestyén H 113 C4
Fåborg DK 64 A3
Fabrègues F 130 B2
Fabriano I 136 B1
Fabrizia I 175 C2
Facha P 148 A1
Facinas E 162 B2
Fačkov SK 98 B2
Fadagosa P 155 B3
Fadd H 112 C2
Faédis I 122 A2
Faenza I 135 A4
Fafe P 148 A1
Fagagna I 122 A2
Făgăras RO 17 C6
Fågelberget S 199 A11
Fågelfors S 62 A3
Fågelmara S 63 B3
Fågelsta S 55 B6
Fagerås S 55 A4
Fagerheim N 47 B4
Fagerhøy N 48 A1
Fagerhult S 62 A3
Fagerlund N 48 B2
Fagernes
*Oppland* N 47 B6
*Troms* N 192 C3
Fagersanna S 55 B5
Fagersta S 50 B2
Fåglavik S 55 B4
Fagnano Castello I 174 B2
Fagnières F 91 C4
Faido CH 107 C3
Fains-Véel F 91 C5
Fairford GB 44 B2
Fairlie GB 34 C3
Fajsz H 112 C2
Fakenham GB 41 C4
Fåker S 199 B11
Fakse DK 65 A5
Fakse Ladeplads DK 65 A5
Falaise F 89 B3
Falcade I 121 A4
Falcarragh IRL 26 A2
Falces E 144 B2
Fălciu RO 17 B8
Falconara I 177 B3
Falconara Maríttima I 136 B2
Falcone I 177 A4
Faldingworth GB 40 B3
Falerum S 56 B2
Făleşti MD 17 B7
Falkenberg
*Bayern* D 95 B4
*Bayern* D 95 C4
*Brandenburg* D 83 A5
S 60 C2
Falkensee D 74 B2
Falkenstein
*Bayern* D 95 B4
*Sachsen* D 83 B4
Falkenthal D 74 B2
Falkirk GB 35 B4
Falkland GB 35 B4
Falköping S 55 B4
Fall D 108 B2
Falla S 56 B1
Fallingbostel D 72 B2
Falmouth GB 42 B1
Falset E 147 C1
Fălticeni RO 17 B7
Falun S 50 B2
Famagusta CY 181 A2
Fammestad N 46 B2
Fana N 46 B2
Fanano I 135 A3
Fanari GR 182 D3
Fanjeaux F 146 A3
Fano I 136 B2
Fântânele RO 126 A3
Fão P 148 A1
Fara in Sabina I 168 A2
Faramontanos de Tábara E 149 A4
Fara Novarese I 119 B5
Farasdues E 144 B2
Fårbo S 62 A4
Fareham GB 44 C2
Färentuna S 57 A3
Färgelanda S 54 B2
Färila S 200 E1
Faringdon GB 44 B2
Faringe S 51 C5
Farini I 120 C2
Fariza E 149 A3
Färjestaden S 63 B4
Farkadona GR 182 D4
Farkasfa H 111 C3
Farlete E 153 A3
Färlöv S 61 C4
Farmos H 113 B3
Farnă SK 112 B2
Färnäs S 50 B1
Farnborough GB 44 B3
Farnese I 168 A1
Farnham GB 44 B3
Farnroda D 82 B2
Faro P 160 B2
Fåro S 57 C5
Fårösund S 57 C5
Farra d'Alpago I 122 A1
Farranfore IRL 29 B2
Farre DK 59 B2
Farsala GR 182 D4
Farsø DK 58 B2
Farsund N 52 B2
Farum DK 61 D2
Fårup DK 58 B2
Fasana I 172 B1
Fasano I 173 B3
Fáskrúðsfjörður IS 191 C11
Fassberg D 72 B3
Fastiv UA 13 C8
Fastnäs S 49 B5
Fátima P 154 B2
Fatmomakke S 195 E6
Fättjaur S 195 E6
Faucogney-et-la-Mer F 105 B5
Fauguerolles F 128 B3
Faulenrost D 74 A1
Faulquemont F 92 B2
Fauquembergues F 78 B2
Fauske N 194 C6
Fauville-en-Caux F 89 A4
Fauvillers B 92 B1
Fåvang N 48 A2
Favara
E 159 B3
I 176 B2
Faverges F 118 B3
Faverney F 105 B5
Faversham GB 45 B4
Favignana I 176 B1
Fawley GB 44 C2
Fay-aux-Loges F 103 B4
Fayence F 132 B2
Fayet F 130 B1
Fayl-Billot F 105 B4
Fayón E 153 A4
Fearn GB 32 D3
Fécamp F 89 A4
Feda N 52 B2
Fedje N 46 B1
Feeny GB 27 B3
Fegen S 60 B3
Fegyvernek H 113 B4
Fehrbellin D 74 B1
Fehring A 111 C3
Feichten A 108 B1
Feiring N 48 B3
Feistritz im Rosental A 110 C1
Feketić SRB 126 B1
Felanitx E 167 B3
Feld am See A 109 C4
Feldbach A 110 C2
Feldberg D 74 A2
Feldkirch A 107 B4
Feldkirchen in Kärnten A 109 C5
Feldkirchen-Westerham D 108 B2
Felgueiras P 148 A1
Felitto I 172 B1
Félix E 164 C2
Felixstowe GB 45 B5
Felizzano I 119 C5
Felletin F 116 B2
Fellingsbro S 56 A1
Felnac RO 126 A3
Felnémet H 113 B4
Felpéc H 111 B4
Fels am Wagram A 97 C3
Felsberg D 81 A5
Felsönyék H 112 C2
Felsöszentiván H 126 A1
Felsöszentmárton H 125 B3
Felsözsolca H 113 A4
Felsted DK 64 B2
Feltre I 121 A4
Femsjö S 60 C3
Fenagh IRL 26 B3
Fene E 140 A2
Fenestrelle I 119 B4
Fénétrange F 92 C3
Feneu F 102 B1
Fengersfors S 54 B3
Fenit IRL 29 B2
Fensmark DK 65 A4
Fenwick GB 36 A2
Feolin Ferry GB 34 C1
Ferbane IRL 28 A4
Ferdinandovac HR 124 A3
Ferdinandshof D 74 A2
Fère-Champenoise F 91 C3
Fère-en-Tardenois F 91 B3
Ferentillo I 168 A2
Ferentino I 169 B3
Feres GR 183 C8
Feria E 155 C4
Feričanci HR 125 B3
Ferizli TR 187 B5
Ferla I 177 B3
Ferlach A 110 C1
Ferleiten A 109 B3
Fermil P 148 A2
Fermo I 136 B2
Fermoselle E 149 A3
Fermoy IRL 29 B3
Fernancabellero E 157 A4
Fernán Nuñéz E 163 A3
Fernán Peréz E 164 C2
Fernão Ferro P 154 C1
Fernay-Voltaire F 118 A3
Ferndown GB 43 B5
Ferness GB 32 D3
Fernhurst GB 44 B3
Ferns IRL 30 B2
Ferpécle CH 119 A4
Ferrals-les-Corbières F 146 A3
Ferrandina I 172 B2
Ferrara I 121 C4
Ferrara di Monte Baldo I 121 B3
Ferreira E 141 A3
Ferreira do Alentejo P 160 A1
Ferreira do Zêzere P 154 B2
Ferreras de Abajo E 141 C4
Ferreras de Arriba E 141 C4
Ferreries E 167 B4
Ferreruela E 152 A2
Ferreruela de Tabara E 149 A3
Ferret CH 119 B4
Ferrette F 106 B2
Ferriere I 120 C2
Ferrière-la-Grande F 79 B3
Ferrières
*Hautes-Pyrénées* F 145 A3
*Loiret* F 103 A4
*Oise* F 90 B2
Ferrières-sur-Sichon F 117 A3
Ferrol E 140 A2
Ferryhill GB 37 B5
Fertörakos H 111 B3
Fertöszentmiklós H 111 B3
Ferwerd NL 70 A2
Festieux F 91 B3
Festøy N 198 C3
Festvåg N 194 C5
Feteşti RO 17 C7
Fethard
*Tipperary* IRL 29 B4
*Wexford* IRL 30 B2
Fethiye TR 188 C4
Fetsund N 48 C3
Fettercairn GB 35 B5
Feucht D 95 B3
Feuchtwangen D 94 B2
Feudingen D 81 B4
Feuges F 91 C4
Feuquières F 90 B1
Feurs F 117 B4
Fevik N 53 B4
Ffestiniog GB 38 B3
Fiamignano I 169 A3
Fiano I 119 B4
Ficarazzi I 176 A2
Ficarolo I 121 C4
Fichtelberg D 95 A3
Ficulle I 135 C5
Fidenza I 120 C3
Fidjeland N 52 B2
Fieberbrunn A 109 B3
Fier AL 182 C1
Fiera di Primiero I 121 A4
Fiesch CH 119 A5
Fiesso Umbertiano I 121 C4
Figari F 180 B2
Figeac F 116 C2
Figeholm S 62 A4
Figgjo N 52 B1
Figline Valdarno I 135 B4
Figols E 145 B4
Figueira da Foz P 148 B1
Figueira de Castelo Rodrigo P 149 B3
Figueira dos Caveleiros P 160 A1
Figueiredo P 154 B3
Figueiredo de Alva P 148 B2
Figueiródos Vinhos P 154 B2
Figueres E 147 B3
Figueroles E 153 B3
Figueruela de Arriba E 141 C4
Filadélfia I 175 C2
Fil'akovo SK 99 C3
Filderstadt D 94 C1
Filey GB 41 A3
Filiaşi RO 17 C5
Filiates GR 182 D2
Filiatra GR 184 B2
Filipstad S 55 A5
Filisur CH 107 C4
Fillan N 198 B5
Filotio GR 185 B6
Filottrano I 136 B2
Filskov DK 59 C2
Filton GB 43 A4
Filtvet N 54 A1
Filzmoos A 109 B4
Finale Emília I 121 C4
Finale Lígure I 133 A4
Fiñana E 164 B2
Finby FIN 51 B7
Fincham GB 41 C4
Finchingfield GB 45 B4
Findhorn GB 32 D3
Findochty GB 33 D4
Finike TR 189 C5
Finkenberg A 108 B2
Finnea IRL 27 C3
Finneidfjord N 195 D4
Finnerödja S 55 B5
Finnskog N 49 B4
Finnsnes N 194 A9
Finntorp S 54 A3
Finócchio I 168 B2
Finsjö S 62 A4
Finsland N 52 B3
Finspång S 56 B1
Finsterwalde D 84 A1
Finsterwolde NL 71 A4
Finstown GB 33 B3
Fintona GB 27 B3
Fionnphort GB 34 B1
Fiorenzuola d'Arda I 120 C2
Firenze = Florence I 135 B4
Firenzuola I 135 A4
Firmi F 130 A1
Firminy F 117 B4
Firmo I 174 B2
Fischamend Markt A 111 A3
Fischbach
A 110 B2
D 93 B3
Fischbeck D 73 B5
Fischen D 107 B5
Fishbourne GB 44 C2
Fishguard GB 39 C2
Fiskardo GR 184 A1
Fiskebäckskil S 54 B2
Fiskebøl N 194 B5
Fismes F 91 B3
Fisterra E 140 B1
Fitero E 144 B2
Fitjar N 46 C2
Fiuggi I 169 B3
Fiumata I 169 A3
Fiumefreddo Brúzio I 174 B2
Fiumefreddo di Sicília I 177 B4
Fiumicino I 168 B2
Fivemiletown GB 27 B3
Fivizzano I 134 A3
Fjälkinge S 63 B2
Fjällåsen S 196 B3
Fjällbacka S 54 B2
Fjæra N 46 C3
Fjärdhundra S 56 A2
Fjellerup DK 58 B3
Fjerritslev DK 58 A2
Fjordgard N 194 A8
Fjugesta S 55 A5
Flå N 47 B6
Flåbygd N 53 A4
Flaça E 147 B3
Flace F 117 A4
Fladungen D 82 B2
Flaine F 118 A3
Flaka FIN 51 B7
Flåm N 46 B4
Flamatt CH 106 C2
Flamborough GB 41 A3
Flammersfeld D 81 B3
Flassans-sur-Issole F 132 B2
Flatdal N 53 A4
Flatebø N 46 B3
Flateby N 48 C3
Flateland N 52 A3
Flateyri IS 190 A2
Flatøydegard N 47 B6
Flatråker N 46 C2
Flattach A 109 C4
Flatvarp S 62 A4
Flauenskjold DK 58 A3
Flavigny-sur-Moselle F 92 C2
Flavy-le-Martel F 90 B3
Flawil CH 107 B4
Flayosc F 132 B2
Flechtingen D 73 B4
Fleckeby D 64 B2
Fleet GB 44 B3
Fleetmark D 73 B4
Fleetwood GB 38 A3
Flehingen D 93 B4
Flekke N 46 A2
Flekkefjord N 52 B2
Flen S 56 A2
Flensburg D 64 B2
Fleringe S 57 C4
Flerohopp S 62 B3
Flers F 88 B3
Flesberg N 47 C6
Fleurance F 129 C3
Fleuré F 115 B4
Fleurier CH 105 C5
Fleurus B 79 B4
Fleury
*Hérault* F 130 B2

**Fleury** *continued*
*Yonne* F 104 B2
**Fleury-les-Aubrais**
F 103 B3
**Fleury-sur-Andelle**
F 89 A5
**Fleury-sur-Orne** F 89 A3
**Flieden** D 81 B5
**Flimby** GB 36 B3
**Flims** CH 107 C4
**Flines-lèz-Raches** F 78 B3
**Flint** GB 38 A3
**Flirey** F 92 C1
**Flirsch** A 108 B1
**Flisa** N 49 B4
**Flisby** S 62 A2
**Fliseryd** S 62 A4
**Flix** E 153 A4
**Flixecourt** F 90 A2
**Flize** F 91 B4
**Flobecq** B 79 B3
**Floby** S 55 B4
**Floda** S 60 B2
**Flodden** GB 37 A4
**Flogny-la-Chapelle**
F 104 B2
**Flöha** D 83 B5
**Flonheim** D 93 B4
**Florac** F 130 A2
**Floreffe** B 79 B4
**Florence = Firenze**
I 135 B4
**Florennes** B 79 B4
**Florensac** F 130 B2
**Florentin** F 129 C5
**Florenville** B 91 B5
**Flores de Avila** E 150 B2
**Floresta** I 177 B3
**Floreşti** MD 17 B8
**Florídia** I 177 B4
**Florina** GR 182 C3
**Florø** N 46 A2
**Flörsheim** D 93 A4
**Floss** D 95 B4
**Fluberg** N 48 B2
**Flúðir** IS 190 C5
**Flühli** CH 106 C3
**Flumet** F 118 B3
**Fluminimaggiore** I 179 C2
**Flums** CH 107 B4
**Flyeryd** S 63 B3
**Flygsfors** S 62 B3
**Foča** BIH 139 B4
**Foça** TR 186 D1
**Fochabers** GB 32 D3
**Focşani** RO 17 C7
**Foel** GB 38 B3
**Foeni** RO 126 B2
**Fogdö** S 56 A2
**Fóggia** I 171 B3
**Foglianise** I 170 B2
**Föglö** FIN 51 B7
**Fohnsdorf** A 110 B1
**Foiano della Chiana**
I 135 B4
**Foix** F 146 B2
**Fojnica**
BIH 139 B3
BIH 139 B4
**Fokstua** N 198 C6
**Földeák** H 126 A2
**Foldereid** N 199 A9
**Főldes** H 113 B5
**Folegandros** GR 185 C5
**Folelli** F 180 A2
**Folgaria** I 121 B4
**Folgosinho** P 148 B2
**Folgoso de la Ribera**
E 141 B4
**Folgoso do Courel**
E 141 B3
**Foligno** I 136 C1
**Folkärna** S 50 B3
**Folkestad** N 198 C3
**Folkestone** GB 45 B5
**Follafoss** N 199 B8
**Folldal** N 198 C6
**Follebu** N 48 A2
**Follina** I 121 B5
**Föllinge** S 199 B11
**Follónica** I 135 C3
**Fölsbyn** S 54 A3
**Foncebadón** E 141 B4
**Foncine-le-Bas** F 105 C5
**Fondevila** E 140 C2
**Fondi** I 169 B3
**Fondo** I 121 A4
**Fonelas** E 164 B1
**Fonfría**
*Teruel* E 152 B2
*Zamora* E 149 A3
**Fonn** N 46 A3
**Fonnes** N 46 B1
**Fonni** I 178 B3
**Fontaine** F 91 C4
**Fontainebleau** F 90 C2
**Fontaine de Vaucluse**
F 131 B4
**Fontaine-Française**
F 105 B4
**Fontaine-le-Dun** F 89 A4
**Fontan** F 133 A3
**Fontanarejo** E 157 A3
**Fontane** I 133 A3
**Fontanélice** I 135 A4
**Fontanières** F 116 A2
**Fontanosas** E 157 B3
**Fonteblanda** I 168 A1
**Fontenay-le-Comte**
F 114 B3
**Fontenay-Trésigny**
F 90 C2
**Fontevrault-l'Abbaye**
F 102 B2
**Fontiveros** E 150 B3
**Fontoy** F 92 B1
**Fontpédrouse** F 146 B3
**Font-Romeu** F 146 B3
**Fontstown** IRL 30 A2
**Fonyód** H 111 C4
**Fonz** E 145 B4
**Fonzaso** I 121 A4
**Fóppolo** I 120 A2
**Föra** S 62 A4
**Forbach**
D 93 C4
F 92 B2
**Forcall** E 153 B3
**Forcalquier** F 132 B1
**Forcarei** E 140 B2
**Forchheim** D 94 B3
**Forchtenau** A 111 B3
**Forchtenberg** D 94 B1
**Ford** GB 34 B2
**Førde**
*Hordaland* N 52 A1
*Sogn og Fjordane*
N 46 A2
**Förderstedt** D 83 A3
**Førdesfjorden** N 52 A1
**Fordham** GB 45 A4
**Fordingbridge** GB 44 C2
**Fordon** PL 76 A3
**Fordongiánus** I 179 C2
**Forenza** I 172 B1
**Foresta di Búrgos**
I 178 B2
**Forfar** GB 35 B5
**Forges-les-Eaux** F 90 B1
**Foria** I 172 B1
**Forio** I 170 C1
**Forjães** P 148 A1
**Førland** N 52 B3
**Forlì** I 135 A5
**Forlimpopoli** I 135 A5
**Formazza** I 119 A5
**Formby** GB 38 A3
**Formerie** F 90 B1
**Fórmia** I 169 B3
**Formígine** I 135 A3
**Formigliana** I 119 B5
**Formiguères** F 146 B3
**Fornalutx** E 166 B2
**Fornåsa** S 56 B1
**Fornelli** I 178 B2
**Fornells** E 167 A4
**Fornelos de Montes**
E 140 B2
**Fornes** E 163 B4
**Forneset** N 192 C3
**Forni Avoltri** I 109 C3
**Forni di Sopra** I 122 A1
**Forni di Sotto** I 122 A1
**Forno**
*Piemonte* I 119 B4
*Piemonte* I 119 B5
**Forno Alpi-Gráie** I 119 B4
**Forno di Zoldo** I 121 A5
**Fornos de Algodres**
P 148 B2
**Fornovo di Taro** I 120 C3
**Foros do Arrão** P 154 B2
**Forráskút** H 126 A1
**Forres** GB 32 D3
**Forriolo** E 140 B3
**Fors** S 50 B3
**Forsand** N 52 B2
**Forsbacka** S 51 B3
**Forserum** S 62 A2
**Forshaga** S 55 A4
**Forsheda** S 60 B3
**Forsinain** GB 32 C3
**Førslev** DK 65 A4
**Förslöv** S 61 C2
**Forsmark**
*Uppsala* S 51 B5
*Västerbotten* S 195 E6
**Forsmo** S 200 C3
**Forsnäs** S 195 D9
**Forsnes** N 198 B5
**Forssa** FIN 8 B3
**Forssjöbruk** S 56 B2
**Forst** D 84 A2
**Forsvik** S 55 B5
**Fortanete** E 153 B3
**Fort Augustus** GB 32 D2
**Forte dei Marmi** I 134 B3
**Fortezza** I 108 C2
**Forth** GB 35 C4
**Fort-Mahon-Plage** F 78 B1
**Fortrie** GB 33 D4
**Fortrose** GB 32 D2
**Fortun** N 47 A4
**Fortuna** E 165 A3
**Fortuneswell** GB 43 B4
**Fort William** GB 34 B2
**Forvik** N 195 E3
**Fos** F 145 B4
**Fosdinovo** I 134 A3
**Foss** N 47 B6
**Fossacésia** I 169 A4
**Fossano** I 133 A3
**Fossato di Vico** I 136 B1
**Fossbakken** N 194 B8
**Fosse-la-Ville** B 79 B4
**Fossombrone** I 136 B1
**Fos-sur-Mer** F 131 B3
**Fot** H 112 B3
**Fouchères** F 104 A3
**Fouesnant** F 100 B1
**Foug** F 92 C1
**Fougères** F 88 B2
**Fougerolles** F 105 B5
**Foulain** F 105 A4
**Fountainhall** GB 35 C5
**Fouras** F 114 C2
**Fourchambault** F 104 B2
**Fourmies** F 91 A4
**Fourna** GR 182 D3
**Fournels** F 116 C3
**Fourni** GR 188 B1
**Fournols** F 117 B3
**Fourques** F 146 B3
**Fourquevaux** F 146 A2
**Fours** F 104 C2
**Fowey** GB 42 B2
**Foxdale** GB 36 B2
**Foxford** IRL 26 C1
**Foyers** GB 32 D2
**Foynes** IRL 29 B2
**Foz** E 141 A3
**Foza** I 121 B4
**Foz do Arelho** P 154 B1
**Foz do Giraldo** P 155 B3
**Frabosa Soprana** I 133 A3
**Frades de la Sierra**
E 149 B4
**Fraga** E 153 A4
**Fragagnano** I 173 B3
**Frailes** E 163 A4
**Fraire** B 79 B4
**Fraize** F 106 A1
**Framlingham** GB 45 A5
**Frammersbach** D 94 A1
**Framnes** N 54 A1
**França** P 141 C4
**Francaltroff** F 92 C2
**Francavilla al Mare**
I 169 A4
**Francavilla di Sicília**
I 177 B4
**Francavilla Fontana**
I 173 B3
**Francavilla in Sinni**
I 174 A2
**Francescas** F 129 B3
**Franco** P 148 A2
**Francofonte** I 177 B3
**Francos** E 151 A4
**Frändefors** S 54 B3
**Franeker** NL 70 A2
**Frangy** F 118 A2
**Frankenau** D 81 A4
**Frankenberg**
*Hessen* D 81 A4
*Sachsen* D 83 B5
**Frankenburg** A 109 A4
**Frankenfels** A 110 B2
**Frankenmarkt** A 109 B4
**Frankenthal** D 93 B4
**Frankfurt**
*Brandenburg* D 74 B3
*Hessen* D 81 B4
**Frankrike** S 199 B10
**Fränsta** S 200 D2
**Františkovy Lázně**
CZ 83 B4
**Franzburg** D 66 B1
**Frascati** I 168 B2
**Frasdorf** D 109 B3
**Fraserburgh** GB 33 D4
**Frashër** AL 182 C2
**Frasne** F 105 C5
**Frasnes-lez-Anvaing**
B 79 B3
**Frasseto** F 180 B2
**Frastanz** A 107 B4
**Fratel** P 155 B3
**Fratta Todina** I 135 C5
**Frauenau** D 96 C1
**Frauenfeld** CH 107 B3
**Frauenkirchen** A 111 B3
**Frauenstein** D 83 B5
**Frauental** A 110 C2
**Frayssinet** F 129 B4
**Frayssinet-le-Gélat**
F 129 B4
**Frechas** P 149 A2
**Frechen** D 80 B2
**Frechilla** E 142 B2
**Freckenhorst** D 71 C4
**Fredeburg** D 81 A4
**Fredelsloh** D 82 A1
**Fredeng** N 48 B2
**Fredensborg** DK 61 D2
**Fredericia** DK 59 C2
**Frederiks** DK 59 B2
**Frederikshavn** DK 58 A3
**Frederikssund** DK 61 D2
**Frederiksværk** DK 61 D2
**Fredrika** S 200 B4
**Fredriksberg** S 50 B1
**Fredriksdal** S 62 A2
**Fredrikstad** N 54 A1
**Fregenal de la Sierra**
E 161 A3
**Fregene** I 168 B2
**Freiberg** D 83 B5
**Freiburg**
*Baden-Württemberg*
D 106 B2
*Niedersachsen* D 64 C2
**Freienhagen** D 81 A5
**Freienhufen** D 84 A1
**Freiensteinau** D 81 B5
**Freihung** D 95 B3
**Freilassing** D 109 B3
**Freisen** D 92 B3
**Freising** D 95 C3
**Freistadt** A 96 C2
**Freital** D 84 A1
**Freixedas** P 149 B2
**Freixo de Espada à**
**Cinta** P 149 A3
**Fréjus** F 132 B2
**Fremdingen** D 94 C2
**Frenštát pod**
**Radhoštěm** CZ 98 B2
**Freren** D 71 B4
**Freshford** IRL 30 B1
**Freshwater** GB 44 C2
**Fresnay-sur-Sarthe**
F 89 B4
**Fresneda de la Sierra**
E 152 B1
**Fresneda de la Sierra**
**Tiron** E 143 B3
**Fresnedillas** E 151 B3
**Fresnes-en-Woevre**
F 92 B1
**Fresne-St Mamès**
F 105 B4
**Fresno Alhandiga**
E 150 B2
**Fresno de la Ribera**
E 150 A2
**Fresno de la Vega**
E 142 B1
**Fresno de Sayago**
E 149 A4
**Fresnoy-Folny** F 90 B1
**Fresnoy-le-Grand** F 91 B3
**Fressenville** F 90 A1
**Fresvik** N 46 A3
**Fréteval** F 103 B3
**Fretigney** F 105 B4
**Freudenberg**
*Baden-Württemberg*
D 94 B1
*Nordrhein-Westfalen*
D 81 B3
**Freudenstadt** D 93 C4
**Freux** B 92 B1
**Frévent** F 78 B2
**Freyburg** D 83 A3
**Freyenstein** D 73 A5
**Freyming-Merlebach**
F 92 B2
**Freystadt** D 95 B3
**Freyung** D 96 C1
**Frias de Albarracin**
E 152 B2
**Fribourg** CH 106 C2
**Frick** CH 106 B3
**Fridafors** S 63 B2
**Fridaythorpe** GB 40 A3
**Friedberg**
A 111 B3
*Bayern* D 94 C2
*Hessen* D 81 B4
**Friedeburg** D 71 A4
**Friedewald** D 82 B1
**Friedland**
*Brandenburg* D 74 B3
*Mecklenburg-*
*Vorpommern* D 74 A2
*Niedersachsen* D 82 A1
**Friedrichroda** D 82 B2
**Friedrichsdorf** D 81 B4
**Friedrichshafen** D 107 B4
**Friedrichskoog** D 64 B1
**Friedrichstadt** D 64 B2
**Friedrichswalde** D 74 A2
**Friesach** A 110 C1
**Friesack** D 73 B5
**Friesenheim** D 93 C3
**Friesoythe** D 71 A4
**Friggesund** S 200 E2
**Frigiliana** E 163 B4
**Frihetsli** N 192 D3
**Frillesås** S 60 B2
**Frinnaryd** S 62 A2
**Frinton-on-Sea** GB 45 B5
**Friockheim** GB 35 B5
**Friol** E 140 A3
**Fristad** S 60 B2
**Fritsla** S 60 B2
**Fritzlar** D 81 A5
**Frizington** GB 36 B3
**Frödinge** S 62 A4
**Froges** F 118 B2
**Frohburg** D 83 A4
**Frohnhausen** D 81 B4
**Frohnleiten** A 110 B2
**Froissy** F 90 B2
**Frombork** PL 69 A4
**Frome** GB 43 A4
**Frómista** E 142 B2
**Fröndenberg** D 81 A3
**Fronsac** F 128 B2
**Front** I 119 B4
**Fronteira** P 155 B3
**Frontenay-Rohan-Rohan**
F 114 B3
**Frontenhausen** D 95 C4
**Frontignan** F 130 B2
**Fronton** F 129 C4
**Fröseke** S 62 B3
**Frosinone** I 169 B3
**Frosolone** I 170 B2
**Frosta** N 199 B7
**Frøstrup** DK 58 A1
**Frosunda** S 57 A4
**Frouard** F 92 C2
**Frövi** S 56 A1
**Frøyset** N 46 B2
**Fruges** F 78 B2
**Frutigen** CH 106 C2
**Frýdek-Místek** CZ 98 B2
**Frýdlant** CZ 84 B3
**Frydlant nad Ostravicí**
CZ 98 B2
**Frygnowo** PL 77 A5
**Fryšták** CZ 98 B1
**Fucécchio** I 135 B3
**Fuencaliente**
*Ciudad Real* E 157 A4
*Ciudad Real* E 157 B3
**Fuencemillán** E 151 B4
**Fuendejalón** E 144 C2
**Fuengirola** E 163 B3
**Fuenlabrada** E 151 B4
**Fuenlabrada de los**
**Montes** E 156 A3
**Fuensalida** E 151 B3
**Fuensanta** E 164 B3
**Fuensanta de Martos**
E 163 A4
**Fuente-Álamo** E 158 C2
**Fuente-Álamo de Murcia**
E 165 B3
**Fuentealbilla** E 158 B2
**Fuente al Olmo de Iscar**
E 150 A3
**Fuentecén** E 151 A4
**Fuente Dé** E 142 A2
**Fuente de Cantos**
E 155 C4
**Fuente del Arco** E 156 B2
**Fuente del Conde**
E 163 A3
**Fuente del Maestre**
E 155 C4
**Fuente de Santa Cruz**
E 150 A3
**Fuente el Fresno** E 157 A4
**Fuente el Saz de Jarama**
E 151 B4
**Fuente el Sol** E 150 A3
**Fuenteguinaldo** E 149 B3
**Fuentelapeña** E 150 A2
**Fuentelcésped** E 151 A4
**Fuentelespino de Haro**
E 158 B1
**Fuentelespino de Moya**
E 158 B2
**Fuentenovilla** E 151 B4
**Fuente Obejuna** E 156 B2
**Fuente Palmera** E 162 A2
**Fuentepelayo** E 151 A3
**Fuentepinilla** E 151 A5
**Fuenterroble de**
**Salvatierra** E 150 B2
**Fuenterrobles** E 158 B2
**Fuentes** E 158 B1
**Fuentesauco** E 151 A3
**Fuentesaúco** E 150 A2
**Fuentes de Andalucía**
E 162 A2
**Fuentes de Ebro** E 153 A3
**Fuentes de Jiloca**
E 152 A2
**Fuentes de la Alcarria**
E 151 B5
**Fuentes de León** E 161 A3
**Fuentes de Nava** E 142 B2
**Fuentes de Oñoro**
E 149 B3
**Fuentes de Ropel**
E 142 B1
**Fuentespalda** E 153 B4
**Fuentespina** E 151 A4
**Fuente-Tójar** E 163 A3
**Fuente Vaqueros** E 163 A4
**Fuentidueña** E 151 A4
**Fuentidueña de Tajo**
E 151 B4
**Fuerte del Rey** E 157 C4
**Fügen** A 108 B2
**Fuglebjerg** DK 65 A4
**Fuglevik** N 54 A1
**Fuhrberg** D 72 B2
**Fulda** D 82 B1
**Fulgatore** I 176 B1
**Fully** CH 119 A4
**Fulnek** CZ 98 B1
**Fülöpszállás** H 112 C3
**Fulpmes** A 108 B2
**Fulunäs** S 49 A5
**Fumay** F 91 B4
**Fumel** F 129 B3
**Funäsdalen** S 199 C9
**Fundão** P 148 B2
**Funzie** GB 33 A6
**Furadouro** P 148 B1
**Fure** N 46 A2
**Fürstenau** D 71 B4
**Furstenau** D 81 A5
**Fürstenberg** D 74 A2
**Fürstenfeld** A 111 B3
**Fürstenfeldbruck**
D 108 A2
**Fürstenstein** D 96 C1
**Fürstenwalde** D 74 B3
**Fürstenwerder** D 74 A2
**Fürstenzell** D 96 C1
**Furta** H 113 B5
**Fürth**
*Bayern* D 94 B2
*Hessen* D 93 B4
**Furth im Wald** D 95 B4
**Furtwangen** D 106 A3
**Furuby** S 62 B3
**Furudal** S 50 A2
**Furuflaten** N 192 C4
**Furulund** S 61 D3
**Furusjö** S 60 B3
**Fusa** N 46 B2
**Fuscaldo** I 174 B2
**Fusch an der**
**Grossglocknerstrasse**
A 109 B3
**Fushë Arrëz** AL 182 A2
**Fushë-Krujë** AL 182 B1
**Fusina** I 122 B1
**Fusio** CH 107 C3
**Füssen** D 108 B1
**Fustiñana** E 144 B2
**Futog** SRB 126 B1
**Futrikelv** N 192 C3
**Füzesabony** H 113 B4
**Füzesgyarmat** H 113 B5
**Fužine** HR 123 B3
**Fyllinge** S 61 C2
**Fynshav** DK 64 B2
**Fyresdal** N 53 A4

## G

**Gaaldorf** A 110 B1
**Gabaldón** E 158 B2
**Gabarret** F 128 C2
**Gabčíkovo** SK 111 B4
**Gąbin** PL 77 B4
**Gabriac** F 130 A1
**Gabrovo** BG 17 D6
**Gaby** I 119 B4
**Gacé** F 89 B4
**Gacko** BIH 139 B4
**Gäddede** S 199 A11
**Gadebusch** D 65 C4
**Gadmen** CH 106 C3
**Gádor** E 164 C2
**Gádoros** H 113 C4
**Gael** F 101 A3
**Găeşti** RO 17 C6
**Gaeta** I 169 B3
**Gafanhoeira** P 154 C2
**Gaflenz** A 110 B1
**Gagarin** RUS 9 E9
**Gaggenau** D 93 C4
**Gagliano Castelferrato**
I 177 B3
**Gagliano del Capo**
I 173 C4
**Gagnet** S 50 B2
**Gaibanella** I 121 C4
**Gaildorf** D 94 B1
**Gaillac** F 129 C4
**Gaillefontaine** F 90 B1
**Gaillon** F 89 A5
**Gainsborough** GB 40 B3
**Gairloch** GB 31 B3
**Gairlochy** GB 34 B3
**Gáiro** I 179 C3
**Gaj**
HR 124 B3
SRB 127 C3
**Gaja-la-Selve** F 146 A2
**Gajanejos** E 151 B5
**Gajary** SK 97 C4
**Gajdobra** SRB 126 B1
**Galan** F 145 A4
**Galanta** SK 111 A4
**Galapagar** E 151 B3
**Galápagos** E 151 B4
**Galaroza** E 161 B3
**Galashiels** GB 35 C5
**Galatas** GR 185 B4
**Galaţi** RO 17 C8
**Galatina** I 173 B4
**Galatista** GR 183 C5
**Galátone** I 173 B4
**Galaxidi** GR 184 A3
**Galdakao** E 143 A4
**Galeata** I 135 B4
**Galende** E 141 B4
**Galera** E 164 B2
**Galéria** F 180 A1
**Galgamácsa** H 112 B3
**Galgate** GB 38 A4
**Galgon** F 128 B2
**Galinduste** E 150 B2
**Galinoporni** CY 181 A3
**Galisteo** E 155 B4
**Galizes** P 148 B2
**Galków** PL 87 A3
**Gallarate** I 120 B1
**Gallardon** F 90 C1
**Gallegos de Argañán**
E 149 B3
**Gallegos del Solmirón**
E 150 B2
**Galleguillos de Campos**
E 142 B1
**Galleno** I 135 B3
**Galliate** I 120 B1
**Gallicano** I 134 A3
**Gállio** I 121 B4
**Gallipoli = Gelibolu**
TR 186 B1
**Gallípoli** I 173 B3
**Gällivare** S 196 B3
**Gallizien** A 110 C1

**Gallneukirchen** A . . . 96 C2
**Gällö** S . . . 199 C12
**Gallocanta** E . . . 152 B2
**Gällstad** S . . . 60 B3
**Gallur** E . . . 144 C2
**Galmisdale** GB . . . 31 C2
**Galmpton** GB . . . 43 B3
**Galston** GB . . . 36 A2
**Galta** N . . . 52 A1
**Galtelli** I . . . 178 B3
**Galten** DK . . . 59 B2
**Galtür** A . . . 107 C5
**Galve de Sorbe** E . 151 A4
**Galveias** P . . . 154 B2
**Gálvez** E . . . 157 A3
**Galway** IRL . . . 28 A2
**Gamaches** F . . . 90 B1
**Gámbara** I . . . 120 B3
**Gambárie** I . . . 175 C1
**Gambassi Terme** I . 135 B3
**Gambatesa** I . . . 170 B2
**Gambolò** I . . . 120 B1
**Gaming** A . . . 110 B2
**Gamla Uppsala** S . . 51 C4
**Gamleby** S . . . 62 A4
**Gamlingay** GB . . . 44 A3
**Gammelgarn** S . . . 57 C4
**Gammelstad** S . . . 196 D5
**Gammertingen** D . . 107 A4
**Gams** CH . . . 107 B4
**Gamvik**
*Finnmark* N . . . 192 B6
*Finnmark* N . . . 193 A12
**Gan** F . . . 145 A3
**Gáname** E . . . 149 A3
**Ganda di Martello** I 108 C1
**Gandarela** P . . . 148 A1
**Ganddal** N . . . 52 B1
**Ganderkesee** D . . . 72 A1
**Gandesa** E . . . 153 A4
**Gandía** E . . . 159 C3
**Gandino** I . . . 120 B2
**Gandrup** DK . . . 58 A3
**Ganges** F . . . 130 B2
**Gånghester** S . . . 60 B3
**Gangi** I . . . 177 B3
**Gangkofen** D . . . 95 C4
**Gannat** F . . . 116 A3
**Gannay-sur-Loire**
F . . . 104 C2
**Gänserdorf** A . . . 97 C4
**Ganzlin** D . . . 73 A5
**Gap** F . . . 132 A2
**Gara** H . . . 125 A5
**Garaballa** E . . . 158 B2
**Garaguso** I . . . 172 B2
**Garbayuela** E . . . 156 A2
**Garbhallt** GB . . . 34 B2
**Garbsen** D . . . 72 B2
**Garching** D . . . 109 A3
**Garciaz** E . . . 156 A2
**Garcihernández** E . 150 B2
**Garcillán** E . . . 151 B3
**Garcinarro** E . . . 151 B5
**Garcisobaco** E . . . 162 B2
**Garda** I . . . 121 B3
**Gardanne** F . . . 131 B4
**Gärdås** S . . . 49 B5
**Gårdby** S . . . 63 B4
**Gardeja** PL . . . 69 B3
**Gardelegen** D . . . 73 B4
**Gardermoen** N . . . 48 B3
**Gardiki** GR . . . 182 E3
**Garding** D . . . 64 B1
**Gardone Riviera** I . 121 B3
**Gardone Val Trómpia**
I . . . 120 B3
**Gárdony** H . . . 112 B2
**Gardouch** F . . . 146 A2
**Gårdsjö** S . . . 55 B5
**Gårdskär** S . . . 51 B4
**Gards Köpinge** S . . 63 C2
**Garein** F . . . 128 B2
**Garelochhead** GB . . 34 B3
**Garéoult** F . . . 132 B2
**Garešnica** HR . . . 124 B2
**Garéssio** I . . . 133 A4
**Garforth** GB . . . 40 B2
**Gargaliani** GR . . . 184 B2
**Gargaligas** E . . . 156 A2
**Gargallo** E . . . 153 B3
**Garganta la Olla** E . 150 B2
**Gargantiel** E . . . 156 B3
**Gargellen** A . . . 107 C4
**Gargilesse-Dampierre**
F . . . 103 C3
**Gargnano** I . . . 121 B3
**Gargnäs** S . . . 195 E8
**Gárgoles de Abajo**
E . . . 152 B1
**Gargrave** GB . . . 40 B1
**Garitz** D . . . 73 C5
**Garlasco** I . . . 120 B1
**Garlieston** GB . . . 36 B2
**Garlin** F . . . 128 C2
**Garlitos** E . . . 156 B2
**Garmisch-Partenkirchen**
D . . . 108 B2
**Garnat-sur-Engièvre**
F . . . 104 C2
**Garpenberg** S . . . 50 B3
**Garphyttan** S . . . 55 A5
**Garray** E . . . 143 C4
**Garrel** D . . . 71 B5
**Garriguella** E . . . 146 B4
**Garrison** GB . . . 26 B2
**Garrovillas** E . . . 155 B4
**Garrucha** E . . . 164 B3
**Gars-am-Kamp** A . . 97 C3
**Garsås** S . . . 50 B1
**Garsdale Head** GB . 37 B4
**Gärsnäs** S . . . 63 C2
**Garstang** GB . . . 38 A4
**Gartow** D . . . 73 A4
**Gartz** D . . . 74 A3
**Gærum** DK . . . 58 A3
**Garvagh** GB . . . 27 B4
**Garvão** P . . . 160 B1
**Garve** GB . . . 32 D2
**Garwolin** PL . . . 12 C4
**Garz** D . . . 66 B2
**Garzyn** PL . . . 85 A4
**Gąsawa** PL . . . 76 B2
**Gåsborn** S . . . 49 C6
**Gaschurn** A . . . 107 C5
**Gascueña** E . . . 152 B1
**Gasny** F . . . 90 B1
**Gąsocin** PL . . . 77 B5
**Gastes** F . . . 128 B1
**Gastouni** GR . . . 184 B2
**Gastouri** GR . . . 182 D1
**Gata**
E . . . 149 B3
HR . . . 138 B2
**Gata de Gorgos** E . 159 C4
**Gătaia** RO . . . 126 B3
**Gatchina** RUS . . . 9 C7
**Gatehouse of Fleet**
GB . . . 36 B2
**Gátér** H . . . 113 C3
**Gateshead** GB . . . 37 B5
**Gátova** E . . . 159 B3
**Gattendorf** A . . . 111 A3
**Gatteo a Mare** I . . 136 A1
**Gattinara** I . . . 119 B5
**Gattorna** I . . . 134 A2
**Gaucín** E . . . 162 B2
**Gaulstad** N . . . 199 B9
**Gaupne** N . . . 47 A4
**Gautefall** N . . . 53 A4
**Gauting** D . . . 108 A2
**Gauto** S . . . 195 D7
**Gava** E . . . 147 C3
**Gavardo** I . . . 121 B3
**Gavarnie** F . . . 145 B3
**Gávavencsello** H . . 113 A5
**Gavi** I . . . 120 C1
**Gavião** P . . . 154 B3
**Gavirate** I . . . 120 B1
**Gävle** S . . . 51 B4
**Gavoi** I . . . 178 B3
**Gavorrano** I . . . 135 C3
**Gavray** F . . . 88 B2
**Gavrio** GR . . . 185 B5
**Gävunda** S . . . 49 B6
**Gaweinstal** A . . . 97 C4
**Gaworzyce** PL . . . 85 A3
**Gawroniec** PL . . . 75 A5
**Gaydon** GB . . . 44 A2
**Gayton** GB . . . 41 C4
**Gazipaşa** TR . . . 189 C7
**Gazoldo degli Ippoliti**
I . . . 121 B3
**Gazzuolo** I . . . 121 B3
**Gbelce** SK . . . 112 B2
**Gdańsk** PL . . . 69 A3
**Gdinj** HR . . . 138 B2
**Gdov** RUS . . . 8 C5
**Gdów** PL . . . 99 B4
**Gdynia** PL . . . 69 A3
**Gea de Albarracin**
E . . . 152 B2
**Geary** GB . . . 31 B2
**Géaudot** F . . . 91 C4
**Geaune** F . . . 128 C2
**Gebesee** D . . . 82 A2
**Gebiz** TR . . . 189 B5
**Gebze** TR . . . 187 B4
**Géderlak** H . . . 112 C2
**Gedern** D . . . 81 B5
**Gedinne** B . . . 91 B4
**Gediz** TR . . . 187 D4
**Gèdre** F . . . 145 B4
**Gedser** DK . . . 65 B4
**Gedsted** DK . . . 58 B2
**Geel** B . . . 79 A4
**Geesthacht** D . . . 72 A3
**Geetbets** B . . . 79 B5
**Gefell** D . . . 83 B3
**Gehrden** D . . . 72 B2
**Gehren** D . . . 82 B3
**Geilenkirchen** D . . 80 B2
**Geilo** N . . . 47 B5
**Geinsheim** D . . . 93 B4
**Geisa** D . . . 82 B1
**Geiselhöring** D . . . 95 C4
**Geiselwind** D . . . 94 B2
**Geisenfeld** D . . . 95 C3
**Geisenhausen** D . . 95 C4
**Geisenheim** D . . . 93 B4
**Geising** D . . . 84 B1
**Geisingen** D . . . 107 B3
**Geislingen** D . . . 94 C1
**Geistthal** A . . . 110 B2
**Geiterygghytta** N . . 47 B4
**Geithain** D . . . 83 A4
**Geithus** N . . . 48 C1
**Gela** I . . . 177 B3
**Geldermalsen** NL . . 79 A5
**Geldern** D . . . 80 A2
**Geldrop** NL . . . 80 A1
**Geleen** NL . . . 80 B1
**Gelembe** TR . . . 186 C2
**Gelendost** TR . . . 189 A6
**Gelibolu = Gallipoli**
TR . . . 186 B1
**Gelida** E . . . 147 C2
**Gelnhausen** D . . . 81 B5
**Gelnica** SK . . . 99 C4
**Gelsa** E . . . 153 A3
**Gelse** H . . . 111 C3
**Gelsenkirchen** D . . 80 A3
**Gelsted** DK . . . 59 C2
**Geltendorf** D . . . 108 A2
**Gelterkinden** CH . . 106 B2
**Gelting** D . . . 64 B2
**Gelu** RO . . . 126 A3
**Gelves** E . . . 162 A1
**Gembloux** B . . . 79 B4
**Gemeaux** F . . . 105 B4
**Géménos** F . . . 132 B1
**Gemerská Poloma**
SK . . . 99 C4
**Gemerská Ves** SK . . 99 C4
**Gemert** NL . . . 80 A1
**Gemla** S . . . 62 B2
**Gemlik** TR . . . 186 B4
**Gemmenich** B . . . 80 B1
**Gemona del Friuli** I 122 A2
**Gémozac** F . . . 114 C3
**Gemund** D . . . 80 B2
**Gemünden**
*Bayern* D . . . 94 A1
*Hessen* D . . . 81 B4
*Rheinland-Pfalz* D . . 93 B3
**Genappe** B . . . 79 B4
**Génave** E . . . 164 A2
**Genazzano** I . . . 169 B2
**Gençay** F . . . 115 B4
**Gencsapáti** H . . . 111 B3
**Gendringen** NL . . . 80 A2
**Genelard** F . . . 104 C3
**Genemuiden** NL . . . 70 B3
**Generalski Stol** HR 123 B4
**Geneva = Genève**
CH . . . 118 A3
**Genevad** S . . . 61 C3
**Genève = Geneva**
CH . . . 118 A3
**Genevriéres** F . . . 105 B4
**Gengenbach** D . . . 93 C4
**Genillé** F . . . 103 B3
**Genk** B . . . 80 B1
**Genlis** F . . . 105 B4
**Gennep** NL . . . 80 A1
**Genner** DK . . . 64 A2
**Gennes** F . . . 102 B1
**Genoa = Génova** I . 134 A1
**Genola** I . . . 133 A3
**Génova = Genoa** I . 134 A1
**Genowefa** PL . . . 76 B3
**Gensingen** D . . . 93 B3
**Gent = Ghent** B . . . 79 A3
**Genthin** D . . . 73 B5
**Gentioux** F . . . 116 B1
**Genzano di Lucánia**
I . . . 172 B2
**Genzano di Roma** I 168 B2
**Georgenthal** D . . . 82 B2
**Georgsmarienhütte**
D . . . 71 B5
**Gera** D . . . 83 B4
**Geraards-bergen** B . 79 B3
**Gerace** I . . . 175 C2
**Geraci Sículo** I . . . 177 B3
**Geraki** GR . . . 184 C3
**Gérardmer** F . . . 106 A1
**Geras** A . . . 97 C3
**Gerbéviller** F . . . 92 C2
**Gerbini** I . . . 177 B3
**Gerbstedt** D . . . 83 A3
**Gerði** IS . . . 191 C9
**Gerede** TR . . . 187 B7
**Gerena** E . . . 161 B3
**Geretsried** D . . . 108 B2
**Gérgal** E . . . 164 B2
**Gergy** F . . . 105 C3
**Gerindote** E . . . 150 C3
**Gerjen** H . . . 112 C2
**Gerlos** A . . . 108 B3
**Germay** F . . . 92 C1
**Germencik** TR . . . 188 B2
**Germering** D . . . 108 A2
**Germersheim** D . . . 93 B4
**Gernika-Lumo** E . . 143 A4
**Gernrode** D . . . 82 A3
**Gernsbach** D . . . 93 C4
**Gernsheim** D . . . 93 B4
**Geroda** D . . . 82 B1
**Gerola Alta** I . . . 120 A2
**Geroldsgrun** D . . . 83 B3
**Gerolsbach** D . . . 95 C3
**Gerolstein** D . . . 80 B2
**Gerolzhofen** D . . . 94 B2
**Gerovo** HR . . . 123 B3
**Gerpinnes** B . . . 79 B4
**Gerrards Cross** GB . 44 B3
**Gerri de la Sal** E . 147 B2
**Gersfeld** D . . . 82 B1
**Gerstetten** D . . . 94 C2
**Gersthofen** D . . . 94 C2
**Gerstungen** D . . . 82 B2
**Gerswalde** D . . . 74 A2
**Gerzat** F . . . 116 B3
**Gerze** TR . . . 23 A8
**Gerzen** D . . . 95 C4
**Gescher** D . . . 71 C4
**Geseke** D . . . 81 A4
**Geslau** D . . . 94 B2
**Gespunsart** F . . . 91 B4
**Gesté** F . . . 101 B4
**Gestorf** D . . . 72 B2
**Gesualda** I . . . 170 C3
**Gesunda** S . . . 50 B1
**Gesztely** H . . . 113 A4
**Geta** FIN . . . 51 B6
**Getafe** E . . . 151 B4
**Getinge** S . . . 60 C2
**Getxo** E . . . 143 A4
**Geversdorf** D . . . 64 C2
**Gevgelija** MK . . . 182 B4
**Gevora del Caudillo**
E . . . 155 C4
**Gevrey-Chambertin**
F . . . 105 B3
**Gex** F . . . 118 A3
**Gey** D . . . 80 B2
**Geyikli** TR . . . 186 C1
**Geysir** IS . . . 190 C5
**Geyve** TR . . . 187 B5
**Gföhl** A . . . 97 C3
**Ghedi** I . . . 120 B3
**Ghent = Gent** B . . . 79 A3
**Gheorgheni** RO . . . 17 B6
**Ghigo** I . . . 119 C4
**Ghilarza** I . . . 178 B2
**Ghisonaccia** F . . . 180 A2
**Ghisoni** F . . . 180 A2
**Gialtra** GR . . . 182 E4
**Gianitsa** GR . . . 182 C4
**Giardinetto Vécchio**
I . . . 171 B3
**Giardini Naxos** I . . 177 B4
**Giarratana** I . . . 177 B3
**Giarre** I . . . 177 B4
**Giat** F . . . 116 B2
**Giaveno** I . . . 119 B4
**Giazza** I . . . 121 B4
**Giba** I . . . 179 C2
**Gibellina Nuova** I . . 176 B1
**Gibostad** N . . . 194 A9
**Gibraleón** E . . . 161 B3
**Gibraltar** GBZ . . . 162 B2
**Gic** H . . . 111 B4
**Gideå** S . . . 200 C5
**Gideåkroken** S . . . 200 B3
**Gidle** PL . . . 86 B3
**Giebelstadt** D . . . 94 B1
**Gieboldehausen** D . 82 A2
**Gielniów** PL . . . 87 A4
**Gielow** D . . . 74 A1
**Gien** F . . . 103 B4
**Giengen** D . . . 94 C2
**Giens** F . . . 132 B2
**Giera** RO . . . 126 B2
**Gieselwerder** D . . . 81 A5
**Giessen** D . . . 81 B4
**Gieten** NL . . . 71 A3
**Giethoorn** NL . . . 70 B3
**Giffaumont-**
**Champaubert** F . . . 91 C4
**Gifford** GB . . . 35 C5
**Gifhorn** D . . . 73 B3
**Gige** H . . . 125 A3
**Gignac** F . . . 130 B2
**Gijón = Xixón** E . . 142 A1
**Gilena** E . . . 162 A3
**Gilford** GB . . . 27 B4
**Gillberga** S . . . 55 A3
**Gilleleje** DK . . . 61 C2
**Gilley** F . . . 105 B5
**Gilley-sur-Loire** F . 104 C2
**Gillingham**
*Dorset* GB . . . 43 A4
*Medway* GB . . . 45 B4
**Gilocourt** F . . . 90 B2
**Gilserberg** D . . . 81 B5
**Gilsland** GB . . . 37 B4
**Gilze** NL . . . 79 A4
**Gimåt** S . . . 200 C4
**Gimo** S . . . 51 B5
**Gimont** F . . . 129 C3
**Ginasservis** F . . . 132 B1
**Gingelom** B . . . 79 B5
**Gingst** D . . . 66 B2
**Ginosa** I . . . 171 C4
**Ginzling** A . . . 108 B2
**Giões** P . . . 160 B2
**Gióia dei Marsi** I . . 169 B3
**Gióia del Colle** I . . 173 B2
**Gióia Sannitica** I . . 170 B2
**Gióia Táuro** I . . . 175 C1
**Gioiosa Iónica** I . . 175 C2
**Gioiosa Marea** I . . 177 A3
**Giosla** GB . . . 31 A2
**Giovinazzo** I . . . 171 B4
**Girifalco** I . . . 175 C2
**Giromagny** F . . . 106 B1
**Girona** E . . . 147 C3
**Gironcourt-sur-Vraine**
F . . . 92 C1
**Gironella** E . . . 147 B2
**Gironville-sous-les-**
**Côtes** F . . . 92 C1
**Girvan** GB . . . 36 A2
**Gislaved** S . . . 60 B3
**Gislev** DK . . . 59 C3
**Gisors** F . . . 90 B1
**Gissi** I . . . 170 A2
**Gistad** S . . . 56 B1
**Gistel** B . . . 78 A2
**Gistrup** DK . . . 58 B3
**Giswil** CH . . . 106 C3
**Githio** GR . . . 184 C3
**Giugliano in Campania**
I . . . 170 C2
**Giulianova** I . . . 136 C2
**Giulvăz** RO . . . 126 B2
**Giurgiu** RO . . . 17 D6
**Give** DK . . . 59 C2
**Givet** F . . . 91 A4
**Givors** F . . . 117 B4
**Givry**
B . . . 79 B4
F . . . 104 C3
**Givry-en-Argonne** F 91 C4
**Givskud** DK . . . 59 C2
**Giżalki** PL . . . 76 B2
**Gizeux** F . . . 102 B2
**Giżycko** PL . . . 12 A4
**Gizzeria** I . . . 175 C2
**Gizzeria Lido** I . . . 175 C2
**Gjedved** DK . . . 59 C2
**Gjegjan** AL . . . 182 B2
**Gjendesheim** N . . . 47 A5
**Gjerde** N . . . 46 B3
**Gjerlev** DK . . . 58 B3
**Gjermundshamn** N . 46 B2
**Gjerrild** DK . . . 58 B3
**Gjerstad** N . . . 53 B5
**Gjesås** N . . . 49 B4
**Gjesvær** N . . . 193 A9
**Gjirokastër** AL . . . 182 C2
**Gjøfjell** N . . . 54 A1
**Gjøl** DK . . . 58 A2
**Gjøra** N . . . 198 C6
**Gjøvik** N . . . 48 B2
**Gladbeck** D . . . 80 A2
**Gladenbach** D . . . 81 B4
**Gladstad** N . . . 195 E2
**Glamis** GB . . . 35 B4
**Glamoč** BIH . . . 138 A2
**Glamsbjerg** DK . . . 59 C3
**Gland** CH . . . 105 C5
**Glandorf** D . . . 71 B4
**Glanegg** A . . . 110 C1
**Glanshammar** S . . . 56 A1
**Glarus** CH . . . 107 B4
**Glasgow** GB . . . 35 C3
**Glashütte**
*Bayern* D . . . 108 B2
*Sachsen* D . . . 84 B1
**Glastonbury** GB . . . 43 A4
**Glatzau** A . . . 110 C2
**Glauchau** D . . . 83 B4
**Glava** S . . . 54 A3
**Glavatičevo** BIH . . 139 B4
**Glavičice** BIH . . . 127 C1
**Gŭlŭbovo** BG . . . 183 A7
**Glein**
A . . . 110 B1
N . . . 195 D3
**Gleinstätten** A . . . 110 C2
**Gleisdorf** A . . . 110 B2
**Glenamoy** IRL . . . 26 B1
**Glenarm** GB . . . 27 B5
**Glenavy** GB . . . 27 B4
**Glenbarr** GB . . . 34 C2
**Glenbeigh** IRL . . . 29 B2
**Glenbrittle** GB . . . 31 B2
**Glencoe** GB . . . 34 B2
**Glencolumbkille** IRL 26 B2
**Glendalough** IRL . . 30 A2
**Glenealy** IRL . . . 30 B2
**Glenelg** GB . . . 31 B3
**Glenfinnan** GB . . . 34 B2
**Glengarriff** IRL . . . 29 C2
**Glenluce** GB . . . 36 B2
**Glennamaddy** IRL . . 28 A3
**Glenrothes** GB . . . 35 B4
**Glenties** IRL . . . 26 B2
**Glesborg** DK . . . 58 B3
**Glesien** D . . . 83 A4
**Gletsch** CH . . . 106 C3
**Glewitz** D . . . 66 B1
**Glifada** GR . . . 185 B4
**Glimåkra** S . . . 63 B2
**Glin** IRL . . . 29 B2
**Glina** HR . . . 124 B2
**Glinde** D . . . 72 A3
**Glinojeck** PL . . . 77 B5
**Glinsk** IRL . . . 28 A2
**Gliwice** PL . . . 86 B2
**Glödnitz** A . . . 109 C5
**Gloggnitz** A . . . 110 B2
**Głogoczow** PL . . . 99 B3
**Glogonj** SRB . . . 127 C2
**Glogovac** SRB . . . 127 C3
**Głogów** PL . . . 85 A4
**Głogówek** PL . . . 86 B1
**Glomel** F . . . 100 A2
**Glomfjord** N . . . 195 D4
**Glommen** S . . . 60 C2
**Glommersträsk** S . 196 D2
**Glonn** D . . . 108 B2
**Glorenza** I . . . 108 C1
**Gloria** P . . . 154 B2
**Glosa** GR . . . 183 D5
**Glossop** GB . . . 40 B2
**Gloucester** GB . . . 39 C4
**Głowaczów** PL . . . 87 A5
**Glówczyce** PL . . . 68 A2
**Glöwen** D . . . 73 B5
**Głowno** PL . . . 77 C4
**Gložan** SRB . . . 126 B1
**Głubczyce** PL . . . 86 B1
**Głuchołazy** PL . . . 85 B5
**Głuchów** PL . . . 87 A4
**Głuchowo** PL . . . 75 B5
**Glücksburg** D . . . 64 B2
**Glückstadt** D . . . 64 C2
**Glumina** BIH . . . 139 A5
**Glumsø** DK . . . 65 A4
**Glušci** SRB . . . 127 C1
**Glusk** BY . . . 13 B8
**Głuszyca** PL . . . 85 B4
**Glyngøre** DK . . . 58 B1
**Glyn Neath** GB . . . 39 C3
**Gmünd**
*Karnten* A . . . 109 C4
*Nieder Östereich* A . 96 C2
**Gmund** D . . . 108 B2
**Gmunden** A . . . 109 B4
**Gnarp** S . . . 200 D3
**Gnarrenburg** D . . . 72 A2
**Gnesau** A . . . 109 C4
**Gnesta** S . . . 56 A3
**Gnięchowice** PL . . . 85 A4
**Gniew** PL . . . 69 B3
**Gniewkowo** PL . . . 76 B3
**Gniezno** PL . . . 76 B2
**Gnoien** D . . . 66 C1
**Gnojnice** BIH . . . 139 B3
**Gnojno** PL . . . 87 B4
**Gnosall** GB . . . 40 C1
**Gnosjö** S . . . 60 B3
**Göbel** TR . . . 186 B3
**Göçbeyli** TR . . . 186 C2
**Goch** D . . . 80 A2
**Gochsheim** D . . . 94 A2
**Göd** H . . . 112 B3
**Godalming** GB . . . 44 B3
**Godby** FIN . . . 51 B6
**Goðdalir** IS . . . 190 B6
**Goddelsheim** D . . . 81 A4
**Gódega di Sant'Urbano**
I . . . 122 B1
**Godegård** S . . . 56 B1
**Godelheim** D . . . 81 A5
**Goderville** F . . . 89 A4
**Godiasco** I . . . 120 C2
**Godič** SLO . . . 123 A3
**Godkowo** PL . . . 69 A4
**Godmanchester** GB 44 A3
**Gödöllö** H . . . 112 B3
**Gödre** H . . . 125 A3
**Godshill** GB . . . 44 C2
**Godzikowice** PL . . . 85 B5
**Godziszewo** PL . . . 69 A3
**Goes** NL . . . 79 A3
**Goetzenbrück** F . . . 93 C3
**Góglio** I . . . 119 A5
**Gogolin** PL . . . 86 B2
**Göhren** D . . . 66 B2
**Goirle** NL . . . 79 A5
**Góis** P . . . 148 B1
**Góito** I . . . 121 B3
**Goizueta** E . . . 144 A2
**Gojna Gora** SRB . . 127 D2
**Gójsk** PL . . . 77 B4
**Gökçedağ** TR . . . 186 C3
**Gökçen** TR . . . 188 A2
**Gökçeören** TR . . . 188 A3
**Gökçeyazı** TR . . . 186 C2
**Göktepe** TR . . . 188 B3
**Gol** N . . . 47 B5
**Gola**
HR . . . 124 A3
N . . . 48 A1
**Gołańcz** PL . . . 76 B2
**Gölbaşı** TR . . . 23 B7
**Gölby** FIN . . . 51 B6
**Gölcük**
*Kocaeli* TR . . . 187 B4
*Niğde* TR . . . 23 B8
**Golčův Jenikov** CZ . 97 B3
**Gołczewo** PL . . . 67 C3
**Goldach** CH . . . 107 B4
**Goldbach** D . . . 93 A5
**Goldbeck** D . . . 73 B4
**Goldberg** D . . . 73 A5
**Goldelund** D . . . 64 B2
**Goldenstedt** D . . . 72 B1
**Gołębiewo** PL . . . 69 A3
**Golegã** P . . . 154 B2
**Goleniów** PL . . . 75 A3
**Golfo Aranci** I . . . 178 B3
**Gölhisar** TR . . . 189 B4
**Golina** PL . . . 76 B3
**Gölle** H . . . 112 C2
**Göllersdorf** A . . . 97 C4
**Golling an der Salzach**
A . . . 109 B4
**Gölmarmara** TR . . . 186 D2
**Golnice** PL . . . 84 A3
**Golnik** SLO . . . 123 A3
**Gölova** TR . . . 189 C5
**Gölpazarı** TR . . . 187 B5
**Gols** A . . . 111 B3
**Golspie** GB . . . 32 D3
**Golssen** D . . . 74 C2
**Golub-Dobrzyń** PL . 77 A4
**Golubinci** SRB . . . 127 C2
**Goluchów** PL . . . 86 A1
**Golymin-Ośrodek**
PL . . . 77 B5
**Golzow** D . . . 73 B5
**Gomagoi** I . . . 108 C1
**Gómara** E . . . 152 A1
**Gomaringen** D . . . 93 C5
**Gömbe** TR . . . 189 C4
**Gömeç** TR . . . 186 C1
**Gomel = Homyel** BY 13 B9
**Gomes Aires** P . . . 160 B1
**Gómezserracín** E . 150 A3
**Gommern** D . . . 73 B4
**Gomulin** PL . . . 86 A3
**Gonäs** S . . . 50 B2
**Goncelin** F . . . 118 B2
**Gończyce** PL . . . 87 A5
**Gondomar**
E . . . 140 B2
P . . . 148 A1
**Gondrecourt-le-Château**
F . . . 92 C1

Gondrin F 128 C3
Gönen
Balıkesir TR 186 B2
Isparta TR 189 B5
Gonfaron F 132 B2
Goñi E 144 B2
Goni
GR 182 D4
I 179 C3
Gonnesa I 179 C2
Gonnosfanádiga I 179 C2
Gönyü H 111 B4
Gonzaga I 121 C3
Goodrich GB 39 C4
Goodwick GB 39 B1
Gooik B 79 B4
Goole GB 40 B3
Goor NL 71 B3
Göpfritz an der Wild
A 97 C3
Goppenstein CH 119 A4
Göppingen D 94 C1
Gor E 164 B2
Góra
Dolnośląskie PL 85 A4
Mazowieckie PL 77 B5
Gorafe E 164 B1
Gorawino PL 67 C4
Goražde BIH 139 B4
Gőrbeháza H 113 B5
Gordaliza del Pino
E 142 B1
Gördes TR 186 D3
Gørding DK 59 C1
Górdola CH 120 A1
Gordon GB 35 C5
Gordoncillo E 142 B1
Gorebridge GB 35 C4
Gorenja Vas SLO 123 A3
Gorenje Jelenje
HR 123 B3
Gorey
GB 88 A1
IRL 30 B2
Gorgonzola I 120 B2
Gorica HR 137 A4
Gorican HR 124 A2
Gorinchem NL 79 A4
Goring GB 44 B2
Goritsy RUS 9 D10
Göritz D 74 A2
Gorízia I 122 B2
Górki PL 77 B4
Gorleben D 73 A4
Gorleston-on-sea
GB 41 C5
Gørlev DK 61 D1
Görlitz D 84 A2
Górliz E 143 A4
Görmin D 66 C2
Górna Grupa PL 69 B3
Gorna Oryakhovitsa
BG 17 D6
Gornja Gorevnica
SRB 127 D2
Gornja Ploča HR 137 A4
Gornja Radgona
SLO 110 C2
Gornja Sabanta
SRB 127 D3
Gornja Trešnjevica
SRB 127 C2
Gornja Tuzla BIH 125 C4
Gornje Polje MNE 139 C4
Gornje Ratkovo
BIH 124 C2
Gornji Grad SLO 123 A3
Gornji Humac HR 138 B2
Gornji Jasenjani
BIH 139 B3
Gornji Kamengrad
BIH 124 C2
Gornji Kneginec
HR 124 A2
Gornji Kosinj HR 123 C4
Gornji Milanovac
SRB 127 C2
Gornji Podgradci
BIH 124 B3
Gornji Ravno BIH 138 B3
Gornji Sjenicak HR 124 B1
Gornji Vakuf BIH 138 B3
Górno PL 87 B4
Görömböly H 113 A4
Górowo Iławeckie
PL 69 A5
Gorran Haven GB 42 B2
Gorredijk NL 70 A3
Gorron F 88 B3
Gorseinon GB 39 C2
Gort IRL 28 A3
Gortin GB 27 B3
Görzke D 73 B5
Gorzkowice PL 86 A3
Górzno
Kujawsko-Pomorskie
PL 77 A4
Zachodnio-Pomorskie
PL 75 A4
Gorzów Śląski PL 86 A2
Gorzów Wielkopolski
PL 75 B4
Górzyca PL 74 B3
Gorzyce PL 98 B2
Górzyn PL 84 A2
Gorzyń PL 75 B4
Gorzyno PL 68 A2
Gosaldo I 121 A4
Gosau A 109 B4
Gosberton GB 41 C3
Gościcino PL 68 A3
Gościęcin PL 86 B2
Gościm PL 75 B4
Gościno PL 67 B4
Gosdorf A 110 C2
Gosforth GB 36 B3
Goslar D 82 A2
Goslice PL 77 B4
Gospič HR 137 A4
Gosport GB 44 C2
Gössäter S 55 B4
Gossau CH 107 B4
Goss Ilsede D 72 B3
Gössnitz D 83 B4
Gössweinstein D 95 B3
Gostivar MK 182 B2
Gostkow PL 77 C4
Göstling an der Ybbs
A 110 B1
Gostomia PL 75 A5
Gostycyn PL 76 A2
Gostyń PL 85 A5
Gostynin PL 77 B4
Goszczyn PL 87 A4
Göta S 54 B3
Göteborg = Gothenburg
S 60 B1
Götene S 55 B4
Gotha D 82 B2
Gothem S 57 C4
Gothenburg = Göteborg
S 60 B1
Gotse Delchev BG 183 B5
Gottersdorf D 95 C4
Göttingen D 82 A1
Gottne S 200 C4
Götzis A 107 B4
Gouarec F 100 A2
Gouda NL 70 B1
Goudhurst GB 45 B4
Goumenissa GR 182 C4
Goura GR 184 B3
Gourdon F 129 B4
Gourgançon F 91 C4
Gourin F 100 A2
Gournay-en-Bray F 90 B1
Gourock GB 34 C3
Gouveia P 148 B2
Gouvy B 80 B1
Gouzeacourt F 90 A3
Gouzon F 116 A2
Govedari HR 138 C3
Govérnolo I 121 B3
Gowarczów PL 87 A4
Gowerton GB 39 C2
Gowidlino PL 68 A2
Gowran IRL 30 B1
Goyatz D 74 B3
Göynük
TR 187 B5
Antalya TR 189 C5
Gozdnica PL 84 A3
Gozdowo PL 77 B4
Gozee B 79 B4
Graal-Müritz D 65 B5
Grabenstätt D 109 B3
Grabhair GB 31 A2
Gråbo S 60 B2
Grabovac
HR 138 B2
SRB 127 C2
Grabovci SRB 127 C1
Grabow D 73 A4
Grabów PL 77 B4
Grabow nad Pilicą
PL 87 A5
Grabów nad Prosną
PL 86 A2
Grabowno PL 76 A2
Grabs CH 107 B4
Gračac HR 138 A1
Gračanica BIH 125 C4
Graçay F 103 B3
Grad SLO 111 C3
Gradac
BIH 139 C4
HR 138 B3
MNE 139 B5
Gradačac BIH 125 C4
Gradec HR 124 B2
Gradefes E 142 B1
Grades A 110 C1
Gradil P 154 C1
Gradina
HR 124 B3
MNE 139 B5
Gradisca d'Isonzo
I 122 B2
Gradište HR 125 B4
Grado
E 141 A4
I 122 B2
Grafenau D 96 C1
Gräfenberg D 95 B3
Gräfenhainichen D 83 A4
Grafenschlag A 97 C3
Grafenstein A 110 C1
Gräfenthal D 82 B3
Grafentonna D 82 A2
Grafenwöhr D 95 B3
Grafing D 108 A2
Grafling D 95 C4
Gräfsnäs S 54 B3
Gragnano I 170 C2
Grahovo SLO 122 A2
Graiguenamanagh
IRL 30 B2
Grain GB 45 B4
Grainau D 108 B2
Graja de Iniesta E 158 B2
Grajera E 151 A4
Gram DK 59 C2
Gramais A 108 B1
Gramat F 129 B4
Gramatneusiedl A 111 A3
Grambow D 74 A3
Grammichele I 177 B3
Gramsh AL 182 C2
Gramzow D 74 A3
Gran N 48 B2
Granada E 163 A4
Granard IRL 27 C3
Grañas E 140 A3
Granátula de Calatrava
E 157 B4
Grancey-le-Château
F 105 B4
Grandas de Salime
E 141 A4
Grandcamp-Maisy F 88 A2
Grand-Champ F 100 B3
Grand Couronne F 89 A5
Grand-Fougeray F 101 B4
Grândola P 160 A1
Grandpré F 91 B4
Grandrieu
B 79 B4
F 117 C3
Grandson CH 106 C1
Grandvillars F 106 B1
Grandvilliers F 90 B1
Grañén E 145 C3
Grangärde S 50 B1
Grange IRL 26 B2
Grangemouth GB 35 B4
Grange-over-Sands
GB 36 B4
Grängesberg S 50 B1
Granges-de Crouhens
F 145 B4
Granges-sur-Vologne
F 106 A1
Gräningen D 73 B5
Granitola-Torretta I 176 B1
Granja
Évora P 155 C3
Porto P 148 A1
Granja de Moreruela
E 142 C1
Granja de Torrehermosa
E 156 B2
Gränna S 55 B5
Grannäs
Västerbotten S 195 E7
Västerbotten S 195 E8
Granö S 200 B5
Granollers E 147 C3
Granowiec PL 85 A5
Granowo PL 75 B5
Gransee D 74 A2
Gransherad N 53 A5
Grantham GB 40 C3
Grantown-on-Spey
GB 32 D3
Grantshouse GB 35 C5
Granville F 88 B2
Granvin N 46 B3
Grærup Strand DK 59 C1
Gräsås S 60 C2
Grasbakken N 193 B12
Grasberg D 72 A2
Grasmere GB 36 B3
Gräsmyr S 200 C5
Grasö S 51 B5
Grassano I 172 B2
Grassau D 109 B3
Grasse F 132 B2
Grassington GB 40 A2
Græsted DK 61 C2
Gråsten DK 64 B2
Grästorp S 54 B3
Gratkorn A 110 B2
Gråträsk S 196 D2
Gratwein A 110 B2
Graulhet F 129 C4
Graus E 145 B4
Grávalos E 144 B2
Grävberget N 49 B4
Grave NL 80 A1
Gravedona I 120 A2
Gravelines F 78 A2
Gravellona Toce I 119 B5
Gravendal S 50 B1
Gravens DK 59 C2
Gravesend GB 45 B4
Graveson F 131 B3
Gravina in Púglia I 172 B2
Gray F 105 B4
Grayrigg GB 37 B4
Grays GB 45 B4
Grayshott GB 44 B3
Graz A 110 B2
Grazalema E 162 B2
Grążawy PL 69 B4
Grazzano Visconti
I 120 C2
Greåker N 54 A2
Great Dunmow GB 45 B4
Great Malvern GB 39 B4
Great Torrington
GB 42 B2
Great Waltham GB 45 B4
Great Yarmouth GB 41 C5
Grebbestad S 54 B2
Grebenstein D 81 A5
Grębocice PL 85 A4
Grębocin PL 76 A3
Greding D 95 B3
Gredstedbro DK 59 C1
Greencastle IRL 27 A3
Greenhead GB 37 B4
Greenisland GB 27 B5
Greenlaw GB 35 C5
Greenock GB 34 C3
Greenway GB 39 C2
Greenwich GB 45 B4
Grefrath D 80 A2
Greifenburg A 109 C4
Greiffenberg D 74 A2
Greifswald D 66 B2
Grein A 110 A1
Greipstad N 53 B3
Greiz D 83 B4
Grenaa DK 58 B3
Grenade F 129 C4
Grenade-sur-l'Adour
F 128 C2
Grenchen CH 106 B2
Grendi N 53 B3
Grenivík IS 191 B7
Grenoble F 118 B2
Gréoux-les-Bains
F 132 B1
Gresenhorst D 66 B1
Gressoney-la-Trinité
I 119 B4
Gressoney-St.-Jean
I 119 B4
Gressthal D 82 B2
Gressvik N 54 A1
Gresten A 110 B2
Gretna GB 36 B3
Greussen D 82 A2
Greve in Chianti I 135 B4
Greven
Mecklenburg-
Vorpommern D 73 A3
Nordrhein-Westfalen
D 71 B4
Grevena GR 182 C3
Grevenbroich D 80 A2
Grevenbrück D 81 A4
Grevenmacher L 92 B2
Grevesmühlen D 65 C4
Grevestrand DK 61 D2
Grevie S 61 C2
Greystoke GB 36 B4
Greystones IRL 30 A2
Grez-Doiceau B 79 B4
Grèzec F 129 B4
Grez-en-Bouère F 102 B1
Grezzana I 121 B4
Grgar SLO 122 A2
Grgurevci SRB 127 B1
Gries A 108 B2
Griesbach D 96 C1
Griesheim D 93 B4
Gries in Sellrain A 108 B2
Grieskirchen A 109 A4
Griffen A 110 C1
Grignan F 131 A3
Grignano I 122 B2
Grigno I 121 A4
Grignols F 128 B2
Grignon F 118 B3
Grijota E 142 B2
Grijpskerk NL 71 A3
Grillby S 56 A3
Grimaud F 132 B2
Grimbergen B 79 B4
Grimma D 83 A4
Grimmen D 66 B2
Grimmialp CH 106 C2
Grimsås S 60 B3
Grimsby GB 41 B3
Grimslöv S 62 B2
Grímsstaðir IS 191 B9
Grimstad N 53 B4
Grimstorp S 62 A2
Grindavík IS 190 D3
Grindelwald CH 106 C3
Grindheim N 52 B3
Grindsted DK 59 C1
Griñón E 151 B4
Gripenberg S 62 A2
Gripsholm S 56 A3
Grisolles F 129 C4
Grisslehamn S 51 B5
Gritley GB 33 C4
Grizebeck GB 36 B3
Grndina BIH 124 C2
Gröbming A 109 B4
Gröbzig D 83 A3
Grocka SRB 127 C2
Gröditz D 83 A5
Gródki PL 77 A5
Grodków PL 85 B5
Grodziec PL 76 B3
Grodzisk Mazowiecki
PL 77 B5
Grodzisk Wielkoposki
PL 75 B5
Groenlo NL 71 B3
Groesbeek NL 80 A1
Grohote HR 138 B2
Groitzsch D 83 A4
Groix F 100 B2
Grójec PL 77 C5
Grom PL 77 A5
Gromiljca BIH 139 B4
Grömitz D 65 B3
Gromnik PL 99 B4
Gromo I 120 B2
Gronau
Niedersachsen D 72 B2
Nordrhein-Westfalen
D 71 B4
Grønbjerg DK 59 B1
Grönenbach D 107 B5
Grong N 199 A9
Grönhögen S 63 B4
Groningen
D 73 C4
NL 71 A3
Grønnestrand DK 58 A2
Grono CH 120 A2
Grönskåra S 62 A3
Grootegast NL 71 A3
Gropello Cairoli I 120 B1
Grorud N 48 C2
Grósio I 120 A3
Grošnica SRB 127 D2
Grossalmerode D 82 A1
Grossarl A 109 B4
Gross Beeren D 74 B2
Gross Berkel D 72 B2
Grossbodungen D 82 A2
Gross-botwar D 94 C1
Grossburgwedel D 72 B2
Grosschönau D 84 B2
Gross-Dölln D 74 A2
Grossenbrode D 65 B4
Grossenehrich D 82 A2
Grossengottern D 82 A2
Grossenhain D 83 A5
Grossenkneten D 71 B5
Grossenlüder D 81 B5
Grossensee D 72 A3
Grossenzersdorf A 111 A3
Grosseto I 135 C4
Gross-Gerau D 93 B4
Grossgerungs A 96 C2
Grossglobnitz A 97 C3
Grosshabersdorf D 94 B2
Grossharras A 97 C4
Grosshartmansdorf
D 83 B5
Grosshöchstetten
CH 106 C2
Gross Kreutz D 74 B1
Grosskrut A 97 C4
Gross Lafferde D 72 B3
Gross Leutheb D 74 B3
Grosslohra D 82 A2
Grossmehring D 95 C3
Gross Muckrow D 74 B3
Gross Oesingen D 72 B3
Grossostheim D 93 B5
Grosspertholz A 96 C2
Grosspetersdorf A 111 B3
Grosspostwitz D 84 A2
Grossraming A 110 B1
Grossräschen D 84 A2
Gross Reken D 80 A3
Grossrinderfeld D 94 B1
Grossröhrsdorf D 84 A2
Gross Sarau D 65 C3
Gross Särchen D 84 A2
Grossschirma D 83 B5
Gross Schönebeck
D 74 B2
Grossschweinbarth
A 97 C4
Grosssiegharts A 97 C3
Grosssölk A 109 B4
Gross Umstadt D 93 B4
Grosswarasdorf A 111 B3
Gross Warnow D 73 A4
Gross-Weikersdorf
A 97 C3
Gross-Welle D 73 A5
Grosswilfersdorf A 110 B2
Gross Wokern D 65 C5
Grostenquin F 92 C2
Grosuplje SLO 123 B3
Grotli N 198 C4
Grötlingbo S 57 C4
Grottáglie I 173 B3
Grottaminarda I 170 B3
Grottammare I 136 C2
Grotte di Castro I 168 A1
Grotteria I 175 C2
Gróttole I 172 B2
Grouw NL 70 A2
Grov N 194 B8
Grova N 53 A4
Grove E 140 B2
Grua N 48 B2
Grube D 65 B4
Grubišno Polje HR 124 B3
Grude BIH 138 B3
Grudusk PL 77 A5
Grudziądz PL 69 B3
Grue N 49 B4
Gruissan F 130 B2
Grullos E 141 A4
Grumo Áppula I 171 B4
Grums S 55 A4
Grünau im Almtal
A 109 B4
Grünberg D 81 B4
Grünburg A 110 B1
Grundarfjörður IS 190 C2
Gründau D 81 B5
Gründelhardt D 94 B1
Grundforsen S 49 A4
Grundlsee A 109 B4
Grundsund S 54 B2
Grunewald D 84 A1
Grungedal N 53 A3
Grunow D 74 B3
Grünstadt D 93 B4
Gruvberget S 50 A3
Gruyères CH 106 C2
Gruža SRB 127 D2
Grybów PL 99 B4
Grycksbo S 50 B2
Gryfice PL 67 C4
Gryfino PL 74 A3
Gryfów Śląski PL 84 A3
Gryllefjord N 194 A8
Grymyr N 48 B2
Gryt S 56 B2
Grytgöl S 56 B1
Grythyttan S 55 A5
Grytnäs S 57 B3
Grzmiąca PL 68 B1
Grzybno PL 74 A3
Grzywna PL 76 A3
Gschnitz A 108 B2
Gschwend D 94 C1
Gstaad CH 106 C2
Gsteig CH 119 A4
Guadahortuna E 163 A4
Guadalajara E 151 B4
Guadalaviar E 152 B2
Guadalcanal E 156 B2
Guadalcázar E 162 A3
Guadalix de la Sierra
E 151 B4
Guadálmez E 156 B3
Guadalupe E 156 A2
Guadamur E 151 C3
Guadarrama E 151 B3
Guadiaro E 162 B2
Guadix E 164 B1
Guagnano I 173 B3
Guagno F 180 A1
Guajar-Faragüit E 163 B4
Gualchos E 163 B4
Gualdo Tadino I 136 B1
Gualtieri I 121 C3
Guarcino I 169 B3
Guarda P 149 B2
Guardamar del Segura
E 165 A4
Guardão P 148 B1
Guardavalle I 175 C2
Guardea I 168 A2
Guárdia I 172 B1
Guardiagrele I 169 A4
Guardiarégia I 170 B2
Guárdia Sanframondi
I 170 B2
Guardias Viejas E 164 C2
Guardiola de Bergueda
E 147 B2
Guardo E 142 B2
Guareña E 156 B1
Guaro E 162 B3
Guarromán E 157 B4
Guasila I 179 C3
Guastalla I 121 C3
Gubbhögen S 199 A12
Gúbbio I 136 B1
Guben D 74 C3
Gubin PL 74 C3
Gudå N 199 B8
Gudavac BIH 124 C2
Guddal N 46 A2
Güderup DK 64 B2
Gudhem S 55 B4
Gudhjem DK 67 A3
Gudovac HR 124 B2
Gudow D 73 A3
Güdül TR 187 B7
Gudvangen N 46 B3
Guebwiller F 106 B2
Guéjar-Sierra E 163 A4
Guéméné-Penfao
F 101 B4
Guéméné-sur-Scorff
F 100 A2
Güeñes E 143 A3
Guer F 101 B3
Guérande F 101 B3
Guéret F 116 A1
Guérigny F 104 B2
Guesa E 144 B2
Gueugnon F 104 C3
Guglionesi I 170 B2
Gühlen Glienicke D 74 A1
Guia P 154 B2
Guichen F 101 B4
Guidizzolo I 121 B3
Guidónia-Montecélio
I 168 B2
Guiglia I 135 A3
Guignes F 90 C2
Guijo E 156 B3
Guijo de Coria E 149 B3
Guijo de Santa Bábera
E 150 B2
Guijuelo E 150 B2
Guildford GB 44 B3
Guillaumes F 132 A2
Guillena E 162 A1
Guillestre F 118 C3
Guillos F 128 B2
Guilsfield GB 38 B3
Guilvinec F 100 B1
Guimarães P 148 A1
Guincho P 154 C1
Guînes F 78 B1

Guingamp F 100 A2
Guipavas F 100 A1
Guisborough GB 37 B5
Guiscard F 90 B3
Guiscriff F 100 A2
Guise F 91 B3
Guisona E 147 C2
Guitiriz E 140 A3
Guîtres F 128 A2
Gujan-Mestras F 128 B1
Gulbene LV 8 D5
Gulçayır TR 187 C6
Guldborg DK 65 B4
Gullabo S 63 B3
Gullane GB 35 B5
Gullbrå N 46 B3
Gullbrandstorp S 61 C2
Gulleråsen S 50 A2
Gullhaug N 53 A6
Gullringen S 62 A3
Gullspång S 55 B5
Gullstein N 198 B5
Güllük TR 188 B2
Gülnar TR 23 C7
Gülpınar TR 186 C1
Gülşehir TR 23 B8
Gulsvik N 48 B1
Gumiel de Hizán E 143 C3
Gummersbach D 81 A3
Gümüldür TR 188 A2
Gümüşhaciköy TR 23 A8
Gümüşova TR 187 B5
Gundelfingen D 94 C2
Gundel-fingen D 106 A2
Gundelsheim D 93 B5
Gunderschoffen F 93 C3
Gundertshausen A 109 A3
Gundinci HR 125 B4
Gündoğmuş TR 189 C7
Güney
*Burdur* TR 189 B4
*Denizli* TR 188 A4
Gunja HR 125 C4
Günlüce TR 188 C3
Gunnarn S 195 E8
Gunnarsbyn S 196 C4
Gunnarskog S 49 C4
Gunnebo S 62 A4
Gunnislake GB 42 B2
Günselsdorf A 111 B3
Guntersblum D 93 B4
Guntersdorf A 97 C4
Guntin E 140 B3
Günyüzü TR 187 C6
Günzburg D 94 C2
Gunzenhausen D 94 B2
Güre
*Balıkesir* TR 186 C1
*Uşak* TR 186 D4
Gurk A 110 C1
Gurrea de Gállego
E 144 B3
Gürsu TR 186 B4
Gušće HR 124 B2
Gusev RUS 12 A5
Gùspini I 179 C2
Gusselby S 56 A1
Güssing A 111 B3
Gusswerk A 110 B2
Gustav Adolf S 49 B5
Gustavsberg S 57 A4
Gustavsfors S 54 A3
Güstrow D 65 C5
Gusum S 56 B2
Gutcher GB 33 A5
Gutenstein A 110 B2
Gütersloh D 81 A4
Guttannen CH 106 C3
Guttaring A 110 C1
Guttau D 84 A2
Güttingen CH 107 B4
Gützkow D 66 C2
Guzów PL 77 B5
Gvardeysk RUS 12 A4
Gvarv N 53 A5
Gvozd MNE 139 C5
Gvozdansko HR 124 B2
Gwda Wielka PL 68 B1
Gwennap GB 42 B1
Gy F 105 B4
Gyál H 112 B3
Gyarmat H 111 B4
Gyékényes H 124 A3
Gyé-sur-Seine F 104 A3
Gyljen S 196 C5
Gylling DK 59 C3
Gyoma H 113 C4
Gyömöre H 111 B4
Gyömrö H 112 B3
Gyón H 112 B3
Gyöngyfa H 125 B3
Gyöngyös H 113 B3
Gyöngyöspata H 113 B3
Gyönk H 112 C2
Györ H 111 B4
Györszemere H 111 B4
Gypsera CH 106 C2
Gysinge S 51 B3
Gyttorp S 55 A5
Gyula H 113 C5
Gyulafirátót H 112 B1
Gyulaj H 112 C2

## H

Haacht B 79 B4
Haag
*Nieder Östereich*
A 110 A1
*Ober Östereich* A 109 A4
D 108 A3
Haaksbergen NL 71 B3
Haamstede NL 79 A3
Haan D 80 A3
Haapajärvi FIN 3 E9
Haapsalu EST 8 C3
Haarlem NL 70 B1
Habas F 128 C2
Habay B 92 B1
Habo S 62 A2
Håbol S 54 B3
Habry CZ 97 B3
Habsheim F 106 B2
Hachenburg D 81 B3
Hacıbektaş TR 23 B8
Hacılar TR 23 B8
Hacinas E 143 C3
Hackås S 199 C11
Hacketstown IRL 30 B2
Hackthorpe GB 37 B4
Hadamar D 81 B4
Hädanberg S 200 C4
Haddington GB 35 C5
Hadersdorf am Kamp
A 97 C3
Haderslev DK 59 C2
Haderup DK 59 B1
Hadım TR 23 C7
Hadleigh
*Essex* GB 45 B4
*Suffolk* GB 45 A4
Hadlow GB 45 B4
Hadmersleben D 73 B4
Hadsten DK 59 B3
Hadsund DK 58 B3
Hadžići BIH 139 B4
Hafnarfjörður IS 190 C4
Hafnir IS 190 D3
Hafslo N 47 A4
Haganj HR 124 B2
Hagby S 63 B4
Hage D 71 A4
Hægebostad N 52 B3
Hægeland N 53 B3
Hagen
*Niedersachsen* D 72 A1
*Nordrhein-Westfalen*
D 80 A3
Hagenbach D 93 B4
Hagenow D 73 A4
Hagetmau F 128 C2
Hagfors S 49 B5
Häggenås S 199 B11
Hagondange F 92 B2
Hagsta S 51 B4
Haguenau F 93 C3
Hahnbach D 95 B3
Hahnslätten D 81 B4
Hahót H 111 C3
Haiger D 81 B4
Haigerloch D 93 C4
Hailsham GB 45 C4
Hainburg A 111 A3
Hainfeld A 110 A2
Hainichen D 83 B5
Hajdúböszörmény
H 113 B5
Hajdučica SRB 126 B2
Hajdúdorog H 113 B5
Hajdúnánás H 113 B5
Hajdúszoboszló H 113 B5
Hajnáčka SK 113 A3
Hajnówka PL 13 B5
Hajós H 112 C3
Håkafot S 199 A11
Hakkas S 196 C4
Håksberg S 50 B2
Halaszi H 111 B4
Halberstadt D 82 A3
Halberton GB 43 B3
Hald Ege DK 58 B2
Haldem D 71 B5
Halden N 54 A2
Haldensleben D 73 B4
Halenbeck D 73 A5
Halesowen GB 40 C1
Halesworth GB 45 A5
Halfing D 109 B3
Halhjem N 46 B2
Håliden S 49 B5
Halifax GB 40 B2
Häljelöt S 56 B2
Halkirk GB 32 C3
Hall S 57 C4
Hälla S 200 C3
Hallabro S 63 B3
Hällabrottet S 56 A1
Halland GB 45 C4
Hällaryd S 63 B2
Hallaryd S 61 C3
Hällberga S 56 A2
Hällbybrunn S 56 A2
Halle
B 79 B4
*Nordrhein-Westfalen*
D 72 B1
*Sachsen-Anhalt* D 83 A3
Hålleberga S 62 B3
Hällefors S 55 A5
Hälleforsnäs S 56 A2
Hallein A 109 B4
Hällekis S 55 B4
Hallen S 199 B11
Hållen S 51 B4
Hallenberg D 81 A4
Hällestad S 56 B1
Hällevadsholm S 54 B2
Hällevik S 63 B2
Hälleviksstrand S 54 B2
Hallingby N 48 B2
Hallingeberg S 62 A4
Hallingen N 47 B6
Hall in Tirol A 108 B2
Hällnäs S 195 D9
Hållnäs S 51 B4
Hällnäs S 200 B5
Hallormsstaður
IS 191 B11
Hallsberg S 56 A1
Hållsta S 56 A2
Hallstahammar S 56 A2
Hallstatt A 109 B4
Hallstavik S 51 B5
Halltorp S 63 B4
Halluin F 78 B3
Hallviken S 199 B12
Hallworthy GB 42 B2
Halmstad S 61 C2
Hals DK 58 A3
Halsa N 198 B5
Halstead GB 45 B4
Haltdalen N 199 C8
Haltern D 80 A3
Haltwhistle GB 37 B4
Halvarsgårdarna S 50 B2
Halver D 80 A3
Halvrimmen DK 58 A2
Ham F 90 B3
Hamar N 48 B3
Hamarhaug N 46 B2
Hamarøy N 194 B6
Hambach F 92 B3
Hambergen D 72 A1
Hambergsund S 54 B2
Hambledon GB 44 C2
Hambuhren D 72 B2
Hamburg D 72 A3
Hamdibey TR 186 C2
Hamdorf D 64 B2
Hämeenlinna FIN 8 B4
Hameln = Hamlin D 72 B2
Hamersleben D 73 B4
Hamidiye TR 187 C5
Hamilton GB 36 A2
Hamina FIN 8 B5
Hamlagrø N 46 B3
Hamlin = Hameln D 72 B2
Hamm D 81 A3
Hammar S 55 B5
Hammarland FIN 51 B6
Hammarö S 55 A4
Hammarstrand S 200 C2
Hamme B 79 A4
Hammel DK 59 B2
Hammelburg D 82 B1
Hammelspring D 74 A2
Hammenhög S 66 A3
Hammerdal S 199 B12
Hammerfest N 192 B7
Hammershøj DK 58 B2
Hammerum DK 59 B2
Hamminkeln D 80 A2
Hamnavoe GB 33 A5
Hamneda S 60 C3
Hamningberg N 193 B14
Hamoir B 80 B1
Hamont B 80 A1
Hámor H 113 A4
Hamra
*Gävleborg* S 199 D12
*Gotland* S 57 D4
Hamrångefjärden S 51 B4
Hamstreet GB 45 B4
Hamsund N 194 B6
Han TR 187 C5
Hanaskog S 61 C4
Hanau D 81 B4
Händelöp S 62 A4
Handlová SK 98 C2
Hanerau-Hademarschen
D 64 B2
Hånger S 60 B3
Hanhimaa FIN 197 B8
Hanken S 55 B5
Hankensbüttel D 73 B3
Han Knežica BIH 124 B2
Hanko FIN 8 C3
Hannover D 72 B2
Hannut B 79 B5
Han Pijesak BIH 139 A4
Hansnes N 192 C3
Hanstedt D 72 A3
Hanstholm DK 58 A1
Hantsavichy BY 13 B7
Hanušovice CZ 85 B4
Haparanda S 196 D7
Haradok BY 13 A8
Harads S 196 C4
Häradsbäck S 63 B2
Häradsbygden S 50 B2
Harbo S 51 B4
Harboør DK 58 B1
Harburg
*Bayern* D 94 C2
*Hamburg* D 72 A2
Hårby DK 59 C3
Harc H 112 C2
Hardegarijp NL 70 A2
Hardegsen D 82 A1
Hardelot Plage F 78 B1
Hardenbeck D 74 A2
Hardenberg NL 71 B3
Harderwijk NL 70 B2
Hardheim D 94 B1
Hardt D 106 A3
Hareid N 198 C3
Haren
D 71 B4
NL 71 A3
Harestua N 48 B2
Harfleur F 89 A4
Harg S 51 B5
Hargicourt F 90 B3
Hargnies F 91 A4
Hargshamn S 51 B5
Härja S 55 B4
Harkány H 125 B4
Härkeberga S 56 A3
Harkebrügge D 71 A4
Harlech GB 38 B2
Harleston GB 45 A5
Hårlev DK 65 A5
Harlingen NL 70 A2
Harlösa S 61 D3
Harlow GB 45 B4
Harmancık TR 186 C4
Harmånger S 200 E3
Härnevi S 56 A3
Härnösand S 200 D3
Haro E 143 B4
Haroldswick GB 33 A6
Háromfa H 124 A3
Haroué F 92 C2
Harpenden GB 44 B3
Harplinge S 60 C2
Harpstedt D 72 B1
Harrogate GB 40 A2
Harrow GB 44 B3
Härryda S 60 B2
Harsefeld D 72 A2
Harsewinkel D 71 C5
Hârşova 17 C7
Harstad N 194 B7
Harsum D 72 B2
Harsvik N 199 A7
Harta H 112 C3
Hartberg A 110 B2
Hartburn GB 37 A5
Hartennes F 90 B3
Hartest GB 45 A4
Hartha D 83 A4
Hartland GB 42 B2
Hartlepool GB 37 B5
Hartmanice CZ 96 B1
Hartmannsdorf A 110 B2
Harvassdal N 195 E5
Harwell GB 44 B2
Harwich GB 45 B5
Harzgerode D 82 A3
Häselgehr A 108 B1
Haselünne D 71 B4
Hasköy TR 186 A1
Haslach D 106 A3
Haslach an der Mühl
A 96 C2
Hasle DK 67 A3
Haslemere GB 44 B3
Haslev DK 65 A4
Hasloch D 94 B1
Hasparren F 144 A2
Hassela S 200 D2
Hasselfelde D 82 A2
Hasselfors S 55 A5
Hasselt
B 79 B5
NL 70 B3
Hassfurt D 94 A2
Hassleben D 74 A2
Hässleholm S 61 C3
Hasslö S 63 B3
Hassloch D 93 B4
Hästbo S 51 B4
Hastersboda FIN 51 B7
Hästholmen S 55 B5
Hastière-Lavaux B 79 B4
Hastigrow GB 32 C3
Hastings GB 45 C4
Hästveda S 61 C3
Hasvik N 192 B6
Hatfield
*Hertfordshire* GB 44 B3
*South Yorkshire* GB 40 B3
Hatherleigh GB 42 B2
Hathersage GB 40 B2
Hatlestrand N 46 B2
Hattem NL 70 B3
Hatten
D 71 A5
F 93 C3
Hattfjelldal N 195 E4
Hatting DK 59 C2
Hattingen D 80 A3
Hattstadt F 106 A2
Hattstedt D 64 B2
Hatvan H 112 B3
Hatvik N 46 B2
Hau D 80 A2
Haudainville F 92 B1
Hauganes IS 191 B7
Haugastøl N 47 B4
Hauge N 52 B2
Haugesund N 52 A1
Haughom N 52 B2
Haugsdal N 46 B2
Haugsdorf A 97 C4
Haukedal N 46 A3
Haukeland N 46 B2
Haukeligrend N 52 A3
Haukeliseter N 52 A3
Haukipudas FIN 3 D9
Haulerwijk NL 71 A3
Haunersdorf D 95 C4
Haus N 46 B2
Hausach D 106 A3
Hausham D 108 B2
Hausmannstätten
A 110 C2
Hausvik N 52 B2
Hautajärvi FIN 197 C12
Hautefort F 129 A4
Hauterives F 117 B5
Hauteville-Lompnès
F 118 B2
Haut-Fays B 91 A5
Hautmont F 79 B3
Hautrage B 79 B3
Hauzenberg D 96 C1
Havant GB 44 C3
Havdhem S 57 C4
Havdrup DK 61 D2
Havelange B 79 B5
Havelberg D 73 B5
Havelte NL 70 B3
Haverfordwest GB 39 C2
Haverhill GB 45 A4
Havering GB 45 B4
Håverud S 54 B3
Havířov CZ 98 B2
Havixbeck D 71 C4
Havlíčkův Brod CZ 97 B3
Havndal DK 58 B3
Havneby DK 64 A1
Havnebyen DK 61 D1
Havnsø DK 61 D1
Havøysund N 193 A8
Havran TR 186 C2
Havrebjerg DK 61 D1
Havsa TR 186 A1
Havstenssund S 54 B2
Havza TR 23 A8
Hawes GB 37 B4
Hawick GB 35 C5
Hawkhurst GB 45 B4
Hawkinge GB 45 B5
Haxey GB 40 B3
Hayange F 92 B2
Haydarlı TR 189 A5
Haydon Bridge GB 37 B4
Hayle GB 42 B1
Haymana TR 187 C7
Hay-on-Wye GB 39 B3
Hayrabolu TR 186 A2
Haysyn UA 13 D8
Hayvoron UA 13 D8
Haywards Heath GB 44 C3
Hazebrouck F 78 B2
Hazlov CZ 83 B4
Heacham GB 41 C4
Headcorn GB 45 B4
Headford IRL 28 A2
Heanor GB 40 B2
Héas F 145 B4
Heathfield GB 45 C4
Hebden Bridge GB 40 B1
Heberg S 60 C2
Heby S 51 C3
Hechingen D 93 C4
Hechlingen D 94 C2
Hecho E 144 B3
Hechtel B 79 A5
Hechthausen D 72 A2
Heckelberg D 74 B2
Heckington GB 41 C3
Hecklingen D 82 A3
Hed S 56 A1
Hedalen N 48 B1
Hedared S 60 B2
Heddal N 53 A5
Hédé F 101 A4
Hede S 199 C10
Hedekas S 54 B2
Hedemora S 50 B2
Hedenäset S 196 C6
Hedensted DK 59 C2
Hedersleben D 82 A3
Hedesunda S 51 B4
Hedge End GB 44 C2
Hedon GB 41 B3
Heede D 71 B4
Heek D 71 B4
Heemstede NL 70 B1
Heerde NL 70 B3
Heerenveen NL 70 B2
Heerhugowaard NL 70 B1
Heerlen NL 80 B1
Heeze NL 80 A1
Heggenes N 47 A6
Hegra N 199 B8
Hegyeshalom H 111 B4
Hegyközség H 111 B3
Heia N 199 A9
Heide D 64 B2
Heidelberg D 93 B4
Heiden D 80 A2
Heidenau D 84 B1
Heidenheim D 94 C2
Heidenreichstein A 97 C3
Heikendorf D 64 B3
Heikkilä FIN 197 C12
Heilam GB 32 C2
Heiland N 53 B4
Heilbad Heiligenstadt
D 82 A2
Heilbronn D 93 B5
Heiligenblut A 109 B3
Heiligendamn D 65 B4
Heiligendorf D 73 B3
Heiligengrabe D 73 A5
Heiligenhafen D 65 B3
Heiligenhaus D 80 A2
Heiligenkreuz A 111 C3
Heiligenstadt D 94 B3
Heiloo NL 70 B1
Heilsbronn D 94 B2
Heim N 198 B6
Heimburg D 82 A2
Heimdal N 199 B7
Heinerscheid L 92 A2
Heinersdorf D 74 B3
Heining D 96 C1
Heiningen D 94 C1
Heinola FIN 8 B5
Heinsberg D 80 A2
Heist-op-den-Berg
B 79 A4
Hejde S 57 C4
Hejdeby S 57 C4
Hejls DK 59 C2
Hejnice CZ 84 B3
Hel PL 69 A3
Helchteren B 79 A5
Heldburg D 82 B2
Heldrungen D 82 A3
Helechosa E 156 A3
Helensburgh GB 34 B3
Helfenberg A 96 C2
Helgen N 53 A5
Helgeroa N 53 B5
Hella
IS 190 D5
N 46 A3
Helland N 194 B7
Hellas S 55 B3
Helle N 52 B2
Helleland N 52 B2
Hellendoorn NL 71 B3
Hellenthal D 80 B2
Hellesøy N 46 B1
Hellesylt N 198 C3
Hellevoetsluis NL 79 A4
Helligskogen N 192 C4
Hellin E 158 C2
Hellissandur IS 190 C2
Hellnar IS 190 C2
Hellum DK 58 A3
Hellvi S 57 C4
Hellvik N 52 B1
Helm-brechts D 83 B3
Helmond NL 80 A1
Helmsdale GB 32 C3
Helmsley GB 37 B5
Helmstedt D 73 B3
Hel'pa SK 99 C3
Helsa D 82 A1
Helsby GB 38 A4
Helsingborg S 61 C2
Helsinge DK 61 C2
Helsingør DK 61 C2
Helsinki FIN 8 B4
Helston GB 42 B1
Hemau D 95 B3
Hemavan S 195 E6
Hemel Hempstead
GB 44 B3
Hemer D 81 A3
Héming F 92 C2
Hemmet DK 59 C1
Hemmingstedt D 64 B2
Hemmoor D 64 C2
Hemnes N 54 A2
Hemnesberget N 195 D4
Hemse S 57 C4
Hemsedal N 47 B5
Hemslingen D 72 A2
Hemsworth GB 40 B2
Hen N 48 B2
Henån S 54 B2
Hendaye F 144 A2
Hendek TR 187 B5
Hendungen D 82 B2
Hønfield GB 44 C3
Hengelo
*Gelderland* NL 71 B3
*Overijssel* NL 71 B3
Hengersberg D 95 C5
Hengoed GB 39 C3
Hénin-Beaumont F 78 B2
Henley-on-Thames
GB 44 B3
Hennan S 200 D1
Henneberg D 82 B2
Hennebont F 100 B2
Henne Strand DK 59 C1
Hennigsdorf D 74 B2
Hennset N 198 B5
Hennstedt
*Schleswig-Holstein*
D 64 B2
*Schleswig-Holstein*
D 64 B2
Henrichemont F 103 B4
Henryków PL 85 B5
Henrykowo PL 69 A5
Hensås N 47 A5
Henstedt-Ulzburg D 64 C2
Heppenheim D 93 B4
Herad
*Buskerud* N 47 B6
*Vest-Agder* N 52 B2
Heradsbygd N 48 B3
Heraklion = Iraklio
GR 185 D6

Herálec CZ 97 B4
Herand N 46 B3
Herbault F 103 B3
Herbern D 81 A3
Herbertstown IRL 29 B3
Herbeumont B 91 B5
Herbignac F 101 B3
Herbisse F 91 C4
Herbitzheim F 92 B3
Herbolzheim D 106 A2
Herborn D 81 B4
Herbrechtingen D 94 C2
Herby PL 86 B2
Herceg-Novi MNE 16 D3
Hercegovać HR 124 B3
Hercegszántó H 125 B4
Herchen D 80 B3
Heréd H 112 B3
Hereford GB 39 B4
Herefoss N 53 B4
Hereke TR 187 B4
Herencia E 157 A4
Herend H 111 B4
Herent B 79 B4
Herentals B 79 A4
Hérépian F 130 B2
Herfølge DK 61 D2
Herford D 72 B1
Herguijuela E 156 A2
Héric F 101 B4
Héricourt F 106 B1
Héricourt-en-Caux F 89 A4
Hérimoncourt F 106 B1
Heringsdorf D 65 B4
Herisau CH 107 B4
Hérisson F 103 C4
Herk-de-Stad B 79 B5
Herlufmagle DK 65 A4
Hermagor A 109 C4
Hermannsburg D 72 B3
Hermansverk N 46 A3
Heřmanův Městec CZ 97 B3
Herment F 116 B2
Hermeskeil D 92 B2
Hermisende E 141 C4
Hermonville F 91 B3
Hermsdorf D 83 B3
Hernani E 144 A2
Hernansancho E 150 B3
Herne D 80 A3
Herne Bay GB 45 B5
Hernes N 48 B3
Herning DK 59 B1
Herøya N 53 A5
Herramelluri E 143 B3
Herräng S 51 B5
Herre N 53 A5
Herrenberg D 93 C4
Herrera E 162 A3
Herrera de Alcántara E 155 B3
Herrera del Duque E 156 A2
Herrera de los Navarros E 152 A2
Herrera de Pisuerga E 142 B2
Herreros del Suso E 150 B2
Herrestad S 54 B2
Herrhamra S 57 B3
Herritslev DK 65 B4
Herrlisheim F 93 C3
Herrljunga S 55 B4
Herrnhut D 84 A2
Herrsching D 108 A2
Hersbruck D 95 B3
Hersby S 57 A4
Herscheid D 81 A3
Herselt B 79 A4
Herso GR 182 B4
Herstal B 80 B1
Herstmonceux GB 45 C4
Herten D 80 A3
Hertford GB 44 B3
Hervás E 149 B4
Hervik N 52 A1
Herxheim D 93 B4
Herzberg
*Brandenburg* D 74 B1
*Brandenburg* D 83 A5
*Niedersachsen* D 82 A2
Herzebrock D 81 A4
Herzfelde D 74 B2
Herzlake D 71 B4
Herzogenaurach D 94 B2
Herzogenbuchsee CH 106 B2
Herzogenburg A 110 A2
Herzsprung D 73 A5
Hesby N 52 A1
Hesdin F 78 B2
Hesel D 71 A4
Heskestad N 52 B2
Hessdalen N 199 C8
Hesselager DK 65 A3
Hesseng N 193 C13
Hessisch Lichtenau D 82 A1
Hessisch-Oldendorf D 72 B2
Hestra S 60 B3
Heswall GB 38 A3
Hetlevik N 46 B2
Hettange-Grande F 92 B2
Hetton-le-Hole GB 37 B5
Hettstedt D 82 A3
Heuchin F 78 B2
Heudicourt-sous-les-Côtes F 92 C1
Heunezel F 105 A5
Heuqueville F 89 A4
Heves H 113 B4
Héviz H 111 C4
Hexham GB 37 B4
Heysham GB 36 B4
Heytesbury GB 43 A4
Hidas H 125 A4
Hieflau A 110 B1
Hiendelaencina E 151 A5
Hiersac F 115 C4
High Bentham GB 37 B4
Highclere GB 44 B2
High Hesket GB 37 B4
Highley GB 39 B4
High Wycombe GB 44 B3
Higuera de Arjona E 157 C4
Higuera de Calatrava E 163 A3
Higuera de la Serena E 156 B2
Higuera de la Sierra E 161 B3
Higuera de Vargas E 155 C4
Higuera la Real E 161 A3
Higuers de Llerena E 156 B1
Higueruela E 158 C2
Hijar E 153 A3
Hilchenbach D 81 A4
Hildburghausen D 82 B2
Hilden D 80 A2
Hilders D 82 B1
Hildesheim D 72 B2
Hilgay GB 41 C4
Hillared S 60 B3
Hille D 72 B1
Hillegom NL 70 B1
Hillerød DK 61 D2
Hillerstorp S 60 B3
Hillesheim D 80 B2
Hillestad N 53 A6
Hillmersdorf D 83 A5
Hillsborough GB 27 B4
Hillswick GB 33 A5
Hilpoltstein D 95 B3
Hiltpoltstein D 94 B3
Hilvarenbeek NL 79 A5
Hilversum NL 70 B2
Himarë AL 182 C1
Himbergen D 73 A3
Himesháza H 125 A4
Himmelberg A 109 C5
Himmelpforten D 72 A2
Himód H 111 B4
Hinckley GB 40 C2
Hindås S 60 B2
Hindelang D 108 B1
Hindelbank CH 106 B2
Hinderavåg N 52 A1
Hindhead GB 44 B3
Hinjosa del Valle E 156 B1
Hinnerup DK 59 B3
Hinneryd S 61 C3
Hinojal E 155 B4
Hinojales E 161 B3
Hinojos E 161 B3
Hinojosa del Duque E 156 B2
Hinojosas de Calatrava E 157 B3
Hinterhornbach A 108 B1
Hinterriss A 108 B2
Hintersee
A 109 B4
D 74 A3
Hinterstoder A 110 B1
Hintertux A 108 B2
Hinterweidenthal D 93 B3
Hinwil CH 107 B3
Hios GR 185 A7
Hippolytushoef NL 70 B1
Hirschaid D 94 B2
Hirschau D 95 B3
Hirschfeld D 83 A5
Hirschhorn D 93 B4
Hirsingue F 106 B2
Hirson F 91 B4
Hirtshals DK 58 A2
Hirvaskoski FIN 197 D10
Hirzenhain D 81 B5
Hisarcık TR 186 C4
Hishult S 61 C3
Hissjön S 200 C6
Hitchin GB 44 B3
Hitra N 198 B5
Hittarp S 61 C2
Hittisau A 107 B4
Hittun N 46 A1
Hitzacker D 73 A4
Hjallerup DK 58 A3
Hjällstad S 49 B5
Hjältevad S 62 A3
Hjärnarp S 61 C2
Hjartdal N 53 A4
Hjellestad N 46 B2
Hjelmeland N 52 A2
Hjelset N 198 C4
Hjerkinn N 198 C6
Hjerm DK 58 B1
Hjerpsted DK 64 A1
Hjerting DK 59 C1
Hjo S 55 B5
Hjordkær DK 64 A2
Hjørring DK 58 A2
Hjorted S 62 A4
Hjortkvarn S 56 B1
Hjortnäs S 50 B1
Hjortsberga S 62 B2
Hjukse N 53 A5
Hjuksebø N 53 A5
Hjulsjö S 55 A5
Hliník nad Hronom SK 98 C2
Hlinsko CZ 97 B3
Hlío IS 191 A10
Hlohovec SK 98 C1
Hlubokánad Vltavou CZ 96 B2
Hlučín CZ 98 B2
Hlyboka UA 17 A6
Hlybokaye BY 13 A7
Hniezdne SK 99 B4
Hnilec SK 99 C4
Hnúšťa SK 99 C3
Hobol H 125 A3
Hobro DK 58 B2
Hobscheid L 92 B1
Hocalar TR 189 A4
Hochdonn D 64 B2
Hochdorf CH 106 B3
Hochfelden F 93 C3
Hochspeyer D 93 B3
Höchstadt D 94 B2
Höchstädt D 94 C2
Hochstenbach D 81 B3
Höchst im Odenwald D 93 B5
Höckendorf D 83 B5
Hockenheim D 93 B4
Hoddesdon GB 44 B3
Hodejov SK 99 C3
Hodenhagen D 72 B2
Hodkovice CZ 84 B3
Hódmezövásárhely H 113 C4
Hodnet GB 38 B4
Hodonín CZ 98 C1
Hodslavice CZ 98 B2
Hoedekenskerke NL 79 A3
Hoegaarden B 79 B4
Hoek van Holland NL 79 A4
Hoenderlo NL 70 B2
Hof
D 83 B3
N 53 A6
Hofbieber D 82 B1
Hoff GB 37 B4
Hofgeismar D 81 A5
Hofheim
*Bayern* D 82 B2
*Hessen* D 93 A4
Hofkirchen im Mühlkreis A 96 C1
Höfn IS 191 C10
Hofors S 50 B3
Hofsós IS 190 B6
Hofstad N 199 A7
Höganäs S 61 C2
Högbo S 51 B3
Hogdal S 54 A2
Høgebru N 46 A4
Högfors S 50 C2
Högklint S 57 C4
Högsäter S 54 B3
Högsby S 62 A4
Högsjö S 56 A1
Hogstad S 55 B6
Högyész H 112 C2
Hohenau A 97 C4
Hohenberg A 110 B2
Hohenbucko D 83 A5
Hohenburg D 95 B3
Hohendorf D 66 B1
Hohenems A 107 B4
Hohenhameln D 72 B3
Hohenhausen D 72 B1
Hohenkirchen D 71 A4
Hohenlinden D 108 A2
Hohenlockstedt D 64 C2
Hohenmölsen D 83 A4
Hohennauen D 73 B5
Hohen Neuendorf D 74 B2
Hohenseeden D 73 B5
Hohentauern A 110 B1
Hohentengen D 106 B3
Hohenwepel D 81 A5
Hohenwestedt D 64 B2
Hohenwutzen D 74 B3
Hohenzieritz D 74 A2
Hohn D 64 B2
Hohne D 72 B3
Hohnstorf D 73 A3
Højer DK 64 B1
Højslev Stby DK 58 B2
Hok S 62 A2
Hökerum S 60 B3
Hökhuvud S 51 B5
Hokksund N 53 A5
Hökön S 63 B2
Hol N 47 B5
Hólar IS 190 B6
Holašovice CZ 96 C2
Holbæk
*Aarhus Amt.* DK 58 B3
*Vestsjællands Amt.* DK 61 D1
Holbeach GB 41 C4
Holdenstedt D 73 B3
Holdhus N 46 B2
Holdorf D 71 B5
Holeby DK 65 B4
Hølen N 54 A1
Hølervasseter N 47 B6
Holešov CZ 98 B1
Holguera E 155 B4
Holíč SK 98 C1
Holice
CZ 97 A3
SK 111 B4
Höljes S 49 B4
Hollabrunn A 97 C4
Hollandstoun GB 33 B4
Høllen N 53 B3
Hollfeld D 95 B3
Hollókő H 112 B3
Hollstadt D 82 B2
Hollum NL 70 A2
Höllviksnäs S 66 A1
Holm N 195 E3
Hólmavík IS 190 B4
Holmbukt N 192 B5
Holmedal S 54 A2
Holmegil N 54 A2
Holmen N 48 B2
Holme-on-Spalding-Moor GB 40 B3
Holmes Chapel GB 38 A4
Holmestrand N 54 A1
Holmfirth GB 40 B2
Holmfoss N 193 C14
Holmsbu N 54 A1
Holmsjö S 63 B3
Holmsund S 200 C6
Holmsveden S 50 A3
Holmudden S 57 C5
Hölö S 57 A3
Holøydal N 199 C8
Holsbybrunn S 62 A3
Holseter N 48 A1
Holsljunga S 60 B2
Holstebro DK 59 B1
Holsted DK 59 C1
Holsworthy GB 42 B2
Holt
D 64 B2
*Norfolk* GB 41 C5
*Wrexham* GB 38 A4
IS 190 D6
N 53 B4
Holten NL 71 B3
Holtwick D 71 B4
Holum N 52 B3
Holwerd NL 70 A2
Holycross IRL 29 B4
Holyhead GB 38 A2
Holýšov CZ 95 B5
Holywell GB 38 A3
Holywood GB 27 B5
Holzdorf D 83 A5
Holzhausen D 72 B1
Holzheim D 94 C2
Holzkirchen D 108 B2
Holzminden D 81 A5
Holzthaleben D 82 A2
Homberg
*Hessen* D 81 A5
*Hessen* D 81 B5
Homburg D 93 B3
Hommelstø N 195 E3
Hommersåk N 52 B1
Homokmegy H 112 C3
Homokszentgyörgy H 124 A3
Homyel = Gomel BY 13 B9
Honaz TR 188 B4
Hondarribia E 144 A2
Hondón de los Frailes E 165 A4
Hondschoote F 78 B2
Hönebach D 82 B1
Hønefoss N 48 B2
Honfleur F 89 A4
Høng DK 61 D1
Honiton GB 43 B3
Hönningen D 80 B2
Honningsvåg N 193 B9
Hönö S 60 B1
Honrubia E 158 B1
Hontalbilla E 151 A3
Hontheim D 92 A2
Hontianske-Nemce SK 98 C2
Hontoria de la Cantera E 143 B3
Hontoria del Pinar E 143 C3
Hontoria de Valdearados E 143 C3
Hoofddorp NL 70 B1
Hoogerheide NL 79 A4
Hoogeveen NL 71 B3
Hoogezand-Sappemeer NL 71 A3
Hoogkarspel NL 70 B2
Hoogkerk NL 71 A3
Hoogstede D 71 B3
Hoogstraten B 79 A4
Hook GB 44 B3
Hooksiel D 71 A5
Höör S 61 D3
Hoorn NL 70 B2
Hope GB 38 A3
Hopen N 194 C6
Hope under Dinmore GB 39 B4
Hopfgarten A 108 B3
Hopfgarten in Defereggen A 109 C3
Hopseidet N 193 B11
Hopsten D 71 B4
Hoptrup DK 59 C2
Hora Svatého Sebestiána CZ 83 B5
Horažďovice CZ 96 B1
Horb am Neckar D 93 C4
Horbelev DK 65 B5
Hørby DK 58 A3
Hörby S 61 D3
Horcajada de la Torre E 158 A1
Horcajo de los Montes E 156 A3
Horcajo de Santiago E 151 C4
Horcajo-Medianero E 150 B2
Horche E 151 B4
Horda S 62 A2
Hordabø N 46 B1
Hordalia N 52 A2
Hordvik N 46 B2
Hořesedly CZ 83 B5
Horezu RO 17 C6
Horgen CH 107 B3
Horgoš SRB 126 A1
Horia RO 126 A3
Hořice CZ 84 B3
Horjul SLO 123 A3
Horka D 84 A2
Hörken S 50 B1
Horki BY 13 A9
Hörle S 60 B4
Horn
A 97 C3
D 81 A4
N 48 B2
S 62 A3
Horna E 158 C2
Hornachos E 156 B1
Hornachuelos E 162 A2
Horná Mariková SK 98 B2
Hornanes N 46 C2
Horná Streda SK 98 C1
Horná Štrubna SK 98 C2
Horná Súča SK 98 C1
Hornbæk
*Aarhus Amt.* DK 58 B2
*Frederiksværk* DK 61 C2
Hornberg D 106 A3
Hornburg D 73 B3
Horncastle GB 41 B3
Horndal S 50 B3
Horndean GB 44 C2
Horne
*Fyns Amt.* DK 64 A3
*Ribe Amt.* DK 59 C1
Hörnebo S 55 B5
Horneburg D 72 A2
Hörnefors S 200 C5
Horní Bečva CZ 98 B2
Horni Benešov CZ 98 B1
Horni Cerekev CZ 97 B3
Horní Jiřetín CZ 83 B5
Horní Lomná CZ 98 B2
Horni Maršov CZ 85 B3
Hornindal N 198 D3
Hørning DK 59 B3
Hörningsholm S 57 A3
Horní Planá CZ 96 C2
Horní Slavkov CZ 83 B4
Horní Vltavice CZ 96 C1
Hornnes N 53 B3
Horno D 84 A2
Hornos E 164 A2
Hornoy-le-Bourg F 90 B1
Hornsea GB 41 B3
Hornsjø N 48 A2
Hornslet DK 59 B3
Hornstein A 111 B3
Hörnum D 64 B1
Hornum DK 58 B2
Horný Tisovník SK 99 C3
Horodenka UA 13 D6
Horodnya UA 13 C9
Horodok
*Khmelnytskyy* UA 13 D7
*Lviv* UA 13 D5
Horokhiv UA 13 C6
Horovice CZ 96 B1
Horred S 60 B2
Hörröd S 61 D4
Hörsching A 110 A1
Horsens DK 59 C2
Horsham GB 44 B3
Hørsholm DK 61 D2
Horslunde DK 65 B4
Horšovský Týn CZ 95 B4
Horst NL 80 A2
Horstel D 71 B4
Horsten D 71 A4
Horstmar D 71 B4
Hort H 113 B3
Horta P 148 A2
Horten N 54 A1
Hortezuela E 151 A5
Hortiguela E 143 B3
Hortobágy H 113 B5
Horton in Ribblesdale GB 37 B4
Hørve DK 61 D1
Hörvik S 63 B2
Horwich GB 38 A4
Hosanger N 46 B2
Hösbach D 93 A5
Hosena D 84 A2
Hosenfeld D 81 B5
Hosingen L 92 A2
Hosio FIN 197 D8
Hospental CH 107 C3
Hospital IRL 29 B3
Hossegor F 128 C1
Hosszuhetény H 125 A4
Hostal de Ipiés E 145 B3
Hoštálkova CZ 98 B1
Hostalric E 147 C3
Hostens F 128 B2
Hostěradice CZ 97 C4
Hostinné CZ 85 B3
Hostomice CZ 96 B2
Hostouň CZ 95 B4
Hotagen S 199 B11
Hoting S 200 B2
Hotolisht AL 182 B2
Hotton B 79 B5
Houdain F 78 B2
Houdan F 90 C1
Houdelaincourt F 92 C1
Houeillès F 128 B3
Houffalize B 92 A1
Houghton-le-Spring GB 37 B5
Houlberg DK 59 B2
Houlgate F 89 A3
Hounslow GB 44 B3
Hourtin F 128 A1
Hourtin-Plage F 128 A1
Houthalen B 79 A5
Houyet B 79 B4
Hov
DK 59 C3
N 48 B2
Hova S 55 B5
Høvåg N 53 B4
Hovborg DK 59 C1
Hovda N 47 B6
Hovden N 52 A3
Hove GB 44 C3
Hovedgård DK 59 C2
Hovelhof D 81 A4
Hoven DK 59 C1
Hovet N 47 B5
Hovingham GB 40 A3
Hovmantorp S 62 B3
Hovsta S 56 A1
Howden GB 40 B3
Howe D 72 A3
Höxter D 81 A5
Hoya D 72 B2
Hoya de Santa Maria E 161 B3
Hoya-Gonzalo E 158 C2
Høyanger N 46 A3
Hoyerswerda D 84 A2
Høyjord N 53 A6
Hoylake GB 38 A3
Høylandet N 199 A9
Hoym D 82 A3
Høymyr N 47 C6
Hoyocasero E 150 B3
Hoyo de Manzanares E 151 B4
Hoyo de Pinares E 150 B3
Hoyos E 149 B3
Hoyos del Espino E 150 B2
Hrabusiče SK 99 C4
Hradec Králové CZ 85 B3
Hradec nad Moravicí CZ 98 B1
Hrádek CZ 97 C4
Hrádek nad Nisou CZ 84 B2
Hradište SK 98 C2
Hrafnagil IS 191 B7
Hrafnseyri IS 190 B2
Hranice
*Severomoravsky* CZ 98 B1
*Západočeský* CZ 83 B4
Hranovnica SK 99 C4
Hrasnica BIH 139 B4
Hrastnik SLO 123 A4
Hřensko CZ 84 B2
Hriňová SK 99 C3
Hrisoupoli GR 183 C6
Hrochov CZ 97 B4
Hrochův Tynec CZ 97 B3
Hrodna BY 13 B5
Hrodzyanka BY 13 B8
Hronov CZ 85 B4
Hronský Beňadik SK 98 C2
Hrotovice CZ 97 B4
Hrtkovci SRB 127 C1
Hrun IS 190 A5
Hrušov SK 112 A3
Hrušovany nad Jevišovkou CZ 97 C4
Hřuštin SK 99 B3
Hrvaćani BIH 124 C3
Hrvace HR 138 B2
Hrymayliv UA 13 D7
Huben A 109 C3
Hückel-hoven D 80 A2
Hückeswagen D 80 A3
Hucknall GB 40 B2
Hucqueliers F 78 B1
Huddersfield GB 40 B2
Huddinge S 57 A3

Huddunge S 51 B3
Hude D 72 A1
Hudiksvall S 200 E3
Huélago E 163 A4
Huélamo E 152 B2
Huelgoat F 100 A2
Huelma E 163 A4
Huelva E 161 B3
Huéneja E 164 B2
Huércal de Almería
E 164 C2
Huércal-Overa E 164 B3
Huerta de Abajo E 143 B3
Huerta del Rey E 143 C3
Huerta de Valdecarabanos
E 151 C4
Huertahernando E 152 B1
Huesa E 164 B1
Huesca E 145 B3
Huéscar E 164 B2
Huete E 151 B5
Huétor Tájar E 163 A3
Hüfingen D 106 B3
Hufthamar N 46 B2
Hugh Town GB 42 B1
Huglfing D 108 B2
Huissen NL 70 C2
Huittinen FIN 8 B3
Huizen NL 70 B2
Hulín CZ 98 B1
Hüls D 80 A2
Hulsig DK 58 A3
Hulst NL 79 A4
Hult S 62 A3
Hulta S 56 B2
Hulteby S 55 A5
Hulterstad S 63 B4
Hultsfred S 62 A3
Humanes E 151 B4
Humberston GB 41 B3
Humble DK 65 B3
Humenné SK 12 D4
Humilladero E 163 A3
Humlebæk DK 61 D2
Humlum DK 58 B1
Hummelsta S 56 A2
Humpolec CZ 97 B3
Humshaugh GB 37 A4
Hundåla N 195 E3
Hundested DK 61 D1
Hundorp N 48 A1
Hundvåg N 52 A1
Hundvin N 46 B2
Hunedoara RO 17 C5
Hünfeld D 82 B1
Hungen D 81 B4
Hungerford GB 44 B2
Hunndalen N 48 B2
Hunnebostrand S 54 B2
Hunstanton GB 41 C4
Huntingdon GB 44 A3
Huntley GB 39 C4
Huntly GB 33 D4
Hünxe D 80 A2
Hurbanovo SK 112 B2
Hürbel D 107 A4
Hurdal N 48 B3
Hurezani RO 17 C5
Hurlford GB 36 A2
Hurstbourne Tarrant
GB 44 B2
Hurstpierpoint GB 44 C3
Hürth D 80 B2
Hurum N 47 A5
Hurup DK 58 B1
Húsafell IS 190 C5
Húsavík IS 191 A8
Husbands Bosworth
GB 44 A2
Husby
D 64 B2
DK 59 B1
Husey IS 191 B11
Huşi RO 17 B8
Husina BIH 139 A4
Husinec CZ 96 B1
Husinish GB 31 B1
Huskvarna S 62 A2
Husnes N 46 C2
Husøy N 194 A8
Hustad N 198 C4
Hüsten D 81 A3
Hustopeče CZ 97 C4
Hustopeče nad Bečvou
CZ 98 B1
Husum
D 64 B2
S 200 C5
Husvika N 195 E3
Huta PL 75 B5
Hutovo BIH 139 C3
Hüttenberg A 110 C1
Hüttlingen D 94 C2
Huttoft GB 41 B4
Hutton Cranswick
GB 40 B3
Hüttschlag A 109 B4
Huttwil CH 106 B2
Huy B 79 B5
Hüyük TR 189 B6
Hval N 48 B2
Hvåle N 47 B6
Hvaler N 54 A2
Hvalpsund DK 58 B2
Hvammstangi IS 190 B5
Hvammur IS 190 B6
Hvanneyri IS 190 C4
Hvar HR 138 B2
Hvarnes N 53 A5
Hveragerði IS 190 D4
Hvidbjerg DK 58 B1
Hvide Sande DK 59 C1
Hvittingfoss N 53 A6
Hvolsvöllur IS 190 D5
Hybe SK 99 B3
Hycklinge S 62 A3
Hydra GR 185 B4
Hyen N 198 D2
Hyères F 132 B2
Hyéres Plage F 132 B2
Hylestad N 52 A3
Hylke DK 59 C2
Hyllestad N 46 A2
Hyllstofta S 61 C3
Hyltebruk S 60 B3
Hynnekleiv N 53 B4
Hythe
*Hampshire* GB 44 C2
*Kent* GB 45 B5
Hyvinkää FIN 8 B4

## I

Iam RO 127 B3
Iaşi RO 17 B7
Iasmos GR 183 B7
Ibahernando E 156 A2
Ibarranguelua E 143 A4
Ibbenbüren D 71 B4
Ibeas de Juarros E 143 B3
Ibestad N 194 B8
Ibi E 159 C3
Ibiza = Eivissa E 166 C1
İbradı TR 189 B6
İbriktepe TR 186 A1
Ibros E 157 B4
Ibstock GB 40 C2
İçel TR 23 C8
Ichenhausen D 94 C2
Ichtegem B 78 A3
Ichtershausen D 82 B2
Idanha-a-Novo P 155 B3
Idar-Oberstein D 93 B3
Idd N 54 A2
Idiazábal E 144 B1
Idivuoma S 196 A4
Idkerberget S 50 B2
Idön S 51 B5
Idre S 199 D9
Idrija SLO 123 A3
Idritsa RUS 9 D6
Idstein D 81 B4
Idvor SRB 126 B2
Iecca Mare RO 126 B2
Ielsi I 170 B2
Ieper = Ypres B 78 B2
Ierapetra GR 185 D6
Ierissos GR 183 C5
Ifjord N 193 B11
Ig SLO 123 B3
Igal H 112 C1
Igea E 144 B1
Igea Marina I 136 A1
Igelfors S 56 B1
Igersheim D 94 B1
Iggesund S 200 E3
Iglesias E 143 B3
Iglésias I 179 C2
Igls A 108 B2
Igny-Comblizy F 91 B3
Igorre E 143 A4
Igoumenitsa GR 182 D2
Igries E 145 B3
Igualada E 147 C2
Igüeña E 141 B4
Iguerande F 117 A4
Iharosberény H 124 A3
Ihl'any SK 99 B4
Ihlienworth D 64 C1
Ihringen D 106 A2
Ihrlerstein D 95 C3
İhsaniye TR 187 C5
Ii FIN 197 D8
Iijärvi FIN 193 C11
Iisalmi FIN 3 E10
IJmuiden NL 70 B1
IJsselmuiden NL 70 B2
IJzendijke NL 79 A3
Ikast DK 59 B2
Ikervár H 111 B3
Ilandža SRB 126 B2
Ilanz CH 107 C4
Ilava SK 98 C2
Iława PL 69 B4
il Castagno I 135 B3
Ilche E 145 C4
Ilchester GB 43 B4
Ilfeld D 82 A2
Ilfracombe GB 42 A2
Ilgaz TR 23 A7
Ilgın TR 189 A6
Ílhavo P 148 B1
Ilica TR 186 C2
Ilidža BIH 139 B4
Ilijaš BIH 139 B4
Ilirska Bistrica
SLO 123 B3
Ilkeston GB 40 C2
Ilkley GB 40 B2
Illana E 151 B5
Illano E 141 A4
Illar E 164 C2
Illas E 141 A5
Illats F 128 B2
Illertissen D 94 C2
Illescas E 151 B4
Ille-sur-Têt F 146 B3
Illfurth F 106 B2
Illichivsk UA 17 B9
Illiers-Combray F 89 B5
Illkirch-Graffenstaden
F 93 C3
Illmersdorf D 74 C2
Illmitz A 111 B3
Íllora E 163 A4
Illueca E 152 A2
Ilmajoki FIN 8 A3
Ilmenau D 82 B2
Ilminster GB 43 B4
Ilok HR 126 B1
Ilomantsi FIN 9 A7
Iłow PL 77 B5
Iłowa PL 84 A3
Iłowo-Osada PL 77 A5
Ilsenburg D 82 A2
Ilshofen D 94 B1
Ilz A 110 B2
Iłża PL 87 A5
Imatra FIN 9 B6
Imielin PL 86 B3
Imingen N 47 B5
Immeln S 63 B2
Immenhausen D 81 A5
Immenstadt D 107 B5
Immingham GB 41 B3
Ímola I 135 A4
Imon E 151 A5
Imotski HR 138 B3
Impéria I 133 B4
Imphy F 104 C2
İmroz TR 183 C7
Imsland N 52 A1
Imst A 108 B1
Inagh IRL 28 B2
Inari FIN 193 D10
Inca E 167 B2
Inchnadamph GB 32 C2
Incinillas E 143 B3
Indal S 200 D3
Indjija SRB 127 B2
Indre Arna N 46 B2
Indre Billefjord N 193 B9
Indre Brenna N 193 B9
İğneada TR 186 A2
İnebolu TR 23 A7
İnecik TR 186 B2
İnegöl TR 187 B4
Inerthal CH 107 B3
Infiesto E 142 A1
Ingatorp S 62 A3
Ingedal N 54 A2
Ingelheim D 93 B4
Ingelmunster B 78 B3
Ingelstad S 62 B2
Ingleton GB 37 B4
Ingolfsland N 47 C5
Ingolstadt D 95 C3
Ingrandes
*Maine-et-Loire* F 101 B5
*Vienne* F 102 C2
Ingwiller F 93 C3
Inhisar TR 187 B5
Iniesta E 158 B2
Inishannon IRL 29 C3
Inishcrone IRL 26 B1
Inke H 124 A3
Inndyr N 195 C5
Innellan GB 34 C3
Innerleithen GB 35 C4
Innermessan GB 36 B2
Innertkirchen CH 106 C3
Innervillgraten A 109 C3
Innsbruck A 108 B2
Innset N 194 B9
Innvik N 198 D3
İnönü TR 187 C5
Inowłódz PL 87 A4
Inowrocław PL 76 B3
Ins CH 106 B2
Insch GB 33 D4
Insjön S 50 B2
Ińsko PL 75 A4
Instow GB 42 A2
İntepe TR 186 B1
Interlaken CH 106 C2
Intragna CH 120 A1
Introbio I 120 B2
Inverallochy GB 33 D5
Inveran
GB 32 D2
IRL 28 A2
Inveraray GB 34 B2
Inverbervie GB 35 B5
Invergarry GB 32 D2
Invergordon GB 32 D2
Invergowrie GB 35 B4
Inverkeilor GB 35 B5
Inverkeithing GB 35 B4
Invermoriston GB 32 D2
Inverness GB 32 D2
Inveruno I 120 B1
Inverurie GB 33 D4
Ioannina GR 182 D2
Iolanda di Savoia I 121 C4
Ion Corvin RO 17 C7
Ióppolo I 175 C1
Ios GR 185 C6
Ipati GR 182 E4
İpsala TR 186 B1
Ipswich GB 45 A5
Iraklia GR 183 B5
Iraklio = Heraklion
GR 185 D6
Irdning A 110 B1
Iregszemcse H 112 C2
Irgoli I 178 B3
Irig SRB 127 B1
Ironbridge GB 39 B4
Irpin UA 13 C9
Irrel D 92 B2
Irsina I 172 B2
Irsta S 56 A2
Irthlingborough GB 44 A3
Iruela E 141 B4
Irún E 144 A2
Irurita E 144 A2
Irurzun E 144 B2
Irvine GB 36 A2
Irvinestown GB 27 B3
Isaba E 144 B3
Isabela E 157 B4
Ísafjörður IS 190 A2
Isane N 198 D2
Isaszeg H 112 B3
Isbister GB 33 A5
Iscar E 150 A3
İscehisar TR 187 D5
Ischgl A 107 B5
Íschia I 170 C1
Ischia di Castro I 168 A1
Ischitella I 171 B3
Isdes F 103 B4
Ise N 54 A2
Iselle I 119 A5
Iseltwald CH 106 C2
Isen D 108 A3
Isenbüttel D 73 B3
Iseo I 120 B3
Iserlohn D 81 A3
Isérnia I 170 B2
Isfjorden N 198 C4
Ishëm AL 182 B1
Isigny-sur-Mer F 88 A2
Işıklı TR 189 A4
Ísili I 179 C3
İskilip TR 23 A8
Isla Canela E 161 B2
Isla Cristina E 161 B2
Islares E 143 A3
Isleham GB 45 A4
Isle of Whithorn GB 36 B2
Ismaning D 108 A2
Isna P 154 B3
Isnestoften N 192 B6
Isny D 107 B5
Isoba E 142 A1
Isokylä
FIN 197 C10
S 196 B5
Isola F 132 A3
Isola d'Asti I 119 C5
Isola del Gran Sasso
d'Itália I 169 A3
Ísola della Scala I 121 B4
Isola delle Fémmine
I 176 A2
Ísola del Liri I 169 B3
Ísola di Capo Rizzuto
I 175 C3
Isona E 147 B2
Ispagnac F 130 A2
Isparta TR 189 B5
Isperikh BG 17 D7
Íspica I 177 C3
Isselburg D 80 A2
Issigeac F 129 B3
Issogne I 119 B4
Issoire F 116 B3
Issoncourt F 91 C5
Issoudun F 103 C4
Issum D 80 A2
Is-sur-Tille F 105 B4
Issy-l'Evêque F 104 C2
Istán E 162 B3
İstanbul TR 186 A3
Istebna PL 98 B2
Ístia d'Ombrone I 135 C4
Istiea GR 183 E5
Istres F 131 B3
Istvándi H 125 A3
Itea GR 184 A3
Ithaki GR 184 A1
Itoiz E 144 B2
Ítrabo E 163 B4
Itri I 169 B3
Ittireddu I 178 B2
Íttiri I 178 B2
Itzehoe D 64 C2
Ivalo FIN 193 D11
Iván H 111 B3
Ivanava BY 13 B6
Ivančice CZ 97 B4
Ivančna Gorica
SLO 123 B3
Iváncsa H 112 B2
Ivanec HR 124 A2
Ivanić Grad HR 124 B2
Ivanjska BIH 124 C3
Ivanka SK 98 C2
Ivankovo HR 125 B4
Ivano-Frankivsk UA 13 D6
Ivanovice na Hané
CZ 98 B1
Ivanska HR 124 B2
Ivatsevichy BY 13 B6
Ivaylovgrad BG 183 B8
Iveland N 53 B3
Ivoz Ramet B 79 B5
Ivrea I 119 B4
İvrindi TR 186 C2
Ivry-en-Montagne
F 104 B3
Ivry-la-Bataille F 90 C1
Ivybridge GB 42 B3
Iwaniska PL 87 B5
Iwiny PL 85 A3
Iwuy F 78 B3
Ixworth GB 45 A4
Izarra E 143 B4
Izbica Kujawska PL 76 B3
Izbište SRB 127 B3
Izeda P 149 A3
Izegem B 78 B3
Izernore F 118 A2
Izmayil UA 17 C8
İzmir TR 188 A2
İzmit = Kocaeli TR 187 B4
Iznájar E 163 A3
Iznalloz E 163 A4
Iznatoraf E 164 A1
İznik TR 187 B4
Izola SLO 122 B2
Izsák H 112 C3
Izsófalva H 99 C4
Izyaslav UA 13 C7

## J

Jabalquinto E 157 B4
Jablanac HR 123 C3
Jablanica BIH 139 B3
Jablonec nad Jizerou
CZ 84 B3
Jablonec nad Nisou
CZ 84 B3
Jablonica SK 98 C1
Jablonka PL 99 B3
Jabłonna PL 77 B5
Jablonnénad Orlicí
CZ 97 A4
Jablonne Podještědi
CZ 84 B2
Jablonov nad Turňou
SK 99 C4
Jabłonowo Pomorskie
PL 69 B4
Jablúnka CZ 98 B1
Jablunkov CZ 98 B2
Jabučje SRB 127 C2
Jabugo E 161 B3
Jabuka SRB 127 C2
Jabukovac HR 124 B2
Jaca E 145 B3
Jáchymov CZ 83 B4
Jacobidrebber D 72 B1
Jade D 71 A5
Jäderfors S 50 B3
Jädraås S 50 B3
Jadraque E 151 B5
Jaén E 163 A4
Jagare BIH 124 C3
Jagel D 64 B2
Jagenbach A 96 C3
Jægerspris DK 61 D1
Jagodina SRB 127 D3
Jagodnjak HR 125 B4
Jagodzin PL 84 A3
Jagstheim D 94 B2
Jagstzell D 94 B2
Jahodna SK 111 A4
Jajce BIH 138 A3
Ják H 111 B3
Jakabszálbs H 112 C3
Jäkkvik S 195 D8
Jakobsnes N 193 C14
Jakovlje HR 124 B1
Jakšic HR 125 B3
Jakubany SK 99 B4
Jalance E 159 B2
Jalasjärvi FIN 8 A3
Jalhay B 80 B1
Jaligny-sur-Besbre
F 117 A3
Jallais F 102 B1
Jalón E 159 C3
Jâlons F 91 C4
Jamena SRB 125 C5
Jamilena E 163 A4
Jämjö S 63 B3
Jamnička Kiselica
HR 124 B1
Jamno PL 67 B5
Jamoigne B 92 B1
Jämsä FIN 8 B4
Jämshög S 63 B2
Jamu Mare RO 126 B3
Janakkala FIN 8 B4
Jandelsbrunn D 96 C1
Jänickendorf D 74 B2
Janikowo PL 76 B3
Janja BIH 125 C5
Janjina HR 138 C3
Janki
*Łódzkie* PL 86 A3
*Mazowieckie* PL 77 B5
Jankov CZ 96 B2
Jankowo Dolne PL 76 B2
Jánoshalma H 126 A1
Jánosháza H 111 B4
Jánoshida H 113 B4
Jánossomorja H 111 B4
Janovice nad Uhlavou
CZ 96 B1
Janów PL 86 B3
Janowiec Wielkopolski
PL 76 B2
Janowo PL 77 A5
Jänsmässholmen
S 199 B10
Janville F 103 A3
Janzé F 101 B4
Jarabá SK 99 C3
Jaraczewo PL 76 C2
Jarafuel E 159 B2
Jaraicejo E 156 A2
Jaraíz de la Vera E 150 B2
Jarak SRB 127 C1
Jarandilla de la Vera
E 150 B2
Jaray E 152 A1
Järbo S 50 B3
Jard-sur-Mer F 114 B2
Jaren N 48 B2
Jargeau F 103 B4
Jarkovac SRB 126 B2
Järlåsa S 51 C4
Jarmen D 66 C2
Järna S 57 A3
Jarnac F 115 C3
Järnäs S 200 C5
Järnforsen S 62 A3
Jarny F 92 B1
Jarocin PL 76 C2
Jaroměř CZ 85 B3
Jaroměřice nad
Rokytnou CZ 97 B3
Jaroslav CZ 97 A4
Jaroslavice CZ 97 C4
Jarosław PL 12 C5
Jaroslawiec PL 68 A1
Jarošov nad Nežarkou
CZ 96 B3
Järpås S 55 B3
Järpen S 199 B10
Jarrow GB 37 B5
Järso FIN 51 B6
Järvenpää FIN 8 B4
Jarvorník CZ 85 B4
Järvsö S 200 E2
Jarzé F 102 B1
Jaša Tomic SRB 126 B2
Jasenak HR 123 B4
Jasenica BIH 124 C2
Jasenice HR 137 A4
Jasenovac HR 124 B2
Jasenovo SRB 127 C3
Jasień PL 84 A3
Jasienica PL 84 A2
Jasło PL 12 D4
Jásova SK 112 B2
Jasseron F 118 A2
Jastarnia PL 69 A3
Jastrebarsko HR 123 B4
Jastrowie PL 68 B1
Jastrzębia-Góra PL 68 A3
Jastrzębie Zdrój PL 98 B2
Jászals-Lószentgyörgy
H 113 B4
Jászapáti H 113 B4
Jászárokszállás
H 113 B3
Jászberény H 113 B3
Jászdózsa H 113 B4
Jászfényszaru H 113 B3
Jászjakóhalma H 113 B4
Jászkarajenö H 113 B4
Jászkisér H 113 B4
Jászladány H 113 B4
Jászszentlászló H 113 C3
Jásztelek H 113 B4
Játar E 163 B4
Jättendal S 200 E3
Jatznick D 74 A2
Jaun CH 106 C2
Jausiers F 132 A2
Jávea E 159 C4
Jävenitz D 73 B4
Javerlhac F 115 C4
Javier E 144 B2
Javorani BIH 124 C3
Javorina SK 99 B4
Javron F 89 B3
Jawor PL 85 A4
Jaworzno PL 86 B3
Jaworzyna Śl. PL 85 B4
Jayena E 163 B4
Jaźow PL 84 A2
Jebel RO 126 B3
Jebjerg DK 58 B2
Jedburgh GB 35 C5
Jedlinsk PL 87 A5
Jedlnia PL 87 A5
Jedlnia Letnisko PL 87 A5
Jednorożec PL 77 A6
Jedovnice CZ 97 B4
Jędrychow PL 69 B4
Jędrzejów PL 87 B4
Jedwabno PL 77 A5
Jeesiö FIN 197 B9
Jegłownik PL 69 A4
Jegun F 129 C3
Jēkabpils LV 8 D4
Jektevik N 46 C2
Jektvik N 195 D4
Jelcz-Laskowice PL 85 A5
Jelenec SK 98 C2
Jelenia Góra PL 85 B3
Jelgava LV 8 D3
Jelka SK 111 A4
Jelling DK 59 C2
Jels DK 59 C2

Jelsa
HR 138 B2
N 52 A2
Jelšava SK 99 C4
Jemgum D 71 A4
Jemnice CZ 97 B3
Jena D 82 B3
Jenaz CH 107 C4
Jenbach A 108 B2
Jenikow PL 75 A4
Jennersdorf A 111 C3
Jenny S 62 A4
Jerchel D 73 B4
Jeres del Marquesado
E 164 B1
Jerez de la Frontera
E 162 B1
Jerez de los Caballeros
E 155 C4
Jerica E 159 B3
Jerichow D 73 B5
Jerka PL 75 B5
Jermenovci SRB 126 B3
Jerslev DK 58 A3
Jerte E 150 B2
Jerup DK 58 A3
Jerxheim D 73 B3
Jerzmanowice PL 87 B3
Jerzu I 179 C3
Jerzwałd PL 69 B4
Jesberg D 81 B5
Jesenice
*Středočeský* CZ 83 B5
*Středočeský* CZ 96 B2
SLO 109 C5
Jeseník CZ 85 B5
Jesenké SK 99 C4
Jesi I 136 B2
Jésolo I 122 B1
Jessen D 83 A4
Jessenitz D 73 A4
Jessheim N 48 B3
Jessnitz D 83 A4
Jesteburg D 72 A2
Jeumont F 79 B4
Jeven-stedt D 64 B2
Jever D 71 A4
Jevičko CZ 97 B4
Jevišovice CZ 97 C3
Jevnaker N 48 B2
Jezerane HR 123 B4
Jezero
BIH 138 A3
HR 123 B4
Jezów PL 87 A3
Jičín CZ 84 B3
Jičiněves CZ 84 B3
Jihlava CZ 97 B3
Jijona E 159 C3
Jilemnice CZ 84 B3
Jilové CZ 84 B2
Jilovéu Prahy CZ 96 B2
Jimbolia RO 126 B2
Jimena E 163 A4
Jimena de la Frontera
E 162 B2
Jimera de Libar E 162 B2
Jimramov CZ 97 B4
Jince CZ 96 B1
Jindřichovice CZ 83 B4
Jindřichův Hradec
CZ 96 B3
Jirkov CZ 83 B5
Jistebnice CZ 96 B2
Joachimsthal D 74 B2
João da Loura P 154 C2
Jobbágyi H 112 B3
Jochberg A 109 B3
Jockfall S 196 C5
Jódar E 163 A4
Jodoigne B 79 B4
Joensuu FIN 9 A6
Joesjö S 195 E5
Joeuf F 92 B1
Jõgeva EST 8 C5
Johanngeorgenstadt
D 83 B4
Johannishus S 63 B3
Johanniskirchen D 95 C4
Johansfors S 63 B3
John o'Groats GB 32 C3
Johnshaven GB 35 B5
Johnstone GB 34 C3
Johnstown IRL 30 B1
Jõhvi EST 8 C5
Joigny F 104 B2
Joinville F 91 C5
Jokkmokk S 196 C2
Jöllenbeck D 72 B1
Jomala FIN 51 B6
Jönåker S 56 B2
Jonava LT 13 A6
Jonchery-sur-Vesle
F 91 B3
Jondal N 46 B3
Jondalen N 53 A5
Joniškis LT 8 D3
Jönköping S 62 A2
Jonkowo PL 69 B5
Jønnbu N 53 A5
Jonsberg S 56 B2
Jonsered S 60 B2
Jonstorp S 61 C2
Jonzac F 114 C3
Jorba E 147 C2
Jordanów PL 99 B3
Jordanowo PL 75 B4
Jordanów Śląski PL 85 B4
Jordbro S 57 A4
Jordbrua N 195 D5
Jördenstorf D 66 C1
Jordet N 49 A4
Jordøse DK 59 C3
Jork D 72 A2
Jörlanda S 60 B1
Jormlien S 199 A10
Jormvattnet S 199 A11
Jörn S 200 A6
Jørpeland N 52 A2
Jorquera E 158 B2
Jošan HR 123 C4
Jošavka BIH 124 C3
Josipdol HR 123 B4
Josipovac HR 125 B4
Jössefors S 54 A3
Josselin F 101 B3
Jøssund N 199 A7
Jostedal N 47 A4
Jósvafö H 99 C4
Jou P 148 A2
Jouarre F 90 C3
Joué-lès-Tours F 102 B2
Joué-sur-Erdre F 101 B4
Joure NL 70 B2
Joutseno FIN 9 B6
Joutsijärvi FIN 197 C10
Joux-la-Ville F 104 B2
Jouy F 90 C1
Jouy-le-Châtel F 90 C3
Jouy-le-Potier F 103 B3
Joyeuse F 131 A3
Joze F 116 B3
Juankoski FIN 8 A6
Juan-les-Pins F 132 B3
Jübek D 64 B2
Jubera E 144 B1
Jubrique E 162 B2
Jüchsen D 82 B2
Judaberg N 52 A1
Judenburg A 110 B1
Juelsminde DK 59 C3
Jugon-les-Lacs F 101 A3
Juillac F 129 A4
Juillan F 145 A4
Juist D 71 A4
Jukkasjärvi S 196 B3
Jule N 199 A10
Julianadorp NL 70 B1
Julianstown IRL 30 A2
Jülich D 80 B2
Jullouville F 88 B2
Jumeaux F 117 B3
Jumièges F 89 A4
Jumilhac-le-Grand
F 115 C5
Jumilla E 159 C2
Jumisko FIN 197 C11
Juncosa E 153 A4
Juneda E 147 C1
Jung S 55 B4
Jungingen D 93 C5
Junglingster L 92 B2
Juniville F 91 B4
Junosuando S 196 B5
Junqueira P 149 A2
Junsele S 200 C2
Juoksengi S 196 C6
Juoksenki FIN 196 C6
Juprelle B 80 B1
Jurata PL 69 A3
Jurbarkas LT 12 A5
Jurjevo HR 123 C3
Jūrmala LV 8 D3
Jurmu FIN 197 D10
Juromenha P 155 C3
Jursla S 56 B2
Jussac F 116 C2
Jussey F 105 B4
Jussy F 90 B3
Juta H 125 A3
Jüterbog D 74 C2
Juuka FIN 3 E11
Juuma FIN 197 C12
Juvigny-le-Terte F 88 B2
Juvigny-sous-Andaine
F 89 B3
Juzennecourt F 105 A3
Jyderup DK 61 D1
Jyrkänkoski FIN 197 C12
Jyväskylä FIN 8 A4

K

Kaamanen FIN 193 C11
Kaamasmukka
FIN 193 C10
Kaaresuvanto FIN 192 D6
Kaarssen D 73 A4
Kaatscheuvel NL 79 A5
Kaba H 113 B5
Kåbdalis S 196 C3
Kačarevo SRB 127 C2
Kács H 113 B4
Kadan CZ 83 B5
Kadarkút H 125 A3
Kadınhanı TR 189 A7
Kaduy RUS 9 C10
Kåfalla S 56 A1
Kåfjord N 192 C7
Kåfjordbotn N 192 C4
Kågeröd S 61 D3
Kahl D 93 A5
Kahla D 82 B3
Kainach bei Voitsberg
A 110 B2
Kaindorf A 110 B2
Kainulasjärvi S 196 C5
Kairala FIN 197 B10
Kaisepakte S 192 D3
Kaisersesch D 80 B3
Kaiserslautern D 93 B3
Kaisheim D 94 C2
Kajaani FIN 3 D10
Kajárpéc H 111 B4
Kajdacs H 112 C2
Kakanj BIH 139 A4
Kakasd H 125 A4
Kaklik TR 189 B4
Kakolewo PL 85 A4
Kál H 113 B4
Kalajoki FIN 3 D8
Kalak N 193 B11
Kalamata GR 184 B3
Kalambaka GR 182 D3
Kalamria GR 182 C4
Kalandra GR 183 D5
Kälarne S 200 D2
Kalavrita GR 184 A3
Kalbe D 73 B4
Kalce SLO 123 B3
Káld H 111 B4
Kale
*Antalya* TR 189 C4
*Denizli* TR 188 B3
Kalecik TR 23 A7
Kalefeld D 82 A2
Kalesija BIH 139 A4
Kalety PL 86 B2
Kalevala RUS 3 D12
Kalhovd N 47 B5
Kali HR 137 A4
Kalimnos GR 188 C2
Kaliningrad RUS 69 A5
Kalinkavichy BY 13 B8
Kalinovac HR 124 A3
Kalinovik BIH 139 B4
Kalinovo SK 99 C3
Kalirachi GR 183 C6
Kaliska
*Pomorskie* PL 68 A3
*Pomorskie* PL 68 B3
Kalisko PL 86 A3
Kalisz PL 86 A2
Kalisz Pomorski PL 75 A4
Kaljord N 194 B6
Kalkan TR 189 C4
Kalkar D 80 A2
Kalkım TR 186 C2
Kall
D 80 B2
S 199 B10
Källby S 55 B4
Kållered S 60 B2
Kållerstad S 60 B3
Kallinge S 63 B3
Kallmünz D 95 B3
Kallo FIN 196 B7
Kallsedet S 199 B9
Källvik S 56 B3
Kalmar S 63 B4
Kalmthout B 79 A4
Kalná SK 112 A2
Kalocsa H 112 C2
Kalokhorio CY 181 B2
Kalo Nero GR 184 B2
Kaloni GR 186 C1
Káloz H 112 C2
Kals A 109 B3
Kalsdorf A 110 C2
Kaltbrunn CH 107 B4
Kaltenbach A 108 B2
Kaltenkirchen D 64 C2
Kaltennordheim D 82 B2
Kalundborg DK 61 D1
Kalush UA 13 D6
Kalv S 60 B3
Kalvåg N 198 D1
Kalvehave DK 65 A5
Kalwang A 110 B1
Kalwaria-Zebrzydowska
PL 99 B3
Kalyazin RUS 9 D10
Kam H 111 B3
Kaman TR 23 B7
Kamares GR 185 C5
Kambos CY 181 A1
Kamen D 81 A3
Kamenice CZ 97 B3
Kamenice nad Lipou
CZ 96 B3
Kameničná SK 112 B2
Kamenný Most SK 112 B2
Kamenny Ujezd CZ 96 C2
Kamenska HR 124 B3
Kamensko HR 138 B2
Kamenz D 84 A2
Kamičak BIH 124 C2
Kamień PL 87 A4
Kamieniec Zabk PL 85 B4
Kamienka SK 99 B4
Kamień Krajeński
PL 76 A2
Kamienna Góra PL 85 B4
Kamień Pomorski
PL 67 C3
Kamieńsk PL 86 A3
Kamiros Skala GR 188 C2
Kamnik SLO 123 A3
Kampen NL 70 B2
Kampinos PL 77 B5
Kamp-Lintfort D 80 A2
Kampor HR 123 C3
Kamyanets-Podil's'kyy
UA 13 D7
Kamyanka-Buz'ka
UA 13 C6
Kamýk nad Vltavou
CZ 96 B2
Kanal SLO 122 A2
Kanalia GR 182 D4
Kandalaksha RUS 3 C13
Kandanos GR 185 D4
Kandel D 93 B4
Kandern D 106 B2
Kandersteg CH 106 C2
Kandila GR 184 B3
Kandıra TR 187 A5
Kandyty PL 69 A5
Kanfanar HR 122 B2
Kangasala FIN 8 B4
Kangos S 196 B5
Kangosjärvi FIN 196 B6
Kaniów PL 75 C3
Kanjiža SRB 126 A2
Kankaanpää FIN 8 B3
Kannus FIN 3 E8
Kanturk IRL 29 B3
Kapaklı TR 186 A2
Kapellen
A 110 B2
B 79 A4
Kapellskär S 57 A5
Kapfenberg A 110 B2
Kapfenstein A 110 C2
Kaplice CZ 96 C2
Kapljuh BIH 124 C2
Kápolna H 113 B4
Kápolnásnyék H 112 B2
Kaposfő H 125 A3
Kaposfüred H 125 A3
Kaposszekcsö H 125 A4
Kaposvár H 125 A3
Kapp N 48 B2
Kappel D 93 C3
Kappeln D 64 B2
Kappelshamn S 57 C4
Kappl A 107 B5
Kappstad S 55 A4
Kaprun A 109 B3
Kaptol HR 125 B3
Kapuvár H 111 B4
Karaadilli TR 189 A5
Karabiğa TR 186 B2
Karabük TR 187 A7
Karaburun TR 186 D1
Karacabey TR 186 B3
Karacaköy TR 186 A3
Karacaören TR 189 A5
Karacasu TR 188 B3
Karácsond H 113 B4
Karád H 112 C1
Karahallı TR 189 A4
Karaisali TR 23 C8
Karaman
*Balıkesir* TR 186 C3
*Karaman* TR 23 C7
Karamanlı TR 189 B4
Karamürsel TR 187 B4
Karan SRB 127 D1
Karancslapujto H 113 A3
Karaova TR 188 B2
Karapınar TR 23 C7
Karasjok N 193 C9
Karasu TR 187 A5
Karataş
*Adana* TR 23 C8
*Manisa* TR 188 A3
Karatoprak TR 188 B2
Karavostasi CY 181 A1
Karbenning S 50 B3
Kårberg S 55 B5
Kårböle S 199 D12
Karby
D 64 B2
DK 58 B1
Kårby S 62 A4
Karby S 57 A4
Karcag H 113 B4
Karczów PL 86 B1
Karczowiska PL 85 A4
Kardamena GR 188 C2
Kardamila GR 185 A7
Kardamili GR 184 C3
Kardašova Rečice
CZ 96 B2
Kardis S 196 C6
Karditsa GR 182 D3
Kärdla EST 8 C3
Kardoskút H 113 C4
Karesuando S 192 D6
Kargı TR 23 A8
Kargopol RUS 9 B11
Kargowa PL 75 B4
Karigasniemi FIN 193 C9
Karise DK 65 A5
Karistos GR 185 A5
Karkkila FIN 8 B4
Karlholmsbruk S 51 B4
Karlino PL 67 B4
Karlobag HR 137 A4
Karlovac HR 123 B4
Karlovasi GR 188 B1
Karlovčic SRB 127 C2
Karlovice CZ 85 B5
Karlovo BG 17 D6
Karlovy Vary CZ 83 B4
Karłowice PL 86 B1
Karlsborg S 55 B5
Karlshamn S 63 B2
Karlshöfen D 72 A2
Karlshus N 54 A1
Karlskoga S 55 A5
Karlskrona S 63 B3
Karlsrud N 47 B5
Karlsruhe D 93 B4
Karlstad S 55 A4
Karlstadt D 94 B1
Karlstetten A 110 A2
Karlstift A 96 C2
Karlstorp S 62 A3
Karmacs H 111 C4
Karmin PL 85 A5
Kärna S 60 B1
Karnobat BG 17 D7
Karojba HR 122 B2
Karow D 73 A5
Karpacz PL 85 B3
Karpathos GR 188 D2
Karpenisi GR 182 E3
Karpuzlu TR 188 B2
Kärrbo S 56 A2
Karrebaeksminde
DK 65 A4
Karshult S 60 B3
Karsin PL 68 B2
Kårsta S 57 A4
Karstädt D 73 A4
Kartal TR 186 B4
Kartitsch A 109 C3
Kartuzy PL 68 A3
Karungi S 196 C6
Karunki FIN 196 C7
Karup DK 59 B2
Karviná CZ 98 B2
Kås DK 58 A2
Kaş TR 189 C4
Kasaba TR 189 C4
Kašava CZ 98 B1
Kåseberga S 66 A3
Kasejovice CZ 96 B1
Kasfjord N 194 B7
Kashin RUS 9 D10
Kašina HR 124 B2
Kasina-Wielka PL 99 B4
Kaskinen FIN 8 A2
Kašperské Hory CZ 96 B1
Kassandrino GR 183 C5
Kassel D 81 A5
Kassiopi GR 182 D1
Kastamonu TR 23 A7
Kastav HR 123 B3
Kasteli GR 185 D4
Kastellaun D 93 A3
Kastelli GR 185 D6
Kaštel-Stari HR 138 B2
Kaštel Zegarski
HR 138 A1
Kasterlee B 79 A4
Kastl D 95 B3
Kastlösa S 63 B4
Kastorf D 65 C3
Kastoria GR 182 C3
Kastorio GR 184 B3
Kastraki GR 185 C6
Kastrosikia GR 182 D2
Kastsyukovichy
BY 13 B10
Kaszaper H 113 C4
Katakolo GR 184 B2
Katapola GR 185 C6
Katastari GR 184 B1
Katerbow D 74 B1
Katerini GR 182 C4
Kathikas CY 181 B1
Kätkesuando S 196 A6
Katlenburg-Lindau
D 82 A2
Kato Achaia GR 184 A2
Káto Pyrgos CY 181 A1
Katouna GR 182 E3
Katovice CZ 96 B1
Katowice PL 86 B3
Katrineberg S 50 A3
Katrineholm S 56 B2
Kattarp S 61 C2
Kattavia GR 188 D2
Katthammarsvik S 57 C4
Kattilstorp S 55 B4
Katwijk NL 70 B1
Katymár H 125 A5
Kąty Wrocławskie
PL 85 A4
Katzenelnbogen D 81 B3
Katzhütte D 82 B3
Kaub D 93 A3
Kaufbeuren D 108 B1
Kauhajoki FIN 8 A3
Kauhava FIN 8 A3
Kaukonen FIN 196 B7
Kauliranta FIN 196 C6
Kaulsdorf D 82 B3
Kaunas LT 13 A5
Kaunisvaara S 196 B6
Kaupanger N 47 A4
Kautokeino N 192 C7
Kautzen A 97 C3
Kavadarci MK 182 B4
Kavajë AL 182 B1
Kavakköy TR 186 B1
Kavaklı TR 186 A2
Kavaklıdere TR 188 B3
Kavala GR 183 C6
Kavarna BG 17 D8
Kävlinge S 61 D3
Kawcze PL 68 A1
Kaxås S 199 B10
Kaxholmen S 62 A2
Käylä FIN 197 C12
Kaymakçı TR 188 A3
Kaymaz TR 187 C6
Kaynarca TR 187 A5
Käyrämö FIN 197 C9
Kayseri TR 23 B8
Kaysersberg F 106 A2
Kazanlŭk BG 17 D6
Kazár H 113 A3
Kazimierza Wielka
PL 87 B4
Kazincbarcika H 113 A4
Kaźmierz PL 75 B5
Kcynia PL 76 A2
Kdyně CZ 95 B5
Kea GR 185 B5
Keadew IRL 26 B2
Keady GB 27 B4
Kecel H 112 C3
Keçiborlu TR 189 B5
Kecskemét H 113 C3
Kėdainiai LT 13 A5
Kędzierzyn-Koźle
PL 86 B2
Keel IRL 28 A1
Keenagh IRL 28 A4
Keerbergen B 79 A4
Kefalos GR 188 C1
Kefken TR 187 A5
Keflavík IS 190 C3
Kegworth GB 40 C2
Kehl D 93 C3
Kehrigk D 74 B2
Keighley GB 40 B2
Keila EST 8 C4
Keillmore GB 34 C2
Keiss GB 32 C3
Keith GB 33 D4
Kelankylä FIN 197 D10
Kelberg D 80 B2
Kelbra D 82 A3
Kelč CZ 98 B1
Kelchsau A 108 B3
Këlcyrë AL 182 C2
Keld GB 37 B4
Kelebia H 126 A1
Kelekçi TR 188 B4
Kelemér H 99 C4
Keles TR 186 C4
Kelheim D 95 C3
Kell D 92 B2
Kellas GB 32 D3
Kellinghusen D 64 C2
Kelloselkä FIN 197 C11
Kells
GB 27 B4
IRL 27 C4
Kelmis B 80 B2
Kelokedhara CY 181 B1
Kelottijärvi FIN 192 D6
Kelsall GB 38 A4
Kelso GB 35 C5
Kelsterbach D 93 A4
Keltneyburn GB 35 B3
Kelujärvi FIN 197 B10
Kemaliye TR 188 A3
Kemalpaşa TR 188 A2
Kematen A 108 B2
Kemberg D 83 A4
Kemer
*Antalya* TR 189 C5
*Burdur* TR 189 B5
*Muğla* TR 189 C4
Kemerkaya TR 187 D6
Kemeten A 111 B3
Kemi FIN 196 D7
Kemijärvi FIN 197 C10
Keminmaa FIN 196 D7
Kemnath D 95 B3
Kemnay GB 33 D4
Kemnitz
*Brandenburg* D 74 B1
*Mecklenburg-Vorpommern* D 66 B2
Kempen D 80 A2
Kempsey GB 39 B4
Kempten D 107 B5
Kemptthal CH 107 B3
Kendal GB 37 B4
Kenderes H 113 B4
Kengyel H 113 B4
Kenilworth GB 44 A2
Kenmare IRL 29 C2
Kenmore GB 35 B4
Kennacraig GB 34 C2
Kenyeri H 111 B4
Kenzingen D 106 A2
Kepez TR 186 B1
Kępice PL 68 A1
Kępno PL 86 A2
Kepsut TR 186 C3
Keramoti GR 183 C6
Keräntöjärvi S 196 B6
Keratea GR 185 B4
Kerava FIN 8 B4
Kerecsend H 113 B4
Kerekegyhaza H 112 C3
Kerepestarcsa H 112 B3
Keri GR 184 B1
Kérien F 100 A2
Kerkafalva H 111 C3
Kerken D 80 A2
Kerkrade NL 80 B2
Kerkyra GR 182 D1
Kerlouan F 100 A1
Kernascléden F 100 A2

Kernhof A 110 B2
Kerns CH 106 C3
Kerpen D 80 B2
Kerrysdale GB 31 B3
Kerta H 111 B4
Kerteminde DK 59 C3
Kerzers CH 106 C2
Keşan TR 186 B1
Kesgrave GB 45 A5
Kesh GB 26 B3
Keskin TR 23 B7
Kesselfall A 109 B3
Kestenga RUS 3 D12
Keswick GB 36 B3
Keszthely H 111 C4
Kétegyháza H 113 C5
Kéthely H 111 C4
Kętrzyn PL 12 A4
Kettering GB 44 A3
Kettlewell GB 40 A1
Kęty PL 99 B3
Ketzin D 74 B1
Keula D 82 A2
Keuruu FIN 8 A4
Kevelaer D 80 A2
Kevermes H 113 C5
Kevi SRB 126 B1
Keyingham GB 41 B3
Keynsham GB 43 A4
Kežmarok SK 99 B4
Kharmanli BG 183 B7
Khaskovo BG 183 B7
Khimki RUS 9 E10
Khisinev = Chişinău
MD 17 B8
Khmelnik UA 13 D7
Khmelnytskyy UA 13 D7
Khodoriv UA 13 D6
Kholm RUS 9 D7
Khotyn UA 13 D7
Khoyniki BY 13 C8
Khust UA 17 A5
Khvoynaya RUS 9 C9
Kiato GR 184 A3
Kibæk DK 59 B1
Kiberg N 193 B14
Kicasalih TR 186 A1
Kičevo MK 182 B2
Kidderminster GB 39 B4
Kidlington GB 44 B2
Kidsgrove GB 40 B1
Kidwelly GB 39 C2
Kiefersfelden D 108 B3
Kiel D 64 B3
Kielce PL 87 B4
Kiełczygłów PL 86 A3
Kielder GB 37 A4
Kiełpino PL 68 A3
Kielpiny PL 77 A4
Kierinki FIN 197 B8
Kiernozia PL 77 B4
Kierspe D 81 A3
Kietrz PL 86 B2
Kietz D 74 B3
Kiev = Kyyiv UA 13 C9
Kiezmark PL 69 A3
Kiffisia GR 185 A4
Kifino Selo BIH 139 B4
Kihlanki
FIN 196 B6
S 196 B6
Kiistala FIN 197 B8
Kije PL 87 B4
Kijevo HR 138 B2
Kikallen N 46 B2
Kikinda SRB 126 B2
Kil
N 53 B5
Örebro S 55 A6
Värmland S 55 A4
Kila S 55 A3
Kilafors S 50 A3
Kilbaha IRL 29 B2
Kilbeggan IRL 30 A1
Kilberry GB 34 C2
Kilbirnie GB 34 C3
Kilboghamn N 195 D4
Kilbotn N 194 B7
Kilb Rabenstein A 110 A2
Kilchattan GB 34 C2
Kilchoan GB 34 B1
Kilcock IRL 30 A2
Kilconnell IRL 28 A3
Kilcormac IRL 28 A4
Kilcreggan GB 34 C3
Kilcullen IRL 30 A2
Kilcurry IRL 27 B4
Kildare IRL 30 A2
Kildinstroy RUS 3 B13
Kildonan GB 32 C3
Kildorrery IRL 29 B3
Kilegrend N 53 A4
Kilen N 53 A4
Kilgarvan IRL 29 C2
Kiliya UA 17 C8
Kilkee IRL 29 B2
Kilkeel GB 27 B4
Kilkelly IRL 26 C2
Kilkenny IRL 30 B1
Kilkieran IRL 28 A2
Kilkinlea IRL 29 B2
Kilkis GR 182 B4
Killadysert IRL 29 B2
Killala IRL 26 B1
Killaloe IRL 28 B3
Killarney IRL 29 B2
Killashandra IRL 27 B3
Killashee IRL 28 A4
Killearn GB 34 B3
Killeberg S 61 C4
Killeigh IRL 30 A1
Killenaule IRL 29 B4
Killimor IRL 28 A3
Killin GB 34 B3
Killinaboy IRL 28 B2
Killinge S 196 B3
Killinick IRL 30 B2
Killorglin IRL 29 B2
Killucan IRL 30 A1
Killybegs IRL 26 B2
Killyleagh GB 27 B5
Kilmacrenan IRL 26 A3
Kilmacthomas IRL 30 B1
Kilmaine IRL 28 A2
Kilmallock IRL 29 B3
Kilmarnock GB 36 A2
Kilmartin GB 34 B2
Kilmaurs GB 36 A2
Kilmeadan IRL 30 B1
Kilmeedy IRL 29 B3
Kilmelford GB 34 B2
Kilmore Quay IRL 30 B2
Kilmuir GB 32 D2
Kilnaleck IRL 27 C3
Kilninver GB 34 B2
Kilpisjärvi FIN 192 C4
Kilrea GB 27 B4
Kilrush IRL 29 B2
Kilsmo S 56 A1
Kilsyth GB 35 C3
Kiltoom IRL 28 A3
Kilwinning GB 36 A2
Kimasozero RUS 3 D12
Kimi GR 185 A5
Kimolos GR 185 C5
Kimovsk RUS 9 E10
Kimratshofen D 107 B5
Kimry RUS 9 D10
Kimstad S 56 B1
Kinbrace GB 32 C3
Kincardine GB 35 B4
Kincraig GB 32 D3
Kindberg A 110 B2
Kindelbruck D 82 A3
Kingarrow IRL 26 B2
Kingisepp RUS 9 C6
Kingsbridge GB 43 B3
Kingsclere GB 44 B2
Kingscourt IRL 27 C4
King's Lynn GB 41 C4
Kingsteignton GB 43 B3
Kingston
Greater London
GB 44 B3
Moray GB 32 D3
Kingston Bagpuize
GB 44 B2
Kingston upon Hull
GB 40 B3
Kingswear GB 43 B3
Kingswood GB 43 A4
Kington GB 39 B3
Kingussie GB 32 D2
Kınık
Antalya TR 188 C4
İzmir TR 186 C2
Kinloch
Highland GB 31 B2
Highland GB 32 C2
Kinlochbervie GB 32 C1
Kinlochewe GB 32 D1
Kinlochleven GB 34 B3
Kinlochmoidart GB 34 B2
Kinloch Rannoch
GB 35 B3
Kinloss GB 32 D3
Kinlough IRL 26 B2
Kinn N 48 B2
Kinna S 60 B2
Kinnared S 60 B3
Kinnarp S 55 B4
Kinnegad IRL 30 A1
Kinne-Kleva S 55 B4
Kinnitty IRL 28 A4
Kinrooi B 80 A1
Kinross GB 35 B4
Kinsale IRL 29 C3
Kinsarvik N 46 B3
Kintarvie GB 31 A2
Kintore GB 33 D4
Kinvarra IRL 28 A3
Kioni GR 184 A1
Kiparissia GR 184 B2
Kipfenburg D 95 C3
Kippen GB 35 B3
Kiraz TR 188 A3
Kirazlı TR 186 B1
Kirberg D 81 B4
Kirchbach in Steiermark
A 110 C2
Kirchberg
CH 106 B2
Baden-Württemberg
D 94 B1
Rheinland-Pfalz D 93 B3
Kirchberg am Wechsel
A 110 B2
Kirchberg an der Pielach
A 110 A2
Kirchberg in Tirol
A 109 B3
Kirchbichl A 108 B3
Kirchdorf
Bayern D 96 C1
Mecklenburg-
Vorpommern D 65 C4
Niedersachsen D 72 B1
Kirchdorf an der Krems
A 109 B5
Kirchdorf in Tirol A 109 B3
Kirchenlamitz D 83 B3
Kirchenthumbach D 95 B3
Kirchhain D 81 B4
Kirchheim
Baden-Württemberg
D 94 C1
Bayern D 108 A1
Hessen D 81 B5
Kirchheimbolanden
D 93 B4
Kirchhundem D 81 A4
Kirchlintein D 72 B2
Kirchschlag A 111 B3
Kirchweidach D 109 A3
Kirchzarten D 106 B2
Kircubbin GB 27 B5
Kireç TR 186 C3
Kırıkkale TR 23 B7
Kirillov RUS 9 C11
Kirishi RUS 9 C8
Kırka TR 187 C5
Kırkağaç TR 186 C2
Kirkbean GB 36 B3
Kirkbride GB 36 B3
Kirkby GB 38 A4
Kirkby Lonsdale GB 37 B4
Kirkby Malzeard GB 40 A2
Kirkbymoorside GB 37 B6
Kirkby Stephen GB 37 B4
Kirkcaldy GB 35 B4
Kirkcolm GB 36 B1
Kirkconnel GB 36 A2
Kirkcowan GB 36 B2
Kirkcudbright GB 36 B2
Kirkehamn N 52 B2
Kirke Hyllinge DK 61 D1
Kirkenær N 49 B4
Kirkenes N 193 C14
Kirkham GB 38 A4
Kirkintilloch GB 35 C3
Kirkjubæjarklaustur
IS 191 D7
Kirkkonummi FIN 8 B4
Kırklareli TR 186 A2
Kirkmichael GB 35 B4
Kirk Michael GB 36 B2
Kirkoswald GB 36 A2
Kirkpatrick Fleming
GB 36 A3
Kirkton of Glenisla
GB 35 B4
Kirkwall GB 33 C4
Kirkwhelpington GB 37 A5
Kirn D 93 B3
Kirovsk RUS 3 C13
Kirriemuir GB 35 B5
Kırşehir TR 23 B8
Kirton GB 41 C3
Kirton in Lindsey
GB 40 B3
Kirtorf D 81 B5
Kiruna S 196 B3
Kisa S 62 A3
Kisač SRB 126 B1
Kisbér H 112 B2
Kiseljak BIH 139 B4
Kisielice PL 69 B4
Kisköre H 113 B4
Kiskőrös H 112 C3
Kiskunfélegyháza
H 113 C3
Kiskunhalas H 112 C3
Kiskunlacháza H 112 B2
Kiskunmajsa H 113 C3
Kisláng H 112 C2
Kisslegg D 107 B4
Kissolt H 112 C3
Kissónerga CY 181 B1
Kist D 94 B1
Kistanje HR 138 B1
Kistelek H 113 C3
Kisterenye H 113 A3
Kisújszállás H 113 B4
Kisvárda H 16 A5
Kisvejke H 112 C2
Kiszkowo PL 76 B2
Kiszombor H 126 A2
Kitee FIN 9 A7
Kithnos GR 185 B5
Kiti CY 181 B2
Kitkiöjärvi S 196 B6
Kitkiöjoki S 196 B6
Kittelfjäll S 195 E6
Kittendorf D 74 A1
Kittilä FIN 196 B7
Kittlitz D 84 A2
Kittsee A 111 A4
Kitzbühel A 109 B3
Kitzingen D 94 B2
Kiuruvesi FIN 3 E10
Kivertsi UA 13 C6
Kividhes CY 181 B1
Kivik S 63 C2
Kivotos GR 182 C3
Kıyıköy TR 186 A3
Kızılcabölük TR 188 B4
Kızılcadağ TR 189 B4
Kızılcahamam TR 23 A7
Kızılırmak TR 23 A7
Kızılkaya TR 189 B5
Kızılkuyu TR 187 D6
Kızılören
Afyon TR 189 A5
Konya TR 189 B7
Kjeldebotn N 194 B7
Kjellerup DK 59 B2
Kjellmyra N 49 B4
Kjøllefjord N 193 B11
Kjopmannskjaer N 54 A1
Kjøpsvik N 194 B7
Kl'ačno SK 98 C2
Kladanj BIH 139 A4
Kläden D 73 B4
Klädesholmen S 60 B1
Kladnice HR 138 B2
Kladno CZ 84 B2
Kladruby CZ 95 B4
Klagenfurt A 110 C1
Klågerup S 61 D3
Klagstorp S 66 A2
Klaipėda LT 8 E2
Klaistow D 74 B1
Klaksvík FO 4 A3
Klana HR 123 B3
Klanac HR 123 C4
Klanjec HR 123 A4
Klardorf D 95 B4
Klarup DK 58 A3
Klašnice BIH 124 C3
Klässbol S 55 A3
Klášterec nad Ohří
CZ 83 B5
Kláštor pod Znievom
SK 98 C2
Klatovy CZ 96 B1
Klaus an der Pyhrnbahn
A 110 B1
Klazienaveen NL 71 B3
Kłecko PL 76 B2
Kleczew PL 76 B3
Klein Plasten D 74 A1
Klein Sankt Paul A 110 C1
Kleinsölk A 109 B4
Kleinzell A 110 B2
Klejtrup DK 58 B2
Klek SRB 126 B2
Klemensker DK 67 A3
Klenak SRB 127 C1
Klenci pod Cerchovem
CZ 95 B4
Klenica PL 75 C4
Klenje SRB 127 C1
Klenoec MK 182 B2
Klenovec SK 99 C3
Klenovica HR 123 B3
Klenovnik HR 124 A2
Kleppe N 52 B1
Kleppestø N 46 B2
Kleptow D 74 A2
Kleszewo PL 77 B6
Kleve D 80 A2
Klevshult S 60 B4
Klewki PL 77 A5
Kličevac SRB 127 C3
Kliening A 110 C1
Klietz D 73 B5
Klikuszowa PL 99 B3
Klimkovice CZ 98 B2
Klimontów PL 87 B5
Klimovichi BY 13 B9
Klimpfjäll S 195 E5
Klin RUS 9 D10
Klinča Sela HR 123 B4
Klingenbach A 111 B3
Klingenberg D 93 B5
Klingenmunster D 93 B4
Klingenthal D 83 B4
Klinken D 73 A4
Klintehamn S 57 C4
Kliny PL 87 A4
Kliplev DK 64 B2
Klippan S 61 C3
Klis HR 138 B2
Klitmøller DK 58 A1
Klitten S 49 A6
Klixbüll D 64 B1
Kljajićevo SRB 126 B1
Ključ BIH 138 A2
Klobouky CZ 97 C4
Kłobuck PL 86 B2
Klockestrand S 200 D3
Kłodawa
Lubuskie PL 75 B4
Wielkopolskie PL 76 B3
Kłodzko PL 85 B4
Kløfta N 48 B3
Klokkarvik N 46 B2
Klokkerholm DK 58 A3
Klokočov SK 98 B2
Kłomnice PL 86 B3
Klonowa PL 86 A2
Kloosterzande NL 79 A4
Kłopot PL 74 B3
Klos AL 182 B2
Kloštar Ivanić HR 124 B2
Kloster
D 66 B2
DK 59 B1
Klösterle A 107 B5
Klostermansfeld D 82 A3
Klosterneuburg A 97 C4
Klosters CH 107 C4
Kloten CH 107 B3
Klötze D 73 B4
Klöverträsk S 196 D4
Klövsjö S 199 C11
Kluczbork PL 86 B2
Kluczewo PL 75 A5
Kluisbergen B 79 B3
Klundert NL 79 A4
Klutz D 65 C4
Klwów PL 87 A4
Klyetsk BY 13 B7
Knaben N 52 B2
Knaften S 200 B4
Knapstad N 54 A2
Knäred S 61 C3
Knaresborough GB 40 A2
Knarvik N 46 B2
Knebel DK 59 B3
Knebworth GB 44 B3
Knesebeck D 73 B3
Knesselare B 78 A3
Knežak SLO 123 B3
Kneževi Vinogradi
HR 125 B4
Kneževo HR 125 B4
Knić SRB 127 D2
Knighton GB 39 B3
Knin HR 138 A2
Knislinge S 61 C4
Knittelfeld A 110 B1
Knivsta S 57 A3
Knock IRL 28 A3
Knocktopher IRL 30 B1
Knokke-Heist B 78 A3
Knowle GB 44 A2
Knurów PL 86 B2
Knutby S 51 C5
Knutsford GB 38 A4
Kobarid SLO 122 A2
København =
Copenhagen DK 61 D2
Kobenz A 110 B1
Kobersdorf A 111 B3
Kobiernice PL 99 B3
Kobierzyce PL 85 B4
Kobilje SLO 111 C3
Kobiór PL 86 B2
Koblenz
CH 106 B3
D 81 B3
Kobryn BY 13 B6
Kobylanka PL 75 A3
Kobylin PL 85 A5
Kobylniki PL 77 B5
Kocaali TR 187 A5
Kocaaliler TR 189 B5
Kocaeli = İzmit TR 187 B4
Kočani MK 182 B4
Koçarlı TR 188 B2
Koceljevo SRB 127 C1
Kočerin BIH 138 B3
Kočevje SLO 123 B3
Kočevska Reka
SLO 123 B3
Kochel am see D 108 B2
Kocs H 112 B2
Kocsér H 113 B3
Kocsola H 112 C2
Koczala PL 68 B2
Kodal N 53 A6
Kode S 60 B1
Kodersdorf D 84 A2
Kodrab PL 86 A3
Koekelare B 78 A2
Kofçaz TR 186 A2
Köflach A 110 B2
Køge DK 61 D2
Kohlberg D 95 B4
Kohtla-Järve EST 8 C5
Köinge S 60 B2
Kojetín CZ 98 B1
Kökar FIN 51 C7
Kokava SK 99 C3
Kokkinotrimithia 181 A2
Kokkola FIN 3 E8
Kokori BIH 124 C3
Kokoski PL 69 A3
Koksijde B 78 A2
Kola
BIH 124 C3
RUS 3 B13
Köla S 54 A3
Kołacin PL 87 A3
Kolari FIN 196 B6
Kolárovo SK 112 B1
Kolašin MNE 16 D3
Kolbäck S 56 A2
Kolbacz PL 75 A3
Kolbeinsstaðir IS 190 C3
Kolbermoor D 108 B3
Kolbnitz A 109 C4
Kolbotn N 54 A1
Kolbu N 48 B2
Kolby Kås DK 59 C3
Kolczewo PL 67 C3
Kolczyglowy PL 68 A2
Kolding DK 59 C2
Kölesd H 112 C2
Kolgrov N 46 A1
Kolín CZ 97 A3
Kolind DK 59 B3
Kolinec CZ 96 B1
Koljane HR 138 B2
Kølkær DK 59 B2
Kölleda D 82 A3
Kollum NL 70 A3
Köln = Cologne D 80 B2
Koło PL 76 B3
Kołobrzeg PL 67 B4
Kolochau D 83 A5
Kolomyya UA 13 D6
Kolonowskie PL 86 B2
Koloveč CZ 95 B5
Kolpino RUS 9 C7
Kolrep D 73 A5
Kölsillre S 199 C12
Kolsko PL 75 C4
Kolsva S 56 A1
Kolta SK 112 A2
Kolunič BIH 138 A2
Koluszki PL 87 A3
Kolut SRB 125 B4
Kolvereid N 199 A8
Kølvrå DK 59 B2
Komadi H 113 B5
Komagvær N 193 B14
Komarica BIH 125 C3
Komárno SK 112 B2
Komárom H 112 B2
Komatou Yialou
CY 181 A3
Komboti GR 182 D3
Komen SLO 122 B2
Komin HR 138 B3
Komiža HR 138 B2
Komjáti H 99 C4
Komjatice SK 112 A2
Komletinci HR 125 B4
Komló H 125 A4
Kömlo H 113 B4
Komoča SK 112 B2
Komorniki PL 75 B5
Komorzno PL 86 A2
Komotini GR 183 B7
Konak SRB 126 B2
Konakovo RUS 9 D10
Konarzyny PL 68 B2
Kondias GR 183 D7
Kondopaga RUS 9 A9
Kondorfa H 111 C3
Kondoros H 113 C4
Konevo RUS 9 A11
Køng DK 65 A4
Konga S 63 B3
Köngäs FIN 196 B7
Kongerslev DK 58 B3
Kongsberg N 53 A5
Kongshamn N 53 B4
Kongsmark DK 64 A1
Kongsmoen N 199 A9
Kongsvik N 194 B7
Kongsvinger N 48 B3
Konice CZ 97 B4
Konie PL 77 C5
Koniecpol PL 86 B3
Königsberg D 82 B2
Königsbronn D 94 C2
Königsbrück D 84 A1
Königsbrunn D 94 C2
Konigsdorf D 108 B2
Königsee D 82 B3
Königshorst D 74 B1
Königslutter D 73 B3
Königssee D 109 B3
Königstein
Hessen D 81 B4
Sachsen D 84 B2
Königstetten A 97 C4
Königswartha D 84 A2
Konigswiesen A 96 C2
Königswinter D 80 B3
Königs Wusterhausen
D 74 B2
Konin PL 76 B3
Konispol AL 182 D2
Konitsa GR 182 C2
Köniz CH 106 C2
Konjevići BIH 139 A5
Konjevrate HR 138 B2
Konjic BIH 139 B3
Konjščina HR 124 A2
Könnern D 83 A3
Konnerud N 53 A6
Konopiska PL 86 B2
Konotop PL 75 C4
Końskie PL 87 A4
Konsmo N 52 B3
Konstancin-Jeziorna
PL 77 B6
Konstantynów Łódźki
PL 86 A3
Konstanz D 107 B4
Kontich B 79 A4
Kontiolahti FIN 9 A6
Konya TR 189 B7
Konz D 92 B2
Kópasker IS 191 A9
Kópavogur IS 190 C4
Kopčany SK 98 C1
Koper SLO 122 B2
Kopervik N 52 A1
Kópháza H 111 B3
Kopice PL 85 B5
Kopidlno CZ 84 B3
Köping S 56 A1
Köpingebro S 66 A2
Köpingsvik S 62 B4
Köpmanholmen S 200 C4
Koppang N 48 A3
Koppangen N 192 C4
Kopparberg S 50 C1
Koppelo FIN 193 D11
Koppom S 54 A3
Koprivlen BG 183 B5
Koprivna BIH 125 C4
Koprivnica HR 124 A2
Kopřivnice CZ 98 B2
Köprübaşı TR 186 D3
Koprzywnica PL 87 B5
Kopstal L 92 B2
Kopychyntsi UA 13 D6
Kopytkowo PL 69 B3

Korbach D 81 A4
Körbecke D 81 A4
Korçë AL 182 C2
Korčula HR 138 C3
Korczyców PL 75 B3
Korenita SRB 127 C1
Korets UA 13 C7
Korfantów PL 85 B5
Körfez TR 187 B4
Korgen N 195 D4
Korinth DK 64 A3
Korinthos = Corinth GR 184 B3
Korita
BIH 138 A2
HR 139 C3
Korithi GR 184 B1
Korkuteli TR 189 B5
Körmend H 111 B3
Korne PL 68 A2
Korneuburg A 97 C4
Kornevo RUS 69 A5
Kórnik PL 76 B2
Kornsjø N 54 B2
Környe H 112 B2
Koromačno HR 123 C3
Koroni GR 184 C2
Koronos GR 185 B6
Koronowo PL 76 A2
Körösladány H 113 C5
Köröstarcsa H 113 C5
Korosten UA 13 C8
Korostyshev UA 13 C8
Korpikå S 196 D6
Korpikylä FIN 196 C6
Korpilombolo S 196 C6
Korsberga
*Jönköping* S 62 A3
*Skaraborg* S 55 B5
Korshavn N 54 A1
Korskrogen S 200 E1
Korsnäs S 50 B2
Korsør DK 65 A4
Korsun Shevchenkovskiy UA 13 D9
Korträsk S 196 D3
Kortrijk B 78 B3
Korucu TR 186 C2
Koryčany CZ 98 B1
Korzeńsko PL 85 A4
Korzybie PL 68 A1
Kos GR 188 C2
Kosakowo PL 69 A3
Kosanica MNE 139 B5
Kösching D 95 C3
Kościan PL 75 B5
Kościelec PL 76 B3
Kościerzyna PL 68 A2
Koserow D 66 B2
Košetice CZ 97 B3
Košice SK 12 D4
Kosjerić SRB 127 D1
Koška HR 125 B4
Koskullskulle S 196 B3
Kosovska Mitrovica KOS 16 D4
Kosta S 62 B3
Kostajnica HR 124 B2
Kostajnik SRB 127 C1
Kostanjevica SLO 123 B4
Kostelec nad Černými Lesy CZ 96 B2
Kostelec na Hané CZ 97 B5
Kostice CZ 84 B1
Kostkowo PL 68 A3
Kostojevići SRB 127 C1
Kostolac SRB 127 C3
Kostomłoty PL 85 A4
Kostopil UA 13 C7
Kostów PL 86 A2
Kostrzyn
*Lubuskie* PL 74 B3
*Wielkopolskie* PL 76 B2
Koszalin PL 67 B5
Koszęcin PL 86 B2
Kőszeg H 111 B3
Koszwaly PL 69 A3
Koszyce PL 87 B4
Kot SLO 123 B4
Kotala FIN 197 B11
Kötelek H 113 B4
Köthen D 83 A3
Kotka FIN 8 B5
Kotomierz PL 76 A3
Kotor MNE 16 D3
Kotoriba HR 124 A2
Kotorsko BIH 125 C4
Kotor Varoš BIH 124 C3
Kotovsk UA 17 B8
Kotronas GR 184 C3
Kötschach A 109 C3
Kötzting D 95 B4
Koudum NL 70 B2
Kouřim CZ 96 A2
Kout na Šumave CZ 95 B5
Kouvola FIN 8 B5
Kovačevac SRB 127 C2
Kovačica SRB 126 B2
Kovdor RUS 197 B13
Kovel' UA 13 C6
Kovilj SRB 126 B2
Kovin SRB 127 C2
Kowal PL 77 B4
Kowalewo Pomorskie PL 69 B3
Kowalów PL 75 B3
Kowary PL 85 B3
Köyceğiz TR 188 C3
Kozani GR 182 C3
Kozarac
BIH 124 C2
HR 124 B1
Kozárovce SK 98 C2
Kozelets UA 13 C9
Kozica HR 138 B3
Koziegłowy PL 86 B3
Kozienice PL 87 A5
Kozina SLO 122 B2
Kozje SLO 123 A4
Kozlu TR 187 A6
Kozluk BIH 139 A5
Koźmin PL 85 A5
Koźminek PL 86 A2
Kozolupy CZ 96 B1
Kożuchów PL 84 A3
Kožuhe BIH 125 C4
Kozyatyn UA 13 D8
Kozyürük TR 186 A1
Kräckelbräken S 49 A6
Krackow D 74 A3
Kraddsele S 195 E7
Krąg PL 68 A1
Kragenæs DK 65 B4
Kragerø N 53 B5
Krągi PL 68 B1
Kragujevac SRB 127 C2
Kraiburg D 109 A3
Krajenka PL 68 B1
Krajišnik SRB 126 B2
Krajková CZ 83 B4
Krajné SK 98 C1
Krajnik Dolny PL 74 A3
Krakača BIH 124 B1
Kräklingbo S 57 C4
Kraków = Cracow PL 99 A3
Krakow am See D 73 A5
Králíky CZ 85 B4
Kraljevica HR 123 B3
Kraljevo SRB 16 D4
Kral'ovany SK 99 B3
Král'ov Brod SK 111 A4
Kralovice CZ 96 B1
Kralupy nad Vltavou CZ 84 B2
Králův Dvůr CZ 96 B2
Kramfors S 200 D3
Kramsach A 108 B2
Kramsk PL 76 B3
Krämvik N 53 A4
Kranenburg D 80 A2
Krania GR 182 D3
Krania Elasonas GR 182 D4
Kranichfeld D 82 B3
Kranidi GR 184 B4
Kranj SLO 123 A3
Kranjska Gora SLO 109 C4
Krapanj HR 138 B1
Krapina HR 124 A1
Krapje HR 124 B2
Krapkowice PL 86 B1
Kraselov CZ 96 B1
Krašić HR 123 B4
Krāslava LV 8 E5
Kraslice CZ 83 B4
Krasna PL 87 A4
Krasna Lipa CZ 84 B2
Krasne PL 77 B5
Kraśnik PL 12 C5
Krašnja SLO 123 A3
Krásno SK 98 B2
Krásnohorské Podhradie SK 99 C4
Krasno Polje HR 123 C4
Krasnozavodsk RUS 9 D11
Krasnystaw PL 13 C5
Krasnyy RUS 13 A9
Krasnyy Kholm RUS 9 C10
Krasocin PL 87 B4
Kraszewice PL 86 A2
Kraszkowice PL 86 A2
Kratigos GR 186 C1
Kratovo MK 182 A4
Kraubath A 110 B1
Krausnick D 74 B2
Krautheim D 94 B1
Kravaře CZ 84 B2
Kraváre CZ 98 B2
Kravarsko HR 124 B2
Kraznějov CZ 96 B1
Krčedin SRB 126 B2
Kŭrdzhali BG 183 B7
Krefeld D 80 A2
Kregme DK 61 D2
Krembz D 73 A4
Kremenets UA 13 C6
Kremmen D 74 B2
Kremna SRB 127 D1
Kremnica SK 98 C2
Krempe D 64 C2
Krems A 97 C3
Kremsbrücke A 109 C4
Kremsmünster A 110 A1
Křemže CZ 96 C2
Křenov CZ 97 B4
Krepa PL 76 C3
Krępa Krajeńska PL 75 A5
Krepsko PL 68 B1
Kreševo BIH 139 B4
Kressbronn D 107 B4
Krestena GR 184 B2
Kretinga LT 8 E2
Krettsy RUS 9 C8
Kreuth D 108 B2
Kreuzau D 80 B2
Kreuzlingen CH 107 B4
Kreuztal D 81 B3
Krewelin D 74 B2
Krezluk BIH 138 A3
Krichem BG 183 A6
Krieglach A 110 B2
Kriegsfeld D 93 B3
Kriens CH 106 B3
Krimml A 108 B3
Krimpen aan de IJssel NL 79 A4
Křinec CZ 84 B3
Kristdala S 62 A4
Kristiansand N 53 B4
Kristianstad S 61 C4
Kristiansund N 198 B4
Kristiinankaupunki FIN 8 A2
Kristinefors S 49 B4
Kristinehamn S 55 A5
Kriváň SK 99 C3
Kriva Palanka MK 182 A4
Křivokát CZ 96 A1
Kriź HR 124 B2
Křižanov CZ 97 B4
Križevci HR 124 A2
Krk HR 123 B3
Krka SLO 123 B3
Krnjača SRB 127 C2
Krnjak HR 123 B4
Krnjeuša BIH 124 C2
Krnjevo SRB 127 C3
Krnov CZ 98 A1
Krobia PL 85 A4
Kroczyce PL 86 B3
Krøderen N 48 B1
Krokees GR 184 C3
Krokek S 56 B2
Krokom S 199 B11
Krokowa PL 68 A3
Krokstad-elva N 53 A5
Kroksund N 54 A2
Kroměříž CZ 98 B1
Krommenie NL 70 B1
Krompachy SK 99 C4
Kronach D 82 B3
Kronshagen D 64 B3
Kronshtadt RUS 9 C6
Kröpelin D 65 B4
Kropp D 64 B2
Kroppenstedt D 73 C4
Kropstädt D 74 C1
Krościenko nad Dunajcem PL 99 B4
Kröslin D 66 B2
Krośnice PL 85 A5
Krośniewice PL 77 B4
Krosno PL 12 D4
Krosno Odrzańskie PL 75 B4
Krostitz D 83 A4
Krotoszyn PL 85 A5
Krottendorf A 110 B2
Krouna CZ 97 B4
Krowiarki PL 86 B2
Krrabë AL 182 B1
Kršan HR 123 B3
Krško SLO 123 B4
Krstac MNE 139 B4
Krstur SRB 126 A2
Křtiny CZ 97 B4
Kruft D 80 B3
Kruishoutem B 79 B3
Krujë AL 182 B1
Krulyewshchyna BY 13 A7
Krumbach
A 111 B3
D 94 C2
Krumovgrad BG 183 B7
Krün D 108 B2
Krupá CZ 84 B1
Krupa na Vrbasu BIH 124 C3
Krupanj SRB 127 C1
Krupina SK 99 C3
Krupka CZ 84 B1
Krupki BY 13 A8
Kruså DK 64 B2
Kruščica BIH 139 A3
Kruševac SRB 16 D4
Kruševo MK 182 B3
Kruszwica PL 76 B3
Kruszyn PL 77 B4
Krychaw BY 13 B9
Krynica PL 99 B4
Krynica Morska PL 69 A4
Krzęcin PL 75 A4
Krzelów PL 85 A4
Krzepice PL 86 B2
Krzepielów PL 85 A4
Krzeszowice PL 86 B3
Krzeszyce PL 75 B4
Krzynowlaga Mała PL 77 A5
Krzywiń PL 75 C5
Krzyżanowice PL 98 B2
Krzyżowa PL 99 B3
Krzyż Wielkopolski PL 75 B5
Ksiaz Wielkopolski PL 87 B4
Książ Wielkopolski PL 76 B2
Kłębowiec PL 75 A5
Kübekháza H 126 A2
Küblis CH 107 C4
Kuchary PL 86 A1
Kuchl A 109 B4
Kucice PL 77 B5
Kuciste HR 138 C3
Kuçovë AL 182 C1
Küçükbahçe TR 188 A1
Küçükköy TR 186 C1
Küçükkuyu TR 186 C1
Kucura SRB 126 B1
Kuczbork-Osada PL 77 A5
Kuddby S 56 B2
Kudowa-Zdrój PL 85 B4
Kufstein A 108 B3
Kuggeboda S 63 B3
Kuggörana S 200 E3
Kühbach D 95 C3
Kuhmo FIN 3 D11
Kuhmoinen FIN 8 B4
Kuhnsdorf A 110 C1
Kuhstedt D 72 A1
Kuinre NL 70 B2
Kuivaniemi FIN 197 D8
Kuivastu EST 8 C3
Kukës AL 182 A2
Kuklin PL 77 A5
Kukljica HR 137 A4
Kukujevci SRB 127 B1
Kula
*Srbija* SRB 127 C3
*Vojvodina* SRB 126 B1
TR 188 A3
Kuldīga LV 8 D2
Kulen Vakuf BIH 124 C2
Kulina BIH 125 C4
Kullstedt D 82 A2
Kulmain D 95 B3
Kulmbach D 82 B3
Kuloharju FIN 197 D11
Kulu TR 23 B7
Kumachevo RUS 69 A5
Kumafşarı TR 189 B4
Kumane SRB 126 B2
Kumanovo MK 182 A3
Kumbağ TR 186 B2
Kumdanlı TR 189 A5
Kumkale TR 186 C1
Kumla S 56 A1
Kumlakyrkby S 50 C3
Kumlinge FIN 51 B7
Kumluca TR 189 C5
Kumrovec HR 123 A4
Kunadacs H 112 C3
Kunágota H 113 C5
Kunbaja H 126 A1
Kunda EST 8 C5
Kundl A 108 B2
Kunes N 193 B10
Kunfehértó H 126 A1
Kungälv S 60 B1
Kungsängen S 57 A3
Kungsäter S 60 B2
Kungsbacka S 60 B2
Kungsgården S 50 B3
Kungshamn S 54 B2
Kungs-Husby S 56 A3
Kungsör S 56 A2
Kunhegyes H 113 B4
Kunmadaras H 113 B4
Kunovice CZ 98 B1
Kunów PL 87 B5
Kunowo
*Wielkopolskie* PL 76 C2
*Zachodnio-Pomorskie* PL 74 A3
Kunštát CZ 97 B4
Kunszállás H 113 C3
Kunszentmárton H 113 C4
Kunszentmiklós H 112 B3
Kunžak CZ 97 B3
Künzelsau D 94 B1
Kuolayarvi RUS 197 C12
Kuolio FIN 197 D11
Kuopio FIN 8 A5
Kuosku FIN 197 B11
Kup
H 111 B4
PL 86 B1
Kupferzell D 94 B1
Kupinec HR 123 B4
Kupinečki Kraljevac HR 124 B1
Kupinovo SRB 127 C2
Kupirovo HR 138 A2
Kupjak HR 123 B3
Kuppenheim D 93 C4
Kupres BIH 138 B3
Küps D 82 B3
Kurd H 112 C2
Küre TR 23 A7
Kuressaare EST 8 C3
Kurikka FIN 8 A3
Kuřim CZ 97 B4
Kuřivody CZ 84 B2
Kurki PL 77 A5
Kurort Oberwiesenthal D 83 B4
Kurort Schmalkalden D 82 B2
Kurort Stolberg D 82 A2
Kurort Wippra D 82 A3
Kurów PL 12 C5
Kurowice PL 86 A3
Kurravaara S 196 B3
Kursu FIN 197 C11
Kurşunlu
*Bursa* TR 187 B4
*Çankırı* TR 23 A7
Kurtakko FIN 196 B7
Kürten D 80 A3
Kurucaşile TR 187 A7
Kurvinen FIN 197 D12
Kurzelów PL 87 B3
Kusadak SRB 127 C2
Kuşadası TR 188 B2
Kusel D 93 B3
Kusey D 73 B4
Küsnacht CH 106 B3
Kütahya TR 187 C4
Kutenholz D 72 A2
Kutina HR 124 B2
Kutjevo HR 125 B3
Kutná Hora CZ 97 B3
Kutno PL 77 B4
Kuttara FIN 193 D10
Küttingen CH 106 B3
Kúty SK 98 C1
Kuusamo FIN 197 D12
Kuusankoski FIN 8 B5
Kuvshinovo RUS 9 D9
Kuyucak TR 188 B3
Kuzmin SRB 127 B1
Kuźnia Raciborska PL 86 B2
Kuźnica Czarnkowska PL 75 B5
Kuźnica Żelichowska PL 75 B5
Kvaløysletta N 192 C2
Kvalsund N 192 B7
Kvam
*Nord-Trøndelag* N 199 A8
*Oppland* N 198 D6
Kvamsøy N 46 A3
Kvænangsbotn N 192 C6
Kvanndal N 46 B3
Kvänum S 55 B4
Kværndrup DK 59 C3
Kvås N 52 B3
Kvasice CZ 98 B1
Kvelde N 53 A5
Kvenna N 198 C5
Kvernaland N 52 B1
Kvibille S 60 C2
Kvicksund S 56 A2
Kvidinge S 61 C3
Kvikkjokk S 195 D8
Kvikne
*Hedmark* N 199 C7
*Oppland* N 47 A6
Kvilda CZ 96 B1
Kville S 54 B2
Kvillsfors S 62 A3
Kvinesdal N 52 B2
Kvinlog N 52 B2
Kvinnherad N 46 C3
Kvissel DK 58 A3
Kvissleby S 200 D3
Kviteseid N 53 A4
Kvitsøy N 52 A1
Kwakowo PL 68 A2
Kwidzyn PL 69 B3
Kwilcz PL 75 B5
Kyjov CZ 98 C1
Kyleakin GB 31 B3
Kyle of Lochalsh GB 31 B3
Kylerhea GB 31 B3
Kylestrome GB 32 C1
Kyllburg D 92 A2
Kyllini GR 184 B2
Kynšperk nad Ohří CZ 83 B4
Kyperounda CY 181 B1
Kyrenia CY 181 A2
Kyritz D 73 B5
Kyrkesund S 60 A1
Kyrkhult S 63 B2
Kyrksæterøra N 198 B6
Kysucké Nové Mesto SK 98 B2
Kythira GR 184 C3
Kythréa CY 181 A2
Kyustendil BG 16 D5
Kyyiv = Kiev UA 13 C9
Kyyjärvi FIN 8 A4

## L

Laa an der Thaya A 97 C4
La Adrada E 150 B3
Laage D 65 C5
La Alameda E 157 B4
La Alberca E 149 B3
La Alberca de Záncara E 158 B1
La Albergueria de Argañán E 149 B3
La Albuera E 155 C4
La Aldea del Portillo del Busto E 143 B3
La Algaba E 162 A1
La Aliseda de Tormes E 150 B2
La Almarcha E 158 B1
La Almolda E 153 A3
La Almunia de Doña Godina E 152 A2
Laanila FIN 193 D11
La Antillas E 161 B2
La Arena E 141 A4
Laatzen D 72 B2
La Aulaga E 161 B3
La Balme-de-Sillingy F 118 B3
Laban IRL 28 A3
La Bañeza E 141 B5
La Barca de la Florida E 162 B2
La Barre-de-Monts F 114 B1
La Barre-en-Ouche F 89 B4
La Barrosa E 162 B1
La Barthe-de-Neste F 145 A4
La Bassée F 78 B2
La Bastide-de-Sèrou F 146 A2
La Bastide-des-Jourdans F 132 B1
Labastide-Murat F 129 B4
La Bastide-Puylaurent F 117 C3
Labastide-Rouairoux F 130 B1
Labastide-St Pierre F 129 C4
La Bathie F 118 B3
Lábatlan H 112 B2
La Baule-Escoublac F 101 B3
La Bazoche-Gouet F 102 A2
La Bégude-de-Mazenc F 131 A3
Labenne F 128 C1
La Bernerie-en-Retz F 114 A1
Labin HR 123 B3
La Bisbal d'Empordà E 147 C4
Łabiszyn PL 76 B2
Lablachère F 131 A3
Lábod H 124 A3
Laboe D 64 B3
La Boissière F 89 A4
Labouheyre F 128 B2
La Bourboule F 116 B2
La Bóveda de Toro E 150 A2
Łabowa PL 99 B4
La Brède F 128 B2
La Bresse F 106 A1
La Bridoire F 118 B2
La Brillanne F 132 B1
Labrit F 128 B2
Labros E 152 A2
La Bruffière F 114 A2
Labruguière F 130 B1
Labrujo P 148 A1
L'Absie F 114 B3
La Bussière F 103 B4
Laç AL 182 B1
La Caillère F 114 B3
Lacalahorra E 164 B1
La Caletta
*Cágliari* I 179 C2
*Núoro* I 178 B3
La Calmette F 131 B3
La Calzada de Oropesa E 150 C2
La Campana E 162 A2
La Cañada E 150 B3
Lacanau F 128 B1
Lacanau-Océan F 128 A1
Lacanche F 104 B3
La Canourgue F 130 A2
La Capelle F 91 B3
Lacapelle-Marival F 129 B4
Laćarak SRB 127 B1
La Cardanchosa E 156 B2
La Caridad E 141 A4
La Carlota E 162 A3
La Carolina E 157 B4
Lacaune F 130 B1
La Cava E 153 B4
La Cavalerie F 130 A2
Laceby GB 41 B3
Lacedónia I 172 A1
La Celle-en-Moravan F 104 B3
La Celle-St Avant F 102 B2
La Cerca E 143 B3
Láces I 108 C1
La Chaise-Dieu F 117 B3
La Chaize-Giraud F 114 B2
La Chaize-le-Vicomte F 114 B2
La Chambre F 118 B3
Lachania GR 188 D2
La Chapelaude F 116 A2
La Chapelle-d'Angillon F 103 B4
La Chapelle-en-Aalgaudémar F 118 C3
La Chapelle-en-Vercors F 118 C2
La Chapelle-Glain F 101 B4
La Chapelle-la-Reine F 90 C2

La Chapelle-Laurent F 116 B3
La Chapelle-St Luc F 91 C4
La Chapelle-sur-Erdre F 101 B4
La Chapelle-Vicomtesse F 103 B3
La Charce F 132 A1
La Charité-sur-Loire F 104 B2
La Chartre-sur-le-Loir F 102 B2
La Châtaigneraie F 114 B3
La Châtre F 103 C3
La Chaussée-sur-Marne F 91 C4
La Chaux-de-Fonds CH 106 B1
Lachen CH 107 B3
Lachendorf D 72 B3
La Cheppe F 91 B4
La Chèze F 101 A3
Lachowice PL 99 B3
La Ciotat F 132 B1
Łąck PL 77 B4
Läckeby S 62 B4
Läckö S 55 B4
La Clayette F 117 A4
La Clusaz F 118 B3
Lacock GB 43 A4
La Codosera E 155 B3
La Concha E 143 A3
La Condamine-Châtelard F 132 A2
Láconi I 179 C3
La Contienda E 161 A3
La Coquille F 115 C4
La Coronada E 156 B2
La Côte-St André F 118 B2
La Cotinière F 114 C2
La Courtine F 116 B2
Lacq F 145 A3
La Crau F 132 B2
La Crèche F 115 B3
La Croix F 102 B2
Lacroix-Barrez F 116 C2
Lacroix-St Ouen F 90 B2
Lacroix-sur-Meuse F 92 C1
La Croix-Valmer F 132 B2
La Cumbre E 156 A2
Łącznik PL 86 B1
Lad H 125 A3
Ladbergen D 71 B4
Lądek-Zdrój PL 85 B4
Ladelund D 64 B2
Ladendorf A 97 C4
Ladignac-le-Long F 115 C5
Ladispoli I 168 B2
Ladoeiro P 155 B3
Ladon F 103 B4
La Douze F 129 A3
Ladushkin RUS 69 A5
Ladybank GB 35 B4
Laer D 71 B4
La Espina E 141 A4
La Estrella E 156 A2
La Farga de Moles E 146 B2
La Fatarella E 153 A4
La Felipa E 158 B2
La Fère F 90 B3
La Ferrière
*Indre-et-Loire* F 102 B2
*Vendée* F 114 B2
La Ferrière-en-Parthenay F 115 B3
La-Ferté-Alais F 90 C2
La Ferté-Bernard F 102 A2
La Ferté-Frênel F 89 B4
La Ferté-Gaucher F 90 C3
La Ferté-Imbault F 103 B3
La Ferté-Macé F 89 B3
La Ferté-Milon F 90 B3
La Ferté-sous-Jouarre F 90 C3
La Ferté-St-Aubin F 103 B3
La Ferté-St-Cyr F 103 B3
La Ferté-Vidame F 89 B4
La Ferté Villeneuil F 103 B3
La Feuillie F 90 B1
Lafkos GR 183 D5
La Flèche F 102 B1
La Flotte F 114 B2
Lafnitz A 111 B3
La Font de la Figuera E 159 C3
La Fouillade F 130 A1
Lafrançaise F 129 B4
La Fregeneda E 149 B3
La Fresneda E 153 B4
La Fuencubierta E 162 A3
La Fuente de San Esteban E 149 B3
La Fulioala E 147 C2
La Gacilly F 101 B3
La Galera E 153 B4
Lagan S 60 C3
Laganadi I 175 C1
Lagarde F 146 A2
La Garde-Freinet F 132 B2
Lagares
*Coimbra* P 148 B2
*Porto* P 148 A1
La Garnache F 114 B2
Lagaro I 135 A4
La Garriga E 147 C3
La Garrovilla E 155 C4
Lagartera E 150 C2
La Gaubretière F 114 B2
Lågbol S 51 B5
Lage D 72 C1
Lägerdorf D 64 C2
Lagg GB 34 C2
Laggan GB 32 D2
Laggartorp S 55 A5
Łagiewniki PL 85 B4
La Gineta E 158 B1
Láglio I 120 B2
Lagnieu F 118 B2
Lagny-sur-Marne F 90 C2
Lago
*Calabria* I 175 B2
*Veneto* I 121 B5
Lagôa P 160 B1
Lagoaça P 149 A3
Lagonegro I 174 A1
Lagos
GR 183 B7
P 160 B1
Lagosanto I 121 C5
Łagów
*Lubuskie* PL 75 B4
*Świętokrzyskie* PL 87 B5
La Granadella
*Alicante* E 159 C4
*Lleida* E 153 A4
La Grand-Combe F 131 A3
La Grande-Croix F 117 B4
La Grande-Motte F 131 B3
La Granja d'Escarp E 153 A4
La Granjuela E 156 B2
Lagrasse F 146 A3
La Grave F 118 B3
La Gravelle F 101 A4
Laguardia E 143 B4
La Guardia E 151 C4
La Guardia de Jaén E 163 A4
Laguarres E 145 B4
Laguenne F 116 B1
Laguépie F 129 B4
La Guerche-de-Bretagne F 101 B4
La Guerche-sur-l'Aubois F 104 C1
La Guérinière F 114 B1
Laguiole F 116 C2
Laguna de Duera E 150 A3
Laguna del Marquesado E 152 B2
Laguna de Negrillos E 142 B1
Lagundo I 108 C2
Lagunilla E 149 B3
La Haba E 156 B2
Laharie F 128 B1
La Haye-du-Puits F 88 A2
La Haye-Pesnel F 88 B2
Lahden D 71 B4
La Herlière F 78 B2
La Hermida E 142 A2
La Herrera E 158 C1
Laheycourt F 91 C5
La Higuera E 158 C2
La Hiniesta E 149 A4
Lahnstein D 81 B3
Laholm S 61 C3
La Horcajada E 150 B2
La Horra E 143 C3
Lahr D 93 C3
Lahti FIN 8 B4
La Hulpe B 79 B4
La Hutte F 89 B4
Laichingen D 94 C1
L'Aigle F 89 B4
La Iglesuela E 150 B3
La Iglesuela del Cid E 153 B3
Laignes F 104 B3
Laiguéglia I 133 B4
L'Aiguillon-sur-Mer F 114 B2
Laimbach am Ostrong A 97 C3
Laina E 152 A1
Lainio S 196 B5
Lairg GB 32 C2
La Iruela E 164 B2
Laissac F 130 A1
Laisvall S 195 D8
Láives I 121 A4
La Javie F 132 A2
Lajkovac SRB 127 C2
La Jonchère-St Maurice F 116 A1
La Jonquera E 146 B3
Lajoskomárom H 112 C2
Lajosmizse H 112 B3
Lak H 99 C4
Lakenheath GB 45 A4
Lakitelek H 113 C4
Lakki GR 185 D4
Lakolk DK 64 A1
Łąkorz PL 69 B4
Lakšárska Nová Ves SK 98 C1
Lakselv N 193 B8
Laksfors N 195 E4
Laktaši BIH 124 C3
Lalapaşa TR 186 A1
L'Albagès E 153 A4
Lalbenque F 129 B4
L'Alcudia E 159 B3
L'Aldea E 153 B4
Lalín E 140 B2
Lalinde F 129 B3
La Línea de la Concepción E 162 B2
Lalizolle F 116 A3
La Llacuna E 147 C2
Lalley F 118 C2
Lalling D 95 C5
Lalm N 198 D6
La Londe-les-Maures F 132 B2
La Loupe F 89 B5
La Louvière B 79 B4
L'Alpe-d'Huez F 118 B3
La Luisiana E 162 A2
Laluque F 128 C1
Lam D 95 B5
La Machine F 104 C2
la Maddalena I 178 A3
Lama dei Peligni I 169 A4
Lamadrid E 142 A2
Lamagistére F 129 B3
La Mailleraye-sur-Seine F 89 A4
La Malène F 130 A2
Lama Mocogno I 135 A3
La Mamola E 163 B4
La Manresana dels Prats E 147 C2
Lamarche F 105 A4
Lamarche-sur-Saône F 105 B4
Lamargelle F 105 B3
Lamarosa P 154 B2
Lamarque F 128 A2
Lamas P 148 B1
La Masadera E 145 C3
Lamas de Moaro P 140 B2
Lamastre F 117 C4
La Mata E 150 C3
La Mata de Ledesma E 149 A4
La Mata de Monteagudo E 142 B1
Lambach A 109 A4
Lamballe F 101 A3
Lamberhurst GB 45 B4
Lambesc F 131 B4
Lambia GR 184 B2
Lambley GB 37 B4
Lambourn GB 44 B2
Lamego P 148 A2
La Meilleraye-de-Bretagne F 101 B4
La Ménitré F 102 B1
L'Ametlla de Mar E 153 B4
Lamia GR 182 E4
Lammhult S 62 A2
La Mojonera E 164 C2
La Mole F 132 B2
La Molina E 147 B2
La Monnerie-le-Montel F 117 B3
La Morera E 155 C4
La Mothe-Achard F 114 B2
Lamothe-Cassel F 129 B4
Lamothe-Montravel F 128 B3
La Mothe-St Héray F 115 B3
Lamotte-Beuvron F 103 B4
La Motte-Chalançon F 131 A4
La Motte-du-Caire F 132 A2
La Motte-Servolex F 118 B2
Lampertheim D 93 B4
Lampeter GB 39 B2
L'Ampolla E 153 B4
Lamprechtshausen A 109 B3
Lamsfeld D 74 C3
Lamspringe D 72 C3
Lamstedt D 72 A2
La Mudarra E 142 C2
La Muela E 152 A2
La Mure F 118 C2
Lamure-sur-Azergues F 117 A4
Lana I 108 C2
Lanaja E 145 C3
Lanarce F 117 C3
Lanark GB 36 A3
La Nava E 161 B3
La Nava de Ricomalillo E 156 A3
La Nava de Santiago E 155 B4
Lancaster GB 37 B4
Lanchester GB 37 B5
Lanciano I 169 A4
Lancing GB 44 C3
Lançon-Provence F 131 B4
Lancova Vas SLO 124 A1
Landau
*Bayern* D 95 C4
*Rheinland-Pfalz* D 93 B4
Landeck A 108 B1
Landen B 79 B5
Landerneau F 100 A1
Landeryd S 60 B3
Landesbergen D 72 B2
Landete E 158 B2
Landévant F 100 B2
Landévennec F 100 A1
Landeyjahöfn 190 D5
Landivisiau F 100 A1
Landivy F 88 B2
Landl A 108 B3
Landön S 199 B11
Landos F 117 C3
Landouzy-le-Ville F 91 B4
Landquart CH 107 C4
Landrecies F 91 A3
Landreville F 104 A3
Landriano I 120 B2
Landsberg D 108 A1
Lands-berg D 83 A4
Landsbro S 62 A2
Landscheid D 92 B2
Landshut D 95 C4
Landskrona S 61 D2
Landstuhl D 93 B3
Lanesborough IRL 28 A4
Lanester F 100 B2
Lanestosa E 143 A3
La Neuve-Lyre F 89 B4
La Neuveville CH 106 B2
Langå DK 59 B2
Langada GR 185 A7
Langadas GR 183 C5
Langa de Duero E 151 A4
Langadia GR 184 B3
Langangen N 53 A5
Långared S 60 A2
Långaröd S 61 D3
Långaryd S 60 B3
Långås S 60 C2
Långasjö S 63 B3
Langau A 97 C3
Langeac F 117 B3
Langeais F 102 B2
Langedijk NL 70 B1
Langeln D 73 C3
Langelsheim D 72 C3
Langemark-Poelkapelle B 78 B2
Langen
*Hessen* D 93 B4
*Niedersachsen* D 72 A1
Langenau D 94 C2
Langenberg D 81 A4
Langenbruck CH 106 B2
Langenburg D 94 B1
Längenfeld A 108 B1
Langenfeld D 80 A2
Langenhorn D 64 B1
Langenlois A 97 C3
Langenlonsheim D 93 B3
Langennaudorf D 83 A5
Langenneufnach D 94 C2
Langenthal CH 106 B2
Langenzenn D 94 B2
Langeoog D 71 A4
Langeskov DK 59 C3
Langesund N 53 A5
Langewiesen D 82 B2
Långflon S 49 A4
Langförden D 71 B5
Langhagen D 73 A5
Länghem S 60 B3
Langhirano I 120 C3
Langholm GB 36 A4
Langholt IS 191 D7
Långlöt S 62 B4
Langnau CH 106 C2
Langø DK 65 B4
Langogne F 117 C3
Langon F 128 B2
Langquaid D 95 C4
Långrådna S 56 B2
Langreo E 142 A1
Langres F 105 B4
Långsele S 200 C3
Långserud S 54 A3
Langset N 48 B3
Långshyttan S 50 B3
Langstrand N 192 B7
Långträsk S 196 D3
Langueux F 101 A3
Languidic F 100 B2
Längvik S 57 A4
Langwarden D 71 A5
Langwathby GB 37 B4
Langwedel D 72 B2
Langweid D 94 C2
Langwies CH 107 C4
Lanheses P 148 A1
Lanięta PL 77 B4
Lanildut F 100 A1
Lanjarón E 163 B4
Lanmeur F 100 A2
Lanna
*Jönköping* S 60 B3
*Örebro* S 55 A5
Lännaholm S 51 C4
Lannavaara S 196 A4
Lannéanou F 100 A2
Lannemezan F 145 A4
Lanneuville-sur-Meuse F 91 B5
Lannilis F 100 A1
Lannion F 100 A2
La Nocle-Maulaix F 104 C2
Lanouaille F 115 C5
Lansjärv S 196 C5
Lanškroun CZ 97 B4
Lanslebourg-Mont-Cenis F 119 B3
Lanta F 129 C4
Lantadilla E 142 B2
Lanton F 128 B1
Lantosque F 133 B3
La Nuez de Arriba E 143 B3
Lanusei I 179 C3
Lanúvio I 168 B2
Lanvollon F 100 A3
Lánycsók H 125 A4
Lanz D 73 A4
Lanza E 140 A2
Lanzada E 140 B2
Lanzahita E 150 B3
Lanžhot CZ 97 C4
Lanzo Torinese I 119 B4
Laole SRB 127 C3
Laon F 91 B3
Laons F 89 B5
La Paca E 164 B3
La Pacaudière F 117 A3
Lapalisse F 117 A3
La Palma d'Ebre E 153 A4
La Palma del Condado E 161 B3
La Palme F 146 B4
La Palmyre F 114 C2
La Parra E 155 C4
Łapczyna Wola PL 87 B3
La Pedraja de Portillo E 150 A3
La Peraleja E 152 B1
La Petit-Pierre F 93 C3
Lapeyrade F 128 B2
Lapeyrouse F 116 A2
Lapford GB 42 B3
La Pinilla E 165 B3
Lapithos CY 181 A2
La Plagne F 118 B3
La Plaza E 141 A4
Laplume F 129 B3
La Pobla de Lillet E 147 B2
La Pobla de Vallbona E 159 B3
La Pobla Llarga E 159 B3
La Pola de Gordón E 142 B1
la Porta F 180 A2
La Pouëze F 102 B1
Lapoutroie F 106 A2
La Póveda de Soria E 143 B4
Lapovo SRB 127 C3
Läppe S 56 A1
Lappeenranta FIN 8 B6
Lappoluobbal N 192 C7
Lappträsk S 196 C6
La Preste F 146 B3
La Primaube F 130 A1
Lapseki TR 186 B1
Lapua FIN 8 A3
La Puebla de Almoradie E 157 A4
La Puebla de Cazalla E 162 A2
La Puebla de los Infantes E 162 A2
La Puebla del Río E 162 A1
La Puebla de Montalbán E 150 C3
La Puebla de Roda E 145 B4
La Puebla de Valdavia E 142 B2
La Puebla de Valverde E 152 B3
La Pueblanueva E 150 C3
La Puerta de Segura E 164 A2
La Punt CH 107 C4
L'Áquila I 169 A3
La Quintana E 162 A3
La Quintera E 162 A2
La Rábita
*Granada* E 164 C1
*Jaén* E 163 A3
Laracha E 140 A2
Laragh IRL 30 A2
Laragne-Montéglin F 132 A1
La Rambla E 163 A3
l'Arboç E 147 C2
L'Arbresle F 117 B4
Lärbro S 57 C4
Larceveau F 144 A2
Larche
*Alpes-de-Haute-Provence* F 132 A2
*Corrèze* F 129 A4
Lårdal N 53 A4
Lærdalsøyri N 47 A4
Lardosa P 155 B3
La Reale I 178 A2
Laredo E 143 A3
La Redondela E 161 B2
La Réole F 128 B2
Largentière F 131 A3
L'Argentière-la-Bessée F 118 C3
Largs GB 34 C3
Lari I 134 B3
La Riera E 141 A4
La Riera de Gaià E 147 C2
La Rinconada E 162 A1
Lariño E 140 B1
Larino I 170 B2
Larisa GR 182 D4
La Rivière-Thibouville F 89 A4
Larkhall GB 36 A3
Larkollen N 54 A1
Larmor-Plage F 100 B2
Larnaca CY 181 B2
Larne GB 27 B5
La Robla E 142 B1
La Roca de la Sierra E 155 B4
La Roche CH 106 C2
La Rochebeaucourtet-Argentine F 115 C4
La Roche-Bernard F 101 B3
La Roche-Canillac F 116 B1
La Roche-Chalais F 128 A3
La Roche Derrien F 100 A2
La Roche-des-Arnauds F 132 A1
La Roche-en-Ardenne B 80 B1
La Roche-en-Brénil F 104 B3
La Rochefoucauld F 115 C4
La Roche-Guyon F 90 B1
La Rochelle F 114 B2
La Roche-Posay F 115 B4
La Roche-sur-Foron F 118 A3
La Roche-sur-Yon F 114 B2
Larochette L 92 B2
La Rochette F 131 A4
La Roda
*Albacete* E 158 B1
*Oviedo* E 141 A4
La Roda de Andalucía E 162 A3
Laroquebrou F 116 C2
La Roquebrussanne F 132 B1
Laroque d'Olmes F 146 B2
La Roque-Gageac F 129 B4
La Roque-Ste Marguerite F 130 A2
Laroque-Timbaut F 129 B3
Larouco E 141 B3
Larraga E 144 B2
Larrau F 144 A3
Larrazet F 129 C4
Larsnes N 198 C2
La Rubia E 143 C4
Laruns F 145 A3
Larva E 164 B1
Larvik N 53 A6
La Sagrada E 149 B3
La Salceda E 151 A4
Lasalle F 131 A2
La Salle F 118 C3
la Salute di Livenza I 122 B1
La Salvetat-Peyralés F 130 A1
La Salvetat-sur-Agout F 130 B1
Las Arenas E 142 A2
La Sarraz CH 105 C5
Lasarte E 144 A1
Låsby DK 59 B2
Las Cabezadas E 151 A4
Las Cabezas de San Juan E 162 B2
Las Correderas E 157 B4
Las Cuevas de Cañart E 153 B3
La Seca E 150 A3
La Selva del Camp E 147 C2
La Senia E 153 B4
La Serra E 147 C2
La Seu d'Urgell E 146 B2
La Seyne-sur-Mer F 132 B1
Las Gabias E 163 A4
Las Herencias E 150 C3
Las Herrerias E 161 B2
Łasin PL 69 B4
Lask PL 86 A3
Laska PL 68 B2
Łaskarzow PL 87 A5
Laško SLO 123 A4
Laskowice PL 76 A3
Las Labores E 157 A4
Las Mesas E 158 B1
Las Minas E 164 A3
Las Navas E 163 A3
Las Navas de la Concepción E 156 C2
Las Navas del Marqués E 150 B3
Las Navillas E 157 A3
Las Negras E 164 C3

La Solana E 157 B4
La Souterraine F 116 A1
Las Pajanosas E 161 B3
Laspaules E 145 B4
Las Pedroñas E 158 B1
La Spézia I 134 A2
Las Planes d'Hostoles E 147 B3
Laspuña E 145 B4
Las Rozas
*Cantabria* E 142 B2
*Madrid* E 151 B4
Lassan D 66 C2
Lassay-les-Châteaux F 89 B3
Lasseube F 145 A3
Lassigny F 90 B2
La Storta I 168 B2
Lastovo HR 138 C2
Lastras de Cuéllar E 151 A3
Lästringe S 56 B3
Lastrup D 71 B4
Las Uces E 149 A3
La Suze-sur-Sarthe F 102 B2
Las Veguillas E 149 B4
Las Ventas con Peña Aguilera E 157 A3
Las Ventas de San Julián E 150 B2
Las Villes E 153 B4
Latasa E 144 B2
Látera I 168 A1
Laterza I 171 C4
La Teste F 128 B1
Lathen D 71 B4
Latheron GB 32 C3
La Thuile I 119 B3
Latiano I 173 B3
Latina I 169 B2
Latisana I 122 B2
Látky SK 99 C3
La Toba E 152 B2
La Toledana E 157 A3
La Torre de Cabdella E 146 B1
La Torre de Esteban Hambrán E 151 B3
La Torre del l'Espanyol E 153 A4
La Torresaviñán E 152 B1
La Tour d'Aigues F 132 B1
La Tour de Peilz CH 106 C1
La Tour-du-Pin F 118 B2
La Tranche-sur-Mer F 114 B2
La Tremblade F 114 C2
La Trimouille F 115 B5
La Trinité F 100 B2
La Trinité-Porhoët F 101 A3
Latrónico I 174 A2
Latronquière F 116 C2
Latterbach CH 106 C2
La Turballe F 101 B3
Laubach D 81 B4
Laubert F 117 C3
Laucha D 83 A3
Lauchhammer D 84 A1
Lauchheim D 94 C2
Lauda-Königshofen D 94 B1
Laudal N 52 B3
Lauder GB 35 C5
Lauenau D 72 B2
Lauenburg D 73 A3
Lauf D 95 B3
Laufach D 94 A1
Laufen
CH 106 B2
D 109 B3
Lauffen D 93 B5
Laugar IS 191 B8
Laugarás IS 190 C5
Laugarbakki IS 190 B5
Laugarvatn IS 190 C5
Laugharne GB 39 C2
Lauingen D 94 C2
Laujar de Andarax E 164 C2
Laukaa FIN 8 A4
Lauker S 196 D2
Laukvik N 194 C5
La Uña E 142 A1
Launceston GB 42 B2
La Unión E 165 B4
Launois-sur-Vence F 91 B4
Laupheim D 94 C1
Lauragh IRL 29 C2
Laureana di Borrello I 175 C2
Laurencekirk GB 35 B5
Laurencetown IRL 28 A3
Laurenzana I 172 B1
Lauria I 174 A1
Laurière F 116 A1
Laurieston GB 36 B2
Laurino I 172 B1
Lausanne CH 106 C1
Laussonne F 117 C4
Lauta D 84 A2
Lautenthal D 82 A2
Lauterach A 107 B4
Lauterbach D 81 B5
Lauterbrunnen CH 106 C2
Lauterecken D 93 B3
Lauterhofen D 95 B3
Lautrec F 130 B1
Lauvsnes N 199 A7
Lauvvlk N 52 B2
Lauzerte F 129 B4
Lauzès F 129 B4
Lauzun F 129 B3
Lavagna I 134 A2
Laval F 102 A1
La Vall d'Uixó E 159 B3
Lavamünd A 110 C1
Lavara GR 186 A1
Lavardac F 129 B3
Lavaris P 148 B1
Lavarone I 121 B4
Lavau F 104 B1
Lavaur F 129 C4
La Vecilla de Curueño E 142 B1
La Vega
*Asturias* E 141 A5
*Asturias* E 142 A1
*Cantabria* E 142 A2
Lavelanet F 146 B2
La Velilla E 151 A4
La Velles E 150 A2
Lavello I 172 A1
Lavelsloh D 72 B1
Lavenham GB 45 A4
Laveno I 120 B1
La Ventosa E 152 B1
Lavezzola I 135 A4
Laviano I 172 B1
La Victoria E 162 A3
La Vid E 151 A4
Lavik N 46 A2
La Vilavella E 159 B3
La Vilella Baixa E 147 C1
La Villa de Don Fadrique E 157 A4
Lavilledieu F 131 A3
La Villedieu F 115 B3
La Ville Dieu-du-Temple F 129 B4
Lavinio-Lido di Enea I 168 B2
Lav is I 121 A4
Lavit F 129 C3
Lavoncourt F 105 B4
Lavos P 148 B1
La Voulte-sur-Rhône F 117 C4
Lavoûte-Chilhac F 117 B3
Lavradio P 154 C1
Lavre P 154 C2
Lavrio GR 185 B5
La Wantzenau F 93 C3
Lawers GB 35 B3
Ławy PL 75 B3
Laxå S 55 B5
Laxamýri IS 191 B8
Laxe E 140 A2
Laxey GB 36 B2
Laxford Bridge GB 32 C1
Laxhall S 55 B4
Laxsjö S 199 B11
Laxtjarn S 49 B6
Laxvik S 61 C2
Laxviken S 199 B11
La Yesa E 159 B3
Laza E 141 B3
Lazarevac SRB 127 C2
Lazarevo SRB 126 B2
Lazise I 121 B3
Łaziska Grn. PL 86 B2
Lazkao E 144 A1
Lázně Bělohrad CZ 84 B3
Lázně Bohdaneč CZ 97 A3
Lázně Kynžvart CZ 95 A4
Lazonby GB 37 B4
La Zubia E 163 A4
Łazy PL 67 B5
Lazzaro I 175 D1
Lea GB 40 B3
Leadburn GB 35 C4
Leadhills GB 36 A3
Leap IRL 29 C2
Leatherhead GB 44 B3
Łeba PL 68 A2
Lebach D 92 B2
Le Barp F 128 B2
Le Bar-sur-Loup F 132 B2
Le Béage F 117 C4
Le Beausset F 132 B1
Lebekke B 79 A4
Lébény H 111 B4
Le Bessat F 117 B4
Le Blanc F 115 B5
Le Bleymard F 130 A2
Łebno PL 68 A3
Leboreiro E 140 B3
Lębork PL 68 A2
Le Boullay-Mivoye F 89 B5
Le Boulou F 146 B3
Le Bourg F 129 B4
Le Bourg-d'Oisans F 118 B3
Le Bourget-du-Lac F 118 B2
Le Bourgneuf-la-Forêt F 101 A5
Le Bousquet d'Orb F 130 B2
Le Brassus CH 105 C5
Le Breuil F 117 A3
Le Breuil-en-Auge F 89 A4
Lebrija E 162 B1
Lebring A 110 C2
Le Brusquet F 132 A2
Le Bry CH 106 C2
Le Bugue F 129 B3
Le Buisson F 129 B3
Lebus D 74 B3
Lebusa D 83 A5
Leca da Palmeira P 148 A1
Le Caloy F 128 C2
Le Cap d'Agde F 130 B2
Le Cateau Cambrésis F 91 A3
Le Caylar F 130 B2
Le Cayrol F 116 C2
Lecce I 173 B4
Lecco I 120 B2
Lécera E 153 A3
Lećevica HR 138 B2
Lech A 107 B5
Le Chambon-Feugerolles F 117 B4
Le Chambon-sur-Lignon F 117 B4
Le Château d'Oléron F 114 C2
Le Châtelard F 118 B3
Le Châtelet F 103 C4
Le Chatelet-en-Brie F 90 C2
Lechbruck D 108 B1
Lechena GR 184 B2
Le Chesne F 91 B4
Le Cheylard F 117 C4
Lechlade GB 44 B2
Lechovice CZ 97 C4
Leciñena E 145 C3
Leck D 64 B1
Le Collet-de-Deze F 131 A2
Le Conquet F 100 A1
Le Creusot F 104 C3
Le Croisic F 101 B3
Le Crotoy F 78 B1
Lectoure F 129 C3
Łęczyca
*Łódzkie* PL 77 B4
*Zachodnio-Pomorskie* PL 75 A4
Ledaña E 158 B2
Ledbury GB 39 B4
Lede B 79 B3
Ledečnad Sazavou CZ 97 B3
Ledenice CZ 96 C2
Le Deschaux F 105 C4
Ledesma E 149 A3
Lédignan F 131 B3
Lédigos E 142 B2
Ledmore GB 32 C2
Lednice CZ 97 C4
Lednicke-Rovné SK 98 B2
Le Donjon F 117 A3
Le Dorat F 115 B5
Lędyczek PL 68 B1
Lędziny PL 86 B3
Leeds GB 40 B2
Leek
GB 40 B1
NL 71 A3
Leenaun IRL 28 A2
Leens NL 71 A3
Leer D 71 A4
Leerdam NL 79 A5
Leerhafe D 71 A4
Leese D 72 B2
Leeuwarden NL 70 A2
Leezen D 64 C3
Le Faou F 100 A1
Le Faoüet F 100 A2
Lefka CY 181 A1
Lefkada GR 182 E2
Lefkimis GR 182 D2
Lefkoniko CY 181 A2
Le Folgoet F 100 A1
Le Fossat F 146 A2
Le Fousseret F 146 A2
Le Fugeret F 132 A2
Leganés E 151 B4
Legau D 107 B5
Le Gault-Soigny F 91 C3
Legbąd PL 68 B2
Legé F 114 B2
Lège-Cap-Ferret F 128 B1
Legionowo PL 77 B5
Léglise B 92 B1
Legnago I 121 B4
Legnano I 120 B1
Legnaro I 121 B4
Legnica PL 85 A4
Łęgowo PL 69 A3
Legrad HR 124 A2
Le Grand-Bornand F 118 B3
Le-Grand-Bourg F 116 A1
Le Grand-Lucé F 102 B2
Le Grand-Pressigny F 102 C2
Le Grand-Quevilly F 89 A5
Le Grau-du-Roi F 131 B3
Léguevin F 129 C4
Legutiano E 143 B4
Le Havre F 89 A4
Lehesten D 82 B3
Lehnice SK 111 A4
Lehnin D 74 B1
Le Hohwald F 93 C3
Le Houga F 128 C2
Lehrberg D 94 B2
Lehre D 73 B3
Lehrte D 72 B2
Lehsen D 73 A4
Leibnitz A 110 C2
Leicester GB 40 C2
Leiden NL 70 B1
Leidschendam NL 70 B1
Leigh GB 38 A4
Leighlinbridge IRL 30 B2
Leighton Buzzard GB 44 B3
Leignon B 79 B5
Leikanger N 198 C2
Leimen D 93 B4
Leinefelde D 82 A2
Leinesfjord N 194 C6
Leintwardine GB 39 B4
Leipojärvi S 196 B4
Leipzig D 83 A4
Leira
*Nordland* N 195 D4
*Oppland* N 47 B6
Leirámoen N 195 D5
Leiria P 154 B2
Leirvassbu N 47 A5
Leirvik
*Hordaland* N 52 A1
*Sogn og Fjordane* N 46 A2
Leisach A 109 C3
Leisnig D 83 A4
Leiston GB 45 A5
Leitholm GB 35 C5
Leitrim IRL 26 C2
Leitza E 144 A2
Leitzkau D 73 B4
Lejkowo PL 68 A1
Lekani GR 183 B6
Łękawa PL 86 A3
Łekawica PL 99 B3
Lekeitio E 143 A4
Lekenik HR 124 B2
Lekeryd S 62 A2
Leknes N 194 B4
Łęknica PL 84 A2
Leksand S 50 B1
Leksvik N 199 B7
Lekunberri E 144 A2
Lekvattnet S 49 B4
Le Lardin-St Lazare F 129 A4
Le Lauzet-Ubaye F 132 A2
Le Lavandou F 132 B2
Le Lion-d'Angers F 102 B1
Lelkowo PL 69 A5
Le Locle CH 106 B1
Le Loroux-Bottereau F 101 B4
Le Louroux-Béconnais F 101 B5
Lelów PL 86 B3
Le Luc F 132 B2
Le Lude F 102 B2
Lelystad NL 70 B2
Lem
*Ringkøbing* DK 59 B1
*Viborg Amt.* DK 58 B1
Le Malzieu-Ville F 116 C3
Le Mans F 102 A2
Le Mas-d'Azil F 146 A2
Le Massegros F 130 A2
Le Mayet-de-Montagne F 117 A3
Le May-sur-Evre F 101 B5
Lembach F 93 B3
Lemberg F 93 B3
Lembèye F 145 A3
Lemelerveld NL 71 B3
Le Mêle-sur-Sarthe F 89 B4
Le Ménil F 105 A5
Le Merlerault F 89 B4
Le Mesnil-sur-Oger F 91 C4
Lemförde D 71 B5
Lemgo D 72 B1
Le Miroir F 105 C4
Lemland FIN 51 B7
Lemmer NL 70 B2
Le Molay-Littry F 88 A3
Le Monastier-sur-Gazeille F 117 C3
Le Monêtier-les-Bains F 118 C3
Le Mont-Dore F 116 B2
Le Montet F 116 A3
Le Mont-St Michel F 88 B2
Lempdes F 116 B3
Le Muret F 128 B2
Le Muy F 132 B2
Lemvig DK 58 B1
Lemwerder D 72 A1
Lena N 48 B2
Lenart SLO 110 C2
Lenartovce SK 99 C4
Lenauheim RO 126 B2
Lencloître F 102 C2
Lend A 109 B4
Lendalfoot GB 36 A2
Lendava SLO 111 C3
Lendery RUS 3 E12
Lendinara I 121 B4
Lendorf A 109 C4
Lendum DK 58 A3
Le Neubourg F 89 A4
Lengefeld D 83 B5
Lengerich
*Niedersachsen* D 71 B4
*Nordrhein-Westfalen* D 71 B4
Lenggries D 108 B2
Lengyeltóti H 111 C4
Lenhovda S 62 B3
Lenk CH 106 C2
Lennartsfors S 54 A2
Lennestadt D 81 A4
Lennoxtown GB 35 C3
Leno I 120 B3
Lénola I 169 B3
Le Nouvion-en-Thiérache F 91 A3
Lens
B 79 B3
F 78 B2
Lensahn D 65 B3
Lens Lestang F 117 B5
Lensvik N 198 B6
Lentellais E 141 B3
Lentföhrden D 64 C2
Lenti H 111 C3
Lentini I 177 B3
Lenungshammar S 54 A3
Lenzburg CH 106 B3
Lenzen D 73 A4
Lenzerheide CH 107 C4
Leoben A 110 B2
Leogang A 109 B3
Leominster GB 39 B4
León E 142 B1
Léon F 128 C1
Leonberg D 93 C5
Léoncel F 118 C2
Leonding A 96 C2
Leonessa I 169 A2
Leonforte I 177 B3
Leonidio GR 184 B3
Leopoldsburg B 79 A5
Leopoldsdorf im Marchfeld A 111 A3
Leopoldshagen D 74 A2
Leova MD 17 B8
Le Palais F 100 B2
Le Parcq F 78 B2
Lepe E 161 B2
Le Péage-de-Roussillon F 117 B4
Le Pellerin F 101 B4
Lepenou GR 182 E3
Le Perthus F 146 B3
Le Pertuis F 117 B4
Le Petit-Bornand F 118 B3
Lephin GB 31 B2
L'Epine F 132 A1
Le Poët F 132 A1
Lepoglava HR 124 A2
Le Poirè-sur-Vie F 114 B2
Le Pont CH 105 C5
Le Pont-de-Montvert F 130 A2
Le Porge F 128 B1
Le Porge-Océan F 128 B1
Le Portel F 78 B1
Le Pouldu F 100 B2
Le Pouliguen F 101 B3
Leppäjärvi FIN 192 D7
Leppävirta FIN 8 A5
Leppin D 73 B4
le Prese I 120 A3
Lepsény H 112 C2
Le Puy-en-Velay F 117 B3
Le Puy-Ste Réparade F 131 B4
Le Quesnoy F 79 B3
Léquile I 173 B4
Le Rayol F 132 B2
Lercara Friddi I 176 B2
Lerdal S 54 B2
Leré F 103 B4
Lérici I 134 A2
Lerin E 144 B2
Lerma E 143 B3
Lerm-et-Musset F 128 B2
Lermoos A 108 B1
Le Roeulx B 79 B4
Le Rouget F 116 C2
Lérouville F 92 C1
Le Rozier F 130 A2
Lerum S 60 B2
Le Russey F 106 B1
Lervik N 54 A1
Lerwick GB 33 A5
Lés E 145 B4
Les Abrets F 118 B2
Les Aix-d'Angillon F 103 B4
Lesaka E 144 A2
Les Ancizes-Comps F 116 B2
Les Andelys F 90 B1
Les Arcs
*Savoie* F 119 B3
*Var* F 132 B2
Les-Aubiers F 102 C1
Les Baux-de-Provence F 131 B3
Les Bézards F 103 B4
Les Bois CH 106 B1
Les Bordes F 103 B4
Les Borges Blanques E 147 C1
Les Borges del Camp E 147 C2
Les Brunettes F 104 C2
Lesbury GB 37 A5
Les Cabannes F 146 B2
L'Escala E 147 B4
Lescar F 145 A3
L'Escarène F 133 B3
Lesce SLO 123 A3
Lescheraines F 118 B3
Lesconil F 100 B1
Les Contamines-Montjoie F 118 B3
les Coves de Vinroma E 153 B4
Les Déserts F 118 B2
Les Deux-Alpes F 118 C3
Les Diablerets CH 119 A4
Lesdins F 90 B3
Les Echelles F 118 B2
Le Sel-de-Bretagne F 101 B4
Le Sentier CH 105 C5
Les Escaldes AND 146 B2
Les Essarts F 114 B2
Les Estables F 117 C4
Les Eyzies-de-Tayac F 129 B4
Les Gets F 118 A3
Les Grandes-Ventes F 89 A5
Les Haudères CH 119 A4
Les Herbiers F 114 B2
Les Hôpitaux-Neufs F 105 C5
Lesično SLO 123 A4
Lésina I 171 B3
Lesjaskog N 198 C5
Lesjöfors S 49 C6
Leskovac SRB 16 D4
Leskova Dolina SLO 123 B3
Leskovec
CZ 98 B1
SLO 123 B4
Leskovice CZ 97 B3
Leskovik AL 182 C2
Leslie GB 35 B4
Les Lucs-sur-Boulogne F 114 B2
Les Mages F 131 A3
Lesmahagow GB 36 A3
Les Mazures F 91 B4
Les Mées F 132 A1
Lesmont F 91 C4
Les Mureaux F 90 C1
Leśna PL 84 A3
Lesneven F 100 A1
Leśnica PL 86 B2
Lešnica SRB 127 C1
Leśniów Wielkoplski PL 75 C4
Lesnoye RUS 9 C9
Les Omergues F 132 A1
Les Ormes-sur-Voulzie F 90 C3
Les Orres F 132 A2
Le Souquet F 128 C1
Lesparre-Médoc F 128 A2
l'Espérance F 91 B3
l'Esperou F 130 A2
Les Pieux F 88 A2
Lesponne F 145 A4
Les Ponts-de-Cé F 102 B1
Les Ponts-de-Martel CH 106 C1
Les Praz F 119 B3
L'Espunyola E 147 B2
Les Riceys F 104 B3
Les Roches F 117 B4
Les Rosaires F 101 A3
Les Rosiers F 102 B1
Les Rousses F 105 C5
Les Sables-d'Olonne F 114 B2
Lessach A 109 B4
Lessay F 88 A2
Lessebo S 62 B3
Les Settons F 104 B3
Lessines B 79 B3
L'Estany E 147 C3
Les Ternes F 116 B2
Lesterps F 115 B4
Les Thilliers en-Vexin F 90 B1
Les Touches F 101 B4
Les Trois Moûtiers F 102 B2
Les Vans F 131 A3
Les Verrières CH 105 C5
Les Vignes F 130 A2
Leswalt GB 36 B1
Leszno
*Mazowieckie* PL 77 B5
*Wielkopolskie* PL 85 A4
Leszno Górne PL 84 A3
Letchworth GB 44 B3
Le Teil F 131 A3
Le Teilleul F 88 B3
Le Temple-de-Bretagne F 101 B4
Letenye H 111 C3
Le Theil F 89 B4
Le Thillot F 106 B1
Letino I 170 B2
Letohrad CZ 97 A4

Le Touquet-Paris-Plage F 78 B1
Le Touvet F 118 B2
Letovice CZ 97 B4
Le Translay F 90 B1
Le Tréport F 90 A1
Letschin D 74 B3
Letterfrack IRL 28 A2
Letterkenny IRL 26 B3
Lettermacaward IRL 26 B2
Lettoch GB 32 D3
Letur E 164 A2
Letux E 153 A3
Letzlingen D 73 B4
Leucate F 146 B4
Leuchars GB 35 B5
Leuglay F 105 B3
Leuk CH 119 A4
Leukerbad CH 119 A4
Leumrabhagh GB 31 A2
Leuna D 83 A4
Leusden NL 70 B2
Leutenberg D 82 B3
Leuterschach D 108 B1
Leutershausen D 94 B2
Leutkirch D 107 B5
Leuven B 79 B4
Leuze-en-Hainaut B 79 B3
Le Val F 132 B2
Le Val-André F 101 A3
Le Val-d'Ajol F 105 B5
Levan AL 182 C1
Levanger N 199 B8
Levanjska Varoš HR 125 B4
Lévanto I 134 A2
Levaré F 88 B3
Levata I 120 B3
Leveld N 47 B5
Leven
  *East Yorkshire* GB 41 B3
  *Fife* GB 35 B5
Leverano I 173 B3
Le Verdon-sur-Mer F 114 C2
Leverkusen D 80 A2
Levern D 72 B1
Le Vernet F 132 A2
Levet F 103 C4
Levice SK 112 A2
Lévico Terme I 121 A4
Levie F 180 B2
Levier F 105 C5
Le Vigan F 130 B2
Lévignen F 90 B2
le Ville I 135 B5
Levinovac HR 124 B3
Le Vivier-sur-Mer F 88 B2
Levoča SK 99 B4
Levroux F 103 C3
Lewes GB 45 C4
Lewin Brzeski PL 85 B5
Lewisham GB 44 B3
Leyburn GB 37 B5
Leyland GB 38 A4
Leysdown-on-Sea GB 45 B4
Leysin CH 119 A4
Lezajsk PL 12 C5
Lézardrieux F 100 A2
Lézat-sur-Léze F 146 A2
Lezay F 115 B3
Lezhë AL 182 B1
Lézignan-Corbières F 130 B1
Lezignan-la-Cèbe F 130 B2
Ležimir SRB 126 B1
Lézinnes F 104 B3
Lezoux F 117 B3
Lezuza E 158 C1
Lhenice CZ 96 C2
Lherm F 146 A2
Lhommaizé F 115 B4
L'Hospitalet F 146 B2
L'Hospitalet de l'Infant E 147 D1
L'Hospitalet de Llobregat E 147 C3
L'Hospitalet-du-Larzac F 130 B2
Lhuître F 91 C4
Liancourt F 90 B2
Liart F 91 B4
Liatorp S 63 B2
Liatrie GB 32 D2
Libáň CZ 84 B3
Libceves CZ 84 B1
Liběchov CZ 84 B2
Liber E 141 B3
Liberec CZ 84 B3
Libiąż PL 86 B3
Libina CZ 98 B1
Libochovice CZ 84 B2
Libohovë AL 182 C2
Libourne F 128 B2
Libramont B 92 B1
Librazhd AL 182 B2
Librilla E 165 B3
Libros E 152 B2
Licata I 176 B2
Licciana Nardi I 134 A3
Licenza I 169 A2
Liceros E 151 A4
Lich D 81 B4
Lichères-près-Aigremont F 104 B2
Lichfield GB 40 C2
Lichtenau
  A 97 C3
  D 81 A4
Lichtenberg D 83 B3
Lichtenfels D 82 B3
Lichtensteig CH 107 B4
Lichtenstein D 83 B4
Lichtenvoorde NL 71 C3
Lichtervelde B 78 A3
Lička Jesenica HR 123 B4
Lickershamn S 57 C4
Lički Osik HR 123 C4
Ličko Lešce HR 123 C4
Licodía Eubéa I 177 B3
Licques F 78 B1
Lida BY 13 B6
Lidar N 47 A6
Lidečko CZ 98 B2
Liden S 200 D2
Lidhult S 60 C3
Lidköping S 55 B4
Lido I 122 B1
Lido Azzurro I 173 B3
Lido degli Estensi I 122 C1
Lido degli Scacchi I 122 C1
Lido della Nazioni I 122 C1
Lido di Camaiore I 134 B3
Lido di Casalbordino I 169 A4
Lido di Castél Fusano I 168 B2
Lido di Cincinnato I 168 B2
Lido di Classe I 135 A5
Lido di Fermo I 136 B2
Lido di Fondi I 169 B3
Lido di Jésolo I 122 B1
Lido di Licola I 170 C2
Lido di Metaponto I 174 A2
Lido di Óstia I 168 B2
Lido di Policoro I 174 A2
Lido di Pomposa I 122 C1
Lido di Savio I 135 A5
Lido di Scanzano I 174 A2
Lido di Siponto I 171 B3
Lido di Squillace I 175 C2
Lido di Volano I 122 C1
Lido Riccio I 169 A4
Lidoriki GR 184 A3
Lido Silvana I 173 B3
Lidsjöberg S 199 A12
Lidzbark PL 77 A4
Lidzbark Warmiński PL 69 A5
Liebenau
  A 96 C2
  D 72 B2
Liebenwalde D 74 B2
Lieberose D 74 C3
Liebling RO 126 B3
Lieboch A 110 C2
Liège B 80 B1
Lieksa FIN 3 E12
Lienen D 71 B4
Lienz A 109 C3
Liepāja LV 8 D2
Lier B 79 A4
Lierbyen N 54 A1
Liernais F 104 B3
Liesing A 109 C3
Liestal CH 106 B2
Liétor E 158 C2
Lieurac F 146 B2
Lieurey F 89 A4
Liévin F 78 B2
Liezen A 110 B1
Liffol-le-Grand F 92 C1
Lifford IRL 27 B3
Liffré F 101 A4
Ligardes F 129 B3
Lignano Sabbiadoro I 122 B2
Ligne F 101 B4
Lignières F 103 C4
Ligny-en-Barrois F 92 C1
Ligny-le-Châtel F 104 B2
Ligoła Polska PL 85 A5
Ligourio GR 184 B4
Ligowo PL 77 B4
Ligueil F 102 B2
Likavka SK 99 B3
Likenäs S 49 B5
Likhoslavl RUS 9 D9
Lild Strand DK 58 A1
L'Île-Bouchard F 102 B2
l'Île-Rousse F 180 A1
Lilienfeld A 110 A2
Lilienthal D 72 A1
Lilla Edet S 54 B3
Lilla Tjärby S 61 C3
Lille
  B 79 A4
  F 78 B3
Lillebonne F 89 A4
Lillehammer N 48 A2
Lillerød DK 61 D2
Lillers F 78 B2
Lillesand N 53 B4
Lillestrøm N 48 C3
Lillhärdal S 199 D11
Lillkyrka S 56 A3
Lillo E 157 A4
Lillögda S 200 B3
Lillpite S 196 D4
Lima S 49 B5
Limanowa PL 99 B4
Limassol CY 181 B2
Limavady GB 27 A4
Limbach-Oberfrohna D 83 B4
Limbaži LV 8 D4
Limbourg B 80 B1
Limburg D 81 B4
Lime DK 58 B3
Limedsforsen S 49 B5
Limenaria GR 183 C6
Limenas Chersonisou GR 185 D6
Limerick IRL 29 B3
Limes I 121 B3
Limésy F 89 A4
Limmared S 60 B3
Limni GR 183 E5
Limoges F 115 C5
Limogne-en-Quercy F 129 B4
Limoise F 104 C2
Limone Piemonte I 133 A3
Limone sul Garda I 121 B3
Limons F 117 B3
Limours F 90 C2
Limoux F 146 A3
Linares E 157 B4
Linares de Mora E 153 B3
Linares de Riofrio E 149 B4
Linaria GR 183 E6
Linas de Broto E 145 B3
Lincoln GB 40 B3
Lind DK 59 B1
Lindås N 46 B2
Lindau D 107 B4
Lindberget N 48 A3
Lindelse DK 65 B3
Lindenberg D 74 B3
Lindenberg im Allgäu D 107 B4
Lindern D 71 B4
Linderöd S 61 D3
Lindesberg S 56 A1
Lindesnäs S 50 B1
Lindesnes N 52 C3
Lindholmen S 57 A4
Lindknud DK 59 C2
Lindlar D 80 A3
Lindö S 56 B2
Lindome S 60 B2
Lindos GR 188 C3
Lindoso P 148 A1
Lindow D 74 B1
Lindsdal S 62 B4
Lindshammar S 62 A3
Lindstedt D 73 B4
Lindved DK 59 C2
Líně CZ 96 B1
Lingbo S 50 A3
Lingen D 71 B4
Linghed S 50 B2
Linghem S 56 B1
Linguaglossa I 177 B4
Linia PL 68 A2
Linie PL 74 A3
Liniewo PL 68 A3
Linkenheim D 93 B4
Linköping S 56 B1
Linksness GB 33 C3
Linlithgow GB 35 C4
Linneryd S 63 B3
Linnes Hammarby S 51 C4
Linnich D 80 B2
Linsell S 199 C10
Linslade GB 44 B3
Linthal CH 107 C4
Linyola E 147 C1
Linz
  A 96 C2
  D 80 B3
Liomseter N 47 A6
Lionárisso CY 181 A3
Lioni I 172 B1
Lion-sur-Mer F 89 A3
Lipany SK 99 B4
Lipar SRB 126 B1
Lipari I 177 A3
Lipcani MD 17 A7
Liperi FIN 9 A6
Liphook GB 44 B3
Lipiany PL 75 A3
Lipik HR 124 B3
Lipka PL 68 B2
Lipki Wielkie PL 75 B4
Lipnica PL 68 B2
Lipnica Murowana PL 99 B4
Lipnik PL 87 B5
Lipník nad Bečvou CZ 98 B1
Lipno
  *Kujawsko-Pomorskie* PL 77 B4
  *Łódzkie* PL 86 A2
Liposthey F 128 B2
Lipovac HR 125 B5
Lipovec CZ 97 B4
Lipovets UA 13 D8
Lipovljani HR 124 B2
Lipowiec PL 77 A6
Lipowina PL 69 A4
Lippborg D 81 A4
Lippó H 125 B4
Lippoldsberg D 81 A5
Lippstadt D 81 A4
Lipsko PL 87 A5
Liptál CZ 98 B1
Liptovská-Lúžna SK 99 C3
Liptovská Osada SK 99 C3
Liptovská-Teplička SK 99 C4
Liptovský Hrádok SK 99 B3
Liptovský Milkuláš SK 99 B3
Lipusz PL 68 A2
Lipůvka CZ 97 B4
Liré F 101 B4
Lisac BIH 139 A3
Lisbellaw GB 27 B3
Lisboa = Lisbon P 154 C1
Lisbon = Lisboa P 154 C1
Lisburn GB 27 B4
Liscannor IRL 28 B2
Lisdoonvarna IRL 28 A2
Lisewo PL 69 B3
Lisia Góra PL 87 B5
Lisięcice PL 86 B1
Lisieux F 89 A4
Lisjö S 56 A2
Liskeard GB 42 B2
L'Isle CH 105 C5
L'Isle-Adam F 90 B2
L'Isle-de-Noé F 129 C3
L'Isle-en-Dodon F 145 A4
L'Isle-Jourdain
  *Gers* F 129 C4
  *Vienne* F 115 B4
L'Isle-sur-la-Sorgue F 131 B4
L'Isle-sur-le Doubs F 105 B5
L'Isle-sur-Serein F 104 B3
Lisle-sur-Tarn F 129 C4
Lismore IRL 29 B4
Lisnaskea GB 27 B3
Lišov CZ 96 B2
Lisów
  *Lubuskie* PL 74 B3
  *Śląskie* PL 86 B2
Lisse NL 70 B1
Lissycasey IRL 28 B2
List D 64 A1
Listerby S 63 B3
Listowel IRL 29 B2
Listrac-Médoc F 128 A2
Liszki PL 99 A3
Liszkowo PL 76 A2
Lit S 199 B11
Litava SK 99 C3
Litcham GB 41 C4
Lit-et-Mixe F 128 B1
Litija SLO 123 A3
Litke H 112 A3
Litlabø N 52 A1
Litochoro GR 182 C4
Litoměřice CZ 84 B2
Litomyšl CZ 97 B4
Litovel CZ 98 B1
Litschau A 96 C3
Littlehampton GB 44 C3
Littleport GB 45 A4
Littleton IRL 29 B4
Little Walsingham GB 41 C4
Litvinov CZ 83 B5
Livadero GR 182 C3
Livadhia CY 181 B2
Livadi GR 182 C4
Livadia GR 184 A3
Livarot F 89 B4
Liveras CY 181 A1
Livernon F 129 B4
Liverovici MNE 139 C5
Liverpool GB 38 A4
Livigno I 107 C5
Livingston GB 35 C4
Livno BIH 138 B2
Livo FIN 197 D9
Livold SLO 123 B3
Livorno I 134 B3
Livorno Ferraris I 119 B5
Livron-sur-Drôme F 117 C4
Livry-Louvercy F 91 B4
Lixheim F 92 C3
Lixouri GR 184 A1
Lizard GB 42 C1
Lizy-sur-Ourcq F 90 B3
Lizzano I 173 B3
Lizzano in Belvedere I 135 A3
Ljig SRB 127 C2
Ljørdalen N 49 A4
Ljosland N 52 B3
Ljubija BIH 124 C2
Ljubinje BIH 139 C4
Ljubljana SLO 123 A3
Ljubno ob Savinji SLO 123 A3
Ljubovija SRB 127 C1
Ljubuški BIH 138 B3
Ljugarn S 57 C4
Ljung S 60 B3
Ljunga S 56 B2
Ljungaverk S 200 D2
Ljungby S 60 C3
Ljungbyhed S 61 C3
Ljungbyholm S 63 B4
Ljungdalen S 199 C9
Ljungsarp S 60 B3
Ljungsbro S 56 B1
Ljungskile S 54 B2
Ljusdal S 200 E2
Ljusfallshammar S 56 B1
Ljusne S 51 A4
Ljusterö S 57 A4
Ljutomer SLO 111 C3
Lŭki BG 183 B6
Lladurs E 147 B2
Llafranc E 147 C4
Llagostera E 147 C3
Llanaelhaiarn GB 38 B2
Llanarth GB 39 B2
Llanbedr GB 38 B2
Llanbedrog GB 38 B2
Llanberis GB 38 A2
Llanbister GB 39 B3
Llanbrynmair GB 39 B3
Llançà E 146 B4
Llandeilo GB 39 C3
Llandissilio GB 39 C2
Llandovery GB 39 C3
Llandrillo GB 38 B3
Llandrindod Wells GB 39 B3
Llandudec F 100 A1
Llandudno GB 38 A3
Llandysul GB 39 B2
Llanelli GB 39 C2
Llanerchymedd GB 38 A2
Llanes E 142 A2
Llanfair Caereinion GB 38 B3
Llanfairfechan GB 38 A3
Llanfyllin GB 38 B3
Llangadog GB 39 C3
Llangefni GB 38 A2
Llangollen GB 38 B3
Llangrannog GB 39 B2
Llangurig GB 39 B3
Llanidloes GB 39 B3
Llanilar GB 39 B2
Llanrhystud GB 39 B2
Llanrwst GB 38 A3
Llansannan GB 38 A3
Llansawel GB 39 B2
Llanstephan GB 39 C2
Llanteno E 143 A3
Llanthony GB 39 C3
Llantrisant GB 39 C3
Llantwit-Major GB 39 C3
Llanuwchllyn GB 38 B3
Llanwddyn GB 38 B3
Llanwrda GB 39 C3
Llanwrtyd Wells GB 39 B3
Llanybydder GB 39 B2
Llanymynech GB 38 B3
Llavorsi E 146 B2
Lleida E 153 A4
Llera E 156 B1
Llerena E 156 B1
Lles E 146 B2
Llessui E 146 B2
Llinars E 147 B2
Lliria E 159 B3
Llivia E 146 B2
Llodio E 143 A4
Lloret de Mar E 147 C3
Llosa de Ranes E 159 B3
Lloseta E 167 B2
Llucena del Cid E 153 B3
Llucmajor E 167 B2
Llutxent E 159 C3
Llwyngwril GB 38 B2
Llyswen GB 39 B3
Lnáře CZ 96 B1
Lniano PL 76 A3
Loanhead GB 35 C4
Loano I 133 A4
Loarre E 145 B3
Löbau D 84 A2
Löbejün D 83 A3
Löberöd S 61 D3
Łobez PL 75 A4
Löbnitz D 66 B1
Lobón E 155 C4
Loburg D 73 B5
Łobżenica PL 76 A2
Locana I 119 B4
Locarno CH 120 A1
Loccum D 72 B2
Loče SLO 123 A4
Lochailort GB 34 B2
Lochaline GB 34 B2
Lochans GB 36 B1
Locharbriggs GB 36 A3
Lochau A 107 B4
Loch Baghasdail GB 31 B1
Lochcarron GB 31 B3
Lochearnhead GB 34 B3
Lochem NL 71 B3
Loches F 102 B2
Lochgelly GB 35 B4
Lochgilphead GB 34 B2
Lochgoilhead GB 34 B3
Lochinver GB 32 C1
Loch nam Madadh GB 31 B1
Lochranza GB 34 C2
Ločika SRB 127 D3
Lockenhaus A 111 B3
Lockerbie GB 36 A3
Löcknitz D 74 A3
Locmaria F 100 B2
Locmariaquer F 100 B3
Locminé F 100 B3
Locorotondo I 173 B3
Locquirec F 100 A2
Locri I 175 C2
Locronan F 100 A1
Loctudy F 100 B1
Lodares de Osma E 151 A5
Lodé I 178 B3
Lodeinoye Pole RUS 9 B8
Lodève F 130 B2
Lodi I 120 B2
Løding N 194 C5
Lødingen N 194 B6
Lodosa E 144 B1
Lödöse S 54 B3
Łódź PL 86 A3
Loeches E 151 B4
Løfallstrand N 46 B3
Lofer A 109 B3
Lofsdalen S 199 C10
Loftahammar S 62 A4
Lofthus N 46 B3
Loftus GB 37 B6
Loga N 52 B2
Logatec SLO 123 B3
Lögdeå S 200 C5
Lograto I 120 B3
Logroño E 143 B4
Logrosán E 156 A2
Løgstør DK 58 B2
Løgumgårde DK 64 A1
Løgumkloster DK 64 A1
Lohals DK 65 A3
Lohiniva FIN 197 B8
Lohja FIN 8 B4
Löhlbach D 81 A4
Lohmen
  *Mecklenburg-Vorpommern* D 65 C5
  *Sachsen* D 84 B2
Löhnberg D 81 B4
Lohne D 71 B5
Löhne D 72 B1
Lohr D 94 B1
Lohra D 81 B4
Lohsa D 84 A2
Loiano I 135 A4
Loimaa FIN 8 B3
Lóiri I 178 B3
Loitz D 66 C2
Loivos P 148 A2
Loivos do Monte P 148 A2
Loja E 163 A3
Lojanice SRB 127 C1
Lojsta S 57 C4
Løjt Kirkeby DK 64 A2
Lok SK 112 A2
Lokca SK 99 B3
Løken N 54 A2
Lokeren B 79 A3
Loket CZ 83 B4
Lokka FIN 197 B10
Løkken
  DK 58 A2
  N 198 B6
Loknya RUS 9 D7
Lökösháza H 113 C5
Lokve SRB 126 B3
Lollar D 81 B4
L'Olleria E 159 C3
Lölling-Graben A 110 C1
Lom
  BG 17 D5
  N 198 D5
  SK 99 C3
Lombez F 146 A1
Lomello I 120 B1
Łomianki PL 77 B5
Lomma S 61 D3
Lommaryd S 62 A2
Lommatzsch D 83 A5
Lommel B 79 A5
Lommersum D 80 B2
Lomnice CZ 97 B4
Lomnice nad Lužnici CZ 96 B2
Lomnice-nad Popelkou CZ 84 B3
Lompolo FIN 196 A7
Łomza PL 12 B5
Lönashult S 63 B2
Lønborg DK 59 C1
Londerzeel B 79 A4
Londinières F 89 A5
London GB 44 B3
Lonevåg N 46 B2
Longa GR 184 C2
Longare I 121 B4
Longares E 152 A2
Longarone I 122 A1
Longastrino I 135 A5
Long Bennington GB 40 C3
Longbenton GB 37 A5
Longchamp-sur-Aujon F 105 A3
Longchaumois F 118 A2
Long Eaton GB 40 C2
Longeau F 105 B4
Longecourt-en-Plaine F 105 B4
Longeville-les-St Avold F 92 B2

Longeville-sur-Mer F 114 B2
Longford IRL 28 A4
Longframlington GB 37 A5
Longhope GB 33 C3
Longhorsley GB 37 A5
Longhoughton GB 37 A5
Longi I 177 A3
Long Melford GB 45 A4
Longny-au-Perche F 89 B4
Longobucco I 174 B2
Long Preston GB 40 A1
Longré F 115 B3
Longridge GB 38 A4
Longroiva P 149 B2
Long Sutton GB 41 C4
Longtown
*Cumbria* GB 36 A4
*Herefordshire* GB 39 C4
Longueau F 90 B2
Longué-Jumelles F 102 B1
Longuyon F 92 B1
Longvic F 105 B4
Longvilly B 92 A1
Longwy F 92 B1
Lonigo I 121 B4
Löningen D 71 B4
Lonja HR 124 B2
Lönneberga S 62 A3
Lönsboda S 63 B2
Lønset N 198 C6
Lons-le-Saunier F 105 C4
Lønstrup DK 58 A2
Looe GB 42 B2
Loone-Plage F 78 A2
Loon op Zand NL 79 A5
Loosdorf A 110 A2
Lo Pagán E 165 B4
Lopar HR 123 C3
Lopare BIH 125 C4
Lopera E 157 C3
Lopigna F 180 A1
Loppersum NL 71 A3
Łopuszna PL 99 B4
Łopuszno PL 87 B4
Lor F 91 B4
Lora N 198 C5
Lora de Estepa E 162 A3
Lora del Río E 162 A2
Loranca del Campo E 151 B5
Lorbé 140 A2
Lörby S 63 B2
Lorca E 164 B3
Lorch D 93 A3
Lørenfallet N 48 B3
Lørenskog N 48 C2
Loreo I 122 B1
Loreto I 136 B2
Lorgues F 132 B2
Lorica I 174 B2
Lorient F 100 B2
Lorignac F 114 C3
Lőrinci H 112 B3
Loriol-sur-Drôme F 117 C4
Lormes F 104 B2
Loro Ciuffenna I 135 B4
Lorqui E 165 A3
Lörrach D 106 B2
Lorrez-le-Bocage F 103 A4
Lorris F 103 B4
Lorup D 71 B4
Łoś PL 77 C5
Los S 199 D12
Losacino E 149 A3
Los Alcázares E 165 B4
Los Arcos E 144 B1
Losar de la Vera E 150 B2
Los Barios de Luna E 141 B5
Los Barrios E 162 B2
Los Caños de Meca E 162 B1
Los Cerricos E 164 B2
Los Corrales E 162 A3
Los Corrales de Buelna E 142 A2
Los Dolores E 165 B3
Losenstein A 110 B1
Los Gallardos E 164 B3
Losheim
*Nordrhein-Westfalen* D 80 B2
*Saarland* D 92 B2
Los Hinojosos E 158 B1
Los Isidros E 159 B2
Los Molinos E 151 B3
Los Morales E 162 A2
Los Navalmorales E 156 A3
Los Navalucillos E 156 A3
Losne F 105 B4
Los Nietos E 165 B4
Løsning DK 59 C2
Los Palacios y Villafranca E 162 A2
Los Pozuelos de Calatrava E 157 B3
Los Rábanos E 143 C4
Los Santos E 149 B4
Los Santos de la Humosa E 151 B4
Los Santos de Maimona E 155 C4
Lossburg D 93 C4
Losse F 128 B2
Losser NL 71 B4
Lossiemouth GB 32 D3
Lössnitz D 83 B4
Loštice CZ 97 B4
Los Tijos E 142 A2
Lostwithiel GB 42 B2
Los Villares E 163 A4
Los Yébenes E 157 A4
Løten N 48 B3
Lotorp S 56 B1
Lottefors S 50 A3
Löttorp S 62 A5
Lotyń PL 68 B1
Lotzorai I 179 C3
Louargat F 100 A2
Loudéac F 101 A3
Loudun F 102 B2
Loué F 102 B1
Loughborough GB 40 C2
Loughbrickland GB 27 B4
Loughrea IRL 28 A3
Louhans F 105 C4
Louisburgh IRL 28 A2
Loukhi RUS 3 C13
Loulay F 114 B3
Loulé P 160 B1
Louny CZ 84 B1
Lourdes F 145 A3
Lourenzá E 141 A3
Loures P 154 C1
Loures-Barousse F 145 A4
Louriçal P 154 A2
Lourinhã P 154 B1
Lourmarin F 131 B4
Loury F 103 B4
Lousa
*Bragança* P 149 A2
*Castelo Branco* P 155 B3
Lousã P 148 B1
Lousa P 154 C1
Lousada
E 140 B3
P 148 A1
Louth GB 41 B3
Loutra Edipsou GR 183 E5
Loutraki GR 184 B3
Loutropoli Thermis GR 186 C1
Louverné F 102 A1
Louvie-Juzon F 145 A3
Louviers F 89 A5
Louvigné-du-Désert F 88 B2
Louvois F 91 B4
Lova I 121 B5
Lovasberény H 112 B2
Lövåsen S 49 C5
Lovászpatona H 111 B4
Lövberga S 200 C1
Lovech BG 17 D6
Lövenich D 80 A2
Lóvere I 120 B3
Lövestad S 61 D3
Loviisa FIN 8 B5
Lovikka S 196 B5
Lovinobaňa SK 99 C3
Loviste HR 138 B3
Lovke HR 123 B3
Lovnäs S 49 A5
Lövö H 111 B3
Lovosice CZ 84 B2
Lovozero RUS 3 C14
Lovran HR 123 B3
Lovreć HR 138 B2
Lovrenc na Pohorju SLO 110 C2
Lovrin RO 126 B2
Lövstabruk S 51 B4
Löwenberg D 74 B2
Löwenstein D 94 B1
Lowestoft GB 41 C5
Lowick GB 37 A5
Łowicz PL 77 B4
Loxstedt D 72 A1
Loyew BY 13 C9
Lož SLO 123 B3
Loza CZ 96 B1
Łozina PL 85 A5
Loznica SRB 127 C1
Lozničko Polje SRB 127 C1
Lozorno SK 111 A4
Lozovik SRB 127 C3
Lozoya E 151 B4
Lozoyuela E 151 B4
Lozzo di Cadore I 109 C3
Luanco E 141 A5
Luarca E 141 A4
Lubaczów PL 13 C5
Lubań PL 84 A3
Lubanie PL 76 B3
Lubanów PL 86 A3
Lubars D 73 B5
Lubasz PL 75 B5
Lubawa PL 69 B4
Lubawka PL 85 B4
Lübbecke D 72 B1
Lübben D 74 C2
Lübbenau D 84 A1
Lubczyna PL 74 A3
Lübeck D 65 C3
Lubenec CZ 83 B5
Lubersac F 115 C5
Lübesse D 73 A4
Lubia E 152 A1
Lubian E 141 B4
Lubiatowo PL 75 A4
Lubichowo PL 69 B3
Lubicz Dolny PL 76 A3
Lubień PL 99 B3
Lubienia PL 87 A5
Lubień Kujawski PL 77 B4
Lubieszewo PL 75 A4
Lubin
*Dolnośląskie* PL 85 A4
*Zachodnio-Pomorskie* PL 67 C3
Lublin PL 12 C5
Lubliniec PL 86 B2
Lubmin D 66 B2
Lubniewice PL 75 B4
Lubochnia PL 87 A4
Lubomierz
*Dolnośląskie* PL 84 A3
*Małopolskie* PL 99 B4
Lubomino PL 69 A5
Luboń PL 76 B1
L'ubotín SK 99 B4
Lubowidz PL 77 A4
Łubowo
*Wielkopolskie* PL 76 B2
*Zachodnio-Pomorskie* PL 68 B1
Lubraniec PL 76 B3
Lubrin E 164 B2
Lubrza PL 85 B5
Lubsko PL 84 A2
Lübtheen D 73 A4
Lubuczewo PL 68 A2
Luby CZ 83 B4
Lübz D 73 A5
Luc F 117 C3
Lucainena de las Torres E 164 B2
Lucan IRL 30 A2
Lučani SRB 127 D2
Lúcar E 164 B2
Luçay-le-Mâle F 103 B3
Lucca I 134 B3
Lucciana F 180 A2
Lucé F 90 C1
Luče SLO 123 A3
Lucena
*Córdoba* E 163 A3
*Huelva* E 161 B3
Lucenay-les-Aix F 104 C2
Lucenay-l'Evêque F 104 B3
Luc-en-Diois F 118 C2
Lučenec SK 99 C3
Luceni E 144 C2
Lucens CH 106 C1
Lucera I 171 B3
Luceram F 133 B3
Lüchow D 73 B4
Luciana E 157 B3
Lucignano I 135 B4
Lucija SLO 122 B2
Lucka D 83 A4
Luckau D 84 A1
Luckenwalde D 74 B2
Lückstedt D 73 B4
Luco dei Marsi I 169 B3
Luçon F 114 B2
Luc-sur-Mer F 89 A3
Ludanice SK 98 C2
Ludbreg HR 124 A2
Lüdenscheid D 81 A3
Lüderitz D 73 B4
Lüdersdorf D 65 C3
Ludgershall GB 44 B2
Ludgo S 56 B3
Lüdinghausen D 80 A3
Ludlow GB 39 B4
Ludomy PL 75 B5
Ludvika S 50 B2
Ludweiler Warndt D 92 B2
Ludwigsburg D 94 C1
Ludwigsfelde D 74 B2
Ludwigshafen D 93 B4
Ludwigslust D 73 A4
Ludwigsstadt D 82 B3
Ludza LV 8 D5
Luesia E 144 B2
Luftkurort Arendsee D 73 B4
Lug
BIH 139 C4
HR 125 B4
Luga RUS 9 C6
Lugagnano Val d'Arda I 120 C2
Lugano CH 120 A1
Lugau D 83 B4
Lugnas S 55 B4
Lúgnola I 168 A2
Lugny F 105 C3
Lugo
E 140 A3
I 135 A4
Lugoj RO 16 C4
Lugones E 141 A5
Lugros E 163 A4
Luhačovice CZ 98 B1
Luhe D 95 B4
Luino I 120 B1
Luintra E 140 B3
Lújar E 163 B4
Luka nad Jihlavou CZ 97 B3
Lukavac BIH 125 C4
Lukavika BIH 125 C4
Lukovë AL 182 D1
Lukovica SLO 123 A3
Lukovit BG 17 D6
Lukovo HR 123 C3
Lukovo Šugorje HR 137 A4
Łuków PL 12 C5
Łukowice Brzeskie PL 85 B5
Luksefjell N 53 A5
Łukta PL 69 B5
Lula I 178 B3
Luleå S 196 D5
Lüleburgaz TR 186 A2
Lumbarda HR 138 C3
Lumbier E 144 B2
Lumbrales E 149 B3
Lumbreras E 143 B4
Lumbres F 78 B2
Lummelunda S 57 C4
Lummen B 79 B5
Lumparland FIN 51 B7
Lumpiaque E 152 A2
Lumsås DK 61 D1
Lumsden GB 33 D4
Lumsheden S 50 B3
Lun HR 123 C3
Luna E 144 B3
Lunamatrona I 179 C2
Lunano I 136 B1
Lunas F 130 B2
Lund
N 199 A8
*Skåne* S 61 D3
*Västra Götaland* S 54 A3
Lundamo N 199 B7
Lunde
DK 59 C1
*Sogn og Fjordane* N 46 A3
*Sogn og Fjordane* N 46 A3
*Telemark* N 53 A5
S 200 D3
Lundebyvollen N 49 B4
Lunden D 64 B2
Lunderseter N 49 B4
Lunderskov DK 59 C2
Lundsberg S 55 A5
Lüneburg D 72 A3
Lunel F 131 B3
Lünen D 81 A3
Lunéville F 92 C2
Lungern CH 106 C3
Lungro I 174 B2
Luninyets BY 13 B7
Lünne D 71 B4
Lunner N 48 B2
Lunteren NL 70 B2
Lunz am See A 110 B2
Luogosanto I 178 A3
Łupawa PL 68 A2
Lupión E 157 B4
Lupoglav HR 123 B3
Luppa D 83 A4
Luque E 163 A3
Lurago d'Erba I 120 B2
Lúras I 178 B3
Lurcy-Lévis F 104 C1
Lure F 105 B5
Lurgan GB 27 B4
Luri F 180 A2
Lury-sur-Arnon F 103 B4
Lušci Palanka BIH 124 C2
Lusévera I 122 A2
Lushnjë AL 182 C1
Lusignan F 115 B4
Lusigny-sur-Barse F 104 A3
Lusnić BIH 138 B2
Luso P 148 B1
Lusówko PL 75 B5
Luspebryggan S 196 B2
Luss GB 34 B3
Lussac F 128 B2
Lussac-les-Châteaux F 115 B4
Lussac-les-Eglises F 115 B5
Lussan F 131 A3
Lüssow D 65 C5
Lustenau A 107 B4
Luštěnice CZ 84 B2
Luster N 47 A4
Lutago I 108 C2
Lutherstadt Wittenberg D 83 A4
Lütjenburg D 65 B3
Lutnes N 49 A4
Lutocin PL 77 B4
Lutomiersk PL 86 A3
Luton GB 44 B3
Lutry CH 106 C1
Lutsk UA 13 C6
Lutter am Barenberge D 72 C3
Lutterworth GB 40 C2
Lututów PL 86 A2
Lützen D 83 A4
Lutzow D 73 A4
Luusua FIN 197 C10
Luvos S 196 C1
Luxembourg L 92 B2
Luxeuil-les-Bains F 105 B5
Luxey F 128 B2
Luz
*Évora* P 155 C3
Luz *continued*
*Faro* P 160 B1
*Faro* P 160 B2
Luzarches F 90 B2
Luže CZ 97 B4
Luzech F 129 B4
Luzern CH 106 B3
Luzino PL 68 A3
Luz-St Sauveur F 145 B3
Luzy F 104 C2
Luzzi I 174 B2
L'viv UA 13 D6
Lwówek PL 75 B5
Lwówek Śląski PL 84 A3
Lyakhavichy BY 13 B7
Lybster GB 32 C3
Lychen D 74 A2
Lychkova RUS 9 D8
Lyckeby S 63 B3
Lycksele S 200 B4
Lydd GB 45 C4
Lydford GB 42 B2
Lydney GB 39 C4
Lyepyel BY 13 A8
Lygna N 48 B2
Lykkja N 47 B5
Lykling N 52 A1
Lyme Regis GB 43 B4
Lymington GB 44 C2
Lympne GB 45 B5
Lyndhurst GB 44 C2
Lyneham GB 43 A5
Lyness GB 33 C3
Lyngdal
*Buskerud* N 47 C6
*Vest-Agder* N 52 B3
Lyngør N 53 B5
Lyngsa DK 58 A3
Lyngseidet N 192 C4
Lyngsnes N 199 A8
Lynmouth GB 42 A3
Lynton GB 42 A3
Lyntupy BY 13 A7
Lyon F 117 B4
Lyons-la-Forêt F 90 B1
Lyozna BY 13 A9
Lyrestad S 55 B5
Lysánad Labem CZ 84 B2
Lysápod Makytou SK 98 B2
Lysebotn N 52 A2
Lysekil S 54 B2
Lysice CZ 97 B4
Lysomice PL 76 A3
Lysøysund N 198 B6
Lyss CH 106 B2
Lystrup DK 59 B3
Lysvik S 49 B5
Łyszkowice PL 77 C4
Lytham St Anne's GB 38 A3
Lyuban RUS 9 C7
Lyubertsy RUS 9 E10
Lyubimets BG 183 B8
Lyuboml' UA 13 C6
Lyubytino RUS 9 C8


## M


Maaninkavaara FIN 197 C11
Maarheeze NL 80 A1
Maaseik B 80 A1
Maastricht NL 80 B1
Mablethorpe GB 41 B4
Mably F 117 A4
Macael E 164 B2
Maçanet de Cabrenys E 146 B3
Mação P 154 B2
Macau F 128 A2
Maccagno-Agra I 120 A1
Maccarese I 168 B2
Macchiagódena I 170 B2
Macclesfield GB 40 B1
Macduff GB 33 D4
Maceda E 140 B3
Macedo de Cavaleiros P 149 A3
Maceira
*Guarda* P 148 B2
*Leiria* P 154 B2
Macelj HR 124 A1
Macerata I 136 B2
Macerata Féltria I 136 B1
Machault F 91 B4
Machecoul F 114 B2
Mchowo PL 77 A5
Machrihanish GB 34 C2
Machynlleth GB 39 B3
Macieira P 148 A1
Maciejowice PL 87 A5
Macinaggio F 180 A2
Mackenrode D 82 A2
Mačkovci SLO 111 C3
Macomer I 178 B2
Macon B 91 A4
Mâcon F 117 A4
Macotera E 150 B2
Macroom IRL 29 C3
Macugnaga I 119 B4
Madan BG 183 B6
Madängsholm S 55 B4
Madaras H 126 A1
Maddaloni I 170 B2
Made NL 79 A4
Madeley GB 38 B4
Maderuelo E 151 A4
Madetkoski FIN 197 B9
Madley GB 39 B4
Madocsa H 112 C2
Madona LV 8 D5
Madonna di Campiglio I 121 A3
Madrid E 151 B4
Madridejos E 157 A4
Madrigal de las Altas Torres E 150 A2
Madrigal de la Vera E 150 B2
Madrigalejo E 156 A2
Madrigalejo de Monte E 143 B3
Madriguera E 151 A4
Madrigueras E 158 B2
Madroñera E 156 A2
Maël-Carhaix F 100 A2
Maella E 153 A4
Maello E 150 B3
Maesteg GB 39 C3
Mafra P 154 C1
Magacela E 156 B2
Magallon E 144 C2
Magaluf E 166 B2
Magán E 151 C4
Magaña E 144 C1
Magasa I 121 B3
Magaz E 142 C2
Magdeburg D 73 B4
Magenta I 120 B1
Magescq F 128 C1
Maghera GB 27 B4
Magherafelt GB 27 B4
Maghull GB 38 A4
Magilligan GB 27 A4
Magione I 135 B5
Magioto P 154 C1
Maglaj BIH 125 C4
Maglehem S 63 C2
Magliano de'Marsi I 169 A3
Magliano in Toscana I 168 A1
Magliano Sabina I 168 A2
Maglić SRB 126 B1
Máglie I 173 B4
Maglód H 112 B3
Magnac-Bourg F 115 C5
Magnac-Laval F 115 B5
Magnieres F 92 C2
Magnor N 49 C4
Magnuszew PL 87 A5
Magny-Cours F 104 C2
Magny-en-Vexin F 90 B1
Mágocs H 125 A4
Maguilla E 156 B2
Maguiresbridge GB 27 B3
Magyarbóly H 125 B4
Magyarkeszi H 112 C2
Magyarszék H 125 A4
Mahide E 141 C4
Mahilyow BY 13 B9
Mahmudiye TR 187 C5
Mahora E 158 B2
Mahovo HR 124 B2
Mähring D 95 B4
Maia
E 144 A2
P 148 A1
Maiaelrayo E 151 A4
Maials E 153 A4
Maîche F 106 B1
Máida I 175 C2
Maiden Bradley GB 43 A4
Maidenhead GB 44 B3
Maiden Newton GB 43 B4
Maidstone GB 45 B4
Maienfeld CH 107 B4
Maignelay Montigny F 90 B2
Maijanen FIN 197 B8
Maillezais F 114 B3
Mailly-le-Camp F 91 C4
Mailly-le-Château F 104 B2
Mainar E 152 A2
Mainbernheim D 94 B2
Mainburg D 95 C3
Mainhardt D 94 B1
Maintal D 81 B4
Maintenon F 90 C1
Mainvilliers F 90 C1
Mainz D 93 A4
Maiorca P 148 B1
Mairena de Aljarafe E 162 A1
Mairena del Alcor E 162 A2
Maisach D 108 A2
Maishofen A 109 B3
Maison-Rouge F 90 C3
Maissau A 97 C3
Maisse F 90 C2
Maizières-lès-Vic F 92 C2
Maja HR 124 B2
Majadahonda E 151 B4
Majadas E 150 C2
Majavatn N 195 E4
Majs H 125 B4
Majšperk SLO 123 A4
Makarska HR 138 B3
Makkum NL 70 A2

Maklár H 113 B4
Makó H 126 A2
Makoszyce PL 85 B5
Makov SK 98 B2
Mąkowarsko PL 76 A2
Maków Mazowiecki PL 77 B6
Maków Podhalański PL 99 B3
Makrakomi GR 182 E4
Maksniemi FIN 196 D7
Malá S 195 E9
Mala Bosna SRB 126 A1
Malacky SK 97 C5
Maladzyechna BY 13 A7
Málaga E 163 B3
Malagón E 157 A4
Malaguilla E 151 B4
Malahide IRL 30 A2
Mala Kladuša BIH 124 B1
Mala Krsna SRB 127 C3
Malalbergo I 121 C4
Malá Lehota SK 98 C2
Malanów PL 76 C3
Mala Pijace SRB 126 A1
Mala Subotica HR 124 A2
Malaucène F 131 A4
Malaunay F 89 A5
Malaya Vishera RUS 9 C8
Malborghetto I 109 C4
Malbork PL 69 A4
Malborn D 92 B2
Malbuisson F 105 C5
Malcésine I 121 B3
Malchin D 74 A1
Malching D 96 C1
Malchow D 73 A5
Malcocinado E 156 B2
Malczyce PL 85 A4
Maldegem B 79 A3
Maldon GB 45 B4
Małdyty PL 69 B4
Malè I 121 A3
Malemort F 129 A4
Malente D 65 B3
Måleräs S 62 B3
Males GR 185 D6
Malesherbes F 90 C2
Malesina GR 183 E5
Malestroit F 101 B3
Maletto I 177 B3
Malexander S 56 B1
Malgrat de Mar E 147 C3
Malhadas P 149 A3
Malia
CY 181 B1
GR 185 D6
Malicorne-sur-Sarthe F 102 B1
Malijai F 132 A2
Malildjoš SRB 126 B1
Målilla S 62 A3
Mali Lošinj HR 137 A3
Malin IRL 27 A3
Málinec SK 99 C3
Malingsbo S 50 C2
Maliniec PL 76 B3
Malinska HR 123 B3
Maliq AL 182 C2
Maljevac HR 123 B4
Malkara TR 186 B1
Małki PL 69 B4
Malko Tŭrnovo BG 17 D7
Mallaig GB 34 A2
Mallaranny IRL 28 A2
Mallemort F 131 B4
Mallén E 144 C2
Malléon F 146 A2
Mallersdorf-Pfaffenberg D 95 C4
Málles Venosta I 108 C1
Malling DK 59 B3
Mallnitz A 109 C4
Mallow IRL 29 B3
Mallwyd GB 38 B3
Malm N 199 A8
Malmbäck S 62 A2
Malmberget S 196 B3
Malmby S 56 A3
Malmédy B 80 B2
Malmesbury GB 43 A4
Malmköping S 56 A2
Malmö S 61 D3
Malmon S 54 B2
Malmslätt S 56 B1
Malnate I 120 B1
Malo I 121 B4
Małogoszcz PL 87 B4
Maloja CH 120 A2
Małomice PL 84 A3
Måløy N 198 D2
Malpartida E 155 B4
Malpartida de la Serena E 156 B2
Malpartida de Plasencia E 150 C1
Malpas
E 145 B4
GB 38 A4
Malpica P 155 B3
Malpica de Bergantiños E 140 A2
Malpica de Tajo E 150 C3
Malsch D 93 C4
Malšice CZ 96 B2
Malta A 109 C4
Maltat F 104 C2
Maltby GB 40 B2
Malung S 49 B5
Malungsfors S 49 B5
Maluszów PL 75 B4
Maluszyn PL 87 B3
Malva E 142 C1
Malvaglia CH 120 A1
Malveira P 154 C1
Malvik N 199 B7
Malyn UA 13 C8
Mamarrosa P 148 B1
Mamer L 92 B2
Mamers F 89 B4
Mamirolle F 105 B5
Mammendorf D 108 A2
Mámmola I 175 C2
Mamoiada I 178 B3
Mamonovo RUS 69 A4
Mamuras AL 182 B1
Maňa SK 112 A2
Manacor E 167 B3
Manavgat TR 189 C6
Mancera de Abajo E 150 B2
Mancha Real E 163 A4
Manchester GB 40 B1
Manching D 95 C3
Manchita E 156 B1
Manciano I 168 A1
Manciet F 128 C3
Mandal N 52 B3
Mandanici I 177 A4
Mándas I 179 C3
Mandatoriccio I 174 B2
Mandayona E 151 B5
Mandelieu-la-Napoule F 132 B2
Mandello del Lário I 120 B2
Mandelsloh D 72 B2
Manderfeld B 80 B2
Manderscheid D 80 B2
Mandino Selo BIH 138 B3
Mandoudi GR 183 E5
Mandra GR 185 A4
Mandraki GR 188 C2
Mandúria I 173 B3
Mane
*Alpes-de-Haute-Provence* F 132 B1
*Haute-Garonne* F 145 A4
Manérbio I 120 B3
Mañeru E 144 B2
Manetin CZ 96 B1
Manfredónia I 171 B3
Mangalia RO 17 D8
Manganeses de la Lampreana E 149 A4
Manganeses de la Polvorosa E 141 B5
Mangen N 48 C3
Manger N 46 B2
Mangiennes F 92 B1
Mangotsfield GB 43 A4
Mångsbodarna S 49 A5
Mangualde P 148 B2
Maniago I 122 A1
Manilva E 162 B2
Manisa TR 186 D2
Manises E 159 B3
Mank A 110 A2
Månkarbo S 51 B4
Manlleu E 147 C3
Manna DK 58 A2
Männedorf CH 107 B3
Mannersdorf am Leithagebirge A 111 B3
Mannheim D 93 B4
Manningtree GB 45 B5
Manoppello I 169 A4
Manorbier GB 39 C2
Manorhamilton IRL 26 B2
Manosque F 132 B1
Manowo PL 67 B5
Manresa E 147 C2
Månsarp S 62 A2
Månsåsen S 199 B11
Manschnow D 74 B3
Mansfeld D 82 A3
Mansfield GB 40 B2
Mansilla de Burgos E 143 B3
Mansilla de las Mulas E 142 B1
Manskog S 55 A3
Mansle F 115 C4
Manso F 180 A1
Manteigas P 148 B2
Mantel D 95 B4
Mantes-la-Jolie F 90 C1
Mantes-la-Ville F 90 C1
Manthelan F 102 B2
Mantorp S 56 B1
Mántova I 121 B3
Mänttä FIN 8 A4
Mäntyjärvi FIN 197 C10
Manuel E 159 B3
Manyas TR 186 B2
Manzanal de Arriba E 141 B4
Manzanares E 157 A4
Manzanares el Real E 151 B4
Manzaneda
*León* E 141 B4
*Orense* E 141 B3
Manzanedo E 143 B3
Manzaneque E 157 A4
Manzanera E 153 B3
Manzanilla E 161 B3
Manzat F 116 B2
Manziana I 168 A2
Manziat F 117 A4
Maó E 167 B4
Maoča BIH 125 C4
Maqueda E 150 B3
Mara E 152 A2
Maramaraereğlisi TR 186 B2
Maraña E 142 A1
Maranchón E 152 A1
Maranello I 135 A3
Marano I 170 C2
Marano Lagunare I 122 B2
Marans F 114 B2
Maratea I 174 B1
Marateca P 154 C2
Marathokambos GR 188 B1
Marathonas GR 185 A4
Marathóvouno CY 181 A2
Marazion GB 42 B1
Marbach
*Baden-Württemberg* D 94 C1
*Hessen* D 82 B1
F 92 C2
Marbäck S 60 B3
Mårbacka S 55 A4
Marbella E 162 B3
Marboz F 118 A2
Marburg D 81 B4
Marcali H 111 C4
Marčana HR 122 C2
Marcaria I 121 B3
Marcelová SK 112 B2
Marcenat F 116 B2
March GB 41 C4
Marchamalo E 151 B4
Marchaux F 105 B5
Marche-en-Famenne B 79 B5
Marchegg A 111 A3
Marchena E 162 A2
Marchenoir F 103 B3
Marcheprime F 128 B2
Marciac F 128 C3
Marciana Marina I 134 C3
Marcianise I 170 B2
Marcigny F 117 A4
Marcilla E 144 B2
Marcillac-la-Croisille F 116 B2
Marcillac-Vallon F 130 A1
Marcillat-en-Combraille F 116 A2
Marcille-sur-Seine F 91 C3
Marcilloles F 118 B2
Marcilly-le-Hayer F 91 C3
Marcinkowice PL 75 A5
Marciszów PL 85 B4
Marck F 78 B1
Marckolsheim F 106 A2
Marco de Canevezes P 148 A1
Mårdsele S 200 B5
Mårdsjö S 200 C1
Mareham le Fen GB 41 B3
Marek S 62 A3
Marennes F 114 C2
Maresquel F 78 B1
Mareuil F 115 C4
Mareuil-en-Brie F 91 C3
Mareuil-sur-Arnon F 103 C4
Mareuil-sur-Lay F 114 B2
Mareuil-sur-Ourcq F 90 B3
Margam GB 39 C3
Margariti GR 182 D2
Margate GB 45 B5
Margaux F 128 A2
Margerie-Hancourt F 91 C4
Margès F 117 B5
Margherita di Savóia I 171 B4
Margita SRB 126 B3
Margone I 119 B4
Margonin PL 76 B2
Marguerittes F 131 B3
Margut F 91 B5
Maria E 164 B2
Mariager DK 58 B2
Mariana E 152 B1
Maria Neustift A 110 B1
Mariannelund S 62 A3
Marianópoli I 176 B2
Mariánské Lázně CZ 95 B4
Mariapfarr A 109 B4
Maria Saal A 110 C1
Mariazell A 110 B2
Maribo DK 65 B4
Maribor SLO 110 C2
Marieberg S 56 A1
Mariefred S 56 A3
Mariehamn FIN 51 B6
Marieholm S 61 D3
Mariembourg B 91 A4
Marienbaum D 80 A2
Marienberg D 83 B5
Marienheide D 81 A3
Mariental D 73 B3
Mariestad S 55 B4
Marieux F 90 A2
Marigliano I 170 C2
Marignane F 131 B4
Marigny
*Jura* F 105 C4
*Manche* F 88 A2
Marigny-le-Châtel F 91 C3
Marija Bistrica HR 124 A2
Marijampolė LT 13 A5
Marín E 140 B2
Marina HR 138 B2
Marina del Cantone I 170 C2
Marina di Acquappesa I 174 B1
Marina di Alberese I 168 A1
Marina di Amendolara I 174 B2
Marina di Árbus I 179 C2
Marina di Campo I 134 C3
Marina di Carrara I 134 A3
Marina di Castagneto-Donorático I 134 B3
Marina di Cécina I 134 B3
Marina di Gáiro I 179 C3
Marina di Ginosa I 173 B2
Marina di Gioiosa Iónica I 175 C2
Marina di Grosseto I 135 C3
Marina di Léuca I 173 C4
Marina di Massa I 134 A3
Marina di Nováglie I 173 C4
Marina di Pisa I 134 B3
Marina di Ragusa I 177 C3
Marina di Ravenna I 135 A5
Marina di Torre Grande I 179 C2
Marinaleda E 162 A3
Marina Romea I 135 A5
Marine de Sisco F 180 A2
Marinella I 176 B1
Marinella di Sarzana I 134 A3
Marineo I 176 B2
Marines F 90 B1
Maringues F 116 B3
Marinha das Ondas P 154 A2
Marinha Grande P 154 B2
Marinhas P 148 A1
Marino I 168 B2
Marjaliza E 157 A4
Markabygd N 199 B8
Markaryd S 61 C3
Markdorf D 107 B4
Markelo NL 71 B3
Market Deeping GB 40 C3
Market Drayton GB 38 B4
Market Harborough GB 40 C3
Markethill GB 27 B4
Market Rasen GB 40 B3
Market Warsop GB 40 B2
Market Weighton GB 40 B3
Markgröningen D 93 C5
Markhausen D 71 B4
Marki PL 77 B6
Markina-Xemein E 143 A4
Markinch GB 35 B4
Märkische Buchholz D 74 B2
Markitta S 196 B4
Markkleeberg D 83 A4
Marklohe D 72 B2
Marknesse NL 70 B2
Markneukirchen D 83 B4
Markopoulo GR 185 B4
Markovac
*Srbija* SRB 127 C3
*Vojvodina* SRB 126 B3
Markowice PL 86 B2
Marktranstädt D 83 A4
Marksuhl D 82 B2
Markt Allhau A 111 B3
Markt Bibart D 94 B2
Marktbreit D 94 B2
Markt Erlbach D 94 B2
Markt-heidenfeld D 94 B1
Markt Indersdorf D 95 C3
Marktl D 95 C4
Marktleuthen D 83 B3
Marktoberdorf D 108 B1
Marktredwitz D 95 A4
Markt Rettenbach D 108 B1
Markt Schwaben D 108 A2
Markt-Übelbach A 110 B2
Markusica HR 125 B4
Markušovce SK 99 C4
Marl D 80 A3
Marlborough
*Devon* GB 42 B3
*Wiltshire* GB 44 B2
Marle F 91 B3
Marlieux F 117 A5
Marlow
D 66 B1
GB 44 B3
Marma S 51 B4
Marmagne F 104 C3
Marmande F 128 B3
Marmara TR 186 B2
Marmaris TR 188 C3
Marmelete P 160 B1
Marmolejo E 157 B3
Marmoutier F 93 C3
Marnay F 105 B4
Marne D 64 C2
Marnheim D 93 B4
Marnitz D 73 A4
Maroldsweisach D 82 B2
Marolles-les-Braults F 89 B4
Maromme F 89 A5
Marone I 120 B3
Maronia GR 183 C7
Maroslele H 126 A2
Maróstica I 121 B4
Marotta I 136 B2
Marpisa GR 185 B6
Marquion F 78 B3
Marquise F 78 B1
Marradi I 135 A4
Marrasjärvi FIN 197 C8
Marraskoski FIN 197 C8
Marratxi E 166 B2
Marrúbiu I 179 C2
Marrum NL 70 A2
Marrupe E 150 B3
Marsac F 129 C5
Marsac-en-Livradois F 117 B3
Marságlia I 120 C2
Marsala I 176 B1
Marsberg D 81 A4
Marsciano I 135 C5
Marseillan F 130 B2
Marseille = Marseilles F 131 B4
Marseille en Beauvaisis F 90 B1
Marseilles = Marseille F 131 B4
Mársico Nuovo I 172 B1
Marske-by-the-Sea GB 37 B5
Mars-la-Tours F 92 B1
Marsliden S 195 E6
Marson F 91 C4
Märsta S 57 A3
Marstal DK 65 B3
Marstrand S 60 B1
Marta I 168 A1
Martano I 173 B4
Martel F 129 B4
Martelange B 92 B1
Martfeld D 72 B2
Martfű H 113 B4
Martham GB 41 C5
Marthon F 115 C4
Martiago E 149 B3
Martigné-Briand F 102 B1
Martigné-Ferchaud F 101 B4
Martigne-sur-Mayenne F 102 A1
Martigny CH 119 A4
Martigny-les-Bains F 105 A4
Martigues F 131 B4
Martim-Longo P 160 B2
Martin SK 98 B2
Martina CH 108 C1
Martina Franca I 173 B3
Martinamor E 150 B2
Martin de la Jara E 162 A3
Martinengo I 120 B2
Martin Muñoz de las Posadas E 150 A3
Martinsberg A 97 C3
Martinšćica HR 123 C3
Martinshöhe D 93 B3
Martinsicuro I 136 C2
Martinszell D 107 B5
Mártis I 178 B2
Martofte DK 59 C3
Martonvásár H 112 B2
Martorell E 147 C2
Martos E 163 A4
Martres Tolosane F 146 A1
Martti FIN 197 B11
Marugán E 150 B3
Marúggio I 173 B3
Marvão P 155 B3
Marvejols F 130 A2
Marville F 92 B1
Marwałd PL 77 A4
Marykirk GB 35 B5
Marypark GB 32 D3
Maryport GB 36 B3
Marytavy GB 42 B2
Marzabotto I 135 A4
Marzahna D 74 C1
Marzahne D 73 B5
Marzamemi I 177 C4
Marzocca I 136 B2
Masa E 143 B3
Mas-Cabardès F 146 A3
Máscali I 177 B4
Mascaraque E 157 A4
Mascarenhas P 149 A2
Mascioni I 169 A3
Mas de Barberáns E 153 B4
Mas de las Matas E 153 B3
Masegoso E 158 C1
Masegoso de Tajuña E 151 B5
Masera I 119 A5
Masevaux F 106 B1
Masfjorden N 46 B2
Masham GB 37 B5
Masi N 192 C7
Maside E 140 B2
Maslacq F 144 A3
Maslinica HR 138 B2
Maşloc RO 126 B3
Maslovare BIH 138 A3
Masone I 133 A4
Massa I 134 A3
Massa Fiscáglia I 121 C5
Massafra I 173 B3
Massa Lombarda I 135 A4
Massa Lubrense I 170 C2
Massamagrell E 159 B3
Massa Maríttima I 135 B3
Massa Martana I 136 C1
Massanassa E 159 B3
Massarosa I 134 B3
Massat F 146 B2
Massay F 103 B3
Massbach D 82 B2
Masseret F 116 B1
Masseube F 145 A4
Massiac F 116 B3
Massignac F 115 C4
Massing D 95 C4
Massmechelen B 80 B1
Masterud N 49 B4
Mästocka S 61 C3
Masty BY 13 B6
Masúa I 179 C2
Masueco E 149 A3
Masugnsbyn S 196 B5
Mašun SLO 123 B3
Maszewo
*Lubuskie* PL 75 B3
*Zachodnio-Pomorskie* PL 75 A4
Mata de Alcántara E 155 B4
Matala GR 185 E5
Matalebreras E 144 C1
Matallana de Torio E 142 B1
Matamala E 151 A5
Mataporquera E 142 B2
Matapozuelos E 150 A3
Mataró E 147 C3
Matarocco I 176 B1
Matélica I 136 B2
Matera I 172 B2
Mátészalka H 16 B5
Matet E 159 B3
Matfors S 200 D3
Matha F 115 C3
Mathay F 106 B1
Matignon F 101 A3
Matilla de los Caños del Rio E 149 B4
Matlock GB 40 B2
Matosinhos P 148 A1
Matour F 117 A4
Mátrafüred H 113 B3
Mátraterenye H 113 A3
Matre
*Hordaland* N 46 B2
*Hordaland* N 52 A1
Matrei am Brenner A 108 B2
Matrei in Osttirol A 109 B3
Matrice I 170 B2
Matsdal S 195 E6
Mattarello I 121 A4
Mattersburg A 111 B3
Mattighofen A 109 A4
Mattinata I 171 B4
Mattos P 154 B2
Mattsee A 109 B4
Mattsmyra S 50 A2
Måttsund S 196 D5
Matulji HR 123 B3
Maubert-Fontaine F 91 B4
Maubeuge F 79 B3
Maubourguet F 145 A4
Mauchline GB 36 A2
Maud GB 33 D4
Mauer-kirchen A 109 A4
Mauern D 95 C3
Mauguio F 131 B3
Maulbronn D 93 C4
Maule F 90 C1
Mauléon F 114 B3
Mauléon-Barousse F 145 B4
Mauléon-Licharre F 144 A3
Maulévrier F 114 A3
Maum IRL 28 A2
Maurach A 108 B2
Maure-de-Bretagne F 101 B4
Maureilhan F 130 B2
Măureni RO 126 B3
Mauriac F 116 B2
Mauron F 101 A3
Maurs F 116 C2
Maury F 146 B3
Maussane-les-Alpilles F 131 B3
Mautern A 97 C3
Mauterndorf A 109 B4
Mautern im Steiermark A 110 B1
Mauthausen A 110 A1
Mauthen A 109 C3
Mauvezin F 129 C3

Mauzé-sur-le-Mignon
F. . . . . 114 B3
Maxent F . . . . 101 B3
Maxey-sur-Vaise F . 92 C1
Maxial P . . . . 154 B1
Maxieira P . . . . 154 B2
Maxwellheugh GB. . 35 C5
Mayalde E . . . . 149 A4
Maybole GB . . . . 36 A2
Mayen D . . . . 80 B3
Mayenne F . . . . 88 B3
Mayet F . . . . 102 B2
Mayorga E . . . . 142 B1
Mayres F . . . . 117 C4
Mayrhofen A . . . . 108 B2
Mazagón E . . . . 161 B3
Mazaleón E . . . . 153 A4
Mazamet F . . . . 130 B1
Mazan F . . . . 131 A4
Mazara del Vallo I . 176 B1
Mazarambroz E . . . 157 A3
Mazarete E . . . . 152 B1
Mazaricos E . . . . 140 B2
Mazarrón E . . . . 165 B3
Mažeikiai LT . . . . 8 D3
Mazères F . . . . 146 A2
Mazères-sur-Salat
F. . . . . 145 A4
Mazières-en-Gâtine
F. . . . . 115 B3
Mazin HR . . . . 138 A1
Mazuelo E . . . . 143 B3
Mazyr BY . . . . 13 B8
Mazzarino I . . . . 177 B3
Mazzarrà Sant'Andrea
I . . . . . 177 A4
Mazzo di Valtellina
I . . . . . 120 A3
Mdzewo PL . . . . 77 B5
Mealabost GB . . . . 31 A2
Mealhada P . . . . 148 B1
Méan B . . . . 79 B5
Meana Sardo I . . . . 179 C3
Meaulne F . . . . 103 C4
Meaux F . . . . 90 C2
Mebonden N . . . . 199 B8
Mecerreyes E . . . . 143 B3
Mechelen B . . . . 79 A4
Mechernich D . . . . 80 B2
Mechnica PL . . . . 86 B2
Mechowo PL . . . . 67 C4
Mechterstädt D . . . . 82 B2
Mecidiye TR . . . . 186 B1
Mecikal PL . . . . 68 B2
Mecina-Bombarón
E. . . . . 164 C1
Mecitözü TR . . . . 23 A8
Meckenbeuren D . . 107 B4
Meckenheim
*Rheinland-Pfalz* D . . 80 B3
*Rheinland-Pfalz* D . . 93 B4
Meckesheim D . . . . 93 B4
Mecseknádasd H . 125 A4
Meda
I. . . . . 120 B2
P. . . . . 149 B2
Medak HR . . . . 137 A4
Mede I . . . . 120 B1
Medebach D . . . . 81 A4
Medelim P . . . . 155 A3
Medemblik NL . . . . 70 B2
Medena Selista
BIH. . . . . 138 A2
Medesano I . . . . 120 C3
Medevi S . . . . 55 B5
Medgidia RO . . . . 17 C8
Medgyesháza H . . . 113 C5
Medhamn S . . . . 55 A4
Mediaş RO . . . . 17 B6
Medicina I . . . . 135 A4
Medinaceli E . . . . 152 A1
Medina de las Torres
E. . . . . 155 C4
Medina del Campo
E. . . . . 150 A3
Medina de Pomar
E. . . . . 143 B3
Medina de Ríoseco
E. . . . . 142 C1
Medina Sidonia E . 162 B2
Medinilla E . . . . 150 B2
Medja SRB . . . . 126 B2
Medjedja BIH . . . . 139 B5
Medulin HR . . . . 122 C2
Meduno I . . . . 122 A1
Medveda SRB . . . . 127 C3
Medvedov SK . . . . 111 B4
Medvezhyegorsk
RUS . . . . . 9 A9
Medvide HR . . . . 137 A4
Medvode SLO . . . . 123 A3
Medzev SK . . . . 99 C4
Medžitlija MK . . . . 182 C3
Meerane D . . . . 83 B4
Meerle B . . . . 79 A4
Meersburg D . . . . 107 B4
Meeuwen B . . . . 79 A5
Megalo Horio GR . . 188 C2
Megalopoli GR . . . . 184 B3
Megara GR . . . . 185 A4
Megève F . . . . 118 B3
Meggenhofen A . . . 109 A4
Megra RUS . . . . 9 B10
Megyaszó H . . . . 113 A5
Mehamn N . . . . 193 A11
Mehedeby S . . . . 51 B4
Méhkerék H . . . . 113 C5
Mehun-sur-Yèvre
F. . . . . 103 B4
Meigle GB . . . . 35 B4
Meijel NL . . . . 80 A1
Meilen CH . . . . 107 B3
Meilhan F . . . . 128 C2
Meimôa P . . . . 149 B2
Meina I . . . . 119 B5
Meine D . . . . 73 B3
Meinersen D . . . . 72 B3
Meinerzhagen D . . . 81 A3
Meiningen D . . . . 82 B2
Meira E . . . . 141 A3
Meiringen CH . . . . 106 C3
Meisenheim D . . . . 93 B3
Meissen D . . . . 83 A5
Meitingen D . . . . 94 C2
Meix-devant-Virton
B. . . . . 92 B1
Męka PL . . . . 86 A2
Meka Gruda BIH . . 139 B4
Mel I . . . . 121 A5
Melbu N . . . . 194 B5
Melč CZ . . . . 98 B1
Meldal N . . . . 198 B6
Méldola I . . . . 135 A5
Meldorf D . . . . 64 B2
Melegnano I . . . . 120 B2
Melenci SRB . . . . 126 B2
Melendugno I . . . . 173 B4
Melfi I . . . . 172 B1
Melfjordbotn N . . . 195 D4
Melgaço P . . . . 140 B2
Melgar de Arriba E 142 B1
Melgar de Fernamental
E. . . . . 142 B2
Melgar de Yuso E . 142 B2
Melhus N . . . . 199 B7
Meliana E . . . . 159 B3
Melide
CH. . . . . 120 B1
E . . . . . 140 B2
Melides P . . . . 160 A1
Meligales GR . . . . 184 B2
Melilli I . . . . 177 B4
Melinovac HR . . . . 124 C1
Melisenda I . . . . 179 C3
Melisey F . . . . 105 B5
Mélito di Porto Salvo
I . . . . . 175 D1
Melk A . . . . 110 A2
Melksham GB . . . . 43 A4
Mellakoski FIN . . . . 196 C7
Mellanström S . . . . 195 E9
Mellbystrand S . . . . 61 C2
Melle
B. . . . . 79 A3
D . . . . . 71 B5
F . . . . . 115 B3
Mellendorf D . . . . 72 B2
Mellerud S . . . . 54 B3
Mellieha M . . . . 175 C3
Mellösa S . . . . 56 A2
Mellrichstadt D . . . 82 B2
Mělnické Vtelno CZ. 84 B2
Mělník CZ . . . . 84 B2
Melón E . . . . 140 B2
Melrose GB . . . . 35 C5
Mels CH . . . . 107 B4
Melsungen D . . . . 82 A1
Meltaus FIN . . . . 197 C8
Meltham GB . . . . 40 B2
Melton Mowbray GB 40 C3
Meltosjärvi FIN . . . 196 C7
Melun F . . . . 90 C2
Melvaig GB . . . . 31 B3
Melvich GB . . . . 32 C3
Mélykút H . . . . 126 A1
Melzo I . . . . 120 B2
Memaliaj AL . . . . 182 C1
Membrilla E . . . . 157 B4
Membrio E . . . . 155 B3
Memer F . . . . 129 B4
Memmelsdorf D . . . 94 B2
Memmingen D . . . . 107 B5
Memoria P . . . . 154 B2
Menàggio I . . . . 120 A2
Menai Bridge GB . . . 38 A2
Menasalbas E . . . . 157 A3
Menat F . . . . 116 A2
Mendavia E . . . . 144 B1
Mendaza E . . . . 144 B1
Mende F . . . . 130 A2
Menden D . . . . 81 A3
Menderes TR . . . . 188 A2
Mendig D . . . . 80 B3
Mendiga P . . . . 154 B2
Mendrisio CH . . . . 120 B1
Ménéac F . . . . 101 A3
Menemen TR . . . . 188 A2
Menen B . . . . 78 B3
Menesjärvi FIN . . 193 D10
Menetou-Salon F . . 103 B4
Menfi I . . . . 176 B1
Ménföcsanak H . . . 111 B4
Mengamuñoz E . . . 150 B3
Mengen
D. . . . . 107 A4
TR . . . . . 187 B7
Mengeš SLO . . . . 123 A3
Mengíbar E . . . . 157 C4
Mengkofen D . . . . 95 C4
Menou F . . . . 104 B2
Mens F . . . . 118 C2
Menslage D . . . . 71 B4
Mensträsk S . . . . 200 A5
Mentana I . . . . 168 A2
Menton F . . . . 133 B3
Méntrida E . . . . 151 B3
Méobecq F . . . . 115 B5
Méounes-les-Montrieux
F. . . . . 132 B1
Meppel NL . . . . 70 B3
Meppen D . . . . 71 B4
Mequinenza E . . . . 153 A4
Mer F . . . . 103 B3
Mera
*Coruña* E . . . . 140 A2
*Coruña* E . . . . 140 A3
Meråker N . . . . 199 B8
Merano I . . . . 108 C2
Merate I . . . . 120 B2
Mercadillo E . . . . 143 A3
Mercatale I . . . . 135 B5
Mercatino Conca I . 136 B1
Mercato San Severino
I . . . . . 170 C2
Mercato Saraceno
I . . . . . 135 B5
Merching D . . . . 108 A1
Merchtem B . . . . 79 B4
Merdrignac F . . . . 101 A3
Merdžanići BIH . . . 139 B3
Meré E . . . . 142 A2
Mere GB . . . . 43 A4
Méréville F . . . . 90 C2
Merfeld D . . . . 80 A3
Méribel F . . . . 118 B3
Méribel Motraret F . 118 B3
Meriç TR . . . . 186 A1
Mérida E . . . . 155 C4
Mérignac F . . . . 128 B2
Měřín CZ . . . . 97 B3
Mering D . . . . 94 C2
Merkendorf D . . . . 94 B2
Merklin CZ . . . . 96 B1
Merksplas B . . . . 79 A4
Merlånna S . . . . 56 A2
Merlimont Plage F . . 78 B1
Mern DK . . . . 65 A5
Mernye H . . . . 111 C4
Mersch L . . . . 92 B2
Merseburg D . . . . 83 A3
Mers-les-Bains F . . . 90 A1
Merthyr Tydfil GB . . 39 C3
Mertingen D . . . . 94 C2
Mértola P . . . . 160 B2
Méru F . . . . 90 B2
Merufe P . . . . 140 B2
Mervans F . . . . 105 C4
Merville F . . . . 78 B2
Méry-sur-Seine F . . 91 C3
Merzen D . . . . 71 B4
Merzifon TR . . . . 23 A8
Merzig D . . . . 92 B2
Mesagne I . . . . 173 B3
Mesão Frio P . . . . 148 A2
Mesas de Ibor E . . 156 A2
Meschede D . . . . 81 A4
Meschers-sur-Gironde
F. . . . . 114 C3
Meslay-du-Maine F 102 B1
Mesna N . . . . 48 A2
Mesnalien N . . . . 48 A2
Mesocco CH . . . . 120 A2
Mésola I . . . . 122 C1
Mesologi GR . . . . 184 A2
Mesopotamo GR . . 182 D2
Mesoraca I . . . . 175 B2
Messac F . . . . 101 B4
Messancy B . . . . 92 B1
Messdorf D . . . . 73 B4
Messei F . . . . 88 B3
Messejana P . . . . 160 B1
Messelt N . . . . 48 A3
Messina I . . . . 177 A4
Messingen D . . . . 71 B4
Messini GR . . . . 184 B3
Messkirch D . . . . 107 B4
Messlingen S . . . . 199 C9
Messtetten D . . . . 107 A3
Mesta GR . . . . 185 A6
Mestanza E . . . . 157 B3
Městec Králové CZ . 84 B3
Mestlin D . . . . 73 A4
Město Albrechtice
CZ . . . . . 85 B5
Město Libavá CZ . . . 98 B1
Město Touškov CZ . 96 B1
Mestre I . . . . 122 B1
Mesvres F . . . . 104 C3
Mesztegnyő H . . . . 111 C4
Meta I . . . . 170 C2
Metajna HR . . . . 137 A4
Metelen D . . . . 71 B4
Methana GR . . . . 185 B4
Methlick GB . . . . 33 D4
Methven GB . . . . 35 B4
Methwold GB . . . . 41 C4
Metković HR . . . . 139 B3
Metlika SLO . . . . 123 B4
Metnitz A . . . . 110 C1
Metsäkylä FIN . . . 197 D11
Metslawier NL . . . . 70 A3
Metsovo GR . . . . 182 D3
Metten D . . . . 95 C4
Mettendorf D . . . . 92 B2
Mettet B . . . . 79 B4
Mettingen D . . . . 71 B4
Mettlach D . . . . 92 B2
Mettlen CH . . . . 106 C2
Mettmann D . . . . 80 A2
Metz F . . . . 92 B2
Metzervisse F . . . . 92 B2
Metzingen D . . . . 94 C1
Meulan F . . . . 90 B1
Meung-sur-Loire F 103 B3
Meuselwitz D . . . . 83 A4
Meuzac F . . . . 115 C5
Mevagissey GB . . . 42 B2
Mexborough GB . . . 40 B2
Meximieux F . . . . 118 B2
Mey GB . . . . 32 C3
Meyenburg D . . . . 73 A5
Meyerhöfen D . . . . 71 B5
Meylan F . . . . 118 B2
Meymac F . . . . 116 B2
Meyrargues F . . . . 132 B1
Meyrueis F . . . . 130 A2
Meyssac F . . . . 129 A4
Meysse F . . . . 117 C4
Meyzieu F . . . . 117 B4
Mèze F . . . . 130 B2
Mézériat F . . . . 117 A5
Mežica SLO . . . . 110 C1
Mézidon-Canon F . . 89 A3
Mézières-en-Brenne
F. . . . . 115 B5
Mézières-sur-Issoire
F. . . . . 115 B4
Mézilhac F . . . . 117 C4
Mézilles F . . . . 104 B2
Mézin F . . . . 128 B3
Mezőberény H . . . . 113 C5
Mezőcsát H . . . . 113 B4
Mezőfalva H . . . . 112 C2
Mezőhegyes H . . . . 126 A2
Mezőkeresztes H . . 113 B4
Mezőkomárom H . . 112 C2
Mezőkövácsháza
H . . . . . 113 C4
Mezőkövesd H . . . . 113 B4
Mezőörs H . . . . 111 B4
Mézos F . . . . 128 B1
Mezőszilas H . . . . 112 C2
Mezőtúr H . . . . 113 B4
Mezquita de Jarque
E. . . . . 153 B3
Mezzano
*Emilia Romagna*
I . . . . . 135 A5
*Trentino Alto Adige*
I . . . . . 121 A4
Mezzojuso I . . . . 176 B2
Mezzoldo I . . . . 120 A2
Mezzolombardo I . 121 A4
Mgarr M . . . . 175 C3
Miajadas E . . . . 156 A2
Miały PL . . . . 75 B5
Mianowice PL . . . . 68 A2
Miasteczko Krajeńskie
PL. . . . . 76 A2
Miasteczko Sł. PL . . 86 B2
Miastko PL . . . . 68 A1
Michalovce SK . . . . 12 D4
Michałowice PL . . . 87 B3
Michelau D . . . . 94 B2
Michelbach D . . . . 94 B2
Micheldorf A . . . . 110 B1
Michelhausen A . . . 110 A2
Michelsneukirchen
D . . . . . 95 B4
Michelstadt D . . . . 93 B5
Michendorf D . . . . 74 B2
Mickleover GB . . . . 40 C2
Midbea GB . . . . 33 B4
Middelburg NL . . . . 79 A3
Middelfart DK . . . . 59 C2
Middelharnis NL . . . 79 A4
Middelkerke B . . . . 78 A2
Middelstum NL . . . . 71 A3
Middlesbrough GB . 37 B5
Middleton Cheney
GB . . . . . 44 A2
Middleton-in-Teesdale
GB . . . . . 37 B4
Middletown GB . . . 27 B4
Middlewich GB . . . . 38 A4
Middlezoy GB . . . . 43 A4
Midhurst GB . . . . 44 C3
Midleton IRL . . . . 29 C3
Midlum D . . . . 64 C1
Midsomer Norton
GB . . . . . 43 A4
Midtgulen N . . . . 198 D2
Midtskogberget N . . 49 A4
Midwolda NL . . . . 71 A4
Mid Yell GB . . . . 33 A5
Miechów PL . . . . 87 B4
Miedes de Aragón
E. . . . . 152 A2
Miedes de Atienza
E. . . . . 151 A4
Międzybodzie Bielskie
PL. . . . . 99 B3
Międzybórz PL . . . . 85 A5
Międzychód PL . . . . 75 B4
Międzylesie PL . . . . 85 B4
Międzyrzec Podlaski
PL. . . . . 12 C5
Międzyrzecz PL . . . 75 B4
Międzywodzie PL . . 67 B3
Międzyzdroje PL . . 67 C3
Miejska Górka PL . . 85 A4
Miélan F . . . . 145 A4
Mielec PL . . . . 87 B5
Mielęcin PL . . . . 75 A3
Mielno
*Warmińsko-Mazurskie*
PL. . . . . 77 A5
*Zachodnio-Pomorskie*
PL. . . . . 67 B5
Miengo E . . . . 143 A3
Mieraslompolo
FIN . . . . . 193 C11
Miercurea Ciuc RO . 17 B6
Mieres
*Asturias* E . . . . 141 A5
*Girona* E . . . . 147 B3
Mieroszów PL . . . . 85 B4
Mierzyn PL . . . . 86 A3
Miesau D . . . . 93 B3
Miesbach D . . . . 108 B2
Mieścisko PL . . . . 76 B2
Mieste D . . . . 73 B4
Miesterhorst D . . . . 73 B4
Mieszków PL . . . . 76 B2
Mieszkowice PL . . . 74 B3
Mietków PL . . . . 85 B4
Migennes F . . . . 104 B2
Miggiano I . . . . 173 C4
Migliánico I . . . . 169 A4
Migliarino I . . . . 121 C4
Migliónico I . . . . 172 B2
Mignano Monte Lungo
I . . . . . 169 B3
Migné F . . . . 115 B5
Miguel Esteban E . 157 A4
Miguelturra E . . . . 157 B4
Mihajlovac SRB . . . 127 C2
Mihald H . . . . 111 C4
Mihalgazi TR . . . . 187 B5
Mihaliççık TR . . . . 187 C6
Mihályi H . . . . 111 B4
Mihla D . . . . 82 A2
Mihohnić HR . . . . 123 B3
Miholjsko HR . . . . 123 B4
Mihovljan HR . . . . 124 A1
Mijares E . . . . 150 B3
Mijas E . . . . 163 B3
Mike H . . . . 124 A3
Mikines GR . . . . 184 B3
Mikkeli FIN . . . . 8 B5
Mikkelvik N . . . . 192 B3
Mikleuš HR . . . . 125 B3
Mikołajki Pomorskie
PL. . . . . 69 B4
Mikolów PL . . . . 86 B2
Mikonos GR . . . . 185 B6
Mikorzyn PL . . . . 86 A2
Mikro Derio GR . . . 183 B8
Mikstat PL . . . . 86 A1
Mikulášovice CZ . . . 84 B2
Mikulov CZ . . . . 97 C4
Mikulovice CZ . . . . 85 B5
Milagro E . . . . 144 B2
Miłakowo PL . . . . 69 A5
Milan = Milano I . . . 120 B2
Miland N . . . . 47 C5
Milano = Milan I . . . 120 B2
Milano Marittima I . 135 A5
Milas TR . . . . 188 B2
Milazzo I . . . . 177 A4
Mildenhall GB . . . . 45 A4
Milejewo PL . . . . 69 A4
Milelín CZ . . . . 85 B3
Miletić SRB . . . . 125 B5
Miletićevo SRB . . . 126 B3
Mileto I . . . . 175 C2
Milevsko CZ . . . . 96 B2
Milford IRL . . . . 26 A3
Milford Haven GB . . 39 C1
Milford on Sea GB . . 44 C2
Milhão P . . . . 149 A3
Milići BIH . . . . 139 A5
Miličin CZ . . . . 96 B2
Milicz PL . . . . 85 A5
Milín CZ . . . . 96 B2
Militello in Val di
Catánia I . . . . 177 B3
Miljevina BIH . . . . 139 B4
Milkowice PL . . . . 85 A4
Millançay F . . . . 103 B3
Millares E . . . . 159 B3
Millas F . . . . 146 B3
Millau F . . . . 130 A2
Millesimo I . . . . 133 A4
Millevaches F . . . . 116 B2
Millom GB . . . . 36 B3
Millport GB . . . . 34 C3
Millstatt A . . . . 109 C4
Millstreet
*Cork* IRL . . . . 29 B2
*Waterford* IRL . . . . 29 B4
Milltown
*Galway* IRL . . . . 28 A3
*Kerry* IRL . . . . 29 B1
Milltown Malbay IRL 28 B2
Milly-la-Forêt F . . . 90 C2
Milmarcos E . . . . 152 A2
Milmersdorf D . . . . 74 A2
Milna HR . . . . 138 B2
Milnthorpe GB . . . . 37 B4
Milogórze PL . . . . 69 A5
Miłomłyn PL . . . . 69 B4
Milos GR . . . . 185 C5
Miloševo SRB . . . . 127 C3
Miłosław PL . . . . 76 B2
Milot AL . . . . 182 B1
Milówka PL . . . . 99 B3
Miltach D . . . . 95 B4
Miltenberg D . . . . 94 B1
Milton Keynes GB . . 44 A3
Miltzow D . . . . 66 B2
Milverton GB . . . . 43 A3
Milzyn PL . . . . 76 B3
Mimice HR . . . . 138 B2
Mimizan F . . . . 128 B1
Mimizan-Plage F . . 128 B1
Mimoň CZ . . . . 84 B2
Mina de Juliana P . 160 B1
Mina de São Domingos
P. . . . . 160 B2
Minas de Riotinto
E. . . . . 161 B3
Minateda E . . . . 158 C2
Minaya E . . . . 158 B1
Minde P . . . . 154 B2
Mindelheim D . . . . 108 A1
Mindelstetten D . . . 95 C3
Minden D . . . . 72 B1
Mindszent H . . . . 113 C4
Minehead GB . . . . 43 A3
Mineo I . . . . 177 B3
Minerbe I . . . . 121 B4
Minérbio I . . . . 121 C4
Minervino Murge I . 171 B4
Minglanilla E . . . . 158 B2
Mingorria E . . . . 150 B3
Minnesund N . . . . 48 B3
Miño E . . . . 140 A2
Miño de San Esteban
E. . . . . 151 A4
Minsen D . . . . 71 A4
Minsk BY . . . . 13 B7
Mińsk Mazowiecki
PL. . . . . 12 B4
Minsterley GB . . . . 39 B4
Mintlaw GB . . . . 33 D4
Minturno I . . . . 169 B3
Mionica
BIH . . . . . 125 C4
SRB . . . . . 127 C2
Mios F . . . . 128 B2
Mira
E. . . . . 158 B2
I. . . . . 121 B5
P. . . . . 148 B1
Mirabel E . . . . 155 B4
Mirabel-aux-Baronnies
F. . . . . 131 A4
Mirabella Eclano I . 170 B3
Mirabella Imbáccari
I . . . . . 177 B3
Mirabello I . . . . 121 C4
Miradoux F . . . . 129 B3
Miraflores de la Sierra
E. . . . . 151 B4
Miralrio E . . . . 151 B5
Miramar P . . . . 148 A1
Miramare I . . . . 136 A1
Miramas F . . . . 131 B3
Mirambeau F . . . . 114 C3
Miramont-de-Guyenne
F. . . . . 129 B3
Miranda de Arga E 144 B2
Miranda de Ebro E 143 B4
Miranda do Corvo
P. . . . . 148 B1
Miranda do Douro
P. . . . . 149 A3
Mirande F . . . . 129 C3
Mirandela P . . . . 149 A2
Mirandilla E . . . . 155 C4
Mirándola I . . . . 121 C4
Miranje HR . . . . 137 A4
Mirano I . . . . 121 B5
Miras AL . . . . 182 C2
Miravet E . . . . 153 A4
Miré F . . . . 102 B1
Mirebeau F . . . . 102 C2
Mirebeau-sur-Bèze
F. . . . . 105 B4
Mirecourt F . . . . 105 A5
Mirepoix F . . . . 146 A2
Mires GR . . . . 185 D5
Miribel F . . . . 117 B4
Miričina BIH . . . . 125 C4
Mirina GR . . . . 183 D7
Mirna SLO . . . . 123 B4
Miroslav CZ . . . . 97 C4
Mirosławice PL . . . . 85 B4
Mirosławiec PL . . . . 75 A5
Mirošov CZ . . . . 96 B1
Mirotice CZ . . . . 96 B2
Mirovice CZ . . . . 96 B2
Mirow D . . . . 74 A1
Mirsk PL . . . . 84 B3
Mirzec PL . . . . 87 A5
Misi FIN . . . . 197 C9
Misilmeri I . . . . 176 A2
Miske H . . . . 112 C3
Miskolc H . . . . 113 A4
Mislinja SLO . . . . 110 C2
Missanello I . . . . 174 A2
Missillac F . . . . 101 B3
Mistelbach
A . . . . . 97 C4
D . . . . . 95 B3
Misten N . . . . 194 C5
Misterbianco I . . . . 177 B4
Misterhult S . . . . 62 A4
Mistretta I . . . . 177 B3
Misurina I . . . . 109 C3
Mitchelstown IRL . . 29 B3
Mithimna GR . . . . 186 C1
Mithoni GR . . . . 184 C2
Mitilini GR . . . . 186 C1
Mitilinii GR . . . . 188 B1
Mittelberg
*Tirol* A . . . . 108 C1
*Vorarlberg* A . . . . 107 B5
Mittenwald D . . . . 108 B2
Mittenwalde D . . . . 74 B2
Mitterback A . . . . 110 B2

**Mitterdorf im Mürztal**
A. . . . . . . . . . . .110 B2
Mitter-Kleinarl A . . 109 B4
Mittersheim F . . . . 92 C2
Mittersill A . . . . . 109 B3
Mitterskirchen D . . . 95 C4
Mitterteich D . . . . . 95 B4
Mitton F . . . . . . . 128 B2
Mittweida D . . . . . . 83 B4
Mitwitz D . . . . . . . 82 B3
Mizhhir'ya UA . . . . 13 D5
Mjällby S . . . . . . . 63 B2
Mjåvatn N . . . . . . 53 B4
Mjöbäck S . . . . . . 60 B2
Mjölby S . . . . . . . 56 B1
Mjølfjell N. . . . . . . 46 B3
Mjøndalen N . . . . . 53 A6
Mjørlund N. . . . . . 48 B2
Mladá Boleslav CZ . 84 B2
Mladá Vožice CZ . . 96 B2
Mladé Buky CZ . . . 85 B3
Mladenovac SRB . 127 C2
Mladenovo SRB . . 126 B1
Mladikovine BIH . . 139 A3
Mława PL . . . . . . . 77 A5
Mlinište BIH . . . . . 138 A2
Młodzieszyn PL . . . 77 B5
Młogoszyn PL . . . . 77 B4
Młynary PL . . . . . . 69 A4
Mnichóvice CZ . . . . 96 B2
Mniów PL . . . . . . . 87 A4
**Mnichovo Hradiště**
CZ . . . . . . . . . . . 84 B2
**Mnisek nad Hnilcom**
SK . . . . . . . . . . . 99 C4
**Mníšek pod Brdy**
CZ . . . . . . . . . . . 96 B2
Mniszek PL . . . . . . 87 A4
Mniszków PL . . . . . 87 A4
**Mo**
Hedmark N. . . . . . . 48 B3
Hordaland N. . . . . . 46 B3
Møre og Romsdal
N. . . . . . . . . . . .198 C5
Telemark N . . . . . . 53 A3
Gävleborg S . . . . . 51 A3
Västra Götaland S . 54 B2
Moaña E . . . . . . . 140 B2
Moate IRL . . . . . . . 28 A4
Mocejón E . . . . . . 151 C4
Močenok SK . . . . . 111 A4
Mochales E . . . . . 152 A1
Mochowo PL . . . . . 77 B4
Mochy PL . . . . . . . 75 B5
Möckern D. . . . . . . 73 B4
Mockfjärd S . . . . . . 50 B1
Möckmühl D . . . . . 94 B1
Mockrehna D. . . . . 83 A4
Moclin E . . . . . . . 163 A4
Mocsa F . . . . . . . 112 B2
Möcsény H. . . . . . 125 A4
Modane F . . . . . . 118 B3
Modbury GB . . . . . 42 B3
Módena I . . . . . . . 121 C3
Módica I . . . . . . . 177 C3
Modigliana I . . . . . 135 A4
Modlin PL. . . . . . . 77 B5
Mödling A . . . . . . .111 A3
Modliszewice PL . . . 87 A4
Modliszewko PL . . . 76 B2
Modogno I . . . . . . 171 B4
Modra SK. . . . . . . 98 C1
Modran BIH . . . . . 125 C3
Modriča BIH . . . . . 125 C4
Möðrudalur IS . . 191 B10
Modrý Kamen SK . . 99 C3
Moëlan-sur-Mer F . 100 B2
Moelfre GB. . . . . . 38 A2
Moelv N . . . . . . . . 48 B2
Moen N. . . . . . . . 194 A9
Moena I . . . . . . . 121 A4
Moerbeke B . . . . . 79 A3
Moers D . . . . . . . 80 A2
Móes P . . . . . . . . 148 B2
Moffat GB. . . . . . . 36 A3
Mogadouro P. . . . . 149 A3
Mogata S . . . . . . . 56 B2
Móggio Udinese I . 122 A2
Mogielnica PL . . . . 87 A4
Mogilany PL. . . . . . 99 B3
Mogilno PL. . . . . . 76 B2
Mogliano I . . . . . . 136 B2
Mogliano Véneto I. 122 B1
Mogor E . . . . . . . 140 B2
Mógoro I . . . . . . . 179 C2
Moguer E . . . . . . 161 B3
Mohács H. . . . . . . 125 B4
Moheda S. . . . . . . 62 A2
Mohedas S. . . . . . 149 B3
**Mohedas de la Jara**
E. . . . . . . . . . . . 156 A2
Mohelnice CZ . . . . 97 B4
Mohill IRL. . . . . . . 26 C3
Möhlin CH . . . . . . 106 B2
Moholm S . . . . . . . 55 B5
Mohorn D. . . . . . . 83 A5
**Mohyliv-Podil's'kyy**
UA . . . . . . . . . . . 13 D7
Moi N . . . . . . . . . 52 B2
Moià E . . . . . . . . 147 C3
Móie I . . . . . . . . . 136 B2
**Moimenta da Beira**
P. . . . . . . . . . . . 148 B2
Mo i Rana N . . . . . 195 D5
Moirans F. . . . . . . 118 B2

**Moirans-en-Montagne**
F. . . . . . . . . . . . .118 A2
Moisaküla EST . . . . 8 C4
**Moisdon-la-Rivière**
F . . . . . . . . . . . . 101 B4
Moissac F . . . . . . 129 B4
**Moita**
Coimbra P . . . . . . 148 B1
Guarda P . . . . . . . 149 B2
Santarém P . . . . . 154 B2
Setúbal P . . . . . . . 154 C1
**Moita dos Ferreiros**
P. . . . . . . . . . . . 154 B1
Moixent E . . . . . . 159 C3
Mojacar E . . . . . . 164 B3
Mojados E . . . . . . 150 A3
Mojmírovce SK . . .112 A2
Mojtin SK . . . . . . . 98 C2
Möklinta S . . . . . . 50 B3
Mokošica HR. . . . . 139 C4
Mokronog SLO . . . 123 B4
Mokro Polje HR. . . 138 A2
Mokrzyska PL. . . . . 99 A4
Møkster N . . . . . . 46 B2
**Mol**
B. . . . . . . . . . . . .79 A5
SRB . . . . . . . . . . 126 B2
Mola di Bari I . . . . 173 A3
Molai GR . . . . . . . 184 C3
Molare I . . . . . . . . 133 A4
Molaretto I . . . . . . 119 B4
Molas F . . . . . . . . 145 A4
Molassano I . . . . . 134 A1
Molbergen D . . . . . 71 B4
Mold GB. . . . . . . . 38 A3
Molde N . . . . . . . 198 C4
Møldrup DK . . . . . . 58 B2
**Moledo do Minho**
P. . . . . . . . . . . . 148 A1
Molfetta I . . . . . . . 171 B4
Molfsee D. . . . . . . 64 B3
Moliden S. . . . . . . 200 C4
Molières F . . . . . . 129 B4
**Molina de Aragón**
E . . . . . . . . . . . . 152 B2
**Molina de Segura**
E . . . . . . . . . . . . 165 A3
Molinar E . . . . . . . 143 A3
Molinaseca E . . . . 141 B4
Molinella I . . . . . . 121 C4
Molinet F . . . . . . . 104 C2
Molinicos E . . . . . 158 C1
Molini di Tures I. . . 108 C2
**Molinos de Duero**
E . . . . . . . . . . . . 143 C4
Molins de Rei E . . 147 C3
Moliterno I . . . . . . 174 A1
Molkom S . . . . . . . 55 A4
Möllbrücke A . . . . 109 C4
Mölle S . . . . . . . . 61 C2
Molledo E. . . . . . . 142 A2
Möllenbeck D . . . . 74 A2
Mollerussa E . . . . 147 C1
**Mollet de Perelada**
E . . . . . . . . . . . . 146 B3
Mollina E . . . . . . . 163 A3
Mölln D. . . . . . . . . 73 A3
Molló E . . . . . . . . 146 B3
Mollösund S . . . . . 54 B2
Mölltorp S . . . . . . 55 B5
Mölnbo S . . . . . . . 56 A3
Mölndal S. . . . . . . 60 B2
Mölnlycke S. . . . . . 60 B2
Molompize F . . . . .116 B3
Moloy F . . . . . . . . 105 B3
Molsheim F . . . . . . 93 C3
Moltzow D . . . . . . . 73 A5
Molve HR . . . . . . . 124 A3
Molveno I . . . . . . . 121 A3
Molvizar E . . . . . . 163 B4
Molzbichl A . . . . . 109 C4
Mombaróccio I . . . . 136 B1
Mombeltrán E . . . . 150 B2
Mombris D. . . . . . . 93 A5
Mombuey E . . . . . 141 B4
Momchilgrad BG . . 183 B7
Mommark DK. . . . . 64 B3
Momo I . . . . . . . . .119 B5
Monaghan IRL. . . . 27 B4
Monar Lodge GB . . 32 D2
**Monasterace Marina**
I . . . . . . . . . . . . 175 C2
Monasterevin IRL . . 30 A1
**Monasterio de Rodilla**
E. . . . . . . . . . . . 143 B3
Monastir I . . . . . . . 179 C3
Monbahus F . . . . . 129 B3
Monbazillac F . . . . 129 B3
Moncada E . . . . . . 159 B3
Moncalieri I. . . . . . .119 B4
Moncalvo I. . . . . . . 119 B5
Monção P . . . . . . . 140 B2
Moncarapacho P. . . 160 B2
Moncel-sur-Seille F. 92 C2
Monchegorsk RUS . 3 C13
**Mönchengladbach =**
**Munchen-Gladbach**
D. . . . . . . . . . . . 80 A2
**Mónchio della Corti**
I . . . . . . . . . . . . 134 A3
Monchique P. . . . . 160 B1
**Monclar-de-Quercy**
F . . . . . . . . . . . . 129 C4
Moncofa E . . . . . . 159 B3
Moncontour F . . . . 101 A3
Moncoutant F . . . . 114 B3
Monda E. . . . . . . . 162 B3
Mondariz E . . . . . . 140 B2

Mondavio I. . . . . . 136 B1
Mondéjar E . . . . . 151 B4
Mondello I . . . . . . 176 A2
**Mondim de Basto**
P. . . . . . . . . . . . 148 A2
Mondolfo I . . . . . . 136 B2
Mondoñedo E . . . . 141 A3
Mondorf-les-Bains L 92 B2
Mondoubleau F . . . 102 B2
Mondov`ì I . . . . . . 133 A3
Mondragon F. . . . . 131 A3
Mondragone I . . . . 170 B1
Mondsee A . . . . . . 109 B4
Monéglia I . . . . . . 134 A2
Monegrillo E . . . . . 153 A3
Monein F . . . . . . . 145 A3
Monemvasia GR . . 184 C4
Mónesi I . . . . . . . 133 A3
Monesiglio I . . . . . 133 A4
Monesterio E . . . . 161 A3
**Monestier-de-Clermont**
F. . . . . . . . . . . . 118 C2
Monestiés F. . . . . 130 A1
Monéteau F . . . . . 104 B2
Moneygall IRL. . . . 28 B4
Moneymore GB . . . 27 B4
Monfalcone I . . . . . 122 B2
Monfero E . . . . . . 140 A2
Monflanquin F . . . . 129 B3
Monflorite E . . . . . 145 B3
Monforte P. . . . . . 155 B3
**Monforte da Beira**
E . . . . . . . . . . . .155 B3
P . . . . . . . . . . . . 155 B3
Monforte d'Alba I . 133 A3
Monforte del Cid E 165 A4
**Monforte de Lemos**
E . . . . . . . . . . . . 140 B3
**Monforte de Moyuela**
E . . . . . . . . . . . . 152 A2
Monghidoro I. . . . . 135 A4
Mongiana I. . . . . . 175 C2
Monguelfo I . . . . . 108 C3
Monheim D . . . . . . 94 C2
Moniaive GB . . . . . 36 A3
Monifieth GB . . . . . 35 B5
Monikie GB . . . . . . 35 B5
**Monistrol-d'Allier**
F. . . . . . . . . . . . 117 C3
**Monistrol de Montserrat**
E . . . . . . . . . . . . 147 C2
**Monistrol-sur-Loire**
F. . . . . . . . . . . .117 B4
Mönkebude D . . . . 74 A2
Monkton GB . . . . . 36 A2
Monmouth GB. . . . 39 C4
Monnaie F . . . . . . 102 B2
Monnerville F . . . . 90 C2
Monnickendam NL . 70 B2
Monolithos GR . . . 188 C2
Monópoli I . . . . . . 173 B3
Monor H . . . . . . . .112 B3
Monóvar E . . . . . . 159 C3
Monpazier F. . . . . 129 B3
**Monreal**
D. . . . . . . . . . . . .80 B3
E . . . . . . . . . . . . 144 B2
**Monreal del Campo**
E . . . . . . . . . . . . 152 B2
Monreale I . . . . . . 176 A2
Monroy E . . . . . . . 155 B4
Monroyo E . . . . . . 153 B3
Mons B . . . . . . . . 79 B3
Monsaraz P . . . . . 155 C3
Monschau D . . . . . 80 B2
Monségur F . . . . . 128 B3
Monsélice I . . . . . . 121 B4
Mønshaug N . . . . . 46 B3
Monster NL . . . . . . 70 B1
Mönsterås S . . . . . 62 A4
**Monsummano Terme**
I . . . . . . . . . . . . 135 B3
Montabaur D . . . . . 81 B3
Montafia I . . . . . . . 119 C5
Montagnac F. . . . . 130 B2
Montagnana I . . . . 121 B4
Montaigu F . . . . . .114 B2
**Montaigu-de-Quercy**
F. . . . . . . . . . . . 129 B4
**Montaiguët-en-Forez**
F. . . . . . . . . . . .117 A3
Montaigut F . . . . . .116 A2
**Montaigut-sur-Save**
F. . . . . . . . . . . . 129 C4
Montainville F . . . . 90 C1
Montalbán E . . . . . 153 B3
**Montalbán de Córdoba**
E . . . . . . . . . . . . 163 A3
**Montalbano Elicona**
I . . . . . . . . . . . . 177 A4
**Montalbano Iónico**
I . . . . . . . . . . . . 174 A2
Montalbo E . . . . . . 158 B1
Montalcino I . . . . . 135 B4
**Montaldo di Cósola**
I . . . . . . . . . . . . 120 C2
Montalegre P. . . . . 148 A2
**Montalieu-Vercieu**
F. . . . . . . . . . . . 118 B2
**Montalivet-les-Bains**
F. . . . . . . . . . . . 114 C2
Montallegro I . . . . 176 B2
**Montalto delle Marche**
I . . . . . . . . . . . . 136 C2
**Montalto di Castro**
I . . . . . . . . . . . . 168 A1
Montalto Pavese I. 120 C2
Montalto Uffugo I . 174 B2

Montalvão P. . . . . 155 B3
Montamarta E . . . . 149 A4
Montana BG. . . . . 17 D5
**Montana-Vermala**
CH . . . . . . . . . . .119 A4
Montánchez E . . . . 156 A1
Montanejos E . . . . 153 B3
Montano Antília I. . 172 B1
Montans F . . . . . . 129 C4
Montargil P . . . . . . 154 B2
Montargis F . . . . . 103 B4
**Montastruc-la-**
**Conseillère** F. . . . 129 C4
Montauban F . . . . . 129 B4
**Montauban-de-Bretagne**
F. . . . . . . . . . . . 101 A3
Montbard F . . . . . . 104 B3
Montbarrey F. . . . . 105 B4
Montbazens F . . . . 130 A1
Montbazon F . . . . . 102 B2
Montbéliard F . . . . 106 B1
Montbenoit F . . . . 105 C5
Montbeugny F . . . . 104 C2
Montblanc E . . . . . 147 C2
Montbozon F . . . . . 105 B5
Montbrison F . . . . .117 B4
Montbron F . . . . . . 115 C4
**Montbrun-les-Bains**
F. . . . . . . . . . . . 131 A4
**Montceau-les-Mines**
F. . . . . . . . . . . . 104 C3
Montcenis F . . . . . 104 C3
Montchanin F . . . . 104 C3
Montcornet F. . . . . 91 B4
Montcuq F . . . . . . 129 B4
Montdardier F . . . . 130 B2
Mont-de-Marsan F. 128 C2
Montdidier F . . . . . 90 B2
Monteagudo E . . . 165 A3
**Monteagudo de las**
**Vicarias** E . . . . . 152 A1
Montealegre E . . . 142 C2
**Montealegre del Castillo**
E . . . . . . . . . . . . 159 C2
**Montebello Iónico**
I . . . . . . . . . . . . 175 D1
**Montebello Vicentino**
I . . . . . . . . . . . . 121 B4
Montebelluna I . . . 121 B5
Montebourg F . . . . 88 A2
Montebruno I. . . . . 134 A2
Monte-Carlo MC . . 133 B3
Montecarotto I . . . . 136 B2
Montecassiano I . . 136 B2
Montecastrilli I . . . 168 A2
**Montecatini Terme**
I . . . . . . . . . . . . 135 B3
Montécchio I . . . . . 136 B1
**Montécchio Emilia**
I . . . . . . . . . . . . 121 C3
**Montécchio Maggiore**
I . . . . . . . . . . . . 121 B4
Montech F . . . . . . 129 C4
**Montechiaro d'Asti**
I . . . . . . . . . . . . 119 B5
Monte Clara P. . . . 155 B3
Monte Clérigo P . . 160 B1
Montecórice I . . . . 170 C2
**Montecorvino Rovella**
I . . . . . . . . . . . . 170 C2
Monte da Pedra P. 155 B3
Monte de Goula P. 155 B3
Montederramo E. . 141 B3
Montedoro I . . . . . 176 B2
Monte do Trigo P.. 155 C3
Montefalco I . . . . . 136 C1
**Montefalcone di Val**
**Fortore** I. . . . . . . 170 B3
**Montefalcone nel**
**Sánnio** I. . . . . . . 170 B2
Montefano I . . . . . 136 B2
Montefiascone I . . 168 A2
Montefiorino I . . . . 134 A3
Montefortino I . . . . 136 C2
Montefranco I . . . . 168 A2
Montefrío E . . . . . 163 A4
**Montegiordano Marina**
I . . . . . . . . . . . . 174 A2
Montegiórgio I . . . . 136 B2
Monte Gordo P . . . 160 B2
Montegranaro I . . . 136 B2
Montehermoso E . . 149 B3
Montejicar E . . . . . 163 A4
**Montejo de la Sierra**
E . . . . . . . . . . . . 151 A4
**Montejo de Tiermes**
E . . . . . . . . . . . . 151 A4
Monte Juntos P.. . 155 C3
Montel-de-Gelat F .116 B2
**Monteleone di Púglia**
I . . . . . . . . . . . . 171 B3
**Monteleone di Spoleto**
I . . . . . . . . . . . . 169 A3
**Monteleone d'Orvieto**
I . . . . . . . . . . . . 135 C5
Montelepre I . . . . . 176 A2
Montelibretti I . . . . 168 A2
Montelier F . . . . . . 117 C5
Montélimar F . . . . 131 A3
**Montella**
E . . . . . . . . . . . .146 B2
I . . . . . . . . . . . . 170 C3
Montellano E . . . . 162 A2
**Montelupo Fiorentino**
I . . . . . . . . . . . . 135 B4
**Montemaggiore Belsito**
I . . . . . . . . . . . . 176 B2
Montemagno I . . . . 119 C5

Montemayor E. . . . 163 A3
**Montemayor de Pinilla**
E. . . . . . . . . . . . 150 A3
Montemésola I. . . . 173 B3
Montemilleto I . . . . 170 B2
Montemilone I . . . . 172 A1
Montemolin E . . . . 161 A3
Montemónaco I . . . 136 C2
**Montemor-o-Novo**
P. . . . . . . . . . . . 154 C2
**Montemor-o-Velho**
P. . . . . . . . . . . . 148 B1
Montemurro I . . . . 174 A1
Montendre F . . . . . 128 A2
**Montenegro de Cameros**
E . . . . . . . . . . . . 143 B4
**Montenero di Bisáccia**
I . . . . . . . . . . . . 170 B2
Monteneuf F . . . . . 101 B3
Monteparano I . . . . 173 B3
Montepescali I . . . 135 C4
Montepiano I . . . . . 135 A4
Monte Porzio I . . . 136 B2
Montepulciano I . . 135 B4
Monte Real P. . . . . 154 B2
Montereale I . . . . . 169 A3
**Montereale Valcellina**
I . . . . . . . . . . . . 122 A1
**Montereau-Faut-Yonne**
F. . . . . . . . . . . . 90 C2
Monte Redondo P . 154 B2
Monterénzio I . . . . 135 A4
Monte Romano I . . 168 A1
**Monteroni d'Árbia**
I . . . . . . . . . . . . 135 B4
**Monteroni di Lecce**
I . . . . . . . . . . . . 173 B4
**Monterosso al Mare**
I . . . . . . . . . . . . 134 A2
Monterosso Almo I 177 B3
**Monterosso Grana**
I . . . . . . . . . . . . 133 A3
Monterotondo I . . . 168 A2
**Monterotondo Maríttimo**
I . . . . . . . . . . . . 135 B3
Monterrey E. . . . . 141 C3
Monterroso E . . . . 140 B3
**Monterrubio de la**
**Serena** E . . . . . . 156 B2
Monterubbiano I . . 136 B2
Montesa E . . . . . . 159 C3
Montesalgueiro E . 140 A2
**Monte San Giovanni**
**Campano** I. . . . . . 169 B3
**Montesano sulla**
**Marcellana** I. . . . 174 A1
**Monte San Savino**
I . . . . . . . . . . . . 135 B4
**Monte Sant'Ángelo**
I . . . . . . . . . . . . 171 B3
Montesárchio I . . . 170 B2
Montescaglioso I . 171 C4
Montesclaros E. . . 150 B3
Montesilvano I . . . 169 A4
Montespértoli I . . . 135 B4
**Montesquieu-Volvestre**
F. . . . . . . . . . . . 146 A2
Montesquiou F . . . 129 C3
**Montestruc-sur-Gers**
F. . . . . . . . . . . . 129 C3
Montes Velhos P . . 160 B1
Montevarchi I . . . . 135 B4
Montevéglio I . . . . 135 A4
Monte Vilar P. . . . . 154 B1
Montfaucon F . . . . 101 B4
**Montfaucon-d'Argonne**
F. . . . . . . . . . . . 91 B5
**Montfaucon-en-Velay**
F. . . . . . . . . . . .117 B4
**Montferrat**
Isère F . . . . . . . . 118 B2
Var F . . . . . . . . . 132 B2
**Montfort-en-Chalosse**
F. . . . . . . . . . . . 128 C2
Montfort-l'Amaury F 90 C1
**Montfort-le-Gesnois**
F. . . . . . . . . . . . 102 A2
**Montfort-sur-Meu**
F. . . . . . . . . . . . 101 A4
Montfort-sur-Risle F 89 A4
Montgai E . . . . . . 147 C1
Montgaillard F . . . . 145 A4
Montgenèvre F . . . 118 C3
Montgiscard F. . . . 146 A2
Montgomery GB . . 39 B3
Montguyon F. . . . . 128 A2
Monthermé F . . . . 91 B4
Monthey CH. . . . . 119 A3
Monthois F . . . . . . 91 B4
**Monthureux-sur-Saône**
F. . . . . . . . . . . . 105 A4
Monti I . . . . . . . . . 178 B3
**Monticelli d'Ongina**
I . . . . . . . . . . . . 120 B2
Montichiari I . . . . . 120 B3
Monticiano I . . . . . 135 B4
Montiel E . . . . . . . 158 C1
Montier-en-Der F . . 91 C4
Montieri I . . . . . . . 135 B4
Montíglio I . . . . . . .119 B5
Montignac F . . . . . 129 A4
Montigny-le-Roi F . 105 B4
**Montigny-lès-Metz**
F. . . . . . . . . . . . 92 B2
**Montigny-sur-Aube**
F. . . . . . . . . . . . 105 B3
**Montijo**
E . . . . . . . . . . . .155 C4

**Montijo** continued
P. . . . . . . . . . . . .154 C2
Montilla E. . . . . . . 163 A3
Montillana E . . . . . 163 A4
Montilly F . . . . . . . 104 C2
Montivilliers F . . . . 89 A4
Montjaux F. . . . . . 130 A1
**Montjean-sur-Loire**
F. . . . . . . . . . . . 102 B1
Montlhéry F . . . . . 90 C2
**Montlieu-la-Garde**
F. . . . . . . . . . . . 128 A2
Mont-Louis F. . . . . 146 B3
**Montlouis-sur-Loire**
F. . . . . . . . . . . . 102 B2
Montluçon F . . . . . 116 A2
Montluel F. . . . . . . 117 B5
Montmarault F . . . . 116 A2
**Montmartin-sur-Mer**
F. . . . . . . . . . . . 88 B2
Montmédy F . . . . . 92 B1
Montmélian F . . . . 118 B3
Montmeyan F . . . . 132 B2
Montmeyran F . . . 117 C4
**Montmirail**
Marne F . . . . . . . 91 C3
Sarthe F . . . . . . . 102 A2
Montmiral F . . . . . 118 B2
Montmirat F . . . . . 131 B3
**Montmirey-le-Château**
F. . . . . . . . . . . . 105 B4
**Montmoreau-St Cybard**
F. . . . . . . . . . . . 115 C4
Montmorency F . . . 90 C2
Montmorillon F . . . 115 B4
Montmort-Lucy F . . 91 C3
**Montoir-de-Bretagne**
F. . . . . . . . . . . . 101 B3
**Montoire-sur-le-Loir**
F. . . . . . . . . . . . 102 B2
Montoito P. . . . . . . 155 C3
Montólieu F . . . . . 146 A3
**Montório al Vomano**
I . . . . . . . . . . . . 169 A3
Montoro E . . . . . . 157 B3
Montpellier F . . . . 131 B2
**Montpezat-de-Quercy**
F. . . . . . . . . . . . 129 B4
**Montpezat-sous-Bouzon**
F. . . . . . . . . . . .117 C4
**Montpon-Ménestérol**
F. . . . . . . . . . . . 128 A3
**Montpont-en-Bresse**
F. . . . . . . . . . . . 105 C4
**Montréal**
Aude F . . . . . . . . 146 A3
Gers F . . . . . . . . 128 C3
**Montredon-Labessonnié**
F. . . . . . . . . . . . 130 B1
Montréjeau F . . . . 145 A4
Montrésor F . . . . . 103 B3
Montresta I . . . . . . 178 B2
Montret F . . . . . . . 105 C4
**Montreuil**
Pas de Calais F. . . 78 B1
Seine St Denis F . . 90 C2
**Montreuil-aux-Lions**
F. . . . . . . . . . . . 90 B3
Montreuil-Bellay F . 102 B1
Montreux CH . . . . 106 C1
Montrevault F . . . . 101 B4
**Montrevel-en-Bresse**
F. . . . . . . . . . . . 118 A2
Montrichard F . . . . 103 B3
Montricoux F . . . . 129 B4
**Mont-roig del Camp**
E . . . . . . . . . . . . 147 C1
**Montrond-les-Bains**
F. . . . . . . . . . . .117 B4
Montrose GB. . . . . 35 B5
Montroy E . . . . . . 159 B3
Montsalvy F. . . . . . 116 C2
**Montsauche-les-Settons**
F. . . . . . . . . . . . 104 B3
Montseny E . . . . . 147 C3
Montsoreau F . . . . 102 B2
**Mont-sous-Vaudrey**
F. . . . . . . . . . . . 105 C4
**Monts-sur-Guesnes**
F. . . . . . . . . . . . 102 C2
Mont-St Aignan F . 89 A5
Mont-St Vincent F . 104 C3
Montsûrs F. . . . . . 102 A1
Montuenga E . . . . 150 A3
Montuïri E . . . . . . 167 B3
Monturque E . . . . 163 A3
Monza I . . . . . . . . 120 B2
Monzón E . . . . . . 145 C4
**Monzón de Campos**
E . . . . . . . . . . . . 142 B2
**Moorbad Lobenstein**
D . . . . . . . . . . . . 83 B3
Moordorf D . . . . . . 71 A4
Moorslede B . . . . . 78 B3
Moos D. . . . . . . . 107 B3
Moosburg D. . . . . 95 C3
**Moosburg im Kärnten**
A. . . . . . . . . . . . 110 C1
Mór H . . . . . . . . . .112 B2
Mora E . . . . . . . . 157 A4
Móra P . . . . . . . . 154 C2
Mora S . . . . . . . . 50 A1
Moraby S . . . . . . . 50 B2
Mòra d'Ebre E . . . 153 A4
**Mora de Rubielos**
E . . . . . . . . . . . . 153 B3
Moradillo de Roa E 151 A4
Morąg PL . . . . . . . 69 B4

Mórahalom H 126 A1
Moraime E 140 A1
Morais P 149 A3
Móra la Nova E 153 A4
Moral de Calatrava E 157 B4
Moraleda de Zafayona E 163 A4
Moraleja E 149 B3
Moraleja del Vino E 150 A2
Morales del Vino E 150 A2
Morales de Toro E 150 A2
Morales de Valverde E 141 C5
Moralina E 149 A3
Morano Cálabro I 174 B2
Mörarp S 61 C2
Morasverdes E 149 B3
Morata de Jalón E 152 A2
Morata de Jiloca E 152 A2
Morata de Tajuña E 151 B4
Moratalla E 164 A3
Moravče SLO 123 A3
Moravec CZ 97 B4
Moraviţa RO 126 B3
Morávka CZ 98 B2
Moravská Třebová CZ 97 B4
Moravské Budějovice CZ 97 B3
Moravské Lieskové SK 98 C1
Moravske Toplice SLO 111 C3
Moravský-Beroun CZ 98 B1
Moravský Krumlov CZ 97 B4
Moravský Svätý Ján SK 98 C1
Morawica PL 87 B4
Morawin PL 86 A2
Morbach D 92 B3
Morbegno I 120 A2
Morbier F 105 C5
Mörbisch am See A 111 B3
Mörbylånga S 63 B4
Morcenx F 128 B2
Morciano di Romagna I 136 B1
Morcone I 170 B2
Morcuera E 151 A4
Mordelles F 101 A4
Mordoğan TR 188 A1
Moréac F 100 B3
Morebattle GB 35 C5
Morecambe GB 36 B4
Moreda
*Granada* E 163 A4
*Oviedo* E 142 A1
Morée F 103 B3
Moreles de Rey E 141 B5
Morella E 153 B3
Moreruela de los Infanzones E 149 A4
Morés E 152 A2
Móres I 178 B2
Morestel F 118 B2
Moretonhampstead GB 43 B3
Moreton-in-Marsh GB 44 B2
Moret-sur-Loing F 90 C2
Moretta I 119 C4
Moreuil F 90 B2
Morez F 105 C5
Mörfelden D 93 B4
Morgat F 100 A1
Morges CH 105 C5
Morgex I 119 B4
Morgongåva S 51 C3
Morhange F 92 C2
Morhet B 92 B1
Mori I 121 B3
Morialmé B 79 B4
Morianes P 160 B2
Moriani Plage F 180 A2
Mórichida H 111 B4
Moriles E 163 A3
Morille E 150 B2
Moringen D 82 A1
Morjärv S 196 C5
Morkarla S 51 B4
Mørke DK 59 B3
Mørkøv DK 61 D1
Morkovice-Slížany CZ 98 B1
Morlaàs F 145 A3
Morlaix F 100 A2
Morley F 91 C5
Mörlunda S 62 A3
Mormanno I 174 B1
Mormant F 90 C2
Mornant F 117 B4
Mornay-Berry F 103 B4
Morón de Almazán E 152 A1
Morón de la Frontera E 162 A2
Morović SRB 125 B5
Morozzo I 133 A3
Morpeth GB 37 A5
Morphou CY 181 A1
Mörrum S 63 B2
Morsbach D 81 B3
Mörsch D 93 C4
Mörsil S 199 B10
Morsum D 64 B1
Mørsvikbotn N 194 C6
Mortagne-au-Perche F 89 B4
Mortagne-sur-Gironde F 114 C3
Mortagne-sur-Sèvre F 114 B3
Mortágua P 148 B1
Mortain F 88 B3
Mortara I 120 B1
Morteau F 105 B5
Mortegliano I 122 B2
Mortelle I 177 A4
Mortemart F 115 B4
Mortimer's Cross GB 39 B4
Mortrée F 89 B4
Mörtschach A 109 C3
Mortsel B 79 A4
Morud DK 59 C3
Morwenstow GB 42 B2
Moryń PL 74 B3
Morzeszczyn PL 69 B3
Morzewo PL 69 B4
Morzine F 118 A3
Mosbach D 93 B5
Mosbjerg DK 58 A3
Mosby N 53 B3
Mosca P 149 A3
Moscavide P 154 C1
Moščenica HR 124 B2
Mošćenice HR 123 B3
Moščenicka Draga HR 123 B3
Mosciano Sant'Ángelo I 136 C2
Mościsko PL 85 B4
Moscow = Moskva RUS 9 E10
Mosina PL 75 B5
Mosjøen N 195 E4
Moskog N 46 A3
Moskorzew PL 87 B3
Moskosel S 196 D2
Moskuvarra FIN 197 B9
Moskva = Moscow RUS 9 E10
Moslavina Podravska HR 125 B3
Moşniţa Nouă RO 126 B3
Moso in Passiria I 108 C2
Mosonmagyaróvár H 111 B4
Mošorin SRB 126 B2
Mošovce SK 98 C2
Mosqueruela E 153 B3
Moss N 54 A1
Mossfellsbær IS 190 C4
Mössingen D 93 C5
Møsstrand N 47 C5
Most CZ 83 B5
Mosta M 175 C3
Mostar BIH 139 B3
Mosterhamn N 52 A1
Mostki PL 75 B4
Most na Soči SLO 122 A2
Móstoles E 151 B4
Mostová SK 111 A4
Mostowo PL 68 A1
Mostuéjouls F 130 A2
Mosty PL 75 A3
Mostys'ka UA 13 D5
Mosvik N 199 B7
Mota del Cuervo E 158 B1
Mota del Marqués E 150 A2
Motala S 55 B6
Motherwell GB 35 C4
Möthlow D 74 B1
Motilla del Palancar E 158 B2
Motnik SLO 123 A3
Motovun HR 122 B2
Motril E 163 B4
Motta I 121 B4
Motta di Livenza I 122 B1
Motta Montecorvino I 170 B3
Motta Visconti I 120 B1
Mottisfont GB 44 B2
Móttola I 173 B3
Mou DK 58 B3
Mouchard F 105 C4
Moudon CH 106 C1
Moudros GR 183 D7
Mougins F 132 B2
Mouilleron en-Pareds F 114 B3
Mouliherne F 102 B2
Moulinet F 133 B3
Moulins F 104 C2
Moulins-Engilbert F 104 C2
Moulins-la-Marche F 89 B4
Moulismes F 115 B4
Moult F 89 A3
Mountain Ash GB 39 C3
Mountbellew IRL 28 A3
Mountfield GB 27 B3
Mountmellick IRL 30 A1
Mountrath IRL 30 A1
Mountsorrel GB 40 C2
Moura P 160 A2
Mourão P 155 C3
Mourenx F 145 A3
Mouriés F 131 B3
Mourmelon-le-Grand F 91 B4
Mouronho P 148 B1
Mourujärvi FIN 197 C11
Mouscron B 78 B3
Mousehole GB 42 B1
Moussac F 131 B3
Moussey F 92 C2
Mousteru F 100 A2
Moustey F 128 B2
Moustiers-Ste Marie F 132 B2
Mouthe F 105 C5
Mouthier-Haute-Pierre F 105 B5
Mouthoumet F 146 B3
Moutier CH 106 B2
Moûtiers F 118 B3
Moutiers-les-Mauxfaits F 114 B2
Mouy F 90 B2
Mouzaki GR 182 D3
Mouzon F 91 B5
Møvik N 46 B2
Moville IRL 27 A3
Moy
*Highland* GB 32 D2
*Tyrone* GB 27 B4
Moycullen IRL 28 A2
Moyenmoutier F 92 C2
Moyenvic F 92 C2
Moylough IRL 28 A3
Mózar E 141 C5
Mozhaysk RUS 9 E10
Mozirje SLO 123 A3
Mözs H 112 C2
Mozzanica I 120 B2
Mramorak SRB 127 C2
Mrčajevci SRB 127 D2
Mrkonjić Grad BIH 138 A3
Mrkopalj HR 123 B3
Mrocza PL 76 A2
Mroczeń PL 86 A1
Mroczno PL 69 B4
Mrzezyno PL 67 B4
Mšec CZ 84 B1
Mšeno CZ 84 B2
Mstów PL 86 B3
Mstsislaw BY 13 A9
Mszana Dolna PL 99 B4
Mszczonów PL 77 C5
Muć HR 138 B2
Múccia I 136 B2
Much D 80 B3
Mücheln D 83 A3
Much Marcle GB 39 C4
Muchów PL 85 A4
Much Wenlock GB 39 B4
Mucientes E 142 C2
Muckross IRL 29 B2
Mucur TR 23 B8
Muda P 160 B1
Mudanya TR 186 B3
Mudau D 93 B5
Müden D 72 B3
Mudersbach D 81 B3
Mudurnu TR 187 B6
Muel E 152 A2
Muelas del Pan E 149 A4
Muess D 73 A4
Muff IRL 27 A3
Mugardos E 140 A2
Muge P 154 B2
Mügeln
*Sachsen* D 83 A5
*Sachsen-Anhalt* D 83 A5
Múggia I 122 B2
Mugnano I 135 B5
Mugron F 128 C2
Mugueimes E 140 C3
Muhi H 113 B4
Mühlacker D 93 C4
Mühlbach am Hochkönig A 109 B4
Mühlberg
*Brandenburg* D 83 A5
*Thüringen* D 82 B2
Mühldorf
A 109 C4
D 95 C4
Muhleberg CH 106 C2
Mühleim D 107 A3
Muhlen-Eichsen D 65 C4
Mühlhausen
*Bayern* D 94 B2
*Thüringen* D 82 A2
Mühltroff D 83 B3
Muhos FIN 3 D10
Muhr A 109 B4
Muine Bheag IRL 30 B2
Muirkirk GB 36 A2
Muir of Ord GB 32 D2
Muirteira P 154 B1
Mukacheve UA 12 D5
Muker GB 37 B4
Mula E 165 A3
Muğla TR 188 B3
Mulben GB 32 D3
Mulegns CH 107 C4
Mules I 108 C2
Mülheim D 80 A2
Mulhouse F 106 B2
Muljava SLO 123 B3
Mullanys Cross IRL 26 B2
Müllheim D 106 B2
Mullhyttan S 55 A5
Mullinavat IRL 30 B1
Mullingar IRL 30 A1
Mullion GB 42 B1
Müllrose D 74 B3
Mullsjö S 60 B3
Mulseryd S 60 B3
Munaðarnes IS 190 A4
Munana E 150 B2
Muñás E 141 A4
Münchberg D 83 B3
Müncheberg D 74 B3
München = Munich D 108 A2
Munchen-Gladbach = Mönchengladbach D 80 A2
Münchhausen D 81 B4
Mundaka E 143 A4
Münden D 82 A1
Munderfing A 109 A4
Munderkingen D 107 A4
Mundesley GB 41 C5
Munera E 158 B1
Mungia E 143 A4
Munich = München D 108 A2
Muñico E 150 B2
Muniesa E 153 A3
Munka-Ljungby S 61 C2
Munkebo DK 59 C3
Munkedal S 54 B2
Munkflohögen S 199 B11
Munkfors S 49 C5
Munktorp S 56 A2
Münnerstadt D 82 B2
Muñopepe E 150 B3
Muñotello E 150 B2
Münsingen
CH 106 C2
D 94 C1
Munsö S 57 A3
Münster
CH 106 C3
*Hessen* D 93 B4
Münster D 72 B3
Münster D 71 C4
Munster F 106 A2
Muntibar E 143 A4
Münzkirchen A 96 C1
Muodoslompolo S 196 B6
Muonio FIN 196 B6
Muotathal CH 107 C3
Muradiye TR 186 D2
Murakeresztúr H 124 A2
Murán SK 99 C4
Murano I 122 B1
Muras E 140 A3
Murat F 116 B2
Muratlı TR 186 A2
Murato F 180 A2
Murat-sur-Vèbre F 130 B1
Murau A 109 B5
Muravera I 179 C3
Murazzano I 133 A4
Murça P 148 A2
Murchante E 144 B2
Murchin D 66 C2
Murcia E 165 B3
Murczyn PL 76 B2
Mur-de-Barrez F 116 C2
Mur-de-Bretagne F 100 A2
Mur-de-Sologne F 103 B3
Mureck A 110 C2
Mürefte TR 186 B2
Muret F 146 A2
Murg CH 107 B4
Murguia E 143 B4
Muri CH 106 B3
Murias de Paredes E 141 B4
Muriedas E 143 A3
Muriel Viejo E 143 C4
Murillo de Rio Leza E 143 B4
Murillo el Fruto E 144 B2
Murjek S 196 C3
Murlaggan GB 34 B2
Murmansk RUS 3 B13
Murmashi RUS 3 B13
Murnau D 108 B2
Muro
E 167 B3
F 180 A1
Muro de Alcoy E 159 C3
Murol F 116 B2
Muro Lucano I 172 B1
Muron F 114 B3
Muros E 140 B1
Muros de Nalón E 141 A4
Murowana Goślina PL 76 B2
Mürren CH 106 C2
Murrhardt D 94 C1
Murska Sobota SLO 111 C3
Mursko Središce HR 111 C3
Murtas E 164 C1
Murten CH 106 C2
Murter HR 137 B4
Murtiçi TR 189 C6
Murtosa P 148 B1
Murtovaara FIN 197 D12
Murvica HR 137 A4
Murviel-lès-Béziers F 130 B2
Mürzsteg A 110 B2
Murzynowo PL 75 B4
Mürzzuschlag A 110 B2
Musculdy F 144 A3
Muskö S 57 A4
Mušov CZ 97 C4
Musselburgh GB 35 C4
Musselkanaal NL 71 B4
Mussidan F 129 A3
Mussomeli I 176 B2
Musson B 92 B1
Mussy-sur-Seine F 104 B3
Mustafakemalpaşa TR 186 B3
Muszaki PL 77 A5
Muszyna PL 99 B4
Mut TR 23 C7
Muta SLO 110 C2
Muthill GB 35 B4
Mutné SK 99 B3
Mutriku E 143 A4
Muttalip TR 187 C5
Mutterbergalm A 108 B2
Muurola FIN 197 C8
Muxía E 140 A1
Muxilka-Ugarte E 143 A4
Muzillac F 101 B3
Mužla SK 112 B2
Muzzano del Turgnano I 122 B2
Mybster GB 32 C3
Myckelgensjö S 200 C3
Myennes F 104 B1
Myjava SK 98 C1
Myking N 46 B2
Mykland N 53 B4
Myra N 53 B5
Myrdal N 46 B4
Myre
*Nordland* N 194 A6
*Nordland* N 194 B6
Myresjö S 62 A2
Mýri IS 191 B8
Myrtou CY 181 A2
Mysen N 54 A2
Mysłakowice PL 85 B3
Myślenice PL 99 B3
Myślibórz PL 75 B3
Mysłowice PL 86 B3
Myszków PL 86 B3
Mytishchi RUS 9 E10
Mýtna SK 99 C3
Mýtne Ludany SK 112 A2
Mýto CZ 96 B1

## N

Nå N 46 B3
Naaldwijk NL 79 A4
Naantali FIN 8 B2
Naas IRL 30 A2
Nabais P 148 B2
Nabbelund S 62 A5
Nabburg D 95 B4
Načeradec CZ 96 B2
Náchod CZ 85 B4
Nacław PL 68 A1
Nadarzyce PL 75 A5
Nadarzyn PL 77 B5
Nádasd H 111 C3
Nădlac RO 126 A2
Nádudvar H 113 B5
Nadvirna UA 13 D6
Näfels CH 107 B4
Nafpaktos GR 184 A2
Nafplio GR 184 B3
Nagel D 95 B3
Nagele NL 70 B2
Naggen S 200 D2
Nagłowice PL 87 B4
Nagold D 93 C4
Nagore E 144 B2
Nagyatád H 124 A3
Nagybajom H 124 A3
Nagybaracska H 125 A4
Nagybátony H 113 B3
Nagyberény H 112 C2
Nagybörzsöny H 112 B2
Nagycenk H 111 B3
Nagycserkesz H 113 B5
Nagydorog H 112 C2
Nagyfüged H 113 B4
Nagyhersány H 125 B4
Nagyigmánd H 112 B2
Nagyiván H 113 B4
Nagykanizsa H 111 C3
Nagykáta H 113 B3
Nagykonyi H 112 C2
Nagykörös H 113 B3
Nagykörü H 113 B4
Nagylóc H 112 A3
Nagymágocs H 113 C4
Nagymányok H 125 A4
Nagymaros H 112 B2
Nagyoroszi H 112 A3
Nagyrábé H 113 B5
Nagyréde H 113 B3
Nagyszékely H 112 C2
Nagyszénás H 113 C4
Nagyszokoly H 112 C2
Nagytöke H 113 C4
Nagyvázsony H 111 C4
Nagyvenyim H 112 C2
Naharros E 152 B1
Nahe D 64 C3
Naila D 83 B3
Nailloux F 146 A2
Nailsworth GB 43 A4
Naintré F 115 B4
Nairn GB 32 D3
Najac F 129 B4
Nájera E 143 B4
Nak H 112 C2
Nakksjø N 53 A5
Nakło nad Notecią PL 76 A2
Nakskov DK 65 B4
Nalda E 143 B4
Nälden S 199 B11
Nálepkovo SK 99 C4
Nalliers F 114 B2
Nallıhan TR 187 B6
Nalzen F 146 B2
Nalžouské Hory CZ 96 B1
Namdalseid N 199 A8
Náměšt'nad Oslavou CZ 97 B4
Námestovo SK 99 B3
Namnå N 49 B4
Namsos N 199 A8
Namsskogan N 199 A10
Namur B 79 B4
Namysłów PL 86 A1
Nançay F 103 B4
Nanclares de la Oca E 143 B4
Nancy F 92 C2
Nangis F 90 C3
Nannestad N 48 B3
Nant F 130 A2
Nanterre F 90 C2
Nantes F 101 B4
Nanteuil-le-Haudouin F 90 B2
Nantiat F 115 B5
Nantua F 118 A2
Nantwich GB 38 A4
Naoussa
*Cyclades* GR 185 B6
*Imathia* GR 182 C4
Napajedla CZ 98 B1
Napiwoda PL 77 A5
Naples = Nápoli I 170 C2
Nápoli = Naples I 170 C2
Nar S 57 C4
Nara N 46 A1
Naraval E 141 A4
Narberth GB 39 C2
Nærbø N 52 B1
Narbonne F 130 B1
Narbonne-Plage F 130 B2
Narbuvollen N 199 C8
Narcao I 179 C2
Nardò I 173 B4
Narkaus FIN 197 C9
Narken S 196 C5
Narmo N 48 B3
Narni I 168 A2
Naro I 176 B2
Naro Fominsk RUS 9 E10
Narón E 140 A2
Narros del Castillo E 150 B2
Narta HR 124 B2
Naruszewo PL 77 B5
Narva EST 8 C6
Narvik N 194 B8
Narzole I 133 A3
Näs FIN 51 B7
Nås S 50 B1
Näs S 57 C4
Näsåker S 200 C2
Năsăud RO 17 B6
Nasavrky CZ 97 B3
Nasbinals F 116 C3
Næsbjerg DK 59 C1
Näshull S 62 A3
Našice HR 125 B4
Nasielsk PL 77 B5
Naso I 177 A3
Nassau D 81 B3
Nassenfels D 95 C3
Nassenheide D 74 B2
Nassereith A 108 B1
Nässjö S 62 A2
Nastätten D 81 B3
Næstved DK 65 A4
Näsum S 63 B2
Näsviken S 199 B12
Natalinci SRB 127 C2
Naters CH 119 A5
Nater-Stetten D 108 A2
Nattavaara S 196 C3
Natters A 108 B2
Nattheim D 94 C2
Nättraby S 63 B3
Naturno I 108 C1
Naucelle F 130 A1
Nauders A 108 C1
Nauen D 74 B1
Naul IRL 30 A2
Naumburg D 83 A3
Naundorf D 83 B5
Naunhof D 83 A4
Naustdal N 46 A2
Nautijaur S 196 C2
Nautsi RUS 193 D13
Nava E 142 A1
Navacerrada E 151 B3
Navaconcejo E 149 B4
Nava de Arévalo E 150 B3
Nava de la Asunción E 150 A3
Nava del Rey E 150 A2

Navafriá E 151 A4
Navahermosa E 157 A3
Navahrudak BY 13 B6
Naval E 145 B4
Navalacruz E 150 B3
Navalcán E 150 B2
Navalcarnero E 151 B3
Navaleno E 143 C3
Navalmanzano E 151 A3
Navalmoral E 150 B3
Navalmoral de la Mata E 150 C2
Naválón E 159 C3
Navalonguilla E 150 B2
Navalperal de Pinares E 150 B3
Navalpino E 157 A3
Navaltalgordo E 150 B3
Navaltoril E 156 A3
Navaluenga E 150 B3
Navalvillar de Pela E 156 A2
Navan IRL 30 A2
Navaperal de Tormes E 150 B2
Navapolatsk BY 13 A8
Navarclés E 147 C2
Navarredonda de Gredos E 150 B2
Navarrenx F 144 A3
Navarrés E 159 B3
Navarrete E 143 B4
Navarrevisca E 150 B3
Navás E 147 C2
Navascués E 144 B2
Navas del Madroño E 155 B4
Navas del Rey E 151 B3
Navas del Sepillar E 163 A3
Navas de Oro E 150 A3
Navas de San Juan E 157 B4
Navasfrias E 149 B3
Nave I 120 B3
Nave de Haver P 149 B3
Nävekvarn S 56 B2
Navelli I 169 A3
Navenby GB 40 B3
Näverkärret S 56 A1
Naverstad S 54 B2
Navés E 147 C2
Navezuelas E 156 A2
Navia E 141 A4
Navia de Suarna E 141 B4
Navilly F 105 C4
Năvodari RO 17 C8
Naxos GR 185 B6
Nay F 145 A3
Nazaré P 154 B1
Nazarje SLO 123 A3
Nazilli TR 188 B3
Nazza D 82 A2
Nea Anchialos GR 182 D4
Nea Epidavros GR 184 B4
Nea Flippias GR 182 D2
Nea Kalikratia GR 183 C5
Nea Makri GR 185 A4
Nea Moudania GR 183 C5
Neap GB 33 A5
Nea Peramos GR 183 C6
Neapoli
*Kozani* GR 182 C3
*Kriti* GR 185 D6
*Lakonia* GR 184 C4
Nea Stira GR 185 A5
Neath GB 39 C3
Nea Visa GR 186 A1
Nea Zichni GR 183 B5
Nebljusi HR 124 C1
Neblo SLO 122 A2
Nebolchy RUS 9 C8
Nebra D 82 A3
Nebreda E 143 C3
Nechanice CZ 84 B3
Neckargemünd D 93 B4
Neckarsulm D 94 B1
Neda E 140 A2
Neded SK 112 A1
Nedelišće HR 124 A2
Nederweert NL 80 A1
Nedreberg N 48 B3
Nedre Gärdsjö S 50 B2
Nedre Soppero S 196 A4
Nedstrand N 52 A1
Nedvědice CZ 97 B4
Nędza PL 86 B2
Neede NL 71 B3
Needham Market GB 45 A5
Needingworth GB 44 A3
Neermoor D 71 A4
Neeroeteren B 80 A1
Neerpelt B 79 A5
Neesen D 72 B1
Neetze D 73 A3
Nefyn GB 38 B2
Negotin SRB 16 C5
Negotino MK 182 B4
Negrar I 121 B3
Negredo E 151 A5
Negreira E 140 B2
Nègrepelisse F 129 B4
Negru Vodă RO 17 D8
Negueira de Muñiz E 141 A4
Neheim D 81 A3
Neila E 143 B4
Néive I 119 C5
Nejdek CZ 83 B4
Nekla PL 76 B2
Neksø DK 67 A4
Nelas P 148 B2
Nelaug N 53 B4
Nelidovo RUS 9 D8
Nelim FIN 193 D12
Nellingen D 94 C1
Nelson GB 40 B1
Neman RUS 12 A5
Nemea GR 184 B3
Nemesgörzsöny H 111 B4
Nemeskér H 111 B3
Nemesnádudvar H 125 A5
Nemesszalók H 111 B4
Németkér H 112 C2
Nemours F 103 A4
Nemška Loka SLO 123 B4
Nemšová SK 98 C2
Nenagh IRL 28 B3
Nenince SK 112 A3
Nenita GR 185 A7
Nenzing A 107 B4
Neochori GR 182 D3
Neo Chori GR 184 A2
Neon Petritsi GR 183 B5
Nepi I 168 A2
Nepomuk CZ 96 B1
Nérac F 129 B3
Neratovice CZ 84 B2
Nerchau D 83 A4
Néré F 115 C3
Neresheim D 94 C2
Nereto I 136 C2
Nerezine HR 123 C3
Nerežišća HR 138 B2
Neringa LT 12 A4
Néris-les Bains F 116 A2
Nerito I 169 A3
Nerja E 163 B4
Néronde F 117 B4
Nérondes F 103 C4
Nerpio E 164 A2
Nersingen D 94 C2
Nerva E 161 B3
Nervesa della Battáglia I 121 B5
Nervi I 134 A2
Nes
*Buskerud* N 48 B1
*Hedmark* N 48 B2
NL 70 A2
*Sogn og Fjordane* N 46 A3
*Sør-Trøndelag* N 198 B6
Nesbyen N 47 B6
Neset N 199 D7
Nesflaten N 52 A2
Nesjahverfi IS 191 C10
Neskaupstaður IS 191 B12
Nesland N 53 A3
Neslandsvatn N 53 B5
Nesle F 90 B2
Nesna N 195 D4
Nesoddtangen N 48 C2
Nesovice CZ 98 B1
Nesselwang D 108 B1
Nesslau CH 107 B4
Nessmersiel D 71 A4
Nesso I 120 B2
Nesterov UA 13 C5
Nestorio GR 182 C3
Nesttun N 46 B2
Nesvady SK 112 B2
Nesvatnstemmen N 53 B4
Nether Stowey GB 43 A3
Netland N 52 B2
Netolice CZ 96 B2
Netphen D 81 B4
Netstal CH 107 B4
Nettancourt F 91 C4
Nettetal D 80 A2
Nettlingen D 72 B3
Nettuno I 168 B2
Neualbenreuth D 95 B4
Neubeckum D 81 A4
Neubrandenburg D 74 A2
Neubruchhausen D 72 B1
Neubukow D 65 B4
Neuburg D 94 C3
Neuchâtel CH 106 C1
Neu Darchau D 73 A3
Neudau A 111 B3
Neudietendorf D 82 B2
Neudorf D 93 B4
Neuenbürg D 93 C4
Neuenburg D 71 A4
Neuendorf D 66 B2
Neuenhagen D 74 B2
Neuenhaus D 71 B3
Neuenkirchen
*Niedersachsen* D 71 B5
*Niedersachsen* D 72 A2
*Nordrhein-Westfalen* D 71 B4
*Nordrhein-Westfalen* D 81 B3
Neuenrade D 81 A3
Neuenwalde D 64 C1
Neuerburg D 92 A2
Neufahrn
*Bayern* D 95 C3
*Bayern* D 95 C4
Neuf-Brisach F 106 A2
Neufchâteau
B 92 B1
F 92 C1
Neufchâtel-en-Bray F 90 B1
Neufchâtel-sur-Aisne F 91 B4
Neuflize F 91 B4
Neugersdorf D 84 B2
Neuhardenberg D 74 B3
Neuharlingersiel D 71 A4
Neuhaus
*Bayern* D 95 B3
*Bayern* D 96 C1
*Niedersachsen* D 64 C2
*Niedersachsen* D 73 A3
*Niedersachsen* D 81 A5
Neuhaus a Rennweg D 82 B3
Neuhausen
CH 107 B3
D 83 B5
Neuhausen ob Eck D 107 B3
Neuhof
*Bayern* D 94 B2
*Hessen* D 82 B1
Neuhofen an der Krems A 110 A1
Neuillé-Pont-Pierre F 102 B2
Neuilly-en-Thelle F 90 B2
Neuilly-le-Réal F 104 C2
Neuilly-l'Évêque F 105 B4
Neuilly-St Front F 90 B3
Neu-Isenburg D 93 A4
Neukalen D 66 C1
Neu Kaliss D 73 A4
Neukirch D 84 A2
Neukirchen
A 109 A4
*Hessen* D 81 B5
*Schleswig-Holstein* D 64 B1
Neukirchen am Grossvenediger A 109 B3
Neukirchen bei Heiligen Blut D 95 B4
Neukloster D 65 C4
Neulengbach A 110 A2
Neulise F 117 B4
Neu Lübbenau D 74 B2
Neum BIH 139 C3
Neumagen D 92 B2
Neumarkt D 95 B3
Neumarkt am Wallersee A 109 B4
Neumarkt im Hausruckkreis A 109 A4
Neumarkt im Mühlkreis A 96 C2
Neumarkt im Steiermark A 110 B1
Neumarkt Sankt Veit D 95 C4
Neumünster D 64 B2
Neunburg vorm Wald D 95 B4
Neung-sur-Beuvron F 103 B3
Neunkirch
*Luzern* CH 106 B3
*Schaffhausen* CH 107 B3
Neunkirchen
A 111 B3
*Nordrhein-Westfalen* D 80 B3
*Saarland* D 92 B3
Neunkirchen am Brand D 94 B3
Neuötting D 95 C4
Neupetershain D 84 A2
Neuravensburg D 107 B4
Neureut D 93 B4
Neuruppin D 74 B1
Neusäss D 94 C2
Neusiedl A 111 B3
Neuss D 80 A2
Neussargues-Moissac F 116 B2
Neustadt
*Bayern* D 94 B2
*Bayern* D 95 B4
*Bayern* D 95 C3
*Brandenburg* D 73 B5
*Hessen* D 81 B5
*Niedersachsen* D 72 B2
*Rheinland-Pfalz* D 93 B4
*Sachsen* D 84 A2
*Schleswig-Holstein* D 65 B3
*Thüringen* D 82 B3
*Thüringen* D 83 B3
Neustadt-Glewe D 73 A4
Neustift im Stubaital A 108 B2
Neustrelitz D 74 A2
Neutal A 111 B3
Neutrebbin D 74 B3
Neu-Ulm D 94 C2
Neuves-Maisons F 92 C2
Neuvic
*Corrèze* F 116 B2
*Dordogne* F 129 A3
Neuville-aux-Bois F 103 A4
Neuville-de-Poitou F 115 B4
Neuville-les-Dames F 117 A5
Neuville-sur-Saône F 117 B4
Neuvy-le-Roi F 102 B2
Neuvy-Santour F 104 A2
Neuvy-St Sépulchre F 103 C3
Neuvy-sur-Barangeon F 103 B4
Neuwied D 80 B3
Neuzelle D 74 B3
Névache F 118 B3
Neveklov CZ 96 B2
Nevel RUS 9 D6
Neverfjord N 192 B7
Nevers F 104 C2
Nevesinje BIH 139 B4
Névez F 100 B2
Nevlunghavn N 53 B5
Nevşehir TR 23 B8
New Abbey GB 36 B3
New Aberdour GB 33 D4
New Alresford GB 44 B2
Newark-on-Trent GB 40 B3
Newbiggin-by-the-Sea GB 37 A5
Newbliss IRL 27 B3
Newborough GB 38 A2
Newbridge IRL 30 A2
Newbridge on Wye GB 39 B3
Newburgh
*Aberdeenshire* GB 33 D4
*Fife* GB 35 B4
Newbury GB 44 B2
Newby Bridge GB 36 B4
Newcastle GB 27 B5
Newcastle Emlyn GB 39 B2
Newcastleton GB 37 A4
Newcastle-under-Lyme GB 40 B1
Newcastle upon Tyne GB 37 B5
Newcastle West IRL 29 B2
Newchurch GB 39 B3
New Costessey GB 41 C5
New Cumnock GB 36 A2
Newent GB 39 C4
New Galloway GB 36 A2
Newham GB 45 B4
Newhaven GB 45 C4
Newington GB 45 B5
Newinn IRL 29 B4
Newlyn GB 42 B1
Newmachar GB 33 D4
Newmarket
*Suffolk* GB 45 A4
*Western Isles* GB 31 A2
IRL 29 B3
Newmarket-on-Fergus IRL 28 B3
New Mills GB 40 B2
New Milton GB 44 C2
New Pitsligo GB 33 D4
Newport
*Isle of Wight* GB 44 C2
*Newport* GB 39 C4
*Pembrokeshire* GB 39 B2
*Telford & Wrekin* GB 38 B4
*Mayo* IRL 28 A2
*Tipperary* IRL 29 B3
Newport-on-Tay GB 35 B5
Newport Pagnell GB 44 A3
Newquay GB 42 B1
New Quay GB 39 B2
New Radnor GB 39 B3
New Romney GB 45 C4
New Ross IRL 30 B2
Newry GB 27 B4
New Scone GB 35 B4
Newton Abbot GB 43 B3
Newton Arlosh GB 36 B3
Newton Aycliffe GB 37 B5
Newton Ferrers GB 42 B2
Newtonhill GB 33 D4
Newtonmore GB 32 D2
Newton Stewart GB 36 B2
Newtown
*Herefordshire* GB 39 B4
*Powys* GB 39 B3
Newtownabbey GB 27 B5
Newtownards GB 27 B5
Newtownbutler GB 27 B3
Newtown Cunningham IRL 27 B3
Newtownhamilton GB 27 B4
Newtownmountkennedy IRL 30 A2
Newtown St Boswells GB 35 C5
Newtown Sands IRL 29 B2
Newtownstewart GB 27 B3
Nexon F 115 C5
Neyland GB 39 C2
Nibbiano I 120 C2
Nibe DK 58 B2
Nicastro I 175 C2
Niccone I 135 B5
Nice F 133 B3
Nickelsdorf A 111 B4
Nicolosi I 177 B4
Nicosia
CY 181 A2
I 177 B3
Nicótera I 175 C1
Nidda D 81 B5
Niğde TR 23 C8
Nidzica PL 77 A5
Niebla E 161 B3
Nieborów PL 77 B5
Niebüll D 64 B1
Niechanowo PL 76 B2
Niechorze PL 67 B4
Niedalino PL 67 B5
Niederaula D 82 B1
Niederbipp CH 106 B2
Niederbronn-les-Bains F 93 C3
Niederfischbach D 81 B3
Niedergörsdorf D 74 C1
Niederkrüchten D 80 A2
Niederndorf A 108 B3
Nieder-Olm D 93 B4
Niedersachswerfen D 82 A2
Niederstetten D 94 B1
Niederurnen CH 107 B4
Niederwölz A 110 B1
Niedoradz PL 85 A3
Niedzica PL 99 B4
Niegosławice PL 85 A3
Nieheim D 81 A5
Niemcza PL 85 B4
Niemegk D 74 B1
Niemisel S 196 C5
Niemodlin PL 85 B5
Nienburg
*Niedersachsen* D 72 B2
*Sachsen-Anhalt* D 83 A3
Niepołomice PL 99 A4
Nierstein D 93 B4
Niesky D 84 A2
Niestronno PL 76 B2
Nieświń PL 87 A4
Nieszawa PL 76 B3
Nieul-le-Dolent F 114 B2
Nieul-sur-Mer F 114 B2
Nieuw-Amsterdam NL 71 B3
Nieuw-Buinen NL 71 B3
Nieuwegein NL 70 B2
Nieuwe Niedorp NL 70 B1
Nieuwe-Pekela NL 71 A3
Nieuwerkerken B 79 B5
Nieuwe-schans NL 71 A4
Nieuwolda NL 71 A3
Nieuwpoort B 78 A2
Nieuw-Weerdinge NL 71 B3
Nigrita GR 183 C5
Nigüelas E 163 B4
Níjar E 164 C2
Nijemci HR 125 B5
Nijkerk NL 70 B2
Nijlen B 79 A4
Nijmegen NL 80 A1
Nijverdal NL 71 B3
Nikel RUS 193 C14
Nikinci SRB 127 C1
Nikiti GR 183 C5
Nikitsch A 111 B3
Nikkaluokta S 196 B2
Nikla H 111 C4
Niklasdorf A 110 B2
Nikšić MNE 139 C4
Nilivaara S 196 B4
Nîmes F 131 B3
Nimis I 122 A2
Nimtofte DK 58 B3
Nin HR 137 A4
Nindorf D 64 B2
Ninemilehouse IRL 30 B1
Ninove B 79 B4
Niort F 114 B3
Niš SRB 16 D4
Nisa P 155 B3
Niscemi I 177 B3
Niskala FIN 197 D10
Nissafors S 60 B3
Nissan-lez-Ensérune F 130 B2
Nissedal N 53 A4
Nissumby DK 58 B1
Nisterud N 53 A5
Niton GB 44 C2
Nitra SK 98 C2
Nitrianske-Pravno SK 98 C2
Nitrianske Rudno SK 98 C2
Nitry F 104 B2
Nittedal N 48 B2
Nittenau D 95 B4
Nittendorf D 95 B3
Nivala FIN 3 E9
Nivelles B 79 B4
Nivnice CZ 98 C1
Nižná SK 99 B3
Nižná Boca SK 99 C3
Nižne Repaše SK 99 B4
Nizza Monferrato I 119 C5
Njarðvík IS 190 D3
Njegůsevo SRB 126 B1
Njivice HR 123 B3
Njurundabommen S 200 D3
Njutånger S 200 E3
Noailles F 90 B2
Noain E 144 B2
Noale I 121 B5
Noalejo E 163 A4
Noblejas E 151 C4
Noceda E 141 B4
Nocera Inferiore I 170 C2
Nocera Terinese I 175 B2
Nocera Umbra I 136 B1
Noceto I 120 C3
Noci I 173 B3
Nociglia I 173 B4
Nodeland N 53 B3
Nödinge S 60 B2
Nods F 105 B5
Noé F 146 A2
Noépoli I 174 A2
Noeux-les-Mines F 78 B2
Noez E 157 A3
Nogales E 155 C4
Nogara I 121 B4
Nogarejas E 141 B4
Nogaro F 128 C2
Nogent F 105 A4
Nogent l'Artaud F 90 C3
Nogent-le-Roi F 90 C1
Nogent-le-Rotrou F 89 B4
Nogent-sur-Seine F 91 C3
Nogent-sur-Vernisson F 103 B4
Nogersund S 63 B2
Noguera E 152 B2
Noguerones E 163 A3
Nohfelden D 92 B3
Nohn D 80 B2
Noia E 140 B2
Noicáttaro I 173 A2
Noirétable F 117 B3
Noirmoutier-en-l'Île F 114 A1
Noja E 143 A3
Nojewo PL 75 B5
Nokia FIN 8 B3
Nol S 60 B2
Nola I 170 C2
Nolay F 104 C3
Noli I 133 A4
Nolnyra S 51 B4
Nombela E 150 B3
Nomeny F 92 C2
Nomexy F 92 C2
Nonancourt F 89 B5
Nonant-le-Pin F 89 B4
Nonántola I 121 C4
Nonaspe E 153 A4
None I 119 C4
Nontron F 115 C4
Nonza F 180 A2
Noordhorn NL 71 A3
Noordwijk NL 70 B1
Noordwijkerhout NL 70 B1
Noordwolde NL 70 B3
Noppikoski S 50 A1
Nora S 55 A6
Nørager DK 58 B2
Norberg S 50 B2
Norboda S 51 B5
Nórcia I 136 C2
Nordagutu N 53 A5
Nordanås S 200 B4
Nordausques F 78 B2
Nordborg DK 64 A2
Nordby
*Aarhus Amt.* DK 59 C3
*Ribe Amt.* DK 59 C1
Norddeich D 71 A4
Norddorf D 64 B1
Norden D 71 A4
Nordenham D 72 A1
Norderhov N 48 B2
Norderney D 71 A4
Norderstapel D 64 B2
Norderstedt D 64 C3
Nordfjord N 193 B14
Nordfjordeid N 198 D3
Nordfold N 194 C6
Nordhalben D 82 B3
Nordhausen D 82 A2
Nordheim vor der Rhön D 82 B2
Nordholz D 64 C1
Nordhorn D 71 B4
Nordingrå S 200 D4
Nordkjosbotn N 192 C3
Nordli N 199 A10
Nördlingen D 94 C2
Nordmaling S 200 C5
Nordmark S 49 C6
Nordmela N 194 A6
Nord-Odal N 48 B3
Nordre Osen N 48 A3
Nordsinni N 48 B1
Nørdstedalsseter N 198 D4
Nordstemmen D 72 B2
Nordvågen N 193 B10
Nordwalde D 71 B4
Noreña E 142 A1
Noresund N 48 B1
Norg NL 71 A3
Norheimsund N 46 B3
Norie S 63 B2
Norma I 169 B2
Nornäs S 49 A5
Norrahammar S 62 A2
Norråker S 200 B1
Norrala S 51 A3
Norra Vi S 62 A3
Nørre Aaby DK 59 C2

Nørre Alslev DK 65 B4
Nørre Lyndelse DK 59 C3
Nørre Nebel DK 59 C1
Norrent-Fontes F 78 B2
Nørre Snede DK 59 C2
Nørresundby DK 58 A2
Nørre Vorupør DK 58 B1
Norrfjärden S 196 D4
Norrhed S 196 C3
Norrhult Klavreström S 62 A3
Norrköping S 56 B2
Norrskedika S 51 B5
Norrsundet S 51 B4
Norrtälje S 57 A4
Nors DK 58 A1
Norsbron S 55 A4
Norsholm S 56 B1
Norsjö S 200 B5
Nörten-Hardenberg D 82 A1
Northallerton GB 37 B5
Northampton GB 44 A3
North Berwick GB 35 B5
North Charlton GB 37 A5
Northeim D 82 A2
Northfleet GB 45 B4
North Frodingham GB 40 B3
North Kessock GB 32 D2
Northleach GB 44 B2
North Molton GB 42 A3
North Petherton GB 43 A3
Northpunds GB 33 B5
North Somercotes GB 41 B4
North Tawton GB 42 B3
North Thoresby GB 41 B3
North Walsham GB 41 C5
Northwich GB 38 A4
Norton GB 40 A3
Nortorf D 64 B2
Nort-sur-Erdre F 101 B4
Nörvenich D 80 B2
Norwich GB 41 C5
Norwick GB 33 A6
Nøsen N 47 B5
Nossa Senhora do Cabo P 154 C1
Nossebro S 55 B3
Nössemark S 54 A2
Nossen D 83 A5
Notaresco I 169 A3
Noto I 177 C4
Notodden N 53 A5
Nottingham GB 40 C2
Nottuln D 71 C4
Nouan-le-Fuzelier F 103 B4
Nouans-les-Fontaines F 103 B3
Nougaroulet F 129 C3
Nouvion F 78 B1
Nouzonville F 91 B4
Nova H 111 C3
Nová Baňa SK 98 C2
Nová Bystrica SK 99 B3
Nová Bystřice CZ 97 B3
Nova Crnja SRB 126 B2
Novafeltria I 135 B5
Nova Gorica SLO 122 B2
Nova Gradiška HR 124 B3
Nováky SK 98 C2
Novalaise F 118 B2
Novales E 145 B3
Nova Levante I 108 C2
Novalja HR 137 A3
Nová Paka CZ 84 B3
Nova Pazova SRB 127 C2
Nová Pec CZ 96 C1
Novara I 120 B1
Novara di Sicília I 177 A4
Nova Siri I 174 A2
Novate Mezzola I 120 A2
Nova Topola BIH 124 B3
Novaya Ladoga RUS 9 B8
Nova Zagora BG 17 D6
Nové Hrady CZ 96 C2
Novelda E 165 A4
Novellara I 121 C3
Nové Město SK 98 C1
Nové Město nad Metují CZ 85 B4
Nové Město na Moravě CZ 97 B4
Nové Město pod Smrkem CZ 84 B3
Nové Mitrovice CZ 96 B1
Noventa di Piave I 122 B1
Noventa Vicentina I 121 B4
Novés E 151 B3
Noves F 131 B3
Nové Sady SK 98 C1
Novés de Segre E 147 B2
Nové Strašeci CZ 84 B1
Nové Zámky SK 112 B2
Novgorod RUS 9 C7
Novi Bečej SRB 126 B2
Novi di Módena I 121 C3
Novigrad *Istarska* HR 122 B2
*Zadarsko-Kninska* HR 137 A4
Novigrad Podravski HR 124 A2
Novi Kneževac SRB 126 A2
Novi Lígure I 120 C1
Noville B 92 A1
Novi Marof HR 124 A2
Novion-Porcien F 91 B4
Novi Pazar BG 17 D7
SRB 16 D4
Novi Sad SRB 126 B1
Novi Slankamen SRB 126 B2
Novi Travnik BIH 139 A3
Novi Vinodolski HR 123 B3
Novohrad-Volynskyy UA 13 C7
Novo Mesto SLO 123 B4
Novo Miloševo SRB 126 B2
Novorzhev RUS 9 D6
Novo Selo BIH 125 B3
Novoselytsya UA 17 A7
Novosokolniki RUS 9 D6
Novoveská Huta SK 99 C4
Novovolynsk UA 13 C6
Novska HR 124 B2
Nový Bor CZ 84 B2
Nový Bydžov CZ 84 B3
Novy-Chevrières F 91 B4
Novy Dwór Mazowiecki PL 77 B5
Nový-Hrozenkov CZ 98 B2
Nový Jičín CZ 98 B2
Novy Knin CZ 96 B2
Nowa Cerekwia PL 86 B1
Nowa Dęba PL 87 B5
Nowa Karczma PL 68 A3
Nowa Kościoł PL 85 A3
Nowa Ruda PL 85 B4
Nowa Słupia PL 87 B5
Nowa Sól PL 85 A3
Nowa Wieś PL 69 B4
Nowa-Wieś Wielka PL 76 B3
Nowe PL 69 B3
Nowe Brzesko PL 87 B4
Nowe Grudze PL 77 B4
Nowe Kiejkuty PL 77 A6
Nowe Miasteczko PL 85 A3
Nowe Miasto *Mazowieckie* PL 77 B5
*Mazowieckie* PL 87 A4
Nowe Miasto Lubawskie PL 69 B4
Nowe Miasto nad Wartą PL 76 B2
Nowe Skalmierzyce PL 86 A2
Nowe Warpno PL 74 A3
Nowica PL 69 A4
Nowogard PL 75 A4
Nowogród Bobrzanski PL 84 A3
Nowogrodziec PL 84 A3
Nowosolna PL 86 A3
Nowy Dwór Gdański PL 69 A4
Nowy Korczyn PL 87 B4
Nowy Sącz PL 99 B4
Nowy Staw PL 69 A4
Nowy Targ PL 99 B4
Nowy Tomyśl PL 75 B5
Nowy Wiśnicz PL 99 B4
Noyalo F 101 B3
Noyal-Pontivy F 100 A3
Noyant F 102 B2
Noyelles-sur-Mer F 78 B1
Noyen-sur-Sarthe F 102 B1
Noyers F 104 B2
Noyers-sur-Cher F 103 B3
Noyers-sur-Jabron F 132 A1
Noyon F 90 B2
Nozay F 101 B4
Nuaillé F 102 B1
Nuaillé-d'Aunis F 114 B3
Nuars F 104 B2
Nubledo E 141 A5
Nuéno E 145 B3
Nuestra Señora Sa Verge des Pilar E 166 C1
Nueva E 142 A2
Nueva Carteya E 163 A3
Nuevalos E 152 A2
Nuits F 104 B3
Nuits-St Georges F 105 B3
Nule I 178 B3
Nules E 159 B3
Nulvi I 178 B2
Numana I 136 B2
Numansdorp NL 79 A4
Nümbrecht D 81 B3
Nunchritz D 83 A5
Nuneaton GB 40 C2
Nunnanen FIN 196 A7
N Unnaryd S 60 B3
Nuñomoral E 149 B3
Nunspeet NL 70 B2
Nuorgam FIN 193 B11
Núoro I 178 B3
Nurallao I 179 C3
Nuremberg = Nürnberg D 94 B3
Nurmes FIN 3 E11
Nürnberg = Nuremberg D 94 B3
Nurri I 179 C3
Nürtingen D 94 C1
Nus I 119 B4
Nusnäs S 50 B1
Nusplingen D 107 A3
Nuštar HR 125 B4
Nuupas FIN 197 C9
Nyáker S 200 C5
Nyáregyháza H 112 B3
Nyarlörinc H 113 C3
Nyasvizh BY 13 B7
Nybble S 55 A5
Nybergsund N 49 A4
Nybøl DK 64 B2
Nyborg DK 59 C3
S 196 D6
Nybro S 62 B3
Nybster GB 32 C3
Nyby DK 65 B5
Nye S 62 A3
Nyékládháza H 113 B4
Nyergesujfalu H 112 B2
Nyhammar S 50 B1
Nyhyttan S 55 A5
Nyirád H 111 B4
Nyirbátor H 16 B5
Nyíregyháza H 16 B4
Nyker DK 67 A3
Nykil S 56 B1
Nykirke N 48 B2
Nykøbing *Falster* DK 65 B4
*Vestsjællands Amt.* DK 61 D1
Nykøbing Mors DK 58 B1
Nyköping S 56 B3
Nykroppa S 55 A5
Nykvarn S 56 A3
Nykyrke S 55 B5
Nyland S 200 C3
Nylars DK 67 A3
Nymburk CZ 84 B3
Nynäshamn S 57 B3
Nyon CH 118 A3
Nyons F 131 A4
Nýřany CZ 96 B1
Nýrsko CZ 95 B5
Nyrud N 193 C13
Nysa PL 85 B5
Nysäter S 55 A3
Nyseter N 198 C5
Nyskoga S 49 B4
Nysted DK 65 B4
Nystrand N 53 A5
Nyúl H 111 B4
Nyvoll N 192 B7

## O

Oadby GB 40 C2
Oakengates GB 38 B4
Oakham GB 40 C3
Oanes N 52 B2
Obalj BIH 139 B4
Oban GB 34 B2
O Barco E 141 B4
Obbola S 200 C6
Obdach A 110 B1
Obejo E 156 B3
Oberammergau D 108 B2
Oberasbach D 94 B2
Oberau D 108 B2
Oberaudorf D 108 B3
Oberbruck F 106 B1
Oberdiessbach CH 106 C2
Oberdorf CH 106 B2
Oberdrauburg A 109 C3
Oberelsbach D 82 B2
Obere Stanz A 110 B2
Ober Grafendorf A 110 A2
Obergünzburg D 108 B1
Obergurgl A 108 C2
Oberhausen D 80 A2
Oberhof D 82 B2
Oberkirch D 93 C4
Oberkirchen D 81 A4
Oberkochen D 94 C2
Obermassfeld-Grimmenthal D 82 B2
Ober-Morlen D 81 B4
Obermünchen D 95 C3
Obernai F 93 C3
Obernberg A 96 C1
Obernburg D 93 B5
Oberndorf D 93 C4
Oberndorf bei Salzburg A 109 B3
Obernkirchen D 72 B2
Oberort A 110 B2
Oberpullendorf A 111 B3
Oberriet CH 107 B4
Oberröblingen D 82 A3
Oberrot D 94 B1
Oberstaufen D 107 B5
Oberstdorf D 107 B5
Obertauern A 109 B4
Obertilliach A 109 C3
Obertraubling D 95 C4
Obertraun A 109 B4
Obertrubach D 95 B3
Obertrum A 109 B4
Oberursel D 81 B4
Obervellach A 109 C4
Oberviechtach D 95 B4
Oberwart A 111 B3
Oberwesel D 93 A3
Oberwinter D 80 B3
Oberwölzstadt A 110 B1
Oberzell D 96 C1
Obice PL 87 B4
Óbidos P 154 B1
Obing D 109 B3
Objat F 129 A4
Objazda PL 68 A2
Öblarn A 109 B5
Obninsk RUS 9 E10
O Bolo E 141 B3
Oborniki PL 75 B5
Oborniki Śląskie PL 85 A4
Obornjača SRB 126 B1
Obrenovac SRB 127 C2
Obrež SRB 127 C1
Obrigheim D 93 B5
Obrov SLO 123 B3
Obrovac HR 137 A4
SRB 126 B1
Obrovac Sinjski HR 138 B2
Obruk TR 23 B7
Obrzycko PL 75 B5
Obudovac BIH 125 C4
Ocaña E 151 C4
O Carballiño E 140 B2
Occhiobello I 121 C4
Occimiano I 119 B5
Očevlja BIH 139 A4
Ochagavía E 144 B2
Ochiltree GB 36 A2
Ochla PL 84 A3
Ochotnica-Dolna PL 99 B4
Ochotnica-Górna PL 99 B4
Ochsenfurt D 94 B2
Ochsenhausen D 107 A4
Ochtendung D 80 B3
Ochtrup D 71 B4
Ocieka PL 87 B5
Ockelbo S 50 B3
Öckerö S 60 B1
Ocniţa MD 17 A7
O Corgo E 141 B3
Očová SK 99 C3
Ócsa H 112 B3
Öcseny H 125 A4
Öcsöd H 113 C4
Octeville F 88 A2
Ocypel PL 69 B3
Ödåkra S 61 C2
Odby DK 58 B1
Odda N 46 B3
Odder DK 59 C3
Ödeborg S 54 B2
Odeceixe P 160 B1
Odechów PL 87 A5
Odeleite P 160 B2
Odemira P 160 B1
Ödemiş TR 188 A2
Odensbacken S 56 A1
Odense DK 59 C3
Odensjö *Jönköping* S 62 A2
*Kronoberg* S 60 C3
Oderberg D 74 B3
Oderzo I 122 B1
Odesa = Odessa UA 17 B9
Ödeshög S 55 B5
Odessa = Odesa UA 17 B9
Odiáxere P 160 B1
Odie GB 33 B4
Odiham GB 44 B3
Odintsovo RUS 9 E10
Odivelas P 160 A1
Odolanów PL 85 A5
Odón E 152 B2
Odorheiu Secuiesc RO 17 B6
Odrowaz PL 87 A4
Odry CZ 98 B1
Odrzywół PL 87 A4
Ødsted DK 59 C2
Odžaci SRB 126 B1
Odžak BIH 125 B4
Oebisfelde D 73 B3
Oederan D 83 B5
Oeding D 71 C3
Oegstgeest NL 70 B1
Oelde D 81 A4
Oelsnitz D 83 B4
Oer-Erkenschwick D 80 A3
Oerlinghausen D 72 C1
Oettingen D 94 C2
Oetz A 108 B1
Oeventrop D 81 A4
Offanengo I 120 B2
Offenbach D 81 B4
Offenburg D 93 C3
Offida I 136 C2
Offingen D 94 C2
Offranville F 89 A5
Ofte N 53 A4
Ofterschwang D 107 B5
Oggiono I 120 B2
Ogihares E 163 A4
Ogliastro Cilento I 170 C3
Ogliastro Marina I 170 C2
Ogmore-by-Sea GB 39 C3
Ogna N 52 B1
Ogre LV 8 D4
Ogrodzieniec PL 86 B3
Ogulin HR 123 B4
Ögur IS 190 A3
Ohanes E 164 B2
Ohey B 79 B5
Ohlstadt D 108 B2
Ohrdorf D 73 B3
Ohrdruf D 82 B2
Ohrid MK 182 B2
Öhringen D 94 B1
Oia E 140 B2
Oiã P 148 B1
Oiartzun E 144 A2
Oijärvi FIN 197 D8
Oilgate IRL 30 B2
Oimbra E 148 A2
Oiselay-et-Grachoux F 105 B4
Oisemont F 90 B1
Oisterwijk NL 79 A5
Öja S 57 C4
Öje S 49 B5
Ojén E 162 B3
Ojrzeń PL 77 B5
Ojuelos Altos E 156 B2
Okalewo PL 77 A4
Okány H 113 C5
Okehampton GB 42 B2
Oklaj HR 138 B2
Økneshamn N 194 B6
Okoč SK 111 B4
Okoličné SK 99 B3
Okonek PL 68 B1
Okonin PL 69 B3
Okřisky CZ 97 B3
Oksa PL 87 B4
Oksbøl DK 59 C1
Oksby DK 59 C1
Øksfjord N 192 B6
Øksna N 48 B3
Okučani HR 124 B3
Okulovka RUS 9 C8
Ólafsfjörður IS 191 A7
Ólafsvík IS 190 C2
ÖLagnö S 57 A4
Olagüe E 144 B2
Oland N 53 B4
Olargues F 130 B1
Oława PL 85 B5
Olazagutia E 144 B1
Olbernhau D 83 B5
Ólbia I 178 B3
Olching D 108 A2
Oldbury GB 43 A4
Oldcastle IRL 27 C3
Old Deer GB 33 D4
Oldeberkoop NL 70 B3
Oldeboorn NL 70 A2
Olden N 198 D3
Oldenbrok D 71 A5
Oldenburg *Niedersachsen* D 71 A5
*Schleswig-Holstein* D 65 B3
Oldenzaal NL 71 B3
Olderdalen N 192 C4
Olderfjord N 193 B9
Oldersum D 71 A4
Oldervik N 192 C2
Oldham GB 40 B1
Oldisleben D 82 A3
Oldmeldrum GB 33 D4
Olea E 142 B2
Oleby S 49 B5
Olechów PL 87 A5
Oledo P 155 B3
Oléggio I 120 B1
Oleiros *Coruña* E 140 A2
*Coruña* E 140 B1
P 154 B3
Oleksandriya UA 13 C7
Olen B 79 A4
Ølen N 52 A1
Olenegorsk RUS 3 B13
Olenino RUS 9 D8
Olesa de Montserrat E 147 C2
Oleśnica PL 85 A5
Olešnice CZ 97 B4
Olesno PL 86 B2
Oletta F 180 A2
Olette F 146 B3
Olevsk UA 13 C7
Olfen D 80 A3
Olgiate Comasco I 120 B1
Olginate I 120 B2
Ølgod DK 59 C1
Olgrinmore GB 32 C3
Olhão P 160 B2
Olhava FIN 197 D8
Olhavo P 154 B1
Oliana E 147 B2
Olias del Rey E 151 C4
Oliena I 178 B3
Oliete E 153 B3
Olimbos GR 188 D2
Olite E 144 B2
Oliva E 159 C3
Oliva de la Frontera E 155 C4
Oliva de Mérida E 156 B1
Oliva de Plasencia E 149 B3
Olivadi I 175 C2
Olival P 154 B2
Olivar E 163 B4
Olivares E 161 B3
Olivares de Duero E 142 C2
Olivares de Júcar E 158 B1
Oliveira de Azeméis P 148 B1
Oliveira de Frades P 148 B1
Oliveira do Conde P 148 B2
Oliveira do Douro P 148 A1
Oliveira do Hospital P 148 B2
Olivenza E 155 C3
Olivet F 103 B3
Olivone CH 107 C3
Öljehult S 63 B3
Olkusz PL 86 B3
Ollerton GB 40 B2
Ollerup DK 65 A3
Olliergues F 117 B3
Ölmbrotorp S 56 A1
Ölme S 55 A4
Olmedilla de Alarcón E 158 B1
Olmedillo de Roa E 143 C3
Olmedo E 150 A3
I 178 B2
Olmeto F 180 B1
Olmillos de Castro E 149 A3
Olmos de Ojeda E 142 B2
Olney GB 44 A3
Ołobok PL 86 A2
Olocau del Rey E 153 B3
Olofström S 63 B2
Olomouc CZ 98 B1
Olonets RUS 9 B8
Olonne-sur-Mer F 114 B2
Olonzac F 130 B1
Oloron-Ste Marie F 145 A3
Olost E 147 C3
Olot E 147 B3
Olovo BIH 139 A4
Olpe D 81 A3
Olsberg D 81 A4
Olsene B 79 B3
Olserud S 55 A4
Olshammar S 55 B5
Olshanka UA 13 D9
Olszanica PL 85 A3
Olsztyn *Śląskie* PL 86 B3
*Warmińsko-Mazurskie* PL 69 B5
Olsztynek PL 77 A5
Olszyna PL 84 A3
Olszyny PL 77 A6
Oltedal N 52 B2
Olten CH 106 B2
Olteniţa RO 17 C7
Olula del Rio E 164 B2
Ølve N 46 B2
Olvega E 144 C2
Olvera E 162 B2
Olympia GR 184 B2
Olzai I 178 B3
Omagh GB 27 B3
Omalos GR 185 D4
Omegna I 119 B5
Omiš HR 138 B2
Omišalj HR 123 B3
Ommen NL 71 B3
Omodhos CY 181 B1
Omoljica SRB 127 C2
On B 79 B5
Oña E 143 B3
Onano I 168 A1
O Näsberg S 49 B5
Oñati E 143 A4
Onda E 159 B3
Ondara E 159 C4
Ondarroa E 143 A4
Onesse-et-Laharie F 128 B1
Oneşti RO 17 B7
Onhaye B 79 B4
Onich GB 34 B2
Onil E 159 C3
Onis E 142 A2
Önnestad S 61 C4
Onsala S 60 B2
Ontinyent E 159 C3
Ontur E 158 C2
Onzain F 103 B3
Onzonilla E 142 B1
Oostburg NL 79 A3
Oostende B 78 A2
Oosterend NL 70 A2
Oosterhout NL 79 A4
Oosterwolde NL 71 B3
Oosterzele B 79 B3
Oosthuizen NL 70 B2
Oostkamp B 78 A3
Oostmalle B 79 A4
Oost-Vlieland NL 70 A2
Oostvoorne NL 79 A4
Ootmarsum NL 71 B3
Opalenica PL 75 B5
O Páramo E 140 B3
Opařany CZ 96 B2
Opatija HR 123 B3
Opatów *Śląskie* PL 86 B2
*Świętokrzyskie* PL 87 B5
*Wielkopolskie* PL 86 A2

Opatówek PL 86 A2
Opatowiec PL 87 B4
Opava CZ 98 B1
O Pedrouzo E 140 B2
Opeinde NL 70 A3
Oper Thalkirchdorf
D 107 B5
Opglabbeek B 80 A1
Opicina I 122 B2
O Pino E 140 B2
Oplotnica SLO 123 A4
Opmeer NL 70 B1
Opochka RUS 9 D6
Opočno CZ 85 B4
Opoczno PL 87 A4
Opole PL 86 B1
Oporów PL 77 B4
O Porriño E 140 B2
Opovo SRB 127 B2
Oppach D 84 A2
Oppdal N 198 C6
Oppeby
Östergötland S 56 B1
Södermanland S 56 B2
Oppedal N 46 A2
Oppegård N 54 A1
Oppenau D 93 C4
Oppenberg A 110 B1
Oppenheim D 93 B4
Óppido Lucano I 172 B1
Óppido Mamertina
I 175 C1
Opponitz A 110 B1
Oppstad N 48 B3
Oprtalj HR 122 B2
Opsaheden S 49 B5
Ópusztaszer H 113 C4
Opuzen HR 138 B3
Ora
CY 181 B2
I 121 A4
Orada P 155 C3
Oradea RO 16 B4
Oradour-sur-Glane
F 115 C5
Oradour-sur-Vayres
F 115 C4
Oragonja SLO 122 B2
Orah BIH 139 C4
Orahova BIH 138 A3
Orahovica HR 125 B3
Orahovo BIH 124 B3
Oraison F 132 B1
Orajärvi FIN 196 C7
Orange F 131 A3
Orani I 178 B3
Oranienbaum D 83 A4
Oranienburg D 74 B2
Oranmore IRL 28 A3
Orašac SRB 127 C2
Orašje BIH 125 B4
Oravská Lesná SK 99 B3
Oravská Polhora
SK 99 B3
Oravské Veselé SK 99 B3
Oravsky-Podzámok
SK 99 B3
Orba E 159 C3
Orbacém P 148 A1
Orbais F 91 C3
Ørbæk DK 59 C3
Orbassano I 119 B4
Orbe CH 105 C5
Orbec F 89 A4
Orbetello I 168 A1
Orbetello Scalo I 168 A1
Orbigny F 103 B3
Ørby DK 59 B3
Örbyhus S 51 B4
Orce E 164 B2
Orcera E 164 A2
Orchamps-Vennes
F 105 B5
Orches F 102 C2
Orchete E 159 C3
Orchies F 78 B3
Orchowo PL 76 B3
Orcières F 118 C3
Ordes E 140 A2
Ordhead GB 33 D4
Ordino AND 146 B2
Ordizia E 144 A1
Orduña E 143 B4
Ore S 50 A2
Orea E 152 B2
Orebić HR 138 C3
Örebro S 56 A1
Öregcsertő H 112 C3
Öregrund S 51 B5
Orehoved DK 65 B4
Orellana E 156 A2
Orellana de la Sierra
E 156 A2
Ören TR 188 B2
Örencik TR 187 C4
Orestiada GR 186 A1
Organyà E 147 B2
Orgaz E 157 A4
Orgelet F 105 C4
Ørgenvika N 48 B1
Orgères-en-Beauce
F 103 A3
Orgibet F 145 B4
Orgnac-l'Aven F 131 A3
Orgon F 131 B4
Orgósolo I 178 B3
Orhaneli TR 186 C3
Orhangazi TR 187 B4
Orhei MD 17 B8
Orhomenos GR 184 A3
Oria E 164 B2
Ória I 173 B3
Origny-Ste Benoite
F 91 B3
Orihuela E 165 A4
Orihuela del Tremedal
E 152 B2
Orikum AL 182 C1
Oriola P 154 C3
Oriolo I 174 A2
Oriovac HR 125 B3
Orissaare EST 8 C3
Oristano I 179 C2
Öriszentpéter H 111 C3
Ørje N 54 A2
Orjiva E 163 B4
Orkanger N 198 B6
Örkelljunga S 61 C3
Örkény H 112 B3
Orlamünde D 82 B3
Orléans F 103 B3
Orlová CZ 98 B2
Orlovat SRB 126 B2
Ormea I 133 A3
Ormelet N 54 A1
Ormemyr N 53 A5
Ormilia GR 183 C5
Ormos GR 185 B5
Ormož SLO 124 A2
Ormskirk GB 38 A4
Ornans F 105 B5
Ornäs S 50 B2
Ørnes N 195 D4
Orneta PL 69 A5
Ørnhøj DK 59 B1
Ornö S 57 A4
Örnsköldsvik S 200 C4
Orolik HR 125 B4
Orom SRB 126 B1
Oron-la-Ville CH 106 C1
Oronsko PL 87 A4
Oropa I 119 B4
Oropesa
Castellón de la Plana
E 153 B4
Toledo E 150 C2
O Rosal E 140 C2
Orosei I 178 B3
Orosháza H 113 C4
Oroslavje HR 124 B1
Oroszlány H 112 B2
Oroszlo H 125 A4
Orotelli I 178 B3
Orozko E 143 A4
Orphir GB 33 C3
Orpington GB 45 B4
Orreaga-Roncesvalles
E 144 A2
Orrefors S 62 B3
Orrviken S 199 B11
Orsa S 50 A1
Orsara di Púglia I 171 B3
Orsay F 90 C2
Orscholz D 92 B2
Orsennes F 103 C3
Orserum S 55 B5
Orsha BY 13 A9
Orsières CH 119 A4
Örsjö S 63 B3
Ørslev DK 65 A4
Örslösa S 55 B3
Orsogna I 169 A4
Orsomarso I 174 B1
Orşova RO 16 C5
Ørsta N 198 C3
Ørsted DK 58 B3
Örsundsbro S 56 A3
Ortaca TR 188 C3
Ortakent TR 188 B2
Ortaklar TR 188 B2
Ortaköy TR 23 B8
Orta Nova I 171 B3
Orte I 168 A2
Ortenburg D 96 C1
Orth A 111 A3
Orthez F 128 C2
Ortigueira E 140 A3
Ortilla E 145 B3
Ortisei I 108 C2
Orţişoara RO 126 B3
Ortnevik N 46 A3
Orton GB 37 B4
Ortona I 169 A4
Ortrand D 84 A1
Orubica HR 124 B3
Ørum DK 58 B2
Orune I 178 B3
Orusco E 151 B4
Orvalho P 155 A3
Orvault F 101 B4
Ørvella N 53 A5
Orvieto I 168 A2
Orvínio I 169 A2
Oryakhovo BG 17 D5
Orzesze PL 86 B2
Orzinuovi I 120 B2
Orzivécchi I 120 B2
Orzyny PL 77 A6
Os
Hedmark N 48 B3
Hedmark N 199 C8
Osann-Monzel D 92 B2
Osbruk S 62 A2
Øsby DK 59 C2
Osby S 61 C3
Oščadnica SK 98 B2
Oschatz D 83 A5
Oschersleben D 73 B4
Óschiri I 178 B3
Oscilowo PL 77 B5
Osdorf D 64 B3
Osečina SRB 127 C1
Osečná CZ 84 B2
Oseja de Sajambre
E 142 A1
Osek CZ 84 B1
Osen N 199 A7
Osera de Ebro E 153 A3
Osidda I 178 B3
Osie PL 69 B3
Osieczna
Pomorskie PL 68 B3
Wielkopolskie PL 75 C5
Osieczno PL 75 A4
Osiek
Kujawsko-Pomorskie
PL 76 B3
Kujawsko-Pomorskie
PL 77 A4
Pomorskie PL 69 B3
Świętokrzyskie PL 87 B5
Osiek nad Notecią
PL 76 A2
Osielsko PL 76 A3
Osijek HR 125 B4
Osilnica SLO 123 B3
Ósilo I 178 B2
Ósimo I 136 B2
Osinja BIH 125 C3
Osintorf BY 13 A9
Osipaonica SRB 127 C3
Osjaków PL 86 A2
Oskamull GB 34 B1
Oskarshamn S 62 A4
Oskarström S 60 C2
Oslany SK 98 C2
Oslavany CZ 97 B4
Ošlje HR 139 C3
Oslo N 48 C2
Øsløs DK 58 A1
Osmancık TR 23 A8
Osmaneli TR 187 B4
Ösmo S 57 B3
Osmolin PL 77 B4
Osnabrück D 71 B5
Ośno Lubuskie PL 75 B3
Osoblaha CZ 85 B5
Osor HR 123 C3
Osorno E 142 B2
Øsoyra N 46 A2
Osøyro N 46 B2
Ospakseyri IS 190 B4
Os Peares E 140 B3
Ospedaletti I 133 B3
Ospitaletto I 120 B3
Oss NL 80 A1
Ossa de Montiel E 158 C1
Ossi I 178 B2
Ossjøen N 47 B5
Ossun F 145 A3
Ostanå S 61 C4
Ostanvik S 50 A2
Ostashkov RUS 9 D8
Östavall S 200 D1
Ostbevern D 71 B4
Østborg N 199 A10
Østby N 49 A4
Osted DK 61 D1
Ostenfeld D 64 B2
Oster UA 13 C9
Øster Assels DK 58 B1
Osterburg D 73 B4
Osterburken D 94 B1
Österbybruk S 51 B4
Østerbyhavn DK 58 A4
Österbymo S 62 A3
Ostercappeln D 71 B5
Österfärnebo S 51 B3
Osterfeld D 83 A3
Österforse S 200 C3
Osterhever D 64 B1
Osterhofen D 95 C5
Osterholz-Scharmbeck
D 72 A1
Øster Hornum DK 58 B2
Øster Hurup DK 58 B3
Østerild DK 58 A1
Øster Jølby DK 58 B1
Österlövsta S 51 B4
Øster-marie DK 67 A4
Ostermiething A 109 A3
Osterode am Harz D 82 A2
Ostersiel D 64 B1
Östersund S 199 B11
Øster Tørslev DK 58 B3
Östervåla S 51 B4
Östervallskog S 54 A2
Østervrå DK 58 A3
Osterwieck D 73 C3
Osterzell D 108 B1
Ostffyasszonyfa H 111 B4
Östfora S 51 C4
Östhammar S 51 B5
Ostheim F 106 A2
Ostheim vor der Rhön
D 82 B2
Osthofen D 93 B4
Ostiano I 120 B3
Ostíglia I 121 B4
Ostiz E 144 B2
Östmark S 49 B4
Östnor S 50 A1
Ostojićevo SRB 126 B2
Ostra I 136 B2
Östra Amtervik S 55 A4
Östraby S 61 D3
Ostrach D 107 B4
Östra Husby S 56 B2
Östra Ljungby S 61 C3
Östra Ryd S 56 B2
Ostrau D 83 A5
Ostrava CZ 98 B2
Østre Halsen N 53 A6
Ostrhauderfehn D 71 A4
Ostritz D 84 A2
Ostróda PL 69 B4
Ostroh UA 13 C7
Ostrołęka PL 12 B4
Ostropole PL 68 B1
Ostroróg PL 75 B5
Ostrošovac BIH 124 C1
Ostrov
CZ 83 B4
RUS 8 D6
Ostrov nad Oslavou
CZ 97 B3
Ostrówek PL 86 A2
Ostrowiec PL 68 A1
Ostrowiec-Świętokrzyski
PL 87 B5
Ostrowite PL 77 A4
Ostrów Mazowiecka
PL 12 B4
Ostrowo PL 76 B3
Ostrów Wielkopolski
PL 86 A1
Ostrožac BIH 139 B3
Ostrzeszów PL 86 A1
Ostseebad
Kühlungsborn D 65 B4
Ostuni I 173 B3
Osuna E 162 A2
Osvětimany CZ 98 B1
Oswestry GB 38 B3
Oświęcim PL 86 B3
Osztopán H 111 C4
Oteiza E 144 B2
Otelec RO 126 B2
Oteo E 143 A3
Oterbekk N 54 A1
Otero de Herreros
E 151 B3
Otero de O Bodas
E 141 C4
Othem S 57 C4
Otley GB 40 B2
Otmuchów PL 85 B5
Otočac HR 123 C4
Otok
Splitsko-Dalmatinska
HR 138 B2
Vukovarsko-Srijemska
HR 125 B4
Otoka BIH 124 C2
Otranto I 173 B4
Otrić HR 138 A2
Otrícoli I 168 A2
Otrokovice CZ 98 B1
Otta N 198 D6
Ottana I 178 B3
Ottaviano I 170 C2
Ottenby S 63 B4
Ottendorf-Okrilla D 84 A1
Ottenhöfen D 93 C4
Ottenschlag A 97 C3
Ottensheim A 96 C2
Otterbach D 93 B3
Otterbäcken S 55 B5
Otterberg D 93 B3
Otterburn GB 37 A4
Otter Ferry GB 34 B2
Otterndorf D 64 C1
Ottersburg D 72 A2
Ottersweier D 93 C4
Otterup DK 59 C3
Ottery St Mary GB 43 B3
Ottignies B 79 B4
Ottmarsheim F 106 B2
Ottobeuren D 107 B5
Öttömös H 126 A1
Ottone I 120 C2
Ottsjö S 199 B10
Ottweiler D 92 B3
Otveşti RO 126 B3
Ötvöskónyi H 124 A3
Otwock PL 12 B4
Ouanne F 104 B2
Ouarville F 90 C1
Oucques F 103 B3
Oud-Beijerland NL 79 A4
Ouddorp NL 79 A3
Oudemirdum NL 70 B2
Oudenaarde B 79 B3
Oudenbosch NL 79 A4
Oudenburg B 78 A3
Oude-Pekela NL 71 A4
Oude-Tonge NL 79 A4
Oudewater NL 70 B1
Oud Gastel NL 79 A4
Oudon F 101 B4
Oue DK 58 B2
Oughterard IRL 28 A2
Ouguela P 155 B3
Ouistreham F 89 A3
Oulainen FIN 3 D9
Oulchy-le-Château
F 91 B3
Oullins F 117 B4
Oulmes F 114 B3
Oulton GB 41 C5
Oulton Broad GB 41 C5
Oulu FIN 3 D9
Oulx I 119 B3
Oundle GB 40 C3
Ouranopoli GR 183 C6
Ourém P 154 B2
Ourense E 140 B3
Ourique P 160 B1
Ourol E 140 A3
Ouroux-en-Morvan
F 104 B2
Ousdale GB 32 C3
Oust F 146 B2
Outakoski FIN 193 C10
Outeiro P 148 B1
Outeiro de Rei E 140 A3
Outes E 140 B2
Outokumpu FIN 9 A6
Outreau F 78 B1
Outwell GB 41 C4
Ouzouer-le-Marché
F 103 B3
Ouzouer-sur-Loire
F 103 B4
Ovada I 133 A4
Ovar P 148 B1
Ovelgönne D 72 A1
Overath D 80 B3
Overbister GB 33 B4
Øverbygd N 192 D3
Overdinkel NL 71 B4
Överenhörna S 56 A3
Overhalla N 199 A8
Overijse B 79 B4
Over-jerstal DK 59 C2
Overlade DK 58 B2
Överlida S 60 B2
Överö FIN 51 B7
Overpelt B 79 A5
Overton GB 38 B4
Övertorneå S 196 C6
Överum S 62 A4
Ovidiopol UA 17 B9
Oviedo E 141 A5
Oviglio I 119 C5
Ovíndoli I 169 A3
Ovodda I 178 B3
Øvre Årdal N 47 A4
Øvrebygd N 52 B2
Øvre Rendal N 199 D8
Øvre Sirdal N 52 B2
Övre Soppero S 196 A4
Övre Ullerud S 55 A4
Ovruch UA 13 C8
Ovtrup DK 59 C1
Owińska PL 76 B1
Oxaback S 60 B2
Oxberg S 49 A6
Oxelösund S 56 B3
Oxenholme GB 37 B4
Oxford GB 44 B2
Oxie S 61 D3
Oxilithos GR 185 A5
Oxted GB 45 B4
Oyaca TR 187 C7
Øye N 47 A5
Øyenkilen N 54 A1
Øyer N 48 A2
Øyeren N 49 B4
Oyfiell N 53 A4
Øygärdslia N 53 B4
Oykel Bridge GB 32 D2
Øymark N 54 A2
Oyonnax F 118 A2
Øyslebø N 52 B3
Øystese N 46 B3
Oyten D 72 A2
Øyuvsbu N 52 A3
Ozaeta E 143 B4
Ozalj HR 123 B4
Ożarów PL 87 B5
Ożarów Maz PL 77 B5
Ožbalt SLO 110 C2
Ózd H 113 A4
Ožďany SK 99 C3
Ozieri I 178 B3
Ozimek PL 86 B2
Ozimica BIH 139 A4
Ozora H 112 C2
Ozorków PL 77 C4
Ozzano Monferrato
I 119 B5

P

Paakkola FIN 196 D7
Paal B 79 A5
Pabianice PL 86 A3
Pacanów PL 87 B5
Paceco I 176 B1
Pachino I 177 C4
Pačir SRB 126 B1
Pack A 110 B2
Paços de Ferreira
P 148 A1
Pacov CZ 96 B3
Pacsa H 111 C4
Pacy-sur-Eure F 89 A5
Paczków PL 85 B5
Padany RUS 3 E13
Padborg DK 64 B2
Padej SRB 126 B2
Padene HR 138 A2
Paderborn D 81 A4
Paderne P 160 B1
Padiham GB 40 B1
Padina SRB 126 B2
Padinska Skela
SRB 127 C2
Padornelo P 148 A1
Pádova I 121 B4
Padragkút H 111 B4
Padria I 178 B2
Padrón E 140 B2
Padru I 178 B3
Padstow GB 42 B2
Padul E 163 A4
Padula I 172 B1
Paduli I 170 B2
Paesana I 119 C4
Paese I 121 B5
Pag HR 137 A4
Pagani I 170 C2
Pagánica I 169 A3
Pagánico I 135 C4
Pagl ieta I 169 A4
Pagny-sur-Moselle
F 92 C2
Páhi H 112 C3
Pahkakumpu FIN 197 C11
Pahl D 108 B2
Paide EST 8 C4
Paignton GB 43 B3
Pailhès F 146 A2
Paimboeuf F 101 B3
Paimpol F 100 A2
Paimpont F 101 A3
Painswick GB 43 A4
Painten D 95 C3
Paisley GB 34 C3
Pajala S 196 B6
Pajares E 141 A5
Pajares de los Oteros
E 142 B1
Pajęczno PL 86 A2
Páka H 111 C3
Pakość PL 76 B3
Pakosławice PL 85 B5
Pakoštane HR 137 B4
Pakrac HR 124 B3
Paks H 112 C2
Palacios de la Sierra
E 143 C3
Palaciòs de la
Valduerna E 141 B5
Palacios del Sil E 141 B4
Palacios de Sanabria
E 141 B4
Palaciosrubios E 150 A2
Palafrugell E 147 C4
Palagiano I 173 B3
Palagonía I 177 B3
Paláia I 135 B3
Palaiokastritsa GR 182 D1
Palaiseau F 90 C2
Palamas GR 182 D4
Palamòs E 147 C4
Påläng S 196 D5
Palanga LT 8 E2
Palanzano I 134 A3
Palárikovo SK 112 A2
Palas de Rei E 140 B3
Palata I 170 B2
Palau I 178 A3
Palavas-les-Flots F 131 B2
Palazuelos de la Sierra
E 143 B3
Palazzo Adriano I 176 B2
Palazzo del Pero I 135 B4
Palazzolo Acréide
I 177 B3
Palazzolo sull Oglio
I 120 B2
Palazzo San Gervásio
I 172 B1
Palazzuolo sul Senio
I 135 A4
Paldiski EST 8 C4
Pale BIH 139 B4
Palekastro GR 185 D7
Palena I 169 B4
Palencia E 142 B2
Palenciana E 163 A3
Paleochora GR 185 D4
Paleometokho CY 181 A2
Palermo I 176 A2
Paleros GR 182 E2
Palestrina I 169 B2
Pálfa H 112 C2
Palfau A 110 B1
Palhaça P 148 B1
Palheiros da Tocha
P 148 B1
Palheiros de Quiaios
P 148 B1
Paliaopoli GR 185 B5
Palić SRB 126 A1
Palidoro I 168 B2
Palinuro I 172 B1
Paliouri GR 183 D5
Paliseul B 91 B5
Pallanza I 119 B5
Pallares E 161 A3
Pallaruelo de Monegros
E 153 A3
Pallas Green IRL 29 B3
Pallerols E 146 B2
Palling D 109 A3
Palluau F 114 B2
Palma P 154 C2
Palma Campánia I 170 C2
Palma del Rio E 162 A2
Palma de Mallorca
E 166 B2

Palma di Montechiaro I 176 B2
Palmádula I 178 B2
Palmanova I 122 B2
Palma Nova E 166 B2
Palmela P 154 C2
Palmerola E 147 B3
Palmi I 175 C1
Pälmonostora H 113 C3
Palo del Colle I 171 B4
Palojärvi FIN 192 D7
Palojoensuu FIN 196 A6
Palomares E 164 B3
Palomares del Campo E 158 B1
Palomas E 156 B1
Palombara Sabina I 168 A2
Palos de la Frontera E 161 B3
Palotaboszok H 125 A4
Palotás H 112 B3
Pals E 147 C4
Pålsboda S 56 A1
Paluzza I 109 C4
Pamhagen A 111 B3
Pamiers F 146 A2
Pamiętowo PL 76 A2
Pampaneira E 163 B4
Pamparato I 133 A3
Pampilhosa
*Aveiro* P 148 B1
*Coimbra* P 148 B2
Pampliega E 143 B3
Pamplona E 144 B2
Pampow D 73 A4
Pamukçu TR 186 C2
Pamukkale TR 188 B4
Pamukova TR 187 B5
Panagyurishte BG 17 D6
Pancalieri I 119 C4
Pančevo SRB 127 C2
Pancey F 91 C5
Pancorvo E 143 B3
Pancrudo E 152 B2
Pandino I 120 B2
Pandrup DK 58 A2
Panenský-Týnec CZ 84 B1
Panes E 142 A2
Panevėžys LT 8 E4
Pangbourne GB 44 B2
Panissières F 117 B4
Panki PL 86 B2
Pannes F 103 A4
Panningen NL 80 A1
Pannonhalma H 111 B4
Pano Lefkara CY 181 B2
Pano Panayia CY 181 B1
Panormos GR 185 B6
Panschwitz-Kuckau D 84 A2
Pansdorf D 65 C3
Pantano de Cíjara E 156 A3
Panticosa E 145 B3
Pantín E 140 A2
Pantoja E 151 B4
Pantón E 140 B3
Panxon E 140 B2
Páola I 174 B2
Paola M 175 C3
Pápa H 111 B4
Papasídero I 174 B1
Pápateszér H 111 B4
Papenburg D 71 A4
Paphos CY 181 B1
Pappenheim D 94 C2
Paprotnia PL 77 B5
Parábita I 173 B4
Paraćin SRB 127 D3
Parád H 113 B4
Parada
*Bragança* P 149 A3
*Viseu* P 148 B1
Paradas E 162 A2
Paradela E 140 B3
Parades de Rubiales E 150 A2
Paradinas de San Juan E 150 B2
Paradiso di Cevadale I 108 C1
Paradyż PL 87 A4
Parainen FIN 8 B3
Parakhino Paddubye RUS 9 C8
Parakka S 196 B4
Paralimni CY 181 A2
Parallo Astros GR 184 B3
Paramé F 88 B2
Paramithia GR 182 D2
Páramo E 141 A4
Páramo del Sil E 141 B4
Parandaça P 148 A2
Paravadella E 141 A3
Paray-le-Monial F 104 C3
Parceiros P 154 B2
Parcey F 105 B4
Parchim D 73 A4
Parciaki PL 77 A6
Parcice PL 86 A2
Pardilla E 151 A4
Pardubice CZ 97 A3
Paredes
E 151 B5
P 148 A1
Paredes de Coura P 140 C2
Paredes de Nava E 142 B2
Paredes de Siguenza E 151 A5
Pareja E 151 B5
Parennes F 102 A1
Parenti I 175 B2
Parentis-en-Born F 128 B1
Parey D 73 B4
Parfino RUS 9 D7
Parga GR 182 D2
Pargny-sur-Saulx F 91 C4
Pari-Gagné F 117 A4
Parigné-l'Évêque F 102 B2
Parikkala FIN 9 B6
Paris F 90 C2
Parisot F 129 B4
Parkalompolo S 196 B5
Parkano FIN 8 A3
Parknasilla IRL 29 C2
Parla E 151 B4
Parlavá E 147 B4
Parma I 120 C3
Parndorf A 111 B3
Párnica SK 99 B3
Parnu EST 8 C4
Parolis E 164 A2
Paros GR 185 B6
Parrillas E 150 B2
Parsberg D 95 B3
Parstein D 74 B3
Partakko FIN 193 C11
Partanna I 176 B1
Parthenay F 102 C1
Partinico I 176 A2
Partizani SRB 127 C2
Partizánske SK 98 C2
Partney GB 41 B4
Påryd S 63 B3
Parzymiechy PL 86 A2
Paşcani RO 17 B7
Pasewalk D 74 A2
Pašina Voda MNE 139 B5
Påskallavik S 62 A4
Pasłęk PL 69 A4
Pašman HR 137 B4
Passage East IRL 30 B2
Passail A 110 B2
Passais F 88 B3
Passau D 96 C1
Passegueiro P 148 B1
Passignano sul Trasimeno I 135 B5
Passo di Tréia I 136 B2
Passopisciaro I 177 B4
Passow D 74 A3
Passy F 118 B3
Pastavy BY 13 A7
Pástena I 170 B2
Pastrana E 151 B5
Pastrengo I 121 B3
Pasym PL 77 A5
Pásztó H 113 B3
Pata SK 98 C1
Patay F 103 A3
Pateley Bridge GB 40 A2
Paterek PL 76 A2
Paterna E 159 B3
Paterna del Campo E 161 B3
Paterna del Madera E 158 C1
Paterna de Rivera E 162 B2
Paternion A 109 C4
Paternò I 177 B3
Paternópoli I 170 C3
Patersdorf D 95 B4
Paterswolde NL 71 A3
Patitiri GR 183 D5
Patmos GR 188 B1
Patna GB 36 A2
Pątnow PL 76 B3
Patoniva FIN 193 C11
Patopirtti FIN 197 B12
Patos AL 182 C1
Patra = Patras GR 184 A2
Patras = Patra GR 184 A2
Patreksfjörður IS 190 B2
Patrickswell IRL 29 B3
Patrimonio F 180 A2
Patrington GB 41 B3
Pattada I 178 B3
Pattensen
*Niedersachsen* D 72 A3
*Niedersachsen* D 72 B2
Patterdale GB 36 B4
Patti I 177 A3
Páty H 112 B2
Pau F 145 A3
Pauillac F 128 A2
Paularo I 109 C4
Paulhaguet F 117 B3
Paulhan F 130 B2
Paulilátino I 178 B2
Paulström S 62 A3
Paullo I 120 B2
Paulstown IRL 30 B1
Pausa D 83 B3
Pauträsk S 200 B3
Pavia
I 120 B2
P 154 C2
Pavias E 159 B3
Pavilly F 89 A4
Pāvilosta LV 8 D2
Pavullo nel Frignano I 135 A3
Pawłowice PL 86 A1
Pawlowice PL 98 B2
Paxi GR 182 D2
Payallar TR 189 C6
Payerne CH 106 C1
Paymogo E 161 B2
Payrac F 129 B4
Pazardzhik BG 183 A6
Pazaryeri TR 187 B4
Pazin HR 122 B2
Paziols F 146 B3
Pčelić HR 124 B3
Peal de Becerro E 164 B1
Peasmarsh GB 45 C4
Peć KOS 16 D4
Péccioli I 135 B3
Pécel H 112 B3
Pechao P 160 B2
Pechenga RUS 3 B12
Pechenizhyn UA 13 D6
Pecica RO 126 A3
Pećinci SRB 127 C1
Pecka SRB 127 C1
Peckelsheim D 81 A5
Pečory RUS 8 D5
Pécs H 125 A4
Pécsvárad H 125 A4
Peczniew PL 86 A2
Pedaso I 136 B2
Pedavena I 121 A4
Pedérobba I 121 B4
Pedersker DK 67 A3
Pedescala I 121 B4
Pedrafita E 141 B3
Pedrajas de San Esteban E 150 A3
Pedralba E 159 B3
Pedralba de la Praderia E 141 B4
Pedraza E 151 A4
Pedreguer E 159 C4
Pedrera E 162 A3
Pedro Abad E 157 C3
Pedro Bernardo E 150 B3
Pedroche E 156 B3
Pedrógão P 160 A2
Pedrogao P 149 B2
Pedrógão P 154 B2
Pedrógão Grande P 154 B2
Pedrola E 144 C2
Pedro-Martinez E 164 B1
Pedro Muñoz E 158 B1
Pedrosa del Rey E 150 A2
Pedrosa del Rio Urbel E 143 B3
Pedrosa de Tobalina E 143 B3
Pedrosillo de los Aires E 150 B2
Pedrosillo el Ralo E 150 A2
Pędzewo PL 76 A3
Peebles GB 35 C4
Peel GB 36 B2
Peenemünde D 66 B2
Peer B 79 A5
Pega P 149 B2
Pegalajar E 163 A4
Pegau D 83 A4
Peggau A 110 B2
Pegli I 133 A4
Pegnitz D 95 B3
Pego E 159 C3
Pegões-Estação P 154 C2
Pegões Velhos P 154 C2
Pęgów PL 85 A4
Pegswood GB 37 A5
Peguera E 166 B2
Pehlivanköy TR 186 A1
Peine D 72 B3
Peisey-Nancroix F 118 B3
Peissenberg D 108 B2
Peiting D 108 B1
Peitz D 84 A2
Péjo I 121 A3
Pelagićevo BIH 125 C4
Pelahustán E 150 B3
Pełczyce PL 75 A4
Pelhřimov CZ 97 B3
Pélissanne F 131 B4
Pelkosenniemi FIN 197 B10
Pellegrino Parmense I 120 C2
Pellegrue F 128 B3
Pellérd H 125 A4
Pellestrina I 122 B1
Pellevoisin F 103 C3
Pellizzano I 121 A3
Pello
FIN 196 C7
S 196 C6
Peloche E 156 A2
Pelplin PL 69 B3
Pelussin F 117 B4
Pély H 113 B4
Pembroke GB 39 C2
Pembroke Dock GB 39 C2
Peñacerrada E 143 B4
Penacova P 148 B1
Peña de Cabra E 149 B4
Peñafiel E 151 A3
Penafiel P 148 A1
Peñaflor E 162 A2
Peñalba de Santiago E 141 B4
Peñalsordo E 156 B2
Penalva do Castelo P 148 B2
Penamacôr P 149 B2
Peñaparda E 149 B3
Peñaranda de Bracamonte E 150 B2
Peñaranda de Duero E 143 C3
Peñarroya de Tastavins E 153 B4
Peñarroya-Pueblonuevo E 156 B2
Peñarrubla E 141 B3
Penarth GB 39 C3
Peñascosa E 158 C1
Peñas de San Pedro E 158 C2
Peñausende E 149 A4
Penc H 112 B3
Pencoed GB 39 C3
Pendalofos GR 182 C3
Pendeen GB 42 B1
Pendine GB 39 C2
Pendueles E 142 A2
Penedono P 148 B2
Penela P 154 A2
Pénestin F 101 B3
Penhas Juntas P 149 A2
Peniche P 154 B1
Penicuik GB 35 C4
Penig D 83 B4
Penilhos P 160 B2
Peñíscola E 153 B4
Penistone GB 40 B2
Penkridge GB 40 C1
Penkun D 74 A3
Penmarch F 100 B1
Pennabilli I 135 B5
Penne I 169 A3
Penne-d'Agenais F 129 B3
Pennes I 108 C2
Pennyghael GB 34 B1
Peno RUS 9 D8
Penpont GB 36 A3
Penrhyndeudraeth GB 38 B2
Penrith GB 37 B4
Penryn GB 42 B1
Pentraeth GB 38 A2
Penybontfawr GB 38 B3
Penygroes
*Carmarthenshire* GB 39 C2
*Gwynedd* GB 38 A2
Penzance GB 42 B1
Penzberg D 108 B2
Penzlin D 74 A2
Pepinster B 80 B1
Peqin AL 182 B1
Pér H 111 B4
Pera Boa P 148 B2
Perachora GR 184 A3
Perafita P 148 A1
Peraleda de la Mata E 150 C2
Peraleda del Zaucejo E 156 B2
Peraleda de San Román E 156 A2
Perales de Alfambra E 152 B2
Perales del Puerto E 149 B3
Perales de Tajuña E 151 B4
Peralta E 144 B2
Peralta de la Sal E 145 C4
Peralva P 160 B2
Peralveche E 152 B1
Perama GR 185 D5
Peranka FIN 197 D12
Perbál H 112 B2
Perchtoldsdorf A 111 A3
Percy F 88 B2
Perdasdefogu I 179 C3
Perdiguera E 145 C3
Peredo P 149 A3
Peregu Mare RO 126 A2
Pereiro
*Faro* P 160 B2
*Guarda* P 149 B2
*Santarém* P 154 B2
Pereiro de Aguiar E 140 B3
Perelada E 147 B4
Perelejos de las Truchas E 152 B2
Pereña E 149 A3
Pereruela E 149 A4
Pérfugas I 178 B2
Perg A 110 A1
Pérgine Valsugana I 121 A4
Pérgola I 136 B1
Pergusa I 177 B3
Periam RO 126 A2
Periana E 163 B3
Périers F 88 A2
Périgueux F 129 A3
Perino I 120 C2
Perjasica HR 123 B4
Perkáta H 112 B2
Perković HR 138 B2
Perleberg D 73 A4
Perlez SRB 126 B2
Përmet AL 182 C2
Pernarec CZ 95 B5
Pernek SK 98 C1
Pernes P 154 B2
Pernes-les-Fontaines F 131 A4
Pernik BG 17 D5
Pernink CZ 83 B4
Pernitz A 110 B2
Pernu FIN 197 C10
Peroguarda P 160 A1
Pérols F 131 B2
Péronne F 90 B2
Péronnes B 79 B4
Pero Pinheiro P 154 C1
Perorrubio E 151 A4
Perosa Argentina I 119 C4
Perozinho P 148 A1
Perpignan F 146 B3
Perranporth GB 42 B1
Perranzabuloe GB 42 B1
Perrecy-les-Forges F 104 C3
Perrero I 119 C4
Perrignier F 118 A3
Perros-Guirec F 100 A2
Persan F 90 B2
Persberg S 55 A5
Persenbeug A 110 A2
Pershore GB 44 A1
Persön S 196 D5
Perstorp S 61 C3
Perth GB 35 B4
Pertisau A 108 B2
Pertoča SLO 111 C3
Pertuis F 131 B4
Perućac SRB 127 D1
Perúgia I 136 B1
Perušić HR 123 C4
Péruwelz B 79 B3
Pervomaysk UA 13 D9
Perwez B 79 B4
Pesadas de Burgos E 143 B3
Pesaguero E 142 A2
Pésaro I 136 B1
Pescantina I 121 B3
Pescara I 169 A4
Pescasséroli I 169 B3
Peschici I 171 B4
Peschiera del Garda I 121 B3
Péscia I 135 B3
Pescina I 169 A3
Pescocostanzo I 169 B4
Pescopagano I 172 B1
Pesco Sannita I 170 B2
Peshkopi AL 182 B2
Peshtera BG 183 A6
Pesmes F 105 B4
Pesnica SLO 110 C2
Peso da Régua P 148 A2
Pesquera de Duero E 142 C2
Pessac F 128 B2
Pestovo RUS 9 C9
Petäjäskoski FIN 197 C8
Petalidi GR 184 C2
Pétange L 92 B1
Petas GR 182 D3
Peteranec HR 124 A2
Peterborough GB 41 C3
Peterculter GB 33 D4
Peterhead GB 33 D5
Peterlee GB 37 B5
Petersfield GB 44 B3
Petershagen
*Brandenburg* D 74 B2
*Brandenburg* D 74 B3
*Nordrhein-Westfalen* D 72 B1
Petershausen D 95 C3
Peterswell IRL 28 A3
Pétervására H 113 A4
Petília Policastro I 175 B2
Petín E 141 B3
Pětipsy CZ 83 B5
Petkus D 74 C2
Petlovac HR 125 B4
Petlovača SRB 127 C1
Petöfiszallás H 113 C3
Petra E 167 B3
Petralia Sottana I 177 B3
Petrčane HR 137 A4
Petrella Tifernina I 170 B2
Petrer E 159 C3
Petreto-Bicchisano F 180 B1
Petrich BG 183 B5
Petrijevci HR 125 B4
Petrinja HR 124 B2
Petrodvorets RUS 9 C6
Pétrola E 158 C2
Petronà I 175 B2
Petronell A 111 A3
Petroşani RO 17 C5
Petrovac SRB 127 C3
Petrovaradin SRB 126 B1
Petrovice
BIH 139 A4
CZ 84 B1
Petrovo RUS 69 A5
Petrozavodsk RUS 9 B9
Pettenbach A 109 B5
Pettigo IRL 26 B3
Petworth GB 44 C3
Peuerbach A 96 C1
Peuntenansa E 142 A2
Peurasuvanto FIN 197 B9
Pevensey Bay GB 45 C4
Peveragno I 133 A3
Pewsey GB 44 B2
Pewsum D 71 A4
Peyrat-le-Château F 116 B1
Peyrehorade F 128 C1
Peyriac-Minervois F 146 A3
Peyrins F 117 B5
Peyrissac F 116 B1
Peyrolles-en-Provence F 132 B1
Peyruis F 132 A1
Pézarches F 90 C2
Pézenas F 130 B2
Pezinok SK 111 A4
Pezuls F 129 B3
Pfaffenhausen D 108 A1
Pfaffenhofen
*Bayern* D 94 C2
*Bayern* D 95 C3
Pfaffenhoffen F 93 C3
Pfäffikon CH 107 B3
Pfarrkirchen D 95 C4
Pfeffenhausen D 95 C3
Pfetterhouse F 106 B2
Pforzheim D 93 C4
Pfreimd D 95 B4
Pfronten D 108 B1
Pfullendorf D 107 B4
Pfullingen D 94 C1
Pfunds A 108 C1
Pfungstadt D 93 B4
Pfyn CH 107 B3
Phalsbourg F 92 C3
Philippeville B 79 B4
Philippsreut D 96 C1
Philippsthal D 82 B1
Piacenza I 120 B2
Piacenza d'Adige I 121 B4
Piádena I 120 B3
Piana F 180 A1
Piana Crixia I 133 A4
Piana degli Albanesi I 176 B2
Piana di Monte Verna I 170 B2
Piancastagnáio I 135 C4
Piandelagotti I 134 A3
Pianella
*Abruzzi* I 169 A4
*Toscana* I 135 B4
Pianello Val Tidone I 120 C2
Pianoro I 135 A4
Pians A 108 B1
Pías E 141 B4
Pias P 160 A2
Piaseczno PL 77 B6
Piasek PL 74 B3
Piaski PL 69 A4
Piastów PL 77 B5
Piaszczyna PL 68 A2
Piątek PL 77 B4
Piatra Neamţ RO 17 B7
Piazza al Sérchio I 134 A3
Piazza Armerina I 177 B3
Piazza Brembana I 120 B2
Piazze I 135 C4
Piazzola sul Brenta I 121 B4
Picassent E 159 B3
Piccione I 136 B1
Picerno I 172 B1
Picher D 73 A4
Pickering GB 40 A3
Pico I 169 B3
Picón E 157 A3
Picquigny F 90 B2
Piechowice PL 84 B3
Piecnik PL 75 A5
Piedicavallo I 119 B4
Piedicroce F 180 A2
Piedimonte Etneo I 177 B4
Piedimonte Matese I 170 B2
Piedimulera I 119 A5
Piedipaterno I 136 C1
Piedrabuena E 157 A3
Piedraescrita E 156 A3
Piedrafita E 142 A1
Piedrahita E 150 B2
Piedralaves E 150 B3
Piedras Albas E 155 B4
Piedras Blancas E 141 A5
Piegaro I 135 C5
Piekary Śl. PL 86 B2
Piekoszów PL 87 B4
Pieksämäki FIN 8 A5
Pielenhofen D 95 B3
Pielgrzymka PL 85 A3
Pieniężno PL 69 A5
Pieńsk PL 84 A3
Pienza I 135 B4
Piera E 147 C2
Pieranie PL 76 B3
Pierowall GB 33 B4
Pierre-Buffière F 115 C5
Pierrecourt F 105 B4
Pierre-de-Bresse F 105 C4
Pierrefeu-du-Var F 132 B2
Pierrefitte-Nestalas F 145 B3

Pierrefitte-sur-Aire F 92 C1
Pierrefonds F 90 B2
Pierrefontaine-les-Varans F 105 B5
Pierrefort F 116 C2
Pierrelatte F 131 A3
Pierrepont
*Aisne* F 91 B3
*Meurthe-et-Moselle* F 92 B1
Piesendorf A 109 B3
Pieštany SK 98 C1
Pieszkowo PL 69 A5
Pieszyce PL 85 B4
Pietarsaari FIN 3 E8
Pietragalla I 172 B1
Pietra Ligure I 133 A4
Pietralunga I 136 B1
Pietramelara I 170 B2
Pietraperzia I 177 B3
Pietrasanta I 134 B3
Pietravairano I 170 B2
Pieve del Cáiro I 120 B1
Pieve di Bono I 121 B3
Pieve di Cadore I 122 A1
Pieve di Cento I 121 C4
Pieve di Soligo I 121 B5
Pieve di Teco I 133 A3
Pievepélago I 134 A3
Pieve Santo Stefano I 135 B5
Pieve Torina I 136 B2
Piges GR 182 D3
Píglio I 169 B3
Pigna I 133 B3
Pignan F 130 B2
Pignataro Maggiore I 170 B2
Piittisjärvi FIN 197 C9
Pijnacker NL 70 B1
Pikalevo RUS 9 C9
Piła PL 75 A5
Pilar de la Horadada E 165 B4
Pilas E 161 B3
Pilastri I 121 C4
Piława Górna PL 85 B4
Piławki PL 69 B4
Pilchowice PL 86 B2
Pilea GR 183 C5
Pilgrimstad S 199 C12
Pili
*Dodekanisa* GR 188 C2
*Trikala* GR 182 D3
Pilica PL 86 B3
Pilis H 112 B3
Piliscaba H 112 B2
Pilisszántó H 112 B2
Pilisvörösvár H 112 B2
Pilos GR 184 C2
Pilsting D 95 C4
Pilszcz PL 98 A1
Pilterud N 48 C2
Pilu RO 113 C5
Pina de Ebro E 153 A3
Piñar E 163 A4
Pınarbaşı TR 186 C1
Pınarhisar TR 186 A2
Pinas F 145 A4
Pincehely H 112 C2
Pinchbeck GB 41 C3
Pińczów PL 87 B4
Pineda de la Sierra E 143 B3
Pineda de Mar E 147 C3
Pinerella I 135 A5
Pinerolo I 119 C4
Pineta Grande I 170 C1
Pineto I 169 A4
Piney F 91 C4
Pinggau A 111 B3
Pinhal Novo P 154 C2
Pinhão P 148 A2
Pinheiro
*Aveiro* P 148 A1
*Aveiro* P 148 B1
Pinheiro Grande P 154 B2
Pinhel P 149 B2
Pinhoe GB 43 B3
Pinilla E 158 C2
Pinilla de Toro E 150 A2
Pinkafeld A 111 B3
Pinneberg D 72 A2
Pinnow D 74 C3
Pino F 180 A2
Pino del Rio E 142 B2
Pino de Val E 140 B2
Pinofranqueado E 149 B3
Pinols F 117 B3
Piñor E 140 B2
Pinos del Valle E 163 B4
Pinoso E 159 C2
Pinos Puente E 163 A4
Pinsk BY 13 B7
Pintamo FIN 197 D10
Pinto E 151 B4
Pinzano al Tagliamento I 122 A1
Pinzio P 149 B2
Pinzolo I 121 A3
Piòbbico I 136 B1
Piombino I 134 C3
Pionki PL 87 A5
Pionsat F 116 A2
Pióraco I 136 B1
Piornal E 150 B2
Piotrkowice PL 87 B4
Piotrków-Kujawski PL 76 B3
Piotrków Trybunalski PL 86 A3
Piotrowo PL 75 B5
Piove di Sacco I 121 B5
Piovene I 121 B4
Piperskärr S 62 A4
Pipriac F 101 B4
Piraeus = Pireas GR 185 B4
Piran SLO 122 B2
Pireas = Piraeus GR 185 B4
Piré-sur-Seiche F 101 A4
Pirgi GR 185 A6
Pirgos
*Ilia* GR 184 B2
*Kriti* GR 185 D6
Piriac-sur-Mer F 101 B3
Piringsdorf A 111 B3
Pirmasens D 93 B3
Pirna D 84 B1
Pirnmill GB 34 C2
Pirot SRB 16 D5
Pirovac HR 137 B4
Pirttivuopio S 196 B2
Pisa I 134 B3
Pisany F 114 C3
Pisarovina HR 124 B1
Pischelsdorf in der Steiermark A 110 B2
Pişchia RO 126 B3
Pisciotta I 172 B1
Písek CZ 96 B2
Pisogne I 120 B3
Pissos F 128 B2
Pissouri CY 181 B1
Pisticci I 174 A2
Pistóia I 135 B3
Piteå S 196 D4
Piteşti RO 17 C6
Pithiviers F 103 A4
Pitigliano I 168 A1
Pitkyaranta RUS 9 B7
Pitlochry GB 35 B4
Pitomača HR 124 B3
Pitres E 163 B4
Pittentrail GB 32 D2
Pitvaros H 126 A2
Pivka SLO 123 B3
Pivnice SRB 126 B1
Piwniczna PL 99 B4
Pizarra E 163 B3
Pizzano I 121 A3
Pizzighettone I 120 B2
Pizzo I 175 C2
Pízzoli I 169 A3
Pizzolungo I 176 A1
Pjätteryd S 61 C4
Plabennec F 100 A1
Placencia E 143 A4
Plaffeien CH 106 C2
Plaisance
*Gers* F 128 C3
*Haute-Garonne* F 129 C4
*Tarn* F 130 B1
Plaka GR 183 D7
Plan E 145 B4
Planá CZ 95 B4
Planánad Lužnici CZ 96 B2
Plaňany CZ 96 A3
Planchez F 104 B3
Plancoët F 101 A3
Plancy-l'Abbaye F 91 C3
Plan-de-Baix F 118 C2
Plandište SRB 126 B3
Plan-d'Orgon F 131 B3
Plánice CZ 96 B1
Planina
SLO 123 A4
SLO 123 B3
Plankenfels D 95 B3
Plasencia E 149 B3
Plasenzuela E 156 A1
Plaški HR 123 B4
Plassen
*Buskerud* N 47 B4
*Hedmark* N 49 A4
Plášt'ovce SK 112 A3
Plasy CZ 96 B1
Platamona Lido I 178 B2
Platania I 175 B2
Platanos GR 185 D4
Platí I 175 C2
Platičevo SRB 127 C1
Platja d'Aro E 147 C4
Plattling D 95 C4
Plau D 73 A5
Plaue
*Brandenburg* D 73 B5
*Thüringen* D 82 B2
Plauen D 83 B4
Plavecký Mikuláš SK 98 C1
Plavinas LV 8 D4
Plavna SRB 125 B5
Plavnica SK 99 B4
Plavno HR 138 A2
Playben F 100 A2
Pléaux F 116 B2
Pleine-Fougères F 88 B2
Pleinfeld D 94 B2
Pleinting D 95 C5
Plélan-le-Grand F 101 B3
Plémet F 101 A3
Pléneuf-Val-André F 101 A3
Plentzia E 143 A4
Plérin F 101 A3
Plešivec SK 99 C4
Plessa D 83 A5
Plessé F 101 B4
Plestin-les-Grèves F 100 A2
Pleszew PL 76 C2
Pleternica HR 125 B3
Plettenberg D 81 A3
Pleubian F 100 A2
Pleumartin F 115 B4
Pleumeur-Bodou F 100 A2
Pleurs F 91 C3
Pleven BG 17 D6
Plevnik-Drienové SK 98 B2
Pleyber-Christ F 100 A2
Pliego E 165 B3
Pliešovce SK 99 C3
Plitvička Jezera HR 123 C4
Plitvički Ljeskovac HR 123 C4
Ploaghe I 178 B2
Ploče HR 138 B3
Plochingen D 94 C1
Płock PL 77 B4
Ploemeur F 100 B2
Ploërmel F 101 B3
Ploeuc-sur-Lie F 101 A3
Plogastel St Germain F 100 B1
Plogoff F 100 A1
Ploieşti RO 17 C7
Plomari GR 186 D1
Plombières-les-Bains F 105 B5
Plomin HR 123 B3
Plön D 65 B3
Plonéour-Lanvern F 100 B1
Płonia PL 74 A3
Płoniawy PL 77 B6
Płońsk PL 77 B5
Płoskinia PL 69 A4
Plössberg D 95 B4
Płoty PL 67 C4
Plouagat F 100 A2
Plouaret F 100 A2
Plouarzel F 100 A1
Plouay F 100 B2
Ploubalay F 101 A3
Ploubazlanec F 100 A2
Ploudalmézeau F 100 A1
Ploudiry F 100 A1
Plouescat F 100 A1
Plouézec F 100 A3
Plougasnou F 100 A2
Plougastel-Daoulas F 100 A1
Plougonven F 100 A2
Plougonver F 100 A2
Plougrescant F 100 A2
Plouguenast F 101 A3
Plouguerneau F 100 A1
Plouha F 100 A3
Plouhinec F 100 A1
Plouigneau F 100 A2
Ploumanach F 100 A2
Plounévez-Quintin F 100 A2
Plouray F 100 A2
Plouzévédé F 100 A1
Plovdiv BG 183 A6
Plozévet F 100 B1
Plumbridge GB 27 B3
Pluméliau F 100 B3
Plumlov CZ 97 B5
Plungė LT 8 E2
Pluty PL 69 A5
Pluvigner F 100 B3
Plužine
BIH 139 B4
MNE 139 B4
Płużnica PL 69 B3
Plymouth GB 42 B2
Plymstock GB 42 B2
Płytnica PL 68 B1
Plyusa RUS 9 C6
Plzeň CZ 96 B1
Pniewy PL 75 B5
Pobes E 143 B4
Poběžovice CZ 95 B4
Pobiedziska PL 76 B2
Pobierowo PL 67 B3
Pobla de Segur E 145 B4
Pobladura del Valle E 142 B1
Pobla-Tornesa E 153 B4
Pobra de Trives E 141 B3
Pobra do Brollón E 141 B3
Pobra do Caramiñal E 140 B2
Pobudje BIH 139 A5
Počátky CZ 97 B3
Poceirão P 154 C2
Pöchlarn A 110 A2
Pociecha PL 87 A4
Pockau D 83 B5
Pocking D 96 C1
Pocklington GB 40 B3
Podbořany CZ 83 B5
Podbrdo SLO 122 A2
Podbrezová SK 99 C3
Podčetrtek SLO 123 A4
Poddębice PL 76 C3
Poděbrady CZ 84 B3
Podence P 149 A3
Podensac F 128 B2
Podenzano I 120 C2
Podersdorf am See A 111 B3
Podgaje PL 68 B1
Podgora HR 138 B3
Podgóra PL 87 A5
Podgorač HR 125 B4
Podgorica MNE 16 D3
Podgorie AL 182 C2
Podgrad SLO 123 B3
Podhájska SK 112 A2
Podkova BG 183 B7
Podlapača HR 123 C4
Podlejki PL 69 B5
Podlužany SK 98 C2
Podnovlje BIH 125 C4
Podolie SK 98 C1
Podolínec SK 99 B4
Podolsk RUS 9 E10
Podporozhy RUS 9 B9
Podromanija BIH 139 B4
Podturen HR 111 C3
Podvín CZ 97 C4
Podwilk PL 99 B3
Poetto I 179 C3
Poggendorf D 66 B2
Poggiardo I 173 B4
Poggibonsi I 135 B4
Póggio a Caiano I 135 B4
Poggio Imperiale I 171 B3
Póggio Mirteto I 168 A2
Póggio Moiano I 169 A2
Póggio Renatico I 121 C4
Póggio Rusco I 121 C4
Pöggstall A 97 C3
Pogny F 91 C4
Pogorzela PL 85 A5
Pogorzelice PL 68 A2
Pogradec AL 182 C2
Pogrodzie PL 69 A4
Pohorelá SK 99 C4
Pohořelice CZ 97 C4
Pohronská Polhora SK 99 C3
Poiares P 148 B1
Poio E 140 B2
Poirino I 119 C4
Poisson F 117 A4
Poissons F 91 C5
Poissy F 90 C2
Poitiers F 115 B4
Poix-de-Picardie F 90 B1
Poix-Terron F 91 B4
Pokka FIN 197 A8
Pokój PL 86 B1
Pokupsko HR 124 B1
Pol E 141 A3
Pola RUS 9 D7
Pol a Charra GB 31 B1
Pola de Allande E 141 A4
Pola de Laviana E 142 A1
Pola de Lena E 141 A5
Pola de Siero E 142 A1
Pola de Somiedo E 141 A4
Polaincourt-et-Clairefontaine F 105 B5
Połajewo PL 75 B5
Polán E 151 C3
Polanica-Zdrój PL 85 B4
Połaniec PL 87 B5
Polanów PL 68 A1
Polatlı TR 187 C7
Polatsk BY 13 A8
Polch D 80 B3
Polcirkeln S 196 C4
Pólczno PL 68 A2
Połczyn-Zdrój PL 67 C5
Polegate GB 45 C4
Poleñino E 145 C3
Polesella I 121 C4
Polessk RUS 12 A4
Polgár H 113 B5
Polgárdi H 112 B2
Polhov Gradec SLO 123 A3
Police PL 74 A3
Police nad Metují CZ 85 B4
Polichnitos GR 186 C1
Polička CZ 97 B4
Poličnik HR 137 A4
Policoro I 174 A2
Policzna PL 87 A5
Poligiros GR 183 C5
Polignano a Mare I 173 B3
Poligny F 105 C4
Polis CY 181 A1
Polístena I 175 C2
Polizzi Generosa I 176 B3
Poljana SRB 127 C3
Poljanák HR 123 C4
Poljčane SLO 123 A4
Polje BIH 125 C3
Poljice
BIH 138 A2
BIH 139 A4
Polkowice PL 85 A4
Polla I 172 B1
Pollas E 150 A2
Pöllau A 110 B2
Polleben D 82 A3
Pollença E 167 B3
Pollenfeld D 95 C3
Pollfoss N 198 D4
Póllica I 170 C3
Polminhac F 116 C2
Polná CZ 97 B3
Polna RUS 8 C6
Polne PL 75 A5
Polomka SK 99 C3
Polonne UA 13 C7
Polperro GB 42 B2
Polruan GB 42 B2
Pöls A 110 B1
Polska Cerekiew PL 86 B2
Poltár SK 99 C3
Põltsamaa EST 8 C4
Polyarny RUS 3 B13
Polyarnyye Zori RUS 3 C13
Polzela SLO 123 A4
Pomarance I 135 B3
Pomarez F 128 C2
Pomárico I 172 B2
Pomáz H 112 B3
Pombal P 154 B2
Pomeroy GB 27 B4
Pomézia I 168 B2
Pommard F 105 B3
Pommelsbrunn D 95 B3
Pomonte I 134 C3
Pomorie BG 17 D7
Pomos CY 181 A1
Pompei I 170 C2
Pompey F 92 C2
Pomposa I 122 C1
Poncin F 118 A2
Pondorf D 95 C3
Ponferrada E 141 B4
Poniec PL 85 A4
Ponikva SLO 123 A4
Poniky SK 99 C3
Pons F 114 C3
Ponsacco I 134 B3
Pont I 119 B4
Pont-a-Celles B 79 B4
Pontacq F 145 A3
Pontailler-sur-Saône F 105 B4
Pont-a-Marcq F 78 B3
Pont-à-Mousson F 92 C2
Pontão P 154 B2
Pontardawe GB 39 C3
Pontarddulais GB 39 C2
Pontarion F 116 B1
Pontarlier F 105 C5
Pontassieve I 135 B4
Pontaubault F 88 B2
Pont-Audemer F 89 A4
Pontaumur F 116 B2
Pont-Aven F 100 B2
Pont Canavese I 119 B4
Pontcharra F 118 B3
Pontcharra-sur-Turdine F 117 B4
Pontchâteau F 101 B3
Pont-Croix F 100 A1
Pont-d'Ain F 118 A2
Pont-de-Beauvoisin F 118 B2
Pont-de-Buis-lès-Quimerch F 100 A1
Pont-de-Chéruy F 118 B2
Pont de Dore F 117 B3
Pont-de-Labeaume F 117 C4
Pont-de-l'Arche F 89 A5
Pont de Molins E 147 B3
Pont-de-Roide F 106 B1
Pont-de-Salars F 130 A1
Pont-d'Espagne F 145 B3
Pont de Suert E 145 B4
Pont-de-Vaux F 117 A4
Pont-de-Veyle F 117 A4
Pont d'Ouilly F 89 B3
Pont-du-Château F 116 B3
Pont-du-Navoy F 105 C4
Ponte a Moriano I 134 B3
Ponte Arche I 121 A3
Ponteareas E 140 B2
Pontebba I 109 C4
Ponte Cáffaro I 121 B3
Pontecagnano I 170 C2
Ponte-Caldelas E 140 B2
Ponteceso E 140 A2
Pontecesures E 140 B2
Pontecorvo I 169 B3
Ponte da Barca P 148 A1
Pontedássio I 133 B4
Pontedécimo I 133 A4
Ponte de Lima P 148 A1
Ponte dell'Ólio I 120 C2
Pontedera I 134 B3
Ponte de Sor P 154 B2
Pontedeume E 140 A2
Ponte di Barbarano I 121 B4
Ponte di Legno I 121 A3
Ponte di Nava I 133 A3
Ponte di Piave I 122 B1
Ponte Felcino I 136 B1
Pontefract GB 40 B2
Ponte Gardena I 108 C2
Ponteginori I 135 B3
Pontelagoscuro I 121 C4
Ponteland GB 37 A5
Pontelandolfo I 170 B2
Ponte-Leccia F 180 A2
Pontelongo I 121 B5
Ponte nelle Alpi I 122 A1
Pont-en-Royans F 118 B2
Pontenure I 120 C2
Pontenx-les-Forges F 128 B1
Ponterwyd GB 39 B3
Ponte San Giovanni I 136 B1
Ponte San Pietro I 120 B2
Pontevedra E 140 B2
Pontevico I 120 B3
Pont Farcy F 88 B2
Pontfaverger-Moronvillers F 91 B4
Pontgibaud F 116 B2
Ponticino I 135 B4
Pontigny F 104 B2
Pontijou F 103 B3
Pontinia I 169 B3
Pontinvrea I 133 A4
Pontivy F 100 A3
Pont-l'Abbé F 100 B1
Pont-l'Évêque F 89 A4
Pontlevoy F 103 B3
Pontoise F 90 B2
Pontones E 164 A2
Pontonx-sur-l'Abour F 128 C2
Pontoon IRL 26 C1
Pontorson F 88 B2
Pontrémoli I 134 A2
Pont-Remy F 90 A1
Pontresina CH 107 C4
Pontrhydfendigaid GB 39 B3
Pontrieux F 100 A2
Ponts E 147 C2
Ponts-aux-Dames F 90 C2
Pont Scorff F 100 B2
Pöntsö FIN 196 B7
Pont-Ste Maxence F 90 B2
Pont-St Esprit F 131 A3
Pont-St Mamet F 129 B3
Pont-St Martin
F 101 B4
I 119 B4
Pont-St Vincent F 92 C2
Pont-sur-Yonne F 104 A2
Pontvallain F 102 B2
Pontypool GB 39 C3
Pontypridd GB 39 C3
Ponza I 169 C2
Poo E 142 A2
Poole GB 43 B5
Poolewe GB 31 B3
Poperinge B 78 B2
Pópoli I 169 A3
Popovac SRB 127 D3
Popovača HR 124 B2
Popow PL 77 B4
Poppel B 79 A5
Poppenhausen
*Bayern* D 82 B2
*Hessen* D 82 B1
Poppi I 135 B4
Poprad SK 99 B4
Popučke SRB 127 C1
Pópulo P 148 A2
Populónia I 134 C3
Pörböly H 125 A4
Porcuna E 163 A3
Pordenone I 122 B1
Pordic F 100 A3
Poręba PL 86 B3
Poreč HR 122 B2
Pori FIN 8 B2
Porjus S 196 C2
Porkhov RUS 9 D6
Porlezza I 120 A2
Porlock GB 43 A3
Pörnbach D 95 C3
Pornic F 101 B3
Pornichet F 101 B3
Porodin SRB 127 C3
Poronin PL 99 B3
Poros
*Attiki* GR 185 B4
*Kefalonia* GR 184 A1
Poroszló H 113 B4
Porozina HR 123 B3
Porquerolles F 132 C2
Porrentruy CH 106 B2
Porreres E 167 B3
Porretta Terme I 135 A3
Porsgrunn N 53 A5
Porspoder F 100 A1
Port-a-Binson F 91 B3
Portacloy IRL 26 B1
Portadown GB 27 B4
Portaferry GB 27 B5
Portaje E 155 B4
Portalegre P 155 B3
Portarlington IRL 30 A1
Port Askaig GB 34 C1
Portavadie GB 34 C2
Portavogie GB 27 B5
Portbail F 88 A2
Port Bannatyne GB 34 C2
Port-Barcarès F 146 B4
Portbou E 146 B4
Port-Camargue F 131 B3
Port Charlotte GB 34 C1
Port d'Andratx E 166 B2
Port-de-Bouc F 131 B3
Port-de-Lanne F 128 C1
Port de Pollença E 167 B3

Port-des-Barques
F 114 C2
Port de Sóller E 166 B2
Portegrandi I 122 B1
Portel P 155 C3
Portela P 148 B1
Port Ellen GB 34 C1
Portelo P 141 C4
Portemouro E 140 B2
Port-en-Bessin F 88 A3
Port'Ercole I 168 A1
Port Erin GB 36 B2
Portes-lès-Valence
F 117 C4
Portets F 128 B2
Port Eynon GB 39 C2
Portezuelo E 155 B4
Port Glasgow GB 34 C3
Portglenone GB 27 B4
Porthcawl GB 39 C3
Port Henderson GB 31 B3
Porthleven GB 42 B1
Porthmadog GB 38 B2
Porticcio F 180 B1
Portici I 170 C2
Portico di Romagna
I 135 A4
Portilla de la Reina
E 142 A2
Portillo E 150 A3
Portimao P 160 B1
Portinatx E 166 B1
Portinho da Arrabida
P 154 C1
Port Isaac GB 42 B2
Portishead GB 43 A4
Port-Joinville F 114 B1
Portknockie GB 33 D4
Port-la-Nouvelle F 130 B2
Portlaoise IRL 30 A1
Portlethen GB 33 D4
Port Logan GB 36 B2
Port Louis F 100 B2
Portmagne IRL 29 C1
Portmahomack GB 32 D3
Portman E 165 B4
Port Manech F 100 B2
Portnacroish GB 34 B2
Portnahaven GB 34 C1
Port Nan Giuran GB 31 A2
Port-Navalo F 100 B3
Port Nis GB 31 A2
Porto
F 180 A1
P 148 A1
Porto-Alto P 154 C2
Porto Azzurro I 134 C3
Portocannone I 170 B3
Porto Cerésio I 120 B1
Porto Cervo I 178 A3
Porto Cesáreo I 173 B3
Porto Colom E 167 B3
Porto Covo P 160 B1
Porto Cristo E 167 B3
Porto d'Áscoli I 136 C2
Porto de Lagos P 160 B1
Porto de Mos P 154 B2
Porto de Rei P 154 C2
Porto do Son E 140 B2
Porto Empédocle I 176 B2
Portoferráio I 134 C3
Portofino I 134 A2
Porto Garibaldi I 122 C1
Portogruaro I 122 B1
Portokhelion GR 184 B4
Portomaggiore I 121 C4
Portomarin E 140 B3
Porton GB 44 B2
Portonovo E 140 B2
Portopalo di Capo
Passero I 177 C4
Porto Petro E 167 B3
Porto Pino I 179 D2
Porto Potenza Picena
I 136 B2
Portør N 53 B5
Porto Recanati I 136 B2
Porto San Giórgio
I 136 B2
Porto Sant'Elpídio
I 136 B2
Porto Santo Stéfano
I 168 A1
Portoscuso I 179 C2
Porto Tolle I 122 C1
Porto Tórres I 178 B2
Porto-Vecchio F 180 B2
Portovénere I 134 A2
Portpatrick GB 36 B1
Portreath GB 42 B1
Portree GB 31 B2
Portroe IRL 28 B3
Portrush GB 27 A4
Port St Mary GB 36 B2
Portsall F 100 A1
Portsmouth GB 44 C2
Portsoy GB 33 D4
Port-Ste Marie F 129 B3
Portstewart GB 27 A4
Port-St-Louis-du-Rhône
F 131 B3
Port-sur-Saône F 105 B5
Port Talbot GB 39 C3
Portugalete E 143 A4
Portumna IRL 28 A3
Port-Vendres F 146 B4
Port William GB 36 B2
Porvoo FIN 8 B4
Porzuna E 157 A3
Posada
*Oviedo* E 141 A5
*Oviedo* E 142 A2
I 178 B3
Posada de Valdeón
E 142 A2
Posadas E 162 A2
Poschiavo CH 120 A3
Posedarje HR 137 A4
Posio FIN 197 C11
Positano I 170 C2
Possagno I 121 B4
Posseck D 83 B4
Possesse F 91 C4
Pössneck D 83 B3
Posta I 169 A3
Postal I 108 C2
Posta Piana I 172 A1
Postbauer-Heng D 95 B3
Posterholt NL 80 A2
Postioma I 121 B5
Postira HR 138 B2
Postojna SLO 123 B3
Postoloprty CZ 84 B1
Postomino PL 68 A1
Posušje BIH 138 B3
Potamos
*Attiki* GR 184 C3
*Attiki* GR 184 D4
Potegowo PL 68 A2
Potenza I 172 B1
Potenza Picena I 136 B2
Potes E 142 A2
Potigny F 89 B3
Potočari BIH 127 C1
Potoci
BIH 138 A2
BIH 139 B3
Potony H 125 B3
Potries E 159 C3
Potsdam D 74 B2
Potštát CZ 98 B1
Pottenbrunn A 110 A2
Pottendorf A 111 B3
Pottenstein
A 111 B3
D 95 B3
Potters Bar GB 44 B3
Pöttmes D 94 C3
Pöttsching A 111 B3
Potworów PL 87 A4
Pouancé F 101 B4
Pougues-les-Eaux
F 104 B2
Pouilly-en-Auxois
F 104 B3
Pouilly-sous Charlieu
F 117 A4
Pouilly-sur-Loire F 104 B1
Poujol-sur-Orb F 130 B2
Poullaouen F 100 A2
Poulton-le-Fylde GB 38 A4
Poundstock GB 42 B2
Pourcy F 91 B3
Pourrain F 104 B2
Poussu FIN 197 D12
Pouyastruc F 145 A4
Pouy-de-Touges F 146 A2
Pouzauges F 114 B3
Pova de Santa Iria
P 154 C1
Považská Bystrica
SK 98 B2
Povedilla E 158 C1
Povenets RUS 9 A9
Povlja HR 138 B2
Povljana HR 137 A4
Póvoa
*Beja* P 161 A2
*Santarém* P 154 B2
Póvoa de Lanhoso
P 148 A1
Póvoa de Varzim
P 148 A1
Póvoa e Meadas P 155 B3
Powidz PL 76 B2
Poyales del Hoyo
E 150 B2
Poynton GB 40 B1
Poyntz Pass GB 27 B4
Poysdorf A 97 C4
Poza de la Sal E 143 B3
Pozaldez E 150 A3
Pozán de Vero E 145 B4
Pozanti TR 23 C8
Požarevac SRB 127 C3
Požega
HR 125 B3
SRB 127 D2
Poznań PL 76 B1
Pozo Alcón E 164 B2
Pozoantiguo E 150 A2
Pozoblanco E 156 B3
Pozo Cañada E 158 C2
Pozo de Guadalajara
E 151 B4
Pozo de la Serna E 157 B4
Pozohondo E 158 C2
Pozondón E 152 B2
Poźrzadło Wielkie
PL 75 A4
Pozuel del Campo
E 152 B2
Pozuelo de Alarcón
E 151 B4
Pozuelo de Calatrava
E 157 B4
Pozuelo del Páramo
E 142 B1
Pozuelo de Zarzón
E 149 B3
Pozzallo I 177 C3
Pozzomaggiore I 178 B2
Pozzo San Nicola I 178 B2
Pozzuoli I 170 C2
Pozzuolo I 135 B4
Prabuty PL 69 B4
Prača BIH 139 B4
Prachatice CZ 96 B1
Prada E 141 B3
Pradelle F 118 C2
Pradelles F 117 C3
Prades
E 147 C1
F 146 B3
Pradła PL 86 B3
Prado
E 142 A1
P 148 A1
Prado del Rey E 162 B2
Pradoluengo E 143 B3
Pragelato I 119 B3
Pragersko SLO 123 A4
Prägraten A 109 B3
Prague = Praha CZ 84 B2
Praha = Prague CZ 84 B2
Prahecq F 115 B3
Praia P 154 B1
Práia a Mare I 174 B1
Praia da Rocha P 160 B1
Praia da Viera P 154 B2
Praia de Mira P 148 B1
Praiano I 170 C2
Pralboino I 120 B3
Pralognan-la-Vanoise
F 118 B3
Pramanda GR 182 D3
Pranjani SRB 127 C2
Prapatnica HR 138 B2
Præstø DK 65 A5
Praszka PL 86 A2
Prat F 146 A1
Prata I 135 B3
Prata di Pordenone
I 122 B1
Pratau D 83 A4
Prat de Compte E 153 B4
Pratdip E 147 C1
Pratella I 170 B2
Prato I 135 B4
Prátola Peligna I 169 A3
Pratola Serra I 170 C2
Prats-de-Mollo-la-Preste
F 146 B3
Prauthoy F 105 B4
Pravia E 141 A4
Praxmar A 108 B2
Prayssac F 129 B4
Prazzo I 132 A3
Prebold SLO 123 A4
Préchac F 128 B2
Précy-sur-Thil F 104 B3
Predáppio I 135 A4
Predazzo I 121 A4
Předin CZ 97 B3
Preding A 110 C2
Predjame SLO 123 B3
Predlitz A 109 B4
Predmeja SLO 122 B2
Predoi I 108 B3
Pré-en-Pail F 89 B3
Prees GB 38 B4
Preetz D 64 B3
Préfailles F 101 B3
Pregarten A 96 C2
Pregrada HR 123 A4
Preignan F 129 C3
Preiļi LV 8 D5
Preitenegg A 110 C1
Prekaja BIH 138 A2
Preko HR 137 A4
Preljina SRB 127 D2
Prelog HR 124 A2
Prelošćica HR 124 B2
Přelouč CZ 97 A3
Prem SLO 123 B3
Premantura HR 122 C2
Prémery F 104 B2
Prémia I 119 A5
Premiàde Mar E 147 C3
Premnitz D 73 B5
Prémont F 91 A3
Prenzlau D 74 A2
Preodac BIH 138 A2
Přerov CZ 98 B1
Prerow D 66 B1
Presencio E 143 B3
Presicce I 173 C4
Presly F 103 B4
Prešov SK 12 D4
Pressac F 115 B4
Pressath D 95 B3
Pressbaum A 111 A3
Prestatyn GB 38 A3
Prestebakke N 54 B2
Presteigne GB 39 B3
Přeštice CZ 96 B1
Preston
*Lancashire* GB 38 A4
*Scottish Borders*
GB 35 C5
Prestonpans GB 35 C5
Prestwick GB 36 A2
Prettin D 83 A4
Preturo I 169 A3
Pretzchendorf D 83 B5
Pretzier D 73 B4
Pretzsch D 83 A4
Preuilly-sur-Claise
F 115 B4
Prevalje SLO 110 C1
Prevenchères F 131 A2
Préveranges F 116 A2
Preveza GR 182 E2
Prevršac HR 124 B2
Prezid HR 123 B3
Priaranza del Bierzo
E 141 B4
Priay F 118 A2
Pribeta SK 112 B2
Priboj
BIH 125 C4
SRB 16 D3
Příbor CZ 98 B2
Příbram CZ 96 B2
Pribylina SK 99 B3
Přibyslav CZ 97 B3
Pričević SRB 127 C1
Pridjel BIH 125 C4
Priego E 152 B1
Priego de Córdoba
E 163 A3
Priekule LV 8 D2
Prien D 109 B3
Prienai LT 13 A5
Prievidza SK 98 C2
Prigradica HR 138 C2
Prigrevica SRB 125 B5
Prijeboj HR 123 C4
Prijedor BIH 124 C2
Prijepolje SRB 16 D3
Prilep MK 182 B3
Priluka BIH 138 B2
Primda CZ 95 B4
Primel-Trégastel F 100 A2
Primišje HR 123 B4
Primorsk
*Kaliningrad* RUS 69 A5
*Severo-Zapadnyy*
RUS 9 B6
Primošten HR 138 B1
Primstal D 92 B2
Princes Risborough
GB 44 B3
Princetown GB 42 B2
Principina a Mare I 135 C4
Priolo Gargallo I 177 B4
Prioro E 142 B2
Priozersk RUS 9 B7
Prirechnyy RUS 193 C14
Prisoje BIH 138 B3
Priština KOS 16 D4
Pritzerbe D 73 B5
Pritzier D 73 A4
Pritzwalk D 73 A5
Privas F 117 C4
Priverno I 169 B3
Privlaka
*Vukovarsko-Srijemska*
HR 125 B4
*Zadarska* HR 137 A4
Prizna HR 123 C3
Prizren KOS 16 D4
Prizzi I 176 B2
Prnjavor
BIH 125 C3
HR 124 B1
SRB 127 C1
Proaza E 141 A4
Probstzella D 82 B3
Probus GB 42 B2
Prócchio I 134 C3
Prochowice PL 85 A4
Prócida I 170 C2
Prodhromos CY 181 B1
Prodo I 135 C5
Proença-a-Nova P 154 B3
Proença-a-Velha P 155 A3
Profondeville B 79 B4
Prokuplje SRB 16 D4
Propriano F 180 B1
Prosec CZ 97 B4
Prösen D 83 A5
Prosenjakovci
SLO 111 C3
Prosotsani GR 183 B5
Prostějov CZ 98 B1
Prószków PL 86 B1
Proszowice PL 87 B4
Protić BIH 138 A2
Protivanov CZ 97 B4
Protivín CZ 96 B2
Prötzel D 74 B2
Provins F 90 C3
Prozor BIH 139 B3
Prrenjas AL 182 B2
Prudhoe GB 37 B5
Prudnik PL 85 B5
Pruggern A 109 B4
Prügy H 113 A5
Prüm D 80 B2
Pruna E 162 B2
Prunelli-di-Fiumorbo
F 180 A2
Prunetta I 135 A3
Pruniers F 103 C4
Prusice PL 85 A4
Pruské SK 98 B2
Pruszcz PL 76 A3
Pruszcz Gdański PL 69 A3
Pruszków PL 77 B5
Prutz A 108 B1
Prüzen D 65 C5
Pruzhany BY 13 B6
Pružina SK 98 B2
Pŭrvomay BG 183 A7
Pryzlęg PL 75 B4
Przasnysz PL 77 A5
Przechlewo PL 68 B2
Przecław PL 87 B5
Przedbórz PL 87 A3
Przedecz PL 76 B3
Przejęslav PL 84 A3
Przemków PL 85 A3
Przemocze PL 75 A3
Przemyśl PL 12 D5
Przerąb PL 87 A3
Przewodnik PL 69 B3
Przewodowo Parcele
PL 77 B5
Przewóz PL 84 A2
Przezmark PL 69 B4
Przodkowo PL 68 A3
Przybiernów PL 75 A3
Przyborowice PL 77 B5
Przybyszew PL 87 A4
Przybyszów PL 86 A3
Przylęg PL 75 B4
Przysucha PL 87 A4
Przytóczna PL 75 B4
Przytyk PL 87 A4
Przywidz PL 68 A3
Psachna GR 185 A4
Psara GR 185 A6
Psary PL 76 C3
Pskov RUS 8 D6
Pszczew PL 75 B4
Pszczółki PL 69 A3
Pszczyna PL 98 B2
Pszów PL 86 B2
Pteleos GR 182 D4
Ptolemaida GR 182 C3
Ptuj SLO 124 A1
Ptusza PL 68 B1
Puch A 109 B4
Puchberg am
Schneeberg A 110 B2
Puchevillers F 90 A2
Puchheim D 108 A2
Púchov SK 98 B2
Pučišća HR 138 B2
Puck PL 69 A3
Puçol E 159 B3
Puconci SLO 111 C3
Pudasjärvi FIN 197 D10
Puderbach D 81 B3
Pudozh RUS 9 B10
Puebla de Albortón
E 153 A3
Puebla de Alcocer
E 156 B2
Puebla de Beleña
E 151 B4
Puebla de Don Fadrique
E 164 B2
Puebla de Don Rodrigo
E 156 A3
Puebla de Guzmán
E 161 B2
Puebla de la Calzada
E 155 C4
Puebla de la Reina
E 156 B1
Puebla de Lillo E 142 A1
Puebla del Maestre
E 161 A3
Puebla del Principe
E 158 C1
Puebla de Obando
E 155 B4
Puebla de Sanabria
E 141 B4
Puebla de Sancho Pérez
E 155 C4
Puente Almuhey E 142 B2
Puente de Domingo
Flórez E 141 B4
Puente de Génave
E 164 A2
Puente del Congosto
E 150 B2
Puente de Montañana
E 145 B4
Puente Duero E 150 A3
Puente-Genil E 162 A3
Puente la Reina E 144 B2
Puente la Reina de Jaca
E 144 B3
Puentelarra E 143 B3
Puente Mayorga E 162 B2
Puente Viesgo E 143 A3
Puertas
*Asturias* E 142 A2
*Salamanca* E 149 A3
Puerto de Mazarrón
E 165 B3
Puerto de Santa Cruz
E 156 A2
Puerto de San Vicente
E 156 A2
Puerto-Lápice E 157 A4
Puertollano E 157 B3
Puerto Lumbreras
E 164 B3
Puerto Moral E 161 B3
Puerto Real E 162 B1
Puerto Rey E 156 A2
Puerto Seguro E 149 B3
Puerto Serrano E 162 B2
Puget-Sur-Argens
F 132 B2
Puget-Théniers F 132 B2
Puget-ville F 132 B2
Pugnochiuso I 171 B4
Puigcerdà E 146 B2
Puigpunyent E 166 B2
Puig Reig E 147 C2
Puillon F 128 C2
Puimichel F 132 B2
Puimoisson F 132 B2
Puiseaux F 103 A4
Puisieux F 90 A2
Puisserguier F 130 B2
Puivert F 146 B3
Pujols F 128 B2
Pukanec SK 98 C2
Pukavik S 63 B2
Pukë AL 182 A1
Pula
HR 122 C2
I 179 C2
Puławy PL 12 C4
Pulborough GB 44 C3
Pulfero I 122 A2
Pulgar E 157 A3
Pulheim D 80 A2
Pulkau A 97 C3
Pulpi E 164 B3
Pulsano I 173 B3
Pulsnitz D 84 A2
Pułtusk PL 77 B6
Pumpsaint GB 39 B3
Punat HR 123 B3
Punta Marina I 135 A5
Punta Prima E 167 B4
Punta Sabbioni I 122 B1
Puntas de Calnegre
E 165 B3
Punta Umbría E 161 B3
Puolanka FIN 3 D10
Puoltikasvaara S 196 B4
Puoltsa S 196 B2
Puračić BIH 125 C4
Purbach am Neusiedler
See A 111 B3
Purchena E 164 B2
Purfleet GB 45 B4
Purgstall A 110 A2
Purkersdorf A 111 A3
Purmerend NL 70 B1
Purullena E 164 B1
Pushkin RUS 9 C7
Pushkino RUS 9 D10
Püspökladány H 113 B5
Pusté Ulany SK 111 A4
Pustoshka RUS 9 D6
Puszcza Mariańska
PL 77 C5
Puszczykowo PL 76 B1
Pusztamagyaród
H 111 C3
Pusztamonostor H 113 B3
Pusztaszabolcs H 112 B2
Pusztavám H 112 B2
Putanges-Pont-Ecrepin
F 89 B3
Putbus D 66 B2
Putignano I 173 B3
Putlitz D 73 A5
Putnok H 99 C4
Putte B 79 A4
Puttelange-aux-Lacs
F 92 B2
Putten NL 70 B2
Puttgarden D 65 B4
Püttlingen D 92 B2
Putzu Idu I 179 B2
Puy-Guillaume F 117 B3
Puylaroque F 129 B4
Puylaurens F 146 A3
Puy-l'Évêque F 129 B4
Puymirol F 129 B3
Puyôo F 128 C2
Puyrolland F 114 B3
Pwllheli GB 38 B2
Pyetrikaw BY 13 B8
Pyhäjärvi FIN 3 E9
Pyhäkylä FIN 197 D11
Pyla CY 181 A2
Pyla-sur-Mer F 128 B1
Pyrzyce PL 75 A3
Pysely CZ 96 B2
Pyskowice PL 86 B2
Pytalovo RUS 8 D5
Pyzdry PL 76 B2

## Q

Quakenbrück D 71 B4
Quargnento I 119 C5
Quarré-les-Tombes
F 104 B2
Quarteira P 160 B1
Quartu Sant'Élena
I 179 C3
Quatre-Champs F 91 B4
Quedlinburg D 82 A3
Queensferry
*Edinburgh* GB 35 C4
*Flintshire* GB 38 A3
Queige F 118 B3
Queipo E 161 B3
Queixans E 146 B2
Quel E 144 B1

Quelaines-St-Gault F 102 B1
Queljada P 148 A1
Quemada E 143 C3
Queralbs E 147 B3
Quercianella I 134 B3
Querfurt D 82 A3
Quérigut F 146 B3
Quero
E 157 A4
I 121 B4
Querqueville F 88 A2
Quesada E 164 B1
Questembert F 101 B3
Quettehou F 88 A2
Quevauvillers F 90 B2
Quevy B 79 B4
Quiaois P 148 B1
Quiberon F 100 B2
Quiberville F 89 A4
Quickborn D 64 C2
Quiévrain B 79 B3
Quillan F 146 B3
Quillebeuf F 89 A4
Quimper F 100 A1
Quimperlé F 100 B2
Quincampoix F 89 A5
Quincoces de Yuso E 143 B3
Quincy F 103 B4
Quinéville F 88 A2
Quingey F 105 B4
Quinson F 132 B2
Quinssaines F 116 A2
Quinta-Grande P 154 C2
Quintana de la Serena E 156 B2
Quintana del Castillo E 141 B4
Quintana del Marco E 141 B5
Quintana del Puenta E 142 B2
Quintana-Martin Galindez E 143 B3
Quintanaortuño E 143 B3
Quintanapalla E 143 B3
Quintanar de la Orden E 157 A4
Quintanar de la Sierra E 143 C3
Quintanar del Rey E 158 B2
Quintanilla de la Mata E 143 C3
Quintanilla del Coco E 143 C3
Quintanilla de Onésimo E 150 A3
Quintanilla de Somoza E 141 B4
Quintas de Valdelucio E 142 B2
Quintela P 148 B2
Quintin F 100 A3
Quinto E 153 A3
Quinzano d'Oglio I 120 B3
Quiroga E 141 B3
Quismondo E 150 B3
Quissac F 131 B2
Quistello I 121 B3

## R

Raab A 96 C1
Raabs an der Thaya A 97 C3
Raahe FIN 3 D9
Raajärvi FIN 197 C9
Raalte NL 71 B3
Raamsdonksveer NL 79 A4
Raanujarvi FIN 196 C7
Raattama FIN 196 A7
Rab HR 123 C3
Rabac HR 123 B3
Rábade E 140 A3
Rábafüzes H 111 C3
Rábahidvég H 111 B3
Rabanales E 149 A3
Rábapatona H 111 B4
Rabapordány H 111 B4
Rabastens F 129 C4
Rabastens-de-Bigorre F 145 A4
Rabat = Victoria M 175 C3
Rabat M 175 C3
Rabča SK 99 B3
Rabe SRB 126 A2
Rabi CZ 96 B1
Rabino PL 67 C4
Rabka PL 99 B3
Rabrovo SRB 127 C3
Rača SRB 127 C3
Rácale I 173 C4
Rácalmás H 112 B2
Racalmuto I 176 B2
Racconigi I 119 C4
Rače SLO 123 A4
Rachecourt-sur-Marne F 91 C5
Raciąż PL 77 B5
Racibórz PL 86 B2
Račinovci HR 125 C4
Ráckeve H 112 B2
Racławice PL 87 B4
Racławice Śląskie PL 86 B1
Racot PL 75 B5
Råda
*Skaraborg* S 55 B4
*Värmland* S 49 B5
Radalj SRB 127 C1
Rădăuţi RO 17 B6
Radda in Chianti I 135 B4
Raddusa I 177 B3
Radeberg D 84 A1
Radebeul D 84 A1
Radeburg D 84 A1
Radeče SLO 123 A4
Radekhiv UA 13 C6
Radenci SLO 111 C3
Radenthein A 109 C4
Radevormwald D 80 A3
Radicófani I 135 C4
Radicóndoli I 135 B4
Radišići BIH 138 B3
Radizel SLO 110 C2
Radków PL 85 B4
Radlje ob Dravi SLO 110 C2
Radlów PL 87 B4
Radmer an der Stube A 110 B1
Radnejaur S 195 E9
Radnice CZ 96 B1
Radohova BIH 138 A3
Radojevo SRB 126 B2
Radolfzell D 107 B3
Radom PL 87 A5
Radomice PL 77 B4
Radomin PL 77 A4
Radomsko PL 86 A3
Radomyshl UA 13 C8
Radomyśl Wielki PL 87 B5
Radošina SK 98 C1
Radošovce SK 98 C1
Radoszewice PL 86 A2
Radoszyce PL 87 A4
Radotin CZ 96 B2
Radovets BG 186 A1
Radoviš MK 182 B4
Radovljica SLO 123 A3
Radowo Wielkie PL 75 A4
Radstadt A 109 B4
Radstock GB 43 A4
Raduc HR 137 A4
Raduša MK 182 A3
Radviliškis LT 8 E3
Radzanów
*Mazowieckie* PL 77 B5
*Mazowieckie* PL 87 A4
Radziejów PL 76 B3
Radziejowice PL 77 B5
Radzovce SK 113 A3
Radzyń Chełmiński PL 69 B3
Raeren B 80 B2
Raesfeld D 80 A2
Raffadali I 176 B2
Rafina GR 185 A4
Rafsbotn N 192 B7
Ragachow BY 13 B9
Ragály H 99 C4
Rågeleje DK 61 C2
Raglan GB 39 C4
Ragnitz A 110 C2
Ragusa I 177 C3
Rahden D 72 B1
Råholt N 48 B3
Raiano I 169 A3
Raigada E 141 B3
Rain D 94 C2
Rainbach im Mühlkreis A 96 C2
Rainham GB 45 B4
Rairiz de Veiga E 140 B3
Raisdorf D 64 B3
Raisio FIN 8 B3
Raiskio FIN 197 D9
Raiva
*Aveiro* P 148 A1
*Coimbra* P 148 B1
Raja-Jooseppi FIN 193 D12
Rajala FIN 197 B9
Rajcza PL 99 B3
Rajec SK 98 B2
Rájec-Jestřebi CZ 97 B4
Rajecké Teplice SK 98 B2
Rajevo Selo HR 125 C4
Rajhrad CZ 97 B4
Rajić HR 124 B3
Rajka H 111 B4
Rakaca H 99 C4
Rakamaz H 113 A5
Rakek SLO 123 B3
Rakhiv UA 17 A6
Rakitna SLO 123 B3
Rakitovo BG 183 B6
Rakkestad N 54 A2
Rákóczifalva H 113 B4
Rakoniewice PL 75 B5
Rakoszyce PL 85 A4
Raková SK 98 B2
Rakovac BIH 125 B3
Rakovica HR 123 C4
Rakovník CZ 96 A1
Rakow D 66 B2
Raków PL 87 B5
Rakvere EST 8 C5
Ralja SRB 127 C2
Rälla S 62 B4
Ramacastañas E 150 B2
Ramacca I 177 B3
Ramales de la Victoria E 143 A3
Ramberg N 194 B4
Rambervillers F 92 C2
Rambouillet F 90 C1
Rambucourt F 92 C1
Ramdala S 63 B3
Ramerupt F 91 C4
Ramingstein A 109 B4
Ramirás E 140 B2
Ramiswil CH 106 B2
Ramkvilla S 62 A2
Ramme DK 58 B1
Rämmen S 49 B6
Ramnäs S 56 A2
Ramnes N 54 A1
Râmnicu Vâlcea RO 17 C6
Ramonville-St Agne F 129 C4
Rampside GB 36 B3
Ramsau D 109 B3
Ramsbeck D 81 A4
Ramsberg S 56 A1
Ramsele S 200 C2
Ramsey
*Cambridgeshire* GB 44 A3
*Isle of Man* GB 36 B2
Ramseycleuch GB 36 A3
Ramsgate GB 45 B5
Ramsjö S 200 D1
Ramstein-Meisenbach D 93 B3
Ramsund N 194 B7
Ramundberget S 199 C9
Ramvik S 200 D3
Ranalt A 108 B2
Rånäs S 51 C5
Rånåsfoss N 48 B3
Rance B 91 A4
Ránchio I 135 B5
Randaberg N 52 A1
Randalstown GB 27 B4
Randan F 117 A3
Randazzo I 177 B3
Rånddalen S 199 C10
Randegg A 110 A1
Randers DK 58 B3
Randijaur S 196 C2
Randin E 140 C3
Randsverk N 198 D6
Råneå S 196 D5
Rânes F 89 B3
Rångedala S 60 B3
Ranis D 82 B3
Rankweil A 107 B4
Rånnaväg S 60 B3
Ränneslöv S 61 C3
Rannoch Station GB 34 B3
Ranovac SRB 127 C3
Ransäter S 55 A4
Ransbach-Baumbach D 81 B3
Ransta S 56 A2
Ranttila FIN 193 C9
Ranua FIN 197 D9
Ranum DK 58 B2
Ranvalhal P 154 B1
Raon-l'Étape F 92 C2
Ráossi I 121 B4
Rapallo I 134 A2
Rapla EST 8 C4
Rapness GB 33 B4
Rapolano Terme I 135 B4
Rapolla I 172 B1
Raposa P 154 B2
Rapperswil CH 107 B3
Raša HR 123 B3
Rasal E 145 B3
Rascafria E 151 B4
Rasdorf D 82 B1
Raseiniai LT 13 A5
Rašica SLO 123 B3
Rasines E 143 A3
Rasquera E 153 A4
Rássina I 135 B4
Rastatt D 93 C4
Rastede D 71 A5
Rastenberg D 82 A3
Rastošnica BIH 125 C4
Rastovac MNE 139 C4
Rasueros E 150 A2
Rasy PL 86 A3
Raszków PL 86 A1
Rätan S 199 C11
Rateče SLO 109 C4
Ratekau D 65 C3
Ratež SLO 123 B4
Rathangan IRL 30 A2
Rathcoole IRL 30 A2
Rathcormack IRL 29 B3
Rathdrum IRL 30 B2
Rathebur D 74 A2
Rathenow D 73 B5
Rathfriland GB 27 B4
Rathkeale IRL 29 B3
Rathmelton IRL 27 A3
Rathmolyon IRL 30 A2
Rathmore IRL 29 B2
Rathmullan IRL 27 A3
Rathnew IRL 30 B2
Rathvilly IRL 30 B2
Ratibořské Hory CZ 96 B2
Ratingen D 80 A2
Ratková SK 99 C4
Ratkovo SRB 126 B1
Ratne UA 13 C6
Rattelsdorf D 94 A2
Ratten A 110 B2
Rattosjärvi FIN 196 C7
Rattray GB 35 B4
Rättvik S 50 B2
Ratvika N 199 B7
Ratzeburg D 65 C3
Rätzlingen D 73 B4
Raucourt-et-Flaba F 91 B4
Raudeberg N 198 D2
Raufarhöfn IS 191 A10
Raufoss N 48 B2
Rauhala FIN 196 B7
Rauland N 53 A4
Raulhac F 116 C2
Raulia N 195 E5
Rauma FIN 8 B2
Raundal N 46 B3
Raunds GB 44 A3
Rauris A 109 B4
Rautas S 196 B2
Rautavaara FIN 3 E11
Rauville-la-Bigot F 88 A2
Rauzan F 128 B2
Ravanusa I 176 B2
Rava-Rus'ka UA 13 C5
Ravča HR 138 B3
Ravels B 79 A4
Rävemåla S 63 B3
Ravenglass GB 36 B3
Ravenna I 135 A5
Ravensburg D 107 B4
Rävlanda S 60 B2
Ravna Gora HR 123 B3
Ravne na Koroškem SLO 110 C1
Ravnje SRB 127 C1
Ravno BIH 139 C3
Ravno Selo SRB 126 B1
Rawa Mazowiecka PL 87 A4
Rawicz PL 85 A4
Rawtenstall GB 40 B1
Rayleigh GB 45 B4
Ražana SRB 127 C1
Ražanac HR 137 A4
Razboj BIH 124 B3
Razes F 115 B5
Razgrad BG 17 D7
Razkrižje SLO 111 C3
Razlog BG 183 B5
Razo E 140 A2
Reading GB 44 B3
Réalmont F 130 B1
Rebais F 90 C3
Reboly RUS 3 E12
Rebordelo P 149 A2
Recanati I 136 B2
Recas E 151 B4
Recco I 134 A2
Recess IRL 28 A2
Recey-sur-Ource F 105 B3
Recezinhos P 148 A1
Rechnitz A 111 B3
Rechytsa BY 13 B9
Recke D 71 B4
Recklinghausen D 80 A3
Recoaro Terme I 121 B4
Recogne B 92 B1
Recoules-Prévinquières F 130 A1
Recsk H 113 B4
Recz PL 75 A4
Reda PL 69 A3
Redalen N 48 B2
Redange L 92 B1
Redcar GB 37 B5
Redditch GB 44 A2
Redefin D 73 A4
Redhill GB 44 B3
Redics H 111 C3
Redkino RUS 9 D10
Redland GB 33 B3
Redlin D 73 A5
Redon F 101 B3
Redondela E 140 B2
Redondo P 155 C3
Red Point GB 31 B3
Redruth GB 42 B1
Redzikowo PL 68 A2
Reepham GB 41 C5
Rees D 80 A2
Reeth GB 37 B5
Reetz D 73 A4
Reftele S 60 B3
Regalbuto I 177 B3
Regen D 95 C5
Regensburg D 95 B4
Regenstauf D 95 B4
Reggello I 135 B4
Réggio di Calábria I 175 C1
Reggiolo I 121 C3
Réggio nell'Emilia I 121 C3
Reghin RO 17 B6
Régil E 144 A1
Regna S 56 B1
Regniéville F 92 C1
Regny F 117 B4
Rego da Leirosa P 154 A2
Regöly H 112 C2
Regueiro E 140 B2
Reguengo
*Portalegre* P 155 B3
*Santarém* P 154 B2
Reguengos de Monsaraz P 155 C3
Rehau D 83 B4
Rehburg D 72 B2
Rehden D 72 B1
Rehna D 65 C4
Reichelsheim D 93 B4
Reichelshofen D 94 B2
Reichenau A 110 B2
Reichenbach
*Sachsen* D 83 B4
*Sachsen* D 84 A2
Reichenfels A 110 B1
Reichensachsen D 82 A2
Reichertshofen D 95 C3
Reichshoffen F 93 C3
Reiden CH 106 B2
Reigada
E 141 A4
P 149 B3
Reigate GB 44 B3
Reillanne F 132 B1
Reillo E 158 B2
Reims F 91 B4
Reinach CH 106 B3
Reinbek D 72 A3
Reinberg D 66 B2
Reine N 194 C4
Reinfeld D 65 C3
Reinheim D 93 B4
Reinli N 47 B6
Reinosa E 142 A2
Reinstorf D 65 C4
Reinsvoll N 48 B2
Reisach A 109 C4
Reiss GB 32 C3
Reitan N 199 C8
Reit im Winkl D 109 B3
Rejmyre S 56 B1
Rekavice BIH 124 C3
Rekovac SRB 127 D3
Relleu E 159 C3
Rém H 125 A5
Remagen D 80 B3
Rémalard F 89 B4
Rembercourt-aux-Pots F 91 C5
Remedios P 154 B1
Remels D 71 A4
Remetea Mare RO 126 B3
Remich L 92 B2
Rémilly F 92 B2
Remiremont F 105 A5
Remolinos E 144 C2
Remoulins F 131 B3
Remscheid D 80 A3
Rémuzat F 131 A4
Rena N 48 A3
Renaison F 117 A3
Renazé F 101 B4
Renchen D 93 C4
Rencurel F 118 B2
Rende I 174 B2
Rendina GR 182 D3
Rendsburg D 64 B2
Renedo E 150 A3
Renens CH 105 C5
Renfrew GB 34 C3
Rengsjö S 50 A3
Reni UA 17 C8
Rennebu N 198 C6
Rennerod D 81 B4
Rennertshofen D 94 C3
Rennes F 101 A4
Rennes-les-Bains F 146 B3
Rennweg A 109 B4
Rens DK 64 B2
Rensjön S 196 A2
Rentería E 144 A2
Rentjärn S 200 A4
Répcelak H 111 B4
Repojoki FIN 193 D9
Repvåg N 193 B9
Requena E 159 B2
Réquista F 130 A1
Rerik D 65 B4
Resana I 121 B4
Resarö S 57 A4
Reschen = Résia I 108 C1
Resen MK 182 B3
Resende P 148 A2
Résia = Reschen I 108 C1
Reşiţa
RO 16 C4
RO 126 B3
Resko PL 67 C4
Resnik SRB 127 C2
Ressons-sur-Matz F 90 B2
Restábal E 163 B4
Resuttano I 177 B3
Retamal E 155 C4
Retford GB 40 B3
Rethel F 91 B4
Rethem D 72 B2
Rethimno GR 185 D5
Retie B 79 A5
Retiers F 101 B4
Retortillo E 149 B3
Retortillo de Soria E 151 A4
Retournac F 117 B4
Rétság H 112 B3
Rettenegg A 110 B2
Retuerta del Bullaque E 157 A3
Retz A 97 C3
Retzbach D 94 B1
Reuden D 73 B5
Reuilly F 103 B4
Reus E 147 C2
Reusel NL 79 A5
Reuterstadt Stavenhagen D 74 A1
Reuth D 95 B4
Reutlingen D 94 C1
Reutte A 108 B1
Reuver NL 80 A2
Revel F 146 A2
Revello I 119 C4
Revenga E 151 B3
Revest-du-Bion F 132 A1
Révfülöp H 111 C4
Revigny-sur-Ornain F 91 C4
Revin F 91 B4
Řevnice CZ 96 B2
Řevničov CZ 84 B1
Revo I 121 A4
Revsnes N 47 A4
Revúca SK 99 C4
Rewa PL 69 A3
Rewal PL 67 B4
Rexbo S 50 B2
Reyðarfjörður IS 191 B11
Reyero E 142 B1
Reykhólar IS 190 B3
Reykholt
*Árnessýsla* IS 190 C5
*Borgarfjarðarsýsla* IS 190 C4
Reykjahlið IS 191 B9
Reykjavík IS 190 C4
Rezé F 101 B4
Rēzekne LV 8 D5
Rezovo BG 17 E8
Rezzato I 120 B3
Rezzoáglio I 134 A2
Rhade D 72 A2
Rhaunen D 93 B3
Rhayader GB 39 B3
Rheda-Wiedenbrück D 81 A4
Rhede
*Niedersachsen* D 71 A4
*Nordrhein-Westfalen* D 80 A2
Rheinau D 93 C3
Rheinbach D 80 B2
Rheinberg D 80 A2
Rheine D 71 B4
Rheinfelden D 106 B2
Rheinsberg D 74 A1
Rhêmes-Notre-Dame I 119 B4
Rhenen NL 70 C2
Rhens D 81 B3
Rheydt D 80 A2
Rhiconich GB 32 C2
Rhinow D 73 B5
Rhiw GB 38 B2
Rho I 120 B2
Rhoden D 81 A5
Rhodes GR 188 C3
Rhondda GB 39 C3
Rhosllanerchrugog GB 38 A3
Rhosneigr GB 38 A2
Rhossili GB 39 C2
Rhubodach GB 34 C2
Rhuddlan GB 38 A3
Rhyl GB 38 A3
Rhynie GB 33 D4
Riala S 57 A4
Riallé F 101 B4
Riaño E 142 B1
Riano I 168 A2
Rians F 132 B1
Rianxo E 140 B2
Riaza E 151 A4
Riba E 143 A3
Ribadavia E 140 B2
Ribadeo E 141 A3
Riba de Saelices E 152 B1
Ribadesella E 142 A1
Ribaflecha E 143 B4
Ribaforada E 144 C2
Ribare SRB 127 C3
Riba-roja d'Ebre E 153 A4
Riba-Roja de Turia E 159 B3
Ribe DK 59 C1
Ribeauvillé F 106 A2
Ribécourt-Dreslincourt F 90 B2
Ribeira da Pena P 148 A2
Ribeira de Piquín E 141 A3
Ribemont F 91 B3
Ribera I 176 B2
Ribérac F 129 A3
Ribera de Cardós E 146 B2
Ribera del Fresno E 156 B1
Ribesalbes E 159 A3
Ribes de Freser E 147 B3
Ribiers F 132 A1
Ribnica
BIH 139 A4
SLO 123 B3

**Ribnica na Potorju** SLO 110 C2
**Ribnik** HR 123 B4
**Ribniţa** MD 17 B8
**Ribnitz-Damgarten** D 66 B1
**Ribolla** I 135 C4
**Říčany** CZ 97 B4
**Ričany** CZ 96 B2
**Riccia** I 170 B2
**Riccione** I 136 A1
**Ricco Del Golfo** I 134 A2
**Richebourg** F 105 A4
**Richelieu** F 102 B2
**Richisau** CH 107 B3
**Richmond**
*Greater London* GB 44 B3
*North Yorkshire* GB 37 B5
**Richtenberg** D 66 B1
**Richterswil** CH 107 B3
**Rickling** D 64 B3
**Rickmansworth** GB 44 B3
**Ricla** E 152 A2
**Riddarhyttan** S 50 C2
**Ridderkerk** NL 79 A4
**Riddes** CH 119 A4
**Ridjica** SRB 125 B5
**Riec-sur-Bélon** F 100 B2
**Ried** A 109 A4
**Riedenburg** D 95 C3
**Ried im Oberinntal** A 108 B1
**Riedlingen** D 107 A4
**Riedstadt** D 93 B4
**Riegersburg** A 110 C2
**Riego de la Vega** E 141 B5
**Riego del Camino** E 149 A4
**Riello** E 141 B5
**Riemst** B 80 B1
**Rienne** B 91 B4
**Riénsena** E 142 A2
**Riesa** D 83 A5
**Riese Pio X** I 121 B4
**Riesi** I 177 B3
**Riestedt** D 82 A3
**Rietberg** D 81 A4
**Rieti** I 169 A2
**Rietschen** D 84 A2
**Rieumes** F 146 A2
**Rieupeyroux** F 130 A1
**Rieux-Volvestre** F 146 A2
**Riez** F 132 B2
**Rīga** LV 8 D4
**Riggisberg** CH 106 C2
**Rignac** F 130 A1
**Rignano Gargánico** I 171 B3
**Rigolato** I 109 C3
**Rigside** GB 36 A3
**Rigutino** I 135 B4
**Riihimäki** FIN 8 B4
**Rijeka** HR 123 B3
**Rijen** NL 79 A4
**Rijkevorsel** B 79 A4
**Rijssen** NL 71 B3
**Rila** BG 183 A5
**Rilić** BIH 138 B3
**Rilievo** I 176 B1
**Rillé** F 102 B2
**Rillo de Gallo** E 152 B2
**Rimavská Baňa** SK 99 C3
**Rimavská Seč** SK 99 C4
**Rimavská Sobota** SK 99 C4
**Rimbo** S 57 A4
**Rimforsa** S 56 B1
**Rimini** I 136 A1
**Rîmnicu Sărat** RO 17 C7
**Rimogne** F 91 B4
**Rimpar** D 94 B1
**Rimske Toplice** SLO 123 A4
**Rincón de la Victoria** E 163 B3
**Rincón de Soto** E 144 B2
**Rindal** N 198 B6
**Rinde** N 46 A3
**Ringarum** S 56 B2
**Ringaskiddy** IRL 29 C3
**Ringe** DK 59 C3
**Ringebu** N 48 A2
**Ringkøbing** DK 59 B1
**Ringsaker** N 48 B2
**Ringsted** DK 61 D1
**Ringwood** GB 44 C2
**Rinkaby** S 63 C2
**Rinkabyholm** S 63 B4
**Rinlo** E 141 A3
**Rinn** A 108 B2
**Rinteln** D 72 B2
**Rio** E 140 B3
**Riobo** E 140 B2
**Riodeva** E 152 B2
**Rio do Coures** P 154 B2
**Rio Douro** P 148 A2
**Riofrio** E 150 B3
**Rio Frio** P 154 C2
**Riofrio de Aliste** E 149 A3
**Rio frio de Riaza** E 151 A4
**Riogordo** E 163 B3
**Rioja** E 164 C2
**Riola** I 135 A4
**Riola Sardo** I 179 C2
**Riolobos** E 155 B4
**Riom** F 116 B3
**Riomaggiore** I 134 A2
**Rio Maior** P 154 B2
**Rio Marina** I 134 C3
**Riom-ès-Montagnes** F 116 B2
**Rion-des-Landes** F 128 C2
**Rionegro del Puente** E 141 B4
**Rionero in Vúlture** I 172 B1
**Riopar** E 158 C1
**Riós** E 141 C3
**Rioseco** E 142 A1
**Rioseco de Tapia** E 141 B5
**Rio Tinto** P 148 A1
**Riotord** F 117 B4
**Riotorto** E 141 A3
**Rioz** F 105 B5
**Ripač** BIH 124 C1
**Ripacándida** I 172 B1
**Ripanj** SRB 127 C2
**Ripatransone** I 136 C2
**Ripley** GB 40 B2
**Ripoll** E 147 B3
**Ripon** GB 40 A2
**Riposto** I 177 B4
**Ripsa** S 56 B2
**Risan** MNE 16 D3
**Risbäck** S 200 B1
**Risca** GB 39 C3
**Rischenau** D 81 A5
**Riscle** F 128 C2
**Risebo** S 56 B2
**Risnes** N 46 A2
**Rišňovce** SK 98 C1
**Risør** N 53 B5
**Risøyhamn** N 194 B6
**Rissna** S 199 B12
**Ritsem** S 194 C8
**Ritterhude** D 72 A1
**Riutula** FIN 193 D10
**Riva del Garda** I 121 B3
**Riva Ligure** I 133 B3
**Rivanazzano** I 120 C2
**Rivarolo Canavese** I 119 B4
**Rivarolo Mantovano** I 121 B3
**Rive-de-Gier** F 117 B4
**Rivedoux-Plage** F 114 B2
**Rivello** I 174 A1
**Rivergaro** I 120 C2
**Rives** F 118 B2
**Rivesaltes** F 146 B3
**Rivignano** I 122 B2
**Rivne** UA 13 C7
**Rivoli** I 119 B4
**Rivolta d'Adda** I 120 B2
**Rixheim** F 106 B2
**Rixo** S 54 B2
**Riza** GR 183 C5
**Rizokarpaso** CY 181 A3
**Rjukan** N 47 C5
**Rø** DK 67 A3
**Rö** S 57 A4
**Roa**
E 143 C3
N 48 B2
**Roade** GB 44 A3
**Roager** DK 59 C1
**Roaldkvam** N 52 A2
**Roanne** F 117 A4
**Röbäck** S 200 C6
**Robakowo** PL 69 B3
**Róbbio** I 120 B1
**Röbel** D 73 A5
**Roberton** GB 35 C5
**Robertsfors** S 200 B6
**Robertville** B 80 B2
**Robin Hood's Bay** GB 37 B6
**Robleda** E 149 B3
**Robledillo de Trujillo** E 156 A2
**Robledo**
*Albacete* E 158 C1
*Orense* E 141 B4
**Robledo de Chavela** E 151 B3
**Robledo del Buey** E 156 A3
**Robledo del Mazo** E 156 A3
**Robledollano** E 156 A2
**Robles de la Valcueva** E 142 B1
**Robliza de Cojos** E 149 B4
**Robres** E 145 C3
**Robres del Castillo** E 144 B1
**Rocafort de Queralt** E 147 C2
**Rocamadour** F 129 B4
**Roccabernarda** I 175 B2
**Roccabianca** I 120 B3
**Roccadáspide** I 172 B1
**Rocca di Mezzo** I 169 A3
**Rocca di Papa** I 168 B2
**Roccagorga** I 169 B3
**Rocca Imperiale** I 174 A2
**Roccalbegna** I 135 C4
**Roccalumera** I 177 B4
**Roccamena** I 176 B2
**Roccamonfina** I 170 B1
**Roccanova** I 174 A2
**Roccapalumba** I 176 B2
**Roccapassa** I 169 A3
**Rocca Priora** I 136 B2
**Roccaraso** I 169 B4
**Rocca San Casciano** I 135 A4
**Roccasecca** I 169 B3
**Rocca Sinibalda** I 169 A2
**Roccastrada** I 135 B4
**Roccatederighi** I 135 B4
**Roccella Iónica** I 175 C2
**Rocchetta Sant'António** I 172 A1
**Rocester** GB 40 C2
**Rochdale** GB 40 B1
**Rochechouart** F 115 C4
**Rochefort**
B 79 B5
F 114 C3
**Rochefort-en-Terre** F 101 B3
**Rochefort-Montagne** F 116 B2
**Rochefort-sur-Nenon** F 105 B4
**Roche-lez-Beaupré** F 105 B5
**Rochemaure** F 131 A3
**Rocheservière** F 114 B2
**Rochester**
*Medway* GB 45 B4
*Northumberland* GB 37 A4
**Rochlitz** D 83 A4
**Rociana del Condado** E 161 B3
**Rockenhausen** D 93 B3
**Rockhammar** S 56 A1
**Rockneby** S 62 B4
**Ročko Polje** HR 123 B3
**Ročov** CZ 84 B1
**Rocroi** F 91 B4
**Rodach** D 82 B2
**Roda de Bara** E 147 C2
**Roda de Ter** E 147 C3
**Rodalben** D 93 B3
**Rødberg** N 47 B5
**Rødby** DK 65 B4
**Rødbyhavn** DK 65 B4
**Rødding**
*Sonderjyllands Amt.* DK 59 C2
*Viborg Amt.* DK 58 B1
**Rödeby** S 63 B3
**Rodeiro** E 140 B3
**Rødekro** DK 64 A2
**Roden** NL 71 A3
**Ródenas** E 152 B2
**Rodenkirchen** D 72 A1
**Rödental** D 82 B3
**Rödermark** D 93 B4
**Rodewisch** D 83 B4
**Rodez** F 130 A1
**Rodi Gargánico** I 171 B3
**Roding** D 95 B4
**Rödjebro** S 51 B4
**Rødkærsbro** DK 59 B2
**Rodolivas** GR 183 C5
**Rodoñá** E 147 C2
**Rødvig** DK 65 A5
**Roermond** NL 80 A1
**Roesbrugge** B 78 B2
**Roeschwoog** F 93 C4
**Roeselare** B 78 B3
**Roetgen** D 80 B2
**Roffiac** F 116 B3
**Röfors** S 55 B5
**Rofrano** I 172 B1
**Rogač** HR 138 B2
**Rogačica** SRB 127 C1
**Rogalinek** PL 76 B1
**Rogaška Slatina** SLO 123 A4
**Rogatec** SLO 123 A4
**Rogatica** BIH 139 B5
**Rogatyn** UA 13 D6
**Rogätz** D 73 B4
**Roggendorf** D 65 C4
**Roggiano Gravina** I 174 B2
**Roghadal** GB 31 B2
**Rogliano**
F 180 A2
I 175 B2
**Rognan** N 195 C6
**Rogne** N 47 A6
**Rognes** F 131 B4
**Rogny-les-7-Ecluses** F 103 B4
**Rogowo** PL 76 B2
**Rogoznica** HR 138 B1
**Rogoźnica** PL 85 A4
**Rogoźno** PL 76 B1
**Rohan** F 101 A3
**Röhlingen** D 94 C2
**Rohožnik** SK 98 C1
**Rohr** D 82 B2
**Rohrbach** A 96 C1
**Rohrbach-lès-Bitche** F 92 B3
**Rohrberg** D 73 B4
**Rohr im Gebirge** A 110 B2
**Röhrnbach** D 96 C1
**Roisel** F 90 B3
**Roja** LV 8 D3
**Rojales** E 165 A4
**Röjeråsen** S 50 B1
**Rojewo** PL 76 B3
**Rokiciny** PL 87 A3
**Rokietnica** PL 75 B5
**Rokiškis** LT 8 E4
**Rokitki** PL 85 A3
**Rokycany** CZ 96 B1
**Rolampont** F 105 B4
**Rold** DK 58 B2
**Røldal** N 52 A2
**Rolde** NL 71 B3
**Rolfs** S 196 D6
**Rollag** N 47 B6
**Rollán** E 149 B4
**Rolle** CH 105 C5
**Roma = Rome** I 168 B2
**Roma** S 57 C4
**Romagnano Sésia** I 119 B5
**Romagné** F 88 B2
**Romakloster** S 57 C4
**Roman** RO 17 B7
**Romana** I 178 B2
**Romanèche-Thorins** F 117 A4
**Romano di Lombardia** I 120 B2
**Romanshorn** CH 107 B4
**Romans-sur-Isère** F 118 B2
**Rombas** F 92 B2
**Rome = Roma** I 168 B2
**Romeán** E 141 B3
**Romenay** F 105 C4
**Romeral** E 157 A4
**Römerstein** D 94 C1
**Rometta** I 177 A4
**Romford** GB 45 B4
**Romhány** H 112 B3
**Römhild** D 82 B2
**Romilly-sur-Seine** F 91 C3
**Romont** CH 106 C1
**Romorantin-Lanthenay** F 103 B3
**Romrod** D 81 B5
**Romsey** GB 44 C2
**Rømskog** N 54 A2
**Rønbjerg** DK 58 B1
**Roncal** E 144 B3
**Ronce-les-Bains** F 114 C2
**Ronchamp** F 106 B1
**Ronchi dei Legionari** I 122 B2
**Ronciglione** I 168 A2
**Ronco Canavese** I 119 B4
**Ronco Scrivia** I 120 C1
**Ronda** E 162 B2
**Rønde** DK 59 B3
**Rone** S 57 C4
**Ronehamn** S 57 C4
**Rong** N 46 B1
**Rönnäng** S 60 B1
**Rønne** DK 67 A3
**Ronneburg** D 83 B4
**Ronneby** S 63 B3
**Rönneshytta** S 55 B6
**Rönninge** S 57 A3
**Rönnöfors** S 199 B10
**Rönö** S 56 B2
**Ronov nad Doubravou** CZ 97 B3
**Ronse** B 79 B3
**Roosendaal** NL 79 A4
**Roosky** IRL 26 C3
**Ropczyce** PL 87 B5
**Ropeid** N 52 A2
**Ropinsalmi** FIN 192 D5
**Ropuerelos del Páramo** E 141 B5
**Roquebilière** F 133 A3
**Roquebrun** F 130 B2
**Roquecourbe** F 130 B1
**Roquefort** F 128 B2
**Roquemaure** F 131 A3
**Roquesteron** F 132 B3
**Roquetas de Mar** E 164 C2
**Roquetes** E 153 B4
**Roquevaire** F 132 B1
**Røra** N 199 B8
**Rörbäcksnäs** S 49 A4
**Rørbæk** DK 58 B2
**Rore** BIH 138 A2
**Röro** S 60 B1
**Røros** N 199 C8
**Rorschach** CH 107 B4
**Rørvig** DK 61 D1
**Rørvik** N 199 A8
**Rörvik** S 62 A2
**Rosà** I 121 B4
**Rosal de la Frontera** E 161 B2
**Rosalina Mare** I 122 B1
**Rosa Marina** I 173 B3
**Rosans** F 132 A1
**Rosário** P 160 B1
**Rosarno** I 175 C1
**Rosbach** D 81 B3
**Rosche** D 73 B3
**Rościszewo** PL 77 B4
**Roscoff** F 100 A2
**Roscommon** IRL 28 A3
**Roscrea** IRL 28 B4
**Rosdorf** D 82 A1
**Rose** I 174 B2
**Rosegg** A 109 C5
**Rosehall** GB 32 D2
**Rosehearty** GB 33 D4
**Rosel** GB 88 A1
**Rosell** E 153 B4
**Roselló** E 153 A4
**Rosendal** N 46 C3
**Rosenfeld** D 93 C4
**Rosenfors** S 62 A3
**Rosenheim** D 108 B3
**Rosenow** D 74 A2
**Rosenthal** D 81 A4
**Rosersberg** S 57 A3
**Roses** E 147 B4
**Roseto degli Abruzzi** I 169 A4
**Roseto Valfortore** I 170 B3
**Rosheim** F 93 C3
**Rosia** I 135 B4
**Rosice** CZ 97 B4
**Rosières-en-Santerre** F 90 B2
**Rosignano Marittimo** I 134 B3
**Rosignano Solvay** I 134 B3
**Roşiori-de-Vede** RO 17 C6
**Roskhill** GB 31 B2
**Roskilde** DK 61 D2
**Roskovec** AL 182 C1
**Röslau** D 83 B3
**Roslev** DK 58 B1
**Rosmaninhal** P 155 B3
**Rosnowo** PL 67 B5
**Rosolini** I 177 C3
**Rosova** MNE 139 B5
**Rosoy** F 104 A2
**Rosporden** F 100 B2
**Rosquete** P 154 B2
**Rosrath** D 80 B3
**Rossa** CH 120 A2
**Rossano** I 174 B2
**Rossas**
*Aveiro* P 148 B1
*Braga* P 148 A1
**Rossdorf** D 82 B2
**Rossett** GB 38 A4
**Rosshaupten** D 108 B1
**Rossiglione** I 133 A4
**Rossignol** B 92 B1
**Rossla** D 82 A3
**Rosslare** IRL 30 B2
**Rosslare Harbour** IRL 30 B2
**Rosslau** D 83 A4
**Rosslea** GB 27 B3
**Rossleben** D 82 A3
**Rossön** S 200 C2
**Ross-on-Wye** GB 39 C4
**Rossoszyca** PL 86 A2
**Rosswein** D 83 A5
**Röstånga** S 61 C3
**Roštár** SK 99 C4
**Rostock** D 65 B5
**Rostrenen** F 100 A2
**Røsvik** N 194 C6
**Rosvik** S 196 D4
**Rosyth** GB 35 B4
**Röszke** H 126 A2
**Rot** S 49 A6
**Rota** E 161 C3
**Rota Greca** I 174 B2
**Rot am See** D 94 B2
**Rotberget** N 49 B4
**Rotella** I 136 C2
**Rotenburg**
*Hessen* D 82 B1
*Niedersachsen* D 72 A2
**Roth**
*Bayern* D 94 B3
*Rheinland-Pfalz* D 81 B3
**Rothbury** GB 37 A5
**Rothemühl** D 74 A2
**Röthenbach** D 95 B3
**Rothenburg** D 84 A2
**Rothenburg ob der Tauber** D 94 B2
**Rothéneuf** F 88 B2
**Rothenklempenow** D 74 A3
**Rothenstein** D 94 C3
**Rotherham** GB 40 B2
**Rothes** GB 32 D3
**Rothesay** GB 34 C2
**Rothwell** GB 44 A3
**Rotnes** N 48 B2
**Rotonda** I 174 B2
**Rotondella** I 174 A2
**Rotova** E 159 C3
**Rott**
*Bayern* D 108 B1
*Bayern* D 108 B3
**Rottach-Egern** D 108 B2
**Röttenbach** D 94 B3
**Rottenbuch** D 108 B1
**Rottenburg**
*Baden-Württemberg* D 93 C4
*Bayern* D 95 C4
**Rottenmann** A 110 B1
**Rotterdam** NL 79 A4
**Rotthalmünster** D 96 C1
**Rottingdean** GB 44 C3
**Röttingen** D 94 B1
**Rottleberode** D 82 A2
**Rottne** S 62 A2
**Rottneros** S 55 A4
**Rottofreno** I 120 B2
**Rottweil** D 107 A3
**Rötz** D 95 B4
**Roubaix** F 78 B3
**Roudnice nad Labem** CZ 84 B2
**Roudouallec** F 100 A2
**Rouen** F 89 A5
**Rouffach** F 106 B2
**Rougé** F 101 B4
**Rougemont** F 105 B5
**Rougemont le-Château** F 106 B1
**Rouillac** F 115 C3
**Rouillé** F 115 B4
**Roujan** F 130 B2
**Roulans** F 105 B5
**Roundwood** IRL 30 A2
**Rousínov** CZ 97 B4
**Roussac** F 115 B5
**Roussennac** F 130 A1
**Rousses** F 130 A2
**Roussillon** F 117 B4
**Rouvroy-sur-Audry** F 91 B4
**Rouy** F 104 B2
**Rovanieman maalaiskunta** FIN 197 C8
**Rovaniemi** FIN 197 C8
**Rovato** I 120 B2
**Rovensko pod Troskami** CZ 84 B3
**Roverbella** I 121 B3
**Rovereto** I 121 B4
**Rövershagen** D 65 B5
**Roverud** N 49 B4
**Rovigo** I 121 B4
**Rovinj** HR 122 B2
**Rovišce** HR 124 B2
**Rów** PL 74 B3
**Rowy** PL 68 A2
**Royal Leamington Spa** GB 44 A2
**Royal Tunbridge Wells** GB 45 B4
**Royan** F 114 C2
**Royat** F 116 B3
**Roybon** F 118 B2
**Roybridge** GB 34 B3
**Roye** F 90 B2
**Royère-de-Vassivière** F 116 B1
**Røykenvik** N 48 B2
**Royos** E 164 B2
**Røyrvik** N 199 A10
**Royston** GB 44 A3
**Rozadas** E 141 A4
**Rozalén del Monte** E 151 C5
**Rózańsko** PL 75 B3
**Rozay-en-Brie** F 90 C2
**Roždalovice** CZ 84 B3
**Rozdilna** UA 17 B9
**Rozental** PL 69 B4
**Rozhyshche** UA 13 C6
**Rožmitál pod Třemšínem** CZ 96 B1
**Rožňava** SK 99 C4
**Rožnov pod Radhoštěm** CZ 98 B2
**Rozoy-sur-Serre** F 91 B4
**Rozprza** PL 86 A3
**Roztoky** CZ 84 B2
**Rozvadov** CZ 95 B4
**Rozzano** I 120 B2
**Rrëshen** AL 182 B1
**Rrogozhine** AL 182 B1
**Ruanes** E 156 A2
**Rubbestadnesset** N 46 C2
**Rubi** E 147 C3
**Rubiá** E 141 B4
**Rubiacedo de Abajo** E 143 B3
**Rubielos Bajos** E 158 B1
**Rubielos de Mora** E 153 B3
**Rubiera** I 121 C3
**Rubik** AL 182 B1
**Rucandio** E 143 B3
**Rud**
*Akershus* N 48 B3
*Buskerud* N 48 B2
**Ruda**
PL 86 A2
S 62 A4
**Rudabánya** H 99 C4
**Ruda Maleniecka** PL 87 A4
**Ruda Pilczycka** PL 87 A4
**Ruda Śl.** PL 86 B2
**Ruddervorde** B 78 A3
**Ruden** A 110 C1
**Rudersberg** D 94 C1
**Rudersdorf** A 111 B3
**Rüdersdorf** D 74 B2
**Ruderting** D 96 C1
**Rüdesheim** D 93 B3
**Rudkøbing** DK 65 B3
**Rudmanns** A 97 C3
**Rudna**
CZ 96 A2
PL 85 A4
**Rudnik** SRB 127 C2
**Rudniki**
*Opolskie* PL 86 A2
*Śląskie* PL 86 B3
**Rudno**
*Dolnośląskie* PL 85 A4
*Pomorskie* PL 69 B3
**Rudnya** RUS 13 A9
**Rudolstadt** D 82 B3
**Rudowica** PL 84 A3
**Rudozem** BG 183 B6
**Rudskoga** S 55 A5
**Rudston** GB 40 A3
**Ruds Vedby** DK 61 D1
**Rudy** PL 86 B2

Rue F 78 B1
Rueda E 150 A3
Rueda de Jalón E 152 A2
Ruelle-sur-Touvre F 115 C4
Ruerrero E 143 B3
Ruffano I 173 C4
Ruffec F 115 B4
Rufina I 135 B4
Rugby GB 44 A2
Rugeley GB 40 C2
Ruggstrop S 62 B4
Rugles F 89 B4
Rugozero RUS 3 D13
Rühen D 73 B3
Ruhla D 82 B2
Ruhland D 84 A1
Ruhle D 71 B4
Ruhpolding D 109 B3
Ruhstorf D 96 C1
Ruidera E 158 C1
Ruillé-sur-le-Loir F 102 B2
Ruinen NL 71 B3
Ruiselede B 78 A3
Ruka FIN 197 C12
Rulles B 92 B1
Rülzheim D 93 B4
Rum H 111 B3
Ruma SRB 127 B1
Rumboci BIH 138 B3
Rumburk CZ 84 B2
Rumenka SRB 126 B1
Rumia PL 69 A3
Rumigny F 91 B4
Rumilly F 118 B2
Rumma S 56 B2
Rumney GB 39 C3
Rumont F 91 C5
Runa P 154 B1
Runcorn GB 38 A4
Rundmoen N 195 D5
Rungsted DK 61 D2
Runhällen S 51 B3
Runowo PL 69 A5
Runtuna S 56 B3
Ruokojärvi FIN 196 B7
Ruokolahti FIN 9 B6
Ruokto S 196 B2
Ruoms F 131 A3
Ruoti I 172 B1
Rupa HR 123 B3
Ruppichteroth D 80 B3
Rupt-sur-Moselle F 106 B1
Rus E 157 B4
Ruse BG 17 D7
Ruše SLO 110 C2
Rusele S 200 B4
Ruševo HR 125 B4
Rush IRL 30 A2
Rushden GB 44 A3
Rusiec PL 86 A2
Rusinowo
*Zachodnio-Pomorskie* PL 67 C4
*Zachodnio-Pomorskie* PL 75 A5
Ruskele S 200 B4
Ruski Krstur SRB 126 B1
Ruskington GB 40 B3
Rusovce SK 111 A4
Rüsselsheim D 93 B4
Russelv N 192 C4
Russi I 135 A5
Rust A 111 B3
Rustefjelbma N 193 B12
Rustrel F 131 B4
Ruszki PL 77 B5
Ruszów PL 84 A3
Rute E 163 A3
Rüthen D 81 A4
Rutherglen GB 35 C3
Ruthin GB 38 A3
Ruthven GB 32 D2
Ruthwell GB 36 B3
Rüti CH 107 B3
Rutigliano I 173 A3
Rutledal N 46 A2
Rutvik S 196 D5
Ruurlo NL 71 B3
Ruuvaoja FIN 197 B11
Ruvo del Monte I 172 B1
Ruvo di Púglia I 171 B4
Ruynes-en-Margeride F 116 C3
Ružic HR 138 B2
Ružomberok SK 99 B3
Ruzsa H 126 A1
Ry DK 59 B2
Rybany SK 98 C2
Rybina PL 69 A4
Rybnik PL 86 B2
Rychliki PL 69 B4
Rychlocice PL 86 A2
Rychnov nad Kněžnou CZ 85 B4
Rychnowo PL 77 A5
Rychtal PL 86 A1
Rychwał PL 76 B3
Ryczywół PL 87 A5
Ryczywól PL 75 B5
Ryd S 63 B2
Rydaholm S 62 B2
Rydal S 60 B2
Rydbo S 57 A4
Rydboholm S 60 B2
Ryde GB 44 C2
Rydöbruk S 60 C3
Rydsgård S 66 A2
Rydsnäs S 62 A3
Rydultowy PL 86 B2
Rydzyna PL 85 A4
Rye GB 45 C4
Rygge N 54 A1
Ryjewo PL 69 B3
Rykene N 53 B4
Rymań PL 67 C4
Rýmařov CZ 98 B1
Rynarzewo PL 76 A2
Ryomgård DK 59 B3
Rypefjord N 192 B7
Rypin PL 77 A4
Rysjedalsvika N 46 A2
Ryssby S 60 C4
Rytel PL 68 B2
Rytinki FIN 197 D10
Rytro PL 99 B4
Rywociny PL 77 A5
Rzeczenica PL 68 B2
Rzeczniów PL 87 A5
Rzeczyca PL 87 A4
Rzęgnowo PL 77 A5
Rzejowice PL 87 A3
Rzemień PL 87 B5
Rzepin PL 75 B3
Rzesznikowo PL 67 C4
Rzeszów PL 12 C4
Rzgów PL 86 A3
Rzhev RUS 9 D9

## S

Saal
*Bayern* D 82 B2
*Bayern* D 95 C3
Saalbach A 109 B3
Saalburg D 83 B3
Saales F 92 C3
Saalfeld D 82 B3
Saalfelden am Steinernen Meer A 109 B3
Saanen CH 106 C2
Saarbrücken D 92 B2
Saarburg D 92 B2
Saarijärvi FIN 8 A4
Saari-Kämä FIN 197 C9
Saarlouis D 92 B2
Saas-Fee CH 119 A4
Šabac SRB 127 C1
Sabadell E 147 C3
Sabáudia I 169 B3
Sabbioneta I 121 C3
Sabero E 142 B1
Sabiñánigo E 145 B3
Sabiote E 157 B4
Sables-d'Or-les-Pins F 101 A3
Sablé-sur-Sarthe F 102 B1
Sabóia P 160 B1
Saborsko HR 123 B4
Sæbøvik N 52 A1
Sabres F 128 B2
Sabrosa P 148 A2
Sabugal P 149 B2
Sabuncu TR 187 C5
Sæby DK 58 A3
Săcălaz RO 126 B3
Sacecorbo E 152 B1
Saceda del Rio E 151 B5
Sacedón E 151 B5
Săcele RO 17 C6
Saceruela E 156 B3
Sachsenburg A 109 C4
Sachsenhagen D 72 B2
Sacile I 122 B1
Sacramenia E 151 A4
Sada E 140 A2
Sádaba E 144 B2
Saddell GB 34 C2
Sadernes E 147 B3
Sadki PL 76 A2
Sadkowice PL 87 A4
Sadlinki PL 69 B3
Sadów PL 75 B3
Sadská CZ 84 B2
Saelices E 151 C5
Saelices de Mayorga E 142 B1
Saerbeck D 71 B4
Saeul L 92 B1
Safaalan TR 186 A3
Safara P 161 A2
Säffle S 55 A3
Saffron Walden GB 45 A4
Safranbolu TR 187 A7
Säfsnäs S 50 B1
Şag RO 126 B3
Sagard D 66 B2
S'Agaro E 147 C4
Sågmyra S 50 B2
Sagone F 180 A1
Sagres P 160 C1
Ságújfalu H 113 A3
Sagunt E 159 B3
Sagvåg N 52 A1
Ságvár H 112 C2
Sagy F 105 C4
Sahagún E 142 B1
Šahy SK 112 A2
Saignelégier CH 106 B1
Saignes F 116 B2
Saija FIN 197 B11
Saillagouse F 146 B3
Saillans F 118 C2
Sains Richaumont F 91 B3
St Abb's GB 35 C5
St Affrique F 130 B1
St Agnan F 104 C2
St Agnant F 114 C3
St Agnes GB 42 B1
St Agrève F 117 B4
St Aignan F 103 B3
St Aignan-sur-Roë F 101 B4
St Albans GB 44 B3
St Alban-sur-Limagnole F 117 C3
St Amand-en-Puisaye F 104 B2
St Amand-les-Eaux F 79 B3
St Amand-Longpré F 103 B3
St Amand-Montrond F 103 C4
St Amans F 117 C3
St Amans-Soult F 130 B1
St Amant-Roche-Savine F 117 B3
St Amarin F 106 B1
St Ambroix F 131 A3
St Amé F 106 A1
St Amour F 118 A2
St André-de-Corcy F 117 B4
St André-de-Cubzac F 128 B2
St André-de-l'Eure F 89 B5
St André-de-Roquepertuis F 131 A3
St André-de-Sangonis F 130 B2
St Andre-de-Valborgne F 130 A2
St André-les-Alpes F 132 B2
St Andrews GB 35 B5
St Angel F 116 B2
St Anthème F 117 B3
St Antoine F 180 A2
St Antoine-de-Ficalba F 129 B3
St Antönien CH 107 C4
St Antonin-Noble-Val F 129 B4
St Août F 103 C3
St Armant-Tallende F 116 B3
St Arnoult F 90 C1
St Asaph GB 38 A3
St Astier F 129 A3
St Athan GB 39 C3
St Auban F 132 B2
St Aubin
CH 106 C1
F 105 B4
GB 88 A1
St Aubin-d'Aubigne´ F 101 A4
St Aubin-du-Cormier F 101 A4
St Aubin-sur-Aire F 92 C1
St Aubin-sur-Mer F 89 A3
St Aulaye F 128 A3
St Austell GB 42 B2
St Avit F 116 B2
St Avold F 92 B2
St Aygulf F 132 B2
St Bauzille-de-Putois F 130 B2
St Béat F 145 B4
St Beauzély F 130 A1
St Bees GB 36 B3
St Benim-d'Azy F 104 C2
St Benoît-du-Sault F 115 B5
St Benoit-en-Woëvre F 92 C1
St Berthevin F 102 A1
St Blaise-la-Roche F 92 C3
St Blazey GB 42 B2
St Blin F 105 A4
St Bonnet F 118 C3
St Bonnet Briance F 115 C5
St Bonnet-de-Joux F 104 C3
St Bonnet-le-Château F 117 B4
St Bonnet-le-Froid F 117 B4
St Brévin-les-Pins F 101 B3
St Briac-sur-Mer F 101 A3
St Brice-en-Coglès F 88 B2
St Brieuc F 101 A3
St Bris-le-Vineux F 104 B2
St Broladre F 88 B2
St Calais F 102 B2
St Cannat F 131 B4
St Cast-le-Guildo F 101 A3
St Céré F 129 B4
St Cergue CH 118 A3
St Cergues F 118 A3
St Cernin F 116 B2
St Chamant F 116 B1
St Chamas F 131 B4
St Chamond F 117 B4
St Chély-d'Apcher F 116 C3
St Chély-d'Aubrac F 116 C2
St Chinian F 130 B1
St Christol F 131 A4
St Christol-lès-Alès F 131 A3
St Christoly-Médoc F 114 C3
St Christophe-du-Ligneron F 114 B2
St Christophe-en-Brionnais F 117 A4
St Ciers-sur-Gironde F 128 A2
St Clair-sur-Epte F 90 B1
St Clar F 129 C3
St Claud F 115 C4
St Claude F 118 A2
St Clears GB 39 C2
St Columb Major GB 42 B2
St Come-d'Olt F 130 A1
St Cosme-en-Vairais F 89 B4
St Cyprien
*Dordogne* F 129 B4
*Pyrenées-Orientales* F 146 B4
St Cyr-sur-Loire F 102 B2
St Cyr-sur-Mer F 132 B1
St Cyr-sur-Methon F 117 A4
St David's GB 39 C1
St Denis F 90 C2
St Denis-d'Oléron F 114 B2
St Denis d'Orques F 102 A1
St Didier F 117 A4
St Didier-en-Velay F 117 B4
St Dié F 92 C2
St Dier-d'Auvergne F 117 B3
St Dizier F 91 C4
St Dizier-Leyrenne F 116 A1
St Dogmaels GB 39 B2
Ste Adresse F 89 A4
Ste Anne F 89 B4
Ste Anne-d'Auray F 100 B3
Ste Croix CH 105 C5
Ste Croix-Volvestre F 146 A2
Ste Engrâce F 144 A3
Ste Enimie F 130 A2
St Efflam F 100 A2
Ste Foy-de-Peyrolières F 146 A2
Ste Foy-la-Grande F 128 B3
Ste Foy l'Argentiere F 117 B4
Ste Gauburge-Ste Colombe F 89 B4
Ste Gemme la Plaine F 114 B2
Ste Geneviève F 90 B2
St Égrève F 118 B2
Ste Hélène F 128 B2
Ste Hélène-sur-Isère F 118 B3
Ste Hermine F 114 B2
Ste Jalle F 131 A4
Ste Livrade-sur-Lot F 129 B3
St Eloy-les-Mines F 116 A2
Ste Marie-aux-Mines F 106 A2
Ste Marie-du-Mont F 88 A2
Ste Maure-de-Touraine F 102 B2
Ste Maxime F 132 B2
Ste Ménéhould F 91 B4
Ste Mère-Église F 88 A2
St Emiland F 104 C3
St Émilion F 128 B2
St Enoder GB 42 B2
Sainteny F 88 A2
Ste Ode B 92 A1
Saintes F 114 C3
Ste Savine F 91 C4
Ste Sévère-sur-Indre F 103 C4
Ste Sigolène F 117 B4
St Esteben F 144 A2
St Estèphe F 128 A2
Ste Suzanne F 102 A1
St Étienne F 117 B4
St Etienne-de-Baigorry F 144 A2
St Étienne-de-Cuines F 118 B3
St Etienne-de-Fursac F 116 A1
St Etienne-de-Montluc F 101 B4
St Etienne-de-St Geoirs F 118 B2
St Étienne-de-Tinée F 132 A2
St Étienne-du-Bois F 118 A2
St Étienne-du-Rouvray F 89 A5
St Etienne-les-Orgues F 132 A1
Ste Tulle F 132 B1
St Fargeau F 104 B2
St Félicien F 117 B4
St Felix-de-Sorgues F 130 B1
St Félix-Lauragais F 146 A2
Saintfield GB 27 B5
St Fillans GB 35 B3
St Firmin F 118 C3
St Florent F 180 A2
St Florentin F 104 B2
St Florent-le-Vieil F 101 B4
St Florent-sur-Cher F 103 C4
St Flour F 116 B3
St Flovier F 103 C3
St Fort-sur-le-Né F 115 C3
St Fulgent F 114 B2
St Galmier F 117 B4
St Gaudens F 145 A4
St Gaultier F 115 B5
St Gély-du-Fesc F 130 B2
St Genest-Malifaux F 117 B4
St Gengoux-le-National F 104 C3
St Geniez F 132 A2
St Geniez-d'Olt F 130 A1
St Genis-de-Saintonge F 114 C3
St Genis-Pouilly F 118 A3
St Genix-sur-Guiers F 118 B2
St Georges Buttavent F 88 B3
St Georges-d'Aurac F 117 B3
St Georges-de-Commiers F 118 B2
St Georges-de-Didonne F 114 C3
St Georges-de-Luzençon F 130 A1
St Georges-de Mons F 116 B2
St Georges-de-Reneins F 117 A4
St Georges d'Oléron F 114 C2
St Georges-en-Couzan F 117 B3
St Georges-lès-Baillargeaux F 115 B4
St Georges-sur-Loire F 102 B1
St Georges-sur-Meuse B 79 B5
St Geours-de-Maremne F 128 C1
St Gérand-de-Vaux F 117 A3
St Gérand-le-Puy F 117 A3
St Germain F 105 B5
St Germain-Chassenay F 104 C2
St Germain-de-Calberte F 130 A2
St Germain-de-Confolens F 115 B4
St Germain-de-Joux F 118 A2
St Germain-des-Fossés F 117 A3
St Germain-du-Bois F 105 C4
St Germain-du-Plain F 105 C3
St Germain-du Puy F 103 B4
St Germain-en-Laye F 90 C2
St Germain-Laval F 117 B4
St Germain-Lembron F 116 B3
St Germain-les-Belles F 116 B1
St Germain-Lespinasse F 117 A3
St Germain-l'Herm F 117 B3
St Gervais-d'Auvergne F 116 A2
St Gervais-les-Bains F 118 B3
St Gervais-sur-Mare F 130 B2
St Gildas-de-Rhuys F 100 B3
St Gildas-des-Bois F 101 B3
St Gilles
*Gard* F 131 B3
*Ille-et-Vilaine* F 101 A4
St Gilles-Croix-de-Vie F 114 B2
St Gingolph F 119 A3
St Girons
*Ariège* F 146 B2
*Landes* F 128 C1
St Girons-Plage F 128 C1
St Gobain F 91 B3
St Gorgon-Main F 105 B5
St Guénolé F 100 B1
St Harmon GB 39 B3
St Helens GB 38 A4
St Helier GB 88 A1
St Herblain F 101 B4
St Hilaire
*Allier* F 104 C2
*Aude* F 146 A3
St Hilaire-de-Riez F 114 B2
St Hilaire-des-Loges F 114 B3
St Hilaire-de-Villefranche F 114 C3
St Hilaire-du-Harcouët F 88 B2
St Hilaire-du-Rosier F 118 B2
St Hippolyte
*Aveyron* F 116 C2
*Doubs* F 106 B1
St Hippolyte-du-Fort F 130 B2
St Honoré-les-Bains F 104 C2
St Hubert B 92 A1
St Imier CH 106 B2
St Issey GB 42 B2
St Ives
*Cambridgeshire* GB 44 A3
*Cornwall* GB 42 B1
St Izaire F 130 B1
St Jacques-de-la-Lande F 101 A4
St Jacut-de-la-Mer F 101 A3
St James F 88 B2
St Jaume d'Enveja E 153 B4
St Jean-Brévelay F 101 B3
St Jean-d'Angély F 114 C3
St Jean-de-Belleville F 118 B3
St Jean-de-Bournay F 118 B2
St Jean-de-Braye F 103 B3
St Jean-de-Côle F 115 C4
St Jean-de-Daye F 88 A2
St Jean de Losne F 105 B4
St Jean-de-Luz F 144 A2
St Jean-de-Maurienne F 118 B3
St Jean-de-Monts F 114 B1
St Jean-d'Illac F 128 B2
St Jean-du-Bruel F 130 A2
St Jean-du-Gard F 131 A2
St Jean-en-Royans F 118 B2
St Jean-la-Riviere F 133 B3
St Jean-Pied-de-Port F 144 A2
St Jean-Poutge F 129 C3
St Jeoire F 118 A3
St Joachim F 101 B3
St Johnstown IRL 27 B3
St Jorioz F 118 B3
St Joris Winge B 79 B4
St Jouin-de-Marnes F 102 C1
St Juéry F 130 B1
St Julien F 118 A2
St Julien-Chapteuil F 117 B4
St Julien-de-Vouvantes F 101 B4
St Julien-du-Sault F 104 A2
St Julien-du-Verdon F 132 B2
St Julien-en-Born F 128 B1
St Julien-en-Genevois F 118 A3
St Julien-l'Ars F 115 B4
St Julien la-Vêtre F 117 B3
St Julien-Mont-Denis F 118 B3
St Julien-sur-Reyssouze F 118 A2
St Junien F 115 C4
St Just
F 131 A3
GB 42 B1
St Just-en-Chaussée F 90 B2
St Just-en-Chevalet F 117 B3
St Justin F 128 C2
St Just-St Rambert F 117 B4
St Keverne GB 42 B1
St Lary-Soulan F 145 B4
St Laurent-d'Aigouze F 131 B3
St Laurent-de-Chamousset F 117 B4
St Laurent-de-Condel F 89 A3
St Laurent-de-la-Cabrerisse F 146 A3

St Laurent-de-la-Salanque F 146 B3
St Laurent-des-Autels F 101 B4
St Laurent-du-Pont F 118 B2
St Laurent-en-Caux F 89 A4
St Laurent-en-Grandvaux F 105 C4
St Laurent-Médoc F 128 A2
St Laurent-sur-Gorre F 115 C4
St Laurent-sur-Mer F 88 A3
St Laurent-sur-Sèvre F 114 B3
St Leger B 92 B1
St Léger-de-Vignes F 104 C2
St Léger-sous-Beuvray F 104 C3
St Léger-sur-Dheune F 104 C3
St Léonard-de-Noblat F 116 B1
St Leonards GB 45 C4
St Lô F 88 A2
St Lon-les-Mines F 128 C1
St Louis F 106 B2
St Loup F 117 A3
St Loup-de-la-Salle F 105 C3
St Loup-sur-Semouse F 105 B5
St Lunaire F 101 A3
St Lupicin F 118 A2
St Lyphard F 101 B3
St Lys F 146 A2
St Macaire F 128 B2
St Maclou F 89 A4
St Maixent-l'École F 115 B3
St Malo F 88 B1
St Mamet-la-Salvetat F 116 C2
St Mandrier-sur-Mer F 132 B1
St Marcel
*Drôme* F 117 C4
*Saône-et-Loire* F 105 C3
St Marcellin F 118 B2
St Marcellin sur Loire F 117 B4
St Marcet F 145 A4
St Mards-en-Othe F 104 A2
St Margaret's-at-Cliffe GB 45 B5
St Margaret's Hope GB 33 C4
St Mars-la-Jaille F 101 B4
St Martin-d'Ablois F 91 C3
St Martin-d'Auxigny F 103 B4
St Martin-de-Belleville F 118 B3
St Martin-de-Bossenay F 91 C3
St Martin-de-Crau F 131 B3
St Martin-de-Londres F 130 B2
St Martin-d'Entraunes F 132 A2
St Martin-de-Queyrières F 118 C3
St Martin-de-Ré F 114 B2
St Martin des Besaces F 88 A3
St Martin-d'Estreaux F 117 A3
St Martin-de-Valamas F 117 C4
St Martin-d'Hères F 118 B2
St Martin-du-Frêne F 118 A2
St Martin-en-Bresse F 105 C4
St Martin-en-Haut F 117 B4
St Martin-la-Méanne F 116 B1
St Martin-Osmonville F 90 B1
St Martin-sur-Ouanne F 104 B2
St Martin-Valmeroux F 116 B2
St Martin-Vésubie F 133 A3
St Martory F 145 A4
St Mary's GB 33 C4
St Mathieu F 115 C4
St Mathieu-de-Tréviers F 131 B2
St Maurice CH 119 A3
St Maurice-Navacelles F 130 B2
St Maurice-sur-Moselle F 106 B1
St Mawes GB 42 B1
St Maximin-la-Ste Baume F 132 B1
St Méard-de-Gurçon F 128 B3
St Médard-de-Guizières F 128 A2
St Médard-en-Jalles F 128 B2
St Méen-le-Grand F 101 A3
St Menges F 91 B4
St Merløse DK 61 D1
St Město CZ 85 B4
St M'Hervé F 101 A4
St Michel
*Aisne* F 91 B4
*Gers* F 145 A4
St Michel-Chef-Chef F 101 B3
St Michel-de-Castelnau F 128 B2
St Michel-de-Maurienne F 118 B3
St Michel-en-Grève F 100 A2
St Michel-enl'Herm F 114 B2
St Michel-Mont-Mercure F 114 B3
St Mihiel F 92 C1
St Monance GB 35 B5
St Montant F 131 A3
St Moritz CH 107 C4
St Nazaire F 101 B3
St Nazaire-en-Royans F 118 B2
St Nazaire-le-Désert F 131 A4
St Nectaire F 116 B2
St Neots GB 44 A3
St Nicolas-de-Port F 92 C2
St Nicolas-de-Redon F 101 B3
St Nicolas-du-Pélem F 100 A2
St Niklaas B 79 A4
St Omer F 78 B2
St Pair-sur-Mer F 88 B2
St Palais F 144 A2
St Palais-sur-Mer F 114 C2
St Pardoux-la-Rivière F 115 C4
St Paul-Cap-de-Joux F 129 C4
St Paul-de-Fenouillet F 146 B3
St Paul-de-Varax F 118 A2
St Paulien F 117 B3
St Paul-le-Jeune F 131 A3
St Paul-lès-Dax F 128 C1
St Paul-Trois-Châteaux F 131 A3
St Pé-de-Bigorre F 145 A3
St Pée-sur-Nivelle F 144 A2
St Péravy-la-Colombe F 103 B3
St Péray F 117 C4
St Père-en-Retz F 101 B3
St Peter Port GB 88 A1
St Petersburg = Sankt-Peterburg RUS 9 C7
St Philbert-de-Grand-Lieu F 114 A2
St Pierre F 130 B1
St Pierre-d'Albigny F 118 B3
St Pierre-d'Allevard F 118 B3
St Pierre-de-Chartreuse F 118 B2
St Pierre-de-Chignac F 129 A3
St Pierre-de-la-Fage F 130 B2
St Pierre-d'Entremont F 118 B2
St Pierre-d'Oléron F 114 C2
St Pierre-Eglise F 88 A2
St Pierre-en-Port F 89 A4
St Pierre-le-Moûtier F 104 C2
St Pierre Montlimart F 101 B4
St Pierre-Quiberon F 100 B2
St Pierre-sur-Dives F 89 A3
St Pierreville F 117 C4
St Pieters-Leeuw B 79 B4
St Plancard F 145 A4
St Poix F 101 B4
St Pol-de-Léon F 100 A2
St Polgues F 117 B3
St Pol-sur-Ternoise F 78 B2
St Pons-de-Thomières F 130 B1
St Porchaire F 114 C3
St Pourçain-sur-Sioule F 116 A3
St Priest F 117 B4
St Privat F 116 B2
St Quay-Portrieux F 100 A3
St Quentin F 90 B3
St Quentin-la-Poterie F 131 A3
St Quentin-les-Anges F 102 B1
St Rambert-d'Albon F 117 B4
St Rambert-en-Bugey F 118 B2
St Raphaël F 132 B2
St Rémy-de-Provence F 131 B3
St Rémy-du-Val F 89 B4
St Remy-en-Bouzemont F 91 C4
St Renan F 100 A1
St Révérien F 104 B2
St Riquier F 90 A1
St Romain-de-Colbosc F 89 A4
St Rome-de-Cernon F 130 A1
St Rome-de-Tarn F 130 A1
St Sadurní-d'Anoia E 147 C2
St Saëns F 89 A5
St Sampson GB 88 A1
St Samson-la-Poterie F 90 B1
St Saturnin-de-Lenne F 130 A2
St Saturnin-lès-Apt F 131 B4
St Sauflieu F 90 B2
St Saulge F 104 B2
St Sauveur
*Finistère* F 100 A2
*Haute-Saône* F 105 B5
St Sauveur-de-Montagut F 117 C4
St Sauveur-en-Puisaye F 104 B2
St Sauveur-en-Rue F 117 B4
St Sauveur-Lendelin F 88 A2
St Sauveur-le-Vicomte F 88 A2
St Sauveur-sur-Tinée F 132 A3
St Savin
*Gironde* F 128 A2
*Vienne* F 115 B4
St Savinien F 114 C3
St Savournin F 131 B4
St Seine-l'Abbaye F 105 B3
St Sernin-sur-Rance F 130 B1
St Sevan-sur-Mer F 88 B1
St Sever F 128 C2
St Sever-Calvados F 88 B2
St Sorlin-d'Arves F 118 B3
St Soupplets F 90 B2
St Sulpice F 129 C4
St Sulpice-Laurière F 116 A1
St Sulpice-les-Feuilles F 115 B5
St Symphorien F 128 B2
St Symphoriende-Lay F 117 B4
St Symphorien d'Ozon F 117 B4
St Symphoriensur-Coise F 117 B4
St Teath GB 42 B2
St Thégonnec F 100 A2
St Thiébault F 105 A4
St Trivier-de-Courtes F 118 A2
St Trivier sur-Moignans F 117 A4
St Trojan-les-Bains F 114 C2
St Tropez F 132 B2
St Truiden B 79 B5
St Vaast-la-Hougue F 88 A2
St Valérien F 104 A2
St Valery-en-Caux F 89 A4
St Valéry-sur-Somme F 78 B1
St Vallier
*Drôme* F 117 B4
*Saône-et-Loire* F 104 C3
St Vallier-de-Thiey F 132 B2
St Varent F 102 C1
St Vaury F 116 A1
St Venant F 78 B2
St Véran F 119 C3
St Vincent I 119 B4
St Vincent-de-Tyrosse F 128 C1
St Vit F 105 B4
St Vith B 80 B2
St Vivien-de-Médoc F 114 C2
St Yan F 117 A4
St Ybars F 146 A2
St Yorre F 117 A3
St Yrieix-la-Perche F 115 C5
Saissac F 146 A3
Saja E 142 A2
Sajan SRB 126 B2
Šajkaš SRB 126 B2
Sajókaza H 99 C4
Sajószentpéter H 113 A4
Sajóvámos H 113 A4
Sakarya TR 187 B5
Šakiai LT 13 A5
Sakskøbing DK 65 B4
Sakule SRB 126 B2
Sala S 50 C3
Šal'a SK 111 A4
Sala Baganza I 120 C3
Sala Consilina I 172 B1
Salakovac SRB 127 C3
Salamanca E 150 B2
Salamina GR 185 B4
Salandra I 172 B2
Salaparuta I 176 B1
Salar E 163 A3
Salardú E 145 B4
Salas E 141 A4
Salas de los Infantes E 143 B3
Salau F 146 B2
Salavaux CH 106 C2
Salbertrand I 119 B3
Salbohed S 50 C3
Salbris F 103 B4
Salbu N 46 A2
Salce E 141 B4
Salching D 95 C4
Salcombe GB 43 B3
Saldaña E 142 B2
Saldus LV 8 D3
Sale I 120 C1
Saleby S 55 B4
Salem D 107 B4
Salemi I 176 B1
Salen
*Argyll & Bute* GB 34 B2
*Highland* GB 34 B2
N 199 A8
Sälen S 49 A5
Salernes F 132 B2
Salerno I 170 C2
Salers F 116 B2
Salford GB 40 B1
Salgótarján H 113 A3
Salgueiro P 155 B3
Salhus N 46 B2
Sali HR 137 B4
Sálice Salentino I 173 B3
Salientes E 141 B4
Salies-de-Béarn F 144 A3
Salies-du-Salat F 145 A4
Salignac-Eyvigues F 129 B4
Saligney-sur-Roudon F 104 C2
Salihli TR 188 A3
Salihorsk BY 13 B7
Salinas
*Alicante* E 159 C3
*Huesca* E 145 B4
Salinas de Medinaceli E 152 A1
Salinas de Pisuerga E 142 B2
Salindres F 131 A3
Saline di Volterra I 135 B3
Salins-les-Bains F 105 C4
Salir P 160 B1
Salisbury GB 44 B2
Salla
A 110 B1
FIN 197 C11
Sallachy GB 32 C2
Sallanches F 118 B3
Sallent E 147 C2
Sallent de Gállego E 145 B3
Salles F 128 B2
Salles-Curan F 130 A1
Salles-sur-l'Hers F 146 A2
Sallins IRL 30 A2
Sällsjö S 199 B10
Salmerón E 152 B1
Salmiech F 130 A1
Salmivaara FIN 197 C11
Salmoral E 150 B2
Salo FIN 8 B3
Salò I 121 B3
Salobreña E 163 B4
Salon-de-Provence F 131 B4
Salonica = Thessaloniki GR 182 C4
Salonta RO 16 B4
Salorino E 155 B3
Salornay-sur-Guye F 104 C3
Salorno I 121 A4
Salou E 147 C2
Šalovci SLO 111 C3
Salsbruket N 199 A8
Salses-le-Chateau F 146 B3
Salsomaggiore Terme I 120 C2
Salt E 147 C3
Saltaire GB 40 B2
Saltara I 136 B1
Saltash GB 42 B2
Saltburn-by-the-Sea GB 37 B6
Saltcoats GB 34 C3
Saltfleet GB 41 B4
Salto P 148 A2
Saltrød N 53 B4
Saltsjöbaden S 57 A4
Saltvik
FIN 51 B7
S 62 A4
Saludécio I 136 B1
Salussola I 119 B5
Saluzzo I 119 C4
Salvacañete E 152 B2
Salvada P 160 B2
Salvagnac F 129 C4
Salvaleon E 155 C4
Salvaterra de Magos P 154 B2
Salvaterra do Extremo P 155 B4
Salvatierra
*Avila* E 143 B4
*Badajoz* E 155 C4
Salvatierra de Santiago E 156 A1
Salviac F 129 B4
Salzburg A 109 B4
Salzgitter D 72 B3
Salzgitter Bad D 72 B3
Salzhausen D 72 A3
Salzhemmendorf D 72 B2
Salzkotten D 81 A4
Salzmünde D 83 A3
Salzwedel D 73 B4
Samadet F 128 C2
Samandıra TR 186 B4
Samassi I 179 C2
Samatan F 146 A1
Sambiase I 175 C2
Sambir UA 13 D5
Samborowo PL 69 B4
Sambuca di Sicilia I 176 B2
Samedan CH 107 C4
Samer F 78 B1
Sami GR 184 A1
Şamlı TR 186 C2
Sammichele di Bari I 173 B2
Samnaun CH 107 C5
Samobor HR 123 B4
Samoëns F 118 A3
Samogneux F 92 B1
Samokov BG 17 D5
Samora Correia P 154 C2
Šamorín SK 111 A4
Samos
E 141 B3
GR 188 B1
Samoš SRB 126 B2
Samothraki GR 183 C7
Samper de Calanda E 153 A3
Sampéyre I 133 A3
Sampieri I 177 C3
Sampigny F 92 C1
Samplawa PL 69 B4
Samproniano I 168 A1
Samtens D 66 B2
Samugheo I 179 C2
San Adrián E 144 B2
San Agustín E 164 C2
San Agustin de Guadalix E 151 B4
Sanaigmore GB 34 C1
San Alberto I 135 A5
San Amaro E 140 B2
Sânandrei RO 126 B3
San Andrês del Rabanedo E 142 B1
San Antanio di Santadi I 179 C2
San Antolín de Ibias E 141 A4
San Arcángelo I 174 A2
Sanary-sur-Mer F 132 B1
San Asensio E 143 B4
San Bartoloméde las Abiertas E 150 C3
San Bartoloméde la Torre E 161 B2
San Bartoloméde Pinares E 150 B3
San Bartolomeo in Galdo I 170 B3
San Benedetto del Tronto I 136 C2
San Benedetto in Alpe I 135 B4
San Benedetto Po I 121 B3
San Benito E 156 B3
San Benito de la Contienda E 155 C3
San Biágio Plátani I 176 B2
San Biágio Saracinisco I 169 B3
San Bonifacio I 121 B4
San Calixto E 156 C2
San Cándido I 109 C3
San Carlo
CH 119 A5
I 176 B2
San Carlos del Valle E 157 B4
San Casciano dei Bagni I 135 C4
San Casciano in Val di Pesa I 135 B4
San Cataldo
*Puglia* I 173 B4
*Sicilia* I 176 B2
San Cebrián de Castro E 149 A4
Sancergues F 104 B1
Sancerre F 103 B4
San Cesário di Lecce I 173 B4
Sancey-le-Long F 105 B5
Sanchiorian E 150 B3
San Chírico Raparo I 174 A2
Sanchonuño E 151 A3
San Cibrao das Viñas E 140 B3
San Cipirello I 176 B2
San Ciprián E 141 A3
San Clemente E 158 B1
San Clodio E 141 B3
Sancoins F 104 C1
San Colombano al Lambro I 120 B2
San Costanzo I 136 B2
San Crisóbal de Entreviñas E 142 B1
San Cristóbal de la Polantera E 141 B5
San Cristóbal de la Vega E 150 A3
San Cristovo E 141 C3
Sancti-Petri E 162 B1
Sancti-Spiritus E 149 B3
Sand
*Hedmark* N 48 B3
*Rogaland* N 52 A2
Sanda S 57 C4
San Damiano d'Asti I 119 C5
San Damiano Macra I 133 A3
Sandane N 198 D3
San Daniele del Friuli I 122 A2
Sandanski BG 183 B5
Sandared S 60 B2
Sandarne S 51 A4
Sandau D 73 B5
Sandbach
D 96 C1
GB 38 A4
Sandbank GB 34 C3
Sandbanks GB 43 B5
Sandbukt N 192 C5
Sandby DK 65 B4
Sande
D 71 A5
*Sogn og Fjordane* N 46 A2
*Vestfold* N 54 A1
Sandefjord N 54 A1
Sandeid N 52 A1
San Demétrio Corone I 174 B2
San Demétrio né Vestini I 169 A3
Sandersleben D 82 A3
Sanderstølen N 47 B6
Sandes N 53 B3
Sandesneben D 65 C3
Sandhead GB 36 B2
Sandhem S 60 B3
Sandhorst D 71 A4
Sandhurst GB 44 B3
Sandıklı TR 189 A5
Sandillon F 103 B4
Sandl A 96 C2
Sandnes N 52 B1
Sandness GB 33 A5
Sandnessjøen N 195 D3
Sando E 149 B3
Sandomierz PL 87 B5
San Dónaci I 173 B3
San Donàdi Piave I 122 B1
San Donato Val di Comino I 169 B3
Sándorfalva H 126 A2
Sandown GB 44 C2
Sandøysund N 54 A1
Sandrigo I 121 B4
Sandsele S 195 E8
Sandset N 194 B5
Sandsjöfors S 62 A2
Sandstad N 198 B6
Sandvatn N 52 B2
Sandvig-Allinge DK 67 A3
Sandvika
*Akershus* N 48 C2
*Hedmark* N 48 B3
*Nord-Trøndelag* N 199 B9
Sandviken S 51 B3
Sandvikvåy N 46 C2
Sandwich GB 45 B5
Sandy GB 44 A3
San Emiliano E 141 B5
San Enrique E 162 B2
San Esteban E 141 A4
San Esteban de Gormaz E 151 A4
San Esteban de la Sierra E 149 B4
San Esteban de Litera E 145 C4
San Esteban del Molar E 142 C1
San Esteban del Valle E 150 B3
San Esteban de Valdueza E 141 B4
San Fele I 172 B1
San Felice Circeo I 169 B3

San Felices E 143 B3
San Felices de los Gallégos E 149 B3
San Felice sul Panaro I 121 C4
San Ferdinando di Púglia I 171 B4
San Fernando E 162 B1
San Fernando de Henares E 151 B4
San Fili I 174 B2
San Foca I 173 B4
San Fratello I 177 B3
Sangatte F 78 B1
San Gavino Monreale I 179 C2
San Gémini Fonte I 168 A2
Sangerhausen D 82 A3
San Germano Vercellese I 119 B5
San Giácomo
*Trentino Alto Adige* I 108 C2
*Umbria* I 136 C1
San Gimignano I 135 B4
San Ginésio I 136 B2
Sangineto Lido I 174 B1
San Giórgio a Liri I 169 B3
San Giorgio della Richinvelda I 122 A1
San Giórgio del Sánnio I 170 B2
San Giórgio di Lomellina I 120 B1
San Giórgio di Nogaro I 122 B2
San Giorgio di Piano I 121 C4
San Giórgio Iónico I 173 B3
San Giovanni a Piro I 172 B1
San Giovanni Bianco I 120 B2
San Giovanni di Sinis I 179 C2
San Giovanni in Croce I 120 B3
San Giovanni in Fiore I 174 B2
San Giovanni in Persiceto I 121 C4
San Giovanni Reatino I 169 A2
San Giovanni Rotondo I 171 B3
San Giovanni Suérgiu I 179 C2
San Giovanni Valdarno I 135 B4
Sangis S 196 D6
San Giuliano Terme I 134 B3
San Giustino I 135 B5
San Godenzo I 135 B4
Sangonera la Verde E 165 B3
San Gregorio Magno I 172 B1
Sangüesa E 144 B2
Sanguinet F 128 B1
San Guiseppe Jato I 176 B2
Sanica BIH 124 C2
Sanitz D 65 B5
San Javier E 165 B4
San Jorge P 154 B2
San José E 164 C2
San Juan E 143 B3
San Juan de Alicante E 165 A4
San Juan de la Nava E 150 B3
San Justo de la Vega E 141 B4
Sankt Aegyd am Neuwalde A 110 B2
Sankt Andrä A 110 C1
Sankt Andreasberg D 82 A2
Sankt Anna S 56 B2
Sankt Anna am Aigen A 110 C2
Sankt Anton am Arlberg A 107 B5
Sankt Anton an der Jessnitz A 110 B2
Sankt Augustin D 80 B3
Sankt Blasien D 106 B3
Sankt Englmar D 95 B4
Sankt Gallen
A 110 B1
CH 107 B4
Sankt Gallenkirch A 107 B4
Sankt Georgen
A 96 C2
D 106 A3
Sankt Georgen am Reith A 110 B1
Sankt Georgen ob Judenburg A 110 B1
Sankt Georgen ob Murau A 109 B5
Sankt Gilgen A 109 B4
Sankt Goar D 81 B3
Sankt Goarshausen D 81 B3
Sankt Ingbert D 92 B3
Sankt Jacob A 109 C5
Sankt Jakob in Defereggen A 109 C3
Sankt Johann am Tauern A 110 B1
Sankt Johann am Wesen A 109 A4
Sankt Johann im Pongau A 109 B4
Sankt Johann in Tirol A 109 B3
Sankt Katharein an der Laming A 110 B2
Sankt Kathrein am Hauenstein A 110 B2
Sankt Lambrecht A 110 B1
Sankt Leonhard am Forst A 110 A2
Sankt Leonhard im Pitztal A 108 B1
Sankt Lorenzen A 109 C3
Sankt Marein
*Steiermark* A 110 B2
*Steiermark* A 110 B2
Sankt Margarethen im Lavanttal A 110 C1
Sankt Margrethen CH 107 B4
Sankt Michael A 110 B2
Sankt Michael im Burgenland A 111 B3
Sankt Michael im Lungau A 109 B4
Sankt Michaelisdonn D 64 C2
Sankt Niklaus CH 119 A4
Sankt Nikolai im Sölktal A 109 B5
Sankt Olof S 63 C2
Sankt Oswald D 96 C1
Sankt Paul
A 110 C1
F 132 A2
Sankt Peter D 106 A3
Sankt Peter am Kammersberg A 110 B1
Sankt-Peterburg = St Petersburg RUS 9 C7
Sankt Peter-Ording D 64 B1
Sankt Pölten A 110 A2
Sankt Radegund A 110 B2
Sankt Ruprecht an der Raab A 110 B2
Sankt Salvator A 110 C1
Sankt Stefan A 110 C1
Sankt Stefan an der Gail A 109 C4
Sankt Stefan im Rosental A 110 C2
Sankt Valentin A 110 A1
Sankt Veit an der Glan A 110 C1
Sankt Veit an der Gölsen A 110 A2
Sankt Veit in Defereggen A 109 C3
Sankt Wendel D 92 B3
Sankt Wolfgang
A 109 B4
D 108 A3
San Lazzaro di Sávena I 135 A4
San Leo I 135 B5
San Leonardo de Yagüe E 143 C3
San Leonardo in Passiria I 108 C2
San Lorenzo al Mare I 133 B3
San Lorenzo a Merse I 135 B4
San Lorenzo Bellizzi I 174 B2
San Lorenzo de Calatrava E 157 B4
San Lorenzo de El Escorial E 151 B3
San Lorenzo de la Parrilla E 158 B1
San Lorenzo di Sebato I 108 C2
San Lorenzo in Campo I 136 B1
San Lorenzo Nuovo I 168 A1
San Lourenco P 160 A1
San Luca I 175 C2
Sanlúcar de Barrameda E 161 C3
Sanlúcar de Guadiana E 160 B2
Sanlúcar la Mayor E 161 B3
San Lúcido I 174 B2
Sanluri I 179 C2
San Marcello I 136 B2
San Marcello Pistoiese I 135 A3
San Marcial E 149 A4
San Marco I 170 C2
San Marco Argentano I 174 B2
San Marco dei Cavoti I 170 B2
San Marco in Lámis I 171 B3
San Marino RSM 136 B1
San Martin de Castañeda E 141 B4
San Martín de la Vega E 151 B4
San Martin de la Vega del Alberche E 150 B2
San Martín del Tesorillo E 162 B2
San Martin de Luiña E 141 A4
San Martin de Montalbán E 157 A3
San Martin de Oscos E 141 A4
San Martin de Pusa E 150 C3
San Martin de Unx E 144 B2
San Martín de Valdeiglesias E 150 B3
San Martino di Campagna I 122 A1
San Martino di Castrozza I 121 A4
San-Martino-di-Lota F 180 A2
San Martino in Pénsilis I 170 B3
San Mateo de Gallego E 144 C3
San Máuro Forte I 172 B2
San Michele all'Adige I 121 A4
San Michele di Ganzaria I 177 B3
San Michele Mondov i I 133 A3
San Miguel de Aguayo E 142 A2
San Miguel de Bernuy E 151 A4
San Miguel del Arroyo E 150 A3
San Miguel de Salinas E 165 B4
Sânmihaiu Roman RO 126 B3
San Millán de la Cogolla E 143 B4
San Miniato I 135 B3
San Muñoz E 149 B3
Sänna S 55 B5
Sannazzaro de'Burgondi I 120 B1
Sanne D 73 B4
Sannicandro di Bari I 171 B4
Sannicandro Gargánico I 171 B3
San Nicola del'Alto I 174 B2
San Nicolás del Puerto E 156 C2
Sânnicolau Mare RO 126 A2
San Nicolò I 121 C4
San Nicolò Gerrei I 179 C3
Sannidal N 53 B5
Sanniki PL 77 B4
Sanok PL 12 D5
San Pablo de los Montes E 157 A3
San Pancrázio Salentino I 173 B3
San Pantaleo I 178 A3
San Páolo di Civitate I 171 B3
San Pawl il-Bahar M 175 C3
San Pedro
*Albacete* E 158 C1
*Oviedo* E 141 A4
San Pedro de Alcántara E 162 B3
San Pedro de Ceque E 141 B4
San Pedro del Arroyo E 150 B3
San Pedro de Latarce E 142 C1
San Pedro del Pinatar E 165 B4
San Pedro del Romeral E 143 A3
San Pedro de Merida E 156 B1
San Pedro de Valderaduey E 142 B2
San Pedro Manrique E 144 B1
San Pellegrino Terme I 120 B2
San Piero a Sieve I 135 B4
San Piero in Bagno I 135 B4
San Piero Patti I 177 A3
San Pietro I 177 B3
San Pietro in Casale I 121 C4
San Pietro in Gu I 121 B4
San Pietro in Palazzi I 134 B3
San Pietro in Volta I 122 B1
San Pietro Vara I 134 A2
San Pietro Vernótico I 173 B3
San Polo d'Enza I 121 C3
Sanquhar GB 36 A3
San Quírico d'Órcia I 135 B4
San Rafael del Rio E 153 B4
San Remo I 133 B3
San Román de Cameros E 143 B4
San Roman de Hernija E 150 A2
San Román de la Cuba E 142 B2
San Roman de los Montes E 150 B3
San Romao P 155 C3
San Roque E 162 B2
San Roque de Riomera E 143 A3
San Rufo I 172 B1
San Sabastián de los Ballesteros E 162 A3
San Salvador de Cantamuda E 142 B2
San Salvo I 170 A2
San Salvo Marina I 170 A2
San Sebastián de los Reyes E 151 B4
San Sebastiano Curone I 120 C2
San Secondo Parmense I 120 C3
Sansepolcro I 135 B5
San Serverino Marche I 136 B2
San Severino Lucano I 174 A2
San Severo I 171 B3
San Silvestre de Guzmán E 161 B2
Sanski Most BIH 124 C2
San Sosti I 174 B2
San Stéfano di Cadore I 109 C3
San Stino di Livenza I 122 B1
Santa Agnès E 166 B1
Santa Amalia E 156 A1
Santa Ana
*Cáceres* E 156 A2
*Jaén* E 163 A4
Santa Ana de Pusa E 150 C3
Santa Barbara E 153 B4
Santa Bárbara P 160 B1
Santa Barbara de Casa E 161 B2
Santa Bárbara de Padrões P 160 B2
Santacara E 144 B2
Santa Catarina P 160 B2
Santa Caterina di Pittinuri I 178 B2
Santa Caterina Villarmosa I 177 B3
Santa Cesárea Terme I 173 B4
Santa Clara-a-Nova P 160 B1
Santa Clara-a-Velha P 160 B1
Santa Clara de Louredo P 160 B2
Santa Coloma de Farners E 147 C3
Santa Coloma de Gramenet E 147 C3
Santa Coloma de Queralt E 147 C2
Santa Colomba de Curueño E 142 B1
Santa Colomba de Somoza E 141 B4
Santa Comba E 140 A2
Santa Comba Dáo P 148 B1
Santa Comba de Rossas P 149 A3
Santa Cristina I 120 B2
Santa Cristina de la Polvorosa E 141 B5
Santa Croce Camerina I 177 C3
Santa Croce di Magliano I 170 B2
Santa Cruz
E 140 A2
P 154 B1
Santa Cruz de Alhama E 163 A4
Santa Cruz de Campezo E 143 B4
Santa Cruz de Grio E 152 A2
Santa Cruz de la Salceda E 151 A4
Santa Cruz de la Sierra E 156 A2
Santa Cruz de la Zarza E 151 C4
Santa Cruz del Retamar E 151 B3
Santa Cruz del Valle E 150 B2
Santa Cruz de Moya E 159 B2
Santa Cruz de Mudela E 157 B4
Santa Cruz de Paniagua E 149 B3
Santadi I 179 C2
Santa Doménica Talao I 174 B1
Santa Doménica Vittória I 177 B3
Santa Elena E 157 B4
Santa Elena de Jamuz E 141 B5
Santaella E 162 A3
Santa Eufemia E 156 B3
Santa Eufémia d'Aspromonte I 175 C1
Santa Eulalia E 152 B2
Santa Eulália P 155 C3
Santa Eulalia de Oscos E 141 A3
Santa Eulàlia des Riu E 166 C1
Santa Fe E 163 A4
Santa Fiora I 135 C4
Sant'Ágata dei Goti I 170 B2
Sant'Ágata di Ésaro I 174 B1
Sant'Ágata di Puglia I 171 B3
Sant'Agata Feltria I 135 B5
Sant'Ágata Militello I 177 A3
Santa Gertrude I 108 C1
Santa Giustina I 121 A5
Sant Agust ìde Lluçanès E 147 B3
Santa Iria P 160 B2
Santa Leocadia P 148 A1
Santa Lucia del Mela I 177 A4
Santa Lucia-de-Porto-Vecchio F 180 B2
Santa Luzia P 160 B1
Santa Maddalena Vallalta I 108 C3
Santa Magdalena de Polpis E 153 B4
Santa Margalida E 167 B3
Santa Margarida P 154 B2
Santa Margarida do Sado P 160 A1
Santa Margaridao de Montbui E 147 C2
Santa Margherita I 179 D2
Santa Margherita di Belice I 176 B2
Santa Margherita Ligure I 134 A2
Santa Maria
CH 108 C1
E 144 B3
Santa Maria al Bagno I 173 B3
Santa Maria Cápua Vétere I 170 B2
Santa Maria da Feira P 148 B1
Santa Maria de Cayón E 143 A3
Santa Maria de Corco E 147 B3
Santa Maria de Huerta E 152 A1
Santa Maria de la Alameda E 151 B3
Santa Maria de las Hoyas E 143 C3
Santa Maria del Camí E 167 B2
Santa Maria del Campo E 143 B3
Santa Maria del Campo Rus E 158 B1
Santa Maria della Versa I 120 C2
Santa Maria del Páramo E 142 B1
Santa Maria del Taro I 134 A2
Santa Maria de Mercadillo E 143 C3
Santa Maria de Nieva E 164 B3
Santa Maria de Trassierra E 156 C3
Santa Maria di Licodia I 177 B3
Santa Maria-di-Rispéscia I 168 A1
Santa Maria la Palma I 178 B2
Santa María la Real de Nieva E 150 A3
Santa Maria Maggiore I 119 A5
Santa Maria Ribarredonda E 143 B3
Santa Marina del Rey E 141 B5
Santa Marinella I 168 A1
Santa Marta
*Albacete* E 158 B1
*Badajoz* E 155 C4
Santa Marta de Magasca E 156 A1
Santa Marta de Penaguião P 148 A2
Santa Marta de Tormes E 150 B2
Santana
*Évora* P 154 C2
*Setúbal* P 154 C1
Sântana RO 126 A3
Santana da Serra P 160 B1
Sant'Ana de Cambas P 160 B2
Santana do Mato P 154 C2
Sant'Anastasia I 170 C2
Santander E 143 A3
Sant'Andrea Frius I 179 C3
Sant'Ángelo dei Lombardi I 172 B1
Sant'Angelo in Vado I 136 B1
Sant'Angelo Lodigiano I 120 B2
Santa Ninfa I 176 B1
Sant'Antíoco I 179 C2
Sant Antoni de Calonge E 147 C4
Sant Antoni de Portmany E 166 C1
Sant'Antonio-di-Gallura I 178 B3
Santanyí E 167 B3
Santa Olalla
*Huelva* E 161 B3
*Toledo* E 150 B3
Santa Pau E 147 B3
Santa Pola E 165 A4
Santa Ponça E 166 B2
Santarcángelo di Romagna I 136 A1
Santarém P 154 B2
Santa Severa
F 180 A2
I 168 A1
Santa Severina I 175 B2
Santas Martas E 142 B1
Santa Sofia I 135 B4
Santa Susana P 154 C2
Santa Suzana P 155 C3
Santa Teresa di Riva I 177 B4
Santa Teresa Gallura I 178 A3
Santa Uxía E 140 B2
Santa Valburga I 108 C1
Santa Vittória in Matenano I 136 B2
Sant Boi de Llobregat E 147 C3
Sant Carles de la Ràpita E 153 B4
Sant Carlos E 166 B1
Sant'Caterina I 135 C4
Sant Celoni E 147 C3
Sant Climent E 167 B4
Santed E 152 A2
Sant'Egídio alla Vibrata I 136 C2
Sant'Elia a Pianisi I 170 B2
Sant'Elia Fiumerapido I 169 B3
Santelices E 143 A3
San Telmo E 161 B3
Sant'Elpídio a Mare I 136 B2
Santéramo in Colle I 171 C4
Santervas de la Vega E 142 B2
Sant' Eufemia Lamezia 175 C2
Sant Feliu E 147 C3
Sant Feliu de Codines E 147 C3
Sant Feliu de Guíxols E 147 C4
Sant Feliu Sasserra E 147 C3
Sant Ferran E 166 C1
Sant Francesc de Formentera E 166 C1
Sant Francesc de ses Salines E 166 C1
Santhià I 119 B5
Sant Hilari Sacalm E 147 C3
Sant Hipòlit de Voltregà E 147 B3
Santiago de Alcántara E 155 B3
Santiago de Calatrava E 163 A3
Santiago de Compostela E 140 B2
Santiago de la Espade E 164 A2
Santiago de la Puebla E 150 B2
Santiago de la Ribera E 165 B4
Santiago del Campo E 155 B4
Santiago de Litem P 154 B2

Santiago do Cacém P 160 B1
Santiago do Escoural P 154 C2
Santiago Maior P 155 C3
Santibáñez de Béjar E 150 B2
Santibáñez de la Peña E 142 B2
Santibáñez de Murias E 142 A1
Santibáñez de Vidriales E 141 B4
Santibáñez el Alto E 149 B3
Santibáñez el Bajo E 149 B3
Santillana E 142 A2
Santiponce E 162 A1
San Tirso de Abres E 141 A3
Santisteban del Puerto E 157 B4
Santiuste de San Juan Bautiste E 150 A3
Santiz E 149 A4
Sant Jaume dels Domenys E 147 C2
Sant Joan Baptista E 166 B1
Sant Joan de les Abadesses E 147 B3
Sant Jordi E 153 B4
Sant Josep de sa Talaia E 166 C1
Sant Juliàde Loria AND 146 B2
Sant'Ilario d'Enza I 121 C3
Sant Llorençde Morunys E 147 B2
Sant Llorençdes Carctassar E 167 B3
Sant Llorenç Savall E 147 C3
Sant Luis E 167 B4
Sant Mart ide Llemaná E 147 B3
Sant Marti de Maldá E 147 C2
Sant Marti Sarroca E 147 C2
Sant Mateu E 153 B4
Sant Miquel E 166 B1
Santo Aleixo P 161 A2
Santo Amado P 161 A2
Santo Amaro P 155 C3
Santo André P 160 A1
Santo Domingo E 155 C3
Santo Domingo de la Calzada E 143 B4
Santo Domingo de Silos E 143 C3
Santo Estêvão
*Faro* P 160 B2
*Santarém* P 154 C2
Santok PL 75 B4
Santomera E 165 A3
Santoña E 143 A3
Santo-Pietro-di Tenda F 180 A2
Sant'Oreste I 168 A2
Santo Spirito I 171 B4
Santo Stefano d'Aveto I 134 A2
Santo Stéfano di Camastra I 177 A3
Santo Stefano di Magra I 134 A2
Santo Stéfano Quisquina I 176 B2
Santo Tirso P 148 A1
Santotis E 142 A2
Santo Tomé E 164 A1
Santovenia
*Burgos* E 143 B3
*Zamora* E 142 C1
Sant Pau de Segúries E 147 B3
Santpedor E 147 C2
Sant Pere de Riudebitlles E 147 C2
Sant Pere Pescador E 147 B4
Sant Pere Sallavinera E 147 C2
Sant Quirze de Besora E 147 B3
Sant Rafel E 166 C1
Sant Ramon E 147 C2
Santu Lussurgiu I 178 B2
Santutzi E 143 A3
Sant Vincençde Castellet E 147 C2
San Valentino alla Muta I 108 C1
San Venanzo I 135 C5
San Vicente de Alcántara E 155 B3
San Vicente de Arana E 144 B1
San Vicente de la Barquera E 142 A2
San Vicente de la Sonsierra E 143 B4
San Vicente de Toranzo E 143 A3
San Vietro E 149 A3
San Vigilio I 108 C2
San Vincente del Raspeig E 165 A4
San Vincenzo I 134 B3
San Vito I 179 C3
San Vito al Tagliamento I 122 B1
San Vito Chietino I 169 A4
San Vito dei Normanni I 173 B3
San Vito di Cadore I 108 C3
San Vito lo Capo I 176 A1
San Vito Romano I 169 B2
Sanxenxo E 140 B2
Sanza I 172 B1
São Aleixo P 155 C3
São Barnabé P 160 B1
São Bartoloméda Serra P 160 A1
São Bartolomeu de Messines P 160 B1
São Bento P 140 C2
São Brás P 160 B2
São Brás de Alportel P 160 B2
São Braz do Reguedoura P 154 C2
São Cristóvão P 154 C2
São Domingos P 160 B1
São Geraldo P 154 C2
São Jacinto P 148 B1
São João da Madeira P 148 B1
São João da Pesqueira P 148 A2
São João da Ribeira P 154 B2
São João da Serra P 148 B1
São João da Venda P 160 B2
São João dos Caldeireiros P 160 B2
São Julião P 155 B3
São Leonardo P 155 C3
São Luis P 160 B1
São Manços P 155 C3
São Marcos da Ataboeira P 160 B2
Saõ Marcos da Serra P 160 B1
São Marcos de Campo P 155 C3
São Martinho da Cortiça P 148 B1
São Martinho das Amoreiras P 160 B1
São Martinho do Porto P 154 B1
São Matias
*Beja* P 160 A2
*Évora* P 154 C2
São Miguel d'Acha P 155 A3
São Miguel de Machede P 155 C3
São Pedro da Torre P 140 C2
São Pedro de Cadeira P 154 B1
São Pedro de Moel P 154 B1
São Pedro de Solis P 160 B2
São Pedro do Sul P 148 B1
Saorge F 133 B3
São Romão P 154 C2
São Sebastião dos Carros P 160 B2
São Teotónio P 160 B1
São Torcato P 148 A1
Sapataria P 154 C1
Sapes GR 183 B7
Sapiãos P 148 A2
Sa Pobla E 167 B3
Sappada I 109 C3
Sappen N 192 C5
Sapri I 174 A1
Sarajärvi FIN 197 D10
Sarajevo BIH 139 B4
Saramon F 129 C3
Sarandë AL 182 D2
Saranovo SRB 127 C2
Saraorci SRB 127 C3
Sa Rapita E 167 B3
Saray TR 186 A2
Saraycık TR 187 C4
Sarayköy TR 188 B3
Saraylar TR 186 B2
Sarayönü TR 189 A7
Sarbia PL 75 B5
Sarbinowo
*Zachodnio-Pomorskie* PL 67 B4
*Zachodnio-Pomorskie* PL 74 B3
Sárbogárd H 112 C2
Sarcelles F 90 B2
Sarche I 121 A3
Sardara I 179 C2
Sardoal P 154 B2
Sardón de Duero E 150 A3
Sare F 144 A2
S'Arenal E 166 B2
Šarengrad HR 125 B5
Sarentino I 108 C2
Sarezzo I 120 B3
Sargans CH 107 B4
Sári H 112 B3
Sarıbeyler TR 186 C2
Sarıcakaya TR 187 B5
Sari-d'Orcino F 180 A1
Sarıgöl TR 188 A3
Sarıkaya TR 23 B8
Sarıköy TR 186 B2
Sarilhos Grandes P 154 C2
Sariñena E 145 C3
Sarıoba TR 187 C7
Sárisáp H 112 B2
Sariyer TR 186 A4
Sarkad H 113 C5
Sárkeresztes H 112 B2
Sárkeresztúr H 112 B2
Särkijärvi FIN 196 B6
Şarkikaraağaç TR 189 A6
Şarköy TR 186 B2
Sarlat-la-Canéda F 129 B4
Sarliac-sur-l'Isle F 129 A3
Sármellék H 111 C4
Särna S 199 D10
Sarnadas P 155 B3
Sarnano I 136 B2
Sarnen CH 106 C3
Sarnesfield GB 39 B4
Sárnico I 120 B2
Sarno I 170 C2
Sarnonico I 121 A4
Sarnow D 74 A2
Sarny UA 13 C7
Särö S 60 B1
Saronno I 120 B2
Sárosd H 112 B2
Šarovce SK 112 A2
Sarpoil F 117 B3
Sarpsborg N 54 A2
Sarracín E 143 B3
Sarral E 147 C2
Sarralbe F 92 B3
Sarrancolin F 145 B4
Sarras F 117 B4
Sarre I 119 B4
Sarreaus E 140 B3
Sarrebourg F 92 C3
Sarreguemines F 92 B3
Sárrétudvari H 113 B5
Sarre-Union F 92 C3
Sarria E 141 B3
Sarriàde Ter E 147 B3
Sarrión E 153 B3
Sarroca de Lleida E 153 A4
Sarroch I 179 C3
Sarron F 128 C2
Sársina I 135 B5
Særslev DK 59 C3
Sarstedt D 72 B2
Sárszentlörinc H 112 C2
Sárszentmihaly H 112 B2
Sárszentmiklós H 112 C2
Sarteano I 135 C4
Sartène F 180 B1
Sartilly F 88 B2
Sartirana Lomellina I 120 B1
Saruhanlı TR 186 D2
Sárvár H 111 B3
Sarvisvaara S 196 C4
Sarzana I 134 A2
Sarzeau F 101 B3
Sarzedas P 155 B3
Sasalli TR 188 A1
Sasamón E 142 B2
Sa Savina E 166 C1
Sásd H 125 A4
Sasino PL 68 A2
Sássari I 178 B2
Sassello I 133 A4
Sassenberg D 71 C5
Sassetta I 134 B3
Sassnitz D 66 B2
Sassocorvaro I 136 B1
Sasso d'Ombrone I 135 C4
Sassoferrato I 136 B1
Sassoleone I 135 A4
Sasso Marconi I 135 A4
Sassuolo I 135 A3
Sástago E 153 A3
Šaštinske Stráže SK 98 C1
Sas van Gent NL 79 A3
Såtåhaugen N 199 C7
Satão P 148 B2
Såtenäs S 55 B3
Säter S 50 B2
Sätila S 60 B2
Satillieu F 117 B4
Satnica Đakovačka HR 125 B4
Sátoraljaújhely H 16 A4
Satow D 65 C4
Sätra-brunn S 50 C3
Sætre N 54 A1
Satrup D 64 B2
Satteins A 107 B4
Satu Mare RO 17 B5
Saturnia I 168 A1
Saucats F 128 B2
Saucelle E 149 A3
Sauda N 52 A2
Sauðarkrókur IS 190 B6
Saudasjøen N 52 A2
Sauerlach D 108 B2
Saugues F 117 C3
Sauherad N 53 A5
Saujon F 114 C3
Sauland N 53 A4
Saulces Monclin F 91 B4
Saulgau D 107 A4
Saulgrub D 108 B2
Saulieu F 104 B3
Saulnot F 106 B1
Sault F 131 A4
Sault-Brénaz F 118 B2
Sault-de-Navailles F 128 C2
Saulx F 105 B5
Saulxures-sur-Moselotte F 106 B1
Saulzais-le-Potier F 103 C4
Saumos F 128 B1
Saumur F 102 B1
Saunavaara FIN 197 B10
Saundersfoot GB 39 C2
Saurat F 146 B2
Saurbær
*Borgarfjarðarsýsla* IS 190 C4
*Dalasýsla* IS 190 B4
*Eyjafjarðarsýsla* IS 191 B7
Sáuris I 109 C3
Sausset-les-Pins F 131 B4
Sauteyrargues F 131 B2
Sauvagnat F 116 B2
Sauve F 131 B2
Sauveterre-de-Béarn F 144 A3
Sauveterre-de-Guyenne F 128 B2
Sauviat-sur-Vige F 116 B1
Sauxillanges F 117 B3
Sauzet
*Drôme* F 117 C4
*Lot* F 129 B4
Sauzé-Vaussais F 115 B4
Sauzon F 100 B2
Sava I 173 B3
Sävar S 200 C6
Sævareid N 46 B2
Savarsin RO 16 B5
Sävast S 196 D4
Savaştepe TR 186 C2
Savci SLO 111 C3
Säve S 60 B1
Savelletri I 173 B3
Savelli I 174 B2
Savenay F 101 B4
Saverdun F 146 A2
Saverne F 93 C3
Savières F 91 C3
Savigliano I 119 C4
Savignac-les-Eglises F 129 A3
Savignano Irpino I 171 B3
Savignano sul Rubicone I 136 A1
Savigny-sur-Braye F 102 B2
Saviñán E 152 A2
Savines-le-lac F 132 A2
Savino Selo SRB 126 B1
Savio I 135 A5
Sävja S 51 C4
Šavnik MNE 139 C5
Savognin CH 107 C4
Savona I 133 A4
Savonlinna FIN 9 B6
Savournon F 132 A1
Sævråsvåg N 46 B2
Sävsjö S 62 A2
Savsjön S 50 C1
Sävsjöström S 62 A3
Savudrija HR 122 B2
Savukoski FIN 197 B11
Sawbridgeworth GB 45 B4
Sawtry GB 44 A3
Sax E 159 C3
Saxdalen S 50 B1
Saxilby GB 40 B3
Saxmundham GB 45 A5
Saxnäs S 195 F6
Saxthorpe GB 41 C5
Sayalonga E 163 B3
Sayatón E 151 B5
Sayda D 83 B5
Säytsjärvi FIN 193 C11
Sázava CZ 97 B3
Sázava CZ 96 B2
Scaër F 100 A2
Scafa I 169 A4
Scalasaig GB 34 B1
Scalby GB 40 A3
Scalea I 174 B1
Scaletta Zanclea I 177 A4
Scalloway GB 33 A5
Scamblesby GB 41 B3
Scandale I 175 B2
Scandiano I 121 C3
Scandicci I 135 B4
Scandolara Ravara I 120 B3
Scanno I 169 B3
Scansano I 168 A1
Scanzano Jónico I 174 A2
Scarborough GB 40 A3
Scardovari I 122 C1
Scardoy GB 32 D2
Scarperia I 135 B4
Scarriff IRL 28 B3
Scey-sur-Saône et St Albin F 105 B4
Schachendorf A 111 B3
Schaffhausen CH 107 B3
Schafstädt D 83 A3
Schafstedt D 64 B2
Schäftlarn D 108 B2
Schagen NL 70 B1
Schalkau D 82 B3
Schangnau CH 106 C2
Schapbach D 93 C4
Scharbeutz D 65 B3
Schärding A 96 C1
Scharnitz A 108 B2
Scharrel D 71 A4
Schattendorf A 111 B3
Scheemda NL 71 A3
Scheessel D 72 A2
Schéggia I 136 B1
Scheibbs A 110 A2
Scheibenberg D 83 B4
Scheidegg D 107 B4
Scheifling A 110 B1
Scheinfeld D 94 B2
Schelklingen D 94 C1
Schenefeld
*Schleswig-Holstein* D 64 B2
*Schleswig-Holstein* D 72 A2
Schenklengsfeld D 82 B1
Scherfede D 81 A5
Schermbeck D 80 A2
Scherpenzeel NL 70 B2
Schesslitz D 94 B3
Scheveningen NL 70 B1
Schiedam NL 79 A4
Schieder-Schwalenberg D 72 C2
Schierling D 95 C4
Schiers CH 107 C4
Schildau D 83 A4
Schillingen D 92 B2
Schillingsfürst D 94 B2
Schilpário I 120 A3
Schiltach D 93 C4
Schiltigheim F 93 C3
Schio I 121 B4
Schirmeck F 92 C3
Schirnding D 83 B4
Schkeuditz D 83 A4
Schkölen D 83 A3
Schlabendorf D 84 A1
Schladen D 73 B3
Schladming A 109 B4
Schlangen D 81 A4
Schleiden D 80 B2
Schleiz D 83 B3
Schleswig D 64 B2
Schleusingen D 82 B2
Schlieben D 83 A5
Schliengen D 106 B2
Schliersee D 108 B2
Schlitz D 81 B5
Schloss Neuhans D 81 A4
Schlossvippach D 82 A3
Schlotheim D 82 A2
Schluchsee D 106 B3
Schlüchtern D 81 B5
Schmallenberg D 81 A4
Schmelz D 92 B2
Schmidmühlen D 95 B3
Schmiedeberg D 84 B1
Schmiedefeld D 82 B2
Schmirn A 108 B2
Schmölln
*Brandenburg* D 74 A3
*Sachsen* D 83 B4
Schnaittach D 95 B3
Schneeberg D 83 B4
Schneizlreuth D 109 B3
Schneverdingen D 72 A2
Schöder A 109 B5
Schoenburg B 80 B2
Schollene D 73 B5
Schöllkrippen D 81 B5
Schomberg D 107 A3
Schönach D 95 C4
Schönau
*Baden-Württemberg* D 106 B2
*Bayern* D 95 C4
Schönbeck D 74 A2
Schönberg
*Bayern* D 96 C1
*Mecklenburg-Vorpommern* D 65 C3
*Schleswig-Holstein* D 65 B3
Schönebeck D 73 B4
Schöneck D 83 B4
Schönecken- D 80 B2
Schönermark D 74 A2
Schönewalde D 83 A5
Schongau D 108 B1
Schöngrabern A 97 C4
Schönhagen D 81 A5
Schönhausen D 73 B5
Schöningen D 73 B3
Schönkirchen D 64 B3
Schönsee D 95 B4
Schöntal D 94 B1
Schönthal D 95 B4
Schonungen D 94 A2
Schönwalde D 65 B3
Schoondijke NL 79 A3
Schoonebeek NL 71 B3
Schoonhoven NL 79 A4
Schopfheim D 106 B2
Schöppenstedt D 73 B3
Schörfling A 109 B4
Schorndorf D 94 C1
Schortens D 71 A4
Schotten D 81 B5
Schramberg D 106 A3
Schraplau D 83 A3
Schrattenberg A 97 C4
Schrecksbach D 81 B5
Schrems A 96 C3
Schrobenhausen D 95 C3
Schröcken A 107 B5
Schrozberg D 94 B1
Schruns A 107 B4
Schüpfheim CH 106 C3
Schüttorf D 71 B4
Schwaan D 65 C5
Schwabach D 94 B3
Schwäbisch Gmünd D 94 C1
Schwäbisch Hall D 94 B1
Schwabmünchen D 108 A1
Schwadorf A 111 A3
Schwagstorf D 71 B4
Schwaigern D 93 B5
Schwalmstadt D 81 B5
Schwanberg A 110 C2
Schwanden CH 107 C4
Schwandorf D 95 B4
Schwanebeck D 73 C4
Schwanenstadt A 109 A4
Schwanewede D 72 A1
Schwanfeld D 94 B2
Schwangau D 108 B1
Schwarmstedt D 72 B2
Schwarza D 82 B2
Schwarzach im Pongau A 109 B4
Schwarzau im Gebirge A 110 B2
Schwarzenau A 97 C3
Schwarzenbach D 83 B3
Schwarzenbach am Wald D 83 B3
Schwarzenbek D 72 A3
Schwarzenberg D 83 B4
Schwarzenburg CH 106 C2
Schwarzenfeld D 95 B4
Schwarz-heide D 84 A1
Schwaz A 108 B2
Schwechat A 111 A3
Schwedt D 74 A3
Schwei D 71 A5
Schweich D 92 B2
Schweighausen D 106 A2
Schweinfurt D 94 A2
Schweinitz D 83 A5
Schweinrich D 74 A1
Schwelm D 80 A3
Schwemsal D 83 A4
Schwendt A 109 B3
Schwenningen D 107 A3
Schwepnitz D 84 A1
Schwerin D 73 A4
Schwerte D 81 A3
Schweskau D 73 B4
Schwetzingen D 93 B4
Schwyz CH 107 B3
Sciacca I 176 B2
Scicli I 177 C3
Ściechów PL 75 B3
Scigliano I 175 B2
Scilla I 175 C1
Ścinawa PL 85 A4
Scionzier F 118 A3
Scoglitti I 177 C3
Scole GB 45 A5
Sconser GB 31 B2
Scopello
*Piemonte* I 119 B5
*Sicilia* I 176 A1
Scordia I 177 B3
Scorzè I 121 B5
Scotch Corner GB 37 B5
Scotter GB 40 B3
Scourie GB 32 C1
Scousburgh GB 33 B5
Scrabster GB 32 C3
Screeb IRL 28 A2
Scremerston GB 37 A5
Scritto I 136 B1
Scunthorpe GB 40 B3
Scuol CH 107 C5
Scúrcola Marsicana I 169 A3
Seaford GB 45 C4
Seaham GB 37 B5
Seahouses GB 37 A5
Seascale GB 36 B3
Seaton GB 43 B3
Sebazac-Concourès F 130 A1
Seben TR 187 B6
Sebersdorf A 110 B2
Sebezh RUS 8 D6
Sebnitz D 84 B2
Seborga I 133 B3
Seby S 63 B4
Seč
*Vychodočeský* CZ 97 B3
*Západočeský* CZ 96 B1

Sečanj SRB 126 B2
Secemin PL 87 B3
Séchault F 91 B4
Seckau A 110 B1
Seclin F 78 B3
Secondigny F 114 B3
Seda P 155 B3
Sedan F 91 B4
Sedano E 143 B3
Sedbergh GB 37 B4
Sedella E 163 B3
Séderon F 131 A4
Sedgefield GB 37 B5
Sedico I 121 A5
Sédilo I 178 B2
Sédini I 178 B2
Sedlarica HR 124 B3
Sedlčany CZ 96 B2
Sedlec-Prčice CZ 96 B2
Sedlice CZ 96 B1
Sędziejowice PL 86 A3
Sędziszów PL 87 B4
Sędziszów Małapolski
PL 87 B5
Seebach F 93 C3
Seeboden A 109 C4
Seefeld
*Brandenburg* D 74 B2
*Niedersachsen* D 71 A5
Seefeld in Tirol A 108 B2
Seeg D 108 B1
Seehausen
*Sachsen-Anhalt* D 73 B4
*Sachsen-Anhalt* D 73 B4
Seeheim-Jugenheim
D 93 B4
Seelbach D 93 C3
Seelow D 74 B3
Seelze D 72 B2
Seerhausen D 83 A5
Sées F 89 B4
Seesen D 82 A2
Seeshaupt D 108 B2
Seewalchen A 109 B4
Seferihisar TR 188 A1
Sefkerin SRB 127 B2
Segård N 48 B2
Segerstad S 55 A4
Segesd H 124 A3
Seglinge FIN 51 B7
Segmon S 55 A4
Segonzac F 115 C3
Segorbe E 159 B3
Segovia E 151 B3
Segré F 101 B5
Segura
E 144 B1
P 155 B3
Segura de León E 161 A3
Segura de los Baños
E 152 B3
Ségur-les-Villas F 116 B2
Segurrilla E 150 B3
Sehnde D 72 B2
Seia P 148 B2
Seiches-sur-le-Loir
F 102 B1
Seifhennersdorf D 84 B2
Seignelay F 104 B2
Seijo E 140 C2
Seilhac F 116 B1
Seilles B 79 B5
Seim N 46 B2
Seinäjoki FIN 8 A3
Seissan F 145 A4
Seitenstetten Markt
A 110 A1
Seixal P 154 C1
Seiz A 110 B1
Seizthal A 110 B1
Sejerslev DK 58 B1
Seksna RUS 9 C11
Selárdalur IS 190 B1
Selárgius I 179 C3
Selb D 83 B4
Selby GB 40 B2
Selca HR 138 B2
Selce HR 123 B3
Selçuk TR 188 B2
Selde DK 58 B2
Selenča SRB 126 B1
Selendi
*Manisa* TR 186 D2
*Manisa* TR 186 D3
Selenicë AL 182 C1
Sélestat F 106 A2
Seleuš SRB 126 B2
Selevac SRB 127 C2
Selfoss IS 190 D5
Selgua E 145 C4
Selice SK 112 A1
Seligenstadt D 93 A4
Seligenthal D 82 B2
Selimiye TR 188 B2
Selizharovo RUS 9 D8
Selja S 50 A1
Selje N 198 C2
Seljeivnes N 192 C3
Seljord N 53 A4
Selkirk GB 35 C5
Sellano I 136 C1
Selles-St Denis F 103 B3
Selles-sur-Cher F 103 B3
Sellières F 105 C4
Sellin D 66 B2
Sellye H 125 B3
Selm D 80 A3
Selnica ob Dravi
SLO 110 C2
Selongey F 105 B4
Selonnet F 132 A2
Selow D 65 C4
Selsey GB 44 C3
Selsingen D 72 A2
Selters D 81 B3
Seltz F 93 C4
Selva E 167 B2
Selva di Cadore I 108 C3
Selva di Val Gardena
I 108 C2
Selvik
*Sogn og Fjordane*
N 46 A2
*Vestfold* N 54 A1
Selvino I 120 B2
Selyatyn UA 17 B6
Sem N 54 A1
Semeljci HR 125 B4
Semič SLO 123 B4
Semide
F 91 B4
P 148 B1
Semily CZ 84 B3
Seminara I 175 C1
Semlac RO 126 A2
Semlacu Mare RO 126 B3
Semmen-stedt D 73 B3
Šempeter SLO 123 A4
Semriach A 110 B2
Semur-en-Auxois
F 104 B3
Sena E 145 C3
Sena de Luna E 141 B5
Senarpont F 90 B1
Sénas F 131 B4
Senćanski Trešnjevac
SRB 126 B1
Sencelles E 167 B2
Senčur SLO 123 A3
Senden
*Bayern* D 94 C2
*Nordrhein-Westfalen*
D 80 A3
Sendenhorst D 81 A3
Sendim P 149 A3
Senec SK 111 A4
Seneffe B 79 B4
Séneghe I 178 B2
Senés E 164 B2
Senez F 132 B2
Senftenberg D 84 A1
Sengouagnet F 145 B4
Sengwarden D 71 A5
Senica SK 98 C1
Senice na Hané CZ 98 B1
Senigállia I 136 B2
Senirkent TR 189 A5
Sénis I 179 C2
Senise I 174 A2
Senj HR 123 C3
Senje SRB 127 D3
Senjehopen N 194 A8
Senjski Rudnik
SRB 127 D3
Senlis F 90 B2
Sennan S 60 C2
Sennecey-le-Grand
F 105 C3
Sennen GB 42 B1
Senno BY 13 A8
Sénnori I 178 B2
Sennwald CH 107 B4
Sennybridge GB 39 C3
Senohrad SK 99 C3
Senonches F 89 B5
Senones F 92 C2
Senorbì I 179 C3
Senovo SLO 123 A4
Senožeče SLO 123 B3
Senožeti SLO 123 A3
Sens F 104 A2
Sens-de-Bretagne
F 101 A4
Senta SRB 126 B2
Senterada E 145 B4
Šentilj SLO 110 C2
Šentjernej SLO 123 B4
Šentjur SLO 123 A4
Senumstad N 53 B4
Seoane E 141 B3
Seon CH 106 B3
Sépeaux F 104 B2
Sépey CH 119 A4
Sepino I 170 B2
Sępólno Krajeńskie
PL 76 A2
Seppenrade D 80 A3
Seppois F 106 B2
Septemvri BG 183 A6
Septeuil F 90 C1
Sepúlveda E 151 A4
Sequals I 122 A1
Sequeros E 149 B3
Seraincourt F 91 B4
Seraing B 80 B1
Seravezza I 134 B3
Sered' SK 98 C1
Seredka RUS 8 C6
Şereflikoçhisar TR 23 B7
Seregélyes H 112 B2
Seregno I 120 B2
Sérent F 101 B3
Serfaus A 108 B1
Sergiyev Posad
RUS 9 D11
Seriate I 120 B2
Sérifontaine F 90 B1
Serifos GR 185 B5
Sérignan F 130 B2
Serik TR 189 C6
Serina I 120 B2
Serinhisar TR 188 B4
Sermaises F 90 C2
Sermaize-les-Bains
F 91 C4
Sérmide I 121 C4
Sermoneta I 169 B2
Sernache de Bonjardim
P 154 B2
Sernancelhe P 148 B2
Serock PL 77 B6
Serón E 164 B2
Serón de Najima E 152 A1
Serooskerke NL 79 A3
Seròs E 153 A4
Serpa P 160 B2
Serracapriola I 171 B3
Serrada E 150 A3
Serra de Outes E 140 B2
Serradifalco I 176 B2
Serradilla E 155 B4
Serradilla del Arroyo
E 149 B3
Serradilla del Llano
E 149 B3
Serramanna I 179 C2
Serramazzoni I 135 A3
Serranillos E 150 B3
Serrapetrona I 136 B2
Serra San Bruno I 175 C2
Serra San Quírico I 136 B2
Serrastretta I 175 B2
Serravalle
*Piemonte* I 119 B5
*Umbria* I 136 C2
Serravalle di Chienti
I 136 B1
Serravalle Scrívia I 120 C1
Serre I 172 B1
Serrejón E 150 C2
Serres
F 132 A1
GR 183 B5
Serrières F 117 B4
Serrières-de-Briord
F 118 B2
Sersale I 175 B2
Sertã P 154 B2
Sertig Dörfli CH 107 C4
Servance F 106 B1
Serverette F 117 C3
Servia GR 182 C4
Servian F 130 B2
Serviers F 131 A3
Servigliano I 136 B2
Serzedelo P 148 A1
Seseña Nuevo E 151 B4
Sesimbra P 154 C1
Seskarö S 196 D6
Seskinore GB 27 B3
Sesma E 144 B1
Sessa Aurunca I 170 B1
Ses Salines E 167 B3
Sesta Godano I 134 A2
Šestanovac HR 138 B2
Sestao E 143 A4
Sestino I 135 B5
Sesto I 109 C3
Sesto Calende I 120 B1
Sesto Fiorentino I 135 B4
Séstola I 135 A3
Sesto San Giovanni
I 120 B2
Sestriere I 119 C3
Sestri Levante I 134 A2
Sestroretsk RUS 9 B7
Sestu I 179 C3
Sesvete HR 124 B2
Setcases E 146 B3
Sète F 130 B2
Setenil E 162 B2
Setermoen N 194 B9
Šetonje SRB 127 C3
Setskog N 54 A2
Settalsjølia N 199 C7
Séttimo Torinese I 119 B4
Settimo Vittone I 119 B4
Settle GB 40 A1
Setúbal P 154 C2
Seubersdort D 95 B3
Seúi I 179 C3
Seúlo I 179 C3
Seurre F 105 C4
Sevel DK 58 B1
Sevenoaks GB 45 B4
Sévérac-le-Château
F 130 A2
Sever do Vouga P 148 B1
Severin HR 123 B4
Severomorsk RUS 3 B13
Séveso I 120 B2
Ševětin CZ 96 B2
Sevettijärvi FIN 193 C12
Sévigny F 91 B4
Sevilla = Seville E 162 A2
Sevilla la Nueva E 151 B3
Seville = Sevilla E 162 A2
Sevilleja de la Jara
E 156 A3
Sevlievo BG 17 D6
Sevnica SLO 123 A4
Sevojno SRB 127 D1
Sevrier F 118 B3
Sexdrega S 60 B3
Seyches F 129 B3
Seyda D 83 A4
Seydişehir TR 189 B6
Seyðisfjörður IS 191 B12
Seyitgazi TR 187 C5
Seyitömer TR 187 C4
Seymen TR 186 A2
Seyne F 132 A2
Seynes F 131 A3
Seyssel F 118 B2
Sežana SLO 122 B2
Sézanne F 91 C3
Sezulfe P 149 A2
Sezze I 169 B3
Sfântu Gheorghe
RO 17 C6
Sforzacosta I 136 B2
Sgarasta Mhor GB 31 B1
's-Gravendeel NL 79 A4
's-Gravenhage = The
Hague NL 70 B1
's-Gravenzande NL 79 A4
Shaftesbury GB 43 A4
Shaldon GB 43 B3
Shalskiy RUS 9 B9
Shanagolden IRL 29 B2
Shanklin GB 44 C2
Shap GB 37 B4
Sharpness GB 43 A4
Shawbury GB 38 B4
's-Heerenberg NL 80 A2
Sheerness GB 45 B4
Sheffield GB 40 B2
Shefford GB 44 A3
Shëmri AL 182 A2
Shenfield GB 45 B4
Shëngjergj AL 182 B2
Shepetivka UA 13 C7
Shepshed GB 40 C2
Shepton Mallet GB 43 A4
Sherborne GB 43 B4
Shercock IRL 27 C4
Sheringham GB 41 C5
's-Hertogenbosch
NL 79 A5
Shiel Bridge GB 32 D1
Shieldaig GB 31 B3
Shijak AL 182 B1
Shillelagh IRL 30 B2
Shimsk RUS 9 C7
Shipston-on-Stour
GB 44 A2
Shklow BY 13 A9
Shkodër AL 182 A1
Shoeburyness GB 45 B4
Shoreham-by-Sea
GB 44 C3
Shotley Gate GB 45 B5
Shrewsbury GB 38 B4
Shugozero RUS 9 C9
Shumen BG 17 D7
Siabost GB 31 A2
Siamanna I 179 C2
Sianów PL 67 B5
Siatista GR 182 C3
Siauges-St Romain
F 117 B3
Šiauliai LT 8 E3
Sibari I 174 B2
Sibbhult S 63 B2
Šibenik HR 138 B1
Siberstedt D 64 B2
Sibinj HR 125 B3
Sibiu RO 17 C6
Sibnica SRB 127 C2
Sibsey GB 41 B4
Siculiana I 176 B2
Šid SRB 125 B5
Sidari GR 182 D1
Siddeburen NL 71 A3
Sidensjö S 200 C4
Siderno I 175 C2
Sidirokastro GR 183 B5
Sidmouth GB 43 B3
Sidzina PL 99 B3
Siebe N 192 D7
Siebenlehn D 83 A5
Siedlce PL 12 B5
Siedlice PL 75 A4
Siedlinghausen D 81 A4
Siedlisko PL 75 B5
Siegburg D 80 B3
Siegen D 81 B4
Siegenburg D 95 C3
Sieghartskirchen A 111 A3
Siegsdorf D 109 B3
Siekierki PL 74 B3
Sielpia PL 87 A4
Siemiany PL 69 B4
Siena I 135 B4
Sieniawka PL 84 B2
Sienno PL 87 A5
Sieppijärvi FIN 196 B7
Sieradz PL 86 A2
Sieraków
*Śląskie* PL 86 B2
*Wielkopolskie* PL 75 B5
Sierakowice PL 68 A2
Sierck-les-Bains F 92 B2
Sierentz F 106 B2
Sierning A 110 A1
Sierpc PL 77 B4
Sierra de Fuentes
E 155 B4
Sierra de Luna E 144 B3
Sierra de Yeguas E 162 A3
Sierre CH 119 A4
Siestrzeń PL 77 B5
Sietamo E 145 B3
Siewierz PL 86 B3
Sigdal N 48 B1
Sigean F 130 B1
Sigerfjord N 194 B6
Sighetu-Marmatiei
RO 17 B5
Sighişoara RO 17 B6
Sigillo I 136 B1
Siglufjörður IS 191 A7
Sigmaringen D 107 A4
Signa I 135 B4
Signes F 132 B1
Signy-l'Abbaye F 91 B4
Signy-le-Petit F 91 B4
Sigogne F 115 C3
Sigri GR 183 D7
Sigtuna S 57 A3
Sigueiro E 140 B2
Sigüenza E 151 A5
Sigües E 144 B2
Sigulda LV 8 D4
Siilinjärvi FIN 8 A5
Sikenica SK 112 A2
Sikfors S 196 D4
Sikia GR 183 C5
Sikinos GR 185 C6
Sikkilsdalseter N 47 A6
Siklós H 125 B4
Sikórz PL 77 B4
Sikselet S 195 D8
Silandro I 108 C1
Silánus I 178 B2
Silbaš SRB 126 B1
Şile TR 187 A4
Siles E 164 A2
Silgueiros P 148 B2
Silifke TR 23 C7
Silíqua I 179 C2
Silistra BG 17 C7
Silivri TR 186 A3
Siljan N 53 A5
Siljansnäs S 50 B1
Silkeborg DK 59 B2
Silla E 159 B3
Sillamäe EST 8 C5
Silleda E 140 B2
Sillé-le-Guillaume
F 102 A1
Sillenstede D 71 A4
Sillerud S 54 A3
Sillian A 109 C3
Silloth GB 36 B3
Silno PL 68 B2
Silnowo PL 68 B1
Silo HR 123 B3
Sils E 147 C3
Silsand N 194 A8
Silte S 57 C4
Šilute LT 12 A4
Silvalen N 195 E3
Silvaplana CH 107 C4
Silvares P 148 B2
Silvberg S 50 B2
Silverdalen S 62 A3
Silvermines IRL 28 B3
Silverstone GB 44 A2
Silverton GB 43 B3
Silves P 160 B1
Silvi Marina I 169 A4
Simandre F 105 C3
Šimanovci SRB 127 C2
Simard F 105 C4
Simat de Valldigna
E 159 B3
Simav TR 186 C3
Simbach
*Bayern* D 95 C4
*Bayern* D 95 C5
Simbário I 175 C2
Simeonovgrad BG 183 A7
Simeria RO 17 C5
Simi GR 188 C2
Simićevo SRB 127 C3
Simitli BG 183 B5
Simlångsdalen S 60 C3
Simmerath D 80 B2
Simmerberg D 107 B4
Simmern D 93 B3
Simo FIN 197 D8
Šimonovce SK 99 C4
Simonsbath GB 43 A3
Simonstorp S 56 B2
Simontornya H 112 C2
Simplon CH 119 A5
Simrishamn S 63 C2
Sinaia RO 17 C6
Sinalunga I 135 B4
Sinarcas E 159 B2
Sincan TR 187 C7
Sincanlı TR 187 D5
Sindal DK 58 A3
Sindelfingen D 93 C5
Sindia I 178 B2
Sındırgı TR 186 C3
Sinekli TR 186 A3
Sines P 160 B1
Sinetta FIN 197 C8
Sineu E 167 B3
Singen D 107 B3
Singleton GB 44 C3
Singsås N 199 C7
Siniscóla I 178 B3
Sinj HR 138 B2
Sinlabajos E 150 A3
Sinn D 81 B4
Sinnai I 179 C3
Sinnes N 52 B2
Sinop TR 23 A8
Sins CH 106 B3
Sinsheim D 93 B4
Sint Annaland NL 79 A4
Sint Annaparochie
NL 70 A2
Sint Athonis NL 80 A1
Sint Nicolaasga NL 70 B2
Sint Oedenrode NL 79 A5
Sintra P 154 C1
Sinzheim D 93 C4
Sinzig D 80 B3
Siófok H 112 C2
Sion CH 119 A4
Sion Mills GB 27 B3
Siorac-en-Périgord
F 129 B3
Šipanska Luka HR 139 C3
Šipovo BIH 138 A3
Sira N 52 B2
Siracusa I 177 B4
Siret RO 17 B7
Sirevåg N 52 B1
Sirig SRB 126 B1
Sirkka FIN 196 B7
Sirmione I 121 B3
Sirniö FIN 197 D11
Sirok H 113 B4
Široké SK 99 C4
Široki Brijeg BIH 139 B3
Sirolo I 136 B2
Siruela E 156 B2
Sisak HR 124 B2
Sisante E 158 B1
Šišljavić HR 123 B4
Sissach CH 106 B2
Sissonne F 91 B3
Sistelo P 140 C2
Sisteron F 132 A1
Sistiana I 122 B2
Sistranda N 198 B5
Sitasjaurestugorna
S 194 C8
Sitges E 147 C2
Sitia GR 185 D7
Sittard NL 80 A1
Sittensen D 72 A2
Sittingbourne GB 45 B4
Sitzenroda D 83 A4
Sivac SRB 126 B1
Sivaslı TR 189 A4
Siverić HR 138 B2
Sivrihisar TR 187 C6
Sixt-Fer-á-Cheval
F 119 A3
Siziano I 120 B2
Sizun F 100 A1
Sjenica SRB 16 D3
Sjoa N 198 D6
Sjøåsen N 199 A8
Sjöbo S 61 D3
Sjøenden
*Hedmark* N 48 A3
*Hedmark* N 48 B3
Sjøholt N 198 C3
Sjøli N 48 A3
Sjølstad N 199 A9
Sjölunda S 56 A1
Sjømarken S 60 B2
Sjørring DK 58 B1
Sjötofta S 60 B3
Sjötorp S 55 B4
Sjoutnäset S 199 A11
Sjøvegan N 194 B8
Sjuntorp S 54 B3
Skåbu N 47 A6
Skafså N 53 A4
Skaftafell IS 191 D9
Skagaströnd IS 190 B5
Skagen DK 58 A3
Skagersvik S 55 B5
Skaiå N 53 B3
Skaidi N 193 B8
Skala GR 184 A1
Skała PL 87 B3
Skaland N 194 A8
Skala Oropou GR 185 A4
Skala-Podilska UA 13 D7
Skalat UA 13 D6
Skalbmierz PL 87 B4
Skålevik N 53 B4
Skalica SK 98 C1
Skalité SK 98 B2
Skällinge S 60 B2
Skalná CZ 83 B4
Skals DK 58 B2
Skælskør DK 65 A4
Skalstugan S 199 B9
Skanderborg DK 59 B2
Skånes-Fagerhult S 61 C3
Skåne-Tranås S 61 D3
Skånevik N 52 A1
Skänninge S 55 B6
Skanör med Falsterbo
S 66 A1
Skåpafors S 54 A3
Skąpe PL 75 B4
Skara S 55 B4
Skærbæk DK 64 A1
Skarberget N 194 B7
Skärblacka S 56 B1
Skarð IS 190 B3
Skarda S 200 B4
Skare N 46 C3
Skåre S 55 A4

**Skärhamn** S 60 B1
**Skarnes** N 48 B3
**Skärplinge** S 51 B4
**Skarpnatö** FIN 51 B6
**Skarp Salling** DK 58 B2
**Skarrild** DK 59 C1
**Skarstad** N 194 B7
**Skärstad** S 62 A2
**Skarsvåg** N 193 A9
**Skarszewy** PL 69 A3
**Skårup** DK 65 A3
**Skärvången** S 199 B11
**Skarvsjöby** S 195 F8
**Skaryszew** PL 87 A5
**Skarżysko-Kamienna** PL 87 A4
**Skarzysko Ksiazece** PL 87 A4
**Skatøy** N 53 B5
**Skattkärr** S 55 A4
**Skattungbyn** S 50 A1
**Skatval** N 199 B7
**Skaulo** S 196 B4
**Skave** DK 59 B1
**Skawina** PL 99 B3
**Skebobruk** S 51 C5
**Skebokvarn** S 56 A2
**Skedala** S 61 C2
**Skedevi** S 56 B1
**Skedsmokorset** N 48 B3
**Skee** S 54 B2
**Skegness** GB 41 B4
**Skei** N 46 A3
**Skela** SRB 127 C2
**Skelani** BIH 127 D1
**Skellefteå** S 2 D7
**Skelleftehamn** S 2 D7
**Skelmersdale** GB 38 A4
**Skelmorlie** GB 34 C3
**Skelund** DK 58 B3
**Skender Vakuf** BIH 138 A3
**Skene** S 60 B2
**Skępe** PL 77 B4
**Skepplanda** S 60 B2
**Skeppshult** S 60 B3
**Skerries** IRL 30 A2
**Ski** N 54 A1
**Skiathos** GR 183 D5
**Skibbereen** IRL 29 C2
**Skibotn** N 192 C4
**Skidra** GR 182 C4
**Skien** N 53 A5
**Skierniewice** PL 77 C5
**Skillingaryd** S 60 B4
**Skillinge** S 63 C2
**Skillingmark** S 49 C4
**Skilloura** CY 181 A2
**Skinnardai** S 57 A4
**Skinnskatteberg** S 50 C2
**Skipmannvik** N 195 C6
**Skipness** GB 34 C2
**Skipsea** GB 41 B3
**Skipton** GB 40 B1
**Skiptvet** N 54 A2
**Skiros** GR 183 E6
**Skivarp** S 66 A2
**Skive** DK 58 B2
**Skjånes** N 193 B12
**Skjærhalden** N 54 A2
**Skjeberg** N 54 A2
**Skjeggedal** N 46 B3
**Skjeljanger** N 46 B1
**Skjeljavik** N 46 C2
**Skjern** DK 59 C1
**Skjervøy** N 192 B4
**Skjold**
*Rogaland* N 52 A1
*Troms* N 192 C3
**Skjoldastraumen** N 52 A1
**Skjolden** N 47 A4
**Skjønhaug** N 54 A2
**Skjøtningsberg** N 193 A11
**Škocjan** SLO 123 B4
**Skoczów** PL 98 B2
**Skodborg** DK 59 C2
**Škofja Loka** SLO 123 A3
**Škofljica** SLO 123 B3
**Skog** S 51 A3
**Skoganvarre** N 193 C9
**Skogen** S 54 A3
**Skogfoss** N 193 C13
**Skoghall** S 55 A4
**Skogly** N 193 C13
**Skogn** N 199 B8
**Skognes** N 192 C3
**Skogstorp**
*Halland* S 60 C2
*Södermanland* S 56 A2
**Skoki** PL 76 B2
**Skokloster** S 57 A3
**Sköldinge** S 56 A2
**Skole** UA 13 D5
**Skollenborg** N 53 A5
**Sköllersta** S 56 A1
**Skomlin** PL 86 A2
**Skonseng** N 195 D5
**Skopelos** GR 183 D5
**Skopje** MK 182 A3
**Skoppum** N 54 A1
**Skórcz** PL 69 B3
**Skorogoszcz** PL 86 B1
**Skoroszów** PL 85 A5
**Skorovatn** N 199 A10
**Skorped** S 200 C3
**Skørping** DK 58 B2
**Skotfoss** N 53 A5
**Skotniki** PL 87 A3
**Skotselv** N 48 C1
**Skotterud** N 49 C4
**Skottorp** S 61 C2
**Skovby** DK 64 B2
**Skövde** S 55 B4
**Skovsgård** DK 58 A2
**Skrad** HR 123 B3
**Skradin** HR 138 B1
**Skradnik** HR 123 B4
**Skråmestø** N 46 B1
**Škrdlovice** CZ 97 B3
**Skrea** S 60 C2
**Skreia** N 48 B2
**Skrolsvik** N 194 A7
**Skruv** S 63 B3
**Skrwilno** PL 77 A4
**Skrydstrup** DK 59 C2
**Skucani** BIH 138 B2
**Skudeneshavn** N 52 A1
**Skui** N 48 C2
**Skulsk** PL 76 B3
**Skultorp** S 55 B4
**Skultuna** S 56 A2
**Skuodas** LT 8 D2
**Skurup** S 66 A2
**Skute** N 48 B2
**Skuteč** CZ 97 B3
**Skutskär** S 51 B4
**Skutvik** N 194 B6
**Skvyra** UA 13 D8
**Skwierzyna** PL 75 B4
**Skýcov** SK 98 C2
**Skyllberg** S 55 B5
**Skyttmon** S 200 C1
**Skyttorp** S 51 B4
**Sládkovičovo** SK 111 A4
**Slagelse** DK 61 D1
**Slagharen** NL 71 B3
**Slagnäs** S 195 E9
**Slaidburn** GB 40 B1
**Slane** IRL 30 A2
**Slangerup** DK 61 D2
**Slano** HR 139 C3
**Slantsy** RUS 8 C6
**Slaný** CZ 84 B2
**Slap** SLO 122 A2
**Šlapanice** CZ 97 B4
**Slåstad** N 48 B3
**Slatina**
BIH 139 B3
HR 125 B3
RO 17 C6
**Slatiňany** CZ 97 B3
**Slatinice** CZ 98 B1
**Slättberg** S 50 A1
**Slattum** N 48 C2
**Slavičin** CZ 98 B1
**Slavkov** CZ 98 C1
**Slavkovica** SRB 127 C2
**Slavkov u Brna** CZ 97 B4
**Slavonice** CZ 97 C3
**Slavonski Brod** HR 125 B4
**Slavonski Kobas** HR 125 B3
**Slavošovce** SK 99 C4
**Slavskoye** RUS 69 A5
**Slavuta** UA 13 C7
**Sława**
*Lubuskie* PL 85 A4
*Zachodnio-Pomorskie* PL 67 C4
**Slawharad** BY 13 B9
**Sławków** PL 86 B3
**Sławno**
*Wielkopolskie* PL 76 B2
*Zachodnio-Pomorskie* PL 68 A1
**Sławoborze** PL 67 C4
**Sl'ažany** SK 98 C2
**Sleaford** GB 40 C3
**Sleðbrjótur** IS 191 B11
**Sledmere** GB 40 A3
**Sleights** GB 37 B6
**Slemmestad** N 54 A1
**Ślesin** PL 76 B3
**Sliač** SK 99 C3
**Sliema** M 175 C3
**Sligo** IRL 26 B2
**Slite** S 57 C4
**Slitu** N 54 A2
**Sliven** BG 17 D7
**Śliwice** PL 68 B3
**Slobozia** RO 17 C7
**Slochteren** NL 71 A3
**Slöinge** S 60 C2
**Słomniki** PL 87 B4
**Slonim** BY 13 B6
**Słońsk** PL 75 B3
**Slootdorp** NL 70 B1
**Slottsbron** S 55 A4
**Slough** GB 44 B3
**Slövag** N 46 B2
**Slovenj Gradec** SLO 110 C2
**Slovenska Bistrica** SLO 123 A4
**Slovenská L'upča** SK 99 C3
**Slovenská-Ves** SK 99 B4
**Slovenské Darmoty** SK 112 A3
**Slovenske Konjice** SLO 123 A4
**Słubice** PL 74 B3
**Sluderno** I 108 C1
**Sluis** NL 78 A3
**Šluknov** CZ 84 A2
**Slunj** HR 123 B4
**Słupca** PL 76 B2
**Słupia** PL 87 A3
**Słupiec** PL 85 B4
**Słupsk** PL 68 A2
**Slutsk** BY 13 B7
**Smålandsstenar** S 60 B3
**Smalåsen** N 195 E4
**Smardzewo** PL 75 B4
**Smarhon** BY 13 A7
**Smarje** SLO 123 A4
**Šmarjeta** SLO 123 B4
**Šmartno** SLO 123 A3
**Smečno** CZ 84 B2
**Smedby** S 63 B4
**Smědec** CZ 96 C2
**Smederevo** SRB 127 C2
**Smederevska Palanka** SRB 127 C2
**Smedjebacken** S 50 B2
**Smęgorzów** PL 87 B5
**Smeland** N 53 B4
**Smidary** CZ 84 B3
**Śmigiel** PL 75 B5
**Smilde** NL 71 B3
**Smiřice** CZ 85 B3
**Smithfield** GB 36 B4
**Śmitowo** PL 75 A5
**Smögen** S 54 B2
**Smogulec** PL 76 A2
**Smołdzino** PL 68 A2
**Smolenice** SK 98 C1
**Smolensk** RUS 13 A10
**Smolník** SK 99 C4
**Smolyan** BG 183 B6
**Smuka** SLO 123 B3
**Smygehamn** S 66 A2
**Smykow** PL 87 A4
**Snainton** GB 40 A3
**Snaith** GB 40 B2
**Snaptun** DK 59 C3
**Snarby** N 192 C3
**Snarum** N 48 B1
**Snåsa** N 199 A9
**Snedsted** DK 58 B1
**Sneek** NL 70 A2
**Sneem** IRL 29 C2
**Snejbjerg** DK 59 B1
**Snillfjord** N 198 B6
**Šnjegotina** BIH 125 C3
**Snøde** DK 65 A3
**Snøfjord** N 193 B8
**Snogebaek** DK 67 A4
**Snyatyn** UA 13 D6
**Soave** I 121 B4
**Sober** E 140 B3
**Sobernheim** D 93 B3
**Soběslav** CZ 96 B2
**Sobota**
*Dolnośląskie* PL 85 A3
*Łódzkie* PL 77 B4
**Sobotište** SK 98 C1
**Sobotka** CZ 84 B3
**Sobótka**
*Dolnośląskie* PL 85 B4
*Wielkopolskie* PL 86 A1
**Sobra** HR 139 C3
**Sobrado**
*Coruña* E 140 A2
*Lugo* E 141 B3
**Sobral da Adica** P 161 A2
**Sobral de Monte Agraço** P 154 C1
**Sobreira Formosa** P 154 B3
**Søby** DK 64 B3
**Soca** SLO 122 A2
**Sochaczew** PL 77 B5
**Sochos** GR 183 C5
**Socodor** RO 113 C5
**Socol** RO 127 C3
**Socovos** E 164 A3
**Socuéllamos** E 158 B1
**Sodankylä** FIN 197 B9
**Soderåkra** S 63 B4
**Söderala** S 51 A3
**Söderås** S 50 B2
**Söderbärke** S 50 B2
**Söderby-Karl** S 51 C5
**Söderfors** S 51 B4
**Söderhamn** S 51 A4
**Söderköping** S 56 B2
**Söderö** S 56 B1
**Södertälje** S 57 A3
**Södingberg** A 110 B2
**Södra Finnö** S 56 B2
**Södra Ny** S 55 A4
**Södra Råda** S 55 A5
**Södra Sandby** S 61 D3
**Södra Vi** S 62 A3
**Sodražica** SLO 123 B3
**Sodupe** E 143 A3
**Soengas** P 148 A1
**Soest**
D 81 A4
NL 70 B2
**Sofades** GR 182 D4
**Sofia = Sofiya** BG 17 D5
**Sofikon** GR 184 B4
**Sofiya = Sofia** BG 17 D5
**Şofronea** RO 126 A3
**Sögel** D 71 B4
**Sogliano al Rubicone** I 135 A5
**Sogndalsfjøra** N 46 A4
**Søgne** N 53 B3
**Sögütköy** TR 188 C3
**Soham** GB 45 A4
**Sohland** D 84 A2
**Sohren** D 93 B3
**Soignies** B 79 B4
**Soissons** F 90 B3
**Söjtör** H 111 C3
**Sokal'** UA 13 C6
**Söke** TR 188 B2
**Sokna** N 48 B1
**Sokndal** N 52 B2
**Soknedal** N 199 C7
**Soko** BIH 125 C4
**Sokolac** BIH 139 B4
**Sokółka** PL 13 B5
**Sokolov** CZ 83 B4
**Sokołowo** PL 76 B3
**Sokołów Podlaski** PL 12 B5
**Sola** N 52 B1
**Solana de los Barros** E 155 C4
**Solana del Pino** E 157 B3
**Solánas** I 179 C3
**Solares** E 143 A3
**Solarino** I 177 B4
**Solarussa** I 179 C2
**Solas** GB 31 B1
**Solberg** S 200 C3
**Solberga** S 62 A2
**Solber-gelva** N 53 A6
**Solbjørg** N 46 B2
**Solčany** SK 98 C2
**Solčava** SLO 123 A3
**Solda** I 108 C1
**Sölden** A 108 C2
**Solec Kujawski** PL 76 A3
**Soleils** F 132 B2
**Solenzara** F 180 B2
**Solera** E 163 A4
**Solesmes** F 79 B3
**Soleto** I 173 B4
**Solgne** F 92 C2
**Solheim** N 46 B2
**Solheimsvik** N 52 A2
**Solignac** F 115 C5
**Solihull** GB 44 A2
**Solin** HR 138 B2
**Solingen** D 80 A3
**Solivella** E 147 C2
**Solkan** SLO 122 B2
**Söll** A 108 B3
**Sollana** E 159 B3
**Sollebrunn** S 54 B3
**Sollefteå** S 200 C3
**Sollenau** A 111 B3
**Sollen-tuna** S 57 A3
**Sóller** E 166 B2
**Sollerön** S 50 B1
**Søllested** DK 65 B4
**Solliès-Pont** F 132 B2
**Sollihøgda** N 48 C2
**Solnechnogorsk** RUS 9 D10
**Solnice** CZ 85 B4
**Solofra** I 170 C2
**Solomiac** F 129 C3
**Solopaca** I 170 B2
**Solórzano** E 143 A3
**Solothurn** CH 106 B2
**Solre-le-Château** F 79 B4
**Solsona** E 147 C2
**Solsvik** N 46 B1
**Solt** H 112 C3
**Soltau** D 72 B2
**Soltsy** RUS 9 C7
**Soltszentimre** H 112 C3
**Soltvadkert** H 112 C3
**Solumsmoen** N 48 C1
**Solund** N 46 A1
**Solva** GB 39 C1
**Sölvesborg** S 63 B2
**Solymár** H 112 B2
**Soma** TR 186 C2
**Somain** F 78 B3
**Somberek** H 125 A4
**Sombernon** F 104 B3
**Sombor** SRB 125 B5
**Sombreffe** B 79 B4
**Someren** NL 80 A1
**Somero** FIN 8 B3
**Somersham** GB 44 A3
**Somerton** GB 43 A4
**Sominy** PL 68 A2
**Somma Lombardo** I 120 B1
**Sommariva del Bosco** I 119 C4
**Sommarøy** N 192 C2
**Sommarset** N 194 C6
**Sommatino** I 176 B2
**Sommeilles** F 91 C4
**Sommen** S 55 B5
**Sommepy-Tahure** F 91 B4
**Sömmerda** D 82 A3
**Sommerfeld** D 74 B2
**Sommersted** DK 59 C2
**Sommesous** F 91 C4
**Somme-Tourbe** F 91 B4
**Sommières** F 131 B3
**Sommières-du-Clain** F 115 B4
**Somo** E 143 A3
**Somogyfajsz** H 111 C4
**Somogyjád** H 111 C4
**Somogysámson** H 111 C4
**Somogysárd** H 125 A3
**Somogyszil** H 112 C2
**Somogyszob** H 124 A3
**Somogyvár** H 111 C4
**Somontin** E 164 B2
**Somosiero** E 151 A4
**Somoskőújfalu** H 113 A3
**Sompolno** PL 76 B3
**Sompuis** F 91 C4
**Son** N 54 A1
**Son Bou** E 167 B4
**Sonceboz** CH 106 B2
**Soncillo** E 143 B3
**Soncino** I 120 B2
**Sóndalo** I 120 A3
**Søndeled** N 53 B5
**Sønder Bjert** DK 59 C2
**Sønderborg** DK 64 B2
**Sønderby** DK 64 B2
**Sønder Felding** DK 59 C1
**Sønderho** DK 59 C1
**Sønder Hygum** DK 59 C1
**Sønder Omme** DK 59 C1
**Sondershausen** D 82 A2
**Søndersø** DK 59 C3
**Søndervig** DK 59 B1
**Søndre Enningdal Kappel** N 54 B2
**Sóndrio** I 120 A2
**Soneja** E 159 B3
**Son en Breugel** NL 80 A1
**Songe** N 53 B5
**Songeons** F 90 B1
**Sonkamuotka** FIN 196 A6
**Sonkovo** RUS 9 D10
**Sönnarslöv** S 61 D4
**Sonneberg** D 82 B3
**Sonnefeld** D 82 B3
**Sonnewalde** D 84 A1
**Sonnino** I 169 B3
**Sonogno** CH 120 A1
**Sonsbeck** D 80 A2
**Sonseca** E 157 A4
**Son Servera** E 167 B3
**Sønsterud** N 49 B4
**Sonstorp** S 56 B1
**Sonta** SRB 125 B5
**Sontheim** D 94 C2
**Sonthofen** D 107 B5
**Sontra** D 82 A1
**Sopelana** E 143 A4
**Sopje** HR 125 B3
**Šoporňa** SK 111 A4
**Sopot**
PL 69 A3
SRB 127 C2
**Sopotnica** MK 182 B3
**Sopron** H 111 B3
**Šor** SRB 127 C1
**Sora** I 169 B3
**Soragna** I 120 C3
**Söråker** S 200 D3
**Sorano** I 168 A1
**Sorbara** I 121 C4
**Sorbas** E 164 B2
**Sórbolo** I 121 C3
**Sörbygden** S 200 D2
**Sordal** N 52 B3
**Sordale** GB 32 C3
**Sore** F 128 B2
**Sörenberg** CH 106 C3
**Soresina** I 120 B2
**Sorèze** F 146 A3
**Sörforsa** S 200 E3
**Sorges** F 115 C4
**Sórgono** I 179 B3
**Sorgues** F 131 A3
**Sorgun** TR 23 B8
**Soria** E 143 C4
**Soriano Cálabro** I 175 C2
**Soriano nel Cimino** I 168 A2
**Sorihuela del Guadalimar** E 164 A1
**Sorisdale** GB 34 B1
**Sørkjosen** N 192 C4
**Sørli** N 199 A10
**Sormás** H 111 C3
**Sörmjöle** S 200 C6
**Sørmo** N 194 B9
**Sornac** F 116 B2
**Sorø** DK 61 D1
**Soroca** MD 17 A8
**Sørreisa** N 194 A9
**Sorrento** I 170 C2
**Sorsele** S 195 E8
**Sörsjön** S 49 A5
**Sorso** I 178 B2
**Sort** E 146 B2
**Sortavala** RUS 9 B7
**Sortino** I 177 B4
**Sortland** N 194 B6
**Sørum** N 48 B2
**Sørumsand** N 48 C3
**Sorunda** S 57 A3
**Sörup** D 64 B2
**Sørvågen** N 194 C3
**Sørvær** N 192 B6
**Sorvik** S 50 B2
**Sørvika** N 199 C8
**Sos** F 128 B3
**Sösdala** S 61 C3
**Sos del Rey Católico** E 144 B2
**Sošice** HR 123 B4
**Sośnica** PL 75 A5
**Sośnicowice** PL 86 B2
**Sośno** PL 76 A2
**Sosnovyy Bor** RUS 9 C6
**Sosnowiec** PL 86 B3
**Sospel** F 133 B3
**Šoštanj** SLO 123 A4
**Sotaseter** N 198 D4
**Sotillo de Adrada** E 150 B3
**Sotillo de la Ribera** E 143 C3
**Sotin** HR 125 B5
**Sotkamo** FIN 3 D11
**Sotobañado y Priorato** E 142 B2
**Soto de la Marina** E 143 A3
**Soto del Barco** E 141 A4
**Soto de los Infantes** E 141 A4
**Soto de Real** E 151 B4
**Soto de Ribera** E 141 A5
**Sotoserrano** E 149 B3
**Soto y Amío** E 141 B5
**Sotresgudo** E 142 B2
**Sotrondio** E 142 A1
**Sotta** F 180 B2
**Sottomarina** I 122 B1
**Sottrum** D 72 A2
**Sottunga** FIN 51 B7
**Sotuelamos** E 158 B1
**Souain** F 91 B4
**Soual** F 146 A3
**Soucy** F 104 A2
**Souda** GR 185 D5
**Soudron** F 91 C4
**Souesmes** F 103 B4
**Soufflenheim** F 93 C3
**Soufli** GR 186 A1
**Souillac** F 129 B4
**Souilly** F 91 B5
**Soulac-sur-Mer** F 114 C2
**Soulaines-Dhuys** F 91 C4
**Soulatgé** F 146 B3
**Soultz-Haut-Rhin** F 106 B2
**Soultz-sous-Forêts** F 93 C3
**Soumagne** B 80 B1
**Soumoulou** F 145 A3
**Souppes-sur-Loing** F 103 A4
**Souprosse** F 128 C2
**Sourdeval** F 88 B3
**Soure** P 154 A2
**Sournia** F 146 B3
**Souro Pires** P 149 B2
**Sourpi** GR 182 D4
**Sours** F 90 C1
**Sousceyrac** F 116 C2
**Sousel** P 155 C3
**Soustons** F 128 C1
**Söğüt**
*Bilecik* TR 187 B5
*Burdur* TR 189 B4
**Soutelo de Montes** E 140 B2
**Southam** GB 44 A2
**Southampton** GB 44 C2
**Southborough** GB 45 B4
**South Brent** GB 42 B3
**South Cave** GB 40 B3
**Southend** GB 34 C2
**Southend-on-Sea** GB 45 B4
**South Hayling** GB 44 C3
**South Molton** GB 42 A3
**South Ockendon** GB 45 B4
**South Petherton** GB 43 B4
**Southport** GB 38 A3
**South Shields** GB 37 B5
**South Tawton** GB 42 B3
**Southwell** GB 40 B3
**Southwold** GB 45 A5
**South Woodham Ferrers** GB 45 B4
**Söğütlu** TR 187 B5
**Souto** P 148 B2
**Soutochao** E 141 C3
**Souto da Carpalhosa** P 154 B2
**Souvigny** F 104 C2
**Souzay-Champigny** F 102 B1
**Soverato** I 175 C2
**Soveria Mannelli** I 175 B2
**Sövestad** S 66 A2
**Sovetsk** RUS 12 A4
**Sovići** BIH 138 B3
**Sovicille** I 135 B4
**Søvik** N 198 C3
**Sowerby** GB 37 B5
**Soyaux** F 115 C4
**Sozopol** BG 17 D7
**Spa** B 80 B1
**Spadafora** I 177 A4
**Spaichingen** D 107 A3
**Spakenburg** NL 70 B2
**Spalding** GB 41 C3
**Spálené Poříčí** CZ 96 B1
**Spalt** D 94 B2
**Spangenberg** D 82 A1
**Spangereid** N 52 B3
**Spantekow** D 74 A2
**Sparanise** I 170 B2
**Sparbu** N 199 B8
**Sparkær** DK 58 B2
**Sparkford** GB 43 A4
**Sparreholm** S 56 A2
**Sparta = Sparti** GR 184 B3
**Spartà** I 177 A4
**Sparti = Sparta** GR 184 B3

Spean Bridge GB 34 B3
Speicher D 92 B2
Speichersdorf D 95 B3
Speke GB 38 A4
Spello I 136 C1
Spenge D 72 B1
Spennymoor GB 37 B5
Spentrup DK 58 B3
Sperenberg D 74 B2
Sperlinga I 177 B3
Sperlonga I 169 B3
Spetalen N 54 A1
Spetses GR 184 B4
Speyer D 93 B4
Spézet F 100 A2
Spezzano Albanese I 174 B2
Spezzano della Sila I 174 B2
Spiddle IRL 28 A2
Spiegelau D 96 C1
Spiekeroog D 71 A4
Spiez CH 106 C2
Spigno Monferrato I 133 A4
Spijk NL 71 A3
Spijkenisse NL 79 A4
Spilamberto I 135 A4
Spili GR 185 D5
Spilimbergo I 122 A1
Spilsby GB 41 B4
Spinazzola I 172 B2
Spincourt F 92 B1
Spind N 52 B2
Spindleruv-Mlyn CZ 84 B3
Spinoso I 174 A1
Špišjć Bukovica HR 124 B3
Spišská Belá SK 99 B4
Spišská Nová Ves SK 99 C4
Spisská Stará Ves SK 99 B4
Spišské-Hanušovce SK 99 B4
Spišské Podhradie SK 99 C4
Spišské Vlachy SK 99 C4
Spišský-Štvrtok SK 99 C4
Spital A 110 B1
Spital am Semmering A 110 B2
Spittal an der Drau A 109 C4
Spittle of Glenshee GB 35 B4
Spitz A 97 C3
Spjald DK 59 B1
Spjærøy N 54 A1
Spjelkavik N 198 C3
Spjutsbygd S 63 B3
Split HR 138 B2
Splügen CH 107 C4
Spodsbjerg DK 65 B3
Spofforth GB 40 B2
Spohle D 71 A5
Spoleto I 136 C1
Spoltore I 169 A4
Spondigna I 108 C1
Sponvika N 54 A2
Spornitz D 73 A4
Spotorno I 133 A4
Spraitbach D 94 C1
Sprakensehl D 72 B3
Spręcowo PL 69 B5
Spremberg D 84 A2
Spresiano I 122 B1
Sprimont B 80 B1
Springe D 72 B2
Sproatley GB 41 B3
Spydeberg N 54 A2
Spytkowice PL 99 B3
Squillace I 175 C2
Squinzano I 173 B4
Sračinec HR 124 A2
Srbac BIH 124 B3
Srbobran SRB 126 B1
Srebrenica BIH 127 C1
Srebrenik BIH 125 C4
Sredets BG 17 D7
Središče SLO 124 A2
Śrem PL 76 B2
Sremska Mitrovica SRB 127 C1
Sremski Karlovci SRB 126 B1
Srní CZ 96 B1
Srnice Gornje BIH 125 C4
Śrock PL 86 A3
Środa Śląska PL 85 A4
Środa Wielkopolski PL 76 B2
Srpska Crnja SRB 126 B2
Srpski Itebej SRB 126 B2
Srpski Miletić SRB 125 B5
Staatz A 97 C4
Stabbursnes N 193 B8
Staberdorf D 65 B4
Stabroek B 79 A4
Stachy CZ 96 B1
Staðarfell IS 190 B3
Stade D 72 A2
Staden B 78 B3
Stadl an der Mur A 109 B4
Stadskanaal NL 71 B3
Stadtallendorf D 81 B5
Stadthagen D 72 B2
Stadtilm D 82 B3
Stadtkyll D 80 B2
Stadtlauringen D 82 B2
Stadtlengsfeld D 82 B2
Stadtlohn D 71 C3
Stadtoldendorf D 82 A1
Stadtroda D 83 B3
Stadtsteinach D 82 B3
Stäfa CH 107 B3
Staffanstorp S 61 D3
Staffelstein D 82 B2
Staffin GB 31 B2
Stafford GB 40 C1
Stainach A 110 B1
Staindrop GB 37 B5
Staines-upon-Thames GB 44 B3
Stainville F 91 C5
Stainz A 110 C2
Staithes GB 37 B6
Staíti I 175 D2
Stäket S 57 A3
Stakroge DK 59 C1
Štalcerji SLO 123 B3
Stalden CH 119 A4
Stalham GB 41 C5
Stalheim N 46 B3
Stallarholmen S 56 A3
Ställberg S 50 C1
Ställdalen S 50 C1
Stallhofen A 110 B2
Stalon S 195 F6
Stalowa Wola PL 12 C5
Stamford GB 40 C3
Stamford Bridge GB 40 B3
Stamnes N 46 B2
Stams A 108 B1
Stamsried D 95 B4
Stamsund N 194 B4
Stanford le Hope GB 45 B4
Stånga S 57 C4
Stange N 48 B3
Stanghella I 121 B4
Stanhope GB 37 B4
Stanišić SRB 125 B5
Staňkov CZ 95 B5
Stankovci HR 137 B4
Stanley GB 37 B5
Stans CH 106 C3
Stansted Mountfitchet GB 45 B4
Stanzach A 108 B1
Stapar SRB 125 B5
Staphorst NL 70 B3
Staplehurst GB 45 B4
Staporków PL 87 A4
Stara Baška HR 123 C3
Starachowice PL 87 A5
Stara Fužina SLO 122 A2
Stara Kamienica PL 84 B3
Stara Kiszewa PL 68 B3
Stará L'ubovnă SK 99 B4
Stara Moravica SRB 126 B1
Stara Novalja HR 137 A3
Stara Pazova SRB 127 C2
Stará Turá SK 98 C1
Staraya Russa RUS 9 D7
Stara Zagora BG 17 D6
Stärbsnäs S 51 C6
Starčevo SRB 127 C2
Stare Dłutowo PL 77 A4
Staré Hamry CZ 98 B2
Stare Jablonki PL 69 B5
Staré Město CZ 98 B1
Stare Pole PL 69 A4
Stare Sedlo CZ 96 B2
Stare Strącze PL 85 A4
Stargard Szczeciński PL 75 A4
Stårheim N 198 D2
Stari Banovci SRB 127 C2
Starigrad
*Ličko-Senjska* HR 123 C3
*Splitsko-Dalmatinska* HR 138 B2
Stari Gradac HR 124 B3
Starigrad-Paklenica HR 137 A4
Stari Jankovci HR 125 B4
Stari Majdan BIH 124 C2
Stari-Mikanovci HR 125 B4
Staritsa RUS 9 D9
Starkenbach A 108 B1
Starnberg D 108 B2
Starogard PL 75 A4
Starogard Gdański PL 69 B3
Starokonstyantyniv UA 13 D7
Staro Petrovo Selo HR 124 B3
Staro Selo
HR 124 B1
SRB 127 C3
Stary Brzozów PL 77 B5
Stary Dzierzgoń PL 69 B4
Starý Hrozenkov CZ 98 C1
Stary Jaroslaw PL 68 A1
Stary Plzenec CZ 96 B1
Stary Sącz PL 99 B4
Starý Smokovec SK 99 B4
Staryy Chartoriysk UA 13 C6
Staškov SK 98 B2
Stassfurt D 82 A3
Staszów PL 87 B5
Stathelle N 53 A5
Staufen D 106 B2
Staunton GB 39 C4
Stavang N 46 A2
Stavanger N 52 B1
Stavåsnäs S 49 B4
Stavby S 51 B5
Staveley GB 40 B2
Stavelot B 80 B1
Stavenisse NL 79 A4
Stavern N 53 B6
Stavnäs S 55 A3
Stavoren NL 70 B2
Stavros
CY 181 A1
GR 183 C5
Stavroupoli GR 183 B6
Stavseng N 47 A6
Stavsiø N 48 B2
Stavsnäs S 57 A4
Stawiszyn PL 76 C3
Steane N 53 A4
Steblevë AL 182 B2
Stechelberg CH 106 C2
Štechovice CZ 96 B2
Stechow D 73 B5
Steckborn CH 107 B3
Stede Broek NL 70 B2
Steeg A 107 B5
Steenbergen NL 79 A4
Steenvoorde F 78 B2
Steenwijk NL 70 B3
Štefanje HR 124 B2
Steffisburg CH 106 C2
Stegaurach D 94 B2
Stege DK 65 B5
Stegelitz D 74 A2
Stegersbach A 111 B3
Stegna PL 69 A4
Steimbke D 72 B2
Stein GB 31 B2
Steinach
A 108 B2
*Baden-Württemberg* D 106 A3
*Bayern* D 82 B2
*Thüringen* D 82 B3
Stein am Rhein CH 107 B3
Steinau
*Bayern* D 81 B5
*Niedersachsen* D 64 C1
Steinbeck D 74 B2
Steinberg am Rofan A 108 B2
Steindorf A 109 C5
Steine N 46 B2
Steinen D 106 B2
Steinfeld
A 109 C4
D 71 B5
Steinfurt D 71 B4
Steingaden D 108 B1
Steinhagen D 72 B1
Steinheid D 82 B3
Steinheim
*Bayern* D 107 A5
*Nordrhein-Westfalen* D 81 A5
Steinhöfel D 74 B3
Steinhorst D 72 B3
Steinigtwolmsdorf D 84 A2
Steinkjer N 199 A8
Steinsholt N 53 A5
Stekene B 79 A4
Stelle D 72 A3
Stellendam NL 79 A4
Stenåsa S 63 B4
Stenay F 91 B5
Stenberga S 62 A3
Stendal D 73 B4
Stenhammar S 55 B4
Stenhamra S 57 A3
Stenhousemuir GB 35 B4
Stenlose DK 61 D2
Stensätra S 50 B3
Stensele S 195 E8
Stenstorp S 55 B4
Stenstrup DK 65 A3
Stenudden S 195 D8
Stenungsund S 54 B2
Štěpánov CZ 98 B1
Stephanskirchen D 108 B3
Stepnica PL 74 A3
Stepojevac SRB 127 C2
Stepping DK 59 C2
Sterbfritz D 82 B1
Sternberg D 65 C4
Šternberk CZ 98 B1
Sterup D 64 B2
Stes Maries-de-la-Mer F 131 B3
Stęszew PL 75 B5
Štětí CZ 84 B2
Stevenage GB 44 B3
Stewarton GB 36 A2
Steyerburg D 72 B2
Steyning GB 44 C3
Steyr A 110 A1
Stężyca PL 68 A2
Stezzano I 120 B2
Stia I 135 B4
Stibb Cross GB 42 B2
Sticciano Scalo I 135 C4
Stidsvig S 61 C3
Stiens NL 70 A2
Stige DK 59 C3
Stigen S 54 B3
Stigliano I 174 A2
Stigtomta S 56 B2
Stilida GR 182 E4
Stilla N 192 C7
Stillington GB 40 A2
Stilo I 175 C2
Stintino I 178 B2
Stio I 172 B1
Štip MK 182 B4
Stira GR 185 A5
Stirling GB 35 B4
Štítnik SK 99 C4
Štíty CZ 97 B4
Stjärnhov S 56 A3
Stjärnsund S 50 B3
Stjørdalshalsen N 199 B7
Stobnica PL 87 A3
Stobno PL 75 A5
Stobreč HR 138 B2
Stochov CZ 84 B1
Stockach D 107 B4
Stöckalp CH 106 C3
Stockaryd S 62 A2
Stockbridge GB 44 B2
Stockerau A 97 C4
Stockheim D 82 B3
Stockholm S 57 A4
Stockport GB 40 B1
Stocksbridge GB 40 B2
Stockton-on-Tees GB 37 B5
Stod CZ 96 B1
Stöde S 200 D2
Stødi N 195 D6
Stöðvarfjörður IS 191 C12
Stoer GB 32 C1
Stoholm DK 58 B2
Stoke Ferry GB 41 C4
Stoke Fleming GB 43 B3
Stoke Mandeville GB 44 B3
Stoke-on-Trent GB 40 B1
Stokesley GB 37 B5
Stokke N 54 A1
Stokkemarke DK 65 B4
Stokken N 53 B4
Stokkseyri IS 190 D4
Stokkvågen N 195 D4
Stokmarknes N 194 B5
Štoky CZ 97 B3
Stolac BIH 139 B3
Stølaholmen N 46 A3
Stolberg D 80 B2
Stolin BY 13 C7
Stollberg D 83 B4
Stöllet S 49 B5
Stollhamm D 71 A5
Stolno PL 76 A3
Stolpen D 84 A2
Stolzenau D 72 B2
Stompetoren NL 70 B1
Ston HR 139 C3
Stonařov CZ 97 B3
Stone GB 40 C1
Stonehaven GB 33 E4
Stonehouse GB 36 A3
Stongfjorden N 46 A2
Stonndalen N 47 B4
Stony Stratford GB 44 A3
Stopnica PL 87 B4
Storå S 56 A1
Storås N 198 B6
Storby FIN 51 B6
Stordal
*Møre og Romsdal* N 198 C4
*Nord-Trøndelag* N 199 B8
Store GB 33 B4
Storebø N 46 B2
Storebro S 62 A3
Store Damme DK 65 B5
Store Heddinge DK 65 A5
Store Herrestad S 66 A2
Store Levene S 55 B3
Storelv N 192 B6
Store Molvik N 193 B12
Støren N 199 B7
Store Skedvi S 50 B2
Store Vika S 57 B3
Storfjellseter N 199 D7
Storfjord N 192 C3
Storfjorden N 198 C3
Storfors S 55 A5
Storforshei N 195 D5
Storhøliseter N 47 A6
Storjord N 195 D6
Storkow
*Brandenburg* D 74 B2
*Mecklenburg-Vorpommern* D 74 A3
Storli N 198 C6
Storlien S 199 B9
Stornara I 171 B3
Stornoway GB 31 A2
Storo I 121 B3
Storozhynets UA 17 A6
Storrington GB 44 C3
Storseleby S 200 B2
Storsjön S 50 A3
Storslett N 192 C5
Storsteinnes N 192 C3
Storsund S 196 D3
Storuman S 195 E8
Störvattnet S 199 C9
Storvik
N 195 D4
S 50 B3
Storvreta S 51 C4
Štos SK 99 C4
Stössen D 83 A3
Stotel D 72 A1
Stötten D 108 B1
Stotternheim D 82 A3
Stouby DK 59 C2
Stourbridge GB 40 C1
Stourport-on-Severn GB 39 B4
Støvring DK 58 B2
Stow GB 35 C5
Stowbtsy BY 13 B7
Stowmarket GB 45 A5
Stow-on-the-Wold GB 44 B2
Straach D 73 C5
Strabane GB 27 B3
Strachan GB 33 D4
Strachur GB 34 B2
Stracin MK 182 A4
Strackholt D 71 A4
Stradbally IRL 29 B1
Stradella I 120 B2
Straelen D 80 A2
Stragari SRB 127 C2
Strakonice CZ 96 B1
Strålsnäs S 55 B6
Stralsund D 66 B2
Strand N 48 A3
Stranda N 198 C3
Strandby DK 58 A3
Strandebarm N 46 B3
Strandhill IRL 26 B2
Strandlykkja N 48 B3
Strandvik N 46 B2
Strangford GB 27 B5
Strängnäs S 56 A3
Strångsjö S 56 B2
Stráni CZ 98 C1
Stranice SLO 123 A4
Stranorlar IRL 26 B3
Stranraer GB 36 B1
Strasatti I 176 B1
Strasbourg F 93 C3
Strasburg D 74 A2
Strašice CZ 96 B1
Stråssa S 56 A1
Strassburg A 110 C1
Strass im Steiermark A 110 C2
Strasskirchen D 95 C4
Strasswalchen A 109 B4
Stratford-upon-Avon GB 44 A2
Strathaven GB 36 A2
Strathdon GB 32 D3
Strathkanaird GB 32 D1
Strathpeffer GB 32 D2
Strathy GB 32 C3
Strathyre GB 34 B3
Stratinska BIH 124 C2
Stratton GB 42 B2
Straubing D 95 C4
Straulas I 178 B3
Straume N 53 A5
Straumen
*Nordland* N 194 C6
*Nord-Trøndelag* N 199 B8
Straumsjøen N 194 B5
Straumsnes N 194 C6
Straupitz D 74 C3
Strausberg D 74 B2
Straussfurt D 82 A3
Strawczyn PL 87 B4
Straža
SLO 123 B4
SRB 127 C3
Stražnad Nezárkou CZ 96 B2
Strážnice CZ 98 C1
Strážný CZ 96 C1
Stráž Pod Ralskem CZ 84 B2
Štrbské Pleso SK 99 B4
Strečno SK 98 B2
Street GB 43 A4
Strehla D 83 A5
Strekov SK 112 B2
Strem A 111 B3
Stremska-Rača SRB 127 C1
Strengberg A 110 A1
Strengelvåg N 194 B6
Stresa I 119 B5
Streufdorf D 82 B2
Strib DK 59 C2
Striberg S 55 A5
Stříbro CZ 95 B4
Strichen GB 33 D4
Strigno I 121 A4
Štrigova HR 111 C3
Strijen NL 79 A4
Strizivojna HR 125 B4
Strmica HR 138 A2
Strmilov CZ 97 B3
Ströhen D 72 B1
Strokestown IRL 28 A3
Stromberg
*Nordrhein-Westfalen* D 81 A4
*Rheinland-Pfalz* D 93 B3
Stromeferry GB 31 B3
Strömnäs S 200 B2
Stromness GB 33 C3
Strömsberg S 51 B4
Strömsbruk S 200 E3
Strömsfors S 56 B2
Strömsnäsbruk S 61 C3
Strömstad S 54 B2
Strömsund
*Jämtland* S 199 B12
*Västerbotten* S 195 E7
Stronachlachar GB 34 B3
Stróngoli I 174 B3
Stronie Śląskie PL 85 B4
Strontian GB 34 B2
Stroppiana I 119 B5
Stroud GB 43 A4
Stroumbi CY 181 B1
Stróża PL 99 B3
Strücklingen D 71 A4
Struer DK 58 B1
Struga MK 182 B2
Strugi Krasnyye RUS 9 C6
Strumica MK 182 B4
Strumien PL 98 B2
Struy GB 32 D2
Stružec HR 124 B2
Stryków PL 77 C4
Stryn N 198 D3
Stryy UA 13 D5
Strzałkowo PL 76 B2
Strzegocin PL 77 B5
Strzegom PL 85 B4
Strzegowo PL 77 B5
Strzelce PL 77 B4
Strzelce Krajeńskie PL 75 B4
Strzelce Kurowo PL 75 B4
Strzelce Opolskie PL 86 B2
Strzelin PL 85 B5
Strzelno PL 76 B3
Strzepcz PL 68 A3
Strzybnica PL 86 B2
Strzygi PL 77 A4
Stubbekøbing DK 65 B5
Stuben A 107 B5
Stubenberg A 110 B2
Stubline SRB 127 C2
Studená CZ 97 B3
Studenci HR 138 B3
Studenka CZ 98 B2
Studenzen A 110 B2
Studienka SK 98 C1
Studland GB 43 B5
Studley GB 44 A2
Studzienice PL 68 A2
Stuer D 73 A5
Stugudal N 199 C8
Stugun S 200 C1
Stuhr D 72 A1
Stukenbrock D 81 A4
Stülpe D 74 B2
Stupava SK 111 A4
Stupnik HR 124 B1
Stupsk PL 77 A5
Sturkö S 63 B3
Sturminster Newton GB 43 B4
Štúrovo SK 112 B2
Sturton GB 40 B3
Stuttgart D 94 C1
Stvolny CZ 96 A1
Stykkishólmur IS 190 B3
Styri N 48 B3
Stysö S 60 B1
Suances E 142 A2
Subbiano I 135 B4
Subiaco I 169 B3
Subotica SRB 126 A1
Subotište SRB 127 C1
Sučany SK 98 B2
Suceava RO 17 B7
Sucha-Beskidzka PL 99 B3
Suchacz PL 69 A4
Suchań PL 75 A4
Suchdol nad Lužnice CZ 96 C2
Suchedniów PL 87 A4
Suchorze PL 68 A2
Suchteln D 80 A2
Sucina E 165 B4
Suckow D 73 A4
Sućuraj HR 138 B3
Súðavík IS 190 A3
Sudbury GB 45 A4
Suddesjaur S 195 E10
Suden D 64 B1
Süderbrarup D 64 B2
Süderlügum D 64 B1
Sudoměřice u Bechyně CZ 96 B2
Sudovec HR 124 A2
Suðureyri IS 190 A2
Sueca E 159 B3
Suelli I 179 C3
Sugenheim D 94 B2
Sugères F 117 B3
Sugny B 91 B4
Suhl D 82 B2
Suhlendorf D 73 B3
Suhopolje HR 124 B3
Suho Polje BIH 125 C5
Şuhut TR 189 A5
Šuica BIH 138 B3
Suippes F 91 B4
Sukošan HR 137 A4
Sükösd H 125 A4

Suków PL 87 B4
Šul'a SK 99 C3
Suldalsosen N 52 A2
Suldrup DK 58 B2
Sulechów PL 75 B4
Sulęcin PL 75 B4
Sulęczyno PL 68 A2
Sulejów PL 87 A3
Süleymanlı TR 186 D2
Sulgen CH 107 B4
Sulibórz PL 75 A4
Sulina RO 17 C8
Sulingen D 72 B1
Suliszewo PL 75 A4
Sulitjelma N 195 C7
Sułkowice PL 99 B3
Süller TR 189 A4
Sully-sur-Loire F 103 B4
Sulmierzyce
*Łódzkie* PL 86 A3
*Wielkopolskie* PL 85 A5
Sulmona I 169 A3
Süloğlu TR 186 A1
Sułoszowa PL 87 B3
Sulów PL 85 A5
Sulsdorf D 65 B4
Sultandağı TR 189 A6
Sülüklü TR 187 D7
Suluova TR 23 A8
Sulvik S 54 A3
Sülysáp H 112 B3
Sülz D 93 C4
Sulzbach
*Baden-Württemberg* D 94 B1
*Baden-Württemberg* D 94 C1
*Bayern* D 93 B5
*Saarland* D 92 B3
Sulzbach-Rosenberg D 95 B3
Sülze D 72 B3
Sulzfeld D 82 B2
Sumartin HR 138 B2
Sumburgh GB 33 B5
Sümeg H 111 C4
Sumiswald CH 106 B2
Šumná CZ 97 C3
Šumperk CZ 97 B4
Šumvald CZ 98 B1
Sunbilla E 144 A2
Sünching D 95 C4
Sund
FIN 51 B7
S 54 A2
Sundborn S 50 B2
Sundby DK 58 B1
Sunde N 46 C2
Sunde bru N 53 B5
Sunderland GB 37 B5
Sundern D 81 A4
Sundhultsbrunn S 62 A2
Sundnäs S 195 D8
Sundom S 196 D5
Sunds DK 59 B2
Sundsfjord N 195 D5
Sundsvall S 200 D3
Sungurlu TR 23 A8
Suni I 178 B2
Sunja HR 124 B2
Sunnansjö S 50 B1
Sunnaryd S 60 B3
Sunndalsøra N 198 C5
Sunne S 49 C5
Sunnemo S 49 C5
Sunnersberg S 55 B4
Suolovuopmio N 192 C7
Suomussalmi FIN 3 D11
Suoyarvi RUS 9 A8
Super Sauze F 132 A2
Supetar HR 138 B2
Supetarska Draga HR 123 C3
Supino I 169 B3
Šuplja Stijena MNE 139 B5
Surahammar S 56 A2
Šurany SK 112 A2
Surazh BY 13 A9
Surbo I 173 B4
Surčin SRB 127 C2
Surgères F 114 B3
Surhuisterveen NL 70 A3
Sùria E 147 C2
Surin F 115 B4
Surka N 48 B2
Surnadalsøra N 198 C5
Sursee CH 106 B3
Surte S 60 B2
Surwold D 71 B4
Sury-le-Comtal F 117 B4
Susa I 119 B4
Šušara SRB 127 C3
Susch CH 107 C5
Susegana I 122 B1
Süsel D 65 B3
Sušice CZ 96 B1
Šušnjevica HR 123 B3
Sussen D 94 C1
Susurluk TR 186 C3
Susz PL 69 B4
Sütçüler TR 189 B5
Sutivan HR 138 B2
Sutjeska SRB 126 B2
Sutri I 168 A2
Sutton GB 44 B3
Sutton Coldfield GB 40 C2
Sutton-in-Ashfield GB 40 B2
Sutton-on-Sea GB 41 B4
Sutton-on-Trent GB 40 B3
Sutton Scotney GB 44 B2
Sutton Valence GB 45 B4
Suvaja BIH 124 C2
Suvereto I 135 B3
Suwałki PL 12 A5
Suze-la-Rousse F 131 A3
Suzzara I 121 C3
Svabensverk S 50 A2
Svalbarð IS 191 A10
Svalöv S 61 D3
Svanabyn S 200 B2
Svanberga S 51 C5
Svaneke DK 67 A4
Svanesund S 54 B2
Svängsta S 63 B2
Svannäs S 195 D9
Svanskog S 54 A3
Svanstein S 196 C6
Svappavaara S 196 B4
Svärdsjö S 50 B2
Svarstad N 53 A5
Svartå S 55 A5
Svärta S 56 B3
Svartå S 55 A4
Svartbyn S 196 C5
Svärtinge S 56 B2
Svartlå S 196 D4
Svartnäs S 50 B3
Svartnes N 195 C5
Svarttjärn S 195 E7
Svatsum N 48 A1
Svätý Jur SK 111 A4
Svätý Peter SK 112 B2
Svedala S 61 D3
Sveg S 199 C11
Sveindal N 52 B3
Sveio N 52 A1
Svejbæk DK 59 B2
Svelgen N 198 D2
Svelvik N 54 A1
Svendborg DK 65 A3
Svene N 53 A5
Svenljunga S 60 B3
Svennevad S 56 A1
Svenstavik S 199 C11
Svenstrup DK 58 B2
Švermov CZ 84 B2
Sveti Ivan Zabno HR 124 B2
Sveti Ivan Zelina HR 124 B2
Sveti Nikole MK 182 B3
Sveti Rok HR 137 A4
Světla nad Sázavou CZ 97 B3
Svetlyy RUS 69 A5
Svetvinčenat HR 122 B2
Švica HR 123 C4
Svidník SK 12 D4
Švihov CZ 96 B1
Svilajnac SRB 127 C3
Svilengrad BG 183 B8
Svindal N 54 A2
Svinhult S 62 A3
Svinna SK 98 C2
Svinninge
DK 61 D1
S 57 A4
Sviritsa RUS 9 B8
Svishtov BG 17 D6
Svislach BY 13 B6
Svit SK 99 B4
Svitavy CZ 97 B4
Svodin SK 112 B2
Svolvær N 194 B5
Svortemyr N 46 A2
Svortland N 52 A1
Svratka CZ 97 B4
Svrčinovec SK 98 B2
Svullrya N 49 B4
Svyetlahorsk BY 13 B8
Swadlincote GB 40 C2
Swaffham GB 41 C4
Swanage GB 43 B5
Swanley GB 45 B4
Swanlinbar IRL 26 B3
Swansea GB 39 C3
Swarzędz PL 76 B2
Swatragh GB 27 B4
Świątki PL 69 B5
Świdnica
*Dolnośląskie* PL 85 B4
*Lubuskie* PL 84 A3
Świdnik PL 12 C5
Świdwin PL 67 C4
Świebodzice PL 85 B4
Świebodzin PL 75 B4
Świecie PL 76 A3
Świedziebnia PL 77 A4
Świeradów Zdrój PL 84 B3
Świerki PL 85 B4
Swierzawa PL 85 A3
Swierzno PL 67 C3
Swięta PL 74 A3
Swieta Anna PL 86 B3
Świętno PL 75 B5
Swifterbant NL 70 B2
Swindon GB 44 B2
Swineshead GB 41 C3
Swinford IRL 26 C2
Świnoujście PL 66 C3
Swinton GB 35 C5
Swobnica PL 74 A3
Swords IRL 30 A2
Swornegacie PL 68 B2
Sya S 56 B1
Syasstroy RUS 9 B8
Sycewice PL 68 A1
Sychevka RUS 9 E9
Syców PL 86 A1
Sycowice PL 75 B4
Sydnes N 52 A1
Syfteland N 46 B2
Syke D 72 B1
Sykkylven N 198 C3
Sylling N 48 C2
Sylte N 198 C4
Symbister GB 33 A5
Symington GB 36 A3
Symonds Yat GB 39 C4
Sypniewo
*Kujawsko-Pomorskie* PL 76 A2
*Wielkopolskie* PL 68 B1
Syserum S 62 A4
Sysslebäck S 49 B4
Syväjärvi FIN 197 B8
Szabadbattyán H 112 B2
Szabadegyháza H 112 B2
Szabadszállás H 112 C3
Szadek PL 86 A2
Szajol H 113 B4
Szakály H 112 C2
Szakcs H 112 C2
Szakmár H 112 C3
Szalánta H 125 B4
Szałas PL 87 A4
Szalkszentmárton H 112 C3
Szalonna H 99 C4
Szamocin PL 76 A2
Szamotuły PL 75 B5
Szany H 111 B4
Szarvas H 113 C4
Szarvaskő H 113 B4
Szászvár H 125 A4
Százhalombatta H 112 B2
Szczawa PL 99 B4
Szczawnica PL 99 B4
Szczecin PL 74 A3
Szczecinek PL 68 B1
Szczekociny PL 87 B3
Szczerców PL 86 A3
Szczucin PL 87 B5
Szczuczarz PL 75 A5
Szczuki PL 77 B5
Szczurowa PL 87 B4
Szczyrk PL 99 B3
Szczytna PL 85 B4
Szczytno PL 77 A5
Szczyty PL 86 A2
Szécsény H 112 A3
Szederkény H 125 B4
Szedres H 112 C2
Szeged H 126 A2
Szeghalom H 113 B5
Szegvár H 113 C4
Székesfehérvár H 112 B2
Székkutas H 113 C4
Szekszárd H 125 A4
Szemplino Czarne PL 77 A5
Szemud PL 68 A3
Szendehely H 112 B3
Szendrö H 99 C4
Szentendre H 112 B3
Szentes H 113 C4
Szentgotthárd H 111 C3
Szentlászló H 125 A3
Szentlörinc H 125 A3
Szentmártonkáta H 113 B3
Szenyér H 111 C4
Szeremle H 125 A4
Szerencs H 113 A5
Szerep H 113 B5
Szigetszentmiklós H 112 B3
Szigetvár H 125 A3
Szikáncs H 126 A2
Szikszó H 113 A4
Szil H 111 B4
Szilvásvárad H 113 A4
Szklarska Poreba PL 84 B3
Szlichtyngowa PL 85 A4
Szob H 112 B2
Szolnok H 113 B4
Szombathely H 111 B3
Szorosad H 112 C2
Szpetal Graniczny PL 77 B4
Szprotawa PL 84 A3
Szreńsk PL 77 A5
Sztum PL 69 B4
Sztutowo PL 69 A4
Szubin PL 76 A2
Szücsi H 113 B3
Szulmierz PL 77 B5
Szulok H 124 A3
Szumanie PL 77 B4
Szwecja PL 75 A5
Szydłów
*Łódzkie* PL 86 A3
*Świętokrzyskie* PL 87 B5
Szydłowiec PL 87 A4
Szydlowo PL 77 A5
Szydłowo PL 75 A5
Szymanów PL 77 B5
Szynkielów PL 86 A2

## T

Taastrup DK 61 D2
Tab H 112 C2
Tabanera la Luenga E 151 A3
Tabaqueros E 158 B2
Tábara E 149 A4
Tabenera de Cerrato E 142 B2
Taberg S 62 A2
Tabernas E 164 B2
Tabiano Bagni I 120 C3
Taboada E 140 B3
Taboadela E 140 B3
Tábor CZ 96 B2
Táborfalva H 112 B3
Taborište HR 124 B2
Tábua P 148 B1
Tabuaco P 148 A2
Tabuenca E 152 A2
Tabuyo del Monte E 141 B4
Täby S 57 A4
Tác H 112 B2
Tachov CZ 95 B4
Tadcaster GB 40 B2
Tadley GB 44 B2
Tafalla E 144 B2
Tafjord N 198 C4
Taganheira P 160 B1
Tågarp S 61 D2
Tággia I 133 B3
Tagliacozzo I 169 A3
Táglio di Po I 121 B5
Tagnon F 91 B4
Tahal E 164 B2
Tahitótfalu H 112 B3
Tahtaköprü TR 187 C4
Tailfingen D 107 A4
Taillis F 101 A4
Tain GB 32 D2
Tain-l'Hermitage F 117 B4
Taipadas P 154 C2
Taivalkoski FIN 197 D11
Takene S 55 A4
Takovo SRB 127 C2
Taksony H 112 B3
Tal E 140 B2
Talachyn BY 13 A8
Talamello I 135 B5
Talamone I 168 A1
Talant F 105 B3
Talarrubias E 156 A2
Talaván E 155 B4
Talavera de la Reina E 150 C3
Talavera la Real E 155 C4
Talayuela E 150 C2
Talayuelas E 159 B2
Talgarth GB 39 C3
Talgje N 52 A1
Talhadas P 148 B1
Táliga E 155 C3
Talizat F 116 B3
Tálknafjörður IS 190 B2
Talla I 135 B4
Talladale GB 31 B3
Tallaght IRL 30 A2
Tallard F 132 A2
Tällberg S 50 B1
Tallberg S 196 C5
Tallinn EST 8 C4
Talloires F 118 B3
Tallow IRL 29 B3
Tallsjö S 200 B4
Tallvik S 196 C5
Talmay F 105 B4
Talmont-St Hilaire F 114 B2
Talmont-sur-Gironde F 114 C3
Talne UA 13 D9
Talsano I 173 B3
Talsi LV 8 D3
Talvik N 192 B6
Talybont GB 39 B3
Tal-Y-Llyn GB 38 B3
Tamajón E 151 B4
Tamame E 149 A4
Tamames E 149 B3
Tamarit de Mar E 147 C2
Tamarite de Litera E 145 C4
Tamariu E 147 C4
Tamási H 112 C2
Tambach-Dietharz D 82 B2
Tameza E 141 A4
Tammisaari FIN 8 B3
Tampere FIN 8 B3
Tamsweg A 109 B4
Tamurejo E 156 B3
Tamworth GB 40 C2
Tana bru N 193 B12
Tañabueyes E 143 B3
Tanakajd H 111 B3
Tananger N 52 B1
Tanaunella I 178 B3
Tancarville F 89 A4
Tandsjöborg S 199 D11
Tånga S 61 C2
Tangelic H 112 C2
Tangen N 48 B3
Tangerhütte D 73 B4
Tangermünde D 73 B4
Tanhua FIN 197 B10
Taninges F 118 A3
Tankavaara FIN 197 A10
Tann D 82 B2
Tanna D 83 B3
Tannadice GB 35 B5
Tannåker S 60 C3
Tännäs S 199 C9
Tannay
*Ardennes* F 91 B4
*Nièvre* F 104 B2
Tannenbergsthal D 83 B4
Tännesberg D 95 B4
Tannheim A 108 B1
Tannila FIN 197 D8
Tanowo PL 74 A3
Tanum S 54 B2
Tanumshede S 54 B2
Tanus F 130 A1
Tanvald CZ 84 B3
Taormina I 177 B4
Tapa EST 8 C4
Tapfheim D 94 C2
Tapia de Casariego E 141 A4
Tapio F 146 A2
Tápióbicske H 112 B3
Tápiógyörgye H 113 B3
Tápióság H 112 B3
Tápiószecső H 112 B3
Tápiószele H 113 B3
Tápiószentmárton H 113 B3
Tapolca H 111 C4
Tapolcafő H 111 B4
Tar HR 122 B2
Tarabo S 60 B2
Taradell E 147 C3
Taraklı TR 187 B5
Taramundi E 141 A3
Tarancón E 151 B4
Táranto I 173 B3
Tarare F 117 B4
Tarascon F 131 B3
Tarascon-sur-Ariège F 146 B2
Tarashcha UA 13 D9
Tarazona E 144 C2
Tarazona de la Mancha E 158 B2
Tarbena E 159 C3
Tarbert
GB 34 C2
IRL 29 B2
Tarbes F 145 A4
Tarbet GB 34 B3
Tarbolton GB 36 A2
Tarcento I 122 A2
Tarčin BIH 139 B4
Tarczyn PL 77 C5
Tardajos E 143 B3
Tardelcuende E 151 A5
Tardets-Sorholus F 144 A3
Tardienta E 145 C3
Tärendö S 196 B5
Targon F 128 B2
Târgovişte RO 17 C6
Târgu-Jiu RO 17 C5
Târgu Mureş RO 17 B6
Târgu Ocna RO 17 B7
Târgu Secuiesc RO 17 C7
Tarifa E 162 B2
Tariquejas E 161 B2
Tarján H 112 B2
Tárkany H 112 B2
Tarland GB 33 D4
Tarłów PL 87 A5
Tarm DK 59 C1
Tarmstedt D 72 A2
Tärnaby S 195 E6
Tarnalelesz H 113 A4
Tarnaörs H 113 B4
Târnăveni RO 17 B6
Tårnet N 193 C14
Tarnobrzeg PL 87 B5
Tarnos F 128 C1
Tarnów
*Lubuskie* PL 75 B3
*Małopolskie* PL 87 B4
Tarnowo Podgórne PL 75 B5
Tarnowskie Góry PL 86 B2
Tärnsjö S 51 B3
Tårnvik N 194 C6
Tarouca P 148 A2
Tarp D 64 B2
Tarquínia I 168 A1
Tarquínia Lido I 168 A1
Tarragona E 147 C2
Tårrajaur S 196 C2
Tàrrega E 147 C2
Tarrenz A 108 B1
Tårs
*Nordjyllands* DK 58 A3
*Storstrøms* DK 65 B4
Tarsia I 174 B2
Tarsus TR 23 C8
Tartas F 128 C2
Tartu EST 8 C5
Tarves GB 33 D4
Tarvisio I 109 C4
Taşağıl TR 189 C6
Täsch CH 119 A4
Taşköprü TR 23 A8
Tasov CZ 97 B4
Tasovčići BIH 139 B3
Taşucuo TR 23 C7
Tát H 112 B2
Tata H 112 B2
Tatabánya H 112 B2
Tataháza H 126 A1
Tatarbunary UA 17 C8
Tatárszentgyörgy H 112 B3
Tatranská-Lomnica SK 99 B4
Tau N 52 A1
Tauberbischofsheim D 94 B1
Taucha D 83 A4
Taufkirchen D 95 C4
Taufkirchen an der Pram A 96 C1
Taulé F 100 A2
Taulignan F 131 A3
Taulov DK 59 C2
Taunton GB 43 A3
Taunusstein D 81 B4
Tauragė LT 12 A5
Taurianova I 175 C2
Taurisano I 173 C4
Tauste E 144 C2
Tauves F 116 B2
Tavankut SRB 126 A1
Tavannes CH 106 B2
Tavarnelle val di Pesa I 135 B4
Tavas TR 188 B4
Tavaux F 105 B4
Tävelsås S 62 B2
Taverna I 175 B2
Taverne CH 120 A1
Tavernelle I 135 B5
Tavernes de la Valldigna E 159 B3
Tavérnola Bergamasca I 120 B3
Taverny F 90 B2
Tavescan E 146 B2
Taviano I 173 C4
Tavira P 160 B2
Tavistock GB 42 B2
Tavşanlı TR 187 C4
Tayinloan GB 34 C2
Taynuilt GB 34 B2
Tayport GB 35 B5
Tázlár H 112 C3
Tazones E 142 A1
Tczew PL 69 A3
Tczów PL 87 A5
Teangue GB 31 B3
Teano I 170 B2
Teba E 162 B3
Tebay GB 37 B4
Techendorf A 109 C4
Tecklenburg D 71 B4
Tecko-matorp S 61 D3
Tecuci RO 17 C7
Tefenni TR 189 B4
Tegelsmora S 51 B4
Tegernsee D 108 B2
Teggiano I 172 B1
Tegoleto I 135 B4
Teichel D 82 B3
Teignmouth GB 43 B3
Teillay F 101 B4
Teillet F 130 B1
Teisendorf D 109 B3
Teistungen D 82 A2
Teixeiro E 140 A2
Tejada de Tiétar E 150 B2
Tejado E 152 A1
Tejares E 150 B2
Tejn DK 67 A3
Teke TR 187 A4
Tekirdağ TR 186 B2
Tekovské-Lužany SK 112 A2
Telavåg N 46 B1
Telč CZ 97 B3
Telese Terme I 170 B2
Telford GB 38 B4
Telfs A 108 B2
Telgárt SK 99 C4
Telgte D 71 C4
Tellingstedt D 64 B2
Telšiai LT 8 E3
Telti I 178 B3
Teltow D 74 B2
Tembleque E 157 A4
Temelin CZ 96 B2
Temerin SRB 126 B1
Temiño E 143 B3
Témpio Pausánia I 178 B3
Templederry IRL 28 B3
Templemore IRL 28 B4
Temple Sowerby GB 37 B4
Templin D 74 A2
Temse B 79 A4
Tenay F 118 B2
Ten Boer NL 71 A3
Tenbury Wells GB 39 B4
Tenby GB 39 C2
Tence F 117 B4
Tende F 133 A3
Tenhult S 62 A2
Tenja HR 125 B4
Tenneville B 92 A1
Tennevoll N 194 B8
Tensta S 51 B4
Tenterden GB 45 B4

Teo E 140 B2
Teora I 172 B1
Tepasto FIN 196 B7
Tepelenë AL 182 C2
Teplá CZ 95 B4
Teplice CZ 84 B1
Teplička nad Váhom SK 98 B2
Tepsa FIN 197 B8
Tera E 143 C4
Téramo I 169 A3
Ter Apel NL 71 B4
Terborg NL 71 C3
Terchová SK 99 B3
Terebovlya UA 13 D6
Teremia Mare RO 126 B2
Terena P 155 C3
Teresa de Cofrentes E 159 B2
Terešov CZ 96 B1
Terezín CZ 84 B2
Terezino Polje HR 124 B3
Tergnier F 90 B3
Teriberka RUS 3 B14
Terlizzi I 171 B4
Termas de Monfortinho P 155 A4
Terme di Súio I 169 B3
Terme di Valdieri I 133 A3
Termens E 145 C4
Termes F 116 C3
Términi Imerese I 176 B2
Terminillo I 169 A2
Térmoli I 170 B3
Termonfeckin IRL 27 C4
Ternberg A 110 B1
Terndrup DK 58 B3
Terneuzen NL 79 A3
Terni I 168 A2
Ternitz A 111 B3
Ternopil UA 13 D6
Terpni GR 183 C5
Terracina I 169 B3
Terråk N 195 E3
Terralba I 179 C2
Terranova di Pollino I 174 B2
Terranova di Sibari I 174 B2
Terras do Bouro P 148 A1
Terrasini I 176 A2
Terrassa E 147 C3
Terrasson-la-Villedieu F 129 A4
Terrazos E 143 B3
Terriente E 152 B2
Terrugem P 155 C3
Tertenía I 179 C3
Teruel E 152 B2
Tervola FIN 196 C7
Tervuren B 79 B4
Terzaga E 152 B2
Tešanj BIH 125 C3
Tesáske-Mlyňany SK 98 C2
Teslić BIH 125 C3
Tessin D 66 B1
Tessy-sur-Vire F 88 B2
Tét H 111 B4
Tetbury GB 43 A4
Teterchen F 92 B2
Teterow D 65 C5
Teteven BG 17 D6
Tetiyev UA 13 D8
Tetovo MK 182 A2
Tettau D 82 B3
Tettnang D 107 B4
Teublitz D 95 B4
Teuchern D 83 A4
Teulada
E 159 C4
I 179 D2
Teupitz D 74 B2
Teurajärvi S 196 C5
Teutschenthal D 83 A3
Tevel H 112 C2
Teviothead GB 36 A4
Tewkesbury GB 39 C4
Thale D 82 A3
Thalfang D 92 B2
Thalgau A 109 B4
Thalkirch CH 107 C4
Thalmässing D 95 B3
Thalwil CH 107 B3
Thame GB 44 B3
Thann F 106 B2
Thannhausen D 94 C2
Thaon-les-Vosges F 105 A5
Tharandt D 83 B5
Tharsis E 161 B2
Thasos GR 183 C6
Thatcham GB 44 B2
Thaxted GB 45 B4
Thayngen CH 107 B3
Theale GB 44 B2
The Barony GB 33 B3
Thebes = Thiva GR 185 A4
Theding-hausen D 72 B2
Theessen D 73 B5
The Hague = 's-Gravenhage NL 70 B1
Themar D 82 B2
The Mumbles GB 39 C3
Thénezay F 102 C1
Thenon F 129 A4
Therouanne F 78 B2
Thessaloniki = Salonica GR 182 C4
Thetford GB 45 A4
Theux B 80 B1
Thézar-les-Corbières F 146 A3
Thèze F 145 A3
Thiberville F 89 A4
Thibie F 91 C4
Thiéblemont-Farémont F 91 C4
Thiendorf D 84 A1
Thiene I 121 B4
Thierrens CH 106 C1
Thiers F 117 B3
Thiesi I 178 B2
Thiessow D 66 B2
Thiezac F 116 B2
Þingeyri IS 190 B2
Þingvellir IS 190 C4
Thionville F 92 B2
Thira GR 185 C6
Thiron-Gardais F 89 B4
Thirsk GB 37 B5
Thisted DK 58 B1
Thiva = Thebes GR 185 A4
Thivars F 90 C1
Thiviers F 115 C4
Thizy F 117 A4
Tholen NL 79 A4
Tholey D 92 B3
Thomas Street IRL 28 A3
Thomastown IRL 30 B1
Thônes F 118 B3
Thonnance-les-Joinville F 91 C5
Thonon-les-Bains F 118 A3
Thorame-Basse F 132 A2
Thorame-Haute F 132 A2
Thorens-Glières F 118 A3
Thorigny-sur-Oreuse F 91 C3
Thörl A 110 B2
Þorlákshöfn IS 190 D4
Thornaby on Tees GB 37 B5
Thornbury GB 43 A4
Thorne GB 40 B3
Thornhill
*Dumfries & Galloway* GB 36 A3
*Stirling* GB 35 B3
Thornthwaite GB 36 B3
Thornton-le-Dale GB 40 A3
Þórshöfn IS 191 A10
Thouarcé F 102 B1
Thouars F 102 C1
Thrapston GB 44 A3
Threlkeld GB 36 B3
Thrumster GB 32 C3
Thueyts F 117 C4
Thuin B 79 B4
Thuir F 146 B3
Thumau D 95 A3
Thun CH 106 C2
Thuret F 116 B3
Thurey F 105 C4
Thüringen A 107 B4
Thurins F 117 B4
Thürkow D 65 C5
Thurles IRL 29 B4
Thurmaston GB 40 C2
Thurø By DK 65 A3
Thursby GB 36 B3
Thurso GB 32 C3
Thury-Harcourt F 89 B3
Thusis CH 107 C4
Thyborøn DK 58 B1
Þykkvibær IS 190 D5
Thyregod DK 59 C2
Tibi E 159 C3
Tibro S 55 B5
Tidaholm S 55 B4
Tidan S 55 B5
Tidersrum S 62 A3
Tiedra E 150 A2
Tiefenbach D 95 B4
Tiefencastel CH 107 C4
Tiefenort D 82 B2
Tiefensee D 74 B2
Tiel NL 79 A5
Tielmes E 151 B4
Tielt B 78 A3
Tienen B 79 B4
Tiengen D 106 B3
Tiercé F 102 B1
Tierga E 152 A2
Tiermas E 144 B2
Tierp S 51 B4
Tierrantona E 145 B4
Tighina MD 17 B8
Tighnabruaich GB 34 C2
Tignes F 119 B3
Tigy F 103 B4
Tihany H 112 C1
Tijnje NL 70 A2
Tijola E 164 B2
Tikhvin RUS 9 C8
Tilburg NL 79 A5
Til Châtel F 105 B4
Tilh F 128 C2
Tillac F 145 A4
Tillberga S 56 A2
Tille F 90 B2
Tillicoultry GB 35 B4
Tilloy Bellay F 91 B4
Tilly F 115 B5
Tilly-sur-Seulles F 88 A3
Tim DK 59 B1
Timau I 109 C4
Timbaki GR 185 D5
Timi CY 181 B1
Timişoara RO 126 B3
Timmele S 60 B3
Timmendorfer Strand D 65 C3
Timmernabben S 62 B4
Timmersdala S 55 B4
Timoleague IRL 29 C3
Timolin IRL 30 B2
Timrå S 200 D3
Timsfors S 61 C3
Timsgearraidh GB 31 A1
Tinajas E 152 B1
Tinalhas P 155 B3
Tinchebray F 88 B3
Tincques F 78 B2
Tineo E 141 A4
Tinglev DK 64 B2
Tingsryd S 63 B2
Tingstäde S 57 C4
Tingvoll N 198 C5
Tinlot B 79 B5
Tinnoset N 53 A5
Tinos GR 185 B6
Tintagel GB 42 B2
Tinténiac F 101 A4
Tintern GB 39 C4
Tintigny B 92 B1
Tione di Trento I 121 A3
Tipperary IRL 29 B3
Tiptree GB 45 B4
Tirana = Tiranë AL 182 B1
Tiranë = Tirana AL 182 B1
Tirano I 120 A3
Tiraspol MD 17 B8
Tire TR 188 A2
Tires I 108 C2
Tiriez E 158 C1
Tirig E 153 B4
Tiriolo I 175 C2
Tirnavos GR 182 D4
Tirrénia I 134 B3
Tirschenreuth D 95 B4
Tirstrup DK 59 B3
Tirteafuera E 157 B3
Tisno HR 137 B4
Tišnov CZ 97 B4
Tisovec SK 99 C3
Tisselskog S 54 B3
Tistedal N 54 A2
Tistrup DK 59 C1
Tisvildeleje DK 61 C2
Tiszaalpár H 113 C3
Tiszabö H 113 B4
Tiszacsége H 113 B5
Tiszadorogma H 113 B4
Tiszaföldvár H 113 C4
Tiszafüred H 113 B4
Tiszajenö H 113 B4
Tiszakécske H 113 C4
Tiszakeszi H 113 B4
Tiszakürt H 113 C4
Tiszalök H 113 A5
Tiszalúc H 113 A5
Tiszanána H 113 B4
Tiszaörs H 113 B4
Tiszaroff H 113 B4
Tiszasüly H 113 B4
Tiszasziget H 126 A2
Tiszaszőlős H 113 B4
Tiszaújváros H 113 B5
Tiszavasvári H 113 B5
Titaguas E 159 B2
Titel SRB 126 B2
Titisee-Neustadt D 106 B3
Tito I 172 B1
Titova Korenica HR 123 C4
Titran N 198 B5
Tittling D 96 C1
Tittmoning D 109 A3
Titz D 80 A2
Tiurajärvi FIN 196 B7
Tived S 55 B5
Tiverton GB 43 B3
Tivisa E 153 A4
Tívoli I 168 B2
Tizsadob H 113 A5
Tjällmo S 56 B1
Tjåmotis S 195 D9
Tjæreborg DK 59 C1
Tjautjas S 196 B3
Tjøme N 54 A1
Tjong N 195 D4
Tjonnefoss N 53 B4
Tjörn IS 190 B5
Tjörnarp S 61 D3
Tjøtta N 195 E3
Tkon HR 137 B4
Tleń PL 68 B3
Tlmače SK 98 C2
Tłuchowo PL 77 B4
Tlumačov CZ 98 B1
Tóalmas H 112 B3
Toano I 134 A3
Toba D 82 A2
Tobarra E 158 C2
Tobermore GB 27 B4
Tobermory GB 34 B1
Toberonochy GB 34 B2
Tobha Mor GB 31 B1
Tobo S 51 B4
Tocane-St Apre F 129 A3
Tocha P 148 B1
Tocina E 162 A2
Töcksfors S 54 A2
Tocón E 163 A4
Todal N 198 C5
Todi I 136 C1
Todmorden GB 40 B1
Todorici BIH 138 A3
Todtmoos D 106 B3
Todtnau D 106 B2
Toén E 140 B3
Tofta
*Gotland* S 57 C4
*Skaraborg* S 55 B4
Toftbyn S 50 B2
Tofte N 54 A1
Töftedal S 54 B2
Tofterup DK 59 C1
Toftlund DK 59 C2
Tófű H 125 A4
Tohmo FIN 197 C10
Tokaj H 113 A5
Tokarnia PL 87 B4
Tokary PL 76 C3
Tokod H 112 B2
Tököl H 112 B2
Tolastadh bho Thuath GB 31 A2
Toledo E 151 C3
Tolentino I 136 B2
Tolfa I 168 A1
Tolg S 62 A2
Tolga N 199 C8
Tolkmicko PL 69 A4
Tollarp S 61 D3
Tollered S 60 B2
Tølløse DK 61 D1
Tolmachevo RUS 9 C6
Tolmezzo I 122 A2
Tolmin SLO 122 A2
Tolna H 112 C2
Tolnanémedi H 112 C2
Tolob GB 33 B5
Tolosa
E 144 A1
P 155 B3
Tolox E 162 B3
Tolpuddle GB 43 B4
Tolva
E 145 B4
FIN 197 C11
Tolve I 172 B2
Tomar P 154 B2
Tomaševac SRB 126 B2
Tomašica BIH 124 C2
Tomášikovo SK 111 A4
Tomašouka BY 13 C5
Tomášovce SK 99 C3
Tomaszów Mazowiecki PL 87 A4
Tomatin GB 32 D3
Tombeboeuf F 129 B3
Tomdoun GB 32 D1
Tomelilla S 66 A2
Tomellosa E 151 B5
Tomelloso E 157 A4
Tomiño E 140 C2
Tomintoul GB 32 D3
Tomislavgrad BIH 138 B3
Tomisław PL 84 A3
Tomisławice PL 76 B3
Tomnavoulin GB 32 D3
Tompa H 126 A1
Tompaládony H 111 B3
Tomra N 198 C3
Tomter N 54 A1
Tona E 147 C3
Tonara I 179 B3
Tonbridge GB 45 B4
Tondela P 148 B1
Tønder DK 64 B1
Tongeren B 79 B5
Tongue GB 32 C2
Tönisvorst D 80 A2
Tønjum N 47 A4
Tonkopuro FIN 197 C11
Tonnay-Boutonne F 114 C3
Tonnay-Charente F 114 C3
Tonneins F 129 B3
Tonnerre F 104 B2
Tonnes N 195 D4
Tönning D 64 B1
Tonsåsen N 47 B6
Tønsberg N 54 A1
Tonstad N 52 B2
Toomyvara IRL 28 B3
Toormore IRL 29 C2
Topares E 164 B2
Topas E 150 A2
Toplița RO 17 B6
Topola SRB 127 C2
Topolčani MK 182 B3
Topoľčany SK 98 C2
Topoľčianky SK 98 C2
Topolje HR 124 B2
Topólka PL 76 B3
Topoľ'niky SK 111 B4
Topolovăţu Mare RO 126 B3
Toponár H 125 A3
Toporów PL 75 B4
Topsham GB 43 B3
Topusko HR 124 B1
Toques E 140 B3
Torà E 147 C2
Toral de los Guzmanes E 142 B1
Toral de los Vados E 141 B4
Torbalı TR 188 A2
Torbjörntorp S 55 B4
Torbole I 121 B3
Torchiarolo I 173 B4
Torcross GB 43 B3
Torcy-le-Petit F 89 A5
Torda SRB 126 B2
Tørdal N 53 A4
Tordehumos E 142 C1
Tordera E 147 C3
Tordesillas E 150 A2
Tordesilos E 152 B2
Töre S 196 D5
Töreboda S 55 B5
Toreby DK 65 B4
Torekov S 61 C2
Torella dei Lombardi I 170 C3
Torellò E 147 B3
Toreno E 141 B4
Torfou F 114 A2
Torgau D 83 A5
Torgelow D 74 A3
Torgueda P 148 A2
Torhamn S 63 B3
Torhop N 193 B11
Torhout B 78 A3
Torigni-sur-Vire F 88 A3
Torija E 151 B4
Toril E 152 B2
Torino = Turin I 119 B4
Toritto I 171 C4
Torkovichi RUS 9 C7
Torla E 145 B3
Tormac RO 126 B3
Törmänen FIN 193 D11
Tormestorp S 61 C3
Tórmini I 121 B3
Tornada P 154 B1
Tornal'a SK 99 C4
Tornavacas E 150 B2
Tornby DK 58 A2
Tornesch D 72 A2
Torness GB 32 D2
Torniella I 135 B4
Tornimparte I 169 A3
Torning DK 59 B2
Tornio FIN 196 D7
Tornjoš SRB 126 B1
Tornos E 152 B2
Toro E 150 A2
Törökszentmiklós H 113 B4
Toropets RUS 9 D7
Torpa S 61 C3
Torpè I 178 B3
Torphins GB 33 D4
Torpo N 47 B5
Torpoint GB 42 B2
Torpsbruk S 62 A2
Torquay GB 43 B3
Torquemada E 142 B2
Torralba de Burgo E 151 A5
Torralba de Calatrava E 157 A4
Torrão P 154 C2
Torre Annunziata I 170 C2
Torreblacos E 143 C4
Torreblanca E 153 B4
Torreblascopedro E 157 B4
Torrecaballeros E 151 A3
Torrecampo E 156 B3
Torre Canne I 173 B3
Torre Cardela E 163 A4
Torrecilla E 152 B1
Torrecilla de la Jara E 156 A3
Torrecilla de la Orden E 150 A2
Torrecilla del Pinar E 151 A3
Torrecilla en Cameros E 143 B4
Torrecillas de la Tiesa E 156 A2
Torre das Vargens P 154 B3
Torre de Coelheiros P 154 C3
Torre de Dom Chama P 149 A2
Torre de Juan Abad E 157 B4
Torre de la Higuera E 161 B3
Torre del Bierzo E 141 B4
Torre del Burgo E 151 B4
Torre del Campo E 163 A4
Torre del Greco I 170 C2
Torre del Lago Puccini I 134 B3
Torre dell'Orso I 173 B4
Torre del Mar E 163 B3
Torredembarra E 147 C2
Torre de Miguel Sesmero E 155 C4
Torre de Moncorvo P 149 A2
Torre de Santa Maria E 156 A1
Torredonjimeno E 163 A4
Torre do Terranho P 148 B2
Torre Faro I 177 A4
Torregrosa E 147 C1
Torreira P 148 B1
Torrejoncillo E 155 B4
Torrejón de Ardoz E 151 B4
Torrejón de la Calzada E 151 B4
Torrejón del Rey E 151 B4
Torrejon el Rubio E 156 A1
Torrelaguna E 151 B4
Torrelapaja E 152 A2
Torre la Ribera E 145 B4
Torrelavega E 142 A2
Torrelobatón E 150 A2
Torrelodones E 151 B4
Torre los Negros E 152 B2
Torremaggiore I 171 B3
Torremanzanas E 159 C3
Torremayor E 155 C4
Torremezzo di Falconara I 174 B2
Torremocha E 156 A1
Torremolinos E 163 B3
Torrenieri I 135 B4
Torrenostra E 153 B4
Torrenova I 168 B2
Torrent E 159 B3
Torrente de Cinca E 153 A4
Torrenueva
*Ciudad Real* E 157 B4
*Granada* E 163 B4
Torreorgaz E 155 B4
Torre Orsáia I 172 B1
Torre-Pacheco E 165 B4
Torre Péllice I 119 C4
Torreperogil E 157 B4
Torres E 163 A4
Torresandino E 143 C3
Torre Santa Susanna I 173 B3
Torres-Cabrera E 163 A3
Torres de la Alameda E 151 B4
Torres Novas P 154 B2
Torres Vedras P 154 B1
Torrevieja E 165 B4
Torricella I 173 B3
Torri del Benaco I 121 B3
Torridon GB 31 B3
Torriglia I 134 A2
Torrijos E 151 C3
Tørring DK 59 C2
Torrita di Siena I 135 B4
Torroal P 154 C2
Torroella de Montgr i E 147 B4
Torrox E 163 B4
Torrskog S 54 A3
Torsåker S 50 B3
Torsang S 50 B2
Torsås S 63 B4
Torsby S 49 B4
Torsetra N 48 B2
Torshälla S 56 A2
Tórshavn FO 4 A3
Torslanda S 60 B1
Torsminde DK 59 B1
Torsnes N 46 B3
Törtel H 113 B3
Tórtoles E 150 B2
Tórtoles de Esgueva E 142 C2
Tortol i I 179 C3
Tortona I 120 C1
Tórtora I 174 B1
Tortoreto Lido I 136 C2
Tortorici I 177 A3
Tortosa E 153 B4
Tortosendo P 148 B2
Tortuera E 152 B2
Tortuero E 151 B4
Toruń PL 76 A3
Torup S 60 C3
Tor Vaiánica I 168 B2
Torver GB 36 B3
Tørvikbygde N 46 B3
Torviscón E 163 B4
Torzhok RUS 9 D9
Torzym PL 75 B4
Tosbotn N 195 E3
Toscelanor-Maderno I 121 B3
Tosno RUS 9 C7
Tossa de Mar E 147 C3
Tossåsen S 199 C10
Tosse F 128 C1
Tösse S 54 B3
Tossicía I 169 A3
Tostedt D 72 A2
Tosya TR 23 A8
Tószeg H 113 B4
Toszek PL 86 B2
Totana E 165 B3
Totebo S 62 A4
Tôtes F 89 A5
Tótkomlós H 113 C4
Totland N 198 D2
Tøtlandsvik N 52 A2
Totnes GB 43 B3
Tótszerdahely H 124 A2
Tøttdal N 199 A8
Totton GB 44 C2
Touça P 149 A2

Toucy F 104 B2
Toul F 92 C1
Toulon F 132 B1
Toulon-sur-Allier F 104 C2
Toulon-sur-Arroux
F 104 C3
Toulouse F 129 C4
Tourcoing F 78 B3
Tour de la Parata F 180 B1
Tourlaville F 88 A2
Tournai B 78 B3
Tournan-en-Brie F 90 C2
Tournay F 145 A4
Tournon-d'Agenais
F 129 B3
Tournon-St Martin
F 115 B4
Tournon-sur-Rhône
F 117 B4
Tournus F 105 C3
Touro
E 140 B2
P 148 B2
Tourouvre F 89 B4
Tourriers F 115 C4
Tours F 102 B2
Tourteron F 91 B4
Tourves F 132 B1
Toury F 103 A3
Touvedo P 148 A1
Touvois F 114 B2
Toužim CZ 83 B4
Tovačov CZ 98 B1
Tovariševo SRB 126 B1
Tovarnik HR 125 B5
Tovdal N 53 B4
Towcester GB 44 A3
Town Yetholm GB 35 C5
Tråastølen N 47 B4
Trabada E 141 A3
Trabadelo E 141 B4
Trabanca E 149 A3
Trabazos E 149 A3
Traben-Trarbach D 92 B3
Trabia I 176 B2
Tradate I 120 B1
Trädet S 60 B3
Trafaria P 154 C1
Tragacete E 152 B2
Tragwein A 96 C2
Traiguera E 153 B4
Trainel F 91 C3
Traisen A 110 A2
Traismauer A 97 C3
Traitsching D 95 B4
Trákhonas CY 181 A2
Tralee IRL 29 B2
Tramacastilla de Tena
E 145 B3
Tramagal P 154 B2
Tramariglio I 178 B2
Tramatza I 179 B2
Tramelan CH 106 B2
Tramonti di Sopra
I 122 A1
Tramore IRL 30 B1
Trampot F 92 C1
Trana I 119 B4
Tranås S 55 B5
Tranbjerg DK 59 B3
Tranby N 54 A1
Trancoso P 148 B2
Tranebjerg DK 59 C3
Tranekær DK 65 B3
Tranemo S 60 B3
Tranent GB 35 C5
Tranevåg N 52 B2
Trängslet S 49 A5
Tranhult S 60 B3
Trani I 171 B4
Trans-en-Provence
F 132 B2
Transtrand S 49 A5
Tranum DK 58 A2
Tranvik S 57 A4
Trápani I 176 A1
Trappes F 90 C2
Traryd S 61 C3
Trasacco I 169 B3
Trasierra E 156 B1
Träslövsläge S 60 B2
Trasmiras E 140 B3
Traspinedo E 150 A3
Trate SLO 110 C2
Trauchgau D 108 B1
Traun A 110 A1
Traunreut D 109 B3
Traunstein D 109 B3
Traunwalchen D 109 B3
Tråvad S 55 B4
Travemünde D 65 C3
Traversétolo I 120 C3
Travnik
BIH 139 A3
SLO 123 B3
Travo
F 180 B2
I 120 C2
Trawsfynydd GB 38 B3
Trbovlje SLO 123 A4
Trbušani SRB 127 D2
Treban F 116 A3
Třebařov CZ 97 B4
Trebatsch D 74 B3
Trebbin D 74 B2
Třebechovice pod
Orebem CZ 85 B3
Trebel D 73 B4
Třebenice CZ 84 B1
Trébeurden F 100 A2
Třebíč CZ 97 B3
Trebinje BIH 139 C4
Trebisacce I 174 B2
Trebitz D 83 A4
Trebnje SLO 123 B4
Třeboň CZ 96 B2
Třebovice CZ 97 B4
Trebsen D 83 A4
Trebujena E 161 C3
Trecastagni I 177 B4
Trecate I 120 B1
Trecenta I 121 B4
Tredegar GB 39 C3
Tredózio I 135 A4
Treffen A 109 C4
Treffort F 118 A2
Treffurt D 82 A2
Trefnant GB 38 A3
Tregaron GB 39 B3
Trégastel-Plage F 100 A2
Tregnago I 121 B4
Tregony GB 42 B2
Tréguier F 100 A2
Trégunc F 100 B2
Treharris GB 39 C3
Trehörningsjö S 200 C4
Tréia I 136 B2
Treignac F 116 B1
Treignat F 116 A2
Treignes B 91 A4
Treis-Karden D 80 B3
Trekanten S 63 B4
Trélazé F 102 B1
Trelech GB 39 C2
Trélissac F 129 A3
Trelleborg S 66 A2
Trélon F 91 A4
Trélou-sur-Marne F 91 B3
Tremblay-le-Vicomte
F 89 B5
Tremés P 154 B2
Tremezzo I 120 B2
Třemošná CZ 96 B1
Tremp E 145 B4
Trenčianska Stankovce
SK 98 C1
Trenčianska Turná
SK 98 C2
Trenčianske Teplá
SK 98 C2
Trenčianske Teplice
SK 98 C2
Trenčín SK 98 C2
Trendelburg D 81 A5
Trengereid N 46 B2
Trensacq F 128 B2
Trent D 66 B2
Trento I 121 A4
Treorchy GB 39 C3
Trept F 118 B2
Trepuzzi I 173 B4
Trescore Balneário
I 120 B2
Tresenda I 120 A3
Tresfjord N 198 C4
Tresigallo I 121 C4
Trešnjevica SRB 127 D3
Tresnurághes I 178 B2
Trespaderne E 143 B3
Třešť CZ 97 B3
Trestina I 135 B5
Tretower GB 39 C3
Trets F 132 B1
Tretten N 48 A2
Treuchtlingen D 94 C2
Treuen D 83 B4
Treuenbrietzen D 74 B1
Treungen N 53 A4
Trevelez E 163 B4
Trevi I 136 C1
Treviana E 143 B3
Treviglio I 120 B2
Trevignano Romano
I 168 A2
Trevi nel Lázio I 169 B3
Treviso I 122 B1
Trévoux F 117 B4
Treysa D 81 B5
Trézelles F 117 A3
Trezzo sull'Adda I 120 B2
Trhová Kamenice
CZ 97 B3
Trhové Sviny CZ 96 C2
Triacastela E 141 B3
Triaize F 114 B2
Trianda GR 188 C3
Triaucourt-en-Argonne
F 91 C5
Tribanj Kruščica
HR 137 A4
Triberg D 106 A3
Tribsees D 66 B1
Tribuče SLO 123 B4
Tricárico I 172 B2
Tricase I 173 C4
Tricésimo I 122 A2
Trieben A 110 B1
Triebes D 83 B4
Triepkendorf D 74 A2
Trier D 92 B2
Trieste I 122 B2
Trie-sur-Baïse F 145 A4
Triggiano I 173 A2
Triglitz D 73 A5
Trignac F 101 B3
Trigueros E 161 B3
Trigueros del Valle
E 142 C2
Trikala GR 182 D3
Trikeri GR 183 D5
Trikomo CY 181 A2
Trilj HR 138 B2
Trillo E 152 B1
Trilport F 90 C2
Trim IRL 30 A2
Trimdon GB 37 B5
Trindade
*Beja* P 160 B2
*Bragança* P 149 A2
Třinec CZ 98 B2
Tring GB 44 B3
Trinità d'Agultu I 178 B2
Trinitápoli I 171 B4
Trino I 119 B5
Trinta P 148 B2
Triora I 133 B3
Tripoli GR 184 B3
Triponzo I 136 C1
Triptis D 83 B3
Triste E 144 B3
Trittau D 72 A3
Trivento I 170 B2
Trivero I 119 B5
Trivigno I 172 B1
Trn BIH 124 C3
Trnava
HR 125 B4
SK 98 C1
Trnovec SK 112 A1
Trnovo BIH 139 B4
Trnovska vas SLO 110 C2
Troarn F 89 A3
Trochtelfingen D 94 C1
Trödje S 51 B4
Troense DK 65 A3
Trofa P 148 A1
Trofaiach A 110 B2
Trofors N 195 E4
Trogir HR 138 B2
Trøgstad N 54 A2
Tróia P 171 B3
Troia P 154 C2
Troina I 177 B3
Troisdorf D 80 B3
Trois-Ponts B 80 B1
Troisvierges L 92 A2
Trojane SLO 123 A3
Troldhede DK 59 C1
Trollhättan S 54 B3
Trolog BIH 138 B2
Tromello I 120 B1
Tromøy N 53 B4
Tromsø N 192 C3
Trondheim N 199 B7
Tronget F 116 A3
Trönninge S 61 C2
Trönningeby S 60 B2
Trönö S 51 A3
Tronzano-Vercellese
I 119 B5
Trôo F 102 B2
Troon GB 36 A2
Tropea I 175 C1
Tropy Sztumskie PL 69 B4
Trosa S 57 B3
Trösken S 50 B3
Trosly-Breuil F 90 B3
Trossingen D 107 A3
Trostberg D 109 A3
Trouville-sur-Mer F 89 A4
Trowbridge GB 43 A4
Troyes F 104 A3
Trpanj HR 138 B3
Trpinja HR 125 B4
Tršće HR 123 B3
Tršice CZ 98 B1
Trstená SK 99 B3
Trstenci BIH 125 B3
Trsteno HR 139 C3
Trstice SK 111 A4
Trstín SK 98 C1
Trubia E 141 A5
Trubjela MNE 139 C4
Truchas E 141 B4
Trujillanos E 155 C4
Trujillo E 156 A2
Trumieje PL 69 B4
Trun
CH 107 C3
F 89 B4
Truro GB 42 B1
Trusetal D 82 B2
Truskavets' UA 13 D5
Trustrup DK 59 B3
Trutnov CZ 85 B3
Tryserum S 56 B2
Trysil N 49 A4
Tryszczyn PL 76 A2
Trzcianka PL 75 A5
Trzciel PL 75 B4
Trzcińsko Zdrój PL 74 B3
Trzebiatów PL 67 B4
Trzebiel PL 84 A2
Trzebielino PL 68 A2
Trzebień PL 84 A3
Trzebiez PL 74 A3
Trzebinia PL 86 B3
Trzebnica PL 85 A5
Trzebnice PL 85 A4
Trzeciewiec PL 76 A3
Trzemeszno PL 76 B2
Trzemeszno-Lubuskie
PL 75 B4
Trzetrzewina PL 99 B4
Tržič SLO 123 A3
Tsamandas GR 182 D2
Tschagguns A 107 B4
Tschernitz D 84 A2
Tsebrykove UA 17 B9
Tsyelyakhany BY 13 B6
Tua P 148 A2
Tuam IRL 28 A3
Tubbercurry IRL 26 B2
Tubbergen NL 71 B3
Tubilla del Lago E 143 C3
Tübingen D 93 C5
Tubize B 79 B4
Tučapy CZ 96 B2
Tučepi HR 138 B3
Tuchan F 146 B3
Tüchen D 73 A5
Tuchola PL 76 A2
Tuchomie PL 68 A2
Tuchów PL 99 B5
Tuczno PL 75 A5
Tuddal N 53 A4
Tudela E 144 B2
Tudela de Duero E 150 A3
Tudweiliog GB 38 B2
Tuejar E 159 B2
Tuffé F 102 A2
Tufsingdalen N 199 C8
Tuhaň CZ 84 B2
Tui E 140 B2
Tukhkala RUS 197 D13
Tukums LV 8 D3
Tula I 178 B2
Tulcea RO 17 C8
Tul'chyn UA 13 D8
Tulette F 131 A3
Tuliszków PL 76 B3
Tulla IRL 28 B3
Tullamore IRL 30 A1
Tulle F 116 B1
Tullins F 118 B2
Tulln A 97 C4
Tullow IRL 30 B2
Tułowice PL 85 B5
Tulppio FIN 197 B12
Tulsk IRL 28 A3
Tumba S 57 A3
Tummel Bridge GB 35 B3
Tun S 55 B3
Tuna
*Kalmar* S 62 A4
*Uppsala* S 51 B5
Tuna Hästberg S 50 B2
Tunçbilek TR 187 C4
Tunes P 160 B1
Tungelsta S 57 A4
Tunnerstad S 55 B5
Tunnhovd N 47 B5
Tunstall GB 45 A5
Tuohikotti FIN 8 B5
Tuoro sul Trasimeno
I 135 B5
Tupadły PL 76 B3
Tupanari BIH 139 A4
Tupik RUS 9 E8
Tuplice PL 84 A2
Tura H 112 B3
Turanj HR 137 B4
Turany SK 99 B3
Turbe BIH 139 A3
Turbenthal CH 107 B3
Turcia E 141 B5
Turčianske Teplice
SK 98 C2
Turcifal P 154 B1
Turckheim F 106 A2
Turda RO 17 B5
Turégano E 151 A4
Turek PL 76 B3
Tŭrgovishte BG 17 D7
Turgutlu TR 188 A2
Turi I 173 B3
Turin = Torino I 119 B4
Turis E 159 B3
Türje H 111 C4
Turka UA 12 D5
Túrkeve H 113 B4
Türkheim D 108 A1
Türkmenli TR 186 C1
Turku FIN 8 B3
Turleque E 157 A4
Turňa nad Bodvou
SK 99 C4
Turnberry GB 36 A2
Turnhout B 79 A4
Türnitz A 110 B2
Turnov CZ 84 B3
Turnu RO 126 A3
Turnu Măgurele RO 17 D6
Turón E 164 C1
Turoszów PL 84 B2
Turowo PL 77 A5
Turquel P 154 B1
Turri I 179 C2
Turries F 132 A2
Turriff GB 33 D4
Tursi I 174 A2
Turtmann CH 119 A4
Turtola FIN 196 C6
Turze PL 86 A1
Turzovka SK 98 B2
Tusa I 177 B3
Tuscánia I 168 A1
Tuse DK 61 D1
Tušilovic HR 123 B4
Tuszyn PL 86 A3
Tutow D 66 C2
Tutrakan BG 17 C7
Tuttlingen D 107 B3
Tutzing D 108 B2
Tuzla
BIH 125 C4
TR 23 C8
Tuzlukçu TR 189 A6
Tvååker S 60 B2
Tvärålund S 200 B5
Tvärskog S 63 B4
Tvedestrand N 53 B4
Tveit
*Hordaland* N 47 B4
*Rogaland* N 52 A2
Tver RUS 9 D9
Tverrelvmo N 192 D3
Tversted DK 58 A3
Tving S 63 B3
Tvrdošin SK 99 B3
Tvrdošovce SK 112 A2
Twardogóra PL 85 A5
Twatt GB 33 B3
Twello NL 70 B3
Twimberg A 110 C1
Twist D 71 B4
Twistringen D 72 B1
Tworóg PL 86 B2
Twyford
*Hampshire* GB 44 B2
*Wokingham* GB 44 B3
Tyachiv UA 17 A5
Tychówka PL 67 C5
Tychowo PL 67 C5
Tychy PL 86 B2
Tydal N 199 B8
Týec nad Labem CZ 97 A3
Tyfors S 49 B6
Tygelsjö S 61 D2
Tylldal N 199 C7
Tylstrup DK 58 A2
Tymbark PL 99 B4
Tymowa PL 99 B4
Tyndrum GB 34 B3
Týnec nad Sázavou
CZ 96 B2
Tynemouth GB 37 A5
Tyngsjö S 49 B5
Týniště nad Orlicí
CZ 85 B4
Týn nad Vltavou CZ 96 B2
Tynset N 199 C7
Tyresö S 57 A4
Tyringe S 61 C3
Tyrislöt S 56 B2
Tyristrand N 48 B2
Tyrrellspass IRL 30 A1
Tysnes N 46 B2
Tysse N 46 B2
Tyssebotn N 46 B2
Tyssedal N 46 B3
Tystberga S 56 B3
Tysvær N 52 A1
Tywyn GB 39 B2
Tzermiado GR 185 D6
Tzummarum NL 70 A2

## U

Ub SRB 127 C2
Ubby DK 61 D1
Úbeda E 157 B4
Überlingen D 107 B4
Ubidea E 143 A4
Ubli HR 138 C2
Ubrique E 162 B2
Ucero E 143 C3
Uchaud F 131 B3
Uchte D 72 B1
Uckerath D 80 B3
Uckfield GB 45 C4
Ucklum S 54 B2
Uclés E 151 C5
Ucria I 177 A3
Udbina HR 137 A4
Uddebo S 60 B3
Uddeholm S 49 B5
Uddevalla S 54 B2
Uddheden S 49 C4
Uden NL 80 A1
Uder D 82 A2
Udiča SK 98 B2
Údine I 122 A2
Udvar H 125 B4
Ueckermünde D 74 A3
Uelsen D 71 B3
Uelzen D 73 B3
Uetendorf CH 106 C2
Uetersen D 72 A2
Uetze D 72 B3
Uffculme GB 43 B3
Uffenheim D 94 B2
Ugarana E 143 A4
Ugento I 173 C4
Ugerldse DK 61 D1
Uggerby DK 58 A3
Uggerslev DK 59 C3
Uggiano la Chiesa
I 173 B4
Ugíjar E 164 C1
Ugine F 118 B3
Uglejevik BIH 125 C5
Uglenes N 46 B2
Uglich RUS 9 D11
Ugljane HR 138 B2
Ugod H 111 B4
Uherské Hradiště
CZ 98 B1
Uherský Brod CZ 98 B1
Uherský Ostroh CZ 98 C1
Uhingen D 94 C1
Uhlířské-Janovice
CZ 96 B3
Uhříněves CZ 96 A2
Uhyst D 84 A2
Uig GB 31 B2
Uitgeest NL 70 B1
Uithoorn NL 70 B1
Uithuizen NL 71 A3
Uithuizermeeden NL 71 A3
Uivar RO 126 B2
Ujazd
*Łódzkie* PL 87 A3
*Opolskie* PL 86 B2
Ujezd u Brna CZ 97 B4
Ujhartyán H 112 B3
Újkígyós H 113 C5
Ujpetre H 125 B4
Ujście PL 75 A5
Ujsolt H 112 C3
Újszász H 113 B4
Újszentmargita H 113 B5
Ujué E 144 B2
Ukanc SLO 122 A2
Ukmergė LT 13 A6
Ukna S 56 B2
Ula TR 188 B3
Ul'anka SK 99 C3
Ulaş TR 186 A2
Ulássai I 179 C3
Ulbjerg DK 58 B2
Ulbster GB 32 C3
Ulceby GB 40 B3
Ulcinj MNE 16 E3
Uldum DK 59 C2
Ulefoss N 53 A5
Uleila del Campo E 164 B2
Ulëz AL 182 B1
Ulfborg DK 59 B1
Uljma SRB 127 B3
Ullånger S 200 C4
Ullapool GB 32 D1
Ullared S 60 B2
Ullatti S 196 B4
Ullatun N 52 A2
Ulldecona E 153 B4
Ulldemolins E 147 C1
Ullerslev DK 59 C3
Ullervad S 55 B4
Üllés H 126 A1
Üllő H 112 B3
Ulm D 94 C1
Ulme P 154 B2
Ulmen D 80 B2
Ulnes N 47 B6
Ulog BIH 139 B4
Ulricehamn S 60 B3
Ulrichstein D 81 B5
Ulrika S 56 B1
Ulriksfors S 200 C1
Ulrum NL 71 A3
Ulsberg N 198 C6
Ulsta GB 33 A5
Ulsted DK 58 A3
Ulsteinvik N 198 C2
Ulstrup
*Vestsjællands Amt.*
DK 59 C3
*Viborg Amt.* DK 59 B2
Ulsvåg N 194 B6
Ulubey TR 188 A4
Uluborlu TR 189 A5
Ulukışla TR 23 C8
Ulverston GB 36 B3
Ulvik N 46 B3
Umag HR 122 B2
Uman UA 13 D9
Umba RUS 3 C14
Umbértide I 135 B5
Umbriático I 174 B2
Umčari SRB 127 C2
Umeå S 200 C6
Umgransele S 200 B4
Umhausen A 108 B1
Umka SRB 127 C2
Umljanovic HR 138 B2
Umnäs S 195 E7
Umurbey TR 186 B1
Unaðsdalur IS 190 A3
Unapool GB 32 C1
Unari FIN 197 B8
Unbyn S 196 D4
Uncastillo E 144 B2
Undenäs S 55 B5
Undersaker S 199 B10
Undredal N 46 B4
Unešić HR 138 B2
Úněšov CZ 96 B1
Ungheni MD 17 B7
Unhais da Serra P 148 B2
Unhošt CZ 84 B2
Unichowo PL 68 A2
Uničov CZ 98 B1
Uniejów PL 76 C3
Unisław PL 76 A3
Unkel D 80 B3
Unken A 109 B3
Unna D 81 A3
Unnaryd S 60 C3
Unquera E 142 A2
Unterach A 109 B4
Unterägeri CH 107 B3
Unterammergau D 108 B2
Unterhaching D 108 A2

Unteriberg CH 107 B3
Unterkochen D 94 C2
Unter Langkampfen A 108 B3
Unterlaussa A 110 B1
Unterlüss D 72 B3
Untermünkheim D 94 B1
Unterschächen CH 107 C3
Unterschleissheim D 95 C3
Unterschwaningen D 94 B2
Untersiemau D 82 B2
Unter-steinbach D 94 B2
Unterweissenbach A 96 C2
Unterzell D 95 B4
Upavon GB 44 B2
Úpice CZ 85 B4
Upiłka PL 68 B2
Upphärad S 54 B3
Uppingham GB 40 C3
Upplands-Väsby S 57 A3
Uppsala S 51 C4
Uppsjøhytta N 48 A1
Upton-upon-Severn GB 39 B4
Ur F 146 B2
Uras I 179 C2
Uraz PL 85 A4
Urbánia I 136 B1
Urbino I 136 B1
Urçay F 103 C4
Urda E 157 A4
Urdax E 144 A2
Urdilde E 140 B2
Urdos F 145 B3
Urk NL 70 B2
Úrkút H 111 B4
Urla TR 188 A1
Urlingford IRL 30 B1
Urnäsch CH 107 B4
Urnes N 47 A4
Uroševac KOS 16 D4
Urracal E 164 B2
Urries E 144 B2
Urroz E 144 B2
Ursensollen D 95 B3
Urshult S 63 B2
Uršna Sela SLO 123 B4
Urszulewo PL 77 B4
Ury F 90 C2
Urziceni RO 17 C7
Urzulei I 178 B3
Usagre E 156 B1
Uşak TR 187 D4
Usedom D 66 C2
Useldange L 92 B1
Uséllus I 179 C2
Ushakovo RUS 69 A5
Usingen D 81 B4
Usini I 178 B2
Usk GB 39 C4
Uskedal N 46 C2
Üsküdar TR 186 A4
Uslar D 82 A1
Úsov CZ 97 B5
Usquert NL 71 A3
Ussássai I 179 C3
Ussé F 102 B2
Usséglio I 119 B4
Ussel
*Cantal* F 116 B2
*Corrèze* F 116 B2
Usson-du-Poitou F 115 B4
Usson-en-Forez F 117 B3
Usson-les-Bains F 146 B3
Ustaoset N 47 B5
Ustaritz F 144 A2
Uštěk CZ 84 B2
Uster CH 107 B3
Ústi CZ 98 B1
Ustikolina BIH 139 B4
Ústínad Labem CZ 84 B2
Ústínad Orlicí CZ 97 B4
Ustiprača BIH 139 B5
Ustka PL 68 A1
Ust Luga RUS 8 C6
Ustroń PL 98 B2
Ustronie Morskie PL 67 B4
Ustyuzhna RUS 9 C10
Uszód H 112 C2
Utåker N 52 A1
Utansjö S 200 D3
Utebo E 152 A3
Utena LT 13 A6
Utery CZ 95 B5
Uthaug N 198 B6
Utiel E 159 B2
Utne N 46 B3
Utö S 57 B4
Utrecht NL 70 B2
Utrera E 162 A2
Utrillas E 153 B3
Utsjoki FIN 193 C11
Utstein kloster N 52 A1
Uttendorf A 109 B3
Uttenweiler D 107 A4
Utterslev DK 65 B4
Uttoxeter GB 40 C2
Utvälinge S 61 C2
Utvorda N 199 A7
Uusikaarlepyy FIN 3 E8
Uusikaupunki FIN 8 B2
Uvaly CZ 96 A2
Uvdal N 47 B5
Uza F 128 B1
Uzdin SRB 126 B2
Uzdowo PL 77 A5
Uzein F 145 A3
Uzel F 100 A3
Uzerche F 116 B1
Uzès F 131 A3
Uzhhorod UA 12 D5
Uzhok UA 12 D5
Užice SRB 127 D1
Uznach CH 107 B3
Üzümlü
*Konya* TR 189 B6
*Muğla* TR 188 C4
Uzunköprü TR 186 A1

## V

Vaalajärvi FIN 197 B9
Vaas F 102 B2
Vaasa FIN 8 A2
Vaasen NL 70 B2
Vabre F 130 B1
Vác H 112 B3
Vacha D 82 B2
Váchartyán H 112 B3
Väckelsång S 63 B2
Vacqueyras F 131 A3
Vad S 50 B2
Vada I 134 B3
Väddö S 51 C5
Väderstad S 55 B5
Vadheim N 46 A2
Vadillo de la Sierra E 150 B2
Vadillos E 152 B1
Vadla N 52 A2
Vado I 135 A4
Vado Lígure I 133 A4
Vadsø N 193 B13
Vadstena S 55 B5
Vadum DK 58 A2
Vaduz FL 107 B4
Vafos N 53 B5
Vág H 111 B4
Vågåmo N 198 D6
Væggerløse DK 65 B4
Vaggeryd S 62 A2
Vaghia GR 184 A4
Vaglia I 135 B4
Váglio Basilicata I 172 B1
Vagney F 106 A1
Vagnhärad S 57 B3
Vagnsunda S 57 A4
Vagos P 148 B1
Vai GR 185 D7
Vaiano I 135 B4
Vaiges F 102 A1
Vaihingen D 93 C4
Vaillant F 105 B4
Vailly-sur-Aisne F 91 B3
Vailly-sur Sauldre F 103 B4
Vairano Scalo I 170 B2
Vaison-la-Romaine F 131 A4
Vaite F 105 B4
Väjern S 54 B2
Vajszló H 125 B3
Vaksdal N 46 B2
Vál H 112 B2
Valaam RUS 9 B7
Valada P 154 B2
Vålådalen S 199 B10
Valadares P 148 A1
Valado P 154 B1
Valandovo MK 182 B4
Valaská SK 99 C3
Valaská Belá SK 98 C2
Valaská Dubová SK 99 B3
Valašská Polanka CZ 98 B1
Valašské Klobouky CZ 98 B2
Valašské Meziříčí CZ 98 B1
Valberg F 132 A2
Vålberg S 55 A4
Valbo S 51 B4
Valbom P 148 A1
Valbondione I 120 A3
Valbonnais F 118 C2
Valbuena de Duero E 142 C2
Vălcani RO 126 B2
Valdagno I 121 B4
Valdahon F 105 B5
Valdaracete E 151 B4
Valday RUS 9 D8
Valdealgorfa E 153 B3
Valdecaballeros E 156 A2
Valdecabras E 152 B1
Valdecarros E 150 B2
Valdeconcha E 151 B5
Valdeflores E 161 B3
Valdefresno E 142 B1
Valdeganga E 158 B2
Valdelacasa E 150 B2
Valdelacasa de Tajo E 156 A2
Valdelarco E 161 B3
Valdelosa E 149 A4
Valdeltormo E 153 B4
Valdelugeros E 142 B1
Valdemanco de Esteras E 156 B3
Valdemarsvik S 56 B2
Valdemorillo E 151 B3
Valdemoro E 151 B4
Valdemoro Sierra E 152 B2
Valdenoceda E 143 B3
Valdeobispo E 149 B3
Valdeolivas E 152 B1
Valdepeñas E 157 B4
Valdepeñas de Jaén E 163 A4
Valdepiélago E 142 B1
Valdepolo E 142 B1
Valderas E 142 B1
Valdérice I 176 A1
Valderrobres E 153 B4
Valderrueda E 142 B2
Val de San Lorenzo E 141 B4
Val de Santo Domingo E 150 B3
Val d'Esquières F 132 B2
Valdestillas E 150 A3
Valdetorres E 156 B1
Valdetorres de Jarama E 151 B4
Valdeverdeja E 150 C2
Valdevimbre E 142 B1
Valdieri I 133 A3
Valdilecha E 151 B4
Val-d'Isère F 119 B3
Valdobbiádene I 121 B4
Valdocondes E 143 C3
Valdoviño E 140 A2
Valea lui Mihai RO 16 B5
Vale de Açor
*Beja* P 160 B2
*Portalegre* P 154 B3
Vale de Agua P 160 B1
Vale de Cambra P 148 B1
Vale de Lobo P 160 B1
Vale de Prazeres P 148 B2
Vale de Reis P 154 C2
Vale de Rosa P 160 B2
Vale de Santarém P 154 B2
Vale de Vargo P 160 B2
Vale do Peso P 155 B3
Valega P 148 B1
Valéggio sul Mincio I 121 B3
Valeiro P 154 C2
Valença P 140 B2
Valençay F 103 B3
Valence
*Charente* F 115 C4
*Drôme* F 117 C4
Valence d'Agen F 129 B3
Valence d'Albigeois F 130 A1
Valence-sur-Baise F 129 C3
Valencia E 159 B3
Valencia de Alcántara E 155 B3
Valencia de Don Juan E 142 B1
Valencia de las Torres E 156 B1
Valencia del Ventoso E 161 A3
Valencia de Mombuey E 161 A2
Valenciennes F 79 B3
Valensole F 132 B1
Valentano I 168 A1
Valentigney F 106 B1
Valentine F 145 A4
Valenza I 120 B1
Valenzuela E 163 A3
Valenzuela de Calatrava E 157 B4
Våler
*Hedmark* N 48 B3
*Østfold* N 54 A1
Valera de Abajo E 158 B1
Valeria E 158 B1
Valestrand N 52 A1
Valestrandsfossen N 46 B2
Valevåg N 52 A1
Valfabbrica I 136 B1
Valflaunes F 131 B2
Valga EST 8 D5
Valgorge F 131 A3
Valgrisenche I 119 B4
Valguarnera Caropepe I 177 B3
Valhelhas P 148 B2
Valjevo SRB 127 C1
Valka LV 8 D4
Valkeakoski FIN 8 B4
Valkenburg NL 80 B1
Valkenswaard NL 79 A5
Valkó H 112 B3
Valla S 56 A2
Vallada E 159 C3
Vallado E 141 A4
Valladolid E 150 A3
Vallåkra S 61 D2
Vallata I 172 A1
Vallberga S 61 C3
Vall d'Alba E 153 B3
Valldemossa E 166 B2
Valle N 52 A3
Valle Castellana I 136 C2
Valle de Abdalajís E 163 B3
Valle de Cabuérniga E 142 A2
Valle de la Serena E 156 B2
Valle de Matamoros E 155 C4
Valle de Santa Ana E 155 C4
Valledolmo I 176 B2
Valledoria I 178 B2
Vallelado E 150 A3
Vallelunga Pratameno I 176 B2
Valle Mosso I 119 B5
Vallendar D 81 B3
Vallentuna S 57 A4
Vallerås S 49 B5
Valleraugue F 130 A2
Vallermosa I 179 C2
Vallet F 101 B4
Valletta M 175 C3
Valley GB 38 A2
Vallfogona de Riucorb E 147 C2
Valli del Pasúbio I 121 B4
Vallo della Lucánia I 172 B1
Valloire F 118 B3
Vallombrosa I 135 B4
Vallon-Pont-d'Arc F 131 A3
Vallorbe CH 105 C5
Vallouise F 118 C3
Valls E 147 C2
Vallset N 48 B3
Vallsta S 50 A3
Vallstena S 57 C4
Valmadrid E 153 A3
Valmiera LV 8 D4
Valmojado E 151 B3
Valmont F 89 A4
Valmontone I 169 B2
Valö S 51 B5
Valognes F 88 A2
Valonga P 148 B1
Valongo P 148 A1
Válor E 164 C1
Valoria la Buena E 142 C2
Valøy N 199 A7
Valozhyn BY 13 A7
Valpaços P 148 A2
Valpelline I 119 B4
Valpiana I 135 B3
Valpovo HR 125 B4
Valras-Plage F 130 B2
Valréas F 131 A3
Vals CH 107 C4
Valsavarenche I 119 B4
Vålse DK 65 B4
Valsequillo E 156 B2
Valsjöbyn S 199 A11
Vals-les-Bains F 117 C4
Valsonne F 117 B4
Valstagna I 121 B4
Val-Suzon F 105 B3
Valtablado del Rio E 152 B1
Valþjofsstaður IS 191 B11
Val Thorens F 118 B3
Valtice CZ 97 C4
Valtiendas E 151 A4
Valtierra E 144 B2
Valtopina I 136 B1
Valtorta I 120 B2
Valtournenche I 119 B4
Valverde E 144 C2
Valverde de Burguillos E 155 C4
Valverde de Júcar E 158 B1
Valverde de la Vera E 150 B2
Valverde de la Virgen E 142 B1
Valverde del Camino E 161 B3
Valverde del Fresno E 149 B3
Valverde de Llerena E 156 B2
Valverde de Mérida E 156 B1
Valvträsk S 196 C4
Vamberk CZ 85 B4
Vamdrup DK 59 C2
Våmhus S 50 A1
Vamlingbo S 57 D4
Vammala FIN 8 B3
Vamos GR 185 D5
Vámosmikola H 112 B2
Vámosszabadi H 111 B4
Vanault-les-Dames F 91 C4
Vandel DK 59 C2
Vandenesse F 104 C2
Vandenesse-en-Auxois F 104 B3
Vandóies I 108 C2
Väne-Åsaka S 54 B3
Vänersborg S 54 B3
Vänersnäs S 54 B3
Vang N 47 A5
Vänge S 51 C4
Vangsnes N 46 A3
Vänjaurbäck S 200 B4
Vännacka S 54 A3
Vannareid N 192 B3
Vännäs S 200 C5
Vannes F 101 B3
Vannsätter S 51 A3
Vannvåg N 192 B3
Vansbro S 49 B6
Vanse N 52 B2
Vantaa FIN 8 B4
Vanttauskoski FIN 197 C9
Vanviken N 199 B7
Vanyarc H 112 B3
Vaour F 129 B4
Vapnyarka UA 13 D8
Vaprio d'Adda I 120 B2
Vaqueiros P 160 B2
Vara S 55 B3
Varacieux F 118 B2
Varades F 101 B4
Varages F 132 B1
Varaldsøy N 46 B2
Varallo I 119 B5
Varangerbotn N 193 B12
Varano de'Melegari I 120 C3
Varaždin HR 124 A2
Varaždinske Toplice HR 124 A2
Varazze I 133 A4
Varberg S 60 B2
Vardal N 48 B2
Varde DK 59 C1
Vårdö FIN 51 B7
Vardø N 193 B15
Vardomb H 125 A4
Varejoki FIN 196 C7
Varel D 71 A5
Varėna LT 13 A6
Vårenes N 52 A1
Varengeville-sur-Mer F 89 A4
Varenna I 120 A2
Varennes-en-Argonne F 91 B5
Varennes-le-Grand F 105 C3
Varennes-St Sauveur F 105 C4
Varennes-sur-Allier F 117 A3
Varennes-sur-Amance F 105 B4
Vareš BIH 139 A4
Varese I 120 B1
Varese Ligure I 134 A2
Vârfurile RO 16 B5
Vårgårda S 60 A2
Vargas
E 143 A3
P 154 B2
Vargön S 54 B3
Varhaug N 52 B1
Variaş RO 126 A2
Variaşu Mic RO 126 A3
Varilhes F 146 A2
Varin SK 98 B2
Väring S 55 B4
Váriz P 149 A3
Varkaus FIN 8 A5
Varmahlíð IS 190 B6
Varmaland IS 190 C4
Värmlands Bro S 55 A4
Värmskog S 55 A3
Varna
BG 17 D7
SRB 127 C1
Värnamo S 60 B4
Varnhem S 55 B4
Varnsdorf CZ 84 B2
Värö S 60 B2
Varoška Rijeka BIH 124 B2
Városlöd H 111 B4
Várpalota H 112 B2
Varreddes F 90 C2
Vars F 118 C3
Varsi I 120 C2
Varsseveld NL 71 C3
Vårsta S 57 A3
Vartdal N 198 C3
Vartofta S 55 B4
Vårvik S 54 A3
Värvölgy H 111 C4
Varzi I 120 C2
Varzjelas P 148 B1
Varzo I 119 A5
Varzy F 104 B2
Vasad H 112 B3
Väse S 55 A4
Vašica SRB 125 B5
Vasilevichi BY 13 B8
Väskinde S 57 C4
Vaskút H 125 A4
Vaslui RO 17 B7
Vassbotn N 53 B4
Vassenden N 47 A6
Vassieux-en-Vercors F 118 C2
Vassmolösa S 63 B4
Vassy F 88 B3
Västansjö S 195 E6
Västanvik S 50 B1
Västerås S 56 A2
Västerby S 50 B2
Västerfärnebo S 50 C3
Västergarn S 57 C4
Västerhaninge S 57 A4
Västervik S 62 A4
Vasto I 170 A2
Västra Ämtervik S 55 A4
Västra-Bodarne S 60 B2
Västra Karup S 61 C2
Vasvár H 111 B3
Vasylkiv UA 13 C9
Vát H 111 B3
Vatan F 103 B3
Väte S 57 C4
Vathia GR 184 C3
Vatican City = Cittádel Vaticano I 168 B2
Vatili CY 181 A2
Vatin SRB 126 B3
Vatland N 52 B3
Vatnar N 53 A5
Vatnås N 48 C1
Vatne N 53 B3
Vatnestrøm N 53 B4
Vätö S 51 C5
Vatra-Dornei RO 17 B6
Vatry F 91 C4
Vattholma S 51 B4
Vättis CH 107 C4
Vauchamps F 91 C3
Vauchassis F 104 A2
Vaucouleurs F 92 C1
Vaudoy-en-Brie F 90 C3
Vaulen N 52 B1
Vaulruz CH 106 C1
Vaulx Vraucourt F 90 A2
Vaumas F 104 C2
Vausseroux F 115 B3
Vauvenargues F 132 B1
Vauvert F 131 B3
Vauvillers F 105 B5
Vaux-sur-Sure B 92 B1
Vawkavysk BY 13 B6
Vaxholm S 57 A4
Växjö S 62 B2
Våxtorp S 61 C3
Vayrac F 129 B4
Važec SK 99 B3
Veberöd S 61 D3
Vechelde D 72 B3
Vechta D 71 B5
Vecinos E 149 B4
Vecsés H 112 B3
Vedavågen N 52 A1
Veddige S 60 B2
Vedersø DK 59 B1
Vedeseta I 120 B2
Vedevåg S 56 A1
Vedra E 140 B2
Vedum S 55 B3
Veendam NL 71 A3
Veenendaal NL 70 B2
Vega
*Asturias* E 142 A1
*Asturias* E 142 A1
Vega de Espinareda E 141 B4
Vega de Infanzones E 142 B1
Vegadeo E 141 A3
Vega de Pas E 143 A3
Vega de Valcarce E 141 B4
Vega de Valdetronco E 150 A2
Vegårshei N 53 B4
Vegas de Coria E 149 B3
Vegas del Condado E 142 B1
Vegby S 60 B3
Vegger DK 58 B2
Veggli N 47 B6
Veghel NL 80 A1
Veglast D 66 B1
Véglie I 173 B3
Veguillas E 151 B4
Vegusdal N 53 B4
Veidholmen N 198 B4
Veidnes N 193 B10
Veikåker N 48 B1
Veinge S 61 C3
Vejbystrand S 61 C2
Vejen DK 59 C2
Vejer de la Frontera E 162 B2
Vejle DK 59 C2
Vejprty CZ 83 B5
Velada E 150 B3
Vela Luka HR 138 C2
Velayos E 150 B3
Velbert D 80 A3
Velburg D 95 B3
Velde N 199 A8
Velden
*Bayern* D 95 B3
*Bayern* D 95 C4
Velden am Worther See A 109 C5
Velefique E 164 B2
Velen D 80 A2
Velenje SLO 123 A4
Veles MK 182 B3
Velesevec HR 124 B2
Velešin CZ 96 C2
Velestino GR 182 D4
Velez Blanco E 164 B2
Vélez de Benaudalla E 163 B4
Vélez-Málaga E 163 B3
Vélez Rubio E 164 B2
Veliiki Radinci SRB 127 B1
Velika HR 125 B3
Velika Gorica HR 124 B2

Vel–Vil 281


Velika Grdevac HR 124 B3
Velika Greda SRB 126 B3
Velika Ilova BIH 125 C3
Velika Kladuša BIH 124 B1
Velika Kopanica HR 125 B4
Velika Krsna SRB 127 C2
Velika Obarska BIH 125 C5
Velika Pisanica HR 124 B3
Velika Plana SRB 127 C3
Velika Zdenci HR 124 B3
Velike Lašče SLO 123 B3
Velike Središte SRB 126 B3
Veliki Gaj SRB 126 B3
Veliki Popović SRB 127 C3
Velikiye Luki RUS 9 D7
Veliko Gradište SRB 127 C3
Veliko Orašje SRB 127 C3
Veliko Selo SRB 127 C3
Veliko Tŭrnovo BG 17 D6
Velilla del Río Carrió E 142 B2
Velilla de San Antonio E 151 B4
Veli Lošinj HR 137 A3
Velingrad BG 183 A5
Velizh RUS 9 E7
Veljun HR 123 B4
Velká Bíteš CZ 97 B4
Velka Hled'scbe CZ 95 B4
Velká Lomnica SK 99 B4
Velkánad Veličkou CZ 98 C1
Velké Bystřice CZ 98 B1
Velké Heraltice CZ 98 B1
Velké Karlovice CZ 98 B2
Vel'ke'Kostol'any SK 98 C1
Vel'ké Leváre SK 97 C5
Velké Losiny CZ 98 A1
Velké Meziříčí CZ 97 B4
Velké Pavlovice CZ 97 C4
Vel'ké Rovné SK 98 B2
Vel'ké Uherce SK 98 C2
Vel'ké Zálužie SK 98 C1
Vel'ký Blahovo SK 99 C4
Velky Bor CZ 96 B1
Vel'ký Cetin SK 112 A2
Vel'ký Krtíš SK 112 A3
Vel'ký Meder SK 111 B4
Velky Ujezd CZ 98 B1
Vellahn D 73 A3
Vellberg D 94 B1
Velles F 103 C3
Velletri I 168 B2
Vellinge S 66 A2
Vellisca E 151 B5
Velliza E 150 A3
Vellmar D 81 A5
Velp NL 70 B2
Velten D 74 B2
Velvary CZ 84 B2
Velvendos GR 182 C4
Vemb DK 59 B1
Vemdalen S 199 C10
Veme N 48 B2
Véménd H 125 A4
Vemmedrup DK 61 D2
Vena S 62 A3
Venaco F 180 A2
Venafro I 169 B4
Venarey-les-Laumes F 104 B3
Venaría I 119 B4
Venasca I 133 A3
Venčane SRB 127 C2
Vence F 132 B3
Venda Nova
*Coimbra* P 154 A2
*Leiria* P 154 B2
Vendas Novas P 154 C2
Vendays-Montalivet F 114 C2
Vendel S 51 B4
Vendelso S 57 A4
Vendeuil F 91 B3
Vendeuvre-sur-Barse F 104 A3
Vendoeuvres F 115 B5
Vendôme F 103 B3
Venelles F 131 B4
Veness GB 33 B4
Venézia = Venice I 122 B1
Venialbo E 150 A2
Venice = Venézia I 122 B1
Vénissieux F 117 B4
Venjan S 49 B5
Venlo NL 80 A2
Vennesla N 53 B3
Vennesund N 195 E3
Vennezey F 92 C2
Venn Green GB 42 B2
Venosa I 172 B1
Venray NL 80 A1
Vent A 108 C1
Venta de Baños E 142 C2
Venta del Moro E 158 B2
Venta de los Santos E 157 B4
Venta las Ranas E 142 A1
Ventanueva E 141 A4
Ventas de Huelma E 163 A4
Ventas de Zafarraya E 163 B3
Ventavon F 132 A1
Ventimíglia I 133 B3
Ventnor GB 44 C2
Ventosa de la Sierra E 143 C4
Ventosilla E 143 C4
Ventspils LV 8 D2
Venturina I 134 B3
Venzolasca F 180 A2
Venzone I 122 A2
Vép H 111 B3
Vera
E 164 B3
N 199 B9
Vera Cruz P 160 A2
Vera de Bidasoa E 144 A2
Vera de Moncayo E 144 C2
Verbánia I 119 B5
Verberie F 90 B2
Verbicaro I 174 B1
Verbier CH 119 A4
Vercelli I 119 B5
Vercel-Villedieu-le-Camp F 105 B5
Verchen D 66 C1
Vercheny F 118 C2
Verclause F 131 A4
Verdalsøra N 199 B8
Verden D 72 B2
Verdens Ende N 54 A1
Verdikoussa GR 182 D3
Verdille F 115 C3
Verdú E 147 C2
Verdun F 92 B1
Verdun-sur-Garonne F 129 C4
Verdun-sur-le-Doubs F 105 C4
Veresegyház H 112 B3
Verfeil F 129 C4
Vergato I 135 A4
Vergel E 159 C4
Vergeletto CH 120 A1
Verges E 147 B4
Vergiate I 120 B1
Vergt F 129 A3
Veria GR 182 C4
Verín E 141 C3
Veringenstadt D 107 A4
Verl D 81 A4
Verma N 198 C5
Vermand F 90 B3
Vermelha P 154 B1
Vermenton F 104 B2
Vernago I 108 C1
Vernante I 133 A3
Vernantes F 102 B2
Vernár SK 99 C4
Vernasca I 120 C2
Vernayaz CH 119 A4
Vernazza I 134 A2
Vern-d'Anjou F 102 B1
Verneřice CZ 84 B2
Vernet F 146 A2
Vernet-les-Bains F 146 B3
Verneuil F 91 B3
Verneuil-sur-Avre F 89 B4
Vernier CH 118 A3
Vérnio I 135 A4
Vérnole I 173 B4
Vernon F 90 B1
Vernoux-en-Vivarais F 117 C4
Veróce H 112 B3
Verolanuova I 120 B3
Véroli I 169 B3
Verona I 121 B4
Verpelét H 113 B4
Verrabotn N 199 B7
Verrès I 119 B4
Verrey-sous-Salmaise F 104 B3
Verrières F 115 B4
Versailles F 90 C2
Versam CH 107 C4
Verseg H 112 B3
Versmold D 71 B5
Versoix CH 118 A3
Verteillac F 115 C4
Vértesacsa H 112 B2
Vertou F 101 B4
Vertus F 91 C3
Verviers B 80 B1
Vervins F 91 B3
Verwood GB 43 B5
Veryan GB 42 B2
Veržej SLO 111 C3
Verzuolo I 133 A3
Verzy F 91 B4
Vescovato F 180 A2
Vése H 124 A3
Veselínad Lužnicí CZ 96 B2
Veselínad Moravou CZ 98 C1
Veseliy BG 17 D7
Vésime I 119 C5
Veskoniemi FIN 193 D11
Vesoul F 105 B5
Vespolate I 120 B1
Vessigebro S 60 C2
Vestbygd N 52 B2
Vestenanova I 121 B4
Vester Husby S 56 B2
Vester Nebel DK 59 C2
Vesterøhavn DK 58 A3
Vester Torup DK 58 A2
Vester Vedsted DK 59 C1
Vestervig DK 58 B1
Vestfossen N 53 A5
Vestmannaeyjar IS 190 D5
Vestmarka N 48 C3
Vestnes N 198 C4
Vestone I 120 B3
Vestre Gausdal N 48 A2
Vestre Jakobselv N 193 B13
Vestre Slidre N 47 A5
Vesyegonsk RUS 9 C10
Veszprém H 112 B1
Veszprémvarsány H 112 B1
Vésztő H 113 C5
Vetlanda S 62 A3
Vetovo HR 125 B3
Vetralla I 168 A2
Větrný Jeníkov CZ 97 B3
Vétroz CH 119 A4
Vetschau D 84 A2
Vettasjärvi S 196 B4
Vetto I 134 A3
Vetulónia I 135 C3
Veules-les-Roses F 89 A4
Veulettes-sur-Mer F 89 A4
Veum N 53 A4
Veurne B 78 A2
Veverská Bítýška CZ 97 B4
Vevey CH 106 C1
Vevi GR 182 C3
Vevring N 46 A2
Vex CH 119 A4
Veynes F 132 A1
Veyre-Monton F 116 B3
Veyrier F 118 B3
Vézelay F 104 B2
Vézelise F 92 C2
Vézenobres F 131 A3
Vezins F 102 B1
Vézins-de-Lévézou F 130 A1
Vezirhan TR 187 B5
Vezirköprü TR 23 A8
Vezza di Óglio I 120 A3
Vezzani F 180 A2
Vezzano I 121 A4
Vezzano sul Cróstolo I 121 C3
Vi S 200 D3
Viadana I 121 C3
Via Gloria P 160 B2
Viana E 143 B4
Viana do Alentejo P 154 C2
Viana do Bolo E 141 B3
Viana do Castelo P 148 A1
Vianden L 92 B2
Viannos GR 185 D6
Viaréggio I 134 B3
Viator E 164 C2
Vibble S 57 C4
Viborg DK 58 B2
Vibo Valéntia I 175 C2
Vibraye F 102 A2
Vic E 147 C3
Vicar E 164 C2
Vicarello I 134 B3
Vicari I 176 B2
Vicchio I 135 B4
Vicdesses F 146 B2
Vic-en-Bigorre F 145 A4
Vicenza I 121 B4
Vic-Fézensac F 129 C3
Vichy F 117 A3
Vickan S 60 B2
Vickerstown GB 36 B3
Vic-le-Comte F 116 B3
Vico F 180 A1
Vico del Gargano I 171 B3
Vico Equense I 170 C2
Vicopisano I 134 B3
Vicosoprano CH 120 A2
Vicovaro I 169 A2
Vic-sur-Aisne F 90 B3
Vic-sur-Cère F 116 C2
Victoria = Rabat M 175 C3
Vidago P 148 A2
Vidauban F 132 B2
Vide P 148 B2
Videbæk DK 59 B1
Videm SLO 123 B3
Videseter N 198 D4
Vidigueira P 160 A2
Vidin BG 16 D5
Vidlin GB 33 A5
Vidsel S 196 D3
Vidzy BY 13 A7
Viechtach D 95 B4
Vieille-Brioude F 117 B3
Vieira P 154 B2
Vieira do Minho P 148 A1
Vieiros P 155 C3
Vielha E 145 B4
Vielle-Aure F 145 B4
Viellespesse F 116 B3
Viellevigne F 114 B2
Vielmur-sur-Agout F 130 B1
Vielsalm B 80 B1
Viels Maison F 91 C3
Vienenburg D 73 C3
Vienna = Wien A 111 A3
Vienne F 117 B4
Vieritz D 73 B5
Viernheim D 93 B4
Vierraden D 74 A3
Viersen D 80 A2
Vierville-sur-Mer F 88 A3
Vierzon F 103 B4
Vieselbach D 82 B3
Vieste I 171 B4
Vietas S 194 C9
Vieteren B 78 B2
Vietri di Potenza I 172 B1
Vietri sul Mare I 170 C2
Vieux-Boucau-les-Bains F 128 C1
Vif F 118 B2
Vig DK 61 D1
Vigásio I 121 B3
Vigaun A 109 B4
Vigeland N 52 B3
Vigeois F 116 B1
Vigévano I 120 B1
Viggianello I 174 B2
Viggiano I 174 A1
Vigliano I 169 A3
Vigmostad N 52 B3
Vignale I 119 B5
Vignanello I 168 A2
Vigneulles-lès-Hattonchâtel F 92 C1
Vignevieille F 146 B3
Vignola I 135 A4
Vignory F 105 A4
Vignoux-sur Barangeon F 103 B4
Vigo E 140 B2
Vigo di Fassa I 121 A4
Vigone I 119 C4
Vigrestad N 52 B1
Vihiers F 102 B1
Viitasaari FIN 8 A4
Vík IS 190 D6
Vik
*Nordland* N 195 E3
*Rogaland* N 52 B1
*Sogn og Fjordane* N 46 A3
S 63 C2
Vika S 50 B2
Vikajärvi FIN 197 C9
Vikane N 54 A1
Vikarbyn S 50 B2
Vike N 46 B2
Vikedal N 52 A1
Vikeland N 53 B3
Viken
*Jämtland* S 199 A10
*Skåne* S 61 C2
Viker N 48 B2
Vikersund N 48 C1
Vikeså N 52 B2
Vikevåg N 52 A1
Vikingstad S 56 B1
Vikmanshyttan S 50 B2
Vikna N 199 A7
Vikøy N 46 B3
Vikran
*Troms* N 192 C2
*Troms* N 194 B7
Viksjö S 200 D3
Viksøyri N 46 A3
Viksta S 51 B4
Vila Boim P 155 C3
Vila Chãde Ourique P 154 B2
Viladamat E 147 B4
Vila de Cruces E 140 B2
Vila de Rei P 154 B2
Vila do Bispo P 160 B1
Vila do Conde P 148 A1
Viladrau E 147 C3
Vila Flor P 149 A2
Vila Franca das Navas P 149 B2
Vilafranca del Maestrat E 153 B3
Vilafranca del Penedès E 147 C2
Vila Franca de Xira P 154 C1
Vila Fresca P 154 C1
Vilagarcía de Arousa E 140 B2
Vilajuiga E 147 B4
Vilamarin E 140 B3
Vilamartín de Valdeorras E 141 B3
Vila Nogueira P 154 C1
Vila Nova da Baronia P 154 C2
Vilanova de Castelló E 159 B3
Vila Nova de Cerveira P 140 C2
Vila Nova de Famalicão P 148 A1
Vila Nova de Foz Côa P 149 A2
Vila Nova de Gaia P 148 A1
Vila Nova de Milfontes P 160 B1
Vila Nova de Paiva P 148 B2
Vila Nova de São Bento P 161 B2
Vilanova de Sau E 147 C3
Vilanova i la Geltrú E 147 C2
Vilapedre E 140 A3
Vila Pouca de Aguiar P 148 A2
Vila Praja de Ancora P 148 A1
Vilarandelo P 148 A2
Vilar de Santos E 140 B3
Vilardevós E 141 C3
Vila Real P 148 A2
Vila-real de los Infantes E 159 B3
Vila Real de Santo António P 160 B2
Vilar Formosa P 149 B3
Vila-Rodona E 147 C2
Vila Ruiva P 160 A2
Vilasantar E 140 A2
Vilaseca E 147 C2
Vila Seca P 148 B1
Vilassar de Mar E 147 C3
Vilasund S 195 D5
Vila Velha de Ródão P 155 B3
Vila Verde
*Braga* P 148 A1
*Lisboa* P 154 B1
Vila Verde de Filcalho P 161 B2
Vila Viçosa P 155 C3
Vilches E 157 B4
Vildbjerg DK 59 B1
Vilémov CZ 97 B3
Vileyka BY 13 A7
Vilhelmina S 200 B2
Vilia GR 184 A4
Viljandi EST 8 C4
Villabáñez E 150 A3
Villablanca E 161 B2
Villablino E 141 B4
Villabona E 144 A1
Villabragima E 142 C1
Villabuena del Puente E 150 A2
Villacadima E 151 A4
Villacañas E 157 A4
Villacarriedo E 143 A3
Villacarrillo E 164 A1
Villa Castelli I 173 B3
Villacastín E 150 B3
Villach A 109 C4
Villacidro I 179 C2
Villaconejos E 151 B4
Villaconejos de Trabaque E 152 B1
Villa Cova de Lixa P 148 A1
Villada E 142 B2
Villadangos del Páramo E 141 B5
Villadecanes E 141 B4
Villa del Prado E 150 B3
Villa del Rio E 157 C3
Villadepera E 149 A3
Villa de Peralonso E 149 A3
Villa di Chiavenna I 120 A2
Villadiego E 142 B2
Villadompardo E 163 A3
Villadóssola I 119 A5
Villaeles de Valdavia E 142 B2
Villaescusa de Haro E 158 B1
Villafáfila E 142 C1
Villafeliche E 152 A2
Villaflores E 150 A2
Villafrades de Campos E 142 B2
Villafranca
*Avila* E 150 B2
*Navarra* E 144 B2
Villafranca de Córdoba E 157 C3
Villafranca del Bierzo E 141 B4
Villafranca de los Barros E 155 C4
Villafranca de los Caballeros E 157 A4
Villafranca di Verona I 121 B3
Villafranca in Lunigiana I 134 A2
Villafranca-Montes de Oca E 143 B3
Villafranca Tirrena I 177 A4
Villafranco del Campo E 152 B2
Villafranco del Guadalquivir E 161 B3
Villafrati I 176 B2
Villafrechós E 142 C1
Villafruela E 143 C3
Villagarcia de las Torres E 156 B1
Villaggio Mancuso I 175 B2
Villagonzalo E 156 B1
Villagotón E 141 B4
Villagrains F 128 B2
Villaharta E 156 B3
Villahermosa E 158 C1
Villaherreros E 142 B2
Villahoz E 143 B3
Villaines-la-Juhel F 89 B3
Villajoyosa E 159 C3
Villalago I 169 B3
Villalba
E 140 A3
I 176 B2
Villalba de Calatrava E 157 B4
Villalba de Guardo E 142 B2
Villalba del Alcor E 161 B3
Villalba de la Sierra E 152 B1
Villalba de los Alcores E 142 C2
Villalba de los Barros E 155 C4
Villalba del Rey E 151 B5
Villalcampo E 149 A3
Villalcázar de Sirga E 142 B2
Villalengua E 152 A2
Villalgordo del Júcar E 158 B1
Villalgordo del Marquesado E 158 B1
Villalmóndar E 143 B3
Villalón de Campos E 142 B1
Villalonga E 159 C3
Villalonso E 150 A2
Villalpando E 142 C1
Villaluenga E 151 B4
Villalumbroso E 142 B2
Villálvaro E 143 C3
Villamalea E 158 B2
Villamanán E 142 B1
Villamanín E 142 B1
Villamanrique E 157 B5
Villamanrique de la Condesa E 161 B3
Villamanta E 151 B3
Villamantilla E 151 B3
Villamar I 179 C2
Villamartín E 162 B2
Villamartín de Campos E 142 B2
Villamartín de Don Sancho E 142 B1
Villamassárgia I 179 C2
Villamayor E 142 A1
Villamayor de Calatrava E 157 B3
Villamayor de Campos E 142 C1
Villamayor de Santiago E 157 A5
Villamblard F 129 A3
Villamejil E 141 B4
Villamesías E 156 A2
Villaminaya E 157 A4
Villa Minozzo I 134 A3
Villamor de los Escuderos E 150 A2
Villamoronta E 142 B2
Villamuelas E 151 C4
Villamuriel de Cerrato E 142 C2
Villandraut F 128 B2
Villanova I 173 B3
Villanova d'Asti I 119 C4
Villanova del Battista I 171 B3
Villanova Mondov i I 133 A3
Villanova Monteleone I 178 B2
Villante E 143 B3
Villantério I 120 B2
Villanubla E 142 C2
Villanueva de Alcardete E 157 A4
Villanueva de Alcorón E 152 B1
Villanueva de Algaidas E 163 A3
Villanueva de Argaña E 143 B3
Villanueva de Bogas E 157 A4
Villanueva de Córdoba E 156 B3
Villanueva de Gállego E 144 C3
Villanueva del Aceral E 150 A3
Villanueva de la Concepcion E 163 B3
Villanueva de la Fuente E 158 C1
Villanueva de la Jara E 158 B2
Villanueva de la Reina E 157 B4
Villanueva del Arzobispo E 164 A2
Villanueva de la Serena E 156 B2
Villanueva de la Sierra E 149 B3
Villanueva de las Manzanas E 142 B1
Villanueva de las Peras E 141 C5
Villanueva de las Torres E 164 B1

Villanueva de la Vera E 150 B2
Villanueva del Campo E 142 C1
Villanueva del Duque E 156 B3
Villanueva del Fresno E 155 C3
Villanueva del Huerva E 152 A2
Villanueva de los Castillejos E 161 B2
Villanueva de los Infantes E 157 B5
Villanueva del Rey E 156 B2
Villanueva del Rio E 162 A2
Villanueva del Rio y Minas E 162 A2
Villanueva del Rosario E 163 B3
Villanueva del Trabuco E 163 A3
Villanueva de Mesia E 163 A4
Villanueva de Nía E 142 B2
Villanueva de Oscos E 141 A4
Villanueva de San Carlos E 157 B4
Villanueva de San Juan E 162 A2
Villanueva de Tapia E 163 A3
Villanueva de Valdegovia E 143 B3
Villány H 125 B4
Villaputzu I 179 C3
Villaquejida E 142 B1
Villaquilambre E 142 B1
Villaquiran de los Infantes E 142 B2
Villaralto E 156 B3
Villarcayo E 143 B3
Villard-de-Lans F 118 B2
Villar de Barrio E 140 B3
Villar de Cañas E 158 B1
Villar de Chinchilla E 158 C2
Villar de Ciervo E 149 B3
Villardeciervos E 141 C4
Villar de Domingo Garcia E 152 B1
Villardefrades E 142 C1
Villar del Arzobispo E 159 B3
Villar del Buey E 149 A3
Villar del Cobo E 152 B2
Villar del Humo E 158 B2
Villar de los Navarros E 152 A2
Villar del Pedroso E 156 A2
Villar del Rey E 155 B4
Villar del Rio E 143 B4
Villar del Saz de Navalón E 152 B1
Villar de Rena E 156 A2
Villarejo E 151 A4
Villarejo de Fuentes E 158 B1
Villarejo de Orbigo E 141 B5
Villarejo de Salvanes E 151 B4
Villarejo-Periesteban E 158 B1
Villares del Saz E 158 B1
Villaretto I 119 B4
Villargordo del Cabriel E 158 B2
Villarino E 149 A3
Villarino de Conso E 141 B3
Villarluengo E 153 B3
Villarobe E 143 B3
Villarosa I 177 B3
Villar Perosa I 119 C4
Villarramiel E 142 B2
Villarrasa E 161 B3
Villarreal de San Carlos E 150 C1
Villarrin de Campos E 142 C1
Villarrobledo E 158 B1
Villarroya de la Sierra E 152 A2
Villarroya de los Pinares E 153 B3
Villarrubia de los Ojos E 157 A4
Villarrubia de Santiago E 151 C4
Villarrubio E 151 C5
Villars-les-Dombes F 117 A5
Villarta E 158 B2
Villarta de los Montes E 156 A3
Villarta de San Juan E 157 A4
Villasana de Mena E 143 A3
Villasandino E 142 B2
Villa San Giovanni I 175 C1
Villa Santa Maria I 169 B4
Villasante E 143 A3
Villa Santina I 122 A1
Villasarracino E 142 B2
Villasayas E 151 A5
Villasdardo E 149 A3
Villaseca de Henares E 151 B5
Villaseca de Laciana E 141 B4
Villaseca de la Sagra E 151 C4
Villaseco de los Gamitos E 149 A3
Villaseco de los Reyes E 149 A3
Villasequilla de Yepes E 151 C4
Villasimius I 179 C3
Villasmundo I 177 B4
Villasor I 179 C2
Villastar E 152 B2
Villastellone I 119 C4
Villatobas E 151 C4
Villatorp E 150 B2
Villatoya E 158 B2
Villavaliente E 158 B2
Villavelayo E 143 B4
Villavella E 141 B3
Villaver de de Guadalimar E 158 C1
Villaverde del Rio E 162 A2
Villaviciosa E 142 A1
Villaviciosa de Córdoba E 156 B3
Villaviciosa de Odón E 151 B4
Villavieja de Yeltes E 149 B3
Villayón E 141 A4
Villé F 93 C3
Villebois-Lavalette F 115 C4
Villecerf F 90 C2
Villecomtal F 130 A1
Villedieu-les-Poêles F 88 B2
Villedieu-sur-Indre F 103 C3
Ville-di-Pietrabugno F 180 A2
Villedômain F 103 B3
Villefagnan F 115 B4
Villefontaine F 118 B2
Villefort F 131 A2
Villefranche-d'Albigeois F 130 B1
Villefranche-d'Allier F 116 A2
Villefranche-de-Lauragais F 146 A2
Villefranche-de-Lonchat F 128 B3
Villefranche-de-Panat F 130 A1
Villefranche-de-Rouergue F 130 A1
Villefranche-du-Périgord F 129 B4
Villefranche-sur-Cher F 103 B3
Villefranche-sur-Mer F 133 B3
Villefranche-sur-Saône F 117 A4
Villegenon F 103 B4
Villel E 152 B2
Villemaur-sur-Vanne F 104 A2
Villemontais F 117 B3
Villemur-sur-Tarn F 129 C4
Villena E 159 C3
Villenauxe-la-Grande F 91 C3
Villenave-d'Ornon F 128 B2
Villeneuve
CH 119 A3
F 129 B5
Villeneuve-d'Ascq F 78 B3
Villeneuve-de-Berg F 131 A3
Villeneuve-de-Marsan F 128 C2
Villeneuve-de-Rivière F 145 A4
Villeneuve-la-Guyard F 90 C3
Villeneuve-l'Archevêque F 104 A2
Villeneuve-le-Comte F 90 C2
Villeneuve-lès-Avignon F 131 B3
Villeneuve-les-Corbières F 146 B3
Villeneuve-St Georges F 90 C2
Villeneuve-sur-Allier F 104 C2
Villeneuve-sur-Lot F 129 B3
Villeneuve-sur-Yonne F 104 A2
Villeréal F 129 B3
Villerias E 142 C2
Villeromain F 103 B3
Villers-Bocage
*Calvados* F 88 A3
*Somme* F 90 B2
Villers-Bretonneux F 90 B2
Villers-Carbonnel F 90 B2
Villers-Cotterêts F 90 B3
Villersexel F 105 B5
Villers-Farlay F 105 C4
Villers-le-Gambon B 79 B4
Villers-le-Lac F 106 B1
Villers-sur-Mer F 89 A3
Villerupt F 92 B1
Villerville F 89 A4
Villeseneux F 91 C4
Ville-sous-la-Ferté F 105 A3
Ville-sur-Illon F 105 A5
Ville-sur-Tourbe F 91 B4
Villetrun F 103 B3
Villetta Barrea I 169 B3
Villeurbanne F 117 B4
Villeveyrac F 130 B2
Villevocance F 117 B4
Villiers-St Benoit F 104 B2
Villiers-St Georges F 91 C3
Villingen D 106 A3
Villmar D 81 B4
Villoldo E 142 B2
Villon F 104 B3
Villoria E 150 B2
Vilnes N 46 A1
Vilnius LT 13 A6
Vils
A 108 B1
DK 58 B1
Vilsbiburg D 95 C4
Vilseck D 95 B3
Vilshofen D 96 C1
Vilshult S 63 B2
Vilusi MNE 139 C4
Vilvestre E 149 A3
Vilvoorde B 79 B4
Vimeiro P 154 B1
Vimercate I 120 B2
Vimianzo E 140 A1
Vimieiro P 154 C3
Vimioso P 149 A3
Vimmerby S 62 A3
Vimoutiers F 89 B4
Vimperk CZ 96 B1
Vimy F 78 B2
Vinadi CH 108 C1
Vinadio I 133 A3
Vinaixa E 147 C1
Vinarós E 153 B4
Vinäs S 50 B1
Vinay F 118 B2
Vinberg S 60 C2
Vinca F 146 B3
Vinča SRB 127 C2
Vinchiaturo I 170 B2
Vinci I 135 B3
Vindeby DK 65 A3
Vindelgransele S 195 E9
Vindeln S 200 B5
Vinderup DK 58 B1
Vindsvik N 52 A2
Vinets F 91 C4
Vineuil F 103 B3
Vinga RO 126 A3
Vingåker S 56 A1
Vingnes N 48 A2
Vingrau F 146 B3
Vingrom N 48 A2
Vinhais P 149 A3
Vinica
HR 124 A2
MK 182 B4
SK 112 A3
SLO 123 B4
Viniegra de Arriba E 143 B4
Vinje
*Hordaland* N 46 B3
*Sør-Trøndelag* N 198 B6
*Telemark* N 53 A3
Vinkovci HR 125 B4
Vinliden S 200 B3
Vinninga S 55 B4
Vinnytsya UA 13 D8
Vinon F 103 B4
Vinon-sur-Verdon F 132 B1
Vinslöv S 61 C3
Vinstra N 48 A1
Vintjärn S 50 B3
Vintrosa S 55 A5
Viñuela E 163 B3
Viñuela de Sayago E 149 A4
Viñuelas E 151 B4
Vinuesa E 143 C4
Vinzelberg D 73 B4
Viöl D 64 B2
Viola I 133 A3
Violay F 117 B4
Vipava SLO 122 B2
Vipiteno I 108 C2
Vipperow D 74 A1
Vir
BIH 138 B3
Vir *continued*
HR 137 A4
Vira CH 120 A1
Vire F 88 B3
Vireda S 62 A2
Vireux F 91 A4
Virgen A 109 B3
Virgen de la Cabeza E 157 B3
Virginia IRL 27 C3
Virieu F 118 B2
Virieu-le-Grand F 118 B2
Virje HR 124 A2
Virkkunen FIN 197 D10
Virklund DK 59 B2
Virovitica HR 124 B3
Virsbo S 50 C3
Virserum S 62 A3
Virtaniemi FIN 193 D12
Virton B 92 B1
Virtsu EST 8 C3
Viry F 118 A3
Vis HR 138 B2
Visbek D 71 B5
Visby
DK 64 A1
S 57 C4
Visé B 80 B1
Višegrad BIH 139 B5
Viserba I 136 A1
Viseu P 148 B2
Visiedo E 152 B2
Viskafors S 60 B2
Visland N 52 B2
Vislanda S 62 B2
Visnes N 52 A1
Višnja Gora SLO 123 B3
Višnjan HR 122 B2
Višnové CZ 97 C4
Visnums-Kil S 55 A5
Viso del Marqués E 157 B4
Visoko
BIH 139 B4
SLO 123 A3
Visone I 119 C5
Visp CH 119 A4
Vissefjärda S 63 B3
Visselhövede D 72 B2
Vissenbjerg DK 59 C3
Visso I 136 C2
Vistabella del Maestrat E 153 B3
Vistheden S 196 D3
Vita I 176 B1
Vitanje SLO 123 A4
Vitebsk = Vitsyebsk BY 13 A9
Viterbo I 168 A2
Vitez BIH 139 A3
Vithkuq AL 182 C2
Vitigudino E 149 A3
Vitina
BIH 138 B3
GR 184 B3
Vitis A 97 C3
Vítkov CZ 98 B1
Vitoria-Gasteiz E 143 B4
Vitré F 101 A4
Vitrey-sur-Mance F 105 B4
Vitry-en-Artois F 78 B2
Vitry-le-François F 91 C4
Vitry-sur-Seine F 90 C2
Vitsand S 49 B4
Vitsyebsk = Vitebsk BY 13 A9
Vittangi S 196 B4
Vittaryd S 60 C3
Vitteaux F 104 B3
Vittel F 105 A4
Vittinge S 51 C4
Vittória I 177 C3
Vittório Véneto I 122 B1
Vittsjö S 61 C3
Viù I 119 B4
Viul N 48 B2
Vivario F 180 A2
Viveiro E 140 A3
Vivel del Rio Martin E 152 B3
Viver E 159 B3
Viverols F 117 B3
Viveros E 158 C1
Viviers F 131 A3
Vivonne F 115 B4
Vivy F 102 B1
Vize TR 186 A2
Vizille F 118 B2
Viziňada HR 122 B2
Viziru RO 17 C7
Vizovice CZ 98 B1
Vizvár H 124 A3
Vizzavona F 180 A2
Vizzini I 177 B3
Vlachiotis GR 184 C3
Vlachovice CZ 98 B1
Vlachovo SK 99 C4
Vláchovo Březi CZ 96 B1
Vladimirci SRB 127 C1
Vladimirovac SRB 127 B2
Vladislav CZ 97 B3
Vlagtwedde NL 71 A4
Vlajkovac SRB 127 B3
Vlasenica BIH 139 A4
Vlašim CZ 96 B2
Vlatkovići BIH 138 A3
Vledder NL 70 B3
Vlissingen NL 79 A3
Vlkolínec SK 99 B3
Vlorë AL 182 C1
Vlotho D 72 B1
Vnanje Gorice SLO 123 B3
Vobarno I 121 B3
Voćin HR 124 B3
Vöcklabruck A 109 A4
Vöcklamarkt A 109 B4
Vodanj SRB 127 C2
Voderady SK 98 C1
Vodice
*Istarska* HR 123 B3
*Šibenska* HR 137 B4
SLO 123 A3
Vodňany CZ 96 B2
Vodnjan HR 122 C2
Vodskov DK 58 A3
Voe GB 33 A5
Voerså DK 58 A3
Voghera I 120 C2
Vogogna I 119 A5
Vogošća BIH 139 B4
Vogué F 131 A3
Vohburg D 95 C3
Vohenstrauss D 95 B4
Vöhl D 81 A4
Vöhrenbach D 106 A3
Vöhringen D 94 C2
Void-Vacon F 92 C1
Voiron F 118 B2
Voise F 90 C1
Voisey F 105 B4
Voiteg RO 126 B3
Voiteur F 105 C4
Voitsberg A 110 B2
Vojakkala FIN 196 D7
Vojens DK 59 C2
Vojka SRB 127 C2
Vojlovica SRB 127 C2
Vojnić HR 123 B4
Vojnice SK 112 B2
Vojnik SLO 123 A4
Vojvoda Stepa SRB 126 B2
Volada GR 188 D2
Volargne I 121 B3
Volary CZ 96 C1
Volče SLO 122 A2
Volda N 198 C3
Volendam NL 70 B2
Volga RUS 9 C11
Volimes GR 184 B1
Volissos GR 185 A6
Volkach D 94 B2
Völkermarkt A 110 C1
Volkhov RUS 9 C8
Völklingen D 92 B2
Volkmarsen D 81 A5
Voll N 198 C4
Vollenhove NL 70 B2
Vollore-Montagne F 117 B3
Vollsjö S 61 D3
Volodymyr-Volyns'kyy UA 13 C6
Volokolamsk RUS 9 D9
Volos GR 182 D4
Volosovo RUS 9 C6
Volovets UA 13 D5
Voltággio I 120 C1
Volta Mantovana I 121 B3
Volterra I 135 B3
Voltri I 133 A4
Volturara Áppula I 170 B3
Volturara Irpina I 170 C2
Volvic F 116 B3
Volx F 132 B1
Volyně CZ 96 B1
Vonitsa GR 182 E2
Vönöck H 111 B4
Vonsild DK 59 C2
Voorschoten NL 70 B1
Vopnafjörður IS 191 B11
Vorau A 110 B2
Vorbasse DK 59 C2
Vorchdorf A 109 B4
Vorden
D 71 B5
NL 71 B3
Vordernberg A 110 B1
Vordingborg DK 65 A4
Vorë AL 182 B1
Voreppe F 118 B2
Vorey F 117 B3
Vorgod DK 59 B1
Vormsund N 48 B3
Võru EST 8 D5
Voskopojë AL 182 C2
Voss N 46 B3
Votice CZ 96 B2
Voué F 91 C4
Vouillé F 115 B4
Voulx F 90 C2
Voussac F 116 A3
Vouvray F 102 B2
Vouvry CH 119 A3
Vouzela P 148 B1
Vouziers F 91 B4
Voves F 103 A3
Voxna S 50 A2
Voy GB 33 B3
Voynitsa RUS 3 D12
Voznesenye RUS 9 B9
Vrå
DK 58 A2
S 60 C3
Vráble SK 98 C2
Vračenovići MNE 139 C4
Vračev Gaj SRB 127 C3
Vraćevsnica SRB 127 C2
Vrådal N 53 A4
Vrakneika GR 184 A2
Vrana HR 123 C3
Vranduk BIH 139 A3
Vrångö S 60 B1
Vrani RO 127 B3
Vranić SRB 127 C2
Vranići BIH 139 B4
Vranja HR 123 B3
Vranjak BIH 125 C4
Vranje SRB 16 D4
Vranovice CZ 97 C4
Vranov nad Dyje CZ 97 C3
Vransko SLO 123 A3
Vrapčići BIH 139 B3
Vratimov CZ 98 B2
Vratsa BG 17 D5
Vrbanja HR 125 C4
Vrbanjci BIH 124 C3
Vrbas SRB 126 B1
Vrbaška BIH 124 B3
Vrbnik
*Primorsko-Goranska* HR 123 B3
*Zadarsko-Kninska* HR 138 A2
Vrbno pod Pradědem CZ 85 B5
Vrboska HR 138 B2
Vrbov SK 99 B4
Vrbovce SK 98 C1
Vrbové SK 98 C1
Vrbovec HR 124 B2
Vrbovski SRB 127 C2
Vrbovsko HR 123 B4
Vrchlabí CZ 84 B3
Vrčin SRB 127 C2
Vrdy CZ 97 B3
Vrebac HR 137 A4
Vreden D 71 B3
Vreoci SRB 127 C2
Vretstorp S 55 A5
Vrginmost HR 124 B1
Vrgorac HR 138 B3
Vrhnika SLO 123 B3
Vrhovine HR 123 C4
Vrhpolie SRB 127 C1
Vriezenveen NL 71 B3
Vrigne-aux-Bois F 91 B4
Vrigstad S 62 A2
Vrlika HR 138 B2
Vrnograč BIH 124 B1
Vron F 78 B1
Vroomshoop NL 71 B3
Vroutek CZ 83 B5
Vrpolje HR 125 B4
Vršac SRB 126 B3
Vrsar HR 122 B2
Vrsi HR 137 A4
Vrtoče BIH 124 C2
Vrútky SK 98 B2
Všeruby CZ 95 B4
Všestary CZ 85 B3
Vsetín CZ 98 B1
Vučkovica SRB 127 D2
Vught NL 79 A5
Vuillafans F 105 B5
Vukovar HR 125 B5
Vuku N 199 B8
Vulcan RO 17 C5
Vulcăneşti MD 17 C8
Vuoggatjålme S 195 D7
Vuojärvi FIN 197 B9
Vuolijoki FIN 3 D10
Vuollerim S 196 C3
Vuotso FIN 197 A10
Vuzenica SLO 110 C2
Vyartsilya RUS 9 A7
Vyborg RUS 9 B6
Výčapy CZ 97 B3
Výčapy-Opatovce SK 98 C2
Východna SK 99 B3
Vydrany SK 111 A4
Vyerkhnyadzvinsk BY 13 A7
Vyhne SK 98 C2
Vy-lès Lure F 105 B5
Vylkove UA 17 C8
Vynohradiv UA 17 A5
Vyshniy Volochek RUS 9 D9
Vyškov CZ 97 B5
Vysokánad Kysucou SK 98 B2
Vysoké Mýto CZ 97 B4
Vysokovsk RUS 9 D10
Vyšší Brod CZ 96 C2
Vytegra RUS 9 B10

## W

Waabs D 64 B2
Waalwijk NL 79 A5
Waarschoot B 79 A3
Wabern D 81 A5
Wąbrzeźno PL 69 B3
Wąchock PL 87 A5
Wachow D 74 B1
Wachów PL 86 B2
Wächtersbach D 81 B5
Wackersdorf D 95 B4
Waddington GB 40 B3
Wadebridge GB 42 B2
Wadelsdorf D 84 A2

**Wädenswil** CH . . . . 107 B3
**Wadern** D . . . . . . . . . 92 B2
**Wadersloh** D . . . . . . 81 A4
**Wadlew** PL . . . . . . . . 86 A3
**Wadowice** PL . . . . . . 99 B3
**Wagenfeld** D . . . . . . 72 B1
**Wageningen** NL . . . . 70 C2
**Waghäusel** D . . . . . . 93 B4
**Waging** D . . . . . . . . 109 B3
**Wagrain** A . . . . . . . . 109 B4
**Wągrowiec** PL . . . . . 76 B2
**Wahlsdorf** D . . . . . . . 74 C2
**Wahlstedt** D . . . . . . . 64 C3
**Wahrenholz** D . . . . . 73 B3
**Waiblingen** D . . . . . . 94 C1
**Waidhaus** D . . . . . . . 95 B4
**Waidhofen an der Thaya**
A . . . . . . . . . . . . . . . 97 C3
**Waidhofen an der Ybbs**
A . . . . . . . . . . . . . . 110 B1
**Waimes** B . . . . . . . . . 80 B2
**Wainfleet All Saints**
GB . . . . . . . . . . . . . 41 B4
**Waizenkirchen** A . . . 96 C1
**Wakefield** GB . . . . . . 40 B2
**Wałbrzych** PL . . . . . . 85 B4
**Walchensee** D . . . . 108 B2
**Walchsee** A . . . . . . 109 B3
**Wałcz** PL . . . . . . . . . 75 A5
**Wald** CH . . . . . . . . . 107 B3
**Waldaschaff** D . . . . . 94 B1
**Waldbach** A . . . . . . . 110 B2
**Waldböckelheim** D . 93 B3
**Waldbröl** D . . . . . . . . 81 B3
**Waldeck** D . . . . . . . . 81 A5
**Waldenburg** D . . . . . 83 B4
**Waldfischbach-Burgalben** D . . . . . 93 B3
**Waldheim** D . . . . . . . 83 A5
**Waldkappel** D . . . . . 82 A1
**Waldkirch** D . . . . . . 106 A2
**Waldkirchen** D . . . . . 96 C1
**Waldkirchen am Wesen**
A . . . . . . . . . . . . . . . 96 C1
**Waldkraiburg** D . . . 109 A3
**Wald-Michelbach** D. 93 B4
**Waldmohr** D . . . . . . . 93 B3
**Waldmünchen** D . . . 95 B4
**Waldring** A . . . . . . . 109 B3
**Waldsassen** D . . . . . 95 A4
**Waldshut** D . . . . . . 106 B3
**Waldstatt** CH . . . . . 107 B4
**Waldwisse** F . . . . . . 92 B2
**Walenstadt** CH . . . 107 B4
**Walentynów** PL . . . . 87 A5
**Walichnowy** PL . . . . 86 A2
**Walincourt** F . . . . . . 90 A3
**Walkenried** D . . . . . . 82 A2
**Walkeringham** GB . . 40 B3
**Wallasey** GB . . . . . . 38 A3
**Walldürn** D . . . . . . . . 94 B1
**Wallenfells** D . . . . . . 82 B3
**Wallenhorst** D . . . . . 71 B5
**Wallers** F . . . . . . . . . 78 B3
**Wallersdorf** D . . . . . 95 C4
**Wallerstein** D . . . . . . 94 C2
**Wallingford** GB . . . . 44 B2
**Wallitz** D . . . . . . . . . 74 A1
**Walls** GB . . . . . . . . . 33 A5
**Wallsbüll** D . . . . . . . 64 B2
**Walmer** GB . . . . . . . . 45 B5
**Walsall** GB . . . . . . . . 40 C2
**Walshoutem** B . . . . . 79 B5
**Walsrode** D . . . . . . . 72 B2
**Waltenhofen** D . . . . 107 B5
**Waltershausen** D . . . 82 B2
**Waltham Abbey** GB . 45 B4
**Waltham on the Wolds**
GB . . . . . . . . . . . . . 40 C3
**Walton-on-Thames**
GB . . . . . . . . . . . . . 44 B3
**Walton-on-the-Naze**
GB . . . . . . . . . . . . . 45 B5
**Wamba** E . . . . . . . . 142 C2
**Wanderup** D . . . . . . . 64 B2
**Wandlitz** D . . . . . . . . 74 B2
**Wanfried** D . . . . . . . . 82 A2
**Wangen im Allgäu**
D . . . . . . . . . . . . . . 107 B4
**Wangerooge** D . . . . . 71 A4
**Wangersen** D . . . . . . 72 A2
**Wängi** CH . . . . . . . . 107 B3
**Wanna** D . . . . . . . . . . 64 C1
**Wansford** GB . . . . . . 40 C3
**Wantage** GB . . . . . . . 44 B2
**Wanzleben** D . . . . . . 73 B4
**Waplewo** PL . . . . . . . 77 A5
**Wapnica** PL . . . . . . . 75 A4
**Wapno** PL . . . . . . . . . 76 B2
**Warburg** D . . . . . . . . 81 A5
**Wardenburg** D . . . . . 71 A5
**Ware** GB . . . . . . . . . . 44 B3
**Waregem** B . . . . . . . . 79 B3
**Wareham** GB . . . . . . 43 B4
**Waremme** B . . . . . . . . 79 B5
**Waren** D . . . . . . . . . . 74 A1
**Warendorf** D . . . . . . 71 C4
**Warga** NL . . . . . . . . . 70 A2
**Warin** D . . . . . . . . . . 65 C4
**Wark** GB . . . . . . . . . . 37 A4
**Warka** PL . . . . . . . . . 87 A5
**Warkworth** GB . . . . . 37 A5
**Warlubie** PL . . . . . . . 69 B3
**Warminster** GB . . . . 43 A4
**Warnemünde** D . . . . 65 B5
**Warnow** D . . . . . . . . . 65 C4
**Warnsveld** NL . . . . . 70 B3
**Warrenpoint** GB . . . 27 B4
**Warrington** GB . . . . 38 A4
**Warsaw = Warszawa**
PL . . . . . . . . . . . . . 77 B6
**Warsingsfehn** D . . . 71 A4
**Warsow** D . . . . . . . . 73 A4
**Warstein** D . . . . . . . . 81 A4
**Warszawa = Warsaw**
PL . . . . . . . . . . . . . 77 B6
**Warta** PL . . . . . . . . . 86 A2
**Wartberg** A . . . . . . . 110 B1
**Warth** A . . . . . . . . . 107 B5
**Warwick** GB . . . . . . . 44 A2
**Warza** D . . . . . . . . . . 82 B2
**Wasbister** GB . . . . . 33 B3
**Washington** GB . . . . 37 B5
**Wąsosz** PL . . . . . . . . 85 A4
**Wasselonne** F . . . . . 93 C3
**Wassen** CH . . . . . . 107 C3
**Wassenaar** NL . . . . . 70 B1
**Wasserauen** CH . . 107 B4
**Wasserburg** D . . . . 108 A3
**Wassertrüdingen** D. 94 B2
**Wassy** F . . . . . . . . . . 91 C4
**Wasungen** D . . . . . . 82 B2
**Watchet** GB . . . . . . . 43 A3
**Waterford** IRL . . . . . 30 B1
**Watergrasshill** IRL . . 29 B3
**Waterloo** B . . . . . . . . 79 B4
**Waterville** IRL . . . . . 29 C1
**Watford** GB . . . . . . . 44 B3
**Wathlingen** D . . . . . . 72 B3
**Watten**
F . . . . . . . . . . . . . . . 78 B2
GB . . . . . . . . . . . . . 32 C3
**Wattens** A . . . . . . . 108 B2
**Watton** GB . . . . . . . . 41 C4
**Wattwil** CH . . . . . . 107 B4
**Waunfawr** GB . . . . . 38 A2
**Wavignies** F . . . . . . . 90 B2
**Wavre** B . . . . . . . . . . 79 B4
**Wearhead** GB . . . . . 37 B4
**Wechadlow** PL . . . . . 87 B4
**Wedel** D . . . . . . . . . . 72 A2
**Wedemark** D . . . . . . 72 B2
**Weedon Bec** GB . . . 44 A2
**Weener** D . . . . . . . . . 71 A4
**Weert** NL . . . . . . . . . 80 A1
**Weesp** NL . . . . . . . . . 70 B2
**Weeze** D . . . . . . . . . . 80 A2
**Weferlingen** D . . . . . 73 B4
**Wegeleben** D . . . . . . 82 A3
**Weggis** CH . . . . . . . 106 B3
**Węgierska-Górka**
PL . . . . . . . . . . . . . 99 B3
**Wegliniec** PL . . . . . . 84 A3
**Węgorzyno** PL . . . . . 75 A4
**Węgrzynice** PL . . . . 75 B4
**Wegscheid** D . . . . . . 96 C1
**Wehdel** D . . . . . . . . . 72 A1
**Wehr** D . . . . . . . . . . 106 B2
**Weibersbrunn** D . . . . 94 B1
**Weichering** D . . . . . . 95 C3
**Weida** D . . . . . . . . . . 83 B4
**Weiden** D . . . . . . . . . 95 B4
**Weidenberg** D . . . . . 95 B3
**Weidenhain** D . . . . . . 83 A4
**Weidenstetten** D . . . 94 C1
**Weierbach** D . . . . . . 93 B3
**Weikersheim** D . . . . 94 B1
**Weil** D . . . . . . . . . . . 108 A1
**Weil am Rhein** D . . 106 B2
**Weilburg** D . . . . . . . . 81 B4
**Weil der Stadt** D . . . 93 C4
**Weilerswist** D . . . . . 80 B2
**Weilheim**
*Baden-Württemberg*
D . . . . . . . . . . . . . . 94 C1
*Bayern* D . . . . . . . . 108 B2
**Weilmünster** D . . . . . 81 B4
**Weiltensfeld** A . . . . 110 C1
**Weimar** D . . . . . . . . . 82 B3
**Weinberg** D . . . . . . . 94 B2
**Weinfelden** CH . . . 107 B4
**Weingarten**
*Baden-Württemberg*
D . . . . . . . . . . . . . . 93 B4
*Baden-Württemberg*
D . . . . . . . . . . . . . 107 B4
**Weinheim** D . . . . . . . 93 B4
**Weinstadt** D . . . . . . . 94 C1
**Weismain** D . . . . . . . 82 B3
**Weissbriach** A . . . . 109 C4
**Weissenbach** A . . . . 108 B1
**Weissenberg** D . . . . 84 A2
**Weissenbrunn** D . . . 82 B3
**Weissenburg** D . . . . 94 B2
**Weissenfels** D . . . . . 83 A3
**Weissenhorn** D . . . . 94 C2
**Weissenkirchen** A . . 97 C3
**Weissensee** D . . . . . 82 A3
**Weissenstadt** D . . . . 83 B3
**Weisskirchen im Steiermark** A . . . . . 110 B1
**Weisstannen** CH . . . 107 C4
**Weisswasser** D . . . . 84 A2
**Weitendorf** D . . . . . . 65 C5
**Weitersfeld** A . . . . . 97 C3
**Weitersfelden** A . . . . 96 C2
**Weitnau** D . . . . . . . 107 B5
**Wéitra** A . . . . . . . . . . 96 C2
**Weiz** A . . . . . . . . . . . 110 B2
**Wejherowo** PL . . . . . 68 A3
**Welkenraedt** B . . . . . 80 B1
**Wellaune** D . . . . . . . . 83 A4
**Wellin** B . . . . . . . . . . 91 A5
**Wellingborough** GB 44 A3
**Wellington**
*Somerset* GB . . . . . . 43 B3
**Wellington** *continued*
*Telford & Wrekin*
GB . . . . . . . . . . . . . 38 B4
**Wellingtonbridge**
IRL . . . . . . . . . . . . . 30 B2
**Wells** GB . . . . . . . . . . 43 A4
**Wells-next-the-Sea**
GB . . . . . . . . . . . . . 41 C4
**Wels** A . . . . . . . . . . . 109 A5
**Welschenrohr** CH . 106 B2
**Welshpool** GB . . . . . 38 B3
**Welver** D . . . . . . . . . . 81 A3
**Welwyn Garden City**
GB . . . . . . . . . . . . . 44 B3
**Welzheim** D . . . . . . . 94 C1
**Welzow** D . . . . . . . . . 84 A2
**Wem** GB . . . . . . . . . . 38 B4
**Wembury** GB . . . . . . 42 B2
**Wemding** D . . . . . . . 94 C2
**Wenden** D . . . . . . . . 81 B3
**Wendisch Rietz** D . . 74 B3
**Wendlingen** D . . . . . 94 C1
**Weng** A . . . . . . . . . . 109 A4
**Weng bei Admont**
A . . . . . . . . . . . . . . 110 B1
**Wengen** CH . . . . . . 106 C2
**Wenigzell** A . . . . . . . 110 B2
**Wennigsen** D . . . . . . 72 B2
**Wenns** A . . . . . . . . . 108 B1
**Wenzenbach** D . . . . 95 B4
**Weppersdorf** A . . . . 111 B3
**Werben** D . . . . . . . . . 73 B4
**Werbig** D . . . . . . . . . 74 C2
**Werdau** D . . . . . . . . . 83 B4
**Werder** D . . . . . . . . . 74 B1
**Werdohl** D . . . . . . . . 81 A3
**Werfen** A . . . . . . . . 109 B4
**Werkendam** NL . . . . 79 A4
**Werl** D . . . . . . . . . . . 81 A3
**Werlte** D . . . . . . . . . . 71 B4
**Wermelskirchen** D . 80 A3
**Wermsdorf** D . . . . . . 83 A4
**Wernberg Köblitz** D 95 B4
**Werne** D . . . . . . . . . . 81 A3
**Werneck** D . . . . . . . . 94 B2
**Werneuchen** D . . . . . 74 B2
**Wernigerode** D . . . . 82 A2
**Wertach** D . . . . . . . 108 B1
**Wertheim** D . . . . . . . 94 B1
**Wertingen** D . . . . . . 94 C2
**Weseke** D . . . . . . . . . 80 A2
**Wesel** D . . . . . . . . . . 80 A2
**Wesenberg** D . . . . . . 74 A1
**Wesendorf** D . . . . . . 73 B3
**Wesołowo** PL . . . . . . 77 A5
**Wesselburen** D . . . . 64 B1
**Wesseling** D . . . . . . 80 B2
**West Bridgford** GB . 40 C2
**West Bromwich** GB. 40 C2
**Westbury**
*Shropshire* GB . . . . . 38 B4
*Wiltshire* GB . . . . . . 43 A4
**Westbury-on-Severn**
GB . . . . . . . . . . . . . 39 C4
**Westendorf** A . . . . . 108 B3
**Westensee** D . . . . . . 64 B2
**Westerbork** NL . . . . 71 B3
**Westerburg** D . . . . . 81 B3
**Westerhaar** NL . . . . . 71 B3
**Westerholt** D . . . . . . 71 A4
**Westerkappeln** D . . . 71 B4
**Westerland** D . . . . . . 64 B1
**Westerlo** B . . . . . . . . 79 A4
**Westerstede** D . . . . . 71 A4
**West Haddon** GB . . . 44 A2
**Westheim** D . . . . . . . 94 B2
**Westhill** GB . . . . . . . 33 D4
**Westkapelle**
B . . . . . . . . . . . . . . . 78 A3
NL . . . . . . . . . . . . . . 79 A3
**West Kilbride** GB . . . 34 C3
**West Linton** GB . . . . 35 C4
**West Lulworth** GB . . 43 B4
**West Mersea** GB . . . 45 B4
**Westminster** GB . . . 44 B3
**Weston** GB . . . . . . . . 40 C1
**Weston-super-Mare**
GB . . . . . . . . . . . . . 43 A4
**Westport** IRL . . . . . . 28 A2
**Westruther** GB . . . . . 35 C5
**West-Terschelling**
NL . . . . . . . . . . . . . . 70 A2
**Westward Ho!** GB . . 42 A2
**West Woodburn** GB 37 A4
**Wetheral** GB . . . . . . 37 B4
**Wetherby** GB . . . . . . 40 B2
**Wetter**
*Hessen* D . . . . . . . . . 81 B4
*Nordrhein-Westfalen*
D . . . . . . . . . . . . . . 80 A3
**Wetteren** B . . . . . . . . 79 A3
**Wettin** D . . . . . . . . . . 83 A3
**Wettringen** D . . . . . . 71 B4
**Wetzikon** CH . . . . . 107 B3
**Wetzlar** D . . . . . . . . . 81 B4
**Wewelsfleth** D . . . . . 64 C2
**Wexford** IRL . . . . . . . 30 B2
**Weybridge** GB . . . . . 44 B3
**Weyerbusch** D . . . . . 81 B3
**Weyer Markt** A . . . . 110 B1
**Weyersheim** F . . . . . 93 C3
**Weyhe** D . . . . . . . . . . 72 B1
**Weyhill** GB . . . . . . . . 44 B2
**Weymouth** GB . . . . . 43 B4
**Weyregg** A . . . . . . . 109 B4
**Węzyska** PL . . . . . . . 75 B3
**Whalton** GB . . . . . . . 37 A5
**Whauphill** GB . . . . . 36 B2
**Wheatley** GB . . . . . . 44 B2
**Whickham** GB . . . . . 37 B5
**Whipsnade** GB . . . . 44 B3
**Whitburn** GB . . . . . . 35 C4
**Whitby** GB . . . . . . . . 37 B6
**Whitchurch**
*Hampshire* GB . . . . . 44 B2
*Herefordshire* GB . . . 39 C4
*Shropshire* GB . . . . . 38 B4
**White Bridge** GB . . . 32 D2
**Whitegate** IRL . . . . . 29 C3
**Whitehaven** GB . . . . 36 B3
**Whitehead** GB . . . . . 27 B5
**Whithorn** GB . . . . . . 36 B2
**Whitley Bay** GB . . . . 37 A5
**Whitstable** GB . . . . . 45 B5
**Whittington** GB . . . . 38 B4
**Whittlesey** GB . . . . . 41 C3
**Wiązów** PL . . . . . . . . 85 B5
**Wick** GB . . . . . . . . . . 32 C3
**Wickede** D . . . . . . . . 81 A3
**Wickford** GB . . . . . . 45 B4
**Wickham** GB . . . . . . 44 C2
**Wickham Market** GB 45 A5
**Wicklow** IRL . . . . . . . 30 B2
**Wicko** PL . . . . . . . . . 68 A2
**Widawa** PL . . . . . . . . 86 A2
**Widdrington** GB . . . 37 A5
**Widecombe in the Moor**
GB . . . . . . . . . . . . . 42 B3
**Widemouth** GB . . . . 42 B2
**Widnes** GB . . . . . . . . 38 A4
**Widuchowo** PL . . . . . 74 A3
**Więcbork** PL . . . . . . 76 A2
**Wiefelstede** D . . . . . 71 A5
**Wiehe** D . . . . . . . . . . 82 A3
**Wiehl** D . . . . . . . . . . . 81 B3
**Wiek** D . . . . . . . . . . . 66 B2
**Większyce** PL . . . . . 86 B1
**Wielbark** PL . . . . . . . 77 A5
**Wiele** PL . . . . . . . . . . 68 B2
**Wieleń** PL . . . . . . . . . 75 B5
**Wielgie**
*Kujawsko-Pomorskie*
PL . . . . . . . . . . . . . 77 B4
*Łódzkie* PL . . . . . . . . 86 A2
*Mazowieckie* PL . . . . 87 A5
**Wielgomłyny** PL . . . . 87 A3
**Wielichowo** PL . . . . . 75 B5
**Wieliczka** PL . . . . . . 99 B4
**Wielka Łąka** PL . . . . 76 A3
**Wielowies** PL . . . . . . 86 B2
**Wieluń** PL . . . . . . . . . 86 A2
**Wien = Vienna** A . . . 111 A3
**Wiener Neustadt** A . 111 B3
**Wiepke** D . . . . . . . . . 73 B4
**Wierden** NL . . . . . . . 71 B3
**Wieren** D . . . . . . . . . 73 B3
**Wieruszów** PL . . . . . 86 A2
**Wierzbica**
*Mazowieckie* PL . . . . 77 B6
*Mazowieckie* PL . . . . 87 A5
**Wierzbie** PL . . . . . . . 86 A2
**Wierzbięcin** PL . . . . 75 A4
**Wierzchowo** PL . . . . 75 A5
**Wierzchucino** PL . . . 68 A3
**Wierzchy** PL . . . . . . . 86 A2
**Wies** A . . . . . . . . . . . 110 C2
**Wiesau** D . . . . . . . . . 95 B4
**Wiesbaden** D . . . . . . 93 A4
**Wieselburg** A . . . . . . 110 A2
**Wiesen** CH . . . . . . . 107 C4
**Wiesenburg** D . . . . . 73 B5
**Wiesenfelden** D . . . . 95 B4
**Wiesensteig** D . . . . . 94 C1
**Wiesentheid** D . . . . . 94 B2
**Wiesloch** D . . . . . . . 93 B4
**Wiesmath** A . . . . . . 111 B3
**Wiesmoor** D . . . . . . . 71 A4
**Wietmarschen** D . . . 71 B4
**Wietze** D . . . . . . . . . 72 B2
**Wigan** GB . . . . . . . . . 38 A4
**Wiggen** CH . . . . . . . 106 C2
**Wigston** GB . . . . . . . 40 C2
**Wigton** GB . . . . . . . . 36 B3
**Wigtown** GB . . . . . . . 36 B2
**Wijchen** NL . . . . . . . 80 A1
**Wijhe** NL . . . . . . . . . 70 B3
**Wijk bij Duurstede**
NL . . . . . . . . . . . . . . 70 C2
**Wil** CH . . . . . . . . . . 107 B4
**Wilamowice** PL . . . . 99 B3
**Wilczęta** PL . . . . . . . 69 A4
**Wilczkowice** PL . . . . 77 B4
**Wilczna** PL . . . . . . . . 76 B3
**Wilczyn** PL . . . . . . . . 76 B3
**Wildalpen** A . . . . . . 110 B1
**Wildbad** D . . . . . . . . 93 C4
**Wildberg**
*Baden-Württemberg*
D . . . . . . . . . . . . . . 93 C4
*Brandenburg* D . . . . . 74 B1
**Wildegg** CH . . . . . . 106 B3
**Wildendürnbach** A . 97 C4
**Wildeshausen** D . . . 72 B1
**Wildon** A . . . . . . . . 110 C2
**Wilfersdorf** A . . . . . . 97 C4
**Wilhelmsburg**
A . . . . . . . . . . . . . . 110 A2
D . . . . . . . . . . . . . . . 74 A2
**Wilhelmsdorf** D . . . 107 B4
**Wilhelmshaven** D . . 71 A5
**Wilków** PL . . . . . . . . 77 B5
**Willebadessen** D . . . 81 A5
**Willebroek** B . . . . . . 79 A4
**Willgottheim** F . . . . . 93 C3
**Willhermsdorf** D . . . 94 B2
**Willich** D . . . . . . . . . 80 A2
**Willingen** D . . . . . . . 81 A4
**Willington** GB . . . . . 37 B5
**Willisau** CH . . . . . . 106 B3
**Wilmslow** GB . . . . . . 40 B1
**Wilsdruff** D . . . . . . . 83 A5
**Wilster** D . . . . . . . . . 64 C2
**Wilsum** D . . . . . . . . . 71 B3
**Wilton** GB . . . . . . . . 44 B2
**Wiltz** L . . . . . . . . . . . 92 B1
**Wimborne Minster**
GB . . . . . . . . . . . . . 43 B5
**Wimereux** F . . . . . . . 78 B1
**Wimmenau** F . . . . . . 93 C3
**Wimmis** CH . . . . . . 106 C2
**Wincanton** GB . . . . . 43 A4
**Winchcombe** GB . . . 44 B2
**Winchelsea** GB . . . . 45 C4
**Winchester** GB . . . . 44 B2
**Windermere** GB . . . . 36 B4
**Windischeschenbach**
D . . . . . . . . . . . . . . . 95 B4
**Windischgarsten** A . 110 B1
**Windorf** D . . . . . . . . . 96 C1
**Windsbach** D . . . . . . 94 B2
**Windsor** GB . . . . . . . 44 B3
**Wingene** B . . . . . . . . 78 A3
**Wingham** GB . . . . . . 45 B5
**Winkleigh** GB . . . . . 42 B3
**Winklern** A . . . . . . . 109 C3
**Winnenden** D . . . . . . 94 C1
**Winnica** PL . . . . . . . . 77 B5
**Winnigstedt** D . . . . . 73 B3
**Winnweiler** D . . . . . . 93 B3
**Winschoten** NL . . . . 71 A4
**Winsen**
*Niedersachsen* D . . . 72 A3
*Niedersachsen* D . . . 72 B2
**Winsford** GB . . . . . . 38 A4
**Wińsko** PL . . . . . . . . 85 A4
**Winslow** GB . . . . . . . 44 B3
**Winsum**
*Friesland* NL . . . . . . 70 A2
*Groningen* NL . . . . . 71 A3
**Winterberg** D . . . . . . 81 A4
**Winterfeld** D . . . . . . 73 B4
**Winterswijk** NL . . . . 71 C3
**Winterthur** CH . . . . 107 B3
**Wintzenheim** F . . . 106 A2
**Winzer** D . . . . . . . . . 95 C5
**Wipperdorf** D . . . . . . 82 A2
**Wipperfürth** D . . . . . 80 A3
**Wirksworth** GB . . . . 40 B2
**Wisbech** GB . . . . . . 41 C4
**Wischhafen** D . . . . . 64 C2
**Wishaw** GB . . . . . . . 35 C4
**Wisła** PL . . . . . . . . . . 98 B2
**Wisła Wielka** PL . . . . 98 B2
**Wislica** PL . . . . . . . . 87 B4
**Wismar** D . . . . . . . . . 65 C4
**Wisniewo** PL . . . . . . 77 A5
**Wiśniowa** PL . . . . . . 99 B4
**Wissant** F . . . . . . . . . 78 B1
**Wissembourg** F . . . . 93 B3
**Wissen** D . . . . . . . . . 81 B3
**Witanowice** PL . . . . 99 B3
**Witham** GB . . . . . . . 45 B4
**Withern** GB . . . . . . . 41 B4
**Withernsea** GB . . . . 41 B4
**Witkowo** PL . . . . . . . 76 B2
**Witmarsum** NL . . . . . 70 A2
**Witney** GB . . . . . . . . 44 B2
**Witnica** PL . . . . . . . . 75 B3
**Witonia** PL . . . . . . . . 77 B4
**Witry-les-Reims** F . . 91 B4
**Wittdün** D . . . . . . . . . 64 B1
**Wittelsheim** F . . . . 106 B2
**Witten** D . . . . . . . . . . 80 A3
**Wittenberge** D . . . . . 73 A4
**Wittenburg** D . . . . . . 73 A4
**Wittenheim** F . . . . . 106 B2
**Wittichenau** D . . . . . 84 A2
**Wittighausen** D . . . . 94 B1
**Wittingen** D . . . . . . . 73 B3
**Wittislingen** D . . . . . 94 C2
**Wittlich** D . . . . . . . . 92 B2
**Wittmannsdorf** A . . 110 C2
**Wittmund** D . . . . . . . 71 A4
**Wittorf** D . . . . . . . . . 72 A2
**Wittstock** D . . . . . . . 73 A5
**Witzenhausen** D . . . 82 A1
**Wiveliscombe** GB . . 43 A3
**Wivenhoe** GB . . . . . 45 B4
**Władysławowo** PL . . 69 A3
**Wleń** PL . . . . . . . . . . 84 A3
**Włocławek** PL . . . . . 77 B4
**Włodawa** PL . . . . . . . 13 C5
**Włodzimierzów** PL . 87 A3
**Włosień** PL . . . . . . . . 84 A3
**Włostow** PL . . . . . . . 87 B5
**Włoszakowice** PL . . 75 C5
**Włoszczowa** PL . . . . 87 B3
**Wöbbelin** D . . . . . . . 73 A4
**Woburn** GB . . . . . . . 44 B3
**Wodzisław** PL . . . . . 87 B4
**Wodzisław Śląski**
PL . . . . . . . . . . . . . 98 B2
**Woerden** NL . . . . . . . 70 B1
**Woerth** F . . . . . . . . . 93 C3
**Wohlen** CH . . . . . . 106 B3
**Woippy** F . . . . . . . . . 92 B2
**Wojcieszow** PL . . . . 85 B3
**Wojkowice Kościelne**
PL . . . . . . . . . . . . . 86 B3
**Wojnicz** PL . . . . . . . . 99 B4
**Woking** GB . . . . . . . . 44 B3
**Wokingham** GB . . . . 44 B3
**Wola Jachowa** PL . . 87 B4
**Wola Niechcicka** PL 86 A3
**Wolbórz** PL . . . . . . . 87 A3
**Wolbrom** PL . . . . . . . 87 B3
**Wołczyn** PL . . . . . . . 86 A2
**Woldegk** D . . . . . . . . 74 A2
**Wolfach** D . . . . . . . . 93 C4
**Wolfegg** D . . . . . . . 107 B4
**Wolfen** D . . . . . . . . . 83 A4
**Wolfenbüttel** D . . . . 73 B3
**Wolfersheim** D . . . . . 81 B4
**Wolfhagen** D . . . . . . 81 A5
**Wolfratshausen** D . 108 B2
**Wolfsberg** A . . . . . . 110 C1
**Wolfsburg** D . . . . . . 73 B3
**Wolf's Castle** GB . . . 39 C2
**Wolfshagen** D . . . . . 74 A2
**Wolfstein** D . . . . . . . 93 B3
**Wolfurt** A . . . . . . . . 107 B4
**Wolgast** D . . . . . . . . 66 B2
**Wolhusen** CH . . . . 106 B3
**Wolin** PL . . . . . . . . . 67 C3
**Wolka** PL . . . . . . . . . 87 A4
**Wolkenstein** D . . . . . 83 B5
**Wolkersdorf** A . . . . . 97 C4
**Wöllersdorf** A . . . . . 111 B3
**Wollin** D . . . . . . . . . . 73 B5
**Wöllstadt** D . . . . . . . 81 B4
**Wolmirstedt** D . . . . . 73 B4
**Wolnzach** D . . . . . . . 95 C3
**Wołów** PL . . . . . . . . . 85 A4
**Wolsztyn** PL . . . . . . . 75 B5
**Wolvega** NL . . . . . . . 70 B2
**Wolverhampton** GB 40 C1
**Wolverton** GB . . . . . 44 A3
**Wombwell** GB . . . . . 40 B2
**Woodbridge** GB . . . . 45 A5
**Woodhall Spa** GB . . 41 B3
**Woodstock** GB . . . . 44 B2
**Wookey Hole** GB . . . 43 A4
**Wool** GB . . . . . . . . . . 43 B4
**Woolacombe** GB . . . 42 A2
**Wooler** GB . . . . . . . . 37 A4
**Woolwich** GB . . . . . . 45 B4
**Wooperton** GB . . . . . 37 A5
**Worb** CH . . . . . . . . 106 C2
**Worbis** D . . . . . . . . . 82 A2
**Worcester** GB . . . . . 39 B4
**Wördern** A . . . . . . . . 97 C4
**Wörgl** A . . . . . . . . . 108 B3
**Workington** GB . . . . 36 B3
**Worksop** GB . . . . . . 40 B2
**Workum** NL . . . . . . . 70 B2
**Wörlitz** D . . . . . . . . . 83 A4
**Wormer** NL . . . . . . . . 70 B1
**Wormhout** F . . . . . . . 78 B2
**Wormit** GB . . . . . . . . 35 B5
**Worms** D . . . . . . . . . 93 B4
**Worpswede** D . . . . . . 72 A1
**Wörrstadt** D . . . . . . . 93 B4
**Wörschach** A . . . . . 110 B1
**Worsley** GB . . . . . . . 38 A4
**Wörth**
*Bayern* D . . . . . . . . . 93 B5
*Bayern* D . . . . . . . . . 95 B4
*Bayern* D . . . . . . . . . 95 C4
*Rheinland-Pfalz* D . . 93 B4
**Worthing** GB . . . . . . 44 C3
**Woudsend** NL . . . . . 70 B2
**Woumen** B . . . . . . . . 78 A2
**Woźniki** PL . . . . . . . . 86 B3
**Wragby** GB . . . . . . . 41 B3
**Wrangle** GB . . . . . . . 41 B4
**Wręczyca Wlk.** PL . . 86 B2
**Wredenhagen** D . . . . 73 A5
**Wremen** D . . . . . . . . 72 A1
**Wrentham** GB . . . . . 45 A5
**Wrexham** GB . . . . . . 38 A3
**Wriedel** D . . . . . . . . . 72 A3
**Wriezen** D . . . . . . . . 74 B3
**Wrist** D . . . . . . . . . . . 64 C2
**Wróblewo**
*Mazowieckie* PL . . . . 77 B5
*Wielkopolskie* PL . . . 75 B5
**Wrocki** PL . . . . . . . . 69 B4
**Wrocław** PL . . . . . . . 85 A5
**Wronki** PL . . . . . . . . 75 B5
**Wroxham** GB . . . . . . 41 C5
**Września** PL . . . . . . . 76 B2
**Wrzosowo** PL . . . . . . 67 B4
**Wschowa** PL . . . . . . 85 A4
**Wulfen** D . . . . . . . . . 80 A3
**Wülfen** D . . . . . . . . . 83 A3
**Wulkau** D . . . . . . . . . 73 B5
**Wünnenberg** D . . . . 81 A
**Wünsdorf** D . . . . . . . 74
**Wunsiedel** D . . . . . . 95
**Wunstorf** D . . . . . . . . 7
**Wuppertal** D . . . . . .
**Wurmannsquick** D
**Würselen** D . . . . .
**Wurzbach** D . . . .
**Würzburg** D . . .
**Wurzen** D . . . .
**Wust** D . . . . .
**Wusterhause**
**Wusterwitz**
**Wustrau-A**
D . . . .
**Wustrow**
**Wuustw**
**Wye** G
**Wygl**
**Wyk**
**Wy**
**W**
**W**

Wymondham GB 41 C5
Wyrzysk PL 76 A2
Wyśmierzyce PL 87 A4
Wysoka
*Dolnośląskie* PL 85 A3
*Wielkopolskie* PL 76 A2
Wyszanów PL 86 A2
Wyszogród PL 77 B5

## X

Xanten D 80 A2
Xanthi GR 183 B6
Xarrë AL 182 D2
Xátiva E 159 C3
Xeraco E 159 B3
Xert E 153 B4
Xerta E 153 B4
Xertigny F 105 A5
Xilagani GR 183 C7
Xilokastro GR 184 A3
Xinzo de Limia E 140 B3
Xixón = Gijón E 142 A1
Xove E 140 A3
Xubia E 140 A2
Xunqueira de Ambia E 140 B3
Xunqueira de Espadañedo E 140 B3
Xylophagou CY 181 B2

## Y

Yablanitsa BG 17 D6
Yağcılar TR 186 C3
Yahyalı TR 23 B8
Yakoruda BG 183 A5
Yalova TR 187 B4
Yalvaç TR 189 A6
Yambol BG 17 D7
Yampil UA 13 D8
Yaniskoski RUS 193 D12
Yantarnyy RUS 69 A4
Yarbasan TR 186 D3
Yarcombe GB 43 B3
Yaremcha UA 13 D6
Yarm GB 37 B5
Yarmouth GB 44 C2
Yarrow GB 35 C4
Yasinya UA 17 A6
Yatağan TR 188 B3
Yate GB 43 A4
Yatton GB 43 A4
Yavoriv UA 13 D5
Yaxley GB 41 C3
Yazıca TR 187 B6
Yazıköy TR 188 C2
Ybbs A 110 A2
Ybbsitz A 110 B1
Ydby DK 58 B1
Yddal N 46 B2
Ydes F 116 B2
Yealmpton GB 42 B3
Yebra de Basa E 145 B3
Yecla E 159 C2
Yecla de Yeltes E 149 B3
Yelsk BY 13 C8
Yelverton GB 42 B2
Yena RUS 197 B14
Yenice
*Ankara* TR 23 B7
*Aydın* TR 188 B3
*Çanakkale* TR 186 C2
*Edirne* TR 183 C8
Yenifoça TR 186 D1
Yenihisar TR 188 B2
Yeniköy TR 186 D4
Yeniköy Plaji TR 186 B3
Yenipazar TR 188 B3
Yenişarbademli TR 189 B6
Yenişehir TR 187 B4
Yenne F 118 B2
Yeovil GB 43 B4
…oes E 151 C4
…köy TR 23 B8
…akkos CY 181 A2
…ipos CY 181 B1
… NL 79 A4
… 89 A4
… 189 B6
… 23 B8
… 186 B3
… 189 B4
… 188 A3
… 164 A2
… 9 E6
…38 A2
Ygos-St Saturnin F 128 C2
Ygrande F 104 C1
Yialousa CY 181 A3
Yığılca TR 187 B6
Yli-Ii FIN 197 D8
Yli-Kärppä FIN 197 D8
Yli-Muonia FIN 196 A6
Ylitornio FIN 196 C6
Ylivieska FIN 3 D9
Ylläsjärvi FIN 196 B7
Ymonville F 103 A3
Yngsjö S 63 C2
York GB 40 B2
Youghal IRL 29 C4
Yoğuntaş TR 186 A2
Yozgat TR 23 B8
Yport F 89 A4
Ypres = Ieper B 78 B2
Yssingeaux F 117 B4
Ystad S 66 A2
Ystalyfera GB 39 C3
Ystebrød N 52 B1
Ystradgynlais GB 39 C3
Ytre Arna N 46 B2
Ytre Enebakk N 54 A2
Ytre Rendal N 199 D8
Ytteran S 199 B11
Ytterhogdal S 199 C11
Yttermalung S 49 B5
Yunak TR 187 D6
Yuncos E 151 B4
Yunquera E 162 B3
Yunquera de Henares E 151 B4
Yushkozero RUS 3 D13
Yverdon-les-Bains CH 106 C1
Yvetot F 89 A4
Yvignac F 101 A3
Yvoir B 79 B4
Yvonand CH 106 C1
Yxnerum S 56 B2
Yzeure F 104 C2

## Z

Zaamslag NL 79 A3
Zaanstad NL 70 B1
Žabalj SRB 126 B2
Zabar H 113 A4
Žabari SRB 127 C3
Zabiče SLO 123 B3
Zabierzów PL 87 B3
Ząbki PL 77 B6
Ząbkowice Śląskie PL 85 B4
Zablaće HR 138 B1
Žabljak MNE 139 B5
Żabno PL 87 B4
Zabok HR 124 A1
Žabokreky SK 98 C2
Zabor PL 75 C4
Żabowo PL 75 A4
Zabrdje BIH 125 C4
Zábřeh CZ 97 B4
Zabrežje SRB 127 C2
Ząbrowo PL 67 C4
Zabrze PL 86 B2
Zabrzeż PL 99 B4
Zacharo GR 184 B2
Zadar HR 137 A4
Zadzim PL 86 A2
Zafarraya E 163 B3
Zafferana Etnea I 177 B4
Zafra E 155 C4
Žaga SLO 122 A2
Zagajica SRB 127 C3
Żagań PL 84 A3
Zaglav HR 137 B4
Zaglavak SRB 127 D1
Zagnanšk PL 87 B4
Zagora GR 183 D5
Zagorc SLO 110 C2
Zagorićani BIH 138 B3
Zagorje SLO 123 A4
Zagórów PL 76 B2
Zagradje SRB 127 C2
Zagreb HR 124 B1
Zagrilla E 163 A3
Zagvozd HR 138 B3
Zagwiździe PL 86 B1
Zagyvarekas H 113 B4
Zagyvaróna H 113 A3
Zahara E 162 B2
Zahara de los Atunes E 162 B2
Zahinos E 155 C4
Zahna D 83 A4
Záhoří CZ 96 B2
Zahrádka CZ 97 B3
Zahrensdorf D 73 A3
Zaidin E 153 A4
Zaječar SRB 16 D5
Zákamenné SK 99 B3
Zákány H 124 A2
Zákányszék H 126 A1
Zakliczyn PL 99 B4
Zakopane PL 99 B3
Zakroczym PL 77 B5
Zakrzew PL 87 A5
Zakrzewo PL 76 B3
Zakupy CZ 84 B2
Zakynthos GR 184 B1
Zalaapáti H 111 C4
Zalabaksa H 111 C3
Zalaegerszeg H 111 C3
Zalakomár H 111 C4
Zalakoppány H 111 C4
Zalalövő H 111 C3
Zalamea de la Serena E 156 B2
Zalamea la Real E 161 B3
Zalaszentgrót H 111 C4
Zalaszentiván H 111 C3
Zalău RO 17 B5
Zalavár H 111 C4
Zalcsie PL 86 A3
Zaldibar E 143 A4
Žalec SLO 123 A4
Zalesie PL 77 A5
Zalewo PL 69 B4
Zalishchyky UA 13 D6
Zalla E 143 A3
Zaltbommel NL 79 A5
Zamárdi H 112 C1
Zamarte PL 68 B2
Zamberk CZ 85 B4
Zambra E 163 A3
Zambugueira do Mar P 160 B1
Zámoly H 112 B2
Zamora E 149 A4
Zamość PL 13 C5
Zamoście PL 86 A3
Zams A 108 B1
Zandhoven B 79 A4
Žandov CZ 84 B2
Zandvoort NL 70 B1
Zangliveri GR 183 C5
Zánka H 111 C4
Zaorejas E 152 B1
Zaovine SRB 127 D1
Zapadnaya Dvina RUS 9 D8
Zapfend D 94 A2
Zapole PL 86 A2
Zapolyarnyy RUS 193 C14
Zapponeta I 171 B3
Zaprešić HR 124 B1
Zaragoza E 153 A3
Zarasai LT 13 A7
Zarautz E 144 A1
Zarcilla de Ramos E 164 B3
Zaręby PL 77 A6
Žarki PL 86 B3
Zarko GR 182 D4
Žarnovica SK 98 C2
Zarnow PL 87 A4
Zarnowiec PL 68 A3
Zarošice CZ 97 B4
Żarów PL 85 B4
Zarren B 78 A2
Zarrentin D 73 A3
Żary PL 84 A3
Zarza Capilla E 156 B2
Zarza de Alange E 156 B1
Zarza de Granadilla E 149 B3
Zarza de Tajo E 151 B4
Zarzadilla de Totana E 164 B3
Zarza la Mayor E 155 B4
Zarzuela del Monte E 150 B3
Zarzuela del Pinar E 151 A3
Zas E 140 A2
Zasavica SRB 127 C1
Zasieki PL 84 A2
Zásmuky CZ 96 B3
Žatec CZ 83 B5
Zaton HR 139 C4
Zatonie PL 84 A3
Zator PL 99 A3
Zauchwitz D 74 B2
Zavala BIH 139 C3
Zavalje BIH 124 C1
Zavattarello I 120 C2
Zavidovići BIH 139 A4
Zavlaka SRB 127 C1
Zawady PL 77 C5
Zawadzkie PL 86 B2
Zawdy PL 86 A2
Zawidów PL 84 A3
Zawidz PL 77 B4
Zawiercie PL 86 B3
Zawoja PL 99 B3
Zawonia PL 85 A5
Žažina HR 124 B2
Zázrivá SK 99 B3
Zbarazh UA 13 D6
Zbąszyń PL 75 B4
Zbąszynek PL 75 B4
Zbehy SK 98 C2
Zbiersk PL 76 C3
Zbiroh CZ 96 B1
Zblewo PL 69 B3
Zbójno PL 77 A4
Zbrachlin PL 76 A3
Zbraslav CZ 96 B2
Zbraslavice CZ 97 B3
Ždala HR 124 A3
Ždánice CZ 98 B1
Žďár nad Sázavov CZ 97 B3
Zdbice PL 75 A5
Zdenci HR 125 B3
Ždiar SK 99 B4
Zdice CZ 96 B1
Zdirec nad Doubravou CZ 97 B3
Zdolbuniv UA 13 C7
Zdounky CZ 98 B1
Ždrelo SRB 127 C3
Zduńska Wola PL 86 A2
Zduny
*Łódzkie* PL 77 B4
*Wielkopolskie* PL 85 A5
Żdżary PL 87 A4
Zdziechowice
*Opolskie* PL 86 A2
*Wielkopolskie* PL 76 B2
Zdziszowice PL 86 B2
Zeberio E 143 A4
Žebrák CZ 96 B1
Zebreira P 155 B3
Zebrzydowa PL 84 A3
Zechlin D 74 A1
Zechlinerhütte D 74 A1
Zederhaus A 109 B4
Žednik SRB 126 B1
Zeebrugge B 78 A3
Zegrze PL 77 B6
Zehdenick D 74 B2
Zehren D 83 A5
Zeil D 94 A2
Zeilarn D 95 C4
Zeist NL 70 B2
Zeithain D 83 A5
Zeitz D 83 A4
Želatava CZ 97 B3
Želazno PL 68 A2
Zele B 79 A4
Zelenoborskiy RUS 3 C13
Zelenogorsk RUS 9 B6
Zelenograd RUS 9 D10
Zelenogradsk RUS 12 A4
Železná Ruda CZ 96 B1
Železnice CZ 84 B3
Železnik SRB 127 C2
Zelezniki SLO 123 A3
Železny Brod CZ 84 B3
Zelhem NL 71 B3
Želiezovce SK 112 A2
Želkowo PL 68 A2
Zell
CH 106 B2
*Baden-Württemberg* D 93 C4
*Baden-Württemberg* D 106 B2
*Rheinland-Pfalz* D 92 A3
Zella-Mehlis D 82 B2
Zell am See A 109 B3
Zell am Ziller A 108 B2
Zell an der Pram A 96 C1
Zell bei Zellhof A 96 C2
Zellerndorf A 97 C3
Zellingen D 94 B1
Želovce SK 112 A3
Zelów PL 86 A3
Zeltweg A 110 B1
Zelzate B 79 A3
Zemberovce SK 98 C2
Zembrzyce PL 99 B3
Zemianske-Kostol'any SK 98 C2
Zemitz D 66 C2
Zemné SK 112 B1
Zemst B 79 B4
Zemun SRB 127 C2
Zemunik Donji HR 137 A4
Zenica BIH 139 A3
Zennor GB 42 B1
Žepa BIH 139 B5
Žepče BIH 139 A4
Zepponami I 168 A2
Zerbst D 73 C5
Zerf D 92 B2
Zerind RO 113 C5
Żerków PL 76 B2
Zermatt CH 119 A4
Zernez CH 107 C5
Zerpen-schleuse D 74 B2
Zestoa E 144 A1
Zetel D 71 A4
Zeulenroda D 83 B3
Zeven D 72 A2
Zevenaar NL 70 C3
Zevenbergen NL 79 A4
Zévio I 121 B4
Zeytinbaği TR 186 B3
Zeytindağ TR 186 D2
Zgierz PL 86 A3
Zgorzelec PL 84 A3
Zgošča BIH 139 A4
Zhabinka BY 13 B6
Zharkovskiy RUS 9 E8
Zhashkiv UA 13 D9
Zhlobin BY 13 B9
Zhmerynka UA 13 D8
Zhodzina BY 13 A8
Zhytomyr UA 13 C8
Žiar nad Hronom SK 98 C2
Zicavo F 180 B2
Zickhusen D 65 C4
Zidani Most SLO 123 A4
Ziddorf D 73 A5
Židlochovice CZ 97 B4
Ziębice PL 85 B5
Ziegendorf D 73 A4
Ziegenrück D 83 B3
Zieleniec
*Dolnośląskie* PL 85 B4
*Warmińsko-Mazurskie* PL 77 A6
*Zachodnio-Pomorskie* PL 75 A4
Zielona PL 77 A4
Zielona Góra PL 75 C4
Zieluń-Osada PL 77 A4
Ziemetshausen D 94 C2
Zierenberg D 81 A5
Zierikzee NL 79 A3
Ziersdorf A 97 C3
Zierzow D 73 A4
Ziesar D 73 B5
Ziesendorf D 65 C5
Ziethen D 74 B2
Žihle CZ 96 A1
Žilina SK 98 B2
Ziltendorf D 74 B3
Zimandu Nou RO 126 A3
Zimna Woda PL 77 A5
Zimnicea RO 17 D6
Zinal CH 119 A4
Zinasco I 120 B2
Zingst D 66 B1
Zinkgruvan S 55 B6
Žinkovy CZ 96 B1
Zinnowitz D 66 B2
Zirc H 112 B1
Žiri SLO 123 A3
Zirl A 108 B2
Zirndorf D 94 B2
Žirovnica SRB 127 C3
Žirovnice CZ 97 B3
Zisterdorf A 97 C4
Žitište SRB 126 B2
Zitsa GR 182 D2
Zittau D 84 B2
Živaja HR 124 B2
Živinice BIH 139 A4
Zlatar HR 124 A2
Zlatar Bistrica HR 124 A2
Zlate Hory CZ 85 B5
Zlaté Klasy SK 111 A4
Zlaté Moravce SK 98 C2
Zlatnána Ostrove SK 112 B1
Zlatniky SK 98 C2
Zlatograd BG 183 B7
Žlebič SLO 123 B3
Zlín CZ 98 B1
Złocieniec PL 75 A5
Złoczew PL 86 A2
Zlonice CZ 84 B2
Złotniki Kujawskie PL 76 B3
Złotoryja PL 85 A3
Złotów PL 68 B2
Złoty Stok PL 85 B4
Zlutice CZ 83 B5
Zmajevac BIH 124 C2
Zmajevo SRB 126 B1
Żmigród PL 85 A4
Zmijavci HR 138 B3
Žminj HR 122 B2
Żnin PL 76 B2
Znojmo CZ 97 C4
Zöblitz D 83 B5
Zocca I 135 A3
Zoetermeer NL 70 B1
Zofingen CH 106 B2
Zogno I 120 B2
Zohor SK 111 A3
Zolling D 95 C3
Zolochiv UA 13 D6
Zomba H 112 C2
Zomergem B 79 A3
Zoñán E 141 A3
Zonguldak TR 187 A6
Zonhoven B 79 B5
Zonza F 180 B2
Zörbig D 83 A4
Zorita E 156 A2
Żory PL 98 A2
Zossen D 74 B2
Zottegem B 79 B3
Zoutkamp NL 71 A3
Zovi Do BIH 139 B4
Zreče SLO 123 A4
Zrenjanin SRB 126 B2
Žrnovica HR 138 B2
Zručnad Sazavou CZ 97 B3
Zsadány H 113 C5
Zsámbék H 112 B2
Zsámbok H 112 B3
Zsana H 126 A1
Zschopau D 83 B5
Zuberec SK 99 B3
Zubieta E 144 A2
Zubiri E 144 B2
Zubtsov RUS 9 D9
Zucaina E 153 B3
Zudar D 66 B2
Zuera E 144 C3
Zufre E 161 B3
Zug CH 107 B3
Zuheros E 163 A3
Zuidhorn NL 71 A3
Zuidlaren NL 71 A3
Zuidwolde NL 71 B3
Zújar E 164 B2
Żukowo PL 69 A3
Žuljana HR 138 C3
Žulová CZ 85 B5
Zülpich D 80 B2
Zumaia E 144 A1
Zumárraga E 143 A4
Zundert NL 79 A4
Županja HR 125 B4
Zurgena E 164 B2
Zürich CH 107 B3
Żuromin PL 77 A4
Zurzach CH 106 B3
Zusmarshausen D 94 C2
Zusow D 65 C4
Züssow D 66 C2
Žuta Lovka HR 123 C4
Zutphen NL 70 B3
Žužemberk SLO 123 B3
Zvenyhorodka UA 13 D9
Zvikovské Podhradi CZ 96 B2
Zvolen SK 99 C3
Zvolenská Slatina SK 99 C3
Zvornik BIH 139 A5
Zwartsluis NL 70 B3
Zweibrücken D 93 B3
Zweisimmen CH 106 C2
Zwettl A 97 C3
Zwettl an der Rodl A 96 C2
Zwickau D 83 B4
Zwiefalten D 107 A4
Zwieryn PL 75 B4
Zwierzno PL 69 A4
Zwiesel D 96 B1
Zwieselstein A 108 C2
Zwoleń PL 87 A5
Zwolle NL 70 B3
Zwönitz D 83 B4
Żychlin PL 77 B4
Zydowo
*Wielkopolskie* PL 76 B2
*Zachodnio-Pomorskie* PL 68 A1
Żyrardów PL 77 B5
Żytno PL 86 B3
Żywiec PL 99 B3
Zyyi CY 181 B2